STATUTORY INSTRUMENTS 1974

PART I

(in three Sections)

SECTION 3

Published by Authority

LONDON
HER MAJESTY'S STATIONERY OFFICE
1975

ISBN 11 840128 9*

Contents of the Volume

PART I, Section 1

PART I, Section 2

PART I, Section 3

PART II

PART III

STATUTORY INSTRUMENTS

1974 No. 519

LOCAL GOVERNMENT, ENGLAND AND WALES

The Local Authority (Stocks and Bonds) Regulations 1974

Made- - - -	*21st March* 1974
Laid before Parliament	*22nd March* 1974
Coming into Operation	*1st April* 1974

The Secretary of State for the Environment, in exercise of the powers conferred upon him by paragraph 4(1) of Schedule 13 to the Local Government Act 1972(a) and of all other powers enabling him in that behalf, with the consent of the Treasury, hereby makes the following regulations:—

Title, commencement and interpretation

1.—(1) These regulations may be cited as the Local Authority (Stocks and Bonds) Regulations 1974 and shall come into operation on 1st April 1974.

(2) The Interpretation Act 1889(b) shall apply for the interpretation of these regulations as it applies for the interpretation of an Act of Parliament.

(3) In these regulations—

"bonds" shall not include bonds transferable by delivery;

"local authority" has the same meaning as in section 270(1) of the Local Government Act 1972;

"negotiable bonds" means any bonds in respect of which application has been or is to be made to the Council of the Stock Exchange for admission to the Official List, or any bonds which are to be issued in whole or in part to a bank, discount house, issuing house, or broker in the City of London;

"registrar", in relation to any description of stock or bonds, means the local authority or other person appointed by the local authority to act as registrar for the purposes of these regulations in respect of that stock or those bonds; and

"stock" shall not include stock transferable by delivery.

Issue of stock and bonds

2. A local authority who propose to raise money by the issue of stock shall, in their resolution to raise money by that method, specify, or indicate the procedure by which may be determined—

    (*a*) the amount of stock to be issued;

    (*b*) the price at which the stock is to be issued;

(a) 1972 c.70.   (b) 1889 c.63.

    (*c*) the rate of interest;

    (*d*) the dates on which interest is payable; .

    (*e*) the date after which the stock may be redeemed at par at the option of the local authority; and

    (*f*) the date by which the stock must be redeemed.

3.—(1) Bonds issued by a local authority shall, subject to the next following paragraph—

    (*a*) bear interest at such rate as the local authority shall determine at the time of issue of the bonds; and

    (*b*) if they are negotiable bonds, be issued for periods of not less than one year.

(2) The period for which any bonds, other than negotiable bonds, are issued may be extended upon such rate of interest and for such period as the local authority and the holder agree.

Conversion of other securities

4.—(1) Where a local authority has raised money by means of any security and have the power, with the consent of the holder, or otherwise, to redeem, they may redeem that security with money raised by the issue of stock or, with the consent of the holder, substitute stock for that security.

(2) A local authority may, in money or stock or both, make a reasonable payment to the holder referred to in paragraph (1) above for his consent or for otherwise compensating him for the redemption or substitution of his security.

Register of stock and bonds

5.—(1) The registrar shall keep a register relating to each description of stock or bonds and in that register he shall enter the name and address of each person who is for the time being a holder of stock or bonds of that description and the amount of such stock or bonds which he holds.

(2) The registrar may keep any register by recording the matters in question otherwise than in legible form so long as they are capable of being reproduced in that form.

(3) Any such register or a reproduction thereof in legible form shall be *prima facie* evidence of any matters directed or authorised by these regulations to be entered in the register and of the title of the persons whose names are entered therein as holders of stock or bonds.

(4) Where two or more persons are registered as holders of any stock or bonds they shall be deemed to be joint holders with right of survivorship between them.

(5) The provisions of the Bankers' Books Evidence Act 1879(a) shall apply for the purpose of proving an entry in a register as if the registrar were a bank and a banker within the meaning of the Act, and as if such entry in a register were an entry in a banker's book.

(a) 1879 c.11.

Certificates

6.—(1) The registrar shall issue to every person whose name is entered in a register as a holder of stock or bonds a certificate representing such stock or bonds which shall include the following particulars—

(*a*) the name of the local authority;

(*b*) the name of the registrar, if not the local authority itself;

(*c*) the name of the holder;

(*d*) the statutory authority under which the stock or bonds are issued;

(*e*) the amount of stock or bonds represented by the certificate;

(*f*) the redemption date and, in the case of stock, the earliest redemption date after which the local authority may exercise its option (if any) to redeem;

(*g*) the rate of interest;

(*h*) the dates on which interest is payable; and

(*i*) the serial number of the certificate.

(2) Where the names of two or more persons are entered in a register as joint holders of any stock or bonds it shall be sufficient for the registrar to issue one certificate in respect thereof to one of the joint holders.

(3) A certificate issued under this regulation shall be *prima facie* evidence of the title of the person named therein as holder of the stock or bonds specified therein.

(4) If a certificate is defaced, lost or destroyed the registrar may, on receipt of such evidence and indemnity as he may require, and on the surrender of the certificate in a case where it is defaced, issue a replacement.

(5) Where the holder of any stock or bonds transfers part of his holding he shall be entitled to a certificate representing the part he retains.

Transfer and transmission

7. Stock or bonds shall be transferable by instrument in writing in accordance with the Stock Transfer Act 1963**(a)** delivered to the registrar who may retain any such instrument.

8. The registrar may decline to give effect to a transfer of any stock or bonds unless—

(*a*) there is furnished to him such evidence as he may require of the right of the transferor to make the transfer; and

(*b*) the transfer is accompanied by a certificate showing that the transferor is the holder of that stock or those bonds; or

(*c*) there is furnished to him such evidence as he may require that a certificate showing that the transferor is the holder of that stock or those bonds has been lost or destroyed and such indemnity in respect thereof as he may require; or

---

(a) 1963 c. 18.

(*d*) the transfer is accompanied by a certificate showing that the transferor is the holder of part of that stock or those bonds and as to the residue thereof there is furnished to him such evidence and indemnity as he may require under paragraph (*c*) above.

9.—(1) Any stock or bonds entered in a register in the name of a deceased person shall be transferable by his personal representative.

(2) The registrar may decline to give effect to a transfer of any stock or bonds entered in a register in the name of a deceased person who has two or more personal representatives unless the transfer is executed by all of them.

(3) The production to the registrar of any document which is by law sufficient evidence of probate of the will, or letters of administration of the estate, of a deceased person having been granted to some person, shall be accepted by the registrar as sufficient evidence of the grant.

10.—(1) A person becoming entitled to any stock or bonds by any lawful means other than—

(i) by transfer by instrument in writing in accordance with regulation 7 above; or

(ii) upon the death of the stock or bond holder;

shall, on production of such evidence as the registrar may require, either be registered as holder of that stock or those bonds or be able to make such transfer of that stock or those bonds as the previous holder could have made.

(2) Until such evidence is furnished the registrar may decline to give effect to the transmission of that stock or those bonds.

11. The certification by the registrar of a transfer of any stock or bonds shall be taken as a representation by him to any person acting on the faith of the certification that there has been furnished to the registrar evidence to show a *prima facie* title to that stock or those bonds in the transferor named in the transfer, but not as a representation that the transferor has any title thereto.

12. Where a person executes an instrument relating to stock or bonds otherwise than by signature, the registrar may decline to recognise that instrument unless there is furnished to him such evidence as he may require that the effect of the instrument was understood by that person.

13.—(1) The transferor of any stock or bonds shall remain the holder thereof until the registrar has given effect to the transfer.

(2) The registrar shall not be required to give effect to a transfer until the expiration of fifteen clear days after the first day on which he has in his possession the transfer and such other evidence as he may require under these regulations.

(3) The registrar shall give effect to a transfer or transmission by entering in the register such particulars as are necessary to show the effect thereof.

Trustees and persons holding offices

14.—(1) The registrar may enter in the register such designation of the holder of any stock or bonds as that holder may specify and, in particular, the holder may be described as trustee of a specified trust or as trustee without specifying a trust or in any other manner indicating the capacity in which he holds the stock or bonds.

(2) Where the holder of any stock or bonds occupies an office or official position, his official description may be entered in the register instead of his name and thereupon any transfer shall be treated as properly executed if executed by the person for the time being occupying that office or official position and any payment of interest or redemption money to that person in accordance with regulation 18 below shall be a sufficient discharge to the local authority and the registrar for that interest or redemption money.

(3) Except as provided in the preceding provisions of this regulation no notice of any trust shall be entered in any register or certificate or be receivable by the registrar and, notwithstanding that the holder of any stock or bonds is described as mentioned in those provisions, the registrar shall not be affected with notice of any trust and it shall not be necessary for him to enquire concerning the propriety of anything done in relation to that stock or those bonds or any part thereof.

Payment of interest and redemption

15.—(1) A local authority who issue stock or bonds shall make a scheme in accordance with paragraph 15 of Schedule 13 to the Local Government Act 1972 to establish and operate a loans fund for the purpose of defraying expenditure which they are authorised to meet out of money borrowed by them and for the redemption of such stock or bonds.

(2) Where the local authority issue stock or bonds at a discount, the difference between the issue price and nominal value shall form part of the loan.

(3) The expenses of the local authority incurred in the issue of stock or bonds may be charged to capital and may be deemed money raiseable under a statutory borrowing power and may, if the issue was at a premium, be wholly or partly defrayed out of the monies received by way of premium.

16.—(1) The registrar, with the approval of the local authority where the registrar is not the local authority, may close a register relating to stock or bonds of any description during the whole or any part of the period of one month preceding the day on which the interest or redemption money is payable.

(2) Instead of closing a register in the manner aforesaid the registrar may strike the balance for interest on stock or bonds of any description on any day not being more than 37 days before the day on which the interest on such stock or bonds is payable.

(3) Any person who, on the date on which a register is closed or the balance is struck as aforesaid, is entered in that register as the holder of any stock or bonds shall, as between himself and any transferee of such stock or bonds, be entitled to the then current interest thereon.

17. Subject to the provisions of regulation 3(2) above stock and bonds shall be redeemed by payment of any amount equal to the denomination thereof at the redemption date specified in the certificate issued in respect of them; but

(*a*) bonds, other than negotiable bonds, may be so redeemed at any time before the date so specified where the local authority and the holder so agree; and

(*b*) stock may be so redeemed at the option of the local authority at any time after the earliest redemption date specified in the certificate issued in respect thereof.

18.—(1) Unless the holder of any stock or bonds otherwise requests in writing the local authority or, where the local authority is not the registrar, the local authority by the registrar shall pay interest and any redemption money due on any stock or bonds by sending a cheque or warrant to the holder by post to his registered address and the posting of that cheque or warrant in a pre-paid letter directed to his address shall be a sufficient discharge to the local authority and the registrar for that interest or redemption money.

(2) Before sending any cheque or warrant in payment of redemption money the registrar may, if he thinks fit, require the holder of any stock or bonds upon which redemption money is to be paid to specify in writing the person to whom the redemption money is to be paid and the address to which the cheque or warrant is to be sent and upon receipt of that specification the registrar shall make the payment of redemption money in accordance therewith.

(3) Before making any payment the registrar may, if he thinks fit, require evidence of the title of any person claiming a right to receive such payment and in particular may require the surrender of the certificate representing the stock or bonds upon which redemption money is to be paid or such indemnity as he may require if the certificate is lost or destroyed.

(4) If any cheque or warrant has not been encashed and has become defaced, lost or destroyed the registrar shall, on receipt of such evidence and indemnity as he may require, and on the surrender of the cheque or warrant where it is defaced, pay the money due.

(5) Every warrant so sent by post shall be deemed to be a cheque and the local authority and the registrar shall, in relation thereto, be deemed a banker within the Bills of Exchange Act 1882(**a**).

(6) For the purpose of this regulation the holder means the person whose name is recorded as the holder of the stock or bonds at the date on which the interest or redemption money is payable, or if the register was closed or a balance struck under regulation 16 above, at the date on which the register was closed or the balance struck, and in the case of joint holders the registrar may treat as holder that one of them who is first named in the register or such other of them as they all may in writing direct, but any request or specification in writing given under paragraphs (1) or (2) above must be given by all of the joint holders.

(7) Where the person who would otherwise be the holder of any stock or bonds is deceased his personal representative or personal representatives shall, for the purposes of this regulation, be deemed to be the holder or joint holders of that stock or those bonds.

(**a**) 1882 c. 61.

(8) Where two or more joint holders of any stock or bonds have given a request as to the payment of interest thereon and one of them becomes of unsound mind, such request shall not thereby become void.

(9) Nothing in the preceding provisions of this regulation shall prevent the registrar and any banker from making special arrangements for the payment of any interest or redemption money payable to the holder of any stock or bonds which is receivable by that banker, either on his own behalf, or as nominee of the holder, or otherwise.

19. Any stock or bonds redeemed by the registrar shall thereupon be cancelled and together with all interest thereon which has not become payable shall be extinguished.

Unclaimed redemption money and interest

20.—(1) Subject to paragraph (2) below if—

    (a) at the end of a period of one year from the date of redemption of any stock or bonds (including redemption at the option of the local authority) the registrar for any reason is unable to make payment of any redemption money or any cheque or warrant issued for that payment has not been encashed; or

    (b) at the end of a period of three years from the date for payment of any interest due on any stock or bonds the registrar for any reason is unable to make that payment or any cheque or warrant issued for that payment has not been encashed;

the registrar, if a local authority or one of its officers may, and if some other person shall, carry, transfer, or pay, an amount equivalent to that payment to the credit of a consolidated loans fund, mortgage pool, or such other account standing in the name of the local authority as the local authority may think fit and in such manner as it may direct but without prejudice to the rights and entitlement of any person at any time to be paid and to recover the same.

(2) Where the registrar is not the local authority or one of its officers the periods of one year and three years in sub-paragraphs (a) and (b) above may be reduced to such shorter periods as the registrar and the local authority may agree.

(3) No interest shall be payable on any sum due in respect of interest on stock or bonds or the redemption of stock or bonds after the date on which the interest or redemption money became payable.

(4) Where an account has been credited in accordance with paragraph (1) above with an amount equivalent to payment of redemption money in respect of any stock or bonds that stock or those bonds shall, for the purpose of regulation 19 above, be deemed to have been redeemed by the registrar.

Rectification of the register

21.—(1) If the name of any person is without sufficient cause entered in or omitted from a register or default is made or unnecessary delay takes place in making any entry required to be made therein, the High Court or, where the sum involved does not exceed five thousand pounds, the County Court may, on application by the person aggrieved or by the registrar, make an order for the rectification of the register.

(2) On any proceedings under this regulation the court may decide any question relating to the title of any party thereto to have his name entered in or omitted from a register and generally any question which it may be necessary or expedient to decide for the purpose of the rectification of a register.

Appointment of Receiver

22.—(1) Except as provided in paragraph (2) below, if at any time any money due in respect of any stock or bonds issued by a local authority remains unpaid for a period of two months after demand in writing, the person entitled thereto may, without prejudice to any other remedy, apply to the High Court for the appointment of a Receiver, and the Court may, if they think fit, appoint a Receiver on such terms and with such powers as the Court think fit.

(2) No such application shall be entertained unless the money due to the applicant, or in the case of a joint application by two or more persons the aggregate monies due to them, amount to not less than five hundred pounds.

(3) The Court may confer upon the Receiver any such powers of collecting, receiving and recovering the revenues of the local authority, and of making, collecting and recovering rates, and of issuing and enforcing precepts, as are possessed by the local authority or their officers.

Revocation

23.—(1) The regulations specified in the Schedule hereto are hereby revoked.

(2) Nothing in these regulations shall affect the continued operation of the London County Council Stock Order 1965(a) with respect to stock to which that order relates.

SCHEDULE

The Local Authorities (Stock) Regulations 1934	S.R. & O. 1934/619 (Rev XII, p.482: 1934 I, p.980)
The Local and Other Authorities (Transfer of Stock) Regulations 1949	S.I. 1949/1562 (1949 I, p.2482)
The Transfer of Stock (Exemption) Order 1949	S.I. 1949/2413 (1949 I, p.2489)
The Local Authorities (Stock) Regulations 1956	S.I. 1956/327 (1956 I, p.1171)
The Local and Other Authorities (Transfer of Stock) Regulations 1956	S.I. 1956/328 (1956 I, p.1172)
The Local Authority Bonds Regulations 1964	S.I. 1964/983 (1964 II, p.2221)
The London County Council Stock Order 1965	S.I. 1965/655 (1965 I, p.2093)

Anthony Crosland,

19th March 1974.   Secretary of State for the Environment.

We consent to these regulations.

James Hamilton,

T. Pendry,

Two of the Lords Commissioners of
21st March 1974.   Her Majesty's Treasury.

(a) S.I. 1965/655 (1965 I, p. 2093).

EXPLANATORY NOTE

(This Note is not part of the Regulations.)

These Regulations provide for the manner in which stock or bonds shall be issued by a local authority, including the terms on which they are to be issued. They regulate the manner of transfer, dealing with and redeeming any stock or bonds issued (other than stock or bonds transferable by delivery).

STATUTORY INSTRUMENTS

1974 No. 520

PENSIONS

The Local Government Superannuation Regulations 1974

Made – – – –	*22nd March* 1974
Laid before Parliament	*25th March* 1974
Coming into Operation	*1st April* 1974

ARRANGEMENT OF REGULATIONS

PART A

PRELIMINARY

PART B

SUPERANNUATION FUNDS AND CONTRIBUTORS THERETO

PART C

CONTRIBUTIONS AND CERTAIN OTHER PAYMENTS TO SUPERANNUATION FUNDS

PART D

SERVICE

PART G

SPECIAL PROVISIONS FOR CERTAIN CASES

PART H

DETERMINATION OF QUESTIONS AND APPEALS

PART J

TRANSITIONAL PROVISIONS AND TRANSITORY PROVISIONS FOR LOCAL GOVERNMENT REORGANISATION, ETC.

PART K

PERSONS CEASING TO BE EMPLOYED AFTER 30TH MARCH 1972 AND BEFORE THE APPOINTED DAY

PART L

MISCELLANEOUS AND SUPPLEMENTAL

PART M

AMENDMENTS, REVOCATIONS AND REPEALS

SCHEDULES

SCHEDULE 15

Transfer of superannuation funds

SCHEDULE 16

Apportionment of superannuation funds

SCHEDULE 17

Modifications to Parts A, D and E and regulations J9 and J16 in their application to persons ceasing to be employed after 30th March 1972 and before the appointed day

SCHEDULE 18—AMENDMENTS

Part I   Enactments

Part II   Instruments

SCHEDULE 19—REVOCATIONS AND REPEALS

Part I   Enactments having effect as regulations under section 7 or 8(2) of the Act of 1972

Part II   Other enactments

Part III   Instruments having effect as regulations under section 7 or 8(2) of the Act of 1972

Part IV   Other instruments

The Secretary of State for the Environment—

(a) after consultation with such associations of local authorities as appeared to him to be concerned, the local authorities with whom consultation appeared to him to be desirable, the local Act authority concerned and such representatives of other persons likely to be affected by the regulations as appeared to him to be appropriate, in exercise of his powers under sections 7, 8 and 12 of the Superannuation Act 1972(a), as read with paragraph 5(1) of Schedule 7 to that Act, and of all other powers enabling him in that behalf, hereby makes the following regulations, except regulations F1 to F19 and Schedule 13; and

(b) being the appropriate Minister for the purposes of section 110 of the National Insurance Act 1965(b) in relation to the schemes for the provision of pensions and other benefits under regulations made under section 7 of the Superannuation Act 1972, in exercise of his powers under the said section 110, and of all other powers enabling him in that behalf, hereby makes regulations F1 to F19 and Schedule 13 of the following regulations:—

(a) 1972 c. 11.   (b) 1965 c.51.

PART A

PRELIMINARY

Title and commencement

A1. These regulations may be cited as the Local Government Superannuation Regulations 1974 and shall come into operation on 1st April 1974.

General interpretation

A2.—(1) In these regulations, unless the context otherwise requires—

(*a*) any reference to any enactment or instrument shall be construed as a reference to that enactment or instrument as amended, modified, extended, applied or re-enacted by or under any other enactment or instrument;

(*b*) any reference to any enactment applying to England and Wales listed in the table in paragraph 5 of Schedule 7 to the Act of 1972, or any instrument (including a scheme) made under any enactment so listed or any provision of any such enactment or instrument shall, additionally, be construed as a reference to that enactment, instrument or provision as having effect by virtue of sub-paragraph (1) of that paragraph and as amended by the Miscellaneous Provisions regulations and the Local Government Superannuation (Miscellaneous Provisions) (No. 2) Regulations 1973**(a)**; and

(*c*) in any case where immediately before the appointed day the provisions of the Acts of 1937 to 1953 and the regulations made thereunder applied to a person as modified or extended by the provisions of any local Act or scheme, any reference to a specified provision of the Act of 1937 or the Act of 1953 or of such regulations shall, where a corresponding provision of a local Act or scheme applied to that person in lieu of the specified provision, be construed in relation to him as a reference to that corresponding provision.

(2) In these regulations, unless the context otherwise requires, any reference to a regulation or to a Part or to a schedule shall be construed as a reference to a regulation contained in, or to a Part of or to a schedule to, these regulations, as the case may be, any reference to a paragraph shall be construed as a reference to a paragraph in the same regulation or, as the case may be, the same schedule and any reference to a sub-paragraph shall be construed as a reference to a sub-paragraph contained in the same paragraph.

(3) The Interpretation Act 1889**(b)** shall apply for the interpretation of these regulations as it applies for the interpretation of an Act of Parliament and as if these regulations and the former regulations were Acts of Parliament.

Definitions

A3.—(1) For the purposes of these regulations, any enactment or group of enactments referred to in regulation A4 has the meaning assigned to it thereby, and unless the context otherwise requires—

(a) S.I. 1973/1996 (1973 III, p. 6872).   (b) 1889 c. 63.

"actuary" means a Fellow of the Institute of Actuaries or of the Faculty of Actuaries;

"added period payment" means a payment made for the purposes of—

(*a*) regulation D10, D12 or D13; or

(*b*) section 2(1) of the Act of 1953 as originally enacted or as having effect as mentioned in regulation A2(1)(*b*), or any similar provision contained in a local Act scheme;

"added years", in relation to any person, means—

(*a*) any additional period of reckonable service which that person is entitled to reckon under regulation D10; and

(*b*) any years added to his service under—

   (i) regulation 12 of the Benefits regulations; or

   (ii) regulation 5 of the Local Government Superannuation (Reckoning of Service on Transfer) Regulations 1954(**a**); or

   (iii) regulation 15(2)(b) of the Local Government Superannuation (England and Scotland) Regulations 1948(**b**) as amended (**c**); or

   (iv) any similar provision contained in a local Act scheme;

"additional contributory payment" means a payment made—

(*a*) for the purposes of—

   (i) regulation D6 or D7; or

   (ii) section 2(3) of the Act of 1953 as originally enacted or as having effect as mentioned in regulation A2(1)(*b*); or

(*b*) under the Act of 1937 as originally enacted, or under the Act of 1922 or under a local Act scheme, as a condition of being entitled to reckon any service, either as service generally or as service of a particular character; or

(*c*) for the purposes of proviso (ii) to section 8(2)(*b*) of the Act of 1937;

"administering authority" means any body which is required to maintain a superannuation fund under these regulations;

"admission agreement" means an agreement made under, or continued in force as if made under, section 15 of the Act of 1953 or made under section 7 of the Act of 1948 or under any provision of a local Act similar in effect to either of those sections;

"appointed day" means 1st April 1974;

"appropriate administering authority", in relation to a pensionable employee and to the employing authority, means the body maintaining the superannuation fund which is, in relation to him and to the employing authority, the appropriate superannuation fund;

"appropriate superannuation fund", in relation to a pensionable employee and to the employing authority, means the superannuation fund maintained under these regulations in the benefits of which the pensionable employee is entitled to participate;

"child" means a person who—

(**a**) S.I. 1954/1211 (1954 II, p. 1676).
(**b**) S.I. 1948/1131 (Rev. XVII, p. 813: 1948 I, p. 3304).
(**c**) The relevant amending instrument is S.I. 1954/1250 (1954 II, p. 1531).

(*a*) is under the age of 16 years; or

(*b*) having attained the age of 16 years, is receiving full-time education or undergoing full-time training for a trade, profession or calling, which training is for a period of not less than 2 years, and up till then there has been no time since he attained that age when he was not receiving such education or undergoing such training; or

(*c*) having attained the age of 16 years, is an incapacitated person by reason of ill-health or infirmity of mind or body which arose either before he attained that age or while receiving such education or undergoing such training as mentioned in paragraph (*b*) of this definition,

and includes a person in respect of whom, as respects any period during which that person is not receiving full-time education or full-time training as mentioned in that paragraph, the appropriate administering authority are satisfied that that person's full-time education or full-time training, as the case may be, ought not to be regarded as completed and, in their discretion, determine either—

(i) that the period shall be disregarded for the purposes of that paragraph; or

(ii) that that period shall be so disregarded and shall also be treated as part of the period during which that person is receiving such full-time education or full-time training as aforesaid;

"combined police authority" has the same meaning as in the Police Act 1964(a);

"the Common Council" means the Common Council of the City of London;

"contributory employee" means a person who was entitled to participate in the benefits of a superannuation fund maintained under Part I of the Act of 1937;

"death gratuity" means a death gratuity payable under regulation E11;

"designated employee" means a person who before 1st April 1939 had been, or had been treated by a local authority as being, an officer or servant to whom the Act of 1922 applied;

"disqualifying break of service", in relation to any person, means a continuous period of 12 months or longer during no part of which he was a pensionable employee, contributory employee or local Act contributor or subject to the Act of 1922;

"eligible child" means—

(*a*) where a person has become entitled to a retirement pension, whether or not he has become entitled to receive payments in respect of that pension,—

(i) a legitimate child of a marriage of that person which took place before the date on which that person became entitled to the retirement pension, born before the expiration of one year after the date on which that person became entitled to that pension;

(ii) an adopted child of that person, adopted before that person became entitled to the retirement pension; or

(iii) a step-child or illegitimate child of that person, an adopted child of the wife of a marriage of that person which took place before that person became entitled to the retirement pension or a child

---

(a) 1964 c. 48.

accepted by that person as a member of the family, being a child wholly or mainly dependent on that person both before he becomes entitled to that pension and at the time of his death;

(b) where a person dies in an employment in which he is a pensionable employee—

   (i) a legitimate child of that person, born before the expiration of one year after the date of the death of that person;

   (ii) an adopted child of that person; or

   (iii) a step-child or illegitimate child of that person, an adopted child of the wife of a marriage of that person or a child accepted by that person as a member of the family, being a child wholly or mainly dependent on that person at the time of his death;

"employee" means an employee whether permanent or temporary, other than a person appointed to a post in a temporary capacity for a period of not more than 3 months or whose employment is of a casual nature;

"employer's contribution" means a sum payable under regulation C5;

"employing authority", in relation to a pensionable employee, means the body in whose employment the pensionable employee is;

"employment" includes office;

"enactment" includes any instrument made under an Act;

"former local authority" means a local authority within the meaning of the Act of 1937 (other than a scheduled body) and includes a metropolitan borough;

"inner London area" has the same meaning as in section 2 of the Administration of Justice Act 1964(a);

"judicially separated" means judicially separated in circumstances in which the husband is not required by the order of any competent court to contribute to the support of his wife, and any such reference to judicial separation includes a reference to separation by a matrimonial order made under the Matrimonial Proceedings (Magistrates' Courts) Act 1960(b) and having by virtue of section 2 of that Act effect as a decree of judicial separation;

"justices' clerk (inner London area)" means a person who, under section 15 of the Administration of Justice Act 1964, is appointed or deemed to have been appointed by the committee of magistrates for the inner London area to be a justices' clerk;

"justices' clerk (outside the inner London area)" means a person who, under Part III of the Justices of the Peace Act 1949(c), is appointed or deemed to have been appointed by a magistrates' courts committee to be a justices' clerk, other than any such person whose remuneration is paid by a local Act authority;

"local Act authority" has the same meaning as in section 8 of the Act of 1972;

"local Act contributor" means a person who is, or has been, entitled to participate in the benefits of a superannuation fund maintained under a local Act scheme;

"local Act scheme" has the same meaning as in section 8 of the Act of 1972;

(a) 1964 c. 42.   (b) 1960 c. 48.   (c) 1949 c. 101.

"local education authority" has the same meaning as in the Education Act 1944(a);

"manual worker" means an employee who is not an officer;

"national service", in relation to any person, means service of a description specified in Schedule 1 to the Reserve and Auxiliary Forces (Protection of Civil Interests) Act 1951(b), and includes any period immediately following the termination thereof during which (with the consent, in the case of a justices' clerk of the authority by whom he was appointed, and in the case of any other person, of the authority or person by whom he was employed before undertaking that service) the person continued in similar service;

"officer" means an employee whose duties are wholly or mainly administrative, professional, technical or clerical;

"old modification scheme" means a scheme made pursuant to section 28(3) of the Widows', Orphans' and Old Age Contributory Pensions Act 1936(c);

"participating employment" means, in relation to any period which is reckonable as service for the purposes of these regulations, any employment in which a person—

(a) is required to pay graduated contributions under the paragraph (c) inserted in section 4(1) of the Insurance Act by section 1(2) of the National Insurance Act 1969(d), as amended by section 2(2) of the National Insurance and Supplementary Benefit Act 1973(e); or

(b) would be required to pay such contributions if the amount which was paid in any income tax week on account of his remuneration (or which would have been paid but for any suspension of remuneration due to leave of absence) exceeded the amount first mentioned in section 4(1) of the Insurance Act as so amended,

and includes any similar period of employment in which a person is, or would be, required to pay graduated contributions under the Northern Ireland Act or the Isle of Man Act; but the expression does not include any period of national service in respect of which contributions were paid under the Superannuation (Local Government Staffs) (National Service) Rules 1949 to 1954(f) if immediately prior to entering national service the person had been in non-participating employment;

"part-time employee" means an employee, other than a whole-time employee or variable-time employee;

"passenger transport executive" means the Executive for a designated area within section 9(1) of the Transport Act 1968(g);

"payment in lieu of contributions" means a payment in lieu of contributions under Part III of the Insurance Act;

"pensionable employee" means a person who is for the time being entitled under regulation B2 to participate in the benefits of the appropriate superannuation fund;

"pensionable remuneration" has the meaning assigned to it by regulation E1;

"police authority" has the same meaning as in the Police Act 1964;

(a) 1944 c. 31.   (b) 1951 c. 65.   (c) 1936 c. 33.   (d) 1969 c. 44.   (e) 1973 c. 42.
(f) S.I. 1949/545, 1951/2145, 1954/1228 (1949 I, p. 3105; 1951 II p. 164; 1954 II, p. 1760).
(g) 1968 c. 73.

"probation and after-care committee" has the same meaning as in the Criminal Justice Act 1948(a);

"probation officer" means a person who is a probation officer appointed under Part I of the Criminal Justice Act 1925(b) or under Schedule 5 to the Criminal Justice Act 1948;

"qualifying service", in relation to any person, means the service, previous periods of employment and any other periods which he is entitled to reckon as qualifying service in accordance with regulation D2;

"reckonable service", in relation to any person, means the service, previous periods of employment and any other periods which he is entitled to reckon as reckonable service in accordance with regulation D1;

"registration officer" means a superintendent registrar or registrar of births and deaths, and includes a registrar of births and deaths exercising any of the functions of a registrar of marriages and a person provided by and at the expense of a local authority to act as a deputy superintendent registrar or deputy registrar of births and deaths;

"regular fireman" means a member of a fire brigade maintained under the Fire Services Act 1947(c) of a class prescribed by a scheme for the time being in operation under section 26 of that Act for the purposes of section 2 of the Fire Services Act 1951(d);

"remuneration" means all the salary, wages, fees, poundage and other payments paid or made to an employee as such for his own use, and includes the money value of any apartments, rations or other allowances in kind appertaining to his employment, but does not include—

(a) payments for non-contractual overtime;

(b) any allowance paid to him to cover cost of office accommodation or clerk's assistance;

(c) any travelling or subsistence allowance or other moneys to be spent, or to cover expenses incurred by him, for the purposes of his employment;

(d) any payment made to him on his ceasing to hold his employment in consideration of loss of holidays; or

(e) any payment accepted by him in lieu of notice to terminate his contract of employment;

"rent officer" and "deputy rent officer" mean respectively any person who, in pursuance of a scheme under section 40 of the Rent Act 1968(e), is or has been appointed a rent officer or deputy rent officer, other than any such person whose remuneration is paid by a local Act authority;

"retiring allowance" means a retiring allowance payable under regulation E2;

"retirement pension" means a retirement pension payable under regulation E2;

"scheduled body" means a body described in column (1) of Part I of Schedule 1 and a body described in column (3) of Part II of that schedule;

"service" means service which is rendered to any scheduled body (other than service as a regular fireman), or to any other body or person as a local Act contributor;

"variable-time employee" means an employee who has no contractual hours of employment;

(a) 1948 c. 58.   (b) 1925 c. 86.   (c) 1947 c. 41.   (d) 1951 c. 27.   (e) 1968 c. 23.

"war service", in relation to any person, means war service within the meaning of the Local Government Staffs (War Service) Act 1939(a) and any period after the termination thereof during which (with the consent, in the case of a justices' clerk of the authority by whom he was appointed, and in the case of any other person of the authority or person by whom he was employed before undertaking that service) the person continues in similar service;

"water authority" has the same meaning as in the Water Act 1973(b); and

"whole-time employee" means an employee whose contractual minimum hours of employment regularly or usually amount to 30 hours or more in each week; and "whole-time officer" and "whole-time manual worker" shall be construed accordingly.

(2) For the purposes of these regulations service rendered by an employee of a scheduled body whose services are placed at the disposal of a Minister of the Crown or a government department in pursuance of any enactment is service rendered to the scheduled body by whom he is employed.

Definition of enactments

A4. In these regulations—

"the Act of 1922" means the Local Government and other Officers' Superannuation Act 1922(c);

"the Act of 1937" means the Local Government Superannuation Act 1937(d);

"the Act of 1948" means the Superannuation (Miscellaneous Provisions) Act 1948(e);

"the Act of 1953" means the Local Government Superannuation Act 1953(f);

"the Acts of 1937 to 1953" means the Local Government Superannuation Acts 1937 to 1953(g);

"the Act of 1972" means the Superannuation Act 1972;

"the Benefits regulations" means the Local Government Superannuation (Benefits) Regulations 1954(h);

"the English Property Order" means the Local Authorities (England) (Property etc.) Order 1973(j);

"the former regulations" means—

(a) (i) the provisions of the enactments listed in the table in paragraph 5 of Schedule 7 to the Act of 1972 as applying to England and Wales; and

(ii) the provisions of any instrument (including a scheme) made under any enactment so listed, being provisions in force immediately before the appointed day,

as having effect, by virtue of sub-paragraph (1) of the said paragraph 5, as provisions of regulations under section 7 of the Act of 1972;

(b) the Miscellaneous Provisions regulations; and

(c) the Local Government Superannuation (Miscellaneous Provisions) (No. 2) Regulations 1973.

But where the expression is used together with a reference to revocation, the expression means such of the provisions mentioned in paragraph (a) of this definition as are specified in column (2) of Part I or II of Schedule 19 and the regulations referred to in paragraphs (b) and (c) of this definition;

(a) 1939 c. 94.   (b) 1973 c. 37.   (c) 1922 c. 59.   (d) 1937 c. 68.
(e) 1948 c. 33.   (f) 1953 c. 25.   (g) 1937 c. 68; 1939 c. 18; 1953 c. 25.
(h) S.I. 1954/1048 (1954 II, p. 1595).   (j) S.I. 1973/1861 (1973 III, p. 6401).

"the Insurance Act" means the National Insurance Act 1965;

"the Insurance Acts" means the National Insurance Acts 1965 to 1973;

"insurance code" means the Insurance Act, the Northern Ireland Act or the Isle of Man Act;

"interchange rules" means rules made under section 2 of the Act of 1948 (which provides for the pensions of persons transferring to different employment) and includes any similar instrument made, or having effect as if made, under any other Act which makes similar provision;

"the Isle of Man Act" means the National Insurance (Isle of Man) Act 1961 (an Act of Tynwald);

"the Local Government Act" means the Local Government Act 1972(a);

"the Miscellaneous Provisions regulations" means the Local Government Superannuation (Miscellaneous Provisions) Regulations 1973(b);

"the Northern Ireland Act" means the National Insurance Act (Northern Ireland) 1959(c); and

"the Welsh Property Order" means the Local Authorities (Wales) (Property etc.) Order 1973 (d).

Application of regulations to Isles of Scilly

A5. These regulations shall apply to the Isles of Scilly as if the Isles of Scilly were a district in the county of Cornwall and the Council of the Isles of Scilly were the council of that district.

Persons treated as employees of a scheduled body

A6.—(1) For the purposes, and subject to the provisions, of these regulations any person of a class described in column (1) of the following table shall be deemed to be an officer in the employment of the body described opposite thereto in column (2).

TABLE

(1) Class	(2) Deemed employing body
Justices' clerks (outside the inner London area)	The magistrates' courts committee by whom he was appointed or is deemed to have been appointed
Registration officers	The local authority who made the scheme under section 14 of the Registration Service Act 1953(e) for the district in or for which the officer acts
Rent officers and deputy rent officers	The local authority for whose area the relevant scheme is made, or has effect as if made, under section 40 of the Rent Act 1968

(a) 1972 c. 70.   (b) S.I. 1973/313 (1973 I, p. 1100).   (c) 1959 c. 21. (N.I.).
(d) S.I. 1973/1863 (1973 III, p. 6452).   (e) 1953 c. 37.

(2) For the purposes, and subject to the provisions, of these regulations every employee of a subsidiary of a passenger transport executive shall be deemed to be an employee of that executive.

Treatment of certain additional duties

A7. Where the duties of an officer in the whole-time employment of a scheduled body include the additional duty of a returning officer at local government elections or of an acting returning officer then—

(a) in the case of a person who became a pensionable employee on the appointed day and who immediately before that day was in the employment mentioned above and whose duties therein immediately before the appointed day included one such additional duty or both such additional duties, these regulations shall, unless the context otherwise requires, apply as respects him in relation to each additional duty as if each additional duty were a separate variable-time employment held by him under a scheduled body, other than the scheduled body under whom he holds the whole-time employment mentioned above; and

(b) in any other case, these regulations shall, unless the context otherwise requires, apply as respects him in relation to the additional duty or, if the duties of his whole-time employment include more than one additional duty, in relation to both those additional duties as if that additional duty or, as the case may be, those additional duties were a separate variable-time employment held by him under a scheduled body, other than the scheduled body under whom he holds the whole-time employment mentioned above.

Deemed employments

A8. In these regulations, unless the context otherwise requires, references to employees of a scheduled body shall be construed as including references to persons who are deemed for the purposes of these regulations to be in the employment of a scheduled body, and other provisions relating to employment by or under a scheduled body shall be construed accordingly.

Treatment of certain separate employments

A9. Where an employee holds under a scheduled body two or more separate employments, the provisions of these regulations shall, unless the context otherwise requires, apply as respects him in relation to each of those separate employments as if the other or others were an employment or employments held by him under another scheduled body.

PART B

SUPERANNUATION FUNDS AND CONTRIBUTORS THERETO

Superannuation funds

B1. A superannuation fund shall be established and administered for the purposes of these regulations by each of the following bodies, that is to say—

(a) every county council;

(b) the Greater London Council;

(c) every London borough council; and

(d) the National Water Council.

Pensionable employees

B2.—(1) The following persons shall, subject to the provisions of this regulation, be entitled to participate in the benefits of the appropriate superannuation fund maintained under these regulations—

(*a*) every whole-time officer of a body described in column (1) of Part I of Schedule 1 (other than any such person as may be specified in respect of such body in column (2));

(*b*) every whole-time manual worker of such a body as aforesaid who either—

(i) has completed 12 months' continuous whole-time employment with his employing authority; or

(ii) entered or re-entered the employment of his employing authority, without a disqualifying break of service, after other employment in which he was a contributory employee, pensionable employee or local Act contributor and in respect of which he has not, before so entering or re-entering, received a return of contributions under the former regulations, or under these regulations, or under a local Act scheme,

other than any such person as may be specified in respect of such body as aforesaid in column (2) of Part I of Schedule 1 or any person who elected under paragraph 2 of Part VI of Schedule 2 to the Act of 1937 not to become a contributory employee and in whose case the election had not before the appointed day ceased to have effect, but so long only as he continues without any break of service as a whole-time manual worker in the employment of the body to whom he gave notice under that paragraph;

(*c*) every variable-time employee of a body described in column (1) of Part I of Schedule 1 (other than any such person as may be specified in respect of such body in column (2)), who is also in the whole-time employment of such a body as aforesaid in virtue of which he is a pensionable employee;

(*d*) every employee described in column (1) of Part II of Schedule 1 of such a body as is described opposite thereto in column (3) (other than any such person as may be specified in respect of such body in column (2)), whom that body have by a statutory resolution specified as a pensionable employee or who belongs to a class which the body have by such a resolution as aforesaid specified as a class the members of which are to be pensionable employees;

(*e*) every whole-time employee of—

(i) the governors of any voluntary school maintained but not provided by a local education authority for such education as may be provided by a local education authority in the exercise of their functions under Part I of the Education Act 1944; or

(ii) the governing body of any polytechnic, technical institute or other similar institution which is for the time being aided by a local education authority under the said Act of 1944,

being an employee whom the local education authority have, with the consent, given either generally or in a particular case, of the governors or, as the case may be, of the governing body, by a statutory resolution specified as a pensionable employee or who belongs to a class which the authority have, with the consent, given either generally or in relation to a class of employee, of the governors, or, as the case may be, of the governing body, by such a resolution as aforesaid specified as a class the members of which are to be pensionable employees;

(*f*) every person employed as a medical inspector of immigrants appointed under the Immigration Act 1971(**a**) who receives his remuneration in that appointment from a local authority (other than a local Act authority) and who, when not employed as aforesaid, is engaged wholly or partly in employment by that or some other local authority in which he is a pensionable employee or local Act contributor;

(*g*) every whole-time member of a passenger transport executive and every whole-time director of a subsidiary thereof, whom that passenger transport executive have, in the case of a member thereof with the consent of the council of the metropolitan county for which that passenger transport executive is the Executive, by a statutory resolution specified as a pensionable employee;

(*h*) every person who immediately before the appointed day was a contributory employee in the employment of any such governors or governing body as are mentioned in sub-paragraph (*e*), but so long only as he continues without a break in the employment of those governors or, as the case may be, that body;

(*i*) every person who immediately before the appointed day was a member of a passenger transport executive or a director of a subsidiary thereof and who immediately before that day was in that position a contributory employee, but so long only as he continues without a break in that position;

(*j*) every person who immediately before the appointed day was in the employment of the Common Council and who immediately before that day was by virtue of article 15 of the London Authorities (Superannuation) Order 1965(**b**) entitled to participate in the benefits of the superannuation fund maintained under Part I of the Act of 1937 by the Greater London Council, but so long only as he continues without a break in the employment of the Common Council;

(*k*) every person who immediately before the appointed day was in the employment of the London Transport Executive and who immediately before that day was by virtue of section 18(4) of the Transport (London) Act 1969(**c**) entitled to participate in the benefits of the superannuation fund maintained under Part I of the Act of 1937 by the Greater London Council or Newham London borough council, but so long only as he continues in the employment of that body, whether in the same post or in some other post, and subject to any order made by the Secretary of State under section 74 of the Transport Act 1962(**d**);

(*l*) every justices' clerk (inner London area) or other officer employed by the committee of magistrates for the inner London area who was on the appointed day such a justices' clerk or other officer so employed and who immediately before that day was by virtue of regulation 2(1) of the Superannuation (Inner London Magistrates' Courts) Regulations 1965(**e**) entitled to superannuation rights corresponding with those to which he was entitled in respect of his service before 1st April 1965 as a justices' clerk in the county of London or an officer employed by the County of London Magistrates' Courts Committee, but so long only as

---

(**a**) 1971 c. 77.   (**b**) S.I. 1965/621 (1965 I, p. 1970).   (**c**) 1969 c. 35.
(**d**) 1962 c. 46.   (**e**) S.I. 1965/537 (1965 I, p. 1550).

he continues as a justices' clerk (inner London area) or as an officer employed by the committee of magistrates for the inner London area without a break of 12 months or more; and

(*m*) every other person who on the appointed day was in the employment of a scheduled body, and who immediately before that day held a post in virtue of which he was a contributory employee (other than an officer of a scheduled body who was employed by them for part only of his time but who immediately before the appointed day was in that employment a contributory employee by reason of devoting substantially the whole of the rest of his time to employment by one or more scheduled bodies or former local authorities), but so long only as he continues without any break of service in the employment of that body, whether in the same post or some other post.

(2) A person who by virtue of paragraph (1)(*c*) became a pensionable employee under a body described in column (1) of Part I of Schedule 1 shall, notwithstanding that he ceases to hold the whole-time employment referred to in that paragraph, continue to be a pensionable employee so long as he continues without any break of service in the variable-time employment of that body.

(3) A body described in column (1) of Part I of Schedule 1 may resolve that a person who falls within paragraph (1)(*a*), (*b*) or (*c*) shall not become a pensionable employee unless he has undergone a medical examination to their satisfaction; and a resolution under this paragraph may apply to any specified person or to any specified class of persons.

(4) The following persons shall not become pensionable employees by virtue of the foregoing provisions of this regulation, that is to say—

(*a*) a person who is under the age of 18 years;

(*b*) a person who has attained the age of 65 years:

Provided that this sub-paragraph shall not apply to a person—

(i) to whom a pension has become payable which is liable to be reduced or suspended under regulation E15 or a short service grant became payable under the former regulations; or

(ii) who, if he were to become a pensionable employee, would be entitled to reckon any previous service, period of employment or other period as reckonable service or qualifying service; or

(iii) who has suffered loss of employment or loss or diminution of emoluments which was attributable to the provisions of any enactment and who under or by virtue of any enactment has received or is entitled to receive compensation for such loss or diminution which compensation is liable to be reduced or suspended in consequence of his taking up employment under a scheduled body in the like manner and to the like extent as it would have been reduced or suspended in consequence of his taking up such employment under the pension scheme to which he was subject immediately before suffering such loss;

(*c*) a person who under regulation 25 of the Miscellaneous Provisions regulations elected not to become a contributory employee and in whose case the election had not before the appointed day ceased to have effect, so long as he remains in the employment of the body to whom he gave notice under that regulation;

(*d*) a person who is entitled to participate in the benefits of any other superannuation scheme provided by or under any enactment (including an enactment in a local Act), other than section 7 of the Act of 1972;

(*e*) a chaplain who is a person to whom the Clergy Pensions Measure 1961(a) applies;

(*f*) an employee of a scheduled body in respect of whom contributions to the Merchant Navy Officers Pension Fund are made;

(*g*) an employee of a scheduled body in respect of whom contributions to the Port Employers and Registered Dock Workers Pension Fund are made; or

(*h*) an employee of the Kingston upon Hull district council employed by that council in connection with their telephone undertaking during such period as that employee is entitled to benefits under a trust deed dated 27th January 1925 and made between the lord mayor, aldermen and citizens of the city of Kingston upon Hull of the one part and Edwin Ombler, Thomas Hayes Toogood and Thomas George Milner of the other part, or any amendment or modification thereof or any new trust deed substituted therefor, or subject to the Post Office Staff Superannuation Scheme.

(5) In this regulation—

"statutory resolution" means, in relation to a scheduled body, a resolution passed in the manner in which an ordinary resolution of the body may be passed, except that 28 days' notice of the meeting at which the resolution is passed and of the terms of the resolution and of the fact that it is to be proposed at that meeting, must have been given in the manner in which notice for convening ordinary meetings of the body may be given; and

"short service grant" means a short service grant as defined in regulation 2 of the Benefits regulations.

Appropriate superannuation fund

B3.—(1) Subject to paragraph (2), the appropriate superannuation fund in relation to the pensionable employees of an employing authority who are an administering authority shall be the superannuation fund maintained by that authority.

(2) The appropriate superannuation fund in relation to any pensionable employee of a London borough council who immediately before the appointed day was by virtue of article 14 of the London Authorities (Superannuation) Order 1965 entitled to participate in the benefits of the superannuation fund maintained under Part I of the Act of 1937 by the Greater London Council shall be the superannuation fund maintained by the Greater London Council, so long as he continues in the employment of that London borough council.

(3) The appropriate superannuation fund in relation to the pensionable employees of an employing authority who are a water authority shall be the superannuation fund maintained by the National Water Council.

(4) The appropriate superannuation fund in relation to such a person as is mentioned in regulation B2(1)(*k*) shall, where immediately before the appointed day the person was entitled to participate in the benefits of the superannuation fund maintained under Part I of the Act of 1937 by the Greater London Council or Newham London borough council, be the superannuation fund maintained by that council.

(a) 1961 No. 3.

(5) The appropriate superannuation fund in relation to such persons as are mentioned in regulation B2(1)(*j*) or (*l*) or to the pensionable employees of the probation and after-care committee for any area in Greater London shall be the superannuation fund maintained by the Greater London Council.

(6) Subject to paragraph (7), in any case not falling within the preceding paragraphs, the appropriate superannuation fund in relation to the pensionable employees of an employing authority shall be the superannuation fund maintained by the county council or the London borough council within whose area the area, or the greater part of the area, of the employing authority is situate.

(7) In any case falling within paragraph (6), if the Secretary of State, on an application made to him, is satisfied, after consultation with the bodies appearing to him to be concerned, that it is expedient so to do, he may from time to time direct that all or any of the pensionable employees of the employing authority concerned shall be entitled to participate in the benefits of the superannuation fund maintained by some other administering authority and where he gives such a direction he shall give such further directions as he deems necessary for the making of financial adjustments, whether by way of a transfer of an apportioned part of the assets comprised in the fund in the benefits of which, but for that direction, those employees would have been entitled to participate, or the making of a payment out of that fund or both, for the transfer of any liabilities of that fund, and with respect to other consequential and incidental matters.

Power to admit employees of other bodies

B4.—(1) If application for the purpose is made to an administering authority by a body specified in paragraph (4), the authority may, if they think fit and on such terms and conditions as, subject to paragraph (2), they think proper, admit any employee (other than an employee who is under the age of 18 years or who has attained the age of 65 years and is not such a person as is mentioned in the proviso to regulation B2(4)(*b*)) of the body to participate in the benefits of the superannuation fund maintained by them, and in that event these regulations shall have effect as if the body were a scheduled body and the employee were a pensionable employee and the body shall have all such powers as may be necessary for the purpose of giving effect to the aforesaid terms and conditions.

(2) The terms and conditions of any agreement made under this regulation—

    (*a*) shall contain provision that any question which may arise between the administering authority and the body concerned relating to the construction of the agreement or to the rights and obligations thereunder of either party thereto shall be determined by the Secretary of State;

    (*b*) may not contain provision (other than provision that any previous period of employment by the body concerned of an employee admitted under the agreement shall be reckonable as reckonable service to such extent as may be agreed between the administering authority and the body) conferring on any employee admitted under the agreement any greater or lesser rights under these regulations or subjecting him to any greater or lesser liabilities thereunder than those which he would have enjoyed or to which he would have been subject respectively had he become a pensionable employee by virtue of regulation B2.

(3) An administering authority shall forthwith upon the making of an agreement under this regulation notify the Secretary of State that the agreement has been made and furnish him with the name of the body concerned and with the date as from which the agreement takes effect.

(4) The bodies referred to in paragraph (1) are—

    (*a*) a voluntary organisation engaged in the provision of services—

        (i) under section 22 of the National Health Service Act 1946**(a)**; or

        (ii) under Part III of the National Assistance Act 1948**(b)**; or

        (iii) under the Disabled Persons (Employment) Act 1958**(c)**; or

        (iv) under the Mental Health Act 1959**(d)**; or

        (v) under section 12 or 45 of the Health Services and Public Health Act 1968**(e)**,

    other than such of those services as under section 2(2) of the National Health Service Reorganisation Act 1973**(f)** the Secretary of State considers are appropriate as part of the health service established in pursuance of the National Health Service Act 1946;

    (*b*) a body representative of local authorities or of local authorities and officers of local authorities or a body representative of officers of local authorities formed for the purpose of consultation as to the common interests of those authorities and the discussion of matters relating to local government;

    (*c*) statutory undertakers;

    (*d*) non-statutory undertakers approved for the purposes of this regulation by the Secretary of State;

    (*e*) a body which provides a public service in the United Kingdom otherwise than for the purposes of gain or to whose funds any local authority contribute or to whom any grant is made out of moneys provided by Parliament;

    (*f*) the Housing Corporation;

    (*g*) the Commission for the New Towns;

    (*h*) a development corporation established under the New Towns Act 1965**(g)**;

    (*i*) the Maplin Development Authority.

(5) In relation to any person who immediately before the appointed day was subject to the former regulations by virtue of an admission agreement continued in force by regulation J8 as if made under this regulation, these regulations shall have effect as if he were a pensionable employee.

(6) Paragraph (1) shall not apply in the case of the governors or managers of a voluntary school within the meaning of the Education Act 1944 and, without prejudice to the rights of any such person as is mentioned in paragraph (5), no employee of any such managers or governors shall be admitted to participate in the benefits of a superannuation fund by virtue of anything contained in an admission agreement continued in force as mentioned in paragraph (5).

(7) In this regulation—

"statutory undertakers" means a body authorised by any enactment to carry on any railway, light railway, tramway, road transport, water transport, canal, inland navigation, dock, harbour, pier, lighthouse or airport, or any undertaking for the supply of electricity, gas, hydraulic power or water;

"non-statutory undertakers" means a body who are primarily engaged in carrying on any railway, light railway, tramway, road transport, water transport, canal, inland navigation, dock, harbour, pier, lighthouse or airport

---

(a) 1946 c. 81.   (b) 1948 c. 29.   (c) 1958 c. 33.   (d) 1959 c. 72.

(e) 1968 c. 46.   (f) 1973 c. 32.   (g) 1965 c. 59.

undertaking, or any undertaking for the supply of electricity, gas, hydraulic power or water, though not authorised by any enactment to carry on such an undertaking;

"voluntary" means not carried on for profit and not provided by a local or public authority;

and any reference to an employee shall, in the case of the Housing Corporation, the Commission for the New Towns and the London Transport Executive, include a reference to a member of any such body.

Management of superannuation fund

B5. There shall be carried and credited in each year to every superannuation fund maintained under this Part—

(*a*) the amounts contributed during the year by pensionable employees entitled to participate in the benefits of the fund;

(*b*) the employer's contributions payable into the fund by employing authorities;

(*c*) all dividends and interest arising during the year out of the investment or use of the fund or any part thereof, and any capital moneys resulting from the realisation of investments, or from the repayment of moneys used temporarily for other authorised purposes;

(*d*) the amount of any additional contributory payments received by the administering authority under these regulations;

(*e*) any other sums which the administering authority may become liable to carry to the fund under these regulations.

Use and investment of superannuation fund's moneys

B6.—(1) If any moneys forming part of a superannuation fund maintained under this Part are not for the time being required to meet payments to be made out of the fund under these regulations, the administering authority shall invest the moneys and for that purpose the Trustee Investments Act 1961(**a**) shall apply subject to Schedule 2, or, in lieu of such investment may, subject to paragraph (2), use the moneys for any purpose for which they have a statutory borrowing power, or may lend the moneys to any other employing authority contributing to the fund for use for any purpose for which that authority have a statutory borrowing power, subject to the conditions specified in paragraph (3).

(2) An administering authority shall not under paragraph (1) use—

(*a*) any further moneys forming part of the superannuation fund maintained by them for any purpose for which they have a statutory borrowing power other than for the purpose of defraying expenses (including, if the administering authority is a local authority, those payable by them to meet the expenses of other local authorities) pending the receipt of revenues receivable by them in respect of the financial year in which those expenses are chargeable, so long as the aggregate amount for the time being not repaid of any moneys, which formed part of the superannuation fund the authority, or a body from whom a superannuation fund is by regulation J2 transferred to that authority, were maintaining immediately before the appointed day and which were used by that authority, or such a body, under section 21(3) of the Act of 1937, or a similar provision contained in a local Act or local Act scheme, for any purpose for which

(a) 1961 c. 62.

3b

the authority have on or after the appointed day a statutory borrowing power, equals or exceeds 25% of the value at cost for the time being of the fund maintained by that authority under this Part;

(b) any moneys for any such purpose, so as to bring the aggregate amount of all moneys so used by them to an amount which exceeds 25% of that value.

(3) The conditions mentioned in paragraph (1) shall be—

(a) interest shall be paid to the fund on any moneys used as mentioned in that paragraph and for the time being not repaid at such rate per cent. per annum as may be determined by the administering authority to be equal, as nearly as may be, to the rate of interest which would be payable on a loan raised on a mortgage under the statutory borrowing power; and

(b) the statutory borrowing power for the purpose of which the moneys are so used shall be deemed to be exercised by such use as fully in all respects as if a loan of the same amount had been raised in exercise of the power.

(4) Such costs, charges and expenses incurred by an administering authority in exercising the powers conferred upon them by paragraph (1) as may be determined by the authority may be paid out of the superannuation fund maintained by them under this Part.

Periodical valuation of superannuation fund

B7.—(1) Every administering authority shall obtain from an actuary, within the period specified in paragraph (2), an actuarial valuation—

(a) as at 1st April 1974, and

(b) as at 31st March 1979, and

(c) as at 31st March in each fifth year thereafter,

of the assets and liabilities of the superannuation fund maintained by them under this Part and a report thereon.

(2) The period referred to in paragraph (1) shall be the period of 21 months after the date as at which the superannuation fund maintained by an administering authority is, in accordance with the provisions of that paragraph, to be valued by an actuary or such extended period as the Secretary of State may allow.

(3) The administering authority shall, within 9 months after the date referred to in paragraph (2) or within such extended period as the Secretary of State may allow, furnish the actuary who is to consider the condition of the fund with such information as he may require.

(4) Forthwith upon receipt of any valuation or report under this regulation, an administering authority shall—

(a) send a copy thereof to the Secretary of State and copies thereof to all employing authorities (other than any magistrates' courts committee) interested in the superannuation fund maintained by the administering authority; and

(b) furnish to the Secretary of State a copy of the consolidated revenue account of the fund furnished to the actuary for the purposes of that valuation and report; and

(c) unless that report contains a summary of the assets of the fund as at the date when that valuation was made, send to the Secretary of State such a summary.

Actuary's certificates

B8.—(1) Every administering authority shall—

(*a*) as soon as is reasonably practicable after the appointed day obtain from an actuary; and

(*b*) as soon as is reasonably practicable after they obtain under regulation B7 an actuarial valuation of, and a report on, the assets and liabilities of the superannuation fund maintained by them under this Part, obtain from the actuary who made that valuation,

a certificate specifying—

(i) in respect of all the bodies interested in the superannuation fund maintained by that authority under this Part, the rate per cent. which in his opinion, taking into consideration where the certificate is required to be obtained under sub-paragraph (*a*) the matters mentioned in paragraph (2), the amount of the employer's contribution payable in each year of the period specified in paragraph (3) should bear to the total remuneration on which contributions will during that year be payable to that fund under regulation C1 or C2 by such a body's pensionable employees, so that such rate shall at all times be as nearly constant as may be and so that the fund shall be solvent, having regard to the then existing and prospective liabilities of the fund arising from circumstances common to all the bodies interested in the fund; and

(ii) in respect of any such body interested in the fund as may be named in the certificate, the amount (expressed as a rate per cent. or in money terms) by which in his opinion, taking into consideration, where the certificate is required to be obtained under sub-paragraph (*a*) the matters mentioned in paragraph (2), the amount of the employer's contribution should in any such year of the period mentioned in sub-paragraph (i) as is specified in the certificate be increased to take account of the then existing or prospective liabilities of the fund arising from circumstances peculiar to that body or be reduced to take account of the then existing or prospective benefits accruing to that fund arising from such circumstances.

(2) The matters referred to in paragraph (1)(i) and (ii) are the following matters—

(*a*) the last valuation (if any) under the Act of 1937 of the superannuation fund maintained under Part I of that Act by the administering authority and the last valuation under that Act of any superannuation fund transferred by regulation J2 to that authority; and

(*b*) the financial progression of each such fund as is mentioned in sub-paragraph (*a*) during the period beginning with the day following the date as at which that fund was last valued as therein mentioned and ending with the day immediately before the appointed day; and

(*c*) the termination under regulation J3 of the liability to pay equal annual charges; and

(*d*) the differences between the nature and scale of the benefits provided under these regulations and the nature and scale of the benefits provided under the former regulations.

(3) The period referred to in paragraph (1)(i) is—

(*a*) where the certificate is required to be obtained under paragraph (1)(*a*), the period of 2 years beginning with the appointed day;

(b) where the certificate is required to be obtained under paragraph (1)(b), the period of 5 years beginning—

    (i) where the actuarial valuation there mentioned was made as at 1st April 1974, with 1st April 1976;

    (ii) where the actuarial valuation was made at a date subsequent to 1st April 1974, with 1st April third following the date as at which that valuation was made.

(4) Forthwith upon receipt of any certificate under this regulation an administering authority shall send a copy thereof to the Secretary of State and copies thereof to all employing authorities (other than any magistrates' courts committee) interested in the superannuation fund maintained by the administering authority.

Accounts and audit

B9. As soon as may be after any audit of the superannuation fund maintained by them, every administering authority shall furnish to all employing authorities (other than any magistrates' courts committee) interested therein copies of the revenue account and balance sheet of the fund and of any report of the auditor on his audit of the fund.

PART C

CONTRIBUTIONS AND CERTAIN OTHER PAYMENTS TO SUPERANNUATION FUNDS

Payment and amount of employee's contributions

C1.—(1) Subject to the provisions of these regulations, a pensionable employee (not being a pensionable employee mentioned in paragraph (2)) of an employing authority shall, at such intervals as the administering authority may determine, contribute to the appropriate superannuation fund—

    (a) in the case of a manual worker, an amount equal to 5% of his remuneration under that employing authority;

    (b) in the case of an officer being a designated employee who, without a disqualifying break of service, is at any time a pensionable employee of an employing authority and is not a person who, before entering employment with that authority,—

        (i) has, on ceasing on or after the appointed day to hold another employment, become entitled (other than by virtue of paragraph (1)(c) of regulation E2) to benefits under these regulations; or

        (ii) has, on so ceasing, become entitled by virtue of that paragraph to benefits under these regulations and gives notice under paragraph (4)(e) of that regulation to that authority,

    an amount equal to 5% of such remuneration as aforesaid;

    (c) in the case of an officer (not being such an officer as is mentioned in sub-paragraph (b)) an amount equal to 6% of such remuneration as aforesaid.

(2) The reference in paragraph (1) to a pensionable employee mentioned in this paragraph is a reference to a pensionable employee who has completed not less than 45 years' reckonable service, disregarding reckonable service before attaining the age of 60 years beyond a total of 40 years.

Leave of absence from duty

C2. A pensionable employee of an employing authority who is on leave of absence from duty, otherwise than by reason of illness or injury, with reduced remuneration or without remuneration, shall—

    (*a*) for the period of 30 days beginning with the date on which he went on leave of absence; and

    (*b*) if he gives, or has given, notice in writing for the purpose to that employing authority not later than 30 days after the day before the date on which he went on leave of absence, for the period beginning with the day after the expiration of the period specified in sub-paragraph (*a*) and ending—

        (i) where the absence from duty is by reason of receiving full-time education or undergoing full-time training which will enable the employee to discharge his duties more efficiently, with the expiration of 36 months from the day before the date on which he went on leave of absence; and

        (ii) in any other case, with the expiration of 12 months from that day,

make contributions to the appropriate superannuation fund on such remuneration as he would have received during that period in his employment under that employing authority but for that leave of absence from duty.

Statement of remuneration received otherwise than from employing authority

C3. A pensionable employee who receives any part of his remuneration otherwise than from the employing authority shall render to that authority within one month after the first day of each financial half-year a written statement of his receipts in respect of that part of his remuneration during the preceding financial half-year and, if so requested in writing by the employing authority, as soon as is reasonably practicable after receipt of the request shall render to that authority a statutory declaration verifying the correctness of the statement.

Deduction from remuneration of employee's contributions and recovery thereof

C4. An employing authority may deduct from the remuneration payable by them to a pensionable employee the contributions payable by him under regulation C1 or C2 to the appropriate superannuation fund and, if and so far as deductions are not made from the remuneration of a pensionable employee, the appropriate administering authority may recover any contributions payable by him as a simple contract debt in any court of competent jurisdiction or may deduct any sum remaining due on account thereof from any payment by way of benefits under these regulations.

Employer's contributions

C5.—(1) An employing authority shall contribute to the appropriate superannuation fund—

    (*a*) in each year of the period specified in paragraph (3)(*a*) of regulation B8, a sum of an amount equal to the rate per cent. specified, in relation to the employer's contribution payable in each year of that period, in the certificate obtained under paragraph (1)(*a*) of that regulation by the appropriate administering authority, increased or, as the case may be, reduced by any such amount as is, in respect of the employing authority, specified in that certificate as the amount by which the employer's contribution should in that year be increased or, as the case may be, reduced;

(*b*) in each year of any period of 5 years mentioned in paragraph (3)(*b*) of regulation B8, a sum of an amount equal to the rate per cent. specified in relation to the employer's contribution payable in each year of that period, in the certificate obtained under paragraph (1)(*b*) of that regulation by the appropriate administering authority, increased or, as the case may be, reduced by any such amount as is, in respect of the employing authority, specified in that certificate as the amount by which the employer's contribution should in that year be increased or, as the case may be, reduced.

(2) An employing authority shall, during the period beginning with the appointed day and ending with the day immediately before the day on which such a certificate as is mentioned in paragraph (1)(*a*) is received by the appropriate administering authority, pay to the appropriate superannuation fund, at such intervals, not longer than 12 months, as the appropriate administering authority may determine, on account of the contributions payable by that employing authority under paragraph (1)(*a*), an amount equal to 130% of the sum which during that period has been contributed to the fund under regulation C1 or C2 by the employing authority's pensionable employees.

Employer's additional contributions

C6. Where a consent is given under regulation D10 in respect of an employee or was given under regulation 12 of the Benefits regulations in respect of an employee who is such a person as is mentioned in regulation D11, the employing authority shall be liable, so long as the employee remains in their employment, to contribute to the appropriate superannuation fund—

(*a*) contributions equal to the amount of the added period payments payable by the employee under that regulation; and

(*b*) contributions equal to any amounts by which, under the proviso to Schedule 6 or proviso (ii) to regulation 12(3) of the Benefits regulations, the amounts payable by the employee as aforesaid have been reduced.

Where the amounts payable by an employee have been reduced as aforesaid or an employee is required by Schedule 4 to satisfy his liability in respect of the excess over 15% by payment in the manner therein mentioned, the amounts payable by the employing authority in respect of their liability under paragraph (*a*) shall be amounts equal to those which would have been payable by the employee but for the reduction or the requirements of that schedule.

Employer's further payments

C7. Where an employing authority have—

(*a*) made a determination under regulation D4; or

(*b*) passed a resolution under regulation D9 or D14; or

(*c*) granted an additional benefit under regulation E13;

any extra charge on the appropriate superannuation fund resulting from that determination or resolution or, as the case may be, the amount of that additional benefit shall be repaid to the fund by that authority.

Return of employee's contributions in certain cases

C8.—(1) This regulation shall apply to a pensionable employee of an employing authority—

(*a*) who before becoming entitled to any benefit under these regulations ceases to be employed by that authority; and

(b) whose remuneration on which contributions were paid under regulation C1 or C2, or under Part I of the Act of 1937 or under a local Act scheme, or were paid under some other superannuation scheme in respect of service or employment which became, by virtue of interchange rules, reckonable for the purposes of the former regulations, has not at any time exceeded the annual rate of £5,000.

(2) A person to whom this regulation applies who—

(a) is entitled to reckon an aggregate of less than 5 years' reckonable service and qualifying service; or

(b) is entitled to reckon an aggregate of not less than 5 years' reckonable service and qualifying service and elects that this paragraph shall apply in his case by notice in writing given to the appropriate administering authority within 12 months after the date on which he ceases to be employed as mentioned in paragraph (1)(a),

shall be entitled—

(i) if he so ceases to be employed for any reason other than his voluntary resignation, or his resignation or dismissal in consequence of inefficiency or an offence of a fraudulent character or misconduct, to receive out of the appropriate superannuation fund a sum equal to the aggregate amount of his contributions to the fund, together with compound interest thereon, calculated, to the date on which he ceased to hold his employment, for any period before 1st April 1972, at the rate of 3% per annum with half-yearly rests on 31st March and 30th September and, for any period after 31st March 1972, at the rate of 4% per annum with yearly rests on 31st March;

(ii) if he so ceases to be employed by reason of his voluntary resignation, or his resignation or dismissal in consequence of inefficiency or an offence of a fraudulent character or misconduct (not being such an offence or grave misconduct in connection with the duties of, or otherwise in relation to, his employment) to receive out of the appropriate superannuation fund a sum equal to the aggregate amount of his contributions to the fund.

(3) Where a person to whom this regulation applies ceases to be employed as mentioned in paragraph (1)(a) in consequence of an offence of a fraudulent character or of grave misconduct, being such an offence or such misconduct in connection with the performance of the duties of, or otherwise in relation to, his employment, the employing authority may, if they think fit, direct the return to him out of the appropriate superannuation fund of a sum equal to the whole or a part of the aggregate amount of his contributions to the fund or, if he so ceases to be employed in consequence of such an offence of a fraudulent character as aforesaid, the payment out of that fund of an equivalent sum to his spouse or any dependant of his.

(4) Notwithstanding anything in the foregoing provisions of this regulation, no payment shall be made thereunder to a person who, having ceased to be employed by the employing authority in the circumstances mentioned in regulation E2(1)(c) and before giving a notice under paragraph (2)(b), again becomes a pensionable employee and gives notice under regulation E2(4)(e).

(5) An administering authority shall not make any payment under paragraph (2) to such a person as is mentioned in sub-paragraph (a) of that paragraph before the expiration of a year from the date on which that person ceases to be employed or until a claim for payment has been made to them, whichever event first occurs.

(6) On making any repayment of contributions (with or without interest) under this regulation, the administering authority shall deduct from the repayment any tax to which they may become chargeable under paragraph 2 of Part II of Schedule 5 to the Finance Act 1970(a) (which relates to charge to tax on repayment of employee's contributions).

(7) For the purposes of this regulation a pensionable employee who ceases to be employed in the circumstances mentioned in regulation E2(1)(c) (other than a person who elects under regulation E2(4)(a)(iv) to receive benefits from the date on which he so ceased or to whom, on so ceasing, regulation E2(4)(ii) applies), shall be treated as not being entitled to any benefit under these regulations.

(8) In this regulation, references to the aggregate amount of an employee's contributions to a superannuation fund include references to—

    (a) any contributions paid by him to any superannuation fund under regulation C1 or C2, or under Part I of the Act of 1937, or under the Act of 1922 or under a local Act scheme;

    (b) any contributions which, if the former regulations had not been revoked by these regulations and he had immediately before ceasing to be employed as mentioned in paragraph (1)(a) been a contributory employee, he would, by virtue of interchange rules, have been deemed to have made to the appropriate superannuation fund within the meaning of the Act of 1937;

    (c) any amount—

        (i) which, if the former regulations had not been revoked as aforesaid and he had immediately before so ceasing been a contributory employee, would, by virtue of interchange rules, have been included in any amount which would, on his so ceasing, have become payable to him by way of a return of contributions under section 10 of the Act of 1937; or

        (ii) by which, if the former regulations had not been revoked as aforesaid and he had immediately before so ceasing been a contributory employee, the last-mentioned amount would, by virtue of interchange rules, have been deemed to have been increased;

    (d) any sum paid by him into a superannuation fund under an old modification scheme;

    (e) any sum paid by him by way of additional contributory payments; and

    (f) any amount paid by him by way of added period payments, but only in so far as any such contribution, sum or amount—

        (i) has not been returned to the person or, if it has been returned, has subsequently been repaid by him;

        (ii) is attributable to service which might have been reckoned under Part D in relation to the employment he has ceased to hold; and

        (iii) is not attributable to any earlier period of service in respect of which a benefit under Part E has been paid.

Reduction of returned contributions following payment in lieu of contributions

C9.—(1) Subject to the provisions of this regulation, where a pensionable employee leaves employment in circumstances in which returned contributions are due and a payment in lieu of contributions has previously been

---

(a) 1970 c. 24.

made in respect of him in circumstances in which returned contributions were not due, those returned contributions shall be reduced by a sum equal to the amount, or the aggregate of the amounts, by which under section 60(5) of the Insurance Act (which defines an employer's rights against an insured person in respect of payments in lieu of contributions) they could have been reduced if returned at the time when the previous payment in lieu of contributions was made.

(2) Paragraph (1) shall also apply for the reduction of returned contributions where a payment in lieu of contributions has been made under any insurance code in respect of any period of former employment which is reckonable as service as a pensionable employee if—

(a) that payment in lieu was made in circumstances not involving the return of any superannuation contributions made by him in that employment; and

(b) the transfer value payable in respect of that employment has been adjusted to take account of that payment in lieu,

and where no superannuation contributions were payable in that employment, any amount returnable in respect of contributions deemed to have been made therein shall be reduced by a sum equal to one half of that payment in lieu.

(3) No payment in lieu of contributions shall be taken into account for the purposes of this regulation—

(a) on more than one occasion; or

(b) if the payment is one which has been reduced under regulation 13 of the National Insurance (Non-participation—Assurance of Equivalent Pension Benefits) Regulations 1960(a) or any corresponding enactment in force in Northern Ireland or the Isle of Man.

(4) Where returned contributions are due in the circumstances mentioned in paragraph (1) on the cessation of two or more concurrently held employments, the reduction required by that paragraph shall be made by such one of the authorities paying the returned contributions as they may agree or, in default of agreement, as is determined by the Secretary of State, and where those employments were held under the same employing authority, the reduction shall be made in relation to such one only of the employments as is determined by the authority.

(5) Where returned contributions are reduced under paragraph (1) or under section 60(5) of the Insurance Act or any corresponding provision of the Northern Ireland Act or the Isle of Man Act, any sum so deducted shall not form part of any amount payable to or in respect of him, either as returned contributions or as a benefit ascertained by reference to the amount of the contributions paid by him, on the occasion of any later cessation of his employment.

(6) In this regulation "returned contributions" means an amount payable under regulation C8 to or in respect of a pensionable employee by way of a return of contributions.

(a) S.I. 1960/1103 (1960 II, p. 2244).

PART D

SERVICE

Reckonable service

D1.—(1) Subject to paragraph (2) and regulation D3, a pensionable employee shall be entitled to reckon as reckonable service, in relation to the employment in respect of which he is a pensionable employee—

(a) service on or after the appointed day in respect of which he has made or is deemed to have made the contributions required by these regulations;

(b) in the case of a person who became a pensionable employee on the appointed day, any service, employment or period which immediately before the appointed day he was, or for the purposes of these regulations is treated as having been, entitled under or by virtue of the former regulations or any other enactment, or would have been entitled upon payment of the amount mentioned in the proviso to section 13(1) of the Act of 1937 or repayment of the sum mentioned in subsection (2) of that section, to reckon as or aggregate with the service he was entitled to reckon as contributing service in relation to that employment or non-contributing service for the purposes of the former regulations;

(c) in the case of a person who became a pensionable employee on the appointed day by virtue of regulations A7(a) and B2(1)(c), any service, employment or period which immediately before the appointed day he was, or for the purposes of these regulations is treated as having been, entitled under or by virtue of the former regulations or any other enactment to reckon as or aggregate with service he was entitled to reckon as contributing service in relation to the whole-time employment mentioned in regulation A7(a) or non-contributing service for the purposes of the former regulations;

(d) in the case of a person who was a contributory employee under a scheduled body or a former local authority, ceased to be employed by that body or authority before the appointed day and on or after that day but within 12 months of so ceasing becomes a pensionable employee, any service, employment or period which immediately before he ceased to be employed by them he was, or for the purposes of these regulations is treated as having been, entitled under or by virtue of the former regulations or any other enactment to reckon as or aggregate with service he was entitled to reckon as contributing service in relation to his employment under that body or authority or non-contributing service for the purposes of the former regulations;

(e) in the case of a person who before the appointed day was a local Act contributor under a local authority or other body, ceased to be employed by that authority or body before the appointed day and on or after that day but within 12 months of so ceasing becomes a pensionable employee, any service, employment or period which he would have been entitled to reckon as service or a period of contribution for the purpose of calculating a benefit payable to him under the local Act scheme if at the date when he ceased to be employed by that authority or body he had been entitled to a benefit payable under that scheme;

(f) any employment which by virtue of regulation D4 is, in relation to the employment in which he is a pensionable employee, to be treated for the purposes of these regulations as service which immediately before the appointed day or, as the case may be, ceasing to be employed as mentioned in paragraph (*d*) he was entitled to reckon or, as the case may be, which he would have been entitled to reckon as non-contributing service for the purposes of the former regulations; and

(*g*) any other service or period which under or by virtue of regulation D10, D11, D12, D13 or D14 is, in relation to that employment, to be reckoned as reckonable service.

(2) In the case of a pensionable employee who—

(*a*) is such a person as is mentioned in paragraph (1)(*b*), (*d*) or (*e*); and

(*b*) if the former regulations had not been revoked by these regulations, would in the employment in respect of which he is a pensionable employee have been a contributory employee and would only have been entitled in relation to that employment to reckon under section 12(2) or 13 of the Act of 1937 previous service upon payment of the amount mentioned in the proviso to subsection (1) of the said section 13 or upon repayment of the sum mentioned in subsection (2) of that section,

then, unless he is such a person as is mentioned in paragraph (1)(*b*) and before the appointed day paid that amount or, as the case may be, that sum, he shall only be entitled to reckon such previous service as reckonable service if, within 12 months after the appointed day or within 3 months after he becomes a pensionable employee, whichever is the later, he pays that amount or, as the case may be, repays that sum to the appropriate administering authority.

Qualifying service

D2. Subject to regulation D3, a pensionable employee shall be entitled to reckon as qualifying service—

(*a*) in the case of a person who became a pensionable employee on the appointed day, any service, employment or period which immediately before the appointed day he was entitled under or by virtue of the former regulations or any other enactment to reckon for the purpose of determining whether he was entitled to a benefit under the former regulations, but for no other purpose;

(*b*) in the case of a person who was a contributory employee under a scheduled body or former local authority, ceased to be employed by that body or authority before the appointed day and on or after that day but within 12 months of so ceasing becomes a pensionable employee, any service, employment or period which immediately before he so ceased he was entitled under or by virtue of the former regulations or any other enactment to reckon for the purpose of determining whether he was, in relation to that employment, entitled to receive a benefit under the former regulations, but for no other purpose;

(*c*) in the case of a person who before the appointed day was a local Act contributor under a local authority or other body, ceased to be employed by that authority or body before the appointed day and on or after that day but within 12 months of so ceasing becomes a pensionable employee, any service, employment or period which immediately before he so ceased he was entitled to reckon for the purpose of determining whether he was entitled to receive a benefit under the local Act scheme, but for no other purpose; and

(*d*) any other service, employment or period which by virtue of regulation D15 or D16 is to be reckoned as qualifying service.

Exclusion from reckonable service and qualifying service

D3.—(1) Subject to regulation E16, a pensionable employee shall not be entitled to reckon as reckonable service—

    (*a*) where he has entered the employment of a scheduled body or former local authority—

        (i) after becoming entitled to receive payment of or payments in respect of any superannuation benefit, under Part E or otherwise, other than a superannuation benefit under the Insurance Act; or

        (ii) after becoming entitled to a benefit under paragraph (1)(*c*) of regulation E2, if he gives notice under paragraph (4)(*e*) of that regulation; or

    (*b*) where, by virtue of regulation K1—

        (i) he becomes entitled to receive payment of or payments in respect of any benefit under these regulations; or

        (ii) he becomes entitled to a benefit under paragraph (1)(*c*) of regulation E2 and gives notice under paragraph (4)(*e*) of that regulation,

any service, employment or period of which account has been taken for the purpose of determining whether he was entitled to that benefit or has been, or is to be, taken for the purpose of calculating the amount of that benefit.

(2) A pensionable employee shall not be entitled to reckon as reckonable service or qualifying service—

    (*a*) any service, employment or period in respect of which he has received a return of contributions under these regulations; or

    (*b*) where before entering the employment in respect of which he is a pensionable employee he was previously a pensionable employee under a scheduled body, or a contributory employee under a scheduled body or former local authority or a local Act contributor under a local authority or other body and ceased to be a pensionable employee, contributory employee or local Act contributor, as the case may be, under that body or authority in such circumstances that a transfer value was paid by the body or authority maintaining the superannuation fund in the benefits of which he was as such an employee or contributor entitled to participate to some body or person (other than an administering authority, or a body or authority maintaining a superannuation fund under Part I of the Act of 1937 or a local Act authority), any service, employment or period in respect of which that transfer value was paid.

Previous employment under an officer

D4.—(1) This regulation shall apply to a pensionable employee who—

    (*a*) has been for a period before the appointed day in previous employment and subsequently entered before that day the employment of a scheduled body or former local authority;

    (*b*) either—

        (i) was a contributory employee immediately before the appointed day and became a pensionable employee on that day; or

        (ii) was a contributory employee under a scheduled body or former local authority, ceased to be employed by that body or authority before the appointed day and on or after that day, but within 12 months of so ceasing, becomes a pensionable employee; and

    (*c*) is not such a person as is mentioned in regulation K1(1).

(2) The appropriate employing authority may, if application for the purpose is made to them in writing by a person to whom this regulation applies within 12 months after the date on which he first becomes a pensionable employee, within 12 months after receipt of the application determine that for the purposes of these regulations the whole or part of the period of previous employment shall, in relation to his employment under them, be treated as service which immediately before the appointed day or, as the case may be, ceasing to be employed as mentioned in paragraph (1)(b)(ii) he was entitled to reckon as non-contributing service for the purposes of the former regulations.

(3) In this regulation—

(a) "appropriate employing authority" means—

(i) in the case of a person to whom paragraph (1)(b)(i) applies, the employing authority under whom that person was a pensionable employee on the appointed day; or

(ii) in the case of a person to whom paragraph (1)(b)(ii) applies, the body or authority mentioned in that paragraph; and

(b) "previous employment", in relation to a person, means employment before the appointed day under an officer of a scheduled body or former local authority, being employment in which he was engaged wholly or mainly in the performance of duties relating to the functions of that body, and includes, in the case of a person who has been in such employment and left that employment in order—

(i) to become a person under training within the meaning of the Military Training (Consequential Provisions) Order 1939(a); or

(ii) to enter upon war service; or

(iii) to enter upon national service (other than such service as is mentioned in sub-paragraph (b)(i)),

in the case of such a person as is mentioned in sub-paragraph (b)(i), his period of training within the meaning of the order there mentioned and, in any other case, the service mentioned in sub-paragraph (b)(ii) or, as the case may be, sub-paragraph (b)(iii), but does not include, in a case where a determination was made in pursuance of section 12(6) of the Act of 1937 or section 7(3) of the Act of 1953, any service, employment or period reckonable by virtue of that determination as non-contributing service for the purposes of the former regulations.

Treatment of certain contributing service as non-contributing service

D5.—(1) This regulation shall apply to a pensionable employee who—

(a) either—

(i) was a contributory employee immediately before the appointed day and became a pensionable employee on that day; or

(ii) was a contributory employee under a scheduled body or former local authority, ceased to be employed by that body or authority before the appointed day and on or after that day, but within 12 months of so ceasing, becomes a pensionable employee;

(b) became a contributory employee before 1st October 1954;

(c) was entitled to the benefit of section 13(1)(b) of the Act of 1937;

(a) S.R. & O. 1939, 718 (Rev. XVI, p 583: 1939 II, p. 2064).

(*d*) from the day on which he so became a contributory employee until immediately before the appointed day or, as the case may be, he ceased to be employed as mentioned in sub-paragraph (*a*)(ii), remained a contributory employee; and

(*e*) is not such a person as is mentioned in regulation K1(1).

(2) For the purposes of these regulations any service of a person to whom this regulation applies which immediately before the appointed day or, as the case may be, the day on which he ceased to be employed as mentioned in paragraph (1)(*a*)(ii), he was, by virtue of regulation 3(*b*) of the Local Government Superannuation (Reckoning of Service on Transfer) Regulations 1939(a), entitled to reckon as contributing service for the purposes of the former regulations in relation to the employment in respect of which he was a contributory employee shall, subject to regulations D6, D7 and D9, be treated as service which immediately before the appointed day or so ceasing he was entitled to reckon as non-contributing service for the purposes of the former regulations.

Non-contributing service treated as contributing service on payment of additional contributory payments

D6.—(1) This regulation shall apply to a pensionable employee who—
(*a*) either—
   (i) became a contributory employee within the period of 3 months before the appointed day; or
   (ii) having become a contributory employee before the commencement of that period, did not before the commencement of that period receive a notification of the decision of the scheduled body or former local authority under whom he was a contributory employee, required to be given under regulations made under section 36(6) of the Act of 1937, that he was a contributory employee or that he was entitled to reckon a period of employment as non-contributing service, as the case may be, or where he appealed, notification of the decision of the Secretary of State thereon;
(*b*) from the day on which he so became a contributory employee until immediately before the appointed day remained a contributory employee; and
(*c*) became a pensionable employee on the appointed day.

(2) If a person to whom this regulation applies, within 12 months after the appointed day, gives notice in writing to the employing authority that he intends to make a payment for the purpose, he shall, if he pays a sum calculated in the manner provided in Part I of Schedule 3, be entitled, in relation to the employment in respect of which the payment is made, to have the whole or part of any service, employment or period which—
(*a*) he is entitled to reckon as reckonable service by virtue of regulation D1(1)(*b*); and
(*b*) is service, employment or a period which immediately before the appointed day he was entitled to reckon as non-contributing service for the purposes of the former regulations,
treated for the purposes of these regulations as service, employment or a period which immediately before that day he was entitled to reckon as contributing service for the purposes of the former regulations in relation to that employment.

(a) S.R. & O. 1939 55 (Rev. XVII, p. 829: 1939 II, p. 2584).

(3) Any such sum may be paid upon the employee giving notice in writing under paragraph (2), in such manner (whether by a lump sum or instalments or partly in one way and partly in the other) and at such times as may be agreed between the employee and the employing authority, subject however to Part II of Schedule 3.

(4) Any amount payable by an employee under this regulation shall be paid to the employing authority and on receipt by the employing authority shall be paid by them to the appropriate administering authority.

Previous employment treated under regulation D4 or service treated under regulation D5 as non-contributing service to be treated as contributing service on payment of additional contributory payments

D7.—(1) If a pensionable employee, within 12 months of a notification under regulation L4 of a determination under regulation D4, gives notice in writing to the employing authority that he intends to make a payment for the purpose, he shall, if he pays a sum calculated in the manner provided in Part I of Schedule 3, be entitled, in relation to the employment in respect of which the payment is made, to have the whole or part of any service, employment or period which—

(a) he is entitled to reckon as reckonable service; and

(b) is treated under regulation D4 as service which immediately before the appointed day or, as the case may be, ceasing to be employed before that day he was entitled to reckon as non-contributing service for the purposes of the former regulations,

treated for the purposes of these regulations as service, employment or a period which immediately before that day or so ceasing he was entitled to reckon as contributing service for the purposes of the former regulations in relation to that employment.

(2) If a pensionable employee, within 12 months of a notification under regulation L4, gives notice in writing to the employing authority that he intends to make a payment for the purpose, he shall, if he pays a sum calculated in the manner provided in Part I of Schedule 3, be entitled, in relation to the employment in respect of which the payment is made, to have the whole or part of any service which—

(a) he is entitled to reckon as reckonable service; and

(b) is treated under regulation D5 as service which immediately before the appointed day or, as the case may be, ceasing to be employed before that day he was entitled to reckon as non-contributing service for the purposes of the former regulations,

treated for the purposes of these regulations as service which immediately before that day or so ceasing he was entitled to reckon as contributing service for the purposes of the former regulations in relation to that employment.

(3) Any such sum as is mentioned in paragraph (1) or (2) may be paid, upon the employee giving notice in writing under paragraph (1) or, as the case may be, paragraph (2) in such manner (whether by a lump sum or instalments or partly in one way and partly in the other) and at such times as may be agreed between the employee and the employing authority, subject however to Part II of Schedule 3.

(4) Any amount payable by an employee under this regulation shall be paid to the employing authority and on receipt by the employing authority shall be paid by them to the appropriate administering authority.

Continuation of additional contributory payments commenced under the former regulations

D8. Where immediately before the appointed day a person, in pursuance of section 2(3) of the Act of 1953, was in the process of paying any sum wholly or partly by instalments under Schedule 2 to the Benefits regulations, the outstanding instalments shall be deemed to be instalments of an amount payable under regulation D6.

Non-contributing service treated at discretion of employing authority as contributing service

D9. The employing authority under whom a person (not being such a person as is mentioned in regulation K1(1)) first became a pensionable employee may, at any time within 12 months after the appointed day, resolve that the whole or a specified part of any service, employment or period which—

(a) that person is entitled to reckon as reckonable service by virtue of regulation D1(1)(b), (c) or (d); and

(b) is, or is treated under regulation D4 or D5 as, service which immediately before the appointed day or, as the case may be, ceasing to be employed before that day, he was entitled to reckon or, as the case may be, which he would have been entitled to reckon, as non-contributing service for the purposes of the former regulations,

shall, in relation to his employment under them, be treated for the purposes of these regulations as service which immediately before that day or, as the case may be, so ceasing, he was entitled to reckon or, as the case may be, which he would have been entitled to reckon, as contributing service for the purposes of the former regulations in relation to the employment in respect of which he was a contributory employee.

Added years reckonable on payment as reckonable service

D10.—(1) This regulation shall apply to a pensionable employee who—

(a) either—

(i) was a contributory employee immediately before the appointed day and became a pensionable employee on that day; or

(ii) was a contributory employee under a scheduled body or former local authority, ceased to be employed by that body or authority before the appointed day and on or after that day, but within 12 months of so ceasing, becomes a pensionable employee;

(b) at the time of his first becoming a contributory employee (or, if he had previously become a designated employee or local Act contributor, at the time of his first becoming such an employee or contributor) had reached the age of 25 years but was not over the age of 35 years; and

(c) for the efficient discharge of his duties in the employment in which he was a contributory employee was required to possess such professional or other qualifications and possessed such qualifications which he had not acquired during employment with a scheduled body or former local authority.

(2) If application for the purpose is made in writing by a person to whom this regulation applies, within 12 months after the date on which he first becomes a pensionable employee, to the employing authority under whom he was a pensionable employee on the appointed day or, as the case may be, the day on which he first became a pensionable employee after the appointed day and the employing authority within 12 months after receipt of the application

in their discretion consent to the reckoning of a number of years, not exceeding the number of years determined in accordance with paragraph (3), as reckonable service, he shall, in relation to his employment under that authority, be entitled to reckon, if he completes payments under this regulation, the number of years in respect of which the employing authority gave their consent under this paragraph and, in any other case, such an additional period (if any) as is determined in accordance with Schedule 5, as reckonable service.

(3) The number of years reckonable under this regulation shall not exceed the number of years by which the age of the pensionable employee at the time of his first becoming a contributory employee, designated employee or local Act contributor, as the case may be, exceeds the age of 20 years, or 10 years, whichever is the less.

(4) The amount payable by an employee in respect of whom such a consent as is mentioned in paragraph (2) has been given shall, in respect of each year of the period in respect of which that consent was given, be calculated in accordance with Schedule 6 and shall, subject to Schedule 4, be paid by way of additional contributions to the appropriate superannuation fund, at such intervals as the administering authority may determine.

(5) The provisions of regulation C4 shall apply in relation to any amount payable by an employee under this regulation as they apply in relation to contributions payable by a pensionable employee under regulation C1.

Continuation of payments for added years commenced under the former regulations

D11. Where immediately before the appointed day a person was in the process of making payments under regulation 12 of the Benefits regulations, the outstanding payments shall be deemed to be payments of an amount payable under regulation D10.

Increase of reckonable service on lump sum payment

D12.—(1) If a pensionable employee (not being a pensionable employee mentioned in paragraph (2)) elects, by notice in writing given to the appropriate administering authority within 12 months after the date on which he first became a pensionable employee, to make a payment to the appropriate superannuation fund in order to be entitled to reckon an additional period, not exceeding the maximum length determined in accordance with Schedule 7, as reckonable service he shall, if he pays by a lump sum to that fund an amount calculated in accordance with Part I of Schedule 8 within the period of 12 months referred to above, be entitled, in relation to the employment in respect of which he is a pensionable employee, to reckon that additional period as reckonable service.

(2) The reference in paragraph (1) to a pensionable employee mentioned in this paragraph is a reference to—

(a) a pensionable employee who, on first becoming a pensionable employee, had attained the age of 59 years; or

(b) a pensionable employee who—

   (i) is such a person as is mentioned in paragraph (1)(a) of regulation E19; and

   (ii) was entitled as mentioned in paragraph (1)(b)(i) of that regulation; and

   (iii) has not made on election under paragraph (2) of that regulation.

Increase of reckonable service on the making of periodical payments

D13.—(1) A pensionable employee (not being a pensionable employee mentioned in paragraph (5)) may, by notice in writing to the appropriate administering authority, elect to make payments to the appropriate superannuation fund in order to be entitled, in relation to the employment in respect of which he is a pensionable employee, to reckon an additional period, not exceeding the maximum length determined in accordance with Schedule 7, as reckonable service.

Where the appropriate administering authority are not the employing authority, the employee shall, when giving a notice under this paragraph, send a copy of that notice to the employing authority.

(2) The amount payable by an employee who has made an election under this regulation shall be calculated and paid in accordance with Part II of Schedule 8 and shall, subject to Schedule 4, be paid by way of additional contributions to the appropriate superannuation fund, at such intervals as the administering authority may determine, which contributions shall commence to be payable on the employee's birthday next following the day on which the election is made under this regulation and shall cease to be payable on the day immediately before the birthday of the employee at which or, as the case may be, the birthday immediately preceding the date at which he would become entitled by virtue of regulation E2(1)(*a*) or (*b*)(ii), if he then ceased to be employed, to a retirement pension.

(3) An employee who has completed payments under this regulation shall be entitled, in relation to the employment mentioned in paragraph (1), to reckon the additional period in respect of which those payments were made as reckonable service and an employee who is in the course of making payments under this regulation shall be entitled to reckon such additional period (if any) as is determined in accordance with Schedule 5 as reckonable service.

(4) The provisions of regulation C4 shall apply in relation to any amount payable by an employee under this regulation as they apply in relation to contributions payable by a pensionable employee under regulation C1.

(5) The reference in paragraph (1) to a pensionable employee mentioned in this paragraph is a reference to—

(*a*) a pensionable employee who has attained the age of 59 years; or

(*b*) such a pensionable employee as is mentioned in regulation D12(2)(*b*).

Increase of reckonable service at discretion of employing authority in the case of certain late entrants

D14.—(1) Subject to paragraph (2), where a person enters the employment of a scheduled body or has been offered an employment under such a body and is, or will be, in that employment a pensionable employee under that body, the scheduled body may, if satisfied that, having regard to the interests of the efficient exercise of their functions, there are exceptional reasons for so doing, not later than 6 months after the person enters their employment, resolve that he shall be entitled, in relation to that employment, to reckon an additional period, not exceeding the maximum length determined in accordance with Schedule 7, as reckonable service and in that case the person shall be entitled to reckon such an additional period as is determined in accordance with paragraph (3).

(2) A scheduled body may not pass a resolution under this regulation in respect of a person who at the time of his entering the employment under them mentioned in paragraph (1) or of the resolution there mentioned, whichever is the earlier, has attained the age of 59 years.

(3) A pensionable employee who remains in the employment of the employing authority by whom a resolution in respect of him was passed under this regulation until he attains the earliest age at which he is entitled by virtue of regulation E2(1)(a) or (b)(ii) to benefits under these regulations shall be entitled to reckon the additional period specified in that resolution as reckonable service and a pensionable employee who leaves the employment of that authority before he attains that age shall be entitled to reckon as reckonable service such an additional period as is determined in accordance with the following formula, namely:—

$$\frac{A \times T}{R}$$

where

A is the length of the additional period specified in the resolution under this regulation;

T is the period during which the employee has been in the employment of the authority who passed that resolution; and

R is the period during which the employee would have been in the employment of that authority had he remained in their employment until attaining the earliest age at which he would have become entitled by virtue of regulation E2(1)(a) or (b)(ii) to benefits under these regulations.

Previous service of certain variable-time employees

D15.—(1) This regulation shall apply to a person who—

(a) on or after the appointed day becomes or has become a variable-time employee of a scheduled body, other than by virtue of regulation A7(a);

(b) is in that employment a pensionable employee; and

(c) on the day on which he entered that employment or, if in that employment he did not become a pensionable employee on that day, during the period beginning with that day and ending with the day on which he became in that employment a pensionable employee, was a whole-time employee of a scheduled body and was in that whole-time employment a pensionable employee.

(2) A person to whom this regulation applies shall be entitled to reckon as qualifying service, in relation to the variable-time employment mentioned in paragraph (1), any service, employment or period which on the day on which he became in that employment a pensionable employee he was entitled to reckon as reckonable service or qualifying service in relation to the whole-time employment mentioned in paragraph (1)(c).

Previous service of certain re-employed pensioners

D16.—(1) Where a person—

(a) either—

(i) has become entitled to a retirement pension and has entered further employment with any scheduled body or former local authority or enters further employment with any scheduled body; or

> (ii) is in receipt of a pension payable out of public funds or under a local Act scheme, enters the employment of any scheduled body and his pension is on that account liable to be reduced or suspended; and

(*b*) is in his new employment a pensionable employee,

then, on ceasing to hold that employment, he shall be entitled to reckon as qualifying service any service, employment or period in respect of which he became entitled to the retirement pension or, as the case may be, the pension referred to in sub-paragraph (*a*)(ii) was granted.

(2) For the purposes of this regulation "retirement pension" includes a superannuation allowance under Part I of the Act of 1937 and an annual pension under the former regulations.

Calculation of part-time service

D17. For the purpose of calculating the amount of any benefit under these regulations which is or will become payable to or in respect of a pensionable employee who has served as a part-time employee, the period of part-time service shall be treated as though it were whole-time service for a proportionately reduced period.

Counting of non-contributing service

D18.—(1) For the purposes of these regulations (other than for a purpose mentioned in paragraph (3)) any reckonable service of a pensionable employee which is, or is treated under these regulations as, service, employment or a period which immediately before the appointed day or, as the case may be, ceasing to be employed he was entitled to reckon as non-contributing service for the purposes of the former regulations shall be counted at half its length unless and until it is treated under or by virtue of regulation D6, D7 or D9 as service, employment or a period which immediately before the appointed day or, as the case may be, ceasing to be employed he was entitled to reckon as contributing service for the purposes of the former regulations.

(2) Where any part of a period of part-time service of a pensionable employee reduced under regulation D17 was non-contributing service, for the purpose of calculating the amount of any benefit under these regulations which is or will become payable to or in respect of him this regulation shall apply to that part as reduced under regulation D17.

(3) The purposes mentioned in paragraph (1) are the following purposes:—

(*a*) determining whether a pensionable employee is entitled to a benefit under these regulations or any such benefit is payable in respect of him; and

(*b*) reckoning the period of reckonable service a pensionable employee would be entitled to reckon as mentioned in paragraph 1 of Schedule 7, in a case where he gave a notice under Schedule 2 to the Benefits regulations or he gave a notice under regulation D6 or D7 before the date on which he gives a notice under regulation D12 or D13 or, as the case may be, the date on which the resolution is passed under regulation D14.

Disregard of certain reckonable service in determining entitlement to benefits

D19. For the purpose of determining whether a pensionable employee is entitled to a benefit under these regulations or any such benefit is payable in respect of him, no account shall be taken of—

(a) any added years;

(b) any additional period reckonable as reckonable service under regulation D12 or D13;

(c) any additional period reckonable as reckonable service at the discretion of the employing authority under regulation D14;

(d) any other period which on entering an employment before the appointed day in which he was a contributory employee he became entitled, by virtue of interchange rules, to reckon as or aggregate with service for the purpose of calculating the amount of any benefit under the former regulations, but for no other purpose.

Counting of certain reckonable service and qualifying service in determining entitlement to benefits

D20. For the purpose of determining whether a pensionable employee is entitled to a benefit under these regulations or any such benefit is payable in respect of him, any reckonable service and qualifying service of his which—

(a) if he became a pensionable employee on the appointed day, was service, employment or a period which immediately before that day he was entitled under or by virtue of the former regulations or any other enactment to reckon for the purpose of determining whether he was entitled to receive a benefit under the former regulations; or

(b) if he was a contributory employee, ceased before the appointed day to be subject to the former regulations but, on or after the appointed day and within 12 months of so ceasing, becomes a pensionable employee, was service, employment or a period which immediately before he so ceased to be employed he was entitled under or by virtue of the former regulations or any other enactment to reckon for the purpose referred to in paragraph (a),

shall be counted at the same length as it would have been counted for the purpose of determining whether he was entitled to receive a benefit under the former regulations.

Disregard of certain reckonable service in calculating the amount of any benefit

D21.—(1) For the purpose of calculating the amount of any benefit under these regulations which is or will become payable to or in respect of a pensionable employee, no account shall be taken of any period of his reckonable service by which that period, together with—

(a) any period of reckonable service which was taken into account in the calculation of a retirement pension; and

(b) any service and any period in respect of which any pension was granted under a local Act scheme,

exceeds 45 years, disregarding reckonable service before attaining the age of 60 years beyond a total of 40 years.

(2) In this regulation—

"retirement pension" includes a superannuation allowance under Part I of the Act of 1937 and an annual pension under the former regulations; and

"reckonable service" includes any period by reference to which an additional benefit has been granted under regulation E13.

Counting of certain reckonable service in calculating the amount of any benefit

D22. For the purpose of calculating the amount of any benefit under these regulations—

(*a*) any reckonable service of an employee which—

(i) if he became a pensionable employee on the appointed day, was service, employment or a period which immediately before that day he was entitled under or by virtue of the former regulations or any other enactment to reckon as or aggregate with contributing service for the purposes of the former regulations;

(ii) if he was a contributory employee, ceased before the appointed day to be subject to the former regulations but, on or after the appointed day and within 12 months of so ceasing, becomes a pensionable employee, was service, employment or a period which immediately before he so ceased he was entitled under or by virtue of the former regulations or any other enactment to reckon as or aggregate with contributing service for the purposes of the former regulations,

shall be counted at the same length as it would have been counted for the purpose of calculating the amount of any benefit under the former regulations;

(*b*) such part (if any) of the reckonable service of an employee as does not amount to a number of complete years shall be counted as a fraction of a year, of which fraction the denominator shall be 365 and the numerator shall be the number of completed days comprised in that part.

PART E

BENEFITS

Pensionable remuneration

E1.—(1) For the purposes of these regulations, the pensionable remuneration of a pensionable employee in relation to an employment under a scheduled body which he ceases to hold shall be taken to be, subject to paragraph (3) and regulation J9, the remuneration of that employment in respect of service rendered to that body in that employment during the relevant period specified in paragraph (2) which is reckonable by him as reckonable service in relation to that employment, and (where that employment commenced after the commencement of the relevant period) the remuneration of any previous employment under a scheduled body, former local authority or local Act authority or national service during the relevant period which is reckonable by him as reckonable service in relation to that employment.

(2) The relevant period for the purpose of calculating the pensionable remuneration of a pensionable employee shall be—

(*a*) the year ending with the day on which he ceases to hold his employment or the day on which he completes 45 years' reckonable service, disregarding reckonable service before attaining the age of 60 years beyond a total of 40 years, whichever is the earlier; or

(*b*) (i) where contributions by and in respect of him have not been made in respect of the whole of the year specified in sub-paragraph (*a*) by reason of absence from duty, otherwise than by reason of illness or injury, without remuneration and notice for the purpose is, or has been, given by him in accordance with paragraph (4) or, as the case may be, a determination for the purpose is made in accordance with paragraph (5), the total of the 365 days immediately preceding the day following the end of the year specified in sub-paragraph (*a*) and in respect of which contributions were made or deemed to have been made by and in respect of him;

(ii) where his remuneration has been reduced and the employing authority have certified under regulation L11 that the reduction in his remuneration was in consequence of a material change in his circumstances—

(*i*) if the reduction was made during the 5 years immediately preceding the day following the end of the year specified in sub-paragraph (*a*) and notice for the purpose is, or has been, given by him in accordance with paragraph (4) or, as the case may be, a determination for the purpose is made in accordance with paragraph (5), such one of the 5 years as is specified in the notice or, as the case may be, determined;

(*ii*) if the reduction was made during the 13 years immediately preceding the day following the end of the year specified in sub-paragraph (*a*) and notice for the purpose is, or has been, given by him in accordance with paragraph (4) or, as the case may be, a determination for the purpose is made in accordance with paragraph (5), such consecutive 3 years of those 13 years as is specified in the notice or, as the case may be, determined.

(3) For the purposes of this regulation—

(*a*) (i) in the case of an employee whose remuneration was, during the 10 years immediately preceding the day following the end of the year specified in sub-paragraph (2) (*a*), reduced or discontinued by reason.of his absence from duty owing to illness or injury;

(ii) in the case of an employee whose remuneration was, during the period mentioned in sub-paragraph (*a*) (i), discontinued during absence from duty, otherwise than by reason of illness or injury, but who made contributions in accordance with regulation C2; and

(iii) in the case of an employee who, during that period, on reduction or discontinuance of his remuneration contributed under section 6 (5) of the Act of 1937,

he shall be deemed to have received the remuneration which he would have received but for the reduction or discontinuance;

(*b*) the remuneration of a pensionable employee in respect of any period of part-time employment shall be deemed to be the remuneration which would have been paid in respect of a single comparable whole-time employment under a scheduled body;

(*c*) if a pensionable employee after ceasing to be in the employment of a single scheduled body or former local authority became an employee in the employment of two or more scheduled bodies or former local authorities or becomes an employee in the employment of two or more scheduled bodies, then if his remuneration in the first-mentioned employment becomes material for the purpose of calculating the benefit payable to him on his ceasing to hold one of the second-mentioned employments, that remuneration shall for the purpose of the calculation be treated as attributable to those employments and apportioned between them;

(*d*) in a case where the relevant period is that specified in paragraph 2(*b*) (ii)(*ii*), the aggregate of the remuneration of the pensionable employee during the relevant period shall be divided by 3;

(*e*) in calculating for the purposes of these regulations the pensionable remuneration of a pensionable employee by whom fees or other variable payments in the nature of fees were earned as part of his remuneration, the amount in respect of fees or other variable payments to be included in his remuneration for the relevant period referred to in paragraph (1) shall be the annual average of the fees or other payments earned by him during the period of 3 years ending with the last day of the relevant period or such longer period, not exceeding 5 years and ending with the last day of the relevant period, as the body who paid the remuneration of the employment he ceased to hold may, if satisfied there are sufficient reasons for so doing, allow or, if he was entitled during part only of the above-mentioned period of 3 years to receive fees or other variable payments in the nature of fees, the annual average of the fees or other payments earned by him during that shorter period;

(*f*) in the case of a pensionable employee whose service rendered as mentioned in paragraph (1) which is reckonable as therein mentioned, previous employment and national service as mentioned in that paragraph was for part only of the year specified in paragraph (2)(*a*), his pensionable remuneration shall be deemed to be the remuneration of his employment during that part of that year and the remuneration of any such previous employment or national service during that part of that year which is reckonable by him as reckonable service in relation to the employment which he ceases to hold multiplied by the reciprocal of the fraction of that year for which he was in receipt of remuneration as mentioned above; and

(*g*) in a case where the relevant period is the year specified in paragraph (2)(*a*), if the amount of the pensionable remuneration of the pensionable employee is less than the amount it would have been had the relevant period been one of the 2 years immediately preceding the year so specified (whichever one of those 2 years yields the higher amount) and notice for the purpose is, or has been, given by him in accordance with paragraph (4) or, as the case may be, a determination for the purpose is made in accordance with paragraph (5), it shall be increased by the difference between the two said amounts.

(4) A notice by a person for the purposes of this regulation shall be made in writing to the appropriate administering authority not later than one month after notification under regulation L8 of his entitlement to a benefit out of the appropriate superannuation fund.

(5) If a person—

(*a*) dies while still in an employment in which he was a pensionable employee; or

(*b*) dies before the expiration of the period within which he is entitled to give a notice under this regulation, without giving notice thereunder,

a determination for the purposes of this regulation may be made by the appropriate administering authority.

(6) In its application for the purposes of regulation E6(1)(*b*), E7, E9(1)(*b*), E10 or E11(2) this regulation shall have effect as if paragraph (3)(*b*) were omitted.

Entitlement to retirement pension and retiring allowance

E2.—(1) Subject to paragraph (4) and as hereafter in these regulations provided, a pensionable employee of an employing authority shall, on ceasing to hold an employment under them, be entitled in relation to that employment to an annual retirement pension and a lump sum retiring allowance if—

(*a*) he has attained the age of 60 years and the reckonable service and qualifying service he is entitled to reckon amounts in aggregate to not less than 25 years; or

(*b*) the reckonable service and qualifying service he is entitled to reckon amounts in aggregate to not less than 5 years and either—

   (i) he is incapable of discharging efficiently the duties of that employment by reason of permanent ill-health or infirmity of mind or body; or

   (ii) he has attained the age of 65 years; or

   (iii) he has attained the age of 50 years and one of the conditions prescribed in paragraph (3) is applicable to his case; or

(*c*) he is not entitled to a benefit under sub-paragraph (*a*) or (*b*) and either the reckonable service and qualifying service he is entitled to reckon amounts in aggregate to not less than 5 years or he is not a person who is entitled on so ceasing to a return of contributions under regulation C8.

(2) A pensionable employee of an employing authority who—

(*a*) was a contributory employee immediately before the appointed day to whom immediately before that day there applied either—

   (i) provisions corresponding to section 16 of the Act of 1937 (modifications applicable to female nursing, etc. staff) as originally enacted by virtue of an option to retain existing benefits under regulation 17 of the Benefits regulations, or regulation 21 or 23 of those regulations; or

   (ii) article 38 of the London County Council (Superannuation) Scheme 1958 (modifications applicable to certain female staff), by virtue of article 21 of the London Authorities (Superannuation) Order 1965 (protection of rights and obligations)**(a)**;

(*b*) became a pensionable employee on the appointed day;

(*c*) ceases to hold an employment under that authority in which on so ceasing, if the former regulations had not been revoked by these regulations and he had been a contributory employee, he would have been a person to whom there applied such a provision of the former regulations as is specified in sub-paragraph (*a*);

(*d*) ceases to hold that employment after attaining—

   (i) in the case of a female nurse, female physiotherapist, midwife or health visitor or a person to whom, if the former regulations had not been revoked by these regulations, provisions corresponding to section 16 of the Act of 1937 would have applied by virtue of section 9 of the Act of 1953 or article 38 of the London County Council (Superannuation) Scheme 1958 would have applied, the age of 55 years;

   (ii) in any other case the age of 60 years;

(a) S.I. 1965/621 (1965 I, p. 1970).

(e) continued to be a pensionable employee without a disqualifying break of service throughout the period beginning with the appointed day and ending with the day on which he so ceased as mentioned above;

(f) is entitled on so ceasing to reckon—

(i) in the case of a person to whom immediately before the appointed day regulation 21 of the Benefits regulations applied, not less than 5 years' (in aggregate) reckonable service and qualifying service;

(ii) in any other case, not less than 25 years' (in aggregate) reckonable service and qualifying service; and

(g) is not entitled on so ceasing to benefits under these regulations by virtue of paragraph (1)(a) or (1)(b)(i) or (ii),

shall be deemed to have ceased to hold the employment mentioned in sub-paragraph (c) in the circumstances mentioned in paragraph (1)(b)(iii).

(3) For the purposes of paragraph (1)(b)(iii) the prescribed conditions shall be—

(a) that the employing authority mentioned in paragraph (1) certify that the employee has ceased to hold his employment by reason of redundancy or in the interests of the efficient exercise of their functions; or

(b) that the employee was one of the holders of a joint appointment whose appointment has been terminated by reason that the other ceased to hold his appointment; or

(c) that the employee is a person duly entitled to benefits payable under regulations made under section 260(3) of the Local Government Act (premature retirement of certain officers).

(4) A pensionable employee who ceases to be employed in the circumstances mentioned in paragraph (1)(c) shall not on that account be entitled to receive payment of or payments in respect of a benefit under this regulation—

(a) in the case of a male pensionable employee—

(i) until he attains the earliest age at which he would, apart from paragraph (1)(b)(iii), have become entitled to receive a benefit under these regulations if he had remained in the employment he ceased to hold in the circumstances referred to above; or

(ii) until, before attaining the age mentioned in sub-paragraph (a)(i), he becomes incapable of discharging efficiently the duties of the employment he so ceased to hold by reason of permanent ill-health or infirmity of mind or body; or

(iii) until he attains or has attained the age of 50 years and the body who, in relation to the employment he so ceased to hold, was immediately before he so ceased the employing authority determine on compassionate grounds that a benefit under this regulation should be paid before the date on which he attains the earliest age as aforesaid; or

(iv) unless he so ceases to be employed after attaining the age of 60 years and not later than one month after so ceasing by notice in writing to the employing authority elects to be entitled to receive benefits under this regulation from the date on which he so ceased;

(b) in the case of a female pensionable employee—

    (i) until she attains the earliest age at which she would, apart from paragraph (1)(b)(iii), have become entitled to receive a benefit under these regulations if she had remained in the employment she ceased to hold in the circumstances referred to above; or

    (ii) until, before attaining the earliest age mentioned in sub-paragraph (b)(i), she retires and attains or has attained the age of 60 years; or

    (iii) until, before attaining the earliest age as aforesaid, she becomes incapable of discharging efficiently the duties of the employment she so ceased to hold by reason of permanent ill-health or infirmity of mind or body; or

    (iv) until she attains or has attained the age of 50 years and the body who, in relation to the employment she so ceased to hold, was immediately before she so ceased the employing authority determine on compassionate grounds that a benefit under this regulation should be paid before the date on which she attains the earliest age as aforesaid;

(c) if contributions have been returned to the pensionable employee under regulation C8;

(d) if, after so ceasing to be employed but before becoming entitled to receive payment of or payments in respect of a benefit under paragraph (1)(c), rights in respect of the reckonable service he was entitled to reckon in relation to the employment he ceased to hold in the circumstances referred to above have been transferred to another pension scheme by virtue of interchange rules; or

(e) if, after so ceasing to be employed but before becoming entitled to receive payment of or payments in respect of a benefit under paragraph (1)(c), he becomes a pensionable employee and does not within 3 months after so becoming a pensionable employee, or such longer period as the appropriate administering authority, if the superannuation fund concerned is the same in the case of both employments, or the authority maintaining the fund relating to the former employment and the authority maintaining the fund relating to the latter employment, may in a particular case allow, give to the authority maintaining the fund relating to the latter employment notice in writing that he wishes to retain the rights to benefits under these regulations to which he had under paragraph (1)(c) already become entitled.

Amount of retirement pension and retiring allowance

E3.—(1) Subject to paragraphs (2), (9) and (10) and as hereafter in this Part provided, the rate of the retirement pension to be paid to a person shall be the amount ascertained by multiplying one eightieth of his pensionable remuneration by the length in years of his reckonable service.

(2) In the case of a person entitled under regulation D12, D13 or D14 to reckon an additional period as reckonable service who had at the appropriate time attained the age of 45 years or over, the amount of the retirement pension shall be increased by the amount ascertained by multiplying one two hundred and fortieth of his pensionable remuneration by the length in years of that additional period.

(3) Subject to the succeeding provisions of this regulation and as hereafter in this Part provided, the retiring allowance to be paid to a person shall be the amount ascertained by multiplying three eightieths of his pensionable remuneration by the length in years of his reckonable service:

Provided that in the case of a person entitled under regulation D12, D13 or D14 to reckon an additional period as reckonable service who had at the appropriate time attained the age of 45 years or over, in calculating the amount of the retiring allowance no account shall be taken of that additional period.

(4) The amount, calculated in accordance with paragraph (3), of the retiring allowance to be paid to an employee who, if the former regulations had not been revoked by these regulations and he had become entitled under regulation 6 of the Benefits regulations to a lump sum grant, would have been entitled under regulation 14 of the Benefits regulations or regulation 21(4) or (5) of those regulations to an increase of the amount of that grant, shall be increased by the amount ascertained by multiplying $\frac{1}{2}\%$ of the amount of the retiring allowance, calculated as aforesaid, by the length in years of his reckonable service ending with the relevant date:

Provided that in the case of a person in the employment of a single scheduled body to whom, in consequence of having been in the part-time employment of each of two or more scheduled bodies or former local authorities, the provisions of more than one of paragraphs (a), (b) and (c) of regulation 14 of the Benefits regulations or, as the case may be, of more than one of paragraphs (4), (5) and (6) of regulation 21 of those regulations would have applied if the former regulations had not been revoked by these regulations, the amount of the increase shall be ascertained by aggregating the amounts which would be payable by way of increase if he had continued in each of the part-time employments until the date on which he ceased to hold the first-mentioned employment and his pensionable remuneration in respect of each part-time employment had been an amount which bears the same proportion to his pensionable remuneration in the employment which he ceased to hold as the remuneration of the part-time employment bears to the aggregate of the remuneration of the part-time employments.

In this paragraph "relevant date" means—

(a) in the case of a person to whom, if the former regulations had not been revoked by these regulations, paragraph (4) or (5) of regulation 21 of the Benefits regulations would have applied, the last day of the period in respect of which he would have been entitled under paragraph (4) or (5) of that regulation to an increase of the amount of the lump sum grant referred to above; and

(b) in any other case—

(i) 30th September 1950, being the date specified in proviso (ii) to regulation 14 of the Benefits regulations; or

(ii) where a date other than 30th September 1950 but corresponding to that date would have been applicable under that proviso to the person's service, that corresponding date.

(5) In the case of a married male employee in respect of whose reckonable service and qualifying service a pension may become payable under regulation E5, the amount of the retiring allowance calculated in accordance with paragraphs (3) and (4) shall be reduced by the amount ascertained by multiplying two eightieths of his pensionable remuneration by the length in years of his reckonable service (if any) before 1st April 1972.

(6) Where at the time when a pensionable employee ceases to be employed—

(a) he is a widower; or

(b) he and his wife are judicially separated; or

(c) he is a person whose marriage has been dissolved,

and the death of his wife or the separation or the dissolution of the marriage, as the case may be, occurred after the relevant date, the amount of the retiring allowance calculated in accordance with paragraphs (3) and (4) shall be reduced by the amount ascertained by multiplying two eightieths of his pensionable remuneration by the length in years of his reckonable service before the death, separation or dissolution occurred or before 1st April 1972, whichever is the earlier.

In this paragraph "relevant date" means—

(i) 30th September 1950; or

(ii) in any case where before the appointed day the former regulations applied to a person as modified or extended by or under the provisions of any local Act or scheme and, if the former regulations had not been revoked by these regulations and that person had become entitled to a retirement grant under the former regulations, that grant would have fallen to be reduced under regulation 6(4) of the Benefits regulations, as modified or extended as aforesaid, or under provisions corresponding to those of that regulation contained in the local Act or scheme by reference to a date other than 30th September 1950, being the date specified in that regulation, the date corresponding to 30th September 1950 specified in those provisions.

(7) Where a pensionable employee becomes entitled to benefits under these regulations by virtue of regulation E2(1)(b)(i), for the purpose of calculating the amount of a benefit under this regulation he shall be treated as being entitled to reckon as reckonable service such an additional period as is determined in accordance with Schedule 9.

(8) In the case of a person to whom regulation E19 applies, who has exercised his right of election under that regulation, paragraph (4) shall apply as if he had at no time been entitled as mentioned in sub-paragraph (b)(i) or (ii) of regulation E19(1) and was immediately before the appointed day or, as the case may be, before ceasing to be employed as mentioned in regulation E19(1)(a)(ii) such a person as is mentioned in paragraph (a) or (b), as the case may be, of regulation 14 of the Benefits regulations.

(9) Where a pensionable employee becomes entitled to benefits under these regulations by virtue of regulation E2(1)(c) and—

(a) in the case of a male pensionable employee having ceased to be employed after attaining the age of 60 years, elects as mentioned in regulation E2(4)(a)(iv) to be entitled to receive benefits from the date on which he so ceased; or

(b) in the case of a female pensionable employee having retired before attaining the earliest age at which she would, apart from regulation E2(1)(b)(iii), have become entitled to receive a benefit under these regulations, has attained the age of 60 years,

the amount of any benefit calculated under the preceding provisions of this regulation shall be reduced according to the age at which the person ceased to hold the employment by the percentage shown in the appropriate column of the relevant table set out in Schedule 10:

Provided that a retirement pension payable in respect of any period of reckonable service shall not be reduced under this paragraph to less than the minimum rate of equivalent pension benefits applicable in respect of that period under the Insurance Acts.

(10) Subject to paragraphs (11) to (13), for the purpose of calculating the amount of any benefit under the preceding provisions of this regulation no account shall be taken of reckonable service before attaining the age of 60 years beyond a total of 40 years.

(11) In the case of a person to whom paragraph (7) applies, paragraph (10) shall apply to his reckonable service as increased by virtue of paragraph (7).

(12) Where the amount of the retiring allowance to be paid to a person falls to be reduced under paragraph (5) or (6), any reckonable service to be disregarded by virtue of paragraph (10) shall be taken from the beginning of the period of his reckonable service.

(13) Where the amount of the retiring allowance to be paid to a person falls to be increased under paragraph (4), any reckonable service to be disregarded by virtue of paragraph (10) shall be taken from the end of the period of his reckonable service.

(14) In this regulation "appropriate time" has the meaning assigned thereto by paragraph 1(2) of Schedule 7.

Allocation of part of retirement pension

E4.—(1) Subject to regulations F19 and K9 and Schedule 11 and in accordance with the provisions of that schedule, a pensionable employee who—

(*a*) on ceasing to hold his employment becomes entitled to a retirement pension; or

(*b*) would, if he were to retire from his employment, become entitled, on so retiring, to and to receive payments in respect of such a pension,

shall if he so desires be allowed by the appropriate administering authority to surrender, as from the date on which he ceases to hold his employment, a part of the retirement pension to which he would otherwise be entitled in consideration of the grant to the spouse or any dependant of his of a pension on his death of such value as, according to tables to be prepared from time to time by the Government Actuary, is actuarially equivalent at the date aforesaid to the value of that part of the retirement pension which is surrendered.

(2) For the purposes of a surrender by virtue of paragraph (1)(*b*), it shall be assumed—

(*a*) that there will be no change in the employee's state of health between the date on which he is allowed to make the surrender and the date on which he ceases to hold his employment; and

(*b*) if he ceases to hold his employment by reason of his death, that he had retired from his employment immediately before he died.

(3) Notwithstanding that a person has already made a surrender of a part of a retirement pension, he may, subject to regulations F19 and K9 and Schedule 11 and in accordance with the provisions of that schedule, surrender a further part or parts of that retirement pension:

Provided that the aggregate of the parts surrendered shall conform with the limits imposed by paragraph 1 of that schedule on the surrender of a single part of a retirement pension.

(4) Where a person was allowed to surrender under section 16 of the Act of 1953 and that surrender did not have effect before the appointed day, the person shall be deemed to have been allowed to surrender part of a retirement pension under this regulation and the provisions of this regulation shall, as nearly as may be, apply to that surrender accordingly:

Provided that—

(a) if the person in whose favour such a surrender was allowed is living and, where that person was at the time the surrender was allowed the spouse of the person who made the surrender, remains the spouse and the husband and wife are not judicially separated, the person who made the surrender may, within 3 months after the appointed day, give notice in writing to the appropriate administering authority—

(i) that he does not wish this paragraph to apply to that surrender, in which event this paragraph shall not apply, and shall be deemed never to have applied, thereto; or

(ii) that he wishes to be deemed to have been allowed to surrender under this regulation such part of the retirement pension to which he would otherwise be entitled as is specified in that notice (such part being of a smaller amount than the amount specified in the notification of surrender given by him under the rules made under section 16 of the Act of 1953), in which event he shall be deemed to have been allowed to surrender under this regulation such part of the retirement pension as is specified in the said notice; and

(b) in determining under paragraph 2 of Schedule 11 the amount of pension payable the tables to be used shall be the tables which were prepared for the purposes of section 16 of the Act of 1953 and in force at the date on which the surrender was allowed under that section.

(5) For the purposes of this regulation a pensionable employee who ceases to be employed in the circumstances mentioned in regulation E2(1)(c) shall not be treated as ceasing to hold his employment until the date immediately preceding the date (if any) on which he becomes entitled to receive payments in respect of the retirement pension or as having become entitled to a retirement pension until the last-mentioned date.

Entitlement to widow's short-term pension and widow's long-term pension

E5.—(1) Subject to paragraph (2) and as hereafter in this Part provided, if a male person dies who—

(a) was entitled at the time of his death to receive payments in respect of a retirement pension; or

(b) was at the time of his death employed in an employment in which he was a pensionable employee and the reckonable and qualifying service he was entitled to reckon amounted in aggregate to not less than 5 years; or

(c) was entitled at the time of his death to a retirement pension, but was not entitled at that time to receive payments in respect of that pension, and he is survived by a widow, his widow shall be entitled—

(i) if he was such a person as is mentioned in sub-paragraph (a) or (b), to a widow's short-term pension in respect of the period of 3 months after the day of his death and to an annual widow's long-term pension; and

(ii) if he was such a person as is mentioned in sub-paragraph (c), to an annual widow's long-term pension:

Provided that—

(a) a widow shall not be entitled to a widow's short-term pension (if any) or to a widow's long-term pension—

    (i) by virtue of sub-paragraph (a) or (c), if the marriage took place on or after the date on which her husband became entitled to the retirement pension; or

    (ii) if at the date on which her husband became entitled to the retirement pension or at the date of his death the husband and wife were judicially separated; and

(b) in the case of the widow of such a person as is mentioned in sub-paragraph (a) or (b), that widow shall not be entitled to receive payment in respect of a widow's long-term pension until the day following the expiration of the period of 3 months after the day of her husband's death.

(2) A widow's short-term pension and a widow's long-term pension shall not be payable to a widow—

(a) if she re-marries, in respect of any period after re-marriage;

(b) if on the day of the death of her husband she is then cohabiting with another man as his wife, in respect of any period after that day; or

(c) if after that day she commences to cohabit with a man as his wife, in respect of any period after so commencing:

Provided that if at any time after her re-marriage she has again become a widow or that marriage has been dissolved or the cohabitation has been terminated, the appropriate administering authority may, in their discretion, bring the widow's long-term pension into payment as from that time.

Amount of widow's short-term pension and widow's long-term pension

E6.—(1) Subject as hereafter in this Part provided, a widow's short-term pension shall be at an annual rate—

(a) in the case of the widow of a person who was entitled at the time of his death to receive payments in respect of a retirement pension, equal to the rate payable to him immediately before his death of that pension; and

(b) in the case of the widow of a person who was at the time of his death employed in an employment in which he was a pensionable employee, equal to his pensionable remuneration.

(2) Subject to paragraph (3) and as hereafter in this Part provided, the amount of a widow's long-term pension shall be—

(a) in the case of the widow of such a person as is mentioned in paragraph (1)(a), one half of the retirement pension to which he was entitled at the time of his death;

(b) in the case of the widow of such a person as is mentioned in paragraph (1)(b), one half of the retirement pension to which he would have been entitled if he had been at the time of his death a person such as is mentioned in regulation E2(1)(b)(i); and

(c) in the case of the widow of a person who was entitled at the time of his death to a retirement pension, but was not entitled at that time to receive payments in respect of that pension, one half of the retirement pension to which he would have been entitled if he had been at the time of his death a person such as is mentioned in regulation E2(1)(b)(ii).

(3) For the purposes of paragraph (2)—

  (*a*) any such retirement pension as is mentioned in paragraph (2)(*a*) shall be deemed to be the retirement pension that would have been payable but for—

    (i) any increase under regulation E3(2);

    (ii) any reduction under regulation E3(9) or E15 or Part F; and

    (iii) any surrender of part thereof under regulation E4; and

  (*b*) if any such retirement pension as is mentioned in paragraph (2)(*b*) or (*c*)—

    (i) would have been increased under regulation E3(2), no account shall be taken of that increase;

    (ii) would have been reduced under Part F, no account shall be taken of that reduction,

and any such retirement pension shall be deemed to be the retirement pension that would have been payable but for any surrender of part thereof under regulation E4.

Widow's special short-term pension

E7. If a male person dies who was at the time of his death employed in an employment in which he was a pensionable employee and the reckonable service and qualifying service he was entitled to reckon amounted in aggregate to less than 5 years and he is survived by a widow, his widow shall be entitled to a widow's special short-term pension—

  (*a*) where her husband is not survived by an eligible child or there is no eligible child in her care, in respect of the period of 3 months after the day of his death; or

  (*b*) where he is survived by an eligible child or eligible children—

    (i) if and so long as one such eligible child is in her care, in respect of the period of $4\frac{1}{2}$ months after that day;

    (ii) if and so long as two or more such eligible children are in her care, in respect of the period of 6 months after that day,

at an annual rate equal to his pensionable remuneration:

Provided that a widow shall not be entitled to a widow's special short-term pension—

    (i) if at the date of the death of her husband the husband and wife are judicially separated; or

    (ii) if on the day of the death of her husband she is then cohabiting with another man as his wife.

Entitlement to children's short-term pension and children's long-term pension

E8.—(1) Subject to paragraph (2) and as hereafter in this Part provided, if a male person dies who—

  (*a*) was entitled at the time of his death to receive payments in respect of a retirement pension; or

  (*b*) was at the time of his death employed in an employment in which he was a pensionable employee and the reckonable service and qualifying service he was entitled to reckon amounted in aggregate to not less than 5 years; or

  (*c*) was entitled at the time of his death to a retirement pension, but was not entitled at that time to receive payments in respect of that pension, and he is survived by an eligible child or eligible children, there shall be payable to or for the benefit of his eligible child or eligible children—

(i) if he was such a person as is mentioned in sub-paragraph (a) or (b), a children's short-term pension in respect of the period of 3 months after the day of his death and an annual children's long-term pension; and

(ii) if he was such a person as is mentioned in sub-paragraph (c), a children's long-term pension:

Provided that—

(a) where a widow's short-term pension is payable to the widow of the deceased person, a children's short-term pension shall not be payable during the period the widow's short-term pension is payable; and

(b) if the deceased person was such a person as is mentioned in sub-paragraph (a) or (b), the children's long-term pension shall not be payable until the day following the expiration of the period of 3 months after the death of the deceased person.

(2) A children's short-term pension and a children's long-term pension shall not be paid to or for the benefit of a female eligible child—

(a) if on the day of the death of the deceased person she is married or cohabiting with another man as his wife, in respect of any period after that day; or

(b) if after that day she marries or commences to cohabit with a man as his wife, in respect of any period after marriage or so commencing:

Provided that if at any time after the marriage she has become a widow or the marriage has been dissolved or the cohabitation has been terminated, the appropriate administering authority may, in their discretion, pay the children's short-term pension or, as the case may be, the children's long-term pension to her or for her benefit as from that time.

Amount of children's short-term pension and children's long-term pension

E9.—(1) A children's short-term pension shall be at an annual rate—

(a) where the deceased person was entitled at the time of his death to receive payments in respect of a retirement pension, equal to the rate payable to him immediately before his death of that pension; and

(b) where the deceased person was at the time of his death employed in an employment in which he was a pensionable employee, equal to his pensionable remuneration.

(2) Subject to paragraph (3), the amount of a children's long-term pension shall be—

(a) where the deceased person is survived by a widow to whom there is payable, or would be payable, apart from proviso (a)(ii) to paragraph (1) of regulation E5 or paragraph (2) of that regulation, a pension under that regulation, the amount which, opposite to the number of eligible children in respect of whom it is for the time being payable specified in column (1) of the following table, is specified in column (2) thereof; or

(b) where the deceased person is not survived by such a widow as is mentioned in sub-paragraph (a) or in respect of any period after the death of such a widow, the amount which, opposite to the number of eligible children in respect of whom it is for the time being payable specified as aforesaid, is specified in column (3) of that table:—

TABLE

(1)	(2)	(3)
Number of eligible children	Annual amount of children's long-term pension where there is a surviving widow of the deceased person	Annual amount of children's long-term pension where there is not a surviving widow of the deceased person
1 child	One quarter of the retirement pension to which the deceased person was entitled	One third of the retirement pension to which the deceased person was entitled
2 or more children ...	One half of the retirement pension to which the deceased person was entitled	Two thirds of the retirement pension to which the deceased person was entitled

(3) For the purposes of paragraph (2)—

(a) the retirement pension of a deceased person shall be deemed to be—

(i) if he was at the time of his death employed in an employment in which he was a pensionable employee, the retirement pension to which he would have been entitled if he had been at that time such a person as is mentioned in regulation E2(1)(b)(i); or

(ii) if he was entitled at the time of his death to a retirement pension, but was not entitled at that time to receive payments in respect of that pension, the retirement pension to which he would have been entitled if he had been at that time such a person as is mentioned in regulation E2(1)(b)(ii);

(b) the retirement pension of a deceased person who was entitled at the time of his death to receive payments in respect of that pension shall be deemed to be the retirement pension that would have been payable but for—

(i) any increase under regulation E3(2);

(ii) any reduction under regulation E3(9) or E15 or Part F; and

(iii) any surrender of part thereof under regulation E4; and

(c) in any case other than that mentioned in sub-paragraph (b), if the retirement pension of a deceased person—

(i) would have been increased under regulation E3(2), no account shall be taken of that increase;

(ii) would have been reduced under Part F, no account shall be taken of that reduction,

and the retirement pension shall be deemed to be the retirement pension that would have been payable but for any surrender of part thereof under regulation E4.

(4) If an eligible child who has attained the age of 16 years and to whom, or for whose benefit, a children's long-term pension is payable is in receipt of remuneration in respect of full-time training for a trade, profession or calling, at an annual rate in excess of £250, increased from time to time by the amount, (if any) by which an annual pension of the amount of £250 would be increased under the Pensions (Increase) Act 1971(a), if the eligible child were in receipt of

(a) 1971 c. 56.

such a pension and that pension were specified in Part II of Schedule 1 to that Act and were one which began for the purposes of the said Act on the appointed day, the annual amount of the children's long-term pension shall be reduced by the amount of the excess or, if it would result in a smaller reduction of the children's long-term pension, the child shall be disregarded for the purpose of calculating the amount of that pension.

(5) The children's short-term pension and the children's long-term pension shall be payable to, or among, the eligible children in respect of whom it is for the time being payable in such proportions as the appropriate administering authority think fit:

Provided that that authority may if they think fit pay any such pension or any part thereof to such other person as they may, in their discretion, determine and any person to whom any such pension or part thereof is so paid shall apply it in accordance with any directions given by the administering authority for the benefit of the eligible children in respect of whom that pension is for the time being payable.

Children's special short-term pension

E10. If a male person dies who was at the time of his death employed in an employment in which he was a pensionable employee and the reckonable service and qualifying service he was entitled to reckon amounted in aggregate to less than 5 years, and he is survived by an eligible child or eligible children and any such eligible child is in the care of a person (other than any surviving widow of his who is entitled to a widow's special short-term pension) (hereafter in this regulation referred to as the "guardian"), a children's special short-term pension shall be paid to the guardian in respect of such eligible child or, as the case may be, eligible children—

(*a*) where the deceased person is survived by a widow who is entitled to a widow's special short-term pension but there is no such eligible child in her care—
    (i) if and so long as one such eligible child is in the care of the guardian, in respect of the period of $1\frac{1}{2}$ months after the day of the deceased person's death;
    (ii) if and so long as two or more such eligible children are in the care of the guardian, in respect of the period of 3 months after that day;

(*b*) where the deceased person is survived by a widow who is entitled to a widow's special short-term pension and so long as there are one or more such eligible children in her care, in respect of the period of $1\frac{1}{2}$ months after that day;

(*c*) where the deceased person is not survived by a widow who is entitled to a widow's special short-term pension—
    (i) if one such eligible child is in the care of the guardian, in respect of the period of 2 months after that day;
    (ii) if two or more such eligible children are in the care of the guardian, in respect of the period of 4 months after that day,

at an annual rate equal to the deceased person's pensionable remuneration.

Death gratuity

E11.—(1) Subject as hereafter in this Part provided, if—

(*a*) a person who is employed in an employment in which he is a pensionable employee dies; or

(*b*) a person dies after having become entitled to a retirement pension and retiring allowance (other than a person who became entitled thereto by virtue of regulation E2(1)(*c*)) and either—

(i) the reckonable service by reference to which the retirement pension was calculated amounted in aggregate to less than 10 years and he had been entitled for a period of less than 5 years to receive payments in respect of that pension; or

(ii) the reckonable service by reference to which the retirement pension was calculated amounted in aggregate to not less than 10 years; or

(c) a person dies who was entitled at the time of his death to a retirement pension and retiring allowance, but was not entitled at that time to receive payments in respect of that pension or payment of that allowance,

his personal representatives shall be entitled to receive a lump sum death gratuity.

(2) Subject to the succeeding provisions of this regulation and as hereafter in these regulations provided, the amount of a death gratuity shall be as follows:—

(a) in respect of such a person as is mentioned in paragraph (1)(a) or (b)(ii), whichever of the following two amounts is the greater:—

(i) the amount ascertained by multiplying three eightieths of his pensionable remuneration by the length in years of his reckonable service by reference to which, in the case of such a person as is mentioned in paragraph (1)(a), the retirement pension would have been calculated had he become entitled to a retirement pension under regulation E2(1)(b)(i) on the day of his death or, in the case of such a person as is mentioned in paragraph (1)(b)(ii), the retirement pension was calculated; or

(ii) the amount of his pensionable remuneration;

(b) in respect of such a person as is mentioned in paragraph (1)(b)(i), an amount equal to five times the rate of the retirement pension mentioned in that paragraph; and

(c) in respect of such a person as is mentioned in paragraph (1)(c), the amount ascertained by multiplying three eightieths of his pensionable remuneration by the length in years of his reckonable service by reference to which the retirement pension was calculated.

(3) In the case of such a person as is mentioned in paragraph (1)(a), (b)(ii) or (c) in respect of whose death a pension under regulation E5 is payable to his widow, the amount of the death gratuity shall be reduced by the amount ascertained by multiplying two eightieths of his pensionable remuneration by the length in years of his reckonable service (if any) before 1st April 1972.

(4) In the case of such a person as is mentioned in paragraph (1)(a) who was entitled to reckon reckonable service and qualifying service amounting in aggregate to not less than 5 years, the amount of the death gratuity shall be calculated as if he had become entitled to a retirement pension on the day of his death by virtue of regulation E2(1)(b)(i).

(5) In the case of such a person as is mentioned in paragraph (1)(b)(i), the amount of the death gratuity calculated under the preceding provisions of this regulation shall be reduced by an amount equal to the aggregate amount of any payments made to him in respect of the retirement pension mentioned in that paragraph and, if the person had surrendered a part of that retirement pension, by an amount equal to the amount which would have been paid in respect thereof but for the surrender.

(6) In the case of such a person as is mentioned in paragraph (1)(b)(ii), the amount of the death gratuity calculated under the preceding provisions of this

regulation shall be reduced by an amount equal to the aggregate amount of any payments made to him in respect of the retirement pension and retiring allowance mentioned in that paragraph and, if the person had surrendered a part of that retirement pension, by an amount equal to the amount which would have been paid in respect thereof but for the surrender.

(7) Subject to paragraph (8), for the purpose of calculating the amount of a death gratuity under the preceding provisions of this regulation no account shall be taken of reckonable service before attaining the age of 60 years beyond a total of 40 years.

(8) Where the amount of a death gratuity to be paid in respect of a person falls to be reduced under paragraph (3), any reckonable service to be disregarded by virtue of paragraph (7) shall be taken from the beginning of the period of his reckonable service.

Pensions of widowers, etc.

E12. Subject as hereafter in this Part provided, a female pensionable employee who—

(*a*) either—

(i) has a husband who is permanently incapacitated by reason of ill-health or infirmity of mind or body and who is wholly or mainly dependent on her; or

(ii) has no husband but has an eligible child or eligible children; and

(*b*) notifies the appropriate administering authority in writing that she wishes to have the provisions of this regulation applied to her,

shall participate in the benefits provided by these regulations as if references in this Part to a male, a married male employee or a male person who was a pensionable employee, or was entitled to receive payments in respect of a retirement pension or was entitled to a retirement pension, but was not in receipt of payments in respect of that pension, included references to her and as if any reference to the wife or widow of such a person included a reference to her husband or her widower:

Provided that if, after giving a notification under paragraph (*b*), she marries or re-marries, the subsequent marriage and—

(i) the legitimate children of the subsequent marriage;

(ii) any adopted child of hers, adopted after re-marriage;

(iii) any legitimate child of hers, born after the expiration of one year after the date of the death;

(iv) any step-child of hers, being a child of an earlier marriage of her husband by the subsequent marriage; and

(v) any adopted child of her husband by the subsequent marriage,

shall be left out of account for all the purposes of this Part unless her husband by the subsequent marriage is permanently incapacitated by reason of ill-health or infirmity of mind or body and wholly or mainly dependent on her.

Additional benefits granted at discretion of employing authority in the case of certain female nursing, etc. staff

E13.—(1) This regulation shall apply to a person who—

(*a*) was a contributory employee immediately before the appointed day to whom immediately before that day section 16(1) of the Act of 1937 applied;

(*b*) became a pensionable employee on the appointed day;

(*c*) ceases to hold an employment in which on so ceasing, if the former regulations had not been revoked by these regulations and she had been a contributory employee, she would have been a person to whom section 16 of the Act of 1937 applied;

(*d*) ceases to hold that employment on or after attaining the age of 60 years but before she has completed 40 years' reckonable service and becomes entitled on so ceasing to a retirement pension; and

(*e*) continued to be a pensionable employee without a disqualifying break of service throughout the period beginning with the appointed day and ending with the day on which she so ceases as mentioned above.

(2) The employing authority of a person to whom this regulation applies may grant to her an additional benefit not exceeding the difference between the benefit to which she is entitled and the benefit to which she would have been entitled if she had remained in the employment of the authority until she attained the age of 65 years receiving an annual remuneration equal to her pensionable remuneration.

Reduction of retirement pension in the case of certain former teachers

E14.—(1) Where a person becomes entitled to a retirement pension in the calculation of the amount of which account is taken of service which he was entitled to reckon under section 17 of the Act of 1937 (which related to teachers), the amount receivable by him in any year in respect of that pension shall be reduced by a sum equivalent to the amount (if any) which is receivable by him in that year by virtue of the Teachers (Superannuation) Acts 1918 to 1945 (in this regulation referred to as "the Teachers Acts"), or would have been so receivable by him in that year but for any deduction made by the Secretary of State under section 7 of the Teachers (Superannuation) Act 1925(a), and the sums (if any) payable to him under the Teachers' Superannuation Regulations 1967 to 1974 (in this regulation referred to as "the Teachers regulations"), or which would be so payable but for any deduction made under regulation 52 of the Teachers' Superannuation Regulations 1967.

(2) In computing the reduction to be made under paragraph (1), account shall be taken of any sum paid or payable at any time under the Teachers Acts or the Teachers regulations which was or is in the nature of a capital payment or which represents a return of contributions in respect of a period of service which has been taken into account in calculating the amount of the retirement pension, in the following manner, that is to say— ·

(*a*) the amount of any sum paid under the Teachers Acts or the Teachers regulations on or before the date on which the person became entitled to that retirement pension or becoming payable under the Teachers Acts or the Teachers regulations at any time thereafter which was or is in the nature of a capital payment shall be divided by the factor shown in the following table in relation to the class of the person and to his age at the date on which the sum was paid or becomes payable, and the resulting amount shall be treated as a sum receivable by him by virtue of the Teachers Acts or the Teachers regulations in any year;

(a) 1925 c. 59.

(b) the amount representing any balance of his contributions under the Teachers Acts or the Teachers regulations which he has become entitled to be repaid at the date on which he became entitled to the retirement pension in respect of a period of service which has been taken into account in calculating the amount of the retirement pension shall be divided by the factor shown in the table in relation to the class of the person and to his age at the date on which he became entitled to the retirement pension, and the resulting amount shall be treated as a sum receivable by him by virtue of the Teachers Acts or payable to him by virtue of the Teachers regulations in any year;

(c) the amount representing any balance of his contributions under the Teachers Acts or the Teachers regulations which he may become entitled to be repaid after the date on which he became entitled to the retirement pension in respect of a period of service which has been taken into account in calculating the amount of the retirement pension shall be divided by the factor shown in the table in relation to the class of the person and to his age at the date on which he so becomes entitled to be repaid that balance of his contributions, and the resulting amount shall be treated as a sum receivable by him by virtue of the Teachers Acts or payable to him by virtue of the Teachers regulations in any year:

Provided that if, after the provisions of either sub-paragraph (b) or (c) have become applicable in relation to any person, a superannuation allowance under the Teachers regulations is granted to him then, if the aggregate amount of the deductions made from his retirement pension by reason of the previous operation of those provisions is less than the amount granted to him by way of lump sum under the Teachers Acts or the Teachers regulations, such latter amount for the purpose of the application of sub-paragraph (a) shall be deemed to be the difference between that amount and such aggregate amount as aforesaid and sub-paragraphs (b) and (c) shall cease to have any further effect in relation to him.

(3) If, after the provisions of either paragraph (2)(b) or (c) have become applicable in relation to any person, a repayment of the amount representing the balance of the person's contributions under the Teachers Acts or the Teachers regulations is made to him, those provisions shall, in respect of the amount so repaid, continue to apply in the same manner as they had previously applied in relation to him for the purpose of computing the reduction to be made in his retirement pension in any year under paragraph (1) and no further account for that purpose shall be taken of that amount.

(4) If a person surrenders or has surrendered in accordance with Part VI of the Teachers' Superannuation Regulations 1967 part of the annual sum payable to him by way of superannuation allowance under the Teachers Acts or the Teachers regulations, the annual sum receivable in any year by virtue of the Teachers Acts or the Teachers regulations shall for the purpose of paragraph (1) be deemed to be the annual sum which would have been receivable by him in that year but for the surrender.

(5) Any reference in this regulation to the date on which a person becomes entitled to a retirement pension shall, in relation to a person who ceased to be employed in the circumstances mentioned in regulation E2(1)(c), be construed as a reference to the date on which he becomes entitled to receive payments in respect of that pension.

TABLE

Age	Men A.	Men B.	Women A.	Women B.
Under 60 years	10	—	12·5	—
60 years but under 61 years	10	11·6	12·5	13·4
61 " " " 62 "	10	11·2	12·5	13
62 " " " 63 "	10	10·8	12·5	
63 " " " 64 "	10	10·4	12·1	
64 " " " 65 "	10		11·7	
65 " " " 66 "	9·7		11·2	
66 " " " 67 "	9·3		10·8	
67 " " " 68 "	8·9		10·3	
68 " " " 69 "	8·5		9·9	
69 " " " 70 "	8·1		9·5	
70 " " " 71 "	7·7		9	

A. Applicable to persons who ceased to be employed in the circumstances mentioned in regulation E2(1)(b)(i).

B. Applicable to persons who ceased to be employed in the circumstances mentioned in regulation E2(1), other than sub-paragraph (b)(i).

Reduction of retirement pension, etc., in the case of certain re-employed local government pensioners

E15.—(1) Subject to paragraph (2) and regulation J9, this regulation shall apply to a person who has become entitled to a retirement pension and since becoming entitled to that pension has entered further employment with any scheduled body, former local authority or local Act authority or enters further employment with any scheduled body or local Act authority (other than employment by virtue of which he is entitled to participate in benefits provided under regulations made under section 9 of the Act of 1972) (in this regulation referred to as "new employment").

(2) This regulation shall not apply to a person who has become entitled to a retirement pension payable to him in respect of service rendered without a disqualifying break of service as a designated employee and a contributory employee or as a designated employee, a contributory employee and a pensionable employee unless he, within one month after entering the further employment or within one month after the appointed day, whichever period ends the later, by notice in writing to the authority under whom he holds that employment, elects that this regulation shall apply to him.

(3) The rate of retirement pension payable to a person to whom this regulation applies during the period, or part thereof, during which he holds the new employment shall not exceed the amount (if any) by which the annual rate of remuneration of the new employment falls short of the annual rate of remuneration of the employment in relation to which he became entitled to the retirement pension (in this regulation referred to as "former employment"), increased by the amount (if any) by which an annual pension of an amount equal to the annual rate of remuneration of the former employment would have been increased under the Pensions (Increase) Act 1971 in respect of the period ending with the day immediately preceding the day on which the person entered the new

employment if the person were in receipt of such a pension and that pension were specified in Part II of Schedule 1 to that Act and were one which began for the purposes of the said Act on the day immediately following the day on which the person ceased to hold his former employment and the person had on the day on which he so ceased attained the age of 55 years:

Provided that if concurrently with the former employment he held, within the period of 12 months ending on the day on which he ceased to hold that employment, any other employment with any scheduled body, former local authority or local Act authority (in this regulation referred to as "concurrent employment") then if either—

(a) before so ceasing he ceased to hold a concurrent employment without having become entitled in relation thereto to a retirement pension and after ceasing to hold the former employment has entered further employment with any scheduled body, former local authority or local Act authority, or enters further employment with any scheduled body or local Act authority, within 12 months after ceasing to hold the concurrent employment; or

(b) after ceasing to hold the former employment he has ceased or ceases to hold a concurrent employment without having become entitled in relation thereto to a retirement pension and thereafter has entered further employment with any scheduled body, former local authority or local Act authority or enters further employment with any scheduled body or local Act authority,

the retirement pension shall—

(i) not be reduced in relation to his new employment unless he spends in his new employment a time materially greater than the time which he spent in the concurrent employment during the year ending on the day on which he ceased to hold that concurrent employment;

(ii) if he spends in his new employment a time materially greater than the time which he spent in the concurrent employment during the year ending on the day on which he ceased to hold that concurrent employment, be reduced only to the extent by which the aggregate of the aforesaid pension and the annual rate of remuneration of his new employment exceeds the aggregate of the annual rate of remuneration of the former employment, increased as mentioned above, and the annual rate of remuneration of the concurrent employment during the year ending on the day on which he ceased to hold that concurrent employment, increased by the amount (if any) by which an annual pension of an amount equal to the annual rate of remuneration of the concurrent employment would have been increased under the Pensions (Increase) Act 1971 in respect of the period ending with the day immediately preceding the day on which the person entered the new employment if the person were in receipt of such a pension and that pension were specified in Part II of Schedule 1 to that Act and were one which began for the purposes of the said Act on the day immediately following the day on which he ceased to hold his concurrent employment and the person had on the day on which he so ceased attained the age of 55 years.

(4) Where a person who has become entitled to a retirement pension proposes to accept any further employment with any scheduled body or local Act authority, he shall inform that body that he is so entitled and, if he enters their employment, shall forthwith give notice in writing that he is so employed to the body from whom he receives the pension.

(5) For the purposes of this regulation a person's annual rate of remuneration of his former employment shall be computed—

(a) in so far as it consisted of or comprised salary, wages or other emoluments, whether in money or in kind, receivable by the employee at a fixed rate—

(i) in the case of a person entitled in respect of that employment to a retirement pension under these regulations, at the rate at which it was payable on the last day of the relevant period in relation to that employment mentioned in regulation E1(1):

Provided that where the pensionable remuneration of the former employment was increased under paragraph (3)(g) of that regulation, the rate shall be computed at the rate at which it was payable on the last day of such of the 2 years mentioned in that paragraph as yielded the higher amount there mentioned; and

(ii) in any other case, at the rate at which it was payable immediately before he ceased to hold his employment; and

(b) in so far as it consisted of or comprised fees or other emoluments in the nature of fees—

(i) in the case of a person entitled in respect of that employment to a retirement pension under these regulations, at the average rate at which he earned those fees and other emoluments during the period of 3 years mentioned in paragraph (3)(e) of regulation E1 or, where under that paragraph a longer period was allowed, during such longer period as was allowed under that paragraph or, if he was entitled during part only of that period of 3 years to receive those fees and other emoluments, at the average rate for the period during which, within the said period of 3 years, he was entitled to receive them; and

(ii) in any other case, at the average rate at which he earned those fees and other emoluments during the 3 years immediately before he ceased to hold the former employment or, if he was entitled during part only of that period to receive those fees or other emoluments, at the average rate for the period during which, within the said period of 3 years, he was entitled to receive them.

(6) For the purposes of this regulation—

(a) a person entitled in respect of his former employment to a retirement pension (other than a retirement pension under these regulations) who, on reduction or discontinuance of the remuneration of that employment, contributed under section 6(5) of the Act of 1937 as if his remuneration had not been reduced or discontinued;

(b) a person entitled in respect of his former employment to a retirement pension under these regulations whose remuneration of that employment was discontinued during leave of absence from duty, otherwise than by reason of illness or injury, but who made contributions in accordance with regulation C2; and

(c) a person whose remuneration of his former employment was reduced or discontinued by reason of his absence from duty owing to illness or injury,

shall, in so far as the remuneration of his former employment at the time of its reduction or discontinuance consisted of or comprised salary, wages or other emoluments, whether in money or in kind, receivable at a fixed rate, be deemed to have received the remuneration which he would have received but for the reduction or discontinuance and, in so far as the remuneration of his former employment at the time aforesaid consisted of or comprised fees and other emoluments in the nature of fees, be deemed to have continued to receive those fees or other emoluments—

    (i) in the case of a person entitled in respect of his former employment to a retirement pension under these regulations, at the average rate at which he received them during the 3 years immediately before the said reduction or discontinuance or, where under paragraph (3)(*e*) of regulation E1 such a longer period as is mentioned in that paragraph was on his ceasing to hold his former employment allowed, during a period of the same length as the said longer period and ending immediately before the said reduction or discontinuance or, if he was not entitled during the whole of that period of 3 years or, as the case may be, such longer period as was allowed as aforesaid to receive those fees or other emoluments, at the average rate for the period during which, within the said period of 3 years or such longer period as was allowed, he was entitled to receive them; and

    (ii) in any other case, at the average rate at which he received them during the 3 years immediately before the said reduction or discontinuance or, if he was not entitled during the whole of that period to receive those fees and other emoluments, at the average rate for the period during which, within the said period of 3 years, he was entitled to receive them.

(7) For the purposes of this regulation a person's annual rate of remuneration of his new employment—

    (*a*) in so far as it consists of or comprises salary, wages or other emoluments, whether in money or in kind, receivable by the employee at a fixed rate, shall be computed at the rate at which it was payable on the day on which he entered that employment; and

    (*b*) where under paragraph (8)(*a*) the remuneration of the new employment is deemed to consist of or comprise such fees or other emoluments as are mentioned in that paragraph, in so far as that remuneration is deemed to consist of or comprise such fees or other emoluments, shall be computed at the average rate applicable in his case under paragraph (5)(*b*) and, if the person's annual rate of remuneration of his former employment is greater than his annual rate of remuneration of his new employment, shall be reduced by deducting therefrom an amount ascertained by multiplying the said average rate by the fraction of which the numerator is the annual rate of remuneration of his new employment and the denominator is the annual rate of remuneration of his former employment.

(8) For the purposes of this regulation, where a person's annual rate of remuneration of his new employment will consist of or comprise fees and other emoluments in the nature of fees, the person's annual rate of remuneration of his new employment shall be deemed not to consist of or comprise those fees and other emoluments and shall be deemed—

    (*a*) if the person's annual rate of remuneration of his former employment consisted of or comprised fees and other emoluments in the nature of fees, to consist of or comprise those fees and other emoluments;

    (*b*) if the person's annual rate of remuneration of his former employment did not consist of or comprise fees and other emoluments in the nature of fees, to consist of or comprise such an amount in respect of those fees and other emoluments as the employing authority and the employee may agree or, in default of agreement, as is determined by the Secretary of State.

(9) For the purposes of this regulation—

(*a*) where the terms and conditions of a person's part-time employment are changed so as to alter the hours of that employment, this regulation shall, on and after the date on which that increase takes effect, apply as if on that date he had entered new employment;

(*b*) where a person is transferred to another post at an altered remuneration this regulation shall, on and after the date on which he is so transferred, apply as if on that date he had entered new employment.

(10) Where in relation to any person two or more retirement pensions fall to be reduced under the provisions of this regulation each such pension shall be reduced in proportion to its amount.

(11) Notwithstanding any previous provision of this regulation, where an instalment of a retirement pension is payable in respect of a period beginning before but ending on or after the appointed day that instalment shall be subject to the like reduction (if any) as it would have been subject to if these regulations had not been made.

(12) For the purposes of this regulation "retirement pension" includes a superannuation allowance under Part I of the Act of 1937 and an annual pension under the former regulations.

Combined benefits in the case of certain re-employed local government pensioners

E16.—(1) This regulation shall apply to a person—

(*a*) who has become entitled to a retirement pension (other than a retirement pension falling to be reduced under regulation E3(9));

(*b*) who after becoming so entitled entered further whole-time employment with any scheduled body and was in that further employment (in this regulation referred to as "further pensionable employment") a pensionable employee;

(*c*) who ceases to hold the further pensionable employment;

(*d*) whose above-mentioned retirement pension was, during the period, or part thereof, during which he held the further pensionable employment, liable to be reduced or suspended; and

(*e*) who becomes, on ceasing to hold the further pensionable employment, entitled to a retirement pension.

(2) If a person to whom this regulation applies, by notice in writing given to the appropriate administering authority not later than one month after he ceases to hold his further pensionable employment or within one month after the appointed day, whichever period ends the later, so elects, he shall, subject to paragraph (4), be entitled on so ceasing to a benefit (in this regulation referred to as a "combined benefit") calculated under these regulations by reference to both his reckonable service in the further pensionable employment and to the reckonable service taken into account in the calculation of the retirement pension mentioned in paragraph (1)(*a*):

Provided that if in conjunction with the retirement pension mentioned in paragraph (1)(*a*) the person received a retiring allowance and the amount of that allowance exceeds the amount of the lump sum payment which, apart from paragraph (4), would be included in the combined benefit (in this regulation referred to as a "lump sum payment"), the person shall not be entitled to a combined benefit unless he pays to the appropriate administering authority, within 3 months after the date on which he gave the notice under this paragraph, a sum equal to the amount by which the retiring allowance exceeds the lump sum payment.

(3) For the purposes of paragraph (2), "reckonable service" includes any period by reference to which an additional benefit has been granted under regulation E13.

(4) Where a person to whom this regulation applies has made an election under paragraph (2) and has paid such sum (if any) as is mentioned in the proviso to that paragraph then—

(a) if in conjunction with the retirement pension mentioned in paragraph (1)(a) the person received a retiring allowance—

    (i) if in calculating that allowance no account was taken by virtue of the proviso to regulation E3(3) of such an additional period as is mentioned in that proviso, no account shall be taken of that additional period in calculating the amount of the lump sum payment;

    (ii) if the amount of that allowance equals or exceeds the amount of the lump sum payment, a lump sum payment shall not be payable under paragraph (2);

    (iii) if the amount of the lump sum payment exceeds the amount of that allowance, the amount of the lump sum payment shall be reduced by the amount of the allowance;

(b) if in calculating the retirement pension mentioned in paragraph (1)(a) the annual pension which would otherwise have been payable was reduced pursuant to the provisions of Part F and, in his further pensionable employment, he was not, apart from the provisions of this sub-paragraph, subject to any provisions in Part F modifying any benefit payable to him in respect of that employment, the combined benefit shall be reduced by the amount by which the retirement pension was reduced;

(c) the retirement pension mentioned in paragraph (1)(a) shall cease to be paid;

(d) if under regulation E4 he has surrendered part of the retirement pension to which, but for the surrender, he would have become entitled on ceasing to hold his former employment, the surrender so made shall have effect in relation to the combined benefit as, but for sub-paragraph (c), it would have had effect in relation to the retirement pension in respect of which it was made, and any pension which becomes payable by virtue of that surrender shall be paid by the authority by whom the combined benefit is payable.

(5) For the purposes of this regulation a person who ceases to hold his further pensionable employment in the circumstances mentioned in regulation E2(1)(c) shall not be treated as having become entitled in relation to that employment to a retirement pension until the date (if any) on which he becomes entitled to receive payments in respect of that pension or as ceasing to hold that employment until the date immediately preceding the first-mentioned date.

Separate benefits in the case of certain re-employed local government pensioners

E17.—(1) This regulation shall apply to a person who—

(a) has become entitled to a retirement pension or a pension payable under a local Act scheme (in this regulation referred to as a "first pension");

(b) after becoming so entitled entered further employment with any scheduled body or former local authority and was in that further employment (in this regulation referred to as "further pensionable employment") a contributory employee and a pensionable employee or a pensionable employee;

(c) ceases to hold the further pensionable employment;

(d) becomes, on so ceasing, entitled to a retirement pension; and

(e) is not a person who, on so ceasing, makes an election under regulation E16 and pays such sum (if any) as is mentioned in the proviso to paragraph (2) of that regulation.

(2) Where a person to whom this regulation applies—

(a) is a person who ceased to hold the employment in relation to which he became entitled to the first pension in the circumstances mentioned in regulation E2(1)(b)(i) and gave a notice under paragraph 3 of Schedule 9, then on ceasing to hold the further pensionable employment regulation E3(7) and Schedule 9 shall not apply;

(b) is a person who ceased to hold the employment in relation to which he became entitled to the first pension in circumstances other than those mentioned in paragraph (1)(b)(i) of regulation E2 and ceases to hold the further pensionable employment in the circumstances mentioned in that paragraph, then on ceasing to hold the new pensionable employment paragraph 1 of Schedule 9, in its application to him, shall have effect as if for the words from "the period specified" to "thereof" there were substituted the words "$6\frac{243}{365}$ years" and paragraph 3 of that schedule shall not apply;

(c) dies, regulation E11(2)(a)(ii) shall not apply to the death gratuity payable in relation to the further pensionable employment.

(3) For the purposes of this regulation "retirement pension" includes a superannuation allowance under Part I of the Act of 1937 and an annual pension under the former regulations.

Adjustment of superannuation rights on death of certain re-employed local government pensioners

E18.—(1) Where a person who—

(a) had become entitled to a retirement pension (other than a retirement pension falling to be reduced under regulation E3(9)); and

(b) after becoming so entitled entered further employment with any scheduled body and was in that further employment a pensionable employee,

dies while still in the employment mentioned in sub-paragraph (b) and, if he had ceased to be employed otherwise than by reason of his death, would have been a person to whom regulation E16 would have applied, then the benefits (if any) payable under these regulations in respect of him (other than a widow's short-term pension and a children's short-term pension) shall be calculated, and any such surrender as is referred to in regulation E16(4)(d) shall have effect, as if immediately before his death he had become entitled to benefits calculated under regulation E16 or regulation E17, whichever method of calculation is the more favourable to the person entitled to receive them.

(2) Where a person who—

(a) had become entitled to a superannuation allowance under Part I of the Act of 1937 or an annual pension under the former regulations or a pension payable under a local Act scheme; and

(b) after becoming so entitled entered further employment with any scheduled body or former local authority and was in that further employment a contributory employee and a pensionable employee or a pensionable employee, and the pension referred to in sub-paragraph (a) is on that account liable to be reduced or suspended, and the person dies while still in that further employment,

then the benefits (if any) payable under these regulations in respect of him (other than a widow's short-term pension and a children's short-term pension) shall have effect as if immediately before his death he had become entitled to benefits calculated under regulation E17.

Benefits of persons with no entitlement under the former regulations to a retiring allowance and widow's pension or to a widow's pension.

E19.—(1) This regulation shall apply to a person who—

(a) either—

(i) was a contributory employee immediately before the appointed day and became a pensionable employee on that day; or

(ii) was a contributory employee under a scheduled body or former local authority, ceased to be employed by that body or authority before the appointed day and on or after that day, but within 12 months of so ceasing, becomes a pensionable employee;

(b) immediately before the appointed day or, as the case may be, ceasing to be employed as mentioned in sub-paragraph (a)(ii), either—

(i) was entitled under the Acts of 1937 to 1953 and any regulations made thereunder, either without any modification of the provisions thereof by or under any enactment or as modified by or under any enactment, to enjoy rights to benefits which did not include a title to a lump sum retiring allowance and a pension payable to his widow; or

(ii) not being such a person as is mentioned in sub-paragraph (b)(i), was entitled under the Acts of 1937 to 1953 and any regulations made thereunder, either without any modification as mentioned in sub-paragraph (b)(i) or as modified as mentioned in that sub-paragraph, to enjoy rights to benefits which did not include a title to a pension payable to his widow.

(2) This Part of these regulations, in its application to a person to whom this regulation applies, shall have effect, in the case of such a person as is mentioned in paragraph (1)(b)(i), subject to the modifications set out in Parts I and III of Schedule 12 and, in the case of such a person as is mentioned in paragraph (1)(b)(ii), subject to the modifications set out in Parts II and III of that schedule, unless and until he otherwise elects in accordance with the provisions of paragraph (3).

(3) Any election by a person under paragraph (2) shall be made by giving notice in writing to the appropriate administering authority—

(a) in the case of such a person as is mentioned in paragraph (1)(a)(i), within 6 months after the appointed day;

(b) in any other case, within 6 months after the date on which he first becomes a pensionable employee.

PART F

NATIONAL INSURANCE MODIFICATION

Classes of employee

Arrangement of pensionable employees into classes

F1.—(1) The provisions of this Part shall have effect for modifying the contributions and other superannuation payments payable by and the benefits payable to pensionable employees who are or have been insured persons, to take account of contributions payable and benefits receivable under the Insurance Act, and to make provision consequential thereon; and for this purpose pensionable employees shall be divided into four classes, namely—

Case A
Any person who—
    (*a*) is contracted out of the graduated pension scheme and
    (*b*) retains unmodified status;

Case B
Any person who—
    (*a*) is contracted out of the graduated pension scheme and
    (*b*) does not enjoy unmodified status;

Case C
Any person who—
    (*a*) is within the graduated pension scheme and
    (*b*) retains unmodified status;

Case D
Any person who—
    (*a*) is within the graduated pension scheme and
    (*b*) does not enjoy unmodified status.

(2) In this Part—

the expression "unmodified status" refers to the status of a person whose contributions were by virtue of the Modification regulations or of interchange rules not subject immediately before the appointed day to reduction to take into account his entitlement to a flat-rate pension and who remains a pensionable employee without a disqualifying break of service;

"the Modification regulations" means the National Insurance (Modification of Local Government Superannuation Schemes) Regulations 1969**(a)**;

"flat-rate pension" means a retirement pension referred to in section 30 of the Insurance Act;

"graduated pension" means a graduated retirement benefit referred to in section 36 of the Insurance Act;

"modification provision" means any provision of a pension scheme which secures the reduction of pensions under the scheme in connection with the operation of any insurance code;

"non-participating employment" has the same meaning as in section 56(1) of the Insurance Act;

"person contracted out of the graduated pension scheme" means a person in employment which is a non-participating employment; and "person within the graduated pension scheme" means a person who is in participating employment;

(a) S.I. 1969/793 (1969 II, p. 2227).

"Stage I" means the period from 3rd April 1961 to 5th January 1964;

"Stage II" means the period from 6th January 1964.

F2. For the purposes of this Part a person may be treated as falling into different cases in respect of different periods of his service.

Case A

Persons within Case A

F3. The contributions payable by and the benefits payable to any person within Case A shall not be subject to any reduction under this Part.

Case B

Persons within Case B

F4. Regulations F5 to F9 shall apply to any person within Case B.

Reduction of contributions

F5. Contributions shall be reduced at the rate of 6p for each completed week of service and for any additional period less than a completed week.

F6.—(1) Any amount payable—

(*a*) by way of additional contributions in respect of years added under regulation D10; or

(*b*) in accordance with regulations D6 and D7 in respect of service which was reckonable as non-contributing service for the purposes of the former regulations of which account may be taken in calculating the amount of the reduction of a retirement pension,

shall be reduced, in the former case by the annual amount, and in the latter case by the lump sum, obtained by—

(i) ascertaining the sum by which, in respect of the years so added or the period of non-contributing service which may be so taken into account, any retirement pension is liable to be reduced under regulation F7; and

(ii) taking for each pound of the sum so ascertained (and proportionately for any fraction of a pound) the sum shown in the appropriate column of Table I or II, as the case may be, in Schedule 13 in relation to the age which corresponds with the person's age on the date on which the relevant consent or notice was given.

(2) In reckoning the amount of the contributions payable by an employing authority in respect of years added as aforesaid, account shall be taken of any reduction under this paragraph of additional contributions.

Reduction of pension

F7.—(1) A retirement pension shall, subject to the provisions of this regulation, be reduced in respect of any service after 31st August 1947 in relation to which reduced contributions were paid pursuant to any enactment.

(2) The rate of reduction shall be £1·70 in respect of each completed year of service as described in paragraph (1).

(3) Added years shall be treated as service after 31st August 1947 unless they had become reckonable under a local Act or local Act scheme on or before that date.

(4) Where a person's retirement pension has been increased under Schedule 9, he shall be treated for the purposes of this regulation as having paid reduced contributions in respect of the period by which his service has been increased under that paragraph.

(5) If a person, having paid reduced contributions for any period under an old modification scheme, or an earlier enactment corresponding thereto, had paid thereunder a sum representing the difference between those contributions and the sum he would have contributed if both contributions had not been reduced, his service during that period shall not be treated as service in respect of which reduced contributions were paid.

(6) Where before the commencement of these regulations a person became entitled to reckon service by virtue of interchange rules, and there has been paid in respect of him a transfer value any part of which has been reduced by reason of modification provisions in his previous pension scheme, the service in respect of which the reduction was made shall be treated for the purposes of this regulation as service after 31st August 1947 for which his contributions were reduced.

(7) Reduction shall take effect on the date on which a retirement pension becomes payable unless the person has not then reached pensionable age within the meaning of the Insurance Act; and in that case the reduction shall take effect on the date on which he reaches that age.

(8) No retirement pension shall be reduced under this regulation by more than £67·75 per annum.

Persons in concurrent, etc. employments

F8.—(1) Where a person within Case B is during any period a pensionable employee in the employment of one or more scheduled bodies concurrently and is also in other employment in which he is not a pensionable employee, then if his employer in that other employment is treated as his employer for the purposes of section 3 of the Insurance Act, regulations F5 and F6 shall not apply to him.

(2) Where an insured person is a pensionable employee in the employment of two or more employing authorities concurrently, regulations F5 and F6 shall only apply in relation to him in his employment under the authority (if any) which is treated as his employer for the purposes of section 3 of the Insurance Act.

(3) Where an insured person is a pensionable employee in each of two or more separate employments under the same employing authority then, subject to paragraphs (1) and (2), regulations F5 and F6 shall apply in relation to him only in whichever of those employments occupies the greater part of his time or, if this cannot readily be ascertained, in whichever the authority may determine.

Old modification schemes

F9.—(1) This regulation applies to any person to whom an old modification scheme applied or was deemed to apply immediately before 1st September 1947 and to whom regulation 14(1) of the Modification regulations applied immediately before the appointed day.

(2) The provisions of Part C with respect to the payment of contributions shall continue to apply in relation to any person to whom this regulation applies subject to modifications corresponding to any which were applicable in relation to him by virtue of the old modification scheme.

(3) Where this regulation applies to any person immediately before he becomes entitled to a retirement pension, that pension shall be subject to modifications corresponding to those which were applicable in relation to him by virtue of the old modification scheme; and if he is entitled to a retiring allowance the amount thereof shall be reduced by the amount ascertained by—

(a) multiplying three eightieths of the amount which, by the said scheme, was required to be deducted from the annual average of his remuneration in calculating his superannuation allowance by the number of years of reckonable service in respect of which his pension is by virtue of the said modifications reduced;

(b) increasing the product by $\frac{1}{2}\%$ for any year of reckonable service in respect of which his retiring allowance is increased under regulation E3(4):

Provided that—

(i) where the old modification scheme contained provision that the superannuation allowance should not be reduced below a sum calculated by reference to a fraction of a person's average remuneration, that provision shall apply to the reduction of a retirement pension as if the reference were to sixty eightieths of the said fraction;

(ii) so much of this paragraph as relates to the reduction of a retiring allowance shall not apply to any person unless under the said scheme the amount of the reduction of benefit was calculated by reference to the annual average of his remuneration;

(iii) where under the said scheme the reduction was subject to a maximum amount in respect of each year or other shorter period of payment, the retiring allowance shall not be reduced by any greater amount than the amount by which the capital value of the said maximum amount or, as the case may be, of the annual equivalent of the maximum amount exceeds the capital value of the amount by which the pension is reduced.

(4) This regulation shall cease to apply to a person who receives a return of contributions.

Cases C and D

Persons within Cases C and D

F10. Regulations F11 to F17 shall apply to any person within Case C or D.

Reduction of contributions

F11. Contributions shall be reduced at the appropriate rate per annum specified in the following table:—

TABLE

Case	Rate per annum
Person within Case C	1% of remuneration up to £936, *less*— 6p for each completed week of service or additional period less than a completed week
Person within Case C to whom regulation F9 applies	A rate calculated as for Case C, *plus*— the amount by which his contributions are required to be reduced under regulation F9
Person within Case D	1% of remuneration up to £936

Reduction of payments for added years and additional contributory payments

F12.—(1) Any amounts payable by way of additional contributions in respect of years added under regulation D10 shall be reduced throughout the period for which they are payable in accordance with the provisions of paragraph (3).

(2) Where in respect of any period of participating employment, or any period of non-participating employment at the end of which a payment in lieu of contributions is required to be made, additional contributory payments as referred to in regulations D6 and D7 are made by a person within Case C or D, those payments shall be reduced in accordance with the provisions of paragraph (4).

(3) The additional contributions referred to in paragraph (1) shall be—

(*a*) where consent to the making of the payments was given during Stage I, at the rate of three quarters of the appropriate percentage of remuneration specified in column 2 of the table in Schedule 6 for so much of the remuneration as does not exceed £780 per annum, and at the appropriate percentage so specified for so much of the remuneration (if any) as exceeds that amount; or

(*b*) where such consent was given during Stage II, at the like rate so specified for so much of the remuneration as does not exceed £936 per annum, and at the appropriate percentage so specified for so much of the remuneration (if any) as exceeds that amount.

(4) The payments referred to in paragraph (2) shall be—

(*a*) at the rate of three quarters of the appropriate percentage of remuneration specified in column 2 or 3 of the table in Part I of Schedule 3 in respect of the specified remuneration; and

(*b*) at the full rate so specified in respect of any part of the remuneration which exceeds the specified remuneration.

(5) In this regulation the expression "specified remuneration" means—

(*a*) in respect of any period of employment during Stage I, the remuneration received, up to a maximum of £780;

(*b*) in respect of any period of employment during Stage II, the remuneration received, up to a maximum of £936,

but where the payments are begun during Stage II in respect of any period of employment at the end of which a payment in lieu of contributions is or was required to be made, the expression means—

(i) in respect of any period of employment during Stage I, £780 per annum;

(ii) in respect of any period of employment during Stage II, £936 per annum.

(6) The reduction required by this regulation in respect of a person within Case D shall not be less than any reduction which would have been required if regulation F6 had been applicable to him.

Reduction of pension

F13.—(1) Where any period of service reckonable in calculating the amount of a retirement pension was in participating employment and modified contributions were paid during it, the part of the pension which is attributable to that period shall be reduced in accordance with the provisions of this regulation.

(2) The rate of reduction shall be 1p for each completed 3 months of that service in respect of each £10 of specified remuneration as defined in regulation F12(5).

(3) The reduction required by this regulation in respect of a person within Case D shall not be less than any reduction which would have been required if regulation F7 had been applicable.

(4) Reduction shall take effect on the date when a retirement pension becomes payable unless the person has not then reached pensionable age within the meaning of the Insurance Act, in which case the reduction shall take effect on the date on which he reaches that age.

(5) No account shall be taken under this regulation of any part of a period of service in respect of which a retirement pension is reduced by virtue of interchange rules.

(6) No account shall be taken under this regulation of any period of participating employment as a pensionable employee during an income tax year if no graduated contributions had been paid under the Insurance Act in respect of any such period during that year unless at the end of that period a payment in lieu of contributions was required to be made.

(7) Where a person becomes entitled to a retirement pension on ceasing to be employed in a non-participating employment, or would have become entitled to a pension in those circumstances had he not continued in employment for more than 5 years after attaining pensionable age within the meaning of the Insurance Act, no account shall be taken, in respect of any period of participating employment, of retiring remuneration in excess of that specified during the period in a certificate of non-participation issued under section 56 of the Insurance Act as the level of his remuneration at which his employment would have become non-participating employment.

Reduction of death gratuity

F14.—(1) Where a death gratuity is payable under regulation E11 in respect of a person within Case C or D and either—

(*a*) a payment in lieu of contributions is required to be made by reason of the cessation of his employment, or such a payment has previously been made in respect of him as a pensionable employee or contributory employee or local Act contributor in circumstances not involving a return of contributions; or

(*b*) a payment in lieu of contributions had been made under any insurance code upon the termination of any period of employment which, by virtue of interchange rules, is reckonable in any manner and to any extent as service as a pensionable employee, and—

(i) the transfer value payable in respect of that employment has been adjusted to take account of the payment in lieu of contributions; and

(ii) where superannuation contributions had been made by him in that employment, the payment in lieu of contributions was made in circumstances not involving the return of those superannuation contributions,

the employing authority may resolve that the death gratuity shall be reduced by a sum not exceeding one half of the payment in lieu of contributions, or the aggregate of such payments if more than one has been made, and in that case the amount of the gratuity shall be calculated accordingly.

(2) No payment in lieu of contributions shall be taken into account for the purposes of this regulation—

  (*a*) on more than one occasion; or

  (*b*) if the payment is one which has been reduced under regulation 13 of the National Insurance (Non-participation—Assurance of Equivalent Pension Benefits) Regulations 1960(a) or any corresponding enactment in force in Northern Ireland or the Isle of Man.

(3) Where a death gratuity is payable on the cessation of two or more concurrently held employments, the power conferred by this regulation shall be exercisable—

  (*a*) in relation to any payment in lieu of contributions then required to be made, by the employing authority making that payment, and

  (*b*) in relation to any such payment previously made, by whichever of the employing authorities lately employing the person as they may agree or, in default of agreement, as is determined by the Secretary of State, and when the said employments were held under the same employing authority, the power shall be exercised in relation to such one only of the gratuities as the authority may determine.

Reduction of benefit attributable to added years, etc.

F15. Where any payments referred to in regulation F12 of these regulations or regulation 20 of the Modification regulations were being reduced in accordance with those regulations, the period to which any such payment relates shall be treated as a period of service (rendered, if any requisite consent was given during Stage II, during that stage) in participating employment in respect of which graduated contributions have been paid; and the part of the pension to which the person concerned subsequently becomes entitled which is attributable to that period shall be reduced in accordance with the provisions of this Part.

Calculation of ill-health pension

F16. Where the period of service on which a retirement pension is based has been increased under Schedule 9, the amount by which that pension exceeds the pension which would otherwise have been payable shall not be subject to reduction under regulation F13; but if in respect of any period of service reckonable for his pension the person falls to be treated within Case B, the amount of that excess shall be reduced under regulation F7.

Persons in concurrent, etc. employments

F17.—(1) Where a person within Case C or D in the employment of one or more employing authorities concurrently is also in other employment in which he is not a pensionable employee, then if his employer in that other employment is treated as his employer for the purposes of section 3 of the Insurance Act, regulations F11 and F12 shall not apply to him.

(2) The provisions of regulation F8(2) and (3) shall apply to a person within Case C or D as they apply to a person within Case B, subject to the modification that references to regulations F5 and F6 shall be construed as references to regulations F11 and F12.

(a) S.I. 1960/1103 (1960 II, p. 2244).

Miscellaneous and consequential

Contributions deemed to have been made

F18. If in respect of any period a pensionable employee pays no contributions under these regulations because the amount of the reduction in his contributions provided for by this Part equals or exceeds the amount of his contributions, he shall nevertheless be deemed for the purposes of regulation D1(1)(*a*) to have made the contributions required in respect of that period.

Limitations on surrender, termination, etc., of pensions

F19. No provision in these regulations—

(*a*) for the surrender or assignment of a pension; or

(*b*) for the reduction, termination or suspension of a pension, where the provision is invoked for any cause other than one prescribed by regulations made or deemed to have been made under section 57(1)(*c*) of the Insurance Act (which section describes equivalent pension benefits),

shall apply so as to reduce a pension payable in respect of any period of service to an employee who attains the age of 65 years in the case of a man, or 60 years in the case of a woman, below the minimum rate of equivalent pension benefits applicable in respect of that period under the Insurance Acts; and for this purpose "service" means service in a non-participating employment which is reckonable for the purpose of calculating the amount of any benefit payable to him, except any earlier period of such service in respect of which—

(i) a payment in lieu of contributions had been made; or

(ii) equivalent pension benefits satisfying the requirements of the Insurance Acts had already been assured to him.

PART G

Special Provisions for Certain Cases

Persons employed in voluntary schools, polytechnics, etc.

G1. Where—

(*a*) a local education authority have, by a resolution passed under and for the purpose of regulation B2(1)(*e*), specified an employee of the governors of a voluntary school as a pensionable employee; or

(*b*) (i) a local education authority, by a resolution passed under and for the purpose of section 3(2)(*f*) of the Act of 1937, specified such an employee as a contributory employee; or

(ii) the Greater London Council, under section 7 of the London County Council (General Powers) Act 1938(**a**), resolved that such an employee should be a contributory employee,

and that employee was immediately before the appointed day a contributory employee and became on the appointed day a pensionable employee; or

---

(a) 1938 c. xxxviii.

(c) a local education authority have, by a resolution passed under and for the purpose of regulation B2(1)(e), specified an employee of the governing body of a polytechnic, technical institute or other similar institution as a pensionable employee; or

(d) the Greater London Council, under section 53 of the London County Council (General Powers) Act 1929(a), resolved that such an employee should be a contributory employee and that employee was immediately before the appointed day a contributory employee and became on the appointed day a pensionable employee,

the employee shall be deemed for the purposes of these regulations, except regulation L15, to be in the employment of that authority.

Employees of magistrates' courts committees

G2. In their application to persons employed by a magistrates' courts committee these regulations shall have effect subject to the modifications set out in paragraphs 1 to 6 of Part I of Schedule 14 and in their application to any justices' clerk (outside the inner London area) shall have effect subject to the further modifications in paragraphs 7 and 8 of that part of that schedule.

Certain employees of the committee of magistrates for the inner London area

G3. Where a justices' clerk (inner London area) or any other officer employed by the committee of magistrates for the inner London area is in that employment a pensionable employee, in their application to him these regulations shall have effect subject to the modifications set out in paragraphs 1 to 3 of Part II of Schedule 14 and as if the committee of magistrates for the inner London area were a scheduled body and in their application to any such justices' clerk shall have effect subject to the further modifications in paragraphs 3 and 4 of that part of that schedule.

Employees of probation and after-care committees

G4. In their application to persons employed by a probation and after-care committee these regulations shall have effect subject to the modifications set out in Part III of Schedule 14.

Medical inspectors of immigrants

G5. Where a person is employed as a medical inspector of immigrants appointed under the Immigration Act 1971 and is in that employment a pensionable employee, he shall in that employment be deemed for the purposes of these regulations to be an officer in the employment of the local authority from whom he receives his remuneration in that appointment.

Members of passenger transport executives and directors of subsidiaries thereof

G6. Where a passenger transport executive—

(a) have, by a resolution passed for the purpose of regulation B2(1)(g), specified a member of that executive or a director of a subsidiary thereof as a pensionable employee; or

(b) by a resolution passed for the purpose of a corresponding provision contained in an order made under section 9(1) of the Transport Act 1968(b),

---

(a) 1929 c. lxxxvii.   (b) 1968 c. 73.

specified such a member or director as a contributory employee and that employee was immediately before the appointed day a contributory employee and became on the appointed day a pensionable employee,

that person shall be deemed for the purposes of these regulations to be in the employment of that executive and, in their application to such a person, these regulations shall have effect as if service as such a member or director were service in the employment of that executive.

Certain employees of the London Transport Executive

G7. In their application to such persons employed by the London Transport Executive as are mentioned in regulation B2(1)(*k*) these regulations shall have effect as if that Executive were a scheduled body:

Provided that nothing in these regulations shall impose upon the London Transport Executive any liability to make any payments to a local authority under the Pensions (Increase) Act 1971.

Certain employees of the Common Council

G8. In their application to such persons employed by the Common Council as are mentioned in regulation B2(1)(*j*) these regulations shall have effect as if that council were a scheduled body.

PART H

DETERMINATION OF QUESTIONS AND APPEALS

Initial determination of questions

H1. Any question concerning—

(*a*) the rights or liabilities of an employee of a scheduled body, or of a person claiming to be treated as such an employee, under any of the provisions of these regulations; or

(*b*) the rights of a person who has been an employee of a scheduled body, or the rights of the widow, dependants or the personal representatives of such a person, under any of those provisions,

shall be decided in the first instance by the body concerned.

Appeal by employee, etc.

H2.—(1) If—

(*a*) an employee of a scheduled body or person claiming to be treated as such an employee is dissatisfied with any decision made under these regulations by the body concerned as to his rights or liabilities or with the body's failure to make any such decision; or

(*b*) a person who has been an employee of a scheduled body or the widow, any dependant or the personal representatives of that person is or are dissatisfied with any decision made under these regulations by the body concerned as to his or their rights or with the body's failure to make any such decision,

and the person or persons serve on the Secretary of State written notice of appeal within the period specified in paragraph (2), the question shall be determined by the Secretary of State and his decision thereon shall be final.

(2) The period referred to in paragraph (1) for service of a notice of appeal shall be—

(a) if the person is dissatisfied with a decision made under these regulations by the body concerned, 3 months from the date on which he receives from such body a written notification of that decision;

(b) if the person is dissatisfied with the failure of the body concerned to make a decision, 3 months from that failure,

or, if the Secretary of State is satisfied that there are reasonable grounds for not serving the notice within that period, such longer period as the Secretary of State may in the particular case allow.

(3) For the purposes of this regulation the body concerned shall be deemed to have failed to give a decision if, after the expiration of 3 months from the date on which they have been requested by notice in writing served on them by any such person as is mentioned in paragraph (1)(a) or (b) to decide any question, they have not decided that question.

Appeal by administering authority

H3.—(1) Subject to paragraph (2), an administering authority may, in accordance with the provisions of paragraph (3), appeal to the Secretary of State against—

(a) any decision made under these regulations by any employing authority whose employees are entitled to participate in the benefits of the super-annuation fund maintained by the administering authority; or

(b) any failure or refusal to make any such decision by any such authority.

(2) The right of appeal provided by paragraph (1) shall not extend to any decision made by an employing authority in exercise of a discretion conferred by or under these regulations solely on that authority.

(3) An administering authority who wish to appeal under the provisions of this regulation shall serve on the Secretary of State written notice of appeal within the period specified in paragraph (4).

(4) The period referred to in paragraph (3) for service of a notice of appeal shall be—

(a) if the appeal is against a decision of an employing authority, 3 months from the date on which the administering authority receive from the employing authority written notice of that decision;

(b) if the appeal is against the failure or refusal of an employing authority to make a decision, 3 months from that failure or refusal.

(5) For the purposes of this regulation an employing authority shall be deemed to have failed to give a decision if, after the expiration of 3 months from the date on which they have been requested by notice in writing served on them by the administering authority to decide any question, they have not decided that question.

Deemed service of notices

H4. Where a notice under regulation H2 or H3 is served by post in a properly addressed pre-paid envelope it shall be deemed to be served at the time at which a letter would be delivered in the ordinary course of post.

PART J

Transitional Provisions and Transitory Provisions for Local Government Reorganisation, etc.

Definitions

J1. In this Part and in Schedule 16, unless the context otherwise requires—

"Health Service regulations" means the National Health Service (Superannuation) Regulations 1961(a);

"transferred employee" means—

(a) a person transferred on or after the appointed day—

    (i) by or under an order made under section 84 of the London Government Act 1963(b) or an agreement made under section 24(7) of that Act; or

    (ii) by virtue of a scheme made under Part I of the Police Act 1964; or

    (iii) by the operation of the Public Libraries and Museums Act 1964(c); or

    (iv) by or under an order made under section 17 of the Transport Act 1968; or

    (v) by or under an order made under section 46 of the Children and Young Persons Act 1969(d); or

    (vi) by or under an order or regulations made under the Local Government Act which, in accordance with the provisions of section 255 of that Act, contains a provision as to the transfer of that person;

(b) any person appointed by a local authority, or the National Water Council or a water authority to hold any office or employment before, or as from, the appointed day who, but for the appointment, would be transferred on that day under section 255 of the Local Government Act; and

(c) any person who at the appointed day remains in the employment of the same body as immediately before that day but who in consequence of the Local Government Act, or anything done thereunder or of these regulations becomes entitled to participate in the benefits of a superannuation fund maintained under Part B by a body different from the body which maintained the superannuation fund in the benefits of which he was immediately before the appointed day entitled to participate;

"new employment" means employment to which a person is so transferred or appointed;

"new employing body" means the body which becomes the employing authority in relation to a person so transferred or appointed;

"transferor body" means the body from which a superannuation fund is transferred by regulation J2;

"transferee body" means the body to which that superannuation fund is so transferred;

and in relation to a person appointed as aforesaid his taking up of the office or employment to which he is appointed shall for the purposes of this Part be deemed to be a transfer.

(a) 1961/1441 (1961 II, p. 2824).   (b) 1963 c. 33.   (c) 1964 c. 75.   (d) 1969 c. 54.

Closure and transfer of superannuation funds maintained under the former regulations, etc.

J2.—(1) Every administering authority shall close the superannuation fund they were maintaining immediately before the appointed day under Part I of the Act of 1937 and transfer any balance standing to the credit thereof to the superannuation fund which they are required to establish and administer under Part B, and all liabilities of, or liabilities of any body or individual to, the former fund shall become liabilities of or, subject to regulation J3, to the latter fund.

(2) Every joint committee established by a scheme of combination made under section 2 of the Act of 1937 and in force immediately before the appointed day shall cease to exist and where any person is a trustee of a superannuation fund maintained by such a committee he shall cease to be a trustee thereof.

(3) The superannuation fund maintained by any body specified in column (1) of Schedule 15 shall by virtue of these regulations be transferred to and vest in the body specified opposite thereto in column (2) of that schedule and any such fund shall, subject to the provisions of regulation J6, be carried by the transferee body to the fund which they are required to maintain under Part B.

(4) All liabilities attaching to a transferor body in respect of their superannuation fund shall, subject to the provisions of this Part, attach to the transferee body in respect of their superannuation fund.

(5) Any liability of any body or person to make payments into the superannuation fund of a transferor body shall, subject to regulation J3, become a liability to make payments into the superannuation fund of the transferee body.

(6) Subject to regulation J8, all contracts, deeds, bonds, agreements and other instruments subsisting in favour of, or against, and all notices in force which were given by or to any transferor body or any other body on their behalf for the purposes of their superannuation fund shall be of full force and effect in favour of, or against, the transferee body.

(7) Any action or proceeding or cause of action or proceeding pending or existing at the appointed day by or against a transferor body in respect of their superannuation fund shall be of full force and effect in favour of, or against, the transferee body.

(8) Where a transferor body would have become liable, or would have been empowered, on the happening of any event, to make a payment out of their superannuation fund or take any other action in respect of any person who has ceased to participate in the benefits of the fund before the appointed day, then on the happening of that event such payment or action shall, or as the case may be may, be made out of the superannuation fund of the transferee body or taken by that body.

(9) Where a person has ceased to contribute to the superannuation fund of a transferor body before the appointed day and has not become a contributor to any other superannuation fund maintained under Part I of the Act of 1937 or a local Act, the superannuation fund of the transferee body shall on and after that date be deemed to be the fund to which he was last a contributor.

(10) The accounts of any body or of their committees or officers relating to any superannuation fund transferred by this regulation shall be made up to 31st March 1974 and shall be audited in the like manner and subject to the like incidents and consequences as if these regulations had not been made:

Provided that any sum certified by a district auditor at any such audit as due from any person shall be paid to the transferee body.

(11) All legal proceedings pending on the appointed day may be amended in such manner as may be necessary or proper in consequence of these regulations.

Cessation of liability for equal annual charges

J3. Any liability of any body to make payments into a superannuation fund maintained under Part I of the Act of 1937 of any sums payable into that fund by that body, or of the share properly attributable to them of any sums payable into that fund, in pursuance of an actuary's certificate given, or a scheme made, under section 22 of the Act of 1937 shall cease.

Discharge of administering authority's liability to make annual payments existing by reason of apportionment before the appointed day of a superannuation fund

J4.—(1) As soon as is reasonably practicable after the commencement of these regulations an administering authority who are liable by virtue of regulation J2 to make annual payments in respect of a fraction of a sum which was certified by an actuary, on an apportionment under an instrument mentioned in paragraph (3) of a superannuation fund maintained under Part I of the Act of 1937, to be equivalent in value to the aggregate of future payments of annual charges and certain liabilities specified in the instrument, shall obtain from an actuary a certificate specifying an amount representing the capital value, at the date hereinafter in this paragraph mentioned, of the aggregate of such of those annual payments as are outstanding at the date on which payment in discharge of those annual payments is made under paragraph (2).

(2) Not later than 3 months after they obtain a certificate under paragraph (1), an administering authority shall pay out of the superannuation fund maintained by them, in discharge of their liability in respect of the annual payments mentioned in that paragraph, to the body entitled by virtue of regulation J2 to receive those payments a lump sum equal in amount to the amount specified in relation to those payments in that certificate, which sum shall be deemed to have formed immediately before the appointed day part of the superannuation fund maintained under Part I of the Act of 1937 by the body which immediately before the appointed day was entitled to receive those annual payments.

(3) The reference in paragraph (1) to an instrument mentioned in this paragraph is a reference to—

(a) an order made under Part II of the Local Government Act 1958(a), section 84 of the London Government Act 1963 or section 17 of the Transport Act 1968; or

(b) directions given under paragraph 5(3) of Schedule 4 to the Police Act 1964.

Valuation of closed or transferred superannuation funds

J5.—(1) An administering authority shall not be required to obtain any actuarial valuation of, or report on, the assets and liabilities of any superannuation fund maintained by them immediately before the appointed day under Part I of the Act of 1937 which was due at 31st March 1973 or 31st March 1974.

(a) 1958 c. 55.

(2) A transferee body shall not be required to obtain any actuarial valuation of, or report on, the assets and liabilities of any superannuation fund transferred by regulation J2(3) which was due at 31st March 1973 or 31st March 1974, but shall arrange for the completion of any such valuation of, and report on, such a fund as at a date prior to 31st March 1973.

Apportionment of superannuation fund

J6.—(1) Where in consequence of any enactment mentioned in paragraph (*a*) of the definition of "transferred employee" in regulation J1 or of these regulations transferred employees who immediately before the appointed day were entitled to participate in the benefits of a superannuation fund maintained by a transferor body become on the appointed day entitled to participate in the benefits of a superannuation fund maintained under Part B (other than the superannuation fund maintained by the transferee body), an apportioned part of the fund of the transferor body in respect of those transferred employees shall be transferred by the transferee body to the body maintaining the fund in the benefits of which those transferred employees become on the appointed day entitled to participate and shall be carried by them to that fund.

(2) Where by or under an order made under section 18(1) of the National Health Service Reorganisation Act 1973(**a**) persons who immediately before the appointed day were entitled to participate in the benefits of a superannuation fund maintained under Part I of the Act of 1937 are on the appointed day transferred to the employment of new health authorities and in consequence become officers within the meaning of the Health Service regulations, an apportioned part of that fund in respect of those persons shall be transferred—

(*a*) where the body which maintained that fund is a body specified in column (1) of Schedule 15, by the body specified opposite thereto in column (2) of that schedule;

(*b*) in any other case, by the body which were immediately before the appointed day maintaining that fund,

to the Secretary of State.

In this paragraph the expression "new health authorities" has the same meaning as in section 18 of the said Act of 1973.

(3) The body maintaining a superannuation fund under Part B comprising a superannuation fund falling to be apportioned shall obtain from an actuary as soon as is reasonably practicable after the appointed day a report on the apportionment of the last-mentioned superannuation fund.

(4) The provisions set out in Schedule 16 shall have effect for the purposes of the apportionment required by paragraph (1) or (2).

(5) Where at any time after the appointed day and before the date of transfer as defined in paragraph 9 of Schedule 16 there is paid to any body receiving an apportioned part of a superannuation fund under paragraph (1) any sum by way of transfer value which became payable, or a repayment of contributions returned, under the former regulations in respect of any period of service of a transferred employee in respect of whom the apportionment is required to be made, the sum shall be paid to the body making the apportionment and shall be deemed to have formed part of the apportioned superannuation fund immediately before the appointed day.

(**a**) 1973 c. 32.

Certain persons employed on the appointed day in voluntary schools maintained by local education authorities for areas outside Greater London

J7. Where an employee of the governors of a voluntary school which as from the appointed day is maintained by any local education authority for any area outside Greater London—

(*a*) was immediately before the appointed day in that employment a contributory employee; and

(*b*) became on that day a pensionable employee,

the employee shall be deemed for the purposes of these regulations, except regulation L15, to be in the employment of that authority.

Admission agreements

J8. Any admission agreement whereby the employees of any body specified in regulation B4(4) are, or can be, admitted to participate in the benefits of a superannuation fund and in force immediately before the appointed day, shall, notwithstanding the revocation effected by regulation M2 of the provision under which that agreement was made, or continued in force as if made—

(*a*) continue in force as if it were an agreement made under regulation B4; and

(*b*) where by the admission agreement the employees of that body are, or can be, admitted to participate in the benefits of a superannuation fund maintained by a body specified in column (1) of Schedule 15, have effect as an agreement between the first-mentioned body or, if that body ceases to exist on the appointed day, the body succeeding to its functions, and the body specified opposite to the second-mentioned body in column (2) of that schedule,

subject, however, to such modifications and adaptations as the parties concerned may agree to be necessary for bringing it into accordance with the provisions of these regulations or, in default of agreement, as the Secretary of State shall determine.

Preservation of rights and liabilities of certain persons to whom the Acts of 1937 to 1953, etc., applied as modified, etc., by a local Act or scheme

J9.—(1) This regulation shall apply to a person who—

(*a*) immediately before the appointed day was a contributory employee to whom the Acts of 1937 to 1953 and the regulations made thereunder applied either as modified or extended by any local Act or scheme or together with any such provisions (in this regulation referred to as "his former superannuation scheme"); and

(*b*) became on the appointed day a pensionable employee under a scheduled body.

(2) Where any right or liability conferred by or under a provision of a regulation specified in the following table would, in relation to a person to whom this regulation applies, be less beneficial than any right or liability conferred by any similar provision contained in his former superannuation scheme, these regulations shall have effect in relation to him, for the appropriate period, as if they conferred on him a right or, as the case may be, a liability corresponding to that previously enjoyed by him or to which he was previously subject under that similar provision in lieu of the right or liability conferred by or under the first-mentioned provision.

TABLE

1. Paragraph (*a*) of the definition in regulation A3(1) of "remuneration".

2. Regulation C1.

3. Regulation E1.

4. Regulation E2(1)(a).

5. Regulation E15.

6. Regulation L15.

(3) Where a person to whom this regulation applies—

(*a*) becomes entitled under regulation C8, on ceasing to be employed during the appropriate period by reason of his voluntary resignation, to receive a return of contributions; and

(*b*) would, if the former regulations had not been revoked by these regulations and he had become entitled on so ceasing to receive a return of contributions, have been entitled under a similar provision contained in his former superannuation scheme, to receive interest on the sum paid to him by way of a return of contributions,

he shall be entitled to receive out of the appropriate superannuation fund interest (calculated, to the date on which he ceased to hold his employment, at the like rate and with the like rests as it would have been calculated under that similar provision) on such part of the sum payable to him under that regulation as is equal to the amount of his contributions payable before 1st April 1972 to any superannuation fund under Part I of the Act of 1937, or under the Act of 1922 or under a local Act scheme.

(4) Where the right to surrender conferred by regulation E4 would, in relation to a person to whom this regulation applies, be less beneficial than any right to surrender conferred by a similar provision contained in his former superannuation scheme and the person does not make an election under regulation E19, these regulations shall have effect in relation to him, for the appropriate period, as if they conferred on him a right to surrender corresponding to that previously enjoyed by him under that similar provision in lieu of the right to surrender conferred by regulation E4.

(5) Where—

(*a*) a person to whom this regulation applies dies during the appropriate period; and

(*b*) if the former regulations had not been revoked by these regulations, any death gratuity payable under a similar provision contained in his former superannuation scheme would have been calculated by reference to a fraction of his average remuneration greater than three eightieths,

the amount of the death gratuity payable in respect of him under these regulations shall be increased by the amount ascertained by multiplying the appropriate fraction of his pensionable remuneration by the length in years of his reckonable service before 1st April 1972.

In this paragraph—

"appropriate fraction" means the fraction mentioned in sub-paragraph (*b*) reduced by three eightieths; and

"average remuneration" has the same meaning as in the Benefits regulations.

3d.

(6) In this regulation the appropriate period during which any provision mentioned in paragraph (2) or (4) is to continue to apply to such a person as is therein mentioned or during which paragraphs (3) and (5) are to apply to or in respect of him means the period of application specified in the similar provision contained in his former superannuation scheme or, if no period is so specified, the period during which that person continues in the employment of the scheduled body mentioned in paragraph (1)(*b*).

Contributions of former clerks of the peace, etc.

J10.—(1) This regulation shall apply to a person who—

(*a*) was immediately before the appointed day, under paragraph 13(2) of Schedule 10 to the Courts Act 1971(**a**), contributing to a superannuation fund maintained under Part I of the Act of 1937 the amount specified in that paragraph; and

(*b*) became on the appointed day a pensionable employee under a scheduled body.

(2) A person to whom this regulation applies shall, so long as he continues in the employment of the scheduled body mentioned in paragraph (1)(*b*), be entitled to contribute to the superannuation fund maintained under Part B by the body which before the appointed day maintained the superannuation fund to which he was contributing as mentioned in paragraph (1)(*a*) or, as the case may be, to whom the superannuation fund to which he was so contributing is transferred by regulation J2(3) the amount which he would have been entitled to contribute under the said paragraph 13(2) if the former regulations had not been revoked by these regulations and, if the person is a transferred employee who is transferred to his new employment on the appointed day, he had remained in the employment of the body from which he was transferred.

(3) For the purpose of determining the amount of any benefit which becomes payable to or in respect of a person to whom this regulation applies and who, by virtue of paragraph (2), paid contributions of the amount there mentioned, that person shall be treated as having received the remuneration which he would have received but for the reduction thereof in consequence of the abolition of his office under section 44(1) of the Courts Act 1971 or cessation of his employment for the purpose of any function as a result of any matters referred to in paragraphs (*a*) to (*c*) of section 44(2) of that Act.

Certain liabilities of former local authorities

J11.—(1) Where at any time before the appointed day a gratuity or allowance, by way of periodical payments or an annuity—

(*a*) has been granted to any person by any authority described in column (1) of Part I or II of Schedule 4 to the English Property Order or in column (1) of Part I or II of Schedule 4 to the Welsh Property Order on his ceasing to be employed by them; or

(*b*) has been granted to the widow or any dependant of a person who died while in or after leaving the employment of such an authority or during the currency of a gratuity or allowance granted to him as mentioned in sub-paragraph (*a*),

and, if payment in respect of the gratuity or allowance had continued in accordance with the terms of the grant and of any subsequent increase, one

---

(**a**) 1971 c. 23.

or more payments would have been made on or after the appointed day (whether under legal obligation or otherwise), those payments shall be made by the authority specified in respect of such authority in column (2) of that Part.

(2) Without prejudice to paragraph (1), where, if these regulations had not been made, any authority described in column (1) of Part I or II of Schedule 4 to the English Property Order or in column (1) of Part I or II of Schedule 4 to the Welsh Property Order would for the purposes of any enactment relating to pensions have been the employing authority or former employing authority in relation to a person who died before the appointed day in the employment of that authority or otherwise ceased to be employed by them, or the widow or any dependant of such a person, the authority specified in respect of such first-mentioned authority in column (2) of that Part shall be treated as being at that time the employing authority or former employing authority for those purposes in relation to that person, his widow or dependant.

Policy schemes

J12. Any agreement or trust deed made for the purposes of any scheme of superannuation by a body employing a transferred employee and having effect immediately prior to his transfer shall, so far as it relates to that employee, have effect thereafter as if it had been made with the new employing body; and any policies of insurance which are held for the purposes mentioned in this regulation for the benefit of any transferred employee shall be held for the like purposes by the new employing body.

Continuity of employment and preservation of status

J13.—(1) Subject to paragraph (2)—

   (*a*) any provision of these regulations and any enactment, instrument or other document contained in or made or issued under Part III of the Insurance Act shall have effect in relation to a transferred employee to whom it applies, as if his new employment and his former employment were one continuous employment; and

   (*b*) notwithstanding anything in these regulations, where such a transferred employee is—

       (i) transferred on the appointed day and was immediately before that day a contributory employee or local Act contributor and does not otherwise on that day become a pensionable employee, he shall become a pensionable employee in his new employment;

       (ii) transferred after the appointed day and is immediately before the date on which he is transferred a pensionable employee or local Act contributor and does not otherwise on that date become or continue to be a pensionable employee, he shall become or continue to be a pensionable employee in his new employment.

(2) Paragraph (1) shall not affect the operation of regulations J6 and J14 in relation to any transferred employee.

Discretionary powers

J14. Where immediately before a transferred employee is transferred it is the prevailing practice of the body employing him, in relation to employees of that description, to exercise beneficially (that is to say, to secure the payment of gratuities, allowances or pensions, or of increased pensions or lump sum benefits) any discretionary power exercisable by them by virtue of any enactment relating to pensions, it shall be the duty of the new employing body in relation to that transferred employee, if he has continued in their employment, to exercise any corresponding power under these regulations or any other enactment relating to pensions for the time being in force in a way which is not less beneficial than the general character of that practice; and Part H shall apply to any question arising under this regulation:

Provided that in exercising any such power as respects any widow or child of a transferred employee, the new employing authority shall have regard to any pension to which the widow is entitled under regulation E5 or which is payable to or for the benefit of the child under regulation E8.

Contributions of transferred manual workers

J15. Any transferred employee who was paying superannuation contributions immediately before his transfer at a rate appropriate to a manual worker shall continue to contribute at the like rate so long as he continues to be employed by the new employing body on duties reasonably comparable to those on which he was engaged immediately before his transfer.

Modification of the regulations in their application to certain transferred employees previously employed by the Manchester Corporation, etc.

J16.—(1) Where a transferred employee—

(a) (i) being a transferred employee who was transferred before the appointed day, was immediately before he was so transferred a contributor to the Manchester pension fund; or

(ii) not being such a transferred employee as is mentioned in sub-paragraph (i), was immediately before the appointed day such a contributor as is therein mentioned; and

(b) becomes on the appointed day a pensionable employee under a scheduled body,

these regulations shall, so long as he remains in the employment of that body, have effect in relation to him as if for any reference to an expression in column (1) of the following table (which lists certain expressions used in these regulations) there were substituted a reference to the expression appearing opposite thereto in column (2):—

TABLE

(1)	(2)
1. the Acts of 1937 to 1953, or the regulations made thereunder the Acts of 1937 to 1953, or the regulations made thereunder applying as amended or extended by any local Act or scheme or together with any such provisions	the Manchester pension provisions

[Table continued on page 2077

TABLE—*continued*

(1)	(2)
2. the appropriate superannuation fund within the meaning of the Act of 1937 a superannuation fund maintained under Part I of the Act of 1937	the Manchester pension fund
3. contributory employee	contributor to the Manchester pension fund
4. (*a*) contributing service and (*b*) non-contributing service for the purposes of the former regulations	service for purposes of the Manchester pension provisions
5. the former regulations	the Manchester pension provisions
6. a provision in the former regulations	the corresponding or similar provision in the Manchester pension provisions

(2) Regulation B2(1)(*a*) and (*b*) (i) shall not apply to a whole-time officer or manual worker who—

(*a*) immediately before the appointed day was a whole-time officer or manual worker of the Manchester Corporation or of any other body any of whose employees were immediately before that day entitled to participate in the benefits of the Manchester pension fund; and

(*b*) was not immediately before the appointed day a contributor to that fund but would have become such a contributor upon the completion of 6 months' continuous service under the Manchester Corporation or, as the case may be, the body by whom he was employed as mentioned in sub-paragraph (*a*); and

(*c*) was on the appointed day in the employment of a scheduled body, and, notwithstanding anything in these regulations, such an officer or manual worker shall become a pensionable employee on completion by him of 6 months' continuous whole-time employment with his employing authority or a total of 6 months' continuous whole-time employment with the body by whom he was employed immediately before the appointed day and his employing authority.

(3) In this regulation—

"the Manchester pension fund" means the pension fund maintained immediately before the appointed day by the Manchester City Council for the officers and servants of the Manchester Corporation; and

"the Manchester pension provisions" means the provisions of the enactments, and of the schemes and other instruments in force thereunder immediately before the appointed day, which relate to the Manchester pension fund (including the provisions of the Acts of 1937 to 1953 and of any relevant instruments thereunder so far as applicable to that fund).

Persons transferred to scheduled bodies under section 18(4)(a) of the National Health Service Reorganisation Act 1973

J17.—(1) This regulation shall apply to a person who—

(a) is by or under an order made under section 18(4)(a) of the National Health Service Reorganisation Act 1973 transferred to the employment of a scheduled body; and

(b) immediately before he was so transferred was in an employment in which he was an officer within the meaning of the Health Service regulations.

(2) Where immediately before he was transferred as mentioned in paragraph (1)(a) a person to whom this regulation applies was a person in respect of whom the Secretary of State paid contributions under regulation 45 of the Health Service regulations (persons subject to non-statutory superannuation schemes and arrangements) or carried out any such scheme or arrangements as are referred to in that regulation, that person shall not be subject to any provisions of these regulations except those contained in this regulation, and the body to which that person is transferred shall—

(a) where immediately before the appointed day the Secretary of State was under the first-mentioned regulation paying in respect of that person the contributions authorised or required by the relevant scheme to be paid by the employer, pay those contributions; and

(b) deduct from the person's remuneration the amount of any contribution required by the scheme or under the arrangements to be paid by the employee.

(3) A person to whom this regulation applies (other than a person mentioned in paragraph (2))—

(a) who does not otherwise on the date on which he is transferred as mentioned in paragraph (1)(a) become a pensionable employee, shall become a pensionable employee in the employment to which he is so transferred;

(b) subject to sub-paragraph (e), shall be entitled to reckon—

(i) as reckonable service any service which for the purposes of the Health Service regulations he was entitled to reckon in relation to the employment mentioned in paragraph (1)(b) as, or as a period of, contributing service; and

(ii) as qualifying service any service which for the purposes of those regulations he was entitled to reckon in relation to that employment for the purpose of determining whether he was entitled to a benefit under those regulations, but for no other purpose:

Provided that for the purposes of this sub-paragraph any period of part-time service shall be treated as though it was whole-time service for a proportionately reduced period and, except for the purposes referred to in regulation D18(3), any service which was reckonable under the Health Service regulations for all purposes (other than for the purpose of determining whether any benefit was payable) as a period of contributing service at half its length shall, subject to paragraph (c), be counted at half its length;

(c) where immediately before he is so transferred he was in the process of making payments which were or were deemed to be payments under Schedule 2 to the Health Service regulations he shall, subject to sub-paragraph (e), be entitled to make the outstanding payments as if they were instalments of an amount payable under regulation D6 and, if he completes the payments in the manner provided in Schedule 4, to have the service in respect of which they were made counted for all the purposes of these regulations at its full length;

(*d*) where immediately before he is so transferred he was in the process of making payments in respect of added years he shall, subject to sub-paragraph (*e*), be entitled to make the outstanding payments as if they were payments of an amount payable under regulation D10 and in respect of the added years in respect of which those payments are made shall enjoy rights and be subject to liabilities as if those years were added years reckonable under that regulation in the employment to which he is so transferred;

(*e*) may, within 6 months after the date on which he is so transferred, give notice in writing to the employing authority that he does not wish to avail himself of the benefits provided under these regulations and in that event these regulations shall have effect in relation to him as if they conferred on him rights corresponding with those which he would have enjoyed if he had remained subject to the provisions of the Health Service regulations, and these regulations shall continue so to apply so long as he is employed without a disqualifying break of service by a scheduled body on duties reasonably comparable to those on which he was engaged immediately before he was so transferred.

PART K

Persons Ceasing to be Employed After 30th March 1972 and Before the Appointed Day

Retrospective application

K1.—(1) If a person—

(*a*) ceased on or after 31st March 1972 to hold an employment in which he was a contributory employee and, where he was a person to whom the provisions of regulation 7 of the Miscellaneous Provisions regulations would otherwise have applied, did not elect under regulation 25 of those regulations that those provisions should not so apply; or

(*b*) died on or after that date while still in such an employment,

subject to paragraph (7), he shall be entitled to or there shall be payable in respect of him such of the benefits conferred by these regulations to which he would have been entitled or as would have been payable in respect of him if these regulations had been in operation at the time he so ceased or died and any benefit to which he may be so entitled or which may be so payable in respect of him shall be in substitution for any benefit (including a return of contributions, any pension payable to a widow or any dependant of his by virtue of a surrender and, unless the employing authority determine otherwise. a gratuity granted to him, but excluding an injury allowance) which may have become payable to or in respect of him under or by virtue of the former regulations in respect of the employment he ceased to hold as mentioned in sub-paragraph (*a*) or, as the case may be, in which he died.

(2) For the purpose of determining whether such a person as is mentioned in paragraph (1) is by virtue of that paragraph entitled to a benefit under these regulations (in substitution for any benefit under the former regulations), or

whether he is entitled to receive payment of or payments in respect of such a benefit or any such benefit is by virtue of that paragraph payable in respect of him and for the purpose of calculating the amount of any such benefit, the provisions of Parts A, D and E and regulation J9, subject to the modifications set out in Schedule 17, and in so far as they are applicable to that person in relation to the employment he ceased to hold as mentioned in paragraph (1)(a) or, as the case may be, in which he died, the provisions of Part G shall apply to or in respect of him as if—

(a) the expression "the appointed day" (except where used in relation to a specified period after that day and in regulations E2(4)(e), E4(1)(i) and (4), E12, E15(11), paragraphs (3) and (4) of this regulation and paragraph 2(a) of Schedule 11) meant the day on which that person so ceased or, as the case may be, died;

(b) that person had become a pensionable employee on that day; and

(c) the body under whom that person was a contributory employee as mentioned in paragraph (1) had on that day been a scheduled body,

and Part H shall apply to any question concerning any right or liability arising under or by virtue of this regulation.

(3) In the case of such a person as is mentioned in paragraph (1)(a), who has died before the appointed day or dies before the expiration of any period within which an application, election or notice is required under any provision of Part D or E, as applied by paragraph (2), to be made or given, without making or giving, as the case may be, the application, election or notice which that person was entitled to make or give, and of such a person as is mentioned in paragraph (1)(b), such an application, election or notice (other than a notice for the purposes of regulation E1, E2(4)(a)(iv), E4 or E15(2)) may be given—

(a) if that person was a male and leaves a widow, by her;

(b) if that person was a male and does not leave a widow or his widow has died before the appointed day or dies before the expiration of any period mentioned above without making or giving, as the case may be, that application, election or notice, by his personal representatives; and

(c) if that person was a female, by her personal representatives.

(4) Where as respects such a person as is mentioned in paragraph (1)(a) a period is treated under regulation D4 by virtue of this regulation as service that person was entitled to reckon as non-contributing service for the purposes of the former regulations, if such a person again became a contributory employee but before the appointed day ceased to hold the employment in which he was a contributory employee or died before that day, then the period treated under that regulation as mentioned above shall be aggregated with any service and any period he was entitled to reckon as non-contributing service for the purposes of the former regulations at the time he first ceased on or after 31st March 1972 to hold an employment in which he was a contributory employee.

(5) Where the body under whom such a person as is mentioned in paragraph (1)(a) or (b) was a contributory employee is an authority described in column (1) of Part I or II of Schedule 4 to the English Property Order or in column (1) of Part I or II of Schedule 4 to the Welsh Property Order—

(a) any provision of these regulations which imposes a liability, or confers a power, on an employing authority to take any action in respect of any such person, shall have effect as if it imposed that liability or, as the case may be, conferred that power on the authority specified in respect of the first-mentioned authority in column (2) of that part of that schedule;

(*b*) any such application, election or notice as is mentioned in paragraph (3) shall be made or given to the authority so specified.

(6) Where immediately before such a person as is mentioned in paragraph (1)(*a*) or (*b*) ceased to hold his employment as mentioned in paragraph (1)(*a*) or, as the case may be, died it was the prevailing practice of the body employing him, in relation to employees of that description, to exercise beneficially any discretionary power under section 12(6) of the Act of 1937, or section 2(2) of the Act of 1953 or regulation 13 of the Benefits regulations, it shall be the duty of the body by whom any discretionary power is exercisable under regulation D4, D9 or E13 in relation to him in respect of the employment he so ceased to hold or in which he died to exercise that power in a way which is not less beneficial than the general character of that practice and the provisions of Part H shall apply to any question arising under this paragraph.

(7) The aggregate amount of any benefits payable to or in respect of a person under these regulations by virtue of paragraph (1) shall be reduced by an amount equal to the aggregate amount of any payments which have been made under the former regulations for which benefits under these regulations are substituted under paragraph (1).

Right to opt out

K2. No provision of these regulations shall apply to any person to whom at any time from 1st April 1972 to 31st March 1974 (both dates inclusive) any benefit (including a return of contributions and any pension payable to a widow or any dependant by virtue of a surrender) was or is being paid or became or may become payable if—

(*a*) he is placed by that provision in a worse position than he would have been if it had not applied in relation to that benefit; and

(*b*) that provision relates to a benefit paid or payable in respect of such a person as is mentioned in regulation K1(1)(*a*) or (*b*) in respect of the employment he ceased to hold as mentioned in regulation K1(1)(*a*) or, as the case may be, in which he died; and

(*c*) the first-mentioned person, by notice in writing given to the appropriate administering authority within 3 months after the appointed day, elects that that provision shall not apply to him.

PART L

MISCELLANEOUS AND SUPPLEMENTAL

Information to be supplied by certain employees

L1.—(1) Every scheduled body shall (unless the circumstances described in paragraph (2) apply) for the purposes of this Part—

(*a*) in the case of a person described in regulation L2(4)(*a*), as soon as is reasonably practicable after the commencement of these regulations;

(*b*) in the case of a person described in regulation L2(4)(*b*), within 3 months after that person has entered that employment; and

(*c*) in the case of a person described in regulation L2(4)(*c*), within 6 months after any resolution, determination or other change mentioned therein, request him to furnish—

>> (i) a statement in writing of all his previous periods of employment (whether by a scheduled body, or by any other body or person), war service and national service (if any); and

>> (ii) a copy of all previous notifications given to him under these regulations, the Local Government Superannuation (Administration) Regulations 1954(a), or the Local Government Superannuation (Administration) Regulations 1938(b),

and the administering authority shall so far as it appears to them necessary to do so verify from any previous employer or administering authority the information given by that person.

(2) A scheduled body who are satisfied that a person in their employment is not a pensionable employee or that they or the administering authority already have in their possession a complete and accurate record of all of his previous service (if any) relevant for the purposes of this Part, shall not be under a duty to request that person to furnish the documents described in paragraph (1).

(3) A request by a scheduled body under paragraph (1) shall be in writing and shall include a conspicuous statement directing the attention of the employee to the importance of supplying full and accurate information on all matters to which the request relates and warning that person that any inaccuracy in or omission from the information which he supplies may prejudice the ascertainment of his rights under these regulations.

Decisions to be taken by scheduled bodies as to status of employees

L2.—(1) In relation to every person employed by a scheduled body, that body shall consider and decide the questions in paragraph (2) and, if appropriate, the questions in paragraph (3) when described in paragraph (4).

(2) The questions referred to in paragraph (1) are—

>> (a) whether the employee is an officer or manual worker;

>> (b) whether his employment is whole-time, variable-time or part-time;

>> (c) where the employee has been required by the body concerned under regulation B2(3) to undergo a medical examination, whether he has undergone that examination to their satisfaction; and

>> (d) whether or not he is a pensionable employee.

(3) Where a scheduled body decide under paragraph (2)(d) that an employee is a pensionable employee they shall also consider and decide the following questions—

>> (a) in the case of an employee whose remuneration does not wholly or partly consist of fees, the remuneration upon which contributions are payable;

>> (b) in the case of an employee whose remuneration does wholly or partly consist of fees, the remuneration upon which contributions are or may become payable;

>> (c) the source of all fees described in sub-paragraph (b); and

>> (d) in the case of an employee whose employment is part-time employment, the proportion which his contractual minimum hours of employment

---

(a) S.I. 1954/1192 (1954 II, p. 1570).
(b) S.R. & O. 1938/574 (Rev. XVII, p. 791: 1938 II, p. 2791).

each week in that part-time employment bear to the number of hours which would have been his contractual minimum hours of employment had he, in that employment, served whole-time.

(4) The questions specified in paragraphs (2) and (3) shall be considered and decided by the scheduled body—

    (*a*) in the case of a person in the employment of that body on the appointed day, as soon as is reasonably practicable after the commencement of these regulations;

    (*b*) in the case of a person entering the employment of that body after the appointed day, within 3 months after he has entered that employment; and

    (*c*) in the case of a person described in sub-paragraph (*a*) or (*b*), if any of the following events occur—

        (i) any statutory resolution is passed by that body for the purposes of regulation B2(1)(*d*);

        (ii) the number of his regular or usual hours of employment is changed;

        (iii) any determination is made under regulation D4 or any resolution is passed under regulation D9; or

        (iv) any other change occurs in, or in relation to, his employment, being a resolution, determination or other change which (either in the opinion of the scheduled body or in the opinion of the employee notified by him in writing to that body within 6 months after the event) is material for the purposes of these regulations, as soon as is reasonably practicable after the change or, as the case may be, after receipt by that body of notification by the employee.

Decisions to be taken by administering authorities as to status of employees

L3.—(1) In relation to every person employed by a scheduled body and, in accordance with regulation L2(2)(*d*), decided by that body to be a pensionable employee, the appropriate administering authority shall, upon receipt of the documents specified in regulation L1(1), consider and decide the questions in paragraph (2) when described in paragraph (3).

(2) The questions referred to in paragraph (1) are—

    (*a*) (i) what previous service or employment (if any) he is entitled to reckon;

        (ii) whether that service counts as reckonable service or qualifying service;

        (iii) whether any (and if so, what period or periods) of that service or employment was part-time service or employment and, if it was, what proportion of whole-time service or employment it represents;

        (iv) what period or periods of that service or employment were in participating employment or non-participating employment for the purposes of Part F;

        (v) whether any such period of participating employment falls to be disregarded under regulation F13(6);

        (vi) whether a payment in lieu of contributions has been made or equivalent pension benefits have been assured under Part III of the Insurance Act in respect of any such period of non-participating employment; and

        (vii) the amount of any payment in lieu of contributions;

(b) what rate of contribution the employee is liable to pay to the appropriate superannuation fund;

(c) whether the rate referred to in sub-paragraph (b) is (by virtue of Part F) a reduced rate, and, if it is, details of the reduction in the rate and the date from which that reduction has effect;

(d) whether the employee is entitled to reckon any added years or additional period as reckonable service, and if so, the number of years or the period of service and the period during which any added period payment or additional contributory payment is payable.

(3) The questions specified in paragraph (2) shall be considered and decided by the appropriate administering authority as soon as is reasonably practicable after—

(a) 1st April 1975, or

(b) the date on which the person in relation to whom the decision is to be made becomes subject to these regulations,

whichever shall last occur; but if the information necessary in order to enable that authority to give a decision on any question is not then immediately available, that authority may postpone their decision on that question for a period not exceeding 6 months.

Notification of decisions as to status

L4.—(1) (a) A scheduled body (unless the circumstances described in paragraph (2) apply), as soon as is reasonably practicable after they have decided any question in accordance with regulation L2; and

(b) an administering authority, as soon as is reasonably practicable after they have decided any question in accordance with regulation L3,

shall send a written notification of their decision to the employee as described in paragraph (3).

(2) A scheduled body shall not be under a duty to send a written notification as described in paragraph (1) if the employee in relation to whom the decision was made has before the appointed day received from the body in whose employment he was immediately before the appointed day, a notification under regulation 7 of the Local Government Superannuation (Administration) Regulations 1954 that he was a contributory employee or local Act contributor and there has been no change in the conditions of his employment.

(3) The written notification mentioned in paragraph (1) shall include a conspicuous statement directing the attention of the employee—

(a) to the place at which he may obtain information about details in the notification or about calculation of service or benefits;

(b) to his right under regulation H2(1), if he is dissatisfied with any decision notified in the notification, to refer the question to which the decision relates for determination by the Secretary of State; and

(c) to the provisions of regulation H2(2) with respect to the time within which notice of any such appeal must be served on the Secretary of State.

(4) Every scheduled body in whose employment there is any pensionable employee shall cause a record to be kept in such form as the body thinks fit for the purpose of making readily available at all times information as to the name of every employee who is a pensionable employee and such other particulars relating to the employee as are referred to in regulation L2(2) and (3).

(5) Every administering authority shall cause a record to be kept in such form as the authority think fit for the purpose of making readily available at all times information as to the name of every person in respect of whom the authority are required to consider and decide as mentioned in regulation L3(2), and such other particulars relating to that person as are referred to in paragraphs (2) and (3) of that regulation.

Payments by employing authorities to administering authorities

L5.—(1) Every employing authority (not being an administering authority) shall pay to the appropriate administering authority at such intervals, not longer than 12 months, as the appropriate administering authority may determine—

(a) all amounts from time to time deducted from the remuneration of their pensionable employees under these regulations; and

(b) a contribution towards the cost of the administration of the appropriate superannuation fund of such annual amount as may be agreed between the employing authority and the administering authority or, in default of agreement, as is determined by the Secretary of State.

(2) Payments made in pursuance of paragraph (1)(a) shall be paid into the appropriate superannuation fund.

(3) The payment by an employing authority of any sum due under paragraph (1)(a) shall, unless the appropriate administering authority direct as mentioned in paragraph (4), be accompanied by a statement showing—

(a) the names and remuneration of each of the pensionable employees in relation to whom the payment is made;

(b) the amounts comprised in the payment which represent deductions from the remuneration of each of those employees, the periods in respect of which such deductions were made and the amounts (if any) by which any contributions to which the statement relates have been reduced by virtue of any provisions in Part F;

(c) the amount of the remuneration of those employees from or in respect of whom deductions have not been made; and

(d) the names of any pensionable employees from whose remuneration no deductions have been made.

(4) The appropriate administering authority may direct that, in lieu of complying with the requirements in paragraph (3), the employing authorities interested in the appropriate superannuation fund are to furnish the information provided for in that paragraph in such form and at such intervals, not being longer than 12 months, as the authority may specify.

(5) If any sum due under the provisions of this regulation remains unpaid beyond a period of one month after the date on which it becomes due, the sum shall bear interest at the rate of 5% per annum as from the expiration of that period.

Transmission of documents and information between authorities

L6.—(1) Every employing authority (not being an administering authority) shall forward to the appropriate administering authority—

(a) when notifying an employee of a decision made under regulation L2, a copy of the notification and a copy of all information supplied by the employee in accordance with regulation L1; ′

(b) as soon as is reasonably practicable upon receipt of every statement rendered by a pensionable employee under regulation C3 and of any statutory declaration, that statement and declaration; and

(c) from time to time, such other documents and information as the administering authority may reasonably require for the purpose of discharging their functions under these regulations.

(2) Every employing authority (not being an administering authority) shall from time to time notify the appropriate administering authority of—

(a) the amount of any payment in lieu of contributions which becomes payable under the Insurance Act in respect of a pensionable employee, and the period to which such payment relates;

(b) details of the amount (if any) by which the employing authority have resolved under regulation F14 to reduce the amount of any death gratuity payable in respect of a pensionable employee; and

(c) details of any amount which the employing authority concerned is entitled to recover under section 60(1) of the Insurance Act in respect of any payment in lieu of contributions made under that Act.

(3) The payment by an administering authority of any amount referred to in paragraph (2)(c) shall be accompanied by a statement showing—

(a) the names of the pensionable employees in relation to whom the payment is made; and

(b) the amounts which have been deducted from any death gratuity pursuant to a resolution referred to in paragraph (2)(b).

(4) Every administering authority, when notifying a person of a decision under regulation L3, shall (if that person is not in their employment) forward to the employing authority a copy of that notification.

Further provisions as to transmission of documents and information

L7.—(1) Without prejudice to the generality of regulation L6, an employing authority (not being an administering authority)—

(a) on receiving from a pensionable employee notice of his intended retirement;

(b) on giving to an employee notice to terminate his services in circumstances in which he may become entitled to a return of contributions or to a benefit payable out of the appropriate superannuation fund; or

(c) on becoming aware of any other circumstances which may necessitate any payment out of the appropriate superannuation fund,

shall, as soon as is reasonably practicable, comply with the requirements in paragraph (2).

(2) The requirements mentioned in paragraph (1) are—

(a) to inform the appropriate administering authority of the notice or other circumstances described in that paragraph;

(b) to forward to that authority particulars of the employee's remuneration during the period that is relevant to a decision on the benefit which may become payable to or in respect of that employee; and

(c) to forward to that authority a copy of any relevant medical or death certificate or of any certificate issued by the employing authority under regulation L11.

Decisions to be taken by employing authorities as to benefits and notification thereof

L8.—(1) Any question as to entitlement to a benefit (including a return of contributions) under these regulations (other than a question as to the amount thereof) shall, subject to the right of appeal to the Secretary of State conferred by regulation H2 or H3, be decided by the authority employing the person in respect of whom the question arises.

(2) The employing authority by whom a decision as to a person's entitlement has been made in accordance with paragraph (1) shall send to that person a written notification of their decision.

(3) A notification sent in pursuance of paragraph (2) shall include—

(*a*) if the decision is adverse to the person, the grounds for the decision; and

(*b*) a statement of the kind required by regulation L4(3).

(4) The employing authority shall send to the appropriate administering authority a copy of every notification sent in accordance with the foregoing provisions of this regulation.

Decisions to be taken by administering authorities as to benefits and notification thereof

L9.—(1) Where a decision is made under regulation L8 that a payment should be made to a person, the appropriate administering authority shall, as soon as is reasonably practicable on receipt of the document described in regulation L8(4) or, if they are themselves the employing authority, as soon as is reasonably practicable on reaching a decision under regulation L8(1), consider and decide the amount of any benefit which is or may become payable out of the fund.

(2) An authority by whom a decision has been made in accordance with paragraph (1) shall send to the person in respect of whom the decision was made a written notification of their decision.

(3) A notification sent in pursuance of paragraph (2) shall include—

(*a*) if the decision under regulation L8 is that a benefit is immediately payable to the person, a statement showing how that payment is computed;

(*b*) in any other case, a statement of any benefit to which the person is entitled; and

(*c*) a statement of the kind required by regulation L4(3).

Payments due in respect of deceased persons

L10. Where any sum not exceeding £500 is due under these regulations to a person who has died or to his personal representatives, the appropriate administering authority may, without requiring the production of probate or letters of administration of the estate of the deceased person, pay out of the superannuation fund maintained by them under Part B the whole or any part of that sum to the person's personal representatives or to the person, or to or among any one or more of any persons, appearing to the authority to be beneficially entitled to the estate of the deceased person, and any person to whom such a payment is made, and not the administering authority, shall be liable to account for the sum paid to him under this paragraph.

Certificates as to reduction in remuneration

L11.—(1) Where it appears to an employing authority that a pensionable employee has, in consequence of a material change in circumstances, suffered a reduction in the remuneration of his employment, that authority—

(*a*) on the application of that employee, shall, or

(*b*) on their own initiative, may,

issue to that employee a certificate that there has been a material change in circumstances.

(2) A certificate issued under this regulation shall specify the date when the material change in circumstances occurred and shall be issued within 12 months of the material change or within such longer period as the Secretary of State may in any such case approve.

(3) An employing authority shall, for a period of not less than 10 years from the date of every material change in respect of which a certificate is issued under this regulation, cause a record to be kept of that certificate in such form as the authority shall think fit, and the record shall include the information that is required for a calculation to be made under regulation E1(2)(*b*)(ii).

Provision as to payments in lieu of contributions

L12. Where a payment in lieu of contributions is made in respect of any pensionable employee, the authority responsible for making the payment shall be entitled to recover out of the superannuation fund to which that person was a contributor or, if that authority is an administering authority, themselves to retain out of that fund a sum not exceeding the lesser of the following amounts—

(*a*) the amount of the payment in lieu of contributions, less the amount (if any) which the authority could recover or retain under section 60 of the Insurance Act in respect of that payment or, in the case of a person to whom regulation F14 applies but the power thereby conferred is not invoked, the amount of the payment in lieu of contributions less the amount by which the death gratuity could have been reduced under that regulation; and

(*b*) the amount paid into that fund in respect of that person (less any sum returnable to him as contributions) together with compound interest at the rate of 4% per annum with yearly rests on 31st March.

Forfeiture of rights

L13. If a pensionable employee is dismissed or resigns, or otherwise ceases to hold his employment, in consequence of an offence of a fraudulent character or grave misconduct, being such an offence or such misconduct in connection with the performance of the duties of, or otherwise in relation to, his employment, the employing authority may direct that all or any of the rights enjoyed by or in respect of him with respect to his previous service, being rights under Parts C, D, E, F and J shall be forfeited.

Benefits not assignable

L14. A benefit under these regulations shall be payable to, or in trust for, the person to whom that benefit is granted by these regulations, and shall not be assignable or chargeable with his debts or other liabilities.

Age of compulsory retirement

L15. When a pensionable employee attains the age of 65 years he shall cease to hold his employment; except that the employing authority may, with his consent, extend his service for one year or any less period, and so from time to time as they deem expedient.

PART M

AMENDMENTS, REVOCATIONS AND REPEALS

Amendments

M1.—(1) The enactments specified in Part I of Schedule 18 shall have effect subject to the amendments set out therein.

(2) The provisions of the instruments specified in Part II of Schedule 18 shall have effect subject to the amendments set out therein.

Revocations and repeals

M2.—(1) The provisions of the enactments set out in column (2) of Part I of Schedule 19, so far as they apply to England and Wales and have effect—

    (*a*) as provisions of regulations made under section 7 of the Act of 1972; or

    (*b*) as provisions of regulations made under section 8(2) of the Act of 1972 relating to the local Act scheme administered immediately before the appointed day by the Manchester City Council,

shall cease to have effect to the extent mentioned in column (2).

(2) The provisions of the enactments set out in column (2) of Part II of Schedule 19 are hereby repealed to the extent mentioned in column (2).

(3) The provisions of the instruments set out in column (2) of Part III of Schedule 19, so far as they have effect as provisions of such regulations as are mentioned in paragraph (1)(*a*) or (*b*) are hereby revoked to the extent mentioned in column (2).

(4) The provisions of the instruments set out in column (2) of Part IV of Schedule 19 are hereby revoked to the extent mentioned in column (2).

SCHEDULE 1

PENSIONABLE EMPLOYEES

Regulations A3 and B2 (1)(a) to (c)   PART I

BODIES WHOSE WHOLE-TIME EMPLOYEES ARE TO BE COMPULSORILY SUPERANNUABLE

(1) Body	(2) Excepted employees
A county council, the Greater London Council, a district council, a London borough council	
A joint board or joint committee appointed under any Act, or any statutory order or statutory scheme, if all the constituent authorities are such councils as aforesaid	
A fire authority constituted by a combination scheme made under the Fire Services Act 1947	
A local valuation panel constituted under the General Rate Act 1967**(a)**	
A magistrates' courts committee	A person who gave notice under the proviso to section 20(1) of the Act of 1937 electing that that Act should not apply to his clerkship
The National Water Council	
A police authority or combined police authority	
A probation and after-care committee, other than the probation and after-care committee for the City of London probation and after-care area	A person who gave notice in accordance with article 1 of the Probation Officers (Superannuation) Order 1948 **(b)**
A water authority	
The Chichester Harbour Conservancy	
The Lee Valley Regional Park Authority	

(a) 1967 c. 9.

(b) S.I. 1948/1220 (Rev. XVIII, p.685: 1948 I, p. 3330).

PART II　　　Regulations A3 and B2 (1)(d)

CERTAIN PERSONS WHO MAY BE SUPERANNUABLE

(1) Employee	(2) Excepted employees	(3) Body
A variable-time employee	A variable-time employee who is also in the whole-time employment of such a body as is described in column (1) of Part I of this schedule	A body described in column (1) of Part I of this schedule
A whole-time employee or a variable-time employee		Any other body being a local authority for the purposes of the Local Loans Act 1875(a)
A whole-time employee		A passenger transport executive

SCHEDULE 2　　　　Regulation B6

MODIFICATIONS TO THE TRUSTEE INVESTMENTS ACT 1961 IN ITS APPLICATION TO INVESTMENT OF SUPERANNUATION FUND'S MONEYS

1. In this schedule—
"the Act of 1961" means the Trustee Investments Act 1961; and

"narrower-range part" and "wider-range part" have the same meanings as they have for the purposes of the Act of 1961.

2. In its application to investment by an administering authority under regulation B6(1) the Act of 1961 shall have effect as if—

(a) in section 2—
　(i) in subsection (1), for the words "equal in value at the time of division" there were substituted the words "so that the wider-range part at the time of the division bears to the then value of the narrower-range part the proportion of 3 to 1 (in this Act referred to as "the prescribed proportion")";
　(ii) after subsection (1) there were inserted the following subsection—
　　"(1A) For the purpose of making a division of a fund in pursuance of subsection (1) of this section the value of the fund may be determined by reference to all such relevant evidence of that value as is available at the time the division is made.";
　(iii) in subsection (3)(b), for the words from "each" to the end there were substituted the words "the wider-range part of the fund is increased by an amount which bears the prescribed proportion to the amount by which the value of the narrower-range part of the fund is increased.";

(b) in section 4(3), for the words "so as either" to "each other" there were substituted the words "so as to bear to each other either the prescribed proportion or";

(c) section 13 were omitted;

(a) 1875 c. 83.

(*d*) in Part II of Schedule 1—

    (i) for paragraphs 3 and 4 there were substituted the following—

        "3. In fixed-interest securities issued by any public, municipal or local authority, or any publicly controlled or nationalised industry or undertaking, whether established within or outside the United Kingdom.

        4. In fixed-interest securities issued by the government of any territory outside the United Kingdom.";

    (ii) for paragraph 6 there were substituted the following—

        "6. In debentures issued by a company incorporated in the United Kingdom or established under the law of any territory outside the United Kingdom.";

    (iii) in paragraph 9—

        (*i*) the words "in the United Kingdom", where first occurring, were omitted;

        (*ii*) at the end of the paragraph there were added the following sub-paragraph—

            "(*g*) any public, municipal or local authority established outside the United Kingdom.";

    (iv) at the end of the part there were added the following paragraph—

        "15. In the advance of money upon the security of—

            (*a*) immovable property of any tenure or kind in the United Kingdom, Isle of Man or the Channel Islands; or

            (*b*) any legal estate or interest in immovable property comprised in a building agreement as specified in paragraph 5 of Part III of this Schedule;

        and in any such case whether the security be taken by a separate and distinct mortgage or security made exclusively to the administering authority, or by a mortgage or security made jointly to that authority and any other person.";

(*e*) in Part III of Schedule 1—

    (i) in paragraph 3, the words from "in the case" to the end were omitted;

    (ii) at the end of the part there were added the following paragraphs—

        "4. In any securities issued by a company established under the law of any territory outside the United Kingdom and not being securities falling within Part II of this Schedule.

        5. In the acquisition, development or management of land situated in the United Kingdom, or in any territory outside the United Kingdom, or any interest in such land, including any interest in such land comprised in a building agreement providing for the grant of a lease of such land contingent on the erection or completion of the building specified in such agreement and whether alone or in association with any other person:

        For the purposes of this paragraph an investment in the units of a unit trust scheme or in participation certificates or in any form of participation under any trust or scheme established in the United Kingdom, or in any territory outside the United Kingdom, having the effect of enabling persons to participate in the profits and income arising from the acquisition, development or management of land, whether alone or in association with any other person, shall be deemed to be an investment in such land.";

(*f*) in Part IV of Schedule 1, paragraphs 1 to 3 were omitted;

(*g*) in paragraph 3(b) of Schedule 2, for the words from "each" to the end there were substituted the words "the wider-range part of the fund is increased by an amount which bears the prescribed proportion to the amount by which the value of the narrower-range part of the fund is increased.".

3. No further moneys forming part of a superannuation fund shall be invested in the manner specified in paragraphs 4 and 5 of Part III of Schedule 1 to the Act of 1961 as modified by these regulations, so long as the value of the investments for the time being made under those paragraphs equals or exceeds 33⅓% of the value of the wider-range part of the superannuation fund.

4. No moneys forming the narrower-range part, or the wider-range part, of a superannuation fund shall be invested in securities of companies the price of which is not quoted on a recognised stock exchange within the meaning of the Prevention of Fraud (Investments) Act 1958(a), if such investment would result in more than 10% of the value of the investments for the time being belonging to that part being invested in such securities.

5. For the purposes of paragraphs 3 and 4 the value of any investment shall be deemed to be the value of the investment at the time it was made.

SCHEDULE 3

ADDITIONAL CONTRIBUTORY PAYMENTS

PART I   Regulations D6 and D7

CALCULATION OF SUM PAYABLE

1. For the purpose of calculating the sum payable by a pensionable employee who, in pursuance of regulation D6 or D7, desires to have any service or period which is, or is treated under regulation D4 or D5 as, service which immediately before the appointed day or, as the case may be, ceasing to be employed before that day he was entitled to reckon as non-contributing service for the purposes of the former regulations treated for the purposes of these regulations as service or a period which immediately before the appointed day or so ceasing he was entitled to reckon as contributing service for the purposes of the former regulations the following table shall be used in accordance with the provisions of this part of this schedule.

2. References in this part of this schedule to the age of an employee or the remuneration of an employee are references to his age at the time when the notice under regulation D6 or, as the case may be, D7 is given or to the annual remuneration on which he is paying contributions at that time:

Provided that if for the purposes of this paragraph account is required to be taken of any fees payable to an employee in respect of any service, the amount thereof shall be taken to be the annual average of the fees payable to him in respect of that service during the 5 years immediately preceding the giving of the notice referred to above or, if that service was of shorter duration, such shorter period.

3. The sum payable by an employee for each year of non-contributing service which he wishes to have treated as service or a period which immediately before the appointed day he was entitled to reckon as contributing service is a sum equal to that percentage of his remuneration which is specified in column (2) or (3) of the table mentioned above, whichever shall be appropriate, opposite to his age specified in column (1), and so proportionately for any period of less than a year:

Provided that if at the time when the notice under regulation D6 or, as the case may be, D7 is given the employee is in whole-time employment, non-contributing service which was part-time shall be reckoned for the purposes of this paragraph as if it were whole-time service for a proportionately reduced period.

(a) 1958 c. 45.

TABLE

	Percentage of remuneration payable per year of non-contributing service	
Age (1)	Officers (2)	Manual workers (3)
Under 26		4·1
26 and under 27 ...		4·15
27 ,, ,, 28 ...		4·2
28 ,, ,, 29 ...		4·25
29 ,, ,, 30 ...		4·3
30 ,, ,, 31 ...		4·35
31 ,, ,, 32 ...	6·5	4·45
32 ,, ,, 33 ...		4·55
33 ,, ,, 34 ...		4·65
34 ,, ,, 35 ...		4·75
35 ,, ,, 36 ...		4·85
36 ,, ,, 37 ...		4·95
37 ,, ,, 38 ...		5·05
38 ,, ,, 39	6·55	5·15
39 ,, ,, 40	6·6	5·25
40 ,, ,, 41	6·65	5·35
41 ,, ,, 42	6·7	5·5
42 ,, ,, 43	6·75	5·65
43 ,, ,, 44	6·85	5·8
44 ,, ,, 45	6·95	5·95
45 ,, ,, 46	7·05	6·1
46 ,, ,, 47	7·15	6·3
47 ,, ,, 48	7·25	6·5
48 ,, ,, 49	7·4	6·7
49 ,, ,, 50	7·55	6·9
50 ,, ,, 51	7·7	7·1
51 ,, ,, 52	7·85	7·35
52 ,, ,, 53	8·05	7·6
53 ,, ,, 54	8·25	7·85
54 ,, ,, 55	8·45	8·1
55 ,, ,, 56	8·7	8·4
56 ,, ,, 57	9·0	8·75
57 ,, ,, 58	9·35	9·15
58 ,, ,, 59	9·75	9·65
59 ,, ,, 60	10·25	10·25
60 and over	10·25, less 0·25 for each completed year by which the employee's age exceeds 60.	10·25 less 0·25 for each completed year by which the employee's age exceeds 60.

Regulations D6 to D8   PART II

PROVISIONS APPLICABLE WHILE ANY SUM OUTSTANDING

1. While any sum payable under regulation D6 or D7 remains outstanding the provisions of this part of this schedule shall have effect.

2. Compound interest shall be payable as from the giving of the notice under the regulation applicable in the particular case upon the amount for the time being outstanding, and shall be calculated at the rate of 3% per annum with half-yearly rests.

3. If the pensionable employee becomes entitled to receive payment of or payments in respect of a benefit under these regulations or a benefit under these regulations becomes payable in respect of him and the amount of any such benefit is calculated by reference to the length of his reckonable service, the amount outstanding shall be recovered by deductions from any payments on account of any such benefit or otherwise.

4. If the employee becomes entitled to receive payment of or payments in respect of benefits under these regulations or any benefit under these regulations becomes payable in respect of him and no such benefit is calculated by reference to the length of his reckonable service, all liability in respect of the amount outstanding shall cease.

5. If the employee ceases to hold his employment without having become entitled to receive payment of or payments in respect of any benefit under these regulations, his liability in respect of any amount outstanding shall cease, save as provided in paragraphs 6 and 7.

6. If, while any sum remains outstanding under the regulation applicable in the particular case, the employee on ceasing to hold his employment under an employing authority becomes entitled to benefits under these regulations by virtue of regulation E2(1)(c), but is not entitled to receive payment of or payments in respect of those benefits and does not elect under sub-paragraph (b) of regulation C8(2) that that regulation should apply in his case, he may, by notice in writing given within 3 months of so ceasing to that authority, elect to pay in a lump sum to that authority the amount outstanding.

7.—(1) If, while any sum such as is mentioned in paragraph 6 remains outstanding, the employee ceases to hold his employment under an employing authority without having become entitled to receive payment of or payments in respect of any benefit under these regulations and, on ceasing to hold his employment, he has paid all such instalments as have then accrued due under his agreement with the employing authority and within 12 months after so ceasing, without having in the meantime elected under sub-paragraph (b) of regulation C8(2) that that regulation should apply in his case or having made such a claim for payment as is mentioned in regulation C8(5) or having become a local Act contributor, he becomes a pensionable employee in the employment of any employing authority, then, subject to the succeeding provisions of this paragraph, he may pay the amount outstanding to the employing authority or, as the case may be, the employing authorities by whom he is employed in the like manner in which it would have been payable if he had not ceased to hold the employment.

(2) Where an employee is employed by two or more scheduled bodies he may pay to each such body which is an employing authority such proportion of the amount outstanding as bears to the whole thereof the same proportion as the annual remuneration of the employment under that body bears to the aggregate of the remuneration of all the employments.

(3) Any apportionment made under this paragraph shall take effect as if the employee had entered all the employments to which the apportionment relates on the date on which he entered the first of them, and any payments made by an employee under this paragraph before the apportionment shall be adjusted accordingly.

SCHEDULE 4   Regulations D10 and D13

LIMITATION ON PAYMENT BY WAY OF ADDITIONAL CONTRIBUTIONS

If the aggregate of any amount payable by a pensionable employee under regulation D10 or D13 and the amount payable by him by way of contributions under regulation C1 exceeds 15% of his remuneration he shall satisfy his liability in respect of the excess over 15% by payment in a lump sum of a sum calculated by the Government Actuary to represent the capital value of the excess.

\

PROVISIONS APPLICABLE AS RESPECTS ADDITIONAL CONTRIBUTIONS WHILE ANY AMOUNT REMAINS OUTSTANDING

1. While any amount payable under regulation D10 or D13 remains to be paid the provisions of this schedule shall have effect.

2. If the employee ceases to hold his employment on the ground that he is incapable of discharging efficiently the duties of the employment by reason of permanent ill-health or infirmity of mind or body or dies, he shall be, or shall be treated as having been immediately before his death, entitled to reckon as reckonable service the number of years or, as the case may be, the additional period for which immediately before so ceasing, or his death, he was paying by way of additional contributions under regulation D10 or, as the case may be, D13.

3. If the employee ceases to hold his employment, other than in the circumstances mentioned in paragraph 2, and the reckonable service and qualifying service he is entitled to reckon amounts in aggregate to not less than 5 years, then he shall be entitled, subject to paragraph 6, in respect of payments made by him on account of the debt to reckon such an additional period as is determined in accordance with the formula in paragraph 4 and his liability in respect of the balance of the debt shall cease.

4. The formula mentioned in paragraph 3 is—

$$\frac{P \times T}{I}$$

where

    P   is the length of the period during which additional contributions have been paid under the appropriate regulation;

    T   is the length of the additional period or, as the case may be, number of years for which the employee was paying by way of additional contributions; and

    I   is the length of the period during which, if the employee had remained in the employment he ceases to hold as mentioned in paragraph 3, additional contributions would have been payable under the appropriate regulation.

5. If the employee ceases to hold his employment and the reckonable service and qualifying service he is entitled to reckon amount in aggregate to less than 5 years then, after the expiration of 12 months, he shall not be entitled to any rights in respect of payments made by him on account of the debt except a right to a return of the amount of such payments, and his liability in respect of the balance of the debt shall cease.

6. If the employee ceases to hold his employment under the employing authority in the circumstances mentioned in paragraph 3 and within 12 months after so ceasing, without having in the meantime elected under sub-paragraph (b) of regulation C8(2) that that regulation should apply in his case or having made such a claim for payment as is mentioned in regulation C8(5) or having become a local Act contributor becomes a pensionable employee in the employment of any employing authority and does not give such a notice as is mentioned in regulation E2(4)(e) then, subject to the succeeding provisions of this paragraph, if, within 3 months after the date on which he again becomes a pensionable employee, he pays to the employing authority or, as the case may be, the employing authorities by whom he is employed an amount equal to the additional contributions (if any) which would have been payable by him during the period between so ceasing to hold his employment and again becoming a pensionable employee, if during that period he had remained in his former employment, paragraph 3 shall cease to apply and his liability in respect of the balance of the debt shall continue.

SCHEDULE 6   Regulation D10

AMOUNT TO BE PAID FOR ADDED YEARS

1. The amount payable by a pensionable employee, by way of additional contributions, in respect of each year in respect of which consent was given under regulation D10(2), shall be—

(*a*) if the employee has not reached the age of 55 years at the time of the giving of that consent, an amount in respect of all service thereafter up to the age of 60 years equal to such percentage of his remuneration for the time being as is shown in column (2) of the following table opposite the age shown in column (1) which corresponds to his age at the time of the giving of the consent;

(*b*) if he has reached the age of 55 years at the time of the giving of that consent, an amount in respect of all service thereafter up to such age, and equal to such percentage of his remuneration for the time being, as the Government Actuary may determine:

Provided that the employing authority may if they think fit reduce by not more than one third the percentage applicable in the case of the employee, and if they do so the reduction shall operate so long as he remains liable to make payments under this paragraph.

TABLE

(1) Age at date of giving consent	(2) Percentage of remuneration payable by the employee in respect of each year desired to be reckoned as reckonable service
25 and under 27	0·15
27 ,, ,, 28	0·16
28 ,, ,, 29	0·17
29 ,, ,, 30	0·18
30 ,, ,, 31	0·19
31 ,, ,, 32	0·20
32 ,, ,, 33	0·21
33 ,, ,, 34	0·22
34 ,, ,, 35	0·23
35 ,, ,, 36	0·24
36 ,, ,, 37	0·25
37 ,, ,, 38	0·26
38 ,, ,, 39	0·28
39 ,, ,, 40	0·30
40 ,, ,, 41	0·32
41 ,, ,, 42	0·34
42 ,, ,, 43	0·36
43 ,, ,, 44	0·38
44 ,, ,, 45	0·41
45 ,, ,, 46	0·44
46 ,, ,, 47	0·48
47 ,, ,, 48	0.53
48 ,, ,, 49	0·58
49 ,, ,, 50	0·64
50 ,, ,, 51	0·72
51 ,, ,, 52	0·81
52 ,, ,, 53	0·92
53 ,, ,, 54	1·07
54 ,, ,, 55	1·28

Regulations D12 to D14   SCHEDULE 7

MAXIMUM LENGTH OF ADDITIONAL PERIODS PURCHASED BY EMPLOYEE OR GRANTED AT DISCRETION OF EMPLOYING AUTHORITY

1.—(1) Subject to paragraph 2, the maximum length of any additional period which a pensionable employee wishes to be entitled under regulation D12 or D13 to reckon as reckonable service or the employing authority resolve under regulation D14 that a person should be entitled so to reckon shall not exceed such period as, together with the period of reckonable service he would be entitled to reckon if he remained in the employment in which he is a pensionable employee until attaining the age of 65 years, amounts to the number of years which, in column (2) of the following table, is specified opposite to the age specified in column (1) which the person had attained at the appropriate time.

TABLE

(1) Age	(2) Number of years
Under 55	40
55 and under 56	32
56 ,, ,, 57	24
57 ,, ,, 58	16
58 ,, ,, 59	8

(2) In this paragraph the expression "appropriate time"—

(*a*) in relation to a person who is entitled to reckon as reckonable service—

(i) any such period as is mentioned in regulation D4; or

(ii) any period which was taken into account under section 12(6) of the Act of 1937, or section 7(3) of the Act of 1953, in reckoning his non-contributing service; or

(iii) any period which was taken into account under any provision of a local Act scheme corresponding to either of those sections; or

(iv) any period of service or employment he was entitled to reckon for the purposes of the former regulations by virtue of interchange rules (other than any of the interchange rules mentioned in paragraph (3)),

means the day on which he first became a contributory employee or, as the case may be, a pensionable employee after the end of the last of any such periods; and

(*b*) in relation to any other person, means the day on which the earliest service or period which he is entitled to reckon as reckonable service actually began,

but, where after that day the person entered an employment (other than an employment in which he was a contributory employee or, as the case may be, a pensionable employee or an employment which he entered in such circumstances that a transfer value was payable in respect of him under interchange rules) and, on ceasing to hold that employment, became entitled to superannuation benefits, the expression means the day on which the earliest service or period which he is entitled to reckon as reckonable service actually began.

(3) The reference in paragraph (2) to the interchange rules mentioned in this paragraph are references to—

(*a*) the Superannuation (Local Government and National Health Service) Interchange Rules 1955(**a**);

(*b*) the Superannuation (Civil Service and Local Government) Interchange Rules 1968(**b**);

(a) S.I. 1955/1494 (1955 II, p. 1758).   (b) S.I. 1968/72 (1968 I, p. 182).

(c) the Superannuation (Teaching and Local Government) Interchange Rules 1970(a);

(d) any earlier interchange rules which contained provisions corresponding to the provisions of any of the interchange rules mentioned above.

2.—(1) In the case of a person who, on the day on which the earliest service, employment or period which he is entitled to reckon as reckonable service in relation to the employment mentioned in paragraph 1(1) (other than any period he is entitled to reckon as reckonable service under regulation D4, or any period which was taken into account in pursuance of a determination under section 12(6) of the Act of 1937 or section 7(3) of the Act of 1953 in reckoning his non-contributing service or any period which was taken into account under any provision of a local Act scheme corresponding to either of those sections) actually began, whether or not it is so reckonable or counted under these regulations at its actual length, was entitled to or had received superannuation benefits (including a return of contributions and any benefit by way of a lump sum payment) in respect of any former trade, profession, vocation or office, the number of years specified in column (2) of the table in paragraph 1 applicable in his case shall be reduced to such extent as will ensure that—

(a) the aggregate annual amount of—

(i) the actuarial value, expressed as an annuity payable to him, of such superannuation benefits;

(ii) the part of the retirement pension attributable to reckonable service before attaining the relevant age; and

(iii) the actuarial value, expressed as an annuity payable to him, of the part of the retiring allowance payable to him attributable to reckonable service before attaining the relevant age,

shall not exceed two-thirds of his pensionable remuneration; and

(b) the aggregate amount of—

(i) the retiring allowance; and

(ii) any such superannuation benefit by way of lump sum payment,

shall not exceed one hundred and twenty eightieths of his pensionable remuneration.

(2) The extent to which the number of years referred to in sub-paragraph (1) are to be reduced shall be certified by an actuary.

(3) For the purposes of sub-paragraph (1)—

(a) it shall be assumed that the person will, until he attains the relevant age, continue to be employed in the same employment and on the same scale of remuneration as at the date of the election under the regulation applicable in the particular case or, as the case may be, the date of the passing of the resolution in respect of him under regulation D14; and

(b) in calculating the reduction (if any) to be made there shall be disregarded any service or period which the person becomes, on or after the date of the election under the regulation applicable in the particular case or, as the case may be, the date of the passing of the resolution in respect of him under regulation D14, entitled to reckon as reckonable service.

(4) In this paragraph "relevant age", in relation to a person, means the earliest age at which the person would have become entitled by virtue of regulation E2(1)(a) or (b)(ii) to a benefit under these regulations.

(5) A person who at the date of the passing of a resolution in respect of him under regulation D14 has not entered the employment mentioned in that regulation shall be treated for the purposes of this schedule as if he had entered that employment on that date and on the scale of remuneration at which the employment is then offered to him.

(a) S.I. 1970/1646 (1970 III, p. 5404).

SCHEDULE 8

AMOUNT TO BE PAID FOR ADDITIONAL PERIOD

Regulation D12   PART I

LUMP SUM PAYMENT

1. The amount payable by a pensionable employee in respect of each year of the additional period which, in pursuance of regulation D12, he desires to reckon as reckonable service shall be determined in accordance with the formula in paragraph 2 and so proportionately for any period of less than a year.

2. The formula mentioned in paragraph 1 is—

$$\frac{T \times R \times F}{100}$$

where

  T   is the number of complete years the employee desires to reckon as reckonable service;

  R   is the remuneration of the employee at the time he made the election under regulation D12; and

  F   is the figure specified in column (2) or column (3) of the following table, whichever shall be appropriate, opposite to the age of the employee on his birthday next following the date on which he made that election specified in column (1).

TABLE

(1) Age	(2) Men	(3) Women	(1) Age	(2) Men	(3) Women
			40	12·60	13·20
			41	12·70	13·30
22	11·20	11·20	42	12·80	13·40
23	11·20	11·20	43	12·80	13·60
24	11·30	11·30	44	12·90	13·70
25	11·40	11·40	45	13·00	13·90
26	11·50	11·50	46	13·10	14·10
27	11·60	11·60	47	13·20	14·20
28	11·60	11·70	48	13·40	14·40
29	11·70	11·70	49	13·50	14·50
30	11·80	11·80	50	13·70	14·70
31	11·90	12·00	51	13·80	14·90
32	11·90	12·10	52	14·00	15·00
33	12·00	12·20	53	14·20	15·20
34	12·10	12·40	54	14·50	15·50
35	12·20	12·50	55	14·80	15·70
36	12·30	12·60	56	15·10	16·00
37	12·40	12·70	57	15·50	16·30
38	12·40	12·90	58	15·90	16·60
39	12·50	13·00	59	16·30	17·10

PART II   Regulation D13

PERIODICAL PAYMENTS

3. The amount payable by a pensionable employee, by way of additional contributions, in respect of each year of the additional period which, in pursuance of regulation D13, he desires to reckon as reckonable service shall be determined in accordance with the formula in paragraph 4 and so proportionately for any period of less than a year.

4.—(1) The formula mentioned in paragraph 3 is—

$$\frac{T \times R \times F}{100}$$

where

T   is the number of complete years the employee desires to reckon as reckonable service;

R   is the remuneration for the time being of the employee; and

F   is the figure specified, opposite to the age of the employee on his birthday next following the date on which he made an election under regulation D13, in the relevant column of Table I or II below appropriate to his pensionable age as defined in sub-paragraph (2).

PENSIONS

TABLE I

MALES

Age on birthday next following election	Figure to be used by reference to the under-mentioned pensionable age							
	Employees to whom on retirement regulation E3(2) would apply	Others						
	65	60	Over 60 and under 61	61 and under 62	62 and under 63	63 and under 64	64 and under 65	65
22		0·40						
23		0·41						
24		0·42						
25		0·43						
26		0·44						
27		0·46						
28		0·48						
29		0·49						
30		0·51						
31		0·53						
32		0·56						
33		0·58						
34		0·61						
35		0·64						
36		0·67	0·66					
37		0·71	0·70	0·66				
38		0·74	0·73	0·69	0·65			
39		0·79	0·78	0·73	0·69	0·65		
40		0·83	0·82	0·77	0·73	0·69	0·65	
41		0·88	0·87	0·82	0·77	0·73	0·69	0·66
42		0·94	0·93	0·87	0·82	0·77	0·73	0·70
43		1·01	0·99	0·93	0·87	0·81	0·77	0·74
44		1·08	1·07	0·99	0·92	0·87	0·82	0·78
45		1·17	1·15	1·06	0·99	0·92	0·87	0·83
46	0·89	1·26	1·24	1·15	1·06	0·99	0·92	0·88
47	0·95	1·38	1·36	1·24	1·14	1·06	0·99	0·94
48	1·01	1·50	1·48	1·35	1·24	1·14	1·06	1·00
49	1·09	1·66	1·63	1·48	1·35	1·24	1·14	1·08
50	1·17	1·84	1·82	1·63	1·47	1·34	1·24	1·16
51	1·27	2·07	2·04	1·81	1·62	1·47	1·34	1·25
52	1·38	2·34	2·31	2·02	1·80	1·62	1·47	1·36
53	1·50	2·70	2·66	2·30	2·01	1·79	1·61	1·49
54	1·65	3·17	3·12	2·64	2·28	2·00	1·78	1·63
55	1·83	3·84	3·77	3·10	2·62	2·27	2·00	1·81
56	2·04	4·83	4·75	3·74	3·08	2·61	2·26	2·02
57	2·31	6·47	6·36	4·70	3·71	3·06	2·59	2·28
58	2·65	—	—	6·29	4·66	3·68	3·04	2·62
59	3·11	—	—	—	6·23	4·62	3·66	3·07

TABLE II

FEMALES

| Age on birthday next following election | Employees to whom on retirement regulation E3(2) would apply | Figure to be used by reference to the under-mentioned pensionable age | | | | | | |
| | | Others | | | | | | |
	65	60	Over 60 and under 61	61 and under 62	62 and under 63	63 and under 64	64 and under 65	65
22		0·39						
23		0·40						
24		0·42						
25		0·43						
26		0·45						
27		0·46						
28		0·48						
29		0·50						
30		0·52						
31		0·54						
32		0·57						
33		0·59						
34		0·62						
35		0·65						
36		0·69	0·68					
37		0·72	0·71	0·67				
38		0·76	0·75	0·70	0·66			
39		0·81	0·80	0·74	0·69	0·65		
40		0·86	0·84	0·78	0·73	0·69	0·65	
41		0·91	0·89	0·83	0·78	0·73	0·68	0·65
42		0·97	0·95	0·88	0·82	0·77	0·72	0·69
43		1·04	1·02	0·94	0·87	0·81	0·76	0·73
44		1·11	1·09	1·01	0·93	0·86	0·81	0·77
45		1·20	1·18	1·08	1·00	0·92	0·86	0·82
46	0·93	1·30	1·27	1·16	1·07	0·99	0·92	0·87
47	0·99	1·41	1·38	1·26	1·15	1·06	0·98	0·93
48	1·06	1·54	1·51	1·37	1·24	1·14	1·05	0·99
49	1·14	1·70	1·67	1·50	1·35	1·23	1·14	1·07
50	1·23	1·89	1·85	1·65	1·48	1·34	1·23	1·15
51	1·33	2·12	2·08	1·83	1·63	1·47	1·34	1·24
52	1·44	2·40	2·36	2·05	1·81	1·62	1·46	1·35
53	1·58	2·77	2·72	2·33	2·03	1·79	1·61	1·48
54	1·73	3·26	3·20	2·68	2·30	2·01	1·78	1·63
55	1·92	3·94	3·86	3·15	2·65	2·28	1·99	1·80
56	2·15	4·95	4·86	3·81	3·11	2·62	2·26	2·01
57	2·43	6·64	6·51	4·78	3·75	3·07	2·59	2·28
58	2·79	—	—	6·40	4·71	3·70	3·04	2·62
59	3·27	—	—	—	6·30	4·64	3·66	3·06

(2) In this paragraph "pensionable age" means the earliest age at which, if the employee were to remain a pensionable employee without any break of service, he would become entitled by virtue of regulation E2(1)(*a*) or (*b*)(ii), if he then ceased to be employed, to a retirement pension.

Regulations E3(7) and E11(4)   SCHEDULE 9

INCREASE OF RECKONABLE SERVICE ON ACCOUNT OF ILL-HEALTH OR DEATH IN SERVICE

1. In this schedule—
"relevant reckonable service", in relation to any person, means the person's reckonable service, other than—

(*a*) any years or any additional period reckonable as reckonable service under regulation D10, D12 or D13;

(*b*) any years added to the person's service under regulation 12 of the Benefits regulations or under that regulation as applied by or under any enactment and reckonable as reckonable service by virtue of regulation D1;

(*c*) any years added to the person's service under any provision of a local Act scheme corresponding to that regulation or that regulation as applied by or under any enactment and reckonable as reckonable service by virtue of regulation D1; and

(*d*) any additional period by which the person's reckonable service was increased by virtue of paragraph 2; and

"relevant service", in relation to any person, means the person's contributing service and non-contributing service, other than—

(*a*) any years added to the person's service under regulation 12 of the Benefits regulations or under that regulation as applied by or under any enactment; and

(*b*) any years added to the person's service under any provision of a local Act scheme corresponding to that regulation or that regulation as applied by or under any enactment; and

(*c*) any period by which his relevant service is under paragraph 3 deemed to have been increased under regulation 5(3) of the Benefits regulations.

2. Subject to paragraphs 3 and 4, the additional period a pensionable employee is to be treated under regulation E3(7) as being entitled to reckon as reckonable service for the purpose of calculating the amount of any benefit under regulation E3 shall be the period specified in column (2) of the following table opposite to the length in years of his relevant reckonable service specified in column (1), but not exceeding the period by which his reckonable service would have been increased if he had remained in the employment in which he was a pensionable employee until attaining the age of 65 years or completing 40 years' reckonable service, whichever would have first occurred.

TABLE

(1) Period of reckonable service	(2) Additional period
Not exceeding 10 years	A period equal to his relevant reckonable service
Exceeding 10 years but not exceeding $13\frac{121}{365}$ years	The period by which his relevant reckonable service is less than 20 years
Exceeding $13\frac{121}{365}$ years	$6\frac{243}{365}$ years

3.—(1) Subject to paragraph 4, where a person, on ceasing to hold an employment (hereafter in this paragraph referred to as the "first employment"), became entitled to benefits under these regulations by virtue of regulation E2(1)(*b*)(i), or under the corresponding provision of the former regulations, entered after he became so entitled further employment with a scheduled body and was in that employment a pensionable employee and, on ceasing to hold that further employment, becomes entitled to benefits under these regulations by virtue of regulation E2(1)(*b*)(i), the additional period (if any) he is, on so ceasing, to be treated under regulation E3(7) as being entitled to reckon as reckonable service for the purpose of calculating the amount of a benefit under regulation E3 shall be the additional period which he would have been entitled under paragraph 2 to reckon as reckonable service if his relevant reckonable service in relation to that further employment had included his relevant reckonable service or, as the case may be, his relevant service in relation to the first employment, reduced by the period (if any) by which his relevant reckonable service or, as the case may be, his relevant service in relation to the first employment was increased by virtue of paragraph 2 or, as the case may be, is deemed to have been increased under regulation 5(3) of the Benefits regulations.

(2) For the purposes of this paragraph, where a person is in respect of the first employment entitled to an annual pension under the former regulations calculated under regulation 5(3) of the Benefits regulations by reference to a minimum fraction of remuneration, his relevant service shall be deemed to have been increased by a period equal to the difference between the period of his relevant service and 20 years and where a person is in respect of the first employment entitled to an annual pension under the former regulations increased under the said regulation 5(3) by reference to the continuation of his employment, his relevant service shall be deemed to have been increased by a period equal to the period by which his relevant service would have been increased if he had remained in the first employment until attaining the age of 65 years.

4.—(1) Where a person—

    (*a*) either—

        (i) was a contributory employee immediately before the appointed day and became a pensionable employee on that day; or

        (ii) was a contributory employee under a scheduled body or former local authority, ceased to be employed by that body before the appointed day and on or after that day, but within 12 months of so ceasing, becomes a pensionable employee; and

    (*b*) was in relation to the employment in which he was a pensionable employee entitled to reckon not less than 10 years' reckonable service,

and a notice for the purpose is given in accordance with sub-paragraph (2), paragraphs 2 and 3 shall not apply and the additional period he is to be treated as being entitled to reckon as reckonable service for the purpose of calculating the amount of any benefit under regulation E3 shall be the period by which his reckonable service would have been increased if he had remained in the employment in which he was a pensionable employee until attaining the age of 65 years or such period as together with his reckonable service would entitle him to reckon 20 years' reckonable service, whichever is the less.

(2) A notice for the purposes of this paragraph shall be made in writing to the appropriate administering authority—

    (*a*) within one month after the day on which, on ceasing to hold an employment in which the person is a pensionable employee, the employee first becomes entitled to benefits under these regulations by virtue of regulation E2(1)(*b*)(i); or

    (*b*) if the employee dies in an employment in which the person is a pensionable employee and a notice has not been previously given under sub-paragraph (*a*), within one month after the day of that person's death,

or such longer period as that authority may in the particular case allow, and may be given—

3e

    (i) in the case of such a person as is mentioned in sub-paragraph (*a*), by that person;

    (ii) if such a person as is referred to in sub-paragraph (i) dies before the expiration of the period in which a notice under this paragraph is required to be given without giving that notice or in the case of such a person as is mentioned in sub-paragraph (*b*), if that person was a male and leaves a widow, by her or, if that person was a male and does not leave a widow or his widow dies before the expiration of the afore-mentioned period without giving that notice or that person was a female, by that person's personal representatives.

Regulation E3(9)   **SCHEDULE 10**

REDUCTION OF BENEFITS UNDER REGULATION E3(9)

TABLE I

RETIREMENT PENSION

Age of person on ceasing to be employed	Percentage reduction to be made under regulation E3(9) by reference to the under-mentioned earliest age at which, if the person were to remain a pensionable employee without any break in service, the person would become entitled by virtue of regulation E2(1)(*a*) or (*b*)(ii), on ceasing to be employed, to a retirement pension									
	61		62		63		64		65	
	Male	Female	Male	Female	Male	Female	Male	Female	Male	Female
60	9	7	17	14	24	20	31	26	37	31
61	—	—	9	7	17	14	25	20	31	26
62	—	—	—	—	9	7	17	14	25	21
63	—	—	—	—	—	—	9	8	18	15
64	—	—	—	—	—	—	—	—	10	8

TABLE II

RETIRING ALLOWANCE

Age of person on ceasing to be employed	Percentage reduction to be made under regulation E3(9) by reference to the under-mentioned earliest age at which, if the person were to remain a pensionable employee without any break in service, the person would become entitled by virtue of regulation E2(1)(*a*) or (*b*)(ii), on ceasing to be employed, to a retiring allowance									
	61		62		63		64		65	
	Male	Female	Male	Female	Male	Female	Male	Female	Male	Female
60	5	4	10	9	15	12	20	16	24	20
61	—	—	5	4	11	9	15	13	20	16
62	—	—	—	—	6	4	11	9	16	13
63	—	—	—	—	—	—	6	5	11	9
64	—	—	—	—	—	—	—	—	6	5

SCHEDULE 11   Regulation E4

ALLOCATION OF PART OF RETIREMENT PENSION

1. A person shall not surrender—

(a) more than one third of the retirement pension to which he would otherwise be entitled;

(b) any such part as would make the amount of the retirement pension payable to him, or which would be payable to him if he were to retire from his employment immediately after the surrender is allowed, less than the amount of the pension which might become payable under this schedule to the person in whose favour the allocation is made (in this schedule referred to as "the beneficiary");

(c) a smaller part than would secure for the beneficiary a pension of £39 per annum;

(d) any part which is not an exact number of pounds;

(e) in the case of a person in the calculation of whose retirement pension account is taken (or would be taken if he were to retire from his employment immediately after the surrender) of service which he was entitled to reckon under section 17 of the Act of 1937, a larger part than one third of the retirement pension, after deduction therefrom of any annual sum which by virtue of regulation E14 will be required to be deducted from the amount receivable in any year in respect of the retirement pension.

2. The amount of pension payable in return for each one pound of a retirement pension surrendered by a person shall be the amount, based on the age and sex of that person and the age and sex of the beneficiary, shown in the tables in force at the date on which the surrender is allowed.

3. Upon a person's becoming eligible to notify his wish to surrender part of his retirement pension the appropriate administering authority shall send him a notice stating that provision has been made by these regulations for the surrender of part of a retirement pension to a spouse or dependant and informing the person to whom the notice is addressed that he may on application to the authority obtain further information on the subject.

4. Where a person wishes to make a surrender he may—

(a) in the case of a pensionable employee who on ceasing to hold his employment becomes entitled to a retirement pension (in this schedule referred to as "a retiring employee") not more than 2 months before or within one month after the date on which he ceases to be employed; and

(b) in the case of a pensionable employee who would, if he were to retire from his employment, become entitled to a retirement pension (in this schedule referred to as "a continuing employee"), within 2 months before or at any time after becoming a continuing employee and while he is still employed,

notify his desire to surrender a part of that retirement pension by completing a copy of the form specified at the end of this schedule, or a form to the like effect, and sending it to the appropriate administering authority:

Provided that where the appropriate administering authority are satisfied that it has not been reasonably practicable for a retiring employee to notify his desire to surrender a part of a retirement pension within the time limit imposed by sub-paragraph (a), owing to circumstances beyond his control, they may at their discretion extend that limit to a date not more than 6 months after the date on which he ceases to be employed.

5. On receipt by the appropriate administering authority of a notification given by a person under paragraph 4 that authority shall—

(a) forthwith arrange for the person to be examined by a registered medical practitioner nominated by them and for a report to be given to them by the practitioner stating whether, in his opinion, the person is in good health, regard being had to his age; and if the opinion stated in such report is that the person is not in good health, the appropriate administering authority shall notify him accordingly and offer him an opportunity of a further examination by some other registered medical practitioner nominated by them with a view to that practitioner reporting to them on the state of the person's health;

(b) require the person to furnish at his own expense—

(i) a certificate of his birth, except where the date of birth has been duly recorded by the authority and is not disputed;

(ii) in respect of a beneficiary who is the person's spouse a birth certificate and a marriage certificate;

(iii) in respect of a beneficiary who is a dependant a birth certificate and such evidence as may be appropriate to prove dependency,

and any other information or evidence which the authority consider necessary:

Provided that if for any reason a birth or marriage certificate cannot be supplied the authority may accept such other evidence of birth or marriage as they think fit in order to determine the age or the question of marriage of the person concerned, as the case may be.

6. Any fee payable to a practitioner in respect of an examination and report under paragraph 5 shall be paid by the person examined at the time of the examination.

7.—(1) Subject to the provisions of this schedule, unless the appropriate administering authority are of opinion, on consideration of a report obtained by them under paragraph 5, that the person to whom the report relates is not in good health or they are of opinion that the evidence produced in regard to marriage or dependency is not satisfactory, they shall allow the surrender of such part of the retirement pension as is specified in the person's notification and as is in conformity with this schedule and shall grant to the beneficiary named in the notification a pension, payable in the event of the beneficiary's surviving the person and to be calculated in accordance with the provisions of paragraph 2:

Provided that a decision by an appropriate administering authority to allow a surrender by a retiring employee shall not be made before the date on which he ceases to be employed and a decision by an appropriate administering authority to allow a surrender by a continuing employee shall not be made before the date on which he becomes such an employee.

(2) Notwithstanding anything in sub-paragraph (1), the appropriate administering authority shall, if they are dissatisfied with the evidence of marriage, but are nevertheless satisfied on the evidence already before them or after making such further enquiries as they think necessary that a person named as spouse in the notification given under paragraph 4 is a dependant of the person who gave the notification, treat the notification as if the person named therein as spouse had been named as a dependant of the person giving the notification.

(3) As soon as is reasonably practicable after coming to a decision in regard to a notification given by a person, the appropriate administering authority shall notify him that they have allowed a surrender in favour of the person named in his notification or that they have decided not to allow a surrender of any part of the retirement pension, as the case may be, and if the appropriate administering authority have allowed a surrender they shall also furnish him with a statement as to the amount of the pension to which the beneficiary may become entitled after his death and, if the person who gave the notification under paragraph 4 is a retiring employee, with a statement as to the amount of the reduced retirement pension to which he is entitled.

(4) A notification of a decision not to allow a surrender shall state the grounds for the decision.

(5) A notification sent to an employee in pursuance of sub-paragraph (3) shall, if it has been posted in a prepaid envelope addressed to the employee by the appropriate administering authority, be deemed to have been received by the employee at the time at which a letter would be delivered in the ordinary course of post.

8. A person who has given a notification of his desire to surrender a part of his retirement pension under paragraph 4 may cancel or amend the notification by a notice in writing addressed to the appropriate administering authority and posted in a prepaid envelope to or left at the principal office of the authority at any time before he has received notification from the authority that his surrender has been allowed.

9.—(1) A notification given by a person under paragraph 4 shall become null and void if—

(a) the beneficiary dies before the person receives notification from the appropriate administering authority that his surrender has been allowed; or

(b) the person dies at any time before midnight on the day on which the appropriate administering authority decide to allow the surrender.

(2) Subject as aforesaid a surrender allowed in pursuance of a notification given by a person shall have effect as from the date on which the person ceases to hold his employment.

FORM OF NOTIFICATION OF SURRENDER
LOCAL GOVERNMENT SUPERANNUATION REGULATIONS
(Regulation E4 and Schedule 11)

SURRENDER OF RETIREMENT PENSION

To(¹) ....

....

Name of employing authority or
former employing authority ....

Particulars relating to person
desiring to make the surrender

    (*a*) Name in full ....

    (*b*) Date of birth ....

    (*c*) Address (private) ....

    ....

    ....

Particulars relating to
beneficiary

    (*a*) Name in full ....

    (*b*) Date of birth ....

    (*c*) Address (private) ....

    ....

    ....

    (*d*) Sex ....

    (*e*) Relationship of beneficiary to person desiring
    to make the surrender ....

    ....

    (*f*) If the beneficiary is spouse of person desiring
    to make the surrender, date of marriage ....

    ....

A.(²) In pursuance of paragraph 4(*a*) of Schedule 11 to the above-mentioned regulations I hereby notify my desire to surrender in favour of the above-named beneficiary the under-mentioned part of the retirement pension to which, on ....19............ I/became/expect to become (³)/entitled to receive payments in respect thereof.

B.(²) In pursuance of paragraph 4(*b*) of Schedule 11 to the above-mentioned regulations I hereby notify my desire to surrender in favour of the above-named beneficiary the under-mentioned part of the retirement pension to which, if I were to retire [immediately] [on ....19............], (³) I would become entitled.

                                                      £   p

(1) Amount of retirement pension to be surrendered(⁴) ...

(2) Amount of retirement pension expected after deduction of
amount surrendered(⁵) ... ...

(3) Pension to beneficiary expected in return for amount
surrendered(⁶) ... ...

                                      Signature..............................

                                      Date.............................

(¹) Insert name of local authority administering the superannuation fund.
(²) Delete paragraph A or B, whichever does not apply.
(³) Delete the word or words which do not apply.
(⁴) This must be an exact number of pounds.
(⁵) This must not be less than the pension payable under the above-mentioned regulations to
    the beneficiary.
(⁶) This must not be less than £39.

SCHEDULE 12   Regulation E19

MODIFICATIONS TO PART E IN ITS APPLICATION TO PERSONS WITH NO ENTITLEMENT UNDER THE FORMER REGULATIONS TO A RETIRING ALLOWANCE AND WIDOW'S PENSION OR TO A WIDOW'S PENSION

PART I

1. In regulation E2(1), the words "and a lump sum retiring allowance" shall be omitted.

2. In regulation E3—

   (a) in paragraph (1), for the words "one eightieth" there shall be substituted the words "one sixtieth"; and

   (b) paragraphs (2) to (6) shall be omitted.

3. In regulation E11—

   (a) in paragraph (1)(b), the words "and retiring allowance" and, in paragraph (1)(c), the words "and retiring allowance" and the words "or payment of that allowance" shall be omitted;

   (b) in paragraph (5), for the expression "paragraph (1)(b)(i)" there shall be substituted the expression "paragraph (1)(b)"; and

   (c) paragraph (6) shall be omitted.

PART II

1. In regulation E3, paragraphs (4) to (6) shall be omitted.

2. In regulation E11—

   (a) paragraph (5) shall be omitted; and

   (b) in paragraph (6), for the words "paragraph (1)(b)(ii)" there shall be substituted the words "paragraph (1)(b)".

PART III

1. In regulation E3—

   (a) in paragraph (10), for the words "Subject to paragraphs (11) to (13)," there shall be substituted the words "Subject to paragraph (11),"; and

   (b) paragraphs (12) and (13) shall be omitted.

2. In regulation E6, for paragraphs (2) and (3) there shall be substituted the following—

"(2) Subject to paragraph (3), the amount of a widow's long-term pension shall be the aggregate of—

   (a) the amount ascertained by multiplying one four hundred and eightieth of the pensionable remuneration of the husband of the widow by the length in years of his reckonable service before 1st April 1972; and

   (b) the amount ascertained by multiplying one one hundred and sixtieth of the pensionable remuneration of the husband of the widow by the length in years of his reckonable service after 31st March 1972.

(3) For the purpose of calculating the amount of a widow's long-term pension under paragraph (2) no account shall be taken of reckonable service before attaining the age of 60 years beyond a total of 40 years and any reckonable service to be disregarded by virtue of this paragraph shall be taken from the beginning of the period of the reckonable service.".

3. In regulation E8—

    (*a*) in paragraph (1)—

        (i) sub-paragraph (*c*) shall be omitted;

        (ii) for sub-paragraphs (i) and (ii) there shall be substituted the words "a children's short-term pension in respect of the period of 3 months after the day of his death";

        (iii) in proviso (*a*), the word "and" shall be omitted; and

        (iv) proviso (*b*) shall be omitted; and

    (*b*) in paragraph (2)—

        (i) the words "and a children's long-term pension" shall be omitted; and

        (ii) in the proviso, the words from "or, as" to "pension" shall be omitted.

4. In regulation E11—

    (*a*) in paragraph (1)(*b*), the words from "and either" to the end shall be omitted;

    (*b*) in paragraph (2)(*a*)—

        (i) for the words "or (*b*)(ii)" there shall be substituted the words "or (*b*)"; and

        (ii) for the words "paragraph (1)(*b*)(ii)" there shall be substituted the words "paragraph (1)(*b*)";

    (*c*) paragraphs (2)(*b*), (3) and (8) shall be omitted; and

    (*d*) in paragraph (7), the words "Subject to paragraph (8)," shall be omitted.

5. In regulation E12, the words "a married male employee" shall be omitted.

SCHEDULE 13 |Regulation F6

FLAT-RATE REDUCTION OF VOLUNTARY PAYMENTS

TABLE I

PAYMENTS IN RESPECT OF ADDED YEARS

(1) Age at date of giving consent	(2) Men	(3) Women
	p	p
25 and under 26	6	9
26 ,, ,, 27	6	10
27 ,, ,, 28	7	10
28 ,, ,, 29	7	11
29 ,, ,, 30	8	13
30 ,, ,, 31	8	13
31 ,, ,, 32	8	15
32 ,, ,, 33	9	15
33 ,, ,, 34	9	17
34 ,, ,, 35	10	18
35 ,, ,, 36	10	19
36 ,, ,, 37	11	20
37 ,, ,, 38	12	22
38 ,, ,, 39	13	24
39 ,, ,, 40	13	25
40 ,, ,, 41	14	27
41 ,, ,, 42	15	30
42 ,, ,, 43	16	32
43 ,, ,, 44	17	35
44 ,, ,, 45	19	37
45 ,, ,, 46	21	41
46 ,, ,, 47	23	45
47 ,, ,, 48	25	50
48 ,, ,, 49	28	55
49 ,, ,, 50	32	61
50 ,, ,, 51	35	68
51 ,, ,, 52	40	78
52 ,, ,, 53	47	90
53 ,, ,, 54	55	105
54 ,, ,, 55	66	126

TABLE II

ADDITIONAL CONTRIBUTORY PAYMENTS

(1) Age at date of giving notice	(2) Men	(3) Women
	£ p	£ p
Under 20	2·00	1·00
20 and under 21	2·05	1·10
21 ,, ,, 22	2·15	1·20
22 ,, ,, 23	2·25	1·35
23 ,, ,, 24	2·30	1·50
24 ,, ,, 25	2·40	1·65
25 ,, ,, 26	2·50	1·85
26 ,, ,, 27	2·60	2·10
27 ,, ,, 28	2·70	2·40
28 ,, ,, 29	2·80	2·75
29 ,, ,, 30	2·90	3·10
30 ,, ,, 31	3·00	3·45
31 ,, ,, 32	3·10	3·85
32 ,, ,, 33	3·20	4·05
33 ,, ,, 34	3·30	4·60
34 ,, ,, 35	3·45	5·00
35 ,, ,, 36	3·55	5·40
36 ,, ,, 37	3·65	5·75
37 ,, ,, 38	3·75	6·15
38 ,, ,, 39	3·85	6·55
39 ,, ,, 40	4·00	6·90
40 ,, ,, 41	4·10	7·25
41 ,, ,, 42	4·20	7·65
42 ,, ,, 43	4·35	8·00
43 ,, ,, 44	4·50	8·35
44 ,, ,, 45	4·65	8·65
45 ,, ,, 46	4·80	8·95
46 ,, ,, 47	4·95	9·25
47 ,, ,, 48	5·10	9·55
48 ,, ,, 49	5·25	9·85
49 ,, ,, 50	5·45	10·20
50 ,, ,, 51	5·65	10·65
51 ,, ,, 52	5·85	10·90
52 ,, ,, 53	6·05	11·25
53 ,, ,, 54	6·25	11·60
54 ,, ,, 55	6·50	12·00
55 ,, ,, 56	6·75	12·40
56 ,, ,, 57	7·00	12·80
57 ,, ,, 58	7·30	13·25
58 ,, ,, 59	7·60	13·70
59 ,, ,, 60	7·90	14·15
60 ,, ,, 61	8·20	
61 ,, ,, 62	8·55	
62 ,, ,, 63	8·95	
63 ,, ,, 64	9·40	
64 ,, ,, 65	9·85	

SCHEDULE 14

MODIFICATIONS TO THE REGULATIONS IN THEIR APPLICATION TO SPECIAL CASES

PART I   Regulation G2

EMPLOYEES OF MAGISTRATES' COURTS COMMITTEES

1. A person's remuneration for any employment where he has more than one and does not receive separate remuneration for that employment shall be taken to be that part of his entire remuneration which is paid by the council or, where the remuneration for more than one employment is paid by the same council, such part of that remuneration as may be agreed between him and the council or, in default of agreement, as is determined by the Secretary of State; and the definition of "remuneration" in regulation A3(1) shall have effect accordingly.

2. Regulation A9 shall have effect as if there were inserted at the end thereof the following paragraph—

"Without prejudice to the preceding paragraph, a person who holds two or more clerkships under a magistrates' courts committee or is employed by a magistrates' courts committee to assist a justices' clerk or clerks in two or more clerkships shall be deemed for the purposes of these regulations (except regulation B3) to be in separate employments under separate authorities as respects any clerkships for which the remuneration is paid by different councils.".

3. Regulation C3 shall not apply and regulation E3(4) shall not apply to a person who first became superannuable under Part I of the Act of 1937 by virtue of the Justices of the Peace Act 1949.

4. In regulations B5(b) and C4 to C7 references to an employing authority shall be construed as references to the council paying the person's remuneration from that employment.

5. Regulations C8(3), D4, D9, D10, D14, K1 and L13 shall have effect as if they—

(a) required the magistrates' courts committee to report to the council paying the remuneration of the person's employment any decision taken by them thereunder; and

(b) provided that if the aforesaid council are dissatisfied with the decision they may within one month of receiving the report appeal to the Secretary of State, whose determination shall be final, and that if that council appeal the decision of the committee shall not be effective until the appeal is determined.

6. In the case of a person who—

(a) was, on 30th March 1939, subject to the Act of 1922 by virtue of a local Act or an order made by the Secretary of State under a local Act; and

(b) was, on 30th September 1954, a person to whom paragraph (h) of Part III of Schedule 2 to the Act of 1937 applied, the rate of contribution to be paid by him shall be 5%.

7. Regulation L15 shall have effect as if for the reference to 65 years there were substituted a reference to the age of 70 years or any lesser age (not being less than 65 years) at which the justices' clerk completes 45 years' reckonable service.

8. Any reference in paragraphs 2, 3(2) and 4(1) of Schedule 9 to the age of 65 years shall be construed as a reference to the age of 70 years.

PART II

CERTAIN EMPLOYEES OF THE COMMITTEE OF MAGISTRATES FOR THE INNER LONDON AREA

1. In regulations C4 to C7 references to an employing authority shall be construed as references to the Receiver for the Metropolitan Police District.

2. Regulations C8(3), D4, D9, D10, D14, K1 and L13 shall have effect as if they—

(a) required the committee of magistrates to report to the Secretary of State any decision taken by them thereunder; and

(b) provided that the decision shall not have effect until it has been approved by the Secretary of State.

3. Regulation L15 shall have effect as if for the reference to 65 years there were substituted a reference to the age of 70 years or any lesser age (not being less than 65 years) at which the justices' clerk completes 45 years' reckonable service.

4. Any reference in paragraphs 2, 3(2) and 4(1) of Schedule 9 to the age of 65 years shall be construed as a reference to the age of 70 years.

PART III

EMPLOYEES OF PROBATION AND AFTER-CARE COMMITTEES

1. Notwithstanding anything in the definition of "employee" in regulation A3(1), a probation officer shall not be deemed to have been appointed in a temporary capacity for a period of not more than 3 months by reason only of the fact that his appointment is determinable within the said period unless it is confirmed by the Secretary of State.

2. In relation to pensionable employees of the probation and after-care committee for the inner London area, in regulation C3 references to an employing authority shall be construed as references to the Receiver for the Metropolitan Police District.

3. The powers conferred by regulation C4 shall, in the case of pensionable employees employed by the probation and after-care committee for the inner London area, be exercisable by the Receiver for the Metropolitan Police District; and any sum payable by that committee under regulation C5, C6 or C7 shall be payable by the said Receiver.

4. Regulations C8(3), D4, D9, D10, D14, K1 and L13 shall have effect—

(a) in relation to an employee or former employee of the probation and after-care committee for the inner London area, as if they—

(i) required the committee to report to the Secretary of State any decision taken by them thereunder; and

(ii) provided that the decision shall not have effect until it has been approved by the Secretary of State; and

(b) in relation to an employee or former employee of the probation and after-care committee for any other area, as if they—

(i) required the committee to report to the council responsible for defraying the expenses of the committee or, where two or more councils contribute to the defraying of those expenses, each of those councils any decision taken by them thereunder; and

(ii) provided that if such a council are dissatisfied with the decision they may within one month of receiving the notice appeal to the Secretary of State, whose determination shall be final, and that if such a council appeal the decision of the committee shall not be effective until the appeal is determined.

5.--(1) In the application of regulation D17 to part-time service as a probation officer, the proportionately reduced period for which such part-time service shall be treated as though it were whole-time service shall—

    (*a*) be determined by making a separate calculation in respect of each year of part-time service;

    (*b*) be in respect of any year of part-time service the period which bears to a period of one year the same proportion as the remuneration received by the probation officer in the year of part-time service bears to the mean of the scale of annual salary for probation officers prescribed by rules made under Schedule 5 to the Criminal Justice Act 1948 (disregarding the scale for probation officers who have not attained the age specified in such rules) in respect of that year,

and the provisions of this paragraph shall apply proportionately to any period of part-time service of less than a year.

(2) In relation to any period of part-time service performed before 1st April 1965, sub-paragraph (1) (*b*) shall have effect as if for the reference to the aforesaid mean there were substituted a reference to the notional whole-time salary of a probation officer determined in relation to any year in accordance with sub-paragraph (3).

(3) The notional whole-time salary of a probation officer in respect of any year of part-time service commencing before 1st April 1965 shall be the amount set out in column (2) or (3), as the case may be, of the following table opposite the entry in column (1) which includes the date on which the year of service commenced.

TABLE

(1) Date on which year of service commenced	(2) Men	(3) Women
1st July 1926 to 30th June 1937 ...	275	210
1st July 1937 to 30th June 1944 ...	330	290
1st July 1944 to 30th November 1946...	375	330
1st December 1946 to 31st March 1954	485	420
1st April 1954 to 31st March 1965 ...	620	555

Regulation J2   **SCHEDULE 15**

TRANSFER OF SUPERANNUATION FUNDS

(1) Transferor body	(2) Transferee body
The council of the administrative county of Glamorgan The Mid Glamorgan (Superannuation) Joint Committee	The County Council of Mid Glamorgan
The council of the administrative county of Yorkshire, West Riding The West Riding (Local Authorities) Superannuation Joint Committee	The County Council of West Yorkshire
The Bucklow (Superannuation) Joint Committee	The County Council of Cheshire
The Central Lancashire (Local Authorities) Joint Superannuation Committee The East Cheshire (Local Authorities) Joint Superannuation Committee The South-East Lancashire (Local Authorities) Superannuation Joint Committee	The County Council of Greater Manchester
The Cotswold District Joint Superannuation Committee	The County Council of Gloucestershire
The Durham (Local Authorities) Superannuation Joint Committee	The County Council of Durham
The Lichfield (Superannuation) Joint Committee	The County Council of Staffordshire
The Northumberland (Local Authorities) Superannuation Joint Committee	The County Council of Northumberland
The West Lancashire (Superannuation) Joint Committee	The County Council of Merseyside
The council of any other administrative county, any other joint committee established by a scheme of combination made under section 2 of the Act of 1937 and the council of a county borough or county district	The council of the county within which the area, or the greater part of the area, of the authority specified in column (1) is situate or, in the case of a joint committee so specified, the areas, or the greater part of the areas, of the constituent authorities thereof are situate
The Upper Tame Main Drainage Authority The Derwent Valley Water Board The Durham County Water Board The Fylde Water Board The Staffordshire Potteries Water Board The West Lancashire Water Board The Wirral Water Board The Metropolitan Water Board	The National Water Council

SCHEDULE 16   Regulation J6

APPORTIONMENT OF SUPERANNUATION FUNDS

1. In this schedule—

the body maintaining a superannuation fund comprising a superannuation fund falling to be apportioned is referred to as "the paying body";

the Secretary of State or other body receiving an apportioned part of the fund falling to be apportioned is referred to as "the receiving body"; and

references to "transferred employees" shall be construed as references to transferred employees in respect of whom an apportionment falls to be made and, in the case where an apportionment falls to be made in respect of any such persons as are mentioned in regulation J6(2), shall include those persons.

2. The paying body shall obtain from the actuary making the report on the apportionment of the superannuation fund falling to be apportioned (in this schedule referred to as "the fund") required by regulation J6(3) a certificate specifying the share of the fund (in this schedule referred to as "the apportioned share") referable to the receiving body.

3. The apportioned share shall be—

(a) an amount which is the same proportion of the amount of the basic apportionable assets of the fund as the part of the accrued actuarial liabilities of the fund determined by the actuary to relate to the transferred employees (other than such of those employees as are mentioned in sub-paragraph (b)) is of the accrued actuarial liabilities of the fund; and

(b) an amount equal to the aggregate amount of the contributions made to the fund under section 6(1) or (2) of the Act of 1937 by or in respect of such of the transferred employees as became contributors to the fund in consequence of the amendments effected to the Act of 1937 by regulations 5(1)(a) and 13 of the Miscellaneous Provisions regulations, together with interest thereon calculated at such rate as is determined by the Government Actuary,

less—

(i) an amount equal to such proportion of the amount determined by the actuary under paragraph 5(b) as is determined by the actuary to be referable to the receiving body; and

(ii) an amount equal to such proportion of any amount certified under regulation J4 to represent the capital value of the annual payments therein mentioned to the fund as is determined by the actuary to be referable to the receiving body.

4. The amount of the basic apportionable assets of the fund shall be the amount by which the aggregate amount of the apportionable assets of the fund at 31st March 1974 exceeds the aggregate of the liabilities of the fund specified in paragraph 6.

5. The apportionable assets of the fund at 31st March 1974 shall be—

(a) any cash, securities, loans or other assets held in the fund at 31st March 1974;

(b) an amount determined by the actuary as representing the capital value at that date of any future payments to the fund in pursuance of an actuary's certificate given, or a scheme made, under section 22 of the Act of 1937;

(c) any amount certified by an actuary under regulation J4 to represent the capital value of the annual payments therein mentioned to the fund; and

(d) any sums due to the fund from sundry debtors at 31st March 1974,

less any sums due from the fund to sundry creditors at that date.

6. The liabilities of the fund referred to in paragraph 4 shall be—

(a) an amount equal to the aggregate amount of the contributions made to the fund under section 6(1) or (2) of the Act of 1937 by or in respect of persons who became contributors thereto in consequence of the amendments effected to the Act of 1937 by regulations 5(1)(a) and 13 of the Miscellaneous Provisions regulations, together with interest thereon calculated at such rate as is determined by the Government Actuary;

(*b*) an amount determined by the actuary as representing as at 31st March 1974 the part of the apportionable assets of the fund at 31st March 1974 referable to the then existing and prospective liabilities of the fund in respect of persons who on that date were, or on the appointed day became, entitled to benefits and the prospective liabilities of the fund in respect of any widow or any dependant of any such person.

7. The accrued actuarial liabilities of the fund referred to in paragraph 3(*a*) are the liabilities of the fund in respect of any service, employment or period before the appointed day which would have been taken into account under the former regulations for the purpose of calculating the amount of any benefit which may have become payable thereunder if the Miscellaneous Provisions regulations had not been made and the former regulations had not been revoked by these regulations to or in respect of persons who immediately before the appointed day were contributory employees (other than such persons as are referred to in paragraph 6).

8. The paying body shall furnish the actuary with such information as is necessary to enable him to calculate the apportioned share and shall keep such accounts as will enable the assets of the fund to be distinguished. A copy of the report required by regulation J6(3) and of the certificate referred to in paragraph 2 shall be sent to the receiving body.

9. The paying body shall transfer to the receiving body—

(*a*) where the date on which the certificate is given under paragraph 2 is not more than 6 months after the appointed day, the amount of the apportioned share of the fund, together with interest thereon calculated at such rate as the paying and receiving bodies may agree or, in default of agreement, as is determined by the Government Actuary;

(*b*) where the date on which the certificate is given under paragraph 2 is more than 6 months after the appointed day, the apportionment fraction of the apportionable assets of the fund at the date on which the transfer is effected (in this schedule referred to as "the date of transfer").

10. The apportionment fraction referred to in paragraph 9(*b*) shall be a fraction of which—

(*a*) the numerator is the amount of the apportioned share of the fund; and

(*b*) the denominator is the amount of the apportionable assets of the fund at 31st March 1974 (other than the amounts mentioned in paragraph 5(*b*) or (*c*)), less the amount of any share of the fund which has before the date of transfer to the receiving body been transferred under paragraph 9(*a*) to any other body.

11. The apportionable assets of the fund at the date of transfer shall be—

(*a*) any cash, securities, loans or other assets held in the fund at that date; and

(*b*) any sums due to the fund from sundry debtors at that date,

less any sums due from the fund to sundry creditors at that date.

12.—(1) The apportionable assets of the fund at 31st March 1974 which consist of Stock Exchange securities shall be valued by reference to their market value at that date, and the remainder of the apportionable assets of the fund at that date shall be valued by the actuary as at that date.

(2) The apportionable assets of the fund at the date of transfer which consist of Stock Exchange securities shall be valued by reference to their market value at that date, and the remainder of the apportionable assets of the fund at that date shall be valued by the actuary as at that date.

(3) Where the receiving body is the Secretary of State the transfer under paragraph 9 shall be effected by way of a payment in cash and in any other case the transfer shall be effected by way of a transfer of assets of the fund, unless the paying and receiving bodies agree that it shall be effected by way of a transfer of an equivalent amount in cash.

MODIFICATIONS TO PARTS A, D AND E AND REGULATIONS J9 AND J16 IN THEIR APPLICATION TO PERSONS CEASING TO BE EMPLOYED AFTER 30TH MARCH 1972 AND BEFORE THE APPOINTED DAY

1. Regulation A3(1) shall have effect as if in the definition of "remuneration" for the words from "(d)" to the end there were substituted the words "and also, in the case of an employee who held his employment on or after 30th March 1973, does not include any payment made to him on his ceasing to hold his employment in consideration of loss of holidays or any payment accepted by him in lieu of notice to terminate his contract of employment.".

2. Regulation D4 shall have effect as if—

    (a) paragraph (1)(c) were omitted; and

    (b) in paragraph (2), for the words from "the date" to "employee" there were substituted the words "the appointed day".

3. Regulation D5(1) shall have effect as if sub-paragraph (e) were omitted.

4. Regulations D6 to D8 shall not apply.

5. Regulation D9 shall have effect as if the words from "not being" to "regulation K1(1)" were omitted.

6. Regulations D10 to D14 shall not apply.

7. Regulation E1(3)(e) shall have effect as if at the end there were added—

    "Provided that if any such person as is mentioned in regulation E2(3)(c), by whom fees were at any time during the years 1967 to 1973 earned in respect of work done by him as returning officer at local government elections as part of his remuneration, gives notice for the purpose in accordance with paragraph (4), in calculating for the purposes of these regulations his pensionable remuneration the amount of those fees to be included in his remuneration during the relevant period referred to in paragraph (1) shall be the annual average of those fees earned during such consecutive 3 years of the years 1967 to 1973 as are specified in the notice;".

8. Regulation E2(4) shall have effect as if—

    (a) in sub-paragraph (a)(iv), for the words from "not" to "authority" there were substituted the words "by notice in writing to the appropriate administering authority, given within one month after the appointed day, or such longer period as that authority may in a particular case allow"; and

    (b) in sub-paragraph (e)—

    (i) the words "after so ceasing to be employed but" were omitted; and

    (ii) for the words "so becoming a pensionable employee" there were substituted the words "the appointed day".

9. Regulation E4 shall have effect as if—

    (a) in paragraph (1)—

    (i) after the words "retirement pension", where they first occur, there were inserted the words "(other than a person who ceased to hold his employment before 1st March 1974 and was, in relation to that employment, entitled to an annual pension under the Acts of 1937 to 1953 and the regulations made thereunder)"; and

(ii) for the words from "according" to "Actuary" there were substituted the following—

"(i) where the person is such a person as is mentioned in paragraph (5) and does not become entitled to receive payments in respect of the retirement pension until on or after the appointed day, according to tables to be prepared from time to time by the Government Actuary;

(ii) in any other case, according to the tables which were prepared for the purposes of section 16 of the Act of 1953,"; and

(b) in paragraph (4)—

(i) for the words from "did not" to "deemed to have been allowed to surrender part of a retirement pension under this regulation" there were substituted the words "had effect before the appointed day, the person shall be deemed to have surrendered part of a retirement pension under this regulation"; and

(ii) in proviso (a), for the words "was allowed", in both places where they occur, there were substituted the words "had effect" and for the words "been allowed to surrender", in both places where they occur, there were substituted the word "surrendered".

10. Regulation E12 shall have effect as if—

(a) for the words from "a female" to "regulations" there were substituted the following—

"if—

(a) a female, being such a person as is mentioned in regulation K1(1), on ceasing to hold an employment as mentioned in sub-paragraph (a) of that regulation or, as the case may be, immediately before her death as mentioned in sub-paragraph (b) of that regulation, either—

(i) had a husband who was permanently incapacitated by reason of ill-health or infirmity of mind or body and who was wholly or mainly dependent on her; or

(ii) had no husband but had an eligible child or eligible children; and

(b) a notice for the purpose is given in accordance with the succeeding provisions of this regulation,

this Part shall apply"; and

(b) at the end there were added—

"A notice for the purposes of this regulation may be given—

(i) in the case of a female, being such a person as is mentioned in regulation K1(1)(a), by her, or, if she has died before the appointed day or dies before the expiration of the period within which a notice under this regulation is required to be given without giving such a notice and leaves a widower, by him or, if she does not leave a widower or her widower has died before the appointed day or dies before the expiration of the period within which such a notice as aforesaid is required to be given without giving such a notice, by her personal representatives; and

(ii) in the case of a female, being such a person as is mentioned in regulation K1(1)(b), by her widower or, if her widower has died before the appointed day or dies before the expiration of the period within which a notice for the purposes of this regulation is required to be given without giving such a notice, by her personal representatives,

and shall be given in writing to the appropriate administering authority within 3 months after the appointed day or such longer period as that authority may in a particular case allow.".

11. Regulation J9 shall have effect as if—

(*a*) in paragraphs (2) and (4), the words "for the appropriate period"; and

(*b*) in paragraphs (3) and (5), the words "during the appropriate period"; and

(*c*) paragraph (6),

were omitted.

12. Regulation J16(1) shall have effect as if for the words from the beginning to "that body" there were substituted the following—

"Where a person, being such a person as is mentioned in regulation K1(1), was immediately before the appointed day a contributor to the Manchester pension fund, these regulations shall".

13. Schedule 11 shall have effect as if—

(*a*) in paragraph 2, for the words from "shown" to the end there were substituted the following—

"(*a*) where the person is such a person as is mentioned in regulation E4(5) and does not become entitled to receive payments in respect of the retirement pension until on or after the appointed day, shown in the tables prepared by the Government Actuary under regulation E4 and in force at the date on which the surrender is allowed;

(*b*) in any other case, shown in the tables which were prepared for the purposes of section 16 of the Act of 1953 and in force at the date of his ceasing to hold his employment.";

(*b*) in paragraph 4, for sub-paragraphs (*a*) and (*b*) there were substituted the following—

"(*a*) in the case of such a person as is mentioned in regulation E4(5), within 2 months before or within one month after the date on which he ceases to be employed or within 3 months after the appointed day, whichever period ends the later; and

(*b*) in any other case, within 3 months after the appointed day,";

(*c*) in the proviso to paragraph 4—

(i) for the words "a retiring employee" there were substituted the words "a person";

(ii) for the words "sub-paragraph (*a*)" there were substituted the words "this paragraph"; and

(iii) for the words from "the date" to the end there were substituted the following—

"(i) in the case of such a person as is referred to in paragraph 4(*a*), the date on which he ceases to be employed or, as the case may be, the appointed day; and

(ii) in any other case, the appointed day.";

(*d*) in paragraph 7—

(i) in the proviso to sub-paragraph (1), for the words "a retiring employee" there were substituted the words "a person referred to in paragraph 4(*a*)" and the words from "and" to the end were omitted; and

(ii) in sub-paragraph (3), the words from "if the person" to "employee" were omitted; and

(*e*) in paragraph B of the form specified at the end of the schedule, for the words from "if" to the end there were substituted the words "as from

19 , I became entitled.".

Regulation M1 SCHEDULE 18

AMENDMENTS

PART I

ENACTMENTS

1. In section 2 of the Local Elections and Register of Electors (Temporary Provisions) Act 1940**(a)**, so far as it applies to England and Wales—

(*a*) in subsection (1), the words "contributory employee or", in the first place where they occur, and the words from "computing" to "or of" shall be omitted and for the words "appropriate superannuation fund" there shall be substituted the words "the superannuation fund in the benefits of which he is entitled to participate"; and

(*b*) in subsection (2), for the words from the beginning to "participate" there shall be substituted the words "In this section the expressions "local Act contributor" and "local Act scheme" have the same meanings as in section 8 of the Superannuation Act 1972".

2. In section 2 of the Local Elections and Register of Electors (Temporary Provisions) Act 1943**(b)**, so far as it applies to England and Wales—

(*a*) in subsection (1), the words from "under" to "(Scotland) Act, 1937" and the words "contributory employee or" shall be omitted; and

(*b*) in subsection (3), for the words from "he shall" to "said remuneration" there shall be substituted the words "the remuneration received by him (otherwise than as part of an inclusive salary) in respect of work done by him in that year under the Act of 1943" and the words from "computing" to "or of" shall be omitted.

3. In section 34 of the Representation of the People Act 1945**(c)**, so far as it applies to England and Wales—

(*a*) in subsection (1), the words "contributory employee or" and the words from "computing" to "or of" shall be omitted and for the words "appropriate superannuation fund" there shall be substituted the words "the superannuation fund in the benefits of which he is entitled to participate";

(*b*) in subsection (3), for the words from "he shall" to "said remuneration" there shall be substituted the words "the remuneration received by him (otherwise than as part of an inclusive salary) in respect of work done by him in that year under the Act of 1943 or this Act" and the words from "computing" to "or of" shall be omitted; and

(*c*) in subsection (4), for the words from the beginning to "participate" there shall be substituted the words "In this section the expressions "local Act contributor" and "local Act scheme" have the same meanings as in section 8 of the Superannuation Act 1972".

4. In section 1 of the Act of 1953, so far as it applies to England and Wales—

(*a*) in subsection (1), for the words from "contributory" to the end of the subsection there shall be substituted the words "pensionable employee";

(*b*) in subsection (2), in paragraph (*c*) for the words "contributory employees" there shall be substituted the words "pensionable employees" and in paragraph (*d*) for the words "contributory employee" there shall be substituted the words "pensionable employee";

(*c*) at the end of the section there shall be added the following subsection—

"(6) In this section "appropriate administering authority", "appropriate superannuation fund", "employing authority" and "pensionable employee" have the same meanings as in the Local Government Superannuation Regulations 1974.".

(a) 4 & 5 Geo. 5. c. 3.   **(b)** 7 & 8 Geo. 6. c. 2.   **(c)** 1945 c. 5.

5. In section 18 of the Act of 1953, so far as it applies to England and Wales and has effect as provisions of regulations under section 7 of the Act of 1972—

 (*a*) in subsection (1), for the words "local authority" there shall be substituted the words "scheduled body" and for the words "contributory employee" there shall be substituted the words "pensionable employee";

 (*b*) in subsection (2), for the word "authority", wherever occurring, there shall be substituted the word "body"; and

 (*c*) at the end of the section there shall be added the following subsection—

  "(5) In this section "employee", "scheduled body" and "pensionable employee" have the same meanings as in the Local Government Superannuation Regulations 1974.".

6. In section 15(1)(*a*) of the Superannuation (Miscellaneous Provisions) Act 1967(a), for the words from "sub-paragraph (ii)" to the end there shall be substituted the words "regulation B2(1)(*l*) of the Local Government Superannuation Regulations 1974;".

7. In Schedule 6 to the Pensions (Increase) Act 1971 for the words "service to which regulation 2(1) of the Superannuation (Inner London Magistrates' Courts) Regulations 1965 applies;" there shall be substituted the words "other than a justices' clerk or other officer such as is mentioned in regulation B2(1)(*l*) of the Local Government Superannuation Regulations 1974;".

PART II

INSTRUMENTS

1. In regulation 7 of the Benefits regulations—

 (*a*) for words "contributory employee", wherever occurring, there shall be substituted the words "pensionable employee";

 (*b*) in paragraph (1), for the words "average remuneration" there shall be substituted the words "pensionable remuneration";

 (*c*) in paragraph (2), for the words beginning "(not" to "applies)" there shall be substituted the words "(not being such a person as is described in proviso (*a*)(ii) to E5(1) or E5(2)(*b*) or (*c*) of the Local Government Superannuation Regulations 1974)"; and

 (*d*) at the end of the regulation there shall be added the following sub-paragraph—

  "(6) In this regulation "appropriate superannuation fund", "employing authority", "pensionable employee" and "pensionable remuneration" have the same meanings as in the Local Government Superannuation Regulations 1974.".

2. In article 26 of the London Authorities (Superannuation) Order 1965(b), for the words from "and section 35" to the end there shall be substituted the words "and any question arising under this article shall be determined by the Secretary of State whose decision shall be final:

Provided that the Secretary of State may at any time before the question is determined, and shall, if so directed by the High Court, state in the form of a special case for the opinion of the High Court any question of law arising in those proceedings.".

3. In article 8 of the London Courts and Probation (Superannuation) Order 1965(c), for the words from "and section 35" to the end there shall be substituted the words "and any question arising under this article shall be determined by the Secretary of State whose decision shall be final:

Provided that the Secretary of State may at any time before the question is determined, and shall, if so directed by the High Court, state in the form of a special case for the opinion of the High Court any question of law arising in those proceedings.".

(a) 1967 c. 28. **(b)** S.I. 1965/621 (1965 I, p. 1970). (c) S.I. 1965/645 (1965 I, p.2030).

Regulations A4 and M2   SCHEDULE 19

REVOCATIONS AND REPEALS

PART I

ENACTMENTS HAVING EFFECT AS REGULATIONS UNDER SECTION 7 OR 8(2) OF THE ACT OF 1972

Chapter	Enactments ceasing to have effect
1 Edw. 8. & 1 Geo.6. c. 68	The Local Government Superannuation Act 1937, except sections 13, 28, 29, 30(3), 35, 36(6), 38, 40(1) and 42 and Part V of Schedule 2.
2 & 3 Geo.6. c. 94	Sections 3 to 9 of the Local Government Staffs (War Service) Act 1939.
11 & 12 Geo.6. c. 33	Sections 6 and 7 of the Superannuation (Miscellaneous Provisions) Act 1948 and the definitions in section 17(1) of that Act of "contributory employee", "local Act scheme", "local Act contributor" and "local authority".
11 & 12 Geo.6. c. 65	Section 72 of the Representation of the People Act 1948.
12, 13 & 14 Geo.6. c. 101	Paragraph 8(6) of Schedule 2 to the Justices of the Peace Act 1949.
1 & 2 Eliz.2. c. 25	The Local Government Superannuation Act 1953, except sections 1(1), (3)(c) and (d), (4)(c) and (5), 18, 21, 27 and 29, in Part I of Schedule 3, paragraph 2(1), and Schedule 4.
1963 c. 33	Section 77(3) of the London Government Act 1963.
1963 c. 38	Section 97(1) of the Water Resources Act 1963.
1964 c. 48	Paragraph 5(5) of Schedule 4 to the Police Act 1964.
1964 c. 75	Paragraph 2 of Schedule 1 to the Public Libraries and Museums Act 1964.
1970 c. li	Section 32 of the Manchester Corporation Act 1970.
1971 c. 23	Paragraphs 13 and 14 of Schedule 10 to the Courts Act 1971.

Part II

OTHER ENACTMENTS

Chapter	Enactments repealed
10 & 11 Geo.5. c. xcvii	Part VII of the Manchester Corporation Act 1920, except the definitions in section 57 of "officer and servant", "superannuation fund" and "contributor" and section 66(1).
17 & 18 Geo.5. c. ciii	Section 29 of the Manchester Corporation Act 1927.
20 & 21 Geo.5. c. clxxviii	Part VI of the Manchester Corporation (General Powers) Act 1930.
24 & 25 Geo.5. c. xcvii	Part IX of, and Schedule 1 to, the Manchester Corporation Act 1934.
2 & 3 Geo.6.c. 18	The Local Government Superannuation Act 1939, so far as unrepealed.
4 & 5 Geo.6. c. 3	In section 2 of the Local Elections and Register of Electors (Temporary Provisions) Act 1940, so far as it applies to England and Wales, in subsection (1) the words "contributory employee or", where they first occur, and the words from "computing" to "or of".
7 & 8 Geo.6. c. 2	In section 2 of the Local Elections and Register of Electors (Temporary Provisions) Act 1943, so far as it applies to England and Wales, in subsection (1) the words from "under" to "(Scotland) Act, 1937", and the words "contributory employee or" and in subsection (3) the words from "computing" to "or of".
8 & 9 Geo.6. c. 5	In section 34 of the Representation of the People Act 1945, so far as it applies to England and Wales, in subsection (1) the words "contributory employee or", where they first occur, and the words from "computing" to "or of" and in subsection (3) the words from "computing" to "or of".
9 & 10 Geo.6. c. xxxviii	Part VII of the Manchester Corporation Act 1946, except section 46.
2 & 3 Eliz.2. c. xlviii	Section 79 of the Manchester Corporation Act 1954.
4 & 5 Eliz.2. c. lxxxiii	In section 9 of the Manchester Corporation Act 1956, in subsection (1) the words from "a contributor" to "fund") or", the words "shall continue to contribute to the superannuation fund or" and the words "(as the case may be)" and subsection (2).
7 Eliz.2. c. vii	Part VII of the Manchester Corporation Act 1958, except section 48.
10 & 11 Eliz.2. c. xxx	Section 37 of the Manchester Corporation Act 1962.

Chapter	Enactments repealed
1964 c. 48	Paragraphs 5(1) to (3) and (6) and 7 of Schedule 4, and paragraph 3 of Schedule 11, to the Police Act 1964, except so far as they apply to a person who by virtue of a scheme made under Part I of that Act was transferred before 1st April 1974, or is transferred to the employment of the Common Council after 31st March 1974.
1964 c. 75	Paragraphs 1(1) to (3) and 3, and the definition of "pensions" in paragraph 5, of Schedule 1 to the Public Libraries and Museums Act 1964, except so far as those paragraphs and that definition apply to a person who by the operation of that Act was transferred before 1st April 1974, or is transferred to the employment of the Common Council after 31st March 1974.
1965 c. xlii	Part VIII of the Manchester Corporation Act 1965.
1967 c. xl	Part VII and section 44(8) of the Manchester Corporation Act 1967.
1968 c. 69	Paragraph 13(4) of Schedule 3 to the Justices of the Peace Act 1968.
1969 c. 27	In section 2(4) of the Vehicle and Driving Licences Act 1969 the words from "and in section 6(5)" to the end of the first paragraph and the words "or either of the said sections 6(5) or such a scheme" and "or a reduction of remuneration occurred".
1970 c. li	In the Manchester Corporation Act 1970, the definition in section 3(2) of "unit trust scheme", sections 28 to 31, 33(1) and (5), 34 and 35.
1971 c. lxvii	In the Manchester Corporation (General Powers) Act 1971, the definition in section 3(2) of "the Manchester pension provisions" and Part VI.

PART III

INSTRUMENTS HAVING EFFECT AS REGULATIONS UNDER SECTION 7
OR 8(2) OF THE ACT OF 1972

References	Instruments or provisions thereof ceasing to have effect
—	The Manchester Corporation Superannuation Scheme 1938 approved by the Minister of Health on 21st February 1939.
S.R.&O. 1939/54 (Rev. XVII, p.839: 1939 II, p.2581)	The Local Government Superannuation (Sum in lieu of Transfer Value) Regulations 1939.
S.R.&O. 1939/57 (Rev. XVII, p.834: 1939 II, p.2667)	The Local Government Superannuation (Service of Registration Officers) Regulations 1939.
S.I.1949/628 (1949 I, p.3054)	The Local Government Superannuation (Break of Service) Regulations 1949.
S.I.1954/879 (1954 II, p.1701)	The Local Government Superannuation (Surrender of Superannuation Allowance) Rules 1954.
S.I.1954/1048 (1954 II, p.1595)	The Local Government Superannuation (Benefits) Regulations 1954, except regulations 1 and 7.
S.I.1954/1049 (1954 II, p.1749)	The Probation Officers and Clerks (Superannuation) Regulations 1954, except so far as they apply and amend section 18 of the Local Government Superannuation Act 1953 and regulation 7 of the Local Government Superannuation (Benefits) Regulations 1954.
S.I.1954/1050 (1954 II, p.1525)	The Justices Clerks and Assistants (Superannuation) Regulations 1954, except so far as they amend section 18 of the Local Government Superannuation Act 1953 and regulation 7 of the Local Government Superannuation (Benefits) Regulations 1954.
S.I.1954/1192 (1954 II, p.1570)	The Local Government Superannuation (Administration) Regulations 1954.
S.I.1954/1224 (1954 II, p.1537)	The Local Government Superannuation (Actuarial Valuations) Regulations 1954.
S.I.1954/1229 (1954 II, p.1715)	The Local Government (Teachers) Regulations 1954.
S.I.1954/1237 (1954 II, p.1672)	The Local Government Superannuation (Limitation on Service) Regulations 1954.
S.I.1954/1238 (1954 II, p.1683)	The Local Government Superannuation (Reduction and Adjustment of Superannuation Allowance) Regulations 1954.
S.I.1955/1041 (1955 II, p.1825)	The Local Government Superannuation (Benefits) (Amendment) Regulations, except regulations 1 and 15.

References	Instruments or provisions thereof ceasing to have effect
S.I.1955/1347	The Manchester Superannuation (Benefits) Scheme Approval Instrument 1955, together with the scheme approved thereby.
S.I.1955/1496	The Justices' Clerks and Assistants (Manchester) Regulations 1955.
S.I.1957/1685	The Manchester Superannuation (Service) Scheme Approval Instrument 1957, together with the scheme approved thereby.
S.I.1958/1273 (1958 II, p.1806)	The Local Government Superannuation (Benefits) (New Towns Staffs) Regulations 1958.
S.I.1962/43	The Manchester Corporation Scheme Approval Instrument 1962, together with the scheme approved thereby.
S.I.1962/2682 (1962 III, p.3649)	The Local Government Superannuation (Benefits) (New Towns Staffs) Regulations 1962.
S.I.1964/1126 (1964 II, p.2512)	The London Authorities (Appropriate Superannuation Funds) Order 1964.
S.I.1965/422 (1965 I, p.1119)	The Probation Officers and Clerks (Superannuation) (Amendment) Regulations 1965, except so far as they amend, or amend provisions contained in the Probation Officers and Clerks (Superannuation) Regulations applying and amending, section 18 of the Local Government Superannuation Act 1953 or regulation 7 of the Local Government Superannuation (Benefits) Regulations 1954.
S.I.1965/537 (1965 I, p. 1550)	The Superannuation (Inner London Magistrates' Courts) Regulations 1965, except so far as they apply or amend section 18 of the Local Government Superannuation Act 1953, or regulation 7 of the Local Government Superannuation (Benefits) Regulations 1954 or have effect for the purposes of that section, or regulation, as so applied.
S.I.1965/621 (1965 I, p.1970)	The London Authorities (Superannuation) Order 1965, except articles 1 to 3 and 26.
S.I.1965/645 (1965 I, p.2030)	The London Courts and Probation (Superannuation) Order 1965.
S.I.1965/1288 (1965 II, p.3660)	The Local Government Superannuation (Administration) (Amendment) Regulations 1965 except articles 8 and 10 to 13.
S.I.1967/1330 (1967 III, p.3975)	The London Authorities (Superannuation) (Amendment) Order 1967, except articles 1 to 3.
S.I.1969/413 (1969 I, p.1163)	The London Authorities (Superannuation) (Amendment) Order 1969.
S.I.1969/793 (1969 II, p.2227)	The National Insurance (Modification of Local Government Superannuation Schemes) Regulations 1969.
S.I.1970/1125 (1970 II, p.3554)	The Local Government Superannuation (Teachers) (Amendment) Regulations 1970.

PART IV

OTHER INSTRUMENTS

References	Instruments or provisions thereof ceasing to have effect
S.I.1957/1685	The Manchester Superannuation (Service) Scheme Approval Instrument 1957 together with the scheme approved thereby, so far as not hereinbefore in Part III of this schedule revoked.
S.I.1965/645 (1965 I, p.2030)	The London Courts and Probation (Superannuation) Order 1965, except articles 8 and 10 to 13 and so far as not hereinbefore in Part III of this schedule revoked.
S.I.1966/1216 (1966 III, p.3273)	Article 5 of the London Authorities (Staff) Order 1966.
S.I.1968/488 (1968 I,p. 1194)	Article 5 of the London Authorities (Staff) Order 1968.
S.I.1969/793 (1969 II, p.2227)	The National Insurance (Modification of Local Government Superannuation Schemes) Regulations 1969, except so far as they apply to the local Act scheme administered by the Common Council and so far as not hereinbefore in Part III of this schedule revoked.
S.I.1973/313 (1973 III, p.1100)	The Local Government Superannuation (Miscellaneous Provisions) Regulations 1973.
S.I.1973/1996 (1973 III, p.6872)	The Local Government Superannuation (Miscellaneous Provisions) (No. 2) Regulations 1973.

22nd March 1974.

Anthony Crosland,

Secretary of State for the Environment.

EXPLANATORY NOTE

(This Note is not part of the Regulations.)

These Regulations, with a small number of exceptions, supersede the provisions of the enactments and instruments constituting the local government superannuation scheme, namely, (i) the provisions of the enactments which, although repealed by the Superannuation Act 1972 ("the Act of 1972"), had effect, together with the provisions of any instrument made under any such enactment, by virtue of paragraph 5(1) of Schedule 7 to that Act as Regulations made under section 7 of that Act, (ii) the Local Government Superannuation (Miscellaneous Provisions) Regulations 1973 and (iii) the Local Government Superannuation (Miscellaneous Provisions) (No. 2) Regulations 1973. The principal of the exceptions referred to above are provisions relating to the granting of gratuities and the payment of injury allowances.

Although considerable drafting changes have been made from the existing provisions, in general the Regulations reproduce the effect of those provisions (Parts A to H and L). There is, however, a number of changes and improvements, including—

(1) Contributions to a superannuation fund will continue to be made by all employees in the scheme until completion of 45 years' service reckonable for the purpose of calculating the amount of benefits (instead of being discontinued on the attainment, before such completion, of a certain age) (Regulation C1).

(2) Benefits are no longer exclusively to be calculated by reference to the remuneration in the final year of pensionable employment; a number of variations are permitted (Regulation E1).

(3) Employees who leave their employment after 5 years' service reckonable for the purpose of determining entitlement to benefits but before qualifying for immediate benefits or who have no right to a return of contributions may have their accrued benefits deferred until the age at which they would normally qualify for immediate benefits, or earlier in certain cases, e.g., by reason of incapacity or on compassionate grounds (Regulation E2(1)(c) and (4)); those employees who have a right to a return of contributions may have their contributions returned instead if they prefer.

(4) The introduction of children's pensions where the father was an employee (Regulations E8 to E10).

(5) Short-term pensions are provided for the widows and the children of deceased male employees or former male employees (other than those who were at death entitled to, but not in receipt of, a pension); long-term pensions are provided on the cessation of payment of short-term pensions for the widows and the children of male employees who die in employment with 5 years' service reckonable for the purpose of determining entitlement to benefits, or of former male employees who were at the time of death in receipt of pension, and long-term pensions, payable as from a man's death, are also provided for the widows and children of men who were at death entitled to, but not in receipt of, a pension (Regulations E5 to E10).

(6) Where a female employee, having a husband who is incapacitated, or children but no husband, gives a notice for the purpose, the same benefits will be payable to her, her husband and children as are payable to a male employee and his family (Regulation E12).

Under the power in section 12 of the Act of 1972, the provisions of Parts D (service) and E (benefits), and other provisions in the regulations incidental to those parts, are (with certain exceptions and modifications) applied to employees who retired or died in employment after 30th March 1972 and before 1st April 1974; provision is made for opting out if a person is thereby placed in a worse position (Part K).

In addition the Regulations—

(a) supersede the National Insurance (Modification of Local Government Superannuation Schemes) Regulations 1969 (Part F);

(b) include (in Part M) the revocation of the Manchester local Act scheme and, in the provision for the transfer of existing superannuation funds, provision for the winding up and transfer of the Manchester pension fund (Regulation J2); the Common Council of the City of London will be the only authority in England and Wales administering a local Act scheme;

(c) make provision for the apportionment of existing superannuation funds consequential on certain statutory reorganisations taking effect on 1st April 1974 (the principal reorganisations being those under the Local Government Act 1972, the Water Act 1973 and the National Health Service Reorganisation Act 1973) or on these Regulations (Regulation J6);

(d) provide for the preservation of certain special rights enjoyed by a number of persons under the existing scheme or by persons entitled to participate in the benefits of the Manchester pension fund and for the protection of the superannuation position of persons who are transferred to new employment by reason of certain statutory reorganisations (Regulations J9, J10 and J12 to J17).

STATUTORY INSTRUMENTS

1974 No. 521 (S.46)

NATIONAL HEALTH SERVICE, SCOTLAND
The National Health Service (Enforceability of Rights and Liabilities of Executive Councils and Joint Committees of Executive Councils) (Scotland) Order 1974

Made - - -	*19th March* 1974
Laid before Parliament	*29th March* 1974
Coming into Operation	*1st April* 1974

In exercise of the powers conferred on me by sections 26(3) and 61(1) of the National Health Service (Scotland) Act 1972(**a**), and of all other powers enabling me in that behalf, I hereby make the following order:—

Citation and commencement

1. This order may be cited as the National Health Service (Enforceability of Rights and Liabilities of Executive Councils and Joint Committees of Executive Councils) (Scotland) Order 1974 and shall come into operation on 1st April 1974.

Interpretation

2.—(1) In this order, unless the context otherwise requires—

"the Act" means the National Health Service (Scotland) Act 1972;

"the Agency" means the Common Services Agency for the Scottish Health Service constituted under section 19 of the Act;

"the appointed day" means 1st April 1974;

"Committee" means a Joint Ophthalmic Services Committee established under the National Health Service (Joint Ophthalmic Services Committees) (Scotland) Regulations 1972(**b**);

"Council" means an Executive Council constituted under section 32 of the National Health Service (Scotland) Act 1947(**c**);

"enactment" includes a provision in a statutory instrument;

"Health Board" means a Health Board constituted under section 13 of the Act.

(2) In this order, unless the context otherwise requires, any reference to a right or liability is a reference to a right or liability transferred to the Secretary of State by virtue of section 26(2) of the Act.

(3) Unless the context otherwise requires, references in this order to any enactment shall be construed as references to that enactment as amended or re-enacted by any subsequent enactment.

(**a**) 1972 c. 58.   (**b**) S.I. 1972/828 (1972 II, p. 2662).
(**c**) 1947 c. 27.

(4) The Interpretation Act 1889(**a**) shall apply for the interpretation of this order as it applies for the interpretation of an Act of Parliament.

Enforceability of rights and liabilities by or against Health Boards

3.—(1) Subject to the following provision of this article, any right or liability enforceable by or against a Council or Committee immediately before the appointed day shall on and after that day be enforceable by or against the Health Board within whose area the office of the Council or Committee is situated immediately before the appointed day.

(2) Any right or liability which was enforceable by or against a Council or Committee in respect of any property held by them shall be enforceable by or against the Health Board which controls and manages such property on the appointed day on behalf of the Secretary of State.

(3) Any right or liability which was enforceable by or against a Council or Committee in respect of the provision by a person of general medical services, general dental services, pharmaceutical services or general ophthalmic services shall be enforceable by or against the Health Board in whose area are situated the practice premises, relevant to the case, of the person undertaking to provide such services.

Enforceability of rights and liabilities by or against the Agency

4. Any right or liability which, immediately before the appointed day, was enforceable by or against the Drug Accounts Committee established by the National Health Service (Drug Accounts Committee) (Scotland) Order 1948(**b**) shall on that day be enforceable by or against the Agency.

Sgnd. *William Ross*
One of Her Majesty's Principal
Secretaries of State.

St. Andrews House,
Edinburgh.
19th March 1974.

EXPLANATORY NOTE

(*This Note is not part of the Order.*)

This Order provides for the rights and liabilities of Executive Councils and Joint Ophthalmic Services Committees to be enforceable by or against Health Boards and for the rights and liabilities of the Drug Accounts Committee to be enforceable by or against the Common Services Agency.

(**a**) 1889 c. 63.   (**b**) S.I. 1948/1596 (Rev. XV, p. 989: 1948 I, p. 2321).

1974 No. 522   (S.47)

NATIONAL HEALTH SERVICE, SCOTLAND

The National Health Service (Charges) (Scotland) Regulations 1974

Made - - - -	19*th March* 1974
Laid before Parliament	29*th March* 1974
Coming into Operation	1*st April* 1974

In exercise of the powers conferred on me by sections 39 and 42 of the National Health Service (Scotland) Act 1947(a) (as amended by sections 11 and 14 of the National Health Service (Amendment) Act 1949(b), by section 78 of and Schedule 4 to the Health Services and Public Health Act 1968(c) and by section 64 of and Schedule 6 to the National Health Service (Scotland) Act 1972(d)), by section 1 of, and the Schedule to, the National Health Service Act 1951(e) (as amended by section 1 of the National Health Service Act 1961 (f), by section 64 of and Schedules 6 and 7 to the National Health Service (Scotland) Act 1972 and by section 57 of and Schedule 4 to the National Health Service Reorganisation Act 1973(g)), by sections 1, 2 and 7 of the National Health Service Act 1952(h) (as amended by sections 1 and 2 of the National Health Service Act 1961, by section 39 of and Schedule 8 to the Ministry of Social Security Act 1966(i), by section 36 of and Schedule 8 to the Finance Act 1970(j), and by section 64 of and Schedule 6 to the National Health Service (Scotland) Act 1972), by section 2 of the National Health Service Act 1961, and of all other powers enabling me in that behalf, I hereby make the following regulations:—

Citation and commencement

1. These regulations may be cited as the National Health Service (Charges) (Scotland) Regulations 1974 and shall come into operation on 1st April 1974.

Interpretation

2.—(1) In these regulations, unless the context otherwise requires—

"the Act of 1947" means the National Health Service (Scotland) Act 1947;

"the Act of 1951" means the National Health Service Act 1951;

"the Act of 1952" means the National Health Service Act 1952;

(a) 1947 c. 27. (b) 1949 c. 93. (c) 1968 c. 46. (d) 1972 c. 58. (e) 1951 c. 31.
(f) 1961 c. 19. (g) 1973 c. 32. (h) 1952 c. 25. (i) 1966 c. 20. (j) 1970 c. 24.

"the Act of 1961" means the National Health Service Act 1961;

"the Act of 1972" means the National Health Service (Scotland) Act 1972;

"Board" means a Health Board constituted under section 13 of the Act of 1972;

"current authorised fee" has the meaning assigned to it in regulation 5(3) of these regulations;

"dentist" means a registered dental practitioner;

"Estimates Board" means the Scottish Dental Estimates Board constituted under Part III of the National Health Service (General Dental Services) (Scotland) Regulations 1974(a);

"Health Service Acts" means the National Health Service (Scotland) Acts 1947 to 1973;

"out-patient" means a person receiving treatment under the Health Service Acts otherwise than under Part IV of the Act of 1947 and who is not for the purpose of receiving that treatment resident in a hospital.

(2) References in any other regulations to the regulations revoked by these regulations or to any provision thereof shall be construed as references to these regulations and to the corresponding provisions hereof as the case may be.

(3) The Interpretation Act 1889(b) shall apply for the interpretation of these regulations as it applies for the interpretation of an Act of Parliament.

Charges

3. The charges specified in these regulations shall insofar as they relate to the supply, otherwise than under Part IV of the Act of 1947, of dental and optical appliances and of the appliances specified in Schedule 2 to these regulations shall be made by, and shall be recoverable by, the appropriate Board.

Acknowledgement

4. Every Board supplying an appliance for which a charge may be made under these regulations shall, before supplying the appliance, obtain an acknowledgement signed by the patient, or by some person competent to sign the acknowledgement on his behalf, of his obligation to pay the said charge.

Dental treatment and appliances

5.—(1) Subject to paragraph (5) below, the authorised charges specified in the Schedule to the Act of 1951 as varied in terms of section 2(1) of the Act of 1952 in respect of the supply of dentures (including bridges) as described in the said Schedule (as amended by section 5(1) of the Act of 1952) shall be one-half of the current authorised fee for the supply of dentures, or £10.00 whichever is the less.

(2) The amount of the charge authorised by section 2 of the Act of 1952 for such general dental services provided under Part IV of the Act of 1947 as are subject to a charge under the said section 2 or under the Act of 1951 shall be one-half of the current authorised fee, or £10.00, whichever is the less.

(3) For the purpose of this regulation "the current authorised fee" has, subject to the exemptions contained in section 2(1) and (4) of the Act of 1952 and to paragraph (4) below, the meaning assigned to it in section 2(5) of the said Act

---

(a) S.I. 1974/505(1974 I. p. 1842). **(b)** 1889 c. 63.

3f

of 1952, that is to say, in relation to any services, the fee authorised in accordance with the Statement of Dental Remuneration made under regulations for the time being in force under the Act of 1947 as the fee payable to the practitioner in respect of those services but does not include any fee or charge mentioned in section 2(5)(*a*) or (*b*) (exemption from charges) of the Act of 1952, so, however, that in relation to bridges, "the current authorised fee" shall be the current authorised fee for a denture having the same number of teeth and made of the same material as the bridge.

(4) Where the current authorised fee payable in respect of the provision of general dental services is such amount as the Estimates Board may in their discretion approve, whether or not subject to a maximum, the current authorised fee shall be—

(a) if the Estimates Board have approved a fee for the services to be provided, the amount of that fee so approved, notwithstanding any subsequent increase of the amount of that fee on appeal; or

(b) if the Estimates Board have not approved a fee for the services to be provided, the amount of the fee authorised on appeal for the provision of those services.

(5) Where a denture to which paragraph (1) above refers is supplied otherwise than under Part IV of the Act of 1947 then,

(a) if the current authorised fee payable is such amount as the Estimates Board may in their discretion approve, the Board shall refer the matter to the Estimates Board and the current authorised fee shall be such amount as the Estimates Board may approve;

(b) if the denture is so supplied as part of a course of treatment begun under general dental services and a person has already become liable to pay a charge to the dentist who began that course of treatment, the maximum amount chargeable by the Board under this regulation shall be less than £10.00 by the amount payable to the dentist who began the course of treatment, and, if a dentist, after beginning as part of the general dental services a course of treatment for a person refers that person for dental services provided by a Board otherwise than under Part IV of the Act of 1947, he shall give to that Board a statement of the amount paid to him by that person under these regulations.

(6) No charge, which would otherwise be payable under section 1 of the Act of 1951, shall be payable in respect of the supply (including the replacement) of a dental appliance otherwise than under Part IV of the Act of 1947 to a person who has undergone operative procedures affecting the mandible, the maxilla, or the soft tissues of the mouth as part of treatment for invasive tumours.

Supply of lenses

6.—(1) The description of lenses (not forming part of children's glasses as described in the Schedule to the Act of 1951) for which charges are authorised under section 1(1) of and the Schedule to that Act shall be varied so as to consist of the descriptions of lenses shown in the several parts of Schedule 1 to these regulations.

(2) The charge authorised in respect of the supply under the Health Service Acts of a lens of any description mentioned in the first column of any part of Schedule 1 to these regulations shall, if it is also of a description mentioned at

the head of any other column in the same part of the Schedule be the amount specified in that column opposite the description of that lens, but, where more than one pair of glasses is supplied following a new prescription, or a change of prescription, the charge for each lens supplied after the first two shall be reduced by 40p.

Supply of wigs and fabric supports to out-patients

7.—(1) Subject to section 1(2) of the Act of 1952 (exemptions from the charges which may be imposed under the section) and to these regulations any out-patient who is supplied by or on behalf of the Board with an appliance of a description specified in column 1 of Schedule 2 to these regulations, shall be liable to pay to the Board the sum specified in column 2 of that Schedule in respect of that appliance.

(2) No charge shall be payable under this regulation by—

(a) a person to whom the Secretary of State has issued an exemption certificate in respect of treatment for accepted war disablement or, as the case may be, for accepted service disablement and who requires an appliance mentioned in this regulation for the purpose of treatment of that disablement; and

(b) a person who is receiving a supplementary pension or supplementary allowance under the Ministry of Social Security Act 1966, or a dependant of such person; and

(c) a person who is receiving a family income supplement under the Family Income Supplements Act 1970(a) or a dependant of such person.

(3) A Board who receive any charge payable to them for any appliance mentioned in Schedule 2 to these regulations shall, if asked to do so, supply a receipt for any charge so received.

(4) Any person to whom paragraph (2) above applies may claim a refund of any charge he has paid by presenting the receipt for such charge obtained from the Board and any refund made shall be made in such manner and subject to such conditions as the Secretary of State may determine but no payment shall be made unless a claim is submitted within one month of the date on which the charge was paid.

Conditions of exemption

8. It shall be a condition of exemption under subsection (3) or subsection (4) of section 1 of the Act of 1961 from a charge payable under section 1 of the Act of 1951 that a declaration in support of the claim is made on a form provided for that purpose by the appropriate Board and that such documentary evidence of age, attendance at school, pregnancy or confinement is produced to the Board as the Board may require.

Recovery of charges

9. Any sum payable or recoverable in consequence of these regulations may, without prejudice to any other method of recovery, be recoverable as a debt.

Revocations

10. The regulations named in Schedule 3 to these regulations are hereby revoked.

St. Andrew's House,	(Sgd.) *William Ross*
Edinburgh.	One of Her Majesty's Principal
19th March 1974	Secretaries of State.

(a) 1970 c. 55.

Regulation 6

SCHEDULE 1

LENSES

PART I

SINGLE VISION (EXCLUDING LENTICULAR) LENSES

Spherical Power	Plano or Spherical	Cylindrical or Sphero-Cylindrical	
		Where neither spherical nor cylindrical power exceeds 2.00D	All other cases
	£	£	£
Not exceeding 6.00D	1.20	1.30	1.35
Exceeding 6.00D but not exceeding 10.00D	1.55	—	1.80
Exceeding 10.00D	1.95	—	2.10

PART II

GLASS BIFOCAL (EXCLUDING LENTICULAR) LENSES

Type	Plano or Spherical	Cylindrical or Sphero-Cylindrical
	£	£
Fused or Cemented	2.45	2.75
Solid (38mm segment)	2.80	3.10
Solid (other segments)	3.40	3.50

PART III

PLASTICS BIFOCAL (EXCLUDING LENTICULAR) LENSES

Spherical Power	Plano or Spherical	Cylindrical or Sphero-Cylindrical Cylindrical Power	
		Not exceeding 2.00D	Exceeding 2.00D
	£	£	£
Not exceeding 4.00D	2.90	3.15	3.50
Exceeding 4.00D but not exceeding 9.00D	3.10	3.35	3.50
Exceeding 9.00D	3.30	3.35	3.50

PART IV

LENTICULAR LENSES

Type (and Spherical Power)	Plano or Spherical	Cylindrical or Sphero-Cylindrical Cylindrical Power		
		Not exceeding 2.00D	Exceeding 2.00D but not exceeding 4.00D	Exceeding 4.00D
	£	£	£	£
Single Vision:— Concave: Glass	2.25	2.40	2.40	2.40
Concave: Plastics Not exceeding 13.00D	2.30	2.45	2.60	2.75
Exceeding 13.00D	2.75	2.95	3.05	3.20
Convex (Glass or Plastics)	2.60	2.75	2.80	3.10
Bifocal	3.50	3.50	3.50	3.50

PART V

OTHER LENSES

Type	Of any Description
	£
Frosted	1.25
Chavasse	1.25
Multifocal	3.50
Varifocal	3.50
Aspherical	3.50
Contact	3.85

Regulation 7

SCHEDULE 2

CHARGES FOR FABRIC SUPPORTS AND WIGS

Column 1	Column 2
Fabric support	each £2.00
Bespoke wig	each £7.50
Stock wig	each £2.50

SCHEDULE 3

REGULATIONS REVOKED

The National Health Service (Charges for Appliances)
(Scotland) Regulations 1951   S.I. 1951/862 (1951 I, p.1411).

The National Health Service (Charges for Appliances)
(Scotland) Amendment Regulations 1961   S.I. 1961/917 (1961 II, p.1771).

The National Health Service (Charges for Appliances)
(Scotland) Regulations 1969   S.I. 1969/918 (1969 II, p.2797).

The National Health Services (Charges)
(Scotland) Regulations 1971   S.I. 1971/420 (1971 I, p.1240).

EXPLANATORY NOTE

(This Note is not part of the Regulations.)

These Regulations consolidate the provisions for the making and recovery of charges for dental, optical and certain other appliances and for dental treatment with amendments principally to take account of the transfer of responsibilities of Regional Hospital Boards and Executive Councils to Health Boards.

STATUTORY INSTRUMENTS

1974 No. 525

WATER, ENGLAND AND WALES

The Statutory Water Undertakers (Pension Schemes) Order 1974

Made - - -	*22nd March* 1974
Coming into Operation	*1st April* 1974

The Secretary of State for the Environment, in exercise of the powers conferred upon him by section 27(3) of the Water Act 1973**(a)** and of all other powers enabling him in that behalf, hereby makes the following order:—

Title and commencement

1. This order may be cited as the Statutory Water Undertakers (Pension Schemes) Order 1974, and shall come into operation on 1st April 1974.

Interpretation

2.—(1) In this order—

"the Act" means the Water Act 1973;

"standard water authority scheme", "standard water company scheme", and "statutory water company" have the same meaning as in the Act.

(2) The Interpretation Act 1889**(b)** shall apply for the interpretation of this order as it applies for the interpretation of an Act of Parliament.

(3) Any reference in this order to a numbered section shall be construed as a reference to the section bearing that number in the Act.

Standard water authority scheme

3.—(1) In this article, "at a material date" means at the date by reference to which this article falls to be applied for the purposes of section 27 in any particular case.

(a) 1973 c. 37.   **(b)** 1889 c. 63.

(2) The scheme designated as the standard water authority scheme for the purposes of section 27(3) (*a*) shall be the scheme contained in such regulations under section 7 of the Superannuation Act 1972(**a**) as have effect at a material date.

Corporation to manage standard water company scheme

4. The corporation designated to manage the standard water company scheme for the purposes of section 27(3) (*b*) shall be the Water Companies (Pension Fund) Trustee Company, a company incorporated on 18th March 1974 in pursuance of the provisions of the Companies Acts 1948 to 1967(**b**).

Date before which option may be exercised

5.—(1) In this article—
"entitled employee" means a person—

(*a*) who is in the employment of a statutory water company on 31st March 1974, and

(*b*) who intends to remain in the employment of such a company after that date, and

(*c*) for whom on that date superannuation arrangements will be in operation;

"relevant terms of transfer", in relation to an entitled employee, means a statement in writing, furnished to him by the statutory water company by whom he is employed, and setting out details of the rights and obligations which would be applicable to him if he were to become a member of the standard water company scheme.

(2) The date prescribed for the purposes of section 27(3) (*c*) (that is to say, the date before which an entitled employee may opt that the standard water company scheme shall not apply to him) shall be, in relation to any entitled employee, the day immediately after the expiration of a period of three months beginning with the date on which he receives the relevant terms of transfer from the statutory water company by whom he is employed.

Anthony Crosland,
Secretary of State for the Environment.

22nd March 1974.

(**a**) 1972 c. 11.   (**b**) 1948 c. 38; 1961 c. 46; 1967 c. 81.

EXPLANATORY NOTE

(This Note is not part of the Order.)

The Water Act 1973 empowers statutory water undertakers to establish and administer pension arrangements for their employees, and requires all statutory water companies to participate in a superannuation scheme (called in the Act "the standard water company scheme") which is to offer to their employees terms and benefits not less favourable than those offered by a corresponding superannuation scheme ("the standard water authority scheme") to employees of water authorities.

This Order, which applies to England and Wales—

(a) designates the scheme contained in Regulations under section 7 of the Superannuation Act 1972 as the standard water authority scheme (Article 3);

(b) designates a corporation to manage the standard water company scheme (Article 4); and

(c) prescribes a date before which certain existing employees of statutory water companies may opt that the standard water company scheme shall not apply to them (Article 5).

STATUTORY INSTRUMENTS

1974 No. 526

TRANSPORT

PENSIONS AND COMPENSATION

The London Transport (Male Wages Grades Pensions) (Amendment) Order 1974

Made - - - -	*21st March* 1974
Laid before Parliament	*1st April* 1974
Coming into Operation	*22nd April* 1974

The Secretary of State for the Environment, in exercise of powers conferred by section 74 of the Transport Act 1962(a) and section 18 of the Transport (London) Act 1969(b) and now vested in him(c), and of all other enabling powers, hereby makes the following Order on the application which the London Transport Executive have made with the approval of the Greater London Council:—

1.—(1) This Order shall come into operation on 22nd April 1974, and may be cited as the London Transport (Male Wages Grades Pensions) (Amendment) Order 1974.

(2) The Interpretation Act 1889(d) shall apply for the interpretation of this Order as it applies for the interpretation of an Act of Parliament.

2. The Rules of the London Transport (Male Wages Grades) Pension Scheme as set out in the Schedule to the London Transport (Male Wages Grades Pensions) Order 1966(e), as amended(f), (as those Rules and that Scheme now have effect subject to the provisions of any orders made under section 74 of the Transport Act 1962) shall be amended as follows:—

(1) In Rule 12, after the words "ill-health retirement pensions and benefits" there shall be added the words "supplementary pensions".

(2) After Rule 16 there shall be inserted the following Rule:—

at-rate
plement
basic
sion

16A (*a*) This Rule applies to every person who
      (i) is entitled on 1st January 1974, or
      (ii) becomes entitled after 1st January 1974 but before 7th April 1975, or
      (iii) having been born before 7th April 1910, becomes entitled on or after 7th April 1975,

---

(a) 1962 c. 46. (b) 1969 c. 35.
(c) S.I. 1970/1681 (1970 III, p. 5551). (d) 1889 c. 63.
(e) S.I. 1966/1164 (1966 III, p. 2789). (f) S.I. 1966/1556 (1966 III, p. 4756).

to receive any age or ill-health retirement pension under the provisions of Rule 13, 14, 15(*b*) or 16(*b*).

(*b*) A person to whom this Rule applies shall be entitled to receive with effect from 1st January 1974 or the date on which entitlement to his basic pension arises, whichever is later, a supplementary pension at a flat-rate of 74p a week, to be paid as an addition to his basic pension and to be payable so long as his basic pension continues.

(*c*) For the purposes of Rule 31 the said supplementary pension shall be disregarded but, save as aforesaid, the provisions of these Rules about pensions payable under these Rules shall apply in relation to the said supplementary pension as they apply in relation to any pension payable under any of the Rules mentioned in paragraph (*a*) of this Rule.

(*d*) Where a person to whom this Rule applies is entitled under the provisions of this Rule to receive the said supplementary pension in respect of a period before the date of the coming into operation of the London Transport (Male Wages Grades Pensions) (Amendment) Order 1974, payment of the said pension to or for the benefit of that person for that period and for any further period between that date and the commencement of the first of the four-weekly periods specified in Rule 19 which begins after that date shall be made as soon as possible after that date.

(*e*) In making any calculation of the sum to be paid to or for the benefit of any person in respect of the said supplementary pension for a fraction of a week such a pension shall be treated as accruing due at the rate of 13p a day, except a Sunday which for the purpose of this paragraph shall be disregarded.

(*f*) In this Rule "basic pension", in relation to a person to whom this Rule applies, means the pension, or the aggregate of the pensions, payable to or for the benefit of that person under any one or more of Rules 13, 14, 15(*b*) and 16(*b*)."

Signed by authority of the Secretary of State.

21st March 1974.

Fred Mulley,
Minister for Transport,
Department of the Environment.

EXPLANATORY NOTE

(This Note is not part of the Order.)

This Order amends the Rules of the London Transport (Male Wages Grades) Pension Scheme so as to make provision for a supplementary pension of 74p a week for persons who are entitled on 1st January 1974, or who become entitled after that date but before 7th April 1975, or who become entitled on or after 7th April 1975 but are over age 65 on that date, to receive a basic pension from the Scheme. The supplementary pension will be payable as from 1st January 1974 or the date of commencement of the basic pension, whichever is the later.

STATUTORY INSTRUMENTS

1974 No. 527

NATIONAL HEALTH SERVICE, ENGLAND AND WALES

The National Health Service (General Ophthalmic Services) (Amendment) Regulations 1974

Made - - -		*22nd March* 1974
Laid before Parliament		*25th March* 1974
Coming into Operation		*1st April* 1974

The Secretary of State for Social Services in exercise of the powers conferred by section 44(1)(*b*) of the National Health Service Act 1946**(a)** (as amended by sections 17(1) and 39(1) of the Health Services and Public Health Act 1968**(b)**) and now vested in her**(c)**, and of all other powers enabling her in that behalf, hereby makes the following regulations:—

Citation, commencement and interpretation

1.—(1) These regulations may be cited as the National Health Service (General Ophthalmic Services) (Amendment) Regulations 1974, and shall come into operation on 1st April 1974.

(2) The rules for the construction of Acts of Parliament contained in the Interpretation Act 1889**(d)** shall apply for the purposes of the interpretation of these regulations as they apply for the purposes of the interpretation of an Act of Parliament.

Amendments to regulations

2. For regulation 16(1) of the National Health Service (General Ophthalmic Services) Regulations 1974**(e)** there shall be substituted:—

"(1) Subject to the provisions of paragraphs (2) and (3), a patient, other than a person—

(*a*) for whom medical inspection or treatment is provided under or by virtue of the provisions of section 3 of the National Health Service Reorganisation Act 1973**(f)**, and

(*b*) in respect of whom evidence to that effect is produced to the Committee—

shall be liable to pay for the replacement or repair under the general ophthalmic services of the whole or part of an optical appliance, the charges in respect thereof for which provision is made in the Statement."

Barbara Castle,

Secretary of State for Social Services.

22nd March 1974.

(a) 1946 c. 81.   **(b)** 1968 c. 46.
(c) *See* Secretary of State for Social Services Order 1968 (S.I. 1968/1699(1968 III, p. 4585)) Article 2.
(d) 1889 c. 63.   **(e)** S.I. 1974/287(1974 I, p. 994).
(f) 1973 c. 32.

EXPLANATORY NOTE

(This Note is not part of the Regulations.)

These Regulations amend the National Health Service (General Ophthalmic Services) Regulations 1974. They provide that pupils attending maintained schools or certain other educational establishments or being educated under special arrangements, do not have to pay certain charges for the replacement or repair under the general ophthalmic services of their optical appliances.

STATUTORY INSTRUMENTS

1974 No. 528

CIVIL AVIATION

The Carriage by Air (Sterling Equivalents) Order 1974

Made - - -	*21st March* 1974
Coming into Operation	*12th April* 1974

The Secretary of State in exercise of the powers conferred by section 4(4) of the Carriage by Air Act 1961(a) and under that provision as applied by Article 6 of the Carriage by Air Acts (Application of Provisions) Order 1967(b) and now vested in him(c) and of all other powers enabling him in that behalf hereby orders as follows:

1. This Order may be cited as the Carriage by Air (Sterling Equivalents) Order 1974 and shall come into operation on 12th April 1974.

2. This Order supersedes the Carriage by Air (Sterling Equivalents) Order 1973(d).

3. The amounts shown in column 2 of the following Table are hereby specified as amounts to be taken for the purposes of Article 22 in the First Schedule to the Carriage by Air Act 1961 and of that Article as applied by the Carriage by Air Acts (Application of Provisions) Order 1967 as equivalent to the sums respectively expressed in francs on the same line in column 1 of that Table:

TABLE

Amount in francs	Sterling equivalent
	£
250	8.73
5,000	174.47
125,000	4,361.60
250,000	8,723.20
875,000	30,531.20

G. R. Sunderland,

An Assistant Secretary of the Department of Trade.

21st March 1974.

(a) 1961 c. 27.　　　　　　　　(b) S.I. 1967/480 (1967 I, p. 1475).
(c) S.I. 1966/741, 1970/1537 (1966 II, p. 1732; 1970 III, p. 5293).
(d) S.I. 1973/1189 (1973 II, p. 3562).

EXPLANATORY NOTE

(This Note is not part of the Order.)

This Order specifies the sterling equivalents of amounts, expressed in gold francs as the limit of the air carrier's liability under the Warsaw Convention of 1929, and under that Convention as amended by the Hague Protocol of 1955, as well as under corresponding provisions applying to carriage by air to which the Convention and Protocol do not apply. It supersedes the Carriage by Air (Sterling Equivalents) Order 1973.

The sterling equivalents have been calculated on the basis of current market rates for sterling in terms of the US dollar on the basis of the valuation of gold at $42.2222 per fine ounce.

STATUTORY INSTRUMENTS

1974 No. 529

PROBATION AND AFTER-CARE

The Combined Probation and After-Care Areas Order 1974

Made - - - -   *20th March* 1974

Laid before Parliament   *29th March* 1974

Coming into Operation   in accordance with Article 1(1)

In exercise of the powers conferred upon me by section 254 of the Local Government Act 1972**(a)**, I hereby make the following Order:—

1.—(1) This Order may be cited as the Combined Probation and After-Care Areas Order 1974 and shall come into operation on 1st April 1974, except that for the purpose of making any appointment under Article 5 below or of making any arrangements to come into effect on and after 1st April 1974 this Order shall come into operation forthwith.

(2) This Order does not extend to Greater London.

2.—(1) The Interpretation Act 1889**(b)** shall apply for the interpretation of this Order as it applies for the interpretation of an Act of Parliament and as if this Order and the Orders revoked thereby were Acts of Parliament.

(2) In this Order any reference to any enactment includes a reference to that enactment as amended or extended by, or under, any other enactment.

(3) The Orders specified in Schedule 1 to this Order are hereby revoked.

3. Any provision contained in, or made under, any enactment which relates to a combined probation and after-care area shall have effect as if this Order were made under Schedule 5 to the Criminal Justice Act 1948**(c)**, and section, 76(3) thereof, and as if any such area and any committee therefor constituted hereby were constituted under that Schedule and, accordingly, the provisions of this Order relating to combined probation and after-care areas and committees therefor may be amended or revoked under the said Schedule 5 and section 76(3).

4. Each of the petty sessions areas specified in column 1 of Schedule 2 to this Order shall form part of the combined probation and after-care area specified opposite to that petty sessions area in column 2 of the said Schedule.

(a) 1972 c. 70.   (b) 1889 c. 63.
(c) 1948 c. 58.

5. The probation and after-care committee for each of the said combined probation and after-care areas (hereafter in this Order referred to as "a committee") shall, subject to the provisions of paragraph 2(3) of Schedule 5 to the Criminal Justice Act 1948 and section 95(2) and (3) of the Criminal Justice Act 1967**(a)** (which provide for the co-option of persons by such committees) and section 57(1) of the Criminal Justice Act 1972**(b)** (which provides for the, appointment of certain judges and justices to be members of such committees) consist of such number of justices appointed by the justices acting for each petty sessions area or, as the case may be, group of petty sessions areas from amongst their number as may be specified in column 3 of the said Schedule 2 opposite to that petty sessions area or group of petty sessions areas, as the case may be.

6. Subject to the provisions of Rule 3 of the Probation Rules 1965**(c)** (which relates to the term of office of a member of a probation and after-care committee appointed to fill a vacancy) members of a committee appointed under Article 5 of this Order shall, without prejudice to any subsequent appointment, be appointed to hold office for a term of eight months reckoned from 1st April 1974 and thereafter for the term of three years reckoned from 1st December next following the date on which they are appointed as aforesaid.

7. The quorum of a committee shall be such number, being not less than three nor more than eight, as the committee shall from time to time determine.

8. The secretary of a committee shall be—

(*a*) in the case of each of the Hampshire, Northumbria and North Wales probation and after-care areas, such officer of one of the councils of the counties comprised in the committee's area as may be agreed between the committee and those councils, and,

(*b*) in any other case, such officer of the council of the county which is coterminous with the committee's area as may be agreed between the committee and that council,

or, in default of agreement under this Article, such person as may be determined by the Secretary of State.

Roy Jenkins,
One of Her Majesty's Principal
Secretaries of State.

Home Office,
Whitehall.
20th March 1974.

(a) 1967 c. 80.   (b) 1972 c. 71.
(c) S.I. 1965/723 (1965 I, p. 2236).

SCHEDULE 1

REVOCATIONS

Orders revoked	References
The Combined Probation and After-Care Areas Order 1972	S.I. 1972/518 (1972 I, p. 1776).
The Combined Probation and After-Care Areas (No. 2) Order 1972	S.I. 1972/519 (1972 I, p. 1781).
The Combined Probation and After-Care Areas (Amendment) Order 1972	S.I. 1972/1728 (1972 III, p. 5035).
The Bedfordshire Probation and After-Care Area Order 1964	S.I. 1964/1584
The Bedfordshire Probation and After-Care Order 1969	S.I. 1969/197
The Berkshire Probation and After-Care Area Order 1972	S.I. 1972/1828
The Buckinghamshire Probation and After-Care Area Order 1951	S.I. 1951/1284
The Cambridgeshire and Isle of Ely Probation and After-Care Area Order 1964	S.I. 1964/1606
The Cheshire Probation and After-Care Area Order 1969	S.I. 1969/1054
The Cornwall Probation and After-Care Area Order 1955	S.I. 1955/1882
The Cumberland Probation and After-Care Area Order 1955	S.I. 1955/280
The Cumberland Probation and After-Care Area (Amendment) Order 1965	S.I. 1965/1014
The Derbyshire Probation and After-Care Area Order 1957	S.I. 1957/1428
The Devon, Exeter and Torbay Probation and After-Care Area Order 1967	S.I. 1967/1031
The Dorset Probation and After-Care Area Order 1953	S.I. 1953/1033
The Durham Probation and After-Care Area Order 1969	S.I. 1969/37
The Essex Probation and After-Care Area Order 1963	S.I. 1963/2076
The Essex Probation and After-Care Area (Amendment) Order 1969	S.I. 1969/38
The Gloucestershire Probation and After-Care Area Order 1952	S.I. 1952/405
The Gloucestershire Probation and After-Care Area (Amendment) Order 1965	S.I. 1965/1016
The Hampshire Probation and After-Care Area Order 1968	S.I. 1968/371
The Herefordshire Probation and After-Care Area Order 1954	S.I. 1954/332
The Hertfordshire Probation and After-Care Area Order 1953	S.I. 1953/1759
The Huntingdon and Peterborough Provision and After-Care Area Order 1964	S.I. 1964/1615
The Kent Probation and After-Care Area Order 1951	S.I. 1951/1855
The Kent Probation and After-Care Area Order 1962	S.I. 1962/2017
The Lancashire Probation and After-Care Areas Order 1959	S.I. 1959/119
The Leicestershire and Rutland (Combined Probation and After-Care Areas) Order 1926	S.R. & O. 1927/948
The Lincolnshire Probation and After-Care Area Order 1956	S.I. 1956/299
The Manchester and Salford Probation and After-Care Area Order 1969	S.I. 1969/525
The Newcastle and Northumberland Probation and After-Care Area Order 1969	S.I. 1969/268
The Norfolk Probation and After-Care Area Order 1964	S.I. 1964/407
The Northampton and County Probation and After-Care Area Order 1964	S.I. 1964/319
The Nottingham City and County Probation and After-Care Area Order 1967	S.I. 1967/1799
The Oxfordshire Probation and After-Care Area Order 1954	S.I. 1954/350
The Oxfordshire Probation and After-Care Area Order 1966	S.I. 1966/1197
The Shropshire Probation and After-Care Area Order 1954	S.I. 1954/436
The Shropshire Probation and After-Care Area Order 1960	S.I. 1960/41

SCHEDULE 1—Revocations—(*continued*)

Orders revoked	References
The Somerset and Bath Probation and After-Care Area Order 1957	S.I. 1957/395
The Staffordshire Probation and After-Care Area Order 1955	S.I. 1955/279
The Suffolk Probation and After-Care Area Order 1955	S.I. 1955/383
The Suffolk Probation and After-Care Area Order 1960	S.I. 1960/747
The Suffolk Probation and After-Care Area Order 1969	S.I. 1969/165
The Surrey Probation and After-Care Area Order 1950	S.I. 1950/1794
The East Sussex Probation and After-Care Area Order 1953	S.I. 1953/1419
The East Sussex Probation and After-Care Area (Amendment) Order 1968	S.I. 1968/611
The West Sussex Probation and After-Care Area Order 1953	S.I. 1953/1488
The Warwickshire Probation and After-Care Area Order 1964	S.I. 1964/389
The West Midlands Probation and After-Care Area Order 1966	S.I. 1966/35
The West Midlands Probation and After-Care Area Order 1970	S.I. 1970/1514
The Westmorland Probation and After-Care Area Order 1962	S.I. 1962/1213
The Wiltshire Probation and After-Care Area Order 1953	S.I. 1953/1441
The Worcester City and County Probation and After-Care Area Order 1963	S.I. 1963/1143
The East Riding and York City Probation and After-Care Area Order 1966	S.I. 1966/325
The North Riding Probation and After-Care Area Order 1953	S.I. 1953/1411
The West Riding Probation and After-Care Area Order 1952	S.I. 1952/924
The West Riding Probation and After-Care Area Order 1955	S.I. 1955/608
The Brecknock Probation and After-Care Area Order 1950	S.I. 1950/ 1351
The Cardiganshire Combined Probation and After-Care Areas Order 1927	S.R. & O. 1927/974
The Carmarthenshire Probation and After-Care Area Order 1956	S.I. 1956/1329
The Flintshire Probation and After-Care Area Order 1953	S.I. 1953/1587
The Flintshire Probation and After-Care Area Order 1966	S.I. 1966/285
The Glamorgan Probation and After-Care Area Order 1966	S.I. 1966/286
The Merioneth Probation and After-Care Area Order 1952	S.I. 1952/1965
The County of Monmouth Probation and After-Care Area Order 1952	S.I. 1952/958
The Montgomeryshire Probation and After-Care Area Order 1964	S.I. 1964/1634
The North Wales(Combined Probation and After-Care Area) Order 1943	S.R. & O. 1943/1149
The North Wales (Combined Probation and After-Care Area) Order 1952	S.I. 1952/2116
The Pembrokeshire Probation and After-Care Area Order 1954	S.I. 1954/1552
The Radnorshire Probation and After-Care Area Order 1964	S.I. 1964/295

SCHEDULE 2

Column 1 Petty Sessions Area	Column 2 Probation and After-Care Area	Column 3 Number of justices on probation and after-care committee
Bath	Avon	2
Bristol		9
Lawford's Gate		3
Long Ashton		2
Sodbury		1
Thornbury		1
Wansdyke		2
Weston-super-Mare		2
Ampthill	Bedfordshire	1
North Bedfordshire		4
Biggleswade		2
Dunstable		2
Leighton Buzzard		1
Luton		4
Bradfield and Sonning	Berkshire	1
Forest		1
Hungerford and Lambourn		1
Maidenhead		1
Newbury		2
New Windsor		1
Reading		4
Slough		2
Windsor		1
Amersham	Buckinghamshire	2
Aylesbury		2
Brill		2
Buckingham		2
Burnham		2
Chesham		2
Fenny Stratford		2
High Wycombe		2
Linslade		2
Marlow		2
Newport Pagnell		2
Stony Stratford		2
Winslow		2
Wycombe (County)		2
Arrington and Melbourn	Cambridgeshire	1
Bottisham		1
Cambridge		1
Cambridge City		2
Caxton		1
Ely		1
Huntingdon Borough and Leightonstone		1
Hurstingstone		1
Linton		1
Newmarket		1
Norman Cross		1

Column 1 Petty Sessions Area	Column 2 Probation and After-Care Area	Column 3 Number of justices on probation and after-care committee
North Witchford	Cambridgeshire (*Contd.*)	1
Ramsey		1
Soke of Peterborough		2
Toseland		1
Whittlesey		1
Wisbech (Borough)		1
Wisbech (Isle)		1
Chester	Cheshire	2
Congleton		2
Crewe and Nantwich		2
Ellesmere Port		2
Halton		2
Macclesfield		3
Vale Royal		2
Warrington		3
Hartlepool	Cleveland	4
Langbaurgh		2
Teesside		13
Bodmin and Trigg	Cornwall	1
Dunheved		1
East Middle		1
East Penwith		1
East Powder		1
East South		1
Falmouth		1
Helston and Kerrier		1
Isles of Scilly		1
Lesnewth		1
Liskerrett		1
Penryn		1
Penwith		2
Powder Tywardreath		1
Pydar		1
South Powder		1
Stratton		1
Truro and West Powder		1
Wadebridge		1
Alston	Cumbria	1
Ambleside and Windermere		1
Barrow-in-Furness		3
Bootle		1
Carlisle		4
Cockermouth		1
East Ward		1
Hawkshead		1
Kendal		2
Keswick		1
Lonsdale Ward		1
Maryport		1
North Lonsdale		1
Penrith		1
West Ward		1

Column 1 Petty Sessions Area	Column 2 Probation and After-Care Area	Column 3 Number of justices on probation and after-care committee
Whitehaven	Cumbria (*Contd.*)	3
Wigton		1
Workington		2
Alfreton	Derbyshire	2
Ashbourne		1
Bakewell		1
Belper		1
Chesterfield		5
Derby		5
Derby County and Appletree		1
Glossop		1
High Peak		2
Ilkeston		3
Matlock		1
South Derbyshire		1
Axminster	Devon	1
Barnstaple		1
Bideford and Great Torrington		1
Cullompton		1
Exeter		3
Exmouth		1
Honiton		1
Kingsbridge		1
Okehampton		1
Plymouth		8
Plympton		1
South Molton		1
Tavistock		1
Teignbridge		2
Tiverton		1
Torbay		3
Totnes		1
Wonford		1
Blandford	Dorset	1
Bournemouth		6
Bridport		1
Christchurch		1
Dorchester		1
Poole		4
Shaftesbury		1
Sherborne		1
Sturminster		1
Wareham		1
Weymouth and Portland		2
Wimborne		1
Chester-le-Street	Durham	2
Darlington		3
Derwentside		3
Durham		3
Easington		4
Sedgfield		3
Teesdale and Wear Valley		4

Column 1 Petty Sessions Area	Column 2 Probation and After-Care Area	Column 3 Number of justices on probation and after-care committee
Battle and Rye	East Sussex	1
Bexhill		1
Brighton		3
Crowborough		1
Eastbourne		1
Hailsham		1
Hastings		1
Hove		1
Lewes		1
Billericay	Essex	2
Brentwood		1
Chelmsford		2
Colchester		2
Dengie and Maldon		1
Dunmow		1
Epping and Ongar		2
Freshwell and South Hinck- ford		1
Halstead		1
Harlow		1
Harwich		1
North Hinckford		1
Rochford		2
Saffron Walden		1
Southend-on-Sea		2
Tendring		1
Thurrock		2
Witham		1
Berkeley	Gloucestershire	1
Campden		1
Cheltenham		2
Cirencester		1
Coleford		1
Dursley		1
Fairford		1
Gloucester (City)		2
Gloucester (County)		1
Lydney		1
Newent		1
Newnham		1
Northleach		1
Stow-on-the-Wold		1
Stroud		1
Tetbury		1
Tewkesbury		1
Whitminster		1
Winchcombe		1
Alton	Hampshire	1
Andover		1
Basingstoke		2
Droxford		1
Eastleigh		1
Fareham		2

Column 1 Petty Sessions Area	Column 2 Probation and After-Care Area	Column 3 Number of justices on probation and after-care committee
Gosport	Hampshire (*Contd.*)	1
Havant		2
Hythe		1
Lymington		1
Odiham		2
Petersfield		1
Portsmouth		4
Ringwood		1
Romsey		1
Southampton		4
Totton and New Forest		1
Winchester		2
Isle of Wight		3
Bewdley Borough	Hereford and Worcester	1
Bromsgrove		2
Bromyard		1
Dore and Bredwardine		1
Droitwich		1
Evesham		1
Hereford (Borough)		2
Hereford (County)		1
Hundred House		1
Kidderminster		2
Kington		1
Ledbury		1
Leominster and Wigmore		1
Malvern		1
Pershore		1
Redditch		2
Ross		1
Stourport		1
Tenbury		1
Upton on Severn		1
Worcester (Borough)		2
Worcester (County)		1
Bishop's Stortford	Hertfordshire	2
Buntingford		1
Cheshunt		2
Dacorum		2
Hatfield		2
Hertford and Ware		2
Hitchin		2
Odsey		1
St. Albans		4
South Mimms		2
Stevenage		1
Watford		2
Welwyn		1
Bainton Beacon	Humberside	1
Barton on Humber		1
Beverley		1
Brigg		1
Dickering		1

Column 1 Petty Sessions Area	Column 2 Probation and After-Care Area	Column 3 Number of justice son probation and after-care committee
Epworth and Goole	Humberside (*Contd.*)	2
Grimsby (Borough)		4
Grimsby (County)		2
Holme Beacon		1
Howdenshire		1
Kingston upon Hull		13
Middle Holderness		1
North Holderness		1
Scunthorpe		4
South Holderness		1
South Hunsley Beacon		2
Wilton Beacon		1
Ashford and Tenterden	Kent	2
Canterbury and St. Augustine		2
Dartford		2
Dover and East Kent		2
Faversham		2
Folkestone and Hythe		2
Gravesham		2
Maidstone		2
Margate		2
Medway		3
Ramsgate		2
Sevenoaks		2
Sittingbourne		2
Tonbridge and Malling		2
Tunbridge Wells and Cranbrook		2
Accrington	Lancashire	1
Blackburn		3
Blackpool		3
Burnley		2
Chorley		2
Church		2
Darwen		1
Fylde		1
Lancaster		3
Ormskirk		2
Pendle		3
Preston		4
Ribble Valley		1
Rossendale		2
South Ribble		2
Wyre		3
Ashby de la Zouch	Leicestershire	1
Leicester (City)		5
Leicester (County)		2
Loughborough		1
Lutterworth		1
Market Bosworth		1
Market Harborough		1
Melton and Belvoir		1
Rutland		1

Column 1 Petty Sessions Area	Column 2 Probation and After-Care Area	Column 3 Number of justices on probation and after-care committee
Alford	Lincolnshire	1
Boston		2
Bourne		1
Caistor		1
East Elloe		1
Gainsborough		1
Grantham		2
Horncastle		1
Lincoln (City)		3
Lincoln (Kesteven)		2
Lindsey (Lincoln and Wragby)		1
Louth		1
Market Rasen		1
Sleaford		1
Spilsby		1
Stamford		1
West Elloe		1
Wigan	Greater Manchester	2
Makerfield		2
Leigh		2
Bolton		4
Bury		2
Rochdale		2
Middleton and Heywood		2
Salford		2
Eccles		2
Manchester		12
Oldham		3
Trafford		3
Stockport		4
Ashton-under-Lyne		2
South Tameside		2
North Sefton	Merseyside	3
South Sefton		3
Liverpool		12
St. Helens		3
Knowsley		3
Wirral		8
Blofield and Walsham	Norfolk	1
Clackclose		1
Depwade		1
Diss		1
Earsham		1
Eynsford		1
Fakenham		1
Forehoe		1
Great Yarmouth		3
Guiltcross and Shropham		1
Holt		1
King's Lynn		3
Loddon and Clavering		1
Mitford and Launditch		1

Column 1 Petty Sessions Area	Column 2 Probation and After-Care Area	Column 3 Number of justices on probation and after-care committee
North Erpingham	Norfolk (*Contd.*)	1
Norwich		5
Smithdon and Brothercross		1
South Erpingham		1
Swaffham		1
Taverham		1
Thetford and Grimshoe		1
Tunstead and Happing		1
Brackley	Northamptonshire	1
Corby		2
Daventry		1
Kettering		3
Mid Northants		1
Northampton		6
Oundle and Thrapston		1
Towcester		1
Wellingborough		4
Bamburgh Ward	Northumbria	
Berwick-Upon-Tweed		1
Glendale Ward		
Bellingham		1
Hexham		
Blyth Valley		2
East Coquetdale Ward		1
West Coquetdale Ward		
Morpeth Ward		1
Wansbeck		2
Newcastle-Upon-Tyne		8
North Tyneside		5
Gateshead		6
South Tyneside		4
Houghton-le-Spring		2
Sunderland		5
Allertonshire	North Yorkshire	1
Birdforth		1
Buckrose		1
Bulmer East		1
Bulmer West		1
Claro		5
Gilling East		1
Hallikeld		1
Hang East		1
Hang West		1
Malton		1
Richmond and Gilling West		1
Ripon Liberty		1
Ryedale		1
Scarborough		4
Selby		3
Staincliffe		2
Stokesley		1
Whitby Strand		1
York		5

Column 1 Petty Sessions Area	Column 2 Probation and After-Care Area	Column 3 Number of justices on probation and after-care committee
Bingham	Nottinghamshire	1
East Retford		1
Mansfield (Borough)		1
Mansfield (County)		3
Newark		2
Nottingham (City)		7
Nottingham (County)		4
Southwell		1
Worksop		1
Abingdon (Borough)	Oxfordshire	1
Abingdon (County)		1
Bampton East		1
Bampton West		1
Bicester		1
Bullingdon		2
Chipping Norton		1
Faringdon		1
Henley		1
Moreton and Wallingford		1
North Oxfordshire		2
Oxford		3
Wantage		1
Watlington		1
Woodstock		1
Bridgnorth	Salop	2
Drayton		3
Ludlow		2
Oswestry		2
Shifnal		1
Shrewsbury		5
The Wrekin		5
Wenlock		2
Barnsley	South Yorkshire	3
Doncaster		3
Sheffield		6
Rotherham		3
Frome	Somerset	1
Ilminster		1
Sedgemoor		3
Shepton Mallet		1
Somerton		1
Taunton Deane		3
Wells		1
West Somerset		1
Wincanton		1
Yeovil		2
Burton upon Trent	Staffordshire	2
Cannock		2
Cheadle		1
Eccleshall		1
Leek		1

Column 1 Petty Sessions Area	Column 2 Probation and After-Care Area	Column 3 Number of justices on probation and after-care committee
Lichfield	Staffordshire (*Contd.*)	1
Newcastle-under-Lyme		2
Pirehill North		1
Rugeley		1
Seisdon		1
Stafford		2
Stoke-on-Trent		6
Stone		1
Tamworth		1
Uttoxeter		1
Beccles	Suffolk	1
Blything		1
Felixstowe		1
Hartismere		1
Ipswich		5
Lackford		1
Lowestoft		3
Newmarket		1
Orwell		1
Risbridge		1
St. Edmundsbury		2
Stow		1
Sudbury and Cosford		1
Woodbridge		1
Chertsey	Surrey	1
Dorking		1
Epsom		1
Esher and Walton		1
Farnham		1
Godstone		1
Guildford		1
Reigate		1
Staines and Sunbury-on- Thames		1
Woking		1
Alcester	Warwickshire	1
Atherstone		2
Kineton		1
Nuneaton		3
Rugby		2
Shipston on Stour		1
Southam		1
Stratford-upon-Avon		2
Warwick		3
Arundel	West Sussex	3
Chichester		3
Crawley		3
Horsham		3
Midhurst		3
Mid Sussex		3
Petworth		3
Steyning		3

Column 1 Petty Sessions Area	Column 2 Probation and After-Care Area	Column 3 Number of justices on probation and after-care committee
Worthing	West Sussex (*Contd.*)	3
Aldridge and Brownhills	West Midlands	2
Birmingham		12
Coventry		5
Dudley		3
Halesowen		2
Solihull		3
Stourbridge		2
Sutton Coldfield		2
Walsall		3
Warley		3
West Bromwich		3
Wolverhampton		4
Bradford	West Yorkshire	6
Keighley		3
Brighouse		1
Calder		1
Halifax		2
Todmorden		1
Batley		1
Dewsbury		2
Huddersfield		4
Leeds		10
Morley		1
Pudsey and Otley		2
Skyrack and Wetherby		2
Pontefract		3
Wakefield		3
Bradford	Wiltshire	1
Calne		1
Chippenham		1
Cricklade		1
Devizes		2
Everley and Pewsey		1
Malmesbury		1
Marlborough		1
Melkesham		1
Salisbury		3
Swindon		3
Tisbury and Mere		1
Trowbridge		1
Warminster		1
Westbury		1
Whorwellsdown		1
Aberaryon	Dyfed	1
Aberystwyth		2
Amman Valley		1
Cardigan		1
Carmarthen		2
Cemaes		1
Dewsland		1
Fishguard		1

Column 1 Petty Sessions Area	Column 2 Probation and After-Care Area	Column 3 Number of justices on probation and after-care committee
Haverfordwest	Dyfed (*Contd.*)	1
Lampeter		1
Llandeilo		1
Llandovery		1
Llandyssul		1
Llanelli		3
Milford Haven		1
Narberth		1
Newcastle Emlyn		1
Pembroke		1
Pencader		1
Rhydlewis		1
St. Clears		1
Tenby		1
Tregaron		1
Whitland		1
Abergavenny	Gwent	1
Bedwellty		13
Caerleon		2
Chepstow		1
Monmouth		1
Newport		9
Pontypool		2
Raglan		1
Skenfrith		1
Trelleck		1
Usk		1
Berwyn	North Wales	1
Colwyn		1
Dyffryn Clwyd		1
Flint		1
Hawarden		1
Mold		1
Rhuddlan		1
Wrexham Maelor		2
Ardudwy-is-Artro } Ardudwy-uwch-Artro }		1
Bangor		1
Caernarvon } Gwyrfai }		1
Conwy and Llandudno } Nant Conwy }		1
Eifionydd } Pwllheli }		1
Estimaner } Penllyn } Talybont }		1
North Anglesey		1
South Anglesey		1
Cynon Valley	Mid-Glamorgan	2
Lower Rhymney Valley		2
Merthyr Tydfil		2

Column 1 Petty Sessions Area	Column 2 Probation and After-Care Area	Column 3 Number of justices on probation and after-care committee
Miskin Newcastle and Ogmore Upper Rhymney Valley	Mid-Glamorgan (*Contd.*)	4 3 1
Brecon Builth Colwyn Crickhowell Defynock Deytheur Knighton Llandrindod Wells Llanfyllin Llanidloes Machynlleth Mathrafal Montgomery New Radnor Newtown Painscastle Presteigne Rhayader Talgarth Welshpool Ystradgynlais	Powys	1 1 1 1 1 1 1 1 1 1 1 1 1 1 1 1 1 1 1 1 1
Cardiff Vale of Glamorgan	South Glamorgan	12 4
Afan Lliw Valley Neath Swansea	West Glamorgan	2 2 2 5

EXPLANATORY NOTE

(This Note is not part of the Order.)

This Order, which is made under the Local Government Act 1972, constitutes new combined probation and after-care areas in England and Wales outside London. The Order comes into operation on 1st April 1974, the date that local government re-organisation takes effect under the 1972 Act and, with three exceptions, the new combined probation and after-care areas are the same as the areas of the new counties established by that Act. The exceptions are the Hampshire, Northumbria and North Wales combined probation and after-care areas where, in each case, two new counties will be combined. The Order makes provision regarding the constitution of a committee for each new combined probation and after-care area and the appointment of a secretary for each such committee.

STATUTORY INSTRUMENTS

1974 No. 530

JUSTICES OF THE PEACE

The Justices' Allowances (Amendment) Regulations 1974

Made - - -	*22nd March* 1974
Laid before Parliament	*29th March* 1974
Coming into Operation	*1st April* 1974

In exercise of the powers conferred upon me by section 8(6) and (7) of the Justices of the Peace Act 1949(**a**) as amended by section 31 of the Administration of Justice Act 1964(**b**) and section 4 of the Justices of the Peace Act 1968(**c**), I hereby make the following Regulations: —

1. These Regulations may be cited as the Justices' Allowances (Amendment) Regulations 1974 and shall come into operation on 1st April 1974.

2. In paragraph 3(2) of Schedule 1 to the Justices' Allowances Regulations 1971(**d**), as amended (**e**), for the words "5·5p", "6·2p" and "6·9p" there shall be substituted the words "6·4p", "6·9p" and "7·8p" respectively.

Roy Jenkins,
One of Her Majesty's Principal
Secretaries of State.

Home Office,
Whitehall.
22nd March 1974.

EXPLANATORY NOTE

(This Note is not part of the Regulations.)

These Regulations amend the Justices' Allowances Regulations 1971 by increasing the rates of travelling allowance payable to justices of the peace in respect of the use of a private motor car or tri-car.

(**a**) 1949 c. 101.   (**b**) 1964 c. 42.
(**c**) 1968 c. 69.   (**d**) S.I. 1971/413 (1971 I, p. 1217).
(**e**) The relevant amending Regulations are S.I. 1972/1401 (1972 III, p. 4262).

STATUTORY INSTRUMENTS

1974 No. 533

LOCAL GOVERNMENT, ENGLAND AND WALES
The Transfer of Police Civilian Staff and Probation Staff
Order 1974

Made - - -	*22nd March* 1974
Laid before Parliament	*28th March* 1974
Coming into Operation	*29th March* 1974

In exercise of the powers conferred on me by sections 254 and 255 of the Local Government Act 1972**(a)**, I hereby make the following Order:—

1.—(1) This Order may be cited as the Transfer of Police Civilian Staff and Probation Staff Order 1974 and shall come into operation on 29th March 1974.

(2) This Order shall not extend to Greater London.

2.—(1) In this Order, except where the context otherwise requires, the following expressions have the following meanings respectively, that is to say:—

"Appeals Memorandum" means the Memorandum on Staff Appeals enclosed with Circular LGSC 15/73 (Local Government Staff Commission for England) or, as the case may be, LGSC(W) 12/73 (Local Government Staff Commission for Wales), both dated 13th December 1973;

"existing" in relation to any authority means that authority as it existed on 1st January 1973;

"new" in relation to any authority means that authority as established on 1st April 1974;

"officer" in relation to any authority includes the holder of any office or employment under that authority, including a traffic warden and a school crossing patrol.

(2) The Interpretation Act 1889**(b)** shall apply for the interpretation of this Order as it applies for the interpretation of an Act of Parliament.

3. In the case of an officer transferred by this Order who is not in the whole-time employment of an authority immediately before 1st April 1974 the transfer effected by this Order in its application to the authority is limited to the extent of his employment by that authority.

(a) 1972 c.70.   **(b)** 1889 c.63.

4.—(1) Every traffic warden, school crossing patrol and other officer employed by an existing police authority, and every officer employed by the council of an existing county or county borough wholly or mainly for police purposes (excluding a school crossing patrol) who is employed by such authority immediately before 1st April 1974 shall, on 1st April 1974, be transferred to the employment of the new police authority for the area in which is situate the premises in which he is wholly or mainly employed or from which he wholly or mainly operates.

(2) Nothing in this Article shall apply to a person—

(*a*) who will, by virtue of an agreement entered into between him and any authority before 1st April 1974, enter into the employment of that authority on 1st April 1974, or

(*b*) who is transferred by a scheme made under the Local Government (Staff Transfer Schemes) Order 1973**(a)**, as amended **(b)**, on or before 1st April 1974, or

(*c*) as respects any employment which, otherwise than by virtue of the abolition of authorities effected by the Local Government Act 1972 is to be terminated on 31st March 1974.

5.—(1) Every probation officer employed and every other officer employed by an existing probation and after-care committee to assist probation officers in the performance of their duties who is employed by such committee immediately before 1st April 1974 shall on 1st April 1974 be transferred to the employment of the probation and after-care committee for the area in which is situate the premises in which he is wholly or mainly employed or from which he wholly or mainly operates.

(2) Nothing in this Article shall apply to a person—

(*a*) who will, by virtue of any agreement entered into between him and a probation and after-care committee or other authority before 1st April 1974, enter into the employment of that committee or authority on 1st April 1974, or

(*b*) as respects any employment which, otherwise than by virtue of the abolition of authorities effected by the Local Government Act 1972 is to be terminated on 31st March 1974.

6.—(1) Where on 31st March 1974 any officer has not taken up the duties of his employment, he shall be deemed, in the application of Articles 4 and 5 above, to be employed in, or to be operating from, the premises in which he would be employed or from which he would be operating if he had taken up such duties.

(2) Where any officer is on 31st March 1974 absent from his normal duties for the purpose of undergoing training, Articles 4 and 5 shall apply—

(*a*) if it was part of the arrangements under which he is so absent that at the completion of such training he should be employed in a place, situation or employment different from the place, situation or employ-

---

(a) S.I. 1973/1847 (1973 III p. 6377).   **(b)** S.I. 1974/147 (1974 I, p. 482).

ment which he occupied prior to the commencement of the training, as if he was, immediately before 1st April 1974, occupying such different place, situation or employment;

(*b*) otherwise as if he was, immediately before 1st April 1974, occupying the place, situation or employment which he occupied immediately prior to the commencement of such training.

(3) Where any officer is, on 31st March 1974, absent from his normal duties otherwise than for the purpose of undergoing training, he shall be deemed, in the application of Articles 4 and 5 to be discharging such duties, and to be discharging them in, or from, the premises in, or from, which he normally discharges them.

7.—(1) Any question by any officer whether he is or is not employed in any manner specified in Article 4 or 5 above shall be determined in accordance with—

(*a*) except in relation to persons transferred by Article 5, the arrangements set out in the Appeals Memorandum;

(*b*) in relation to such persons, the arrangements made by the Secretary of State.

(2) An existing police authority and the council of any existing county or county borough shall ensure that every officer transferred by Article 4 of this Order is informed as to the provisions of the Appeals Memorandum which are applicable.

8. Appeals may be made by officers and shall be determined in accordance with—

(*a*) except in relation to persons transferred by Article 5 above, the arrangements set out in the Appeals Memorandum,

(*b*) in relation to such persons, the arrangements made by the Secretary of State.

9.—(1) Every officer transferred under Article 4 or 5 above to the employment of any authority shall, so long as he continues in that employment by virtue of the transfer and until he is served with a statement in writing referring to this Order and specifying new terms and conditions of employment, enjoy terms and conditions of employment not less favourable than those which he enjoyed immediately before 1st April 1974.

(2) In the case of an officer who has appealed on grounds of hardship in accordance with the arrangements for appeal, a statement of new terms and conditions of employment shall not be served—

(*a*) if the appeal is allowed, until an alternative transfer or employment has been arranged, or, if no alternative transfer or employment is arranged, until the expiration of three months from the date of the decision of the appellate authority or 30th September 1974, whichever is the later,

(*b*) in any other case, until the date of the decision.

(3) A statement of new terms and conditions of employment shall be served on every officer transferred by this Order before 1st April 1975, and subject to paragraph (2) may be served before 1st April 1974.

(4) If after service of a statement of new terms and conditions of employment upon him an officer appeals on grounds of hardship as aforesaid, the statement shall cease to have effect, paragraph (1) above shall have effect as if the statement had not been served, and a new statement shall be served only in accordance with paragraph 2 above.

(5) The new terms and conditions of employment shall be such that—

(a) so long as the officer is engaged in duties reasonably comparable to those in which he was engaged immediately before 1st April 1974, the scale of his salary or remuneration is not less favourable than that which he enjoyed immediately before 1st April 1974; and

(b) the other terms and conditions of his employment are not less favourable than those which he enjoyed immediately before 1st April 1974.

(6) Where between 1st April 1974 and the service of the statement of new terms and conditions of employment upon any officer the scale of the salary or remuneration which he enjoyed immediately before 1st April 1974 is improved, paragraph (5)(a) above shall have effect as if the scale as improved had been so enjoyed.

(7) Where the new terms and conditions of employment involve any diminution of the scale of the salary or remuneration of an officer, they shall not come into effect until the date specified in the statement of the new terms and conditions, being a date not earlier than the expiration of three months from the date of service of that statement.

(8) Any question whether the duties of an officer are reasonably comparable within the meaning of paragraph (5) above shall be determined in accordance with—

(a) except in the case of a person transferred by Article 5, the arrangements set out in the Appeals Memorandum;

(b) in the case of such a person, the arrangements made by the Secretary of State.

(9) An officer may appeal in respect of new terms and conditions of employment in accordance with—

(a) except in the case of a person transferred by Article 5, the arrangements set out in the Appeals Memorandum;

(b) in the case of such a person, the arrangements made by the Secretary of State.

(10) Any statement of new terms and conditions of employment shall contain a statement of the provisions of paragraphs (8) and (9) above.

(11) In this Article, "terms and conditions of employment" include any restriction arising under any Act or any instrument made under any Act on the termination of the employment of any officer.

(12) A written statement given in accordance with section 4(1) of the Contracts of Employment Act 1972(a) shall not be regarded as a statement of new terms

---

(a) 1972 c.53.

and conditions of employment for the purposes of this Article unless the statement so indicates.

10.—(1) Any officer transferred by this Order to the employment of any authority may, before 1st January 1975 or the expiration of two months from the service upon him of the statement of new terms and conditions of employment under Article 9 above, whichever is the later, be transferred by the said authority to the employment of any other authority, with the consent of the latter authority and of the officer; and Article 9 shall thereupon apply to such officer as it applies to other officers so transferred.

(2) The council of a county which is not a constituent authority of a combined police authority may, by a resolution passed before 1st January 1975, transfer to its own employment every officer other than a traffic warden who was transferred by Article 4 above to the employment of the police authority for that county and who remains in the employment of that police authority; and Article 9 shall thereupon apply to such officer as it applies to other officers transferred by Article 4.

11. Where an officer transferred by this Order is undergoing training under arrangements which have not been discharged before 1st April 1974, those arrangements shall continue to apply with the substitution, for the authority in whose employment he was immediately before the commencement of the training, of the authority to whose employment he has been transferred by this Order.

12. Any dispensation from the requirement of any regulation granted to the authority from whom any officer is transferred by this Order shall have effect, in relation to such officer, as if it had been granted to the authority to whose employment he has been transferred by this Order.

13. Any extension of service under section 7(1) of the Local Government Superannuation Act 1937**(a)** effective on 1st April 1974 in relation to an officer transferred by this Order shall continue to have effect as if it had been made by the authority to whose employment he is transferred by this Order.

14. Any additional travelling expenses and any removal or incidental expenses reasonably incurred by any officer in consequence of his transfer by this Order shall be reimbursed by the authority to whose employment he is transferred by this Order.

15.—(1) This Article applies to contracts of employment resulting from the operation of Article 4 or 5 above.

(2) Notice to terminate any contract of employment to which this Article applies may, with his consent, be given to any officer before 1st April 1974 by the authority to whose authority he would be transferred on that date.

(3) A notice to terminate any contract of employment to which this Article applies shall, unless the officer to whom it is given otherwise agrees, not come into operation earlier than the expiration of three months from the service thereof.

(a) 1937 c. 68.

16. Where, in relation to any officer—

(*a*) on the scale of salary or remuneration applicable to him immediately before 1st April 1974 he would have become entitled to an increment on that date; and

(*b*) by reason of any appointment effective as from 1st April 1974 made by the authority to whom he is transferred, any other scale of salary or remuneration becomes applicable to him as from that date,

any term of his employment as to his commencing point on such other scale shall be applicable as if his employment before, and on and after, the said date were continuous employment under one authority.

Roy Jenkins,

One of Her Majesty's Principal

Secretaries of State.

Home Office,

Whitehall.

22nd March 1974.

EXPLANATORY NOTE

(*This Note is not part of the Order.*)

This Order makes provision for the transfer of traffic wardens, school crossing patrols and police civilian staff employed by police authorities, police civilian staff employed by an existing county or county borough council and probation staff to new police authorities or, as the case may be, new probation and after-care committees, and for the protection of the interests of those persons.

1974 No. 536

MERCHANT SHIPPING

The Merchant Shipping (Limitation of Liability) (Sterling Equivalents) Order 1974

Made - - -	*21st March* 1974
Coming into Operation	*12th April* 1974

The Secretary of State, in exercise of the powers conferred by section 1(3) of the Merchant Shipping (Liability of Shipowners and Others) Act 1958(**a**) and now vested in him (**b**) and of all other powers enabling him in that behalf, hereby orders as follows: —

1. This Order may be cited as the Merchant Shipping (Limitation of Liability) (Sterling Equivalents) Order 1974 and shall come into operation on 12th April 1974.

2. The Interpretation Act 1889(**c**) shall apply to the interpretation of this Order as it applies to the interpretation of an Act of Parliament and as if this Order and the Order hereby revoked were Acts of Parliament.

3. For the purposes of section 1 of the Merchant Shipping (Liability of Shipowners and Others) Act 1958, £108·1677 and £34·8928 are hereby specified as the amounts which shall be taken as equivalent to 3,100 and 1,000 gold francs respectively.

4. The Merchant Shipping (Limitation of Liability) (Sterling Equivalents) Order 1973(**d**) is hereby revoked.

J. K. T. Frost,
An Assistant Secretary of
the Department of Trade.

21st March 1974.

(**a**) 1958 c. 62.

(**c**) 1889 c. 63.

(**b**) S.I. 1970/1537 (1970 III, p. 5293).

(**d**) S.I. 1973/1190 (1973 II, p.3564).

EXPLANATORY NOTE

(This Note is not part of the Order.)

Under section 503 of the Merchant Shipping Act 1894 (c.60), and section 2 of the Merchant Shipping (Liability of Shipowners and Others) Act 1900 (c.32) as amended by the Merchant Shipping (Liability of Shipowners and Others) Act 1958, shipowners, harbour authorities and others may limit their liability at amounts expressed in gold francs. This Order specifies the sterling equivalents of the gold franc amounts. These have been calculated on the basis of current market rates for sterling in terms of the US dollar on the basis of the valuation of gold at $42·2222 per fine ounce.

STATUTORY INSTRUMENTS

1974 No. 537

WAGES COUNCILS

The Wages Regulation (Ostrich and Fancy Feather and Artificial Flower) Order 1974

Made - - - -	*22nd March* 1974
Coming into Operation	*24th April* 1974

Whereas the Secretary of State has received from the Ostrich and Fancy Feather and Artificial Flower Wages Council (Great Britain) the wages regulation proposals set out in the Schedule hereto;

Now, therefore, the Secretary of State in exercise of powers conferred by section 11 of the Wages Councils Act 1959(a), as modified by Article 2 of the Counter-Inflation (Modification of Wages Councils Act 1959) Order 1973(b), and now vested in him(c), and of all other powers enabling him in that behalf, hereby makes the following Order:—

1. This Order may be cited as the Wages Regulation (Ostrich and Fancy Feather and Artificial Flower) Order 1974.

2.—(1) In this Order the expression "the specified date" means the 24th April 1974, provided that where, as respects any worker who is paid wages at intervals not exceeding seven days, that date does not correspond with the beginning of the period for which the wages are paid, the expression "the specified date" means, as respects that worker, the beginning of the next such period following that date.

(2) The Interpretation Act 1889(d) shall apply to the interpretation of this Order as it applies to the interpretation of an Act of Parliament and as if this Order and the Order hereby revoked were Acts of Parliament.

3. The wages regulation proposals set out in the Schedule hereto shall have effect as from the specified date and as from that date the Wages Regulation (Ostrich and Fancy Feather and Artificial Flower) Order 1973(e) shall cease to have effect.

Signed by order of the Secretary of State.

22nd March 1974.

W. H. Marsh,

Assistant Secretary,
Department of Employment.

(a) 1959 c. 69.   (b) S.I. 1973/661 (1973 I, p. 2141).
(c) S.I. 1959/1769, 1968/729 (1959 I, p. 1795; 1968 II, p. 2108).
(d) 1889 c. 63.   (e) S.I. 1973/521 (1973 I, p. 1682).

Article 3

SCHEDULE 1

The following minimum remuneration shall be substituted for the statutory minimum remuneration set out in the Wages Regulation (Ostrich and Fancy Feather and Artificial Flower) Order 1973 (Order O.F. (49)).

STATUTORY MINIMUM REMUNERATION

PART I

GENERAL

1. The minimum remuneration payable to a worker to whom this Schedule applies for all work except work to which a minimum overtime rate applies under Part III is:—

(1) in the case of a time worker, the hourly general minimum time rate payable to the worker under Part II of this Schedule;

(2) in the case of a worker employed on piece work, piece rates each of which would yield, in the circumstances of the case, to an ordinary worker at least the same amount of money as the piece work basis time rate applicable to the worker under Part II of this Schedule.

PART II

GENERAL MINIMUM TIME RATES

2. The general minimum time rates payable to all workers other than workers employed as heavy duty warehouse operators are as follows:—

	Age of worker on first entering the trade		
	Under 17 years	17 and under 18 years	18 years or over
	Per hour	Per hour	Per hour
	p	p	p
Aged:			
Under 17 years	26.625	—	—
17 years and under 18 years ...	29.125	28.625	—
18 years or over	32.125	32.125	32.125

3. The general minimum time rates payable to workers employed as heavy duty warehouse operators are as follows:—

								per hour p
Aged—								
21 years or over	...	...	...	...	...	...	...	40.625
20 and under 21 years	...	...	...	...	...	...	38.125
19 ,, ,, 20 ,,	...	...	...	...	...	...	35.125
18 ,, ,, 19 ,,	...	...	...	...	...	...	33.125
17 ,, ,, 18 ,,	...	...	...	...	...	...	32.125
under 17 years	...	...	...	...	...	...	29.625

PIECE WORK BASIS TIME RATE

4. The piece work basis time rate applicable to all workers (including homeworkers), employed on piece work shall be a rate equal to the general minimum time rate which would be payable if the worker were a time worker, increased by 12½ per cent.

PART III

OVERTIME AND WAITING TIME
NORMAL NUMBER OF HOURS

5. Subject to the provisions of this Part of this Schedule the minimum overtime rates set out in paragraph 6 are payable to any worker in respect of any time worked:—

(1) in excess of the hours following, that is to say:

    (a) in any week ... ...   40 hours

    (b) on any day other than a Saturday, Sunday or customary holiday—where the normal working hours exceed 8½ ..   9 hours

    or

    where the normal working hours are more than 8 but not more than 8½ ... ...   8½ hours

    or where the normal working hours are not more than 8..   8 hours

(2) on a Saturday, Sunday or customary holiday.

MINIMUM OVERTIME RATES

6. Minimum overtime rates are payable to any worker as follows:—

(1) on any day other than a Sunday or customary holiday—

    (a) for the first 2 hours of overtime worked ...   time-and-a-quarter

    (b) for the next 2 hours .. ..   time-and-a-half

    (c) thereafter ... ...   double time

(2) on a Sunday or customary holiday—
    for all time worked ... ...   double time

(3) in any week, exclusive of any time in respect of which any minimum overtime rate is payable under the foregoing provisions of this paragraph—

    for all time worked in excess of 40 hours ... ...   time-and-a-quarter

    Provided that where it is the practice in a Jewish undertaking for the employer to require attendance on Sunday instead of Saturday the provisions of this paragraph shall apply as if in such provisions the word "Saturday" were substituted for "Sunday" except where such substitution is unlawful.

7. In this Part of this Schedule—

(1) the expression "customary holiday" means:—

    (a)   (i) in England and Wales—

Christmas Day; 26th December if it be not a Sunday; 27th December in a year when 25th or 26th December is a Sunday; *New Year's Day if it be not a Sunday or, if it be a Sunday, 2nd January*; Good Friday; Easter Monday; the last Monday in May; and the last Monday in August; or

where a day is substituted for any of the above days by national proclamation, that day;

       (ii) in Scotland—

New Year's Day if it be not a Sunday or, if it be a Sunday, 2nd January;

the local Spring holiday;

the local Autumn holiday; and

four other days (being days on which the worker normally works for the employer) in the course of a calendar year to be fixed by the employer and notified to the worker not less than three weeks before the holiday; or

    (b) in the case of each of the said days (other than a day fixed by the employer in Scotland and notified to the worker as aforesaid) a day substituted by the employer therefor, being a day recognised by local custom as a day of holiday in substitution for the said day.

(2) The expressions "time-and-a-quarter", "time-and-a-half" and "double time" mean respectively:—

    (a) in the case of a time worker, one and a quarter times, one and a half times and twice the hourly general minimum time rate otherwise applicable to the worker;

    (b) in the case of a worker employed on piece work—

       (i) a time rate equal respectively to one-quarter, one-half and the whole of the piece work basis time rate otherwise applicable to the worker, and, in addition thereto,

       (ii) the piece rates otherwise applicable to the worker under paragraph 1(2).

WAITING TIME

8.—(1) A worker is entitled to payment of the minimum remuneration specified in this Schedule for all time during which he is present on the premises of his employer unless he is present thereon in any of the following circumstances:—

    (a) without the employer's consent, express or implied;

    (b) for some purpose unconnected with his work and other than that of waiting for work to be given to him to perform;

    (c) by reason only of the fact that he is resident thereon;

    (d) during normal meal times in a room or place in which no work is being done, and he is not waiting for work to be given to him to perform.

(2) The minimum remuneration payable under sub-paragraph (1) of this paragraph to a piece worker when not engaged on piece work is that which would be applicable if he were a time worker.

PART IV

INTERPRETATION

9. In this Schedule—

(1) the expression "homeworker" means a worker who works in his own home or any other place not under the control or management of the employer.

(2) "the trade" means the ostrich and fancy feather and artificial flower trade.

(3) "heavy duty warehouse operator" means a worker wholly or mainly engaged in manually moving goods exceeding 28lbs. *or 12.7 kilogrammes* in weight at any one time in or about a warehouse or similar place.

PART V

APPLICABILITY OF STATUTORY MINIMUM REMUNERATION

10. This Schedule applies to workers in relation to whom the Ostrich and Fancy Feather and Artificial Flower Wages Council (Great Britain) operates, that is to say, workers employed in Great Britain in the Ostrich and Fancy Feather and Artificial Flower trade as specified in the Schedule to the Regulations made by the Minister of Labour, dated 3rd February 1921, with respect to the constitution and proceedings of the Trade Board for the Ostrich and Fancy Feather and Artificial Flower Trade (Great Britain)(a), which Schedule reads as follows:—

"The Ostrich and Fancy Feather and Artificial Flower Trade, that is to say:—

1. The preparation throughout of ostrich or fancy feathers from the natural condition to the finished feather product.

2. The making of artificial flowers, fruit, foliage, grasses, mosses, seeds or pods from paper, wax, textile materials, porcelain, glass, plaster, metal composition, rubber, leather, raffia, celiphane and similar materials.

3. The preservation of natural flowers, foliage, grasses, mosses, ferns, seeds or pods.

4. The making of hats of any of the articles specified in paragraphs 1, 2 and 3 above, when made in or in association with or in conjunction with any business or establishment or branch or department or workroom mainly engaged in any of the operations specified in those paragraphs.

5. The making of feather garments (including neckwear and muffs), feather trimmings for dresses, feather fans or feather mountings of any description, when made in or in association with or in conjunction with any business or establishment or branch or department or workroom mainly engaged in the preparation of ostrich or fancy feathers.

6. The cleaning, dyeing or renovating of any of the articles specified in paragraphs 1, 2 and 3 above, when carried on as a main business or in association with or in conjunction with any business or establishment or branch or department or workroom mainly engaged in any of the operations specified in these paragraphs.

Including:—

7. A. Any of the following and similar operations or processes known in the trade as:—

   (i) The sorting, stringing, washing, bleaching, dyeing, beating, scraping, laying-up, sewing, curling, finishing, sticking, twisting, mounting of ostrich or fancy feathers;

   (ii) Pattern-making, dyeing, stiffening, waterproofing, waxing, cutting, stamping, shading, veining, goffing, mould making, mounting, in connection with the manufacture of artificial flowers, fruits, foliage, grasses, mosses, seeds or pods;

   (iii) The dyeing, preserving, painting, varnishing or decorating of natural flowers, foliage, grasses, mosses, ferns, seeds or pods.

   B. The making of any of the articles specified in paragraph 2 above by needle-work processes, when carried on in or in association with or in conjunction with a business or establishment or branch or department or workroom mainly engaged in any of the operations specified in that paragraph.

(a) S.R. & O. 1921/170 (1921, p. 1371).

C. The making or mounting of any of the articles specified in paragraphs 1, 2 and 3 above for cakes or cracker ornaments, except when made or mounted in or in association with or in conjunction with an establishment or business or branch or department or workroom which is mainly engaged in the making of crackers.

D. The mounting (whether singly or in festoons or garlands) or assembling of any of the articles specified in paragraphs 1, 2 and 3 above for the purpose of decoration, when mounted or assembled in a business or establishment or branch or department or workroom mainly engaged in these operations.

E. The warehousing of, the packing of, and similar operations in regard to any of the articles specified in paragraphs 1 to 5 above when carried on in or in association with or in conjunction with a business or establishment or branch or department or workroom mainly engaged in any of the operations specified in paragraphs 1 to 6 above.

But excluding:—

8. A. The making of any of the articles mentioned in paragraph 2 above in a business or establishment or branch or department or workroom which is mainly engaged in the manufacture of the materials specified in that paragraph, and not of the articles therein specified.

B. The preparation, making or preservation of any of the articles specified in paragraphs 1, 2 and 3 above, when carried out in a business or establishment or branch or department or workroom mainly engaged in the manufacture of stationers' sundries.

C. The stiffening or preparation of textile materials for the making of any of the articles mentioned in paragraph 2 above, when carried on in a business or establishment or branch or department or workroom mainly engaged in the preparation of textile materials for other purposes.

D. The making of any of the articles specified in paragraph 2 above wholly from metal, or the mounting thereof when so made or the making or mounting of plaster flowers, fruits or foliage, except when made or mounted:—

   (i) For funeral tokens, wreaths or crosses.

   (ii) In association with, or in conjunction with the making of any of the articles specified in paragraph 2, from any of the materials specified therein.

   (iii) For cake or cracker ornaments as specifically mentioned in the operations and processes included in the trade.

E. The making from rubber of any of the articles mentioned in paragraph 2 above, or the mounting thereof when so made, where carried on in or in association with or in conjunction with a business or establishment or branch or department or workroom mainly engaged in the manufacture of other rubber articles.

F. All operations covered by the following orders:—

   (i) The Trade Boards (Sugar Confectionery and Food Preserving) Order, 1913(a).

   (ii) The Trade Boards (Hat, Cap and Millinery) Order, 1919(b).

   (iii) The Trade Boards (Women's Clothing) Order, 1919(c).

   (iv) The Trade Boards (Toy) Order, 1920(d)."

(a) Confirmed by 3 & 4 Geo. 5 c. clxii.   (b) S.R. & O. 1919/1262 (1919 II, p. 515).
(c) S.R. & O. 1919/1263 (1919 II, p. 531).   (d) S.R. & O. 1920/470 (1920 II, p. 792).

EXPLANATORY NOTE

(This Note is not part of the Order.)

This Order which has effect from 24th April 1974, sets out the increased statutory minimum remuneration payable to workers in relation to whom the Ostrich and Fancy Feather and Artificial Flower Wages Council (Great Britain) operates, in substitution for that fixed by the Wages Regulation (Ostrich and Fancy Feather and Artificial Flower) Order 1973 (Order O.F. (49)). Order O.F. (49) is revoked.

New provisions are printed in italics.

STATUTORY INSTRUMENTS

1974 No. 538

WAGES COUNCILS

The Wages Regulation (Ostrich and Fancy Feather and Artificial Flower) (Holidays) Order 1974

Made - - -	*22nd March* 1974
Coming into Operation	*24th April* 1974

Whereas the Secretary of State has received from the Ostrich and Fancy Feather and Artificial Flower Wages Council (Great Britain) the wages regulation proposals set out in the Schedule hereto;

Now, therefore, the Secretary of State in exercise of powers conferred by section 11 of the Wages Councils Act 1959(a), as modified by Article 2 of the Counter-Inflation (Modification of Wages Councils Act 1959) Order 1973(b), and now vested in him(c), and of all other powers enabling him in that behalf, hereby makes the following Order:— ·

1. This Order may be cited as the Wages Regulation (Ostrich and Fancy Feather and Artificial Flower) (Holidays) Order 1974.

2.—(1) In this Order the expression "the specified date" means the 24th April 1974, provided that where, as respects any worker who is paid wages at intervals not exceeding seven days, that date does not correspond with the beginning of the period for which the wages are paid, the expression "the specified date" means, as respects that worker, the beginning of the next such period following that date.

(2) The Interpretation Act 1889(d) shall apply to the interpretation of this Order as it applies to the interpretation of an Act of Parliament and as if this Order and the Order hereby revoked were Acts of Parliament.

3. The wages regulation proposals set out in the Schedule hereto shall have effect as from the specified date and as from that date the Wages Regulation (Ostrich and Fancy Feather and Artificial Flower) (Holidays) Order 1968(e) shall cease to have effect.

Signed by order of the Secretary of State.
22nd March 1974.

W. H. Marsh,
Assistant Secretary,
Department of Employment.

(a) 1959 c. 69. (b) S.I. 1973/661 (1973 I, p. 2141).
(c) S.I. 1959/1769, 1968/729 (1959 I, p. 1795; 1968 II, p. 2108).
(d) 1889 c. 63. (e) S.I. 1968/1927 (1968 III, p. 5226).

SCHEDULE   Article 3

The following provisions as to holidays and holiday remuneration shall be substituted for the provisions as to holidays and holiday remuneration set out in the Wages Regulation (Ostrich and Fancy Feather and Artificial Flower) (Holidays) Order 1968 (hereinafter referred to as "Order O.F.(43)").

Part I

APPLICATION

1.—(1) This Schedule applies to every worker (other than a homeworker) for whom statutory minimum remuneration has been fixed.

(2) For the purposes of this Schedule a homeworker is a worker who works in his own home or in any other place not under the control or management of the employer.

Part II

CUSTOMARY HOLIDAYS

2.—(1) An employer shall allow to every worker to whom this Schedule applies a holiday (hereinafter referred to as a "customary holiday") in each year on the days specified in the following sub-paragraph provided that the worker has been in his employment for a period of not less than two weeks immediately preceding the customary holiday and (unless excused by the employer or absent by reason of the proved illness of the worker) has worked for the employer throughout the last working day on which work was available to him immediately preceding the customary holiday.

(2) The said customary holidays are:—

(a) (i) in England and Wales—
        Christmas Day; 26th December if it be not a Sunday, 27th December in a year when 25th or 26th December is a Sunday; *New Year's Day if it be not a Sunday or if it be a Sunday,* 2nd January; Good Friday; Easter Monday; the last Monday in May; and the last Monday in August; or where a day is substituted for any of the above days by national proclamation, that day;

    (ii) in Scotland—
        New Year's Day *if it be not a Sunday or, if it be a Sunday,* 2nd January; the local Spring holiday;
        the local Autumn holiday; and
        four other days (being days on which the worker normally works for the employer) in the course of a calendar year to be fixed by the employer and notified to the worker not less than three weeks before the holiday;

or (b) in the case of each of the said days (other than a day fixed by the employer in Scotland and notified to the worker as aforesaid) a day substituted by the employer therefor, being a day recognised by local custom as a day of holiday in substitution for the said day.

(3) Notwithstanding the preceding provisions of this paragraph, an employer may (except where in the case of a woman or young person such a requirement would be unlawful) require a worker who is otherwise entitled to any customary holiday under the foregoing provisions of this Schedule to work thereon and, in lieu of any holiday on which he so works, the employer shall allow to the worker a day's holiday (hereinafter referred to as a "holiday in lieu of a customary holiday") on a week day on which he would normally work for the employer, within the period of eight weeks next ensuing.

(4) A worker who is required to work on a customary holiday shall be paid:—

(a) for all time worked thereon, the statutory minimum remuneration then appropriate to the worker for work on a customary holiday; and

(b) in respect of the holiday in lieu of the customary holiday, holiday remuneration in accordance with paragraph 6.

PART III

ANNUAL HOLIDAY

3.—(1) Subject to the provisions of this paragraph and of paragraph 4, in addition to the holidays specified in Part II of this Schedule an employer shall, between 1st May 1974 and 30th September 1974 and in each succeeding year between 1st May and 30th September, allow a holiday (hereinafter referred to as an "annual holiday") to every worker in his employment to whom this Schedule applies who has been employed by him during the 12 months ended on 5th April immediately preceding the commencement of the holiday season for any of the periods of employment (calculated in accordance with the provisions of paragraph 10) specified below and the duration of the annual holiday shall, in the case of each such worker, be related to his period of employment during that 12 months as follows:—

Period of employment	Duration of annual holiday
At least 48 weeks	15 days
,, ,, 45 ,,	14 ,,
,, ,, 44 ,,	13 ,,
,, ,, 42 ,,	13 ,,
,, ,, 40 ,,	12 ,,
,, ,, 39 ,,	12 ,,
,, ,, 36 ,,	11 ,,
,, ,, 33 ,,	10 ,,
,, ,, 32 ,,	9 ,,
,, ,, 30 ,,	9 ,,
,, ,, 28 ,,	8 ,,
,, ,, 27 ,,	8 ,,
,, ,, 24 ,,	7 ,,
,, ,, 21 ,,	6 ,,
,, ,, 20 ,,	5 ,,
,, ,, 18 ,,	5 ,,
,, ,, 16 ,,	4 ,,
,, ,, 15 ,,	4 ,,
,, ,, 12 ,,	3 ,,
,, ,, 8 ,,	2 ,,
,, ,, 4 ,,	1 day

(2) Notwithstanding the provisions of the last foregoing sub-paragraph, the number of days of annual holiday which an employer is required to allow to a worker in respect of a period of employment during the 12 months ending on 5th April 1974 and during the 12 months ending on 5th April in any succeeding year shall not exceed in the aggregate three times the number of days constituting the worker's normal working week;

(3) In this Schedule the expression "holiday season" means in relation to the year 1974 the period commencing on 1st May 1974 and ending on 30th September 1974 and, in each succeeding year, the period commencing on 1st May and ending on 30th September of the same year.

4.—(1) Subject to the provisions of this paragraph an annual holiday shall be allowed on consecutive working days being days on which the worker is normally called upon to work for the employer, and days of annual holiday shall be treated as consecutive notwithstanding that a Sunday, a customary holiday on which the worker is not required to work for the employer or a holiday in lieu of a customary holiday intervenes.

(2) (*a*) Where the number of days of annual holiday for which a worker has qualified exceeds the number of days constituting his normal working week but does not exceed twice that number, the holiday may, by agreement between the employer and the worker or his representative, be allowed in two separate periods of consecutive working days; so, however, that when a holiday is so allowed, one of the periods shall consist of a number of such days not less than the number of days constituting the worker's normal working week;

   (*b*) Where the number of days of annual holiday for which a worker has qualified exceeds twice the number of days constituting his normal working week the holiday may be allowed as follows:—

      (i) as to two periods of consecutive working days, each such period not being less than the period constituting the worker's normal working week, during the holiday season; and

      (ii) as to any additional days, on working days which need not be consecutive, to be fixed by the employer after consultation with the worker, either during the holiday season or before the beginning of the next following holiday season.

(3) Where a day of holiday allowed to a worker under Part II of this Schedule immediately precedes a period of annual holiday or occurs during such a period then, notwithstanding the foregoing provisions of this paragraph, the duration of that period of annual holiday may be reduced by one day and in such a case one day of annual holiday may be allowed on any working day in the holiday season, or by agreement between the employer and the worker or his representative, on any working day before the beginning of the next following holiday season.

(4) Subject to the provisions of this paragraph, any day of annual holiday under this Schedule may be allowed on a day on which the worker is entitled to a day of holiday or to a half-holiday under any enactment other than the Wages Councils Act 1959.

5. An employer shall give to a worker reasonable notice of the commencing date or dates and duration of the period or periods of his annual holiday. Such notice may be given individually to the worker or by the posting of a notice in the place where the worker is employed.

Part IV

HOLIDAY REMUNERATION

A—CUSTOMARY HOLIDAYS AND HOLIDAYS IN LIEU OF CUSTOMARY HOLIDAYS

6.—(1) For each day of holiday to which a worker is entitled under Part II of this Schedule he shall be paid by the employer as holiday remuneration whichever of the following amounts is the greater:—

   (*a*) the appropriate proportion (as defined in paragraph 11) of the average weekly earnings of the worker during the 12 months ended on 5th April immediately preceding the holiday, such average weekly earnings to be determined by dividing, by the number of weeks of employment with the employer during the said period, the total remuneration paid to him by the employer during that period:

Provided that when Good Friday or Easter Monday in England and Wales or the local Spring holiday in Scotland (or days substituted therefor under the provisions of sub-paragraph (2) (*b*) of paragraph 2 or holidays in lieu of such customary holidays) fall after 5th April in any year, the holiday remuneration for any such holiday under this sub-paragraph shall be the appropriate proportion of the average weekly earnings of the worker during the 12 months ended on 5th April in the preceding calendar year; or

(*b*) the appropriate statutory minimum remuneration to which he would have been entitled as a time worker if the day had not been a day of holiday and he had been employed on work for which statutory minimum remuneration is payable for the time usually worked by him on that day of the week.

(2) Notwithstanding the provisions of sub-paragraph (1) of this paragraph, payment of the said holiday remuneration is subject to the condition that the worker (unless excused by the employer or absent by reason of the proved illness of, or accident to, the worker) presents himself for employment at the usual starting hour on the first working day following the holiday:

Provided that when two customary holidays occur on successive days (or so that no working day intervenes) the said condition shall apply only to the second customary holiday.

(3) Holiday remuneration in respect of any customary holiday shall be paid by the employer to the worker on the pay day on which the wages for the pay week including the holiday are paid.

(4) Holiday remuneration in respect of any holiday in lieu of a customary holiday shall be paid on the pay day on which the wages for the week including the holiday in lieu of a customary holiday are paid:

Provided that the said payment shall be made immediately upon the termination of the worker's employment if he ceases to be employed before being allowed such holiday in lieu of a customary holiday and in that case the condition specified in sub-paragraph (2) of this paragraph shall not apply.

B—ANNUAL HOLIDAY

7.—(1) Subject to the provisions of paragraph 8, a worker qualified to be allowed an annual holiday under this Schedule shall be paid as holiday remuneration by his employer in respect thereof, on the last pay day preceding such annual holiday, whichever of the following sums is the greater:—

(*a*) in respect of the annual holiday to be allowed during the period of 12 months commencing on 1st May 1974 and during the period of 12 months commencing on 1st May in each succeeding year an amount equal to three fifty-seconds of the total remuneration paid by the employer to the worker in the 12 months ended on 5th April immediately preceding the holiday season; or

(*b*) one day's holiday pay (as defined in paragraph 11) in respect of each day of annual holiday.

(2) Where, under the provisions of paragraph 4, an annual holiday is allowed in more than one period the holiday remuneration shall be apportioned accordingly.

8. Where any accrued holiday remuneration has been paid by the employer to the worker (in accordance with the provisions of paragraph 9 of this Schedule or under Order O.F. (43)) in respect of employment during any of the periods referred to in that paragraph or that Order respectively, the amount of holiday remuneration payable by the employer in respect of any annual holiday for which the worker has qualified by reason of employment during the said period shall be reduced by the amount of the said accrued holiday remuneration unless that remuneration has been deducted from a previous payment of holiday remuneration made under the provisions of this Schedule or of Order O.F. (43).

ACCRUED HOLIDAY REMUNERATION PAYABLE ON
TERMINATION OF EMPLOYMENT

9. Where a worker ceases to be employed by an employer after the provisions of this Schedule become effective the employer shall, immediately on the termination of the employment, pay to the worker as accrued holiday remuneration:—

(1) in respect of employment in the 12 months up to the preceding 5th April, a sum equal to the holiday remuneration to which the worker would have been entitled under the provisions of (b) of sub-paragraph (1) of paragraph 7 for any days of annual holiday for which he has qualified, except days of annual holiday which he has been allowed or has become entitled to be allowed before leaving the employment; and

(2) in respect of any employment since the said 5th April, a sum equal to the holiday remuneration which would have been payable to him under the provisions of (b) of sub-paragraph (1) of paragraph 7 if he could have been allowed an annual holiday in respect of that employment at the time of leaving it.

(3) Notwithstanding the provisions of sub-paragraphs (1) and (2) of this paragraph, the accrued holiday remuneration payable to a worker who has been employed by the employer for the whole of the 12 months ended on 5th April immediately preceding the termination of his employment shall be as follows:—

(a) in respect of the 12 months ended on 5th April preceding the termination of his employment, whichever of the following amounts is the greater—

(i) an amount equal to three fifty-seconds of the total remuneration as defined in paragraph 11 paid by the employer to the worker during any such period; or

(ii) the amount calculated in accordance with the provisions of sub-paragraph (1) of this paragraph; and

(b) in respect of any period of employment after such 5th April, the amount calculated in accordance with the provisions of sub-paragraph (2) of this paragraph.

Part V

GENERAL

10. For the purposes of calculating any period of employment qualifying a worker for an annual holiday or for any accrued holiday remuneration under this Schedule, the worker shall be treated:—

(1) as if he were employed for a week in respect of any week in which—

(a) he has worked for the employer for not less than 20 hours and has performed some work for which statutory minimum remuneration is payable;

(b) he has been absent throughout the week by reason of the proved illness of, or accident to, the worker but not exceeding four weeks in the aggregate in the period of 12 months immediately preceding the commencement of the holiday season;

(c) he has been suspended throughout the week owing to shortage of work but not exceeding six weeks in the aggregate in such period as aforesaid; and

(2) as if he were employed on any day of holiday allowed under the provisions of this Schedule or of Order O.F. (43), and for the purposes of the provisions of sub-paragraph (1) of this paragraph, a worker who is absent on such a

holiday shall be treated as having worked thereon the number of hours ordinarily worked by him for the employer on that day of the week on work for which statutory minimum remuneration is payable.

11. In this Schedule, unless the context otherwise requires, the following expressions have the meanings hereby respectively assigned to them, that is to say:—

"appropriate proportion" means—

where the worker's normal working week is five days.. .. one-fifth
where the worker's normal working week is four days or less .. one-quarter

"appropriate rate of statutory minimum remuneration" means—

(a) in the case of a time worker, the rate or rates of statutory minimum remuneration applicable to the worker, and

(b) in the case of a piece worker, the rate or rates of statutory minimum remuneration which would be applicable to the worker if he were a time worker.

"normal working week" means the number of days on which it has been usual for the worker to work in a week in the employment of the employer during the 12 months immediately preceding the commencement of the holiday season or, where under paragraph 9 accrued holiday remuneration is payable on the termination of the employment, during the 12 months immediately preceding the date of the termination of the employment:

Provided that—

(i) part of a day shall count as a day;

(ii) no account shall be taken of any week in which the worker did not perform any work for which statutory minimum remuneration has been fixed.

"one day's holiday pay" means the appropriate proportion (as defined in this paragraph) of the remuneration which the worker would be entitled to receive from his employer at the date of the annual holiday (or where the holiday is allowed in more than one period at the date of the first period) or at the termination of the employment, as the case may require, for one week's work if working his normal working week and the number of daily hours normally worked by him (exclusive of overtime) and if paid at the appropriate rate of statutory minimum remuneration for work for which statutory minimum remuneration is payable and at the same rate for any work for which such remuneration is not payable.

"statutory minimum remuneration" means minimum remuneration (other than holiday remuneration) fixed by a wages regulation order made by the Secretary of State to give effect to proposals submitted to him by the Wages Council.

"total remuneration" means any payments paid or payable to the worker under his contract of employment, for time worked or piece work done by him, holiday remuneration, any productivity, long service or other bonus payable to the worker on a weekly, fortnightly or monthly basis and merit payments so payable but does not include any other payments.

"week" in paragraphs 2, 3 and 10 means "pay week".

12. The provisions of this Schedule are without prejudice to any agreement for the allowance of any further holidays with pay or for the payment of additional holiday remuneration.

13. The revocation by this Order of Order O.F. (43) and the coming into effect of the provisions of this Schedule shall not affect the right of a worker to be allowed, and to receive holiday remuneration for, any such days of annual holiday which his employer was required to allow him before 1st May 1974 under the provisions of paragraph 4 of the Schedule to Order O.F. (43).

EXPLANATORY NOTE
(This Note is not part of the Order.)

This Order which has effect from 24th April 1974, sets out the holidays which an employer is required to allow to workers in relation to whom the Ostrich and Fancy Feather and Artificial Flower Wages Council (Great Britain) operates and the remuneration payable for those holidays in substitution for the holidays and holiday remuneration fixed by the Wages Regulation (Ostrich and Fancy Feather and Artificial Flower) (Holidays) Order 1968 (Order O.F.(43)) as amended by Schedule 2 of The Wages Regulation (Ostrich and Fancy Feather and Artificial Flower) Order 1973 (S.I. 1973/521) (Order O.F. (49)). Order O.F. (43) is revoked.

New provisions are printed in italics.

STATUTORY INSTRUMENTS

1974 No. 539

TOWN AND COUNTRY PLANNING, ENGLAND AND WALES

The Land Compensation Development Order 1974

Made - - - -	*22nd March* 1974
Laid before Parliament	*28th March* 1974
Coming into Operation	*1st April* 1974

The Secretary of State for the Environment, in exercise of his powers under section 24 of the Town and Country Planning Act 1971(a) and section 20 of the Land Compensation Act 1961(b) and of all other powers enabling him in that behalf, hereby makes the following order:—

Citation and commencement

1. This order may be cited as the Land Compensation Development Order 1974 and shall come into operation on 1st April 1974.

Interpretation

2.—(1) In this order—

"the Act of 1961" means the Land Compensation Act 1961; and

"the parties directly concerned" has the meaning assigned to that expression by section 22(1) of the Act of 1961.

(2) A section referred to by number in this order means the section so numbered in the Act of 1961.

(3) The Interpretation Act 1889(c) shall apply for the interpretation of this order as it applies for the interpretation of an Act of Parliament.

Application for and issue of certificates

3.—(1) An application to a local planning authority for a certificate under section 17 of the Act of 1961 shall be in writing and shall (as well as complying with the requirements of section 17(3)) include a plan or map sufficient to identify the land to which the application relates.

(2) The time within which a certificate is to be issued by a local planning authority shall, subject to the provisions of section 17(4), be two months of the receipt of such an application by them.

(a) 1971 c. 78. (b) 1961 c. 33. (c) 1889 c. 63.

(3) If a local planning authority issue a certificate otherwise than for the class or classes of development specified in the application made to them, or contrary to representations in writing made to them by a party directly concerned, they shall in that certificate include a statement in writing of their reasons for so doing and give particulars of the manner in which and the time within which an appeal may be made to the Secretary of State under section 18 and this order.

(4) The county planning authority shall send a copy of every certificate issued by them to the council of every district in which any part of the land to which the certificate relates is situated and a district planning authority shall, if the certificate issued by them specifies a class or classes of development relating to a county matter, send a copy of that certificate to the county planning authority, and where any part of the land is situated within Greater London the council of a London borough or the Common Council of the City of London, as the case may be, shall, where the certificate issued by them specifies a class or classes of development for which a planning application would fall to be dealt with by the Greater London Council, send a copy of that certificate to that authority.

Appeals

4.—(1) The time for giving notice of an appeal under section 18 shall be within one month of—

(a) receipt of the certificate, or

(b) the expiry of the time or extended period mentioned in sub-section (4) of that section,

as the case may be.

(2) Notice of appeal shall be given in writing to the Secretary of State and a copy of such notice shall be sent by the appellant to the other of the parties directly concerned and to the local planning authority who issued the certificate under section 17, or if no certificate has been issued, to the local planning authority to whom the application for a certificate was made, and where the issue of a certificate falls to be determined by a local planning authority other than that to which the application was made, the copy notice of appeal shall be forwarded to the local planning authority concerned.

(3) The appellant shall within one month of giving notice of appeal, or such longer period as the Secretary of State may in any particular case allow, furnish to the Secretary of State one copy of the application to the local planning authority, and of the certificate (if any) issued by the local planning authority, together with a statement of the grounds of appeal.

(4) If an appellant does not within the time limited under the last preceding paragraph furnish to the Secretary of State the copies of the documents thereby required, the appeal shall be treated as withdrawn.

Information as to certificates, etc.

5. Where a written request is made to a local planning authority by any person appearing to them to have an interest in the land which is the subject of a certificate under section 17 for—

(a) the name and address of the applicant for the certificate and the date of the application, and

(b) a copy of the certificate,

the local planning authority shall furnish such person with such information and a copy of the certificate, if any, or shall pass the written request to the local planning authority whose function it is to issue the certificate, which authority shall then comply with such request.

Publication of general requirements

6. If a local planning authority, on issuing a certificate, specify conditions by reference to general requirements formulated by them under section 17(6), that authority shall supply with such certificate and every copy thereof a copy of such requirements (or of so much thereof as is relevant to the certificate) unless, before the certificate is issued, the requirements in question have been made available to the public by depositing them for public inspection at all reasonable hours both at their office and at the office of the county or district planning authority in which the land is situate, or in the case of Greater London, at the office of the Greater London Council, as the case may be.

Revocation

7. The Land Compensation Development Order 1963**(a)** is hereby revoked provided that any application for, any appeal against, or any request for information as to a certificate under section 17 which is outstanding at the coming into operation of this order shall have effect as if made and shall be dealt with under and in accordance with the provisions of this order.

Anthony Crosland,

Secretary of State for
the Environment.

22nd March 1974.

(a) S.I. 1963/749 (1963 I, p. 899).

EXPLANATORY NOTE

(This Note is not part of the Order.)

This Order revokes and replaces the Land Compensation Development Order 1963. The Order prescribes the procedure for determining, and for appealing against, certificates under section 17 of the Land Compensation Act 1961 and for obtaining information as to such certificates. It requires a county planning authority to send a copy of every certificate issued by them to the district planning authority in which part of the land is situated and requires a district planning authority to send a copy of every certificate it issues to the county planning authority if the certificate specifies a class or classes of development which is a county matter within the meaning of the Local Government Act 1972 (c.70). A duty is also imposed on a London borough and the Common Council of the City of London to send to the Greater London Council a copy of every certificate they issue specifying a class of development for which a planning application would be determined by that Council. The Order also prescribes the procedure for securing that where conditions in such certificates are specified by reference to general requirements copies of such requirements shall be supplied, unless the requirements have previously been made public at the offices of both the county and district planning authority or, in the case of certificates relating to land in Greater London, at the office of the London borough or Common Council of the City of London and the Greater London Council.

STATUTORY INSTRUMENTS

1974 No. 540

LOCAL GOVERNMENT, ENGLAND AND WALES

The Fire Services (Compensation) Regulations 1974

Made - - -	*20th March* 1974
Laid before Parliament	*29th March* 1974
Coming into Operation	*1st April* 1974

ARRANGEMENT OF REGULATIONS

PART VI

ADJUSTMENT, REVIEW AND COMPOUNDING OF COMPENSATION

PART VII

PROCEDURE AND MISCELLANEOUS

Whereas the Secretary of State is the appropriate Minister for the purposes of section 259 of the Local Government Act 1972(a) in relation to members of fire brigades of a class prescribed by the Firemen's Pension Scheme in pursuance of section 2 of the Fire Services Act 1951(b):

Now, therefore, in exercise of the powers conferred on me by the said section 259 and by section 24 of the Superannuation Act 1972(c), I hereby, with the consent of the Minister for the Civil Service so far as the exercise of powers conferred by the said section 24 are concerned, make the following Regulations—

(a) 1972 c. 70.   (b) 1951 c. 27.   (c) 1972 c. 11.

PART I
PRELIMINARY
Title and commencement
1. These Regulations may be cited as the Fire Services (Compensation) Regulations 1974 and shall come into operation on 1st April 1974.

Interpretation
2.—(1) In these Regulations, unless the context otherwise requires—

"the Act" means the Local Government Act 1972;

"age of compulsory retirement" means, in relation to a regular fireman, the age at which he would become liable to be required to retire on account of age under the Firemen's Pension Scheme;

"compensating authority" in relation to any person who suffers loss of employment or loss or diminution of emoluments as specified in Regulation 4, means the fire authority by whom he was last employed prior to the loss or diminution or, if that authority has ceased to exist, the authority to whom the residue of their property and liabilities has been transferred under the Act;

"compensation question" means a question arising under these Regulations—

(a) as to a person's entitlement to compensation for loss of employment, or for loss or diminution of emoluments; or

(b) as to the manner of a person's employment or the comparability of his duties;

"emoluments" has the meaning given by Regulation 36(1) and "annual rate of emoluments" has the meaning given by Regulation 36(3);

"enactment" means any Act or any instrument made under an Act;

"existing authority" has the meaning given by section 270(1) of the Act;

"Firemen's Pension Scheme" means the Scheme from time to time in force under section 26 of the Fire Services Act 1947**(a)**;

"fund authority", in relation to any person, means the authority maintaining the superannuation fund or account in relation to that person;

"instrument" includes an Order in Council, regulation, order, rule, scheme or direction;

"interchange rules" means rules made under section 2 of the Superannuation (Miscellaneous Provisions) Act 1948**(b)** (which provides for the pensions of persons transferring to different employment) and includes any similar instrument made, or having effect as if made, under any other Act which makes similar provision;

"local authority" means—

(a) the council of a county, county borough, borough (whether or not included in a rural district) and an urban or rural district; a county council and a district council described in section 2 or 21 of the Act; a parish council, a community council; a parish meeting, a representative body of a parish and a common parish council;

(b) the council of a metropolitan borough or London borough, the Common Council of the City of London, the Greater London Council and the council of the Isles of Scilly;

(c) any burial board or joint burial board established under the Burial Acts 1852 to 1906;

(d) any joint board or joint body constituted by or under any enactment for the purpose of exercising the functions of two or more authorities described in (a), (b) or (c) above;

(a) 1947 c. 41.   (b) 1948 c. 33.

(e) any other authority or body, not specified in (a), (b), (c) or (d) above, established by or under any enactment for the purpose of exercising the functions of or advising one or more of the authorities specified in (a), (b), (c) or (d) above;

(f) any committee (including a joint committee) established by or under any enactment for the purpose of exercising the functions of, or advising, two or more authorities described in (a), (b), (c) or (d) above;

(g) any two or more authorities described in (a), (b), (c), (d), (e) or (f) above acting jointly or as a combined authority;

(h) a police authority for a county, a borough or a combined area;

" long-term compensation" means compensation payable in accordance with the provisions of Part IV of these Regulations for loss of employment or loss or diminution of emoluments;

"material date" means—

(a) in relation to any person affected by any provision of the Act or the National Health Service Reorganisation Act 1973(a), 1st April 1974 or the date on which the loss of employment or loss or diminution of emoluments occurred, whichever is the earlier;

(b) in relation to a person affected by any provision of an instrument made under either of those Acts, the date on which the instrument was made or, if some other date is specified therein, that other date;

"national service", in relation to any person, means compulsory national service and service which is relevant service within the meaning of the Reserve and Auxiliary Forces (Protection of Civil Interests) Act 1951(b) and any similar service immediately following such service entered into with the consent of the authority or person under whom he held his last relevant employment, or, where appropriate, the authority by whom he was appointed, and service otherwise than as a member of a fire brigade maintained under the Fire Services Act 1947 which is pensionable under the Firemen's Pension Scheme;

"pensionable pay" and "average pensionable pay" have the same meanings, respectively, as in the Firemen's Pension Scheme;

"pension scheme", in relation to any person, means any form of arrangement associated with his employment for the payment of superannuation benefits, whether subsisting by virtue of an Act of Parliament, trust, contract or otherwise;

"pensionable service" has the same meaning as in the Firemen's Pension Scheme;

"reckonable service", in relation to any person, means any period of whole-time or part-time employment in any relevant employment and includes any period of war service or national service undertaken on his ceasing to hold such an employment;

"regular fireman" means a member of a fire brigade of a class prescribed by the Firemen's Pension Scheme for the purposes of section 2 of the Fire Services Act 1951;

"relevant employment" means employment—

(a) under the Crown or by any person, authority or body for the purposes of the Crown;

(b) under any officer employed as mentioned in (a) above for the purposes of the functions of that person, authority or body;

(c) by any person, authority or body specified in the Schedule to these Regulations;

(a) 1973 c. 32.   (b) 1951 c. 65.

(d) preceding any of the foregoing employment which was reckonable for the purposes of the last relevant pension scheme; or

(e) such other employment as the Secretary of State may, in the case of any named person, approve;

but, except for national service and war service, does not include service in the armed forces of the Crown;

"resettlement compensation" means compensation payable in accordance with Part III of these Regulations for loss of employment;

"retirement compensation" means compensation payable in accordance with the provisions of Regulation 19, 20 or 21;

"tribunal" means a tribunal established under section 12 of the Industrial Training Act 1964**(a)**;

"war service" means war service within the meaning of the Local Government Staffs (War Service) Act 1939**(b)**, the Teachers' Superannuation (War Service) Act 1939**(c)**, the Education (Scotland) (War Service Superannuation) Act 1939**(d)**, the Police and Firemen (War Service) Act 1939**(e)** or employment for war purposes within the meaning of the Superannuation Schemes (War Service) Act 1940**(f)**, and includes any period of service in the first world war in the armed forces of the Crown or in the forces of the Allied or Associated Powers if that service immediately followed a period of relevant employment and was undertaken either compulsorily or with the permission of the employer in that employment.

(2) The holder of any office, appointment, place, situation or employment shall, for the purposes of these Regulations, be regarded as an officer employed in that office, appointment, place, situation or employment, and the expressions "officer" and "employment" shall be construed accordingly.

(3) Where under any provision of these Regulations an annual value is to be assigned to a capital sum or a capital value to an annual amount, the annual or capital value shall be calculated by the Government Actuary.

(4) In these Regulations, unless the context otherwise requires, references to any enactment shall be construed as references thereto as amended, re-enacted, applied or modified by any subsequent enactment.

(5) References in these Regulations to a numbered Regulation shall, unless the reference is to a regulation of specified regulations, be construed as references to the Regulation bearing that number in these Regulations.

(6) References in any of these Regulations to a numbered paragraph shall, unless the reference is to a paragraph of a specified Regulation, be construed as references to the paragraph bearing that number in the first mentioned Regulation.

(7) The Interpretation Act 1889**(g)** shall apply for the interpretation of these Regulations as it applies for the interpretation of an Act of Parliament.

PART II

ENTITLEMENT TO COMPENSATION

Persons to whom the Regulations apply

3.—(1) Subject to the provisions of paragraph (2), these Regulations shall apply to any person who—

(a) was serving immediately before the material date as a regular fireman; or

(b) would have been so serving at that time but for any national service on which he was then engaged.

(a) 1964 c. 16.   (b) 1939 c. 94.   (c) 1939 c. 95.   (d) 1939 c. 96.   (e) 1939 c. 103.
(f) 1940 c. 26.   (g) 1889 c. 63.

(2) These Regulations shall not apply to a person duly entitled within the meaning of the Fire Services (Retirement of Senior Officers) Regulations 1973(**a**).

Grounds of entitlement to compensation

4.—(1) Subject to the provisions of these Regulations, any person to whom these Regulations apply and who suffers loss of employment or loss or diminution of emoluments which is attributable to any provision of the Act or of the National Health Service Reorganisation Act 1973 or of any instrument made under either of those Acts shall be entitled to have his case considered for the payment of compensation under these Regulations, and such compensation shall be determined in accordance with these Regulations.

(2) Without prejudice to the generality of these Regulations, paragraph (1) shall apply to a person who—

(*a*) for the purposes of entering on employment described in sub-paragraph (*b*) of this paragraph, terminates his employment as a regular fireman;

(*b*) at any time before 1st April 1974 entered the employment of a local authority described in section 2 or 21 of the Act; and

(*c*) would, but for his entry into the employment described in the said sub-paragraph (*b*), be transferred on 1st April 1974 in accordance with the provisions of section 255 of the Act to the employment of a local authority;

and in determining the compensating authority for the purposes of these Regulations, any loss or diminution of emoluments suffered by him which is attributable thereto shall be assumed to have occurred on the day after that on which he enters the employment described in the said sub-paragraph (*b*).

National service

5.—(1) Where any person to whom these Regulations apply would have been serving immediately before the material date as a regular fireman but for any national service on which he was then engaged, then if before the expiry of two months after ceasing to be so engaged, or if prevented by sickness or other reasonable cause, as soon as practicable thereafter, he gives notice to the compensating authority that he is available for employment, that person shall be entitled to have his case considered for the payment of compensation on the ground—

(*a*) if he is not given or offered re-employment as a regular fireman in his former rank or in any reasonably comparable employment, of loss of employment;

(*b*) if he is so re-employed with reduced emoluments as compared with the emoluments which he would have enjoyed had he continued to serve as a regular fireman in his former rank, of diminution of emoluments.

(2) The loss of employment which is the ground of a claim for compensation under sub-paragraph (*a*) of paragraph (1) shall be treated as having occurred on the earlier of the two following dates, that is to say, the date of the refusal of re-employment or a date one month after the date on which the person gave notice that he was available for employment, and the claimant shall be deemed to have been entitled to the emoluments which he would have enjoyed at such earlier date had he continued to serve as a regular fireman in his former rank.

(**a**) S.I. 1973/1951 (1973 III, p. 6772).

PART III
RESETTLEMENT COMPENSATION

Resettlement compensation for loss of employment

6. The compensating authority shall, subject to the provisions of these Regulations, pay resettlement compensation to any person to whom these Regulations apply and who satisfies the conditions set out in Regulation 7.

Conditions for payment of resettlement compensation

7.—(1) Without prejudice to any other requirement of these Regulations, the conditions for the payment of resettlement compensation to any person are that—

(a) he has suffered loss of employment attributable to any provision of the Act or of any instrument made under the Act not later than 10 years after the material date;

(b) he had not at the date of the loss attained the age of compulsory retirement;

(c) he had been for a period of 2 years immediately before the material date continuously engaged (disregarding breaks not exceeding in the aggregate 6 months) for the whole or part of his time in relevant employment;

(d) he has made a claim for such compensation in accordance with the provisions of Part VII of these Regulations not later than 13 weeks after the loss of employment which is the cause of his claim, or 13 weeks after the coming into operation of these Regulations, whichever is the later, or within any longer period which the compensating authority allow in any particular case where they are satisfied that the delay in making the claim was due to ill health or other circumstances beyond the claimant's control;

(e) the loss of employment which is the cause of his claim has occurred for some reason other than misconduct or incapacity to perform the duties that, immediately before the loss, he was performing or might reasonably have been required to perform;

(f) he has not, subject to paragraphs (2) and (3), on or after the employer either informs him in writing that his employment is to be terminated or is likely to be terminated or gives him written notice of termination of his employment, been offered in writing—

    (i) any relevant employment which is reasonably comparable with the employment which he has lost, or

    (ii) any employment by a fire authority which is suitable for him and is at the same place or in the same locality as that where he was employed immediately before the loss.

(2) In ascertaining for the purposes of this Regulation whether a person has been offered employment which is reasonably comparable with the employment which he has lost, no account shall be taken of the fact that the duties of the employment offered are in relation to a different service from that in connection with which his employment was held or are duties which involve a transfer of his employment from one place to another within England and Wales.

(3) For the purposes of this Regulation, where the compensating authority are satisfied—

(a) that acceptance of an offer would have involved undue hardship to the person,

(b) that he was prevented from accepting an offer by reason of ill-health or other circumstances beyond his control, or *(c)* that, before the commencement of these Regulations, an offer—

    (i) has not been accepted by him, and

    (ii) has lapsed or otherwise terminated,

no account shall be taken of that offer.

Amount of resettlement compensation

8. The amount of resettlement compensation which may be paid to a person shall, subject to the provisions of Regulation 9, be the amount described in paragraph (*a*) or (*b*) of this Regulation whichever is the greater—

  (*a*) an amount equal to 13 weeks' emoluments and, in the case of a person who has attained the age of 45 years, one additional week's emoluments for every year of his age after attaining the age of 45 years and before the loss of employment, subject to a maximum addition of 13 such weeks;

  (*b*) subject to the provisions of Regulation 35, an amount equal to—

    (i) $1\frac{1}{2}$ weeks' emoluments for each completed year of reckonable service in which the person was not below the age of 41 years.

    (ii) 1 week's emoluments for each completed year of reckonable service (not falling within (i) of this paragraph) in which the person was not below the age of 22 years, and

    (iii) $\frac{1}{2}$ week's emoluments for each completed year of reckonable service not falling within either (i) or (ii) of this paragraph.

Special factors relating to calculation of amount of resettlement compensation

9.—(1) For the purposes of paragraph (*a*) of Regulation 8, if the loss of employment takes place within 3 years of the date on which he would have become entitled to retire with an ordinary pension under the Firemen's Pension Scheme, the amount shall be reduced by the fraction of which—

  (*a*) the denominator is 6, and

  (*b*) the numerator is the number of complete periods of 6 months in the period beginning with the date 3 years before that on which he would have become so entitled and ending on the date of loss of employment;

but the amount payable to a person who, on the material date, has not been continuously engaged in relevant employment as described in Regulation 12(1)(*c*) shall not by this paragraph be reduced to less than the equivalent of 13 weeks' emoluments.

(2) For the purposes of paragraph (*b*) of Regulation 8—

  (*a*) in the case of a person who has completed more than 20 years' reckonable service, only the period of 20 years immediately prior to the loss of employment shall be taken into account, and

  (*b*) if the loss of employment takes place within the period of one year prior to the date on which the person would have attained the age of compulsory retirement, the amount shall be reduced by the fraction of which the denominator is 12 and of which the numerator is the number of whole months in the period commencing at the beginning of the said period of one year and ending with the date of loss of employment.

(3) For the purposes of Regulation 8 and this Regulation, the weekly rate of emoluments shall be deemed to be seven-three hundred and sixty-fifths of the annual rate of emoluments.

Adjustment of resettlement compensation

10. A person who is entitled to—

(*a*) a redundancy payment under the Redundancy Payments Act 1965**(a)**, or

(*b*) any similar payment in consequence of the loss of his employment under any other enactment or under any contract or arrangement with the authority by whom he was employed (other than payments by way of a return of contributions under a pension scheme), or

(*c*) any payment under or by virtue of the provisions of any enactment relating to the reinstatement in civil employment of persons who have been in the service of the Crown, shall—

   (i) if the amount of any resettlement compensation that would, apart from this Regulation, be payable exceeds the payment or payments specified in (*a*), (*b*) or (*c*) above, be entitled to resettlement compensation equal to that excess, or

   (ii) if the amount of any resettlement compensation that would apart from this Regulation be payable is equal to or less than the said payment or payments, not be entitled to resettlement compensation.

PART IV
LONG-TERM COMPENSATION

Long-term compensation for loss of employment or loss or diminution of emoluments

11. The compensating authority shall, subject to the provisions of these Regulations, pay long-term compensation to any person to whom these Regulations apply and who satisfies the conditions set out in Regulation 12.

Conditions for payment of long-term compensation

12.—(1) Without prejudice to any other requirement of these Regulations, the conditions for the payment of long-term compensation to any person are that—

(*a*) he has suffered loss of employment or loss or diminution of emoluments attributable to any provision of the Act or of any instrument under the Act not later than 10 years after the material date;

(*b*) he had not at the date of the loss or diminution attained the age of compulsory retirement;

(*c*) he had been, for a period of not less than 5 years immediately before the material date, continuously engaged (without a break of more than 12 months at any one time) for the whole or part of his time in relevant employment;

(*d*) he has made a claim for such compensation in accordance with the provisions of Part VII of these Regulations not later than 2 years after the loss or diminution which is the cause of the claim or 2 years after the coming into operation of these Regulations whichever is the later; and

(*e*) if the cause of the claim for compensation is loss of employment—

   (i) the loss has occurred for some reason other than misconduct or incapacity to perform such duties as, immediately before the loss, he was performing or might reasonably have been required to perform; and

---

(a) 1965 c. 62.

(ii) he has not, subject to paragraph (2), after the employer either informed him in writing that his employment was to be terminated or was likely to be terminated or gave him written notice of termination of his employment, been offered in writing any relevant employment which is reasonably comparable with the employment which he has lost.

(2) Regulation 7(2) and (3) (which relate to offers of employment) shall apply for the purposes of this Regulation in ascertaining whether a person has been offered reasonably comparable employment.

(3) Claims for long-term compensation for loss of employment shall in all respects be treated as claims for such compensation for the loss of emoluments occasioned thereby and the provisions of these Regulations shall apply to all such claims accordingly.

Factors to be considered in determining payment of long-term compensation

13.—(1) For the purpose of determining whether long-term compensation for loss or diminution of emoluments should be paid to any person and, if so, the amount of the compensation (subject to the limits set out in these Regulations) the compensating authority shall, subject to the provisions of paragraphs (2) and (3), have regard to such of the following factors as may be relevant, that is to say:—

(a) the conditions upon which the person held the employment which he has lost, including in particular its security of tenure, whether by law or practice;

(b) the emoluments and other conditions, including security of tenure, whether by law or practice, of any work or employment undertaken by the person as a result of the loss of employment;

(c) the extent to which he has sought suitable employment and the emoluments he might have acquired by accepting other suitable employment which, after the employer either informs him in writing that his employment is to be terminated or is likely to be terminated or gives him written notice of termination of his employment, has been offered to him in writing;

(d) all the other circumstances of his case;

but no account shall be taken of the fact that he entered the employment which he has lost or the emoluments of which have been diminished after—

(i) 26th October 1972, where the loss or diminution was attributable to any provision of the Act,

(ii) after the making of any instrument under the Act, where the loss or diminution was attributable to any provision of that instrument, or

(iii) 18th July 1973, where the loss or diminution was attributable to any provision of the National Health Service Reorganisation Act 1973.

(2) In ascertaining for the purposes of paragraph (1)(b) and (1)(c) the emoluments in respect of any work or employment that gives the employee or his widow, child or other dependant the right to benefit under a pension scheme under which the employee is not under an obligation to pay contributions, the amount of emoluments shall be increased by the amount of contributions which the employee would have to pay to secure equivalent benefits under a pension scheme in respect of which both the employer and the employee are under an obligation to pay equal contributions.

(3) Regulation 7(3) shall apply for the purposes of this Regulation in ascertaining whether a person has been offered suitable employment.

Amount of long-term compensation payable for loss of emoluments

14.—(1) Long-term compensation for loss of emoluments shall, subject to the provisions of these Regulations, be payable until the age of compulsory retirement or death of a person to whom it is payable, whichever first occurs, and shall not exceed a maximum annual sum calculated in accordance with the provisions of paragraphs (2) and (3).

(2) The said maximum annual sum shall, subject to the provisions of paragraph (3) and Regulation 35 as hereinafter provided, be the aggregate of the following sums, namely:-

(a) for every year of the person's reckonable service, one sixtieth of the emoluments which he has lost; and

(b) in the case of a person who has attained the age of 40 years at the date of the loss, a sum calculated in accordance with the provisions of paragraph (3) appropriate to his age at that date,

but the said maximum annual sum shall in no case exceed two thirds of the emoluments which the person has lost.

(3) The sum referred to in paragraph (2)(b) shall be—

(a) in the case of a person who has attained the age of 40 years but has not attained the age of 50 years at the date of the loss, the following fraction of the emoluments which he has lost—

(i) where his reckonable service is less than 10 years, one sixtieth for each year of that service after attaining the age of 40 years; or

(ii) where his reckonable service amounts to 10 years but is less than 15 years, one sixtieth for each year of that service after attaining the age of 40 years and an additional one sixtieth; or

(iii) where his reckonable service amounts to 15 years but is less than 20 years, one sixtieth for each year of that service after attaining the age of 40 years and an additional two sixtieths; or

(iv) where his reckonable service amounts to 20 years or more, one sixtieth for each year of that service after attaining the age of 40 years and an additional three sixtieths;

but the sum so calculated shall not in any case exceed one sixth of the said emoluments;

(b) in the case of a person who has attained the age of 50 years but has not attained the age of 60 years at the date of the loss, one sixtieth of the said emoluments for each year of his reckonable service after attaining the age of 40 years, up to a maximum of 15 years.

(4) The amount of long-term compensation, which apart from this paragraph would become payable to a person, shall be reduced by the amount by which the aggregate of—

(a) the emoluments of any work or employment undertaken by him as a result of the loss of employment, and

(b) the long-term compensation which, apart from this Regulation and any reduction under Regulation 26,

exceeds the emoluments of the employment which has been lost.

(5) Long-term compensation shall be payable to a person at intervals equivalent to those at which the emoluments of his employment were previously paid or at such other intervals as may be agreed between the person and the compensating authority.

Long-term compensation for diminution of emoluments

15.—(1) Long-term compensation for the diminution of emoluments in respect of any employment shall, subject to the provisions of these Regulations consist of an annual sum calculated in accordance with the provisions of paragraph (2).

(2) The said annual sum shall not exceed the sum that would be the annual sum under the provisions of Regulations 14(1) to (4) calculated on the assumptions—

(a) that there was a loss of employment, and

(b) that emoluments after diminution were emoluments of any work or employment undertaken as a result of a loss of employment within the meaning of Regulation 13(1)(b).

(3) Long-term compensation for diminution of emoluments shall be payable to a person at intervals equivalent to those at which the emoluments of his employment are or were previously paid or at such other intervals as may be agreed between the person and the compensating authority.

Period during which long-term compensation is to be payable

16.—(1) Long-term compensation shall be payable with effect from the date of the claim or from any earlier date permitted by the succeeding provisions of this Regulation.

(2) Where a claim for long-term compensation is duly made within 13 weeks of the commencement of these Regulations or occurrence of the loss or diminution which is the cause of the claim (whichever is the later), the award shall be made retrospective to the date on which the loss or diminution occurred.

(3) Where a claim for long-term compensation is made after the expiry of the period mentioned in paragraph (2), the compensating authority may—

(a) in its discretion make the award retrospective to a date not earlier than 13 weeks prior to the date on which the claim was made, or

(b) if it is satisfied that the failure to make the claim within the period mentioned in paragraph (2) was due to ill-health or other circumstances beyond the claimant's control, make the award retrospective to a date not earlier than that on which the loss or diminution occurred.

(4) Long-term compensation shall not be payable to a person for any period in respect of which compensation under Part V of these Regulations is payable to him.

Part V

Retirement Compensation and Payments on Death

Entitlement to retirement compensation and other payments

17.—(1) The compensating authority shall, subject to the provisions of these Regulations, pay retirement compensation to any person to whom these Regulations apply and who satisfies the conditions set out in Regulation 12, and shall make the other payments for which provision is made in Regulation 24.

(2) Regulation 13 shall apply in relation to compensation under this Part of these Regulations as it applies in relation to compensation under Part IV.

Additional factors governing payment of retirement compensation

18.—(1) Where retirement compensation is payable under any one of Regulations 19, 20 and 21, compensation shall not be payable under any other of these Regulations.

(2) If a person has attained the age of 40 years at the date on which he lost his employment or suffered a diminution of his emoluments, the compensating authority, in calculating the amount of the retirement compensation payable to him, shall credit him with an additional period of service on the following basis, namely—

(*a*) 2 years, whether or not he has completed any years of service after attaining the age of 40 years,

(*b*) 2 years for each of the first 4 completed years of his reckonable service between the date when he attained the age of 40 years and the date of the loss or diminution, and

(*c*) 1 year for each year of that reckonable service after the fourth, but the additional period so credited shall not exceed the shortest of the following periods, namely—

(i) the number of years that, when added to his pensionable service, would amount to the maximum period of service which would have been reckonable by him had he continued in his employment until attaining the age of compulsory retirement, or

(ii) the period of his reckonable service, or

(iii) 15 years;

and in calculating the amount of any retirement compensation payable to him he shall be regarded as having served as a regular fireman, before 1st April 1972, for the additional period so credited.

In this paragraph the expression "reckonable service" includes any period of service or employment which has been taken into account for the purposes of any award under the Firemen's Pension Scheme to which the person concerned has become entitled.

(3) The benefit in respect of the additional period described in paragraph (2) shall be calculated at the same rate as is applicable for the day immediately preceding the loss or diminution.

(4) When retirement compensation is awarded, or when an award is reviewed under Regulation 30, the additional compensation payable in consequence of any period credited to a person under paragraph (2) may be reduced or withheld to the extent that the compensating authority may think reasonable having regard to the pension scheme (if any) associated with any further employment obtained by him.

(5) The provisions of the Firemen's Pension Scheme relating to the allocation of a pension, that is to say to the surrender by a regular fireman of a portion of his pension in favour of his wife or such other person as is substantially dependent on him, shall, subject to any necessary modifications have effect in relation to any retirement compensation as they have effect in relation to an ordinary or ill-health pension under the Firemen's Pension Scheme; and without prejudice to the generality of the preceding provisions of this paragraph—

(a) where before the date of the loss or diminution a regular fireman has, under the Firemen's Pension Scheme, allocated an ordinary pension and the allocation has taken effect, the said provisions shall apply as if the retirement compensation were an ordinary pension; and

(b) the said provisions shall apply as if any reference to the fire authority included a reference to the compensating authority and as if any reference to retirement included a reference to a person becoming entitled to retirement compensation.

(6) In calculating for the purpose of Regulation 19 or 20 the amount of a pension under the Firemen's Pension Scheme, no account shall be taken of any reduction falling to be made in that pension by reason of the provisions of any Act relating to National Insurance until the person concerned reaches the age at which under the Firemen's Pension Scheme the pension would have been so reduced.

Retirement compensation for loss of emoluments payable to a person on attainment of the age of compulsory retirement

19. Subject to the provisions of these Regulations, when a person to whom these Regulations apply reaches the age of compulsory retirement the retirement compensation payable to him for loss of emoluments shall be an annual sum equal to the amount of the short service pension which would have been payable under the provisions of the Firemen's Pension Scheme calculated in accordance with Regulation 18(2).

Retirement compensation payable to a person who would have become entitled to a pension

20.—(1) Where a person to whom these Regulations apply and who has suffered loss of employment before attaining what would have been the age of compulsory retirement—

(a) becomes incapacitated in circumstances in which, if he had continued to serve as a regular fireman, he would have become entitled to retire with an ill-health pension under the Firemen's Pension Scheme, or

(b) attains the age at which, had he continued to serve as a regular fireman, he would have been entitled to retire with an ordinary pension, he shall be entitled on the happening of either event to claim—

(i) in the case mentioned in head (a) of this paragraph, an annual sum equal to the amount of the ill-health pension which would have been payable under the Firemen's Pension Scheme calculated in accordance with Regulation 18(2), and

(ii) in the case mentioned in head (b) of this paragraph, an annual sum equal to the amount of the ordinary pension which would have been payable under the Firemen's Pension Scheme calculated in accordance with Regulation 18(2),

in both cases calculated by reference to his average pensionable pay (or where appropriate pensionable pay) immediately before he ceased to serve as a regular fireman, subject however to paragraph (7).

(2) On receipt of a claim under paragraph (1) the compensating authority shall consider whether the claimant is a person to whom that paragraph applies, and within 13 weeks after the date of the receipt of the claim—

(a) if they are satisfied that he is not such a person, they shall notify him in writing accordingly, or

(b) if they are satisfied that he is such a person, they shall assess the amount of compensation payable to him and notify him in writing accordingly;

and notification as described in (a) or (b) above shall, for the purposes of these Regulations, be deemed to be a notification by the authority of a decision on a claim for compensation.

(3) A compensating authority may require any person who makes a claim under paragraph (1)(a) to submit himself to a medical examination by a registered medical practitioner selected by that authority, and if they do so, they shall also offer the person an opportunity of submitting a report from his own medical adviser as a result of an examination by him, and the authority shall take that report into consideration together with the report of the medical practitioner selected by them.

(4) If a person wishes to receive compensation under this Regulation, he shall so inform the compensating authority in writing within one month from the receipt of a notification under paragraph (2) or, where the claim has been the subject of an appeal, from the decision of the tribunal thereon; and the compensation shall be payable as from the date on which the compensating authority received the claim.

(5) If the compensating authority so agree, in the case of a person who would have become entitled to retire with an ordinary pension, as aforesaid, if his notice of retirement were given with the permission of the fire authority, it shall be assumed for the purposes of this Regulation that he would have obtained such permission.

(6) If the compensating authority so agree, in the case of a person in whose case the Firemen's Pension Scheme had effect subject to the modifications set out in section 27(3) of the Fire Services Act 1947, no account shall be taken, for the purposes of this Regulation, of any modification which has the effect that—

(a) a person's entitlement to a pension is conditional on the chief officer of the fire brigade concerned giving a certificate that he has served with zeal and fidelity, or

(b) the grant of a pension may be refused on account of misconduct or on account of any of the grounds on which the pension, if granted, would be liable to be forfeited or withdrawn.

(7) In calculating the amount of any compensation under this Regulation, where the compensating authority, by virtue of Regulation 18(2), have credited the person with an additional period of service, no account shall be taken of any additional period beyond the period which he could have served, had he not lost his employment, before the date on which the claim was received by the compensating authority.

Retirement compensation for diminution of emoluments

21.—(1) A person to whom these Regulations apply and who has suffered a diminution of his emoluments shall be entitled to receive retirement compensation in accordance with the provisions of this Regulation.

(2) The provisions of Regulations 19 and 20 shall apply to any such person as if he had suffered loss of employment immediately before the diminution occurred; but the amount of retirement compensation payable shall be the amount which would have been payable in respect of loss of employment multiplied by a fraction of which—

(a) the numerator is the amount by which his pensionable emoluments have been diminished, and (*b*) the denominator is the amount of his pensionable emoluments immediately before they were diminished;

but in calculating, for the purpose of Regulation 19 or 20, the amount of a pension under the Firemen's Pension Scheme, no account shall be taken of any provision of that Scheme by which a pension would be reduced beyond the age of 65 years.

Superannuation contributions

22.—(1) A person entitled to retirement compensation under Regulation 19 or 20 shall pay to the compensating authority an amount equal to any award by way of repayment of aggregate contributions received by him under the Firemen's Pension Scheme on ceasing to be a regular fireman but, where he has made the said payment to the compensating authority before becoming entitled to retirement compensation as aforesaid, that authority may, at his request before he becomes so entitled, refund the payment to him; and if the said payment is not made to the compensating authority, or is refunded by them, the compensation shall be reduced by an annual amount the capital value of which is equal to the amount of the said award under the Firemen's Pension Scheme.

(2) In the case of a person who undertook, for the purposes of the Firemen's Pension Scheme, to make payments by regular instalments in respect of previous service, the compensating authority shall be empowered to deduct the balance of the sum outstanding under the undertaking when he ceased to serve as a regular fireman, if any, from any payments to him of retirement compensation.

(3) Any sums paid to a compensating authority under this Regulation, in respect of returned contributions under the Firemen's Pension Scheme shall be applied for the payment of compensation which the authority is liable to pay under this part of these Regulations.

Retirement compensation of a person who obtains further pensionable employment

23.—(1) Where a person to whom these Regulations apply, after suffering loss of employment or diminution of emoluments as a regular fireman, enters employment in which he is subject to a pension scheme and thereafter becomes entitled to reckon for the purposes of that scheme any service or period of contribution which falls to be taken into account for the purpose of assessing the amount of any retirement compensation payable to him, his entitlement to retirement compensation shall be reviewed, and, subject to the provisions of this Regulation, no retirement compensation shall be payable in respect of that service or period unless the annual rate of the emoluments to which he was entitled immediately before the loss or diminution exceeds the annual rate on entry of the emoluments of the new employment, and any retirement compensation so payable to him shall, insofar as it is calculated by reference to remuneration, be calculated by reference to the difference between the said annual rates.

(2) The provisions of this Regulation shall not operate to increase the amount of any retirement compensation payable in respect of diminution of emoluments beyond the amount which would have been payable if the person had attained the age of compulsory retirement immediately before he ceased to hold the employment in which he suffered the diminution of emoluments.

Compensation payable on the death of a claimant

24.—(1) Where a person to whom this part of these Regulations applies dies, payments in accordance with this Regulation shall be made to or for the benefit of his widow or child or to his personal representatives or as the case may be, to trustees empowered by him to stand possessed of any benefit under the Firemen's Pension Scheme.

(2) Where the widow or child has become, or but for the person's loss of employment as a regular fireman would have become, entitled to benefits under the Firemen's Pension Scheme, the widow or child, as the case may be, shall (subject to the provisions of this Regulation) be entitled to compensation calculated from time to time in accordance with the methods prescribed by the Firemen's Pension Scheme modified as follows:—

(a) where the person dies before becoming entitled to receive retirement compensation, and the Firemen's Pension Scheme provides that when he dies in service his widow or child shall be entitled for any period to a benefit equal to his pensionable pay, the annual rate of compensation for that period shall be equal to the annual amount of his long-term compensation calculated in accordance with paragraphs (1) to (3) of Regulation 14;

(b) where the person dies before becoming entitled to receive retirement compensation and the Firemen's Pension Scheme provides that when he dies in service his widow or child shall be entitled for any period to a benefit calculated by reference to the pension or ill-health pension which would have been payable to him if he had retired immediately before his death, the compensation for that period shall be calculated by reference to the retirement compensation to which he would have been entitled under Regulation 20 if that Regulation had been applied to him immediately before his death;

(c) where a person dies after becoming entitled to receive retirement compensation and the Firemen's Pension Scheme provides that when he dies after having retired his widow or child shall be entitled for any period to a benefit equal to his pension, the annual rate of compensation for that period shall be equal to the annual amount of retirement compensation;

(d) where a person dies after he has become entitled to receive retirement compensation and the Firemen's Pension Scheme provides that when he dies after having retired his widow or child shall be entitled for any period to a benefit calculated by reference to his pension, the annual rate of compensation for that period shall be calculated by reference to the annual amount of retirement compensation that would have been payable to him but for any reduction or suspension under Regulation 28(1).

(3) Calculation of the amounts described in paragraph (2) shall be subject to the following adjustments, that is to say—

(a) where any retirement compensation has been surrendered under Regulation 18(5) or compounded under Regulation 31 any sum payable under paragraph (2)(b) or (d) shall be calculated as if such surrender or compounding had not taken place;

(b) if immediately before his death the person's long-term compensation was reduced under Regulation 14(4) or 30 or his retirement compensation was reduced or suspended under Regulation 28(1) by reason of employment in which he was subject to a pension scheme and the widow or child is entitled under that scheme for any period to a benefit equal to his pensionable remuneration, regard shall be had to any such reduction or suspension for the purpose of sub-paragraphs (a) and (c).

(4) If the person in question suffered a diminution of emoluments, the provisions of paragraph (2) shall apply with the substitution of references to diminution of emoluments for references to loss of employment, and the sums payable to his widow or child shall be calculated, as if he had suffered loss of employment and as if the loss of emoluments occasioned thereby had been equivalent to the amount of the diminution.

(5) Compensation payable in accordance with this Regulation shall be payable on the like conditions in all respects as a widow's pension or, as the case may be, a child's allowance under the Firemen's Pension Scheme and, accordingly, the provisions of that Scheme (including any provision for the commutation of a pension or allowance for a gratuity) shall apply, subject to any necessary modifications, in relation to such compensation as they apply in relation to such a pension or allowance.

(6) Except where retirement compensation payable to the deceased person has been reduced under Regulation 22(1), the payments by way of compensation under this Regulation shall, in the aggregate, be reduced by an amount the capital value whereof is equal to the amount of any award by way of repayment of aggregate contributions received by him under the Firemen's Pension Scheme and either not paid to the compensating authority in accordance with Regulation 22(1) or refunded to him by that authority; and, where payments under this Regulation are made to or for the benefit of two or more persons, the said reduction shall be apportioned between those payments according to the capital value thereof.

(7) Where a person to whom this part of these Regulations applies dies and, but for his loss of employment as a regular fireman, the fire authority would have had discretion to grant a gratuity to a person who was substantially dependent on him immediately before his death, the compensating authority shall have a like discretion to grant a gratuity calculated in accordance with the methods prescribed by the Firemen's Pension Scheme.

(8) In this Regulation and in Regulation 26 the expression "child" has the same meaning as in the Firemen's Pension Scheme and related expressions shall be construed accordingly.

Intervals for payment of compensation under Part V

25. Any compensation awarded under this Part of these Regulations to or in respect of any person, shall be payable in advance at intervals equivalent to those at which the corresponding benefit would have been payable under the Firemen's Pension Scheme or at such other intervals as may be agreed between the person entitled to receive the compensation and the compensating authority.

PART VI
ADJUSTMENT, REVIEW AND COMPOUNDING OF COMPENSATION

Abatement of compensation by award under the Firemen's Pension Scheme

26.—(1) Where compensation under these Regulations is payable to a person who has lost employment as a regular fireman or to or for the benefit of his widow or child and a pension or allowance under the Firemen's Pension Scheme is also so payable, the annual amount of the compensation shall be abated by the annual amount of the corresponding pension or allowance.

(2) For the purposes of this Regulation in its application to the payment of long-term compensation, where a pension has been reduced under the provisions of the Firemen's Pension Scheme—

(a) relating to the allocation of a portion of a pension and mentioned in Regulation 18(5), or

(b) relating to the commutation of a portion of a pension for a lump sum, or

(c) relating to payments under the Firemen's Pension Scheme for the purpose of qualifying for benefits in respect of previous service or for an improved widow's pension,

the annual amount of that pension shall be deemed to be the annual amount which would have been payable but for the said reduction.

(3) For the purposes of this Regulation no account shall be taken of a pension payable to a widow or child under the Firemen's Pension Scheme by reason of the allocation by the husband or father of a portion of his pension.

Adjustment of compensation where superannuation benefit is also payable

27.—(1) Where any period of service of which account was taken in calculating the amount of any compensation payable under Part IV or V of these Regulations is subsequently taken into account for the purpose of calculating the amount of any superannuation benefit payable to or in respect of any person in accordance with a pension scheme associated with any employment undertaken subsequent to the loss of employment or diminution of emoluments which was the subject of the claim for compensation, the compensating authority may in accordance with this Regulation withhold or reduce the compensation payable.

(2) If the part of any superannuation benefit which is attributable to a period of service mentioned in paragraph (1) equals or exceeds the part of any compensation which is attributable to the same period, that part of the compensation may be withheld, or if the part of the superannuation benefit is less than the part of the compensation, the compensation may be reduced by an amount not exceeding that part of the superannuation benefit.

(3) In addition to any reduction authorised by paragraph (2), if, in the circumstances mentioned in paragraph (1), compensation is attributable in part to any provision of the Firemen's Pension Scheme for a minimum benefit, the compensation may be reduced by an amount not exceeding that part.

(4) Where any additional period of service has been credited to a person under Regulation 18(2), and that period is equal to or less than the period spent in the subsequent employment mentioned in paragraph (1), the compensation may be reduced (in addition to any other reduction authorised by this Regulation) by an amount not exceeding that attributable to the additional period of service credited or, if the period is greater than the period spent in the subsequent employment, by the proportion of that amount which the period spent in the subsequent employment bears to the additional period so credited.

(5) In making any reduction under paragraphs (2) to (4), the amount of pension to be taken into account relating to the subsequent employment shall be the amount of such pension reduced by a fraction of that pension, where—

(i) the numerator of the fraction is equivalent to the aggregate of the amount of increases which would have been awarded under the provisions of the Pensions (Increase) Act 1971**(a)**, during the period beginning with the day following loss of the employment for which compensation is payable and ending on the day the subsequent employment terminated, on an official pension (within the meaning of that Act) of £100 a year which commenced from the first mentioned day, and

(a) 1971 c. 56.

(ii) the denominator of the fraction is equivalent to the aggregate of an official pension of £100 a year and the amount of the increases so determined.

(6) Where compensation has been calculated in accordance with Regulation 23, the provisions of this Regulation shall only apply in relation to the part (if any) of the superannuation benefit which is attributable to annual emoluments in excess of those to which the person was entitled on entering the new employment referred to in Regulation 23.

(7) Where compensation is payable in respect of diminution of emoluments, the provisions of this Regulation shall apply only in relation to the part (if any) of the superannuation benefit which is attributable to annual emoluments in excess of those to which the person was entitled immediately prior to the diminution.

Reduction of compensation in certain cases

28.—(1) If under the Firemen's Pension Scheme any benefit payable to a person under the Scheme would have been subject to reduction or suspension on his taking up other specified employment, any retirement compensation to which he is entitled for loss of employment or diminution of emoluments shall, where such an employment is taken up, be reduced or suspended in the like manner and to the like extent.

(2) There shall be deducted from any long-term compensation or retirement compensation payable to any person any contributory payments remaining unpaid at the date when he suffered loss of employment that are not recovered in accordance with the provisions of the Firemen's Pension Scheme.

(3) Where in any week a person entitled to long-term compensation for loss or diminution of emoluments is also entitled to a National Insurance benefit, there shall be deducted from the long-term compensation payable in respect of that week a sum equal to the amount by which the aggregate of—

(i) the National Insurance benefit that would be payable in respect of that week if calculated at the rate applicable at the date of loss or diminution, and

(ii) the weekly rate at which the long-term compensation would be payable but for this Regulation,

exceeds two thirds of the weekly rate of the emoluments of the employment which he has lost or in which the emoluments have been diminished.

(4) No deduction shall be made under paragraph (3) insofar as—

(*a*) an equivalent sum is deducted from the emoluments of his current employment, and

(*b*) that deduction from those emoluments has not occasioned an increase in his long-term compensation.

(5) (*a*) In paragraph (2) the expression "contributory payments" in relation to any person means any payments which he undertook to make under the Firemen's Pension Scheme for the purpose of qualifying for benefits in respect of previous service or for an improved widow's pension.

(*b*) In paragraph (3) the expression "weekly rate" means seven-three hundred and sixty-fifths of the relevant annual rate, and the expression "National Insurance benefit" means any unemployment, sickness, invalidity or injury benefit or retirement pension payable under any enactment relating to National Insurance, other than a benefit claimable by him in respect of a dependant.

Notification of change of circumstances

29. Where a person to whom these Regulations apply—

(a) after suffering loss of employment or diminution of emoluments enters any employment referred to in Regulation 23 or becomes entitled to any superannuation benefit on ceasing to hold such an employment, or

(b) being entitled to long-term compensation, whilst that compensation is liable to review in accordance with the provisions of Regulation 30, enters any employment, or ceases to hold an employment, or receives any increase in his emoluments in an employment, or

(c) being entitled to retirement compensation, enters employment in which the compensation is subject to reduction or suspension under Regulation 28 or ceases to hold such an employment, or

(d) being entitled to long-term compensation, starts to receive any benefit, any increase in benefit or any further benefit, under any enactment relating to National Insurance,

he shall forthwith in writing inform the compensating authority of that fact.

Review of awards of long-term or retirement compensation

30.—(1) The compensating authority shall—

(a) on the expiry of 6 months from the decision date, or

(b) on the occurrence of any material change in the circumstances of the case,

whichever shall first occur, and thereafter within a period of 2 years after the decision date, or within any longer period specified in the subsequent provisions of this Regulation, and at intervals of not more than 6 months, review its decision or, where the claim has been the subject of an appeal, the decision of the tribunal, and (subject to paragraph (7)) these Regulations shall apply in relation to such a review as they apply in relation to the initial determination of the claim; and on such a review, in the light of any material change in the circumstances of the case, compensation may be awarded, or compensation previously awarded may be increased, reduced or discontinued, subject to the limits set out in these Regulations.

(2) The person to whom the decision relates may require the compensating authority to carry out the review mentioned in paragraph (1) at any time mentioned in that paragraph if he considers that there has been a change in the circumstances of his case which is material for the purposes of these regulations.

(3) The compensating authority shall carry out a review in accordance with paragraph (1), notwithstanding the expiration of the period of 2 years mentioned in that paragraph, if—

(a) the emoluments of employment or work undertaken as a result of the loss of employment had been taken into account in determining the amount of any compensation awarded, and

(b) that employment or work has been lost or the emoluments thereof reduced, otherwise than by reason of misconduct or incapacity to perform the duties which the person might reasonably have been required to perform, and

(c) the compensating authority is satisfied that the loss or reduction is causing him hardship,

and where any decision is so reviewed, the decision shall be subject to further review in accordance with paragraph (1) as if the review carried out under this paragraph had been the initial determination of the claim.

(4) Paragraphs (1) and (2) shall apply in relation to any decision on a claim for long-term or retirement compensation in respect of diminution of emoluments as they apply in relation to any decision mentioned in paragraph (1) and as if in paragraph (1) "decision date" means the date on which any decision on a claim for long-term compensation for diminution of emoluments is notified to the claimant, but—

(a) where the person to whom the decision relates ceases to hold the employment in which his emoluments were diminished, a review shall be held within 3 months after that date, but no further review shall be held after the expiry of that period, and

(b) while that person continues to hold that employment, there shall be no limit to the period within which a review may take place.

(5) Notwithstanding anything contained in the foregoing provisions of this Regulation, the compensating authority shall review a decision, whether of the authority or the tribunal, on a claim for long-term compensation for loss of employment or diminution of emoluments after the expiration of any period within which a review is required to be made if at any time—

(a) the person to whom the decision relates becomes engaged in any employment (hereinafter referred to as "his current employment") the emoluments of which are payable out of public funds and which he had undertaken subsequent to the loss or diminution, and

(b) the aggregate of the emoluments of his current employment, any pension under the Firemen's Pension Scheme and the long-term compensation payable to him exceeds the emoluments of the employment which he has lost or, as the case may be, in which the emoluments have been diminished.

(6) The compensating authority shall further review any decision reviewed under paragraph (5) whenever the emoluments of the person's current employment are increased.

(7) If on any review under this Regulation the compensation is reduced it shall not be reduced below the amount by which the emoluments of the work or employment undertaken as a result of the loss of employment or diminution of emoluments, together with any pension under the Firemen's Pension Scheme falls short of the emoluments of the employment which he has lost, or, as the case may be, in which the emoluments have been diminished.

(8) The compensating authority shall give to a person to whom a decision relates not less than 14 days' notice of any review of that decision to be carried out under this Regulation unless the review is carried out at his request.

(9) In this Regulation the expression "decision date" means the date on which any decision on a claim for long-term or retirement compensation for loss of employment is notified to a claimant under Regulation 32.

(10) For the purpose of Regulations 14(4), 23(1) and 27(6) and (7) and any review under this Regulation, no account shall be taken of any increase in the emoluments of any work or employment undertaken as a result of the loss of employment or diminution of emoluments, or of any superannuation benefit attributable to such an increase, if any such increase is effective from any date after the date of the loss or diminution, and is attributable to a rise in the cost of living.

(11) Nothing in this Regulation shall preclude the making of any adjustment of compensation required by Regulation 27 or 28.

Compounding of awards

31.—(1) In the case where an annual sum which has been or might be awarded under these Regulations does not exceed £35, the compensating authority may, at its discretion, compound its liability in respect thereof by paying a lump sum equivalent to the capital value of the annual sum.

(2) In any other case, if the person who has been awarded long-term or retirement compensation requests it to do so, the compensating authority may, after having regard to the state of health of that person and the other circumstances of the case, compound up to one quarter of their liability to make payments under the award (other than payments to a widow, child or other dependant under Regulation 24) by the payment of an equivalent amount as a lump sum.

(3) The making of a composition under paragraph (2) in relation to an award of long-term or retirement compensation shall not prevent the subsequent making of a composition under paragraph (1) in relation to that award but, subject as aforesaid, not more than one composition may be made in relation to any award.

PART VII
PROCEDURE AND MISCELLANEOUS

Procedure on making claims

32.—(1) Every claim for compensation under these Regulations and every request for a review of an award of long-term or retirement compensation shall be made in accordance with this Regulation.

(2) Every such claim or request shall be made to the compensating authority in writing and shall state whether any other claim for compensation has been made by the claimant under these Regulations.

(3) Resettlement compensation shall be claimed separately from any other form of compensation claimable under these Regulations.

(4) The compensating authority shall consider any such claim or request in accordance with the relevant provisions of these Regulations and shall notify the claimant in writing of their decision—

   (*a*) in the case of a claim for resettlement compensation, not later than 1 month after the receipt of the claim,

   (*b*) in the case of a claim for, or request for the review of an award of, compensation under Part IV or V of these Regulations, not later than 1 month after the receipt of the claim or request, and

   (*c*) in any other case, as soon as possible after the decision;

but the decision of the compensating authority shall not be invalidated by reason of the fact that notice of the decision is given after the expiry of the period mentioned in this paragraph.

(5) Every notification of a decision by the compensating authority (whether granting or refusing compensation or reviewing an award, or otherwise affecting any compensation under these Regulations) shall contain a statement—

   (*a*) giving reasons for the decision;

   (*b*) showing how any compensation has been calculated and, in particular, if the amount is less than the maximum which could have been awarded under these Regulations, showing the factors taken into account in awarding that amount; and (*c*) directing the attention of the claimant to his right under **Regulation 39**, if he is aggrieved by the decision, to institute proceedings before a tribunal and giving him the address to which any application instituting those proceedings should be sent.

Claimants to furnish information

33.—(1) Any person claiming or receiving compensation or whose award of compensation is being reviewed shall furnish all such information that the compensating authority may at any time reasonably require; and he shall verify that information in such manner, including the production of documents in his possession or control, as may be reasonably so required.

(2) Such a person shall, on receipt of reasonable notice, present himself for interview at any place that the compensating authority may reasonably require; and any person who attends for interview may, if he so desires be represented by his adviser.

Procedure on death of claimant

34.—(1) In the event of the death of a claimant or of a person who, if he had survived, could have been a claimant, a claim for compensation under these Regulations may be continued or made, as the case may be, by his personal representatives.

(2) Where any such claim is continued or made as aforesaid by personal representatives, the personal representatives shall, as respects any steps to be taken or thing to be done by them in order to continue or make the claim, be deemed for the purposes of these Regulations to be the person entitled to claim, but, save as aforesaid, the person in whose right they continue or make the claim shall be deemed for the purposes of these Regulations to be that person, and the relevant provisions of these Regulations shall be construed accordingly.

(3) The compensating authority may in any case where a person who, if he had survived could have been a claimant, has died, extend the period within which a claim under Regulation 7 or 12 is to be made by his personal representatives.

Calculation of service

35. For the purpose of making any calculation under these Regulations in respect of a person's reckonable service, all periods of that service shall be aggregated, and except where reference is made to completed years of service if the aggregated service includes a fraction of a year, that fraction shall, if it equals or exceeds 6 months, be treated as a year, and shall, in any other case be disregarded.

Emoluments

36.—(1) In these Regulations, subject to the provisions of paragraph (2) and Regulation 37 (temporary variation of emoluments) the expression "emoluments" means all salary, wages, fees and other payments paid or made to an officer as such for his own use, and also the money value of any accommodation or other allowances in kind appertaining to his employment, but does not include payments for overtime which are not a usual incident of his employment, or any allowances payable to him to cover the cost of providing office accommodation or clerical or other assistance, or any travelling or subsistence allowance or other moneys to be spent, or to cover expenses incurred, by him for the purposes of his employment.

(2) Where fees or other variable payments were paid to an officer as part of his emoluments during any period immediately preceding the loss or diminution, the amount in respect of fees or other variable payments to be included in the annual rate of emoluments shall be the annual average of the fees or other payments paid to him during the period of 5 years immediately preceding the loss or diminution, or such other period as the compensating authority may think reasonable in the circumstances.

(3) For the purposes of these Regulations the annual rate of emoluments in relation to any employment which has been lost or the emoluments whereof have been lost or diminished shall be the amount described in (a), (b) or (c) of this paragraph, whichever is the greater—

(a) the emoluments received by him in the period of 12 months immediately preceding the loss or diminution;

(b) in the case of emoluments payable monthly, the emoluments payable in respect of the last complete month immediately preceding the loss or diminution multiplied by 12; or

(c) in the case of emoluments payable weekly, the emoluments payable in respect of the last complete week immediately preceding the loss or diminution multiplied by 52.

Temporary variation of emoluments

37. In calculating for the purposes of these Regulations the amount of any emoluments lost, or the amount by which any emoluments have been diminished and in determining the resettlement and long-term compensation of any person who has suffered such a loss or diminution—

(a) no account shall be taken of any temporary increase or decrease in the amount of the person's emoluments which is attributable to the passing or making of any provision mentioned in Regulation 4 and otherwise than in the ordinary course of his employment, and

(b) in any case where an office becomes vacant by reason of the last holder thereof either becoming a person duly entitled, in respect of the same employment, to benefits payable under regulations made under section 260(3) of the Local Government Act 1972(a) (early retirement of Chief Officers) or entering an employment to which Article 10 of the Local Government (New Councils etc.) Order 1973(b) applies, any increase in the amount of a person's emoluments which is, after the date of commencement of the regulations or the order relating to that person, attributable to—

(i) his filling that office in an acting or temporary capacity, or

(ii) his performance of, or responsibility for, the duties of that office, shall be disregarded.

Compensation not assignable

38.—(1) Subject to any statutory provision in that behalf, any compensation under these Regulations shall be paid by the compensating authority and (except in the case of compensation payable in accordance with Regulation 24(4)) shall be payable to, or in trust for, the person who is entitled to receive it, and shall not be assignable.

(a) 1972 c. 70.   (b) S.I. 1973/444 (1973 I, p. 1535).

(2) Without prejudice to any other right of recovery, any compensation paid in error may be recovered by the compensating authority by deduction from any compensation payable under these Regulations.

Right of appeal from decision of compensating authority

39.—(1) Every person who is aggrieved by any decision of the compensating authority with respect to a compensation question or by any failure on the part of the compensating authority to notify him of any such decision within the appropriate time prescribed by these Regulations, may within 13 weeks of the notification to him of the decision or the expiry of the prescribed time, as the case may be, institute proceedings for the determination of the question by a tribunal in accordance with the Industrial Tribunals (Industrial Relations, etc.) Regulations 1972**(a)** and these Regulations; and the tribunal shall determine the question accordingly.

(2) Every interested authority aggrieved by any decision of the compensating authority with respect to a compensation question may, within 13 weeks of the notification to them of the decision, institute proceedings for the determination of the question by a tribunal in accordance with the Industrial Tribunals (Industrial Relations etc.) Regulations 1972 and these Regulations; and the tribunal shall determine the question accordingly.

(3) For the purpose of any proceedings described in paragraph (1) a person or persons may be appointed to sit with the tribunal as assessor or assessors.

(4) The compensating authority shall give effect to the decision of a tribunal subject to any modifications that may be required in consequence of any appeal from that decision on a point of law.

Roy Jenkins,
One of Her Majesty's Principal
Secretaries of State.

Home Office,
   Whitehall.
18th March 1974.

Consent of the Minister for the Civil Service, so far as the exercise of powers conferred by section 24 of the Superannuation Act 1972 are concerned, given under his official seal on 20th March 1974.

(L.S.)   *K. H. McNeill,*
Authorised by the Minister
for the Civil Service.

(a) S.I. 1972/38 (1972 I, p. 91).

Regulation 2   **SCHEDULE**

1. An officer of a local authority.

2. An officer of a water authority.

3. An officer of an association—
 (i) which is representative of local authorities,
 (ii) which is established by one or more of the associations described in
     (i) above for the purpose of disseminating information concerning local
     government, or
 (iii) being the Association of River Authorities or the British Waterworks
     Association.

4. The holder of the office of justices' clerk or a person employed in assisting
the holder of such an office in the performance of his duties.

5. An officer of a probation and after-care committee.

6. An officer of a Local Valuation Panel.

7. A person employed by managers of an approved school, remand home,
approved probation hostel or approved probation home (which has not been
taken over by a local authority or by a joint committee representing two or
more local authorities) to whom a certificate of approval under section 79 of the
Children and Young Persons Act 1933(a) has been issued by the Secretary of
State for Health and Social Security.

8. A person employed by a voluntary organisation described in section 30
of the National Assistance Act 1948(b).

9. A person employed by the Central Council for the Education and Training
in Social Work and the Courses for the Education and Training of Health
Visitors.

10. A person employed by a Passenger Transport Executive.

11. A person employed by or under (and for the purpose of the functions of)
any person described in paragraphs 1-3 and 5-10 above.

(a) 1933 c. 12.   (b) 1948 c. 29.

EXPLANATORY NOTE

(This Note is not part of the Regulations.)

1. These Regulations provide for the payment of compensation to or in respect of regular firemen who suffer loss of employment or loss or diminution of emoluments in consequence of the provisions of the Local Government Act 1972 or the National Health Service Reorganisation Act 1973 or any instrument made thereunder.

2. Part I of the Regulations contains definitions. Part II specifies the persons to whom the Regulations apply and the grounds of entitlement to compensation.

3. The compensation payable is—

(*a*) resettlement compensation for loss of employment (Part III);

(*b*) long-term compensation for loss of employment or loss or diminution of emoluments (Part IV);

(*c*) retirement compensation for loss of employment or loss or diminution of emoluments (Part V);

(*d*) compensation payable on the death of a claimant who was a regular fireman (Part V).

4. Resettlement compensation is payable in a lump sum to firemen with at least 2 years' service in relevant employment. The qualifying conditions and factors to be considered are set out in Regulation 7 and the methods of calculation are set out in Regulations 8, 9 and 10.

5. Long-term and retirement compensation is payable to officers with at least 5 years' service in relevant employment. The qualifying conditions and factors to be considered are set out in Regulations 12 and 13.

6. The method of calculating the amount of long-term compensation is laid down in Regulation 14 (loss of emoluments) and 15 (diminution of emoluments).

The compensation is payable from the date determined under Regulation 16, but is not payable for any period in respect of which retirement compensation is payable.

7. Retirement compensation payable to a regular fireman is based upon his accrued pension rights (Regulations 18 and 20) supplemented in the case of persons aged 40 years or over at the date of the loss or diminution by the addition of notional years of service (Regulation 18). Retirement compensation is ordinarily payable from the age of compulsory retirement but in certain circumstances is payable earlier (Regulations 19 and 20).

8. Compensation is payable to the widow, child or other dependant or to the personal representatives or trustees of a claimant who dies where such persons would have benefited under the relevant pension scheme (Regulation 24).

9. Part VI provides for long-term and retirement compensation to be reviewed and for awards to be varied in the light of changing circumstances. It also contains provisions for the adjustment, suspension and compounding of compensation in certain circumstances.

10. Part VII contains provisions relating to the procedure for making claims and notifying decisions. A right is given to a claimant who is aggrieved by a decision on a compensation question or the failure of the compensating authority to notify its decision to refer the question for determination by a tribunal in accordance with the Industrial Tribunals (Industrial Relations, etc.) Regulations 1972.

STATUTORY INSTRUMENTS

1974 No. 541

NATIONAL HEALTH SERVICE, ENGLAND AND WALES

The National Health Service Financial (No. 2) Regulations 1974

Made - - - -	*25th March* 1974
Laid before Parliament	*29th March* 1974
Coming into Operation	*1st April* 1974

The Secretary of State for Social Services as respects England, and the Secretary of State for Wales as respects Wales, in exercise with the approval of the Treasury of powers conferred by section 54(6) of the National Health Service Act 1946(**a**) (as amended by section 57 of, and paragraph 30 of Schedule 4 to, the National Health Service Reorganisation Act 1973(**b**)), and in exercise of powers conferred by section 40(2) of the said Act of 1946 (as amended by paragraphs 25(3) and (4) of the said Schedule), sections 28(2) and 29(1) of the Health Services and Public Health Act 1968(**c**) (as amended by paragraphs 114 and 115 respectively of the said Schedule), and now vested in them(**d**), and of powers conferred on them by sections 7(4), 9(6) and 47(1) and (2) of the said Act of 1973, and of all other powers enabling them in that behalf hereby make the following regulations :—

Citation and commencement

1. These regulations may be cited as the National Health Service Financial (No. 2) Regulations 1974 and shall come into operation on 1st April 1974.

Interpretation

2.—(1) In these regulations, unless the context otherwise requires—

" the Act " means the National Health Service Act 1946 ;

" the Reorganisation Act " means the National Health Service Reorganisation Act 1973 ;

" auditor " means an auditor appointed by the Secretary of State under section 55(2) of the Act ;

" enactment " includes a provision in a Statutory Instrument ;

" Health Authority " means a Regional or Area Health Authority ;

" Prescription Pricing Authority " means the special health authority constituted by the Prescription Pricing Authority (Establishment and Constitution) Order 1974(**e**) ;

" Welsh Health Technical Services Organisation " means the special health authority constituted by the Welsh Health Technical Services Organisation (Establishment and Constitution) Order 1973(**f**).

(**a**) 1946 c. 81. (**b**) 1973 c. 32. (**c**) 1968 c. 46.
(**d**) *See* Secretary of State for Social Services Order 1968 (S.I.1968/1699 (1968 III, p.4585)) Article 2, and Transfer of Functions (Wales) Order 1969 (S.I. 1969/388 (1969 I, p.1070)) Article 2.
(**e**) S.I. 1974/9 (1974 I, p. 14).
(**f**) S.I. 1973/1624 (1973 III, p. 5070).

(2) Unless the context otherwise requires, references in these regulations to an enactment shall be construed as references to that enactment as amended by any subsequent enactment.

(3) Unless the context otherwise requires, any reference in these regulations to a numbered regulation is a reference to the regulation bearing that number in these regulations, and any reference in a regulation to a numbered paragraph is a reference to the paragraph bearing that number in that regulation.

(4) References in any other regulations to the regulations revoked by these regulations or to any provision thereof shall be construed as references to these regulations or to the corresponding provision hereof, as the case may be.

(5) The rules for the construction of Acts of Parliament contained in the Interpretation Act 1889(a) shall apply for the purposes of the interpretation of these regulations as they apply for the purposes of the interpretation of an Act of Parliament.

Estimates

3.—(1) Subject to paragraph (5), each Regional Health Authority shall submit to the Secretary of State such estimates of such expenditure, income and capital receipts in such form, by such dates, for such financial years and accompanied by such relevant information as he may specify.

(2) The Secretary of State may approve any such estimates with or without modification and subject to such conditions as he thinks fit and may at any time vary such approval or conditions.

(3) Subject to paragraph (5), each Area Health Authority in England shall submit to the Regional Health Authority in whose region it is included, and each Area Health Authority in Wales shall submit to the Secretary of State, such estimates of such expenditure, income and capital receipts in such form, by such dates, for such financial years and accompanied by such relevant information as the Regional Health Authority or the Secretary of State may specify.

(4) Subject to regulation 4, the Regional Health Authority or the Secretary of State may approve any such estimates with or without modification and subject to such conditions as the Regional Health Authority or the Secretary of State thinks fit and may at any time vary such approval or conditions.

(5) A Regional Health Authority shall not be required to submit to the Secretary of State, an Area Health Authority in England shall not be required to submit to a Regional Health Authority, and in Wales shall not be required to submit to the Secretary of State, estimates of payments to be made by a Family Practitioner Committee to persons for the provision of services under Part IV of the Act or estimates of any sums which may be due from such persons in respect of that provision.

Community Health Councils

4. Modification under regulation 3(4) by a Regional Health Authority or the Secretary of State of the estimates of an Area Health Authority may include modification by the incorporation in or addition to those estimates

---

(a) 1889 c. 63.

of the approved estimates of such Community Health Council as they may respectively specify ; and may incorporate arrangements with that Area Health Authority for the payment of sums equal to such expenses of that Community Health Council as are included in such approved estimates.

Standing Financial Instructions

5.—(1) Each Health Authority shall make and may from time to time vary Standing Financial Instructions for the regulation of the conduct of its members and officers in relation to all financial matters with which it is concerned including those relating to the provision of services to a Family Practitioner Committee.

(2) Each Health Authority shall incorporate in such Standing Financial Instructions such requirements as the Secretary of State may direct and may not vary such requirements otherwise than as such directions may provide.

Annual Accounts

6.—(1) Each Health Authority and body of Special Trustees shall transmit its annual accounts (including in the case of a Health Authority accounts in respect of any property held on trust, and in the case of an Area Health Authority the annual accounts of any Family Practitioner Committee which it has established and the annual accounts of any Community Health Council whose approved estimates were the subject of a modification under regulation 4 of the estimates of that Area Health Authority) to the Secretary of State by such date after the end of each financial year and in such form as he, with the approval of the Treasury, may direct and each Area Health Authority and each body of Special Trustees in England shall send a copy of such accounts to the Regional Health Authority in whose region it is included.

(2) Each Health Authority and body of Special Trustees shall maintain such records relating to its accounts and shall comply with such conditions as to certificates relating to such accounts as the Secretary of State may direct.

Audit of accounts

7.—(1) Each Health Authority and body of Special Trustees shall make available to an auditor at all reasonable times such books, accounts, vouchers and other documents of the Health Authority or body and their officers as the auditor may require on giving reasonable notice thereof in writing to the Health Authority or body.

(2) Each Health Authority shall require such member or officer (including an officer whose services are placed at the disposal of a Family Practitioner Committee or Community Health Council), each body of Special Trustees shall require such Special Trustee, and each Family Practitioner Committee shall require such member to attend before the auditor to give such information relating to the affairs of such Authority, body or Committee for the purpose of an audit as he may require on giving reasonable notice thereof in writing to such Authority, body or Committee.

Losses and damages

8. Where a loss occurs or a claim for damages or compensation is made against a Health Authority that Authority shall follow such procedures, maintain such records and make such reports in relation thereto as the Secretary of State may require.

Treasurer

9.—(1) Each Regional Health Authority shall appoint an officer as Regional Treasurer and each Area Health Authority shall appoint an officer as Area Treasurer.

(2) Without prejudice to the generality of the functions of officers of Health Authorities, the duties of the Regional Treasurer and the Area Treasurer shall include the provision of financial advice to the Health Authority and its officers, supervision of the implementation of the Health Authority's financial policies, the design, implementation and supervision of systems of financial control and the preparation and maintenance of such accounts, certificates, estimates, records and reports as the Health Authority may require for the purpose of carrying out its duties under these regulations, and in the case of an Area Treasurer the like provision to the Family Practitioner Committee established by the Health Authority of which he is the Area Treasurer.

Dental Estimates Board

10.—(1) The Dental Estimates Board shall appoint as Finance Officer such person as may be approved by the Secretary of State.

(2) Without prejudice to the generality of the functions of officers of the Dental Estimates Board, the duties of the Finance Officer shall include the provision of financial advice to the Dental Estimates Board or any of its committees, the design, implementation and supervision of systems of financial control, and the preparation and maintenance of such accounts, certificates, estimates, records and reports as the Board may require for the purpose of carrying out its duties under these regulations.

(3) Regulations 3, 5, 6, 7 and 8 shall apply to the Dental Estimates Board as if it were a Regional Health Authority.

Prescription Pricing Authority

11. Regulation 10 shall apply to the Prescription Pricing Authority with the substitution of the words " Prescription Pricing Authority " for the words " Dental Estimates Board ".

Welsh Health Technical Services Organisation

12.—(1) The Welsh Health Technical Services Organisation shall appoint its Chief Administrator as its Chief Financial Officer.

(2) Regulation 9(2) shall apply to the Chief Financial Officer as if he were the Area Treasurer of an Area Health Authority in Wales.

(3) Regulations 3, 5, 6, 7 and 8 shall apply to the Welsh Health Technical Services Organisation as they apply to an Area Health Authority in Wales.

Revocation

13. Part III of the National Health Service (Executive Councils and Dental Estimates Board) Financial Regulations 1969(**a**) and the National Health Service Financial Regulations 1974(**b**) are hereby revoked.

Barbara Castle,

Secretary of State for Social Services.

21st March 1974.

John Morris,

Secretary of State for Wales.

21st March 1974.

We approve these regulations.

T. Pendry,

James Hamilton,

Two of the Lords Commissioners
of Her Majesty's Treasury.

25th March 1974.

EXPLANATORY NOTE

(This Note is not part of the Regulations.)

These Regulations supersede with corrections the National Health Service Financial Regulations 1974 which have not yet come into operation. They provide for the preparation, the submission for approval and the approval of estimates of income and expenditure by Area Health Authorities and Regional Health Authorities. They also provide for any approvals to be subject to conditions and modifications ; require annual accounts to be kept and audited and standing financial instructions to be prepared to govern the conduct of members and staff of those authorities. Provision is also made to apply the Regulations as appropriate to Special Trustees, the Prescription Pricing Authority and the Welsh Health Technical Services Organisation as well as to the Dental Estimates Board. The Health Authorities are also required to appoint a Treasurer whose duties are set out and to keep such accounts of losses or claims for damages as they may be required to do.

(**a**) S.I. 1969/1581 (1969 III, p. 5047).   (**b**) S.I. 1974/282.(1974 I, p.972).

1974 No. 542

VALUE ADDED TAX

The Value Added Tax (General) (No. 1) Order 1974

Made - - - -	*26th March* 1974
Laid before the House of Commons	*26th March* 1974
Coming into Operation	*1st April* 1974

The Treasury, in exercise of the powers conferred on them by sections 12(4) and 43(1) of the Finance Act 1972(**a**) and of all other powers enabling them in that behalf, hereby make the following Order:—

1. This Order may be cited as the Value Added Tax (General) (No. 1) Order 1974 and shall come into operation on 1st April 1974.

2.—(*a*) The Interpretation Act 1889(**b**) shall apply for the interpretation of this Order as it applies for the interpretation of an Act of Parliament.

(*b*) In this Order the words " the Schedule " shall mean Schedule 4 to the Finance Act 1972 as amended(**c**).

3. The Value Added Tax (Food) Order 1973(**d**) is hereby revoked.

4. The following shall be substituted for Group 2 of the Schedule:—

" GROUP 2—WATER
Item No.
1.　　Water other than—
　　　　　(*a*) distilled water, deionised water and water of similar purity; and
　　　　　(*b*) water comprised in the excepted items set out in Group 1.".

5. The following shall be substituted for Group 7 of the Schedule:—

" GROUP 7—FUEL AND POWER
Item No.
1.　　Coal, coke and other solid mineral fuels.
2.　　Coal gas, water gas, producer gases and similar gases.
3.　　Petroleum gases and other gaseous hydrocarbons, whether in a gaseous or liquid state.
4.　　Hydrocarbon oil within the meaning of the Hydrocarbon Oil (Customs & Excise) Act 1971(**e**).
5.　　Electricity, heat and air-conditioning.
6.　　Lubricating oils other than those included in item 4.

(**a**) 1972 c. 41.　　　　　　　　　　　　　　　(**b**) 1889 c. 63.
(**c**) The relevant amending instruments are S.I. 1973/324, 386, 2151 (1973 I, pp. 1128, 1325; III, p. 7429).
(**d**) S.I. 1973/386 (1973 I, p. 1325).　　　　　(**e**) 1971 c. 12.

Notes:

(1) " Lubricating oils " means agents for lubrication which are neither:—

(*a*) solid or semi-solid at a temperature of 60° F, nor

(*b*) gaseous at a temperature of 60° F and under a pressure of one atmosphere.

(2) Items 2 and 3 do not include any gas (within the meaning of section 3 of the Finance Act 1971)(**a**) for use as fuel in road vehicles and on which a duty of excise has been charged or is chargeable.

(3) Item 4 does not include hydrocarbon oil on which a duty of customs or excise has been or is to be charged without relief from, or rebate of, such duty by virtue of the provisions of the Hydrocarbon Oil (Customs & Excise) Act 1971.".

Harold Wilson,
Denis Healey,
Two of the Lords Commissioners
of Her Majesty's Treasury.

26th March 1974.

EXPLANATORY NOTE

(This Note is not part of the Order.)

This Order imposes value added tax at the standard rate on certain food products and drinks, including:—

(*a*) Ice cream, ice lollies, frozen yoghurt, similar frozen products and preparations for making such products;

(*b*) Chocolates, sweets, similar confectionery and chocolate biscuits;

(*c*) Manufactured non-alcoholic beverages, including fruit juices and bottled waters, and products for the preparation of beverages; and cider, perry, etc., not specifically chargeable with customs or excise duty;

(*d*) Potato crisps and similar products, salted and roasted nuts.

The Order also imposes value added tax at the standard rate on all hydrocarbon oils on which revenue duty at the unrebated rate (at present 22½p per gallon), has been or is to be charged, on any gas to be used as road fuel, on petrol substitutes and on power methylated spirits.

(**a**) 1971 c. 68.

STATUTORY INSTRUMENTS

1974 No. 543

COUNTER-INFLATION

The Counter-Inflation (Notification of Increases in Prices and Charges) (Amendment) Order 1974

Made - - -	*26th March* 1974
Laid before Parliament	*26th March* 1974
Coming into Operation	*27th March* 1974

The Secretary of State, in exercise of powers conferred on her by sections 5 and 15 of, and paragraphs 1(1) and (2), 2(4) and 3 of Schedule 2 to and paragraphs 1(1), (2), (4) and (6) and 2(2) of Schedule 3 to, the Counter-Inflation Act 1973(**a**), and of all other powers enabling her in that behalf, hereby makes the following Order:—

1.—(1) This Order may be cited as the Counter-Inflation (Notification of Increases in Prices and Charges) (Amendment) Order 1974 and shall come into operation on 27th March 1974.

(2) The Interpretation Act 1889(**b**) shall apply for the interpretation of this Order as it applies for the interpretation of an Act of Parliament and as if this Order and the Order hereby varied were Acts of Parliament.

2. The Counter-Inflation (Notification of Increases in Prices and Charges) (No. 3) Order 1973(**c**) is hereby varied by the insertion after article 4(5) of the following paragraph—

" (6) A price or charge shall not be treated for the purposes of this Order as an increased price or charge only because it exceeds an earlier price or charge if the increase does not exceed the cash amount of any increase (including a change from a nil amount) in—

(*a*) excise duties, customs duties or car tax on, or on anything comprised in, the goods in question which, whether by virtue of a contract or otherwise, is, or is to be, borne in the particular case by the person intending to implement the increase; or

(*b*) value added tax chargeable by that person on the supply of the goods or services in question."

Shirley Williams,
Secretary of State for Prices and
Consumer Protection.

26th March 1974.

EXPLANATORY NOTE

(*This Note is not part of the Order.*)

This Order provides that an increase in a price or a charge resulting solely from a change in a customs or excise duty, car tax or value added tax need not be notified to the Price Commission before it is implemented, provided it does not exceed the cash amount of the tax increase.

(**a**) 1973 c. 9.　　(**b**) 1889 c. 63.　　(**c**) S.I. 1973/1786 (1973 III, p. 5488).

STATUTORY INSTRUMENTS

1974 No. 544

DENTISTS

The Ancillary Dental Workers (Amendment) Regulations 1974

Laid before Parliament in draft

Made - - - -	*19th March* 1974
Coming into Operation	*1st May* 1974

The General Dental Council in exercise of the powers conferred upon them by section 41 of the Dentists Act 1957(a) and of all other powers enabling them in that behalf hereby make the following regulations:

1. These regulations may be cited as the Ancillary Dental Workers (Amendment) Regulations 1974 and shall come into force on 1st May 1974.

2. The Ancillary Dental Workers Regulations 1968(b) shall be amended as follows:

(1) In paragraphs (1) and (3) of regulation 4 for the word "March" wherever it appears there shall be substituted the word "December".

(2) In paragraph (2) of regulation 4 for the words "fourteenth day of March" there shall be substituted the words "first day of December".

(3) For regulation 6 there shall be substituted the following:
"*Fees Payable for Enrolments, etc.*

6. The following are the fees prescribed by the Council under subsection (7) of section 41 of the Act:

For first enrolment of a name	£2
For the retention of a name under regulation 4 of these regulations	£1·50
For restoration of a name under regulation 5 of these regulations	£1 "

(4) For regulation 23(1)(c) there shall be substituted the following:
"(c) the application to the teeth of such prophylactic materials as the Council may from time to time determine;"

(5) For regulation 28(1)(*e*) there shall be substituted the following:

"(*e*) the application to the teeth of such prophylactic materials as the Council may from time to time determine;"

The Common Seal of the General Dental Council was hereto affixed in the presence of:

Robert Bradlaw,
President.

David Hindley-Smith,
Registrar.

(L.S.)

this 19th day of March 1974.

EXPLANATORY NOTE

(*This Note is not part of the Regulations.*)

These Regulations amend the Ancillary Dental Workers Regulations 1968 as follows:

The fee for the retention of a name in a Roll is increased from £1 to £1·50. The date by which the fee must be paid for the next following year is amended from 31st March to 31st December. The coming into operation of the amending Regulations has been postponed until 1st May 1974, so that the fee to be paid for retention in the Rolls for the period 31st March to 31st December 1974 is £1.

The definition of the material which may be applied to the teeth by dental hygienists and dental auxiliaries for the prevention of dental disease has been widened to permit the use of such prophylactic materials as the General Dental Council may from time to time determine.

The Regulations were approved in draft:—

(*a*) by the Privy Council on the 9th day of November 1973.

(*b*) by a resolution of the House of Lords on the 8th day of February 1974·

(*c*) by a resolution of the House of Commons on the 8th day of February 1974.

STATUTORY INSTRUMENTS

1974 No. 545

NORTHERN IRELAND

The Northern Ireland Assembly (Bye-Elections) Order 1974

Made - - -	25*th March* 1974
Laid before Parliament	2*nd April* 1974
Coming into Operation	24*th April* 1974

In exercise of the powers conferred on me by section 2(5) of the Northern Ireland Assembly Act 1973(a) and section 29 of the Northern Ireland Constitution Act 1973(b) and of all other powers enabling me in that behalf, I hereby make the following Order:—

Citation and commencement

1. This Order may be cited as the Northern Ireland Assembly (Bye-Elections) Order 1974 and shall come into operation on 24th April 1974.

Interpretation

2.—(1) In this Order—

"the Assembly" means the Northern Ireland Assembly;

"bye-election" means an election to fill one or more casual vacancies in the Assembly;

"the principal Act" means the Electoral Law Act (Northern Ireland) 1962(c);

"the principal Order" means the Northern Ireland Assembly (Election) Order 1973(d);

and any expression used in this Order and in the principal Act and the principal Order has the same meaning as in that Act and Order.

(2) The Interpretation Act (Northern Ireland) 1954(e) shall apply to Article 1 and the following provisions of this Order as it applies to a Measure of the Assembly.

Bye-elections

3.—(1) As soon as possible after the presiding officer informs the Assembly, in accordance with the provisions of section 26(7) of the Northern Ireland Constitution Act 1973 that a seat has become vacant or, where the presiding officer has so informed the Assembly before the date of the coming into operation of this Order, as soon as possible after that date, the Clerk to the Assembly shall send written notification of the vacancy to the Secretary of State.

(2) Within a period of ninety days from the day on which he receives a notification under paragraph (1), the Secretary of State shall, having consulted such persons (if any) as he considers appropriate, inform the Chief Electoral

(a) 1973 c. 17.   (b) 1973 c. 36.   (c) 1962 c. 14 (N.I.).
(d) S.I. 1973/890 (1973 II, p. 2704).   (e) 1954 c. 33 (N.I.).

Officer of the vacancy and a bye-election to fill the vacancy shall then be conducted in accordance with the time-table contained in Schedule 1 to this Order and with the rules contained in Parts II to VI of Schedule 2 to the principal Order but with the amendments specified in Schedule 2 to this Order.

(3) The provisions of the principal Act as adapted and applied by Article 3 of and Schedule 1 to the principal Order to the first election to the Assembly and to persons entitled to vote and voting at that election shall apply in like manner to a bye-election held in accordance with paragraph (2) and to persons entitled to vote and voting at a bye-election.

(4) Articles 5 and 6 of the principal Order shall apply to a bye-election in like manner as they applied to the first election to the Assembly.

(5) The forms contained in Schedule 3 to the principal Order shall, with any necessary adaptation, be used at a bye-election.

Death of a candidate

4.—(1) If at any time before the commencement of the poll (or where no poll is to be taken, before the declaration of the result of the election) at a bye-election proof is given to the satisfaction of the returning officer of the death of a candidate standing validly nominated, the returning officer—

(*a*) if notice of the poll has been given, shall forthwith publicly countermand that notice;

(*b*) whether or not notice of the poll has been given, shall forthwith publish a notice stating that all notices given and acts done in connection with the election (other than the nomination of any surviving candidates) are void and of no effect, and that a fresh election will be held;

(*c*) shall, taking all necessary precautions to ensure the secrecy of the ballot, destroy any postal ballot papers received by him from voters at the election;

and the principal Order and this Order shall have effect in relation to such fresh election as if it were a bye-election to fill a vacancy notified to the Chief Electoral Officer under Rule 3 of this Order on the day on which proof of the death was given to the returning officer.

(2) Where a fresh election is to be held under paragraph (1)—

(*a*) any surviving candidates standing validly nominated for the countermanded election shall be deemed to have been duly nominated for such fresh election;

(*b*) the countermanded election and the fresh election shall be regarded as separate elections for the purposes of sections 22, 40 and 42 of the principal Act;

(*c*) the references in sections 41, 43 and 46 of the principal Act to the day on which the result of the election is declared shall, in relation to the countermanded election, be construed as the day on which a notice is published under paragraph (1)(*b*);

(*d*) for the purposes of Part IX of the principal Act, the countermanded election and the fresh election shall be regarded as one election.

Postal voting at bye-elections

5.—(1) A person entitled to vote at a bye-election may vote by post if he—

(*a*) obtains from the returning officer and completes and has duly certified an application in the form set out in Schedule 3 and returns it to the returning officer to reach him not later than the twelfth day before the day of the poll; and

(b) gives an address in the United Kingdom to which a ballot paper may be sent.

(2) Where the returning officer receives an application duly made under paragraph (1) by a person entitled to vote at a bye-election and that person gives an address within the United Kingdom to which a ballot paper may be sent, the returning officer shall place that person's name on the postal voting list for that bye-election.

M. Rees,
One of Her Majesty's Principal
Secretaries of State.

Northern Ireland Office.
25th March 1974.

SCHEDULE 1 — Article 3(2)

TIME-TABLE FOR BYE-ELECTION TO FILL CASUAL VACANCY
IN NORTHERN IRELAND ASSEMBLY

Proceeding	Time fixed or allowed
1. Publication of notice of election.	Within two days after the day on which the Chief Electoral Officer is informed of the vacancy by the Secretary of State.
2. Delivery of nomination papers.	Subject to Rule 12 of Schedule 2 to the Northern Ireland Assembly (Election) Order 1973 during the period between the hours of 10 in the morning and 5 in the evening of such day, as the Chief Electoral Officer shall fix, not being later than 28 days after the day on which the Chief Electoral Officer is informed of the vacancy by the Secretary of State.
3. Delivery of withdrawal of candidature.	Within the period allowed for proceeding 2 above.
4. The making of objections to nomination papers.	Within the time specified in Rule 11(11) of Schedule 2 to the Northern Ireland Assembly (Election) Order 1973.
5. Notice to candidates (a) of valid nomination; (b) of invalid nomination.	As soon as practicable after the expiration of the time allowed for making objections to nomination papers.
6. Publication of statement of candidates validly nominated.	As soon as practicable after the time allowed for proceeding 4 above has expired and the validity of all nomination papers has been determined.
7. Despatch of Polling Information Cards.	As soon as possible after the time allowed for proceedings 4 or 5 and not later than the day following the delivery of nomination papers.
8. Notice of poll.	Not later than the fifth day before polling day.
9. Poll.	Between the hours of 8 a.m. and 8 p.m. on the fourteenth day after nomination day.

SCHEDULE 2 — Article 3(2)

AMENDMENTS OF SCHEDULE 2 TO PRINCIPAL ORDER IN ITS
APPLICATION TO BYE-ELECTIONS

1. Rules 15, 21(3) and 22 shall not apply.

2. In rule 43(1) in sub-paragraphs (a)(ii) and (b)(ii) the words "or any other constituency" shall be omitted.

3. Where there is only one vacancy to be filled at a bye-election—

   (a) rule 56 shall not apply; and

   (b) in rule 57(1) for the words from the beginning to the words "Rule 56" there shall be substituted the words "Where after the first stage has been completed in accordance with Rule 54.".

Article 5(1)   **SCHEDULE 3**
                   FORM PVL 1

NORTHERN IRELAND ASSEMBLY BYE-ELECTION
CONSTITUENCY OF...........................

This Form, completed and certified, must be posted to reach the
Returning Officer not later than....................

APPLICATION TO VOTE BY POST

I ....
Surname (Block letters)

....
Other Names (Block letters)

am registered as an elector at the following address:

....
(Block letters in full)

....

Where the address is in a rural area state the townland......................

Please state Polling District and number on register (if known)...............

* I apply to vote by post at the Election to be held on ....

*(If an applicant has moved from his address
as stated above he must indicate below his
full postal address in the United Kingdom
to which the Ballot Paper is to be sent.)*

Address ....
(Block letters)

....

* I apply to vote by post as proxy for the elector named overleaf.

....
(Block letters)

Signature (or mark) .... Date..................
* Delete whichever is inapplicable.

CERTIFICATION   I certify that the above applicant, who has satisfied me as
to his identity, has signed (or marked) the application in my
presence.

Signature..

Address ....

....

Telephone Number (Day) ....

Telephone Number (Night) ....

Date ....

                   (See notes overleaf)

Tick your qualification and add any additional information requested

☐ Justice of the Peace

☐ Minister of Religion

☐ Member of a Police Force (Sergeant or above)

☐ Established Civil Servant in the Civil Service of the United Kingdom or of Northern Ireland (specify the Department)

....

☐ Member of the Houses of Parliament of the United Kingdom

☐ Member of the Northern Ireland Assembly

☐ Officer employed by a Local Authority or Public Authority in Northern Ireland (specify the Authority)

....

☐ Teacher or Lecturer employed in a school, college or institution of further education (specify school etc.)

....

☐ Commissioned officer in H.M. Forces

TO BE COMPLETED ONLY WHERE APPLICANT IS THE APPOINTED PROXY FOR A QUALIFIED REGISTERED ELECTOR.

Name of Elector ....

Qualifying Address on Register ....

Polling District (if known) ....

Electoral Number on Register ....

NOTES

1. This application when completed must be returned by post in the envelope provided to the office of the Returning Officer so as to reach his office NOT LATER THAN

2. This application cannot be allowed if the applicant is not included in the Register of Electors as a voter entitled to vote at an election to the Northern Ireland Assembly.

3. Postal ballot papers can be issued only to qualified applicants with an address in the United Kingdom.

4. All applicants must submit their applications to the Deputy Returning Officer appointed for the constituency in which the bye-election is being held.
The Deputy Returning Officer's Principal Office is:—

EXPLANATORY NOTE

(This Note is not part of the Order.)

This Order makes provision for the holding of bye-elections in relation to casual vacancies occurring amongst the members of the Northern Ireland Assembly.

1974 No. 548 (S.48)

NATIONAL HEALTH SERVICE, SCOTLAND

The National Health Service (Supply of Goods at Clinics) (Scotland) Regulations 1974

Made – – –	*22nd March* 1974
Laid before Parliament	*29th March* 1974
Coming into Operation	*1st April* 1974

In exercise of the powers conferred on me by sections 5(2) and 8(2) of the National Health Service (Scotland) Act 1972(a), and of all other powers enabling me in that behalf, I hereby make the following regulations:—

Citation and commencement

1. These regulations may be cited as the National Health Service (Supply of Goods at Clinics) (Scotland) Regulations 1974, and shall come into operation on 1st April 1974.

Interpretation

2.—(1) In this order unless the context otherwise requires—

"cost price" means the actual cost of an article payable by a Health Board after any deductions in respect of discount or rebate but including any transport or delivery charges due to the supplier by that Health Board in respect of the article;

"enactment" includes a provision in a statutory instrument;

"family planning clinic" means a clinic at which services are provided under section 8 of the National Health Service (Scotland) Act 1972 and includes such a clinic situated in a health centre or a hospital;

"Health Board" means a board constituted under section 13 of the National Health Service (Scotland) Act 1972;

"hospital" has the meaning assigned to it by section 4(3) of the National Health Service (Scotland) Act 1972;

"local health authority" has the meaning assigned to it by section 20(1) of the National Health Service (Scotland) Act 1947(b);

"maternity or child health clinic" means such a clinic which, before 1st April 1974, was the responsibility of a local health authority and includes such a clinic situated in a health centre or a hospital.

(2) In these regulations, unless the context otherwise requires, references to any enactment shall be construed as references to that enactment as amended or re-enacted by any subsequent enactment.

(a) 1972 c. 58.   (b) 1947 c. 27.

(3) The Interpretation Act 1889(a) shall apply for the interpretation of these regulations as it applies for the interpretation of an Act of Parliament.

Supply of goods at maternity or child health clinics

3. Without prejudice to regulation 4 of these regulations or to the provisions of the Welfare Food Order 1971(b), a Health Board shall on and after 1st April 1974 make and recover for the supply at a clinic of goods appropriate to the promotion of the health of nursing and expectant mothers and young children (not being a drug, a medicine or an appliance of a type normally supplied), charges equal to the cost price of each article to the Health Board plus a sum in respect of handling charges of ten per cent of the cost price; but so that such charge shall be calculated to the nearest half penny.

Exemption from charge

4. Where before 1st April 1974, having regard to the means of those concerned a local health authority exempted from its charges under section 22(2) of the National Health Service (Scotland) Act 1947 proprietary brands of milk for babies supplied in respect of a child at any clinic, the Health Board whose responsibility that clinic becomes on 1st April 1974 shall likewise exempt the supply of such milk for that child from the charges required to be made and recovered under these regulations.

Supply of contraceptive substances and appliances

5. A Health Board shall make and recover, for the supply at or through a family planning clinic of contraceptive substances or appliances otherwise than following consultation with and advice from a doctor or nurse employed by the Board or on prescription, charges equal to the cost price of each article to the Health Board plus a sum in respect of handling charges of ten per cent of the cost price; but so that such charge shall be calculated to the nearest half penny.

Revocations

6.—(1) The National Health Service (Local Health Authority Charges) (Scotland) Regulations 1948(c) and the National Health Service (Local Health Authority Charges) (Scotland) Amendment Regulations 1951(d) are hereby revoked.

(2) Section 38 of the Interpretation Act 1889 shall apply as if these regulations were an Act of Parliament and as if the regulations revoked by paragraph (1) above were Acts of Parliament repealed by an Act of Parliament.

William Ross,

One of Her Majesty's Principal Secretaries of State.

St. Andrew's House,
Edinburgh.
22nd March 1974.

(a) 1889 c. 63.
(c) S.I. 1948/1677 (Rev. XV, p. 1030: 1948 I, p. 2436).
(b) S.I. 1971/457 (1971 I, p. 1358).
(d) S.I. 1951/1464 (1951 I. p. 1426).

EXPLANATORY NOTE

(This Note is not part of the Regulations.)

These Regulations provide that where goods suitable for expectant or nursing mothers and young children are sold in maternity or child welfare clinics, or contraceptive substances or appliances are sold in family planning clinics, the charge made by the Health Board is normally to be the cost price plus a handling charge of 10 per cent. The Regulations make provision for continued exemption from charges in respect of the supply of proprietary brands of milk for babies where a free supply was being provided before 1st April 1974.

STATUTORY INSTRUMENTS

1974 No. 549 (S. 49)

NATIONAL HEALTH SERVICE, SCOTLAND

The National Health Service (Professions Supplementary to Medicine) (Scotland) Regulations 1974

Made - - -	*18th March* 1974
Laid before Parliament	*2nd April* 1974
Coming into Operation	*3rd April* 1974

In exercise of the powers conferred on me by paragraph 8 of Part I of Schedule 1 to the National Health Service (Scotland) Act 1972(a) and of all other powers enabling me in that behalf, I hereby make the following regulations:—

Citation and commencement

1. These regulations may be cited as the National Health Service (Professions Supplementary to Medicine) (Scotland) Regulations 1974 and shall come into operation on 3rd April 1974.

Interpretation

2.—(1) In these regulations, "Health Board" means a board constituted under section 13 of the National Health Service (Scotland) Act 1972.

(2) For the purposes of these regulations a person is registered in respect of a profession if his name is on the register maintained under the Professions Supplementary to Medicine Act 1960(b) by the Board for that profession.

(3) Unless the context otherwise requires, references in these regulations to any enactment shall be construed as references to that enactment as amended or re-enacted by any subsequent enactment.

(4) The Interpretation Act 1889(c) shall apply for the interpretation of these regulations as it applies for the interpretation of an Act of Parliament.

(a) 1972 c. 58.   (b) 1960 c. 66.   (c) 1889 c. 63.

Employment of officers

3. No person shall be employed as an officer of a Health Board in the capacity of chiropodist, dietitian, medical laboratory technician, occupational therapist, orthoptist, physiotherapist, radiographer or remedial gymnast, unless:—

　(*a*) he is registered in respect of the profession appropriate to the work for which he is employed; or

　(*b*) immediately before 1st April 1974 he was an officer employed within the meaning of regulation 2 of the National Health Service (Professions Supplementary to Medicine) (Scotland) Regulations 1964(**a**) as amended (**b**) in the capacity of chiropodist, dietitian, medical laboratory technician, occupational therapist, orthoptist, physiotherapist, radiographer or remedial gymnast.

Revocation

4.—(1) The National Health Service (Professions Supplementary to Medicine) (Scotland) Regulations 1964 and the National Health Service (Professions Supplementary to Medicine) (Scotland) (Amendment) Regulations 1968 are hereby revoked.

(2) Section 38 of the Interpretation Act 1889 shall apply as if these regulations were an Act of Parliament and as if the regulations revoked by these regulations were Acts of Parliament repealed by an Act of Parliament.

William Ross,
One of Her Majesty's Principal
Secretaries of State.

St Andrew's House,
Edinburgh.

18th March 1974.

(**a**) S.I. 1964/995 (1964 II, p. 2233).　　(**b**) S.I. 1968/279 (1968 I, p. 808).

EXPLANATORY NOTE

(This Note is not part of the Regulations.)

These Regulations prohibit the employment for the purpose of providing services under the national health service, as reorganised by the National Health Service (Scotland) Act 1972, of chiropodists, dietitians, medical laboratory technicians, occupational therapists, orthoptists, physiotherapists, radiographers or remedial gymnasts unless they are registered under the Professions Supplementary to Medicine Act 1960 or were employed in such capacity immediately before 1st April 1974 in the national health service.

STATUTORY INSTRUMENTS

1974 No. 550

LOCAL GOVERNMENT, ENGLAND AND WALES

The Rate Support Grant Order 1974

Made - - - -	14*th March* 1974
Laid before the House of Commons	14*th March* 1974
Coming into Operation	26*th March* 1974

The Secretary of State for the Environment, in exercise of the powers conferred upon him by section 3(1) of the Local Government Act 1974(a), and of all other powers enabling him in that behalf, with the consent of the Treasury and after consultation with the associations of local authorities appearing to him to be concerned and the local authority with whom consultation appeared to him to be desirable, hereby makes the following order:—

Title and commencement

1. This order may be cited as the Rate Support Grant Order 1974 and shall come into operation on the day following the day on which it is approved by a resolution of the Commons House of Parliament.

Interpretation

2.—(1) In this order—

"the Act" means the Local Government Act 1974;

"education unit" and "personal social services unit" bear the respective meanings ascribed to them by the Rate Support Grant Regulations 1974(b); and

"Wales" means the area consisting of the counties established by section 20 of the Local Government Act 1972(c) (new local government areas in Wales), and England does not include any area included in any of those counties.

(2) The Interpretation Act 1889(d) shall apply for the interpretation of this order as it applies for the interpretation of an Act of Parliament.

Rate support grants for 1974–5

3. For the purposes of rate support grants for the year 1974–5, this order fixes and prescribes—

(1) As the estimated aggregate of the rate support

grants	£3,076,000,000
divided as follows—	
the aggregate amount of the needs element	£1,907,000,000
the aggregate amount of the domestic element	£446,000,000
the estimated aggregate amount of the resources element	£723,000,000

(a) 1974 c. 7.   (b) S.I. 1974/428 (1974 I, p.1384).

(c) 1972 c. 70.   (d) 1889 c. 63.

(2) As the aggregate amount of supplementary grants under section 7 of the Act (supplementary grants towards expenditure with respect to National Parks) £1,400,000

(3) With respect to the needs element—as the sum to be multiplied by the population of a local authority's area for the purposes of paragraph 1(*a*) of Schedule 2 to the Act ... £16·62

and the additional factors with respect to which additional amounts are to be payable by virtue of paragraph 1(*b*) of that Schedule and the manner in which those amounts are to be determined shall be those set out in the Schedule to this order;

(4) In pursuance of paragraph 5 of Schedule 2 to the Act—

As the amount in the pound for the purposes of section 48 of the General Rate Act 1967(**a**) (reduction of rates on dwellings by reference to domestic element)—
In relation to a rating area in England... 13p
In relation to a rating area in Wales ... 33.5p

(5) In pursuance of paragraph 8 of Schedule 2 to the Act—

As the national standard rateable value per head of population £154

Apportionment of supplementary grants (*National Parks*)

4.—(1) The proportion of the aggregate amount of supplementary grants under section 7 of the Act payable for the year to a county council shall be determined by—

(*a*) multiplying the aggregate amount of supplementary grants as prescribed by article 3(2) of this order by $\frac{x}{X}$, where—

x is the amount of the estimated expenditure of the county council or councils liable for meeting the expenses incurred with respect to a particular National Park and

X is the aggregate amount of the estimated expenditure of county councils incurred with respect to all National Parks,

in order to ascertain the proportion of the aggregate amount referable to that particular National Park and

(*b*) allocating that proportion to the county council or councils responsible for meeting the expenses incurred with respect to that National Park and, where there is more than one such council, dividing it between them in the same manner as the liability for meeting those expenses is divided.

(2) In this article any reference to estimated expenditure refers to so much of the estimated expenditure of a council with respect to National Parks as the Secretary of State, in exercise of his powers under section 7(3) of the Act, determines to be appropriate to be taken into account for purposes of that section.

(**a**) 1967 c. 9.

SCHEDULE

Needs Element—Additional Factors

Additional factor	Manner of determining additional amount

1. In relation to the council of a non-metropolitan county, a metropolitan district or a London borough, the Common Council of the City of London or the Council of the Isles of Scilly—

   (*a*) The number of education units in excess of 200 per 1000 of the population of their area—   Multiplying that number by £112·95.

   (*b*) The acreage of their area in excess of 1·5 per head of the population of their area—   Multiplying that acreage by—
      (*a*) £1·22 if it exceeds 1·5 but does not exceed 3 or
      (*b*) £3·12 if it exceeds 3.

   (*c*) The number by which the population on 30th June 1972 fell short of the population on 30th June 1962 of the area which constitutes their area on 1st April 1974—   Multiplying that number by £44·68.

   (*d*) The number of personal social services units in their area—   Multiplying that number by £600·57.

2. In relation to the county council of Berkshire, Buckinghamshire, Essex, Hertfordshire, Kent or Surrey—

   The number of the population of their area—   Multiplying that number by £5·99.

3. In relation to the county council of Bedfordshire, East Sussex, Hampshire, Isle of Wight, Oxfordshire or West Sussex—

   The number of the population of their area—   Multiplying that number by £1·04.

4. In relation to the county council of Hereford and Worcester, Salop, Staffordshire or Warwickshire—

   The number of the population of their area—   Multiplying that number by £1·44.

5. In relation to a London borough council or the Common Council of the City of London—

   The aggregate of the amounts payable to that council by virtue of article 3(3) above and the preceding provisions of this Schedule—   Multiplying that aggregate by 3%.

Anthony Crosland,
Secretary of State for the
Environment.

14th March 1974.

We consent.

T. Pendry,
Donald R. Coleman,
Two of the Lords Commissioners
of Her Majesty's Treasury.

14th March 1974.

EXPLANATORY NOTE

(*This Note is not part of the Order.*)

This Order, which came into operation on 26th March 1974, fixes and prescribes for the year 1974–5—

(1) The aggregate amount of the rate support grants payable to local authorities in England and Wales under Part I of the Local Government Act 1974;

(2) The division of this amount between the needs element, the resources element and the domestic element;

(3) The amount of the supplementary grants to county councils towards expenditure on national parks;

(4) The amount by which rates on dwelling-houses are to be reduced in each rating area to take account of the domestic element;

(5) Various matters which have to be, or may be, prescribed for purposes of Part I of or Schedule 2 to the Local Government Act 1974 in connection with rate support grants.

The Order is complemented by the Rate Support Grant Regulations 1974, which prescribe how calculations are to be made for various purposes of the Order.

STATUTORY INSTRUMENTS

1974 No. 551

POLICE

The Transfer of Police Officers Order 1974

Made - - -	*22nd March* 1974
Laid before Parliament	*29th March* 1974
Coming into Operation	*1st April* 1974

In exercise of the powers conferred on me by sections 254 and 255 of the Local Government Act 1972 (**a**), I hereby make the following Order:—

1. This Order may be cited as the Transfer of Police Officers Order 1974 and shall come into operation on 1st April 1974.

2.—(1) In this Order, except where the context otherwise requires, the following expressions have the following meanings respectively, that is to say:—

"existing" in relation to a police force or police area, means that force or area as it existed immediately before the passing of the Local Government Act 1972;

"new" in relation to a police area, means that area as established on 1st April 1974;

"police cadet" means a police cadet appointed, or deemed to have been appointed, under Part I of the Police Act 1964 (**b**) and any reference to a police cadet of a force is a reference to a police cadet undergoing training with a view to becoming a member of that force;

"special constable" means a special constable appointed, or deemed to have been appointed, for a police area and any reference to appointment for a police area shall be construed accordingly.

(2) The Interpretation Act 1889 (**c**) shall apply for the interpretation of this Order as it applies for the interpretation of an Act of Parliament.

3. A member of an existing police force, other than a chief constable, or a police cadet undergoing training with a view to becoming a member of that police force, who falls within a category of members or cadets described in column 1 of Schedule 1 to this Order shall, on 1st April 1974, become a member, or, as the case may be, a police cadet undergoing training with a view to becoming a member, of the police force for the new police area specified opposite thereto in column 2 of the said Schedule 1.

4. A special constable falling within a category of special constables described in column 1 of Schedule 2 to this Order shall, on 1st April 1974, become a special constable for the new police area specified opposite thereto in column 2 of the said Schedule 2.

(**a**) 1972 c. 70   (**b**) 1964 c. 48.   (**c**) 1889 c. 63.

5. Where immediately before 1st April 1974 by virtue of—

(a) section 43(1)(a) of the Police Act 1964, or

(b) section 2 of the Police (Overseas Service) Act 1945 (**a**), or

(c) section 2(1)(b) of the Police Act 1969 (**b**),

a person has a right of reversion to an existing police force, that section shall apply to him in relation to any period after 31st March 1974 as if for any reference to the police force to which he was entitled to revert there were substituted a reference to the police force for the new police area designated by the police authority for the new police area, or by agreement between the police authorities for the new police areas, as the case may be, specified in column 2 of Schedule 3 to this Order opposite to the existing police force in column 1 of the said Schedule 3 to which he is entitled to revert immediately before 1st April 1974; and references in that section to the appropriate authority shall be construed accordingly.

6.—(1) Any agreement between the police authorities as to the transfer of persons under the provisions of Article 3 of, and Schedule 1 to, this Order, or of Article 4 of, and Schedule 2 to, this Order, or as to the designation of a police force for a new police area to which a person is entitled to revert under the provisions of Article 5 of, and Schedule 3 to, this Order shall be subject to the approval of the Secretary of State.

(2) In default of such agreement so approved the matters requiring such agreement shall be determined by the Secretary of State.

7.—(1) All members of an existing police force who are transferred under the provisions of Article 3 of, and Schedule 1 to, this Order shall be deemed to have been duly appointed as members of the police force for the new police area to which they are transferred, and to have been duly attested as such, and shall hold in that force the same ranks respectively as they held immediately before 1st April 1974.

(2) All special constables who are transferred under the provisions of Article 4 of, and Schedule 2 to, this Order shall be deemed to have been appointed as special constables for the new police area to which they are transferred, and to have been duly attested as such.

(3) All police cadets who are transferred under the provisions of Article 3 of, and Schedule 1 to, this Order shall be deemed to have been appointed under Part I of the Police Act 1964 to undergo training with a view to becoming members of the police force for the new police area to which they are transferred.

8. Where immediately before 1st April 1974 a member of an existing police force who is transferred under the provisions of Article 3 of, and Schedule 1 to, this Order is entitled to appeal to the Secretary of State under the provisions of section 37 of the Police Act 1964 or where any such member has appealed to the Secretary of State under those provisions before that date but the appeal has not been determined, then, unless the Secretary of State otherwise directs, the disciplinary authority in respect of offences against discipline committed by members of the police force for the new police area to which he is transferred shall, on and after 1st April 1974, be the respondent for the purpose of the appeal.

(**a**) 1945 c. 17 (9 & 10 Geo. 6). (**b**) 1969 c. 63.

9.—(1) Any register, or the appropriate part of any register, kept in pursuance of any enactment by the chief constable of an existing police force members of which are transferred under the provisions of Article 3 of, and Schedule 1 to, this Order shall be transferred by him as soon as may be after 1st April 1974 in accordance with the provisions of paragraph (2) of this Article, and thereafter shall be deemed to form part of the register kept by the chief constable to whom it is transferred.

(2) (*a*) If all the members of an existing police force are transferred to the police force for a new police area, the register shall be transferred to the chief constable of that new police area.

(*b*) If members of an existing police force are transferred to the police forces for two or more new police areas, the register shall be transferred to the chief constable of any one of those new police areas selected by the first mentioned chief constable.

(*c*) In the case of a register transferred under the provisions of paragraph (b) above, the chief constable of a new police area to whom the register is not transferred may request the chief constable to whom it is transferred to transfer to him the part of the register pertaining to his police area.

(*d*) Any dispute concerning the transfer of any register or part thereof may be resolved by the Secretary of State whose determination shall be final.

10. Subject to the foregoing provisions of this Order, anything done before 1st April 1974 by, to or before the chief constable or police authority of an existing police area shall, as from 1st April 1974, be treated as having been done by, to or before the police authority or chief constable for the appropriate new police area.

Roy Jenkins,
One of Her Majesty's Principal
Secretaries of State.

Home Office,
  Whitehall.
22nd March 1974.

SCHEDULE 1

MEMBERS OF POLICE FORCES
AND POLICE CADETS

1 Existing police forces	2 New police areas
1. (a) All members and police cadets of the existing Somerset and Bath constabulary;	1. Avon and Somerset
(b) All members and police cadets of the existing Bristol constabulary;	
(c) Such members and police cadets (if any) of the existing Gloucestershire constabulary as may be agreed between the police authorities for the new police areas of Avon and Somerset and of Gloucestershire.	
2. All members and police cadets of the existing Bedfordshire and Luton constabulary.	2. Bedfordshire
3. All members and police cadets of the existing Mid-Anglia constabulary.	3. Cambridgeshire
4. (a) All members and police cadets of the existing Cheshire constabulary, except those becoming members or police cadets of the police forces for the new police areas of Derbyshire, Greater Manchester and Merseyside;	4. Cheshire
(b) Such members and police cadets (if any) of the existing Lancashire constabulary as may be agreed between the police authorities for the new police areas of Cheshire, Cumbria, Greater Manchester, Lancashire and Merseyside.	
5. (a) All members and police cadets of the existing Teesside police force;	5. Cleveland
(b) Such members and police cadets (if any) of the existing Durham constabulary as may be agreed between the police authorities for the new police areas of Cleveland and Durham;	
(c) Such members and police cadets (if any) of the existing York and North-East Yorkshire police force as may be agreed between the police authorities for the new police areas of Cleveland, Durham, Humberside and North Yorkshire.	
6. (a) All members and police cadets of the existing Cumbria constabulary;	6. Cumbria
(b) Such members and police cadets (if any) of the existing Lancashire constabulary as may be agreed between the police authorities for the new police areas of Cheshire, Cumbria, Greater Manchester, Lancashire and Merseyside;	
(c) Such members and police cadets (if any) of the existing West Yorkshire constabulary as may be agreed between the police authorities for the new police areas of Cumbria, Greater Manchester, Humberside, Lancashire, North Yorkshire, South Yorkshire and West Yorkshire.	

1 Existing police forces	2 New police areas
7. (a) All members and police cadets of the existing Derby county and borough constabulary; (b) Such members and police cadets (if any) of the existing Cheshire constabulary as may be agreed between the police authorities for the new police areas of Cheshire and Derbyshire.	7. Derbyshire
8. All members and police cadets of the existing Devon and Cornwall constabulary.	8. Devon and Cornwall
9. (a) All members and police cadets of the existing Dorset and Bournemouth constabulary; (b) Such members and police cadets (if any) of the existing Hampshire constabulary as may be agreed between the police authorities for the new police areas of Dorset and Hampshire.	9. Dorset
10. (a) All members and police cadets of the existing Durham constabulary, except those becoming members or police cadets of the police forces for the new police police areas of Cleveland and Northumbria; (b) Such members and police cadets (if any) of the existing York and North-East Yorkshire police force as may be agreed between the police authorities for the new police areas of Cleveland, Durham, Humberside and North Yorkshire.	10. Durham
11. All members and police cadets of the existing Dyfed-Powys constabulary, except those becoming members or police cadets of the police forces for the new police areas of Gwent and South Wales.	11. Dyfed-Powys
12. All members and police cadets of the existing Essex and Southend-on-Sea joint constabulary.	12. Essex
13. All members and police cadets of the existing Gloucestershire constabulary, except those becoming members or police cadets of the police force for the new police area of Avon and Somerset.	13. Gloucestershire
14. (a) All members and police cadets of the existing Manchester and Salford police force; (b) Such members and police cadets (if any) of the existing Cheshire constabulary as may be agreed between the police authorities for the new police areas of Cheshire and Greater Manchester; (c) Such members and police cadets (if any) of the existing Lancashire constabulary as may be agreed between the police authorities for the new police areas of Cheshire, Cumbria, Greater Manchester, Lancashire and Merseyside; (d) Such members and police cadets (if any) of the existing West Yorkshire constabulary as may be agreed between the police authorities for the	14. Greater Manchester

1 Existing police forces	2 New police areas
new police areas of Cumbria, Greater Manchester, Humberside, Lancashire, North Yorkshire, South Yorkshire and West Yorkshire.	
15. (*a*) All members and police cadets of the existing Gwent constabulary, except those becoming members or police cadets of the police force for the new police area of South Wales; (*b*) Such members and police cadets (if any) of the existing Dyfed-Powys constabulary as may be agreed between the police authorities for the new police areas of Dyfed-Powys and Gwent.	15. Gwent
16. All members and police cadets of the existing Hampshire constabulary, except those becoming members or police cadets of the police force for the new police area of Dorset.	16. Hampshire
17. All members and police cadets of the existing Hertfordshire constabulary.	17. Hertfordshire
18. (*a*) All members and police cadets of the existing Kingston-upon-Hull police force; (*b*) Such members and police cadets (if any) of the existing York and North-East Yorkshire police force as may be agreed between the police authorities for the new police areas of Cleveland, Durham, Humberside and North Yorkshire; (*c*) Such members and police cadets (if any) of the existing Lincolnshire constabulary as may be agreed between the police authorities for the new police areas of Humberside and Lincolnshire; (*d*) Such members and police cadets (if any) of the existing West Yorkshire constabulary as may be agreed between the police authorities for the new police areas of Cumbria, Greater Manchester, Humberside, Lancashire, North Yorkshire, South Yorkshire and West Yorkshire.	18. Humberside
19. All members and police cadets of the existing Kent police force.	19. Kent
20. (*a*) All members and police cadets of the existing Lancashire constabulary, except those becoming members or police cadets of the police forces for the new police areas of Cheshire, Cumbria, Greater Manchester and Merseyside; (*b*) Such members and police cadets (if any) of the existing West Yorkshire constabulary as may be agreed between the police authorities for the new police areas of Cumbria, Greater Manchester, Humberside, Lancashire, North Yorkshire, South Yorkshire and West Yorkshire.	20. Lancashire
21. All members and police cadets of the existing Leicester and Rutland constabulary.	21. Leicestershire

1 Existing police forces	2 New police areas
22. All members and police cadets of the existing Lincolnshire constabulary, except those becoming members or police cadets of the police force for the new police area of Humberside.	22. Lincolnshire
23. (a) All members and police cadets of the existing Liverpool and Bootle constabulary; (b) Such members and police cadets (if any) of the existing Cheshire constabulary as may be agreed between the police authorities for the new police areas of Cheshire and Merseyside; (c) Such members and police cadets (if any) of the existing Lancashire constabulary as may be agreed between the police authorities for the new police areas of Cheshire, Cumbria, Greater Manchester, Lancashire and Merseyside.	23. Merseyside
24. (a) All members and police cadets of the existing Norfolk joint police; (b) Such members and police cadets (if any) of the existing Suffolk constabulary as may be agreed between the police authorities for the new police areas of Norfolk and Suffolk.	24. Norfolk
25. All members and police cadets of the existing Gwynedd constabulary.	25. North Wales
26. (a) All members and police cadets of the existing York and North-East Yorkshire police, except those becoming members or police cadets of the police forces for the new police areas of Cleveland, Durham and Humberside; (b) Such members and police cadets (if any) of the existing West Yorkshire constabulary as may be agreed between the police authorities for the new police areas of Cumbria, Greater Manchester, Humberside, Lancashire, North Yorkshire, South Yorkshire and West Yorkshire.	26. North Yorkshire
27. All members and police cadets of the existing Northampton constabulary.	27. Northamptonshire
28. (a) All members and police cadets of the existing Northumberland constabulary; (b) Such members and police cadets (if any) of the existing Durham constabulary as may be agreed between the police authorities for the new police areas of Durham and Northumbria.	28. Northumbria
29. All members and police cadets of the existing Nottinghamshire combined constabulary, except those becoming members or police cadets of the police force for the new police area of South Yorkshire.	29. Nottinghamshire
30. (a) All members and police cadets of the existing South Wales constabulary;	30. South Wales

1 Existing police forces	2 New police areas
(b) Such members and police cadets (if any) of the existing Dyfed-Powys constabulary as may be agreed between the police authorities for the new police areas of Dyfed-Powys and South Wales;	
(c) Such members and police cadets (if any) of the existing Gwent constabulary as may be agreed between the police authorities for the new police areas of Gwent and South Wales.	
31. (a) All members and police cadets of the existing Sheffield and Rotherham constabulary;	31. South Yorkshire
(b) Such members and police cadets (if any) of the existing West Yorkshire constabulary as may be agreed between the police authorities for the new police areas of Cumbria, Greater Manchester, Humberside, Lancashire, North Yorkshire, South Yorkshire and West Yorkshire;	
(c) Such members and police cadets (if any) of the existing Nottinghamshire combined constabulary as may be agreed between the police authorities for the new police areas of Nottinghamshire and South Yorkshire.	
32. All members and police cadets of the existing Staffordshire County and Stoke-on-Trent constabulary, except those becoming members or police cadets of the police force for the new police area of West Midlands.	32. Staffordshire
33. All members and police cadets of the existing Suffolk constabulary except those becoming members or police cadets of the police force for the new police area of Norfolk.	33. Suffolk
34. All members and police cadets of the existing Surrey constabulary except those becoming members or police cadets of the police force for the new police area of Sussex.	34. Surrey
35. (a) All members and police cadets of the existing Sussex Police force;	35. Sussex
(b) Such members and police cadets (if any) of the existing Surrey constabulary as may be agreed between the police authorities for the new police areas of Surrey and Sussex.	
36. All members and police cadets of the existing Warwickshire and Coventry constabulary, except those becoming members or police cadets for the new police area of West Midlands.	36. Warwickshire
37. All members and police cadets of the existing West Mercia constabulary except those becoming members or police cadets of the police force for the new police area of West Midlands.	37. West Mercia
38. (a) All members and police cadets of the existing West Midlands constabulary;	38. West Midlands

1 Existing police forces	2 New police areas
(b) All members and police cadets of the existing Birmingham city police force;	
(c) Such members and police cadets (if any) of the existing Staffordshire County and Stoke-on-Trent constabulary as may be agreed between the police authorities for the new police areas of Staffordshire and West Midlands;	
(d) Such members and police cadets (if any) of the existing West Mercia constabulary as may be agreed between the police authorities for the new police areas of West Mercia and West Midlands;	
(e) Such members and police cadets (if any) of the existing Warwickshire and Coventry constabulary as may be agreed between the police authorities for the new police areas of Warwickshire and West Midlands.	
39. (a) All members and police cadets of the existing Bradford city police force;	39. West Yorkshire
(b) All members and police cadets of the existing Leeds city police force;	
(c) All members and police cadets of the existing West Yorkshire constabulary, except those becoming members or police cadets of the police forces for the new police areas of Cumbria, Greater Manchester, Humberside, Lancashire, North Yorkshire and South Yorkshire.	
40. All members and police cadets of the existing Wiltshire constabulary.	40. Wiltshire

SCHEDULE 2

SPECIAL CONSTABLES

1 Special constables for existing police areas	2 New police areas
1. (a) All special constables appointed for the existing Somerset and Bath police area; (b) All special constables appointed for the existing county borough of Bristol police area; (c) Such special constables appointed for the existing Gloucestershire police area as may be agreed between the police authorities for the new police areas of Avon and Somerset and of Gloucestershire.	1. Avon and Somerset
2. All special constables appointed for the existing Bedfordshire and Luton police area.	2. Bedfordshire
3. All special constables appointed for the existing Mid-Anglia police area.	3. Cambridgeshire
4. (a) All special constables appointed for the existing Cheshire police area, except those becoming special constables for the new police areas of Derbyshire, Greater Manchester and Merseyside; (b) Such special constables appointed for the existing Lancashire police area as may be agreed between the police authorities for the new police areas of Cheshire, Greater Manchester and Merseyside.	4. Cheshire
5. (a) All special constables appointed for the existing county borough of Teeside police area; (b) Such special constables appointed for the existing Durham police area as may be agreed between the police authorities for the new police areas of Cleveland and Durham; (c) Such special constables appointed for the existing York and North-East Yorkshire police area as may be agreed between the police authorities for the new police areas of Cleveland and North Yorkshire.	5. Cleveland
6. (a) All special constables appointed for the existing Cumbria police area; (b) Such special constables appointed for the existing Lancashire police area as may be agreed between the police authorities for the new police areas of Cumbria and Lancashire; (c) Such special constables appointed for the existing West Yorkshire police area as may be agreed between the police authorities for the new police areas of Cumbria and North Yorkshire.	6. Cumbria

1 Special constables for existing police areas	2 New police areas
7. (a) All the special constables appointed for the existing Derby county and borough police area; (b) Such special constables appointed for the existing Cheshire police area as may be agreed between the police authorities for the new police areas of Cheshire and Derbyshire.	7. Derbyshire
8. All special constables appointed for the existing Devon and Cornwall police area.	8. Devon and Cornwall
9. (a) All special constables appointed for the existing Dorset and Bournemouth police area; (b) Such special constables appointed for the existing Hampshire police area as may be agreed between the police authorities for the new police areas of Dorset and Hampshire.	9. Dorset
10. (a) All special constables appointed for the existing Durham police area, except those becoming special constables for the new police areas of Cleveland and Northumbria; (b) Such special constables appointed for the existing York and North-East Yorkshire police area as may be agreed between the police authorities for the new police areas of Durham and North Yorkshire.	10. Durham
11. All special constables appointed for the existing Dyfed-Powys police area, except those becoming special constables for the new police areas of Gwent and South Wales.	11. Dyfed-Powys
12. All special constables appointed for the existing Essex and Southend-on-Sea joint police area.	12. Essex
13. All special constables appointed for the existing Gloucestershire police area, except those becoming special constables for the new police area of Avon and Somerset.	13. Gloucestershire
14. (a) All special constables appointed for the existing Manchester and Salford police area; (b) Such special constables appointed for the existing Cheshire police area as may be agreed between the police authorities for the new police areas of Cheshire and Greater Manchester; (c) Such special constables appointed for the existing Lancashire police area as may be agreed between the police authorities for the new police areas of Cheshire Greater Manchester, Lancashire and Merseyside; (d) Such special constables appointed for the existing West Yorkshire police area as may be agreed between the police authorities for	14. Greater Manchester

1 Special constables for existing police areas	2 New police areas
the new police areas of Greater Manchester and West Yorkshire.	
15. (a) All special constables appointed for the existing Gwent police area, except those becoming special constables for the new police area of South Wales; (b) Such special constables appointed for the existing Dyfed-Powys police area as may be agreed between the police authorities for the new police areas of Dyfed-Powys and Gwent.	15. Gwent
16. All special constables appointed for the existing Hampshire police area, except those becoming special constables for the new police area of Dorset.	16. Hampshire
17. All special constables appointed for the existing Hertfordshire police area.	17. Hertfordshire
18. (a) All special constables appointed for the existing county borough of Kingston-upon-Hull police area; (b) Such special constables appointed for the existing York and North-East Yorkshire police area as may be agreed between the police authorities for the new police areas of Humberside and North Yorkshire; (c) Such special constables appointed for the existing Lincolnshire police area as may be agreed between the police authorities for the new police areas of Humberside and Lincolnshire; (d) Such special constables appointed for the existing West Yorkshire police area as may be agreed between the police authorities for the new police areas of Humberside, North Yorkshire and South Yorkshire.	18. Humberside
19. All special constables appointed for the existing Kent police area.	19. Kent
20. (a) All special constables appointed for the existing Lancashire police area, except those becoming special constables for the new police areas of Cheshire, Cumbria, Greater Manchester and Merseyside; (b) Such special constables appointed for the existing West Yorkshire police area as may be agreed between the police authorities for the new police areas of Lancashire and North Yorkshire.	20. Lancashire

1 Special constables for existing police areas	2 New police areas
21. All special constables appointed for the existing Leicester and Rutland police area.	21. Leicestershire
22. All special constables appointed for the existing Lincolnshire police area, except those becoming special constables for the new police area of Humberside.	22. Lincolnshire
23. (a) All special constables appointed for the existing Liverpool and Bootle police area; (b) Such special constables appointed for the existing Cheshire police area as may be agreed between the police authorities for the new police areas of Cheshire and Merseyside; (c) Such special constables appointed for the existing Lancashire police area as may be agreed between the police authorities for the new police areas of Cheshire, Greater Manchester, Lancashire and Merseyside.	23. Merseyside
24. (a) All special constables appointed for the existing Norfolk joint police area; (b) Such special constables appointed for the existing Suffolk police area as may be agreed between the police authorities for the new police areas of Norfolk and Suffolk.	24. Norfolk
25. All special constables appointed for the existing Gwynedd police area.	25. North Wales
26. (a) All special constables appointed for the existing York and North-East Yorkshire police area, except those becoming special constables for the new police areas of Cleveland, Durham and Humberside; (b) Such special constables appointed for the existing West Yorkshire police area as may be agreed between the police authorities for the new police areas of Cumbria, Humberside, Lancashire, North Yorkshire, South Yorkshire and West Yorkshire.	26. North Yorkshire
27. All special constables appointed for the existing Northampton and County police area.	27. Northamptonshire
28. (a) All special constables appointed for the existing Northumberland police area; (b) Such special constables appointed for the existing Durham police area as may be agreed between the police authorities for the new police areas of Durham and Northumbria.	28. Northumbria
29. All special constables appointed for the existing Nottinghamshire combined police area, except those becoming special constables for the new police area of South Yorkshire.	29. Nottinghamshire

1 Special constables for existing police areas	2 New police areas
30. (a) All special constables appointed for the existing South Wales police area; (b) Such special constables appointed for the existing Dyfed-Powys police area as may be agreed between the police authorities for the new police areas of Dyfed-Powys and South Wales; (c) Such special constables appointed for the existing Gwent police area as may be agreed between the police authorities for the new police areas of Gwent and South Wales.	30. South Wales
31. (a) All special constables appointed for the existing Sheffield and Rotherham police area; (b) Such special constables appointed for the existing West Yorkshire police area as may be agreed between the police authorities for the new police areas of Humberside, North Yorkshire, South Yorkshire and West Yorkshire; (c) Such special constables appointed for the existing Nottinghamshire combined police area as may be agreed between the police authorities for the new police areas of Nottinghamshire and South Yorkshire.	31. South Yorkshire
32. All special constables appointed for the existing Staffordshire County and Stoke-on-Trent police area, except those becoming special constables for the new police area of West Midlands.	32. Staffordshire
33. All special constables appointed for the existing Suffolk police area, except those becoming special constables for the new police area of Norfolk.	33. Suffolk
34. All special constables appointed for the existing Surrey police area, except those becoming special constables for the new police area of Sussex.	34. Surrey
35. (a) All special constables appointed for the existing Sussex police area; (b) Such special constables appointed for the existing Surrey police area as may be agreed between the police authorities for the new police areas of Surrey and Sussex.	35. Sussex
36. All special constables appointed for the existing Warwickshire and Coventry police area, except those becoming special constables for the new police area of West Midlands.	36. Warwickshire
37. All special constables appointed for the existing West Mercia police area, except those becoming special constables for the new police area of West Midlands.	37. West Mercia

1 Special constables for existing police areas	2 New police areas
38. (a) All special constables appointed for the existing West Midlands police area;	38. West Midlands
(b) All special constables appointed for the existing county borough of Birmingham police area;	
(c) Such special constables appointed for the existing Staffordshire County and Stoke-on-Trent police area as may be agreed between the police authorities for the new police areas of Staffordshire and West Midlands;	
(d) Such special constables appointed for the existing West Mercia police area as may be agreed between the police authorities for the new police areas of West Mercia and West Midlands;	
(e) Such special constables appointed for the existing Warwickshire and Coventry police area as may be agreed between the police authorities for the new police areas of Warwickshire and West Midlands.	
39. (a) All special constables appointed for the existing county borough of Bradford police area;	39. West Yorkshire
(b) All special constables appointed for the existing county borough of Leeds police area;	
(c) All special constables appointed for the existing West Yorkshire police area, except those becoming special constables for the new police areas of Cumbria, Greater Manchester, Humberside, Lancashire, North Yorkshire and South Yorkshire.	
40. All special constables appointed for the existing Wiltshire police area.	40. Wiltshire

SCHEDULE 3

REVERSIONARY MEMBERS OF HOME POLICE FORCES

1 Existing police forces	2 New police areas
1. Bedfordshire and Luton constabulary	Bedfordshire
2. Birmingham city police force	West Midlands
3. Bristol constabulary	Avon and Somerset
4. City of Bradford police force	West Yorkshire
5. Cheshire constabulary	Cheshire, Derbyshire, Greater Manchester, and Merseyside
6. Cumbria constabulary	Cumbria
7. Derby County and Borough constabulary	Derbyshire
8. Devon and Cornwall constabulary	Devon and Cornwall
9. Dorset and Bournemouth constabulary	Dorset
10. Durham constabulary	Cleveland, Durham and Northumbria
11. Dyfed-Powys constabulary	Dyfed-Powys, Gwent and South Wales
12. Essex and Southend-on-Sea Joint constabulary	Essex
13. Gloucestershire constabulary	Avon and Somerset and Gloucestershire
14. Gwent constabulary	Gwent and South Wales
15. Gwynedd constabulary	North Wales
16. Hampshire constabulary	Dorset and Hampshire
17. Hertfordshire constabulary	Hertfordshire
18. Kent police force	Kent
19. Kingston-upon-Hull city police force	Humberside
20. Lancashire constabulary	Cheshire, Cumbria, Greater Manchester, Lancashire and Merseyside
21. Leeds city police force	West Yorkshire
22. Leicester and Rutland constabulary	Leicestershire
23. Lincolnshire constabulary	Humberside and Lincolnshire
24. Liverpool and Bootle constabulary	Merseyside
25. Manchester and Salford police force	Greater Manchester
26. Mid-Anglia constabulary	Cambridgeshire
27. Norfolk joint police	Norfolk
28. Northampton and County constabulary	Northamptonshire
29. Northumberland constabulary	Northumbria
30. Nottinghamshire combined constabulary	Nottinghamshire and South Yorkshire
31. Sheffield and Rotherham constabulary	South Yorkshire
32. Somerset and Bath constabulary	Avon and Somerset
33. South Wales constabulary	South Wales
34. Staffordshire County and Stoke-on-Trent constabulary	Staffordshire and West Midlands
35. Suffolk constabulary	Norfolk and Suffolk
36. Surrey constabulary	Surrey and Sussex
37. Sussex constabulary	Sussex
38. Teesside police force	Cleveland
39. Warwickshire and Coventry constabulary	Warwickshire and West Midlands
40. West Mercia constabulary	West Mercia and West Midlands
41. West Midlands constabulary	West Midlands
42. West Yorkshire constabulary	Cumbria, Greater Manchester, Humberside, Lancashire, North Yorkshire, South Yorkshire and West Yorkshire

1 Existing police forces	2 New police areas
43. Wiltshire constabulary	Wiltshire
44. York and North-East Yorkshire Constabulary	Cleveland, Durham, Humberside and North Yorkshire

EXPLANATORY NOTE

(This Note is not part of the Order.)

This Order makes provision for the transfer of policemen consequent on changes in police areas arising under the Local Government Act 1972. It does not apply to Greater London. It provides for the transfer of members of police forces, other than chief constables, police cadets and special constables to the new police areas established on 1st April 1974 and for persons having a right of reversion to an existing police force to have a right of reversion to a new police force.

STATUTORY INSTRUMENTS

1974 No. 552
NATIONAL DEBT
The Savings Certificates (Amendment) Regulations 1974

Made - - -	*26th March* 1974
Laid before Parliament	*29th March* 1974
Coming into Operation	*17th June* 1974

The Treasury, in exercise of the powers conferred on them by section 11 of the National Debt Act 1972(**a**) and of all other powers enabling them in that behalf, hereby make the following Regulations:—

1. These Regulations may be cited as the Savings Certificates (Amendment) Regulations 1974, and shall come into operation on 17th June 1974.

2. The Interpretation Act 1889(**b**) shall apply for the interpretation of these Regulations as it applies for the interpretation of an Act of Parliament.

3. The Savings Certificates Regulations 1972(**c**), as amended(**d**), shall be further amended, in Regulation 5(1), by substituting for sub-paragraph (*h*) thereof the following sub-paragraphs:—

" (*h*) 1,500, in the case of certificates issued after 4th October 1970 but not later than 16th June 1974, and

(*i*) 1,000, in the case of certificates issued after 16th June 1974."

4. The Savings Certificates (Amendment) Regulations 1973(**d**) are hereby revoked.

Donald R. Coleman,
James Hamilton,
Two of the Lords Commissioners
of Her Majesty's Treasury.

26th March 1974.

EXPLANATORY NOTE

(This Note is not part of the Regulations.)

These Regulations, which amend the Savings Certificates Regulations 1972, increase the maximum permitted holding of national savings certificates by adding to it 1,000 unit certificates of the 14th issue of national savings certificates, which will be on sale from 17th June 1974.

(**a**) 1972 c. 65.　　(**b**) 1889 c. 63.　　(**c**) S.I. 1972/641 (1972 I, p. 2084).
(**d**) S.I. 1973/389 (1973 I, p. 1329).

STATUTORY INSTRUMENTS

1974 No. 553

SAVINGS BANKS

The National Savings Bank (Amendment) Regulations 1974

Made - - -	*26th March* 1974
Laid before Parliament	*27th March* 1974
Coming into Operation	*1st May* 1974

The Treasury, in exercise of the powers conferred on them by section 2 of the National Savings Bank Act 1971(a), as extended by section 3(2) of that Act, and of all other powers enabling them in that behalf, hereby make the following Regulations:—

1. These Regulations may be cited as the National Savings Bank (Amendment) Regulations 1974, and shall come into operation on 1st May 1974.

2. The Interpretation Act 1889(b) shall apply for the interpretation of these Regulations as it applies for the interpretation of an Act of Parliament.

3. The National Savings Bank Regulations 1972(c) shall be amended, in Regulation 28, by the deletion of paragraphs (3) and (4) thereof.

Donald R. Coleman,

James Hamilton,

Two of the Lords Commissioners
of Her Majesty's Treasury.

26th March 1974.

EXPLANATORY NOTE

(This Note is not part of the Regulations.)

These Regulations, which amend the National Savings Bank Regulations 1972, remove the requirement that a person making an investment deposit in the National Savings Bank shall have ordinary deposits of not less than £50 standing to his credit in the Bank.

(a) 1971 c. 29.   (b) 1889 c. 63.   (c) S.I. 1972/764 (1972 II, p. 2421).

STATUTORY INSTRUMENTS

1974 No. 554

VALUE ADDED TAX

The Value Added Tax (United Kingdom and Isle of Man) Order 1974

Made - - -	*26th March* 1974
Coming into Operation	*26th March* 1974

At the Court at Windsor Castle, the 26th day of March 1974

Present,

The Queen's Most Excellent Majesty in Council

Whereas an Act of Tynwald entitled the Value Added Tax and Other Taxes Act 1973(a) has been passed making, in relation to the Isle of Man, provision similar to the provision made by Part I of the Finance Act 1972(b) with respect to value added tax:

And whereas the Treasury, in exercise of the powers conferred on them by sections 12(4) and 13(2) of the Finance Act 1972, have made the Value Added Tax (General) (No. 2) Order 1973(c):

And whereas the Treasury, in exercise of the powers conferred on them by item 5 of Group 9 in Schedule 4 to the Finance Act 1972, have made the Value Added Tax (Finance and Insurance) (No. 2) Order 1973(d):

And whereas the Finance Board, in exercise of the powers conferred on it by sections 12(4) and 13(2) of the Value Added Tax and Other Taxes Act 1973, has made the Value Added Tax (Isle of Man) (General) Order 1974(e):

And whereas the Finance Board, in exercise of the powers conferred on it by item 5 of Group 9 in Schedule 4 to the Value Added Tax and Other Taxes Act 1973, has made the Value Added Tax (Isle of Man) (Finance and Insurance) Order 1974(f):

Now, therefore, Her Majesty, in pursuance of section 50 of the Finance Act 1972 and all other powers enabling Her in that behalf, is pleased, by and with the advice of Her Privy Council, to order, and it is hereby ordered, as follows—

1.—(1) This Order may be cited as the Value Added Tax (United Kingdom and Isle of Man) Order 1974 and shall come into operation on 26th March 1974.

(a) Acts of Tynwald 1973 Ch. 1. (b) 1972 c. 41.
(c) S.I. 1973/2151 (1973 III, p. 7429). (d) S.I. 1973/2150 (1973 III, p. 7427).
(e) Govt. Circular 16/1974. (f) Govt. Circular 15/1974.

(2) The Interpretation Act 1889(a) shall apply for the interpretation of this Order as it applies for the interpretation of an Act of Parliament.

2.—(1) In the Value Added Tax (General) (No. 2) Order 1973 for the words "United Kingdom" in Article 5(a) and (c) there shall be substituted "United Kingdom or the Isle of Man".

(2) In the Value Added Tax (Isle of Man) (General) Order 1974 for the words "Isle of Man" in Article 5(a) and (c) there shall be substituted "Isle of Man or the United Kingdom".

3. In the Schedule to the Value Added Tax (Finance and Insurance) (No. 2) Order 1973—

(1) For the words "United Kingdom" in the following places where they occur—

    (a) paragraph 1,
    (b) the first place in paragraph 2,
    (c) the first place in paragraph 2(b),
    (d) paragraph 4(a), and
    (e) the second place in paragraph 5(b)

there shall be substituted "United Kingdom or the Isle of Man".

(2) For the words "United Kingdom" in the following places where they occur—

    (a) the second place in paragraph 2(b),
    (b) paragraph 4(b),
    (c) the first place in paragraph 5, and
    (d) the first place in paragraph 5(b)

there shall be substituted "both the United Kingdom and the Isle of Man".

4. In the Schedule to the Value Added Tax (Isle of Man) (Finance and Insurance) Order 1974—

(1) For the words "Isle of Man" in the following places where they occur—

    (a) paragraph 1,
    (b) the first place in paragraph 2,
    (c) the first place in paragraph 2(b),
    (d) paragraph 4(a), and
    (e) the second place in paragraph 5(b)

there shall be substituted "Isle of Man or the United Kingdom".

(2) For the words "Isle of Man" in the following places where they occur—

    (a) the second place in paragraph 2(b),
    (b) paragraph 4(b),
    (c) the first place in paragraph 5, and
    (d) the first place in paragraph 5(b)

there shall be substituted "both the Isle of Man and the United Kingdom".

W. G. Agnew.

(a) 1889 c. 63.

EXPLANATORY NOTE

(This Note is not part of the Order.)

This Order makes the necessary provisions to secure that the zero rating of supplies of certain services as specified in the Orders referred to made under either the Finance Act 1972 (an Act of Parliament) or the Value Added Tax and Other Taxes Act 1973 (an Act of Tynwald) shall apply as if references therein to the United Kingdom or the Isle of Man included both places.

STATUTORY INSTRUMENTS

1974 No. 555

SOCIAL SECURITY

The Family Allowances, National Insurance and Industrial Injuries (Gibraltar) Order 1974

Made - - - *26th March* 1974

At the Court at Windsor Castle, the 26th day of March 1974

Present,

The Queen's Most Excellent Majesty in Council

Whereas by an exchange of Letters (which Letters are set out in the Schedule to this Order) between the Secretary of State for Foreign and Commonwealth Affairs and the Governor of Gibraltar an Agreement on social security was made between the Government of the United Kingdom of Great Britain and Northern Ireland and the Government of Gibraltar:

And Whereas it was provided in the Letters that the Agreement should enter into force forthwith:

And Whereas by section 105(1) of the National Insurance Act 1965(a), as extended by section 22(1) of the Family Allowances Act 1965(b), and section 84(1) of the National Insurance (Industrial Injuries) Act 1965(c), it is provided that Her Majesty may, by Order in Council, make provision for modifying or adapting the said Acts of 1965 in their application to cases affected by agreements with other governments providing for reciprocity in matters specified in those sections:

Now, therefore, Her Majesty, in pursuance of the said section 105(1), as so extended, and the said section 84(1), and all other powers enabling Her in that behalf, is pleased, by and with the advice of Her Privy Council, to order, and it is hereby ordered, as follows:—

Citation and Interpretation

1.—(1) This Order may be cited as the Family Allowances, National Insurance and Industrial Injuries (Gibraltar) Order 1974.

(2) The rules for the construction of Acts of Parliament contained in the Interpretation Act 1889(d) shall apply for the purpose of the interpretation of this Order as they apply to the interpretation of an Act of Parliament.

Modification of Acts

2. The provisions contained in the Letters set out in the Schedule to this Order shall have full force and effect, so far as they relate to England, Wales

---

(a) 1965 c.51.　　(b) 1965 c.53.　　(c) 1965 c.52.　　(d) 1889 c.63.

and Scotland and provide for reciprocity with the Government of Gibraltar in any matters specified in either section 105(1) of the National Insurance Act 1965, as extended by section 22(1) of the Family Allowances Act 1965, or section 84(1) of the National Insurance (Industrial Injuries) Act 1965; and the Family Allowances Acts 1965 to 1969, the National Insurance Acts 1965 to 1973 and the National Insurance (Industrial Injuries) Acts 1965 to 1973 shall have effect subject to such modifications as may be required therein for the purpose of giving effect to any such provisions.

W. G. Agnew.

SCHEDULE

LETTERS EXCHANGED BETWEEN THE SECRETARY OF STATE FOR FOREIGN AND
COMMONWEALTH AFFAIRS AND THE GOVERNOR OF GIBRALTAR

No. 1

The Secretary of State for Foreign and Commonwealth Affairs to the Governor of Gibraltar.

12 December 1973.

Sir,

I have the honour to refer to discussions which have taken place between the Government of the United Kingdom of Great Britain and Northern Ireland and the Government of Gibraltar and to record below the points which have been agreed between the two Governments concerning an Interim Agreement on Social Security arising out of the United Kingdom's Accession to the European Economic Community.

1   Any reference in the following paragraphs to a territory shall be construed as a reference to the territory of the United Kingdom or Gibraltar or both as the case may be and any reference to a child shall be construed as a reference to any person for whom family allowances are payable under the legislation in question.

2(a) Any person shall have the same rights and liabilities in relation to social security other than family allowances, as he would have had if the United Kingdom and Gibraltar had been separate Member States of the European Economic Community.

(b) For the purpose of giving effect to paragraph (a) above the same procedures shall so far as is practicable be adopted in relation to the person and benefit concerned as would have been applicable had the United Kingdom and Gibraltar been such separate Member States.

3   For the purpose of the right to receive payment of a pension for old age, widow's benefit, guardian's allowance, child's special allowance or dependency benefits in respect of any such pension, benefit or allowance, under the legislation applicable to either the United Kingdom, or Gibraltar, any period during which a person, not subject to paragraph 2, was present or ordinarily resident in the other territory shall be treated as a period during which he was present or ordinarily resident, as the case may be, in the territory to which the legislation applies.

4   In relation to family allowances—

(a) where under the legislation applicable to a territory—

(i) the completion of a period of presence in that territory is required, any period during which a person was in the other territory shall be treated as a period during which he was in the territory to which the legislation applies,

    (ii) the place of a person's birth is relevant, a person who was born in the other territory shall be treated as having been born in the territory to which the legislation applies;

   (b) family allowances shall not be payable in respect of the same child under the legislation applicable to both territories and where but for this provision they would have been so payable, they shall be paid under the legislation which applies to the territory in which the child is ordinarily resident.

5   Such administrative and financial arrangements may be made as may be required for the application of this Agreement.

6   The Agreement shall enter into force forthwith and shall remain in force until reviewed at any time by agreement between both parties.

If the Government of Gibraltar agree that the foregoing correctly sets out the points agreed between the two Governments, I have the honour to propose that this despatch and your reply to that effect shall constitute an Agreement between the Government of the United Kingdom of Great Britain and Northern Ireland and the Government of Gibraltar.

I have the honour to be,

Sir,

Your most obedient, humble servant,

Alec Douglas-Home.

No. 2

The Governor of Gibraltar to the Secretary of State for Foreign and Commonwealth Affairs.

30 January 1974.

Sir,
I have the honour to acknowledge receipt of your Despatch of 12 December 1973 and to confirm that this correctly states the understanding between our two Governments concerning an Interim Agreement on Social Security arising out of the UK accession to the European Economic Community.

2. I agree that the Despatch and this reply shall be regarded as placing that understanding on record.

I have the honour to be,

Sir,

Your most obedient humble servant,

John Grandy,

EXPLANATORY NOTE

(This Note is not part of the Order.)

This Order gives effect in England, Wales and Scotland to the Agreement (contained in an exchange of Letters set out in the Schedule) made between the Governments of the United Kingdom and Gibraltar in so far as it relates to the matters for which provision is made by the Family Allowance Acts 1965 to 1969, the National Insurance Acts 1965 to 1973 and the National Insurance (Industrial Injuries) Acts 1965 to 1973.

STATUTORY INSTRUMENTS

1974 No. 556

MAINTENANCE OF DEPENDANTS

The Reciprocal Enforcement of Maintenance Orders (Designation of Reciprocating Countries) Order 1974

Made - - -	*26th March* 1974
Laid before Parliament	*2nd April* 1974
Coming into Operation	*8th May* 1974

At the Court at Windsor Castle, the 26th day of March 1974

Present,

The Queen's Most Excellent Majesty in Council

Whereas Her Majesty is satisfied that, in the event of the benefits conferred by Part I of the Maintenance Orders (Reciprocal Enforcement) Act 1972(a) being applied to, or to particular classes of, maintenance orders made by the courts of each of the countries and territories specified in column (1) of the Schedule to this Order, similar benefits will in that country or territory be applied to, or to those classes of, maintenance orders made by the courts of the United Kingdom:

And whereas Her Majesty considers the provisions contained in Article 4 of this Order expedient for the purpose of securing the matters set out in section 24 of the said Act of 1972:

Now, therefore, Her Majesty, in exercise of the powers conferred by sections 1 and 24 of the Maintenance Orders (Reciprocal Enforcement) Act 1972, is pleased, by and with the advice of Her Privy Council, to order, and it is hereby ordered, as follows:—

1. This Order may be cited as the Reciprocal Enforcement of Maintenance Orders (Designation of Reciprocating Countries) Order 1974 and shall come into operation on 8th May 1974.

2.—(1) In this Order—

"the Act of 1972" means the Maintenance Orders (Reciprocal Enforcement) Act 1972;

"the Act of 1920" means the Maintenance Orders (Facilities for Enforcement) Act 1920(b);

"column (1)" and "column (2)" mean respectively columns (1) and (2) of the Schedule to this Order.

(2) The Interpretation Act 1889(c) shall apply for the interpretation of this Order as it applies for the interpretation of an Act of Parliament.

(a) 1972 c. 18. (b) 1920 c. 33. (c) 1889 c. 63.

3. Each of the countries and territories specified in column (1) is hereby designated as a reciprocating country for the purposes of Part I of the Act of 1972 as regards maintenance orders of the description specified in respect of that country or territory in column (2).

4.—(1) Sections 5, 12 to 15, 17, 18 and 21 of the Act of 1972 shall apply in relation to a maintenance order transmitted under section 2 or 3 of the Act of 1920 to one of the countries and territories specified in column (1), being an order of the description specified in respect of that country or territory in column (2) to which immediately before the coming into operation of this Order the Act of 1920 applied, as they apply in relation to a maintenance order sent to that country or territory in pursuance of section 2 of the Act of 1972 or made by virtue of section 3 or 4 of the Act of 1972 and confirmed by a competent court in that country or territory.

(2) Sections 8 to 21 of the Act of 1972 shall apply in relation to a maintenance order made in one of the countries and territories specified in column (1), being an order of the description specified in respect of that country or territory in column (2) to which immediately before the coming into operation of this Order the Act of 1920 applied and not being an order which immediately before that date is registered in the High Court or the High Court of Justice in Northern Ireland under section 1 of the Act of 1920, as they apply in relation to a registered order.

(3) A maintenance order made by a court in one of the countries and territories specified in column (1) being an order of the description specified in respect of that country or territory in column (2) which has been confirmed by a court in England, Wales or Northern Ireland under section 4 of the Act of 1920 and is in force immediately before the coming into operation of this Order, shall be registered under section 7(5) of the Act of 1972 in like manner as if it had been confirmed by that court in England, Wales or Northern Ireland under subsection (2) of that section.

(4) Any proceedings brought under or by virtue of any provision of the Act of 1920 in a court in England, Wales or Northern Ireland which are pending immediately before the coming into operation of this Order, being proceedings affecting a person resident in one of the countries and territories specified in column (1), shall be continued as if they had been brought under or by virtue of the corresponding provision of the Act of 1972.

W. G. Agnew.

SCHEDULE   Article 3
COUNTRIES AND TERRITORIES DESIGNATED AS RECIPROCATING COUNTRIES

(1) Country or territory	(2) Description of maintenance orders to which designation extends
Australian Capital Territory	Maintenance orders other than— (*a*) provisional affiliation orders, and (*b*) orders obtained by or in favour of a public authority
British Columbia	Maintenance orders generally
Gibraltar	Maintenance orders generally
Manitoba	Maintenance orders other than provisional affiliation orders
New South Wales	Maintenance orders other than— (*a*) provisional affiliation orders, and (*b*) orders obtained by or in favour of a public authority
New Zealand	Maintenance orders other than— (*a*) provisional affiliation orders, and (*b*) maintenance orders of the description contained in paragraph (*b*) of the definition of "maintenance order" in section 21(1) of the Act of 1972 (orders for the payment of birth and funeral expenses of child)
Northern Territory of Australia	Maintenance orders other than— (*a*) provisional affiliation orders, and (*b*) orders obtained by or in favour of a public authority
Nova Scotia	Maintenance orders other than— (*a*) maintenance orders of the description contained in the said paragraph (*b*), and (*b*) orders obtained by or in favour of a public authority
Ontario	Maintenance orders other than— (*a*) provisional affiliation orders, (*b*) maintenance orders of the description contained in the said paragraph (*b*), and (*c*) provisional maintenance orders made by virtue of the Matrimonial Proceedings (Polygamous Marriages) Act 1972(a) or any corresponding legislation in Ontario
Queensland	Maintenance orders other than— (*a*) provisional affiliation orders, and (*b*) orders obtained by or in favour of a public authority
South Australia	Maintenance orders other than— (*a*) provisional affiliation orders, and (*b*) orders obtained by or in favour of a public authority
Tasmania	Maintenance orders other than— (*a*) provisional affiliation orders, and (*b*) orders obtained by or in favour of a public authority
Victoria	Maintenance orders other than— (*a*) provisional affiliation orders, and (*b*) orders obtained by or in favour of a public authority

(a) 1972 c. 38.

EXPLANATORY NOTE

(This Note is not part of the Order.)

This Order designates as reciprocating countries for the purposes of Part I of the Maintenance Orders (Reciprocal Enforcement) Act 1972 the following countries: the Australian Territories and States, except Western Australia; the Canadian Provinces of British Columbia, Manitoba, Nova Scotia and Ontario; Gibraltar; and New Zealand. The Order also contains transitional provisions in respect of maintenance orders and proceedings to which the Maintenance Orders (Facilities for Enforcement) Act 1920 applied before the coming into operation of the Order.

STATUTORY INSTRUMENTS

1974 No. 557

MAINTENANCE OF DEPENDANTS

The Maintenance Orders (Facilities for Enforcement) (Revocation) Order 1974

Made - - -		*26th March* 1974
Coming into Operation		*8th May* 1974

At the Court at Windsor Castle, the 26th day of March 1974

Present,

The Queen's Most Excellent Majesty in Council

Her Majesty, in exercise of the powers conferred by section 19 of the Maintenance Orders Act 1958(a), is pleased, by and with the advice of Her Privy Council, to order, and it is hereby ordered, as follows:—

1. This Order may be cited as the Maintenance Orders (Facilities for Enforcement) (Revocation) Order 1974 and shall come into operation on 8th May 1974.

2.—(1) Insofar as the Maintenance Orders (Facilities for Enforcement) Order 1959(b) provides that the Maintenance Orders (Facilities for Enforcement) Act 1920(c) shall extend to the countries and territories specified in paragraph (2) below, that Order is hereby revoked, and accordingly the names of those countries and territories shall be omitted from the First Schedule to that Order.

(2) The countries and territories referred to in paragraph (1) above are—

(*a*) Australia, Territory for the Seat of Government of the Commonwealth (Australian Capital Territory);

(*b*) British Columbia;

(*c*) Gibraltar;

(*d*) Manitoba;

(*e*) New South Wales;

(*f*) New Zealand;

(*g*) Northern Territory of Australia;

(*h*) Nova Scotia;

(*i*) Ontario;

(*j*) Queensland;

(*k*) South Australia;

(*l*) Tasmania;

(*m*) Victoria.

W. G. Agnew.

(a) 1958 c. 39.　　(b) S.I. 1959/377 (1959 I, p. 1666).　　(c) 1920 c. 33.

EXPLANATORY NOTE

(This Note is not part of the Order.)

This Order revokes the Maintenance Orders (Facilities for Enforcement) Order 1959 insofar as it extends the Maintenance Orders (Facilities for Enforcement) Act 1920 to the Australian Territories and States (except Western Australia), British Columbia, Gibraltar, Manitoba, New Zealand, Nova Scotia and Ontario. Those countries and territories are designated as reciprocating countries for the purposes of Part I of the Maintenance Orders (Reciprocal Enforcement) Act 1972 (c. 18) by the Reciprocal Enforcement of Maintenance Orders (Designation of Reciprocating Countries) Order 1974 (S.I. 1974/556) which comes into operation on the same date as this Order.

1974 No. 558

INCOME TAX

The Double Taxation Relief (Taxes on Income) (Sweden) Order 1974

Laid before the House of Commons in draft

Made - - - *26th March* 1974

At the Court at Windsor Castle, the 26th day of March 1974

Present,

The Queen's Most Excellent Majesty in Council

Whereas a draft of this Order was laid before the Commons House of Parliament in accordance with the provisions of section 497(8) of the Income and Corporation Taxes Act .1970(a), and an Address has been presented to Her Majesty by that House praying that an Order may be made in the terms of this Order:

Now, therefore, Her Majesty, in exercise of the powers conferred upon Her by section 497 of the said Income and Corporation Taxes Act 1970, as amended by section 98 of the Finance Act 1972(b), and of all other powers enabling Her in that behalf, is pleased, by and with the advice of Her Privy Council, to order, and it is hereby ordered, as follows:—

1. This Order may be cited as the Double Taxation Relief (Taxes on Income) (Sweden) Order 1974.

2. It is hereby declared—

    (*a*) that the arrangements specified in the Further Supplementary Protocol set out in the Schedule to this Order have been made with the Government of the Kingdom of Sweden with a view to affording relief from double taxation in relation to income tax or corporation tax and taxes of a similar character imposed by the laws of Sweden varying the arrangements set out in the Schedule to the Double Taxation Relief (Taxes on Income) (Sweden) Order 1961(c) as amended by the arrangements set out in the Schedule to the Double Taxation Relief (Taxes on Income) (Sweden) Order 1968(d) and by the arrangements set out in the Schedule to the Double Taxation Relief (Taxes on Income) (Sweden) (No. 2) Order 1968(e); and

    (*b*) it is expedient that those arrangements should have effect.

W. G. Agnew.

(**a**) 1970 c. 10.
(**c**) S.I. 1961/577 (1961 I, p. 1265).
(**e**) S.I. 1968/2034 (1968 III, p. 5496).

(**b**) 1972 c. 41.
(**d**) S.I. 1968/1105 (1968 II, p. 3057).

SCHEDULE

FURTHER SUPPLEMENTARY PROTOCOL BETWEEN THE GOVERNMENT OF THE UNITED
KINGDOM OF GREAT BRITAIN AND NORTHERN IRELAND AND THE GOVERNMENT
OF THE KINGDOM OF SWEDEN, AMENDING THE CONVENTION FOR THE AVOID-
ANCE OF DOUBLE TAXATION AND THE PREVENTION OF FISCAL EVASION WITH
RESPECT TO TAXES ON INCOME, SIGNED AT LONDON ON 28 JULY, 1960, AS
MODIFIED BY THE PROTOCOL SIGNED AT LONDON ON 25 MARCH, 1966 AND
THE SUPPLEMENTARY PROTOCOL SIGNED AT LONDON ON 27 JUNE, 1968.

The Government of the United Kingdom of Great Britain and Northern Ireland
and the Government of the Kingdom of Sweden;

Desiring to conclude a Further Supplementary Protocol to amend the Convention between the Contracting Parties for the Avoidance of Double Taxation and
the Prevention of Fiscal Evasion with respect to Taxes on Income, signed at
London on 28 July, 1960, as modified by the Protocol signed at London on 25
March, 1966 and the Supplementary Protocol signed at London on 27 June, 1968
(hereinafter referred to as "the Convention");

Have agreed as follows:

ARTICLE 1

Article VII of the Convention shall be deleted and replaced by the following:

"ARTICLE VII

(1) (a) Dividends paid by a company which is a resident of the United Kingdom to a resident of Sweden may be taxed in Sweden.

(b) Where a resident of Sweden is entitled to a tax credit in respect of such
a dividend under paragraph (2) of this Article tax may also be charged in the
United Kingdom and according to the laws of the United Kingdom, on the
aggregate of the amount or value of that dividend and the amount of that tax
credit at a rate not exceeding 15 per cent.

(c) Except as aforesaid dividends paid by a company which is a resident
of the United Kingdom and which are beneficially owned by a resident of
Sweden shall be exempt from any tax in the United Kingdom which is chargeable on dividends.

(2) A resident of Sweden who receives dividends from a company which is
a resident of the United Kingdom shall, subject to the provisions of paragraph (3) of this Article and provided he is the beneficial owner of the dividends, be entitled to the tax credit in respect thereof to which an individual
resident in the United Kingdom would have been entitled had he received those
dividends, and to the payment of any excess of that tax credit over his liability
to United Kingdom tax.

(3) Paragraph (2) of this Article shall not apply where the beneficial owner
of the dividend is a company which either alone or together with one or more
associated companies controls directly or indirectly at least 10 per cent of the
voting power in the company paying the dividend. For the purposes of this
paragraph two companies shall be deemed to be associated if one is controlled
directly or indirectly by the other, or both are controlled directly or indirectly
by a third company.

(4) Dividends paid by a company which is a resident of Sweden and which
are beneficially owned by a resident of the United Kingdom may be taxed in
the United Kingdom. Such dividends may also be taxed in Sweden but the
tax so charged shall not exceed:

(a) 5 per cent of the gross amount of the dividends if the beneficial owner
is a company which controls directly or indirectly at least 10 per cent
of the voting power in the company paying the dividends;

(b) in all other cases 10 per cent of the gross amount of the dividends.

(5) The preceding paragraphs of this Article shall not affect the taxation of the company in respect of the profits out of which the dividends are paid.

(6) Dividends paid before the date of entry into force of the Supplementary Protocol signed at London on 27 June, 1968 by a company which is a resident of one of the territories to a resident of the other territory who is subject to tax there in respect thereof (or would be so subject to tax there but for a provision in the Convention) shall be exempt from any tax which is chargeable in the first-mentioned territory on dividends in addition to the tax chargeable in respect of the profits or income of the company.

(7) The term "dividends" as used in this Article means income from shares, mining shares, founders' shares or other rights, not being debt-claims, participating in profits, as well as income from other corporate rights assimilated to income from shares by the taxation law of the territory of which the company making the distribution is a resident and, in the case of the United Kingdom, includes any item (other than interest exempt from United Kingdom tax under Article VIII of this Convention) which under the law of the United Kingdom is treated as a distribution of a company.

(8) Where the company paying a dividend is a resident of the United Kingdom and the beneficial owner of the dividend, being a resident of Sweden, owns 10 per cent or more of the class of shares in respect of which the dividend is paid, paragraphs (1), (2) and (6) of this Article shall not apply to the dividend to the extent that it can have been paid only out of profits which the company paying the dividend earned or other income which it received in a period ending twelve months or more before the relevant date. For the purposes of this paragraph the term "relevant date" means the date on which the beneficial owner of the dividend became the owner of 10 per cent or more of the class of shares in question. Provided that this paragraph shall not apply if the shares were acquired for *bona fide* commercial reasons and not primarily for the purpose of securing the benefit of this Article.

(9) The provisions of paragraphs (1), (2), (4) and (6) of this Article shall not apply if the recipient of the dividends, being a resident of one of the territories, has in the other territory, of which the company paying the dividends is a resident, a permanent establishment, and the holding by virtue of which the dividends are paid is effectively connected with a trade or business carried on through such permanent establishment. In such a case the provisions of Article III shall apply.

(10) Where a company which is a resident of one of the territories derives profits or income from the other territory, that other territory may not impose any tax on the dividends paid by the company to persons who are not residents of that other territory, or subject the company's undistributed profits to a tax on undistributed profits, even if the dividends paid or the undistributed profits consist wholly or partly of profits or income arising in such other territory."

ARTICLE 2

(1) This Further Supplementary Protocol shall be ratified and the instruments of ratification shall be exchanged at Stockholm as soon as possible.

(2) This Further Supplementary Protocol shall enter into force after the expiration of a month following the date on which the instruments of ratification are exchanged(a) and shall thereupon have effect:

    (*a*) in the United Kingdom in relation only to dividends due and payable on or after 6 April, 1973; and

    (*b*) in Sweden in relation only to dividends due and payable on or after 1 January, 1974.

(a) Instruments of ratification were exchanged on 30th January 1974.

ARTICLE 3

This Further Supplementary Protocol shall remain in force as long as the Convention remains in force.

In witness whereof the undersigned, duly authorised thereto by their respective Governments, have signed this Further Supplementary Protocol.

Done in duplicate at London this 27 day of September 1973 in the English and Swedish languages, both texts being equally authoritative.

For the Government of
the United Kingdom of
Great Britain and
Northern Ireland:

For the Government
of the Kingdom of Sweden:

ANTHONY H. F. ROYLE.

ÖLE JODAHL.

EXPLANATORY NOTE

(This Note is not part of the Order.)

The Further Supplementary Protocol scheduled to this Order makes certain alterations to the Convention with Sweden signed on 28th July 1960 (as amended by Protocols signed on 25th March 1966 and 27th June 1968). These alterations mostly follow from the introduction of the new United Kingdom corporation tax system which, so far as it relates to the tax treatment of dividends paid by a United Kingdom company to an overseas shareholder, came into operation on 6th April 1973. The Protocol provides that where a United Kingdom company pays a dividend to a resident of Sweden other than a company which controls 10 per cent or more of the voting power in the paying company, the recipient is, subject to certain conditions, to receive the tax credit to which an individual resident in the United Kingdom and in receipt of such a dividend would be entitled less income tax at a rate not exceeding 15 per cent on the aggregate of the dividend and the tax credit. The Protocol also provides that the rate of Swedish tax on dividends paid by a Swedish company to a resident of the United Kingdom is not to exceed 5 per cent where the dividend is paid to a United Kingdom company which controls at least 10 per cent of the voting power in the paying company and 10 per cent in all other cases. The Protocol is expressed to take effect in the United Kingdom in relation to dividends due and payable on or after 6th April 1973 and in Sweden in relation to dividends due and payable on or after 1st January 1974.

STATUTORY INSTRUMENTS

1974 No. 559

LAND REGISTRATION

The Registration of Title (No. 2) Order 1974

Made - - -	*26th March* 1974
Coming into Operation	*1st May* 1974

At the Court at Windsor Castle, the 26th day of March 1974

Present,

The Queen's Most Excellent Majesty in Council

Her Majesty, in exercise of the powers conferred on Her by section 120(1) of the Land Registration Act 1925**(a)**, is pleased, by and with the advice of Her Privy Council, to order and declare, and it is hereby ordered and declared, as follows:—

1.—(1) This Order may be cited as the Registration of Title (No. 2) Order 1974 and shall come into operation on 1st May 1974.

(2) The Interpretation Act 1889 **(b)** shall apply to the interpretation of this Order as it applies to the interpretation of an Act of Parliament.

(3) In this Order "remainder of the district" means that part of a district in which registration of title to land is not declared to be compulsory on sale by Article 3 of the Registration of Title Order 1974**(c)**.

2. In addition to the areas specified in column 2 of Schedule 1 to the Registration of Title Order 1974, registration of title to land shall be compulsory on sale—

(*a*) in the areas specified in column 2 of Schedule 1 to this Order (being areas within the counties specified in column 1 of that Schedule), on and after 1st May 1974;

(*b*) in the areas specified in column 2 of Schedule 2 to this Order (being areas within the counties specified in column 1 of that Schedule), on and after 1st September 1974; and

(*c*) in the district of Rotherham in the county of South Yorkshire, on and after 1st November 1974.

W. G. Agnew.

(a) 1925 c. 21.   (b) 1889 c. 63.   (c) S.I. 1974/250 (1974 I, p. 824).

SCHEDULE 1

Column 1 County	Column 2 Areas of compulsory registration
Avon	The district of Bath.
Cambridgeshire	The district of Cambridge.
Cheshire	The remainder of the districts of Chester, and Crewe and Nantwich.
Cleveland	The remainder of the districts of Hartlepool, Langbaurgh and Stockton-on-Tees.
Devon	The districts of Exeter and Torbay.
Durham	The remainder of the districts of Darlington, Durham and Easington.
Gwent	The district of Newport.
Hertfordshire	The district of Stevenage and the remainder of the districts of Hertsmere and Three Rivers.
Lancashire	The remainder of the districts of Blackburn and Preston.
South Glamorgan	The district of Cardiff.
Suffolk	The district of Ipswich.
Tyne and Wear	The district of North Tyneside.

SCHEDULE 2

Column 1 County	Column 2 Areas of compulsory registration
Avon	The remainder of the district of Kingswood.
Bedfordshire	The remainder of the districts of Bedford and South Bedfordshire.
Cheshire	The remainder of the district of Warrington.
Derbyshire	The remainder of the district of Erewash.
Humberside	The district of North Wolds.
Lancashire	The remainder of the district of Burnley.
Nottinghamshire	The remainder of the districts of Broxtowe, Gedling and Rushcliffe.
Oxfordshire	The remainder of the district of South Oxfordshire.
South Yorkshire	The districts of Barnsley and Doncaster.
Warwickshire	The remainder of the districts of Rugby and Warwick.
West Sussex	The remainder of the districts of Crawley and Mid Sussex.
West Yorkshire	The districts of Bradford and Wakefield.

EXPLANATORY NOTE

(This Note is not part of the Order.)

This Order extends the system of compulsory registration of title on sale of land to the areas specified in column 2 of Schedule 1 with effect from 1st May 1974, to those specified in column 2 of Schedule 2 with effect from 1st September 1974 and to the district of Rotherham with effect from 1st November 1974.

STATUTORY INSTRUMENTS

1974 No. 560

PARTNERSHIP

The Limited Partnerships (Amendment) Rules 1974

Made - - - - *22nd March* 1974

Coming into Operation *25th April* 1974

The Secretary of State, in exercise of the powers conferred by section 17(*d*) of the Limited Partnerships Act 1907(**a**) and now vested in him(**b**), hereby makes the following Rules :—

1.—(1) These Rules may be cited as the Limited Partnerships (Amendment) Rules 1974 and shall come into operation on 25th April 1974.

(2) The Interpretation Act 1889(**c**) applies for the interpretation of these Rules as it applies for the interpretation of an Act of Parliament.

2. The Appendix to these Rules shall be substituted for the Appendix to the Limited Partnerships Rules 1907(**d**).

R. C. M. Cooper,
An Under-Secretary of
The Department of Trade.

22nd March 1974.

(**a**) 1907 c. 24.   (**b**) *See* S.I. 1970/1537 (1970 III p. 5293).
(**c**) 1889 c. 63.   (**d**) S.R. & O. 1907/1020 (Rev. XVII, p. 15: 1907 p. 765).

APPENDIX

FORMS TO BE USED FOR THE PURPOSES OF THE ACT AND FOR THE
PURPOSES OF SECTION 47 OF THE FINANCE ACT 1973

Registration No....................   Form No. L.P.5
                                                      (Registration fee £2)
                                                      (Capital duty also payable)

LIMITED PARTNERSHIPS ACT 1907

Application for Registration of a Limited Partnership and

Statement of particulars and of the amounts contributed
(in cash or otherwise) by the Limited Partners

(Pursuant to Section 8 of the Limited Partnerships Act 1907
and Section 47 of the Finance Act 1973)

Name of firm or partnership..

We, the undersigned, being the partners of the above-named firm, hereby apply for registration as a limited partnership and for that purpose supply the following particulars:

The general nature of the business	
The principal place of business	
The term, if any, for which the partnership is entered into	
If no definite term, the conditions of existence of the partnership	
Date of commencement	

The partnership is limited and the full name and address of each of the partners are as follows:

General partners

Limited partners	Amounts Contributed (1)	Capital duty payable (2)
Total		

Signatures of all the partners

Date ....

Presented by:
Presentor's reference:

NOTES

(1) State amount contributed by each limited partner, and whether paid in cash, or how otherwise.

(2) The capital duty is £1 for every £100, or part of £100, contributed by each limited partner.   3k

Registration No...................   Form No. L.P.6

LIMITED PARTNERSHIPS ACT 1907

Statement specifying the nature of a change in the
Limited Partnership

and Statement of increase in the amount contributed (in cash
or otherwise) by limited partners

(Pursuant to Section 9 of the Limited Partnerships Act 1907
and Section 47 of the Finance Act 1973)

Name of firm or partnership..

Notice is hereby given that the changes specified below have occurred in this
limited partnership:

(please see Notes overleaf)

(a) The firm name	{	Previous name
		New name
(b) General nature of the business	{	Business previously carried on
		Business now carried on
(c) Principal place of business	{	Previous place of business
		New place of business
(d) Change in the partners or the name of a partner (Note 1)	{	
(e) Term or character of the partnership (Note 2)	{	Previous term
		New term
(f) Change in the sum contributed by any limited partner (Note 3) (particulars of any increase in capital contributions must be provided at (h) overleaf)	{	
(g) Change in the liability of any partner by reason of his becoming a limited instead of a general partner, or vice versa	{	

(*h*) Statement of increase in capital contributions

Names of Limited Partners	Increase or additional sum now contributed (If otherwise than in cash, that fact, with particulars, must be stated)	Total amount contributed (If otherwise than in cash, that fact, with particulars, must be stated)	Capital duty payable on increase, etc.

Total capital duty payable

Signature of firm ....

Date ....

Presented by :

Presentor's reference :

NOTES

(1) Changes brought about by death, by transfer of interests, by increase in the number of partners, or by change of name of any partner, must be notified here.

(2) If there is, or was, no definite term, then state against " previous term " the conditions under which the partnership was constituted and against " new term " the conditions under which it is now constituted.

(3) Any variation in the sum contributed by any limited partner must be stated at (*f*) overleaf. A statement of any increase in the amount of the partnership capital, whether arising from increase of contributions, or from introduction of fresh partners must also be made at (*h*) above. Capital duty is payable at £1 for every £100, or part of £100, on any increase in the amounts of contributions made, in cash or otherwise, by a limited partner.

(4) Each change must be entered in the proper division (*a*), (*b*), (*c*), (*d*), (*e*), (*f*), (*g*) or (*h*), as the case may be. Provision is made in this form for notifying all the changes required by the Act to be notified, but it will frequently happen that only one item of change has to be notified. In any such case, the word " Nil " should be inserted in the other divisions.

(5) The statement must be signed at the end by the firm, and delivered for registration within seven days of the change or changes taking place.

EXPLANATORY NOTE

(This Note is not part of the Rules.)

These Rules amend the Limited Partnerships Rules 1907. They prescribe new forms for making statements of particulars on the registration of Limited Partnerships and for making statements specifying changes in Limited Partnerships. The new forms provide for the disclosure of the particulars required to be disclosed in these statements under section 47 of the Finance Act 1973 (c.51).

STATUTORY INSTRUMENTS

1974   No. 563

EDUCATION, ENGLAND AND WALES

The Independent Schools Tribunal (Amendment) Rules 1974

Made – – –		*21st March* 1974
Coming into Operation		*25th April* 1974

The Lord Chancellor, in exercise of the powers conferred on him by section 75(1) of the Education Act 1944(a) and with the concurrence of the Lord President of the Council and the consent of the Minister for the Civil Service, in exercise of the powers now vested in him **(b)**, hereby makes the following Rules:—

1.—(1) These Rules may be cited as the Independent Schools Tribunal (Amendment) Rules 1974 and shall come into operation on 25th April 1974.

(2) The Interpretation Act 1889(c) shall apply to the interpretation of these Rules as it applies to the interpretation of an Act of Parliament.

(3) In these Rules a rule referred to by number means a rule so numbered in the Independent Schools Tribunal Rules 1958(d), as amended **(e)**.

2.—(1) In rule 13(1) for the expressions "£22" and "£10.50" there shall be substituted the expressions "£25" and "£12.60" respectively.

(2) In rule 13(3)(i) for the expression "£6" there shall be substituted the expression "£7".

(3) In rule 13(3)(ii) for the expressions "£11" and "£22" there shall be substituted the expressions "£12.50" and "£25" respectively.

Dated 11th March 1974.

Elwyn - Jones, C.

I concur.

Dated 14th March 1974.

Edward Short,
Lord President of the Council.

I consent.

Dated 21st March 1974.

Robert Sheldon,
Minister of State.

(a) 1944 c. 31.
(c) 1889 c. 63.
(b) S.I. 1971/2099 (1971 III, p. 6186).
(d) S.I. 1958/519 (1958 I, p. 1006).
(e) The relevant amending instrument is S.I. 1972/42 (1972 I, p. 120).

EXPLANATORY NOTE

(This Note is not part of the Rules.)

These Rules increase the fees payable to the chairman and members of the Independent Schools Tribunal as follows. For each day on which the Tribunal sits the fee of the chairman is increased from £22 to £25 and that of a member from £10.50 to £12.60. The chairman's fees for interlocutory matters are increased from £22 to £25 where the hearing lasts for more than 3 hours, from £11 to £12.50 where the hearing does not last for more than 3 hours and from £6 to £7 where no party appears.

STATUTORY INSTRUMENTS

1974 No. 564

CIVIL AVIATION

The Civil Aviation (Navigation Services Charges) (Third Amendment) Regulations 1974

Made - - -	*26th March* 1974
Laid before Parliament	*27th March* 1974
Coming into Operation	*1st April* 1974

The Secretary of State, in exercise of his powers under sections 4 and 7 of the Civil Aviation (Eurocontrol) Act 1962(a), as these sections are amended respectively by paragraphs 6 and 7 of Schedule 10 to the Civil Aviation Act 1971(b), and under section 15(3) of the Civil Aviation Act 1968(c) and of all other powers enabling him in that behalf and with the consent of the Treasury hereby makes the following Regulations:

1. These Regulations may be cited as the Civil Aviation (Navigation Services Charges) (Third Amendment) Regulations 1974 and shall come into operation on 1st April 1974.

2. The Interpretation Act 1889(d) shall apply for the purpose of the interpretation of these Regulations as it applies for the purpose of the interpretation of an Act of Parliament.

3. The Civil Aviation (Navigation Services Charges) Regulations 1971(e), as amended(f), shall be further amended as follows:

In Regulation 6A for "seven pounds" there shall be substituted "twelve pounds".

S. Clinton Davis,
Parliamentary Under-Secretary of State
for Companies, Aerospace and Shipping,
Department of Trade.

19th March 1974.

We consent to the making of these Regulations.

Donald R. Coleman,
John Golding,
Lords Commissioners of Her Majesty's
Treasury.

26th March 1974.

(a) 1962 c. 8.   (b) 1971 c. 75.   (c) 1968 c. 61.
(d) 1889 c. 63.   (e) S.I. 1971/1135 (1971 II, p. 3345).
(f) S.I. 1971/1730, 1972/188 (1971 III, p. 4716; 1972 I, p. 670).

EXPLANATORY NOTE

(*This Note is not part of the Regulations.*)

These Regulations further amend the Civil Aviation (Navigation Services Charges) Regulations 1971, as amended, by increasing from seven to twelve pounds the charge payable by the operator of an aircraft which flies within the Shanwick Oceanic Control Area and in respect of which a flight plan is communicated to the appropriate air traffic control unit.

STATUTORY INSTRUMENTS

1974 No. 565

FOOD AND DRUGS

The Milk (Great Britain) (Amendment) Order 1974

Made - - - -	*26th March* 1974
Laid before Parliament	*27th March* 1974
Coming into Operation	*21st April* 1974

The Minister of Agriculture, Fisheries and Food and the Secretary of State, acting jointly in exercise of the powers conferred on them by sections 6 and 7 of the Emergency Laws (Re-enactments and Repeals) Act 1964(a) and of all other powers enabling them in that behalf, hereby make the following order:—

Citation and commencement

1. This order may be cited as the Milk (Great Britain) (Amendment) Order 1974, and shall come into operation on 21st April 1974.

Amendment of the principal order

2. The Milk (Great Britain) Order 1971(b), as amended by the Milk (Great Britain) (Amendment) Order 1972(c), shall be further amended by substituting for Schedules 1 and 2 thereto respectively Schedules 1 and 2 to this order.

In Witness whereof the Official Seal of the Minister of Agriculture, Fisheries and Food is hereunto affixed on 25th March 1974.

(L.S.)

Frederick Peart,
Minister of Agriculture, Fisheries
and Food.

26th March 1974.

William Ross,
Secretary of State for Scotland.

SCHEDULE 1

MAXIMUM PRICES OF MILK IN ENGLAND AND WALES

1. Subject to the provisions of this Schedule, the maximum price of milk on a sale in England and Wales shall be a price in accordance with the following table:—

Milk	Maximum Price (Rate per Pint)
	p
Channel Islands milk	$5\frac{1}{2}$
South Devon milk	$5\frac{1}{2}$
Untreated Milk Farm Bottled	$5\frac{1}{2}$
Ultra Heat Treated milk	5
Sterilised milk	5
Homogenised milk	5
Untreated milk	$4\frac{1}{2}$
Pasteurised milk	$4\frac{1}{2}$
Milk, other than the above mentioned ...	$4\frac{1}{2}$

(a) 1964 c. 60. (b) S.I. 1971/1038 (1971 II, p. 3108). (c) S.I. 1972/367 (1972 I, p. 1440).

2306   FOOD AND DRUGS

2. A reasonable charge may be made by the seller in addition to the appropriate maximum price specified in the above table for milk sold by him as Kosher or Kedassia milk if—

(a) such milk is sold in a container distinctly labelled " Kosher " or " Kedassia ", as the case may be; and

(b) such milk has been prepared for consumption in accordance with the appropriate Jewish practice relating thereto.

SCHEDULE 2

MAXIMUM PRICES OF MILK IN SCOTLAND

1. Subject to the provisions of this Schedule, the maximum price of milk on a sale in Scotland, excluding the islands other than the islands of Islay, Coll and Gigha in the County of Argyll and those in the Counties of Bute and Orkney, shall be a price in accordance with the following table:—

Milk	Maximum Price (Rate per Pint)
	p
Channel Islands milk	5½
South Devon milk	5½
Premium milk	5½
Ultra Heat Treated milk	5
Sterilised milk	5
Homogenised milk	5
Standard milk	4½
Pasteurised milk	4½
Milk, other than the above mentioned ...	4½

2. A reasonable charge may be made by the seller in addition to the appropriate maximum price specified in the above table for milk sold by him as Kosher milk or Kedassia milk if—

(a) such milk is sold in a container distinctly labelled " Kosher " or " Kedassia ", as the case may be; and

(b) such milk has been prepared for consumption in accordance with the appropriate Jewish practice relating thereto.

EXPLANATORY NOTE

(This Note is not part of the Order.)

This amending Order, which comes into operation on 21st April 1974, reduces by 1p per pint the maximum prices of milk on sales in Great Britain.

STATUTORY INSTRUMENTS

1974 No. 566

FOOD AND DRUGS

The Milk (Northern Ireland) (Amendment) Order 1974

Made - - - -	*25th March* 1974
Laid before Parliament	*27th March* 1974
Coming into Operation	*21st April* 1974

The Minister of Agriculture, Fisheries and Food, in exercise of the powers conferred on him by sections 6 and 7 of the Emergency Laws (Re-enactments and Repeals) Act 1964(a) and of all other powers enabling him in that behalf, hereby makes the following order : —

Citation and commencement

1. This order may be cited as the Milk (Northern Ireland) (Amendment) Order 1974, and shall come into operation on 21st April 1974.

Amendment of the principal order

2. The Milk (Northern Ireland) Order 1971(b), as amended by the Milk (Northern Ireland) (Amendment) Order 1972(c), shall be further amended by substituting for the Schedule thereto the Schedule to this order.

In Witness whereof the Official Seal of the Minister of Agriculture, Fisheries and Food is hereunto affixed on 25th March 1974.

(L.S.)

Frederick Peart,
Minister of Agriculture, Fisheries
and Food.

SCHEDULE

MAXIMUM PRICES OF MILK

Milk	Maximum Price (Rate per Pint)
	p
Farm bottled milk	4½
Pasteurised milk	4½

EXPLANATORY NOTE

(This Note is not part of the Order.)

This amending Order, which comes into operation on 21st April 1974, reduces by 1p per pint the maximum prices of milk on sales in Northern Ireland.

(a) 1964 c. 60.   (b) S.I. 1971/1037 (1971 II, p. 3105).   (c) S.I. 1972/366 (1972 I, p. 1438).

STATUTORY INSTRUMENTS

1974 No. 569

LOCAL GOVERNMENT, ENGLAND AND WALES

The Local Government (Successor Parishes) Order 1974

Made - - -	*27th March* 1974
Laid before Parliament	*28th March* 1974
Coming into Operation	*30th March* 1974

The Secretary of State for the Environment, upon consideration of proposals made to him by the Local Government Boundary Commission for England and in exercise of the powers conferred upon him by paragraph 2(1) of Part V of Schedule 1 to the Local Government Act 1972(a) and of all other powers enabling him in that behalf, hereby makes the following order:—

Title, commencement and interpretation

1. This order may be cited as the Local Government (Successor Parishes) Order 1974 and shall come into operation on 30th March 1974.

2. The Interpretation Act 1889(b) shall apply for the interpretation of this order as it applies for the interpretation of an Act of Parliament.

Successor parishes

3. There shall be constituted the parishes named in column (1) of the Schedule to this order, the boundaries of which are coterminous with the boundaries of the existing urban districts or boroughs respectively specified in respect of such parishes in column (2).

Parish councillors

4. In relation to the parishes named in the said column (1), 30th March 1974 is hereby specified as the date for the purposes of sub-paragraphs (2) (aldermen and councillors of boroughs or councillors of urban districts to be parish councillors) and (5) (cessation of provision suspending elections, and filling of casual vacancies) of paragraph 13 of Schedule 3 to the Local Government Act 1972.

(a) 1972 c.70.   (b) 1889 c.63.

SCHEDULE

(1) Parishes	(2) Existing urban districts or boroughs
County of Cheshire Sandbach	The urban district of Sandbach
County of East Sussex Lewes	The borough of Lewes
County of Hertfordshire Hertford	The borough of Hertford
County of Lancashire Adlington	The urban district of Adlington

27th March 1974.

Anthony Crosland,
Secretary of State for the Environment.

EXPLANATORY NOTE

(This Note is not part of the Order.)

Part V of Schedule 1 to the Local Government Act 1972 makes provision for the constitution of parishes for areas of existing boroughs and urban districts in England. A number of parishes were constituted by the Local Government (Successor Parishes) Order 1973 (S.I. 1973/1110) and the Local Government (Successor Parishes) (No. 2) Order 1973 (S.I. 1973/1939). This Order gives effect to further proposals made by the Local Government Boundary Comission for England. It also specifies a date for certain electoral provisions of the 1972 Act (*See* Article 4).

STATUTORY INSTRUMENTS

1974 No. 570

CUSTOMS AND EXCISE

The Import Duties (Temporary Reductions and Exemptions) (No. 4) Order 1974

Made - - - -	*26th March* 1974
Laid before the House of Commons	*27th March* 1974
Coming into Operation	*2nd April* 1974

The Lords Commissioners of Her Majesty's Treasury, by virtue of the powers conferred on them by sections 1, 2, 3(6) and 13 of the Import Duties Act 1958(a), as amended by section 5(5) of, and paragraph 1 of Schedule 4 to, the European Communities Act 1972(b), and of all other powers enabling them in that behalf, on the recommendation of the Secretary of State(c), hereby make the following Order:

Citation, operation, interpretation

1.—(1) This Order may be cited as the Import Duties (Temporary Reductions and Exemptions) (No. 4) Order 1974 and shall come into operation on 2nd April 1974.

(2) In this Order "the relevant date" in relation to goods of a description specified in column 2 of any Schedule hereto means 31st December 1974 or, if an earlier date is there specified in relation to the description, the date so specified.

(3) The Interpretation Act 1889(d) shall apply to the interpretation of this Order as it applies to the interpretation of an Act of Parliament.

Intra-Community trade

2. Up to and including the relevant date, no import duty shall be charged on goods of a heading of the Customs Tariff 1959 specified in column 1 of Schedules 1, 2 or 3 or Part II of Schedule 4 hereto which are of a description specified in column 2 thereof if they satisfy the requisite conditions to benefit from Regulation (EEC) 385/73(e) (relating to goods entitled to benefit from the eventual abolition of customs duties in trade between member States of the European Communities).

The full rate

3.—(1) Up to and including the relevant date, in the case of goods which fall within a heading of the Customs Tariff 1959 specified in column 1 of Schedule 1, 2 or 4 hereto which are of a description specified in column 2 thereof, if a rate

---

(a) 1958 c. 6.   (b) 1972 c. 68.
(c) *See* S.I. 1970/1537 (1970 III, p. 5293).   (d) 1889 c. 63.
(e) O.J. No. L42, 14.2.1973, p. 1.

of duty is shown in column 3 thereof in relation to the goods, import duty shall be charged at the rate so shown instead of any higher rate which would otherwise apply, and if the entry "free" appears in relation to them, no import duty shall be charged.

(2) If no entry appears in column 3 of the said Schedules hereto in relation to goods of a description specified in column 2 thereof, no exemption from or reduction in duty applies to such goods by virtue of this Article.

(3) Paragraph (1) above shall operate without prejudice to the exemptions provided for by Article 2 above or any greater reductions provided for by Articles 4 and 5 below in the case of goods originating in Egypt or Cyprus or goods qualifying for Commonwealth preference.

Egypt and Cyprus

4.—(1) Up to and including the relevant date, any import duty for the time being chargeable on goods of a heading of the Customs Tariff 1959 specified in column 1 of Schedules 1, 2 or 4 hereto which are of a description specified in column 2 thereof shall be charged:

(*a*) at the rate, if any, shown in column 4 thereof in relation to the description if the goods originate in Egypt and

(*b*) at the rate, if any, shown in column 5 thereof in relation to the description if the goods originate in Cyprus.

(2) For the purposes of paragraph (1) above goods shall be regarded as originating:

(*a*) in Egypt if they are to be so regarded under the Agreement, signed on 18th December 1972, between the European Economic Community and Egypt**(a)** and

(*b*) in Cyprus if they are to be so regarded under the Agreement, signed on 19th December 1972, between the Community and Cyprus**(a)**.

(3) If no entry appears in column 4 or 5 of the said Schedules in relation to goods of a description specified in column 2 thereof, no reduction in duty applies by virtue of this Article to goods of that description originating in Egypt or Cyprus.

(4) This Article shall operate without prejudice to any greater reduction in, or to any exemption from, import duties which may be available apart from this Order in the case of goods herein referred to by virtue of their being goods of a developing country or goods qualifying for Commonwealth preference or otherwise.

Goods qualifying for Commonwealth preference

5. Up to and including the relevant date, any import duty for the time being chargeable on goods of a heading of the Customs Tariff 1959 specified in column 1 of Parts I and II of Schedule 4 hereto which are of a description specified in column 2 thereof and which qualify for Commonwealth preference shall be charged at the rate shown in column 6 of the said Parts I and II of Schedule 4 instead of any higher rate which would otherwise apply.

Miscellaneous

6.—(1) Any description in column 2 of any Schedule hereto shall be taken

(a) The Agreement is annexed to Regulation (EEC) 2409/73 (O.J. No. L251, p. 1).
(b) The Agreement is annexed to Regulation (EEC) 1246/73 (O.J. No. L133, p. 1).

to comprise all goods which would be classified under an entry in the same terms constituting a subheading (other than the final subheading) in the relevant heading in the Customs Tariff 1959.

(2) For the purposes of classification under the Customs Tariff 1959, insofar as that depends on the rate of duty, any goods to which this Order applies shall be treated as chargeable with the same duty as if this Order had not been made.

John Golding,
T. Pendry,
Two of the Lords Commissioners
of Her Majesty's Treasury.

26th March 1974.

NOTE: *Where no rate of duty is shown in columns 4 and 5 there is no reduction in the case of goods of Egypt and Cyprus as such.*

SCHEDULE 1

GOODS TEMPORARILY EXEMPT FROM IMPORT DUTY

Tariff Heading (1)	Description (2)	Rates of Duty % Full (3)	Egypt (4)	Cyprus (5)
29.02	Chlorobenzene	14·4	6·4	4·3
29.04	2,2,4-Trimethylpentane-1,3-diol	16·4	7·3	4·9
29·22	Sodium hydrogen 3-aminonaphthalene-1,5-di-sulphonate	12·8	5·7	3·8
29.25	N-(Hydroxymethyl)acrylamide	14·4	6·4	4·3
29.31	2-Chloro-1-phthalimidoethyl OO-diethyl phos-phordithioate	14·4	6·4	4·3
29.35	Temazepam	10·4	4·6	3·1
70.10	Carboys, bottles, jars, pots and similar containers, of glass, of a kind commonly used for the conveyance and packing of goods, excluding tubular containers (up to and including 2nd September 1974)	9·5	4·2	2·8
73.11	Angles, shapes and sections of iron or steel, not further worked than hot-rolled or extruded, and not clad, in the case of I, U, H and Z sections the distance between the outer surfaces of the two parallel planes is to be not less than 70 millimetres in the case of angles the outer length of the leg or of the longest leg is to be not less than 70 millimetres and in all other cases the greatest dimension of the cross-section is to be not less than 70 millimetres —drilled, punched or otherwise fabricated (ECSC) ... ... —other (ECSC) ... ... (up to and including 1st July 1974)	6 6	— —	— —
73.14	Iron or steel wire of circular cross-section and of which the diameter is not less than 0·8 millimetres and not more than 13 millimetres; containing not less than 0·05 per cent. and not more than 0·25 per cent. by weight of carbon, not less than 0·20 per cent. and not more than 1·7 per cent. by weight of manganese, not more than 0·07 per cent. by weight of phosphorus, not more than 0·2 per cent. by weight of silicon and not more than 0·7 per cent. by weight of sulphur; having a tensile strength not greater than 600 newtons per square millimetre (up to and including 1st July 1974)	8	3·6	2·4

Tariff Heading (1)	Description (2)	Rates of Duty %		
		Full (3)	Egypt (4)	Cyprus (5)
73·15	Alloy steel billets containing not less than 0·3 per cent. and not more than 1·7 per cent. by weight of manganese and containing two or more of the following elements, by weight, in the proportions indicated:—			
	Not less than Not More than (per cent.) (per cent.) Chromium 0·3 5·0 Nickel 0·4 5·0 Molybdenum 0·2 2·5 and having a cross-section of which neither the width nor the thickness is less than 50 millimetres nor more than 250 millimetres			
	—forged	5	2·2	1·5
	—other than forged (ECSC) ... ... (up to and including 1st July 1974)	4	—	—
73.18	Steel linepipe, welded, in lengths of not less than 8·0 metres and not more than 16·0 metres with an outside diameter of not less than 1207 millimetres and not more than 1232 millimetres and a wall thickness of not less than 10·0 millimetres and not more than 14·0 millimetres (up to and including 1st July 1974)	10	4·5	3

SCHEDULE 2

GOODS ON WHICH TEMPORARY REDUCTION OF OR EXEMPTION FROM IMPORT DUTY IS EXTENDED

Tariff Heading (1)	Description (2)	Rates of Duty %		
		Full (3)	Egypt (4)	Cyprus (5)
28.33	Ammonium bromide (up to and including 2nd September 1974)	12	5·4	3·6
	Sodium bromide containing not more than 0·05 per cent. by weight of chlorides expressed as Cl (up to and including 1st July 1974)	12	5·4	3·6
29.01	*iso*Butene of a purity not less than 99·0 per cent.			
	—for use as power or heating fuel	17·5	7·8	5·2
	—for other purposes	Free	—	—
29.04	*n*-Butan-1-ol	11·2	5	3·3
	2-Ethylhexan-1-ol	15·8	7·1	4·7
29.06	*o*-Cresol (up to and including 2nd September 1974)	2·4	1	0·7
	Quinol (up to and including 1st July 1974) ...	14·4	6·4	4·3
29.14	Undec-10-enoic acid of a purity not less than 98·0 per cent.	10·4	4·6	3·1

Tariff Heading (1)	Description (2)	Rates of Duty %		
		Full (3)	Egypt (4)	Cyprus (5)
39.02	Polymerisation and copolymerisation products of ethylene, of natural colour, in the forms covered by Note 3(*b*) to Chapter 39, and having a density of not less than 0·940 grammes per cubic centimetre when determined by Method B2 of British Standard 3412: 1966			
	—falling within subheading CI a)2	—	5·5	3·7
	—falling within subheading CXIV a)3bb ...	—	5·7	3·8
	(up to and including 1st July 1974)			
68.13	Asbestos paper, rubber impregnated, in rolls, being not less than 0·55 millimetre and not more than 0·85 millimetre in thickness, weighing not less than 500 grammes and not more than 780 grammes per square metre, and having a loss on ignition at 1,000° centigrade of not less than 24 per cent. by weight and not more than 32 per cent. by weight (up to and including 1st July 1974)	—	4·1	2·7
73.10	Bars and rods of iron or steel, not further worked than hot-rolled or extruded, in straight lengths and having a rectangular cross-section of which the width is not less than 10 millimetres nor more than 210 millimetres and the thickness is not less than 6 millimetres (up to and including 1st July 1974)	6	—	—
	Bars and rods of iron or steel, not further worked than hot-rolled or extruded, in straight lengths or in coils, of circular, square or hexagonal cross-section, or ribbed and of which the greatest cross-sectional dimension does not exceed 156 millimetres; in the case of square cross-section the corners may be either square or rounded (up to and including 1st July 1974)	6	—	—
73.15	Bars and rods of alloy steel, not further worked than hot-rolled or extruded, and in coils, having a circular, square or hexagonal cross-section of which no cross-sectional dimension exceeds 46 millimetres and containing either (*a*) not less than 0·10 per cent. lead; or (*b*) not less than 0·10 per cent. sulphur as the major alloying element other than carbon			
	—wire rod (ECSC)	7	—	—
	—other (ECSC)	6	—	—
	(up to and including 1st July 1974)			

Tariff Heading (1)	Description (2)	Rates of Duty %		
		Full (3)	Egypt (4)	Cyprus (5)
	Bars and rods of alloy steel, not further worked than hot-rolled or extruded, and in straight lengths, having a circular, square or hexagonal cross-section of which no cross-sectional dimension exceeds 156 millimetres and containing either (a) not less than 0·10 per cent. lead; or (b) not less than 0·10 per cent. sulphur as the major alloying element other than carbon			
	—wire rod (ECSC)	7	—	—
	—other (ECSC)	6	—	—
	(up to and including 1st July 1974)			
	Bars and rods of high carbon steel, in coils, not further worked than hot-rolled, of circular cross-section and having a diameter of not less than 13 millimetres and not more than 28·5 millimetres (up to and including 1st July 1974) ...	6	—	—
85.15	The following apparatus for use in aircraft:			
	(a) automatic radio direction finding apparatus covering a frequency range of at least 200 KHz to 850 KHz;	10	4·5	3
	(b) distance measuring apparatus for determining the slant range from aircraft to ground transponder and operating within the frequency range of 960 MHz to 1,215 MHz;	10	4·5	3
	(c) panel-mounted secondary surveillance radar transponder apparatus, operating within a 12 or 24 volt electrical power system, having an integral control panel and capable of interrogation at a frequency of 1,030 MHz on each of the modes A and C and replying on these modes at a frequency of 1,090 MHz;	10	4·5	3
	(d) very high frequency omni-directional radio range apparatus (VOR), instrument landing system localiser apparatus (ILS/LOC), instrument landing system glide path apparatus (ILS/G.PATH);	10	4·5	3
	(e) very high frequency communication apparatus (VHF/COM) (transmitters, receivers, or combined transmitter/receivers) covering a frequency band of at least 118 to 135·95 MHz, with not less than 180 channels and capable of operating in areas where 50 KHz channel spacing is in force;			
	—transmitters	7	3·1	2·1
	—transmitter/receivers	11	4·9	3·3
	—receivers, whether or not combined with a sound recorder or reproducer	—	6·3	4·2
	(f) apparatus combining the functions and capabilities of any of the apparatus specified in (d) and (e) above but excluding apparatus combining any of those functions and capabilities with any other function of capability;	10	4·5	3

Tariff Heading (1)	Description (2)	Rates of Duty % Full (3)	Egypt (4)	Cyprus (5)
	being apparatus of a type approved by the Civil Aviation Authority, at the date of this Order, under Article 14(5) of the Air Navigation Order 1972, for use in aircraft of not more than 5,700 kilogrammes maximum total weight authorised, flying in controlled airspace in accordance with the Instrument Flight Rules as defined in the said Air Navigation Order, but not for use in other aircraft (up to and including 1st July 1974)			

SCHEDULE 3

EXEMPTION FROM DUTY ONLY IN THE CASE OF GOODS IN INTRA-COMMUNITY TRADE

Tariff Heading (1)	Descripton (2)
05.15	Horse mackerel (trachurus trachurus)
	Mackerel (Scomber Scombrus)

SCHEDULE 4

PART I

REDUCTIONS IN DUTY

Tariff Heading (1)	Description (2)	Rates of Duty %			
		Full (3)	Egypt (4)	Cyprus (5)	Common-wealth (6)
08.02	Grapefruit				
	I Fresh	£0·2000 + 0·8	—	—	0·8
	II Dried	8·8	—	—	0·8

PART II

EXEMPTION FROM DUTY IN THE CASE OF GOODS IN INTRA-COMMUNITY TRADE: REDUCTIONS IN OTHER CASES

Tariff Heading (1)	Description (2)	Full (3)	Egypt (4)	Cyprus (5)	Common-wealth (6)
09.10	Saffron:				
	Neither crushed nor ground:				
	—Stigmas and styles dried ...	4	—	—	—
	—Other	10	—	—	4
	(Up to and including 30th June 1974)				
29.01	Vinyltoluene (up to and including 30th June 1974)	6	2·7	1·8	2·4

EXPLANATORY NOTE

(This Note is not part of the Order.)

This Order provides for exemption from or reductions in import duty in the case of goods specified in the Schedules to the Order from 2nd April 1974 until 31st December 1974 or any earlier date appearing in the Schedules.

There is exemption from import duties in the case of all goods in the Schedules, other than those in Part I of Schedule 4, if the goods satisfy the requisite conditions to benefit from the eventual abolition of customs duties in trade between member States of the European Communities.

In the case of other goods, where a rate of duty is specified in column 3 of Schedules 1, 2 or 4, duty is reduced to that rate, instead of any higher rate which would otherwise apply, and where "free" appears in column 3 in relation to the goods, they are exempt from duty.

In the case of goods qualifying for Commonwealth preference or originating in Egypt or Cyprus greater reductions in duty are available in a number of cases than those referred to above. These are shown respectively in column 6 of Schedule 4 and columns 4 and 5 of Schedules 1, 2 and 4.

As regards the exemption for equipment for use in aircraft under heading 85.15, apparatus of a type approved by the Civil Aviation Authority is listed in Civil Aviation Publication CAP 208, Airborne Radio Apparatus Volume 2, published by Her Majesty's Stationery Office. This publication is subject to amendment, and confirmation that apparatus is of a type approved at the date of this Order should be obtained from the Civil Aviation Authority, Controllerate of National Air Traffic Services, Tels. N2(c), 19-29 Woburn Place, London WC1H 0LX.

STATUTORY INSTRUMENTS

1974 No. 571

REGISTRATION OF BIRTHS, DEATHS, MARRIAGES, ETC.
ENGLAND AND WALES

The Registration of Births, Deaths and Marriages (Amendment) Regulations 1974

Made - - -	*26th March* 1974
Coming into Operation	*1st April* 1974

The Registrar General, in exercise of the powers conferred on him by sections 6, 16 and 20 of the Registration Service Act 1953(a) and of all other powers enabling him in that behalf, with the approval of the Secretary of State for Social Services, hereby makes the following regulations:—

Citation and commencement

1.—(1) These regulations may be cited as the Registration of Births, Deaths and Marriages (Amendment) Regulations 1974 and shall come into operation on 1st April 1974.

(2) These regulations, the Registration of Births, Deaths and Marriages Regulations 1968(b), the Registration of Births, Deaths and Marriages (Amendment) Regulations 1969(c), the Marriage (Registrar General's Licence) Regulations 1970(d) and the Registration of Births, Deaths and Marriages (Amendment) Regulations 1971(e) shall be construed as one and may be cited together as the Registration of Births, Deaths and Marriages Regulations 1968 to 1974.

Interpretation

2.—(1) In these regulations, unless the context otherwise requires, "the principal regulations" means the Registration of Births, Deaths and Marriages Regulations 1968 as amended(f).

(2) The Interpretation Act 1889(g) shall apply to the interpretation of these regulations as it applies to the interpretation of an Act of Parliament.

Amendment of Principal Regulations

3.—(1) In regulation 2(1)—

   (*a*) in the definition of "borough" the words "county borough or a" shall be omitted;

   (*b*) the definition of "clerk" shall be omitted;

(a) 1953 c. 37.
(c) S.I. 1969/1811 (1969 III, p. 5623).
(e) S.I. 1971/1218 (1971 II, p. 3551).
(g) 1889 c. 63.

(b) S.I. 1968/2049 (1968 III, p. 5522).
(d) S.I. 1970/1780 (1970 III, p. 5781).
(f) The amending Regulations are not relevant to the subject matter of these Regulations.

(c) in the definition of "council" for the word "county" in both places where it occurs there shall be substituted the words "non-metropolitan county, metropolitan district";

(d) in the definition of "local scheme" for the word "county" there shall be substituted the words "non-metropolitan county, metropolitan district";

(e) after the definition of "principal officer" there shall be inserted the following definition—

' "proper officer" means the officer appointed by the council for the purposes of the Registration Service Act 1953;'.

(2) In regulation 5—

(a) in paragraph (a)—

(i) sub-paragraph (iv) shall be omitted and sub-paragraphs (v) and (vi) shall be re-numbered "(iv)" and "(v)" respectively, and

(ii) after sub-paragraph (v) as re-numbered the following sub-paragraph shall be added—"(vi) if he is an officer or servant of the council appointed by them to exercise the functions of the proper officer;";

(b) in paragraph (c), after the word "coroner" the following shall be added "or is an officer or servant of a local authority employed by them in the performance of duties relating to their functions as a burial authority.".

(3) In regulation 7 for the word "clerk" in both places where it occurs there shall be substituted the words "proper officer".

(4) In regulation 8(1)—

(a) for the word "clerk" where it first occurs there shall be substituted the words "proper officer";

(b) for sub-paragraph (v) there shall be substituted the following sub-paragraph—

"(v) the council of every non-metropolitan district, parish and community wholly or partly situated in the district;";

(c) in sub-paragraph (vii) after the word "persons" there shall be inserted the words "or bodies".

(5) In regulation 85 for the word "clerk" wherever it occurs there shall be substituted the words "proper officer".

Given under my hand on 25th March 1974.

G. Paine,

Registrar General.

I approve.   *Barbara Castle,*

Secretary of State for Social Services.

26th March 1974.

EXPLANATORY NOTE

(This Note is not part of the Regulations.)

These Regulations amend the Registration of Births, Deaths and Marriages Regulations 1968. The amendment of Regulation 2 modifies the definition of words and phrases used in these Regulations in order to comply with the provisions of the Local Government Act 1972(c. 70). The amendments of Regulations 5, 7, 8 and 85 remove all references to the clerk of the council and substitute a reference to the proper officer.

STATUTORY INSTRUMENTS

1974 No. 572

REGISTRATION OF BIRTHS, DEATHS, MARRIAGES, ETC.
ENGLAND AND WALES

The Registration of Births, Still-births and Deaths (Welsh Language) and the Registration of Marriages (Welsh Language) (Amendment) Regulations 1974

Made - - -	*25th March* 1974
Coming into Operation	*1st April* 1974

The Registrar General, in exercise of the powers conferred on him by sections 27, 31, 32, 35, 55 and 74 of the Marriage Act 1949(a), sections 1, 5, 7, 9, 11 (as amended by section 2 of the Population (Statistics) Act 1960)(b), 13, 14, 15, 20 to 25, 29, 33, 39 and 41 of the Births and Deaths Registration Act 1953(c), and section 20 of the Registration Service Act 1953(d), as extended by sections 2(2) and 3 of the Welsh Language Act 1967(e) and of all other powers enabling him in that behalf, with the approval of the Secretary of State for Wales, hereby makes the following regulations:—

Citation and commencement

1. These regulations may be cited as the Registration of Births, Still-births and Deaths (Welsh Language) and the Registration of Marriages (Welsh Language) (Amendment) Regulations 1974 and shall come into operation on 1st April 1974.

Interpretation

2. The Interpretation Act 1889(f) shall apply to the interpretation of these regulations as it applies to the interpretation of an Act of Parliament.

Amendment of the Registration of Births, Still-births and Deaths (Welsh Language) Regulations 1969

3. The Registration of Births, Still-births and Deaths (Welsh Language) Regulations 1969(g) shall be amended as follows—

(a) the words "or Monmouthshire" shall be deleted wherever they occur; and

(b) in regulation 2(2) the following definition shall be inserted after the definition of "the principal regulations":—

' "Wales" means the area consisting of the counties established by section 20 of the Local Government Act 1972(h).'

(a) 1949 c. 76.   (b) 1960 c. 32.   (c) 1953 c. 20.   (d) 1953 c.37.

(e) 1967 c. 66.   (f) 1889 c. 63.   (g) S.I. 1969/203 (1969 I, p. 499).

(h) 1972 c. 70.

Amendment of the Registration of Marriages (Welsh Language) Regulations 1971

4. The Registration of Marriages (Welsh Language) Regulations 1971**(a)** shall be amended as follows—

  (*a*) the words "or Monmouthshire" shall be deleted wherever they occur;

  (*b*) in regulation 2(2), after the words "as amended" there shall be inserted the words " "Wales" means the area consisting of the counties established by section 20 of the Local Government Act 1972";

     and

  (*c*) in Schedule 1 in Forms 6 and 7, the words "county borough" and "bwrdeistref sirol" shall be deleted.

Given under my hand on 25th March 1974.

I approve.

G. Paine,
Registrar General.

John Morris,
Secretary of State for Wales.

25th March 1974.

EXPLANATORY NOTE

(This Note is not part of the Regulations.)

These Regulations amend the Registration of Births, Still-births and Deaths (Welsh Language) Regulations 1969 and the Registration of Marriages (Welsh Language) Regulations 1971 by deleting all references to Monmouthshire and county boroughs as both will cease to exist on 1st April 1974 by virtue of section 20 of the Local Government Act 1972.

(a) S.I. 1971/129 (1971 I, p. 246).

STATUTORY INSTRUMENTS

1974 No. 573

MARRIAGE

The Marriage (Authorised Persons) (Amendment)

Regulations 1974

Made - - -	26th *March* 1974
Coming into Operation	1st *April* 1974

The Registrar General, in exercise of the powers conferred on him by section 74 of the Marriage Act 1949(a) and of all other powers enabling him in that behalf, with the approval of the Secretary of State for Social Services, hereby makes the following regulations:—

Citation and commencement

1.—(1) These regulations may be cited as the Marriage (Authorised Persons) (Amendment) Regulations 1974 and shall come into operation on 1st April 1974.

(2) These regulations, the Marriage (Authorised Persons) Regulations 1952(b), as amended(c), and the Marriage (Authorised Persons) (Amendment) Regulations 1971(d) shall be construed as one and may be cited together as the Marriage (Authorised Persons) Regulations 1952 to 1974.

Interpretation

2. The Interpretation Act 1889(e) shall apply to the interpretation of these regulations as it applies to the interpretation of an Act of Parliament.

Amendment of the Marriage (Authorised Persons) Regulations 1952 (as amended)

3. In regulations 10 and 13(1) of the Marriage (Authorised Persons) Regulations 1952 (as amended), for the words "administrative county, county borough" there shall be substituted the words "non-metropolitan county, metropolitan district".

Given under my hand on 25th March 1974.

G. Paine,
Registrar General.

I approve.

Barbara Castle,
Secretary of State for Social Services.

26th March 1974.

(a) 1949 c. 76.   (b) S.I. 1952/1869 (1952 II, p. 1691).

(c) The relevant amending instrument is S.I. 1965/528 (1965 I, p. 1393).

(d) S.I. 1971/1216 (1971 II, p. 3547).   (e) 1889 c. 63.

EXPLANATORY NOTE

(*This Note is not part of the Regulations.*)

These Regulations amend the Marriage (Authorised Persons) Regulations 1952 by substituting the words non-metropolitan county and metropolitan district for the words administrative county and county borough respectively.

STATUTORY INSTRUMENTS

1974 No. 574

WAGES COUNCILS

The Wages Regulation (Dressmaking and Women's Light Clothing) (England and Wales) Order 1974

Made - - -		*26th March* 1974
Coming into Operation		*3rd May* 1974

Whereas the Secretary of State has received from the Dressmaking and Women's Light Clothing Wages Council (England and Wales) the wages regulation proposals set out in the Schedule hereto;

Now, therefore, the Secretary of State in exercise of powers conferred by section 11 of the Wages Councils Act 1959(a), as modified by Article 2 of the Counter-Inflation (Modification of Wages Councils Act 1959) Order 1973(b), and now vested in him (c), and of all other powers enabling him in that behalf, hereby makes the following Order:—

1. This Order may be cited as the Wages Regulation (Dressmaking and Women's Light Clothing) (England and Wales) Order 1974.

2.—(1) In this Order the expression "the specified date" means the 3rd May 1974, provided that where, as respects any worker who is paid wages at intervals not exceeding seven days, that date does not correspond with the beginning of the period for which the wages are paid, the expression "the specified date" means, as respects that worker, the beginning of the next such period following that date.

(2) The Interpretation Act 1889(d) shall apply to the interpretation of this Order as it applies to the interpretation of an Act of Parliament and as if this Order and the Order hereby revoked were Acts of Parliament.

3. The wages regulation proposals set out in the Schedule hereto shall have effect as from the specified date and as from that date the Wages Regulation (Dressmaking and Women's Light Clothing) (England and Wales) Order 1973(e) shall cease to have effect.

Signed by order of the Secretary of State.

26th March 1974.

W. H. Marsh,

Assistant Secretary,
Department of Employment.

(a) 1959 c. 69.   (b) S.I. 1973/661 (1973 I, p. 2141).
(c) S.I. 1959/1769, 1968/729 (1959 I, p. 1795; 1968 II, p. 2108).
(d) 1889 c. 63.   (e) S.I. 1973/311 (1973 I, p. 1080).

Article 3

SCHEDULE

The following minimum remuneration shall be substituted for the statutory minimum remuneration fixed by the Wages Regulation (Dressmaking and Women's Light Clothing) (England and Wales) Order 1973 (Order W.D. (97)).

STATUTORY MINIMUM REMUNERATION

PART I

GENERAL

1. The minimum remuneration payable to a worker to whom this Schedule applies for all work except work to which a minimum overtime rate applies under Part V of this Schedule is:—

(1) in the case of a time worker, the general minimum time rate;

(2) in the case of a worker employed on piece work, piece rates each of which would yield, in the circumstances of the case, to an ordinary worker at least the same amount of money as the piece work basis time rate or, where no piece work basis time rate is applicable, at least the same amount of money as the general minimum time rate which would be applicable if the worker were a time worker.

PART II

RETAIL BESPOKE BRANCH

FEMALE WORKERS

GENERAL MINIMUM TIME RATES

2. Subject to the provisions of this Schedule, the general minimum time rates applicable to female workers in the retail bespoke branch, in Areas A, B and C respectively, are as follows:—

	Area A Per hour p	Area B Per hour p	Area C Per hour p
(1) BODICE, COAT, SKIRT, GOWN OR BLOUSE HANDS, aged 20 years or over, who—			
having worked for 2½ years in the said branch in one or more of the occupations of learner, apprentice or improver and for at least 2 years in the said branch thereafter, take bodices, coats, skirts, gowns or blouses direct from the fitter in an establishment in which a fitter is employed and make them up without supervision other than the general supervision of the fitter or the workroom foreman or forewoman ..	39·50	40·50	41·50

	Area A Per hour p	Area B Per hour p	Area C Per hour p

(2) LEARNERS (as defined in paragraph 19) during the following periods of employment in the retail bespoke branch:—

	Area A	Area B	Area C
1st year	19·25	20·00	22·00
2nd year	24·50	25·50	27·25
6 months then next ensuing	27·50	28·50	31·50

Provided that a learner who enters, or has entered, the trade for the first time at or over the age of 18 years shall be treated for the purposes of this paragraph as though she had, at the date of her entry, completed her first year's employment as a learner in the said branch.

(3) All other workers .. .. 38·00 39·00 40·50

RECKONING EMPLOYMENT IN THE WHOLESALE MANUFACTURING BRANCH

3. Where a worker has been employed in the wholesale manufacturing branch, one half of the period of such employment shall be treated for the purposes of this Part of this Schedule as employment in the retail bespoke branch.

DEFINITION OF AREAS

4. For the purposes of this Part of this Schedule:—

Area A—comprises each area in England and Wales which at the date of the 1961 census was administered by

(1) a Rural District Council or

(2) a Municipal Borough Council or an Urban District Council having according to the said census a population of less than 10,000, but does not include any area within the Metropolitan Police District.

Area B—comprises the whole of England and Wales except Area A and Area C.

Area C—comprises the Metropolitan Police District, as defined in the London Government Act 1963(a), the City of London, the Inner Temple and the Middle Temple.

(a) 1963 c. 33.

MALE WORKERS

GENERAL MINIMUM TIME RATES

5. Subject to the provisions of this Schedule, the general minimum time rates applicable to male workers in the retail bespoke branch are as follows:—

	Per hour p
Aged 21 years or over	45·25
„ 20 and under 21 years	40·25
„ 19 „ „ 20 „	38·25
„ 18 „ „ 19 „	34·75
„ 17 „ „ 18 „	29·25
„ *under 17 years*	25·50

Provided that the general minimum time rate applicable during his first year's employment in the trade to a worker who enters, or has entered, the trade for the first time at or over the age of 19 years shall be—

During the 1st six months of such employment	34·75
During the 2nd six months of such employment	38·25

PIECE WORK BASIS TIME RATE

	Per hour p
6. The piece work basis time rate applicable to a male worker of any age employed in the retail bespoke branch on piece work is	48·75

PART III

WHOLESALE MANUFACTURING BRANCH
FEMALE WORKERS
GENERAL MINIMUM TIME RATES

7. Subject to the provisions of this Schedule, the general minimum time rates applicable to female workers in the wholesale manufacturing branch are as follows:—

	Per hour p
(1) CONVEYOR BELT MACHINISTS (that is to say, female workers employed in machining any work conveyed directly to and from them on a mechanical conveyor belt) not being learners to whom (2) of this paragraph applies	41·50

(2) LEARNERS (as defined in paragraph 19) during the following periods of employment in the wholesale manufacturing branch—

	1st 6 months Per hour p	2nd 6 months Per hour p	2nd year Per hour p
Entering the trade:			
Aged 15 and under 16 years	21·75	25·50	32·00
„ 16 „ „ 17 „	23·75	27·25	33·75
„ 17 „ „ 18 „	25·50	29·25	33·75
„ 18 years and over	30·75	32·50	38·50

Per hour
p
(3) All other workers   ..   ..   *40·50*

RECKONING EMPLOYMENT IN THE RETAIL BESPOKE BRANCH

8. Where a worker has been employed in the retail bespoke branch, one half of the period of such employment shall be treated for the purposes of this Part of this Schedule as employment in the wholesale manufacturing branch.

PIECE WORK BASIS TIME RATE

Per hour
p
9. The piece work basis time rate applicable to a female worker of any age employed in the wholesale manufacturing branch on piece work is   ..   *44·00*

MALE WORKERS

GENERAL MINIMUM TIME RATES

10. Subject to the provisions of this Schedule, the general minimum time rates applicable to male workers in the wholesale manufacturing branch are as follows:—

Per hour
p
(1) CUTTERS aged 21 years or over who have had at least 4 years' experience as cutters in the wholesale manufacturing branch   ..   *47·25*

(2) All other workers:—

	Per hour p
Aged 21 years or over	*45·25*
„ 20 and under 21 years	*40·25*
„ 19 „ „ 20 „	*38·25*
„ 18 „ „ 19 „	*34·75*
„ 17 „ „ 18 „	*29·25*
„ *under 17 years*	*25·50*

Provided that the general minimum time rate applicable during his first year's employment in the trade to a worker who enters, or has entered, the trade for the first time at or over the age of 19 years shall be—

During the 1st six months of such employment   ..   ..   ..   *34·75*
„   „   2nd „   „   „   „   „   „   ..   ..   ..   *38·25*

PIECE WORK BASIS TIME RATES

11. The piece work basis time rates applicable to male workers employed in the wholesale manufacturing branch on piece work are as follows:—

Per hour
p
(1) CUTTERS aged 21 years or over who have had at least 4 years' experience as cutters in the wholesale manufacturing branch   ..   *50·25*

(2) All other workers..   ..   ..   *48·75*

PART IV

EXPERIENCE UNDER THE GOVERNMENT VOCATIONAL TRAINING SCHEME

12. Where any worker has completed a full course of training as a machinist or as a hand sewer under the Government Vocational Training Scheme for resettlement training such period of training shall, for the purpose of reckoning the period of the worker's employment in the trade, be treated as though it were

(1) in the case of a female worker, a period of three years' employment as a learner in the branch of the trade in which she is employed, or

(2) in the case of a male worker, a period of at least one year's employment in the trade.

PART V

RETAIL BESPOKE BRANCH AND WHOLESALE MANUFACTURING BRANCH

OVERTIME AND WAITING TIME

ALL WORKERS OTHER THAN ALTERATION HANDS WHO ARE NORMALLY REQUIRED TO ATTEND ON 6 DAYS IN THE WEEK

NORMAL NUMBER OF HOURS

13. Subject to the provisions of this Part of this Schedule, the minimum overtime rates set out in paragraph 14 are payable to workers in any branch of the trade, other than alteration hands referred to in paragraphs 15 and 16, in respect of any time worked—

(1) in excess of the hours following, that is to say,

    (a) in any week   ..   ..   40 hours

    (b) on any day other than a Saturday, Sunday or customary holiday—

        where the normal working hours exceed $8\frac{1}{2}$ ..   ..   9 hours

        or

        where the normal working hours are not more than $8\frac{1}{2}$ .. $8\frac{1}{2}$ hours

(2) on a Saturday, Sunday or customary holiday.

MINIMUM OVERTIME RATES

14.—(1) Minimum overtime rates are payable to a worker in any branch of the trade other than an alteration hand referred to in paragraphs 15 and 16 as follows:—

    (a) on any day other than a Sunday or customary holiday—

        (i) for the first 2 hours of overtime worked   ..   time-and-a-quarter

        (ii) for the next 2 hours   ..   ..   time-and-a-half

        (iii) thereafter   ..   ..   double time;

    (b) on a Sunday or customary holiday—

        for all time worked   ..   ..   double time

        Provided that where it is the practice in a Jewish undertaking for the employer to require attendance on Sunday instead of Saturday the provisions of this paragraph shall apply as if in such provisions the word "Saturday" were substituted for "Sunday", except where such substitution is unlawful;

    (c) in any week, exclusive of any time in respect of which any minimum overtime rate is payable under the foregoing provisions of this sub-paragraph—

        for all time worked in excess of 40 hours..   ..   time-and-a-quarter

(2) The minimum overtime rates set out in sub-paragraph (1)(*a*) or (*b*) of this paragraph are payable in any week whether or not the minimum overtime rate set out in sub-paragraph (1)(*c*) is also payable.

(3) Where a worker employed in the retail bespoke branch of the trade normally attends work on a Saturday, instead of on another week-day, for the purposes of this Part of this Schedule that other week-day shall be treated as a Saturday and Saturday as another week-day.

ALTERATION HANDS WHO ARE NORMALLY REQUIRED TO ATTEND ON 6 DAYS IN THE WEEK

NORMAL NUMBER OF HOURS

15. Subject to the provisions of this Part of this Schedule, the minimum overtime rates set out in paragraph 16 are payable to workers in any branch of the trade who are normally required to attend on six days in the week and who are employed solely in the alteration (including repairing and renovating) of any of the articles specified in inclusion (1) in paragraph 21 and who are employed in or about a shop engaged in the retail sale of the articles so specified, as follows:—

(1) in any week,
for all time worked in excess of..   ..   ..   40 hours

(2) on any day other than a Saturday, Sunday or a customary holiday,
for all time worked in excess of..   ..   ..   8 hours

(3) on a Saturday, not being a customary holiday,
for all time worked in excess of..   ..   ..   4 hours

(4) on a Sunday or a customary holiday ..   ..   ..   for all time worked.

MINIMUM OVERTIME RATES

16.—(1) Subject to the provisions of this Part of this Schedule, minimum overtime rates are payable to a worker in any branch of the trade who is normally required to attend on six days in the week and who is employed solely in the alteration (including repairing and renovating) of any of the articles specified in inclusion (1) in paragraph 21 and who is employed in or about a shop engaged in the retail sale of the articles so specified, as follows:—

(*a*) on any day other than a Saturday, Sunday
or customary holiday—

(i) for the first two hours worked in excess of 8 hours   time-and-a-quarter

(ii) for the next two hours ..   ..   time-and-a-half

(iii) thereafter ..   ..   double time

(*b*) on a Saturday, not being a customary holiday—

(i) for the first 4 hours worked in excess of 4 hours..   time-and-a-half

(ii) thereafter ..   ..   double time

(*c*) on a Sunday or a customary holiday—
for all time worked ..   ..   double time

(*d*) in any week, exclusive of any time in respect of which a
minimum overtime rate is payable under the foregoing
provisions of this sub-paragraph—

for all time worked in excess of 40 hours ..   ..   time-and-a-quarter

(2) The minimum overtime rates set out in sub-paragraph (1)(*a*), (*b*) or (*c*) of this paragraph are payable in any week whether or not the minimum overtime rate set out in sub-paragraph (1)(*d*) of this paragraph is also payable.

(3) Where the worker normally attends on Sunday and not on Saturday, for the purposes of this Part of this Schedule (except where such attendance is unlawful) Saturday shall be treated as a Sunday, and, subject to the provisions of sub-paragraph (4) of this paragraph, Sunday as a Saturday.

(4) Where the worker normally attends on six days in the week and an ordinary week-day is substituted for Saturday, or in a case where the provisions of sub-paragraph (3) of this paragraph apply, for Sunday, as the worker's weekly short day, for the purposes of this Part of this Schedule (except where such substitution is unlawful) that ordinary week-day shall be treated as a Saturday and Saturday or Sunday, as the case may be, as an ordinary week-day.

17. In this Part of this Schedule:—

(1) The expression "customary holiday" means—

    (a) Christmas Day; 26th December if it be not a Sunday; 27th December in a year when 25th or 26th December is a Sunday; *New Year's Day if it be not a Sunday, or, if it be a Sunday, 2nd January;* Good Friday; Easter Monday; the last Monday in May; the last Monday in August; (or, where another day is substituted for any of the said days by national proclamation, that day); and one other day (being a day of the week on which the worker normally works for the employer) in the course of each calendar year, to be fixed by consultation between the employer or his representative and the worker or his representative and notified to the worker not less than three weeks before the holiday; or

    (b) in the case of each of the said days a day substituted by the employer therefor, being a day recognised by local custom as a day of holiday in substitution for the said day;

(2) the expressions "time-and-a-quarter", "time-and-a-half" and "double time" mean respectively—

    (a) in the case of a time worker, one and a quarter times, one and a half times and twice the general minimum time rate otherwise payable to the worker;

    (b) in the case of a male worker employed on piece work in either branch or of a female worker employed on piece work in the wholesale manufacturing branch—

        (i) a time rate equal respectively to one quarter, one half and the whole of the piece work basis time rate otherwise applicable to the worker, and, in addition thereto,

        (ii) the piece rates otherwise payable to the worker under paragraph 1(2);

    (c) in the case of a female worker employed on piece work in the retail bespoke branch—

        (i) a time rate equal respectively to one quarter, one half and the whole of the general minimum time rate which would be payable to the worker if she were a time worker and a minimum overtime rate did not apply, and, in addition thereto,

        (ii) the piece rates otherwise payable to the worker under paragraph 1(2).

WAITING TIME

18.—(1) A worker is entitled to payment of the minimum remuneration specified in this Schedule for all time during which he is present on the premises of his employer unless he is present thereon in any of the following circumstances:—

    (a) without the employer's consent, express or implied;

    (b) for some purpose unconnected with his work and other than that of waiting for work to be given to him to perform;

(c) by reason only of the fact that he is resident thereon;

(d) during normal meal times in a room or place in which no work is being done, and he is not waiting for work to be given to him to perform.

(2) The minimum remuneration payable under sub-paragraph (1) of this paragraph to a piece worker when not engaged on piece work is that which would be payable if he were a time worker.

PART VI

INTERPRETATION

19. In this Schedule, unless the context otherwise requires, the following expressions have the meanings hereby respectively assigned to them, that is to say:—

(1) "The trade" means the trade of dressmaking and the making of women's light clothing, that is to say, those branches of the women's clothing trade which are specified in paragraph 21.

(2) The retail bespoke branch means that branch of the trade in which the employer supplies the garment direct to the individual wearer and employs the worker direct.

(3) The wholesale manufacturing branch means any branch of the trade other than the retail bespoke branch.

(4) A cutter means a person who is substantially employed in one or more of the following processes:—

(a) marking-in or marking-out or marking-up materials;

(b) laying-up or hooking-up or folding materials;

(c) cutting materials;

(d) dividing, that is to say, the process ordinarily carried on by cutters or their assistants of dividing, parting or separating parts of garments which are being cut and of assembling them into suitable bundles for making up.

(5) A learner means a female worker who is employed by an employer who provides her with reasonable facilities for learning, practically and efficiently, one of the branches of the trade or the various processes involved in the making of any of the articles specified in the definition of the trade set out in paragraph 21.

PART VII

APPLICABILITY OF STATUTORY MINIMUM REMUNERATION

20. This Schedule shall not apply to—

(a) machinists

(b) hand sewers

during any period in respect of which they are in receipt of allowances as provided under the Government Vocational Training Scheme for resettlement training if they are trainees who have been placed by the Department of Employment with the employer for a period of approved training and if the requirements of the said Scheme are duly complied with.

21. Subject to the provisions of paragraph 20, this Schedule applies to workers in relation to whom the Dressmaking and Women's Light Clothing Wages Council (England and Wales) operates, that is to say, workers employed in England and Wales in those branches of the Women's Clothing Trade which are specified in Regulation 1 of the Trade Boards (Dressmaking and Women's Light Clothing Trade, England and

Wales) (Constitution and Proceedings) Regulations 1928(a), excluding any processes or operations included in the appendix to the Trade Boards (Shirtmaking) Order 1920(b).

The said branches of the women's clothing trade are specified in the said Regulations as follows:—

Those branches of the women's clothing trade that are engaged in the making of non-tailored garments, namely, the making from textile or knitted fabrics of (a) non-tailored wearing apparel (other than handkerchiefs) worn by women or girls, or by children without distinction of sex, or (b) boys' ready-made washing suits or sailor suits, where carried out in association with or in conjunction with the making of garments to be worn by women or girls or by children without distinction of sex;

INCLUDING:—

(1) All operations and processes of cutting, making or finishing by hand or machine of dresses, non-tailored skirts, wraps, blouses, blouse-robes, jumpers, sports-coats, neckwear, tea-gowns, dressing gowns, dressing jackets, pyjamas, under-clothing, underskirts, aprons, overalls, nurses' and servants' caps, juvenile clothing, baby-linen or similar non-tailored articles;

(2) The making of field bonnets, sun-bonnets, boudoir caps or infants' millinery where carried on in association with or in conjunction with the making of any of the articles mentioned in paragraph (1) above;

(3) (a) The altering, repairing, renovating or re-making of any of the above-mentioned articles;

(b) The cleaning of any of the above-mentioned articles, where carried on in association with or in conjunction with the altering, repairing, renovating or re-making of such garments;

(4) All processes of embroidery or decorative needlework where carried on in association with or in conjunction with the making, altering, repairing, renovating or re-making of such articles other than hand embroidery or hand-drawn thread work on articles made of linen or cotton or of mixed linen and cotton;

(5) The following processes if done by machine:—thread-drawing, thread-clipping, top-sewing, scalloping, nickelling and paring;

(6) Laundering, smoothing, folding, ornamenting, boxing, packing, warehousing or other operations incidental to or appertaining to the making, altering, repairing, renovating or re-making of any of the above-mentioned articles;

BUT EXCLUDING:—

(a) The making of knitted articles; the making of under-clothing, socks and stockings, from knitted fabrics; and the making from knitted fabrics of articles mentioned in paragraphs (1) and (2) above, where carried on in association with or in conjunction with the manufacture of the knitted fabrics;

(b) The making of gloves, spats, gaiters, boots, shoes and slippers;

(c) The making of headgear, other than the articles mentioned in paragraph (2) above;

(d) The branches of trade covered by the Trade Boards (Corset) Order 1919(c);

(e) The making of rubberised or oilskin garments;

(a) S.R. & O. 1928/628 (1928 p. 1265).   (b) S.R. & O. 1920/711 (1920 II, p. 790).
(c) S.R. & O. 1919/570 (1919 II, p. 509).

(*f*) The making of women's collars and cuffs and of nurses' stiff washing belts where carried on in association with or in conjunction with the making of men's or boys' shirts or collars;

(*g*) Warehousing, packing and other similar operations carried on in shops mainly engaged in the retail distribution of articles of any description that are not made on the premises.

EXPLANATORY NOTE

(This Note is not part of the Order.)

This Order, which has effect from 3rd May 1974, sets out the increased statutory minimum remuneration payable to workers in relation to whom the Dressmaking and Women's Light Clothing Wages Council (England and Wales) operates, in substitution for that fixed by the Wages Regulation (Dressmaking and Women's Light Clothing) (England and Wales) Order 1973 (Order W.D. (97)). Order W.D. (97) is revoked.

New provisions are printed in italics.

STATUTORY INSTRUMENTS

1974 No. 575

WAGES COUNCILS

The Wages Regulation (Dressmaking and Women's Light Clothing) (England and Wales) (Holidays) Order 1974

Made	-	-	-	*26th March* 1974
Coming into Operation				*3rd May* 1974

Whereas the Secretary of State has received from the Dressmaking and Women's Light Clothing Wages Council (England and Wales) the wages regulation proposals set out in the Schedule hereto;

Now, therefore, the Secretary of State in exercise of powers conferred by section 11 of the Wages Councils Act 1959(a), as modified by Article 2 of the Counter-Inflation (Modification of Wages Councils Act 1959) Order 1973(b), and now vested in him (c), and of all other powers enabling him in that behalf, hereby makes the following Order:—

1. This Order may be cited as the Wages Regulation (Dressmaking and Women's Light Clothing) (England and Wales) (Holidays) Order 1974.

2.—(1) In this Order the expression "the specified date" means the 3rd May 1974, provided that where, as respects any worker who is paid wages at intervals not exceeding seven days, that date does not correspond with the beginning of the period for which the wages are paid, the expression "the specified date" means, as respects that worker, the beginning of the next such period following that date.

(2) The Interpretation Act 1889(d) applies to the interpretation of this Order as it applies to the interpretation of an Act of Parliament and as if this Order and the Order hereby revoked were Acts of Parliament.

3. The wages regulation proposals set out in the Schedule hereto shall have effect as from the specified date and as from that date the Wages Regulation (Dressmaking and Women's Light Clothing) (England and Wales) (Holidays) Order 1973(e) shall cease to have effect.

Signed by order of the Secretary of State.

26th March 1974.

W. H. Marsh,
Assistant Secretary,
Department of Employment.

(a) 1959 c. 69.
(b) S.I. 1973/661 (1973 I, p. 2141).
(c) S.I. 1959/1769, 1968/729 (1959 I, p. 1795; 1968 II, p. 2108).
(d) 1889 c. 63.
(e) S.I. 1973/312 (1973 I, p. 1091).

Article 3

SCHEDULE

HOLIDAYS AND HOLIDAY REMUNERATION

The following provisions as to holidays and holiday remuneration shall be substituted for the provisions as to holidays and holiday remuneration set out in the Wages Regulation (Dressmaking and Women's Light Clothing) (England and Wales) (Holidays) Order 1973 (hereinafter referred to as "Order W.D. (98)").

PART I

APPLICATION

1.—(1) This Schedule applies to every worker (other than a homeworker) for whom statutory minimum remuneration has been fixed.

(2) For the purposes of this Schedule a homeworker is a worker who works in his own home or in any other place not under the control or management of the employer.

PART II

CUSTOMARY HOLIDAYS

2.—(1) An employer shall allow to every worker in his employment to whom this Schedule applies a holiday (hereinafter referred to as a "customary holiday") in each year on the days specified in the following sub-paragraph, provided that the worker has been in his employment for a period of not less than eight weeks immediately preceding the customary holiday and has worked for the employer during the whole or part of that period and is in his employment on the day of the customary holiday.

(2) The said customary holidays are:—

(a) Christmas Day; 26th December if it be not a Sunday; 27th December in a year when 25th or 26th December is a Sunday; *New Year's Day, if it be not a Sunday, or, if it be a Sunday 2nd January;* Good Friday; Easter Monday; the last Monday in May; the last Monday in August; (or, where another day is substituted for any of the said days by national proclamation, that day); and one other day (being a day of the week on which the worker normally works for the employer) in the course of a calendar year, to be fixed by consultation between the employer or his representative and the worker or his representative and notified to the worker not less than three weeks before the holiday, or

(b) in the case of each of the said days, a day substituted by the employer therefor, being a day recognised by local custom as a day of holiday in substitution for the said day.

(3) Notwithstanding the preceding provisions of this paragraph, an employer may (except where in the case of a woman or young person such a requirement would be unlawful) require a worker who is otherwise entitled to any customary holiday under the foregoing provisions of this Schedule to work thereon and, in lieu of any such holiday on which he so works for the employer, the worker shall be entitled to be allowed a day's holiday (hereinafter referred to as a "holiday in lieu of a customary holiday") on a week day within the period of four weeks next ensuing.

(4) A worker who is required to work on a customary holiday shall be paid:—

(a) for all time worked thereon at the minimum rate then appropriate to the worker for work on a customary holiday; and

(b) in respect of the holiday in lieu of the customary holiday, holiday remuneration in accordance with paragraph 6.

PART III

ANNUAL HOLIDAY

3.—(1) Subject to the provisions of this paragraph and of paragraph 4, in addition to the holidays specified in Part II of this Schedule, an employer shall between the date on which the provisions of this Schedule become effective and 30th September 1974, and between 6th April and 30th September in each succeeding year, allow a holiday (hereinafter referred to as an "annual holiday") to every worker in his employment to whom this Schedule applies, who has been employed by him during the 12 months immediately preceding the commencement of the holiday season for any of the periods of employment (calculated in accordance with the provisions of paragraph 10) specified below, and the duration of the annual holiday shall in the case of each such worker be related to that period as follows:—

Workers with a normal working week of 6 days		Workers with a normal working week of 5 days or less	
Period of employment	Duration of annual holiday	Period of employment	Duration of annual holiday
At least 48 weeks	20 days	At least 48 weeks	17 days
„ „ 46 „	19 „	„ „ 46 „	16 „
„ „ 44 „	18 „	„ „ 44 „	15 „
„ „ 42 „	17 „	„ „ 42 „	14 „
„ „ 40 „	16 „	„ „ 40 „	13 „
„ „ 38 „	14 „	„ „ 38 „	12 „
„ „ 36 „	13 „	„ „ 36 „	11 „
„ „ 34 „	12 „	„ „ 33 „	10 „
„ „ 32 „	11 „	„ „ 30 „	9 „
„ „ 30 „	10 „	„ „ 27 „	8 „
„ „ 28 „	9 „	„ „ 24 „	7 „
„ „ 25 „	8 „	„ „ 21 „	6 „
„ „ 22 „	7 „	„ „ 18 „	5 „
„ „ 19 „	6 „	„ „ 15 „	4 „
„ „ 16 „	5 „	„ „ 12 „	3 „
„ „ 13 „	4 „	„ „ 8 „	2 „
„ „ 10 „	3 „	„ „ 4 „	1 day
„ „ 7 „	2 „		
„ „ 4 „	1 day		

(2) Notwithstanding the provisions of the last foregoing sub-paragraph:—

(a) the number of days of annual holiday which an employer is required to allow to a worker in respect of a period of employment during the 12 months immediately preceding 6th April 1974 and during the 12 months immediately preceding 6th April in any succeeding year shall not exceed in the aggregate three times the number of days constituting the worker's normal working week, plus two days;

(*b*) where before 17th September in any holiday season a worker and his employer enter into an agreement in writing that the worker shall be allowed after the end of the holiday season and before 6th April next following, days of holiday not exceeding twice the number of days constituting his normal working week, being all or part of the annual holiday for which he has qualified under this paragraph, any such days of annual holiday may, subject to the provisions of paragraph 4, be allowed in accordance with the agreement and if so allowed shall be treated for the purpose of this Schedule as having been allowed during the holiday season;

(*c*) the duration of the worker's annual holiday during the holiday season *ending on 30th September 1974 shall be reduced by any days of holiday with pay* (*not being days of customary holiday*) *which have been allowed to him by the employer under the provisions of Order W.D.* (*98*), *between 6th April 1974 and the date on which the provisions of this Schedule become effective.*

(3) In this Schedule the expression "holiday season" means in relation to an annual holiday during the year 1974 the period commencing with the date on which the provisions of this Schedule become effective and ending on 30th September 1974, and in relation to each subsequent year, the period commencing on 6th April and ending on 30th September in that year.

4.—(1) Subject to the provisions of this paragraph, an annual holiday under this Schedule shall be allowed on consecutive working days and days of holiday shall be treated as consecutive notwithstanding that a day of holiday allowed to a worker under Part II of this Schedule or a day upon which he does not normally work for the employer intervenes.

(2)(*a*) Where the number of days of annual holiday for which a worker has qualified exceeds the number of days constituting his normal working week, but does not exceed twice that number, the holiday may be allowed in two periods of consecutive working days; so, however, that when a holiday is so allowed, one of the periods shall consist of a number of such days not less than the number of days constituting the worker's normal working week.

(*b*) Where the number of days of annual holiday for which a worker has qualified exceeds twice the number of days constituting his normal working week the holiday may be allowed as follows:—

   (i) as to two periods of consecutive working days, each such period not being less than the period constituting the worker's normal working week, during the holiday season; and

   (ii) as to any additional days, on working days which need not be consecutive, to be fixed by agreement between the employer or his representative and the worker or his representative in relation to the holiday season in 1974 and in each subsequent year, either during the holiday season or on any working day before the beginning of the next following holiday season.

(3) Where a day of holiday allowed to a worker under Part II of this Schedule immediately precedes a period of annual holiday or occurs during such a period then, notwithstanding the foregoing provisions of this paragraph, the duration of that period of annual holiday may be reduced by one day and in such a case one day of annual holiday may be allowed on any working day in the holiday season, or by agreement between the employer and the worker or his representative, on any working day before the beginning of the next following holiday season.

(4) Subject to the provisions of sub-paragraph (1) of this paragraph, any day of annual holiday under this Schedule may be allowed on a day on which the worker is entitled to a day of holiday or to a half-holiday under any enactment other than the Wages Councils Act 1959.

5. An employer shall give to a worker reasonable notice of the commencing date or dates and of the duration of his annual holiday. Such notice may be given individually to the worker or by the posting of a notice in the place where the worker is employed.

PART IV

HOLIDAY REMUNERATION

A—CUSTOMARY HOLIDAYS AND HOLIDAYS IN LIEU OF CUSTOMARY HOLIDAYS

6.—(1) For each day of holiday (including a holiday falling on a Saturday) to which a worker is entitled under Part II of this Schedule he shall be paid by the employer as holiday remuneration whichever of the following amounts is the greater:—

(a) (i) in the case of a worker employed in the retail bespoke branch of the trade whose normal working week exceeds five days, two-elevenths

(ii) in the case of all other workers, one-fifth ..   ..

of the average weekly earnings of the worker during the 12 months ended on 5th April immediately preceding the holiday, such average weekly earnings to be determined by dividing, by the number of weeks of employment with the employer during the said period, the total remuneration paid to him by the employer during that period:

Provided that when Good Friday or Easter Monday (or days substituted therefor under the provisions of sub-paragraph (2)(b) of paragraph 2 or holidays in lieu of such customary holidays) fall after 5th April in any year, the holiday remuneration for any such holiday under this sub-paragraph shall be two-elevenths or one-fifth, as the case may require, of the average weekly earnings of the worker during the 12 months ended on 5th April in the preceding calendar year; or

(b) the appropriate statutory minimum remuneration to which he would have been entitled as a time worker if the day had not been a day of holiday and he had been employed on work for which statutory minimum remuneration is payable:—

(i) in the case of a worker normally employed for more than 30 hours a week, for 8 hours, or

(ii) in the case of a worker normally employed for 30 hours a week or less, for 4 hours.

(2) Notwithstanding the provisions of sub-paragraph (1) of this paragraph, payment of the said holiday remuneration is subject to the condition that the worker (unless excused by the employer or absent by reason of the proved illness of, or accident to, the worker) presents himself for employment at the usual starting hour on the first working day following the holiday:

Provided that when two customary holidays occur on successive days (or so that no working day intervenes) the said condition shall apply only to the second customary holiday.

(3) Where a worker normally works in the week on every week-day except Saturday, he shall be paid in respect of any Saturday on which he would have been entitled to a holiday under Part II of this Schedule if it had been a day on which he normally worked, a sum equivalent to the holiday remuneration he would have been entitled to receive had he been allowed a holiday on that day.

(4) Holiday remuneration in respect of any customary holiday shall be paid by the employer to the worker on the pay-day on which the wages for the first working day following the customary holiday are paid.

(5) Holiday remuneration in respect of any holiday in lieu of a customary holiday shall be paid on the pay-day on which the wages are paid for the first working day following the holiday in lieu of a customary holiday: Provided that the said payment shall be made immediately upon the termination of the worker's employment if he ceases to be employed before being allowed such holiday in lieu of a customary holiday and in that case the condition specified in sub-paragraph (2) of this paragraph shall not apply.

B—ANNUAL HOLIDAY

7.—(1) Subject to the provisions of paragraph 8, a worker qualified to be allowed an annual holiday under this Schedule shall be paid as holiday remuneration by his employer in respect thereof, on the last pay-day preceding such annual holiday, whichever of the following amounts is the greater:—

(a) *in respect of the annual holiday to be allowed during the 1974 holiday season and during the holiday season in each succeeding year, an amount equal to seventeen two-hundred-and-sixtieths of the total remuneration paid by the employer to the worker in the 12 months ending on 5th April immediately preceding the holiday season; or*

(b) one day's holiday pay (as defined in paragraph 11) in respect of each day of annual holiday.

(2) Where, under the provisions of paragraph 4, an annual holiday is allowed in more than one period the holiday remuneration shall be apportioned accordingly.

8. Where any accrued holiday remuneration has been paid by the employer to the worker (in accordance with paragraph 9 of this Schedule or under the provisions of Order W.D. (98)) in respect of employment during any of the periods referred to in that paragraph or that Order, the amount of holiday remuneration payable by the employer in respect of any annual holiday for which the worker has qualified by reason of employment during the said period shall be reduced by the amount of the said accrued holiday remuneration unless that remuneration has been deducted from a previous payment of holiday remuneration made under the provisions of this Schedule or of Order W.D. (98).

ACCRUED HOLIDAY REMUNERATION PAYABLE ON TERMINATION OF EMPLOYMENT

9.—(1) Where a worker ceases to be employed by an employer after the provisions of this Schedule become effective, the employer shall, immediately on the termination of the employment, pay to the worker accrued holiday remuneration in accordance with this paragraph.

(2) Accrued holiday remuneration shall be payable in accordance with the following table if the worker has in the 12 months commencing on 6th April 1973, and thereafter in any period of 12 months commencing on 6th April been employed for any of the periods of employment specified in that table.

(3) Accrued holiday remuneration is not payable in respect of any period of employment for which the worker has been allowed or become entitled to be allowed an annual holiday under this Schedule.

(4) Subject to the provisions of sub-paragraph (5) hereof, where a worker has been allowed in a holiday season part only of the annual holiday for which he has qualified under this Schedule or under Order W.D. (98) and his employment is terminated before he becomes entitled to the rest of that holiday the accrued holiday remuneration payable shall be:—

(a) in the case of a worker who has qualified for days of annual holiday exceeding twice the number of days constituting his normal working week and who has been allowed as days of annual holiday not less than twice the number of days constituting his normal working week, or, where the circumstances in sub-paragraph (3) of paragraph 4 are applicable, that number of days reduced by one:—

(i) in respect of the days of holiday for which he has qualified during the 12 months ended on 5th April immediately preceding the termination of his employment, the holiday remuneration due in respect thereof calculated in accordance with the provisions of paragraph 7 less the amount received by him in respect of the part of the holiday which has been allowed; and

(ii) in respect of any period of employment since the said 5th April, the amount calculated in accordance with the following table;

(b) in the case of any other worker, the appropriate amount under the following table in respect of the qualifying period of employment less the amount received by the worker in respect of that part of the holiday which has been allowed.

(5) Any accrued holiday remuneration payable under the provisions of this paragraph shall be reduced by the amount of any accrued holiday remuneration already paid by the employer to the worker in pursuance of this Order or Order W.D. (98) in respect of the same period of employment or part thereof.

TABLE OF ACCRUED HOLIDAY REMUNERATION

In respect of employment during the 12 months ending on 5th April 1974 and during each succeeding 12 months ending on 5th April.

(i) Workers with a normal working week of 6 days.

Column 1 Period of employment calculated in accordance with the provisions of paragraph 10	Column 2 Accrued holiday remuneration	Column 3
At least 48 weeks	Three and one-third times the amount in Column 3	
„ „ 46 „	Three and one-sixth times the amount in Column 3	The amount which the worker would be entitled
„ „ 44 „	Three times the amount in Column 3	to receive from his em-
„ „ 42 „	Two and five-sixths times the amount in Column 3	ployer, at the date of the termination of his employ-
„ „ 40 „	Two and two-thirds times the amount in Column 3	ment, for one week's work, if working his normal
„ „ 38 „	Two and one-third times the amount in Column 3	working week and the number of daily hours
„ „ 36 „	Two and one-sixth times the amount in Column 3	normally worked by him (exclusive of overtime) and
„ „ 34 „	Twice the amount in Column 3	if paid as a time worker at
„ „ 32 „	One and five-sixths times the amount in Column 3	the appropriate rate of statutory minimum re-
„ „ 30 „	One and two-thirds times the amount in Column 3	muneration for work for which statutory minimum
„ „ 28 „	One and one-half times the amount in Column 3	remuneration is payable and at the same rate for
„ „ 25 „	One and one-third times the amount in Column 3	any work for which such remuneration is not pay-
„ „ 22 „	One and one-sixth times the amount in Column 3	able.
„ „ 19 „	The amount in Column 3	
„ „ 16 „	Five-sixths of the amount in Column 3	
„ „ 13 „	Two-thirds of the amount in Column 3	
„ „ 10 „	One-half of the amount in Column 3	
„ „ 7 „	One-third of the amount in Column 3	
„ „ 4 „	One-sixth of the amount in Column 3	

(ii) Workers with a normal working week of 5 days or less.

Column 1 Period of employment calculated in accordance with the provisions of paragraph 10	Column 2 Accrued holiday remuneration	Column 3
At least 48 weeks	*Three and two-fifths times the amount in Column 3*	The amount which the worker would be entitled to receive from his employer, at the date of the termination of his employment, for one week's work, if working his normal working week and the number of daily hours normally worked by him (exclusive of overtime) and if paid as a time worker at the appropriate rate of statutory minimum remuneration for work for which statutory minimum remuneration is payable and at the same rate for any work for which such remuneration is not payable.
„ „ 46 „	*Three and one-fifth times the amount in Column 3*	
„ „ 44 „	*Three times the amount in Column 3*	
„ „ 42 „	*Two and four-fifths times the amount in Column 3*	
„ „ 40 „	*Two and three-fifths times the amount in Column 3*	
„ „ 38 „	*Two and two-fifths times the amount in Column 3*	
„ „ 36 „	Two and one-fifth times the amount in Column 3	
„ „ 33 „	Twice the amount in Column 3	
„ „ 30 „	One and four-fifths times the amount in Column 3	
„ „ 27 „	One and three-fifths times the amount in Column 3	
„ „ 24 „	One and two-fifths times the amount in Column 3	
„ „ 21 „	One and one-fifth times the amount in Column 3	
„ „ 18 „	The amount in Column 3	
„ „ 15 „	Four-fifths of the amount in Column 3	
„ „ 12 „	Three-fifths of the amount in Column 3	
„ „ 8 „	Two-fifths of the amount in Column 3	
„ „ 4 „	One-fifth of the amount in Column 3	

(6) Notwithstanding the provisions of the foregoing table, the accrued holiday remuneration payable to a worker who has been employed by the employer for the whole of the 12 months ending on 5th April immediately preceding the termination of his employment shall be as follows:—

(a) in respect of that 12 months an amount equal to the holiday remuneration for the days of annual holiday for which he has qualified, calculated in accordance with the provisions of sub-paragraph (1) of paragraph 7; and

(b) in respect of any period of employment since the said 5th April, the amount calculated in accordance with the foregoing table in this paragraph.

PART V

GENERAL

10. For the purpose of calculating any period of employment qualifying a worker for an annual holiday or for any accrued holiday remuneration under this Schedule, the worker shall be treated—

(1) as if he were employed for a week in respect of any week in which—

(a) in the case of a worker other than a part-time worker, he has worked for the employer for not less than 20 hours and has performed some work for which statutory minimum remuneration is payable;

(b) in the case of a part-time worker, he has worked for the employer and has performed some work for which statutory minimum remuneration is payable;

(c) in the case of any worker—

(i) he has worked for the employer for less than 20 hours by reason of the proved illness of, or accident to, the worker or for a like reason has been absent throughout the week (provided that the number of weeks which may be treated as weeks of employment for such reason shall not exceed four in the aggregate in any such period); or

(ii) he has been suspended throughout the week owing to shortage of work (provided that the number of weeks which may be treated as weeks of employment for such reason shall not exceed six in the aggregate in any such period);

(2) as if he were employed on any day of holiday allowed under the provisions of this Schedule, or of Order W.D. (98), and on any other day of holiday with pay, and for the purposes of the provisions of sub-paragraph (1) of this paragraph, a worker who is absent on such a holiday shall be treated as having worked thereon for the employer on work for which statutory minimum remuneration is payable,

(a) where the holiday is a customary holiday, or a holiday in lieu of a customary holiday, for 8 hours if the worker is normally employed for more than 30 hours a week or for 4 hours if he is normally employed for 30 hours a week or less, or

(b) where the holiday is a day of annual holiday or any other day of holiday with pay, for the number of hours ordinarily worked by him on that day of the week.

11. In this Schedule, unless the context otherwise requires, the following expressions have the meanings hereby respectively assigned to them, that is to say:—

"NORMAL WORKING WEEK" means the number of days on which it has been usual for the worker to work in a week in the employment of the employer in the 12 months immediately preceding the commencement of the holiday season or, where under paragraph 9 accrued holiday remuneration is payable on the termination of the employment, in the 12 months immediately preceding the date of the termination of the employment:

Provided that—

(1) part of a day shall count as a day;

(2) no account shall be taken of any week in which the worker did not perform any work for which statutory minimum remuneration has been fixed.

"ONE DAY'S HOLIDAY PAY" means the appropriate proportion of the remuneration which the worker would be entitled to receive from his employer at the date of the annual holiday or at the termination of the employment, as the case may require, for one week's work if working his normal working week and the number of daily hours normally worked by him (exclusive of overtime) and if paid as a time worker at the appropriate rate of statutory minimum remuneration for work for which statutory minimum remuneration is payable and at the same rate for any work for which such remuneration is not payable, and in this definition "appropriate proportion" means—

where the worker's normal working week is six days .. .. one-sixth

where the worker's normal working week is five days .. .. one-fifth

where the worker's normal working week is four days or less .. one-quarter

"PART-TIME WORKER" means a worker who normally works for the employer for less than 20 hours a week by reason only of the fact that he does not hold himself out as normally available for work for more than the number of hours he normally works in the week.

"RETAIL BESPOKE BRANCH OF THE TRADE" means that branch of the trade in which the employer supplies the garment direct to the individual wearer and employs the worker direct.

"STATUTORY MINIMUM REMUNERATION" means minimum remuneration (other than holiday remuneration) fixed by a wages regulation order.

"WAGES REGULATION ORDER" means a wages regulation order made by the Secretary of State to give effect to proposals submitted to him by the Dressmaking and Women's Light Clothing Wages Council (England and Wales).

"WEEK" means "pay week".

12. The provisions of this Schedule are without prejudice to any agreement for the allowance of any further holidays with pay or for the payment of additional holiday remuneration.

EXPLANATORY NOTE

(This Note is not part of the Order.)

This Order, which has effect from 3rd May 1974, sets out the holidays which an employer is required to allow to workers in relation to whom the Dressmaking and Women's Light Clothing Wages Council operates and the remuneration payable for those holidays in substitution for the holidays and holiday remuneration fixed by the Wages Regulation (Dressmaking and Women's Light Clothing) (England and Wales) (Holidays) Order 1973 (Order W.D. (98)). Order W.D. (98) is revoked.

New provisions are printed in italics.

STATUTORY INSTRUMENTS

1974 No. 588

EXCHANGE CONTROL

The Exchange Control (Authorised Dealers and Depositaries) (First Amendment) Order 1974

Made - - - -	*26th March* 1974
Coming into Operation	*30th April* 1974

The Treasury, in exercise of the powers conferred upon them by sections 42(1) and 36(5) of the Exchange Control Act 1947(a), hereby make the following Order.

1.—(1) This Order may be cited as the Exchange Control (Authorised Dealers and Depositaries) (First Amendment) Order 1974, and shall come into operation on 30th April 1974.

(2) The Interpretation Act 1889(b) shall apply for the interpretation of this Order as it applies for the interpretation of an Act of Parliament.

2. Paragraph 2 of Schedule 2 to the Exchange Control (Authorised Dealers and Depositaries) (No. 2) Order 1973(c) (hereinafter called "the said Order") shall be amended as follows:—

(*a*) by deleting the words "Anglo-Israel Bank Ltd.";

(*b*) by inserting the words "Bank Leumi (U.K.) Ltd." after the words "Bank Hapoalim B.M.";

(*c*) by inserting the words "Bank Saderat Iran." and the words "Bank Sepah, Iran." after the words "Bank of Tokyo Trust Company, The.";

(*d*) by inserting the words "European Banking Company Ltd." after the words "Dresdner Bank A.G.";

(*e*) by inserting the words "Hokkaido Takushoku Bank, Ltd., The." after the words "Hoare & Co., C.";

(*f*) by inserting the words "Iran Overseas Investment Bank Ltd." after the words "Ionian Bank Ltd."; and

(*g*) by inserting the words "Saitama Bank, Ltd., The." after the words "Royal Bank of Scotland Ltd., The.".

(a) 1947 c. 14.   (b) 1889 c. 63.
(c) S.I. 1973/1949 (1973 III, p. 6760).

3. Paragraph 6(*a*) of Schedule 3 to the said Order shall be amended as follows:—

(*a*) by inserting the words "Arthur Young McClelland Moores & Co." before the words "Bagshaw & Co.";

(*b*) by inserting the words "Bartrum, Roth & Co." after the words "Bagshaw & Co.";

(*c*) by inserting the words "Hughes, Allen, Soole & Co." after the words "Hope, Agar & Co.";

(*d*) by inserting the words "Matthew Sheppard & Co." after the words "Mallett (E. Churchill) & Co.";

(*e*) by inserting the words "Sydenham, Snowden, Nicholson & Co." after the words "Stubbs, Parkin, South & Phillips.";

(*f*) by inserting the words "Turner, Hutton & Lawson." after the words "Thomson McLintock & Co.";

(*g*) by inserting the words "Watson & Danbury." after the words "Turquands Barton Mayhew & Co."; and

(*h*) by inserting the words "Whittingham Riddell & Co." after the words "Watts, Knowles & Co.".

4. Paragraph 6(*b*) of Schedule 3 to the said Order shall be amended as follows:—

(*a*) by inserting the words "F. E. Dack (of Myers, Davies & Co.)." after the words "J. K. H. Cook (of Cook & Co.).";

(*b*) by inserting the words "J. B. Lockyer-Nibbs (of Allfields)." after the words "Neville A. Joseph (of Wendover, Buckinghamshire)."; and

(*c*) by inserting the words "P. N. Nicholas (of Sunningdale, Berkshire)." after the words "Helen M. Lowe (of Edinburgh).".

5. Paragraph 7 of Schedule 3 to the said Order shall be amended as follows:—

(*a*) by inserting the words "First National Bank of Boston (Guernsey) Ltd., The." after the words "Channel International Bank Ltd.";

(*b*) by deleting the words "Lloyds Bank Executor & Trustee Company (Channel Islands) Ltd." and substituting the words "Lloyds Bank Trust Company (Channel Islands) Ltd.";

(*c*) by inserting the words "Whyte, Gasc & Co. (Channel Islands) Ltd." after the words "Wallace Brothers Sassoon Bank (Jersey) Ltd."; and

(*d*) by inserting the words "Williams Glyn Secretaries & Registrars (C.I.) Ltd." after the words "Williams & Glyn's Bank Investments (Jersey) Ltd.".

6. Paragraph 8 of Schedule 3 to the said Order shall be amended by inserting the words "G. T. Whyte & Company (Isle of Man) Ltd." after the words "Slater, Walker (Isle of Man) Ltd.".

7. Paragraph 9 of Schedule 3 to the said Order shall be amended by inserting the words "British Petroleum Pension Trust Ltd., The." and the words "Central Trustee Savings Bank Ltd." after the words "Bankers' Automated Clearing Services Ltd.".

8. This Order shall extend to the Channel Islands, and any reference in this Order to the Exchange Control Act 1947 includes a reference to that Act as extended by the Exchange Control (Channel Islands) Order 1947(a).

Donald R. Coleman,
John Golding,
Two of the Lords Commissioners
of Her Majesty's Treasury.

26th March 1974.

EXPLANATORY NOTE

(This Note is not part of the Order.)

This Order amends the lists of banks and other persons authorised under the Exchange Control Act 1947 to deal in gold and foreign currencies and to act as authorised depositaries for the purpose of the deposit of securities as required by that Act.

(a) S.R. & O. 1947/2034 (Rev. VI, p. 1001: 1947 I, p. 660).

STATUTORY INSTRUMENTS

1974 No. 593

SOCIAL SECURITY

The National Insurance (Unemployment and Sickness Benefit and Overlapping Benefits) Amendment Regulations 1974

Made - - -		*27th March* 1974
Coming into Operation		*1st April* 1974

The National Insurance Joint Authority, in exercise of powers conferred by sections 20(2) and 50 of the National Insurance Act 1965(a) and now vested in them (b), and of all other powers enabling them in that behalf, and in conjunction with the Treasury so far as relates to matters with regard to which the Treasury have so directed (c), hereby make the following regulations, which are made in consequence of the Employment and Training Act 1973(d) and which accordingly by virtue of section 14(1) of and paragraph 7(3) of Schedule 3 to that Act are exempt from the requirements of sections 107 and 108 of the said Act of 1965 (which relate respectively to the Parliamentary control of regulations and reference to the National Insurance Advisory Committee): —

Citation and commencement

1. These regulations may be cited as the National Insurance (Unemployment and Sickness Benefit and Overlapping Benefits) Amendment Regulations 1974 and shall come into operation on 1st April 1974.

Substitution for regulation 7(1)(g) *of the National Insurance* (*Unemployment and Sickness Benefit*) *Regulations* 1967

2. For sub-paragraph (g) of regulation 7(1) of the National Insurance (Unemployment and Sickness Benefit) Regulations 1967(e), as amended (f) (days of attendance at certain courses not to be treated as days of incapacity for work), there shall be substituted the following sub-paragraph: —

"(g) a day shall not be treated as a day of incapacity for work if on that day a person is attending—

(i) at a training course provided by or on behalf of the Manpower Services Commission, or

---

(a) 1965 c. 51.
(b) *See* S.I. 1948/211 (Rev. XVI, p. 367: 1948 I, p. 2905) and sections 104(4)(b) and 117(1) of the National Insurance Act 1965 (c. 51).
(c) *See* section 106(5) of the National Insurance Act 1965 (c. 51).
(d) 1973 c. 50.　　　　　　　　　　(e) S.I. 1967/330 (1967 I, p. 1131).
(f) The relevant amending instrument is S.I. 1971/1419 (1971 II, p. 3964).

(ii) at a training course or course of instruction provided in pursuance of arrangements made with the said Commission, or with the Training Services Agency, by any public authority, firm or person, or

(iii) at a course of training in agricultural occupations provided by, or in pursuance of arrangements made by, the Minister of Agriculture, Fisheries and Food or the Secretary of State,

and payment of training allowance is made by or on behalf of the said Commission, that Minister or the Secretary of State to the said person for his attendance at the course in question."

Amendment of regulation 1(2) of the National Insurance (Overlapping Benefits) Regulations 1972

3. In regulation 1(2) of the National Insurance (Overlapping Benefits) Regulations 1972(**a**), as amended (**b**) (definitions), in the definition of "training allowance" —

(*a*) after the words "Government department" there shall be inserted the words "or by or on behalf of the Manpower Services Commission";

(*b*) at the end there shall be added the words "or so provided or approved by or on behalf of the said Commission".

Given under the official seal of the National Insurance Joint Authority.

(L.S.)

Barbara Castle,
Secretary of State for Social Services.
A member of the
National Insurance Joint Authority.

26th March 1974.

John Golding,
T. Pendry,
Two of the Lords Commissioners of
Her Majesty's Treasury.

27th March 1974.

(**a**) S.I. 1972/604 (1972 I, p. 1994).
(**b**) There is no amendment which relates expressly to the subject matter of these Regulations.

EXPLANATORY NOTE

(This Note is not part of the Regulations.)

These Regulations amend the National Insurance (Unemployment and Sickness Benefit) Regulations 1967 and the National Insurance (Overlapping Benefits) Regulations 1972. Provisions of those Regulations which have applied hitherto in relation to persons receiving grants from a Government department for attending certain training courses will under these Regulations apply also where the grant is paid by or on behalf of the Manpower Services Commission.

The Regulations are made in consequence of the Employment and Training Act 1973; by virtue of paragraph 7(3) of Schedule 3 to that Act they are not required to be referred to the National Insurance Advisory Committee and no such reference has been made.

STATUTORY INSTRUMENTS

1974 No. 594

HOUSING, ENGLAND AND WALES

The Housing (Transitional Provisions) Order 1974

Made - - -	*27th March* 1974
Laid before Parliament	*28th March* 1974
Coming into Operation	*1st April* 1974

The Secretary of State for the Environment and the Secretary of State for Wales, in exercise of their powers under section 254(1) and (2)(*a*), (*c*) and (*h*) of the Local Government Act 1972(**a**), and under those provisions as extended by section 102(5) of the Housing Finance Act 1972(**b**) and of all other powers enabling them in that behalf, hereby make the following order in relation, respectively, to England and Wales:—

Citation and commencement

1. This order may be cited as the Housing (Transitional Provisions) Order 1974 and shall come into operation on 1st April 1974.

Interpretation

2.—(1) The Interpretation Act 1889(**c**) shall apply to the interpretation of this order as it applies for the interpretation of an Act of Parliament.

(2) In this order, unless the context otherwise requires—

"the Housing Act" means the Housing Finance Act 1972;

"the 1972 Act" means the Local Government Act 1972;

"the English Order" means the Local Authorities (England) (Property etc.) Order 1973(**d**);

"the Welsh Order" means the Local Authorities (Wales) (Property etc.) Order 1973(**e**);

"the appropriate proportion" in relation to any amount, however expressed, means—

　(*a*) in relation to any area comprised in the district of a new authority which immediately before 1st April 1974 was co-extensive with the district of an existing authority, the whole of that amount; and

---

(a) 1972 c. 70.　　　　　　　　　　　　(b) 1972 c. 47.
(c) 1889 c. 63.　　　　　　　　　　　　(d) S.I. 1973/1861 (1973 III, p. 6401).
(e) S.I. 1973/1863 (1973 III, p. 6452).

(*b*) in relation to any area comprised in the district of a new authority and not falling within sub-paragraph (*a*) above, but which immediately before 1st April 1974 formed part of the district of an existing authority, such proportion of that amount as the number of Housing Revenue Account dwellings in that area bore to the total number of such dwellings in the whole of the district of the existing authority on 31st March 1974;

"combined district" means a district of a new authority other than a non-combined district;

"constituent part" in relation to any combined district means any area which immediately before 1st April 1974 constituted a district or part of a district of an existing authority;

"existing authority" means, as respects any area comprised in the district of a new authority, the authority who immediately before 1st April 1974 were the local authority as respects that area (whether or not co-extensive with any local government area) for the purposes of the Housing Acts 1957 to 1973 (disregarding any order made under section 95 of the Housing Act);

"new authority" means the council of a district who are the local authority with respect to that district for the purposes of the Housing Acts 1957 to 1973;

"non-combined district" means a district of a new authority which immediately before 1st April 1974 constituted the district of a single existing authority;

"Wales" means the area consisting of the counties established by section 20 of the 1972 Act (new local government areas in Wales), and England shall not include any area included in any of those counties.

(3) In this order, unless the context otherwise requires, references to any enactment shall be construed as references to that enactment as amended, extended or applied by or under any other enactment.

(4) In this order, unless the context otherwise requires, expressions used which are also used in the Housing Act shall have the same meaning as they have in that Act.

(5) In this order, unless the context otherwise requires, any reference in any article to a numbered paragraph shall, unless the reference is to a paragraph of a specified article, be construed as a reference to the paragraph bearing that number in the first mentioned article.

Residual subsidy

3.—(1) This article has effect for the purposes of establishing the entitlement (if any) of a new authority under section 2 of the Housing Act to residual subsidy for the year 1974-75 and subsequent years.

(2) In the case of a non-combined district, the entitlement of a new authority to residual subsidy for the year 1974-75 and subsequent years shall be the same as that which the existing authority would have had if the 1972 Act had not been passed.

(3) In the case of a combined district, the entitlement of a new authority to residual subsidy for the year 1974-75 and subsequent years shall be the aggregate of the constituent amounts (if any) determined in accordance with paragraph (4).

(4) In the case of a combined district, if for any year beginning 1974-75 an existing authority would, but for the passing of the 1972 Act, have had an entitlement to residual subsidy for that year, the constituent amount for that year as respects any constituent part of that combined district shall be the appropriate proportion of the amount of the residual subsidy to which the existing authority would have been so entitled for that year.

Transition subsidy

4.—(1) Subject to the provisions of this article, the entitlement of a new authority to transition subsidy and their obligation to make an associated rate fund contribution for the year 1974-75 and subsequent years shall be determined in accordance with section 3 of the Housing Act.

(2) In the case of a non-combined district, the entitlement of a new authority to transition subsidy and their obligation to make an associated rate fund contribution for the year 1974-75 and subsequent years shall be the same as that which the existing authority would have had if the 1972 Act had not been passed.

(3) Where, in the case of a combined district, an existing authority were entitled to transition subsidy for any base year beginning before 1st April 1974, by reference to a shortfall for that year, the new authority shall, subject to Part III of Schedule 1 to the Housing Act, be entitled to transition subsidy for the year 1974-75 and each subsequent year consisting of or, as the case may be, comprising an element for that base year equivalent to the appropriate proportion, in relation to any constituent part of the district, of the amount of transition subsidy to which the existing authority were entitled for the relevant base year by reference to the shortfall for that year, or, where more than one existing authority were so entitled, equivalent to the aggregate of such appropriate proportions.

(4) If for the year 1974-75 or any subsequent year the entitlement of a new authority to transition subsidy consists of or, as the case may be, comprises an element for a base year calculated in accordance with paragraph (3), the associated rate fund contribution to be made by the new authority for that year shall, subject to Part III of Schedule 1 to the 1972 Act, consist of or, as the case may be, comprise an element by reference to the shortfall for that base year, equivalent to the appropriate proportion, in relation to any constituent part of the district, of the amount of the associated rate fund contribution which was required to be made by the existing authority, by reference to the shortfall for that base year, or, where more than one existing authority were required to make such a contribution, equivalent to the aggregate of such appropriate proportions.

(5) In ascertaining in the case of a combined district the amount of a new authority's "rent increases" for the year 1974-75 for the purposes of section 3 of the Housing Act, the amount to be taken as the income of the new authority from rents in respect of Housing Revenue Account dwellings for the immediately preceding year shall be the aggregate income from rents (exclusive of any amount as mentioned in subsection (5) of the said section 3) of the existing

authorities for the year 1973-74 in respect of the Housing Revenue Account dwellings of those authorities which were transferred to the new authority by virtue of the English Order or, as the case may be, the Welsh Order.

(6) The requirements of paragraph (5) shall be deemed to be satisfied if the aggregate income from rents (exclusive of any amount as mentioned in the said subsection (5)) of the existing authorities for the year 1973-74 is calculated by reference in the case of any constituent part of a combined district to the appropriate proportion of the income from rents of the existing authority for that year of all that authority's Housing Revenue Account dwellings.

(7) For the purpose of calculating under the provisions of subsection (7) of section 3 of the Housing Act, in the case of a combined district, a new authority's standard amount for the year 1974-75—

(a) the amount which is to be taken as the residual subsidy payable for the immediately preceding year shall be an amount equivalent to the aggregate of the appropriate proportions, in relation to the constituent parts of the district, of the amounts of residual subsidy (if any) to which the existing authorities were entitled for the year 1973-74; and

(b) the withdrawal factor shall be an amount equivalent to the aggregate of the appropriate proportions, in relation to the constituent parts of the district, of the withdrawal factors which applied in relation to the existing authorities.

Rising costs subsidy

5.—(1) Subject to the provisions of this article, the entitlement of a new authority to rising costs subsidy and their obligation to make an associated rate fund contribution for the year 1974-75 and subsequent years shall be determined in accordance with section 4 of the Housing Act.

(2) In the case of a non-combined district, the entitlement of a new authority to rising costs subsidy and their obligation to make an associated rate fund contribution for the year 1974-75 and subsequent years shall be the same as that which the existing authority would have had if the 1972 Act had not been passed.

(3) Where, in the case of a combined district, an existing authority were entitled to rising costs subsidy for any base year beginning before 1st April 1974 by reference to a qualifying amount for that year, the new authority shall, subject to Part III of Schedule 1 to the Housing Act, be entitled to rising costs subsidy for the year 1974-75 and each subsequent year consisting of or, as the case may be, comprising an element for that base year equivalent to the appropriate proportion, in relation to any constituent part of the district, of the amount of rising costs subsidy to which the existing authority were entitled for the relevant base year by reference to the qualifying amount for that year, or, where more than one existing authority were so entitled, equivalent to the aggregate of such appropriate proportions.

(4) If for the year 1974-75 or any subsequent year the entitlement of a new authority to rising costs subsidy consists of or, as the case may be, comprises an element for a base year calculated in accordance with paragraph (3), the associated rate fund contribution to be made by the new authority for that

year shall, subject to Part III of Schedule 1 to the Housing Act, consist of or, as the case may be, comprise an element by reference to the qualifying amount for that base year, equivalent to the appropriate proportion, in relation to any constituent part of the district, of the amount of the associated rate fund contribution which was required to be made by the existing authority by reference to the qualifying amount for that base year, or, where more than one existing authority were required to make such a contribution, equivalent to the aggregate of such appropriate proportions.

(5) In ascertaining in the case of a combined district a new authority's qualifying amount for the year 1974-75 for the purposes of section 4 of the Housing Act, the amount to be taken as the new authority's reckonable expenditure for the year 1973-74 shall be an amount equivalent to the aggregate of the appropriate proportions, in relation to the constituent parts of the district, of the reckonable expenditure of the existing authorities for the year 1973-74.

Operational deficit subsidy

6.—(1) This article has effect for the purposes of establishing the entitlement (if any) of a new authority under section 5 of the Housing Act to operational deficit subsidy and the associated rate fund contribution to be made by the new authority for the year 1974-75 and subsequent years.

(2) In the case of a non-combined district the entitlement of a new authority to operational deficit subsidy and their obligation to make an associated rate fund contribution for the year 1974-75 and subsequent years, shall be the same as that which the existing authority would have had if the 1972 Act had not been passed.

(3) Subject to Part III of Schedule 1 to the Housing Act, in the case of a combined district, the entitlement of a new authority to operational deficit subsidy for the year 1974-75 and subsequent years shall be an amount equivalent to the aggregate of the constituent amounts (if any) determined in accordance with paragraph (4), and the associated rate fund contribution to be made by the new authority shall be the same amount.

(4) The constituent amount in relation to any constituent part of a combined district shall be an appropriate proportion of the amount of operational deficit subsidy to which the existing authority was entitled for the year 1973-74.

Subsidy claims

7. In the case of any subsidy to be paid by the Secretary of State under Part I of the Housing Act to an existing authority for any year beginning before 1st April 1974, in respect of which a claim for payment has not been made before that date by that authority in accordance with section 15 of that Act, that claim may be made—

(*a*) in any case where an authority ("the relevant authority") are required, by virtue of article 36(3) of the English Order or, as the case may be, article 35(3) of the Welsh Order, to take any action in relation to the accounts of an existing authority which, had the 1972 Act not been passed, would have fallen to be taken by that existing authority, by the relevant authority; and

(*b*) in any other case, by the new authority.

Rent rebates and rent allowances

8.—(1) Subject to the following provisions of this article, in the case of a non-combined district, the existing rebate scheme and the existing allowance scheme shall continue in force and have effect as if made by the new authority.

(2) Subject to the following provisions of this article, in the case of a combined district, any existing rebate scheme or existing allowance scheme shall continue in force as respects any constituent part of that district and shall have effect as if made by the new authority.

(3) Nothing in the foregoing provisions of this article shall affect any function of a new authority under Part II of the Housing Act to vary or revoke any existing rebate scheme or any existing allowance scheme.

(4) The foregoing provisions of this article shall not apply or, as the case may be, shall cease to apply in any case where a new authority make a rebate scheme or an allowance scheme under Part II of the Housing Act to come into operation on 1st April 1974 or subsequently as respects the whole of their district replace each existing scheme.

(5) In this article any reference to an existing rebate scheme or to an existing allowance scheme means a rebate scheme or, as the case may be, an allowance scheme of an existing authority which, would, if the 1972 Act had not been passed, have been in operation on 1st April 1974.

Anthony Crosland,
Secretary of State for the Environment.

27th March 1974.

John Morris,
Secretary of State for Wales.

27th March 1974.

EXPLANATORY NOTE

(This Note is not part of the Order.)

This Order, which applies to England and Wales, makes transitional provisions in relation to—

    (*a*) certain subsidies payable to local authorities under Part I of the Housing Finance Act 1972 ("the 1972 Act"); and

    (*b*) claims for payment of subsidies under Part I of the 1972 Act; and

    (*c*) rent rebates and rent allowances under Part II of the 1972 Act,

to take account of the new authorities established by the Local Government Act 1972.

STATUTORY INSTRUMENTS

1974 No. 595

LOCAL GOVERNMENT, ENGLAND AND WALES

The Local Authorities etc. (Miscellaneous Provision) (No. 2) Order 1974

Made - - - -	27th March 1974
Laid before Parliament	29th March 1974
Coming into Operation	1st April 1974

ARRANGEMENT OF ARTICLES

1. Title and commencement.
2. Interpretation.
3. Miscellaneous amendments of public general and other Acts.
4. Miscellaneous provision as to instruments.
5. Statutes of University of Lancaster.
6. Charter of University College of North Wales.
7. Rate relief for charitable and other organisations.
8. Discount in respect of rates.
9. Local land charges.
10. Coroners' superannuation.
11. Franchise and prescriptive rights.
12. Provision as to markets in relation to former boroughs included in rural districts.
13. Alteration of certain parish names.
14. Confederation of the Cinque Ports.
15. Lincolnshire and Yorkshire County Committees.
16. Kingston upon Hull telephone etc. undertaking.
17. Mersey Tunnels.
18. East Riding Deeds Registry.
19. Dissolution of authorities.
20. Amendment of Property etc. orders.
21. Amendment of Staff Transfer and Protection order.

SCHEDULES

1. Repeal of enactments.
2. Statutory harbour undertakings: form of accounts.
3. Contributing local authorities to National Ports Council.
4. Instruments revoked.

The Secretary of State for the Environment, in relation to England, and the Secretary of State for Wales, in relation to Wales, in exercise of the powers conferred upon them by section 254(1)(*a*) and (2)(*a*), (*b*), (*c*), (*e*) and (*i*), 262(6) and 266(2) of the Local Government Act 1972(**a**), section 84(1)(*a*) and (2)(*b*) and (*c*) of the London Government Act 1963(**b**) and section 34(1) of the Water Act 1973(**c**) and of all other powers enabling them in that behalf, hereby make the following order:—

Title and commencement

1. This order may be cited as the Local Authorities etc. (Miscellaneous Provision) (No. 2) Order 1974 and shall come into operation on 1st April 1974.

Interpretation

2.—(1) The Interpretation Act 1889(**d**) shall apply for the interpretation of this order as it applies for the interpretation of an Act of Parliament.

(2) In this order—

"the Act" means the Local Government Act 1972; and

"Wales" means the area consisting of the counties established by section 20 of the Act (new local government areas in Wales), and "England" does not include any area included in any of those counties.

(3) In this order, unless the context otherwise requires, references to any enactment or instrument shall be construed as references to that enactment or instrument as amended, extended or applied by or under any other enactment or instrument.

Miscellaneous amendments of public general and other Acts

3.—(1) In the Telegraph Act 1863(**e**)—

(*a*) for section 9 as amended in Schedule 5 to the Public Utilities Streets Works Act 1950(**f**) there shall be substituted—

"9. The company shall not place a telegraph under any street not being a highway maintainable at the public expense except with the consent of the body having the control of the street."

(*b*) in section 21—

for the words from "Provided" to "large town," there shall be substituted—

"Provided always that if the body having the control of any street";

for the words from "subject nevertheless" to "such telegraph" there shall be substituted—

"subject nevertheless to sections 23 to 29 of this Act and to the following provisions:—"; and

(*c*) in section 23, for the words preceding "they shall publish a notice" there shall be substituted "Before the company proceeds to place a

---

(**a**) 1972 c. 70.   (**b**) 1963 c. 33.   (**c**) 1973 c. 37.
(**d**) 1889 c. 63.   (**e**) 1863 c. 112.   (**f**) 1950 c. 39.

telegraph over, along or across a street or a public road, or to place posts in or upon a street or a public road,".

(2) In the Telegraph Act 1892(a), in section 5(2)(b)—

for "in any urban sanitary district outside Greater London of the urban sanitary authority, and elsewhere of the county council" there shall be substituted "elsewhere of the district council;"

for "county council or urban sanitary authority" there shall be substituted "or district council".

(3) In the Patriotic Fund Reorganisation Act 1903(b), in Schedule 1 (constitution of Royal Patriotic Fund Corporation), in paragraph 1, for items (b), (c) and (d) in their application to England and Wales there shall be substituted—

"(b) The lord-lieutenant for each county and the lord-lieutenant of Greater London.

(c) The chairman for the time being of the council of every county and every metropolitan district and of the Greater London Council:

Provided that any such council may, if the chairman is unable or unwilling to act, appoint some other person to be a member of the Corporation, and any person so appointed shall hold office for one year from the time of his appointment.

(cc) The Lord Mayor of London and the mayor for the time being of every London borough.

(ccc) Any other person for the time being entitled to the style of Lord Mayor.",

and in item (d) as amended by the Transfer of Functions (Local Government, etc.) (Northern Ireland) Order 1973 the words "and the mayor for the time being of every county borough in England and Wales" shall be omitted.

(4) In the Telegraph (Construction) Act 1908(c), for section 2 there shall be substituted—

"2. The provisions of section 21 of the Telegraph Act 1863 shall extend to public roads as well as to streets."

(5) In the Land Drainage Act 1930(d), for section 23(1) (expenses of county councils) as it applies to London boroughs by virtue of paragraph 1 of Schedule 14 to the London Government Act 1963 and paragraph 25(5) of Schedule 29 to the Act, there shall be substituted—

"(1) Any amount due to a water authority from the council of a London borough under the Water Act 1973 shall be defrayed as the council, having regard to the benefit, if any, derived by various areas, think just and equitable as general expenses or as special expenses chargeable on such part or parts of the London borough within the water authority's area as the council think fit.".

(a) 1892 c. 59.   (b) 1903 c. 20.   (c) 1908 c. 33.
(d) 1930 c. 44.

(6) In the Green Belt (London and Home Counties) Act 1938(a)—

(a) in section 2(1), for the definitions of "the area" and "local authority", there shall be substituted—

"the expression "the area" means—

Greater London

the counties of Buckinghamshire, Hertfordshire and Surrey

the county of Essex other than the borough of Southend-on-Sea

the county of Kent other than the area of the former county borough of Canterbury

in the county of Berkshire—

the borough of Slough

in the borough of Windsor and Maidenhead, the parishes of Datchet, Eton, Horton and Wraysbury

in the county of West Sussex, so much of the borough of Crawley as was immediately before 1st April 1974 comprised in the administrative county of Surrey;" and

"the expression "local authority" means the Greater London Council, a London borough council or the council of any county or district wholly or partly within the area;";

(b) the expression "contributing local authority", in relation to any land in relation to which, if the Act had not been passed, any existing council to whom section 1(10) of the Act applies would have been such an authority shall include the council of any county or district whose area includes the whole or any part of the area of that existing council; and

(c) in section 2(2) the words "or the municipal corporation of the county borough" shall be omitted.

(7) In the Representation of the People Act 1949(b)

(a) in section 36(2) for "section seventy-two of the Local Government Act, 1933", there shall be substituted "section 44 of the Local Government Act 1972";

(b) in section 172(1), for the definition of "local government Act" there shall be substituted—

" "local government Act" means the Local Government Act 1972";

and

(c) in Schedule 8, in paragraph 2 (references in other Acts) for "the registration officer or returning officer appointed under this Act" there shall be substituted "the registration officer appointed under section 39, or the returning officer appointed under section 40, of the Local Government Act 1972".

(8) In the Dog Licences Act 1959(c)—

in section 10(1)—

for the words preceding "shall keep", there shall be substituted "The

---

(a) 1 & 2 Geo. 6 c. xciii.   (b) 1949 c. 68.   (c) 1959 c. 55.

proper officer of the council of every district or London borough, and the Town Clerk of the City of London,"; and

for "county or borough", there shall be substituted "area"; and

in section 13, for "county or county borough" there shall be substituted "district or London borough, or of the Common Council of the City of London,".

(9) In the Humber Bridge Act 1959(a), for section 6 (constitution of Humber Bridge Board) there shall be substituted—

"**6.** The Board shall consist of 22 members to be appointed as follows—

12 members to be appointed by the District Council of Kingston upon Hull

2 members to be appointed by the County Council of Humberside;

1 member to be appointed by the County Council of Lincolnshire;

1 member to be appointed by the District Council of Scunthorpe;

3 members to be appointed by the Borough Council of Beverley; and

3 members to be appointed by the Borough Council of Glanford."

and article 20(2) and (3) of the Local Authorities etc. (Miscellaneous Provision) Order 1974(b) shall apply to the Board with the necessary modifications.

(10) In the London Government Act 1963, in Schedule 14 (functions with respect to land drainage), in paragraph 11, after "this Schedule" there shall be inserted "or section 34 of the Act of 1961".

(11) In the Severn Bridge Tolls Act 1965(c), in section 3(7), for the definitions of "the county councils" and "local authority" there shall be substituted—

" "the county councils" means the councils of the counties of Avon and Gwent respectively; "local authority" means the council of a county or district;".

(12) In the Gas Act 1965(d), in section 28(1), in the definition of "local authority" for "the council of a county, county borough or county district" there shall be substituted "the council of a county or district".

(13) In the Docks and Harbours Act 1966(e), in Schedule 1 (Ports and Licensing Authorities), as amended by the Docks and Harbours Act 1966 (Amendment No. 6) Order 1973(f), in respect of any port specified in Column (1) of the following table the authority specified in respect thereof in column (2) shall be substituted as the licensing authority.

(a) 7 & 8 Eliz. 2. c. xlvi.   (b) S.I. 1974/482 (1974 I, p. 1690).   (c) 1965 c. 24.
(d) 1965 c. 36.   (e) 1966 c. 28.   (f) S.I. 1973/94 (1973 I, p. 478).

TABLE

(1) Port	(2) Licensing Authority
Boston	The District Council of Boston
Wisbech	The District Council of Fenland
Whitstable	The City Council of Canterbury
Weymouth	The Borough Council of Weymouth and Portland
Penryn	The District Council of Carrick
Penzance	The District Council of Penwith
Truro	The District Council of Carrick
Bristol	The City Council of Bristol
Preston	The Borough Council of Preston
Sunderland	The Borough Council of Sunderland

(14) In the Post Office Act 1969(a), in section 14(1) (Post Office users' councils) for "a users' council for Wales and Monmouthshire, to be called "the Post Office Users' Council for Wales and Monmouthshire" " there shall be substituted "a users' council for Wales, to be called "the Post Office Users' Council for Wales" ".

(15) In the Courts Act 1971(b), Schedule 3 (premises formerly used for business of abolished courts) shall apply, in respect of any premises being, or being comprised in, any property transferred by the Local Authorities (England) (Property etc.) Order 1973(c) or the Local Authorities (Wales) (Property etc.) Order 1973(d), with the substitution for the authority from whom the property is transferred of the authority to whom it is transferred.

(16) In the Pensions (Increase) Act 1971(e), in Schedule 3, in paragraph 6(1) (definition of local authority"), for sub-paragraph (a) there shall be substituted—

"(a) in England and Wales

(i) the Greater London Council, the Common Council of the City of London and the council of a London borough;

(ii) in respect of any time before 1st April 1974, the council of an administrative county, county borough or county district;

(iii) the council of a county or district established by or under the Local Government Act 1972; and

(iv) any other local authority within the meaning of the Local Loans Act 1875; and".

(17) In the Housing Finance Act 1972(f) in Schedule 9 (minor and consequential amendments)—

in paragraph 2 (1), for the words preceding "Except" there shall be substituted—

"(1) In paragraph 17 of Schedule 13 to the Local Government Act 1972 (local authorities' capital funds) after sub-paragraph (1) there shall be inserted—

(a) 1969 c. 48.   (b) 1971 c. 23.
(c) S.I. 1973/1861 (1973 III, p. 6401).   (d) S.I. 1973/1863 (1973 III, p. 6452).
(e) 1971 c. 56.   (f) 1972 c. 47.

"(1A)".

in paragraph 2(2), for the words preceding "Except" there shall be substituted—

"(2) After the said paragraph 17 there shall be inserted—
"17A."

(18) In the Gas Act 1972(**a**), in section 39(3), for "the council of a county, county borough or county district" there shall be substituted "the council of a county or district".

(19) In the Act, paragraph 6(2)(*b*) and (4) of Schedule 29 (provision for the construction of references to parishes and rural parishes) shall apply to the areas constituting parishes by virtue of article 3(2) of the New Parishes Order 1973(**b**) and article 3 of the New Parishes (Amendment) Order 1973(**c**) as they apply to the areas mentioned in paragraph 3 of Part IV of Schedule 1 to the Act.

(20) Any statutory provision contained in any local or private Act or made under section 30 of the Local Loans Act 1875(**d**) which is inconsistent with the Local Authority (Stocks and Bonds) Regulations 1974(**e**) shall cease to have effect.

(21) Any local statutory provision which would, but for this paragraph, operate so as to empower the council of a district in a metropolitan county to carry on a road passenger transport, ferry or railway undertaking shall cease to have effect, and no such council shall, by virtue of Part V (running of public service vehicles by local authorities) of the Road Traffic Act 1930(**f**), have power to run public service vehicles on any road inside or outside their district.

(22) The enactments specified in Schedule 1 to this order are hereby repealed to the extent mentioned in column (3) thereof.

Miscellaneous provision as to instruments

4.—(1) In the Public Trustee Rules 1912(**g**), in rule 30 (corporate bodies as custodian trustees) as substituted by the Public Trustee (Custodian Trustee) Rules 1971(**h**), for items (g)(ii) and (iii) there shall be substituted—

"(ii) the corporation of any London borough, acting by the council,

(iii) a county council, district council, parish council or community council, or".

(2) The House to House Collections Regulations 1947(**i**) shall continue to have effect on and after 1st April 1974 as if for any reference to a police authority there were substituted a reference to a licensing authority within the meaning of section 2 of the House to House Collections Act 1939(**j**) as amended by Schedule 29 to the Act, and any reference in those regulations to a police area shall be construed accordingly.

(3) In the Bedwellty Order 1951(**k**), section 3 shall cease to have effect.

(4) In the Llanelly Harbour Order 1954(**l**)—

(*a*) in section 4 for the definition of "the Council" there shall be substituted—

(**a**) 1972 c. 60.   (**b**) S.I. 1973/688.
(**c**) S.I. 1973/1466.   (**d**) 1875 c. 83.
(**e**) S.I. 1974/519.(1974 I, p. 1977).   (**f**) 1930 c. 43.
(**g**) S.R. & O. 1912/348 (Rev XXIII p. 311: (1974 I, p. 1977) 1912 p. 1231)
(**h**) S.I. 1971/1894, (1971 III, p. 5142). (**i**) S.I. 1947/2662 (Rev. III, p. 679).
(**j**) 1939 c. 44.   (**k**) S.I. 1951/1222.
(**l**) Confirmed by 2 & 3 Eliz. 2. c. xxxiii.

" "the Council" means the Community Council of Llanelli;"; and

(b) in section 6, for "twenty-four" (being the maximum number of members of the Llanelly Harbour Trust to be appointed by the Council) there shall be substituted "18".

(5) In the Agricultural Lime Scheme 1966(a), in Part I of Schedule 2 (rates of contribution in respect of lime)—

(a) in paragraph (a), for "elsewhere than in the counties of Cornwall, Montgomery, Cardigan, Merioneth and Pembroke" there shall be substituted "elsewhere than in the county of Cornwall, the districts of Ceredigion, Meirionnydd, Montgomery, Preseli and South Pembrokeshire and the communities of Betws Gwerfil Goch, Corwen, Gwyddelwern, Llandrillo, Llangar and Llansantffraid Glyndyfrdwy"; and

(b) in paragraph (c), for "in the counties of Montgomery, Cardigan, Merioneth and Pembroke" there shall be substituted "in any district or community named in paragraph (a) of this Part of this Schedule".

(6) In the Humber Harbour Reorganisation Scheme 1966 Confirmation Order 1967(b), in article 11(2) (members of the Humber Local Board) of the Scheme set out therein, for items (g) and (h) there shall be substituted—

"(g) one shall be appointed on the joint nomination of the Borough Council of Grimsby, the District Council of Cleethorpes and the County Council of Humberside;

(h) one shall be appointed on the joint nomination of the District Council of Boothferry and the County Council of Humberside;".

(7) In the Southampton Harbour Reorganisation Scheme 1967 Confirmation Order 1968(c), in article 11(2) (members of Southampton Local Board) of the Scheme set out therein, for items (h) and (i) there shall be substituted—

"(h) one shall be appointed on the nomination of the City Council of Southampton;

(i) one shall be appointed on the nomination of the County Council of Hampshire;".

(8) In the Statutory Harbour Undertakings (Form of Accounts etc.) (Local Authorities) Regulations 1969(d), for Schedule 1 there shall be substituted the Schedule set out in Schedule 2 to this order.

(9) In the Gaming Clubs (Permitted Areas) Regulations 1971(e)—

(a) for paragraph (a) of regulation 3 (which as amended by the Gaming Clubs (Permitted Areas) (Amendment) Regulations 1971(f) defines certain of the areas in which licences for general gaming may be granted) there shall be substituted—

"(a) the area of every county borough which was shown as having an estimated population of 125,000 or more in any of the annual estimates made by the Registrar General for England and Wales and published between 1st December 1970 and 1st October 1973; and"; and

---

(a) S.I. 1966/794 (1966 II, p. 1840).   (b) S.I. 1968/237.
(c) S.I. 1968/941.   (d) S.I. 1969/1296 (1969 III, p. 3860).
(e) S.I. 1971/1538 (1971 III, p. 4345).   (f) S.I. 1971/2029 (1971 III, p. 5820).

(b) the Schedule (which defines further areas for that purpose) shall not be affected by the abolition of areas effected by section 1(10) of the Act.

(10) In the Housing Finance (North Eastern Housing Association) Order 1972(a)—

(a) article 16 (special provision for Tow Law urban district) shall be omitted; and

(b) for Schedule 1 there shall be substituted—

"SCHEDULE 1

LOCAL AUTHORITIES IN RELATION TO WHICH THE ORDER APPLIES

The District Councils of Allerdale, Blyth Valley, Copeland, Derwentside, Durham, Easington, Gateshead, Hartlepool, North Tyneside, Sedgefield, South Tyneside, Sunderland, Teesdale and Wear Valley.".

(11) In the Poisons Rules 1972(b), Schedule 13 (restriction of sale and supply of strychnine and certain other substances)—

(a) in Part I—

(i) in paragraph 6(1)(a) and (b), for "medical officer of health" there shall be substituted "proper officer"; and

(ii) in paragraph 6(2), in the definition of "local authority", for ", a county borough or a county district" there shall be substituted "or a district"; and

(b) in Part III, in forms A and B for "Medical Officer of Health of" there shall be substituted "The officer appointed for this purpose by".

(12) The abolition of areas effected by sections 1(10) and 20(6) of the Act shall not affect the Schedule to the Grey Squirrels (Warfarin) Order 1973(c) (which sets out the areas in which specified poison may be used only inside a building).

(13) In the National Ports Council Provision of Funds (Variation) Scheme 1973 (Confirmation) Order 1973(d), in the Schedule of third contributing authorities, for each entry set out in column (1) of Schedule 3 to this order there shall be substituted the entry set out in respect thereof in column (2).

(14) Outside Greater London, any order made under section 112(1) of the Local Government Act 1933 or any enactment replaced by that provision, in force immediately before 1st April 1974, shall cease to have effect.

(15) The instruments specified in Schedule 4 to this order are hereby revoked.

Statutes of University of Lancaster

5.—(1) The amendments set out in paragraphs (2) and (3) shall be made in the Statutes of the University of Lancaster.

(2) In Statute 8 (The Court)—

(a) S.I. 1972/1193.
(b) S.I. 1972/1939 (1972 III, p. 5750).
(c) S.I. 1973/744 (1973 I, p. 2376).
(d) S.I. 1973/1620 (1973 III, p. 5060).

(*a*) in paragraph (1)—

(i) in Class II, for clauses (a), (f), (j), (k), (l) and (m) there shall be substituted—

"(a) The Lord-Lieutenants of the Counties of Lancashire and Cumbria (or at the wish of a Lord-Lieutenant a Lieutenant of the County in his place).";

"(f) The High Sheriffs of the Counties of Lancashire and Cumbria."; and

"(j) The members of the Commons House of Parliament elected for the constituencies wholly within the Counties of Lancashire and Cumbria and the Darwen, Morecambe and Lonsdale and Rossendale constituencies.

(k) The Mayor of the City of Lancaster and the chief executive officer of the City Council.

(l) The Chairmen and the chief executive officers of the County Councils of Lancashire and Cumbria.

(m) The Chairmen of the education committees and the chief education officers of the County Councils of Lancashire and Cumbria.", and

(ii) in Class III—

(*a*) for clause (i) there shall be substituted—

" (i) (1) Four persons appointed by the County Council of Lancashire.

(2) Three persons appointed by the County Council of Cumbria.

(3) Five persons appointed by the City Council of Lancaster.

(4) One person appointed by the council of each other district in the counties of Lancashire and Cumbria.

(5) One person appointed by each other local authority which has, during its preceding financial year, contributed from its general fund to the general funds of the University."; and

(*b*) in clause (j) for "Lancashire, Westmorland and Cumberland" there shall be substituted "the Counties of Lancashire and Cumbria";

(*c*) in paragraph (2), for "or Constitution of the Counties, County Boroughs, Municipal Boroughs, Urban Districts and Rural Districts" there shall be substituted "of the Counties and Districts".

(3) In Statute 9 (The Council)—

(a) in paragraph (1), for clauses (e) and (f) there shall be substituted—

"(e) One person appointed by the City Council of Lancaster, who shall be a member of that Council.

(f) One person appointed by the County Council of Lancashire.";
and

(b) in paragraph (2) (holding of office), for clause (ii) there shall be substituted—

"(ii) so long as he remains a member of the City Council, the person appointed under clause (e) shall hold office for such period, being not less than three years, as the City Council may determine, and shall be eligible for reappointment.".

Charter of University College of North Wales

6.—(1) The amendments set out in paragraphs (2) to (4) shall be made in the Supplemental Charter of the University College of North Wales granted on 26th October 1951 and the provisions of paragraph (5) shall have effect for the purposes therein mentioned.

(2) In article 25 (Governors while holding certain office)—

(a) for paragraph (1) there shall be substituted—

"(1) The Lord-Lieutenants of Clwyd, Gwynedd and Powys;";

(b) for paragraph (2) there shall be substituted—

"(2) The members of the Commons House of Parliament elected for constituencies in the counties of Clwyd and Gwynedd and the district of Montgomery;".

(3) In article 26 (the appointment of persons to be members of the Court of Governors—

(a) in paragraph (1) for the words from the beginning to "last preceding census of population;" there shall be substituted—

"(a) Twenty one persons appointed by the County Council of Clwyd;

(b) Sixteen persons appointed by the County Council of Gwynedd;

(c) Four persons appointed by the County Council of Powys;";

(b) paragraph (2) shall cease to have effect;

(c) in paragraph (3) for the words "A person appointed by each District Council in North Wales;" there shall be substituted—

"(a) Five persons appointed by the District Council of Arfon;

(b) Six persons appointed by the District Council of Glyndŵr;

(c) Nine persons appointed by the District Council of Montgomery;

(d) Three persons appointed by each of the district councils of Alyn and Deeside, Rhuddlan and Wrexham Maelor;

(*e*) Four persons appointed by each of the district councils of Colwyn, Delyn and Dwyfor;

(*f*) Eight persons appointed by each of the district councils of Aberconwy, Meirionnydd and Ynys Môn-Isle of Anglesey;".

(4) In article 38 (the appointment of persons to be members of the Council)—

(*a*) for paragraph (9) there shall be substituted—

"(9) One person to be appointed annually by the District Council of Arfon.";

(*b*) in paragraph (11) for the words from the beginning to "the County Council of Montgomery;" there shall be substituted—

"Four representatives to be appointed by the County Council of Clwyd, four by the County Council of Gwynedd and one by the County Council of Powys;".

(5) For the purposes of the first appointments under paragraphs (3) and (4)—

(*a*) the persons so appointed as members of the Court of Governors or the Council shall come into office on 1st April 1974 or as soon as practicable thereafter;

(*b*) the persons so appointed as members of the Court of Governors shall retire on 1st January 1975; and

(*c*) the provisions of Statutes 11 and 40 of the Statutes of the said University College (certain requirements as to the giving of notice to the body making the appointments), so far as they are applicable in relation to the persons so appointed, shall not have effect.

Rate relief for charitable and other organisations

7. Any reduction or remission of payment of rates effected under section 40(5) of the General Rate Act 1967(a) in force immediately before 1st April 1974 in a county borough or county district abolished by section 1 or 20 of the Act shall cease to have effect on that date.

This article is without prejudice to any reduction or remission of payment of rates effected by a district council under the said section 40(5) and taking effect from 1st April 1974.

Discount in respect of rates

8. Any direction for the allowance of a discount in respect of rates under section 51 or 54 of the General Rate Act 1967 in force immediately before 1st April 1974 in a county borough or county district abolished by section 1 or 20 of the Act shall cease to have effect on that date.

This article is without prejudice to any direction of a district council under the said section 51 or 54 taking effect as from 1st April 1974.

(a) 1967 c. 9.

Local land charges

9.—(1) For the purposes of section 212 of the Act, every entry made in a register of local land charges before 1st April 1974 shall be treated as an entry in the register kept by the proper officer of the council of the district in which the land to which the entry relates is situated.

(2) The powers, rights, obligations and liabilities of every proper officer of an authority abolished by section 1(10) or 20(6) of the Act with respect to the register of local land charges shall be transferred to, exercisable by and enforceable against the proper officer required under section 212 of the Act to keep the register in relation to which the power, right or obligation arose.

Coroners' superannuation

10. A person appointed a coroner for a county to hold office from 1st April 1974 who was immediately before that date holding office as a coroner shall be entitled to reckon as service for the purpose of section 6 of the Coroners (Amendment) Act 1926**(a)** in its application to that county the service which he was entitled to reckon for such purpose immediately before that date.

Franchise and prescriptive rights

11.—(1) Any powers to maintain markets exercisable immediately before 1st April 1974 by the corporation or council of the borough of Abingdon, Henley-on-Thames, Okehampton, Wallingford or Wokingham or the council of the urban district of Stowmarket, Wantage or Wymondham under any franchise or by virtue of prescription shall be exercisable by the parish council constituted under Part V of Schedule 1 to the Act for the area of the borough or urban district.

(2) Any powers to hold fairs exercisable immediately before 1st April 1974 by the corporation or council of the borough of Abingdon or Southwold or the council of the urban district of Wantage under any franchise or by virtue of prescription shall be exercisable by the parish council so constituted for the area of the borough or urban district.

(3) Any manorial rights not included in paragraph (1) or (2) above exercisable immediately before 1st April 1974 by the corporation or council of the borough of Henley-on-Thames or Thetford or the council of the urban district of Sidmouth or Wantage shall be exercisable by the parish council of the parish constituted as aforesaid for the area of the borough or urban district.

(4) Any parish council to whom any matter is transferred by paragraph (1), (2) or (3) above shall have the same powers in relation thereto as were exercisable immediately before 1st April 1974 by the corporation or council from whom the matter is transferred.

Provision as to markets in relation to former boroughs included in rural districts

12.—(1) The provision of this article has effect for the continuance as respects the parish councils of parishes which immediately before the passing of the Act were boroughs included in rural districts of provision made in relation to markets as respects the councils of such boroughs.

(a) 1926 c. 59.

(2) The Parish Council of Lostwithiel shall have such rights in relation to markets as were exercised immediately before 1st April 1974 by the council of the borough.

(3) The Parish Council of Much Wenlock shall maintain the Guildhall market and shall be a market authority for the purposes of Part III of the Food and Drugs Act 1955**(a)**.

(4) The Parish Council of Oswestry shall maintain the markets maintained immediately before 1st April 1974 by the council of the borough.

(5) The Parish Council of South Molton shall maintain the Pannier market.

Alteration of certain parish names

13.—(1) The parish of Bollington in the existing rural district of Bucklow shall be renamed Little Bollington.

(2) The parish of Chard constituted by the Local Government (Successor Parishes) Order 1973**(b)** shall be renamed Chard Town.

(3) The parish of Liskeard in the existing rural district of Liskeard shall be renamed Dobwells and Trevidland.

(4) The parish of Murton in the existing rural district of Helmsley shall be renamed Murton Grange.

(5) The parish of Staunton in the existing rural district of West Dean shall be renamed Staunton Coleford.

(6) The parish of Waltham Holy Cross constituted by the said order of 1973 shall be renamed Waltham Abbey.

Confederation of the Cinque Ports

14. The district council, town council or charter trustees for any area being a port, antient town or corporate limb of the Confederation of the Cinque Ports shall exercise the functions in relation to such Confederation which were immediately before 1st April 1974 exercised by the corporation for such area.

In this article "town council" means the council of a parish having the status of a town by virtue of a resolution under section 245(6) of the Act.

Lincolnshire and Yorkshire County Committees

15.—(1) Any functions exercisable immediately before 1st April 1974 by the Lincolnshire County Committee shall be exercisable by the County Council of Lincolnshire.

(2) Any functions so exercisable by the Yorkshire County Committee shall be exercisable by the County Council of North Yorkshire.

Kingston upon Hull telephone etc. undertaking

16. The District Council of Kingston upon Hull may, subject to the conditions and within the limits contained in a licence dated 18th July 1969 and made

---

(a) 4 & 5 Eliz. 2 c. 16.   (b) S.I. 1973/1110 (1973 II, p. 3393).

between the Postmaster General and the Lord Mayor, Aldermen and Citizens of the City and County of Kingston upon Hull and in any licence made between the Post Office and the said District Council, operate a public telephone and other telegraphic business undertaking.

Mersey Tunnels

17.—(1) The functions conferred by the Mersey Tunnels Acts 1925 to 1972 on the corporations of the county boroughs of Birkenhead, Liverpool and Wallasey and the Mersey Tunnel Joint Committee shall be exercised by the County Council of Merseyside, and nothing in subsections (3) and (4) of section 262 of the Act shall apply to the said Acts.

(2) For section 81 of the Mersey Tunnel Act 1925(a) there shall be substituted—

"81. All expenditure in respect of the Mersey Tunnels properly chargeable to revenue shall in so far as moneys received on account of revenue are for the time being in the hands of the County Council of Merseyside be discharged out of such moneys.".

East Riding Deeds Registry

18. Those functions in respect of the East Riding Deeds Registry constituted under section 31 of the Yorkshire Registries Act 1884(b) which, apart from the abolition of authorities effected by section 1(10) of the Act, would have fallen to be discharged by the county council of the East Riding of Yorkshire shall be discharged by the County Council of Humberside; and in any enactment or instrument relating to the Deeds Registry references to a county council shall, unless the context otherwise requires, be construed as references to the County Council of Humberside.

Dissolution of authorities

19.—(1) The following joint committees, which would apart from this article, by virtue of section 263(5) of the Act, continue to exist on and after 1st April 1974, shall cease to exist—

The Breconshire and Radnorshire joint fire services committee

The Denbighshire and Montgomeryshire joint fire services committee.

(2) The following bodies, namely—

The Mersey Tunnel Joint Committee

The Snowdonia Park Joint Advisory Committee

The South Westmorland Joint Pest Control Board

The West Monmouthshire Omnibus Board

shall be dissolved on 1st April 1974.

Amendment of Property etc. orders

20.—(1) Schedule 1 to the Local Authorities (England) (Property etc.) Order 1973 as extended by the Local Authorities etc. (England) (Property etc.:

(a) 15 & 16 Geo. 5 c. cx.   (b) 1884 c. 54.

Further Provision) Order 1974**(a)** shall be further extended by the inclusion of the Schedule "Further extension of Schedule 1 of the Local Authorities (England) (Property etc.) Order 1973" signed by an Assistant Secretary in the Department of the Environment. The Schedule is deposited in the offices of the Secretary of State for the Environment. Copies of the Schedule have been deposited with the councils of counties and districts in England and shall be open to inspection at all reasonable times.

(2) In Schedule 4 to the said order as so extended, there shall be added—

"The Great Ouse Water Authority   The Anglian Water Authority
The Derwent Valley Water Board   The Severn-Trent Water Authority
The South Westmorland Joint Pest   The South Lakeland District Coun-
   Control Board   cil".

(3) Schedule 1 to the Local Authorities (Wales) (Property etc.) Order 1973 as extended by the Local Authorities etc. (Wales) (Property etc.: Further Provision) Order 1974**(b)** shall be further extended by the inclusion of the Schedule "Further extension of Schedule 1 of the Local Authorities (Wales) (Property etc.) Order 1973" signed by an Assistant Secretary in the Welsh Office. The Schedule is deposited in the Cardiff offices of the Secretary of State for Wales. Copies of the Schedule have been deposited with the councils of counties and districts in Wales and shall be open to inspection at all reasonable times.

Amendment of Staff Transfer and Protection order

21.—(1) In Schedule 2 to the Local Authorities etc. (Staff Transfer and Protection) Order 1974**(c)** there shall be added—

"The Great Ouse Water Authority   The Anglian Water Authority".

(2) In Schedule 3 to the said order, in Schedule 3, after the entry for the Peak Park Planning Board there shall be inserted—
"The South Westmorland Joint Pest   The South Lakeland District Coun-
   Control Board   cil".

SCHEDULE 1

Article 3(22)   REPEAL OF ENACTMENTS

PART I—GENERAL

(1) Chapter	(2) Short Title	(3) Extent of Repeal
34 & 35 Hen. 8 c. 26	The Laws in Wales Act 1542	Section 61
6 & 7 Will. 4 c. 103	The Berwick-on-Tweed Act 1836	The whole Act
45 & 46 Vict. c. 56	The Electric Lighting Act 1882	In section 31, the words "county borough, county"
51 & 52 Vict. c. 41	The Local Government Act 1888	Section 64(5)

(a) S.I. 1974/406 (1974 I, p. 1276).   (b) S.I. 1974/404 (1974 I, p. 1264).
                    (c) S.I. 1974/483 (1974 I, p. 1709).

(1) Chapter	(2) Short Title	(3) Extent of Repeal
55 & 56 Vict. c. 59	The Telegraph Act 1892	In section 3 the words to "district; and" In section 9 the definitions of "urban sanitary authority" and "urban sanitary district"
55 & 56 Vict. c. clxxxvii	The Pontypridd Burial Board Act 1892	The whole Act
6 Edw. 7 c. 34	The Prevention of Corruption Act 1906	In section 1(3), the word "municipal"
15 & 16 Geo. 5. c. liv	The Bedwellty Urban District Council Act 1925	Section 40
15 & 16 Geo. 5 c. cii	The Blackpool Improvement Act 1925	Section 110
7 & 8 Geo. 6 c. 31	The Education Act 1944	In section 114(1), in the definition of "local education authority" the words "and, in relation to a county borough, the council of the county borough"
10 & 11 Geo. 6 c. 54	The Electricity Act 1947	In section 67(1), in the definition of "local authority" the words "county borough, county"
12, 13 & 14 Geo. 6 c. 68	The Representation of the People Act 1949	In section 116(5), the words following "election was held." Sections 118(2) and 167(1)(b) except in their application to the City of London
14 Geo. 6 c. 39	The Public Utilities Street Works Act 1950	In Schedule 5, the entry relating to section 9 of the Telegraph Act 1863
14 & 15 Geo. 6 c. 60	The Mineral Workings Act 1951	In section 1(1) the words following "this Act" In section 16(5), paragraph (a) and in paragraph (b) the word "county" where first occurring
1962 c. 58	The Pipe-lines Act 1962	In section 35(6), the words "county borough, county"
1964 c. 48	The Police Act 1964	In Schedule 9, the amendment of the Local Government Act 1933
1967 c. 10	The Forestry Act 1967	In section 40(2)(c)(i) the words "county borough,"
1971 c. 40	The Fire Precautions Act 1971	In section 43(1), in the definition of "local authority", the words "county borough," and "county"
1972 c. 70	The Local Government Act 1972	In paragraph 10 of Schedule 26, the words "and 16"

PART II—LOCAL ACT POWERS FOR ISSUE OF BILLS

(1) Chapter	(2) Short Title	(3) Extent of Repeal
63 & 64 Vict. c. cxxxii	The Nottingham Corporation Act 1900	Section 14
63 & 64 Vict. c. ccxxxiv	The Halifax Corporation Act 1900	Section 170
63 & 64 Vict. c. cclxxxi.	The Southport Corporation Act 1900	Section 138
1 Edw. 7 c. cxxiv	The Kingston-upon-Hull Corporation Act 1901	Section 57
1 Edw. 7 c. cxxviii	The Blackpool Improvement Act 1901	Section 64
1 Edw. 7 c. cxxix	The Burton-upon-Trent Corporation Act 1901	Section 115
1 Edw. 7 c. cxciii	The Manchester Corporation Act 1901	Section 44
2 Edw. 7 c. lxii	The Birkenhead Corporation Act 1902	Section 24
2 Edw. 7 c. clxxvii	The Leicester Corporation Act 1902	Section 105
3 Edw. 7 c. ccxxxiii	The Bradford Corporation Act 1903	Section 54
5 Edw. 7 c. i	The Leeds Corporation (Consolidation) Act 1905	Section 306
8 & 9 Geo. 5 c. lxi	The Sheffield Corporation (Consolidation) Act 1918	Section 418
11 & 12 Geo. 5 c. lxxiv	The Liverpool Corporation Act 1921	Section 561
1966 c. xxx	The Leeds Corporation Act 1966	Section 40
1967 c. xxxiii	The Kingston upon Hull Corporation Act 1967	Section 66
1967 c. xxxv	The Somerset County Council Act 1967	Section 31
1968 c. xxix	The Lancashire County Council (General Powers) Act 1968	Section 20
1968 c. xxxvi	The Cheshire County Council Act 1968	Section 53
1968 c. xxxviii	The Durham County Council Act 1968	Section 71
1968 c. xl	The Leicester Corporation Act 1968	Section 95
1968 c. xlii	The Newcastle upon Tyne Corporation Act 1968	Section 66
1969 c. iii	The Derbyshire County Council Act 1969	Section 3
1969 c. v	The Derby Corporation Act 1969	Section 4
1969 c. vi	The Bournemouth Corporation Act 1969	Section 6
1969 c. vii	The Coventry Corporation Act 1969	Section 3
1969 c. viii	The Northampton County Council Act 1969	Section 4
1969 c. xiv	The Teesside Corporation Act 1969	Section 3
1969 c. xxi	The Luton Corporation Act 1969	Section 3

(1) Chapter	(2) Short Title	(3) Extent of Repeal
1969 c. xxxvii	The Portsmouth Corporation Act 1969	Section 13
1969 c. xxxviii	The York Corporation Act 1969	Section 39
1969 c. xlvii	The Cardiff Corporation Act 1969	Section 68
1969 c. liii	The Dudley Corporation Act 1969	Section 106
1969 c. liv	The Warley Corporation Act 1969	Section 99
1969 c. lv	The Liverpool Corporation Act 1969	Section 30
1969 c. lvi	The Worcestershire County Council Act 1969	Section 56
1969 c. lvii	The Blackpool Corporation Act 1969	Section 14
1969 c. lviii	The Walsall Corporation Act 1969	Section 154
1969 c. lix	The West Bromwich Corporation Act 1969	Section 114
1969 c. lx	The Wolverhampton Corporation Act 1969	Section 142
1970 c. vi	The Warwickshire County Council Act 1970	Section 3.
1970 c. viii	The Doncaster Corporation Act 1970	Section 3
1970 c. ix	The Newport Corporation Act 1970	Section 3
1970 c. x	The Huddersfield Corporation Act 1970	Section 3
1970 c. xi	The Bolton Corporation Act 1970	Section 3
1970 c. xii	The Hampshire County Council Act 1970	Section 3
1970 c. xiv	The Leicestershire County Council Act 1970	Section 10
1970 c. xv	The Swansea Corporation Act 1970	Section 3
1970 c. xvii	The Wallasey Corporation Act 1970	Section 3
1970 c. xviii	The Flintshire County Council Act 1970	Section 12
1970 c. xxii	The Birmingham Corporation Act 1970	Section 5
1970 c. xxiv	The Huntingdon and Peterborough County Council Act 1970	Section 20
1970 c. xxv	The West Riding County Council Act 1970	Section 4
1970 c. xxvii	The Norwich Corporation Act 1970	Section 37
1970 c. xxix	The Stoke-on-Trent Corporation Act 1970	Section 3
1970 c. xxx.	The Southampton Corporation Act 1970	Section 3
1970 c. xli	The North Riding County Council Act 1970	Section 3
1970 c. xlii	The Blackburn Corporation Act 1970	Section 3

(1) Chapter	(2) Short Title	(3) Extent of Repeal
1970 c. xliii	The Kent County Council Act 1970	Section 8
1970 c. xlv	The Cumberland County Council Act 1970	Section 8
1970 c. xlvi	The Gloucestershire County Council Act 1970	Section 3
1970 c. xlvii	The Salop County Council Act 1970	Section 3
1970 c. xlviii	The West Sussex County Council Act 1970	Section 3
1970 c. xlix	The Staffordshire County Council Act 1970	Section 4
1970 c. l.	The Northumberland County Council Act 1970	Section 16
1970 c. li	The Manchester Corporation Act 1970	Section 27 and Schedule 1
1970 c. lxi	The Nottinghamshire County Council Act 1970	Section 3
1970 c. lxii	The Preston Corporation Act 1970	Section 3
1970 c. lxiii	The Lindsey County Council Act 1970	Section 3
1970 c. lxiv	The Northampton Corporation Act 1970	Section 23
1970 c. lxviii	The Gateshead Corporation Act 1970	Section 3
1970 c. lxx	The Gloucester Corporation Act 1970	Section 4
1970 c. lxxii	The East Suffolk County Council Act 1970	Section 12
1970 c. lxxiv	The Southend-on-Sea Corporation Act 1970	Section 7
1970 c. lxxvii	The Monmouthshire County Council Act 1970	Section 74
1970 c. lxxx	The Bootle Corporation Act 1970	Section 73
1970 c. lxxxii	The Grimsby Corporation Act 1970	Section 19
1970 c. lxxxiii	The Oxfordshire County Council Act 1970	Section 25
1970 c. lxxxiv	The Reading Corporation Act 1970	Section 38
1970 c. lxxxv	The Wiltshire County Council Act 1970	Section 11
1971 c. vii	The Nottingham Corporation Act 1971	Section 19
1971 c. viii	The Berkshire County Council Act 1971	Section 26
1971 c. ix	The Bristol Corporation (General Powers) Act 1971	Section 10
1971 c. xi	The Buckinghamshire County Council Act 1971	Section 19
1971 c. xix	The Essex County Council Act 1971	Section 11
1971 c. xxi	The Plymouth Corporation Act 1971	Section 3
1971 c. xxix	The Oldham Corporation Act 1971	Section 3

(1) Chapter	(2) Short Title	(3) Extent of Repeal
1971 c. xxxiii	The Torbay Corporation Act 1971	Section 104
1971 c. xxxvi	The Surrey County Council Act 1971	Section 35
1971 c. xli	The Kesteven County Council Act 1971	Section 4
1971 c. xlvi	The Hertfordshire County Council Act 1971	Section 7
1971 c. l	The Stockport Corporation Act 1971	Section 79
1971 c. liv	The Cornwall County Council Act 1971	Section 73
1971 c. lxv	The Exeter Corporation Act 1971	Section 26
1972 c. xi	The Solihull Corporation Act 1972	Section 3
1972 c. xxii	The Bath Corporation Act 1972	Section 5
1972 c. xxx	The Devon County Council Act 1972	Section 24
1972 c. xxxiv	The Oxford Corporation Act 1972	Section 4
1972 c. xlix	The Port Talbot Corporation Act 1972	Section 94
1972 c. l	The West Sussex County Council Act 1972	Section 70
1973 c. i.	The Glamorgan County Council Act 1973	Section 125

SCHEDULE 2

Article 4(8)

STATUTORY HARBOUR UNDERTAKINGS: FORM OF ACCOUNTS

"SCHEDULE 1

LOCAL AUTHORITIES WHO CARRY ON UNDERTAKINGS TO WHICH THESE
REGULATIONS APPLY

The District Councils of Boston, Bristol, Canterbury, Carrick, Colchester, Exeter, Fenland, Gillingham, Medina, North Devon, Norwich, Penwith, Portsmouth, Preston, Sedgemoor, Southend-on-Sea, Sunderland, Thanet, Torridge, West Dorset, West Somerset and Weymouth and Portland.

The Perth Corporation".

SCHEDULE 3

Article 4(13)

CONTRIBUTING LOCAL AUTHORITIES TO NATIONAL PORTS COUNCIL

(1) Existing local authorities	(2) New local authorities
Anglesey County Council	District Council of Ynys Môn-Isle of Anglesey
Barnstaple Corporation Ilfracombe Urban District Council	District Council of North Devon
Bideford Corporation	District Council of Torridge
Boston Corporation	District Council of Boston
Bridgwater Corporation	District Council of Sedgemoor
Bridport Corporation	District Council of West Dorset
Bristol Corporation	City Council of Bristol
Colchester Corporation	Borough Council of Colchester
Exeter Corporation	City Council of Exeter
Gillingham Corporation	Borough Council of Gillingham
Minehead Urban District Council Watchet Urban District Council	District Council of West Somerset
Newport (Isle of Wight) Corporation	Borough Council of Medina
Norwich Corporation	City Council of Norwich
Penryn Corporation Truro Corporation	District Council of Carrick
Penzance Corporation	District Council of Penwith
Portsmouth Corporation	City Council of Portsmouth
Preston Corporation	Borough Council of Preston
Ramsgate Corporation	District Council of Thanet
Sunderland Corporation	Borough Council of Sunderland
Torbay Corporation	Borough Council of Torbay
Weymouth and Melcombe Regis Corporation	Borough Council of Weymouth and Portland
Whitstable Urban District Council	City Council of Canterbury
Wisbech Corporation	District Council of Fenland

SCHEDULE 4

Article 4(15)

INSTRUMENTS REVOKED

The Birkenhead Order 1915(a)

The Schemes of Divisional Administration (Notices) Regulations 1947(b)

The Snowdonia Park Joint Advisory Committee Order 1953(c)

The Snowdonia Park Joint Advisory Committee (Amendment) Order 1956(d)

The Snowdonia Park Joint Advisory Committee (Amendment) Order 1959(e)

The Public Health Officers Regulations 1959(f)

The Public Health Officers (Port Health Districts) Regulations 1959(g)

The Rural Borough Council Election Rules 1970(h)

The Rural Borough Council Election Rules 1971(i)

The Gaming Clubs (Permitted Areas) (Amendment) Regulations 1971(j)

The Local Government (Allowances to Members) Regulations 1972(k)

The Rural Borough Council Election (Amendment) Rules 1973(l)

The Local Government (Financial Loss Allowance) Regulations 1973(m)

The Local Government (Allowances to Members) (Amendment) Regulations 1974(n)

Anthony Crosland,

Secretary of State for the Environment.

27th March 1974.

John Morris,

Secretary of State for Wales.

27th March 1974.

EXPLANATORY NOTE

(*This Note is not part of the Order.*)

This Order makes miscellaneous provision incidental, consequential, transitional and supplementary to the Local Government Act 1972. The various subject matters are indicated in the table on page 1.

(a) Confirmed by 5 & 6 Geo. 5 c. iii.
(b) S.R. & O. 1947/148 (Rev. VI, p. 399: 1947 I, p. 580).
(c) S.I. 1953/179.   (d) S.I. 1956/711.
(e) S.I. 1959/813.   (f) S.I. 1959/962 (1959 I, p. 1605).
(g) S.I. 1959/963 (1959 II, p. 2125).   (h) S.I. 1970/197 (1970 I, p. 843).
(i) S.I. 1971/547 (1971 I, p. 1542).   (j) S.I. 1971/2029 (1971 III, p. 5820)..
(k) S.I. 1972/1566 (1972 III, p. 4556).   (l) S.I. 1973/229 (1973 I, p. 859).
(m) S.I. 1973/1047 (1973 II, p. 3140).   (n) S.I. 1974/125 (1974 I, p. 417).

STATUTORY INSTRUMENTS

1974 No. 596

TOWN AND COUNTRY PLANNING, ENGLAND AND WALES

The Town and Country Planning General Regulations 1974

Made - - - -	*27th March* 1974
Laid before Parliament	*29th March* 1974
Coming into Operation	*1st April* 1974

ARRANGEMENT OF REGULATIONS

PART I

TITLE, COMMENCEMENT AND INTERPRETATION

PART II

DEVELOPMENT BY LOCAL PLANNING AUTHORITIES

Development Permissions

Supplementary Provisions

PART III

GENERAL

16. Notices and counter-notices relating to planning blight.
17. Advertisement and notice of unopposed order revoking or modifying planning permission.
18. Revocation and savings.

SCHEDULES

SCHEDULE 1—Prescribed forms of blight notices and counter-notice.

SCHEDULE 2—Advertisement and notice of unopposed order revoking or modifying a planning permission.

The Secretary of State for the Environment and the Secretary of State for Wales in exercise of the powers conferred on them by sections 164, 169, 170, 180, 187, 188, 189, 193, 194 and 283 of the Town and Country Planning Act 1971(a) and section 78 of the Land Compensation Act 1973(b) and of all other powers enabling them in that behalf, and the Secretary of State for the Environment also in exercise of the powers conferred on him by sections 46, 91, 177, 201, 212, 219, 270, 287 and 290 of the Town and Country Planning Act 1971 and of all other powers enabling him in that behalf, hereby make the following regulations:—

PART I

TITLE, COMMENCEMENT AND INTERPRETATION

Citation and commencement

1. These regulations may be cited as the Town and Country Planning General Regulations 1974 and shall come into operation on 1st April 1974.

Interpretation

2.—(1) In these regulations, except so far as the context otherwise requires—

"the Act" means the Town and Country Planning Act 1971;

"the Common Council" means the Common Council of the City of London;

"listed building" has the same meaning as in Part IV of the Act;

"local authority" means the council of a county or district, the Common Council, the Greater London Council, the council of a London borough and any other authority (except the Receiver for the Metropolitan Police District) who are a local authority within the meaning of the Local Loans Act 1875(c), and includes any drainage board and any joint board or joint committee if all the constituent authorities are local authorities within the meaning of that Act;

"local planning authority" means the council of a county, district or London borough, the Greater London Council and the Common Council.

(2) The Interpertation Act 1889(d) shall apply for the interpretation of these regulations as it applies for the interpretation of an Act of Parliament.

(a) 1971 c. 78. (b) 1973 c. 26.
(c) 1875 c. 83. (d) 1889 c. 63.

PART II

DEVELOPMENT BY LOCAL PLANNING AUTHORITIES

Development Permissions

Application of Part III of the Act

3. In relation to—

(*a*) development by a local authority, being a local planning authority (other than the Greater London Council, the council of a London borough, the Common Council or, as respects land any part of which is within a National Park, a district council) of land within their area which is vested in them;

(*b*) development by a local authority (other than the Greater London Council, the council of a London borough, the Common Council or, as respects land, any part of which is within a National Park, a district council) of land within their area, being development in respect of which they exercise the functions of local planning authority;

(*c*) development by the Greater London Council which by virtue of paragraph 3 of Schedule 3 to the Act is deemed to be development by that council of land in respect of which they are the local planning authority;

(*d*) development by the Greater London Council or the Inner London Education Authority of land in Greater London which is vested in the Council;

(*e*) development by the council of a London borough or the Common Council of land in their area which is vested in the corporation of the borough or the City, as the case may be, or development in respect of which the council are the local planning authority by virtue of paragraph 2 of Schedule 3 to the Act;

the provisions of Part III of the Act specified in Part V of Schedule 21 to the Act shall have effect subject to the exceptions and modifications prescribed in regulations 4 to 9; and in this part of these regulations "the appropriate Part III provisions" means the provisions of Part III specified in the said Schedule.

Deemed permission and applications to the Secretary of State

4.—(1) Subject to the provisions of regulation 6, and 7 where the authority—

(*a*) require a permission for the development of land which is not granted by a development order (other than a permission for development which does not accord with the provisions of the development plan or consists in or includes works for the alteration or extension of a listed building) and

(*b*) resolve, by a resolution which is expressed to be passed for the purpose of this regulation, to carry out that development,

that permission shall, subject to the provisions of regulations 6 to 9, be deemed to be granted by the Secretary of State unless in the case of any particular development the Secretary of State requires the authority to make an application to him for permission.

(2) If the Secretary of State requires the authority to make an application for permission in accordance with the preceding paragraph, or if the authority seek a

permission for development which consists in or includes works for the alteration or extension of a listed building, the application shall be made in the form of an application to the local planning authority, and shall be deemed to have been referred to the Secretary of State under section 35 of the Act, and the provisions of that section shall apply to the determination of the application by the Secretary of State.

(3) A permission deemed to be granted by virtue of paragraph (1) of this regulation shall be treated for all purposes of the Act as a permission granted by a planning decision given on an application, and as if it had been granted on the date of the authority's resolution to carry out the development.

(4) For the purposes of this regulation, development which does not accord with the development plan shall not include such development for which the local planning authority may grant permission by virtue of a development order or a direction given by the Secretary of State thereunder.

Register of applications

5. Where permission is deemed to be granted by virtue of paragraph (1) of regulation 4, section 34 of the Act (which provides for the keeping of a register with respect to applications for permission) shall apply as if the resolution passed by the authority were an applictaion for planning permission made to the local planning authority and the deemed planning permission were granted on that application; and where an application falls to be made under the provisions of paragraph (2) of regulation 4, the said section 34 shall apply to that application.

Industrial development

6.—(1) No permission shall be deemed to be granted by virtue of paragraph (1) of regulation 4 in a case where an industrial development certificate issued under section 67 of the Act would be required if an application had to be made under sections 25 and 31 of the Act, unless prior to the date of the authority's resolution to carry out the development, the Secretary of State has issued an industrial development certificate in respect of such development; and any planning permission deemed to be granted under regulation 4(1) in respect of such development shall be deemed to have been granted subject to any conditions which may have been attached to such certificate.

(2) Where an application falls to be made under the provisions of regulation 4, the application shall be accompanied by an industrial development certificate issued under section 67 of the Act in any case where such a certificate would have been required if the application had been made to the local planning authority under sections 25 and 31 of the Act.

Office development

7. No permission shall be deemed to be granted by virtue of paragraph (1) of regulation 4 in a case where an office development permit issued under section 74 of the Act would be required if an application had to be made to the local planning authority under sections 25 and 31 of the Act, unless prior to the date of the authority's resolution to carry out the development, the Secretary of State has issued an office development permit in respect of such development; and any planning permission deemed to have been granted under regulation 4(1) in respect of such development shall be deemed to have been granted subject to any conditions which may be attached to such permit.

Consultation and furnishing of information

8.—(1) The authority shall consult with, furnish information to, and notify the terms of any permission granted or deemed to be granted under regulation 4 to any other authority or person in any case where, if an application had been made to them in respect of the development, they would have been required to do so.

(2) A county or district planning authority shall in every case before passing a resolution under regulation 4(1) or making an application under regulation 4(2) consult with any other county or district planning authority, as the case may be, for the area in which the land or any part thereof is situated.

(3) The Greater London Council shall in every case consult with the Common Council or with the council of the London borough in which the land or any part thereof is situate.

(4) The council of a London borough or the Common Council shall consult with the Greater London Council in any case where, if an application had been made in respect of the development, it would have been dealt with by the Greater London Council (by virtue of regulations made by the Secretary of State under paragraph 3 of Schedule 3 to the Act) or the council would have been required (by regulations made by the Secretary of State under paragraph 7 of Schedule 3 to the Act) to refer it to the Greater London Council.

(5) Where under this regulation the authority are required to consult with any other authority or person, they shall give notice to that authority or person that a proposal to carry out the development is to be considered, and shall not resolve to carry out the development except after 21 days from the giving of the notice and after taking into account any representations received from that authority or person.

Directions to local planning authority

9. In any case in which directions have been given to the local planning authority restricting the grant of permission by them, the authority shall observe the terms of those directions in relation to any development projected by them, or shall make an application for permission to the Secretary of State, accompanied by particulars identifying the directions, and paragraph (2) of regulation 4 shall apply to the application as if the Secretary of State had required it to be made.

Supplementary Provisions

Other consents

10. Where an authority require any consent or approval of a local planning authority under any provisions of the Act specified in Part V of Schedule 21 to the Act, other than a permission for development, and that authority are themselves the local planning authority by whom such consent or approval would be given, the application shall be made to the Secretary of State and his decision thereon shall be final and shall take the place of the decision of the local planning authority.

Savings

11. Any application, reference, representation or notice made or given under Part III of the Town and Country Planning General Regulations 1969(a) which

---

(a) S.I. 1969/286 (1969 I, p. 766).

at the coming into operation of these regulations is outstanding shall have effect as if made or given and shall be determined under and in accordance with this part of these regulations.

PART III

GENERAL

Claims for compensation and purchase notices

12.—(1) A claim for compensation made to a local planning authority under sections 164, 165, 169, 170, 177, 187 or 212 of the Act, or a purchase notice served on the council of a district or London borough or on the Common Council under sections 180, 188, 189 or 191 of the Act, shall be in writing and shall be served on that authority or council by delivering it at the offices of the authority or council, or by sending it by pre-paid post.

(2) The time within which any such claim or notice as is mentioned in paragraph (1) of this regulation shall be served shall be—

(*a*) in the case of a claim for compensation, 6 months; and

(*b*) in the case of a purchase notice, 12 months,

from the date of the decision in respect of which the claim or notice is made or given:

Provided that the period may be extended by the Secretary of State in any particular case.

Marking of certain notices and documents

13. The manner in which a notice or document such as is referred to in subsection (2) of section 283 of the Act shall be marked in order that it shall be deemed to be duly served under head (*b*) of that subsection shall be by inscribing clearly and legibly upon the notice or document, and upon the envelope containing it, the words "Important—This Communication affects your property".

Application of the Public Health Act 1936 to enforcement notices

14. The provisions of sections 276, 289 and 294 of the Public Health Act 1936(a) shall apply in relation to steps required to be taken by an enforcement notice, or by a notice under section 65 of the Act, as if—

(*a*) references to a local authority were references to a local planning authority;

(*b*) references (in whatever form) to the execution of works under the said Act of 1936 were references to the taking of steps required to be taken under the notice;

(*c*) references in the said section 289 to the occupier were references to a person having an interest in the premises other than the owner; and

(*d*) the reference in the said section 294 to "expenses under this Act" were a reference to expenses incurred in the taking of such steps as aforesaid.

(a) 1936 c. 49.

Concurrent procedure for acquisition of land and extinguishment of rights of way

15.—(1) Where under section 112 of the Act a compulsory purchase order for the acquisition of any land has been made by a local authority and submitted to the Secretary of State in accordance with the provisions of the Acquisition of Land (Authorisation Procedure) Act 1946**(a)**, or where any land has been acquired by a local authority under section 119 of the Act, the succeeding provisions of this regulation shall apply in relation to the extinguishment of public rights of way over such land and the acquisition of land for the provision of alternative rights of way.

(2) The Secretary of State may on or after any such submission or acquisition publish in accordance with the provisions of section 215(1) of the Act notice of an order proposed to be made under section 214 of the Act relating to the extinguishment of any such right of way.

(3) On or after the publication of any such notice, the Secretary of State may prepare in draft or a local highway authority may make a compulsory purchase order under section 218(1) of the Act for the acquisition of land for providing an alternative right of way.

(4) Any other proceedings required to be taken in connection with the making of an order under section 214 of the Act may be taken concurrently with the proceedings required to be taken in connection with such an order as is mentioned in paragraph (1) of this regulation and any other proceedings for the making or confirmation of such a compulsory purchase order as is referred to in paragraph (3) of this regulation may be taken concurrently with either or both of the said proceedings:

Provided that:—

(*a*) no such order under section 214 shall be made until the land over which the right of way subsists has been acquired by the local authority; and

(*b*) no such compulsory purchase order as is referred to in paragraph (3) of this regulation shall be made by the Secretary of State or confirmed, until the original right of way has been extinguished by an order under section 214.

Notices and counter-notices relating to planning blight

16. The forms set out in Schedule 1 hereto or forms substantially to the like effect are the prescribed forms of blight notice for the purposes of sections 193 and 201 of the Act and section 78 of the Land Compensation Act 1973 and of counter-notice for the purposes of section 194 of the Act.

Advertisement and notice of unopposed order revoking or modifying planning permission

17. The advertisement, for the purposes of section 46(2) of the Act, of an order made under section 45 of the Act shall be in the form set out in Form 1 of Schedule 2 to these regulations or a form substantially to the like effect; and the notice required to be served by section 46(3) of the Act shall be in the form set out in Form 2 of that Schedule or a form substantially to the like effect.

(a) 1946 c. 49.

Revocation and savings

18. The Town and Country Planning General Regulations 1969 are hereby revoked, but without prejudice to the validity of anything done thereunder before the date of the coming into operation of these regulations, and subject to the savings in regulation 11 hereof.

SCHEDULE 1   Regulation 16

FORM 1

TOWN AND COUNTRY PLANNING ACT 1971
LAND COMPENSATION ACT 1973

Blight Notice

To   (*a*)

at   (*b*)

[I] [We]*   (*c*)

pursuant to the provisions of section 193(1) of the Town and Country Planning Act 1971 (hereinafter called "the Act of 1971") HEREBY GIVE YOU NOTICE:—

1. [I am] [We are]* entitled to the interest set out in the First Schedule hereto in the [hereditament] [agricultural unit]* described in the Second Schedule hereto.

2. [The] [Part of the]* [hereditament] [agricultural unit]* has been included in land falling within paragraph (*d*) of section 192(1) of the Act of 1971 [as that paragraph is amended or extended by section   (*e*) of the Land Compensation Act 1973]*.

3. [I] [We]* have made reasonable endeavours to sell [my] [our]* interest and in consequence of the fact that [the] [part of the]* [hereditament] [agricultural unit]* was or was likely to be comprised in land in one of the descriptions set out in section 192(1) of the Act of 1971 (as amended) [I] [We]* have been unable to sell that interest except at a price substantially lower than that for which it might reasonably have been expected to sell if no part of the [hereditament] [agricultural unit]* were, or were likely to be, comprised in such land. Particulars of those endeavours are set out [below] [in the letter accompanying this notice]*. (*f*)

4. [My] [Our]* interest qualifies for protection under sections 192 to 207 of the Act of 1971 because (*g*)

EITHER

[the annual value of the hereditament does not exceed the prescribed limit of annual value and [my] [our]* interest is that of owner-occupier(s) of the hereditament within the meaning of section 203(1) of the Act of 1971.]*

OR

[[my] [our]* interest is that of resident owner-occupier(s) of the hereditament within the meaning of section 203(3) of the Act of 1971.]*

OR

[[my] [our]* interest is that of owner-occupier(s) of the agricultural unit within the meaning of section 203(2) of the Act of 1971.]*

[5. [The] [The part of the] agricultural unit in which [I am] [we are]* entitled to an interest contains land which does not fall within any of the descriptions set out in section 192(1) of the Act of 1971 (as amended) as well as land which does so and that area which is unaffected is not reasonably capable of being farmed either by itself or in conjunction with other relevant land (within the meaning of section 79(2) of the Land Compensation Act 1973), as a separate agricultural unit.]

---

*Delete where inappropriate.

6. [[I] [We]* therefore require you to purchase [my] [our]* interest in the [hereditament] [agricultural unit]*.]

OR

[[I] [We]* therefore require you to purchase [my] [our]* interest in [the whole of the agricultural unit] [the whole of that part of the agricultural unit to which this notice relates]*.]*(*i*)

FIRST SCHEDULE

Particulars of interest in land, together with the names and addresses of any mortgagees thereof and a note of any other encumberances thereon.

SECOND SCHEDULE

Particulars of the [hereditament] [agricultural unit](*j*)

Dated   19   Signed

[On behalf of   ]*

FORM 2

TOWN AND COUNTRY PLANNING ACT 1971
LAND COMPENSATION ACT 1973

Mortgagee's Blight Notice

To   (*a*)

at   (*b*)

[I] [We]*   (*c*)

pursuant to the provisions of section 201(1) of the Town and Country Planning Act 1971 (hereinafter called "the Act of 1971") HEREBY GIVE YOU NOTICE:—

1. [I am] [We are]* entitled as mortgagee(s) (by virtue of a power which has become exercisable) to sell the interest (hereinafter called "the said interest") set out in the First Schedule hereto in the [hereditament] [agricultural unit]* described in the Second Schedule hereto, giving immediate vacant possession of the land.

2. [The] [The part of the]* [hereditament] [agricultural unit]* has been included in land falling within paragraph (*d*) of section 192(1) of the Act of 1971 [as that paragraph is amended or extended by section   (*e*) of the Land Compensation Act 1973].*

3. [I] [We]* have made reasonable endeavours to sell the said interest and in consequence of the fact that [the] [part of the]* [hereditament] [agricultural unit]* was or was likely to be comprised in land in one of the descriptions set out in section 192(1) of the Act of 1971 (as amended) [I] [We]* have been unable to sell that interest except at a price substantially lower than that for which it might reasonably have been expected to sell if no part of the [hereditament] [agricultural unit]* were, or were likely to be, comprised in such land. Particulars of those endeavours are set out [below] [in the letter accompanying this notice]*.(*f*)

4. [I am] [We are]* entitled to take advantage of the provisions of sections 192 to 207 of the Act of 1971 because (*g*)

EITHER

[the annual value of the hereditament does not exceed the prescribed limit of annual value and the person entitled (otherwise than as mortgagee) to the said interest *either* is an owner-occupier of the hereditament within the meaning of section 203(1) of the Act *or* was such an owner-occupier on an earlier date not more than six months before the service of this notice, on which earlier date, namely   19   , the particulars in paragraph 2 above were correct in relation to the hereditament (*h*)]*

---

*Delete where inappropriate.

OR

[the person entitled (otherwise than as mortgagee) to the said interest *either* is a resident owner-occupier of the hereditament within the meaning of section 203(3) of the Act of 1971 *or* was such a resident owner-occupier on an earlier date not more than six months before the service of this notice, on which earlier date, namely   19 , the particulars in paragraph 2 above were correct in relation to the hereditament (*h*)]*

OR

[the person entitled (otherwise than as mortgagee) to the said interest *either* is an owner-occupier of the agricultural unit within the meaning of section 203(2) of the Act of 1971 *or* was such an owner-occupier on an earlier date, not more than six months before the service of this notice, on which earlier date, namely   19 , the particulars in paragraph 2 above were correct in relation to the agricultural unit (*h*)]*

[5. [The] [Part of the] agricultural unit in which the said interest is held contains land which does not fall within any of the descriptions set out in section 192(1) of the Act of 1971 (as amended) as well as land which does so and that area which is un-affected is not reasonably capable of being farmed, either by itself or in conjunction with other relevant land (within the meaning of section 79(2) of the Land Compensation Act 1973), as a separate agricultural unit.]

6. [[I] [We]* therefore require you to purchase the said interest in the [hereditament] [agricultural unit]*.]

OR

[[I] [We] *therefore require you to purchase the said interest in [the whole of the agricultural unit] [the whole of that part of the agricultural unit to which this notice relates.]*]*(*i*).

First Schedule
Particulars of interest in land, together with the names and addresses of any other known mortgagees thereof and a note of any other encumberances thereon known to the claimant

Second Schedule
Particulars of the [hereditament] [agricultural unit](*j*)

Dated   19   Signed

[On behalf of   ]*

Form 3

Town and Country Planning Act 1971
Land Compensation Act 1973

Personal Representative's Blight Notice

To   (*a*)

at   (*b*)

[I] [We]*   (*c*)

pursuant to the provisions of section 78(1) of the Land Compensation Act 1973 (hereinafter called "the Act of 1973") HEREBY GIVE YOU NOTICE:—

1. [I am] [We are]* the personal representative(s) of a person (hereinafter called "the deceased") who at the date of [his] [her]* death was entitled to the interest set out in the First Schedule hereto in the [hereditament] [agricultural unit]* described in the Second Schedule hereto.

*Delete where inappropriate.

2. [The] [Part of the]* [hereditament] [agricultural unit]* has been included in land falling within paragraph   (d) of section 192(1) of the Town and Country Planning Act 1971 (hereinafter called "the Act of 1971") [as that paragraph is amended or extended by section   (e) of the Act of 1973]* and was so included on the date of death of the deceased.

3. Since the date of death of the deceased [I] [We]* have made reasonable endeavours to sell [his] [her]* interest and in consequence of the fact that [the] [part of the]* [hereditament] [agricultural unit]* was or was likely to be comprised in land in one of the descriptions set out in section 192(1) of the Act of 1971 (as amended) [I] [We]* have been unable to sell that interest except at a price substantially lower than that for which it might reasonably have been expected to sell if no part of the [hereditament] [agricultural unit]* were, or were likely to be, comprised in such land. Particulars of those endeavours are set out [below] [in the letter accompanying this notice]* (f).

4. The deceased's interest qualified for protection under sections 192 to 207 of the Act of 1971 because (g)

EITHER

[the annual value of the hereditament does not exceed the prescribed limit of annual value and [his] [her]* interest was that of owner-occupier of the hereditament within the meaning of section 203(1) of the Act of 1971.]*

OR

[[his] [her]* interest was that of resident owner-occupier of the hereditament within the meaning of section 203(3) of the Act of 1971.]*

OR

[[his] [her]* interest was that of owner-occupier of the agricultural unit within the meaning of section 203(2) of the Act of 1971.]*

5. One or more individuals are (to the exclusion of any body corporate) beneficially entitled to the deceased's interest in the [hereditament] [agricultural unit]*.

[6. [The] [The part of the] agricultural unit in which the deceased was entitled to an interest contains land which does not fall within any of the descriptions set out in section 192(1) of the Act of 1971 (as amended) as well as land which does so and that area which is unaffected is not reasonably capable of being farmed, either by itself or in conjunction with other relevant land (within the meaning of section 79(2) of the Act of 1973), as a separate agricultural unit.]

7. [[I] [We]* therefore require you to purchase the deceased's interest in the [hereditament] [agricultural unit]*]*

OR

[[I] [We]* therefore require you to purchase the deceased's interest in [the whole of the agricultural unit] [the whole of that part of the agricultural unit to which this notice relates]*]* (i)

FIRST SCHEDULE

Particulars of deceased's interest in land, together with the names and addresses of any mortgagees thereof and a note of any other encumberances thereon

SECOND SCHEDULE

Particulars of the [hereditament] [agricultural unit](j)*

Dated   19

Signed

[On behalf of   ]*

---

*Delete where inappropriate.

Notes to Forms 1, 2 and 3

(a) Insert name of authority to be served.

(b) Insert principal address of authority.

(c) Insert full name(s) and address(es) of person(s) serving this notice.

(d) Insert letter of the paragraph which is applicable.

(e) Insert (if appropriate) number of the section (and sub-section) of the Act of 1973 which is applicable.

(f) Particulars of the steps taken to sell the land should be given here or in accompanying letter, and should include dates, price asked and any offers received.

(g) The claimant should choose which paragraph is to form part of the notice and delete the other two.

(h) Within the paragraph chosen, underline those words after "either" which are appropriate to the case.

(i) The second alternative paragraph applies only to agricultural units coming within the description set out in the preceding paragraph of the notice (where appropriate). The claimant should choose which alternative is to form part of the notice and delete the other.

(j) A plan should be attached to identify the land, if this is necessary.

FORM 4

TOWN AND COUNTRY PLANNING ACT 1971
LAND COMPENSATION ACT 1973

Counter-notice Objecting to Blight Notice

To   (a)

THE   (b)

HEREBY GIVE YOU NOTICE under section 194(1) of the Town and Country Planning Act 1971 that they OBJECT to the Blight Notice served by you on
           19   under [section 193(1) of that Act] [section 78(1) of the Land Compensation Act 1973]* in respect of the [hereditament] [agricultural unit]* described as (c).

The grounds on which objection is taken are (d)—

Dated   19

On behalf of the (b)

NOTE: If you do not accept this objection, you may require the objection to be referred to the Lands Tribunal, under the provisions of section 195 of the Town and Country Planning Act 1971. In that case you should notify the Registrar, The Lands Tribunal, 3 Hanover Square, London W1R OER, within 2 months of the date of service of this notice.

Notes to Form 4

(a) Insert name and address of addressee.

(b) Insert name of authority.

(c) Insert particulars.

*Delete where inappropriate.

(*d*) These must specify the grounds on which the authority object to the notice (being one or more of the grounds specified in section 194(2) of the Town and Country Planning Act 1971 or, where relevant, in section 80 of the Land Compensation Act 1973). Regard should (where appropriate) be had to the restrictions imposed by sections 73 and 76 of the Act of 1973 on the grounds on which objection may be made to a blight notice served by virtue of one of those sections.

Regulation 17   SCHEDULE 2

FORM 1

TOWN AND COUNTRY PLANNING ACT 1971

Advertisement under section 46(2) of the Making of a Revocation Order or Modification Order

Planning permission for   (*a*)

at   (*b*)

Notice is hereby given that the   (*c*) council have made an order under section 45 of the Town and Country Planning Act 1971 to [revoke the above planning permission] [to the following extent   (*d*)] [modify the above planning permission as follows   (*e*)]*

The council have been notified in writing by the owner and the occupier of the land [and by all other persons who in the council's opinion will be affected by the order]* that they do not object to the order.

Any person who will be affected by the order and who wishes for an opportunity of appearing before, and being heard by, a person appointed by the [Secretary of State for the Environment] [Secretary of State for Wales]* must give notice in writing to that effect to the [Secretary, Department of the Environment, 2 Marsham Street, London SW1P 3EB] [Secretary, Welsh Office, Summit House, Windsor Place, Cardiff]* not later than   19(*f*).

If no such notice has been given by that date, the order will take effect, by virtue of the provisions of section 46 of the Town and Country Planning Act 1971, on 19   (*g*) without being confirmed by the Secretary of State.

FORM 2

TOWN AND COUNTRY PLANNING ACT 1971

Notice under section 46(3) of the Making of a Revocation Order or Modification Order

Planning permission for   (*a*)

at   (*b*)

TAKE NOTICE THAT THE   (*c*) council have made an order under section 45 of the Town and Country Planning Act 1971 to [revoke the above planning permission] [to the following extent (*d*)] [modify the above planning permission as follows   (*e*)]*

The council have been notified in writing by the owner and the occupier of the land [and by all other persons who in the council's opinion will be effected by the order]* that they do not object to the order.

---

*Delete where inappropriate.

If you will be affected by the order and wish for an opportunity of appearing before, and being heard by, a person appointed by the [Secretary of State for the Environment] [Secretary of State for Wales]* you should give notice in writing to that effect to the [Secretary, Department of the Environment, 2 Marsham Street, London SW1P 3EB] [Secretary, Welsh Office, Summit House, Windsor Place, Cardiff]* not later than
19   (*f*)

If no such notice has been given by that date, the order will take effect, by virtue of the provisions of section 46 of the Town and Country Planning Act 1971, on
19   (*g*) without being confirmed by the Secretary of State.

Notes to Forms 1 and 2

(*a*) Insert description of the development for which permission has been granted.

(*b*) Insert site or locality of development.

(*c*) Insert name of council.

(*d*) Insert particulars of extent of revocation.

(*e*) Insert particulars of modification.

(*f*) Insert a date not less than 28 days later than the date on which the relevant advertisement first appears.

(*g*) Insert a date not less than 14 days later than the date to which note (*f*) relates.

Anthony Crosland,
Secretary of State for the Environment.

27th March 1974.

John Morris,
Secretary of State for Wales.

27th March 1974.

EXPLANATORY NOTE

(This Note is not part of the Regulations.)

These Regulations revoke and re-enact the Town and Country Planning General Regulations 1969, with amendments. These take into account the provisions of the Local Government Act 1972 in relation to the creation of county and district planning authorities, and the provisions of the Land Compensation Act 1973 in relation to the service of blight notices.

The principal changes are:—

(*a*) Part II of the Regulations of 1969 is not continued in these Regulations, as from 1st April 1974 there will no longer be provision for the delegation of planning functions;

(*b*) the provisions relating to development by local planning authorities are amended to provide that where county and district councils (except district councils in the National Parks) resolve to carry out development on land within their area which is vested in them, or development in respect of which they exercise the functions of local planning authority, planning permission shall (subject to certain exceptions) be deemed to have been granted by the Secretary of State;

(*c*) the procedure relating to development which does not accord with the development plan has been omitted; applications for such development will now fall to be dealt with under the Development Plans Directions;

(*d*) the requirements relating to office and industrial development have been recast;

(*e*) minor amendments are made to the forms of blight notice and counter-notice prescribed for the purposes of sections 193 and 201 of the Town and Country Planning Act 1971 and a new form called a personal representatives blight notice is prescribed: these amendments take account of changes made by the Land Compensation Act 1973.

STATUTORY INSTRUMENTS

1974 No. 597 (L.8)

SUPREME COURT OF JUDICATURE, ENGLAND
PROCEDURE

The Non-Contentious Probate (Amendment) Rules 1974

Made - - - -	*26th March* 1974
Laid before Parliament	*8th April* 1974
Coming into Operation	*1st May* 1974

The President of the Family Division, in exercise of the powers conferred on him by section 100 of the Supreme Court of Judicature (Consolidation) Act 1925(a), and with the concurrence of the Lord Chancellor and the Lord Chief Justice, hereby makes the following Rules:—

1.—(1) These Rules may be cited as the Non-Contentious Probate (Amendment) Rules 1974 and shall come into operation on 1st May 1974.

(2) The Interpretation Act 1889(b) shall apply to the interpretation of these Rules as it applies to the interpretation of an Act of Parliament.

(3) The amendments set out in these Rules shall be made to the Non-Contentious Probate Rules 1954(c), as amended (d).

2. Rule 2 (interpretation) shall be amended as follows:—

(*a*) in the definition of "Registrar" in paragraph (2), for the words "(except in rules 45 and 46)" there shall be substituted the words "(except in rules 45, 46 and 47)";

(*b*) after paragraph (3) there shall be added the following new paragraph:—
"(4) Unless the context otherwise requires, any reference in these Rules to any rule or enactment shall be construed as a reference to that rule or enactment as amended, extended or applied by any other rule or enactment.".

3. For rule 18 (evidence of foreign law) there shall be substituted the following rule:—

"18. Where evidence as to the law of any country or territory outside England is required on any application for a grant, the registrar may accept an affidavit from any person whom, having regard to the particulars of his knowledge or experience given in the affidavit, he regards as suitably qualified to give expert evidence of the law in question.".

4. Rule 19 (order of priority for a grant where deceased left a will) shall be amended as follows:—

(*a*) in paragraph (iv), after the words "ultimate residuary legatee or devisee" there shall be inserted the words ", including one entitled on the happening of any contingency,"; and after the words "Provided

---

(a) 1925 c. 49.   (b) 1889 c. 63.   (c) S.I. 1954/796 (1954 II, p. 2202).
(d) The relevant amending instruments are S.I. 1967/748, 1969/1689, 1971/1977 (1967 II, p. 2225; 1969 III, p. 5319; 1971 III, p. 5650).

that" there shall be inserted the words "(*a*) unless a registrar otherwise directs a residuary legatee or devisee whose legacy or devise is vested in interest shall be preferred to one entitled on the happening of a contingency; and (*b*)";

(*b*) in paragraph (vi), for the words "Any legatee or devisee, whether residuary or specific," there shall be substituted the words "Any specific legatee or devisee".

5. Rule 36 (consent of administrator of enemy property) is hereby revoked.

6. In rule 47 (citation to propound a will), paragraph (2) shall be omitted and there shall be substituted the following paragraph:—

"(2) If the time limited for appearance has expired, the citor may,—

(*a*) in the case where no person cited has entered an appearance, apply to a registrar for an order for a grant as if the will were invalid;

(*b*) in the case where no person who has entered an appearance proceeds with reasonable diligence to propound the will, apply to a registrar by summons (which shall be served on every person cited who has entered an appearance) for such an order as is mentioned in paragraph (*a*) above.".

Dated 22nd March 1974.

George Baker, P

We concur.

Dated 26th March 1974.

Elwyn-Jones, C.

Dated 22nd March 1974.

Widgery, C. J.

EXPLANATORY NOTE
(This Note is not part of the Rules.)

These Rules make amendments to the Non-Contentious Probate Rules 1954. The changes include—

(1) dispensing with the necessity for a person giving evidence of foreign law to have practised as a qualified lawyer in the country concerned (Rule 18);

(2) minor alterations to the prescribed order of priority of entitlement to a grant of representation in cases where the deceased has left a will (Rule 19);

(3) dispensing with applications by way of summons in cases where persons cited have not entered appearances following the issue of a citation to propound a will (Rule 47).

These Rules come into force on 1st May 1974.

STATUTORY INSTRUMENTS

1974 No. 599 (S.51)

SHERIFF COURT, SCOTLAND

The Union of Offices (Sheriff Courts and Legal Officers (Scotland) Act 1927) Order 1974

Made - - -	*21st March* 1974
Coming into Operation	*1st April* 1974

In exercise of the powers conferred on me by section 11(1) of the Sheriff Courts and Legal Officers (Scotland) Act 1927(**a**), and of all other powers enabling me in that behalf, I hereby make the following order:—

1.—(1) This order may be cited as the Union of Offices (Sheriff Courts and Legal Officers (Scotland) Act 1927) Order 1974 and shall come into operation on 1st April 1974.

(2) The Interpretation Act 1889(**b**) shall apply for the interpretation of this order as it applies for the interpretation of an Act of Parliament.

2. The office of sheriff clerk of chancery shall be united with the office of the sheriff clerk of Midlothian and the office of commissary clerk of Edinburgh to the effect that the offices shall be held and the duties thereof discharged by one and the same person.

William Ross,
One of Her Majesty's Principal
Secretaries of State.

St Andrew's House,
 Edinburgh.
21st March 1974.

EXPLANATORY NOTE

(This Note is not part of the Order.)

This Order unites the office of sheriff clerk of chancery with the (already united) offices of the sheriff clerk of Midlothian and the commissary clerk of Edinburgh.

(**a**) 1927 c. 35.   (**b**) 1889 c. 63.

STATUTORY INSTRUMENTS

1974 No. 600 (S. 52)

RATING AND VALUATION

The Rate Rebate (Scotland) Regulations 1974

Made - - - -	*25th March* 1974
Laid before Parliament	*10th April* 1974
Coming into Operation	*1st May* 1974

In exercise of the powers conferred on me by section 112 of the Local Government (Scotland) Act 1973(a) and of all other powers enabling me in that behalf I hereby, with the consent of the Treasury, make the following regulations:—

Citation and commencement

1. These regulations may be cited as the Rate Rebate (Scotland) Regulations 1974 and shall come into operation on 1st May 1974.

Interpretation

2.—(1) The Interpretation Act 1889(b) shall apply for the interpretation of these regulations as it applies for the interpretation of an Act of Parliament.

(2) References in these regulations to any enactment shall be construed as including references to such enactment as amended or extended by or under any other enactment, order or regulations.

(3) In these regulations—

"the Act" means the Local Government (Scotland) Act 1973;

"the Act of 1972" means the Housing (Financial Provisions) (Scotland) Act 1972(c);

"applicant" includes a person treated as an applicant under regulation 4(3) and any person whose application for a rent rebate or allowance under the Act of 1972 is deemed to be an application for rebate under regulation 22, and "application" shall be interpreted accordingly;

"authority" has the meaning assigned to it by section 22(1) of the Act of 1972 as read with section 78(1) of that Act;

"dependent child" means a person who resides with the applicant and whose requirements are provided for, in whole or in part, by the applicant or his spouse and who is either under the age of sixteen or of or over that age and receiving full-time instruction at any university, college or other educational establishment;

"financial year" means the financial year of the rating authority;

"full-time instruction at an educational establishment" includes a reference to a person undergoing training for any trade, profession or vocation in

---

(a) 1973 c. 65.　　　　　(b) 1889 c. 63.　　　　　(c) 1972 c. 46.

such circumstances that he is required to devote the whole of his time to the training for a period of not less than two years;

"married couple" includes a man and a woman who lives with him as his wife, but does not include a man and wife who are living apart, and "wife" and, save for paragraph 9(2)(*j*) of Schedule 2 to the Act of 1972 in relation to the ascertainment of income, "spouse" shall be construed accordingly;

"non-dependant" means in relation to an applicant, any person who resides with the applicant except a spouse of the applicant and a dependant of the applicant or his spouse;

"pensionable age" has the meaning assigned to it by section 114(1) of the National Insurance Act 1965(a);

"rating authority" has the meaning assigned to it by sections 109(1) and 112(6) of the Act;

"rebate" means a rebate under the standard scheme or an approved variation;

"rent" means the rent payable under a tenancy or a sub-tenancy;

"supplementary benefit" means benefit under Part II of the Ministry of Social Security Act 1966(b) except that it does not include benefit under section 6 (benefit to meet medical and similar requirements) or section 7 (benefit to meet exceptional requirements) of that Act;

"tenant" except where the context otherwise requires includes a joint tenant and a sub-tenant.

(4) Any reference in these regulations to a numbered regulation or to a Schedule other than a Schedule to an Act shall be construed as a reference to the regulation or Schedule bearing that number in these regulations.

General

3. It shall be the duty of every rating authority to operate in respect of rebate periods beginning on or after 16th May 1974 a scheme for the grant by the authority to persons to whom section 112 of the Act applies of rebates from rates calculated by reference to the needs and the resources of such persons in accordance with the provisions of these regulations (hereinafter referred to as "the standard scheme") or the standard scheme varied in accordance with section 114 of the Act (hereinafter referred to as "an approved variation").

Right to rebate

4.—(1) Any person to whom section 112 of the Act applies shall be entitled in respect of any rebate period for which application is made to a rebate under the standard scheme calculated in accordance with these regulations by reference to—

(*a*) an amount to be allowed for the needs of the applicant and of any spouse of the applicant or dependent child of the applicant or his spouse (hereinafter referred to as "the needs allowance");

(*b*) the income of the applicant and of any such spouse;

(*c*) the amount of the reckonable rates;

(*d*) a minimum rate liability;

(*e*) a minimum and a maximum rebate;

(a) 1965 c. 51.   (b) 1966 c. 20.

(*f*) amounts to be deducted for non-dependants;

(*g*) a limit of rateable value—

or under an approved variation thereof.

(2) The amounts listed in regulation 4(1) shall be ascertained in accordance with these regulations and Schedules to these regulations.

(3) If it appears to the rating authority that a person with a higher income than the applicant resides in such lands and heritages as are mentioned in section 113(1) of the Act they may if they consider it reasonable make their calculations under these regulations by reference to the income of that other person and not that of the applicant and for that purpose they may treat that person as the applicant and make such payments of rebate (if any) as ought to be made.

(4) Where the rating authority exercise the power conferred upon them by regulation 4(3), the occupier or tenant as the case may be shall for the purposes of these regulations be treated as a non-dependant but neither the spouse nor a dependent child of the applicant shall be treated as a non-dependant for those purposes.

(5) No person shall be entitled to rebate under the standard scheme or an approved variation in respect of rates in respect of the financial year ending in 1974 or any earlier year.

Conversion to weekly amounts

5. Where any sum which is payable or calculated otherwise than as a weekly amount falls to be taken into account for the purposes of these regulations, it shall be converted into the weekly amount, or as near as may be, which represents it and that amount shall be treated as the relevant amount for those purposes; and accordingly in these regulations references to "weekly rates" and "weekly income" are references to the amount which represents the rates or the income as so converted.

Needs allowance

6. The needs allowance shall be ascertained in accordance with the provisions of Schedule 1.

Assessment of income

7.—(1) If the rating authority are satisfied on an application for a rebate that the applicant is eligible for consideration for a rebate, it shall be their duty to assess the amount which is likely to be the income of the applicant and of any spouse of the applicant during the rebate period.

(2) For any rebate period the income of the applicant and any spouse of the applicant shall, save as otherwise provided, be assessed for the purposes of these regulations as it would be under Schedule 3 to the Act of 1972 for the purpose of calculating rent rebate or allowance under the model scheme within the meaning of section 17(5) of that Act if—

(*a*) the application were for rent rebate or allowance under the model scheme; and

(*b*) the rebate period were a rent rebate or allowance period.

(3) In ascertaining income there shall be disregarded (*a*) any such part of the payments received by the applicant from any other person who is entitled to make an application in respect of part of the lands and heritages as is equal to the amount which, by virtue of regulation 9 or Schedule 3 was or would have been the amount of that person's reckonable rates and (*b*) such part of rent received by the applicant as does not exceed the rent (if any) payable by him and attributable to any part of the lands and heritages which is let or sub-let by him.

Income and disregards

8. The weekly income of the applicant and any spouse of the applicant shall be ascertained for the purpose of these regulations by taking the amount which the rating authority have assessed by virtue of regulation 7 as likely to be their income during any rebate period and disregarding the amount of any item mentioned in regulation 7(3) or paragraph 9 of Schedule 2 to the Act of 1972 except item (*a*) of paragraph 9(2) of that Schedule.

Reckonable rates

9.—(1) If such a person as is mentioned in section 113(1)(*a*) of the Act applies for a rebate the reckonable rates for the purpose of calculating the rebate shall be the amount of rates chargeable on the lands and heritages in which he resides less the amount (if any) which is deemed to be the reckonable rates of any other person entitled to apply for a rebate in respect of any part of those lands and heritages by virtue of section 113(1)(*c*) of the Act.

(2) The reckonable rates of any such person as is mentioned in section 113(1)(*b*) and (*c*) of the Act shall be calculated in accordance with Schedule 3.

10.—(1) If at the time a rebate is to be calculated the amount of rates payable by the applicant for a financial year in which the rebate period or part of the period falls has not been determined and applied for the purposes of collection the rating authority shall calculate the rebate on their estimate of the amount of rates for that period or part of that period and may, at such time as the rates for the financial year are determined and applied for the purposes of collection, recalculate the rebate.

(2) Subject to regulation 27 where rebate is recalculated in accordance with regulation 10(1) any resulting overpayment of rebate shall without prejudice to any other right of recovery be treated as an amount of rebate recoverable in accordance with regulation 28 and any underpayment of rebate shall be paid or allowed in accordance with the provisions of regulation 30.

11. The rates chargeable on lands and heritages, for the purposes of a rebate under these regulations, shall, subject to regulation 10(1), be taken to be—

(*a*) where a rebate period is contained within a single financial year, such proportion of that year's rates on the lands and heritages as the rebate period bears to the whole financial year; or

(*b*) where a rebate period falls partly in one financial year and partly in another, such proportion of each year's rates on the lands and heritages as each part of the rebate period bears to the whole of the year in which that part falls.

Joint occupiers and tenants

12. Where in respect of any lands and heritages two or more persons are joint occupiers or joint tenants within the meaning of section 113(2) of the Act, a rating authority for the purposes of calculating rebate, if any, shall without prejudice to the provisions of regulation 4(3), treat as sole occupier or tenant, as the case may be, one of those joint occupiers or tenants and in that case the reckonable rates shall be the reckonable rates on those lands and heritages ascertained in accordance with regulations 9 to 11 inclusive and every joint occupier or joint tenant who resides in the lands and heritages and is not treated as sole occupier or tenant shall be deemed to be a non-dependant; provided that neither the spouse nor a dependent child of a joint occupier or joint tenant shall be treated as a non-dependant by virtue of this regulation.

Reasonable accommodation

13. Notwithstanding any other provision in these regulations relating to the ascertainment of reckonable rates, it shall be the duty of every rating authority for the purpose of the computation of a rebate, if they consider that an applicant is in occupation of lands and heritages larger than he reasonably requires, to consider whether they ought to treat the reckonable rates of the lands and heritages as reduced by an appropriate amount and if in their opinion they ought to treat the reckonable rates as reduced, to grant a rebate only in respect of the reckonable rates as so reduced.

Weekly rates

14.—(1) In these regulations "minimum weekly rates" means, subject to regulation 14(2) and (3), 33 new pence or 40 per cent of the weekly rates, whichever is greater.

(2) In any case where the weekly income of the applicant and his spouse is less than the needs allowance, "minimum weekly rates" means the amount calculated in accordance with regulation 14(1) less an amount equal to 8 per cent of the difference between the needs allowance and the weekly income.

(3) In any case where the reduction under regulation 14(2) would be equal to or greater than the greater of 33 new pence or 40 per cent of the weekly rates, the minimum weekly rates shall be zero.

Amount of rebate

15.—(1) The amount of rebate to be granted shall be an amount calculated in accordance with this regulation but less any sum in respect of non-dependants as mentioned in Schedule 2, and subject in any event to regulations 16, 17 and 18.

(2) If the weekly income of the applicant and his spouse is equal to or less than the needs allowance, the rebate shall be equal to the amount, if any, by which the weekly rates exceed the minimum weekly rates.

(3) In any case where the weekly income exceeds the needs allowance, the rebate shall be calculated in accordance with regulation 15(4).

(4) In order to ascertain whether any rebate is to be granted there shall be added—

    (*a*) an amount equal to the minimum weekly rates; and

    (*b*) an amount equal to 6 per cent of the difference between the weekly income and the needs allowance;

if the sum so produced is less than the weekly rates the rebate shall be equal to the difference between the weekly rates and that sum subject always to regulations 16 and 17.

16. If the amount of a rebate as calculated in accordance with these regulations would be less than 5 new pence an authority may or may not grant the rebate, as they think fit.

17. If the amount of a rebate as so calculated would exceed £2.15 the excess shall not be granted.

Treatment of fractional amounts

18. The amount of any rebate shall be calculated to the nearest new penny by disregarding an odd amount of half a new penny or less, and by treating an odd amount exceeding half a new penny as a whole new penny.

Applications for rebates

19. When a rating authority receive an application for a rebate it shall be their duty, subject to regulations 20 and 21, to determine whether the applicant is entitled to a rebate and if so, the amount to which he is so entitled: and they shall request him in writing to furnish such information and such evidence as they may reasonably require for that purpose as to the following matters namely—

(*a*) the persons who reside in the lands and heritages occupied by him;

(*b*) the rent and rates, if any, payable to him for any part of the said lands and heritages let by him to a tenant;

(*c*) any income by way of payments made to him or to his spouse in respect of living accommodation or board by any persons who reside with the applicant;

(*d*) his other income and, if he has a spouse, the income of his spouse;

(*e*) the rent, if any, and rates payable by him;

and shall include with the request a notice to the applicant of the duty under regulation 25 to report to the rating authority changes of circumstances such as are mentioned in that regulation.

20. A rating authority shall be under no duty to grant a rebate unless they are satisfied that the applicant has furnished all such information and evidence as they require for the purpose of determining whether he is entitled to a rebate.

21. An application may be withdrawn at any time, and if an application is withdrawn the rating authority shall upon the withdrawal cease to be under any duty to make a determination on it, or to take any further steps in relation to it.

22.—(1) Any copy of an application made to an authority for a rent rebate or rent allowance under the Act of 1972 received by a rating authority shall be deemed to be an application for rate rebate and any copy of a notification of change of circumstances made to an authority under paragraph 5 of Schedule 3 to that Act received by a rating authority shall be deemed to satisfy, as respects the change of circumstances to which it relates, the duty imposed on an applicant by regulation 25.

(2) Where to the knowledge of a rating authority a tenant is on the first day of the financial year 1974-75 in receipt of rent rebate or rent allowance under the Act of 1972 the application by virtue of which rent rebate or allowance is received shall be deemed to be an application for rebate in respect of a rebate period commencing on the first day of the financial year 1974-75 and any notification of change of circumstances made to an authority under paragraph 5 of Schedule 3 to the Act of 1972 on or before that date which comes to the notice of a rating authority shall be deemed to satisfy, as respects the change of circumstances to which it relates, the duty imposed on an applicant by regulation 25.

23.—(1) An applicant to whom a rebate has been granted in respect of any rebate period may apply to the rating authority for a further rebate commencing on the day next following the last day of that rebate period.

(2) An application under regulation 23(1) need not be entertained—

  (*a*) if it is made more than one month before the end of the rebate period during which it is made; or

  (*b*) if at the beginning of the rebate period in respect of which it is made rates to which these regulations apply are neither due and payable nor being paid on account.

(3) If an application is made not later than one month after the end of a rebate period a new rebate period shall commence on the day next following the last day of that rebate period.

(4) If an application is made more than one month after the end of a rebate period the new rebate period shall commence as provided in regulation 24: provided that the rating authority may, if in their opinion the circumstances are exceptional, allow the new rebate period to commence on the day next following the last day of the preceding rebate period, or such later date, being a day not later than that otherwise determined under this regulation, as they consider appropriate.

(5) Subject to this regulation these regulations shall apply on an application for a further rebate as they apply on a first application.

(6) Where, apart from the operation of this regulation, a rebate period would begin before the first day of the financial year 1974-75 it shall begin on that day.

(7) If an application for rebate is made not later than one month after the commencement of the financial year 1974-75 the rebate period shall, save as otherwise provided, commence on the first day of that financial year.

Rebate periods
24. For the purpose of these regulations "rebate period" means—

  (*a*) in relation to an applicant who is receiving or is about to receive a rent rebate or rent allowance under the Act of 1972, the rent rebate or rent allowance period; provided that if the rent rebate or rent allowance period commenced before the first day of the financial year 1974-75, the rebate period shall commence from that day and end with the aforementioned rent rebate or rent allowance period;

  (*b*) in relation to any other applicant a period commencing and terminating on dates determined by the rating authority in accordance with these regulations which period shall not exceed 12 months.

Change of circumstances and general duty of rating authority as to determinations

25.—(1) If at any time between the making of an application for a rebate and any determination made on that application there is a change of circumstances such that the applicant may be reasonably expected to know that it may reduce the amount of rebate to which he is entitled, it shall be the duty of the applicant to notify the rating authority of that change.

(2) If after a rebate has been granted to an applicant and before the end of the rebate period there is a change of circumstances such that the applicant may be reasonably expected to know that it may affect his entitlement or reduce the amount to which he is entitled, it shall be the duty of the applicant to notify the rating authority of that change.

(3) If during a rebate period a rating authority receive a notification of a change of circumstances under regulation 25(2) or consider without receiving such a notification that there has been such a change in the applicant's circumstances as will affect his entitlement or reduce the amount of rebate to which he is entitled, the rating authority shall determine, according to the circumstances, either that the rebate period shall terminate on a date earlier than it would otherwise terminate or that the amount of rebate for that rebate period shall be altered as they consider appropriate.

(4) Where in a case falling within regulation 24(*b*) a rebate period exceeds nine months and the applicant is not at the commencement of the period a person of pensionable age it shall be the duty of the rating authority, not later than nine months after the commencement of the rebate period, to consider whether there has been any change of circumstances as will affect his entitlement to rebate or reduce the amount to which he is entitled and shall make a determination, according to the circumstances, either as provided by regulation 25(3) or 25(5) or that the amount of rebate shall continue unchanged.

(5) If during a rebate period a rating authority receive from an applicant a notification of a change of circumstances relating to him which might entitle him to a higher rebate, the rating authority, if they are of the opinion, after obtaining and considering such information and evidence as they require, that the applicant is entitled to a higher rebate, shall determine, according to the circumstances, either that the rebate period shall terminate on a date earlier than that on which it would otherwise terminate, or that the amount of rebate for the rebate period shall be increased from such date as they may determine.

(6) If a rating authority determine under regulations 25(3) or 25(5) that a rebate period ought to terminate, they shall invite the applicant to submit a further application for a rebate.

(7) Without prejudice to the generality of this regulation if any applicant for any reason ceases to occupy or reside in or be usually resident in the lands and heritages in respect of which an application for rebate has been made or in respect of which a rebate has been granted there shall be deemed to be a change of circumstances in terms of these regulations.

26. If there is such an alteration in the standard scheme or an approved variation, whether by the introduction of a variation or otherwise, or in the rates payable by the applicant as to affect the amount of rebate to which an applicant is entitled, the rating authority shall make such alterations as may be appropriate in the amount of his rebate.

27. It shall not be the duty of a rating authority to alter a rebate under regulations 10, 25(3) or (5) or regulation 26 if the alteration would not exceed 5 new pence.

28. Without prejudice to any other right to recover the amount of any rebate which has been wrongly granted, where any person has received a rebate to which he was not entitled, it may be recovered from him by deduction from sums which would otherwise be granted to him by way of rebate:
Provided that no rebate shall be recovered under this regulation in respect of any rebate period which had ended before the rating authority discovered that excessive rebate had been granted unless they have reason to believe that the excessive grant was attributable to fraud or negligence or wilful default on the part of the applicant.

29.—(1) It shall be the duty of a rating authority to notify an applicant in writing of every determination which they make under their rebate scheme, and every alteration made pursuant to regulation 26, in relation to him.

(2) An applicant may make representations to a rating authority concerning a determination or alteration of rebate which they make in relation to him, and if a rating authority receive such a representation from an applicant within one month of their notification to him of such a determination or alteration they shall consider the representation and may alter or confirm the determination or alteration according to the circumstances, and they shall notify the applicant in writing of their reasons for doing so.

(3) Every notification of a determination or alteration shall include a notice to the applicant explaining the provisions of regulation 29(2).

(4) When a rating authority determine to treat as the applicant, in pursuance of regulation 4(3) or regulation 12, a person who is not the occupier or tenant or, as the case may be, not the sole occupier or tenant, it shall be their duty to notify that determination both to the person who will fall to be treated as the applicant as a result of it and to the person or persons who would have been considered eligible for a rebate but for the determination.

(5) The references to the applicant in regulation 29(2) and (3) shall accordingly be construed as including every person to whom regulation 29(4) applies.

(6) Where a rating authority notify an applicant of a determination to grant him a rebate their notification shall state the amount of the rebate granted, the rebate period and the circumstances in which the amount or the period may be altered, and draw his attention to the duty imposed on him by regulation 25(2).

Payment of rebates

30. A rating authority may pay a rebate at any time and in any manner that they think fit provided that in granting a rebate they shall—

(*a*) comply with such general or particular directions as the Secretary of State may from time to time give as to the frequency of payment; and

(*b*) have regard to the reasonable needs and convenience of the applicant.

31. A rating authority may terminate a rebate period or suspend the granting of rebate if they are satisfied that the applicant is not making payments in respect of rates.

Limit of rateable value

32.—(1) The limit of rateable value referred to in section 113(1)(*a*) and (*c*) of the Act shall be £300.

(2) The limit of rateable value referred to in section 113(1)(*b*) of the Act shall in any particular case be such a sum that the proportion of the rateable value of the lands and heritages as shown in the valuation roll in force at the date of the making of the application which is attributable to the part of the lands and heritages used for the purposes of a private dwelling or private dwellings does not exceed the limit of rateable value prescribed in regulation 32(1).

Persons receiving supplementary benefit

33.—(1) Save as provided in regulation 33(2) and (3) no rebate shall be granted to an applicant who is to the knowledge of the rating authority in receipt of supplementary benefit.

(2) Where in relation to any rebate period a rating authority receive notice from the Supplementary Benefits Commission (in this regulation referred to as "the Commission") that an applicant is in receipt of supplementary benefit of an amount adjusted under paragraph 5 (adjustment of benefit to normal earnings) of Schedule 2 to the Supplementary Benefit Act 1966 (in this regulation referred to as "the Act of 1966") or of an amount which would fall to be so adjusted if a rebate were not granted, then in relation to the grant of rebate for that period—

(*a*) notwithstanding regulation 7(2) but subject to regulations 7(3) and 8 the provisions of paragraph 20(2) and (3) of Schedule 2 to the Act of 1972 shall apply in relation to the assessment of income of the applicant and any spouse of the applicant for the purpose of these regulations as they would for the purpose of calculating rent rebate or allowance under the model schemes;

(*b*) notwithstanding anything in regulation 15 the amount of the rebate shall not exceed any amount, determined by the Commission, by which supplementary benefit would have fallen to be adjusted under paragraph 5 of Schedule 2 to the Act of 1966 in the absence of any rebate; and

(*c*) notwithstanding anything in these regulations—

(i) any notice under this regulation received by a rating authority shall be treated as an application for rebate made by the person to whom it relates and the rebate period shall begin on such date as may be specified by the Commission and shall continue until the rating authority consider that there has been a change of circumstances such as will affect the applicant's entitlement or reduce the amount of rebate to which he is entitled;

(ii) if when a notice under this regulation is received by a rating authority the applicant is already in receipt of a rebate the rebate period then current shall be terminated upon the date specified by the Commission as the commencement of the period for which supplementary benefit falls to be adjusted to normal earnings.

(3) Nothing in regulation 33(1) shall prevent the continued granting of a rebate which was determined and granted before it became known to the rating authority that the applicant was in receipt of supplementary benefit.

(4) For the purposes of this regulation an applicant who is a woman shall be treated as receiving supplementary benefit if her requirements have, under

paragraph 3(1) of Schedule 2 to the Act of 1966, been aggregated with and treated as those of a person who has been awarded supplementary benefit.

St. Andrew's House,
Edinburgh.

22nd March 1974.

William Ross,
One of Her Majesty's
Principal Secretaries of State.

We consent.

Donald R. Coleman,

James Hamilton,

Two of the Lords Commissioners
of Her Majesty's Treasury.

25th March 1974.

SCHEDULE 1

NEEDS ALLOWANCE

1.—(1) Subject to sub-paragraph (2) below, the needs allowance for each week is—

(a) for an individual person who has no dependent children.............. £15.50

(b) for a married couple.. £20.75

(c) for an individual person who has a dependent child or children....... £20.75

(d) for each dependent child of an applicant or his spouse.............. £3.00

(2) The needs allowance for each week is—

(a) for an individual person who has no dependent children and who is a chronically sick or disabled person............................... £16.75

(b) for a married couple, one of whom is a chronically sick or disabled person.. £22.00

(c) for an individual person who is a chronically sick or disabled person and who has a dependent child or children........................ £22.00

(d) for a married couple, both of whom are chronically sick or disabled persons... £22.75

(3) In sub-paragraph (2) above, any reference to a chronically sick or disabled person is a reference to a person in need under section 12 of the Social Work (Scotland) Act 1968(a) as read with section 1 of the Chronically Sick and Disabled Persons (Scotland) Act 1972(b).

SCHEDULE 2

1.—(1) The deductions from a rebate in respect of non-dependants are for each week—

(a) for each person aged 18 years or more, but under 21 years and neither undergoing full-time instruction at an educational establishment nor in receipt of supplementary benefit.................................. £0.35

(b) for each person aged 21 years or more, but under pensionable age and neither undergoing full-time instruction at an educational establishment nor in receipt of supplementary benefit except in the case mentioned in paragraph (e) below.. £0.50

(c) for each person in receipt of supplementary benefit.................. £0.20

(d) for each person of pensionable age not in receipt of supplementary benefit, except in the case mentioned in paragraph (e) below........... £0.20

(e) for a married couple where the husband is of pensionable age and not in receipt of supplementary benefit................................ £0.20

(2) If any person is in receipt of supplementary benefit for himself and also for his spouse, they shall be treated as one person for the purposes of this Schedule.

(a) 1968 c. 49.   (b) 1972 c. 51.

SCHEDULE 3

RECKONABLE RATES

1. If such a person as is mentioned in section 113(1)(*b*) of the Act applies for a rebate the reckonable rates for the purpose of calculating rebate shall be an amount equal to such proportion of the rates chargeable in respect of the lands and heritages as, having regard to the apportionment of the rateable value of the lands and heritages referred to in section 113(3)(*a*) of the Act, the rating authority may determine to be attributable to the part of those lands and heritages used for the purposes of a private dwelling or private dwellings less the amount (if any) which is or would be deemed to be the reckonable rates of any person entitled to apply for a rebate in respect of any part thereof by virtue of section 113(1)(*c*) of the Act.

2. If such a person as is mentioned in section 113(1)(*c*) of the Act applies for a rebate the reckonable rates for the purpose of calculating rebate shall be ascertained by proper apportionment under section 113(4) of the Act as relating to the lands and heritages which are used by him for the purposes of a private dwelling.

EXPLANATORY NOTE

(This Note is not part of the Regulations.)

These Regulations make provision for the standard scheme for the grant of rate rebates.

The Regulations impose on rating authorities a duty to operate, for the year 1974-75, the standard scheme and, for subsequent years the standard scheme or the standard scheme varied in accordance with section 114 of the Act.

The Regulations prescribe rules for the making of applications, for the ascertainment of income and for the calculation and payment of rebate; and for various ancillary purposes.

STATUTORY INSTRUMENTS

1974 No. 601

METROPOLITAN AND CITY POLICE DISTRICTS

CABS

The London Cab Order 1974

Made - - - -		*26th March* 1974
Coming into Operation		*7th April* 1974

In exercise of the powers conferred on me by section 9 of the Metropolitan Public Carriage Act 1869(a) and section 1 of the London Cab and Stage Carriage Act 1907(b) as extended by section 1 of the London Cab Act 1968(c), I hereby order as follows:—

1. This Order may be cited as the London Cab Order 1974 and shall come into operation on 7th April 1974.

2. The London Cab Order 1973(d) (which provides for a surcharge of 3p on each hiring of a motor cab) is hereby revoked.

3.—(1) For paragraph 40 of the London Cab Order 1934(e), as amended(f) (which prescribes the scale of fare charges payable for the hiring of a motor cab) there shall be substituted the following paragraph:—

"40.—(1)(*a*) Subject to the provisions of sub-paragraph (1)(*b*) below, the fare payable for the hiring of a motor cab shall be according to the following scale:—

    (i) a hiring charge of fifteen pence (15p), and

    (ii) in respect of any part of the hiring during which the cab travels at a speed exceeding 6 miles an hour, at the rate of 5p for 560 yards or, if the fare shown on the meter is 115p or more, thereafter at the rate of 5p for 280 yards, and

    (iii) in respect of any part of the hiring during which the cab is stationary or travels at a speed not exceeding 6 miles an hour, at the rate

---

(a) 1869 c. 115.   (b) 1907 c. 55.   (c) 1968 c. 7.
(d) S.I. 1973/519 (1973 I, p. 1680).
(e) S.R. & O. 1934/1346 (Rev. XIV, p. 795: 1934 I, p. 1221).
(f) The relevant amending instruments are S.I. 1951/1352, 1958/2148, 1968/1929, 1971/333 (1951 I, p. 1311; 1958 I, p. 1503; 1968 III, p. 5234; 1971 I, p. 1059).

of 5p for 3 minutes or, if the fare shown on the meter is 115p or more, thereafter at the rate of 5p for $1\frac{1}{2}$ minutes.

(b) in any case where the fare according to the foregoing scale is less than 25p the fare payable shall be 25p, and in any other case where the fare exceeds a multiple of 5p by a sum which is less than 5p the fare payable shall be the next higher multiple of 5p.

(2)(a) Where a motor cab is fitted with a taximeter which is not capable of recording automatically the fare payable according to the scale prescribed in sub-paragraph (1) above the fare payable—

(i) in the case of a fare shown on the meter not exceeding £3·45 shall, so long as a notice in the terms of the notice set out in Schedule E to this Order is kept prominently displayed in the cab in such a manner as to be clearly legible by the hirer, be, as respects a fare shown on the meter and set out in a column of the notice entitled 'Shown on Meter', the sum set out immediately thereunder in the column entitled 'New Fare Charge', and otherwise shall be the fare shown on the meter,

(ii) in the case of a fare shown on the meter exceeding £3·45 but not exceeding £9·99 shall, so long as a notice in the terms of the notice set out in Schedule E to this Order is available on request by the hirer from the driver of the motor cab, be, as respects a fare shown on the meter and set out in a column entitled 'Shown on Meter', the sum set out immediately thereunder in the column entitled 'New Fare Charge', and otherwise shall be the fare shown on the meter,

(iii) where the meter would have recorded a fare of £10 or more if it were capable of recording such a fare shall be the fare payable under the foregoing provisions of this sub-paragraph and in addition £13·35 shall be payable in respect of each occasion that the meter has recorded the maximum sum that it is capable of recording.

(b) In the application of the notice set out in Schedule E to this Order any reference to a fare shown on the meter shall, where the fare shown on the meter exceeds a multiple of 3p by a sum which is less than 3p, be construed as a reference to the next higher multiple of 3p.

(3) Where the taximeter is capable of recording automatically the fare payable according to the scale prescribed in sub-paragraph (1) above but is not capable of recording a total fare which exceeds £9·95 the fare payable shall be the fare shown on the meter (if any) and in addition £10 shall become payable on each occasion when the meter has recorded the maximum possible fare and would record £10 if it were capable of recording such a fare.".

4. For Schedule E to the London Cab Order 1934, as amended (a) (which prescribes increase of fares) there shall be substituted the Schedule set out in the Schedule to this Order.

(a) The relevant amending instrument is S.I. 1971/333 (1971 I, p. 1059).

5. In paragraph 41(1A) of the London Cab Order 1934, as amended **(a)**, (which provides for an extra charge in respect of any hiring commencing or terminating between midnight and six o'clock in the morning) for the words "9p" there shall be substituted the words "12p".

Roy Jenkins,

One of Her Majesty's Principal
Secretaries of State.

Home Office,
    Whitehall.
26th March 1974.

(a) The relevant amending instrument is S.I. 1968/1929 (1968 III, p. 5234).

SCHEDULE

SCHEDULE E

INCREASE OF FARES

For all journeys beginning and ending within the Metropolitan and/or City Police Districts, the fare shown upon the taximeter, excluding extras, is (as authorised by the London Cab Order 1974 made by the Secretary of State) increased as shown in the table.

The fare payable when an amount in excess of £3·45 is shown on the meter is contained in a table in possession of the driver who must produce it for inspection on request.

Shown on Meter	0·15	0·18	0·21	0·24	0·27	0·30	0·33	0·36	0·39	0·42	0·45	0·48	0·51	0·54
New Fare Charge	0·25	0·25	0·30	0·35	0·40	0·40	0·45	0·50	0·55	0·60	0·60	0·65	0·70	0·75
Shown on Meter	0·57	0·60	0·63	0·66	0·69	0·72	0·75	0·78	0·81	0·84	0·87	0·90	0·93	0·96
New Fare Charge	0·80	0·80	0·85	0·90	0·95	1·00	1·00	1·05	1·10	1·10	1·15	1·20	1·25	1·25
Shown on Meter	0·99	1·02	1·05	1·08	1·11	1·14	1·17	1·20	1·23	1·26	1·29	1·32	1·35	1·38
New Fare Charge	1·30	1·35	1·40	1·45	1·50	1·50	1·55	1·60	1·65	1·70	1·70	1·75	1·80	1·85
Shown on Meter	1·41	1·44	1·47	1·50	1·53	1·56	1·59	1·62	1·65	1·68	1·71	1·74	1·77	1·80
New Fare Charge	1·90	1·90	1·95	2·00	2·05	2·10	2·10	2·15	2·20	2·25	2·30	2·30	2·35	2·40
Shown on Meter	1·83	1·86	1·89	1·92	1·95	1·98	2·01	2·04	2·07	2·10	2·13	2·16	2·19	2·22
New Fare Charge	2·45	2·50	2·50	2·55	2·60	2·65	2·70	2·70	2·75	2·80	2·85	2·90	2·90	2·95
Shown on Meter	2·25	2·28	2·31	2·34	2·37	2·40	2·43	2·46	2·49	2·52	2·55	2·58	2·61	2·64
New Fare Charge	3·00	3·05	3·10	3·10	3·15	3·20	3·25	3·30	3·30	3·35	3·40	3·45	3·50	3·50

Shown on Meter	2·67	2·70	2·73	2·76	2·79	2·82	2·85	2·88	2·91	2·94	2·97	3·00	3·03	3·06
New Fare Charge	3·55	3·60	3·65	3·70	3·75	3·75	3·80	3·85	3·90	3·95	3·95	4·00	4·05	4·10
Shown on Meter	3·09	3·12	3·15	3·18	3·21	3·24	3·27	3·30	3·33	3·36	3·39	3·42	3·45	3·48
New Fare Charge	4·15	4·15	4·20	4·25	4·30	4·35	4·35	4·40	4·45	4·50	4·55	4·55	4·60	4·65
Shown on Meter	3·51	3·54	3·57	3·60	3·63	3·66	3·69	3·72	3·75	3·78	3·81	3·84	3·87	3·90
New Fare Charge	4·70	4·75	4·75	4·80	4·85	4·90	4·95	4·95	5·00	5·05	5·10	5·15	5·15	5·20
Shown on Meter	3·93	3·96	3·99	4·02	4·05	4·08	4·11	4·14	4·17	4·20	4·23	4·26	4·29	4·32
New Fare Charge	5·25	5·30	5·35	5·35	5·40	5·45	5·50	5·55	5·55	5·60	5·65	5·70	5·75	5·75
Shown on Meter	4·35	4·38	4·41	4·44	4·47	4·50	4·53	4·56	4·59	4·62	4·65	4·68	4·71	4·74
New Fare Charge	5·80	5·85	5·90	5·95	6·00	6·00	6·05	6·10	6·15	6·20	6·20	6·25	6·30	6·35
Shown on Meter	4·77	4·80	4·83	4·86	4·89	4·92	4·95	4·98	5·01	5·04	5·07	5·10	5·13	5·16
New Fare Charge	6·40	6·40	6·45	6·50	6·55	6·60	6·60	6·65	6·70	6·75	6·80	6·80	6·85	6·90
Shown on Meter	5·19	5·22	5·25	5·28	5·31	5·34	5·37	5·40	5·43	5·46	5·49	5·52	5·55	5·58
New Fare Charge	6·95	7·00	7·00	7·05	7·10	7·15	7·20	7·20	7·25	7·30	7·35	7·40	7·40	7·45
Shown on Meter	5·61	5·64	5·67	5·70	5·73	5·76	5·79	5·82	5·85	5·88	5·91	5·94	5·97	6·00
New Fare Charge	7·50	7·55	7·60	7·60	7·65	7·70	7·75	7·80	7·80	7·85	7·90	7·95	8·00	8·00
Shown on Meter	6·03	6·06	6·09	6·12	6·15	6·18	6·21	6·24	6·27	6·30	6·33	6·36	6·39	6·42
New Fare Charge	8·05	8·10	8·15	8·20	8·25	8·25	8·30	8·35	8·40	8·45	8·45	8·50	8·55	8·60

Shown on Meter	6·84	6·81	6·78	6·75	6·72	6·69	6·66	6·63	6·60	6·57	6·54	6·51	6·48	6·45
New Fare Charge	9·15	9·10	9·05	9·05	9·00	8·95	8·90	8·85	8·85	8·80	8·75	8·70	8·65	8·65
Shown on Meter	7·26	7·23	7·20	7·17	7·14	7·11	7·08	7·05	7·02	6·99	6·96	6·93	6·90	6·87
New Fare Charge	9·70	9·65	9·65	9·60	9·55	9·50	9·45	9·45	9·40	9·35	9·30	9·25	9·25	9·20
Shown on Meter	7·68	7·65	7·62	7·59	7·56	7·53	7·50	7·47	7·44	7·41	7·38	7·35	7·32	7·29
New Fare Charge	10·25	10·25	10·20	10·15	10·10	10·05	10·05	10·00	9·95	9·90	9·85	9·85	9·80	9·75
Shown on Meter	8·10	8·07	8·04	8·01	7·98	7·95	7·92	7·89	7·86	7·83	7·80	7·77	7·74	7·71
New Fare Charge	10·85	10·80	10·75	10·70	10·70	10·65	10·60	10·55	10·50	10·50	10·45	10·40	10·35	10·30
Shown on Meter	8·52	8·49	8·46	8·43	8·40	8·37	8·34	8·31	8·28	8·25	8·22	8·19	8·16	8·13
New Fare Charge	11·40	11·35	11·30	11·30	11·25	11·20	11·15	11·10	11·10	11·05	11·00	10·95	10·90	10·90
Shown on Meter	8·94	8·91	8·88	8·85	8·82	8·79	8·76	8·73	8·70	8·67	8·64	8·61	8·58	8·55
New Fare Charge	11·95	11·90	11·90	11·85	11·80	11·75	11·70	11·70	11·65	11·60	11·55	11·50	11·50	11·45
Shown on Meter	9·36	9·33	9·30	9·27	9·24	9·21	9·18	9·15	9·12	9·09	9·06	9·03	9·00	8·97
New Fare Charge	12 50	12·50	12·45	12·40	12·35	12·30	12·30	12·25	12·20	12·15	12·10	12·10	12·05	12·00
Shown on Meter	9·78	9·75	9·72	9·69	9·66	9·63	9·60	9·57	9·54	9·51	9·48	9·45	9·42	9·39
New Fare Charge	13·10	13·05	13·00	12·95	12·95	12·90	12·85	12·80	12·75	12·75	12·70	12·65	12·60	12·55
Shown on Meter				0·12	0·09	0·06	0·03	9·99	9·96	9·93	9·90	9·87	9·84	9·81
New Fare Charge				0·20	0·15	0·10	0·05	13·35	13·35	13·30	13·25	13·20	13·15	13·15

EXPLANATORY NOTE

(This Note is not part of the Order.)

This Order increases the fares payable for the hiring of a motor cab in the Metropolitan Police District and the City of London in respect of all journeys beginning and ending in London. So long as a cab is not fitted with a meter capable of recording the new fares automatically, only the fare shown on the meter will be chargeable unless a notice in the terms set out in the Schedule is prominently displayed in the cab or is available at the request of the hirer in which case the increased fares shown in the notice will be chargeable. The Order also increases the extra charge payable for the hiring of a cab between midnight and six o'clock in the morning.

STATUTORY INSTRUMENTS

1974 No. 604

NORTHERN IRELAND

FINANCE

The Agriculture Payments (Extension) (Northern Ireland) Order 1974

Made - - -	*7th February* 1974
Laid before Parliament	*12th March* 1974
Coming into Operation	*29th March* 1974

The Minister of Agriculture, Fisheries and Food and the Secretaries of State respectively concerned with agriculture in Scotland and Northern Ireland, acting jointly, in exercise of the powers conferred on them by sections 32(2) and 35(3) of the Agriculture Act 1957(**a**), hereby make the following Order:—

1. This order may be cited as the Agriculture Payments (Extension) (Northern Ireland) Order 1974 and shall come into operation on the day after it has been approved by both Houses of Parliament.

2. The period during which, by virtue of the Payments in Aid of Agricultural Schemes (Extension) Order 1971(**b**), payments not exceeding £1,900,000 a year may be made by the Minister of Agriculture, Fisheries and Food into the Consolidated Fund of Northern Ireland under section 32(1) of the Agriculture Act 1957 (as adapted by paragraph 2(2) of Schedule 5 to the Northern Ireland Constitution Act 1973(**c**)) which would otherwise expire on 31st March 1974, shall be extended until 31st March 1977, and Article 3 of the said Order of 1971 shall have effect accordingly.

(**a**) 1957 c. 57.   (**b**) S.I. 1971/343 (1971 I, p. 1085).
(**c**) 1973 c. 36.

In Witness whereof the Official Seal of the Minister of Agriculture, Fisheries and Food is hereunto affixed on 7th February 1974.

(L.S.)

Joseph Godber,
Minister of Agriculture,
Fisheries and Food.

Gordon Campbell,
7th February 1974.   Secretary of State for Scotland.

Francis Pym,
Secretary of State for
6th February 1974.   Northern Ireland.

EXPLANATORY NOTE

(This Note is not part of the Order.)

This Order extends until 31st March 1977 the period during which payments may be made by the Minister of Agriculture, Fisheries and Food under section 32(1) of the Agriculture Act 1957 in respect of expenses incurred by the Department of Agriculture for Northern Ireland, under approved arrangements, in making payments to or for the benefit of agricultural producers in Northern Ireland.

STATUTORY INSTRUMENTS

1974 No. 605

AGRICULTURE

EGGS MARKETING

The Eggs Authority Levy Scheme (Approval) Order 1974

Made - - - -	14*th March* 1974
Laid before Parliament	14*th March* 1974
Coming into Operation	29*th March* 1974

Whereas the Eggs Authority constituted under section 2 of the Agriculture Act 1970(a) (hereinafter referred to as "the Act"), have prepared and submitted to the Ministers hereinafter named, pursuant to section 16(1) of the Act, a Scheme for imposing and for recovering a levy for the purposes of Part I of the Act (which Scheme is hereinafter referred to as "the Scheme"):

Now, therefore, the Minister of Agriculture, Fisheries and Food, the Secretary of State for Wales, the Secretary of State for Scotland and the Secretary of State concerned with agriculture in Northern Ireland, acting jointly in exercise of powers conferred upon them by section 16(5) of the Act and of all other powers enabling them in that behalf, hereby make the following order:—

Citation and commencement

1. This order may be cited as the Eggs Authority Levy Scheme (Approval) Order 1974, and shall come into operation on the day after it has been approved by a resolution of each House of Parliament.

Approval of scheme under section 16 *of the Agriculture Act* 1970

2. The Scheme is hereby approved with the following modifications:—

(*a*) in paragraph 1 thereof for the figures and word "31st March 1974" there shall be substituted the figures and words "the day on which the order approving it under section 16(5) of the Act comes into operation";

(*b*) in paragraph 2(1) thereof for the definitions " 'chicks' means day-old pullet chicks of domestic fowls" and " 'day-old' in relation to chicks refers not merely to the day of hatching but to any period within 72 hours after hatching" there shall be substituted the following definition:—

" 'chicks' means pullet chicks of domestic fowls being chicks which have been hatched for not more than 72 hours;";

(a) 1970 c. 40.

(*c*) in paragraph 2(1) thereof for the definitions " 'numbers of chicks' in relation to chicks placed by way of sale does not include chicks supplied by way of tolerance (or replacement) for mortality" and " 'place' in relation to chicks, means place by way of sale or in any business of rearing domestic fowls for egg production or for use in any business of egg production and 'placed' shall be construed accordingly" there shall be substituted the following definitions:—

" 'place' in relation to chicks means place by way of sale or in any business of rearing domestic fowls for egg production or for use in any business of egg production but does not include supply, as part of or in connection with any sale, a quantity by way of free replacement, or tolerance not exceeding two per cent. of the quantity ordered by the buyer, in either case to compensate for chick mortality; and 'placed' shall be construed accordingly:";

(*d*) at the beginning of paragraph 3 thereof there shall be inserted the words "Subject to paragraph 4A of this Scheme,";

(*e*) in paragraph 4 thereof there shall be inserted after the words "(whether by the person with whom they are placed or by any other person)" the words "in Great Britain or Northern Ireland";

(*f*) after paragraph 4 thereof there shall be inserted the following paragraph:—

"4A. Where any order under subsection (2)(*b*) of section 13 of the Act specifying the rate of levy for any accounting period comes into operation on a date after the beginning of that accounting period, each hatcher and each importer shall be exempt from the provisions of paragraph 3 of this Scheme in respect of the numbers of chicks placed by him during that accounting period before that date.";

(*g*) in paragraphs 6(1) and 7 thereof for the figures and word "31st March 1974" there shall be substituted the words "the date on which this Scheme comes into operation".

3. The Scheme as so modified and approved is set forth in the Schedule to this order.

In Witness whereof the Official Seal of the Minister of Agriculture, Fisheries and Food is hereunto affixed on 11th March 1974.

(L.S.)   *Frederick Peart,*
                          Minister of Agriculture, Fisheries and Food.

12th March 1974.   *John Morris,*
                               Secretary of State for Wales.

13th March 1974.   *William Ross,*
                               Secretary of State for Scotland.

14th March 1974.   *Merlyn Rees,*
                          Secretary of State for Northern Ireland.

SCHEDULE

Eggs Authority Levy Scheme

under Section 16 of the Agriculture Act 1970

1. This Scheme, which applies in the United Kingdom, may be cited as the Eggs Authority Levy Scheme 1974, and shall come into operation on the day on which the order approving it under section 16(5) of the Act comes into operation.

2.—(1) In this Scheme, unless the context otherwise requires—

"the Act" means the Agriculture Act 1970;

"the Authority" means the Eggs Authority constituted under section 2 of the Act;

"chicks" means pullet chicks of domestic fowls being chicks which have been hatched for not more than 72 hours;

"hatcher" means any person engaged by way of business in the hatching of domestic fowls for egg laying in Great Britain or Northern Ireland other than any person who during any period of twelve months does not place more than 300 chicks for egg laying;

"importer" means any person engaged by way of business in the bringing (otherwise than only as a carrier) of live domestic fowls of laying stock into Great Britain or Northern Ireland from outside those areas other than any person who during any period of twelve months does not place more than 300 chicks for egg laying;

"place" in relation to chicks means place by way of sale or in any business of rearing domestic fowls for egg production or for use in any business of egg production but does not include supply, as part of or in connection with any sale, a quantity by way of free replacement, or tolerance not exceeding two per cent. of the quantity ordered by the buyer, in either case to compensate for chick mortality; and "placed" shall be construed accordingly:

AND other expressions have the same meaning as in the Act.

(2) The Interpretation Act 1889 shall apply to the interpretation of this Scheme as it applies to the interpretation of an Act of Parliament.

3. Subject to paragraph 4A of this Scheme, for each accounting period beginning on or after 31st March 1974, there is hereby imposed on hatchers and importers a levy for the purposes of Part I of the Act at such rate as may be specified in any order for that accounting period made under subsection (2)(b) of section 13 of the Act:

Provided that, where as respects part of an accounting period an order is made under subsection (3) of the said section specifying a rate of additional levy, then in relation to that part the rate of levy hereby imposed shall be the aggregate of the rate specified in the said order for that period made under subsection (2)(b) of section 13 of the Act and the rate of additional levy.

4. Where, in any order under section 13 of the Act—

(a) a rate of levy is specified for any accounting period beginning on or after 31st March 1974, or

(b) an additional rate of levy is specified as respects any part of an accounting period beginning on or after 31st March 1974,

by reference to numbers of chicks, such numbers shall be determined for the purposes of the levy as the numbers of chicks placed in Great Britain or Northern Ireland by each hatcher or each importer for the production (whether by the person with whom they are placed or by any other person) in Great Britain or Northern Ireland of eggs for human consumption, as contained in returns in respect of that accounting period or that part of such an accounting period furnished to the Authority by that hatcher or importer in accordance with paragraph 7(a) of this Scheme:

Provided that if the Authority are unable to obtain from any hatcher or importer a sufficient return of the numbers of chicks placed by him during any period, he shall, if the Authority think fit, be treated as having placed during that period such numbers of chicks as the Authority think proper having regard to such information (if any) as may be in the possession of the Authority, whether in respect of that period or of any earlier period, but, before taking action under this proviso, the Authority shall send the hatcher or importer concerned notice that the Authority propose to do so and shall have regard to any information which may be supplied to the Authority within 21 days of the sending of such notice.

4A Where any order under subsection (2)(*b*) of section 13 of the Act specifying the rate of levy for any accounting period comes into operation on a date after the beginning of that accounting period, each hatcher and each importer shall be exempt from the provisions of paragraph 3 of this Scheme in respect of numbers of chicks placed by him during that accounting period before that date.

5.—(1) Any levy imposed in accordance with this Scheme shall, subject to sub-paragraph (3) of this paragraph, be payable to the Authority on such date or dates (not being sooner than the end of the second month next following the month during which the chicks were placed) and at such place or places as the Authority may from time to time require and shall be recoverable as a debt due to the Authority from the hatcher or importer on whom it is imposed.

(2) Every hatcher and importer on whom a levy is imposed in accordance with this Scheme is hereby empowered (as respects chicks sold by him) to recover as a debt due to him from the person to whom he sells chicks the amount of levy imposed on the hatcher or importer by reference to the chicks so sold.

(3) Every hatcher and importer shall be entitled, as respects chicks sold by him, to deduct from the amount otherwise payable by him by way of the levy, or to be otherwise reimbursed by the Authority, a sum calculated in such manner as the Authority may determine in respect of any expenses incurred by him in recovering that amount in accordance with sub-paragraph (2) of this paragraph.

6.—(1) So far as is necessary for determining the liability of persons to any levy which is or is to be imposed in accordance with this Scheme for any accounting period, the Authority shall as from the date on which this Scheme comes into operation have power to require hatchers and importers to be registered in a register kept by the Authority for the purpose of this Scheme and such power may be exercised in accordance with sub-paragraphs (2) and (3) of this paragraph.

(2) The Authority may, by notice published in at least one newspaper having a national circulation in England and Wales, in Scotland and in Northern Ireland respectively and in such other newspapers and other periodicals as the Authority consider appropriate to bring the matter to the notice of persons affected, from time to time require every hatcher and importer to be registered with the Authority in a register kept by the Authority for the purposes of this Scheme.

(3) Without prejudice to the preceding sub-paragraph, the Authority may by notice served upon any hatcher or importer require him to be registered as aforesaid.

(4) Any hatcher or importer who is required to be registered as aforesaid shall apply to the Authority to be registered upon such form as the Authority may from time to time prescribe; and any person so registered who has ceased to be a hatcher or importer and who desires that his name shall be removed from the register shall apply for such removal upon such form as the Authority may from time to time prescribe.

7. So far as is necessary for determining the liability of any hatcher or importer to any levy which is or is to be imposed in accordance with this Scheme for an accounting period, the Authority may from time to time (as from the date on which this Scheme comes into operation) by notice in writing served upon him require him:—

(*a*) to furnish returns to the Authority at such address and at such time or times as may be specified in the notice:—

(i) in the case of a hatcher, of the numbers of chicks placed by the hatcher during any monthly or other period specified in the notice, whether for use in Great Britain or Northern Ireland or for export therefrom and whether from the hatcher's own production or imported;

      (ii) in the case of an importer, of the numbers of chicks placed by the importer during any monthly or other period specified in the notice;

    (*b*) to keep an accurate record in writing, to be duly completed and dated each day, specifying:—

      (i) in the case of a hatcher, the numbers of chicks placed and where placed, indicating separately the numbers placed for export from Great Britain and Northern Ireland;

      (ii) in the case of an importer, the numbers of chicks placed and where placed;

    (*c*) to retain any such record for such period, not exceeding two years, as may be specified in the notice;

    (*d*) to produce any such record for examination on demand by an authorised officer of the Authority;

    (*e*) if he is a hatcher, to permit authorised officers of the Authority to enter upon any land or premises used by him by way of business for the hatching of domestic fowls and to inspect any domestic fowls found on those premises.

EXPLANATORY NOTE
(*This Note is not part of the Order.*)

By this Order the Ministers approve, with modifications, a Scheme submitted to them by the Eggs Authority under section 16 of the Agriculture Act 1970 ("the Act"). The Scheme, as modified, comes into force on the same day as this Order and provides for the imposition on and recovery from hatchers and importers, as defined in the Scheme, of a levy for the purposes of Part I of the Act at such rate or additional rate as may be specified in any Order under section 13 of the Act. Where such rate or additional rate is specified by reference to numbers of chicks, the Scheme requires those numbers to be determined as the numbers of chicks placed during the relevant accounting period in Great Britain or Northern Ireland by hatchers or importers for production of eggs in those areas for human consumption, as shown in returns furnished by hatchers and importers. Where an Order specifying the rate of levy for an accounting period comes into operation on a date after the beginning of that period, hatchers and importers are exempt from the levy in respect of chicks placed before that date. The Scheme empowers hatchers or importers on whom a levy is imposed to recover from anyone to whom they sell chicks the levy imposed by reference to the chicks so sold.

The Scheme also provides for the registration of hatchers and importers, for the keeping of records by them and for a power of entry to hatchers' premises by authorised officers of the Authority.

The modifications to the Scheme—

    (*a*) provide for the Scheme to come into force on the same day as this Order;

    (*b*) combine the definitions of "chicks" and "day-old" in a revised definition of the former;

    (*c*) substitute for the definitions of "numbers of chicks" and "place" a revised definition of the latter so as to exempt from liability for levy, in specified circumstances, the supply of chicks by way of replacement, or tolerance, for mortality;

    (*d*) limit the numbers of chicks liable in respect of levy, to those placed for production "in Great Britain or Northern Ireland" of eggs for human consumption.

    (*e*) exempt hatchers and importers from liability for levy in respect of numbers of chicks placed during an accounting period but before the operative date of the Order specifying the rate of the levy for that period under section 13(2)(b) of the Act.

STATUTORY INSTRUMENTS

1974 No. 606

AGRICULTURE

EGGS MARKETING

The Eggs Authority (Rates of Levy) Order 1974

Made - - - -	28*th March* 1974
Laid before Parliament	29*th March* 1974
Coming into Operation	31*st March* 1974

Whereas the Eggs Authority (hereinafter referred to as "the Authority"), constituted under section 2 of the Agriculture Act 1970(a) (hereinafter referred to as "the Act"), have prepared and submitted to the Ministers hereinafter named, pursuant to section 13(1) of the Act, an estimate of the amounts required to be raised by levy for the period beginning with 31st March 1974 and ending with 31st March 1975 (hereinafter referred to as "the relevant accounting period") for the purposes of the functions respectively of the Authority under Part I of the Act, subject to section 10 of the Act, referred to in paragraphs (*a*) and (*c*) of the section 13(1):

And whereas, after consultation pursuant to subsection (4) of section 13 of the Act with such organisations appearing to the said Ministers to represent the interests of persons engaged by way of business in the production of eggs (hereinafter referred to as "producers") as those Ministers consider appropriate and with such other organisations as they consider appropriate having regard to the fact that the levy for the relevant accounting period will be imposed on persons other than producers, the said Ministers have pursuant to subsection (2)(*a*) of the said section determined that the respective amounts to be raised by levy for the relevant accounting period shall be £136,946 for the purposes of the functions referred to in paragraph (*a*) of section 13(1) of the Act and £1,229,164 for the purposes of the functions referred to in paragraph (*c*) of that section:

Now, therefore, the Minister of Agriculture, Fisheries and Food, the Secretary of State for Wales, the Secretary of State for Scotland and the Secretary of State concerned with agriculture in Northern Ireland, acting jointly in exercise of the powers conferred upon them by subsections (2)(*b*) and (6) of section 13 of the Act and of all other powers enabling them in that behalf, hereby make the following order:—

Citation and commencement

1. This order may be cited as the Eggs Authority (Rates of Levy) Order 1974, and shall come into operation on 31st March 1974.

(a) 1970 c. 40.

Interpretation

2.—(1) In this order "chicks" means pullet chicks of domestic fowls being chicks which have been hatched for not more than 72 hours.

(2) The Interpretation Act 1889**(a)** shall apply to the interpretation of this order as it applies to the interpretation of an Act of Parliament.

(3) Any reference in this order to any scheme shall be construed as a reference to such scheme as varied by any subsequent scheme.

Rate of levy and related matters

3.—(1) The rate of levy for the relevant accounting period, which appears to the Ministers to be sufficient (but not more than sufficient) to meet the aggregate of the amounts determined by the Ministers under paragraph (*a*) of section 13(2) of the Act for the purposes of the functions referred to in paragraphs (*a*) and (*c*) of section 13(1) of the Act shall be £2·84 per hundred chicks determined in accordance with the provisions of the Eggs Authority Levy Scheme 1974 set forth in the Schedule to the Eggs Authority Levy Scheme (Approval) Order 1974**(b)**.

(2) The rate of levy specified above is attributable as to £0·28 and £2·56 respectively to functions referred to in paragraphs (*a*) and (*c*) of section 13(1) of the Act.

In Witness whereof the Official Seal of the Minister of Agriculture, Fisheries and Food is hereunto affixed on 28th March 1974.

(L.S.)

Frederick Peart,
Minister of Agriculture, Fisheries and Food.

28th March 1974.

John Morris,
Secretary of State for Wales.

28th March 1974.

William Ross,
Secretary of State for Scotland.

28th March 1974.

Merlyn Rees,
Secretary of State for Northern Ireland.

(a) 1889 c. 63.   (b) S.I. 1974/605 (1974 I, p. 2422).

EXPLANATORY NOTE

(This Note is not part of the Order.)

This Order, which comes into operation on 31st March 1974, specifies the rate of levy to be raised in respect of the accounting period beginning with 31st March 1974 and ending with 31st March 1975, to meet the aggregate of the amounts determined by the Ministers for the purpose of financing the functions of the Eggs Authority referred to in paragraphs (*a*) and (*c*) of section 13(1) of the Agriculture Act 1970. It also specifies how much of the rate is attributable to the functions referred to in each respectively of those paragraphs.

The rate of levy is specified per hundred pullet chicks of domestic fowls being chicks which have been hatched for not more than 72 hours, determined in accordance with the Eggs Authority Levy Scheme 1974.

In accordance with section 16(7) of the Agriculture Act 1970, the levy will, from the date of operation of this Order, be imposed under the scheme, in prescribed circumstances and subject to specified exceptions, on persons engaged by way of business in the hatching of domestic fowls for egg laying in Great Britain or Northern Ireland or in the bringing (otherwise than only as a carrier) of live domestic fowls of laying stock into Great Britain or Northern Ireland from outside those areas.

STATUTORY INSTRUMENTS

1974 No. 607

WATER

The Water Authorities etc. (Miscellaneous Provisions) Order 1974

Made - - -	*28th March* 1974
Laid before Parliament	*29th March* 1974
Coming into Operation—	
Article 16	*31st March* 1974
Remainder	*1st April* 1974

The Secretary of State for the Environment and the Secretary of State for Wales, in exercise of the powers conferred upon them by section 254(1)(*a*) and (2)(*c*) of the Local Government Act 1972(**a**), as extended by section 34(1) of the Water Act 1973(**b**), and of the powers so conferred by section 34(2) of, and paragraph 15 of Schedule 6 to, the said Act of 1973, and of all other powers enabling them in that behalf, hereby make the following order:—

Title and commencement

1.—(1) This order may be cited as the Water Authorities etc. (Miscellaneous Provisions) Order 1974.

(2) Article 16 of this order shall come into operation on 31st **March** 1974 and the remaining provisions shall come into operation on 1st April 1974.

Territorial extent of exercise of powers

2.—(1) Articles 4, 8, 10, 11 and 15 are made by the Secretary of State for Wales in relation to the Welsh National Water Development Authority and their area, and by the Secretary of State for the Environment in relation to any other water authority or area.

(2) The remaining articles of this order are made by the Secretary of State for the Environment.

Interpretation

3.—(1) The Interpretation Act 1889(**c**) shall apply for the interpretation of this order as it applies for the interpretation of an Act of Parliament.

(**a**) 1972 c. 70.   (**b**) 1973 c. 37.   (**c**) 1889 c. 63.

(2) In this order—

"the 1945 Act" means the Water Act 1945(**a**);

"the 1963 Act" means the Water Resources Act 1963(**b**);

"the 1972 Act" means the Local Government Act 1972;

"the 1973 Act" means the Water Act 1973;

"the Third Schedule" means the Third Schedule to the 1945 Act.

(3) In this order, unless the context otherwise requires, references to any enactment or instrument shall be construed as references to that enactment or instrument as amended, extended or applied by or under any other enactment or instrument.

Annual reports and accounts of river authorities and kindred authorities

4.—(1) The provisions of this article shall have effect in the case of any authority mentioned in column (1) of the following table; and in this article "the transferor authority" menas any such authority and "the water authority", in relation to that authority, means the authority mentioned in relation to that authority in column (2) of the table.

TABLE

(1)	(2)
The Avon and Dorset River Authority	The Wessex Water Authority
The Essex River Authority	The Anglian Water Authority
The Kent River Authority	The Southern Water Authority
The Severn River Authority	The Severn-Trent Water Authority
Any other river authority	The water authority in whose area the area of the authority mentioned in column (1) is comprised
The Lee Conservancy Catchment Board	The Thames Water Authority
The Isle of Wight River and Water Authority	The Southern Water Authority

(2) In relation to every transferor authority, the water authority shall, before 1st October 1974, send to the Secretary of State and the Minister of Agriculture, Fisheries and Food a report relating to the proceedings of the transferor authority in respect of the year ending on 31st March 1974, and a similar report in respect of any preceding year, if such a report was not sent to the said Ministers by the transferor authority before their dissolution, and shall at the same time send a copy of any such report to the council of any county

(**a**) 1945 c 42.   (**b**) 1963 c. 38.

(within the meaning of the 1972 Act) which was wholly or partly included in the area of the transferor authority immediately before 1st April 1974.

(3) Any such report shall be in the form set out in a direction dated 4th July 1966 given to river authorities by the Minister of Housing and Local Government, the Minister of Agriculture, Fisheries and Food, and the Secretary of State for Wales under section 110(1) of the 1963 Act, and shall contain particulars with respect to the matters specified in the Schedule to that direction.

(4) The Secretary of State shall lay before each House of Parliament a copy of any report sent to him under this article.

(5) As soon as the accounts of the transferor authority have been audited, the water authority shall send a copy of them to the Secretary of State and the Minister of Agriculture, Fisheries and Food, and shall at the same time send a copy to the council of every county mentioned in paragraph (2) above; and a copy of the accounts shall be kept at the office of the water authority and any person interested shall be entitled, without payment, to inspect and take copies of, or extracts from, the copy of the accounts.

(6) Copies of any such report as is mentioned in paragraph (2) of this article and of statements summarising the accounts of the transferor authority shall be furnished to any person on application and on payment of such reasonable sum as the water authority may determine.

Report and accounts of the Conservators of the River Thames

5.—(1) In this article—

"the 1932 Act" means the Thames Conservancy Act 1932(**a**);

"the 1964 Order" means the Thames Conservancy (New Functions of River Authorities in Thames Catchment Area) Order 1964(**b**);

"the Conservators" means the Conservators of the River Thames;

"report", in relation to any year, means the general report of their proceedings during that year which the Conservators are required by section 43 of the 1932 Act to present to Parliament;

"accounts", in relation to any year, means a copy of the accounts of the Conservators for that year in the form in which such a copy is required by the said section 43 to accompany the report for that year when it is presented to Parliament in pursuance of that section.

(2) The report and accounts for the year ended on 31st December 1973 may, for the purposes of the said section 43 and of section 228 (which requires the accounts to be sent to the Secretary of State for the Environment) of the 1932 Act, and of article 13 of the 1964 Order, be so compiled as to relate to the period of fifteen months ending on 31st March 1974.

(3) Everything with respect to the report and accounts relating to any period which by virtue of the said sections 43 and 228, or of the said article 13, is required to be done by the Conservators and which has not been done by them before 1st April 1974 shall be done by the Thames Water Authority.

(**a**) 1932 c. xxxvii.   (**b**) S.I. 1964/1251.

Annual report and accounts of Metropolitan Water Board

6.—(1) The provisions of this article shall have effect in the case of the annual report and accounts required by sections 19 (accounts and audit) and 28 (annual report) of the Metropolis Water Act 1902(**a**) (in this article referred to as "the 1902 Act") to be made, or made up and audited, as the case may be, by the Metropolitan Water Board (in this article referred to as "the Board").

(2) Everything in respect of the accounts of the Board and any committee appointed by them, and of their officers, in relation to the year ending on 31st March 1974 which by virtue of section 19 of the 1902 Act is authorised or required to be done by or to the Board, or an officer of the Board, shall be done by or to the Thames Water Authority or, as the case may be, an officer of that authority, and the provisions of the said section 19 shall have effect accordingly.

(3) In relation to the proceedings of the Board during the year ending on 31st March 1974, it shall be the duty of the Thames Water Authority—

(*a*) to make to the Secretary of State for the Environment a report comprising so much of the annual report of the proceedings of the Board as has not, on that date, been so made by the Board, and

(*b*) to give to the said Secretary of State such returns, statistics and information as he may require with respect to the exercise of the powers of the Board during the said year.

and the provisions of section 28 of the 1902 Act shall have effect accordingly.

Annual report and accounts of Water Supply Industry Training Board

7.—(1) The provisions of this article shall have effect in the case of the report and statement of accounts required by section 8 (report and accounts of industrial training boards) of the Industrial Training Act 1964(**b**) (in this article referred to as "the 1964 Act") to be made and prepared by the Water Supply Industry Training Board (in this article referred to as "the Training Board").

(2) The National Water Council shall, as soon as reasonably practicable after 31st March 1974—

(*a*) prepare, in relation to the financial year ending on that day, a statement of account in respect of the accounts of the Training Board in the form determined in writing on 9th May 1966 by the Minister of Labour in pursuance of section 8(1) of the 1964 Act; and

(*b*) make to the Secretary of State for Employment a report of the activities of the Training Board for the said financial year which shall include the said statement of account together with a copy of any report made on the accounts by auditors appointed in pursuance of section 8(2) of the 1964 Act;

and, notwithstanding the dissolution of the Training Board, the provisions of subsections (2) and (4) of the said section 8 shall have effect in relation to the auditing of the accounts of the Training Board and the laying before Parliament of the report required by sub-paragraph (*b*) above.

(**a**) 1902 c. 41.   (**b**) 1964 c. 16.

Application of Parts VII, IX and XIII of Third Schedule to Water Act 1945

8.—(1) In this article, "water supply area", in relation to a water authority, means the area within which it is the duty of that authority to supply water under Part II of the 1973 Act.

(2) Where, in relation to any area forming part of a water authority's water supply area, there was in operation immediately before 1st April 1974 a local statutory provision which—

(a) applied with modifications some or all of the provisions of Parts VII and IX of the Third Schedule (relating respectively to supply of water for domestic purposes, and duties as to constancy of supply and pressure), or

(b) comprised provisions substantially to the like effect as any such last-mentioned provisions,

notwithstanding anything in section 11(7)(b) of the 1973 Act, that local statutory provision shall continue to have effect in relation to the first-mentioned area instead of the corresponding provisions, as originally enacted, of the said Part VII or IX.

(3) Notwithstanding anything in section 12 of the Local Government (Miscellaneous Provisions) Act 1953(a) water undertakings of water authorities), Part XIII of the Third Schedule (provisions for preventing waste of water) shall not apply within any part of the water supply area of the Thames Water Authority which immediately before 1st April 1974 lay within the limits of supply of the Metropolitan Water Board, but within any such part, on and after that date, any local statutory provision which conferred on the said Board any functions relating to the prevention of waste of water shall have effect as if for any reference therein to the Board there were substituted a reference to the Thames Water Authority.

Application of Third Schedule in place of provisions of Public Health Act 1936

9.—(1) In this article—

"former statutory water undertakers" means statutory water undertakers within the meaning of the 1945 Act as that Act had effect immediately before 1st April 1974;

"water supply area", in relation to a water authority, means the area within which it is the duty of that authority to supply water under Part II of the 1973 Act.

(2) This article shall not apply to the Welsh National Water Development Authority.

(3) Subject to paragraph (2) above, this article shall apply to any of the following areas, that is to say—

(a) any area which forms part of the water supply area of a water authority and within which, immediately before 1st April 1974, a supply of

---

(a) 1953 c. 26.

water was furnished by former statutory water undertakers under powers conferred by Part IV (Water Supply) of the Public Health Act 1936(**a**);

(*b*) the parish of Ulpha in the rural district of Millom.

(4) Subject to the provisions of this article, the Third Schedule shall apply in relation to any area to which this article applies and is hereby incorporated with this order and shall have effect, as so applied, as if it had been applied by virtue of section 32 of the 1945 Act.

(5) For the purposes of paragraph (4) above, the following provisions of the Third Schedule shall be excepted: —

Section 2 (permissible limits of deviation).

Section 7 (power to acquire easements for underground works).

Part XV (Financial Provisions applicable to Water Companies).

(6) The provisions of the Third Schedule as applied and incorporated by this article shall have effect subject to the following modifications: —

(*a*) in section 3 (limit on powers of undertakers to take water) there shall be added at the end the words "(including any enactment passed or made before 1st April 1974)".

(*b*) the following subsection shall be added at the end of section 5 (power of undertakers to lay or erect telephone wires etc.): —

"(6) This section shall apply to any wires, posts, conductors or other apparatus laid or erected before 1st April 1974 for the purposes and in the manner specified in this section or for like purposes and in like manner as if they had been laid or erected under the powers conferred by this section."

(*c*) In subsection (1) of section 19 (power to lay mains), for paragraph (*b*) there shall be substituted the following paragraph: —

"(*b*) in, on or over any land not forming part of a street, after giving reasonable notice to every owner and occupier of that land, and with the consent of—

(i) the highway authority concerned, if the main will be laid within 220 feet of any highway; and

(ii) the electricity or gas board concerned, if the main will be laid in, on or over any land of that board being operational land within the meaning of the Town and Country Planning Act 1971(**b**)"

(*d*) In subsection (1) of section 41 (laying of communication pipes, etc.), for the proviso there shall be substituted the following proviso: —

"Provided that the undertakers may elect to lay a main in lieu of any part of a service pipe which is to be laid in a highway and in that case shall lay a communication pipe from that main and connect it with the supply pipe."

(*e*) In section 41(3), for the proviso there shall be substituted the following proviso:—

"Provided that if under the provisions of this section the undertakers lay a main in lieu of part of a service pipe the additional cost incurred of laying a main instead of that part of a service pipe shall be borne by them."

(*f*) In section 42 (power of undertakers to require separate service pipes) the following paragraph shall be added at the end of subsection (8):—
"(*d*) the owner or occupier of any of the houses has caused or knowingly permitted interference with the existing service pipe, or with any stopcock fixed thereto, in such a way as to interrupt the supply of water to any other house supplied by that pipe".

(*g*) Section 64 (penalty for waste, etc., of water by non-repair of water fittings) shall have effect as set out in the Schedule to the Local Government (Miscellaneous Provisions) Act 1953 and not as originally enacted.

(*h*) At the end of section 70 (meters, etc., to measure water or detect waste) there shall be added the following subsection:—

(2) This section shall apply to any apparatus affixed, maintained or inserted before 1st April 1974 for the purposes and in the manner specified in subsection (1) above as if it had been affixed, maintained or inserted under the powers conferred by this section."

(7) Where by virtue of this article the provisions of the Third Schedule have effect in relation to any area, references in that Schedule to statutory water undertakers shall be construed as referring only to the water authority in whose water supply area that area lies.

Adjustment of amounts raised by precept

10.—(1) In this article, unless the context otherwise requires—

(*a*) "local land drainage district" means a local land drainage district established under section 19 of, and Schedule 5 to, the 1973 Act and any part of a water authority area which is to be treated as a local land drainage district for the purposes of Parts II and III of that Schedule;

"relevant area", in relation to the council of a county or county borough, means so much of the county or county borough existing immediately before 1st April 1974 as was then comprised in the area of a river authority, and "appropriate penny rate product" in relation to the relevant area of the council of any county or county borough or part of such a relevant area means the appropriate penny rate product for that area or part calculated in accordance with the provisions of section 121 of the 1963 Act for the calculation of the appropriate penny rate product of the relevant area of any such council;

"transferee council" means the county council constituted under the 1972 Act for the county in which becomes comprised the relevant area, or part only of the relevant area, of a county or county borough existing immediately before 1st April 1974;

(b) references to a county borough and the council thereof or a transferee council shall be construed as including references respectively to a London borough and the council thereof and the City of London and the Common Council;

(c) references to sections 87 and 121 of the 1963 Act or any part of them shall be construed as references to those enactments as they had effect immediately before the repeal thereof on 1st April 1974 by the 1973 Act.

(2) It shall be the duty of a water authority, as soon as practicable after 31st March 1974, to calculate the amount by which the amount demanded by any precept for the financial year ending on that date issued under section 87 (precepts by river authorities) of the 1963 Act to the council of a county or county borough by a river authority whose area or any part of whose area becomes comprised in the water authority area exceeds, or falls short of, the amount which would have fallen to be so demanded from that council if the apportionment under subsection (3) of that section had been made, in relation to each of the councils referred to in that subsection, on the basis specified in relation to such apportionment in subsection (9) of that section; and if in any case the calculation under that subsection shows an excess, the amount of the excess shall be recoverable by the transferee council from the water authority, or, if it shows a deficiency, the amount of the deficiency shall be recoverable by the water authority from the transferee council:

Provided that where part only of the relevant area of the county or county borough becomes comprised in a water authority area the amount of the excess or deficiency, as the case may be, shall be such sum as bears to the amount of the excess or deficiency calculated in relation to the whole of the relevant area the same proportion as the product of a rate of one new penny in the pound for that part of the relevant area for the year ending on 31st March 1974 (estimated in like manner as that directed by the Secretary of State and the Minister of Agriculture, Fisheries and Food under section 121(2) of the 1963 Act for estimating the amount of the product of a rate of one new penny in the pound for the whole of the relevant area for that year) bears to the product of a rate of one new penny in the pound for the whole of the relevant area for that year estimated as aforesaid.

(3) If before 1st April 1974 a river authority shall not have made in relation to any financial year ending on a date preceding 1st April 1973 the calculation which they are required by section 87(9) of the 1963 Act to make, such calculation in relation to that financial year shall be made by the water authority in whose area becomes comprised the area, or part only of the area, of that river authority as soon as practicable after 31st March 1974; and if such calculation shows an excess, the amount of the excess shall be recoverable by the transferee council from the water authority, or, if it shows a deficiency, the amount of the deficiency shall be recoverable by the water authority from the transferee council:

Provided that where part only of the relevant area of a county or county borough becomes comprised in a water authority area the amount of the excess or deficiency, as the case may be, shall be such sum as bears to the amount of the excess or deficiency calculated in relation to the whole of the relevant area the same proportion as the product of a rate of one new penny in the pound for that part of the relevant area for that financial year (estimated in like manner as that directed by the Secretary of State and the Minister of Agriculture, Fisheries and Food under section 121(2) of the 1963 Act for estimating the amount of the product of a rate of one new penny in the pound for the whole of the relevant area for that year) bears to the product of a rate of one new penny in the pound for the whole of the relevant area for that year estimated as aforesaid.

(4) (*a*) As soon as practicable after 31st March 1974, each water authority shall ascertain the actual amount which was the aggregate amount required to be raised by precept for the year ending on that day by each river authority the whole, or part only, of the area of which becomes comprised in a local land drainage district in the water authority area, and how far, if at all, the aggregate amount for which precepts were issued by such river authority for that year exceeds or falls short of the amount ascertained under this paragraph.

(*b*) Where part only of a river authority area becomes comprised in a local land drainage district, the amount of the excess or deficiency (if any) shall, for the purposes of sub-paragraph (*c*) below, be such sum as bears to the amount of the excess or deficiency calculated in accordance with sub-paragraph (*a*) above in relation to the whole of the river authority area the same proportion as the aggregate of the appropriate penny rate products for the year ending 31st March 1974 for the relevant areas of the councils of counties or county boroughs or, where parts only of one or more such relevant areas were situated within the part of the river authority area which becomes comprised in the local land drainage district, for those parts of such relevant areas, bears to the aggregate of the appropriate penny rate products for the relevant areas of the councils of counties or county boroughs comprised in the river authority area for that year.

(*c*) If the comparison under sub-paragraph (*a*) above in relation to a river authority shows an excess or deficiency, the excess or deficiency so shown in relation to each of the river authorities whose areas become comprised in a local land drainage district and, where that local land drainage district contains a part or parts only of the area of a river authority or parts of the areas of river authorities, the excess or deficiency calculated in relation to each such part in accordance with sub-paragraph (*b*) above, shall be aggregated and, if there shall be both excesses and deficiencies, the difference between the aggregates thereof shall be ascertained and is hereinafter referred to as "the net excess" or "the net deficiency", as the case may be.

(*d*) The aggregate amount of the excesses (if there shall be no deficiencies) or the aggregate amount of the deficiencies (if there shall be no excesses) or the net excess or the net deficiency or such portion thereof as the water authority may determine was attributable to the land drainage functions of the river authority or river authorities shall be taken into account (by deduction, if an excess, or by addition, if a deficiency) by the water authority in ascertaining the aggregate amount required to be raised by precept by the water authority in respect of the local land drainage district for either of the financial years commencing on 1st April 1974 and 1st April 1975 respectively.

Transitional provisions relating to land drainage

11.—(1) In this article, "the 1930 Act" means the Land Drainage Act 1930(**a**) and "the 1961 Act" means the Land Drainage Act 1961(**b**); and, unless the context otherwise requires—

(*a*) any reference to a river authority includes a reference to the Conservators of the River Thames, the Lee Conservancy Catchment Board and the Isle of Wight River and Water Authority; and

(*b*) any reference to the area of a river authority includes a reference to the Thames catchment area, the Lee catchment area and the area of the Isle of Wight River and Water Authority.

(2) Any petition under section 11 of the 1930 Act or section 18 or section 36 of the 1961 Act made by, to or in relation to a river authority before 1st April 1974 shall as from that date be treated as having been made by, to or in relation to the water authority in whose area the land in relation to which that petition was made becomes comprised, and any such petition snall as from that date have effect as if any reference therein to a specified river authority or to the area thereof were a reference to such a water authority as aforesaid or to the area thereof.

(3) Any request made under subsection (3) of section 20 of the 1961 Act to a river authority for the submission to the Minister of Agriculture, Fisheries and Food for confirmation of a scheme under section 8 of the 1930 Act for the revocation, variation or amendment of any provisions affecting or relating to land drainage contained in any award specified in the request which is not complied with by the river authority before 1st April 1974 shall as from that date be treated as a request made to the water authority in whose area the land affected by such a scheme becomes comprised, and in relation to such a request, for the purpose of the said section 20—

(*a*) the period of six months specified in the said subsection (3) shall be calculated from the date of the making of the request to the river authority,

(*b*) the refusal of the river authority to submit the scheme shall be treated as a refusal by the water authority, and

(*c*) if a scheme different from the scheme so requested is submitted by the river authority, it shall be treated as having been submitted by the water authority.

(4) Where before 1st April 1974 the Minister of Agriculture, Fisheries and Food has, in accordance with Part I of Schedule 2 to the 1930 Act, caused notice of the intention to make any order to which the provisions of that Schedule apply to be published and sent to the councils and authorities mentioned in paragraph 1 of that Schedule, and that order has not been made before that date—

(*a*) any reference to a specified river authority in the draft order prepared for the purpose of the said Part I, and in any objection to the draft order, and in any document relating to an inquiry with respect to any objection so made, shall have effect from that date as if it were a reference to the water authority in whose area the river authority area becomes comprised or, if the river authority area becomes comprised partly in the area of one water authority and partly in the area of another water authority, as if it were a reference to the water authority in whose area becomes comprised the lands or the greater part of the land, to which the draft order, or any scheme in respect of which the order is intended to be made, refers, and

(b) in making such an order as aforesaid, the Minister may modify the draft order by substituting for references to any enactment amended or repealed by the 1972 Act or the 1973 Act references to that enactment as so amended or to any other enactment.

(5) Any application which has been made after 1st February 1974 but before 1st April 1974 to a river authority by the council of a county, county borough or county district, or by the Greater London Council or the council of a London borough, under section 34(6) of the 1961 Act for consent to the execution of drainage works, being an application to which consent is neither given nor refused before 1st April 1974, shall be treated and have effect as an application made to the water authority in whose area becomes comprised the land in which those drainage works are intended to be executed; and if the consent of the water authority is neither given nor refused during such period from 1st April 1974 as constitutes the remainder of the period of two months from the date of the making of the application to the river authority, the consent of that water authority shall be deemed to have been given—

(a) in the case of an application made by the council of a county, county borough or county district, to the council established under the 1972 Act to which the relevant functions of the council which made the application have been transferred, and

(b) in the case of an application made by the Greater London Council or a London borough council, to the council which made the application.

Port of London Authority: prevention of pollution, and fisheries matters

12.—(1) Part VI (Prevention of Pollution) of the Port of London Act 1968**(a)** (in this article referred to as "the 1968 Act") is hereby repealed.

(2) Subject to paragraph (3) below, such provisions of the 1968 Act as relate to fish shall cease to have effect in relation to salmon, trout, freshwater fish and eels, and accordingly, in section 2(1) of that Act, the following definition shall be substituted for the definition of "fish" there appearing—

" 'fish' includes shell fish and also the spawn, brood and fry of fish and shell fish, but does not include salmon, trout, freshwater fish or eels, within the meaning of the Salmon and Freshwater Fisheries Act 1923**(b)**."

(3) Any byelaws made by the Port of London Authority in force immediately before 1st April 1974 and relating to salmon, trout, freshwater fish and eels shall continue in force, and in any such byelaws, so far as they so relate, any reference to the Port of London Authority shall have effect as if it were a reference to the Thames Water Authority.

Application of certain enactments within London excluded area

13.—(1) In this article, unless the context otherwise requires—

(a) 1968 c. xxxii.   **(b)** 1923 c. 16.

"inland water" has the same meaning as in the 1963 Act;

"the London excluded area" means so much of Greater London, and of any area adjoining Greater London, as did not on 31st March 1974 lie within the Thames catchment area, the Lee catchment area or the area of any river authority;

"the Licences Regulations" means the Water Resources (Licences) Regulations 1965(**a**) as amended (**b**);

(2) In relation to any inland water which on 31st March 1974 was within the London excluded area, and to the water in or comprising any such inland water, and in relation to the water in or comprising that part of the Thames below low water mark of ordinary spring tides which lies outside that area but within the area of the Thames Water Authority upstream of the boundary between the areas of that authority and the Southern Water Authority, the provisions of the 1963 Act shall, unless the context otherwise requires, have effect as if—

(*a*) the expression "the second appointed day" meant 1st April 1975, and the definition of that expression in section 135(1) were construed accordingly;

(*b*) in section 56(5) for the words " with the coming into operation of a charging scheme prepared by that river authority under Part V of this Act" there were substituted the words "on 1st April 1976";

(*c*) for the words "the passing of this Act" wherever they occur there were substituted "1st April 1974".

(3) In relation to any such inland water, or to any such water, as is specified in paragraph (2) above, the provisions of the Licences Regulations shall, unless the context otherwise requires, have effect as if—

(*a*) in regulation 7 (application for licence of right), regulation 10 (duties of water authority in dealing with applications) and Schedule 1 (Particulars to be included in applications), any reference to the year 1965 were a reference to the year 1975;

(*b*) in regulation 10(4)(*a*), for "31st March 1966" there were substituted "31st March 1976";

(*c*) in Schedule 1, in column (1) of Table V of Model Forms 4 and 5, for "1961", "1962", "1963" and "1964" there were substituted "1971", "1972", "1973" and "1974" respectively;

(*d*) in Schedule 1, in paragraph 11(*a*) and (*b*) of Model Form 5, for "31st July 1963" there were substituted "1st April 1974".

(4) For the purposes of the levying of charges under section 30 or 31 of the 1973 Act in respect of a licence of right granted by virtue of the provisions of this article, the licence shall be treated as not having effect until 1st April 1976.

(**a**) S.I. 1965/534 (1965 I, p. 1479).   (**b**) S.I. 1965/2082 (1965 III, p. 6132).

Coquet Water Board

14.—(1) The Coquet Water Board Order 1959(a) and the Coquet Water Board Order 1963(b) (in this article referred to respectively as "the 1959 Order" and "the 1963 Order") shall have effect subject to the amendments set out in the following provisions of this article.

(2) In the 1959 Order—

(*a*) in section 2(1)—

(i) the definitions of "the borough", "the Corporation" and "the town clerk" shall be omitted;

(ii) in the definition of "the authorities", the reference to the County Council shall be omitted;

(iii) there shall be inserted the following definitions—

" 'the chief executive' means the chief executive of the Water Authority;"

" 'the Water Authority' means the Northumbrian Water Authority".

(*b*) in section 5(4) for the words from "the borough" to "are respectively" there shall be substituted "the area in which the Water Authority are";

(*c*) for section 6 there shall be substituted the following section:—

"6.—(1) The members of the Board holding office on 31st March 1974 shall cease to hold office immediately after that day.

(2) On and after 1st April 1974 the Board shall consist of seven members, of whom four shall be appointed by the Company and three by the Water Authority.

(3) Each authority shall appoint the number of members of the Board to be appointed by them pursuant to this order in accordance with the following provisions:—

(*a*) at a meeting held before 1st April 1974, they shall appoint members to hold office from that date until and including 8th June 1977;

(*b*) at a meeting held in 1977 and in every third year thereafter before 8th June in that year, they shall appoint members to hold office from 9th June in that year for a period of three years;

Provided that if any authority fail to appoint a member within the time herein prescribed, the Minister may, on the application of the authority concerned, extend the time for making the appointment.

(4) Immediately after the appointment of any member of the Board—

(a) S.I. 1959/940.   (b) S.I. 1963/743.

(*a*) in the case of members appointed by the Company, the secretary of the Company, and

(*b*) in the case of members appointed by the Water Authority, the chief executive

shall notify the name, address and description of the member appointed to the clerk of the Board.

(5) Any casual vacancy in the membership of the Board shall be filled as soon as practicable by the appointment by the authority in whose representation the vacancy arises of a new member, and the person so appointed shall come into office upon his appointment and shall, if otherwise qualified, hold office during the remainder of the term of office of the person in whose place he is appointed:

Provided that it shall not be obligatory upon an authority to fill any casual vacancy arising between 1st April and 9th June in the year 1977 or in any third year thereafter."

(*d*) in section 7(1), for paragraph (*a*) there shall be substituted the following paragraph—

"(*a*) A person shall not be qualified to be appointed a member of the Board by the Water Authority unless he is a member of that authority."

(*e*) in the proviso to section 7(2), for the words "the council of the borough or of the County Council" there shall be substituted "the Water Authority"; and for the words "re-elected a member of such council" there shall be substituted "reappointed a member of the Water Authority."

(*f*) in the proviso to section 8(2), the words from "or, if the Clerk" to the end shall be omitted;

(*g*) in section 22, subsection (3) and the proviso to subsection (7) shall be omitted;

(*h*) in section 24(4), the words from "and, in the case" to "the Company" shall be omitted;

(*i*) in section 24(5)(*a*), the words from "and in the case" to "the Company" shall be omitted;

(*j*) in section 24(6)—
   (i) in paragraph (*c*) the words "and the County Council," and
   (ii) in paragraph (*e*)(iii) the words "the County Council" shall be omitted;

(*k*) section 28 shall be omitted;

(*l*) in section 36(2), the words "or the County Council" shall be omitted;

(*m*) in section 42(1), for the words from "the County Council" to "such council" there shall be substituted "the Water Authority authorised by that authority".

(*n*) paragraph 1 of Schedule 2 shall be omitted;

(*o*) Schedules 4 and 5 shall be omitted;

(*p*) throughout the order, for "the Corporation" there shall be substituted "the Water Authority".

(3) In the 1963 Order—

(*a*) in section 6, all references to the County Council shall be omitted;

(*b*) throughout the order, for "the Corporation" there shall be substituted "the Water Authority".

Extension of certain local statutory provisions

15.—(1) The provisions of the Llanelli and District Water Board Orders 1961 to 1971, in so far as those provisions are continued in force on and after 1st April 1974 by virtue of paragraph 11 of Schedule 6 to the 1973 Act, and except in so far as any such provision is expressly restricted so as to apply only to a specified area, thing or person (other than the area of the Llanelli and District Water Board), shall be extended and shall be in force in that part of the area of the Welsh National Water Development Authority which immediately before the said date comprised the limits of supply of the water undertakings of Llandovery Corporation, Cwmamman Urban District Council, Llandeilo Urban District Council, Carmarthen Rural District Council and Llandeilo Rural District Council.

(2) The provisions of the Bucks Water Acts and Orders 1937 to 1973, in so far as those provisions are continued in force on and after 1st April 1974 by virtue of the said paragraph 11, and except in so far as any such provision is expressly restricted so as to apply only to a specified area, thing or person (other than the area of the Bucks Water Board), shall be extended and shall be in force in that part of the area of the Anglian Water Authority which immediately before the said date comprised the limits of supply of Buckingham Corporation.

Savings, etc.

16.—(1) Notwithstanding anything in Schedule 9 to the 1973 Act—

(*a*) subsection (8) of section 35 (sewers and sewage disposal works) of the London Government Act 1963(**a**) shall continue in force, and that subsection, as so saved, shall have effect as if any reference to the Greater London Council included a reference to the Thames Water Authority; and the expression "reconvey" and "the two councils" shall be construed accordingly.

_____

(**a**) 1963 c. 33.

(*b*) in Schedule 13 to the 1963 Act, paragraphs 2 to 5, 7, 8, 10, 11, 14 to 16 and 23 shall continue in force.

(2) Any mains, pipes, or other works transferred to statutory water undertakers by virtue of an order under the 1973 Act shall be deemed to have been laid or constructed by those undertakers.

28th March 1974.
                              Anthony Crosland,
                Secretary of State for the Environment.

28th March 1974.
                              John Morris,
                Secretary of State for Wales.

EXPLANATORY NOTE

(This Note is not part of the Order.)

This Order, which applies to England and Wales, makes certain incidental, consequential, transitional and supplementary provisions for the purposes of the Water Act 1973 and for giving full effect to that Act.

Provision is made in Articles 4 to 7 for the completion and submission of annual reports and accounts of bodies abolished by the Act of 1973.

Articles 8 and 9 continue or modify the application of the Third Schedule to the Water Act 1945 in relation to the areas specified in those articles.

Article 10 adjusts certain amounts raised by precept for land drainage purposes, and Article 11 makes transitional provisions concering petitions, applications and other proceedings relating to land drainage matters.

Article 12 amends and partially repeals the Port of London Authority Act 1968, with a saving for certain byelaws relating to fish.

Article 13 makes supplementary provision with respect to the application to "the London excluded area" (as defined in the Article) of the provisions of the Water Resources Act 1963 relating to the licensing of abstraction of surface water.

Articles 14 and 15 provide for the modification and extension of local statutory provisions relating to the Coquet Water Board, the Llanelli and District Water Board, and the Bucks Water Board.

Article 16 effects savings from certain repeals enacted by the Water Act 1973 and makes provision concerning certain works transferred under that Act.

STATUTORY INSTRUMENTS

1974 No. 608

CUSTOMS AND EXCISE
The Import Duties (General) (No. 2) Order 1974

Made - - - -	*28th March* 1974
Laid before the House of Commons	*29th March* 1974
Coming into Operation	*1st April* 1974

The Lords Commissioners of Her Majesty's Treasury, by virtue of the powers conferred on them by sections 1, 2, 3(6) and 13 of the Import Duties Act 1958**(a)**, as amended **(b)**, and of all other powers enabling them in that behalf, on the recommendation of the Secretary of State **(c)**, hereby make the following Order:—

1.—(1) This Order may be cited as the Import Duties (General) (No. 2) Order 1974, and shall come into operation on 1st April 1974.

(2) The Interpretation Act 1889**(d)** shall apply for the interpretation of this Order as it applies for the interpretation of an Act of Parliament.

(3) This Order does not increase duties of customs otherwise than in pursuance of a Community obligation.

2. The Import Duties (General) (No. 8) Order 1973**(e)**, as amended **(f)**, shall have effect as if, in Schedule 1 thereto, the rates of duty, if any, in columns 3, 4 and 5 of the subheadings of headings 01.02, 02.01, 02.06, 15.02 and 16.02 specified in the Schedule to this Order (being subheadings relating to bovine animals and beef and veal products) were replaced by the rates of duty shown in the said Schedule hereto.

John Golding,
Donald R. Coleman,
Two of the Lords Commissioners
of Her Majesty's Treasury.

28th March 1974.

(a) 1958 c. 6.
(b) *See* section 5(5) of and paragraph 1 of Schedule 4 to the European Communities Act 1972 (c. 68).
(c) *See* S.I. 1970/1537 (1970 III, p. 5293).   (d) 1889 c. 63.
(e) S.I. 1973/1845 (1973 III, p. 5601).
(f) The amending Orders are not relevant to the subject matter of this Order.

SCHEDULE

RATES OF DUTY FROM 1ST APRIL 1974 ON PRODUCTS COVERED
BY THE EUROPEAN ECONOMIC COMMUNITY'S COMMON ORGANIZATION
OF THE MARKET IN BEEF AND VEAL

		3		4		5
01.02 (Live animals of the bovine species)						
01.02 A.II.a)	F	6·4%	M	—	C.1	6·4%
	S	—	E	6·4%	C.2	—
01.02 A.II.b)1.	F	5·2%	M	—	C.1	5·2%
	S	—	E	5·2%	C.2	—
01.02 A.II.b)2.aa)	F	6·4%	M	—	C.1	6·4%
	S	—	E	6·4%	C.2	—
01.02 A.II.b)2.bb)	F	6·4%	M	—	C.1	6·4%
	S	—	E	6·4%	C.2	—
02.01 (Meat and edible offals, fresh chilled or frozen)						
02.01 A.II.a)1.aa)11	F	£0.1866 per cwt. plus 8%	M⎫ D⎭	£0·1866 per cwt.	C.1	8%
	S	£0·3110 per cwt.	E	£0·1866 per cwt. plus 8%	C.2	—
02.01 A.II.a)1.aa)22	F	£0·1866 per cwt. plus 8%	M⎫ D⎭	£0·1866 per cwt.	C.1	8%
	S	£0·3110 per cwt.	E	£0·1866 per cwt. plus 8%	C.2	—
02.01 A.II.a)1.aa)33	F	£0·1866 per cwt. plus 8%	M⎫ D⎭	£0·1866 per cwt.	C.1	8%
	S	£0·3110 per cwt.	E	£0·1866 per cwt. plus 8%	C.2	—
02.01 A.II.a)1.bb)11.aaa)	F	£0·1866 per cwt. plus 8%	M⎫ D⎭	£0·1866 per cwt.	C.1	8%
	S	£0·3110 per cwt.	E	£0·1866 per cwt. plus 8%	C.2	—
02.01 A.II.a)1.bb)11.bbb)	F	£0·1866 per cwt. plus 8%	M⎫ D⎭	£0·1866 per cwt.	C.1	8%
	S	£0·3110 per cwt.	E	£0·1866 per cwt. plus 8%	C.2	—
02.01 A.II.a)1.bb)22.aaa)	F	£0·1866 per cwt. plus 8%	M⎫ D⎭	£0·1866 per cwt.	C.1	8%
	S	£0·3110 per cwt.	E	£0·1866 per cwt. plus 8%	C.2	—
02.01 A.II.a)1.bb)22.bbb)	F	£0·1866 per cwt. plus 8%	M⎫ D⎭	£0·1866 per cwt.	C.1	8%
	S	£0·3110 per cwt.	E	£0·1866 per cwt. plus 8%	C.2	—
02.01 A.II.a)1.bb)33.aaa)	F	£0·1866 per cwt. plus 8%	M⎫ D⎭	£0·1866 per cwt.	C.1	8%
	S	£0·3110 per cwt.	E	£0·1866 per cwt. plus 8%	C.2	—
02.01 A.II.a)1.bb)33.bbb)	F	£0·1866 per cwt. plus 8%	M⎫ D⎭	£0·1866 per cwt.	C.1	8%
	S	£0·3110 per cwt.	E	£0·1866 per cwt. plus 8%	C.2	—
02.01 A.II.a)1.cc)11.	F	£0·1866 per cwt. plus 8%	M⎫ D⎭	£0·1866 per cwt.	C.1	8%
	S	£0·3110 per cwt.	E	£0·1866 per cwt. plus 8%	C.2	—
02.01 A.II.a)1.cc)22	F	11%	M⎫ D⎭	3%	C.1	8%
	S	5%	E	11%	C.2	—
02.01 A.II.a)2.aa)	F	£0·1866 per cwt. plus 8%	M⎫ D⎭	£0·1866 per cwt.	C.1	8%
	S	£0·3110 per cwt.	E	£0·1866 per cwt. plus 8%	C.2	—

		3		4	5	
02.01 A.II.a)2.bb)	F	£0·1866 per cwt. plus 8%	M D	£0·1866 per cwt.	C.1	8%
	S	£0·3110 per cwt.	E	£0·1866 per cwt. plus 8%	C.2	—
02.01 A.II.a)2.cc)	F	£0·1866 per cwt. plus 8%	M D	£0·1866 per cwt.	C.1	8%
	S	£0·3110 per cwt.	E	£0·1866 per cwt. plus 8%	C.2	—
02.01 A.II.a)2.dd)11	F	£0·1866 per cwt. plus 8%	M D	£0·1866 per cwt.	C.1	8%
	S	£0·3110 per cwt.	E	£0·1866 per cwt. plus 8%	C.2	—
02.01 A.II.a)2.dd)22.aaa)	F	11%	M D	3%	C.1	8%
	S	5%	E	11%	C.2	—
02.01 A.II.a)2.dd)22.bbb)	F	11%	M D	3%	C.1	8%
	S	5%	E	11%	C.2	—
02.01 A.II.a)2.dd)22.ccc)	F	11%	M D	3%	C.1	8%
	S	5%	E	11%	C.2	—
02.01 B.II.b)1	F	11·6%	M D	6%	C.1	5·6%
	S	10%	E	11·6%	C.2	—
02.01 B.II.b)2.aa)	F	4·8%	M	—	C.1	4·8%
	S	—	E	4·8%	C.2	—
02.01 B.II.b)2.bb)	F	10·8%	M D	6%	C.1	4·8%
	S	10%	E	10·8%	C.2	—
02.06 (Meat and edible meat offals, salted in brine, dried or smoked) 02.06 C.I.a)1	F	£0·1866 per cwt. plus 9·6%	M D	£0·1866 per cwt.	C.1	9·6%
	S	£0·3110 per cwt.	E	£0·1866 per cwt. plus 9·6%	C.2	—
02.06 C.I.a)2	F	21·6%	M D	12%	C.1	9·6%
	S	20%	E	21·6%	C.2	—
02.06 C.I.b)1	F	9·6%	M	—	C.1	9·6%
	S	—	E	9·6%	C.2	—
02.06 C.I.b)2	F	21·6%	M D	12%	C.1	9·6%
	S	20%	E	21·6%	C.2	—
15.02 (Fats of bovine cattle) 15.02 B.I		8·8%	M D	6%	C.1	2·8%
			E	8·8%	C.2	—
16.02 (Other prepared or preserved meat or meat offal) 16.02 B.III.b)1.aa)11	F	19·4%	M	9%	C.1	10·4%
	S	15%	E	10·4%	C.2	—
16.02 B.III.b)1.aa)22	F	19·4%	M D	9%	C.1	10·4%
	S	15%	E	19·4%	C.2	—
16.02 B.III.b)1.bb)11.aaa)	F	19·4%	M D	9%	C.1	10·4%
	S	15%	E	19·4%	C.2	—
16.02 B.III.b)1.bb)11.bbb)	F	16·4%	M D	6%	C.1	10·4%
	S	10%	E	16·4%	C.2	—
16.02 B.III.b)1.bb)22	F	19·4%	M D	9%	C.1	10·4%
	S	15%	E	19·4%	C.2	—

EXPLANATORY NOTE

(This Note is not part of the Order.)

This Order, which comes into operation on 1st April 1974, further amends the Import Duties (General) (No. 8) Order 1973, which sets out the United Kingdom Customs Tariff and the protective import duties chargeable in accordance with it.

The Order (Article 2 and the Schedule) provides for changes in duty on products covered by the European Economic Community's common organisation of the market in beef and veal in accordance with Articles 59(1)(a) and 59(2) of the Act of Accession with effect from the beginning of the marketing year for those products.

STATUTORY INSTRUMENTS

1974 No. 609

NATIONAL HEALTH SERVICE, ENGLAND AND WALES

The National Health Service (Charges for Appliances) (Amendment) Regulations 1974

Made - - -	*29th March* 1974
Laid before Parliament	*29th March* 1974
Coming into Operation	*1st April* 1974

The Secretary of State for Social Services in exercise of the powers conferred by section 3(2) of the National Health Service Act 1946(a) (as amended by section 39(1) of the Health Services and Public Health Act 1968(b) and by section 57(1) of and paragraph 12(1) of Schedule 4 to the National Health Service Reorganisation Act 1973(c)) and now vested in her (d), and of all other powers enabling her in that behalf, hereby makes the following regulations:—

Citation, commencement and interpretation

1.—(1) These regulations may be cited as the National Health Service (Charges for Appliances) (Amendment) Regulations 1974, and shall come into operation on 1st April 1974.

(2) The rules for the construction of Acts of Parliament contained in the Interpretation Act 1889(e) shall apply for the purposes of the interpretation of these regulations as they apply for the purposes of the interpretation of an Act of Parliament.

Amendments to regulations

2. In regulation 6(1) of the National Health Service (Charges for Appliances) Regulations 1974(f) after the words "when it occurred, then" there shall be inserted—

"unless the person supplied is a person for whom medical inspection or treatment is provided under or by virtue of the provisions of section 3 of the National Health Service Reorganisation Act 1973 and in respect of whom evidence to that effect is produced to the Secretary of State or the Authority as the case may require—"

Barbara Castle,
Secretary of State for Social Services.

29th March 1974.

(a) 1946 c. 81.　　　　(b) 1968 c. 46.　　　　(c) 1973 c. 32.
(d) *See* Secretary of State for Social Services Order 1968 (S.I. 1968/1699 (1968 III, p. 4585)) Article 2.
(e) 1889 c. 63.　　　　(f) S.I. 1974/284 (1974 I, p. 977).

EXPLANATORY NOTE

(This Note is not part of the Regulations.)

These Regulations amend the National Health Service (Charges for Appliances) Regulations 1974. They provide that pupils attending maintained schools or certain other educational establishments or being educated under special arrangements do not have to pay charges for the replacement or repair of appliances supplied to them by the Secretary of State or a Health Authority.

STATUTORY INSTRUMENTS

1974 No. 610

CUSTOMS AND EXCISE

The Customs Duties (Quota Relief) (No. 2) Order 1974

Made	- - -	28th March 1974
Laid before the House of Commons		29th March 1974
Coming into Operation		1st April 1974

The Secretary of State, in exercise of the powers conferred on him by section 5(1) and (4) of, and paragraph 8 of Schedule 3 to, the Import Duties Act 1958(a), as amended (b), and of all other powers enabling him in that behalf, hereby makes the following Order:

1.—(1) This Order may be cited as the Customs Duties (Quota Relief) (No. 2) Order 1974 and shall come into operation on 1st April 1974.

(2) The Interpretation Act 1889(c) shall apply for the interpretation of this Order as it applies for the interpretation of an Act of Parliament.

2.—(1) This Article applies to goods of the following description, namely, fermentation ethyl alcohol or fermentation neutral spirits undenatured, of a strength of 140° proof or higher, not warehoused or warehoused less than three years.

(2) Subject to Article 3 below, up to and including 31st December 1974, any duty of customs for the time being chargeable on goods of subheading 22.08B II of the Customs Tariff 1959 shall be reduced by £0·0750 per proof gallon in the case of a quota consisting of 3,344,000 proof gallons of goods to which this Article applies which satisfy the requisite conditions to benefit from Regulation (EEC) 385/73(d) (relating to goods entitled to benefit from the eventual abolition of customs duties in trade between the United Kingdom and other Member States of the European Economic Community).

3.—(1) Goods shall be treated as forming part of the quota referred to in Article 2(2) above only if they are certified by the Secretary of State as forming part of the quota and any conditions attaching to the certificate issued in respect of the goods are complied with.

(2) Any certificate to the effect that goods form part of the quota may be modified or revoked at any time.

S. Clinton Davis,
Parliamentary Under-Secretary of State
for Companies, Aerospace and Shipping,
Department of Trade.

28th March 1974.

(a) 1958 c.6. (b) *See* section 5(5) of, and paragraph 1 of Schedule 4 to, the European Communities Act 1972 (c.68).

(c) 1889 c.63. (d) O.J. No. L.42. 14.2. 1973. p.1.

EXPLANATORY NOTE

(This Note is not part of the Order.)

This Order, which comes into operation on 1st April 1974, provides for the opening and administration of a tariff quota of 3,344,000 proof gallons of certain fermentation ethyl alcohol and other spirits imported into the United Kingdom from other Member States of the European Economic Community.

The Order specifies the reduced rates of customs duty applicable up to and including 31st December 1974 to imports of the relevant goods within the quota.

The Order also provides that any relevant goods shall be treated as forming part of the quota if they are certified to that effect by the Secretary of State.

STATUTORY INSTRUMENTS

1974 No. 611

CUSTOMS AND EXCISE

The Import Duties (Quota Relief) (No. 2) Order 1974

Made - - -	*29th March* 1974
Laid before the House of Commons	*29th March* 1974
Coming into Operation	*30th March* 1974

The Secretary of State, in exercise of the powers conferred on him by section 5(1) and (4) of, and paragraph 8 of Schedule 3 to, the Import Duties Act 1958(**a**), as amended (**b**), and of all other powers enabling him in that behalf, hereby makes the following Order:—

1.—(1) This Order may be cited as the Import Duties (Quota Relief) (No. 2) Order 1974 and shall come into operation on 30th March 1974.

(2) The Interpretation Act 1889(**c**) shall apply for the interpretation of this Order as it applies for the interpretation of an Act of Parliament.

2. This Order applies to goods falling within subheading 15.12 B IIIa) (certain fats and oils wholly obtained from fish or marine mammals) of the Customs Tariff 1959 other than sperm oil.

3.—(1) Up to and including 31st December 1974 any import duty for the time being chargeable on goods to which this Order applies up to a quantity of 10,000 tonnes (hereinafter referred to as "the quota") shall be reduced to the following rates:—

(*a*) to 10% in the case of goods subject to the full rate and

(*b*) to 4% in the case of goods qualifying for commonwealth preference or goods of Austria, Finland, Iceland, Norway, Portugal, Sweden or Switzerland.

(2) Goods shall be treated as forming part of the quota in the order in wh'ch they are entered for home use (within the meaning of the Customs and Excise Act 1952(**d**)) in the United Kingdom on or after the date of coming into operation of this Order.

4. Up to and including 31st December 1974 any import duty for the time being chargeable on goods to which this Order applies shall be reduced to 4% if the goods satisfy the requisite conditions to benefit from Regulation (EEC) 385/73(**e**) (relating to goods entitled to benefit from the eventual abolition of customs duties in trade between the United Kingdom and the other member States of the Communities).

(**a**) 1958 c. 6.
(**b**) *See* paragraph 1 of Schedule 4 to the European Communities Act 1972 (c.68).
(**c**) 1889 c. 63.   (**d**) 1952 c. 44.
(**e**) O.J. No. L 42, 14.2.73, p. 1.

S. Clinton Davis,

Parliamentary Under-Secretary of State
for Companies, Aerospace and Shipping,
29th March 1974. Department of Trade.

EXPLANATORY NOTE

(This Note is not part of the Order.)

This Order, which comes into operation on 30th March 1974, provides for the implementation and administration of a tariff quota for certain fats and oils of fish or marine mammals (specified in Article 2).

The Order provides for reduced rates of duty (specified in Article 3(1)) applicable up to and including 31st December 1974 to imports of the relevant goods within a quota of 10,000 tonnes and that any goods constitute part of the quota as soon as they are entered with Customs for home use. The Order (Article 4) also provides that up to and including 31st December 1974 a duty of 4% shall be applied on goods satisfying the requisite conditions to benefit from the eventual abolition of Customs duties between the United Kingdom and other member States of the Communities.

STATUTORY INSTRUMENTS

1974 No. 612 (S.53)

LOCAL GOVERNMENT, SCOTLAND

The Rate Support Grant (Scotland) Order 1974

Made - - - -	18*th March* 1974
Laid before the Commons House of Parliament	19*th March* 1974
Coming into Operation	27*th March* 1974

In exercise of the powers conferred on me by section 9(5) of the Local Government (Financial Provisions) (Scotland) Act 1963(a) as amended by section 13(*b*) of the Local Government (Scotland) Act 1966(b) (hereinafter referred to as "the Act"), section 2(4) of the Act and section 3 of the Act as amended by section 120(1)(*a*) of the Local Government (Scotland) Act 1973(c), paragraphs 1 and 3 of Part I of Schedule 1 to the Act, paragraph 4(2) of Part II of Schedule 1 to the Act and paragraph 1 of Part III of Schedule 1 to the Act, and of all other powers enabling me in that behalf, with the consent of the Treasury and after consultation with such associations of local authorities as appear to me to be concerned in accordance with the provisions of section 3 of the Act, I hereby make the following order:—

1. This order may be cited as the Rate Support Grant (Scotland) Order 1974 and shall come into operation on the day following the day on which it is approved by a resolution of the Commons House of Parliament.

2. The Interpretation Act 1889(d) shall apply for the interpretation of this order as it applies for the interpretation of an Act of Parliament.

3. For the purposes of rate support grants for the year 1974-75 I hereby fix and prescribe:

Aggregate grants

(1) As the aggregate amount of the rate support grants and the amounts of the needs element, the resources element and the domestic element, the amounts set out in the following table:—

	£
Aggregate amount of rate support grants comprising—	412,020,000
the needs element	289,780,000
the resources element	96,600,000
the domestic element	25,640,000

(a) 1963 c. 12.	(b) 1966 c. 51.
(c) 1973 c. 65.	(d) 1889 c. 63.

3p

Domestic rate reduction

(2) Under paragraph 1 of Part III of Schedule 1 to the Act and for the purposes of the reduction to be made under section 7(1) of the Act, as the amount in the pound which in my opinion corresponds to the amount of the domestic element for the year—17p;

Apportionment of needs element

(3) Under paragraph 3 of Part I of Schedule 1 to the Act, that such part of the needs element (hereinafter referred to as the "roads portion") for the year as is represented by the proportion which eight-ninths of all reckonable expenditure on roads bears to total reckonable expenditure less all specific grants shall be distributed among the classes of local authorities and on the basis set out in Schedule 1 to this order;

(4) Under paragraph 1 of Part I of Schedule 1 to the Act that the needs element as reduced by the roads portion shall first be apportioned to all counties and those burghs which are counties of cities in proportion to their weighted populations determined as provided in Schedule 2 to this order; and the sums so apportioned shall, subject to adjustment in accordance with paragraph 5 of the said Part I be further apportioned in accordance with paragraph 2 of the said Part I;

Weighted population for resources element

(5) For the purposes of Part II of Schedule 1 to the Act and in particular the calculation of the standard penny rate product for an area, that the weighted population of the area for the year shall be determined as provided in Schedule 3 to this order;

Notional rent income

(6)(a) Under paragraph 4(2) of Part II of Schedule 1 to the Act, that the notional rent income of a county or town council for the year shall be such percentage of the aggregate of the gross annual values of the relevant subjects, as shown in the valuation roll for the year, as is specified in column (1) of Schedule 4 to this order:

Provided that, if I am requested by any council to do so, I shall direct that, in relation to that council this sub-paragraph shall have effect as if references therein to the council's notional rent income for the year were references to such percentage of the aggregate of the gross annual values of the relevant subjects, as shown in the valuation roll for the year, as is specified in column (2) of the said Schedule, less an amount equal to the aggregate of any rent rebates granted in respect of those subjects by the council for the year under a rebates scheme;

(b) in this paragraph—

    (i) references to the relevant subjects, in relation to any council, are references to any house, buildings, land or dwellings let by the council and shown in the valuation roll for the year;

    (ii) references to the aggregate of the gross annual values of the relevant subjects, in relation to any council, are references to that aggregate exclusive of such part of the gross annual value of any house or dwelling comprised in those subjects as may be certified by the assessor to be attributable to any garage provided otherwise than by the council;

(iii) the expression "rebates scheme" means a scheme for the granting of rebates to which Part II of and Schedules 2 and 3 to the Housing (Financial Provisions) (Scotland) Act 1972(a) applies;

(iv) the expression "valuation roll" does not include "supplementary valuation roll".

William Ross,
One of Her Majesty's Principal
Secretaries of State.

St Andrew's House,
Edinburgh.
14th March 1974.

We consent.

James A. Dunn,
T. Pendry,

Two of the Lords Commissioners
of Her Majesty's Treasury.

18th March 1974.

(a) 1972 c. 46.

Article 3(3) **SCHEDULE 1**

DISTRIBUTION OF ROADS PORTION OF NEEDS ELEMENT

1. The roads portion of the needs element, as determined under article 3(3) of this order, shall be divided into 6 equal parts which shall be apportioned to a county share and a large burgh share as follows:—

 (a) 5 parts shall be apportioned in proportion to classified road mileage of all county councils and large burghs; and

 (b) one part shall be apportioned in proportion to the number of thousands in the population of all counties and large burghs.

2. The county share determined in accordance with paragraph 1 of this Schedule shall be apportioned to individual counties in proportion to their adjusted classified road mileage.

For the purpose of this paragraph the adjusted classified road mileage shall be, where the proportion that the total population bears to the number of miles of classified roads is as specified in any line in column (1) of the Table annexed to this Schedule, the number which is derived from applying the percentage specified in the same line in column (2) of that Table to the number of miles of classified roads.

3. The amounts apportioned to individual counties in accordance with paragraph 2 of this Schedule shall be further apportioned among the landward area, or in the case of a combined county the landward areas of the county, and the small burghs in the county in accordance with paragraph 2 of Part I of Schedule 1 to the Act.

4. The large burgh share determined in accordance with paragraph 1 of this Schedule shall be divided into 4 equal parts which shall be further apportioned to individual large burghs as follows:—

 (a) one part shall be apportioned in proportion to classified road mileage;

 (b) one part shall be apportioned in proportion to principal road mileage; and

 (c) two parts shall be apportioned in proportion to population.

5. For the purpose of this Schedule:—

 (a) the population of any county or large burgh shall be calculated by reference to estimates of the Registrar General of Births, Deaths and Marriages in Scotland relating to the 30th day of June in the year immediately preceding the grant year;

 (b) the mileage of classified roads in any county or large burgh shall be calculated by reference to estimates of the Secretary ofState relating to the 16th day of May in the year immediately preceding the grant year; and

 (c) the mileage of principal roads in any county or large burgh shall be calculated by reference to estimates of the Secretary of State relating to the 16th day of May in the year immediately preceding the grant year.

6. In this Schedule:—

 (a) "county" means a county or, in relation to counties combined for the purposes mentioned in section 118(1) of the Local Government (Scotland) Act 1947(a) the combined county, inclusive of any small burgh situated therein;

 (b) "large burgh" has the meaning assigned to it in section 379(1) of the Local Government (Scotland) Act 1947;

 (c) "grant year" in relation to the roads portion of the needs element of rate support grants means the year for which the grants are payable;

 (d) "classified roads" means roads classified within the meaning of section 28(2) of the Act; and

 (e) "principal roads" means roads designated as principal roads within the meaning of section 28(2) of the Act.

(a) 1947 c. 43.

TABLE

PROPORTION OF TOTAL POPULATION TO MILES OF CLASSIFIED ROAD

Column (1)	*Percentage* *Column* (2)
100 to 1 and over	100·00
Under 100 to 1 and not under 85 to 1	110·00
Under 85 to 1 and not under 70 to 1	112·50
Under 70 to 1 and not under 55 to 1	125·00
Under 55 to 1	133·33

SCHEDULE 2   Article 3(4)

DETERMINATION OF WEIGHTED POPULATION FOR APPORTIONMENT OF
NEEDS ELEMENT

1. The weighted population of a county or a burgh, being a county of a city, shall be the sum of the following, calculated by the Secretary of State in relation to the county or burgh, that is to say:—

(a) the total population;

(b) twice the number of children under 15 years of age in excess of 27 per cent of the total population;

(c) twice the number of persons over 65 years of age in excess of 14 per cent of the total population;

(d) the number of education units which shall be the sum of the following:—

(i) the sum of the products of the number of pupils in each of the categories in column (1) of Table 1 annexed to this Schedule and the number specified in the same line in column (2) of that Table; and

(ii) the number formed by multiplying by 6 the number of thousands of midday meals produced by the education authority during the year ending one year before the start of the grant year;

(e) where an increase of population during the 5 years immediately preceding the year in question exceeds 5 per cent of the population in the first year of that period of 5 years, or where a decrease of population during the 5 years immediately preceding the year in question exceeds 8 per cent of the population in the first year of that period of 5 years, twice the number of persons by which the net increase or decrease of the population during the period 10 years immediately preceding the year in question exceeds 5 per cent of the population in the first year of that period of 10 years;

(f) where the proportion which the total population bears to the number of miles of roads is as specified in any line in column (1) of Table 2 annexed to this Schedule, the number which is derived from applying the percentage specified in the same line in column (2) of that Table to the sum of the figures calculated in accordance with sub-paragraphs (a) to (e) of this paragraph; and

(g) in the case of a county, where the proportion which the population of the landward area or, in the case of a combined county, the landward areas, bears to the total population is as specified in any line in column (1) of Table 3 annexed to this Schedule, the number which is derived from applying the percentage specified in the same line in column (2) of that Table to the sum of the figures calculated in accordance with sub-paragraphs (a) to (f) of this paragraph.

2. For the purposes of this Schedule:—

(a) the total population of any county or burgh, the number of children under 15 years of age and the number of persons over 65 years of age in any such population and the population of the landward area or areas of any county shall be calculated by reference to estimates of the Registrar General of Births, Deaths and Marriages in Scotland relating to the 30th day of June in the year immediately preceding the grant year;

(b) the number of primary pupils or secondary pupils shall be the number of pupils who are receiving primary education or secondary education respectively within the meaning of the Education (Scotland) Act 1962(a) in public schools or under special arrangements made by the education authority under section 14 of that Act and who are not attending special schools;

(c) the number of special school pupils shall be the number of pupils attending special schools under the management of the education authority;

(d) the number of pupils in the various categories shall be calculated by reference to certificates of the education authority relating to the year ending on the 31st day of July in the year immediately preceding the grant year; and

(e) the number of miles of roads shall be calculated by reference to estimates of the Secretary of State relating to the 16th day of May in the year immediately preceding the grant year.

3. In this Schedule:—

(a) "county" means a county or, in relation to counties combined for the purposes mentioned in section 118(1) of the Local Government (Scotland) Act 1947 the combined county, inclusive of any burgh situated therein, other than a burgh which is a county of a city;

(b) "grant year" in relation to the needs element of rate support grants means the year for which the grants are payable;

(c) "public school" and "special school" have the respective meanings assigned to them in the Education (Scotland) Act 1962; and

(d) "roads" means roads maintained and managed by the Secretary of State or by a local authority, and includes any sea route between two places in a county which the Secretary of State has determined under section 6(2) of the Act is to be treated as if it were a road in the county.

TABLE 1

Category Column (1)	Weighting Column (2)
Primary pupil	6·0
Secondary pupil under age 16	13·8
age 16 and over	20·7
Special school pupil	16·5

TABLE 2
PROPORTION OF TOTAL POPULATION TO MILES OF ROADS

Column (1)	Percentage Column (2)
Under 19 to 1	60·0
Under 24 to 1 and not under 19 to 1	52·5
Under 32 to 1 and not under 24 to 1	40·0
Under 42 to 1 and not under 32 to 1	32·5
Under 44 to 1 and not under 42 to 1	25·0
Under 46 to 1 and not under 44 to 1	19·0
Under 48 to 1 and not under 46 to 1	15·0
Under 50 to 1 and not under 48 to 1	13·0
Under 52 to 1 and not under 50 to 1	11·5
Under 54 to 1 and not under 52 to 1	10·0
Under 56 to 1 and not under 54 to 1	8·5
Under 58 to 1 and not under 56 to 1	7·0
Under 60 to 1 and not under 58 to 1	6·0
Under 62 to 1 and not under 60 to 1	5·0
Under 64 to 1 and not under 62 to 1	4·0
Under 66 to 1 and not under 64 to 1	3·0
Under 68 to 1 and not under 66 to 1	2·0
Under 70 to 1 and not under 68 to 1	1·0
70 to 1 and over	Nil

(a) 1962 c. 47.

TABLE 3

PROPORTION OF POPULATION IN LANDWARD AREA OF COUNTY TO TOTAL POPULATION

Column (1)	Percentage Column (2)
90 per cent and over	60
Under 90 per cent and not under 82·5 per cent	40
Under 82·5 per cent and not under 72·5 per cent	25
Under 72·5 per cent and not under 52·5 per cent	5
Under 52·5 per cent	Nil

SCHEDULE 3 Article 3(5)

RESOURCES ELEMENT—WEIGHTED POPULATION FOR DETERMINING STANDARD PENNY RATE PRODUCT

1. The weighted population of an area for the year shall be the population thereof plus, if applicable in accordance with this Schedule, the variation weighting for the area.

Variation Weighting

2. For the purposes of paragraph 1 of this Schedule the variation weighting for an area which is a large burgh shall be the number of persons by which the increase or decrease (if any) of the population of the burgh during the period of 5 years immediately preceding the year in question exceeds one-twentieth of the population of the burgh in the first year of that period of 5 years.

3.—(1) For the purposes of paragraph 1 of this Schedule the variation weighting for an area which is a small burgh or the landward area of a county shall be such number as bears to the number ascertained under sub-paragraph (2) of this paragraph the same proportion as the population of the area bears to the population of the county.

(2) The number to be ascertained under this sub-paragraph is the number of persons by which the increase or decrease (if any) of the population of the county during the period of 5 years immediately preceding the year in question exceeds one-twentieth of the population of the county in the first year of that period of 5 years.

Population

4.—(1) The population of any area shall be calculated by reference to estimates of the Registrar General of Births, Deaths and Marriages in Scotland relating to the 30th day of June in the year in respect of which the payment of resources element is made; and, in the case of the variation weighting to estimates of the Registrar General of Births, Deaths and Marriages in Scotland relating to the 30th day of June next after the first and last days respectively of the period of 5 years in question.

(2) In the computation of the population of any area for the purpose of ascertaining the variation weighting for the area under this Schedule no account shall be taken of any members of the armed forces of the Crown, within the meaning of the Crown Proceedings Act 1947(a), or of a visiting force, within the meaning of the Visiting Forces Act 1952(b), who may be located in the area only because of their duty as such.

Supplementary

5. References in this Schedule to a county, in relation to a small burgh or a landward area are references to the county in which the small burgh, or as the case may be, the landward area is situated, excluding any large burgh situated in the county.

(a) 1947 c. 44. (b) 1952 c. 67.

Article 3(6)

SCHEDULE 4

Percentage of Gross Annual Value to be taken as Notional Rent	*Percentage of Gross Annual Value to be taken as Notional Rent*
Column (1)	Column (2)
Percentage referred to in article 3(6)(*a*) 90 per cent	Percentage referred to in the proviso to article 3(6)(*a*) 115 per cent

EXPLANATORY NOTE

(*This Note is not part of the Order.*)

This Order prescribes for the year 1974-75—

(*a*) the aggregate amount of the rate support grants payable under Part I of the Local Government (Scotland) Act 1966 to county and town councils in Scotland, and the division of these amounts between the needs element, the resources element and the domestic element;

(*b*) the amount by which rating authorities are to reduce the amount in the pound of the county or burgh rate which they would otherwise levy on dwelling-houses in their areas so as to take account of the amount of the domestic element for the year; and

(*c*) the formulae for distributing the needs and resources elements of rate support grants among local authorities, so far as not already prescribed in the Act.

STATUTORY INSTRUMENTS

1974 No. 613 (S.54)

LOCAL GOVERNMENT, SCOTLAND

The Rate Support Grant (Increase) (Scotland) Order 1974

Made - - - -	*12th March* 1974
Laid before the Commons House of Parliament	*19th March* 1974
Coming into Operation	*27th March* 1974

In exercise of the powers conferred on me by section 4 of the Local Government (Scotland) Act 1966(a) and of all other powers enabling me in that behalf, since it appears to me that there has been an unforseen increase in the level of prices, costs and remuneration affecting substantially the reckonable expenditure of local authorities for the year 1972-73, with the consent of the Treasury and after consultation with such associations of local authorities as appear to me to be concerned in accordance with the provisions of section 3 of the Act, I hereby make the following order:—

Title, commencement and interpretation

1. (1) This order may be cited as the Rate Support Grant (Increase) (Scotland) Order 1974 and shall come into operation on the day following the day on which it is approved by a resolution of the Commons House of Parliament.

(2) The Interpretation Act 1889(b) shall apply for the interpretation of this order as it applies for the interpretation of an Act of Parliament.

(3) In this order "the Act" means the Local Government (Scotland) Act 1966.

Aggregate grants

2. For the amount prescribed by the Rate Support Grant (Scotland) Order 1971(c) as amended by the Rate Support Grant (Increase) (Scotland) (No. 2) Order 1972(d) and the Rate Support Grant (Increase) (Scotland) Order 1973(e) for the purposes of rate support grants for the year 1972-73 in respect of the matters indicated in column (1) of the following table, being the amounts set out in column (2) thereof, there shall be substituted the amounts specified in column (3) thereof—

(a) 1966 c. 51.   (b) 1889 c. 63.
(c) S.I. 1971/469 (1971 I, p. 1392).   (d) S.I. 1972/263 (1972 I, p. 874).
(e) S.I. 1973/667 (1973 I, p. 2172).

TABLE

Column (1)	Column (2) £	Column (3) £
As the aggregate amount of rate support grants—For the year 1972-73	311,720,000	316,470,000
As the amount of the needs element—For the year 1972-73	220,850,000	224,410,000
As the amount of the resources element—For the year 1972-73	73,610,000	74,800,000

William Ross,
**One of Her Majesty's Principal
Secretaries of State.**

**St Andrew's House,
Edinburgh.**

7th March 1974.

We consent.

James Hamilton,
John Golding,
**Two of the Lords Commissioners
of Her Majesty's Treasury.**

12th March 1974.

EXPLANATORY NOTE
(This Note is not part of the Order.)

This Order increases the aggregate amount of the rate support grants and the amounts of the needs and resources elements payable for the year 1972-73 under Part I of the Local Government (Scotland) Act 1966 to county and town councils in Scotland.

STATUTORY INSTRUMENTS

1974 No. 614 (S.55)

LOCAL GOVERNMENT, SCOTLAND

The Rate Support Grant (Increase) (Scotland) (No. 2) Order 1974

Made - - - -	*12th March* 1974
Laid before the Commons House of Parliament	*19th March* 1974
Coming into Operation	*27th March* 1974

In exercise of the powers conferred on me by section 4 of the Local Government (Scotland) Act 1966(a) and subsections (7), (8) and (9) of section 60 of the National Health Service (Scotland) Act 1972(b) and of all other powers enabling me in that behalf, since it appears to me that there has been an unforeseen increase in the level of prices, costs and remuneration affecting substantially the reckonable expenditure of local authorities for the year 1973-74, with the consent of the Treasury and after consultation with such associations of local authorities as appear to me to be concerned in accordance with the provisions of section 3 of the Act, I hereby make the following order:—

Title, commencement and interpretation.

1.—(1) This order may be cited as the Rate Support Grant (Increase) (Scotland) (No. 2) Order 1974 and shall come into operation on the day following the day on which it is approved by a resolution of the Commons House of Parliament.

(2) The Interpretation Act 1889(c) shall apply for the interpretation of this order as it applies for the interpretation of an Act of Parliament.

(3) In this order "the Act" means the Local Government (Scotland) Act 1966.

Aggregate grants

2. For the amount prescribed by the Rate Support Grant (Scotland) Order 1973(d) for the purposes of rate support grants for the year 1973-74 in respect

---

(a) 1966 c. 51.   (b) 1972 c. 58.

(c) 1889 c. 63   (d) S.I. 1973/666 (1973 I, p. 2164).

of the matters indicated in column (1) of the following table, being the amounts set out in column (2) thereof, there shall be substituted the amounts specified in column (3) thereof—

TABLE

Column (1)	Column (2) £	Column (3) £
As the aggregate amount of rate support grants— For the year 1973-74	362,310,000	396,580,000
As the amount of the needs element— For the year 1973-74	255,270,000	280,880,000
As the amount of the resources element— For the year 1973-74	85,090,000	93,630,000
As the amount of the domestic element— For the year 1973-74	21,950,000	22,070,000

William Ross,

One of Her Majesty's Principal Secretaries of State.

St Andrew's House,
Edinburgh.

7th March 1974.

We consent.

James Hamilton,
John Golding,

Two of the Lords Commissioners of Her Majesty's Treasury.

12th March 1974.

EXPLANATORY NOTE

(This Note is not part of the Order.)

This Order increases the aggregate amount of the rate support grants and the amounts of the needs, resources and domestic elements payable for the year 1973-74 under Part I of the Local Government (Scotland) Act 1966 to county and town councils in Scotland.

STATUTORY INSTRUMENTS

1974 No. 615

LANDLORD AND TENANT

The Regulated Tenancies (Conversion from Control) Order 1974

Made - - -	*27th March* 1974
Coming into Operation	*31st March* 1974

The Secretary of State for the Environment (as respects England, except Monmouthshire) and the Secretary of State for Wales (as respects Wales and Monmouthshire), in exercise of their powers under section 35(3) of the Housing Finance Act 1972(**a**) and of all other powers enabling them in that behalf, hereby make the following order:—

1. This order may be cited as the Regulated Tenancies (Conversion from Control) Order 1974 and shall come into operation on 31st March 1974.

2. The Interpretation Act 1889(**b**) shall apply for the interpretation of this order as it applies for the interpretation of an Act of Parliament.

3. In subsection (2) of section 35 of the Housing Finance Act 1972 (conversion of tenancies from control to regulation) for 1st July 1974 set out in that subsection there shall be substituted 1st January 1975 as the date applicable to a dwelling-house in Greater London of a value of £60 or more but less than £70, and to a dwelling-house elsewhere in England and Wales of a value of £25 or more but less than £35.

27th March 1974.

Anthony Crosland,
Secretary of State
for the Environment.

27th March 1974.

John Morris,
Secretary of State for Wales.

(**a**) 1972 c. 47. (**b**) 1889 c. 63.

EXPLANATORY NOTE

(*This Note is not part of the Order.*)

Section 35 of the Housing Finance Act 1972 provides for the conversion on specified dates into regulated tenancies of controlled tenancies of dwelling-houses according to the rateable value of those dwelling-houses on 31st March 1972. The conversion date in the case of a dwelling-house with a rateable value of £60 or more but less than £70 in Greater London, and of a rateable value of £25 or more but less than £35 elsewhere in England and Wales, is 1st July 1974. This order, which applies to England and Wales, substitutes for that date 1st January 1975.

STATUTORY INSTRUMENTS

1974 No. 616

LIBRARIES

The District Councils in Wales (Libraries) (Temporary Designation) Order 1974

Made - - -	*29th March* 1974
Laid before Parliament	*29th March* 1974
Coming into Operation	*1st April* 1974

Whereas in pursuance of the provisions of section 207(2) of the Local Government Act 1972(**a**) the councils of the boroughs and districts in Wales specified in the Schedule to this order have applied to the Secretary of State for Education and Science for an order constituting each of them a library authority;

And whereas the Secretary of State for Education and Science is considering each such application:

Now, therefore, the Secretary of State for Education and Science in exercise of the powers conferred upon him by section 207(3) of the Local Government Act 1972 hereby makes the following order:—

Citation, commencement and interpretation

1.—(1) This order may be cited as the District Councils in Wales (Libraries) (Temporary Designation) Order 1974 and shall come into operation on 1st April 1974.

(2) In this order "Wales" means the area consisting of the counties established by section 20 of the Local Government Act 1972 (new local government areas in Wales).

(3) The Interpretation Act 1889(**b**) shall apply for the interpretation of this order as it applies for the interpretation of an Act of Parliament.

Constitution of library authorities

2. As from 1st April 1974 each of the councils of the boroughs and districts in Wales specified in the Schedule to this order is constituted a library authority for the purposes of the Public Libraries and Museums Act 1964(**c**) until such a date as is specified by the Secretary of State for Education and Science on deciding to make or not to make an order under section 207(2) of the Local Government Act 1972.

SCHEDULE

The District Council of Llanelli

The District Council of Cynon Valley

The Borough Council of Merthyr Tydfil

The Borough Council of Rhondda

(a) 1972 c. 70.	(b) 1889 c. 63.	(c) 1964 c. 75.

Given under the Official Seal of the Secretary of State for Education and Science on 29th March 1974.

(L.S.)   *Reginald E. Prentice,*
Secretary of State for Education
and Science.

EXPLANATORY NOTE

(This Note is not part of the Order.)

This Order constitutes each of the councils of the boroughs and districts specified in the Schedule a library authority for the purposes of the Public Libraries and Museums Act 1964, as a temporary measure, while the Secretary of State for Education and Science is considering the applications of those councils to be made library authorities. The councils so specified are each constituted a library authority until such time as the Secretary of State decides to make or not to make an Order under section 207(2) of the 1972 Act.

STATUTORY INSTRUMENTS

1974 No. 618

HOUSING, ENGLAND AND WALES
The Slum Clearance Subsidy Regulations 1974

Made - - -	*29th March* 1974
Laid before Parliament	*29th March* 1974
Coming into Operation	*31st March* 1974

ARRANGEMENT OF REGULATIONS

Regulation
No.

1. Citation and commencement.
2. Interpretation.
3. The slum clearance loss.
4. Items not to be taken into account unless approved by the Secretary of State.
5. Items not to be taken into account.
6. Land appropriated to slum clearance functions.
7. Slum clearance land appropriated to other functions.
8. Slum clearance land appropriated for the provision of open space, school playing fields, or allotment gardens.
9. Exchanges of land.
10. Capital expenditure treated as revenue expenditure.
11. Capital items.
12. Apportionment.
13. Land acquired in the six year period ending on 31st March 1971.

The Secretary of State for the Environment and the Secretary of State for Wales, with the concurrence of the Treasury, in exercise of their powers under subsections (3), (4), (5), (6), (8) and (10) of section 11 of the Housing Finance Act 1972(a) and all other powers enabling them in that behalf, hereby make the following regulations:—

Citation and commencement

1. These regulations may be cited as the Slum Clearance Subsidy Regulations 1974 and shall come into operation on 31st March 1974.

Interpretation

2.—(1) The Interpretation Act 1889(b) shall apply for the interpretation of these regulations as it applies for the interpretation of an Act of Parliament.

(a) 1972 c. 47.　　　　　　　(b) 1889 c. 63.

(2) In these regulations, unless the context otherwise requires—

"the 1957 Act" means the Housing Act 1957(a);

"the 1972 Act" means the Housing Finance Act 1972;

"equivalent annual amount" means an equivalent annual amount ascertained in accordance with the provisions of regulation 11;

"expenditure" means any expenditure incurred, or deemed by regulation 6 or 9(1) to be incurred, by the local authority in or in connection with the exercise of their slum clearance functions;

"loans fund" means a consolidated loans fund, a loans fund, or a loans pool;

"receipt" means any receipt due, or deemed by regulation 7 or 9(2) to be due, to the local authority in or in connection with the exercise of their slum clearance functions; and

"slum clearance land" means land for the time being held by the local authority for the purposes of their slum clearance functions.

(3) For the purposes of these regulations, any interest on compensation or purchase-money paid by the local authority in connection with the acquisition of land for the purposes of their slum clearance functions shall be treated as part of such compensation or purchase-money, as the case may be.

(4) In these regulations, any reference to a numbered regulation shall be construed as a reference to the regulation bearing that number in these regulations.

(5) In these regulations, unless the context otherwise requires, any reference to an enactment shall be construed as a reference to that enactment as amended, extended or applied by or under any other enactment.

The slum clearance loss

3.—(1) Subject to the following provisions of these regulations. a local authority incur a loss for any year (beginning with the year 1971-72) in or in connection with the exercise of their slum clearance functions if their aggregate expenditure for that year exceeds their aggregate receipts for that year, and the amount of any such loss shall be equal to the excess.

(2) For the purposes of paragraph (1) of this regulation—

(*a*) a local authority's aggregate expenditure for any year shall be the aggregate of:

(i) their revenue expenditure for that year, including any capital expenditure treated under regulation 10 as revenue expenditure for that year; and

(ii) the equivalent annual amounts for that year in respect of their capital expenditure;

and

(*b*) the local authority's aggregate receipts for any year shall be the aggregate of:

(i) their revenue receipts for that year; and

(ii) the equivalent annual amounts for that year in respect of their capital receipts.

(a) 1957 c. 56.

Items not to be taken into account unless approved by the Secretary of State

4.—(1) No account shall be taken under any of the provisions of these regulations of—

(*a*) any expenditure or receipts in connection with land adjoining a clearance area, which is acquired by agreement or pursuant to a blight notice, or which is appropriated to slum clearance functions, or

(*b*) any expenditure under section 290 of the Local Government Act 1933(**a**) or section 250 of the Local Government Act 1972(**b**) (both of which sections relate to the power to direct inquiries) in respect of the costs of any person other than the Secretary of State,

unless, and except so far as, the expenditure is approved by the Secretary of State.

(2) In this regulation, "blight notice" means a notice served by virtue of section 70 or 73(1) of the Land Compensation Act 1973(**c**).

Items not to be taken into account

5. No account shall be taken under any of the provisions of these regulations of—

(*a*) any expenditure or receipts under section 18 or sections 30 to 32 of the 1957 Act so far as those provisions relate to section 9, section 10 or section 12 of that Act (unfit premises); or

(*b*) any expenditure under section 67 of the 1957 Act (costs of opposing orders) in respect of the expenses of any person other than the Secretary of State; or

(*c*) any expenditure or receipts in connection with land acquired by the local authority before 1st April 1965; or

(*d*) subject to regulation 13, any expenditure or receipts incurred or due before 1st April 1971; or

(*e*) any expenditure in respect of the appropriation to slum clearance functions, or any receipts in respect of the disposal or appropriation from slum clearance functions, of land appropriated to slum clearance functions by the local authority at any time, if the authority acquired that land in the period of six years beginning on 1st April 1965 and ending on 31st March 1971; or

(*f*) any expenditure or receipts in connection with land at any time held by the local authority for the purposes of their slum clearance functions, which is appropriated for the purposes of Part V of the 1957 Act (provision of housing accommodation), if the authority have received or are entitled to receive any subsidy under sections 1 to 10 of the Housing Subsidies Act 1967(**d**) (financial assistance towards the provision of new dwellings) in connection with new dwellings provided by them on that land after the date of that appropriation; or

(*g*) any expenditure or receipts in connection with land which is or was the site of a house, other than any expenditure or receipts in connection with the clearance of that land, if the local authority have received or are entitled to receive any exchequer contribution in respect of that house under section 13 of the Housing (Financial Provisions) Act 1958(**e**) or paragraph 6 of Schedule 8 to the 1972 Act (both of which

---

(**a**) 1933 c. 51.   (**b**) 1972 c. 70.
(**c**) 1973 c. 26.   (**d**) 1967 c. 29.
(**e**) 1958 c. 42.

provisions relate to exchequer contributions for unfit houses retained by local authorities); or

(*h*) subject to regulation 9, any money paid or received by the local authority for equality of exchange in relation to the exchange of any land; or

(*i*) subject to regulation 11, any loan charges incurred by or due to the local authority in connection with any capital expenditure or receipts.

Land appropriated to slum clearance functions

6.—(1) Subject to regulations 4 and 5, where land is appropriated to slum clearance functions, the local authority shall be deemed to have incurred at the date of the appropriation capital expenditure of an amount equal to the relevant amount ascertained in accordance with paragraph (2) of this regulation.

(2) For the purposes of paragraph (1) of this regulation, the relevant amount shall be the amount certified by the District Valuer as the price which the local authority might properly have agreed to pay for the land if they had acquired that land at the date of the appropriation from another local authority as land comprised in or, as the case may be, surrounded by or adjoining the clearance area.

Slum clearance land appropriated to other functions

7.—(1) Subject to regulations 4, 5 and 8, where slum clearance land is appropriated to some other function, the local authority shall be deemed to be entitled to receive at the date of the appropriation a capital receipt of an amount equal to the relevant amount ascertained in accordance with paragraph (2) of this regulation.

(2) For the purposes of paragraph (1) of this regulation the relevant amount shall be—

(*a*) in the case of slum clearance land appropriated for the purposes of Part V of the 1957 Act (provision of housing accommodation), the amount certified by the District Valuer as the market value at the date of the appropriation of that land for the purpose for which it is to be used after that date;

(*b*) in the case of slum clearance land for which the local authority have received, or receive, after the date of the appropriation, any grant under section 7 of the Local Government Act 1966(**a**), section 250 of the Town and Country Planning Act 1971(**b**) (both of which sections relate to grants for development or redevelopment), or section 235 of the Highways Act 1959(**c**) (grants in respect of the construction or improvement of highways etc.), an amount equal to the expenditure originally incurred by the authority in connection with the acquisition of that land, together with the expenditure, if any, incurred before the date of the appropriation by the authority in connection with the clearance of that land; and

(*c*) in any other case, the amount certified by the District Valuer as the price which the local authority might properly have agreed to accept for the land if they had sold that land to another local authority at the date of the appropriation.

(a) 1966 c. 42.   (b) 1971 c. 78.   (c) 1959 c. 25.

(3) For the purposes of this regulation and regulation 8, the local authority shall be treated as having appropriated any land at the date of their resolution to appropriate that land or at the date they first use that land for the purposes of the function to which that land is to be appropriated, whichever is the earlier.

Slum clearance land appropriated for the provision of open space, school playing fields, or allotment gardens

8.—(1) Where in any year any slum clearance land is appropriated for the purposes of providing open space, school playing fields, or allotment gardens, regulation 7 shall not apply to that land, unless—

(a) the aggregate of the relevant amounts (ascertained in accordance with regulation 7(2)(c)) in respect of all slum clearance land appropriated by the local authority for any of those purposes in that year exceeds one-third of the aggregate of the authority's capital receipts in respect of all other slum clearance land disposed of, and appropriated, by the authority in that year, and

(b) the Secretary of State does not approve such excess; but

where regulation 7 does apply to that land it shall apply subject to paragraph (2) of this regulation.

(2) The aggregate amount of the capital receipts deemed by regulation 7 to be due to the local authority in any year in respect of all slum clearance land appropriated by them for the purposes of providing open space, school playing fields, or allotment gardens shall be an amount equal to the excess for that year under paragraph (1)(a) of this regulation.

(3) In this regulation, the expression "open space" has the meaning ascribed to it by section 290(1) of the Town and Country Planning Act 1971, and the expression "allotment gardens" has the meaning ascribed to it by section 22(1) of the Allotments Act 1922(a).

Exchanges of land

9.—(1) Subject to regulations 4 and 5, where land is acquired by a local authority for the purposes of their slum clearance functions in exchange for other land, the authority shall be deemed to have incurred at the date of the contract for the exchange capital expenditure of an amount equal to the amount certified by the District Valuer as the price which the local authority might properly have agreed to pay for the land acquired, if they had acquired it, otherwise than by way of exchange, at the date of the said contract.

(2) Subject to regulations 4 and 5, where slum clearance land is exchanged for other land, the local authority shall be deemed to be entitled to receive at the date of the contract for the exchange a capital receipt of an amount equal to the amount certified by the District Valuer as the price which the local authority might properly have agreed to accept for the slum clearance land, if they had disposed of it, otherwise than by way of exchange, at the date of the said contract.

Capital expenditure treated as revenue expenditure

10.—(1) Subject to paragraph (2) of this regulation and regulations 4, 5 and 11(5), where in any year a local authority charge capital expenditure to

---

(a) 1922 c. 51.

revenue, that expenditure shall be treated, for the purposes of these regulations, as revenue expenditure for that year.

(2) The aggregate amount of capital expenditure treated as revenue expenditure for any year under paragraph (1) of this regulation shall not exceed £10 for each household displaced by the local authority in that year in consequence of the exercise of their slum clearance functions.

(3) In this regulation, "household" means either one person living alone or a group of persons, whether or not related, living at the same address with common housekeeping.

Capital items

11.—(1) Subject to regulation 10, any item of a capital nature shall be converted into equivalent annual amounts in accordance with paragraph (2) of this regulation.

(2) The equivalent annual amount for any year in respect of an item of a capital nature shall be—

(a) if the local authority operate a loans fund, an amount equal to the loan charges for that year which would be made, in accordance with the authority's normal financing and accounting practice, in the case of an advance from the authority's loans fund of an amount equal, subject to paragraphs (5) and (6) of this regulation, to the amount of that item repayable over a period of 60 years from the relevant date for that item; or

(b) if the local authority do not operate a loans fund, an amount equal to the loan charges which would be payable for that year under a loan of an amount equal, subject to paragraphs (5) and (6) of this regulation, to the amount of that item repayable together with interest at the appropriate rate for that item over a period of 60 years from the relevant date for that item by equal annual instalments of principal and interest combined.

(3) Subject to regulation 13, all equivalent annual amounts in respect of an item of a capital nature shall be left out of account from the end of the fifteenth year after the relevant date for that item.

(4) (a) For the purposes of paragraphs (2) and (3) of this regulation, the relevant date for an item specified in column 1 of the following Table shall be 1st April in the year in which the corresponding event for that item specified in column 2 of the Table occurs.

(b) For the purposes of paragraph (2)(b) of this regulation, the appropriate rate of interest for an item specified in column 1 of the following Table shall be the percentage rate of interest expressed by the formula:

$$\frac{X}{Y} \times 100, \text{ where—}$$

X   is the aggregate amount of the relevant amounts of interest in respect of all loans obtained by the local authority in connection with the exercise of their slum clearance functions in the year in which the corresponding event for that item specified in column 2 of the Table occurs, and for the purposes of this formula "the relevant amount of interest" in respect of any such loan is the total interest payable by that authority for the first complete year of that loan, beginning on the date on which that loan was obtained; and

Y   is the aggregate amount of the said loans.

TABLE

1. Item	2. Event
(a) Expenditure deemed by regulation 6 to be incurred in respect of the appropriation of land to slum clearance functions.	(a) Resolution to appropriate the land to slum clearance functions.
(b) Expenditure deemed by regulation 9(1) to be incurred in respect of the exchange of land.	(b) Completion of the exchange.
(c) Receipt deemed by regulation 7 to be due in respect of the appropriation of slum clearance land to some other function.	(c) Resolution to appropriate the slum clearance land to that other function or first use of that land for purposes of that function, whichever is the earlier.
(d) Receipt deemed by regulation 9(2) to be due in respect of the exchange of slum clearance land.	(d) Completion of the exchange.
(e) Expenditure other than expenditure within (a) or (b) above.	(e) Expenditure is paid.
(f) Receipt other than a receipt within (c) or (d) above.	(f) Receipt is received.

(5) Where—

(a) any expenditure is incurred in respect of the acquisition of land, or

(b) any payment is made under section 30 or 60 of the 1957 Act as amended and extended by sections 65, 66 and 67 of the Housing Act 1969(a) (well-maintained houses), or

(c) any payment is made under section 31 or 61 of the 1957 Act or section 68 of the Housing Act 1969 (owner-occupier supplements), or

(d) any payment is made under section 37 of the Land Compensation Act 1973 (disturbance payments to persons without compensatable interests),

the amount to be taken into account in accordance with the provisions of these regulations shall not in any case exceed the amount certified by the District Valuer as properly so incurred or paid.

(6) Where a receipt arises from the disposal of slum clearance land, the amount to be taken into account in accordance with the provisions of these regulations shall not in any case be less than the amount certified by the District Valuer as properly receivable in respect of that land.

Apportionment

12.—(1) Where a local authority incur any expenditure, or are entitled to any receipt, partly in the exercise of their slum clearance functions and partly in the exercise of some other function, only such part of the expenditure or,

---

(a) 1969 c. 33.

as the case may be, such part of the receipt, as may fairly be regarded as attributable to the exercise by the authority of their slum clearance functions, shall be taken into account in accordance with the provisions of these regulations.

(2) Subject to regulation 11(5), where slum clearance land is acquired together with other land, the expenditure incurred by the local authority in connection with such acquisition shall be apportioned by reference to the respective values, certified by the District Valuer, of the slum clearance land and the other land at the date of the acquisition, and the apportioned amount relating to the slum clearance land shall be taken into account in accordance with the provisions of these regulations.

(3) Subject to regulation 11(6), where slum clearance land is disposed of together with other land, the receipt due to the local authority in connection with such disposal shall be apportioned by reference to the respective values, certified by the District Valuer, of the slum clearance land and the other land at the date of the disposal, and the apportioned amount relating to the slum clearance land shall be taken into account in accordance with the provisions of these regulations.

Land acquired in the six year period ending on 31st March 1971

13. Where in the period of six years beginning on 1st April 1965 and ending on 31st March 1971 a local authority have acquired any land for the purposes of their slum clearance functions, and continue to hold that land for those purposes until the end of that period, the appropriate equivalent annual amounts (for the fifteen years beginning with the year 1971-72) in respect of capital expenditure incurred or capital receipts becoming due, in that period in connection with that land shall be taken into account in accordance with the provisions of these regulations; but, all equivalent annual amounts in respect of any such expenditure or receipts shall be left out of account from the beginning of the year 1986-87.

Anthony Crosland,
Secretary of State for the Environment.

29th March 1974.

John Morris,
Secretary of State for Wales.

29th March 1974.

We concur.

John Golding,

T. Pendry,

Two of the Lords Commissioners
of Her Majesty's Treasury.

29th March 1974.

EXPLANATORY NOTE

(This Note is not part of the Regulations.)

Section 11 of the Housing Finance Act 1972 provides for the payment of slum clearance subsidy to a local authority for any year (beginning with the year 1971-72) in which the local authority incur a loss in or in connection with the exercise of their slum clearance functions. The amount of slum clearance subsidy payable to a local authority for the year is to be 75 per cent. of the loss.

These Regulations prescribe the method of determining whether a local authority have incurred a loss in carrying out their sum clearance functions and of determining the amount of any such loss.

STATUTORY INSTRUMENTS

1974 No. 619

ROAD TRAFFIC

The Motor Vehicles (Speed Limits on Motorways) (Amendment) Regulations 1974

Made - - -	20*th March* 1974
Laid before Parliament	21*st March* 1974
Coming into Operation	29*th March* 1974

The Secretary of State for the Environment, in exercise of powers conferred by section 78(2) and (4) of the Road Traffic Regulation Act 1967(a) and now vested in him(b), and of all other enabling powers, and after consultation with representative organisations in accordance with section 107(2) of that Act, hereby makes the following Regulations:—

1.—(1) These Regulations may be cited as the Motor Vehicles (Speed Limits on Motorways) (Amendment) Regulations 1974, and shall come into operation on the day following the day on which they are approved by Parliament.

(2) The Interpretation Act 1889(c) shall apply for the interpretation of these Regulations as it applies for the interpretation of an Act of Parliament, and as if for the purposes of section 38 of that Act these Regulations were an Act of Parliament and the Regulations revoked by Regulation 2 of these Regulations were an Act of Parliament thereby repealed.

2. The Motor Vehicles (Speed Limits on Motorways) (Amendment) Regulations 1973(d) are hereby revoked and the Motor Vehicles (Speed Limits on Motorways) Regulations 1973(e) shall have effect as they were originally made.

Signed by authority of the Secretary of State.

20th March 1974.

Fred Mulley,
Minister for Transport,
Department of the Environment.

(a) 1967 c. 76.   (b) S.I. 1970/1681 (1970 III, p. 5551).   (c) 1889 c. 63.
(d) S.I. 1973/2058 (1973 III, p. 7086).   (e) S.I. 1973/748 (1973 I, p. 2389).

EXPLANATORY NOTE

(This Note is not part of the Regulations.)

These Regulations revoke the Motor Vehicles (Speed Limits on Motorways) (Amendment) Regulations 1973 (which reduced the speed limit on motorways for goods vehicles having an unladen weight exceeding 3 tons from 60 mph to 50 mph in order to save motor fuel) and restore the provisions of the Motor Vehicles (Speed Limits on Motorways) Regulations 1973 to their original form.

STATUTORY INSTRUMENTS

1974 No. 620

CONTROL OF FUEL AND ELECTRICITY

The Motor Fuel (Maximum Retail Prices) (Second Amendment) Order 1974

Made - - -	*29th March* 1974
Laid before Parliament	*29th March* 1974
Coming into Operation	*1st April* 1974

The Secretary of State, in exercise of his powers under Section 2(1)(b) of the Fuel and Electricity (Control) Act 1973(**a**) and Section 7 of the Emergency Laws (Re-enactments and Repeals) Act 1964(**b**) as having effect by virtue of Section 5 of the Fuel and Electricity (Control) Act 1973, hereby orders as follows:—

1. This Order may be cited as the Motor Fuel (Maximum Retail Prices) (Second Amendment) Order 1974 and shall come into operation on 1st April 1974.

2. The Motor Fuel (Maximum Retail Prices) Order 1973(**c**) as varied (**d**) shall be further varied as follows:

    (*a*) by the substitution, for Schedule 1 of that Order, of the Schedule set out in Schedule 1 to this Order;

    (*b*) by the substitution, for Schedule 2 of that Order, of the Schedule set out in Schedule 2 to this Order.

Eric Varley,
Secretary of State for Energy.

29th March 1974.

(**a**) 1973 c. 67.   (**b**) 1964 c. 60.
(**c**) S.I. 1973/2119 (1973 III, p. 7285).   (**d**) S.I. 1974/197 (1974 I, p. 704).

SCHEDULE 1

Article 2(a)

" SCHEDULE 1

Column 1 Grades or subdivisions of a grade of motor spirit and classes of diesel fuel	Column 2 Amount in pence
Motor Spirit	
5 star grade	56
4 star grade	55
3 star grade of not less than 96 minimum RON value	$54\frac{1}{2}$
Other 3 star grade	54
2 star grade of not less than 92 minimum RON value	$53\frac{1}{2}$
Other 2 star grade	53
Diesel Fuel	
Class A1	$54\frac{1}{2}$
Class A2	$54\frac{1}{2}$

"

Article 2(b)   **SCHEDULE 2**

'' SCHEDULE 2

Column 1	Column 2	Column 3
Zone or place	Amount in pence	Grades or subdivisions of a grade of motor spirit or classes of diesel fuel
Zones		
Inner zone	—	—
Outer zone	$\frac{1}{2}$	4 star grade.
General zone	$\frac{1}{2}$	All grades or subdivisions of a grade of motor spirit and classes of diesel fuel.
North Scotland (mainland only) zone	1	All grades or subdivisions of a grade of motor spirit.
	$2\frac{1}{2}$	Both classes of diesel fuel.
Places		
Northern Ireland	$\frac{1}{2}$	4 star grade.
Benbecula, Bute, Harris, Lewis, Millport, Skye, Uist and West Cowal	1	All grades or subdivisions of a grade of motor spirit.
	$2\frac{1}{2}$	Both classes of diesel fuel.
Arran and Mull	2	All grades or subdivisions of a grade of motor spirit except 4 star grade.
	$2\frac{1}{2}$	4 star grade and both classes of diesel fuel.
Colonsay and Islay	3	All grades or subdivisions of a grade of motor spirit except 4 star grade.
	$3\frac{1}{2}$	4 star grade and both classes of diesel fuel.
Orkney Islands (mainland) and Shetland Isles (mainland)	1	All grades or subdivisions of a grade of motor spirit.
	$2\frac{1}{2}$	Both classes of diesel fuel.
Other Orkney Islands and Shetland Isles	$4\frac{1}{2}$	All grades or subdivisions of a grade of motor spirit.
	6	Both classes of diesel fuel.
Barra, Coll, Jura and Tiree	6	All grades or subdivisions of a grade of motor spirit and classes of diesel fuel.

EXPLANATORY NOTE

(This Note is not part of the Order.)

This Order makes further variation to the Motor Fuel (Maximum Retail Prices) Order 1973, as varied, by making further increases in the maximum retail prices imposed in respect of the supply of motor spirit and diesel fuel in consequence of the supply of these fuels ceasing to be zero-rated for value added tax.

STATUTORY INSTRUMENTS

1974 No. 627

NATIONAL HEALTH SERVICE, ENGLAND AND WALES

The National Health Service (Charges for Drugs and Appliances) (Amendment) Regulations 1974

Made - - - -	*29th March* 1974
Laid before Parliament	*2nd April* 1974
Coming into Operation	*8th April* 1974

The Secretary of State for Social Services in exercise of powers conferred by section 38(3)(**a**) of the National Health Service Act 1946(**b**) and section 1(2) of the National Health Service Act 1952(**c**) and now vested in her(**d**), and of all other powers enabling her in that behalf, hereby makes the following regulations : —

Citation and commencement

1. These regulations may be cited as the National Health Service (Charges for Drugs and Appliances) (Amendment) Regulations 1974 and shall come into operation on 8th April 1974.

Amendment to regulations

2. For sub-paragraphs (*a*) and (*b*) of regulation 6(1) of the National Health Service (Charges for Drugs and Appliances) Regulations 1974(**e**), there shall be substituted—

" (*a*) a person who has not attained the age of 16 years ; or

(*b*) a person being a man who has attained the age of 65 years, or being a woman who has attained the age of 60 years ; or ".

Barbara Castle,
Secretary of State for Social Services.

29th March 1974.

EXPLANATORY NOTE

(*This Note is not part of the Regulations.*)

These Regulations amend the National Health Service (Charges for Drugs and Appliances) Regulations 1974 by altering the ages by reference to which is determined the remission to minors and women of the charges imposed by those regulations.

(**a**) *See* section 16 of the National Health Service (Amendment) Act 1949 c. 93.
(**b**) 1946 c. 81.
(**c**) 1952 c. 25.
(**d**) *See* Secretary of State for Social Services Order 1968 (S.I. 1968/1699 (1968 III, p. 4585)) Article 2.
(**e**) S.I. 1974/285.(1974 I, p. 982).

STATUTORY INSTRUMENTS

1974 No. 628

BURIAL, ENGLAND AND WALES

The Local Authorities' Cemeteries Order 1974

Made - - - -	*12th March* 1974
Laid before the House of Commons	18*th March* 1974
Laid before the House of Lords	20*th March* 1974
Coming into Operation	1*st April* 1974

The Secretary of State for the Environment, in relation to England, and the Secretary of State for Wales, in relation to Wales, after consultation with associations appearing to them to be representative of local authorities and with other bodies appearing to them to be concerned, in exercise of the powers conferred upon them by section 214(3) of the Local Government Act 1972(a) and of all other powers enabling them in that behalf, hereby make the following order:—

Title and commencement

1. This order may be cited as the Local Authorities' Cemeteries Order 1974 and shall come into operation on 1st April 1974 or on the day following the day on which it has been approved by a resolution of each House of Parliament, whichever is the later.

Interpretation

2.—(1) The Interpretation Act 1889(b) shall apply for the interpretation of this order as it applies for the interpretation of an Act of Parliament.

(2) In this order, unless the context otherwise requires—

"the Act" means the Local Government Act 1972;

"bishop" means, in relation to any ecclesiastical district or place not subject to the jurisdiction of a bishop, the authority known to the law of the Church of England as "the ordinary";

"burial" includes—

(*a*) the interment of cremated human remains;

(*b*) the interment of the bodies of still-born children or of the cremated remains thereof; and

(*c*) burial in a vault;

(**a**) 1972 c. 70.   (**b**) 1889 c. 63.

"burial authority" means the council of a district, London borough, parish or community, the Common Council of the City of London, the parish meeting of a parish having no parish council, whether separate or common or a joint board established under section 6 of the Public Health Act 1936(a) or by or under any local Act to exercise the functions conferred by section 214 of, and Schedule 26 to, the Act or by any enactment re-replaced by those provisions;

"cemetery" means a cemetery provided and maintained by a burial authority;

"consecration" means consecration according to the rites of the Church of England, and cognate expressions shall be construed accordingly;

"tombstone" includes kerbs;

"Wales" means the area consisting of the counties established by section 20 of the Act (new local government areas in Wales), and "England" does not include any area included in any of those counties; and

"the Welsh Church Act" means the Welsh Church Act 1914(b), and "the area subject to the Welsh Church Act" means the area in which the Church of England was disestablished by the Act.

(3) Any reference in this order to a chapel provided as mentioned in article 6(1)(b) includes a reference to any chapel provided under any enactment replaced by that provision.

(4) For the purposes of this order, subject to the provisions thereof, any power or right to provide anything includes a power or right to maintain it.

(5) For the purposes of this order any railings surrounding a grave, vault, tombstone or other memorial shall be treated as forming part thereof.

(6) In this order, unless the context otherwise requires, references to any enactment shall be construed as references to that enactment as amended, extended or applied by or under any other enactment or by this order.

General powers of management

3.—(1) Subject to the provisions of this order, a burial authority may do all such things as they consider necessary or desirable for the proper management, regulation and control of a cemetery.

(2) Nothing in paragraph (1) shall be construed as authorising—

(a) any action in relation to any chapel provided as mentioned in article 6(1)(b) below; or

(b) any action in relation to any tombstone or other memorial other than action which is necessary to remove a danger which arises by reason of the condition of the tombstone or other memorial itself.

Layout, repair and access

4.—(1) A burial authority may enclose, lay out and embellish a cemetery in such manner as they think fit, and from time to time improve it, and shall keep

---

(a) 1936 c. 49.   (b) 1914 c. 91.

the cemetery in good order and repair, together with all buildings, walls and fences thereon and other buildings provided for use therewith.

Nothing in this paragraph shall be construed as requiring any action in relation to any chapel provided as mentioned in article 6(1)(b) below.

(2) Schedule 1 to this order shall have effect with respect to the provision of access to cemeteries.

Consecration, and setting apart for particular denominations

5.—(1) Subject to paragraphs (2) and (3) below, a burial authority may if they think fit—

(a) apply to the bishop of the diocese in which a cemetery is situated for the consecration of any part thereof;

(b) set apart for the use of a particular denomination or religious body any part of a cemetery which has not been consecrated.

(2) A burial authority in exercising the powers conferred by paragraph (1) above shall satisfy themselves that a sufficient part of the cemetery remains unconsecrated and not set apart for the use of denominations or religious bodies.

(3) Paragraph (1)(a) above does not apply to cemeteries within the area subject to the Welsh Church Act, and any part of such a cemetery which was consecrated before the end of March 1920, or in respect of which a ceremony of consecration has been performed since that time in accordance with the rites of the Church in Wales, shall be treated for the purposes of this order as having been set apart for the use of that Church (and as not having been consecrated).

(4) A burial authority shall mark off any consecrated part of a cemetery in such manner as they consider suitable.

(5) Notwithstanding the consecration or the setting apart for the use of a particular Christian denomination of the part of a cemetery in which any body is to be buried the burial may take place without any religious service or with such Christian and orderly religious service at the grave, conducted by such person or persons, as the person having the charge of or being responsible for the burial may think fit.

(6) A burial authority may at the request of a particular denomination or religious body prohibit the interring or scattering of cremated human remains in or over a part of the cemetery set apart for their use.

(7) Burials in the consecrated part of a cemetery shall be registered in the same way and subject to the same provisions as burials in the unconsecrated part.

Provision of chapels

6.—(1) A burial authority may provide chapels as follows—

(a) on any part of a cemetery which is not consecrated or set apart for the use of a particular denomination or religious body, they may provide any chapel which they consider necessary for the due performance of funeral services, and

(b) on any part of a cemetery which is consecrated or so set apart, they may, subject to paragraph (3) below, provide a chapel for the performance of funeral services according to the rites of the Church of England or other denomination or religious body.

(2) A chapel provided on any part of a cemetery which is neither consecrated nor set apart for the use of a particular denomination or religious body shall not itself be consecrated or reserved for such a use.

(3) A burial authority may provide a chapel as mentioned in paragraph (1)(b) above only at the request of members of the Church of England or other denomination or religious body, and out of funds provided for the purpose otherwise than by the authority; and the authority shall not be required to maintain any chapel so provided except so far as funds provided otherwise than by them are available for that purpose.

(4) At the request of persons appearing to them to be representative of the members of the Church of England or other denomination or religious body at whose request a chapel was provided under paragraph (1)(b) above or under any enactment replaced by that provision, a burial authority may make such chapel available for funeral services according to the rites of any other such body or for the due performance of any funeral services.

(5) Where the cemeteries of any two authorities adjoin each other, the authorities may agree to exercise their powers under paragraph (1) above by providing jointly, on either cemetery or partly on one and partly on the other, one chapel to be used in connection with both cemeteries in accordance with the terms of the agreement.

(6) A burial authority may furnish and equip their chapels in such manner as they think proper, but, in the case of one provided on consecrated ground or on ground set apart for the use of a particular denomination or religious body, only out of funds provided for the purpose otherwise than by the authority.

(7) Where a chapel provided under paragraph (1)(b) above or under any enactment replaced by that provision becomes dangerous, a burial authority may take such action, including removal, in relation thereto as they consider proper.

Provision of mortuaries and biers

7.—(1) A burial authority may if they think fit provide a mortuary for use in connection with a cemetery, and may furnish and equip any mortuary so provided in such manner as they think proper.

(2) A burial authority may provide biers, and such other things as they consider necessary or desirable, for use in connection with burials taking place in a cemetery.

Arrangements for sharing of facilities

8.—(1) A burial authority may enter into such agreements as they think fit for—

(a) the use in connection with burials taking place in a cemetery of chapels, mortuaries, biers and other things provided by persons other than the authority, or (*b*) the use in connection with burials taking place in other places of burial, or in connection with cremations, of any chapel, mortuary, bier or other thing provided for use in connection with burials taking place in the cemetery.

Nothing in this paragraph shall be construed as authorising any action in relation to any chapel provided as mentioned in article 6(1)(*b*) above.

(2) An agreement under this article may include terms as to the services of any staff employed in connection with the subject matter of the agreement.

Grant of burial rights and rights to erect memorials, and agreements for maintenance of graves and memorials

9.—(1) A burial authority may grant, on such terms and subject to such conditions as they think proper—

(*a*) to any person—

(i) the exclusive right of burial in any grave space or grave, or the right to construct a walled grave or vault together with the exclusive right of burial therein; or

(ii) the right to one or more burials in any grave space or grave which is not subject to any exclusive right of burial;

(*b*) to the owner of a right described in (*a*)(i) or (ii) (or to any person who satisfies them that he is a relative of a person buried in the grave, walled grave or vault, or is acting at the request of the person first mentioned, and that it is impractical for such relative to trace the owner of the right so described), the right to place and maintain, or to put any additional inscription on, a tombstone or other memorial on the grave space, grave, walled grave or vault in respect of which the right so described subsists;

(*c*) to any person, the right to place and maintain a memorial in a cemetery otherwise than on a grave space, grave, walled grave or vault in respect of which a right described in (*a*)(i) has been granted, but—

(i) in the case of a memorial to be placed in a chapel provided under article 6(1)(*b*) above or under any enactment replaced by that provision, only at the request of persons appearing to the burial authority to be representative of the Church of England or other denomination or religious body at whose request the chapel was provided; and

(ii) in the case of any other memorial being an additional inscription on an existing memorial, only with the consent of the owner of the right to place and maintain such existing memorial.

(2) A right under paragraph (1) above shall subsist for the period specified in the grant, being a period beginning with the date of the grant and not exceeding 100 years.

(3) A burial authority may from time to time extend the period of any grant under subsection (1) above or under any enactment replaced by that provision (subject if they think fit, to any modification of its terms or conditions) for up to 100 years from the date on which the extension is granted.

(4) No body shall be buried, or cremated human remains interred or scattered, in or over any grave, walled grave or vault in which an exclusive right of burial for the time being subsists except by or with the consent in writing of the owner of the right.

(5) A burial authority shall also have power to agree with any person, on such terms and subject to such conditions as they think proper, to maintain any grave, vault, tombstone or other memorial in a cemetery for a period not exceeding 100 years from the date of the agreement.

Any agreement under section 1(1)(a) of the Parish Councils and Burial Authorities (Miscellaneous Provisions) Act 1970(a) shall have effect as if it had been entered into under this paragraph.

(6) Rights granted under paragraph (1) above or under enactments replaced by that paragraph shall be exercisable subject to and in accordance with the provisions of Part I of Schedule 2 to this order. The provisions of Part II of that Schedule shall have effect with respect to grants under paragraph (1) above and with respect to the registration of, and other matters concerning, rights granted under that paragraph or under enactments replaced by that paragraph. The provisions of Part III of the said Schedule shall have effect for the purpose of enabling a burial authority to terminate certain rights and agreements entered into before 1st April 1974.

Right of bishop to object to inscriptions in consecrated parts

10. A bishop of the Church of England shall, as respects the consecrated part of any cemetery (including any chapel thereon), have the same rights of objecting to, and procuring the removal of, any inscription on a tombstone or other memorial placed, or intended to be placed, therein as he has in the case of churches of the Church of England and the churchyards belonging thereto.

Rites of Church of England

11.—(1) The incumbent of an ecclesiastical parish situated wholly or partly in an area chargeable with the expenses of a cemetery shall, with respect to members of the Church of England who are his own parishioners or who die in his parish, where he is requested to do so, be under the same obligation to perform funeral services in the consecrated part, if any, of the cemetery as he has to perform funeral services in any churchyard of the ecclesiastical parish.

(2) This article does not apply to a cemetery in the area subject to the Welsh Church Act.

Fees and other charges

12.—(1) Subject to the provisions of this article a burial authority may charge such fees as they think proper—

(a) for or in connection with burials in a cemetery;

(b) for any grant of a right to place a tombstone or other memorial in a cemetery otherwise than in a chapel provided as mentioned in article 6(1) (b) above; or

(c) for any grant of a right to put an additional inscription on such a tombstone or other memorial.

In determining the fees to be charged the burial authority shall take into account the effect of any resolution under section 147(3) of, or under paragraph 6 of Schedule 26 to, the Act.

(a) 1970 c. 29.

(2) Fees collected by a burial authority in respect of services rendered by any minister of religion or sexton acting at the request of the authority shall be paid by the authority to the minister of religion or sexton.

(3) A burial authority shall keep a table showing the matters in respect of which fees or other charges are payable to them, and the amount of each such fee or charge, and the table shall be available for inspection by the public at all reasonable times.

(4) No fee shall be payable to an incumbent of an ecclesiastical parish in respect of any burial in a cemetery, or in respect of any other matter connected with a cemetery, except for services rendered by him; and no fee shall be paid to any clerk or other ecclesiastical officer in respect of burial in a cemetery except for services rendered by him.

Cost of removal of unauthorised memorials

13. If a burial authority remove from a cemetery any tombstone or other memorial placed therein otherwise than in the exercise of a right granted by, or otherwise with the approval of, the burial authority or any predecessor of theirs, the burial authority may recover the cost thereby incurred by them—

(a) from the person to whose order the tombstone or memorial was placed;

(b) within two years from the placing of the tombstone or memorial, from the personal representative of such person,

as a simple contract debt in any court of competent jurisdiction.

Offences in cemeteries

14.—(1) No person shall—

(a) wilfully create any disturbance in a cemetery;

(b) commit any nuisance in a cemetery;

(c) wilfully interfere with any burial taking place in a cemetery;

(d) wilfully interfere with any grave, walled grave or vault, any tombstone or other memorial, or any flowers or plants on any such matter; or

(e) play at any game or sport in a cemetery.

(2) No person not being an officer or servant of the burial authority or another person so authorised by or on behalf of the burial authority shall enter or remain in a cemetery at any hour when it is closed to the public.

Penalties

15. Every person who contravenes—

(a) any prohibition under article 5(6) above;

(b) article 9(4) above;

(c) article 14 above;

(d) Part I of Schedule 2 to this order,

shall be liable on summary conviction to a fine not exceeding £20 and in the case of a continuing offence to a fine not exceeding £5 for each day during which the offence continues after conviction therefor.

Commonwealth War Graves Commission

16.—(1) In this article "the Commission" means the Commonwealth War Graves Commission.

(2) A burial authority may grant to the Commission the right to provide any structure or any tree, plant, path or other feature.

(3) Nothing in article 3 above shall be construed as authorising any action in relation to any tombstone or other memorial, any structure or any tree, plant, path or other feature provided by the Commission, except with the consent of the Commission.

(4) In the application of article 9 to the Commission—

the words "and not exceeding 100 years" in paragraph (2);

the words "for up to 100 years from the date on which the extension is granted" in paragraph (3);

the words "for a period not exceeding 100 years from the date of the agreement" in paragraph 5

shall not have effect.

(5) Part III of Schedule 2 to this order shall not apply to the Commission.

Repeals

17. The enactments specified in Schedule 3 to this order are hereby repealed to the extent mentioned in that Schedule except in their application to the Isles of Scilly.

General saving

18. Nothing in this order shall be construed as authorising the disturbance of human remains.

Article 4   SCHEDULE 1

ACCESS TO CEMETERIES

1. A burial authority may construct such roads to a cemetery as they think fit and, subject to the next following paragraph, may widen or otherwise improve any road leading to a cemetery or giving access to such a road.

2. A burial authority shall not widen or otherwise improve any road which is not vested in them except with the consent of the highway authority or other person in whom it is vested.

3. A burial authority shall be responsible as such for maintaining in a proper state of repair any road constructed by them or any predecessor of theirs, not being a highway which is for the time being maintainable at the public expense.

Article 9   SCHEDULE 2

BURIAL RIGHTS, RIGHTS TO ERECT MEMORIALS, AND AGREEMENTS FOR MAINTENANCE OF GRAVES AND MEMORIALS

PART I

EXERCISE OF RIGHTS

1. No burial shall take place, no cremated human remains shall be scattered and no tombstone or other memorial shall be placed in a cemetery, and no additional

inscription shall be made on a tombstone or other memorial, without the permission of the officer appointed for that purpose by the burial authority.

2. No body shall be buried in a grave in such a manner that any part of the coffin is less than three feet below the level of any ground adjoining the grave:

Provided that the burial authority may, where they consider the soil to be of suitable character, permit a coffin made of perishable materials to be placed not less than two feet below the level of any ground adjoining the grave.

3. No body shall be buried in a grave unless the coffin is effectively separated from any coffin interred in the grave on a previous occasion by means of a layer of earth not less than six inches thick.

4. When any grave is reopened for the purpose of making another burial therein, no person shall disturb any human remains interred therein or remove therefrom any soil which is offensive.

5. Every walled grave or vault shall be properly constructed of suitable materials.

6. Within 24 hours of any burial in a walled grave or vault, the coffin shall be—

(a) embedded in concrete, and covered with a layer of concrete not less than six inches thick; or

(b) enclosed in a separate cell or compartment of slate, stone flagging or precast concrete slabs of a 1: 2: 4 mix, in any case not less than two inches thick, in such a manner as to prevent, as far as may be practicable, the escape of any noxious gas from the interior of the cell or compartment.

7. Any person to whose order a body is buried in a grave in respect of which an exclusive right of burial has been granted shall, as soon as conveniently may be after the subsidence of the earth has been completed, cause the surface of the grave to be covered with any tombstone or other memorial in respect of which a right has been granted by the burial authority or any predecessor of theirs, or with fresh turf, or, where the burial authority permits, with such flowers and shrubs, or in such other manner, as may be permitted.

Part II

Provision as to Grants and Matters Concerning Rights

1.—(1) A grant under article 9 of this order shall be in writing signed by the officer appointed for that purpose by the burial authority.

(2) Any extension of the period of such a grant shall also be in writing signed by such an officer.

2.—(1) A burial authority shall—

(a) maintain a register of all rights granted by them or any predecessor of theirs under article 9, which shall show as respects each such right the date on which it was granted, the name and address of the grantee, the consideration for the grant, the place in which it is exercisable and its duration; and

(b) subject to the provision of section 229 of the Act, preserve registers of the rights granted under section 33 of the Burial Act 1852(a), section 40 of the Cemeteries Clauses Act 1847(b), or a corresponding provision in any local Act, transferred to them by the Local Authorities (England) (Property etc.) Order 1973(c) or the Local Authorities (Wales) (Property etc.) Order 1973(d).

(2) A burial authority shall also maintain a plan of any cemetery, showing and allocating a distinguishing number to each place which is subject to a right so granted,

---

(a) 1852 c. 85.
(b) 1847 c. 65.
(c) S.I. 1973/1861 (1973 III, p. 6401).
(d) S.I. 1973/1863 (1973 III, p. 6452).

and a book, setting out the numbers so allocated and specifying in relation to each the name and address of the grantee of the right.

3. Rights to which paragraph 2(1) above applies may be assigned by deed or bequeathed by will.

4. A person to whom any such right is assigned or transmitted shall not be entitled to its exercise until he has notified the assignment or transmission to the burial authority in writing, and, subject to such investigation as they think proper, the authority shall record particulars of the notification in the register under this Schedule.

5. A burial authority may charge such fees as they think proper for the making of searches in, and the provision of certified copies of entries in, a register under this Schedule, and the register shall at all reasonable times be available for inspection by any person free of charge.

Part III

Determination of Rights and Agreements for Periods exceeding 100 Years

1.—(1) This paragraph applies to the following rights and agreements granted or entered into by a burial authority or any predecessor of theirs at a time before this order came into operation—

(a) any right granted in perpetuity, or for a period exceeding 100 years from the date of the grant, under a provision falling within paragraph 2(1)(b) of Part II above, and

(b) any agreement to maintain a grave, vault, tombstone or other memorial in a cemetery either in perpetuity or for a period ending more than 100 years after the date of the agreement.

(2) Where any right to which this paragraph applies has not been exercised during the period of 100 years beginning with the date on which it was granted, the burial authority may at any time thereafter serve notice on the owner of the right of its liability to determination under this paragraph, and the right shall determine by virtue of the notice unless, within 6 months of the date of service, the owner notifies the authority in writing of his intention to retain it.

(3) In the case of any agreement to which this paragraph applies, the burial authority may at any time after the period of 100 years beginning with the date of the agreement serve a like notice on the person entitled to its benefit, and the agreement shall determine by virtue of the notice unless, within 6 months of the date of service, that person notifies the authority in writing of his intention that the agreement should continue in force.

(4) Where a burial authority are entitled to serve a notice under sub-paragraph (2) or (3) above in respect of any right or agreement, but are unable after reasonable inquiry to trace the owner of the right or, as the case may be, the person entitled to the benefit of the agreement, they may instead—

(a) display the notice in a conspicuous position in the cemetery, and

(b) publish the notice in two successive weeks in one or more newspapers circulating in their area and, if the cemetery is situated outside their area and it is not practicable to select a newspaper circulating both in that area and in the locality of the cemetery, in the same two weeks in one or more newspapers circulating in the locality of the cemetery,

and the sub-paragraph in question shall then have effect as if the notice had been duly served thereunder on the date on which it was first published pursuant to item (b) of this sub-paragraph.

SCHEDULE 3

Article 17

REPEAL OF ENACTMENTS

(1) Chapter	(2) Short Title	(3) Extent of Repeal
43 & 44 Vict. c. 41	The Burial Laws Amendment Act 1880	In section 1 the words from "The word 'graveyard' " to the end of the section. In section 10 the words from "or in the case of any burial ground" to "burials in such burial ground or cemetery" and the words "or of such burial ground or cemetery" and "or other such person as aforesaid". In section 12 the words "vested in any burial board, or".
63 & 64 Vict. c. 15	The Burial Act 1900	Sections 1, 2 and 7 to 11.
1970 c. 29	The Parish Councils and Burial Authorities (Miscellaneous Provisions) Act 1970	In section 1(1), sub-paragraph (a) and the words "grave, vault, tombstone".
1972 c. 70	The Local Government Act 1972	In Schedule 26, paragraphs 12, 13 and 18 to 23, and in paragraph 25 the words "the Burial Act 1900 and".

12th March 1974.

Anthony Crosland,
Secretary of State for the Environment.

12th March 1974.

John Morris,
Secretary of State for Wales.

EXPLANATORY NOTE

(This Note is not part of the Order.)

Section 214(3) of the Local Government Act 1972 provides that provision may be made by Order for the management, regulation and control of the cemeteries of local authorities. This Order contains such provision. In accordance with section 214(4) of the Act, this Order was approved by a resolution of the House of Commons on 25th March 1974 and a resolution of the House of Lords on 28th March 1974. It therefore has effect from 1st April 1974.

1974 No. 629

RATING AND VALUATION

The Rating of Minor Structural Alterations to Dwellings (Specified Amount) Order 1974

Made - - -	*7th March* 1974
Laid before Parliament	13*th March* 1974
Coming into Operation	1*st April* 1974

The Secretary of State for the Environment, in exercise of his powers under section 21(1)(*b*) of the Local Government Act 1974 (**a**) and of all other powers enabling him in that behalf, hereby makes the following order:—

1. This order may be cited as the Rating of Minor Structural Alterations to Dwellings (Specified Amount) Order 1974 and shall come into operation on 1st April 1974.

2. The Interpretation Act 1889 (**b**) shall apply for the interpretation of this order as it applies for the interpretation of an Act of Parliament.

3. The amount specified for the purposes of section 21(1)(*b*) of the Local Government Act 1974 is £30.

Anthony Crosland,
Secretary of State for the Environment.

7th March 1974.

(**a**) 1974 c. 7.   (**b**) 1889 c. 63.

EXPLANATORY NOTE

(This Note is not part of the Order.)

Section 21 of the Local Government Act 1974 makes special provision with respect to the alteration of valuation lists on or after 1st April 1974 on account of minor structural alterations to dwellings or mixed hereditaments within the meaning of section 48 of the General Rate Act 1967 (c.9). In a case other than one to which section 21 (1) (*a*) applies (central heating installations), section 21(1) (*b*) of the Act of 1974 provides that no proposal for an alteration may be made if the proposal would be for an increase not exceeding such amount as the Secretary of State may by Order specify. The Order specifies an amount of £30.

STATUTORY INSTRUMENTS

1974 No. 630

AGRICULTURE

LIVESTOCK INDUSTRIES

The Calf Subsidies (United Kingdom) Scheme 1974

Laid before Parliament in draft

Made - - - -		*29th March* 1974
Coming into Operation		*1st April* 1974

The Minister of Agriculture, Fisheries and Food, the Secretary of State for Scotland and the Secretary of State for Wales, acting jointly, being the appropriate Minister in relation to a joint scheme for the whole of the United Kingdom, in exercise of the power conferred by sections 1 and 4 of the Agriculture (Calf Subsidies) Act 1952**(a)**, as amended by section 10 of the Agriculture Act 1967**(b)**, and by the said section 10, and now vested in them **(c)**, and of all other powers enabling them in that behalf, with the approval of the Treasury, hereby make the following scheme:—

Citation, extent and commencement

1. This scheme, which may be cited as the Calf Subsidies (United Kingdom) Scheme 1974, shall apply to the United Kingdom and shall come into operation on 1st April 1974, or on the date on which it is made, whichever is the later.

Interpretation

2.—(1) In this scheme the following expressions have the meanings hereby respectively assigned to them:—

"the Act" means the Agriculture (Calf Subsidies) Act 1952;

"carcases" means carcases of cattle;

"the Minister" means the Minister of Agriculture, Fisheries and Food;

"proper officer" means for any of the purposes of this scheme the person for the time being authorised to act for that purpose, in England by the Minister, in Scotland by the Secretary of State for Scotland, in Wales by the Minister and the Secretary of State for Wales, acting jointly, or by either of them, and in Northern Ireland by the Department of Agriculture for Northern Ireland.

(2) For the purposes of Part I of this scheme the limit of age at which an animal ceases to be a calf shall (subject to paragraph 6(2) below) be the age when it cuts its first permanent incisor tooth.

(a) 1952 c. 62. (b) 1967 c. 22.
(c) *See* S.I. 1969/388 (1969 I, p. 1070).

(3) The Interpretation Act 1889(a) applies to the interpretation of this scheme as it applies to the interpretation of an Act of Parliament.

Applications for subsidy

3. It shall be a condition of the payment of a subsidy under this scheme that any person who desires to be paid in accordance with the provisions of this scheme shall apply in writing in such form applicable to Part I or Part II thereof and at such time as in relation to England the Minister, to Scotland the Secretary of State for Scotland, to Wales the Minister and the Secretary of State for Wales, acting jointly, and to Northern Ireland the Department of Agriculture for Northern Ireland may from time to time respectively require.

PART I

STAGE A—CALVES

Rates of subsidy

4. Subject to the provisions of this scheme, the Minister or the Secretary of State for Scotland may pay to the person who is the owner of a calf to which this part of this scheme applies at the time when the calf is certified to be a calf of the description specified in this part of this scheme—

   (*a*) in the case of a heifer calf, a subsidy of £6.50, or

   (*b*) in the case of a male calf, a subsidy of £8.50.

Eligible calves

5. The description of calf specified in this part of this scheme is any male or heifer calf, except a heifer calf of the Guernsey, Jersey, Friesian or Ayrshire breeds, which has been reasonably well reared and is, or will after further rearing be, suitable for beef production or, if a heifer calf, for use for breeding for beef production, being in any case an animal which, if slaughtered either immediately or after a period of further rearing and fattening, would be likely to yield a carcase of reasonably good quality beef, and which, in the case of an animal in Northern Ireland, is without horns, other than rudimentary or stub horns, and without unhealed wounds caused by the removal of its horns.

Conditions of subsidy

6.—(1) A calf to which this part of this scheme applies is a calf which—

   (*a*) was born in the United Kingdom within the period beginning with 30th October 1973 and ending with 29th October 1976;

   (*b*) has been certified by a proper officer to be of the description specified in paragraph 5 above;

   (*c*) had not been previously so certified under either this scheme or a corresponding provision of any earlier scheme made under the Act; and

   (*d*) had not at the time of certification attained the age at which it ceases to be a calf for the purposes of this part of this scheme.

(2) Sub-paragraph (1)(*d*) above shall not apply where the Minister in the case of an animal in England or Northern Ireland, the Secretary of State for Scotland in the case of an animal in Scotland, or the Minister and the Secretary of State for Wales, acting jointly, in the case of an animal in Wales, is or are satisfied that the animal in question would have been certified under this part of this

---

(a) 1889 c. 63.

scheme before it attained the age referred to in that sub-paragraph had certification not been delayed in order to avoid the risk of the introduction or spread-
ing of animal disease.

(3) It shall be a condition of the payment of a subsidy under this part of this
scheme that any person who desires to be paid in accordance with the provisions
thereof in respect of any calves—

    (*a*) shall collect them at a convenient place for the purposes of examination
and marking in accordance with any order made under section 11 of the
Agriculture Act 1967;

    (*b*) shall so manage and secure them before, during and after their exam-
ination and marking that the person appointed for those purposes may
carry out the examination and marking without risk of injury to himself;
and

    (*c*) shall give to the person appointed for those purposes such assistance
as he may reasonably require in carrying them out.

PART II

STAGE B—CARCASES

Subsidies in respect of carcases

7.—(1) Subject to the provisions of this part of this scheme the Minister or
the Secretary of State for Scotland may pay to the person who is the producer
of a carcase to which this part of this scheme applies a subsidy at the rate
determined in accordance with paragraph 10 below.

(2) This part of this scheme applies to any carcase which—

    (*a*) is eligible for payment of subsidy in accordance with the provisions
of the Schedule to this scheme; and

    (*b*) is not the carcase of an animal in respect of which a subsidy has been
paid under Part I of this scheme (or under any earlier scheme made under
the Act) or which has been imported into the United Kingdom.

(3) In this paragraph "producer" means the person in whose name the carcase
is presented for certification under this part of this scheme.

Conditions of subsidy

8. It shall be a condition of the payment of subsidy under this part of this
scheme that—

    (*a*) the carcase has been presented for certification at the place and in the
manner specified in paragraph 5 of the Schedule to this scheme;

    (*b*) the carcase is certified by a proper officer to be a carcase of the descrip-
tion specified in paragraph 7(2)(*a*) above; and

    (*c*) such proper officer is satisfied that subsidy under any scheme made under
the Act, whether as originally enacted or as amended by sections 10 and
11 of the Agriculture Act 1967, has not previously been paid in respect of
the animal in question, either as a calf or a carcase.

Period for presentation

9. Subsidy shall not be payable under this part of this scheme unless the
carcase is certified in accordance with paragraph 8(*b*) above within the period
beginning with 1st April 1974 or the date on which this scheme comes into
operation, whichever is the later, and ending with 31st March 1977.

Amount of subsidy

10.—(1) The rates of subsidy in respect of carcases of animals eligible for subsidy under this part of this scheme shall be such amounts as the Minister, the Secretary of State for Scotland and the Secretary of State for Wales, acting jointly, with the approval of the Treasury, determine as being approximately equivalent on the average to the rates of subsidy which would have been payable under Part I of this scheme (or the corresponding provisions of any earlier scheme made under the Act) if the animals in question had been certified for subsidy under the said Part I (or the corresponding provisions of any such earlier scheme).

(2) For the purposes of this paragraph the fact that heifer calves of certain breeds are excepted under paragraph 5 of this scheme (or a corresponding provision of any such earlier scheme) shall be disregarded.

Delegation to Meat and Livestock Commission

11. The Minister, the Secretary of State for Scotland and the Secretary of State for Wales, acting jointly, may, to such extent and in such manner as they may from time to time direct, delegate to the Meat and Livestock Commission established under section 1 of the Agriculture Act 1967 any of their functions in relation to Great Britain conferred on them by this part of this scheme.

In Witness whereof the Official Seal of the Minister of Agriculture, Fisheries and Food is hereunto affixed on 28th March 1974.

(L.S.)
Frederick Peart,
Minister of Agriculture, Fisheries and Food.

William Ross,
28th March 1974.
Secretary of State for Scotland.

John Morris,
28th March 1974.
Secretary of State for Wales.

We approve.

John Golding,
T. Pendry,
29th March 1974.
Two of the Lords Commissioners of Her Majesty's Treasury.

SCHEDULE

STAGE B—CARCASES

Carcases eligible for subsidy

1. The carcases of fat cattle of the following kinds, namely fat steers, clean fat heifers, bulls and other male cattle, of the standards, minimum weights and other qualifications set out in paragraphs 2 and 3 below, are eligible for payment of subsidy. The carcases of cattle specified in paragraph 4 below are, subject to the exceptions therein mentioned, not eligible.

QUALIFYING STANDARDS

2. *Steers and Heifers*

(i) *General Class*

The dressed carcase weight must be not less than 450 lb. in the case of a steer and not less than 390 lb. in the case of a heifer. The carcase must be of good conformation, the rounds, loins and ribs being reasonably well fleshed and the chucks and plates reasonably thick, but the neck and foreshanks may be slightly long and thin. However, some slight lack of flesh development in the rounds is acceptable provided the minimum qualifying standards are met in all other respects. The carcases of young animals of such conformation need have only a thin exterior fat covering. Carcases from older animals may possess a rather thicker fat covering but must not be excessively fat or patchy.

(ii) *Lightweight animals*

The dressed carcase weight must be not less than 410 lb. in the case of a steer and not less than 345 lb. in the case of a heifer. The carcase must be moderately compact and moderately thickly fleshed throughout with rounds moderately well developed and rounded, loins and ribs thick and well fleshed. The neck and shanks must be relatively short. Fat covering, which should be smooth and evenly distributed over the exterior of the carcase, may vary in quantity from medium to light. Cod or udder, kidney and aitch fat should be adequate but not excessive. If the loins or ribs are only moderately thick and moderately well fleshed, the carcase will be eligible provided it satisfies these specifications in all other respects.

3. *Bulls*

A bull carcase must conform to either of the following standards:

(i) *General Class*

The dressed carcase weight must be not less than 450 lb. The carcase must be of good conformation, the rounds, loins and ribs being reasonably well fleshed and the shoulders and plates reasonably thick. The shanks may be slightly long. The forequarters may be relatively heavier than in steer carcases but must not be excessively so. The exterior fat covering on carcases of such conformation may vary in quantity from medium to thin but should not be excessive or patchy. Inside, kidney and aitch fat must not be excessive but should be at least in moderate supply. Flesh should be moderately firm. Colour must not be dark but may range from a light cherry red to a slightly darker red. The chine bones should be soft and red and terminate in soft pearly white cartilage.

(ii) *Special lightweight bulls*

The dressed carcase weight must be not less than 410 lb. The carcase must be moderately compact and moderately thickly fleshed throughout with rounds moderately well developed and rounded. Loins, ribs and shoulders should be thick and well fleshed. Shanks and neck must be relatively short. The forequarters may be relatively heavier than in steer carcases but must not be excessively so.

Fat covering, which must be present, should be smooth and evenly distributed over the carcase exterior and may vary in quantity from medium to light. Inside, kidney and aitch fat should be adequate but not excessive.

Flesh must be moderately firm. Colour must not be dark but may range from light cherry red to a slightly darker red. The chine bones should be soft and red and terminate in soft pearly white cartilage.

If the loins or ribs are only moderately thick and moderately well fleshed the carcase will be eligible provided it satisfies these specifications in all other respects.

4. *Ineligible carcases*

The following carcases are not eligible for payment of subsidy:

(a) carcases of bulls or other male cattle showing "bullish" characteristics except for the carcases of bulls and other male cattle meeting the qualifying standards in paragraph 3;

(b) carcases of cows;

(c) carcases of other female cattle which are or have been pregnant, except where, in the opinion of the certifying officer, the quality of the carcase has not been seriously depreciated by the pregnancy;

(d) carcases which have not been sold unless—

    (i) they are for sale by or on behalf of the producer in a butchery business and are not intended for consumption in the producer's household, or

    (ii) they are transferred in special circumstances approved by the Meat and Livestock Commission (in Great Britain) or the Department of Agriculture for Northern Ireland (in Northern Ireland);

(e) carcases which are carcases of affected animals as defined in the Tuberculosis Order 1964(a), the Tuberculosis (Compensation) (Scotland) Order 1964(b), the Bovine Tuberculosis (Northern Ireland) Order 1935(c), the Tuberculosis Control Order (Northern Ireland) 1964(d), the Tuberculosis Control (Amendment) Order (Northern Ireland) 1968(e), the Tuberculosis Control (Amendment) Order (Northern Ireland) 1973(f), or any order amending or re-enacting these orders;

(f) carcases of brucellosis reactor cattle which are slaughtered under terms by which compensation is payable by the Minister, the Secretary of State or the Department of Agriculture for Northern Ireland and the reactor becomes his or their property, except that in Northern Ireland carcases of animals for which the owner receives carcase value only may be presented for certification;

(g) carcases wholly condemned as unfit for human consumption.

5. *Presentation*

Carcases must be presented at deadweight certification centres approved by the Meat and Livestock Commission (in Great Britain) or the Department of Agriculture for Northern Ireland (in Northern Ireland). They must be presented either as whole carcases or in sides, both sides together, and must conform to the following specifications and conditions for dressing and weighing:—

(A) The following offals shall be removed:

    (a) hide;

    (b) head and tongue; but in Northern Ireland, unless the Department of Agriculture agrees to the contrary, the ears must be examined by the certifying officer before slaughter, after which they may be removed. In Great Britain in every case, and in Northern Ireland where the Department has agreed not to inspect before slaughter, the ears must be left naturally attached to the carcase until it has been examined as a carcase to determine eligibility for subsidy, after which they may be removed;

    (c) feet;

(a) S.I. 1964/1151 (1964 II, p. 2634).   (b) S.I. 1964/1152 (1964 II, p. 2643).
(c) S.R. & O. (N.I.)1935/39.   (d) S.R. & O. (N.I.) 1964/31.
(e) S.R. & O. (N.I.)1968/236.   (f) S.R. & O. (N.I.)1973/76.

(*d*) guts and tripes with the accompanying glands:
   (i) liver;
   (ii) spleen;
   (iii) pancreas;
(*e*) caul and gut fat;
(*f*) heart and heart fat;
(*g*) heart bread and neck bread (thymus glands);
(*h*) lights (lungs, trachea and larynx);
(*i*) thick skirt (pillar of diaphragm);
(*j*) tail;
(*k*) genito-urinary organs, excluding kidneys;
(*l*) large blood vessels of abdomen and thorax.

(B) The following specifications shall be observed when offals are removed:
   (*a*) the head shall be removed at the junction of the skull and the spinal column, thereby leaving the entire spinal column on the carcase;
   (*b*) the forefeet shall be removed at the knee joint and the hindfeet at the hock joint;
   (*c*) the "rib skirt" or diaphragm shall be trimmed to leave a margin of at least one half inch of "skin" or membranous portion along the bottom; this will leave the fleshy part of the diaphragm intact;
   (*d*) there shall be no trimming of the neck beyond cutting off the ragged edges; the jugular vein may be removed cleanly but there shall be no trimming of the surrounding fat;
   (*e*) no channel or kidney fat shall be removed unless a corresponding addition to the weight is made;
   (*f*) the tail shall be removed at the second joint from the base bone;
   (*g*) where it is trade practice to leave the thick skirt or tail or both these offals on the carcase, a weight deduction of 3 lb. will be made in respect of the tail and a weight deduction of 2 lb. in respect of the thick skirt.

(C) The following conditions shall apply to the weighing of carcases of cattle:
   (*a*) carcases must be dressed according to the specifications above when they are weighed, except that the ears may be removed before weighing after the carcase has been accepted as being eligible for certification; if they are not so removed, a deduction of 2 lb., i.e. 1 lb. for each ear, will be made;
   (*b*) when the kidneys are removed before the carcase is weighed, an addition of 3 lb. shall be made to the carcase weight;
   (*c*) carcases shall be weighed:
      (i) if weighed "hot", within 1 hour of slaughter;
      (ii) if weighed "cold", within 24 hours of slaughter except when prior approval for an extension of this period has been given;
   (*d*) when carcases are weighed "hot", the "cold" weight will be ascertained by making rebates as follows:

	Hot weight	Rebate
	lb.	lb.
Sides of Beef	250 and under	4
	251 to 300	5
	301 to 400	6
	over 400	7

EXPLANATORY NOTE

(This Note is not part of the Scheme.)

Part I of this Scheme (Stage A) ,which applies to calves born in the United Kingdom between 30th October 1973 and 29th October 1976 continues provision for the payment of calf subsidies under the Agriculture (Calf Subsidies) Act 1952. The amounts payable per head are £6.50 for heifers and £8.50 for male calves.

Part II of the Scheme (Stage B), made under the extended powers conferred by section 10 of the Agriculture Act 1967, provides for the payment of subsidy to producers of certain carcases. Such carcases must satisfy the standards of eligibility for payment of subsidy set out in the Schedule to the Scheme. They must not be of animals in respect of which subsidy has been paid at Stage A, or which have been imported into the United Kingdom. They must be presented for certification at the place and in the manner specified in the Schedule, and they must be certified between 1st April 1974 and 31st March 1977.

The rates of subsidy at Stage B are such amounts as are determined to be approximately equivalent on the average to the rates which would have been payable at Stage A if the animals in question had been certified (while calves) at Stage A.

The Scheme, which applies to the whole of the United Kingdom, contains a provision enabling the Stage B functions in Great Britain to be delegated to the Meat and Livestock Commission.

This Scheme enables subsidy to be paid on live young bulls, and removes the dentition test for Stage B certification of bulls and special lightweight animals. Otherwise, except for changes in the dates and minor and consequential amendments, this Scheme is the same as its predecessor.

STATUTORY INSTRUMENTS

1974 No. 631

WAGES COUNCILS

The Wages Regulation (Made-up Textiles) Order 1974

Made – – – –	29th March 1974
Coming into Operation	30th April 1974

Whereas the Secretary of State has received from the Made-up Textiles Wages Council (Great Britain) the wages regulation proposals set out in the Schedule hereto;

Now, therefore, the Secretary of State in exercise of powers conferred by section 11 of the Wages Councils Act 1959(a), as modified by Article 2 of the Counter-Inflation (Modification of Wages Councils Act 1959) Order 1973(b), and now vested in him(c), and of all other powers enabling him in that behalf, hereby makes the following Order:—

1. This Order may be cited as the Wages Regulation (Made-up Textiles) Order 1974.

2.—(1) In this Order the expression "the specified date" means the 30th April 1974, provided that where, as respects any worker who is paid wages at intervals not exceeding seven days, that date does not correspond with the beginning of the period for which the wages are paid, the expression "the specified date" means, as respects that worker, the beginning of the next such period following that date.

(2) The Interpretation Act 1889(d) shall apply to the interpretation of this Order as it applies to the interpretation of an Act of Parliament and as if this Order and the Order hereby revoked were Acts of Parliament.

3. The wages regulation proposals set out in the Schedule hereto shall have effect as from the specified date and as from that date the Wages Regulation (Made-up Textiles) Order 1973(e) shall cease to have effect.

Signed by order of the Secretary of State.

29th March 1974.

W. H. Marsh,
Assistant Secretary,
Department of Employment.

(a) 1959 c. 69. (b) S.I. 1973/661 (1973 I, p. 2141).
(c) S.I. 1959/1769, 1968/729 (1959 I, p. 1795; 1968 II, p. 2108).
(d) 1889 c. 63. (e) S.I. 1973/175 (1973 I, p. 702).

Article 3

SCHEDULE 1

The following minimum remuneration shall be substituted for the statutory minimum remuneration fixed by the Wages Regulation (Made-up Textiles) Order 1973 (Order M.T. (71)).

STATUTORY MINIMUM REMUNERATION

PART I

GENERAL

1. The minimum remuneration payable to a worker to whom this Schedule applies for all work except work to which a minimum overtime rate applies under Part IV of this Schedule is:—

(1) in the case of a time worker, the general minimum time rate payable to the worker under Part II or Part III of this Schedule;

(2) in the case of a worker employed on piece work, piece rates each of which would yield, in the circumstances of the case, to an ordinary worker at least the same amount of money as the piece work basis time rate applicable to the worker under Part II or Part III of this Schedule.

PART II

MALE WORKERS

GENERAL MINIMUM TIME RATES

2. The general minimum time rates payable to male workers are as follows:—

	Per hour p
(1) Workers aged 21 years or over and employed as awl and needle stitchers (leather and canvas), cutters, letter writers (other than stencillers), machinists (sewing), mixers, palm and needle hands, ropers of tents and coal sacks, or splicers of ropes over $1\frac{1}{2}$ in. in circumference	44
(2) All other workers, being aged—	
21 years or over	41
20 and under 21 years	39
19 ,, ,, 20 ,,	38
18 ,, ,, 19 ,,	37
17 ,, ,, 18 ,,	$32\frac{1}{2}$
under 17 years	$27\frac{1}{2}$

Provided that the general minimum time rate payable during his first six months' employment in the trade to a worker who enters, or has entered, the trade for the first time at or over the age of 18 years shall be $\frac{1}{2}$p per hour less than the rate otherwise payable under sub-paragraph (1) or (2) of this paragraph.

PIECE WORK BASIS TIME RATES

3. *The piece work basis time rates applicable to male workers employed on piece work shall be the appropriate general minimum time rates payable to workers aged 21 years or over (as set out in sub-paragraph (1) or (2) of paragraph 2), increased by $12\frac{1}{2}$ per cent.*

PART III

FEMALE WORKERS

GENERAL MINIMUM TIME RATES

4. The general minimum time rates payable to female workers are as follows:—

Per hour
p

(1) Workers aged 18 years or over and employed as awl and needle stitchers (leather and canvas), cutters, letter writers (other than stencillers), machinists (sewing), mixers, palm and needle hands, ropers of tents and coal sacks, or splicers of ropes over $1\frac{1}{2}$ in. in circumference   ..   .. $39\frac{1}{2}$

(2) All other workers, being aged—
18 years or over   37
17 and under 18 years   ..   .. $32\frac{1}{2}$
under *17* years   ..   .. $27\frac{1}{2}$

Provided that the general minimum time rate payable during her first six months' employment in the trade to a worker who enters, or has entered, the trade for the first time at or over the age of 16 years shall be $\frac{1}{2}$p per hour less than the minimum rate otherwise payable under sub-paragraph (1) or (2) of this paragraph.

PIECE WORK BASIS TIME RATES

5. *The piece work basis time rates applicable to all female workers employed on piece work shall be the appropriate general minimum time rate payable to workers aged 18 years or over (as set out in sub-paragraph (1) or (2) of paragraph 4), increased by $12\frac{1}{2}$ per cent.*

PART IV

OVERTIME AND WAITING TIME

MINIMUM OVERTIME RATES

6. Minimum overtime rates are payable to a worker to whom this Schedule applies as follows:—

(1) on any day except a Saturday, Sunday or customary holiday—

(*a*) for the first 2 hours worked in excess of 8 hours .. time-and-a-quarter

(*b*) thereafter   ..   ..   time-and-a-half

Provided that where it is, or may become, the established practice of the employer to require the worker's attendance on five days only in the week the said minimum overtime rates of time-and-a-quarter and time-and-a-half shall be payable after $8\frac{3}{4}$ and $10\frac{3}{4}$ hours' work respectively;

(2) on a Saturday, not being a customary holiday—

    (a) for the first 2 hours worked in excess of 3 hours ..   time-and-a-quarter

    (b) thereafter   ..   ..   time-and-a-half

Provided that where it is, or may become, the established practice of the employer to require the worker's attendance on five days only in the week, minimum overtime rates shall be payable to the worker for all time worked on a Saturday as follows:—

    (i) for the first 2 hours   ..   ..   time-and-a-quarter

    (ii) thereafter ..   ..   time-and-a-half

(3) on a Sunday or a customary holiday for all time worked   double time

(4) in any week exclusive of any time for which a minimum overtime rate is payable under the foregoing provisions of this paragraph, for all time worked in excess of 40 hours   time-and-a-quarter

7. In this Part of this Schedule—

(1) the expression "customary holiday" means—

    (a) (i) in England and Wales—

        Christmas Day;
        26th December if it be not a Sunday, 27th December in a year when 25th or 26th December is a Sunday;
        New Year's Day, if it be not a Sunday, or if be a Sunday, 2nd January;
        Good Friday;
        Easter Monday;
        the last Monday in May;
        the last Monday in August;
        (or where a day is substituted for any of the above days by national proclamation, that day);

        (ii) in Scotland—

        New Year's Day and the following day:

        Provided that if New Year's Day falls on a Sunday the holidays shall be the following Monday and Tuesday and if New Year's Day falls on a Saturday the holidays shall be New Year's Day and the following Monday;

        the local Spring Holiday;

        the local Autumn Holiday; and

        three other days (being normal working days for the workers concerned) in the course of a calendar year, to be fixed by the employer and notified to the workers not less than three weeks before the holiday; or

    (b) in the case of each of the said days such week day as may be substituted therefor, being either—

      (i) a day which is by local custom recognised as a day of holiday, or

      (ii) a day which falls within three weeks of the day for which it is substituted, and is mutually agreed between the employer and the worker.

(2) the expressions "time-and-a-quarter", "time-and-a-half" and "double time" mean respectively—

(a) in the case of a time worker, one and a quarter times, one and a half times and twice the general minimum time rate otherwise applicable to the worker under Part II or Part III of this Schedule;

(b) in the case of a worker employed on piece work—

(i) a time rate equal respectively to one quarter, one half and the whole of the piece work basis time rate otherwise applicable to the worker under Part II or Part III of this Schedule and, in addition thereto,

(ii) the piece rates otherwise applicable to the worker under paragraph 1(2).

WAITING TIME

8.—(1) A worker is entitled to payment of the minimum remuneration specified in this Schedule for all time during which he is present on the premises of his employer unless he is present thereon in any of the following circumstances—

(a) without the employer's consent, express or implied,

(b) for some purpose unconnected with his work and other than that of waiting for work to be given to him to perform,

(c) by reason only of the fact that he is resident thereon,

(d) during normal meal times in a room or place in which no work is being done, and he is not waiting for work to be given to him to perform.

(2) The minimum remuneration payable under sub-paragraph (1) of this paragraph to a piece worker when not engaged on piece work is that which would be applicable if he were a time worker.

PART V

APPLICABILITY OF STATUTORY MINIMUM REMUNERATION

9. This Schedule does not apply to workers who are persons registered as handicapped by disablement in pursuance of the Disabled Persons (Employment) Acts 1944 and 1958(a), in respect of their employment by Remploy Limited but, save as aforesaid, applies to workers in relation to whom the Made-up Textiles Wages Council (Great Britain) operates, that is to say, workers employed in Great Britain in the trade specified in the Schedule to the Trade Boards (Made-up Textiles Trade, Great Britain) (Constitution and Proceedings) Regulations 1932(b), that is to say:—

(1) The making from woven fabrics of any of the following articles, or the repairing thereof:—

tarpaulins; tents; marquees; rick, cart or wagon covers; nose-bags, oilskin clothing or headgear or linings therefor; flags made of more than one piece; baths, basins, buckets, beds, cots, hammocks, ground sheets or similar articles; girths and articles known in the trade as horse-clothing.

(a) 1944 c. 10; 1958 c. 33.
(b) S.R. & O. 1932/805 (Rev. XXIII, p. 480: 1932, p. 1706).

(2) The making of any of the following articles from fabrics of the kind specified in sub-paragraph (1) above, or the repairing thereof, when carried on in association with or in conjunction with the making or repairing of any of the articles mentioned in the said sub-paragraph:—

rope-bound coal and coke sacks; haversacks or knapsacks; outside and inside blinds or awnings; flags made of one piece; bunting decorations;

including:—

(A) the following operations when carried on in association with or in conjunction with the operations specified in sub-paragraphs (1) and (2) above, viz., operations known in the trade as—

(i) the dyeing, oiling, tarring, chemically treating, or otherwise proofing of the fabrics mentioned in sub-paragraph (1) and the preparation of dressings therefor;

(ii) cutting, sewing, finishing, stencilling or branding by hand or machine;

(B) the following or similar operations performed by hand or machine when incidental to and carried on in association with or in conjunction with the operations specified in sub-paragraphs (1) and (2) above:—

(i) the splicing or braiding of rope, cord or twine;

(ii) the making of fittings of leather or webbing, including the assembling of metal or other parts;

(iii) the sewing or attaching to any of the articles mentioned in sub-paragraph (1) or (2) above of:—

(a) rope, cord or twine;

(b) leather, webbing or metal or fittings made thereof;

(C) the warehousing of, the packing of, and similar operations in regard to any of the articles mentioned in sub-paragraphs (1) and (2) above, when carried on in association with or in conjunction with the operations specified in the said sub-paragraphs;

(D) the warehousing of, the packing of, and similar operations in regard to any other articles when carried on in or in association with or in conjunction with any business, establishment, branch or department mainly engaged in any of the operations mentioned in sub-paragraph (C) above;

but excluding:—

(i) the making of haversacks and knapsacks when made in association with or in conjunction with the making of and as part of military web equipment;

(ii) the making of folding or deck chairs;

(iii) the making or repairing of horse-clothing, girths and nose-bags when carried on in association with or in conjunction with the making or repairing of leather saddlery or harness;

(iv) the making or repairing of rubberised articles;

(v) the making or repairing of tarpaulins or of rope-bound coal and coke sacks in an establishment, business, branch or department in which the making of sails is the main or principal business of the establishment, business, branch or department;

(vi) the printing by hand or machine of flags or parts thereof;

(vii) the operations mentioned in sub-paragraph (C) above, when carried on in or in association with or in conjunction with any business, establishment, branch or department mainly engaged in the warehousing of, the packing of, and similar operations in regard to corn sacks, flour sacks, coal sacks, sugar sacks, cement bags, sand bags, nail bags, potato bags, seed bags and similar sacks or bags;

(viii) operations performed by workers directly employed by railway companies;

(ix) operations included in the Trade Boards (Hat, Cap and Millinery) Order 1919(a);

(x) operations included in the Trade Boards (Linen and Cotton Handkerchief and Household Goods and Linen Piece Goods) Order 1920(b);

(xi) operations included in the Trade Boards (Rope, Twine and Net) Order 1919(c), but not specifically mentioned in the Trade Boards (Made-up Textiles) Order 1920(d).

(a) S.R. & O. 1919/1262 (1919 II, p. 515).   (b) S.R. & O. 1920/103 (1920 II, p. 780).
(c) S.R. & O. 1919/930 (1919 II, p. 524).   (d) S.R. & O. 1920/1901 (1920 II, p. 782).

EXPLANATORY NOTE

(This Note is not part of the Order.)

This Order, which has effect from 30th April 1974, sets out the increased statutory minimum remuneration payable to workers in relation to whom the Made-up Textiles Wages Council (Great Britain) operates, in substitution for that fixed by the Wages Regulation (Made-up Textiles) Order 1973 (Order M.T. (71)), which Order is revoked.

New provisions are printed in italics.

STATUTORY INSTRUMENTS

1974 No. 632

WAGES COUNCILS

The Wages Regulation (Made-up Textiles) (Holidays) Order 1974

Made - - - -	*29th March* 1974
Coming into Operation	*30th April* 1974

Whereas the Secretary of State has received from the Made-up Textiles Wages Council (Great Britain) the wages regulation proposals set out in the Schedule hereto;

Now, therefore, the Secretary of State in exercise of powers conferred by section 11 of the Wages Councils Act 1959(a), as modified by Article 2 of the Counter-Inflation (Modification of Wages Councils Act 1959) Order 1973(b), and now vested in him(c), and of all other powers enabling him in that behalf, hereby makes the following Order:—

1. This Order may be cited as the Wages Regulation (Made-up Textiles) (Holidays) Order 1974.

2.—(1) In this Order the expression "the specified date" means the 30th April 1974, provided that where, as respects any worker who is paid wages at intervals not exceeding seven days, that date does not correspond with the beginning of the period for which the wages are paid, the expression "the specified date" means, as respects that worker, the beginning of the next such period following that date.

(2) The Interpretation Act 1889(d) shall apply to the interpretation of this Order as it applies to the interpretation of an Act of Parliament and as if this Order and the Order hereby revoked were Acts of Parliament.

3. The wages regulation proposals set out in the Schedule hereto shall have effect as from the specified date and as from that date the Wages Regulation (Made-up Textiles) (Holidays) Order 1970(e) as amended by Schedule 2 to the Wages Regulation (Made-up Textiles) Order 1973(f) shall cease to have effect.

Signed by order of the Secretary of State.

29th March 1974.

W. H. Marsh,
Assistant Secretary,
Department of Employment.

(a) 1959 c. 69.　　　　　　　　　　　(b) S.I. 1973/661 (1973 I, p. 2141).
(c) S.I. 1959/1769, 1968/729 (1959 I, p. 1795; 1968 II, p. 2108).
(d) 1889 c. 63.　　　　　　　　　　　(e) S.I. 1970/1228 (1970 II, p. 4062).
(f) S.I. 1973/175 (1973 I, p. 702).

Article 3

SCHEDULE

The following provisions as to holidays and holiday remuneration shall be sub-stituted for the provisions as to holidays and holiday remuneration set out in the Wages Regulation (Made-up Textiles) (Holidays) Order 1970 (Order M.T. (67), as amended by Schedule 2 to the Wages Regulation (Made-up Textiles) Order 1973 (Order M.T. (71)).

PART I

APPLICATION

1. This Schedule applies to every worker (other than a homeworker) for whom statutory minimum remuneration has been fixed.

PART II

CUSTOMARY HOLIDAYS

2.—(1) An employer shall allow to every worker to whom this Schedule applies a holiday (hereinafter referred to as a "customary holiday") in each year on the days specified in the following sub-paragraph, provided that the worker has been in his employment for a period of not less than eight weeks immediately preceding the customary holiday and unless excused by the employer or absent by reason of the proved illness of the worker has worked for the employer throughout the last working day on which work was available to him prior to the holiday.

(2) The said customary holidays are:—

  (a) (i) in England and Wales—

   Christmas Day;
   26th December if it be not a Sunday, 27th December in a year when 25th or 26th December is a Sunday; *New Year's Day, if it be not a Sunday, or if it be a Sunday, 2nd January;*
   Good Friday;
   Easter Monday;
   the last Monday in May; and
   the last Monday in August;
   (or where a day is substituted for any of the above days by national proclamation, that day);

   (ii) in Scotland—

   New Year's Day and the following day:

    Provided that if New Year's Day falls on a Sunday the holidays shall be the following Monday and Tuesday and if New Year's Day falls on a Saturday the holidays shall be New Year's Day and the following Monday;
   the local Spring Holiday;
   the local Autumn Holiday; and

   three other days (being normal working days for the workers concerned) in the course of a calendar year, to be fixed by the employer and notified to the workers not less than three weeks before the holiday;
  or
   (b) in the case of each of the said days such week day as may be substituted therefor, being either—
    (i) a day which is by local custom recognised as a day of holiday, or
    (ii) a day which falls within three weeks of the day for which it is substituted, and is mutually agreed between the employer and the worker.

(3) Where Christmas Day, 26th December, or New Year's Day or the following day (or any day substituted for any one of these days under the provision of (*b*) of sub-paragraph (2) of this paragraph), falls on a Saturday, the employer shall allow:—

(*a*) to a worker who normally works for the employer on five days a week but does not normally work for him on a Saturday, instead of the customary holiday, a holiday on a day on which the worker normally works for the employer during the eight weeks immediately following the customary holiday;

(*b*) to a worker who normally works for the employer on six days a week (including Saturday) but normally works on a Saturday for not more than five hours, in addition to the customary holiday, a holiday on a Saturday during the eight weeks immediately following the customary holiday:

Provided that a worker shall not be entitled to a holiday in pursuance of this sub-paragraph:—

(i) if he is not qualified under sub-paragraph (1) of this paragraph to be allowed the customary holiday and would not be so qualified if he normally worked for the employer on a Saturday; or

(ii) if, in the case of a worker to whom (*a*) of this sub-paragraph applies, he has been allowed a day of holiday (not being a customary holiday or a day of annual holiday) on a day on which he would normally work for the employer in the four weeks immediately preceding the customary holiday and has been paid for that holiday not less than the amount to which he would have been entitled had the day been a customary holiday allowed to him under sub-paragraph (1) of this paragraph; or

(iii) if, in the case of a worker to whom (*b*) of this sub-paragraph applies, he has been allowed not less than 4 hours off from work during his normal working hours on a day on which the worker would normally have worked for the employer (not being a customary holiday or a day of annual holiday) during the ten days immediately preceding the customary holiday and has been paid in respect of the hours off so allowed to him not less than the statutory minimum remuneration to which he would have been entitled as a time worker if he had worked throughout those hours on his usual work.

(4) Notwithstanding the preceding provisions of this paragraph where by reason of the circumstances under which the work is carried on in an establishment the allowing of the customary holiday is rendered impracticable, a worker may be required to work on a customary holiday (except where in the case of a woman or young person such a requirement would be unlawful) and, if so required, shall be paid for all time worked thereon the statutory minimum remuneration appropriate to him for work on a customary holiday.

PART III

ANNUAL HOLIDAY

3.—(1) Subject to the provisions of sub-paragraph (2) of this paragraph and paragraph 4, in addition to the holidays specified in Part II of this Schedule an employer shall, between 1st May 1974 and 30th September 1974, and between 1st May and 30th September in each succeeding year, allow a holiday (hereinafter referred to as an "annual holiday") to every worker in his employment to whom this Schedule applies who has been employed by him during the 12 months ended on 5th April immediately preceding the commencement of the holiday season for any of the periods of employment set out in the table below and the duration of the annual holiday shall, in the case of each such worker, be related to his period of employment during that 12 months as follows:—

Where the worker's normal working week is 6 days		Where the worker's normal working week is 5 days or less	
Period of employment	Duration of annual holiday	Period of employment	Duration of annual holiday
At least 48 weeks	20 days	At least 48 weeks	17 days
,, ,, 46 ,,	19 ,,	,, ,, 45 ,,	16 ,,
,, ,, 43 ,,	18 ,,	,, ,, 42 ,,	15 ,,
,, ,, 40 ,,	17 ,,	,, ,, 39 ,,	14 ,,
,, ,, 38 ,,	16 ,,	,, ,, 36 ,,	13 ,,
,, ,, 35 ,,	15 ,,	,, ,, 32 ,,	11 ,,
,, ,, 32 ,,	13 ,,	,, ,, 29 ,,	10 ,,
,, ,, 30 ,,	13 ,,	,, ,, 26 ,,	9 ,,
,, ,, 27 ,,	11 ,,	,, ,, 23 ,,	8 ,,
,, ,, 24 ,,	10 ,,	,, ,, 20 ,,	7 ,,
,, ,, 22 ,,	9 ,,	,, ,, 16 ,,	6 ,,
,, ,, 19 ,,	8 ,,	,, ,, 13 ,,	5 ,,
,, ,, 16 ,,	7 ,,	,, ,, 10 ,,	4 ,,
,, ,, 14 ,,	6 ,,	,, ,, 7 ,,	2 ,,
,, ,, 11 ,,	5 ,,	,, ,, 4 ,,	1 day
,, ,, 8 ,,	3 ,,		
,, ,, 6 ,,	3 ,,		
,, ,, 3 ,,	1 day		

(2) Notwithstanding the provisions of the last foregoing sub-paragraph, the number of days of annual holiday which an employer is required to allow to a worker in respect of a period of employment during the 12 months immediately preceding 5th April 1974, and during the 12 months immediately preceding 5th April in any succeeding year shall not exceed in the aggregate three times the number of days constituting the worker's normal working week, *plus 2 days.*

(3) In this Schedule the expression "holiday season" means in relation to an annual holiday during the year 1974, the period commencing on 1st May 1974, and ending on 30th September 1974, and in relation to each subsequent year, the period commencing on 1st May and ending on 30th September in that year.

4.—(1) Subject to the provisions of this paragraph, an annual holiday under this Schedule shall be allowed on consecutive working days, being days on which the worker is normally called upon to work for the employer, and days of annual holiday shall be treated as consecutive notwithstanding that a Sunday or a customary holiday on which the worker is not required to work for the employer intervenes.

(2) (a) Where the number of days of annual holiday for which a worker has qualified exceeds the number of days constituting his normal working week, but does not exceed twice that number, the holiday may be allowed in two periods of consecutive working days; so however that when a holiday is so allowed, one of the periods shall consist of a number of such days not less than the number of days constituting the worker's normal working week.

(b) Where the number of days of annual holiday for which a worker has qualified exceeds twice the number of days constituting his normal working week the holiday may be allowed as follows:—

    (i) as to two periods of consecutive working days, each such period not being less than the period constituting the worker's normal working week, during the holiday season; and

    (ii) as to any additional days, on working days, to be fixed by agreement between the employer or his representative, and the worker or his representative, either during the holiday season or within the period ending on 5th April immediately following the holiday season.

(3) Where a day of holiday allowed to a worker under Part II of this Schedule immediately precedes a period of annual holiday or occurs during such a period then, notwithstanding the foregoing provisions of this paragraph, the duration of that period of annual holiday may be reduced by one day and in such a case one day of annual holiday may be allowed on any working day in the holiday season, or by agreement between the employer and the worker or his representative, on any working day before the beginning of the next following holiday season.

(4) Subject to the provisions of this paragraph, any day of annual holiday under this Schedule may be allowed on a day on which the worker is entitled to a day of holiday or to a half-holiday under any enactment other than the Wages Councils Act 1959.

5. An employer shall give to a worker reasonable notice of the commencing date or dates and duration of the period or periods of his annual holiday. Such notice may be given individually to the worker or by the posting of a notice in the place where the worker is employed.

PART IV

HOLIDAY REMUNERATION

CUSTOMARY HOLIDAYS

6.—(1) Subject to the provisions of this paragraph, for each day of holiday to which a worker is entitled under Part II of this Schedule he shall be paid by the employer as holiday remuneration whichever of the following amounts is the greater:—

    (a) one-fifth of the average weekly earnings of the worker during the 12 months ended on the 5th April immediately preceding the holiday, such average weekly earnings to be determined by dividing, by the number of weeks of employment with the employer during the said period, the total remuneration as defined in paragraph 11 paid to him by the employer during that period:

       Provided that when Good Friday or Easter Monday in England and Wales or the local Spring holiday in Scotland (or days substituted therefor under the provisions of sub-paragraph (2)(b) of paragraph 2) fall after 5th April in any year, the holiday remuneration for any such holiday under this sub-paragraph shall be one-fifth of the average weekly earnings of the worker during the 12 months ended on the 5th April in the preceding calendar year; or

    (b) the amount to which he would have been entitled as a time worker, calculated at the appropriate rate of statutory minimum remuneration, if the day had not been a day of holiday and he had worked on that day on work for which statutory minimum remuneration is payable for the time usually worked by him on that day of the week:

       Provided, however, that payment of the said holiday remuneration is subject to the conditions that the worker (a) has worked throughout the last working day on which work was available to him preceding the holiday and (b) that the worker presents himself for employment at the usual starting hour on the first working day following the holiday and works his normal number of hours on that day or, if he fails to do so, failure is by reason of the proved illness of the worker or with the consent of the employer.

(2) Holiday remuneration in respect of any customary holiday shall be paid by the employer to the worker on the pay day on which the wages for the first working day following the customary holiday are paid.

ANNUAL HOLIDAY

7.—(1) Subject to the provisions of paragraph 8, a worker qualified to be allowed an annual holiday under this Schedule shall be paid as holiday remuneration by his employer in respect thereof, on the last pay day preceding such annual holiday, whichever of the following amounts is the greater:—

    (a) an amount equal to three fifty-seconds of the total remuneration as defined in paragraph 11 paid by the employer to the worker during the 12 months ended on 5th April immediately preceding the holiday; or,

    (b) one day's holiday pay (as defined in paragraph 11) in respect of each day of annual holiday.

(2) Where under the provisions of paragraph 4 an annual holiday is taken in more than one period, the holiday remuneration shall be apportioned accordingly.

8. Where any accrued holiday remuneration has been paid by the employer to the worker (in accordance with paragraph 9 of this Schedule or in accordance with the provisions of Order M.T. (67), as amended by Schedule 2 of Order M.T. (71)), in respect of employment during any of the periods referred to in that paragraph or that Order respectively, the amount of holiday remuneration payable by the employer in respect of any annual holiday for which the worker has qualified by reason of employment during the said period shall be reduced by the amount of the said accrued holiday remuneration unless that remuneration has been deducted from a previous payment of holiday remuneration made under the provisions of this Schedule or of Order M.T. (67) as amended.

ACCRUED HOLIDAY REMUNERATION PAYABLE ON TERMINATION OF EMPLOYMENT

9. Where a worker ceases to be employed by an employer after the provisions of this Schedule become effective the employer shall, immediately on the termination of the employment, pay to the worker as accrued holiday remuneration:—

    (1) in respect of employment in the 12 months up to the preceding 5th April, a sum equal to the holiday remuneration to which the worker would have been entitled under the provisions of (b) of sub-paragraph (1) of paragraph 7 for any days of annual holiday for which he has qualified, except days of annual holiday which he has been allowed or has become entitled to be allowed before leaving the employment; and

    (2) in respect of any employment since the said 5th April, a sum equal to the holiday remuneration which would have been payable to him under the provisions of (b) of sub-paragraph (1) of paragraph 7 if he could have been allowed an annual holiday in respect of that employment at the time of leaving it.

    (3) Notwithstanding the provisions of sub-paragraphs (1) and (2) of this paragraph, the accrued holiday remuneration payable to a worker who has been employed by the employer for the whole of the 12 months ended on 5th April immediately preceding the termination of his employment shall be as follows:—

        (a) in respect of the 12 months ended on 5th April preceding the termination of his employment, whichever of the following amounts is the greater—

            (i) an amount equal to three fifty-seconds of the total remuneration as defined in paragraph 11 paid by the employer to the worker during that period; or

            (ii) the amount calculated in accordance with the provisions of sub-paragraph (1) of this paragraph; and

        (b) in respect of any period of employment after such 5th April, the amount calculated in accordance with the provisions of sub-paragraph (2) of this paragraph.

PART V

GENERAL

10. For the purpose of calculating any period of employment qualifying a worker for a holiday or for any accrued holiday remuneration under this Schedule, the worker shall be treated:—

(1) as if he were employed for a week in respect of any week in which—

(a) he has worked for the employer for not less than 24 hours and has performed some work for which statutory minimum remuneration is payable; or

(b) (i) he has been absent throughout the week, or

(ii) he has worked for the employer for less than 24 hours

solely by reason of the proved illness of, or accident to, the worker, provided that the number of weeks which may be treated as weeks of employment for such reasons shall not exceed four in the aggregate in the period of 12 months immediately preceding the customary holiday in the case of a customary holiday or 12 months ended on the 5th April immediately preceding the holiday, in the case of an annual holiday; or

(c) he has been suspended throughout the week owing to shortage of work but not exceeding 4 weeks in the aggregate in any of the periods of 12 months last mentioned;

(2) as if he were employed on any day of holiday allowed under the provisions of this Schedule or of Order M.T. (67), as amended by Schedule 2 of Order M.T. (71) and for the purposes of the provisions of sub-paragraph (1) of this paragraph, a worker who is absent on such a holiday shall be treated as having worked thereon for the employer for the number of hours ordinarily worked by him on that day of the week on work for which statutory minimum remuneration is payable.

11. In this Schedule, unless the context otherwise requires, the following expressions have the meanings hereby respectively assigned to them, that is to say:—

"NORMAL WORKING WEEK" means the number of days on which it has been usual for the worker to work in a week in the employment of the employer during the 12 months immediately preceding the commencement of the holiday season or, where under paragraph 9 accrued holiday remuneration is payable on the termination of the employment, during the 12 months immediately preceding the date of the termination of the employment:

Provided that—

(1) part of a day shall count as a day;

(2) no account shall be taken of any week in which the worker did not perform any work for which statutory minimum remuneration has been fixed.

"ONE DAY'S HOLIDAY PAY" means the appropriate proportion of the remuneration which the worker would be entitled to receive from his employer at the date of the annual holiday (or where the holiday is taken in more than one period, at the date of the first period) or at the termination of the employment, as the case may require, for one week's work if working his normal working week and the number of daily hours normally worked by him (exclusive of overtime) and if paid as a time worker at the appropriate rate of statutory minimum remuneration for work for which statutory minimum remuneration is payable and at the same rate for any work for which such remuneration is not payable, and in this definition "appropriate proportion" means—

where the worker's normal working week is six days	.. ..	one-sixth
where the worker's normal working week is five days	.. ..	one-fifth
where the worker's normal working week is four days	..	one-quarter
where the worker's normal working week is three days	..	one-third.

"STATUTORY MINIMUM REMUNERATION" means minimum remuneration (other than holiday remuneration) fixed by a wages regulation order.

"TOTAL REMUNERATION" means any payments paid or payable to the worker under his contract of employment, for time worked or piece work done by him, holiday remuneration, any productivity, long service or other bonus payable to the worker on a weekly, fortnightly or monthly basis and merit payments so payable but does not include any other payments.

"WAGES REGULATION ORDER" means an order made by the Secretary of State to give effect to wages regulation proposals submitted to him by the Made-up Textiles Wages Council (Great Britain).

"WEEK" in paragraphs 3 and 10 means "pay week".

12. The provisions of this Schedule are without prejudice to any agreement for the allowance of any further holidays with pay or for the payment of additional holiday remuneration.

13. The revocation by this Order of Order M.T. (67), as amended by Schedule 2 of Order M.T. (71) and the coming into effect of the provisions of this Schedule shall not affect the right of a worker:—

(1) to be allowed, and to receive holiday remuneration for, any such days of annual holiday which his employer was required to allow him before 1st May 1974 under the provisions of paragraph 4(2)(b)(ii) of the Schedule to Order M.T. (67) as amended; and

(2) to receive accrued holiday remuneration in respect of employment in the 12 months ended 5th April 1974 under the provisions of paragraph 9 of the Schedule to Order M.T. (67) as amended.

EXPLANATORY NOTE

(This Note is not part of the Order.)

This Order, which has effect from 30th April 1974, sets out the holidays which an employer is required to allow to workers in relation to whom the Made-up Textiles Wages Council (Great Britain) operates, in substitution for the holidays fixed by the Wages Regulation (Made-up Textiles) (Holidays) Order 1970 (Order M.T. (67)) which Order is revoked.

New provisions are printed in italics.

STATUTORY INSTRUMENTS

1974 No. 636 (L.9)

COUNTY COURTS

PROCEDURE

The County Court (Amendment No. 2) Rules 1974

Made - - -   28*th March* 1974

Coming into Operation   1*st May* 1974

1.—(1) These Rules may be cited as the County Court (Amendment No. 2) Rules 1974.

(2) In these Rules an Order and Rule referred to by number means the Order and Rule so numbered in the County Court Rules 1936(**a**), as amended (**b**), and a form referred to by number means the form so numbered in Appendix A to those Rules.

(3) The Interpretation Act 1889(**c**) shall apply for the interpretation of these Rules as it applies for the interpretation of an Act of Parliament.

2. In Order 1, Rule 2(2)(*d*), for the words "the Friday before" there shall be substituted the words "the Tuesday after".

3. Order 45A shall be amended as follows:—

(1) In Rule 1—

    (*a*) for the definition of "the Act of 1970" there shall be substituted the following definition:—

        " "the Act of 1973" means the Matrimonial Causes Act 1973"(**d**);

    (*b*) in the definition of "the deceased", for the words "section 15 of the Act of 1970" there shall be substituted the words "section 36 of the Act of 1973".

(2) In Rules 2, 3 and 7 for the words "section 15 of the Act of 1970", wherever they appear, there shall be substituted the words "section 36 of the Act of 1973".

(**a**) S.R. & O. 1936/626 (1936 I, p. 282).
(**b**) The relevant amending instruments are S.I. 1970/1871, 1971/2127, 1972/1156 (1970 III, p. 6154; 1971 III, p. 6276; 1972 II, p. 3430).
(**c**) 1889 c. 63.   (**d**) 1973 c. 18.

(3) In paragraph 8 of Form 370 for the words from "for a maintenance order" to "*section* 17(2) *of the Act*)" there shall be substituted the words "made or deemed to be made by me during the lifetime of the deceased for any such order as is mentioned in section 26(4)(*c*) of the Act [*Give particulars*".

(4) In paragraph 1 of Form 370A for the words "section 14 of the Matrimonial Proceedings and Property Act 1970" there shall be substituted the words "section 35 of the Matrimonial Causes Act 1973".

4. In Order 46 after Rule 24 there shall be added the following Rule:—

"**25.**—(1) In this Rule a section referred to by number means the section so numbered in the Maintenance Orders (Reciprocal Enforcement) Act 1972**(a)**, and expressions used in this Rule which are used in that Act have the same meaning as in that Act.

(2) For the purpose of sections 2(3), 5(4) and 14 the prescribed officer in relation to a county court shall be the registrar.

(3) An application for a maintenance order made by a county court to be sent to a reciprocating country under section 2 shall be made to the registrar by lodging in the court office:—

(*a*) an affidavit by the applicant stating—

   (i) the applicant's reasons for believing that the payer under the maintenance order is residing in that country, and

   (ii) the amount of any arrears due to the applicant under the order, the date to which the arrears have been calculated, and the date on which the next payment falls due;

(*b*) a statement giving such information as the applicant possesses as to the whereabouts of the payer;

(*c*) a statement giving such information as the applicant possesses for facilitating the identification of the payer (including, if known to the applicant, the name and address of any employer of the payer, his occupation and the date and place of issue of any passport of the payer), and

(*d*) if available to the applicant, a photograph of the payer.

(4) Where a county court makes a provisional order under section 5, the document required by subsection (4) of that section to set out or summarise the evidence given in the proceedings shall be authenticated by a certificate signed by the registrar.

(5)(*a*) On receipt by a county court of a certified copy of a provisional order made in a reciprocating country, together with the document mentioned in section 5(5), the registrar shall fix a time and place for the court to consider whether or not the provisional order should be confirmed, and shall send to the payee under the maintenance order notice of the time and place so fixed, together with a copy of the provisional order and of that document.

(a) 1972 c. 18.

(*b*) The registrar shall send to the court which made the provisional order a certified copy of any order confirming or refusing to confirm that order.

(6)(*a*) A county court shall be the prescribed court for the purpose of taking the evidence of a person residing within its district pursuant to a request by a court in a reciprocating country under section 14 where the request for evidence relates to a maintenance order made by a county court which is not for the time being registered in a magistrates' court under the Maintenance Orders Act 1958(**a**).

(*b*) The evidence may be taken before the judge or registrar of the county court as the court thinks fit, and the provisions of Order 20, Rule 18, shall apply with the necessary modifications as if the evidence were required to be taken pursuant to an order made by the court for the examination of the witness on oath.

(7) Where a county court makes an order (other than a provisional order) varying or revoking a maintenance order a copy of which has been sent to a reciprocating country in pursuance of section 2, the registrar shall send a certified copy of the order to the court in the reciprocating country.

(8) Any document required to be sent to a court in a reciprocating country under section 5(4) or section 14(1), or paragraph (5)(*b*) or (7) of this Rule, shall be sent to the Secretary of State for transmission to that court unless the registrar is satisfied that, in accordance with the law of that country, the document may be sent by him direct to that court.".

We, the undersigned members of the Rule Committee appointed by the Lord Chancellor under section 102 of the County Courts Act 1959(**b**) having by virtue of the powers vested in us in this behalf made the foregoing Rules, do hereby certify the same under our hands and submit them to the Lord Chancellor accordingly.

D. O. McKee.
Conolly H. Gage.
H. S. Ruttle.
David Pennant.
W. Granville Wingate.
E. A. Everett.
A. A. Hibbert.
K. W. Mellor.
Arnold Russell Vick.
D. A. Marshall.
D. P. Tomlin.

I allow these Rules, which shall come into operation on 1st May 1974.

Dated 28th March 1974.

Elwyn-Jones, C.

(**a**) 1958 c. 39.   (**b**) 1959 c. 22.

EXPLANATORY NOTE

(This Note is not part of the Rules.)

These Rules provide for county court offices to be closed on the Tuesday following (instead of the Friday before) the spring holiday and make minor amendments in Order 45A (Family Provision) by reason of the consolidation of the relevant enactments by the Matrimonial Causes Act 1973.

Provision is also made for proceedings under the Maintenance Orders (Reciprocal Enforcement) Act 1972. A new Rule 25 is added to Order 46 to deal with the transmission of a county court maintenance order for enforcement in a reciprocating country, the subsequent variation or revocation of such an order and the taking of evidence by a county court for the purpose of proceedings in a foreign court relating to a county court order.

1974 No. 637 (L.10)

BANKRUPTCY, ENGLAND

The Bankruptcy Fees (Amendment) Order 1974

Made - - - -	26*th March* 1974
Coming into Operation	1*st May* 1974

The Lord Chancellor and the Treasury, in exercise of the powers conferred on them by section 133 of the Bankruptcy Act 1914(a) and sections 2 and 3 of the Public Offices Fees Act 1879(b), hereby make, sanction and consent to the following Order:—

1.—(1) This Order may be cited as the Bankruptcy Fees (Amendment) Order 1974 and shall come into operation on 1st May 1974.

(2) The Interpretation Act 1889(c) shall apply to the interpretation of this Order as it applies to the interpretation of an Act of Parliament.

2. The Bankruptcy Fees Order 1970(d), as amended (e), shall have effect subject to the following amendment:—

in Fee No. 41, in part II of Table A in the Schedule to that Order, for the figures "£0.15s.0d." and "£0.75" there shall be substituted the figures "£0.17s.0d." and "£0.85" respectively.

Dated 20th March 1974.

Elwyn-Jones, C.

Dated 26th March 1974.

John Golding,
T. Pendry,
Two of the Lords Commissioners
of Her Majesty's Treasury.

(a) 1914 c. 59.   (b) 1879 c. 58.
(c) 1889 c. 63.   (d) S.I. 1970/2007 (1970 III, p. 6524).
(e) The relevant amending instrument is S.I. 1971/1017 (1971 II, p. 2958).

EXPLANATORY NOTE

(This Note is not part of the Order.)

This Order increases from 75p to 85p the fee for insertion in the London Gazette of notices in bankruptcy proceedings.

1974 No. 638 (L. 11)

COMPANIES

WINDING-UP

The Companies (Board of Trade) Fees (Amendment) Order 1974

Made - - -	*26th March* 1974
Coming into Operation	*1st May* 1974

The Lord Chancellor and the Treasury, in exercise of the powers conferred on them by section 365(3) of the Companies Act 1948**(a)** and sections 2 and 3 of the Public Offices Fees Act 1879**(b)**, hereby make, sanction and consent to the following Order:—

1.—(1) This Order may be cited as the Companies (Board of Trade) Fees (Amendment) Order 1974 and shall come into operation on 1st May 1974.

(2) The Interpretation Act 1889**(c)** shall apply to the interpretation of this Order as it applies to the interpretation of an Act of Parliament.

2. The Companies (Board of Trade) Fees Order 1969**(d)**, as amended **(e)**, shall have effect subject to the following further amendment:—

in Fee No. 7 in Table A of the Schedule to that Order, for the figure "75p" there shall be substituted the figure "85p".

Elwyn Jones, C.

Dated 20th March 1974.

John Golding,

T. Pendry,

Two of the Lords Commissioners
of Her Majesty's Treasury.

Dated 26th March 1974.

(a) 1948 c. 38.   **(b)** 1879 c. 58.
(c) 1889 c. 63.   **(d)** S.I. 1969/519 (1969 I, p. 1440).
(e) The relevant amending instrument is S.I. 1971/1020 (1971 II, p. 2966).

EXPLANATORY NOTE

(This Note is not part of the Order.)

This Order increases from 75p to 85p the fee payable for insertion in the London Gazette of notices in proceedings for the winding-up of companies.

STATUTORY INSTRUMENTS

1974 No. 645

HIGHWAYS, ENGLAND AND WALES
The New Street Byelaws (Extension of Operation) Order 1974

Made - - - *29th March* 1974

The Secretary of State for the Environment and the Secretary of State for Wales, in exercise of their respective powers under the proviso to section 312(6) of the Highways Act 1959(**a**), as read with the Secretary of State for Wales and Minister of Land and Natural Resources Order 1965(**b**), and of all other powers enabling them in that behalf, hereby order as follows: —

1. This order may be cited as the New Street Byelaws (Extension of Operation) Order 1974.

2. Any byelaws in force on 31st March 1974, being byelaws remaining in force by virtue of the New Street Byelaws (Extension of Operation) Orders 1962(**c**), 1967(**d**) and 1972(**e**) shall remain in force until 31st March 1977 or until they are revoked, whichever date is the earlier.

Signed by authority of the Secretary of State for the Environment.

J. Toohey,
An Under Secretary in the
Department of the Environment.

26th March 1974.

Signed by authority of the Secretary of State for Wales.

J. H. Clement,
An Under Secretary in the Welsh Office.

29th March 1974.

(**a**) 1959 c. 25.
(**c**) S.I. 1962/645 (1962 I. p. 695).
(**e**) S.I. 1972/595 (I. p. 1964).

(**b**) S.I. 1965/319 (1965 I. p. 785).
(**d**) S.I. 1967/512 (1967 I. p. 1684).

EXPLANATORY NOTE

(This Note is not part of the Order.)

1. The Highways Act 1959 repealed certain enactments which had empowered local authorities to make new street byelaws, and provided that existing byelaws made under any of those enactments should cease to have effect on 30th April 1962, unless the Minister of Housing and Local Government extended their period of operation by Order under the Act of 1959.

2. That period was extended until 31st March 1974 by the New Street Byelaws (Extension of Operation) Order 1972, and this Order further extends it until 31st March 1977.

STATUTORY INSTRUMENTS

1974 No. 646

INDUSTRIAL DEVELOPMENT

INVESTMENT GRANTS

Investment Grants Termination (No. 4) Order 1974

Made – – –		*2nd April* 1974
Laid before Parliament		11*th April* 1974
Coming into Operation		6*th May* 1974

The Secretary of State in exercise of his powers under section 1(6) of the Investment and Building Grants Act 1971(**a**), and all other powers in that behalf enabling him, hereby orders as follows:—

Citation, commencement and interpretation

1.—(1) This Order may be cited as the Investment Grants Termination (No. 4) Order 1974 and shall come into force on 6th May 1974.

(2) The Interpretation Act 1889(**b**) shall apply to the interpretation of this Order as it applies to the interpretation of an Act of Parliament.

Dates before which certain applications for grant are to be made

2.—(1) Applications for grant under Part I of the Industrial Development Act 1966(**c**) in respect of expenditure incurred during the period 1st April 1973 to 30th June 1973 (both dates inclusive) are to be made before 1st January 1975.

(2) Such applications in respect of expenditure incurred during the period 1st July 1973 to 30th September 1973 (both dates inclusive) are to be made before 1st April 1975.

(3) Such applications in respect of expenditure incurred during the period 1st October 1973 to 31st December 1973 (both dates inclusive) are to be made before 1st July 1975.

(4) Such applications in respect of expenditure incurred during the period 1st January 1974 to 31st March 1974 (both dates inclusive) are to be made before 1st October 1975.

Form and manner of applications

3. The applications for grant to which this Order applies are to be made in such form and manner, and to contain such particulars and be accompanied by such documents, as the Secretary of State may direct.

Gregor Mackenzie,
Joint Parliamentary Under-Secretary of State,
Department of Industry.

2nd April 1974.

(**a**) 1971 c. 51.   (**b**) 1889 c. 63.   (**c**) 1966 c. 34.

EXPLANATORY NOTE

(This Note is not part of the Order.)

The Investment Grants Termination (No. 1) Order 1971 (S.I. 1971/1275) the Investment Grants Termination (No. 2) Order 1972 (S.I. 1972/34) and the Investment Grants Termination (No. 3) Order 1973 (S.I. 1973/384) each specified certain dates by which applications for investment grant in respect of expenditure incurred before a related date or in related periods must be made. This Order specifies further dates by which such applications in respect of expenditure incurred in further related periods must be made.

The Order also provides for the making of directions as to the form of such applications, the particulars they must contain and the documents to accompany them.

STATUTORY INSTRUMENTS

1974 No. 647 (S.56)

NATIONAL HEALTH SERVICE, SCOTLAND

The National Health Service (Charges for Drugs and Appliances) (Scotland) Amendment Regulations 1974

Made - - -	*1st April* 1974
Laid before Parliament	*5th April* 1974
Coming into Operation	*8th April* 1974

In exercise of the powers conferred on me by sections 34(2), 39(2) and 40 of the National Health Service (Scotland) Act 1947(**a**) (as amended by section 14, 16 and 29 of and the Schedule to the National Health Service (Amendment) Act 1949(**b**), and section 64 of and Schedule 6 to the National Health Service (Scotland) Act 1972(**c**) and section 57 of and Schedule 4 to the National Health Service Reorganisation Act 1973(**d**)), section 1 and 7(6) of the National Health Service Act 1952(**e**) (as amended by section 64 of and Schedule 6 to the National Health Service (Scotland) Act 1972), and of all other powers enabling me in that behalf, I hereby make the following regulations: —

1.—(1) These regulations may be cited as the National Health Service (Charges for Drugs and Appliances) (Scotland) Amendment Regulations 1974 and shall come into operation on 8th April 1974.

(2) The Interpretation Act 1889(**f**) applies for the interpretation of these regulations as it applies for the interpretation of an Act of Parliament.

2. The National Health Service (Charges for Drugs and Appliances) (Scotland) Regulaions 1974(**g**) shall be amended as follows—

(*a*) in regulations 6(1)(*a*), for "15" there shall be substituted "16";

(*b*) for regulation 6(1)(*b*) there shall be substituted—

"(*b*) a woman who has attained the age of 60 years or a man who has attained the age of 65 years; or"

William Ross,

One of Her Majesty's Principal
Secretaries of State.

St. Andrew's House,
Edinburgh.
1st April 1974.

(**a**) 1947 c. 27. (**b**) 1949 c. 93. (**c**) 1972 c. 58. (**d**) 1973 c. 32.
(**e**) 1952 c. 25. (**f**) 1889 c. 63. (**g**) S.I. 1974/508 (1974 I, p. 1934).

EXPLANATORY NOTE

(This Note is not part of the Regulations.)

These Regulations modify the categories of persons who are exempt from charges under the principal Regulations by raising the age of exemption for children from under 15 to under 16 years, and by lowering the age of exemption for women from 65 to 60 years.

STATUTORY INSTRUMENTS

1974 No. 648

REPRESENTATION OF THE PEOPLE

The Representation of the People Regulations 1974

Made - - - -	*6th February* 1974
Laid before Parliament	*8th February* 1974
Coming into Operation	*1st April* 1974

ARRANGEMENT OF REGULATIONS

PART I

GENERAL

PART II

REGISTRATION

The Register

The Electors Lists

Claims and Objections

Receipt of Postal Ballot Papers

PART V

SERVICE VOTERS

PART VI

SUPPLEMENTARY

SCHEDULE

FORMS

Forms for use by registration officers

Forms for use by returning officers

Form E: Elector's official poll card.

Form F: Proxy's official poll card.

Form G: Certificate of employment.

Form H: Declaration of identity.

Forms for use by service voters

Form J: Service declaration and application for appointment of proxy by a member of the forces.

Form K: Service declaration and application for appointment of proxy by the spouse of a member of the forces.

Form L: Service declaration and application for appointment of proxy by a Crown servant or by a person employed by the British Council.

Form M: Service declaration and application for appointment of proxy by the spouse of a Crown servant or of a person employed by the British Council.

Form N: Application by a service voter in the United Kingdom to vote by post.

Forms for use by other persons

Form O: Form of claim to be registered as an elector.

Form P: Form of objection to an entry in the electors lists.

Form Q: Application to be treated as an absent voter for an indefinite period owing to occupation or physical incapacity.

Form R: Application to vote by post owing to change of residence.

Form S: Application to be treated as an absent voter for a particular election.

Form T: Application to be treated as an absent voter for an indefinite period owing to air or sea journey.

Form U: Application for appointment of proxy.

Form V: Application by a proxy to vote by post.

Form W: Application by service voter's spouse for appointment of proxy.

Form X: Return of expenses required by section 63 of the Representation of the People Act 1949 to be authorised by an election agent.

Form Y: Declaration as to expenses required by section 63 of the Representation of the People Act 1949 to be authorised by an election agent.

In exercise of the powers conferred on me by sections 42 and 171(5) of the Representation of the People Act 1949**(a)**, I hereby make the following Regulations:—

PART I

GENERAL

Citation and extent

1.—(1) These Regulations may be cited as the Representation of the People Regulations 1974.

(2) These Regulations shall not extend to Scotland or Northern Ireland.

(a) 1949 c. 68.

Commencement

2. These Regulations shall, subject to their having been approved by resolution of each House of Parliament, come into operation on 1st April 1974.

Revocation and savings

3.—(1) The provisions of the Representation of the People Regulations 1969**(a)**, as amended **(b)**, shall be revoked as from 1st April 1974:

Provided that Regulations 29 to 58 (inclusive), 68, 69(1) and 70(2) and so much of the Schedules to the Regulations of 1969 as relates to the said Regulations, shall continue to have effect in relation to an election notice of which has been published before 1st April 1974.

(2) Section 38 of the Interpretation Act 1889**(c)** shall apply as if these Regulations were an Act of Parliament and as if any Regulations revoked by these Regulations were Acts of Parliament repealed by an Act of Parliament.

(3) Without prejudice to the said section 38 any register, list or record prepared, any application, appointment or declaration made, any proceeding initiated or other thing done under any Regulations revoked by these Regulations shall not be invalidated by the revocation effected by paragraph (1) of this Regulation and shall, in so far as it could have been prepared, made, initiated or done under any provision of these Regulations, have effect as if it had been prepared, made, initiated or done under that provision.

(4) Any reference in any statutory instrument to a Regulation revoked by these Regulations shall be taken as a reference to the corresponding Regulation contained in these Regulations.

Interpretation

4.—(1) For the purpose of these Regulations, unless the context otherwise requires—

the expression "the Act of 1949" means the Representation of the People Act 1949;

the expression "the Act of 1969" means the Representation of the People Act 1969**(d)**;

the expression "postal proxy" means a person entitled to vote by post as proxy at an election;

the expression "registration officer" means an electoral registration officer.

(2) A reference in these Regulations to a rule in the elections rules shall be construed as a reference to a rule in the parliamentary elections rules in Schedule 2 to the Act of 1949 or, as the case may be, to the corresponding rule in the Local Elections (Principal Areas) Rules 1973**(e)**.

(3) A claim or objection includes a claim or objection that a letter or date should or should not be placed against a person's name in the electors lists and the register in accordance with Regulation 9 or Regulation 10(*a*) or (*b*).

(4) A reference in these Regulations to any enactment or statutory instrument shall be construed as including a reference to that enactment or statutory

---

(a) S.I. 1969/904 (1969 II, p. 2602).   (b) S.I. 1973/427 (1973 I, p. 1396).
(c) 1889 c. 63.   (d) 1969 c. 15.
(e) S.I. 1973/79 (1973 I, p. 422).

instrument as amended or replaced by any other enactment or statutory instrument.

(5) A reference in these Regulations to a Regulation shall be construed as a reference to a Regulation contained in these Regulations.

(6) A reference in these Regulations to a form identified by means of a letter shall be construed as a reference to the form so identified in the Schedule to these Regulations.

(7) A reference in these Regulations to the record or list of absent voters, postal proxies or proxies shall be taken as referring to the records kept or lists prepared for parliamentary and local government elections.

(8) The Interpretation Act 1889 shall apply to the interpretation of these Regulations as it applies to the interpretation of an Act of Parliament.

Constituencies not wholly within a district or London borough

5.—(1) Where a constituency is not coterminous with, or wholly contained in, a district or London borough—

(*a*) the registration officer for any part of the constituency shall, if he is not the acting returning officer for the constituency, consult him concerning the form of the register and of the records and lists of absent voters, proxies and postal proxies, or such parts thereof as relate to the constituency, in order to ensure that, so far as is reasonably practicable, they are in a form similar to those in use elsewhere in the constituency;

(*b*) during the period of a parliamentary election the duties or powers of a registration officer in connection with applications to vote by post or by proxy, or otherwise specified in Part III of these Regulations, shall, in relation to each part of the constituency, be exercised by the acting returning officer for the constituency.

(2) For the purposes of paragraph (1)(*b*) of this Regulation, the expression "period of a parliamentary election" means the period ending with the close of the poll and beginning—

(i) at a general election, with the date of the dissolution of Parliament or any earlier time at which Her Majesty's intention to dissolve Parliament is announced; or

(ii) at a by-election, with the date of the issue of the writ for the election or any earlier date on which a certificate of the vacancy is notified in the Gazette in accordance with the Recess Elections Act 1784**(a)** or the Election of Members during Recess Act 1858**(b)**.

PART II

REGISTRATION

The Register

Separate part of register for each parliamentary polling district

6. The register shall be framed in separate parts for each parliamentary polling district, except that, where a parliamentary polling district is contained in more than one electoral area, there shall be a separate part of the register for each part of the polling district which is contained in each electoral area.

(a) 1784 c. 26.   (b) 1858 c. 110.

Separate letter for each parliamentary polling district

7. There shall be a separate letter or letters in the register for each parliamentary polling district and such letter or letters shall be deemed to form part of an elector's number in the register.

Order of names

8.—(1) Subject to paragraph (2) of this Regulation, the names in each separate part of the register shall be arranged in street order unless the council which appointed the registration officer determine for any part of the register that street order is not reasonably practicable in which case the names shall be arranged in alphabetical order or partly in street order and partly in alphabetical order as the council may determine.

(2) The names of every service voter in any separate part of the register who in his service declaration has given an address at which the declarant has resided in the United Kingdom, not being an address at which he would have been residing but for the circumstances entitling him to make the declaration, shall be grouped in alphabetical order at the end of the part of the register beneath a heading indicating that the service voters have so declared.

(3) The names in the register shall be numbered so far as is reasonably practicable consecutively; and there shall be a separate series of numbers (beginning with the number one) for each parliamentary polling district.

Marking of names to indicate at which elections person entitled to vote

9.—(1) To indicate that an elector is not entitled to vote at a parliamentary election the letter "L" shall be placed against his name in the electors lists and the register.

(2) If an elector will attain voting age before the end of the twelve months following the day by which a register is required to be published but will not be of voting age on the first day of those twelve months, the date on which he will attain that age shall be placed against his name in the electors lists as well as in the register.

Marking of names to indicate manner of voting

10. To indicate the manner in which an elector is entitled to vote at an election there shall be placed—

    (*a*) in the electors lists and the register against the name of any elector who is a service voter the letter "S";

    (*b*) in the electors lists and the register against the name of any elector who is a merchant seaman the letter "M";

    (*c*) in any copy of the register or part thereof provided for a polling station against the name of any elector who is, or whose proxy is, entitled to vote by post the letter "A".

The Electors Lists

Form of electors lists

11.—(1) The electors lists shall be framed in separate parts for each parliamentary polling district, except that, where a parliamentary polling district is contained in more than one electoral area, there shall be a separate part of the electors lists for each part of the polling district which is contained in each electoral area.

(2) The electors lists for each separate part shall consist of—

List A—a copy of the register in force for that part;

List B—a list of newly qualified electors, that is to say, persons who are qualified for registration as parliamentary or as local government electors in respect of qualifying addresses for which they are not registered in the register in force or who, since the qualifying date of the register in force, have become entitled to be registered as residents instead of as service voters, or vice versa, in respect of those addresses; and

List C—a list of persons who have ceased to be qualified as electors or whose qualification has been altered, that is to say, persons who, being registered in respect of qualifying addresses in the register in force, have ceased to be qualified for registration as parliamentary or as local government electors in respect of those addresses or who, since the qualifying date for the register in force, have become entitled to be registered as residents instead of as service voters, or vice versa, in respect of those addresses:

Provided that where the area of a parliamentary polling district differs from the area of that polling district as constituted for the purposes of the register in force, the polling district may be treated as having the same area as it had for the purposes of the register in force.

(3) The names in List B need not be numbered.

(4) The names in List C shall have opposite them their numbers in the register in force.

(5) Notwithstanding the provisions of paragraphs (2), (3) and (4) of this Regulation, the electors lists for a separate part may be prepared as a draft register so as to show only the persons appearing to the registration officer to be entitled to be registered, together with their qualifying addresses, and to comply with the provisions of the preceding Regulations:

Provided that the names in the draft register need not be numbered.

Publication of the electors lists

12.—(1) The registration officer shall publish the electors lists by—

    (*a*) making a copy thereof available for inspection at his office:

    (*b*) as soon as practicable making copies of the part of the electors lists relating to each electoral area available for inspection at a specified place in or near that electoral area to which the public have access;

    (*c*) publishing a notice (to be combined with the notice of claims and objections referred to in Regulation 13) specifying the said place.

(2) The electors lists shall be published on or before the twenty-eighth day of November and shall be kept published till the publication of the register prepared from those lists.

Claims and Objections

Notice of claims and objections

13.—(1) The registration officer shall at the time of publishing the electors lists publish a notice in Form C or, in the case of electors lists to which Regulation 11(5) applies, in Form B specifying the manner in which and the time within which claims and objections in respect of the electors lists may be made.

(2) The said notice shall be published in the way the registration officer thinks best calculated to bring the said notice to the attention of the electors.

Time for making claims and objections

14.—(1) A claim or objection in respect of the electors lists which is delivered to the registration officer after the sixteenth day of December shall be disregarded:

Provided that an objection to a claim shall not be disregarded if it is delivered to the registration officer within three days after the claim has been entered in the list of claims.

(2) A service declaration made with reference to a qualifying date and made during the twelve months ending with that date, but received too late for inclusion of the declarant's name in the electors lists, shall, if it is received by the registration officer—

(a) not later than the last day for making claims, be treated as a claim,

(b) after the said last day, be disregarded.

Form of claims and objections

15.—(1) A claim shall be in Form O and may be made by a person either on his own behalf or on behalf of another person.

(2) An objection shall be in Form P.

(3) Claims and objections shall be made available for inspection in the registration officer's office till completion of the hearing of claims and objections.

Entry and preliminary disposal of claims and objections

16.—(1) The registration officer shall keep separate lists of claims and objections and shall, on receipt of a claim or objection, forthwith enter in the appropriate list the name and qualifying address of the claimant or the person in respect of whom the objection is made.

(2) If the registration officer is of opinion—

(a) that the particulars given in a claim or objection are insufficient, he may ask for further information and take no further action until such information is supplied;

(b) that a claim may be allowed without a hearing, he may allow the claim, provided that no objection is made thereto, and shall so inform the person making the claim;

(c) that the objector is not entitled to object, he may disallow the objection and shall so inform the objector;

(*d*) that a claim or objection cannot be allowed because—

(i) the matter has been concluded by the decision of a court, or

(ii) the particulars given in a claim or objection do not entitle the claimant or objector to succeed,

he may send to the person making the claim or objection a notice stating his opinion and the grounds thereof and that he intends to disallow the claim or objection unless that person gives the registration officer notice within three days from the date of the first mentioned notice that he requires the claim or objection to be heard, and, if he receives no such notice within the said time, he may disallow the claim or objection.

(3) The registration officer shall, unless he allows or disallows the claim or objection under paragraph (2) of this Regulation, send a notice, in the case of a claim, to the person making the claim and, in the case of an objection, to the objector and the person objected to, stating the time and place at which he proposes to hear the claim or objection; and the notice sent to a person objected to shall also state the name and address of the objector and the grounds of the objection.

(4) The time fixed for the hearing of a claim or objection shall not be earlier than the third day after the date of the notice referred to in paragraph (3) of this Regulation.

(5) The registration officer shall make available for inspection at his office till completion of the hearing of claims and objections the lists of claims and objections together with the time and place at which he proposes to hear any claim or objection.

Hearing of claims and objections

17.—(1) On the hearing of a claim, the person making the claim and any person who has duly made an objection and, on the hearing of an objection, the objector and the person objected to and, on the hearing of either, any other person who appears to the registration officer to be interested shall be entitled to appear and be heard.

(2) The right to appear and be heard includes the right to make written representations.

(3) Any person entitled to appear and be heard may do so either in person or by any other person on his behalf.

(4) The registration officer may, at the request of any person entitled to appear and be heard or, if he thinks fit, without such a request, require that the evidence tendered by any person shall be given on oath and may administer an oath for the purpose.

Corrections to the electors lists

18. Any alteration to the electors lists which is required—

(*a*) to carry out the registration officer's decision with respect to any claim or objection,

(*b*) to correct any clerical error,

(c) to correct any misnomer or inaccurate description, or

(d) to delete the name of any person who the registration officer is satisfied is dead,

shall be made by the registration officer.

Other corrections to the electors lists

19.—(1) Where it appears to the registration officer that it is necessary to make any alteration (other than an alteration under Regulation 18) to the electors lists in order to ensure that no person shall be incorrectly registered, or registered when not entitled, he shall send to the person affected by the alteration a notice stating the proposed alteration and shall give him an opportunity within five days from the date of such notice of objecting to the alteration and, if necessary, of appearing and being heard in accordance with the provisions of Regulation 17.

(2) After the said five days the registration officer shall make such alteration (if any) as seems to him to be necessary.

Publication and Sale of the Register

Publication of register

20.—(1) The registration officer shall publish the register by making a copy available for inspection at his office and by making copies of the part of the register relating to each electoral area available for inspection as soon as practicable at the place at which copies of the part of the electors lists relating to that electoral area have been made available for inspection.

(2) The register shall be kept published until the coming into force of the next register.

Registration officer to furnish copies of register

21.—(1) A copy of the register shall, on publication, be furnished by the registration officer to the Secretary of State and the British Museum.

(2) An abstract of the contents of the register shall be furnished by the registration officer to the Secretary of State at such times and in such form and giving such particulars as the Secretary of State may require.

Free copies of register

22.—(1) The registration officer who is acting returning officer for a constituency shall on request supply without fee—

(a) one copy of the register for the constituency to the Member of Parliament for that constituency;

(b) four copies of the register for the constituency (which may be printed on one side only) and four copies of Lists B and C of the electors lists therefor, or, in the case of electors lists to which Regulation 11(5) applies, of the draft register therefor, so long as the lists are kept published, to any person who satisfies the registration officer that he requires them for use in connection with his own or some other persons prospective candidature at a parliamentary election for that constituency:

Provided that not more than one person in respect of the same candidature shall be so supplied;

(c) two copies of the register for the constituency to each candidate at a parliamentary election for that constituency or his election agent.

(2) The registration officer for a part of a constituency, where the constituency is not coterminous with, or wholly contained in, a district or London borough, shall, if he is not the acting returning officer for the constituency, supply without fee the registration officer who is the acting returning officer with as many copies of the register, electors lists or draft register for that part as he may require for the purposes of paragraph (1) above.

(3) The registration officer shall on request supply without fee one copy of so much of the register as relates to an electoral area to—

(a) every councillor for that area; and

(b) each candidate at a local government election for that area or his election agent.

Sale of register

23. So long as there are sufficient copies available after allowing for the number which may be required for the purposes of any election (including the purposes of Regulation 22) or for the purposes of section 26(2) of the Criminal Justice Act 1972(a), the registration officer shall supply to any person copies of any part or parts of the register, or of any electors lists therefor, on payment—

(a) in the case of a person who has been supplied in pursuance of Regulation 22 with a copy of any part of the register or who is a returning officer or a local authority, of a fee at the rate of five pence for each thousand (or part of one thousand) names in such copy;

(b) in the case of any other person, of a fee at the rate of twenty-five pence for each one thousand (or part of one thousand) names in such copy.

Supplementary

Declaration as to age and nationality

24.—(1) The registration officer before registering any person (other than a service voter) may, if he thinks it necessary—

(a) require that person either to produce a birth certificate or to make a statutory declaration as to the date of his birth,

(b) require that person either to produce a certificate of naturalisation or a document showing that he has become a British subject by virtue of registration, or to make a statutory declaration that he was a British subject or citizen of the Republic of Ireland on the qualifying date.

(2) Where a declaration is so made, any fee payable in connection therewith shall be paid by the registration officer as part of his registration expenses.

(3) Any such declaration shall be made available for inspection in the registration officer's office till completion of the hearing of claims and objections.

(a) 1972 c. 71.

Information from householders

25. The registration officer may require any householder or person owning or occupying any premises within the area for which he acts or the agent or factor of any such person to give information required for the purposes of his registration duties or the purposes of his duties under section 26(2) of the Criminal Justice Act 1972.

Adaptation of electors lists and register in consequence of altered polling districts

26.—(1) Where the Secretary of State directs a local authority to make or himself makes any alteration of parliamentary polling districts, he may also direct that—

(*a*) the register in force be adapted to the alteration;

(*b*) if the alteration takes place between the publication of any electors lists and the coming into force of the register prepared from those lists, the form of that register be framed in accordance with the alterations.

(2) Where any alteration of parliamentary polling districts is made otherwise than by virtue of section 11(4) of the Act of 1949 (which relates to powers exercisable by the Secretary of State), the council of the district or London borough which appointed the registration officer may direct him to make the adaptations set out in paragraph (1) of this Regulation.

(3) Except as otherwise provided by this Regulation an alteration of parliamentary polling districts shall not be effective until the coming into force of the first register prepared from the electors lists published after the alteration is made.

Corrupt and illegal practices list

27.—(1) The registration officer shall, at the same time as he publishes the electors lists, prepare and publish the corrupt and illegal practices list (if any) required by section 40(1) of the Act of 1949 by making a copy thereof available for inspection at the same places as he makes available copies of the electors lists or any part thereof.

(2) A person named in the corrupt and illegal practices list may claim to be omitted therefrom and any person may object to the omission of any person from such list, and paragraph (1) of Regulation 14, paragraph (3) of Regulation 15 and Regulations 16 and 17 shall apply to any such claim and objection as they apply to a claim or objection in respect of the electors lists.

(3) A claim may be made by a person either on his own behalf or on behalf of another person and shall give particulars of the grounds on which the person concerned should be omitted, and an objection to the omission of any person shall give the name and address of the objector and the person in respect of whom the objection is made and the grounds on which such person should be entered in the corrupt and illegal practices list including particulars of the alleged conviction by a court or of the alleged report of any election court.

(4) The registration officer shall make such alterations to the corrupt and illegal practices list as are required to carry out his decisions on any claims or objections or to correct any clerical error, misnomer or inaccurate description.

(5) Where it appears to the registration officer that a person not named in the corrupt and illegal practices list should be entered therein, he shall send to that person a notice that he intends to enter him therein and shall give him an opportunity within five days from the date of such notice of objecting and being heard in accordance with the provisions of Regulation 17, and after the said five days he shall make such alteration as seems to him to be necessary.

(6) The registration officer shall publish the corrected corrupt and illegal practices list (if any) at the same time as he publishes the register and in the same manner as he publishes each part of the register.

(7) A copy of the corrected corrupt and illegal practices list shall, on publication, be furnished by the registration officer to the Secretary of State and the British Museum.

(8) The corrupt and illegal practices list as first published and as corrected shall be kept published for the same length of time as the electors lists and the register.

Correction of Register

Correction of register

28.—(1) When a registration officer makes an alteration in a register pursuant to section 7(2) of the Act of 1969, he shall—

(*a*) send to the person affected by the alteration and, if he gives effect to a decision on an objection made with respect to the electors lists, to the objector a notice stating the alteration;

(*b*) make a copy of the alteration available for inspection at his office;

(*c*) make copies of the alteration available for inspection at the place at which copies of the part of the register to which the alteration relates have been made available for inspection;

(*d*) furnish a copy of the alteration to the Secretary of State and the British Museum;

(*e*) supply without a fee a copy of the alteration to each person to whom he has supplied a copy of the part of the register to which the alteration relates in pursuance of Regulation 22 or 23(*a*).

(2) The registration officer who is acting returning officer for the constituency shall supply without a fee a copy of the alteration to each person to whom he has supplied a copy of that part of the register to which the alteration relates in pursuance of Regulation 22(1).

(3) Copies of alterations made available for inspection under this Regulation shall be kept available for the same length of time as the register is kept published.

PART III

ABSENT VOTERS, PROXIES AND POSTAL PROXIES

Application to be treated as an absent voter

29.—(1) An application to be treated as an absent voter shall be made in respect of each qualifying address and shall be—

(*a*) in Form S in any case where the application is made for a particular election only;

(b) in Form R in any case where the applicant no longer resides at his qualifying address;

(c) in Form N in any case where the applicant is a service voter;

(d) in Form W in any case where the applicant is the spouse of a service voter, has made a service declaration, but has not yet been registered as a service voter in pursuance of that declaration;

(e) in Form T in any case where the applicant is unable or likely to be unable to go in person from his qualifying address or the polling station without making a journey by air or sea;

(f) in Form Q in any other case.

(2) (a) An application to be treated as an absent voter based on the ground of religious observance shall not be allowed by the registration officer unless it is accompanied by a certificate signed by a minister of the applicant's religious denomination certifying the nature and times of the religious observances and that the applicant is bound to observe them.

(b) An application to be treated as an absent voter based on the ground of physical incapacity shall be allowed by the registration officer if—

(i) the applicant has been registered as a blind person by a local authority under section 29(4)(g) of the National Assistance Act 1948(a); or

(ii) the application is accompanied by a certificate signed by a registered medical practitioner certifying, or a declaration signed by a Christian Science practitioner stating, that the applicant is unable, or likely to be unable, by reason either of blindness or any other physical incapacity to go in person to the polling station or, if able to go, to vote unaided, and estimating for how long the applicant is likely to be so unable.

(3) The registration officer, on disallowing a person's application to be treated as an absent voter, shall notify the applicant of the fact.

(4) Where under section 13(3)(c) or 24(3)(c) of the Act of 1949 the registration officer gives notice to an absent voter that he has reason to believe there has been a material change of circumstances, that person shall cease to be treated as an absent voter seven days after the date on which the registration officer sends such notice.

Application to vote by proxy

30.—(1) An application by a service voter for the appointment of a proxy to vote on his behalf shall be in the form of Part 2 of Form J, K, L or M, as the case may be.

(2) An application by an absent voter who is not a service voter for the appointment of a proxy to vote on his behalf shall be in Form U or W, as the case may be.

Appointment of proxy

31.—(1) For the purpose of ascertaining in pursuance of section 14(4) of the Act of 1949 and of that subsection as applied by section 25(6) of that Act

---

(a) 1948 c. 29.

that a proxy is capable of being and willing to be appointed, the registration officer shall, unless he is satisfied that the person nominated in the application as first choice is not capable of being and willing to be appointed, notify him that a proxy paper will be issued to him unless within five days from the date of such notice the registration officer receives notice from him that he is not capable of being and willing to be appointed.

(2) If the person nominated as first choice is not capable of being and willing to be appointed, the registration officer shall, if another person is nominated as second choice, deal in like manner with such person:

Provided that if the application is received by the registration officer after publication of notice of an election, the registration officer need not do so until after the day of the poll for that election.

(3) If for any reason the registration officer does not issue a proxy paper in pursuance of an application made to him, he shall notify the person making the application why he has not done so.

Proxy paper

32.—(1) The proxy paper to be issued by the registration officer shall be in Form D.

(2) As soon as may be after issue of the proxy paper the registration officer shall send a notice of the fact to the elector stating the name of the person to whom the paper has been issued.

Cancellation of proxy appointment

33.—(1) Where the appointment of a proxy is cancelled by notice given to the registration officer or ceases to be or no longer remains in force under section 14(5) of the Act of 1949 or that subsection as applied by section 25(6) of that Act, the registration officer shall forthwith notify the person whose appointment as proxy has been cancelled or is no longer in force of the fact and remove his name from the record of proxies.

(2) Where a service voter is entitled to vote by post at an election, the registration officer shall forthwith notify his proxy (if any) of the fact and that his appointment will not have effect for that election.

Application by proxy to vote by post

34.—(1) An application by a proxy to vote by post shall be in Form V.

(2) The registration officer on disallowing such an application shall notify the applicant of the fact.

Disregard of applications

35.—(1) An application to be treated as an absent voter, by a proxy to vote by post, or for the issue of a proxy paper shall be disregarded—

(a) for the purposes of a parliamentary election if it is received by the registration officer after the twelfth day before the day of the poll at that election;

(b) for the purposes of a local government election if it is received by the registration officer after the fourteenth day before the day of the poll at that election:

Provided that an application to be treated as an absent voter on the grounds of employment on the day of the poll by a returning officer or as a constable may be allowed after the said twelfth or fourteenth day as the case may be.

(2) An application to be no longer treated as an absent voter, or a notice cancelling the appointment of a proxy, may be disregarded—

(a) for the purposes of a parliamentary election if it is received by the registration officer after the twelfth day before the day of the poll at that election;

(b) for the purposes of a local government election if it is received by the registration officer after the fourteenth day before the day of the poll at that election.

(3) An application under section 15(7)(a) of the Act of 1949 whereby a proxy ceases to be entitled to vote by post may be disregarded for the purposes of a parliamentary election if it is received by the registration officer after the twelfth day before the day of the poll at that election.

Records and lists of absent voters, proxies and postal proxies

36.—(1) Subject to the provisions of this Regulation and Regulation 5(1)(a), the records and lists of absent voters, proxies and postal proxies shall be in such form as the registration officer may decide.

(2) In the absent voters list the address to which a ballot paper is to be sent to an absent voter shall be placed opposite his name and number in the register unless a proxy (other than a service voter's proxy) has been appointed to vote on his behalf, in which case the letter "P" shall be placed opposite his name.

(3) In the proxies list the name and address of the proxy shall be placed opposite the elector's name and number in the register.

(4) In the postal proxies list the name of the proxy and the address to which a ballot paper is to be sent to the postal proxy shall be placed opposite the elector's name and number in the register.

(5) As soon as the lists of absent voters, proxies and postal proxies have been prepared, the registration officer shall publish them by making a copy thereof available for inspection at his office, and as soon as practicable thereafter he shall, on request and without fee, supply a copy thereof to each candidate or his election agent:

Provided that, if such request is made before any issue of postal ballot papers, he shall before that issue supply a copy of the lists of absent voters and postal proxies or a copy of so much thereof as relates to that issue.

(6) The registration officer shall make a copy of the records of absent voters, proxies and postal proxies available for inspection at his office.

Certificate of employment

37. The certificate as to the employment of constables and persons employed by the returning officer on the day of the poll at a parliamentary election (to enable such a constable or person to vote elsewhere than at his own polling station) shall be in Form G and signed, in the case of a constable, by a member of a police force of or above the rank of inspector.

Part IV

Issue and Receipt of Postal Ballot Papers

Interpretation

Interpretation of Part IV

38. For the purpose of this Part of these Regulations, unless the context otherwise requires—

the expression "agent" includes the election agent and a person appointed to attend in the election agent's place;

the expression "issue" includes the original and any subsequent issue;

the expression "postal ballot paper" means a ballot paper issued to a postal voter;

the expression "postal voter" means a person entitled to vote by post at an election as an absent voter or as a proxy.

Issue of Postal Ballot Papers

Form of postal ballot paper

39. The ballot papers to be sent to postal voters shall be in the same form as, and indistinguishable from, the ballot papers delivered to other voters.

Form of declaration of identity

40. The declaration of identity sent with the ballot paper to a postal voter shall be in Form H.

Persons entitled to be present at issue and receipt of postal ballot papers

41.—(1) No person other than—

(*a*) the returning officer and his clerks,

(*b*) a candidate,

(*c*) an election agent or any person appointed by a candidate to attend in his election agent's place,

(*d*) any agents appointed under paragraph (2) of this Regulation,

may be present at the proceedings on the issue or receipt of postal ballot papers.

(2) Where postal ballot papers are to be issued, or the envelopes contained in the postal voters' ballot boxes are to be opened, simultaneously in two or more batches, each candidate may appoint one or more agents up to the number he may be authorised by the returning officer to appoint not exceeding the number of such batches so, however, that the number authorised shall be the same in the case of each candidate.

(3) Notice of the appointment stating the names and addresses of the persons appointed shall be given by the candidate to the returning officer before the time fixed for the issue of the postal ballot papers or the opening of the said postal voters' ballot boxes, as the case may be.

(4) If an agent dies or becomes incapable of acting, the candidate may appoint another agent in his place and shall forthwith give to the returning officer notice in writing of the name and address of the agent appointed.

(5) Agents may be appointed and notice of appointment given to the returning officer by the candidate's election agent instead of by the candidate.

(6) In this Part of these Regulations references to agents shall be taken as references to agents whose appointments have been duly made and notified and, in the case of agents appointed under paragraph (2) of this Regulation, who are within the number authorised by the returning officer.

(7) A candidate may himself do any act or thing which any agent of his, if appointed, would have been authorised to do, or may assist his agent in doing any such act or thing.

(8) Where in this Part of these Regulations any act or thing is required or authorised to be done in the presence of the candidates or their agents, the non-attendance of any such persons or person at the time and place appointed for the purpose shall not, if the act or thing is otherwise duly done, invalidate the act or thing done.

Declaration of secrecy

42.—(1) Every person attending the proceedings on the issue or receipt of postal ballot papers shall make a declaration of secrecy in the form in paragraph (3) of this Regulation, or in a form as near thereto as circumstances admit, before the issue of postal ballot papers:

Provided that if any person attends only the proceedings on the receipt of postal ballot papers, he need not make the declaration before the issue but shall make it before he is permitted to attend the proceedings on the receipt of postal ballot papers.

(2) The returning officer shall make the declaration in the presence of a justice of the peace or a person who is chairman of the Greater London Council, a county council or a district council or mayor of a London borough, and any other person shall make the declaration in the presence either of a justice of the peace or of the returning officer or of a person who is chairman or proper officer of the Greater London Council, a county council or a district council or mayor or proper officer of a London borough, and subsections (4) and (6) of section 53 of the Act of 1949 shall be read to the declarant by the person taking the declaration or shall be read by the declarant in the presence of that person.

(3) The declaration shall be as follows:—

"I solemnly promise and declare that I will not do anything forbidden by subsections (4) and (6) of section 53 of the Representation of the People Act 1949, which have been read to [by] me.".

(4) Any person before whom a declaration is authorised to be made under this Regulation may take the declaration.

Notice of issue of postal ballot papers

43.—(1) The returning officer shall give each candidate not less than two days' notice in writing of the time and place at which he will issue postal ballot papers and of the number of agents he may appoint under Regulation 41(2) to attend the said issue.

(2) Where any subsequent issue of postal ballot papers is made, the returning officer shall notify each candidate as soon as practicable of the time and place at which he will make such subsequent issue and of the number of agents he may appoint under Regulation 41(2) to attend such issue.

Marking of postal ballot paper

44.—(1) Each postal ballot paper issued shall be stamped with the official mark either embossed or perforated, and the name and number in the register of the elector shall be called out, and such number shall be marked on the counterfoil, and a mark shall be placed in the absent voters list or the list of postal proxies against the number of the elector to denote that a ballot paper has been issued to the elector or his proxy but without showing the particular ballot paper issued.

(2) The number of a postal ballot paper shall be marked on the declaration of identity sent with that paper.

Refusal to issue postal ballot paper

45. Where a returning officer is satisfied that two or more entries in the absent voters list or the list of postal proxies relate to the same elector or that a postal proxy has been appointed for a person entered in the absent voters list, he shall not issue more than one ballot paper in respect of the same elector.

Ballot paper envelope

46. The returning officer shall, in addition to the ballot paper, declaration of identity and envelope for their return (hereinafter referred to as a "covering envelope") which he is required by rule 25 of the elections rules to send to a postal voter, send a smaller envelope marked "ballot paper envelope" bearing the number of the ballot paper.

Delivery of postal ballot papers to post office

47.—(1) Envelopes addressed to postal voters shall be counted and forthwith delivered by the returning officer to the nearest head post office, or such other office as may be arranged with the head postmaster, and the postmaster shall stamp with the post office date stamp a form of receipt to be presented by the returning officer stating the number of envelopes so delivered, and shall immediately forward such envelopes for delivery to the persons to whom they are addressed.

(2) At local government elections first-class postage of all such envelopes and all covering envelopes shall be prepaid by the returning officer.

Provision of postal voters' ballot box

48.—(1) The returning officer shall, at the proceedings on the original issue of postal ballot papers, provide a ballot box or ballot boxes for the reception of the covering envelopes when returned by the postal voters.

(2) Every such ballot box shall be shown open and empty to the agents present and shall then be locked by the returning officer and sealed with the

seal of the returning officer and the seals of such of the agents as desire to affix their seals in such manner as to prevent its being opened without breaking the seal.

(3) Every such ballot box shall be marked "postal voters' ballot box" and with the name of the constituency or the electoral area for which the election is held.

(4) The returning officer shall make provision for the safe custody of every such ballot box.

Sealing up of special lists and counterfoils

49.—(1) The returning officer, as soon as practicable after the completion of the issue of the postal ballot papers, and in the presence of the agents, shall make up in separate packets—

> (*a*) the marked copies of the absent voters list and of the list of postal proxies, and
>
> (*b*) the counterfoils of those ballot papers which were issued,

and shall seal such packets.

(2) The sealed packet containing the marked copies of the absent voters list and of the list of postal proxies may be opened by the returning officer for the purposes of a subsequent issue, and on completion of that issue the copies shall be again made up and sealed in accordance with the last foregoing paragraph.

Spoilt postal ballot paper

50.—(1) If a postal voter has inadvertently dealt with his postal ballot paper in such manner that it cannot be conveniently used as a ballot paper (in these Regulations referred to as "a spoilt postal ballot paper") he may return (either by hand or by post) to the returning officer the spoilt postal ballot paper, the declaration of identity, the ballot paper envelope and the covering envelope.

(2) The returning officer, on receipt of the said documents, shall, unless the documents are received too late for another postal ballot paper to be returned before the close of the poll, issue another postal ballot paper and the foregoing provisions of this Part of these Regulations, but not sub-paragraph (*b*), (*c*) or (*d*) of paragraph (1) or paragraphs (2) to (8) of Regulation 41 or Regulation 43, shall apply accordingly.

(3) The spoilt postal ballot paper, the declaration of identity and the ballot paper envelope shall be immediately cancelled.

(4) The returning officer, as soon as practicable after cancelling the said documents, shall make up the said documents in a separate packet and shall seal the packet; and if on any subsequent occasion documents are cancelled as aforesaid, the sealed packet shall be opened and the additional cancelled documents included therein and the packet shall thereupon be again made up and sealed.

Receipt of Postal Ballot Papers

Receipt of covering envelope

51. The returning officer shall, immediately on receipt (whether by hand or by post) of a covering envelope before the close of the poll, place it unopened in a postal voters' ballot box locked and sealed in accordance with Regulation 48.

Opening of postal voters' ballot box

52.—(1) Each postal voters' ballot box shall be opened by the returning officer in the presence of the agents.

(2) So long as the returning officer secures that there is at least one postal voters' ballot box for the reception of covering envelopes up to the time of the close of the poll, the other postal voters' ballot boxes may previously be opened by him.

(3) The returning officer shall give each candidate at least forty-eight hours' notice in writing of the time and place of his opening of each postal voters ballot box and the envelopes contained therein and of the number of agents the candidate may appoint under Regulation 41(2) to be present at each opening.

Opening of covering envelopes

53.—(1) When a postal voters' ballot box has been opened, the returning officer shall count and note the number of covering envelopes, and shall then open each covering envelope separately.

(2) Where a covering envelope does not contain both a declaration of identity and a ballot paper envelope or, there being no ballot paper envelope, a ballot paper, he shall mark the covering envelope "rejected", attach thereto the contents (if any) of the covering envelope and place it is a separate receptacle (hereinafter referred to as "the receptacle for votes rejected"); and if the covering envelope does not contain the declaration separately, the returning officer shall open the ballot paper envelope to ascertain if the declaration is inside that envelope.

(3) On opening a covering envelope, other than one to which paragraph (2) of this Regulation applies, he shall first satisfy himself that the declaration of identity has been duly signed and authenticated and, if he is not so satisfied, he shall mark the declaration "rejected", attach thereto the ballot paper envelope or, if there is no such envelope, the ballot paper, and place it in the receptacle for votes rejected:

Provided that before so doing he shall show the declaration to the agents and, if any objection is made by any agent to his decision, he shall add the words "rejection objected to".

(4) Where the number on the declaration of identity duly signed and authenticated agrees with the number on the ballot paper envelope, he shall place the declaration in a separate receptacle (hereinafter referred to as "the receptacle for declarations of identity") and the ballot paper envelope in another separate receptacle (hereinafter referred to as "the receptacle for ballot paper envelopes").

(5) Where there is no ballot paper envelope or the ballot paper envelope has been opened under paragraph (2) of this Regulation, he shall—

(a) where the number on the declaration of identity duly signed and authenticated agrees with the number on the ballot paper, place the declaration in the receptacle for declarations of identity and the ballot paper in a ballot box previously shown open and empty to the agents present and locked by the returning officer and sealed with the seal of the returning officer and the seals of such of the agents as desire to affix their seals in such manner as to prevent its being opened without breaking the seal, which shall be subsequently treated as a ballot box for the purpose of rule 46 of the elections rules;

(b) where the number on the said declaration does not agree with the number on the ballot paper, mark the declaration "rejected", attach thereto the ballot paper and place it in the receptacle for votes rejected.

(6) Where the number on the declaration of identity duly signed and authenticated does not agree with the number on the ballot paper envelope or that envelope has no number on it, he shall open the envelope and shall—

(a) where the number on the declaration agrees with the number on the ballot paper, place the declaration in the receptacle for declarations of identity and the ballot paper in the ballot box referred to in paragraph (5) of this Regulation;

(b) where the number on the declaration does not agree with the number on the ballot paper or there is no ballot paper, mark the declaration "rejected", attach thereto the ballot paper (if any) and place it in the receptacle for votes rejected.

(7) Except for the purposes of ascertaining under paragraph (2) of this Regulation whether a ballot paper envelope contains a declaration of identity or under paragraph (6) of this Regulation whether the number on the declaration agrees with the number on the ballot paper, the returning officer shall not open the ballot paper envelopes before they are opened under Regulation 55.

Sealing up of rejected votes and declarations of identity

54. On the conclusion of the proceedings under Regulation 53 the returning officer shall put the contents of the receptacle for votes rejected and the contents of the receptacle for declarations of identity into two separate packets and shall seal up such packets.

Opening of ballot paper envelopes

55.—(1) After sealing up the said packets the returning officer shall open separately each ballot paper envelope placed in the receptacle for ballot paper envelopes.

(2) Where a ballot paper envelope does not contain a ballot paper, he shall mark the envelope "rejected".

(3) Where the number on the ballot paper envelope agrees with the number on the ballot paper contained therein, he shall place the ballot paper in the ballot box referred to in Regulation 53(5).

(4) Where the number on the ballot paper envelope does not agree with the number on the ballot paper contained therein, he shall mark the ballot paper "rejected" and attach the ballot paper envelope thereto.

(5) He shall put into a separate packet the envelopes and the ballot papers marked "rejected" under the provisions of this Regulation and shall seal up such packet.

Abandoned poll

56. Where a poll is abandoned, or countermanded after postal ballot papers have been issued, by reason of the death of a candidate, the returning officer—

(*a*) shall not take any step or further step to open covering envelopes or deal with their contents in accordance with the provisions of this Part of these Regulations, and

(*b*) shall, notwithstanding Regulation 54 or 55, treat all unopened covering envelopes and the contents of those which have been opened as if they were counted ballot papers.

Forwarding of documents

57.—(1) The returning officer shall forward, in the case of a parliamentary election, to the Clerk of the Crown in Chancery and, in the case of a local government election, to the proper officer of the authority to which councillors are to be elected, at the same time as he forwards the documents mentioned in rule 56 of the elections rules—

(*a*) any packets referred to in Regulation 49, 50, 54 or 55, subject to the provisions of Regulation 56, endorsing on each packet a description of its contents, the date of the election to which it relates and the name of the constituency or electoral area for which the election was held, and

(*b*) a statement of the number of postal ballot papers issued in such form and giving such other particulars with respect to such papers as the Secretary of State may require.

(2) Where any covering envelopes are received by the returning officer after the close of the poll or any envelopes addressed to postal voters are returned as undelivered too late to be readdressed, or any spoilt ballot papers are returned too late to enable other postal ballot papers to be issued, he shall put them unopened into a separate packet, seal up such packet and forward it at a subsequent date in the manner described in paragraph (1) of this Regulation.

(3) Any packet or statement forwarded under this Regulation shall be deemed to have been forwarded in pursuance of the elections rules.

(4) A copy of the statement referred to in paragraph (1) of this Regulation shall, in the case of a parliamentary election, be furnished by the returning officer to the Secretary of State.

PART V

SERVICE VOTERS

Service declaration by members of the forces and spouses

58.—(1) A service declaration made by a member of the forces shall be in Form J.

(2) A service declaration made by the spouse of a member of the forces shall be in Form K.

(3) A service declaration made by either a member of the forces or his or her spouse shall be attested by a commissioned officer who is a member of the forces or by an officer of a Government department and shall be transmitted by or on behalf of the declarant to the appropriate registration officer.

Qualification for Crown servant

59. A person employed in the service of the Crown in a post outside the United Kingdom the occupant of which is required to devote his whole time to the duties of that post and the remuneration of which is paid wholly out of moneys provided by Parliament (hereinafter referred to as "a Crown servant") shall have a service qualification.

Service declaration by Crown servants, British Council employees and spouses

60.—(1) A service declaration made by a Crown servant or by a person who is employed by the British Council in a post outside the United Kingdom (hereinafter referred to as "a British Council employee") shall be in Form L.

(2) A service declaration made by the spouse of a Crown servant or of a British Council employee shall be in Form M.

(3) A service declaration made by a person who is or will be a Crown servant or by his or her spouse shall be attested by an officer or of designated by the Government department under which that person or his or her spouse is or will be employed or by another person himself having a service qualification through being employed in the service of the Crown in a post outside the United Kingdom.

(4) A service declaration made by a person who is or will be a British Council employee or by his or her spouse shall be attested by an officer of the British Council or by another person himself having a service qualification through being employed in the service of the Crown in a post outside the United Kingdom.

Transmission of service declaration by Crown servants, British Council employees and spouses

61.—(1) A service declaration made by a person who is or will be a Crown servant or by his or her spouse shall be transmitted by the declarant to the Government department under which that person or his or her spouse is or will be employed or to an officer designated by that department and transmitted by that department or officer to the appropriate registration officer.

(2) A service declaration made by a person who is or will be a British Council employee or by his or her spouse shall be transmitted by the declarant to the British Council and transmitted by the British Council to the appropriate registration officer.

Service declaration by person about to leave the United Kingdom

62. A service declaration made by a person about to leave the United Kingdom in such circumstances as to acquire a service qualification shall be made not more than six weeks before the date on which he expects to leave the United Kingdom.

Proceedings by registration officer on receipt of service declaration

63. Subject to Regulation 64, the registration officer on receipt of a service declaration shall notify the declarant that his declaration has been received.

Invalid service declaration

64.—(1) Where a service declaration does not appear—

    (*a*) to be properly made out and attested, or

    (*b*) to have been transmitted in the proper manner to the registration officer,

the registration officer shall return the declaration to the declarant and explain his reasons for so doing.

(2) Where the registration officer has been notified by the appropriate Government department or an officer designated by that department or has been notified by the British Council that a person is not entitled to make a service declaration, he shall not enter that person's name in the electors lists and shall notify that person that he has not done so but that that person may make a claim to be so entered.

Evidence as to service declaration

65. The registration officer shall treat a notice from the appropriate Government department or an officer designated by that department or a notice from the British Council that a person is not entitled to make a service declaration or that a person's service declaration has ceased to be in force as conclusive evidence thereof.

PART VI

SUPPLEMENTARY

Appeals

66.—(1) A person desiring to appeal against the decision of a registration officer must give notice of appeal to the registration officer and to the opposite party (if any) when the decision is given, or within fourteen days thereafter, specifying the grounds of appeal.

(2) The registration officer shall forward any such notice to the county court in the manner directed by rules of court together in each case with a statement of the material facts which in his opinion have been established in the case and of his decision upon the whole case and on any point which may be specified as a ground of appeal, and shall also furnish to the court any further information which the court may require and which he is able to furnish.

(3) Where it appears to the registration officer that any notices of appeal given to him are based on similar grounds, he shall inform the county court of the fact for the purpose of enabling the court (if it thinks fit) to consolidate the appeals or select a case as a test case.

Official poll card at parliamentary elections

67. At parliamentary elections—

(*a*) the official poll card issued to an elector shall be in Form E;

(*b*) the official poll card issued to the proxy of an elector shall be in Form F.

Return and declaration of election expenses

68.—(1) The return and declaration of expenses required by sections 63 of the Act of 1949 to be authorised by an election agent shall be in Forms X and Y.

(2) The fee for inspecting a return or declaration (including any accompanying documents) specified in section 77(1) of, or paragraph 8(1) of Schedule 6 to, the Act of 1949 (which relate to returns and declarations of election expenses) shall be twenty-five pence.

(3) The price of a copy of any such return, declaration or document shall be at the rate of five pence for the contents of each side of each page.

Forms

69.—(1) Form A shall be used for the purpose for which it is expressed to be applicable.

(2) The registration officer shall without fee supply a reasonable number of copies of Forms N to W to any person.

(3) The forms set out in the Schedule to these Regulations or forms substantially to the like effect may be used with such variations as the circumstances may require.

Sending of notices, etc.

70.—(1) Any application, notice, claim or objection which is required by these Regulations to be made to the registration officer or returning officer shall be in writing and sent by post or delivered to his office or to the address specified by him for the purpose.

(2) Where the registration officer or returning officer is required by these Regulations to notify any person, such notification shall be in writing and may be sent by post—

(*a*) in the case of a person other than a service voter, to the address furnished by that person for the purpose of such notification or of any record or, if there is no such address, to the last known place of abode of that person;

(*b*) in the case of a service voter, to any address provided by him for the purpose of such notification or of any record or to the address provided for the purpose by the appropriate Government department or, as the case may be, the British Council.

Publication of documents

71.—(1) Any failure to publish a document in accordance with these Regulations shall not invalidate the document, but this provision shall not relieve the registration officer from any penalty for such a failure.

(2) A document which is made available for inspection in pursuance of these Regulations shall be made available during ordinary business hours.

(3) Where a document is made available for inspection, any person may make a copy of, or take extracts from, such document.

Misnomers

72. No misnomer or inaccurate description of any person or place in any notice, electors list, list of claims or objections, corrupt and illegal practices list, special list or register shall prejudice the operation of that document with respect to that person or place in any case where the description of the person or place is such as to be commonly understood.

Time

73.—(1) Subject to the provisions of the following paragraphs of this Regulation, where the last day of the time allowed by these Regulations for any matter falls on a Sunday, or a day of the Christmas break, of the Easter break or of a bank holiday break, that time shall be extended until the end of the next following day which is not one of the days before mentioned.

(2) In computing for the purposes of Regulation 35 the period of twelve or fourteen days before the day of the poll at a parliamentary or local government election, as the case may be, a Sunday, or a day of the Christmas break, of the Easter break or of a bank holiday break shall be disregarded.

(3) In this Regulation "the Christmas break", "the Easter break" and "a bank holiday break" have the same meanings as in rule 2 of the elections rules, except that in paragraph (1) of this Regulation a bank holiday means a day which is a bank holiday under the Banking and Financial Dealings Act 1971**(a)** in England and Wales.

Penalties

74.—(1) If any person fails to comply with or gives false information in pursuance of any such requisition of the registration officer as is mentioned in Regulation 25, he shall be liable on summary conviction to a fine not exceeding £50.

(2) If any person without lawful authority destroys, mutilates, defaces or removes any notice published by the registration officer in connection with his registration duties or any copies of a document which have been made available for inspection in pursuance of those duties, he shall be liable on summary conviction to a fine not exceeding £20.

Robert Carr,

One of Her Majesty's Principal
Secretaries of State.

Home Office,
  Whitehall.
6th February 1974.

(a) 1971 c. 80.

SCHEDULE

FORMS

Forms for use by registration officers

Regulation 69.

FORM A: RETURN BY OCCUPIER AS TO RESIDENTS

REPRESENTATION OF THE PEOPLE ACTS

REGISTER OF ELECTORS 19

Qualifying date: 10th October 19 . Register in force for twelve months from 16th February 19 .

I have to compile and publish an up-to-date Register of Electors for 19 . To do so, I need information which you, as occupier, are obliged by law to supply.

Registers of Electors are needed so that everyone who is entitled to vote at parliamentary or local elections may do so. A person whose name does not appear in the Register cannot vote.

The notes within tell you how to fill up the form, but if you need further help, I shall be glad to give it.

You should complete the form even if you intend to move house after the qualifying date.

Please complete and sign this form, and return it to me now—there is no need to wait until the qualifying date.

The Electoral Registration Officer.

Address

No. of flat, room or floor (where applicable)	No. of house (or name if not numbered)	Name of street or road	Remainder of address

Residents eligible to be included (*see* notes 1 and 2)

If none, please write "None"

Surname and title (Mr., Mrs., etc.) (BLOCK LETTERS)	Full Christian names or forenames (BLOCK LETTERS)	If 18 or over by 16th February 19 enter a √ in this column	If under 18 on 16th February 19 but 18 by 15th February 19 , give date of birth (see note 1)	If a merchant seaman enter "M" (see notes 1 and 2)	Jury Service (see note 5) If over 65 by 16th February 19 enter a √ in this column

Other residents

Is any part of your house/flat *separately* occupied by persons not entered above?

Please answer Yes or No

Declaration

I declare that to the best of my knowledge and belief the particulars given above are true and accurate, and all those whose names are entered above are British subjects or citizens of the Irish Republic and will be 18 or over by 15th February 19 .

Sign here.. Date..................................

NOTES

1. *You are required to enter* all British subjects (Commonwealth citizens are British subjects) and citizens of the Irish Republic who will be resident at your address on *10th October 19* and who will be 18 or over by 15th February 19 (*this means all those born before 16th February 19 : they may be only 16 or 17 now, but they can vote at elections as soon as they are 18*)—

Including

(*a*) Those who normally live at your address but are temporarily away, e.g. on holiday; as students; in hospital (including informal patients in psychiatric hospitals); or as reservists called up for service or training;

(*b*) Resident guests (but not short-stay visitors);

(*c*) Lodgers and resident domestics;

(*d*) Anyone who is away working, unless his absence will be for more than six months;

(*e*) Merchant seamen who, but for their job, would live at your address (which may be a hostel or club). Mark their names with an "M" and they will be invited to vote by post or proxy.

2. *Do not enter—*

(*a*) Aliens;

(*b*) Members of H.M. Forces;

(*c*) Crown servants employed outside the U.K.;

(*d*) British Council staff employed outside the U.K.;

(*e*) Wives or husbands of members of H.M. Forces, of Crown servants or of British Council staff employed outside the U.K. *if living abroad* to be with their husbands or wives.

Their names will be included in the register if they have made the necessary service declaration; to do this they should apply to their Service or Department or to the British Council.

3. *Electors Lists*

These lists can be checked at council offices etc, from 28th November. Claims in respect of names not included in the lists must be received by 16th December.

4. *Postal voting*

If you think you may be entitled to vote by post, e.g. because you are disabled, because your work takes you away from home, or because you are leaving the area, ask the electoral registration officer for an application form. *Do not wait* for an election before applying.

5. *Jury service*

Electors who are over 65 are ineligible on age grounds for jury service. Those who are ineligible on other grounds, or who are exempt, will be able to indicate this if they receive a jury summons from the Crown Court.

HOW TO RETURN THE FORM

(*a*) Use the addressed envelope if one was supplied; or if you received the form in an envelope marked "Use this envelope for your reply", fold the form so that the electoral registration officer's address shows through the window *and seal the envelope*.

(*b*) If there was no envelope with it the form will be collected from you.

Regulation 13.

FORM B: NOTICE AS TO PUBLICATION OF A DRAFT REGISTER OF ELECTORS AND MAKING OF CLAIMS AND OBJECTIONS

REPRESENTATION OF THE PEOPLE ACTS

DRAFT REGISTER OF ELECTORS

WHAT THE DRAFT REGISTER IS FOR

1. The register of electors for the twelve months beginning on 16th February next will be based on the draft register. Unless your name is on the register of electors you will not be able to vote at parliamentary or local government elections. To make sure that you will be on the new register and able to vote you should therefore look at the draft register to see that your name is included on it.

HOW TO FIND YOUR NAME IN THE DRAFT REGISTER

2. Before you can trace your name in the draft register you must know in which polling district you live. If you do not know, ask whether an index of streets is available showing where your address appears in the register.

WHAT TO DO IF YOU FIND THAT YOUR NAME IS NOT ON THE DRAFT REGISTER

3. If your name is not on the draft register and you think it ought to be, you should submit a claim to the electoral registration officer before 16th December on a form which he will give you.

4. Your name ought to be on the register if you are over 18 now, or your 18th birthday is not later than 15th February in the year after next, and
either   (i) you were resident at an address in the constituency on 10th October last,

    or (ii) you had, as a service voter, made a service declaration on or before 10th October last in respect of an address in the constituency.

OBJECTIONS TO OR ALTERATION OF ENTRIES

5. A request for the alteration of any entry, or an objection to the inclusion of any other person's name, should be submitted to the electoral registration officer before 16th December on a form which he will give you.

Signature ....

Electoral Registration Officer

Address   ....

....

....

Date..

FORM C: NOTICE AS TO PUBLICATIONS OF THE ELECTOR LISTS ^{Regulation 13.} AND MAKING OF CLAIMS AND OBJECTIONS

REPRESENTATIONS OF THE PEOPLE ACTS

ELECTORS LISTS

WHAT THE LISTS ARE FOR

1. The register of electors for the twelve months beginning on 16th February next will be based on these electors lists. Unless your name in on the register of electors you will not be able to vote at parliamentary or local government elections. To make sure that you will be on the new register and able to vote you should therefore look at these lists.

HOW TO FIND YOUR NAME IN THE LISTS

2. Before you can trace your name in the lists you must know in which polling district you live. If you do not know, ask whether an index of streets is available showing where your address appears in the register.

3. There are three lists, marked A, B and C.

List A is the register for the present year.

List B shows the names which will be added to it next year.

List C shows the names which will be removed from it next year.

    (i) Look at List A first.
    (ii) If your name is in List A, look at List C. If your name is not in List C, then it will be included in the new register, and you will be able to vote.
    (iii) If your name is not in List A, look at List B. If your name is in List B, then it will be included in the new register, and you will be able to vote.

WHAT TO DO IF YOU FIND THAT YOUR NAME WILL NOT BE ON THE REGISTER

4. If you think your name ought to be on the register, you should submit a claim to the electoral registration officer before 16th December on a form which he will give you.

5. Your name ought to be on the register if you are over 18 now, or your 18th birthday is not later than 15th February in the year after next, and
either   (i) you were resident at an address in the constituency on 10th October last,

   or (ii) you had, as a service voter, made a service declaration on or before 10th October last in respect of an address in the constituency.

OBJECTIONS TO OR ALTERATION OF ENTRIES

6. A request for the alteration of any entry, or an objection to the inclusion of any other person's name, should be submitted to the electoral registration officer before 16th December on a form which he will give you.

Signature ....
Electoral Registration Officer

Address ....

....

....

Date......................................

Regulation 32.

FORM D: PROXY PAPER

REPRESENTATION OF THE PEOPLE ACTS

Constituency...

Polling District...

Local government electoral area(s)..
....

(Name of proxy)...

(Address) ....

....

....

is hereby appointed as proxy for

(Name of elector)..

who is qualified as a *service voter ———————— to be registered for
resident

(Qualifying address)..

....

*Delete
whichever is
inapplicable

to vote for *him/her at

*the parliamentary election for the above constituency
on ....

*any election for the above parliamentary constituency
or local government electoral area(s) (*see* Note 1)

This proxy appointment is not valid until ....

Signature ....
Electoral Registration Officer

Address   ....

....

....

Date.......................................

NOTES

1. If your appointment as proxy is for a particular parliamentary election, it will be valid for that election only. In other cases your appointment will continue in force until the electoral registration officer informs you to the contrary (e.g. because the elector cancels it).

If the elector is shown on this form as a resident, your appointment will be valid for all parliamentary and local government elections for the constituency and local government electoral area(s) named above, but not for parish or community council elections.

If the elector is shown on this form as a service voter, your appointment will be valid for all parliamentary and local government elections for the constituency and local government electoral area(s) named above (including parish and community council elections) unless the elector applies to vote by post at a particular parliamentary election. If he does this, your appointment will be suspended for that election only and you will be so informed.

If a ballot paper is issued to the elector at the polling station before you apply for a ballot paper on his behalf, you will not be entitled to vote as proxy.

2. To vote as proxy at an election you must go in person to the polling station for the elector's qualifying address unless you are entitled to vote by post as proxy. You are entitled to vote by post as proxy if either—

(*a*) you are entitled to vote by post as an elector in respect of your own vote at the election; or

(*b*) at a parliamentary election (but not at a local government election) your address is in a different area from the address for which the elector is registered.

Where (*b*) applies, the application cannot be allowed if your address and the address for which the elector is registered are—

(*a*) in the same electoral division of Greater London; or

(*b*) in the same electoral division of an English county and, if either address is in a parish, both are in the same parish; or

(*c*) in the same electoral division of a Welsh county and in the same community.

If you wish to vote by post as proxy, you must apply to do so on Form V, which may be obtained from the electoral registration officer.

3. It is an offence to vote, whether in person or by post, as proxy for some other person if you know that that person is subject to a legal incapacity to vote, e.g. if that person has been convicted and is detained in a penal institution in pursuance of his sentence.

Forms for use by returing officers

Regulation 67. ## FORM E: ELECTOR'S OFFICIAL POLL CARD

REPRESENTATION OF THE PEOPLE ACTS

Front of card

OFFICIAL POLL CARD

Constituency

....

Polling Day.....................................

Your polling station will be

....
Polling hours
7 a.m. to 10 p.m.

Number on Register.....................

Name ....

Address ....
....
....
....

Back of card

PARLIAMENTARY ELECTION

You need not take this card with you when you go to the polling station, but it will save time if you take it and show it to the clerk there.

When you go to the polling station, tell the clerk your name and address, as shown on the front of this card. The presiding officer will give you a ballot paper; see that he stamps the official mark on it before he gives it to you.

Mark your vote on the ballot paper secretly in one of the voting compartments. Put one X in the space to the right opposite the name of the candidate for whom you wish to vote. You may vote for only one candidate. If you put any other mark on the ballot paper your vote may not be counted.

Then fold the ballot paper so as to conceal your vote, show the official mark on the back to the presiding officer and put the paper into the ballot box.

If you spoil the ballot paper by mistake, do not destroy it; give it back to the presiding officer and ask for another.

If you have appointed a proxy to vote in person for you, you may nevertheless vote at this election if you do so before your proxy has voted on your behalf.

If you have been granted a postal vote, you will *not* be entitled to vote in person at this election; so please ignore this poll card.

ISSUED BY THE RETURNING OFFICER

FORM F: PROXY'S OFFICIAL POLL CARD

REPRESENTATION OF THE PEOPLE ACTS

Front of card

PROXY'S OFFICIAL POLL CARD

Proxy's name ....

Proxy's address...

....

Back of card

PARLIAMENTARY ELECTION

....CONSTITUENCY

Polling day...

The poll will be open from 7 a.m. to 10 p.m.

The elector named below whose proxy you are is entitled to vote at the polling station—

....

....

To vote as proxy you must go to that polling station. Tell the clerk that you wish to vote as proxy; give the name and qualifying address of the elector, as follows:—

Number on Register...

Name ....

Address ....

....

The presiding officer will give you the elector's ballot paper. The method of voting as proxy is the same as for casting your own vote.

It is an offence to vote as proxy for some other person if you know that that person is subject to a legal incapacity to vote, e.g. if that person has been convicted and is detained in a penal institution in pursuance of his sentence.

The person who appointed you as proxy may himself vote in person at this election if he is able, and wishes, to do so and if he votes before you vote on his behalf.

ISSUED BY THE RETURNING OFFICER

Regulation 37.

FORM G: CERTIFICATE OF EMPLOYMENT

REPRESENTATION OF THE PEOPLE ACTS

ELECTION IN THE

....

CONSTITUENCY

I certify that (name)...

who is numbered.....................................in the register of electors for the

constituency named above, is unlikely to be unable to go in person to the poll-

ing station allotted to him at the election on (date of poll).............................

.........by reason of the particular circumstances of his employment on that date—

*(a) as a constable,

*Delete whichever is inapplicable.

*(b) by me for a purpose connected with the election.

Signature...
*Returning Officer/Police Officer (Inspector or above)

Date...............................

Note.—The person named above is entitled to vote at any polling station of the above constituency on production and surrender of this certificate to the presiding officer.

FORM H: DECLARATION OF IDENTITY

REPRESENTATION OF THE PEOPLE ACTS

Front of form

Ballot Paper No..............................

I hereby declare that I am the person to whom the ballot paper numbered as above was sent.

Voter's signature (or mark)..

The voter, who is personally known to me, has signed (or marked) this declaration in my presence.

Witness's signature....................................

SEE INSTRUCTIONS ON THE BACK OF THIS FORM

Back of form

INSTRUCTIONS TO THE VOTER

1. You must sign (or mark) the declaration of identity in the presence of a person known to you.

2. You may vote for not more than............candidate[s].

3. Place a cross (X) on the right-hand side of the ballot paper opposite the name[s] of the candidate[s] for whom you vote. Do this secretly: if you cannot vote without assistance, the person assisting you must not disclose how you have voted.

4. Put the ballot paper in the small envelope marked "A" and seal it. Then put the envelope marked "A", together with this declaration of identity, in the larger envelope marked "B". Return it without delay. The ballot paper, in order to be counted, must be received by the returning officer not later than the close of the poll.

5. If you receive more than one ballot paper, remember that it is illegal to vote more than once (otherwise than as proxy) at the same election.

6. At this election you cannot vote in person at a polling station, even if you receive an official poll card.

7. If you inadvertently spoil your postal ballot paper, you can apply to the returning officer for another one. With your application you must return, in a fresh envelope, the spoilt ballot paper, the declaration of identity and the envelopes marked "A" and "B". Remember that there is little time available if a fresh postal ballot paper is to be counted.

Forms for use by service voters

Regulation 58.

FORM J: SERVICE DECLARATION AND APPLICATION FOR APPOINTMENT OF PROXY BY A MEMBER OF THE FORCES

REPRESENTATION OF THE PEOPLE ACTS

REGISTER OF ELECTORS 19

Qualifying date: 10th October 19 .

Register in force for twelve months from 16th February 19 .

Part 1.

Surname ....

    (BLOCK LETTERS)

Other names..

    (BLOCK LETTERS)

Service (R.N., Army,   Regiment
R.A.F., etc.).................................or Corps............................

Rank or Rating ....Service No...............................

Present Service address...

    ....

I HEREBY DECLARE—

(1) that I am a British subject or citizen of the Republic of Ireland;

(2) that—

   *(a) I shall be 18 years of age or over on 16th February 19 ;

   OR

*Delete
whichever is
inapplicable.

   *(b) (*if 18th birthday is after 16th February 19 and on or before the
following 15th February*)

Day	Month	Year
:		:

my 18th birthday is on

(3) that I reside, or but for my service would reside, in the United Kingdom, and—

   *(a) reside, or but for my service would reside, at (full postal address in
block letters) ....

      ....

      ....

   OR

   *(b) (*if the declarant cannot give any such address*) have resided in the
United Kingdom at (full postal address in block letters)

      ....

      ....

      ....

I HEREBY CANCEL any previous declaration made by me.

Signature of declarant...............................Date............................

Signature and Rank of attesting officer (*see* Note 3)............................

NOTES

1. This declaration is to be made with a view to registration in the register of electors which will be in force for twelve months from 16th February 19 and with reference to your circumstances on the qualifying date for that register, i.e. 10th October 19 .

2. The declaration is to be made during the twelve months ending with the qualifying date.

3. The declaration must be attested by a commissioned officer or by an officer of a Government Department.

4. When completed and attested, this form should be sent to the electoral registration officer.

Part 2.   Regulation 30.

PROXY APPOINTMENT

(While you are outside the United Kingdom you can vote only by proxy.)

I HEREBY CANCEL ANY PREVIOUS PROXY APPOINTMENT AND APPLY FOR THE APPOINTMENT AS MY PROXY OF—

Names of first choice..
    (BLOCK LETTERS)

Postal address...
    (BLOCK LETTERS)
    ....

Relationship, if any, to elector...

OR IF HE OR SHE IS UNWILLING OR UNABLE TO BE APPOINTED

Names of second choice..
    (BLOCK LETTERS)

Postal address...
    (BLOCK LETTERS)
    ....

Relationship, if any, to elector...

Signature...............................   Date....................

NOTES

1. A person to vote as proxy must be a British subject or citizen of the Republic of Ireland, of voting age and not subject to any legal incapacity to vote. A proxy appointed in consequence of this application will be entitled to vote for you at all parliamentary and local government elections.

2. If the address in paragraph (3) of Part 1 is the same as that in your previous declaration (if any), you need not apply for the appointment of a proxy unless you want to appoint a different one; the previous appointment will remain valid. If, however, the address is different, you will need to apply afresh for the appointment of a proxy.

3. If at any time you wish to cancel the appointment of your proxy, you should notify the electoral registration officer.

Regulation 58.

FORM K: SERVICE DECLARATION AND APPLICATION FOR APPOINTMENT OF PROXY BY THE SPOUSE OF A MEMBER OF THE FORCES

REPRESENTATION OF THE PEOPLE ACTS

REGISTER OF ELECTORS 19

Qualifying date: 10th October 19 .
Register in force for twelve months from 16th February 19 .

Part 1.

Surname ....
    (BLOCK LETTERS)

Other names...
    (BLOCK LETTERS)

Other names of *husband/wife...

Service (R.N., Army,   Regiment
R.A.F., etc.)............................or Corps....................

Rank or Rating ....Service No.......................

Present address of *husband/wife...

....

I HEREBY DECLARE

(1) that I am a British subject or citizen of the Republic of Ireland;

(2) that—

*(a) I shall be 18 years of age or over on 16th February 19 ;

OR

Delete whichever is inapplicable.

*(b) (*if 18th birthday is after 16th February 19 and on or before the following 15th February*)

my 18th birthday is on

Day	Month	Year
:	:	

(3) that I reside, or expect to go abroad within six weeks (*see* Note 2) to reside, outside the United Kingdom to be with my *husband/wife who is a member of the forces;

(4) that but for my *husband's/wife's service I would be residing in the United Kingdom, and—

*(a) would be residing at (full postal address in block letters)

....
....

OR

*(b) (*if the declarant cannot give any such address*) have resided in the United Kingdom at (full postal address in block letters)

....
....
....

I HEREBY CANCEL any previous declaration made by me.

Signature of declarant...Date........................

Signature and Rank of attesting officer (*see* Note 3)...................................

NOTES

1. This declaration is to be made with a view to registration in the register of electors which will be in force for twelve months from 16th February 19   and with reference to your circumstances on the qualifying date for that register, i.e. 10th October 19   .

2. The declaration is to be made during the twelve months ending with the qualifying date, but a person about to leave the United Kingdom must not make it more than six weeks before the expected date of departure.

3. The declaration must be attested by a commissioned officer or by an officer of a Government Department.

4. When completed and attested this form should be sent to the electoral registration officer.

Part 2. Regulation 30.

PROXY APPOINTMENT

(While you are outside the United Kingdom you can vote only by proxy.)

I HEREBY CANCEL ANY PREVIOUS PROXY APPOINTMENT AND APPLY FOR THE APPOINTMENT AS MY PROXY OF

Names of first choice..
    (BLOCK LETTERS)

Postal address..
    (BLOCK LETTERS)

....

Relationship, if any, to elector..

OR IF HE OR SHE IS UNWILLING OR UNABLE TO BE APPOINTED

Names of second choice...
    (BLOCK LETTERS)

Postal address..
    (BLOCK LETTERS)

....

Relationship, if any, to elector..

Signature... Date................

NOTES

1. A person to vote as proxy must be a British subject or citizen of the Republic of Ireland, of voting age and not subject to any legal incapacity to vote. A proxy appointed in consequence of this application will be entitled to vote for you at all parliamentary and local government elections.

2. If the address in paragraph (4) of Part 1 is the same as that in your previous declaration (if any) you need not apply for the appointment of a proxy unless you want to appoint a different one; the previous appointment will remain valid. If, however, the address is different, you will need to apply afresh for the appointment of a proxy.

3. If at any time you wish to cancel the appointment of your proxy, you should notify the electoral registration officer.

Regulation 60.

FORM L: SERVICE DECLARATION AND APPLICATION FOR APPOINTMENT OF PROXY BY A CROWN SERVANT OR BY A PERSON EMPLOYED BY THE BRITISH COUNCIL

REPRESENTATION OF THE PEOPLE ACTS

REGISTER OF ELECTORS 19 .

Qualifying date: 10th October 19 .

Register in force for twelve months from 16th February 19 .

Part 1.

Surname ....
(BLOCK LETTERS)

Other names..
(BLOCK LETTERS)

I HEREBY DECLARE—

(1) that I am a British subject or citizen of the Republic of Ireland;

(2) that—

*(a) I shall be 18 years of age or over on 16th February 19 ;

OR

*(b) (if 18th birthday is after 16th February 19 and on or before the following 15th February)

my 18th birthday is on

Day	Month	Year
:		:

*Delete whichever is inapplicable.

(3) that I am employed, or leaving the United Kingdom to take up employment (see Note 2), in the service of the *Crown/British Council—

Description of post ....

Name of Government Department under which you are employed (if applicable)..

Present address ....
....

(4) that but for my service abroad I would be residing in the United Kingdom, and—

*(a) would be residing at (full postal address in block letters)...........
....
....

OR

*(b) (if the declarant cannot give any such address) have resided in the United Kingdom at (full postal address in block letters)
....
....
....

I HEREBY CANCEL any previous declaration made by me.

Signature of declarant.. Date...........................

Signature of person attesting (see Note 3)...

Rank or official position...

NOTES

1. This declaration is to be made with a view to registration in the register of electors which will be in force for twelve months from 16th February 19   and with reference to your circumstances on the qualifying date for that register, i.e. 10th October 19 .

2. The declaration is to be made during the twelve months ending with the qualifying date, but a person about to leave the United Kingdom must not make it more than six weeks before the expected date of departure.

3. The declaration must be attested by an officer of, or designated by, the Government Department under which you are employed, or, as the case may be, by an officer of the British Council, or by another person who has a service qualification through being employed in the service of the Crown in a post outside the United Kingdom.

4. This form when completed and attested should be returned to the Government Department under which you are employed or to an officer designated by that Department or to the British Council as the case may be.

Part 2. Regulation 30.

PROXY APPOINTMENT

(While you are outside the United Kingdom you can vote only by proxy.)

I HEREBY CANCEL ANY PREVIOUS PROXY APPOINTMENT AND APPLY FOR THE APPOINTMENT AS MY PROXY OF—

Names of first choice...
    (BLOCK LETTERS)
Postal address ....
    (BLOCK LETTERS)
....
Relationship, if any, to elector..

OR IF HE OR SHE IS UNWILLING OR UNABLE TO BE APPOINTED

Names of second choice..
    (BLOCK LETTERS)
Postal address ....
    (BLOCK LETTERS)
....
Relationship, if any, to elector..

Signature.. Date........................

NOTES

1. A person to vote as proxy must be a British subject or citizen of the Republic of Ireland, of voting age and not subject to any legal incapacity to vote. A proxy appointed in consequence of this application will be entitled to vote for you at all parliamentary and local government elections.

2. If the address in paragraph (4) of Part 1 is the same as that in your previous declaration (if any) you need not apply for the appointment of a proxy unless you want to appoint a different one; the previous appointment will remain valid. If, however, the address is different, you will need to apply afresh for the appointment of a proxy.

3. If at any time you wish to cancel the appointment of your proxy, you should notify the electoral registration officer.

Regulation 60.

FORM M: SERVICE DECLARATION AND APPLICATION FOR APPOINTMENT OF PROXY BY THE SPOUSE OF A CROWN SERVANT OR OF A PERSON EMPLOYED BY THE BRITISH COUNCIL

REPRESENTATION OF THE PEOPLE ACTS

REGISTER OF ELECTORS 19

Qualifying date: 10th October 19 .

Register in force for twelve months from 16th February 19 .

Part 1.

Surname ....
    (BLOCK LETTERS)

Other names...
    (BLOCK LETTERS)

Other names of *husband/wife...

I HEREBY DECLARE—

(1) that I am a British subject or citizen of the Republic of Ireland;

(2) that—

*(a) I shall be 18 years of age or over on 16th February 19 ;

OR

*(b) (if 18th birthday is after 16th February 19 and on or before the following 15th February)

my 18th birthday is on

Day	Month	Year
:		:

*Delete whichever is inapplicable.

(3) that I reside, or expect to go abroad within six weeks (see Note 2) to reside, outside the United Kingdom to be with my *husband/wife, who is employed, or is leaving the United Kingdom to take up employment, in the service of the *Crown/British Council—

Description of *husband's/wife's post...

Name of Government Department under which *husband/wife employed (if applicable) ....

Present address of *husband/wife...
....

(4) that but for my *husband's/wife's service I would be residing in the United Kingdom, and—

*(a) would be residing at (full postal address in block letters)
....
....

OR

*(b) (if the declarant cannot give any such address) have resided in the United Kingdom at (full postal address in block letters)
....
....
....

I HEREBY CANCEL any previous declaration made by me.

Signature of declarant.......................................Date.....................

Signature of person attesting (see Note 3) ....

Rank or official position..

Notes

1. This declaration is to be made with a view to registration in the register of electors which will be in force for twelve months from 16th February 19   and with reference to your circumstances on the qualifying date for that register, i.e. 10th October 19   .

2. The declaration is to be made during the twelve months ending with the qualifying date, but a person about to leave the United Kingdom must not make it more than six weeks before the expected date of departure.

3. The declaration must be attested by an officer of, or designated by, the Government Department under which your husband or wife is employed, or, as the case may be, by an officer of the British Council, or by another person who has a service qualification through being employed in the service of the Crown in a post outside the United Kingdom.

4. This form when completed and attested should be returned to the Government Department under which your husband or wife is employed or to an officer designated by that Department or to the British Council as the case may be.

Part 2.   Regulation 30.

Proxy Appointment

(While you are outside the United Kingdom you can vote only by proxy.)

I HEREBY CANCEL ANY PREVIOUS PROXY APPOINTMENT AND APPLY FOR THE APPOINTMENT AS MY PROXY OF—

Names of first choice ....
  (BLOCK LETTERS)

Postal address ....
  (BLOCK LETTERS)

....

Relationship, if any, to elector...

OR IF HE OR SHE IS UNWILLING OR UNABLE TO BE APPOINTED

Names of second choice..
  (BLOCK LETTERS)

Postal address ....
  (BLOCK LETTERS)

....

Relationship, if any, to elector...

Signature.. Date......................

Notes

1. A person to vote as proxy must be a British subject or citizen of the Republic of Ireland, of voting age and not subject to any legal incapacity to vote. A proxy appointed in consequence of this application will be entitled to vote for you at all parliamentary and local government elections.

2. If the address in paragraph (4) of Part 1 is the same as that in your previous declaration (if any), you need not apply for the appointment of a proxy unless you want to appoint a different one; the previous appointment will remain valid. If, however, the address is different, you will need to apply afresh for the appointment of a proxy.

3. If at any time you wish to cancel the appointment of your proxy, you should notify the electoral registration officer.

Regulation 29.

FORM N: APPLICATION BY A SERVICE VOTER IN THE UNITED KINGDOM TO VOTE BY POST

REPRESENTATION OF THE PEOPLE ACTS

I, (Surname)..
　　　(BLOCK LETTERS)

　　(Other names) ....
　　　(BLOCK LETTERS)

　　(Rank or　　　　　　　　　　　(Service
　　Rating) ....　　No.)..

am registered as a service voter for

....
(Give the qualifying address which you gave on your service declaration)
and I apply for a ballot paper for the coming parliamentary election to be sent
to me at

....

....
(Give full postal address in block letters)

　　　　Signature.................................　　　　　Date.............................

NOTES

1. If you have changed your name since completing your service declaration,
put your former name in brackets after your present name.

2. You should send this application to the electoral registration officer at the
address stated on his acknowledgement of your service declaration.

Forms for use by other persons

FORM O: FORM OF CLAIM TO BE REGISTERED AS AN
ELECTOR

Regulation 15.

REPRESENTATION OF THE PEOPLE ACTS

(If the form is sent to the Electoral Registration Officer by post, postage must be prepaid.)

To the Electoral Registration Officer

Qualifications for Registration

An elector must have been resident on 10th October last; a service voter must have made a service declaration on or before that date.

The person must be a British subject or citizen of the Republic of Ireland and must be 18 years of age or over by 15th February in the year after next.

Note. Any false declaration made by a person for the purpose of this claim will render such person liable to a penalty.

1. Surname and...Other............................
    title (Mr., Mrs., etc.)   names
    (BLOCK LETTERS)   (BLOCK LETTERS)

2. Full postal address (in BLOCK LETTERS) of premises for which claimant claims to be qualified to be registered
    ....
    ....

3. (*a*) Will the claimant be 18 years of age or over by 16th February next?
        (Yes or No)..

    (*b*) If not, give date of birth...

4. (*a*) Was claimant resident at the said address on 10th October last?
        (Yes or No)..

    (*b*) Had claimant made a service declaration by 10th October last
        (Yes or No)..

    (*c*) Was claimant a merchant seaman on 10th October last? (Yes or No) ....

DECLARATION

The particulars above are true and correct in all respects. The claimant is a British subject or citizen of the Republic of Ireland; and he claims the parliamentary and/or local government franchise to which such particulars entitle him.

Signature of claimant or person making claim on behalf of claimant

....

Address of person making claim ....

....

....

Date...

Regulation 15.

FORM P: FORM OF OBJECTION TO AN ENTRY IN THE ELECTORS LISTS

REPRESENTATION OF THE PEOPLE ACTS

(If this form is sent to the Electoral Registration Officer by post, postage must be prepaid.)

*Here insert extract from printed electors lists, stating name and address as given in claim.

To the Electoral Registration Officer

I hereby give you notice that I object to the entry of*..............................

....

....

....

†Delete if inapplicable.

as an elector [in accordance with the claim made in that behalf.]†

The grounds of my objection are...

....

....

....

‡Here insert extract from printed electors lists.

I am entered in the electors lists as an elector as follows‡ :—

....

....

Signature   ....

Address   ....

Date...

FORM Q: APPLICATION TO BE TREATED AS AN ABSENT VOTER FOR AN INDEFINITE PERIOD OWING TO OCCUPATION OR PHYSICAL INCAPACITY

Regulation 29.

REPRESENTATION OF THE PEOPLE ACTS

1   I, (Surname) ....

     (BLOCK LETTERS)

     (Other names) ....

     (BLOCK LETTERS)

     am qualified to be registered as an elector for (address in full in block letters)

     ....

     ....

2   I apply to be treated as an absent voter at parliamentary and local government elections because I am likely to be unable to go in person to the polling station (or, where (c) or (d) below applies, to vote unaided)—

     *(a) by reason of the general nature of my occupation, service or employment as

     ....

          (Give full reasons for application)

     *(b) by reason of the general nature of the occupation, service or employment of my *husband/wife as

     ....
          and my resulting absence from my qualifying address until...............
          (insert likely date of return) to be with my *husband/wife

     *(c) by reason of blindness† (in respect of which I have been registered as a blind person by the...
          ....Council)

     *(d) by reason of physical incapacity (see Note 2).

Signature... Date.........................

Address in the United Kingdom (in block letters) to which ballot paper is to be sent (if different from address given above)

         ....

         ....

*Delete whichever is inapplicable.

†If the applicant is not registered as a blind person, the words in brackets should be deleted and the certificate or declaration below should be completed.

MEDICAL CERTIFICATE

I, a registered medical practitioner, certify that the statement at 2(c)/(d)* above is correct, and that the applicant's inability is likely to continue for .... months/indefinitely*.

*Delete whichever is inapplicable.

     Signed   ....
              Registered medical practitioner

     Address   ....

                 ....

     Date...

DECLARATION

*Delete whichever is inapplicable.

I declare that to the best of my knowledge and belief the statement at 2(*c*)/(*d*)* above is correct, and the applicant's inability is likely to continue for .... months/indefinitely*.

Signed ....

Occupation ....

Address ....

....

Date...

NOTES

1. This application, if allowed, will continue in force until you cancel it or cease to be registered for your present qualifying address or become registered in a different capacity or until the electoral registration officer gives you notice to the contrary. This application will be valid for all parliamentary and local government elections at which you are entitled to vote except parish and community council elections. A separate application should be made for each qualifying address.

2. Where the application is made on the ground of physical incapacity, it will be allowed by the electoral registration officer if the medical certificate is given by a registered medical practitioner or if the declaration is made by a Christian Science practitioner. It *may* be allowed if the declaration is made by anyone else.

3. If the ground of the application is the nature of your occupation, service or employment (or that of your husband or wife) and you are likely to be at sea or out of the United Kingdom at the time of an election, you may apply to have a proxy appointed to vote for you. If so, apply on Form U which may be obtained from the electoral registration officer.

4. If you have been appointed proxy for an elector in the same parliamentary constituency or local government electoral area, you may apply on Form V to vote as such by post, but not if you yourself have a proxy appointed for you.

Form V may be obtained from the electoral registration officer.

5. Any change of the address to which ballot papers are to be sent should be notified promptly to the electoral registration officer. If you wait until an election occurs, you may be too late.

FORM R: APPLICATION TO VOTE BY POST OWING TO CHANGE OF RESIDENCE

Regulation 29.

REPRESENTATION OF THE PEOPLE ACTS

I, (Surname)...
    (BLOCK LETTERS)

(Other names)..
    (BLOCK LETTERS)

am qualified to be registered as an elector for (old address in full in block letters)

....

....

....

I apply to be treated as an absent voter at parliamentary elections because I no longer reside there. My new address is (new address in full in block letters)

....

....

....

Signature.. Date........................

NOTES

1. This application, if allowed, will continue in force for all parliamentary elections so long as you remain registered for your old address.

2. Temporary absence, e.g. on holiday, does NOT constitute a change of residence.

3. This application cannot be allowed if the address at which you now reside and the address for which you are registered as an elector are—

(a) in the same electoral division of Greater London; or

(b) in the same electoral division of an English county and, if either address is in a parish, both are in the same parish; or

(c) in the same electoral division of a Welsh county and in the same community.

4. If you have been appointed proxy for an elector you may apply on Form V to vote as such by post at parliamentary elections. Form V may be obtained from the electoral registration officer.

Regulation 29.

FORM S: APPLICATION TO BE TREATED AS AN ABSENT VOTER FOR A PARTICULAR ELECTION

‾‾‾‾‾

REPRESENTATION OF THE PEOPLE ACTS

‾‾‾‾‾

I, (Surname)...
    (BLOCK LETTERS)

(Other names)..
    (BLOCK LETTERS)

am qualified to be registered as an elector for (address in full in block letters)

....

....

and I apply to be treated as an absent voter at the coming parliamentary/local government election (*see* Note 1)

in ....
constituency/local government electoral area because I am likely to be unable to go in person to the polling station allotted to me, owing to—

*(*a*) my service in one of Her Majesty's reserve or auxiliary forces (*see* Note 2)

....;

*(*b*) my employment on polling day

    * (i) as a constable;

    *(ii) by the returning officer in connection with the election in

      ....
      constituency/local government electoral area;

*Delete
whichever is
inapplicale.

*(*c*) my being bound to the following religious observances (*see* Note 3)
....;

*(*d*) my acting as returning officer for...
constituency/local government electoral area;

*(*e*) my/my husband's/my wife's candidature

    in ....constituency.

    Signature................................. Date...................................

Address in the United Kingdom (in block letters) to which ballot paper is to be sent (if different from address given above)

....

....

CERTIFICATE

To be completed where (c) above applies

I certify that the statement at (c) above is correct.

Signature...
(Minister of the elector's religious denomination)

Address   ....

....

Date...

NOTES

1. Where (a), (b) or (c) applies, the application may be made for any parliamentary or local government election except a parish or community council election. Where (d) applies, the application may be made for a parliamentary general election or ordinary local government election (with the same exceptions). Where (e) applies, the application may be made only for a parliamentary general election.

2. Where (a) applies, the application must state the name of the reserve or auxiliary force concerned. If the application is for a particular parliamentary election and you are likely to be at sea or out of the United Kingdom on polling day, you may apply on Form U to have a proxy appointed to vote for you.

3. Where (c) applies, the application must state the nature and times of the religious observances. The certificate must be completed by a minister of your religious denomination.

4. If you have been appointed proxy for an elector in the same constituency or local government electoral area, you may apply on Form V to vote as such by post, but not if you yourself have a proxy appointed for you.

The forms referred to may be obtained from the electoral registration officer.

Regulation 29. FORM T: APPLICATION TO BE TREATED AS AN ABSENT VOTER FOR AN INDEFINITE PERIOD OWING TO AIR OR SEA JOURNEY

———

REPRESENTATION OF THE PEOPLE ACTS

———

I, (Surname)...
(BLOCK LETTERS)

(Other names)...
(BLOCK LETTERS)

am qualified to be registered as an elector for (address in full in block letters)

....

....

and I apply to be treated as an absent voter at parliamentary and local government elections (*see* Note 1) because I am likely to be unable to go in person from the above address to the polling station without making a journey by air or sea.

Signature.. Date................................

Address in the United Kingdom (in block letters) to which ballot paper is to be sent (if different from address given above)

....

....

NOTES

1. The journey in question is the journey necessary to go to the polling station from your qualifying address, not from where you may happen to be at the time of an election.

2. This application, if allowed, will continue in force until you cancel it or cease to be registered for your present qualifying address or become registered in a different capacity or until the electoral registration officer gives you notice to the contrary. It will be valid for all parliamentary and local government elections at which you are entitled to vote except parish and community council elections. A separate application should be made for each qualifying address.

3. If you have been appointed proxy for an elector in the same parliamentary constituency or local government electoral area, you may apply on Form V to vote as such by post, but not if you yourself have a proxy appointed for you.

Form V may be obtained from the electoral registration officer.

4. Any change of the address to which ballot papers are to be sent should be notified promptly to the electoral registration officer. If you wait until an election occurs, you may be too late.

FORM U: APPLICATION FOR APPOINTMENT OF PROXY

Representation of the People Acts

(*Not to be used by service voters*)

I, (Surname)...
(BLOCK LETTERS)

(Other names)...
(BLOCK LETTERS)

am qualified to be registered as an elector for (address in full in block letters)
....
....
....

I have applied to be treated as an absent voter—

  (*a*) at parliamentary and local government elections owing to—

    * (i) the general nature of my occupation, service or employment;

    *(ii) the general nature of the occupation, service, or employment of my *husband/wife and my resulting absence from my qualifying address to be with *him/her;

*Delete whichever is inapplicable.

  *(*b*) at the coming parliamentary election in..
constituency owing to my service in Her Majesty's reserve or auxiliary forces;

and I declare that I am likely to be at sea or outside the United Kingdom on polling day.

I therefore apply for the person named below as first choice (or, if he or she is unwilling or unable to be appointed, the person named as second choice) to be appointed as proxy to vote for me.

Proxy Appointment

1. First choice (the elector must fill this up)

Full names..
(BLOCK LETTERS)

Postal address...
(BLOCK LETTERS)
....

Relationship, if any, to elector
....

2. Second choice (the elector should fill this up as the first choice may be unwilling or unable to be appointed)

Full names..
(BLOCK LETTERS)

Postal addresss..
(BLOCK LETTERS)
....

Relationship, if any, to elector
....

Signature............................   Date...

NOTES

1. A person to vote as proxy must be a British subject or citizen of the Republic of Ireland, of voting age and not subject to any legal incapacity to vote.

2. Where (*a*) applies, a proxy appointed in consequence of your application to be treated as an absent voter will be entitled to vote for you at all parliamentary and local government elections except parish and community council elections. You can cancel the appointment by giving notice to the electoral registration officer.

3. Where (*b*) applies, the proxy's appointment will be for a particular parliamentary election only.

FORM V: APPLICATION BY A PROXY TO VOTE BY POST

Regulation **34.**

REPRESENTATION OF THE PEOPLE ACTS

I, (Surname)..
(BLOCK LETTERS)

(Other names)..
(BLOCK LETTERS)

have been appointed proxy for

(†Name) ....   †As shown on
(BLOCK LETTERS)   proxy paper.

who is registered as an elector for

(†Qualifying address) ....
(BLOCK LETTERS)

....

and I apply to vote by post as proxy for the above-named elector because—

*(a) I am entitled to vote by post as an absent voter: the address for which I
am registered as an elector is   *Delete
(address in full in block letters)   whichever is
                                                                                 inapplicable.

....

....

*(b) the address entered below is in a different area from the address for which
the above named elector is registered (*see* Note 2).

A ballot paper should be sent to me at the following address (block letters) in
the United Kingdom

....

....

....

Signature..   Date................................

NOTES

1. Where (*a*) applies, this application, if allowed, will be valid for all parliamentary and local government elections (except parish and community council elections) for which your application to be treated as an absent voter is valid so long as your appointment as proxy continues. Where (*b*) applies, the application will be valid only for parliamentary elections and will remain in force until you cancel it or cease to be proxy for the elector.

2. Where (*b*) applies, the application cannot be allowed if your address and the address for which the elector is registered are—

(*a*) in the same electoral division of Greater London; or

(*b*) in the same electoral division of an English county and, if either address is in a parish, both are in the same parish; or

(*c*) in the same electoral division of a Welsh county and in the same community.

Regulations,
29, 30.

FORM W: APPLICATION BY SERVICE VOTER'S SPOUSE
FOR APPOINTMENT OF PROXY

REPRESENTATION OF THE PEOPLE ACTS

Part 1.

Surname ....
    (BLOCK LETTERS)

Other names...
    (BLOCK LETTERS)

Other names of *husband/wife...

*(a) Service (R.N.,   Regiment
      Army, R.A.F., etc.).......................or Corps.................................
      Rank or Rating...........................Service No................................

    OR

*Delete
whichever is
inapplicable.

*(b) Name of Government Department under   Description
      which *husband/wife employed ....of post........................

    OR

*(c) British Council   Description
                           of post...................................

Present address of *husband/wife

....
....

(1) I am qualified to be registered as an elector for (address in full in block letters)

....
....

(2) I have made a service declaration on Form K/Form M that I reside, or expect to go abroad within six weeks to reside, outside the United Kingdom to be with my *husband/wife.

(3) I therefore apply to be treated as an absent voter for the person named below as first choice (or, if he or she is unwilling or unable to be appointed, the person named as second choice) to be appointed to vote as proxy for me at parliamentary and local government elections.

Part 2.

PROXY APPOINTMENT

1. First choice (the elector must fill this up)

Full names ....
    (BLOCK LETTERS)

Postal address...
    (BLOCK LETTERS)
....

Relationship, if any, to elector

....

2. Second choice (the elector should fill this up as the first choice may be unwilling or unable to be appointed)

Full names ....
      (BLOCK LETTERS)

Postal address..
      (BLOCK LETTERS)

....

Relationship, if any, to elector

....

Signature.. Date....................................

NOTE

A person to vote as proxy must be a British subject or citizen of the Republic of Ireland, of voting age and not subject to any legal incapacity to vote. A proxy appointed in consequence of this application will be entitled to vote for you at all parliamentary and local government elections, except parish and community council elections, until your service declaration on Form K/Form M takes effect.

Regulation 68.   FORM X: RETURN OF EXPENSES REQUIRED BY SECTION 63 OF
THE REPRESENTATION OF THE PEOPLE ACT 1949 TO BE AUTHO-
RISED BY AN ELECTION AGENT

REPRESENTATION OF THE PEOPLE ACTS

ELECTION IN THE

....
CONSTITUENCY/LOCAL GOVERNMENT ELECTORAL AREA

Date of publication of notice of election...

The expenses incurred at the above election in support of............................

.............................a candidate thereat, by..

....

(*insert name of person or association or body of persons incurring the expenses*)
being expenses required by section 63 of the Representation of the People Act

1949 to be authorised by the election agent, amounted to £..........................

The written authority of the election agent is annexed hereto.

Signature... Date...................................

FORM Y: DECLARATION AS TO EXPENSES REQUIRED BY SECTION
63 OF THE REPRESENTATION OF THE PEOPLE ACT 1949 TO BE
AUTHORISED BY AN ELECTION AGENT

REPRESENTATION OF THE PEOPLE ACTS

ELECTION IN THE

....

CONSTITUENCY/LOCAL GOVERNMENT ELECTORAL AREA

Date of publication of notice of election..

I hereby declare that—

1. I am the person *or* a director, general manager, secretary or similar officer
of the association or body of persons named as incurring expenses in the
accompanying return, marked..................., of expenses required by section 63
of the Representation of the People Act 1949 to be authorised by an election agent.

2. To the best of my knowledge and belief the said return is complete and
correct.

3. The matters for which the expenses referred to in the said return were

incurred were as follows...

....

....

Signature ....

Office held...
(In the case of an association or body of persons)

Date.....................................

EXPLANATORY NOTE

(This Note is not part of the Regulations.)

These Regulations revoke and replace with minor amendments the Representation of the People Regulations 1969 as amended by the Representation of the People Regulations 1973. The main amendments are the following. Regulation 5 requires that, where a constituency is not coterminous with, or wholly contained in, a district or London borough, each registration officer must consult the acting returning officer for the constituency concerning the form of the register and special lists and records for the purpose of ensuring consistency throughout the constituency. The Regulation also provides that during a parliamentary election the functions of each registration officer with respect to voting by post or by proxy are to be exercised by the acting returning officer for the constituency. Regulation 10 does not require the part of a register provided for a polling station to mark electors for whom proxies have been appointed. Regulation 22(3)(*a*) requires every local government councillor to be given a copy of the register for his area. Regulation 22 also requires that, where a constituency is not coterminous with, or wholly contained in, a district or London borough, the acting returning officer for the constituency is to be supplied by each registration officer with copies of the register and electors lists so that he can give copies of them to the Member of Parliament for the constituency, candidates at a parliamentary election and party agents. Regulation 27 no longer requires the proper officer of a local authority, who has to make out a corrupt and illegal practices list for his area in accordance with section 40(2) of the Representation of the People Act 1949, to send a copy to the registration officer.

STATUTORY INSTRUMENTS

1974 No. 649

POLICE

The Police (Amendment) Regulations 1974

Made - - - -	*30th March* 1974
Laid before Parliament	*11th April* 1974
Coming into Operation	*1st May* 1974

In exercise of the powers conferred on me by section 33 of the Police Act 1964(a), and after consulting the Police Council for the United Kingdom in accordance with section 4(4) of the Police Act 1969(b), I hereby make the following Regulations:—

1. These Regulations may be cited as the Police (Amendment) Regulations 1974.

2. These Regulations shall come into operation on 1st May 1974 and shall have effect—

(*a*) for the purposes of Regulation 8 thereof, as from that date;

(*b*) for the purposes of paragraph (3) of Regulation 6 thereof, as respects any period of 6 months ending on or after 1st September 1973 but before 1st March 1974, as provided in the said Regulation 6 and, subject as aforesaid, as from 1st March 1974;

(*c*) for the purposes of Regulation 7 thereof, as respects the year beginning on 1st May 1973 as provided therein and, subject as aforesaid, as from 1st May 1974;

(*d*) for all other purposes, as from 1st September 1973.

3. In these Regulations any reference to the principal Regulations is a reference to the Police Regulations 1971(c), as amended (d).

4.—(1) In paragraph (5) of Regulation 47 of the principal Regulations (removal allowance) for the amount "£15" there shall be substituted the amount "£20".

(a) 1964 c. 48. (b) 1969 c. 63.

(c) S.I. 1971/156 (1971 I, p. 439).

(d) The relevant amending instruments are S.I. 1971/1141, 1901, 1973/1583 (1971 II, p. 3373; III, p. 5156; 1973 III, p. 4960).

(2) For paragraph (6) of the said Regulation 47 there shall be substituted the following paragraphs:—

"(6) In the case of any other member the amount of the allowance under paragraph (3) shall not exceed £250 nor be less than the minimum amount mentioned in paragraph (6A) but, subject as aforesaid, shall equal the aggregate of the following amounts—

(*a*) the amount of the expenditure incidental to the move reasonably incurred by the member, and

(*b*) where he satisfies the police authority that, in consequence of the move, he has failed to benefit, in whole or in part, from expenditure reasonably incurred by him prior to the move (other than such payments as are referred to in paragraph (1)(*d*), the whole or the proportionate part of that expenditure so far as it is not recoverable by him.

(6A) The minimum amount referred to in paragraph (6) shall be—

(*a*) where the member holds, or is transferring to be appointed in, a rank higher than that of chief superintendent, such amount as may be determined by the police authority;

(*b*) where he holds, or is transferring to be appointed in, the rank of superintendent, £95;

(*c*) where he holds, or is transferring to be appointed in, the rank of inspector, £75;

(*d*) where he holds, or is transferring to be appointed in, any rank lower than inspector, £60.".

5. In Regulation 49 of the principal Regulations (boot allowance) for the rate "£0·24 a week" there shall be substituted the rate "£0·29 a week".

6.—(1) For paragraph (2) of Regulation 50 of the principal Regulations (plain clothes allowances) there shall be substituted the following provision:—

"(2) A plain clothes allowance payable under paragraph (1) shall be payable at the rate of—

(*a*) £76 a year in the case of a superintendent;

(*b*) £72 a year in the case of an inspector;

(*c*) £64 a year in the case of a sergeant;

(*d*) £60 a year in the case of a constable.".

(2) In paragraph (3) of the said Regulation 50 for the qualifying period "48 hours" there shall be substituted the qualifying period "40 hours".

(3) For paragraph (4) of the said Regulation 50 there shall be substituted the following provision:—

"(4) A plain clothes allowance payable under paragraph (3) shall be payable at the rate of—

(a) £0·033 an hour in the case of an inspector;

(b) £0·031 an hour in the case of a sergeant;

(c) £0·028 an hour in the case of a constable.".

(4) As respects any period of 6 months ending on or after 1st September 1973 but before 1st March 1974 a plain clothes allowance payable under Regulation 50(3) of the principal Regulations, as amended by paragraph (2) of this Regulation, shall be calculated as hereinafter provided.

(5) So far as the allowance falls to be calculated by reference to duties performed on or after 1st September 1973 it shall be calculated in accordance with Regulation 50(4) of the principal Regulations, as amended by paragraph (3) of this Regulation, and the principal Regulations shall have effect accordingly.

(6) Nothing in this Regulation shall affect the calculation of the allowance so far as it falls to be calculated by reference to duties performed before 1st September 1973.

7.—(1) For Tables A, B, C and D in Schedule 8 to the principal Regulations (motor car allowances) there shall be substituted the Tables set out in Appendix 1 to these Regulations.

(2) As respects the year beginning on 1st May 1973 a motor vehicle allowance in respect of a motor car payable under Regulation 55 of the principal Regulations shall be calculated as hereinafter provided.

(3) So far as the allowance falls to be calculated by reference to completed months of authorised use ending, or mileage of authorised use performed, on or after 1st January 1974, it shall be calculated in accordance with the principal Regulations as amended by this Regulation, and the principal Regulations shall have effect accordingly.

(4) Nothing in this Regulation shall affect the calculation of the allowance so far as it falls to be calculated by reference to completed months of authorised use ending, or mileage of authorised use performed, before 1st January 1974.

8. For the Tables in Schedule 11 to the principal Regulations (issue of uniform and equipment) there shall be substituted the Tables set out in Appendix 2 to these Regulations.

Roy Jenkins,
One of Her Majesty's Principal
Secretaries of State.

Home Office,
Whitehall.
30th March 1974.

APPENDIX 1

TABLES SUBSTITUTED FOR TABLES A, B, C AND D IN
SCHEDULE 8 TO THE PRINCIPAL REGULATIONS

TABLE A

STANDARD AMOUNT

Cylinder capacity	Annual rate of fixed element	Mileage element	
		Basic rate per mile	Reduced rate per mile
	£	£	£
1,200 c.c. or more but less than 1,700 c.c.	129	0·047	0·029
1,000 c.c. or more but less than 1,200 c.c.	117	0·042	0·026
Less than 1,000 c.c.	108	0·038	0·023

TABLE B

ABATED AMOUNT

Cylinder capacity	Annual rate of fixed element	Mileage element	
		Basic rate per mile	Reduced rate per mile
	£	£	£
1,200 c.c. or more but less than 1,700 c.c.	114	0·045	0·029
1,000 c.c. or more but less than 1,200 c.c.	105	0·040	0·026
Less than 1,000 c.c.	99	0·036	0·023

TABLE C

STANDARD AMOUNT

Cylinder capacity	Rate per mile
	£
1,200 c.c. or more but less than 1,700 c.c.	0·087
1,000 c.c. or more but less than 1,200 c.c.	0·077
Less than 1,000 c.c.	0·070

TABLE D

ABATED AMOUNT

Cylinder capacity	Rate per mile
	£
1,200 c.c. or more but less than 1,700 c.c.	0·081
1,000 c.c. or more but less than 1,200 c.c.	0·072
Less than 1,000 c.c.	0·065

APPENDIX 2

TABLES SUBSTITUTED FOR TABLES IN SCHEDULE 11 TO
THE PRINCIPAL REGULATIONS

TABLES

MEN

Article	Issue	Maximum number in issue
Jacket.	1 annually (period of wear 4 years).	4
Trousers.	2 pairs annually (period of wear 2 years).	4 pairs.
Greatcoat.	If the police authority approves the issue of greatcoats to the force, as required.	1
Cape.	As required.	2
Raincoat or mackintosh.	As required.	2
Headdress.	As required.	2
Shirts (either collar attached or complete with 3 separate collars).	After an initial issue of not less than 4 nor more than 6 (as the police authority may determine) 3 annually or, in the case of shirts with separate collars, 2 annually.	—
Ties.	2 annually.	—

WOMEN

Article	Issue	Maximum number in issue
Jacket.	1 annually (period of wear 4 years).	4
Skirt.	2 annually (period of wear 2 years).	4
Greatcoat.	As required.	1 or 2 (as the police authority may determine).
Other outer garments comprising the following items:—		
(a) a coat being a raincoat or mackintosh, or	As required.	2
(b) a cloak, a gaberdine coat and a fully waterproofed coat as the police authority may determine.	As required.	1 of each item.
Headdress.	As required.	2
Shirts (general issue, either collar attached or complete with 3 separate collars).	After an initial issue of not less than 4 nor more than 6 (as the police authority may determine), 2 annually.	—
Shirts (summer issue, for wear with or without ties).	After an initial issue of 3, 2 annually.	—
Ties.	2 annually.	—

EXPLANATORY NOTE

(This Note is not part of the Regulations.)

These Regulations amend the Police Regulations 1971.

Regulation 4 of the present Regulations increases removal allowances in respect of incidental expenditure and, in certain cases and within specified limits, permits of the reimbursement of such expenditure reasonably incurred.

Regulations 5, 6 and 7 increase the rates of boot, plain clothes and motor car allowances.

Regulation 8 makes fresh provision as respects the scale on which uniform is to be issued.

To the extent mentioned in Regulation 2, the Regulations have retrospective effect; this is authorised by section 33(4) of the Police Act 1964.

S T A T U T O R Y   I N S T R U M E N T S

1974 No. 651 (S. 57)

REPRESENTATION OF THE PEOPLE

The Representation of the People (Scotland) Regulations 1974

Made- - - -	11*th March* 1974
Laid before Parliament	20*th March* 1974
Coming into Operation	1*st April* 1974

In exercise of the powers conferred on me by sections 42 and 171(5) of and Schedule 4 to the Representation of the People Act 1949(**a**) and of all other powers enabling me in that behalf, I hereby make the following regulations:—

1.—(1) These regulations may be cited as the Representation of the People (Scotland) Regulations 1974.

(2) These regulations shall come into force on 1st April 1974.

(3) The Interpretation Act 1889(**b**) shall apply for the interpretation of these regulations as it applies for the interpretation of an Act of Parliament.

2. In sub-paragraph (*a*) of paragraph (2) of regulation 38 of the Representation of the People (Scotland) Regulations 1969(**c**) as amended (**d**), for the words "Scottish local elections rules in Schedule 3 to that Act" there shall be substituted the words "Scottish Local Elections Rules 1974(**e**)".

3. In paragraph (1) of regulation 57 of the said regulations for the words "county clerk or the town clerk" there shall be substituted the words "proper officer, within the meaning of rule 53(2) of Schedule 1 to, as read, where appropriate, with Schedule 2 to, the elections rules, of the council to which councillors are elected".

4. In Schedule 2 to the said regulations, in the table of comparison of election rules, for the words "Scottish local elections rules" at the head of the second column there shall be substituted "Schedule 1 to the Scottish Local Elections Rules 1974".

William Ross,

One of Her Majesty's Principal
Secretaries of State.

St. Andrew's House,
Edinburgh.
11th March 1974.

(a) 1949 c. 68. (b) 1889 c.63. (c) S.I. 1969/912 (1969 II, p.2726).
(d) S.I. 1973/1177 (1973 II, p. 3556). (e) S.I. 1974/82 (1974 I, p. 257).

EXPLANATORY NOTE

(This Note is not part of the Regulations.)

These Regulations make further amendments to the Representation of the People (Scotland) Regulations 1969 as amended by the Representation of the People (Scotland) Regulations 1973. Regulations 2 and 4 make provision for Part IV of the Representation of the People (Scotland) Regulations 1969 (issue and receipt of postal ballot papers) to apply to elections of councillors for the new local authorities in Scotland (as defined in section 235 of the Local Government (Scotland) Act 1973 (c. 65)). Regulation 3 makes provision for the disposal of documents relating to postal voting at elections of such councillors.

STATUTORY INSTRUMENTS

1974 No. 652 (S.58)

LOCAL GOVERNMENT, SCOTLAND

The Local Government (Travelling Allowances, etc.) (Scotland) Amendment Regulations 1974

Made - - -	*29th March* 1974
Laid before Parliament	*16th April* 1974
Coming into Operation	*17th April* 1974

In exercise of the powers conferred on me by sections 113 and 117 as read with section 118 of the Local Government Act 1948(a) and of all other powers enabling me in that behalf, I hereby make the following regulations:—

1. These regulations may be cited as the Local Government (Travelling Allowances, etc.) (Scotland) Amendment Regulations 1974 and shall come into operation on 17th April 1974.

2. The Interpretation Act 1889(b) shall apply for the interpretation of these regulations as it applies for the interpretation of an Act of Parliament.

3. In paragraph 3(e) of Schedule 1 to the Local Government (Travelling Allowances, etc.) (Scotland) Regulations 1970(c) as amended (d) for the sums of 5·5p, 6·2p and 6·9p shall be substituted the sums of 6·4p, 6·9p and 7·8p respectively.

William Ross,
One of Her Majesty's Principal
Secretaries of State.

St. Andrew's House,
Edinburgh.
29th March 1974.

(a) 1948 c. 26.   (b) 1889 c. 63.
(c) S.I. 1970/107 (1970 I, p. 458).
(d) S.I. 1971/2131, 1972/ 1572. 1973/1300 (1971 III, p. 6298; 1972 III, p. 4564; 1973 II, p. 3920).

EXPLANATORY NOTE

(This Note is not part of the Regulations.)

These Regulations increase the maximum rates of mileage allowance of certain travelling allowances payable to members of local authorities and other bodies under Part VI of the Local Government Act 1948. Only these rates relating to the use of a motor car or tri-car have been amended.

1974 No. 653 (S. 59)

LOCAL GOVERNMENT, SCOTLAND

The Local Government (New Councils etc.) (Scotland) Order 1974

Made - - -	29th March 1974
Laid before Parliament	16th April 1974
Coming into Operation	7th May 1974

In exercise of the powers conferred on me by section 215 of the Local Government (Scotland) Act 1973(a) and of all other powers enabling me in that behalf, I hereby make the following order:—

Citation, commencement and interpretation

1. This order may be cited as the Local Government (New Councils etc.) (Scotland) Order 1974 and shall come into operation on 7th May 1974.

2.—(1) The Interpretation Act 1889(b) shall apply for the interpretation of this order as it applies for the interpretation of an Act of Parliament.

(2) In this order—

"The Act" means the Local Government (Scotland) Act 1973;

"Local authority" means a regional, islands or district council.

Admission to meetings

3. For the purpose of securing the admission of representatives of the Press and other members of the public to the meetings of local authorities from the coming into office of councillors thereof until 16th May 1975, such local authorities shall be bodies to which the Public Bodies (Admission to Meetings) Act 1960(c) applies.

Allowances to members

4. For the purpose of securing that financial loss, travelling and subsistence allowances are payable, and that the expenses of certain visits and conferences can be defrayed, in respect of members of local authorities or of committees of joint committees thereof, including in either case sub-committees, from their coming into office until 16th May 1975, Part VI of the Local Government Act 1948(d) (Allowances to Members of Local Authorities and other Bodies) as amended by section 36 of the Local Government (Scotland) Act 1966(e) shall apply until the said date as if the said local authorities were local authorities to which the said Part VI applied.

Term of office of provosts, magistrates, etc.

5. Any councillor holding the office of provost, bailie, honorary treasurer, judge of police or dean of guild of a burgh who but for this order would have ceased to hold that office on 6th May 1975 shall continue in office until 16th May 1975.

(a) 1973 c. 65. (b) 1889 c. 63.
(c) 1960 c. 67. (d) 1948 c. 26.
(e) 1966 c. 51.

Appointment of officers before 16th May 1975

6. Where a local authority before 16th May 1975 appoint to hold any office or employment before or as from that date any person (hereinafter referred to as "the officer") who but for the appointment would be transferred on 16th May 1975 under section 216 of the Act to the employment of any local authority, the appointment shall be on such terms and conditions that—

    (*a*)   so long as the officer is engaged in duties reasonably comparable to those in which he was engaged immediately before the appointment, the scale of his salary or remuneration; and

    (*b*)   the other terms and conditions of his employment,

are not less favourable than those he enjoyed immediately before the appointment.

William Ross,
One of Her Majesty's
Principal Secretaries of State.

St. Andrew's House,
Edinburgh.

29th March 1974.

EXPLANATORY NOTE

(This Note is not part of the Order.)

This Order makes provision (Articles 3 and 4)—

(a) for the application of the Public Bodies (Admission to Meetings) Act 1960 to the new regional, islands or district councils;

(b) for the payment of allowances under the Local Government Act 1948 and the expenses of certain visits and conferences, in respect of members of such councils,

in both cases from the coming into office of the councillors until 16th May 1975, when the provisions of the Local Government (Scotland) Act 1973 will be applicable.

This Order also makes transitional provision (Articles 5 and 6)—

(a) for the extension of the term of office of any office-bearer in a burgh between 7th May 1975 and 16th May 1975; and

(b) for the protection of officers appointed to hold office before or as from 16th May 1975.

STATUTORY INSTRUMENTS

1974 No. 654

WAGES COUNCILS
The Boot and Floor Polish Wages Council (Great Britain) (Abolition) Order 1974

Made - - - - -	1st April 1974
Laid before Parliament	10th April 1974
Coming into Operation	13th May 1974

Whereas the Secretary of State in accordance with section 4 of and Schedule 1 to the Wages Councils Act 1959(a) published notice of his intention to make an order abolishing the Boot and Floor Polish Wages Council (Great Britain):

And whereas no objection has been made with respect to the draft order referred to in the said notice:

Now, therefore, the Secretary of State in exercise of powers conferred by section 4(1)(b) of, and paragraph 4 of Schedule 1 to, the said Act and now vested in him (b), and of all other powers enabling him in that behalf, hereby makes the following Order:—

1. The Boot and Floor Polish Wages Council (Great Britain) is hereby abolished.

2.—(1) This Order may be cited as the Boot and Floor Polish Wages Council (Great Britain) (Abolition) Order 1974 and shall come into operation on 13th May 1974.

(2) The Interpretation Act 1889(c) shall apply to the interpretation of this Order as it applies to the interpretation of an Act of Parliament.

Signed by order of the Secretary of State.

1st April 1974.

Harold Walker,
Joint Parliamentary Under Secretary of State,
Department of Employment.

(a) 1959 c. 69.
(b) S.I.1959/1769, 1968/729 (1959 I, p. 1795; 1968 II, p. 2108).
(c) 1889 c. 63.

EXPLANATORY NOTE
(This Note is not part of the Order.)

This Order abolishes the Boot and Floor Polish Wages Council (Great Britain), which was established as a Trade Board under the Trade Boards Acts 1909 and 1918 (c. 22 and c. 32), and became a Wages Council by virtue of the Wages Councils Act 1945 (c. 17).

The abolition of the Council was recommended by the Commission on Industrial Relations on the grounds that the Council is no longer necessary in order to maintain adequate pay and conditions for the workers in the boot and floor polish industry.

STATUTORY INSTRUMENTS

1974 No. 655

WAGES COUNCILS

The Wages Regulation (Pin, Hook and Eye, and Snap Fastener) Order 1974

Made - - -	*2nd April* 1974
Coming into Operation	*30th April* 1974

Whereas the Secretary of State has received from the Pin, Hook and Eye, and Snap Fastener Wages Council (Great Britain) the wages regulation proposals set out in Schedules 1 and 2 hereto;

Now, therefore, the Secretary of State in exercise of powers conferred by section 11 of the Wages Councils Act 1959(**a**), as modified by Article 2 of the Counter-Inflation (Modification of Wages Councils Act 1959) Order 1973(**b**), and now vested in him(**c**), and of all other powers enabling him in that behalf, hereby makes the following Order:—

1. This Order may be cited as the Wages Regulation (Pin, Hook and Eye, and Snap Fastener) Order 1974.

2.—(1) In this Order, the expression "the specified date" means the 30th April 1974, provided that where, as respects any worker who is paid wages at intervals not exceeding seven days, that date does not correspond with the beginning of the period for which the wages are paid, the expression "the specified date" means, as respects that worker, the beginning of the next such period following that date.

(2) The Interpretation Act 1889(**d**) shall apply to the interpretation of this Order as it applies to the interpretation of an Act of Parliament and as if this Order and the Order hereby revoked were Acts of Parliament.

3. The wages regulation proposals set out in Schedules 1 and 2 hereto shall have effect as from the specified date and as from that date the Wages Regulation (Pin, Hook and Eye, and Snap Fastener) Order 1973(**e**) shall cease to have effect.

Signed by order of the Secretary of State.

2nd April 1974.

> *W. H. Marsh,*
> Assistant Secretary,
> Department of Employment.

(**a**) 1959 c. 69.   (**b**) S.I. 1973/661 (1973 I, p. 2141).
(**c**) S.I. 1959/1769, 1968/729 (1959 I, p. 1795; 1968 II, p. 2108).
(**d**) 1889 c. 63.   (**e**) S.I. 1973/1159 (1973 II, p. 3518).

SCHEDULE 1   Article 3

The following minimum remuneration shall be substituted for the statutory minimum remuneration fixed by the Wages Regulation (Pin, Hook and Eye, and Snap Fastener) Order 1973 (Order O.(89)).

STATUTORY MINIMUM REMUNERATION

PART I

GENERAL

1.—(1) Subject to the provisions of paragraph 7, which relate to the guaranteed weekly remuneration, the minimum remuneration payable to a worker (including a home-worker) to whom this Schedule applies is as follows:—

(*a*) for all work other than work to which a minimum overtime rate applies under Part III of this Schedule—

    (i) in the case of a time worker, the hourly general minimum time rate applicable to the worker under the provisions of this Schedule;

    (ii) in the case of a male worker employed on piece work, piece rates each of which would yield, in the circumstances of the case, to an ordinary worker at least the same amount of money as the hourly general minimum time rate which would be applicable under the provisions of this Schedule if the worker were a time worker;

    (iii) in the case of a female worker employed on piece work, piece rates each of which would yield, in the circumstances of the case, to an ordinary worker at least the same amount of money as the hourly piece work basis time rate as defined in sub-paragraph (2) of this paragraph or the piece work basis time rate applicable to the worker under paragraph 4 of this Schedule;

(*b*) for all work to which a minimum overtime rate applies under Part III of this Schedule, that rate.

(2) In this Schedule the expression "per week" in Part II means per week of 40 hours, and the expression "hourly general minimum time rate" and "hourly piece work basis time rate" mean respectively the general minimum time rate and the piece work basis time rate applicable to the worker under paragraphs 2 and 3 of this Schedule divided by 40.

PART II

ALL MALE WORKERS

GENERAL MINIMUM TIME RATES

2. The general minimum time rates payable to male workers are as follows:—

	Per week £
(1) Workers aged 20 years or over—	
(*a*) Artificers (including Pinmakers) in charge of automatic machinery, carrying out if required toolmaking, toolsetting, hardening and minor repairs	25·00
(*b*) Toolsetters, other than workers covered by (*a*) above, who are in charge of automatic machinery but who do not make tools ...	25·00
(*c*) (i) Platers and Finishers carrying out (without technical supervision) one or more of the following processes— electro-deposition ... ... / chemical deposition ... ... / dyeing ... ... / enamelling and lacquering ... ... / barrel polishing	24·30
(ii) Platers and Finishers carrying out under technical supervision, one or more of the processes specified in (i) above ...	22·20
(iii) Plating and Finishing workers, other than those specified in (i) and (ii) above	20·00

Per week
£

(d) Wire Straighteners wholly or mainly engaged in wire straight-
ening; and Assistant Toolsetters working under the supervision
of artificers or toolsetters ... ... 22·20

(e) Workers other than those specified in (a) to (d) above ... 20·00

(2) Workers aged under 20 years, being aged—
19 and under 20 years ... ... 19·00
18 „ „ 19 „ ... ... 16·20
17 „ „ 18 „ ... ... 13·80
Under 17 years ... ... 10·20

ALL FEMALE WORKERS (OTHER THAN HOME-WORKERS)
GENERAL MINIMUM TIME RATES AND PIECE WORK BASIS TIME RATES

3. The general minimum time rates and piece work basis time rates payable to female workers other than home-workers are as follows:—

	General minimum Time Rates Per week £	Piece work basis Time Rates Per week £
(1) Charge hands who are responsible for all work and order in the particular section of which they have charge	20·00	—
(2) All other workers		
Aged 20 years or over	18·00	18·50
„ 19 and under 20 years	16·40	16·66
„ 18 „ „ 19 „	14·58	15·93
„ 17 „ „ 18 „	12·42	14·99
Under 17 years	9·18	14·67

FEMALE HOME-WORKERS

Per hour
p

4. The piece work basis time rate applicable (irrespective of age) to female home-workers is 30½

PART III

ALL WORKERS OTHER THAN HOME-WORKERS
MINIMUM OVERTIME RATES

5.—(1) Minimum overtime rates are payable to any worker (other than a home-worker) as follows:—

(a) on a Sunday or a customary holiday—
for all time worked ... ... double time

(b) on a Saturday, not being a customary holiday—
for all time worked in excess of 4½ hours ... ... time-and-a-half

(c) in any week exclusive of any time in respect of which
a minimum overtime rate is payable under the preceding
provisions of this sub-paragraph—

    (i) for the first 10 hours worked in excess of 40 hours   time-and-a-quarter

    (ii) thereafter ... ...   time-and-a-half

(2) The minimum overtime rates set out in sub-paragraph (1)(a) and (b) of this paragraph are payable in any week whether or not a minimum overtime rate set out in sub-paragraph (1)(c) is also payable.

6. In this Part of this Schedule,

(1) the expression "customary holiday" means—

    (a) (i) in England and Wales—
    Christmas Day;
    26th December if it be not a Sunday; 27th December in a year when 25th or 26th December is a Sunday;
    New Year's Day (or, if New Year's Day falls on a Sunday, the following Monday);
    Good Friday;
    Easter Monday;
    the last Monday in May;
    the last Monday in August; or,
    where a day is substituted for any of the above days by national proclamation, that day;

    (ii) in Scotland—
    New Year's Day (or, if New Year's Day falls on a Sunday, the following Monday);
    the local Spring holiday;
    the local Autumn holiday; and
    four other days (being days on which the worker normally works) in the course of a calendar year, to be fixed by the employer and notified to the worker not less than three weeks before the holiday;

    or (b) in the case of each of the said days (other than a day fixed by the employer and notified to the worker as aforesaid) such weekday as may be substituted therefor by agreement between the employer and the worker.

(2) the expressions "time-and-a-quarter", "time-and-a-half" and "double time" mean respectively—

    (a) in the case of a time worker, one and a quarter times, one and a half times and twice the hourly general minimum time rate otherwise payable to the worker;

    (b) in the case of a worker employed on piece work—

        (i) a time rate equal respectively to one quarter, one half and the whole of the hourly general minimum time rate which would be payable if the worker were a time worker and a minimum overtime rate did not apply, and, in addition thereto,

        (ii) the piece rates otherwise payable to the worker under sub-paragraph (1)(a) of paragraph 1.

PART IV

GUARANTEED WEEKLY REMUNERATION FOR WORKERS OTHER THAN HOME-WORKERS

7.—(1) Subject to the provisions of this paragraph a worker (other than a home-worker) who ordinarily works for the employer at least 34 hours weekly on work to which this Schedule applies shall be paid in respect of any week in which he works for less than 34 hours on such work not less than the guaranteed weekly remuneration.

(2) The guaranteed weekly remuneration is 34 hours' pay calculated at the hourly general minimum time rate ordinarily applicable to the worker.

(3) The guaranteed weekly remuneration in any week shall be reduced by the amount of any holiday remuneration paid, or payable, by the employer to the worker in respect of any holiday allowed to, and taken by, the worker in that week under the provisions of the Wages Councils Act 1959.

(4) In calculating the number of hours worked in any week for the purposes of this paragraph, a worker shall be treated as though he had worked on any holiday allowed to, and taken by, him in that week under the provisions of the Wages Councils Act 1959, the number of hours ordinarily worked by him on that day of the week, provided that a worker shall not be treated as having worked in any week throughout which he is on holiday.

(5) Payment of the guaranteed weekly remuneration in any week is subject to the condition that the worker throughout the period of his ordinary employment in that week, excluding any day allowed to him as a holiday, is—

(a) capable of and available for work; and

(b) willing to perform such duties outside his normal occupation as the employer may reasonably require if his normal work is not available to him in the establishment in which he is employed.

(6) The guaranteed weekly remuneration shall not be payable to a worker—

(a) in any week in which work is not available to him by reason of a strike or lock-out or circumstances outside the employer's control, if he has given the worker not less than four days' notice of his inability to provide such employment and the notice has expired; or

(b) in any week in which the worker has been dismissed on the grounds of serious misconduct; or

(c) if at any time in the week the worker is absent from work by reason of sickness; or

(d) if at any time in the week or during the preceding four weeks the worker has been otherwise absent from work without the leave of the employer.

(7) The guaranteed weekly remuneration payable to a piece worker shall be the sum to which he would be entitled if he were a time worker.

PART V

ALL WORKERS
WAITING TIME

8.—(1) A worker shall be entitled to payment of the minimum remuneration specified in this Schedule for all time during which he is present on the premises of his employer unless he is present thereon in any of the following circumstances : —

(a) without the employer's consent, express or implied;

(b) for some purpose unconnected with his work and other than that of waiting for work to be given to him to perform;

(c) by reason only of the fact that he is resident thereon;

(d) during normal meal times in a room or place in which no work is being done and he is not waiting for work to be given to him to perform.

(2) The minimum remuneration payable under sub-paragraph (1) of this paragraph to a piece worker when not engaged on piece work, is that which would be payable if the worker were a time worker.

APPLICABILITY OF STATUTORY MINIMUM REMUNERATION

9. This Schedule applies to workers in relation to whom the Wages Council operates, that is to say, workers employed in Great Britain in the trade specified in the Schedule to the Trade Boards (Pin, Hook and Eye, and Snap Fastener Trade, Great Britain) (Constitution and Proceedings) Regulations 1935(a), namely:—

"The manufacture of pins, hairpins, hooks and eyes, hair-curlers, snap fasteners, or safety pins, from the following metals in wire or sheet form:— aluminium, copper, iron, lead, steel, tin, zinc, or alloys of any two or more of the above metals;

INCLUDING:—

(a) the capping of safety pins;

(b) the operation of pin sticking;

(c) packeting, boxing, or carding of any of the above articles wherever carried on;

(d) packing, despatching, warehousing or other operations incidental to or appertaining to the manufacture of any of the above articles.

BUT EXCLUDING:—

(e) the manufacture of steel hatpins or shanks for steel toilet pins, wherever carried on."

Article 3

SCHEDULE 2

HOLIDAYS AND HOLIDAY REMUNERATION

The Wages Regulation (Pin, Hook and Eye, and Snap Fastener) (Holidays) Order 1973(b) (Order O. (90)) shall have effect as if in the Schedule thereto:—

1. For sub-paragraph (2) of paragraph 2 (which relates to customary holidays) there were substituted the following:—

"(2) The said customary holidays are:—

(a) (i) In England and Wales—

Christmas Day;

26th December if it be not a Sunday; 27th December in a year when 25th or 26th December is a Sunday;

New Year's Day (or, if New Year's Day falls on a Sunday, the following Monday);

Good Friday;

Easter Monday;

the last Monday in May;

the last Monday in August;

(or where a day is substituted for any of the above days by national proclamation, that day);

(a) S.R. & O. 1935/440 (1935. p. 1680).　　(b) S.I. 1973/1160 (1973 II, p. 3524).

(ii) in Scotland—

New Year's Day (or, if New Year's Day falls on a Sunday, the following Monday);

the local Spring holiday;

the local Autumn holiday; and

four other days (being days on which the worker normally works) in the course of a calendar year, to be fixed by the employer and notified to the worker not less than three weeks before the holiday;

or (*b*) in the case of each of the said days (other than a day fixed by the employer and notified to the worker as aforesaid) such weekday as may be substituted therefor by agreement between the employer and the worker."

2. For paragraph 3 (which relates to annual holiday) there were substituted the following:—

"PART III

ANNUAL HOLIDAY

3.—(1) In addition to the holidays specified in Part II of this Schedule and subject to the provisions of paragraph 4, an employer shall, between 1st May 1974 and 30th September 1974, and in each succeeding year between 1st May and 30th September, allow a holiday (hereinafter referred to as an 'annual holiday') to every worker in his employment to whom this Schedule applies who has been employed by him during the 12 months immediately preceding the commencement of the holiday season for any of the periods of employment specified below, and the duration of the annual holiday shall in the case of each such worker be related to that period as follows:—

Period of employment							Duration of annual holiday
Column 1							Column 2
At least 48 weeks	...	...	...	...	...	...	*17 days*
„ „ 44 „	...	...	...	...	...	...	*15 „*
„ „ 40 „	...	...	...	...	...	...	*14 „*
„ „ 36 „	...	...	...	...	...	...	*12 „*
„ „ 32 „	...	...	...	...	...	...	*11 „*
„ „ 28 „	...	...	...	...	...	...	*10 „*
„ „ 24 „	...	...	...	...	...	...	*9 „*
„ „ 20 „	...	...	...	...	...	...	*7 „*
„ „ 16 „	...	...	...	...	...	...	*5 „*
„ „ 12 „	...	...	...	...	...	...	*4 „*
„ „ 8 „	...	...	...	...	...	...	*2 „*
„ „ 4 „	...	...	...	...	...	...	*1 day*

(2) Notwithstanding the provisions of the last foregoing sub-paragraph the number of days of annual holiday which an employer is required to allow to a worker in any holiday season shall not exceed in the aggregate *three times* the number of days constituting the worker's normal working week, plus *two days*.

(3) In this Schedule the expression 'holiday season' means in relation to the year 1974 the period commencing on 1st May 1974 and ending on 30th September 1974, and in each succeeding year, the period commencing on 1st May and ending on 30th September of the same year."

EXPLANATORY NOTE

(This Note is not part of the Order.)

This Order has effect from 30th April 1974. Schedule 1 sets out the increased statutory minimum remuneration payable to workers in relation to whom the Pin, Hook and Eye, and Snap Fastener Wages Council (Great Britain) operates, in substitution for that fixed by the Wages Regulation (Pin, Hook and Eye, and Snap Fastener) Order 1973 (Order O. (89)), which Order is revoked. Schedule 2 amends the Wages Regulation (Pin, Hook and Eye, and Snap Fastener) (Holidays) Order 1973 (Order O. (90)) by providing for an additional day of customary holiday and one additional day of annual holiday.

New provisions are printed in italics.

STATUTORY INSTRUMENTS

1974 No. 660

COUNTER-INFLATION

The Counter-Inflation (Residential Rents) (Northern Ireland) Order 1974

Made – – –	*4th April* 1974	
Laid before Parliament	*8th April* 1974	
Coming into Operation	*8th April* 1974	

In exercise of the powers conferred on me by sections 11 and 23(2) of, and paragraphs 1 and 3 of Schedule 3 to, the Counter-Inflation Act 1973(a), I hereby make the following Order: —

Citation, commencement and extent

1.—(1) This Order may be cited as the Counter-Inflation (Residential Rents) (Northern Ireland) Order 1974 and shall come into operation on 8th April 1974.

(2) This Order extends to Northern Ireland only.

Interpretation

2.—(1) The Interpretation Act 1889(b) shall apply for the interpretation of this Order as it applies for the interpretation of an Act of Parliament.

(2) In this Order, unless the context otherwise requires—
"dwelling-house" has the same meaning as in the Rent and Mortgage Interest (Restrictions) Acts (Northern Ireland) 1920 to 1967;

"enactment" includes an enactment of the Parliament of Northern Ireland;

"the 1956 Act" means the Housing (Miscellaneous Provisions) and Rent Restriction Law (Amendment) Act (Northern Ireland) 1956(c);

"rent" includes any premium rateably apportioned over the period of a tenancy;

"standstill period" means the period beginning with 8th April 1974 and ending with 31st December 1974;

(3) In this Order, unless the context otherwise requires, references to any enactment shall be construed as references to that enactment as amended, extended or applied by or under any other enactment.

(4) For the purposes of this Order "rent" in section 11(1) of the Counter-Inflation Act 1973 shall include, in relation to any tenancy of a dwelling-house to which this Order applies, any sums payable by the tenant to the landlord for the use of furniture or for services, and which would be treated as rent for any of the purposes of the Rent and Mortgage Interest (Restrictions) Acts (Northern Ireland) 1920 to 1967.

(a) 1973 c. 9.   (b) 1889 c. 63.   (c) 1956 c. 10 (N.I.).

Rent limit for tenancies of certain houses

3.—(1) This Order applies to a tenancy of the following dwelling-houses—

  (*a*) a dwelling-house the net annual value (ascertained in accordance with the Rates (Northern Ireland) Order 1972(**a**)) of which is £50 or over;

  (*b*) a dwelling-house such as is mentioned in section 56(1)(*a*) or (*b*) of the 1956 Act (dwelling-houses erected or converted after the commencement of that Act);

  (*c*) a dwelling-house such as is mentioned in section 58(2)(*a*) or (*b*) of the 1956 Act (dwelling-houses of which the landlord is in possession at or after the commencement of that Act); and

  (*d*) a dwelling-house let at a rent which includes payment for the use of furniture or for services.

(2) The rent recoverable in respect of the standstill period under a tenancy of a dwelling-house to which this Order applies shall not, subject to paragraph (4) below, exceed the counter-inflation limit and, accordingly, the amount of any excess shall, notwithstanding anything in any agreement, be irrecoverable from the tenant.

(3) For the purposes of this Article, the counter-inflation limit shall be determined as follows—

  (*a*) if on 8th April 1974 the dwelling-house is let, the counter-inflation limit is the rent under the tenancy on that date as varied by any agreement made before that date (but not as varied by any later agreement);

  (*b*) if sub-paragraph (a) above does not apply, but the dwelling-house was let at any time within a period of twelve months beginning on 8th April 1973, the counter-inflation limit is the rent under the tenancy (or, if there was more than one tenancy, the last of them) for the last rental period thereof;

  (*c*) if sub-paragraphs (*a*) and (*b*) above do not apply, and the dwelling-house is let after 8th April 1974, the counter-inflation limit is the rent payable under the terms of the tenancy (or if there is more than one tenancy, the first of them) for the first rental period thereof, and not as varied by any agreement made after that date.

(4) The foregoing paragraphs do not prevent the rent recoverable in respect of the standstill period under a tenancy of a dwelling-house to which this Order applies being increased to take account of any increase in rates or of the cost of any improvements to that dwelling-house, and the counter-inflation limit shall be increased accordingly.

(5) Where any notice of increase purporting to increase the rent under a tenancy of a dwelling-house to which this Order applies (other than on account of rates or improvements as permitted by paragraph (4) above) is served whether before on or after 8th April 1974 which would, apart from this Order, take effect during the standstill period, that notice shall be invalid and of no effect.

(a) S.I. 1972/1633 (N.I. 16).

Recovery of excess rent

4.—(1) Subject to paragraph (3) below, where a tenant has paid on account of rent any amount which by virtue of this Order he is not liable to pay, he shall be entitled to recover that amount from the landlord who received it or his personal representatives.

(2) Subject to paragraph (3) below, any amount which a tenant is entitled to recover under paragraph (1) above may, without prejudice to any other method of recovery, be deducted by the tenant from any rent payable by him to the landlord.

(3) No amount which a tenant is entitled to recover under paragraph (1) above shall be recoverable at any time after the expiry of two years from the date of payment.

Adjustments relating to rental periods

5.—(1) In ascertaining for the purposes of this Order whether there is any difference with respect to rents between one rental period and another (whether of the same tenancy or not), or the amount of any such difference, any necessary adjustment shall be made to take account of periods of different lengths.

(2) For the purposes of such an adjustment as is mentioned in paragraph (1) above—

    (*a*) a period of one month shall be treated as equivalent to one-twelfth of a year; and

    (*b*) a period of a week shall be treated as equivalent to one fifty-second of a year.

(3) Where by virtue of this Order any amount of rent is in respect of the standstill period irrecoverable from the tenant, any necessary adjustment shall be made to take account of rental periods which—

    (*a*) begin before the standstill period and end during or after that period; or

    (*b*) begin during the standstill period and end after that period.

Validity of agreements and tenancies

6. Any agreement or tenancy in relation to which this Order has effect—

    (*a*) is not rendered invalid by this Order; but

    (*b*) shall have effect during the standstill period subject to this Order.

Jurisdiction of the county court

7. The county court shall, subject to rules of court, have jurisdiction to determine—

    (*a*) any question as to the applicability of any provision of this Order to any dwelling-house;

    (*b*) any question as to the rent recoverable by virtue of this Order; and

    (*c*) any matter which is or may become material for determining any such question as is mentioned in sub-paragraphs (a) and (b) above,

notwithstanding that by reason of the amount involved the court would not otherwise have jurisdiction.

Transitional

8. Without prejudice to paragraph 4 of Schedule 3 to the Counter-Inflation Act 1973, any right acquired or liability, obligation or penalty incurred by virtue of this Order shall not be affected by Part II of that Act ceasing to be in force and accordingly any legal proceeding or remedy in respect of any such right, liability, obligation or penalty may be instituted, continued or enforced as though that Part had continued in force.

M. Rees,

One of Her Majesty's Principal
Secretaries of State.

Northern Ireland Office.
4th April 1974.

EXPLANATORY NOTE

(This Note is not part of the Order.)

This Order, which applies to Northern Ireland only, prohibits, during the period from 8th April 1974 to 31st December 1974, any increase (other than one reflecting an increase in rates or the cost of improvements) in the rent for any dwelling-house—

    (*a*) with a net annual value of £50 or over;

    (*b*) to which section 56(1)(*a*) or (*b*) or 58(2)(*a*) or (*b*) of the Housing (Miscellaneous Provisions) and Rent Restriction Law (Amendment) Act (Northern Ireland) 1956 applies; or

    (*c*) which is let at a rent which includes payment for the use of furniture or for services.

1974 No. 661

COUNTER-INFLATION

The Counter-Inflation (Price and Pay Code) (Amendment) Order 1974

Made - - - -	*4th April* 1974
Laid before Parliament	*4th April* 1974
Coming into Operation	*5th April* 1974

The Treasury, in exercise of the powers conferred on them by section 2 of the Counter-Inflation Act 1973(**a**) and of all other powers enabling them in that behalf, and having consulted the Price Commission and the Pay Board and representatives of consumers, persons experienced in the supply of goods or services, employers and employees and other persons in accordance with subsection (4) of the said section 2, hereby make the following Order:

1. (1) This Order may be cited as the Counter-Inflation (Price and Pay Code) (Amendment) Order 1974 and shall come into operation on 5 April 1974.

(2) The Interpretation Act 1889(**b**) shall apply for the interpretation of this Order as it applies for the interpretation of an Act of Parliament.

2. The Schedule to the Counter-Inflation (Price and Pay Code) (No. 2) Order 1973(**c**) shall have effect subject to the amendments specified in the Schedule to this Order.

John Golding,

Donald R. Coleman,

Two of the Lords Commissioners
of Her Majesty's Treasury.

4th April 1974.

SCHEDULE

Article 2

1. Insert, next after paragraph 26, the following paragraph—

" 26A (i) Where after 25 March 1974 an indirect tax has been increased, an addition not exceeding the cash amount of the increase borne by the vendor may be made to the prices permitted by other provisions of the Code for goods bearing the increased tax. Where an indirect tax is reduced the reduction must be fully reflected in prices.

(ii) This paragraph applies also to the effects of changes in the coverage of indirect taxes.

(iii) In calculating maximum permitted price increases after 25 March 1974, the figures for total costs per unit and the selling price at the base date must exclude any additions or reductions under this paragraph.

(iv) VAT is not regarded as part of the price for calculating prices and price increases for manufacturing and service enterprises, and this paragraph does not affect the treatment of VAT for this purpose."

(**a**) 1973 c. 9.   (**b**) 1889 c. 63.   (**c**) S.I. 1973/1785 (1973 III, p. 5445).

2. In paragraph 63, 7th line, before " excise " insert " customs and ";
and at the end add—
" and of other changes in those duties. Where indirect taxes have been
increased after 25 March 1974, a deduction should be made from the value
of sales corresponding to the cash value of the extra tax borne by the
goods sold; conversely, where indirect taxes have been reduced after
25 March 1974, a corresponding addition should be made to the value of
sales."

3. Insert, next after paragraph 74, the following paragraph—
" 74A. Where indirect taxes have been increased after 25 March 1974,
an addition not exceeding the cash amount of the increase may be made
to prices charged by distributors. Where indirect taxes are reduced,
the reduction must be fully reflected in prices. The cash amount of the
increase or reduction need not however be applied precisely to the goods
bearing the indirect taxes."

4. In paragraph 75, add at the end—
" In particular the cash value of increases in indirect taxes after
25 March 1974 should be deducted from both sales and costs of sales in
arriving at current gross percentage margins. Similarly the cash equivalent
of any tax reductions should be added to costs and sales."

EXPLANATORY NOTE

(This Note is not part of the Order.)

This Order amends the Counter-Inflation (Price and Pay Code) (No. 2)
Order 1973 by inserting in Part 1 of the Schedule to that Order (which relates
to prices and charges) provisions dealing with the effect of changes in
indirect taxes.

1974 No. 666 (S.60)

JURIES

The Jurors' Allowances (Scotland) Amendment Regulations 1974

Made - - -		*2nd April* 1974
Coming into Operation		*29th April* 1974

In exercise of the powers conferred on me by sections 24(1) and 32(1) of the Juries Act 1949(**a**), as amended by the Juries Act 1954(**b**), and as read with the Minister for the Civil Service Order 1971(**c**), and of all other powers enabling me in that behalf, I hereby, with the consent of the Minister for the Civil Service, make the following regulations : —

1.—(1) These regulations may be cited as the Jurors' Allowances (Scotland) Amendment Regulations 1974 and shall come into operation on 29th April 1974.

(2) The Interpretation Act 1889(**d**) shall apply for the interpretation of these regulations as it applies for the interpretation of an Act of Parliament.

2. In paragraph 3(2) of the Schedule to the Jurors' Allowances (Scotland) Regulations 1971(**e**) as amended (**f**) (which relates to travelling allowances) for the expressions "4·4p", "5·5p" and "6·0p" there shall be substituted the expressions "4·8p", "6·0p" and "6·6p" respectively.

William Ross,
One of Her Majesty's Principal
Secretaries of State.

St. Andrew's House,
Edinburgh.
2nd April 1974.

Consent of the Minister for the Civil Service given under his Official Seal on 2nd April 1974.

P. F. Clifton,
Authorised by the Minister
for the Civil Service.

(**a**) 1949 c. 27. (**b**) 1954 c. 41.
(**c**) S.I. 1971/2099 (1971 III, p. 6186). (**d**) 1889 c. 63.
(**e**) S.I. 1971/220 (1971 I, p. 651).
(**f**) The relevant amending instrument is S.I. 1973/1686 (1973 III, p. 5163).

EXPLANATORY NOTE

(This Note is not part of the Regulations.)

These Regulations amend the Jurors' Allowances (Scotland) Regulations 1971. They increase the rates of travel allowances payable to jurors.

STATUTORY INSTRUMENTS

1974 No. 667 (S.61)

NATIONAL HEALTH SERVICE, SCOTLAND

The National Health Service (Speech Therapists) (Scotland) Regulations 1974

Made - - - -	*2nd April* 1974
Laid before Parliament	18*th April* 1974
Coming into Operation	19*th April* 1974

In exercise of the powers conferred on me by paragraph 8 of Part I of Schedule 1 to the National Health Service (Scotland) Act 1972(**a**) and of all other powers enabling me in that behalf, I hereby make the following regulations:—

Citation and commencement

1. These regulations may be cited as the National Health Service (Speech Therapists) (Scotland) Regulations 1974 and shall come into operation on 19th April 1974.

Interpretation

2.—(1) In these regulations, subject to paragraph (2) of this regulation, expressions to which a meaning is assigned by the National Health Service (Scotland) Act 1947(**b**) have that meaning, and "Health Board" means a board constituted under section 13 of the National Health Service (Scotland) Act 1972.

(2) In these regulations, in relation to England and Wales, expressions to which a meaning is assigned by the National Health Service Act 1946(**c**) have that meaning.

(3) Unless the context otherwise requires, any reference in these regulations to any enactment shall be construed as a reference to that enactment as amended or re-enacted by any subsequent enactment.

(4) The Interpretation Act 1889(**d**) shall apply for the interpretation of these regulations as it applies for the interpretation of an Act of Parliament.

Employment of officers

3. No person shall be employed as an officer of a Health Board in the capacity of a speech therapist unless he satisfies one of the following conditions:—

(*a*) he holds a certificate issued by the College of Speech Therapists (hereinafter referred to as "the College")—

(i) certifying that he has attended a course of training and passed an examination approved by the Secretary of State; or

---

(**a**) 1972 c. 58.
(**c**) 1946 c. 81.
(**b**) 1947 c. 27.
(**d**) 1889 c. 63.

    (ii) certifying that the College are satisfied that he has, in a country or territory outside the United Kingdom, attended a course of training and passed an examination recognised by the College and approved by the Secretary of State;

  (b) his name is included in a list, kept by the Secretary of State, of persons not qualified in accordance with the foregoing provisions of this regulation, who have satisfied him that their training and experience are adequate for employment as speech therapists;

  (c) his name is included in a list of persons suitable for employment as speech therapists kept by the Secretary of State for Social Services, the Secretary of State for Wales, or the Secretary of State for Northern Ireland;

  (d) he was immediately before 1st April 1974 employed as a speech therapist—

    (i) by a Regional Hospital Board, or a Board of Management exercising functions on behalf of a Regional Hospital Board; or

    (ii) by a local health authority or an education authority; or

    (iii) by a Regional Hospital Board or the Welsh Hospital Board, a Board of Governors of a teaching hospital, a local health authority, or a local education authority in England or Wales; or

    (iv) in the Northern Ireland health service.

Revocation

4.—(1) The National Health Service (Speech Therapists) (Scotland) Regulations 1964(a) are hereby revoked.

(2) Section 38 of the Interpretation Act 1889 shall apply as if these regulations were an Act of Parliament and as if the regulations revoked by these regulations were an Act of Parliament repealed by an Act of Parliament.

William Ross,
One of Her Majesty's Principal
Secretaries of State.

St Andrew's House,
Edinburgh.
2nd April 1974.

EXPLANATORY NOTE

(This Note is not part of the Regulations.)

These Regulations prescribe the conditions under which a speech therapist may be employed for the purpose of providing services under the national health service, as reorganised by the National Health Service (Scotland) Act 1972.

(a) S.I. 1964/997 (1964 II, p. 2237).

STATUTORY INSTRUMENTS

1974 No. 668 (L.12)

MAGISTRATES' COURTS
PROCEDURE

The Magistrates' Courts (Reciprocal Enforcement of Maintenance Orders) Rules 1974

Made - - -	*4th April* 1974
Laid before Parliament	*17th April* 1974
Coming into Operation	*8th May* 1974

The Lord Chancellor, in exercise of the powers conferred on him by section 15 of the Justices of the Peace Act 1949(**a**), as extended by section 122 of the Magistrates' Courts Act 1952(**b**) and sections 2(3) and (4), 3(5)(*b*) and (*c*), 5(4) and (9)(*a*), 6(2) and (3), 7(2) and (5), 8(5) and (6), 9(5) and (10), 10(1) to (5) and (7), 11(1)(*b*), 14(1), 16(1), 18(1) and 23(3) of the Maintenance Orders (Reciprocal Enforcement) Act 1972(**c**), after consultation with the Rule Committee appointed under the said section 15, hereby makes the following Rules:—

1. These Rules may be cited as the Magistrates' Courts (Reciprocal Enforcement of Maintenance Orders) Rules 1974 and shall come into operation on 8th May 1974.

2.—(1) In these Rules, unless the context otherwise requires—

"the Act" means the Maintenance Orders (Reciprocal Enforcement) Act 1972; and

"his register", in relation to a justices' clerk, means the register kept by that clerk in pursuance of rule 54 of the Magistrates' Courts Rules 1968(**d**).

(2) The Interpretation Act 1889(**e**) shall apply for the interpretation of these Rules as it applies for the interpretation of an Act of Parliament.

3. The officer of any court, by or in relation to whom anything is to be done in pursuance of any provision of Part I of the Act shall, where that court is a magistrates' court, be the justices' clerk.

4.—(1) An application under section 2 of the Act (transmission of maintenance order made in the United Kingdom for enforcement in reciprocating country) may, where the court which made the maintenance order to which the application relates is a magistrates' court, be made in writing by or on behalf of the payee under the order.

(2) Any application made in pursuance of paragraph (1) above shall—

(*a*) specify the date on which the order was made;

(**a**) 1949 c. 101.   (**b**) 1952 c. 55.   (**c**) 1972 c. 18.
(**d**) S.I. 1968/1920 (1968 III, p. 5175).   (**e**) 1889 c. 63.

(b) contain such particulars as are known to the applicant of the whereabouts of the payer;

(c) specify any matters likely to assist in the identification of the payer;

(d) where possible, be accompanied by a recent photograph of the payer.

(3) In this rule, "the payer" means the payer under the order to which the application relates.

5. A document setting out or summarising any evidence, required by section 3(5)(b), 5(4) or 9(5) of the Act (provisional orders) to be authenticated shall be authenticated by a certificate, signed by one of the justices before whom that evidence was given, that the document is the original document containing or recording or, as the case may be, summarising that evidence or a true copy of that document.

6.—(1) Subject to paragraph (2) below, any documents required by section 5(4) or 9(5) of the Act to be sent to a court in a reciprocating country shall be sent to that court by post.

(2) Where the court to which the documents are to be sent is in a country specified in Schedule 1 to these Rules, such documents shall be sent to the Secretary of State for transmission to that court.

7.—(1) For the purposes of compliance with section 5(9) of the Act (revocation by United Kingdom court of provisional order) there shall be served on the person on whose application the maintenance order was made a notice which shall—

(a) set out the evidence received or taken, as the case may be, in pursuance of that subsection;

(b) inform that person that it appears to the court that the maintenance order ought not to have been made; and

(c) inform that person that if he wishes to make representations with respect to the evidence set out in the notice he may do so orally or in writing and that if he wishes to adduce further evidence he should notify the clerk of the magistrates' court which made the maintenance order.

(2) Where a justices' clerk receives notification that the person on whose application the maintenance order was made wishes to adduce further evidence, he shall fix a date for the hearing of such evidence and shall send that person written notice of the date fixed.

8.—(1) Where a certified copy of an order, not being a provisional order, is received by a justices' clerk who is required under any provision of Part I of the Act to register the order, he shall cause the order to be registered in his court by means of a minute or memorandum entered and signed by him in his register.

(2) Where any magistrates' court makes or confirms an order which is required under section 7(5) or 9(10) of the Act to be registered, the justices' clerk shall enter and sign a minute or memorandum thereof in his register.

(3) Every minute or memorandum entered in pursuance of paragraph (1) or (2) above shall specify the section of the Act under which the order in question is registered.

9.—(1) Payment of sums due under a registered order shall, while the order is registered in a magistrates' court, be made to the clerk of the registering court during such hours and at such place as that clerk may direct; and a justices' clerk to whom payments are made under this rule shall send those payments by post to the court which made the order or to such other person or authority as that court or the Secretary of State may from time to time direct:

Provided that if the court which made the order is in one of the countries or territories specified in Schedule 2 to these Rules the justices' clerk shall send any such sums to the Crown Agents for Overseas Governments and Administrations for transmission to the person to whom they are due.

(2) Where it appears to a justices' clerk to whom payments under any maintenance order are made by virtue of paragraph (1) above that any sums payable under the order are in arrear he may and, if such sums are in arrear to an amount equal to four times the sum payable weekly under the order, he shall, whether the person for whose benefit the payment should have been made requests him to do so or not, proceed in his own name for the recovery of those sums, unless it appears to him that it is unreasonable in the circumstances to do so.

10.—(1) Subject to paragraph (2) below, where a request is made by or on behalf of a court in a reciprocating country for the taking in England and Wales of the evidence of a person residing therein, the following magistrates' courts shall have power under section 14(1) of the Act (obtaining of evidence needed for purpose of certain proceedings) to take that evidence, that is to say:—

  (a) where the maintenance order to which the proceedings in the court in the reciprocating country relate was made by a magistrates' court, the court which made the order;

  (b) where the maintenance order to which those proceedings relate is registered in a magistrates' court, the court in which the order is registered;

  (c) a magistrates' court which has received such a request from the Secretary of State.

(2) The power conferred by paragraph (1) above may, with the agreement of a court having that power, be exercised by any other magistrates' court which, because the person whose evidence is to be taken resides within its jurisdiction or for any other reason, the first-mentioned court considers could more conveniently take the evidence; but nothing in this paragraph shall derogate from the power of any court specified in paragraph (1) above.

(3) Subject to paragraph (4) below, where the evidence of any person is to be taken by a magistrates' court under the foregoing provisions of this rule—

  (a) the evidence shall be taken in the same manner as if that person were a witness in proceedings on a complaint;

  (b) any oral evidence so taken shall be put into writing and read to the person who gave it, who shall be required to sign the document; and

  (c) the justices by whom the evidence of any person is so taken shall certify at the foot of any document setting out the evidence of, or produced in evidence by, that person that such evidence was taken, or document received in evidence, as the case may be, by them.

(4) Where such a request as is mentioned in paragraph (1) above includes a request that the evidence be taken in a particular manner, the magistrates' court by which the evidence is taken shall, so far as circumstances permit, comply with that request.

(5) Any document such as is mentioned in paragraph (3)(*c*) above shall be sent—

(*a*) where the request for the taking of the evidence was made by or on behalf of a court in a country specified in Schedule 1 to these Rules, to the Secretary of State for transmission to that court;

(*b*) in any other case, to the court in the reciprocating country by or on behalf of which the request was made.

11. Any request under section 14(5) of the Act for the taking or providing of evidence by a court in a reciprocating country shall, where made by a magistrates' court, be communicated in writing to the court in question.

12.—(1) Where a magistrates' court makes an order, not being a provisional order, varying a maintenance order to which section 5 of the Act (variation and revocation of maintenance order made in the United Kingdom) applies, the justices' clerk shall send written notice of the making of the order to the Secretary of State; and where the order is made by virtue of paragraph (*a*) or (*b*) of subsection (3) of that section, he shall send such written notice to the court in a reciprocating country which would, if the order had been a provisional order, have had power to confirm the order.

(2) Where a magistrates' court revokes a maintenance order to which section 5 of the Act applies, the justices' clerk shall send written notice of the revocation to the Secretary of State and to the court in a reciprocating country which has power to confirm that maintenance order, or by which the order has been confirmed, or in which the order is registered for enforcement, as the case may be.

(3) Where under section 9 of the Act (variation and revocation of maintenance order registered in United Kingdom court) a magistrates' court makes an order, not being a provisional order, varying or revoking a registered order, the justices' clerk shall send written notice of the making of the order to the court in a reciprocating country which made the registered order.

(4) Where under section 7(2) of the Act (confirmation by United Kingdom court of provisional maintenance order made in reciprocating country) a magistrates' court confirms an order to which section 7 of the Act applies, the justices' clerk shall send written notice of the confirmation to the court in a reciprocating country which made the order.

13.—(1) Where a justices' clerk—

(*a*) registers under section 6(3) of the Act (registration in United Kingdom court of maintenance order made in reciprocating country) an order to which section 6 of the Act applies; or

(*b*) registers under section 7(5) of the Act an order which has been confirmed in pursuance of section 7(2) of the Act,

he shall send written notice to the Secretary of State that the order has been duly registered.

(2) Where a justices' clerk cancels the registration of a maintenance order under section 10(1) of the Act (cancellation of registration and transfer of order), he shall send written notice of the cancellation to the payer under the order.

(3) Where a justices' clerk registers a maintenance order under section 10(4) of the Act, he shall send written notice to the Secretary of State and to the

payer under the order that the order has been duly registered.

Dated 4th April 1974.

Elwyn-Jones, C.

Rules 6(2) and 10(5)   SCHEDULE 1

RECIPROCATING COUNTRIES TO WHICH DOCUMENTS ARE TRANSMITTED
VIA THE SECRETARY OF STATE

British Columbia

New Zealand

Nova Scotia

Ontario

Rule 9(1)   SCHEDULE 2

COUNTRIES AND TERRITORIES IN WHICH SUMS ARE PAYABLE THROUGH
CROWN AGENTS FOR OVERSEAS GOVERNMENTS AND ADMINISTRATIONS

Gibraltar

EXPLANATORY NOTE

(*This Note is not part of the Rules.*)

These Rules make provision, in relation to magistrates' courts, for the various matters which are to be prescribed under Part I of the Maintenance Orders (Reciprocal Enforcement) Act 1972 and for the giving of notice of things done under that part of the Act.

In particular, the Rules prescribe the manner of applying for a maintenance order to be sent for enforcement to a reciprocating country, the manner in which maintenance orders are to be registered in magistrates' courts, the manner of enforcing orders so registered and the manner in which evidence is to be taken at the request of a foreign court.

STATUTORY INSTRUMENTS

1974 No. 670

CHILDREN AND YOUNG PERSONS

The Cessation of Approved Institutions (St. Benedict's School) Order 1974

Made	-	-	-	5th April 1974
Coming into Operation				1st May 1974

The Secretary of State for Social Services in exercise of her power under section 46 of the Children and Young Persons Act 1969(a) and of all other powers enabling her in that behalf, hereby makes the following order:—

Citation and commencement

1. This order may be cited as the Cessation of Approved Institutions (St. Benedict's School) Order 1974, and shall come into operation on 1st May 1974.

Interpretation

2.—(1) In this order unless the context otherwise requires—

"the specified date" means 1st May 1974;

"the school" means the school approved by the Secretary of State in pursuance of section 79(1) of the Children and Young Persons Act 1933(b) and known as St. Benedict's School;

"the managers" means the managers of the school for the purpose of section 79(1) of the Children and Young Persons Act 1933;

"the tribunal" means a tribunal established under section 12 of the Industrial Training Act 1964(c) and referred to in section 100 of the Industrial Relations Act 1971(d);

"terms and conditions of employment" includes any restriction arising under any Act or any instrument made under any Act on the termination of the employment of any officer;

"the Council" means the council of the London Borough of Brent;

"approved institution" has the meaning assigned to it under section 46 of the Children and Young Persons Act 1969;

"Planning Area No. 8" is the area so designated in the Schedule to the Children and Young Persons (Planning Areas) Order 1974(e).

(2) Any reference in this order to the Local Government Superannuation Acts 1937 to 1953(f), to any provisions thereof or to the provisions of any instrument made under those Acts shall be construed as references to the said provisions as they have effect as regulations made under section 7 of the Superannuation Act 1972(g).

(a) 1969 c. 54.   (b) 1933 c. 12.   (c) 1964 c. 16.
(d) 1971 c. 72.   (e) S.I. 1974/163 (1974 I, p. 545).
(f) 1937 c. 68; 1939 c. 18; 1953 c. 25.   (g) 1972 c. 11.

(3) In this order, unless the context otherwise requires, references to any enactment shall be construed as references to that enactment as amended, extended or applied by or under any other enactment or by this order.

(4) Any reference in this order to a numbered article shall, unless the reference is to an article of a specified order, be construed as a reference to the article bearing that number in this order.

(5) Any reference in any article of this order to a numbered paragraph shall, unless the reference is to a paragraph of a specified article, be construed as a reference to the paragraph bearing that number in the first-mentioned article.

(6) The Interpretation Act 1889(a) shall apply to the interpretation of this order as it applies to the interpretation of an Act of Parliament.

Cessation as an approved institution

3. It having appeared to the Secretary of State that in consequence of the establishment of community homes in Planning Area No. 8, the school is no longer required she hereby orders that it shall cease to be an approved institution as from the specified date.

Transfer of staff and the safeguarding of their interests

4.—(1) Any person who immediately before the specified date is employed by the managers of the school wholly or substantially in respect of the school shall be transferred to the employment of the Council on the specified date.

(2) Any question whether a person is employed as described in paragraph (1) shall where necessary be determined by the tribunal and references to the tribunal may be made as soon as may be and in any case not later than 15th June 1974 and if any question that a person is not, or is, so employed is undecided on the specified date the person shall not be transferred as mentioned in paragraph (1) until the expiration of the second week following that in which the decision of the tribunal is notified.

(3) (*a*) Every person transferred by paragraph (1) to the employment of the Council shall, so long as he continues in that employment by virtue of the transfer, and until he is served with a statement in writing of new terms and conditions of employment, enjoy terms and conditions of employment not less favourable than those he enjoyed immediately before the specified date and the said new terms and conditions shall be such that—

(i) so long as the person is engaged in duties reasonably comparable to those in which he was engaged immediately before the specified date, the scale of his salary or remuneration, and

(ii) the other terms and conditions of his employment, are not less favourable than those he enjoyed immediately before the specified date, and any question whether duties are reasonably comparable or whether terms and conditions of employment are less favourable shall where necessary be determined by the tribunal.

(*b*) A statement of new terms and conditions of employment shall not be served in respect of any person in relation to whom a question has been referred under paragraph (2) until the decision of the tribunal has been notified.

(*c*) Subject to sub-paragraph (*b*), a statement of new terms and conditions of employment may be served before the specified date.

(a) 1889 c. 63.

(*d*) If after service upon a person of a statement of new terms and conditions of employment a question is referred to the tribunal in respect of such person under paragraph (2), the statement shall cease to have effect, sub-paragraph (*a*) of this paragraph shall have effect as if the statement had not been served, and no new statement shall be served until the decision on the question has been notified.

(4) A written statement given in accordance with section 4(1) of the Contracts of Employment Act 1972(**a**) shall not be regarded as a statement of new terms and conditions of employment for the purposes of paragraph (3) unless the statement so indicates.

(5) Any extension of service under section 7(1) of the Local Government Superannuation Act 1937 effective on the specified date in relation to a person transferred by paragraph (1) shall continue to have effect as if it had been made by the Council to whose employment he is transferred as aforesaid.

(6) (*a*) Any determination made by the tribunal as provided under paragraph (2) or (3)(*a*)(ii) shall be made in accordance with the Industrial Tribunals (Industrial Relations, etc.) Regulations 1972(**b**), and this order, and in respect of any hearing of the tribunal for purposes of any such determination a person or persons may be appointed to sit with the tribunal as assessor or assessors.

(*b*) Any determination of the tribunal as mentioned in sub-paragraph (*a*) above shall, subject to any modification that may be required in consequence of any appeal from that determination on a point of law, be given effect to by the Council or the managers as the case may be.

(*c*) The Council shall inform everyone who is employed by the managers on 30th April 1974 of his right to make reference to the tribunal under paragraph (2) and shall inform every employee transferred by this order of his right to make reference to the tribunal under paragraph (3)(*a*)(ii) and shall at the same time give them the address to which the reference may be made, and with respect to a reference under paragraph (2) the Council shall inform the employee not later than 15th May 1974 that he must make reference to the tribunal not later than 15th June 1974, and with respect to a reference under paragraph (3)(*a*)(ii) the Council may inform the employee of his said right by means of an insertion in the statement in writing to be served under paragraph (3)(*a*).

Superannuation

5.—(1) The admission agreement made by or on behalf of the managers and the County Council of the Administrative County of Berkshire on 18th February 1964 and approved by the Minister of Housing and Local Government on 27th February 1964 and by virtue of regulation 10(2) of the Local Government Superannuation (Miscellaneous Provisions) (No. 2) Regulations 1973(**c**) having effect as if made by or on behalf of the managers and the council of the Non-metropolitan County of Berkshire shall cease to have effect on the specified date but without prejudice to accrued rights or any liabilities thereunder.

(2) Any liabilities of the managers arising out of the agreement referred to in the last preceding paragraph shall become the liability of the Council with effect from the specified date.

(3) Where at any time before the specified date a gratuity or allowance by way of periodical payments or an annuity—

(a) 1972 c. 53.   (b) S.I. 1972/38 (1972 I, p. 91).
(c) S.I. 1973/1996 (1973 III, p. 6872).

(*a*) has been granted to any person by the managers on or after his ceasing to be employed by them at or in connection with the school, or

(*b*) has been granted to the widow or other dependant of a person who died while in the employment of the managers at or in connection with the school or during the currency of a gratuity or allowance granted to him as mentioned in sub-paragraph (*a*) above,

and, if payment in respect of the gratuity or allowance or annuity had continued in accordance with the terms of the grant and of any subsequent increase, one or more payments would have been made on or after the specified date (whether under legal obligation or otherwise), such payments shall be made by the Council in place of the managers.

(4) Without prejudice to the last preceding paragraph, where, if this order had not been made, the managers would for the purpose of any statutory provision relating to pensions have been the employing authority or former employing authority in relation to a person who died before the specified date while in the employment of the managers at or in connection with the school or otherwise ceased to be employed by them at or in connection with the school or the widow or other dependant of such a person, the Council shall be treated as being at that time the employing authority or former employing authority for those purposes in relation to that person, his widow or other dependant.

Signed by authority of the Secretary of State for Social Services.

M. G. Russell,
Assistant Secretary,
Department of Health and Social Security.

5th April 1974.

EXPLANATORY NOTE

(This Note is not part of the Order.)

This Order makes provision for the cessation as an approved institution of St. Benedict's School and for the transfer of the staff of the school to the London Borough of Brent Council which is to assume responsibility after the school becomes a community home. The Order also makes provision for the protection of the interests of the staff and pensioners of the school.

STATUTORY INSTRUMENTS

1974 No. 671

CHILDREN AND YOUNG PERSONS

The Cessation of Approved Institutions (St. Laurence's School) Order 1974

Made - - -		*5th April* 1974
Coming into Operation		*6th May* 1974

The Secretary of State for Social Services in exercise of her power under section 46 of the Children and Young Persons Act 1969(**a**) and of all other powers enabling her in that behalf, hereby makes the following order:—

Citation and commencement

1. This order may be cited as the Cessation of Approved Institutions (St. Laurence's School) Order 1974, and shall come into operation on 6th May 1974.

Interpretation

2.—(1) In this order unless the context otherwise requires—

"the specified date" means 6th May 1974;

"the school" means the school approved by the Secretary of State in pursuance of section 79(1) of the Children and Young Persons Act 1933(**b**) and known as St. Laurence's School;

"the managers" means the managers of the school for the purpose of section 79(1) of the Children and Young Persons Act 1933;

"the tribunal" means a tribunal established under section 12 of the Industrial Training Act 1964(**c**) and referred to in section 100 of the Industrial Relations Act 1971(**d**);

"terms and conditions of employment" includes any restriction arising under any Act or any instrument made under any Act on the termination of the employment of any officer;

"the Council" means the council of the London Borough of Greenwich;

"approved institution" has the meaning assigned to it under section 46 of the Children and Young Persons Act 1969;

"Planning Area No. 8" is the area so designated in the Schedule to the Children and Young Persons (Planning Areas) Order 1974(**e**).

(2) Any reference in this order to the Local Government Superannuation Acts 1937 to 1953(**f**), to any provisions thereof or to the provisions of any instrument made under those Acts shall be construed as references to the said provisions as they have effect as regulations made under section 7 of the Superannuation Act 1972(**g**).

(**a**) 1969 c. 54.	(**b**) 1933 c. 12.
(**c**) 1964 c. 16.	(**d**) 1971 c. 72.
(**e**) S.I. 1974/163 (1974 I, p. 545).	(**f**) 1937 c. 68; 1939 c. 18; 1953 c. 25.
(**g**) 1972 c. 11.	

(3) In this order, unless the context otherwise requires, references to any enactment shall be construed as references to that enactment as amended, extended or applied by or under any other enactment or by this order.

(4) Any reference in this order to a numbered article shall, unless the reference is to an article of a specified order, be construed as a reference to the article bearing that number in this order.

(5) Any reference in any article of this order to a numbered paragraph shall, unless the reference is to a paragraph of a specified article, be construed as a reference to the paragraph bearing that number in the first-mentioned article.

(6) The Interpretation Act 1889(a) shall apply to the interpretation of this order as it applies to the interpretation of an Act of Parliament.

Cessation as an approved institution

3. It having appeared to the Secretary of State that in consequence of the establishment of community homes in Planning Area No. 8., the school is no longer required she hereby orders that it shall cease to be an approved institution as from the specified date.

Transfer of staff and the safeguarding of their interests

4.—(1) Any person who immediately before the specified date is employed by the managers of the school wholly or substantially in respect of the school shall be transferred to the employment of the Council on the specified date.

(2) Any question whether a person is employed as described in paragraph (1) shall where necessary be determined by the tribunal and references to the tribunal may be made as soon as may be and in any case not later than 20th June 1974 and if any question that a person is not, or is, so employed is undecided on the specified date the person shall not be transferred as mentioned in paragraph (1) until the expiration of the second week following that in which the decision of the tribunal is notified.

(3) (*a*) Every person transferred by paragraph (1) to the employment of the Council shall, so long as he continues in that employment by virtue of the transfer, and until he is served with a statement in writing of new terms and conditions of employment, enjoy terms and conditions of employment not less favourable than those he enjoyed immediately before the specified date and the said new terms and conditions shall be such that—

(i) so long as the person is engaged in duties reasonably comparable to those in which he was engaged immediately before the specified date, the scale of his salary or remuneration, and

(ii) the other terms and conditions of his employment, are not less favourable than those he enjoyed immediately before the specified date, and any question whether duties are reasonably comparable or whether terms and conditions of employment are less favourable shall where necessary be determined by the tribunal.

(*b*) A statement of new terms and conditions of employment shall not be served in respect of any person in relation to whom a question has been referred under paragraph (2) until the decision of the tribunal has been notified.

(a) 1889 c. 63.

(c) Subject to sub-paragraph (b), a statement of new terms and conditions of employment may be served before the specified date.

(d) If after service upon a person of a statement of new terms and conditions of employment a question is referred to the tribunal in respect of such person under paragraph (2), the statement shall cease to have effect, sub-paragraph (a) of this paragraph shall have effect as if the statement had not been served, and no new statement shall be served until the decision on the question has been notified.

(4) A written statement given in accordance with section 4(1) of the Contracts of Employment Act 1972(**a**) shall not be regarded as a statement of new terms and conditions of employment for the purposes of paragraph (3) unless the statement so indicates.

(5) Any extension of service under section 7(1) of the Local Government Superannuation Act 1937 effective on the specified date in relation to a person transferred by paragraph (1) shall continue to have effect as if it had been made by the Council to whose employment he is transferred as aforesaid.

(6) (a) Any determination made by the tribunal as provided under paragraph (2) or (3)(a)(ii) shall be made in accordance with the Industrial Tribunals (Industrial Relations, etc.) Regulations 1972(**b**), and this order, and in respect of any hearing of the tribunal for purposes of any such determination a person or persons may be appointed to sit with the tribunal as assessor or assessors.

(b) Any determination of the tribunal as mentioned in sub-paragraph (a) above shall, subject to any modification that may be required in consequence of any appeal from that determination on a point of law, be given effect to by the Council or the managers as the case may be.

(c) The Council shall inform everyone who is employed by the managers on 5th May 1974 of his right to make reference to the tribunal under paragraph (2) and shall inform every employee transferred by this order of his right to make reference to the tribunal under paragraph (3)(a)(ii) and shall at the same time give them the address to which the reference may be made, and with respect to a reference under paragraph (2) the Council shall inform the employee not later than 20th May 1974 that he must make reference to the tribunal not later than 20th June 1974, and with respect to a reference under paragraph (3)(a)(ii) the Council may inform the employee of his said right by means of an insertion in the statement in writing to be served under paragraph (3)(a).

Superannuation

5.—(1) The admission agreement made by or on behalf of the managers and the county council of East Sussex on 5th August 1964 and approved by the Minister of Housing and Local Government on 12th August 1964 and by virtue of regulation 10(2) of the Local Government Superannuation (Miscellaneous Provisions) (No. 2) Regulations 1973(**c**) having effect as if made by or on behalf of the managers and the council of the Non-metropolitan County of East Sussex shall cease to have effect on the specified date but without prejudice to accued rights or any liabilities thereunder.

(**a**) 1972 c. 53.   (**b**) S.I. 1972/38 (1972 I, p. 91).
(**c**) S.I. 1973/1996 (1973 III, p. 6872).

(2) Any liabilities of the managers arising out of the agreement referred to in the last preceding paragraph shall become the liability of the Council with effect from the specified date.

(3) Where at any time before the specified date a gratuity or allowance by way of periodical payments or an annuity—

(*a*) has been granted to any person by the managers on or after his ceasing to be employed by them at or in connection with the school, or

(*b*) has been granted to the widow or other dependant of a person who died while in the employment of the managers at or in connection with the school or during the currency of a gratuity or allowance granted to him as mentioned in sub-paragraph (*a*) above,

and, if payment in respect of the gratuity or allowance or annuity had continued in accordance with the terms of the grant and of any subsequent increase, one or more payments would have been made on or after the specified date (whether under legal obligation or otherwise), such payments shall be made by the Council in place of the managers.

(4) Without prejudice to the last preceding paragraph, where, if this order had not been made, the managers would for the purpose of any statutory provision relating to pensions have been the employing authority or former employing authority in relation to a person who died before the specified date while in the employment of the managers at or in connection with the school or otherwise ceased to be employed by them at or in connection with the school or the widow or other dependant of such a person, the Council shall be treated as being at that time the employing authority or former employing authority for those purposes in relation to that person, his widow or other dependant.

Financial provisions

6. The Council shall repay to the Secretary of State before the expiry of 3 months from the specified date such sum as she may determine in accordance with paragraph 9(4) of Schedule 3 to the Children and Young Persons Act 1969, such sum being notified to the Council before the expiry of one month from the specified date.

Signed by authority of the Secretary of State for Social Services.

M. G. Russell,
Assistant Secretary,
Department of Health and Social Security.

5th April 1974.

EXPLANATORY NOTE

(This Note is not part of the Order.)

This Order makes provision for the cessation as an approved institution of St. Laurence's School and for the transfer of the staff of the school to the London Borough of Greenwich Council which is to assume responsibility after the school becomes a community home. The Order also makes provision for the protection of the interests of the staff and pensioners of the school and for the repayment to the Secretary of State by The London Borough of Greenwich Council of grants which had been made to the managers of the school.

STATUTORY INSTRUMENTS

1974 No. 673 (S.62)

JUSTICES OF THE PEACE

The Justices Allowances (Scotland) Amendment Regulations 1974

Made - - -	*2nd April* 1974
Laid before Parliament	*19th April* 1974
Coming into Operation	*29th April* 1974

In exercise of the powers conferred on me by section 8(6) and (7) of the Justices of the Peace Act 1949(a) as extended by section 31 of the Administration of Justice Act 1964(b), and of all other powers enabling me in that behalf, I hereby make the following regulations:—

1.—(1) These regulations may be cited as the Justices Allowances (Scotland) Amendment Regulations 1974 and shall come into operation on 29th April 1974.

(2) The Interpretation Act 1889(c) shall apply for the interpretation of these regulations as it applies for the interpretation of an Act of Parliament.

2. In paragraph 3(*e*) of Schedule 1 to the Justices Allowances (Scotland) Regulations 1971(d) as amended (e), for the sums of 5·5p, 6·2p and 6·9p there shall be substituted the sums of 6·4p, 6·9p and 7·8p respectively.

William Ross,
One of Her Majesty's Principal
Secretaries of State.

St. Andrew's House,
Edinburgh.
2nd April 1974.

EXPLANATORY NOTE

(This Note is not part of the Regulations.)

These Regulations increase the rates of travelling allowance payable to a Justice of the Peace.

(a) 1949 c. 101.
(b) 1964 c. 42.
(c) 1889 c. 63.
(d) S.I. 1971/490 (1971 I, p. 1440).
(e) The relevant amending instrument is S.I. 1972/1425 (1972 III, p. 4292).

1974 No. 674

WAGES COUNCILS

The Wages Regulation (Button Manufacturing) Order 1974

Made	-	-	-	*5th April* 1974

Coming into Operation   *3rd May* 1974

Whereas the Secretary of State has received from the Button Manufacturing Wages Council (Great Britain) the wages regulation proposals set out in the Schedule hereto;

Now, therefore, the Secretary of State in exercise of powers conferred by section 11 of the Wages Councils Act 1959(**a**), as modified by Article 2 of the Counter-Inflation (Modification of Wages Councils Act 1959) Order 1973(**b**), and now vested in him(**c**), and of all other powers enabling him in that behalf, hereby makes the following Order:—

1. This Order may be cited as the Wages Regulation (Button Manufacturing) Order 1974.

2.—(1) In this Order the expression "the specified date" means the 3rd May 1974, provided that where, as respects any worker who is paid wages at intervals not exceeding seven days, that date does not correspond with the beginning of the period for which the wages are paid, the expression "the specified date" means, as respects that worker, the beginning of the next such period following that date.

(2) The Interpretation Act 1889(**d**) shall apply to the interpretation of this Order as it applies to the interpretation of an Act of Parliament and as if this Order and the Order hereby revoked were Acts of Parliament.

3. The wages regulation proposals set out in the Schedule hereto shall have effect as from the specified date and as from that date the Wages Regulation (Button Manufacturing) Order 1970(**e**) shall cease to have effect.

Signed by order of the Secretary of State.

5th April 1974.

W. H. Marsh,

Assistant Secretary,

Department of Employment.

(**a**) 1959 c. 69.   (**b**) S.I. 1973/661 (1973 I, p. 2141).

(**c**) S.I. 1959/1769, 1968/729 (1959 I, p. 1795; 1968 II, p. 2108).

(**d**) 1889 c. 63.   (**e**) S.I. 1970/1478 (1970 III, p. 4813).

Article 3

SCHEDULE

The following minimum remuneration shall be substituted for the statutory minimum remuneration fixed by the Wages Regulations (Button Manufacturing) Order 1970 (Order V.(69)).

STATUTORY MINIMUM REMUNERATION

PART I

GENERAL

1.—(1) The minimum remuneration payable to a worker to whom this Schedule applies for all work except work to which a minimum overtime rate applies under Part V is—

(a) in the case of a worker other than a *homeworker*,

(i) where the worker is employed on time work, the general minimum time rate payable to the worker under Part II or Part III of this Schedule;

(ii) where the worker is employed on piece work, piece rates each of which would yield, in the circumstances of the case, to an ordinary worker at least the same amount of money as the piece work basis time rate applicable to the worker under Part II or Part III of this Schedule;

(b) in the case of a *homeworker*,

(i) where a general minimum piece rate applies under Part IV of this Schedule, that rate;

(ii) where no general minimum piece rate applies, piece rates each of which would yield, in the circumstances of the case, to an ordinary worker at least the same amount of money as the piece work basis time rate applicable to the worker under Part IV of this Schedule.

(2) In this Schedule the expression *"homeworker"* means a worker who works in his own home or in any other place that is not under the control or management of the employer.

ADDITIONAL REMUNERATION
PAYABLE IN CERTAIN CIRCUMSTANCES

2.—(1) *Up to and including 15th November 1974, in addition to the minimum remuneration specified in paragraphs 1(1) (a) and b(ii) of this Schedule, additional remuneration hereinafter referred to as a "cost of living payment" shall be payable to all workers to whom those sub-paragraphs apply in accordance with the following table:—*

		Retail Price Indices				
Cost of living payment to be paid from the first complete pay week following the publication by the Department of Employment of the Index of Retail Prices for All Items containing a figure which is	not less than	198·4	200·2	202·1	203·9	205·8
	and not more than	200·1	202·0	203·8	205·7	207·5
		£	£	£	£	£
Cost of living payment payable to full-time workers in respect of each complete pay week		0·40	0·80	1·20	1·60	2·00
Cost of living payment payable to part-time workers, in respect of each complete pay week, is the amount in the appropriate column multiplied by the number of hours worked (excluding overtime)		0·01	0·02	0·03	0·04	0·05

(2) *The cost of living payment shall not be treated as part of the general minimum time rate for the purposes of calculating payment for overtime under paragraph 9 of this Schedule.*

(3) *On and after 16th November 1974, the cost of living payment to be payable under this paragraph shall be that which was payable in respect of the last complete pay week before that date.*

(4) *In this paragraph—*
"full-time worker" means a worker who normally works for the employer for 40 hours or more a week;
"part-time worker" means a worker who normally works for the employer for less than 40 hours a week.

PART II
MALE WORKERS OTHER THAN *HOMEWORKERS*
GENERAL MINIMUM TIME RATES

3. The general minimum time rates payable to male workers (other than *homeworkers*) are as follows:—

	Up to and including 31st December 1974	On and after 1st January 1975
	Per hour	Per hour
	p	p
Aged 20 years or over	37·5	37·5
,, 19 and under 20 years	36·0	37·5
,, 18 ,, ,, 19 ,, ...	34·5	37·5
,, 17 ,, ,, 18 ,, ...	28·5	28·5
,, under 17 years	25·5	25·5

PIECE WORK BASIS TIME RATE

Per hour
p

4. The piece work basis time rate applicable to a male worker of any
    age (other than a *homeworker*) employed on piece work is .. ..   40·5

PART III
FEMALE WORKERS OTHER THAN *HOMEWORKERS*
GENERAL MINIMUM TIME RATES

5. The general minimum time rates payable to female workers (other than *home-
    workers*) are as follows:—

Per hour
p

Aged 18 years or over   ..   ..   36·0
  „   17 and under 18 years ..   ..   28·5
  „   under *17* years ..   ..   25·5

PIECE WORK BASIS TIME RATE

Per hour
p

6. The piece work basis time rate applicable to a female worker of any
    age employed on piece work (other than *a homeworker*) is   38

PART IV
HOMEWORKERS
GENERAL MINIMUM PIECE RATES

7. The following general minimum piece rates are payable to a *homeworker* where the
    materials for sewing the buttons by hand are provided by the employer and the
    worker actually performs the work:—

    The carding of buttons—

	Per 1,000 buttons	
	Sew through	Shanks
	p	p
12 buttons or over per card..	51	61
5—11 buttons per card	61	65
3—4 „ „ „	74	76
1—2 „ „ „	90	98

Provided that where perforated or sectional cards are used the above rates shall
apply to each section or knotting off or fastening off.

PIECE WORK BASIS TIME RATE

Per hour
p

8. The piece work basis time rate applicable to all *homeworkers*
    employed on piece work, other than those to whom the general
    minimum piece rates set out in paragraph 7 apply, is   25

PART V

OVERTIME AND WAITING TIME

MINIMUM OVERTIME RATES

TIME WORKERS

9.—(1) Subject to the provisions of this paragraph, the following minimum overtime rates are payable to male or female workers (other than *homeworkers*) employed on time work:—

    (*a*) on a Saturday, not being a customary holiday—

            for all time worked ..   ..   ..   time-and-a-quarter

    (*b*) on a Sunday or a customary holiday—

            for all time worked   ..   ..   ..   double time

    (*c*) in any week exclusive of any time in respect of which a minimum overtime rate is payable under the provisions of (*a*) or (*b*) above—

    for all time worked in excess of

        40 hours   ..   ..   time-and-a-quarter

(2) Where the employer normally requires attendance on Sunday instead of Saturday, for the purposes of this paragraph (except where in the case of a woman or young person such substitution is unlawful) Saturday shall be treated as a Sunday and Sunday as a Saturday.

FEMALE PIECE WORKERS

10. The following minimum overtime rates are payable to female workers (other than *homeworkers*) employed on piece work for all time worked in excess of 40 hours in any week:—

    (1) Piece rates each of which would yield, in the circumstances of the case, to an ordinary worker at least the same amount of money as the piece work basis time rate applicable to an ordinary worker, and, in addition thereto,

    (2) a time rate of *1p* per hour.

11. In this Part of this Schedule,

    (1) the expression "customary holiday" means:—

        (*a*) (i) In England and Wales—

            Christmas Day;
            26th December if it be not a Sunday; 27th December in a year when 25th or 26th December is a Sunday;

            Good Friday;

            Easter Monday;

            the last Monday in May;
            the last Monday in August;
            (or where a day is substituted for any of the above days by national proclamation, that day);

        (ii) In Scotland—

            New Year's Day (or, if New Year's Day falls on a Sunday, the following Monday);

            the local Spring holiday;

             the local Autumn holiday; and

            three other days (being days on which the worker normally works) in the course of a calendar year, to be fixed by the employer and notified to the worker not less than three weeks before the holiday; or

(b) in the case of each of the said days (other than a day fixed by the employer in Scotland and notified to the worker as aforesaid) a day substituted by the employer therefor, being a day recognised by local custom as a day of holiday in substitution for the said day;

(2) the expressions "time-and-a-quarter" and "double time" mean, respectively one and a quarter times and twice the general minimum time rate otherwise payable to the worker.

WAITING TIME

12.—(1) A worker is entitled to payment of the minimum remuneration specified in this Schedule for all time during which he is present on the premises of his employer unless he is present thereon in any of the following circumstances:—

(a) without the employer's consent, express or implied;

(b) for some purpose unconnected with his work and other than that of waiting for work to be given to him to perform;

(c) by reason only of the fact that he is resident thereon;

(d) during normal meal times in a room or place in which no work is being done, and he is not waiting for work to be given to him to perform.

(2) The minimum remuneration payable under sub-paragraph (1) of this paragraph to a piece worker when not engaged on piece work is that which would be payable if the worker were a time worker.

PART VI

APPLICABILITY OF STATUTORY MINIMUM REMUNERATION

13. This Schedule applies to workers in relation to whom the Button Manufacturing Wages Council (Great Britain) operates, that is to say, workers employed in Great Britain in the trade specified in the Schedule to the Trade Boards (Button Manufacturing Trade, Great Britain) (Constitution and Proceedings) Regulations 1938(a), which reads as follows:—

"Schedule

1. Subject to the provisions of this Schedule the following operations and processes shall constitute the Button Manufacturing Trade:—

(a) all processes and operations in the making from any material other than precious metals and precious stones of buttons, button-moulds, metal fancy buttons, button-headed studs, upholsterers' buttons or upholsterers' button-headed nails (excluding in all cases, except as hereinafter provided, the making of the shanks), or in the covering of button-moulds;

(b) All processes and operations in the making of the following articles when done in association with or in conjunction with the work specified in sub-paragraph (a) above—

(i) shanks;

(ii) studs, links or parts thereof from any material other than metal;

(iii) clasps, slides, ornaments and similar articles used on wearing apparel when such articles are made—

(1) wholly or mainly from any material other than metal, and

(2) in a branch or department in which articles mentioned in sub-paragraph (a) are made or carded;

(c) (i) the carding wherever carried on of any of the articles specified in sub-paragraph (a) above;

(ii) the carding of any of the articles specified in sub-paragraph (b) above, except when done apart from any of the making which is included in the trade herein specified and from the carding of articles specified in sub-paragraph (a);

(a) S.R. & O. 1938/1497 (1938 II, p. 3238).

(d) The manufacture of metal small-wares as specified in Paragraphs (1) to (6) of the Appendix to the Trade Boards (Stamped or Pressed Metal-Wares) Order 1924(a)*, when carried on in an establishment mainly engaged in any of the processes or operations mentioned above;

(e) All processes and operations in the (i) assembling, or (ii) finishing of articles specified above when done in association with or in conjunction with any of the above-mentioned processes or operations;

(f) All processes and operations in the warehousing, packing or despatching of any of the articles specified above when done in association with or in conjunction with any of the above-mentioned processes or operations.

2. Notwithstanding anything in this Schedule the following processes or operations shall not be processes or operations of the Button Manufacturing Trade:—

(a) The manufacture of wooden button-moulds where not carried on in association with or in conjunction with button-making;

(b) the making of buttons or the covering of button-moulds in an establishment in which (i) such work is performed in association with or in conjunction with the making of wearing apparel and (ii) the majority of the buttons made or of the button-moulds covered are for use on such wearing apparel;

(c) The making of buttons or the covering of button-moulds when done in association with or in conjunction with the manufacture of embroidery and trimmings, unless such making of buttons or covering of button-moulds is done (i) by machine process and (ii) in a separate department by workers exclusively engaged thereon;

(d) The processes or operations specified in Paragraph 1 above when performed in an establishment mainly engaged in the manufacture of articles of real or imitation jewellery except when performed by a worker who during the whole time that he works in any week in such establishment is wholly or mainly employed on such processes or operations;

(e) Any work which by Paragraph (7) of the Appendix to the Trade Boards (Stamped or Pressed Metal-Wares) Order, 1924*, is included in the Stamped or Pressed Metal-Wares Trade."

*(Paragraphs (1) to (7) of the Appendix to the Trade Boards (Stamped or Pressed Metal-Wares) Order 1924, referred to in the Schedule to the Trade Boards (Button Manufacturing Trade, Great Britain) (Constitution and Proceedings) Regulations 1938, set out above are as follows:—

(1) The manufacture from metal in sheet or strip form by cold stamping or cold pressing of articles known in the trade as metal small wares;

(2) the cutting, shearing, annealing and hardening of metal in an establishment in which the metal is used for such manufacture;

(3) the covering of corset steels prior to capping or tipping in an establishment in which the steels are capped or tipped;

(4) finishing (including dipping, nickelling, plating, tinning, japanning, stove-enamelling, lacquering, bronzing, colouring, painting, varnishing, barrelling, burnishing, grinding, planishing, polishing, and the capping, counting, lopping, studding, or tipping of corset busks or steels) and similar operations when done in conjunction with such manufacture;

(5) viewing, inspecting, testing, sorting, boxing, carding, carrying, delivering, despatching, labelling, packeting, packing, portering, warehousing, weighing and similar processes or operations when done in conjunction with such manufacture;

(a) S.R. & O. 1924/832 (1924, p. 1753).

(6) the assembling of the above-mentioned wares or parts thereof, whether the things assembled are made inside or outside Great Britain; and

(7) any process or operation which is included in the Button-making Trade, as defined for the purposes of the Trade Boards Acts, when carried on in an establishment mainly engaged in any of the processes or operations defined in the preceding paragraphs hereof.)

EXPLANATORY NOTE

(*This Note is not part of the Order.*)

This Order, which has effect from 3rd May 1974, sets out the increased statutory minimum remuneration, and, in certain circumstances, cost of living payments, due to workers in relation to whom the Button Manufacturing Wages Council (Great Britain) operates in substitution for that fixed by the Wages Regulation Button Manufacturing Order 1970 (Order V. (69)) which Order is revoked.

New provisions are printed in italics.

STATUTORY INSTRUMENTS

1974 No. 675

WAGES COUNCILS

The Wages Regulation (Button Manufacturing) (Holidays) Order 1974

Made - - - -	*5th April* 1974
Coming into Operation	*3rd May* 1974

Whereas the Secretary of State has received from the Button Manufacturing Wages Council (Great Britain) the wages regulation proposals set out in the Schedule hereto ;

Now, therefore, the Secretary of State in exercise of powers conferred by section 11 of the Wages Councils Act 1959(a), as modified by Article 2 of the Counter-Inflation (Modification of Wages Councils Act 1959) Order 1973(b), and now vested in him(c), and of all other powers enabling him in that behalf, hereby makes the following Order : —

1. This Order may be cited as the Wages Regulation (Button Manufacturing) (Holidays) Order 1974.

2.—(1) In this Order the expression " the specified date " means the 3rd May 1974, provided that where, as respects any worker who is paid wages at intervals not exceeding seven days, that date does not correspond with the beginning of the period for which the wages are paid, the expression " the specified date " means, as respects that worker, the beginning of the next such period following that date.

(2) The Interpretation Act 1889(d) shall apply to the interpretation of this Order as it applies to the interpretation of an Act of Parliament and as if this Order and the Order hereby revoked were Acts of Parliament.

3. The wages regulation proposals set out in the Schedule hereto shall have effect as from the specified date and as from that date the Button Manufacturing Wages Council (Great Britain) Wages Regulation (Holidays) Order 1970(e) shall cease to have effect.

Signed by order of the Secretary of State.

5th April 1974.

W. H. Marsh,

Assistant Secretary,
Department of Employment.

(a) 1959 c. 69.   (b) S.I. 1973/661 (1973 I, p. 2141).
(c) S.I. 1959/1769, 1968/729 (1959 I, p. 1795; 1968 II, p. 2108).
(d) 1889 c. 63.   (e) S.I. 1970/1479 (1970 III, p. 4823).

Article 3

SCHEDULE

The following provisions as to holidays and holiday remuneration shall be substituted for the provisions as to holidays and holiday remuneration set out in Order V. (70).

PART I

APPLICATION

1. This Schedule applies to every worker (other than a homeworker) for whom statutory minimum remuneration has been fixed.

PART II

CUSTOMARY HOLIDAYS

2.—(1) An employer shall allow to every worker to whom this Schedule applies a holiday (hereinafter in this Schedule referred to as a " customary holiday ") in each year on the days specified in the following sub-paragraph, provided that the worker has been in his employment for a period of not less than four weeks immediately preceding the customary holiday and has worked for the employer during the whole or part of that period and (unless excused by the employer or absent by reason of the proved illness of the worker) has worked for the employer throughout the last working day on which work was available to him prior to the customary holiday.

(2) The said customary holidays are:—

(a) (i) In England and Wales—

Christmas Day ;
26th December if it be not a Sunday, 27th December in a year when 25th or 26th December is a Sunday ;

Good Friday ;

Easter Monday ;

the last Monday in May ;

the last Monday in August ;

(or, where a day is substituted for any of the above days by national proclamation, that day) ;

(ii) In Scotland :—

New Year's Day (or, if New Year's Day falls on a Sunday, the following Monday) ;

the local Spring holiday ;

the local Autumn holiday ; and

three other days (being days on which the worker normally works for the employer) in the course of a calendar year to be fixed by the employer and notified to the worker not less than three weeks before the holiday ; or

(b) in the case of each of the said days (other than a day fixed by the employer in Scotland and notified to the worker as aforesaid) a day substituted by the employer therefor, being a day recognised by local custom as a day of holiday in substitution for the said day.

(3) Notwithstanding the preceding provisions of this paragraph, an employer may (except where in the case of a woman or young person such a requirement would be unlawful) require a worker who is otherwise entitled to any customary

holiday under the foregoing provisions of this Schedule to work thereon and, in lieu of any customary holiday on which he so works, the employer shall allow to the worker a day's holiday (hereinafter in this Schedule referred to as a " holiday in lieu of a customary holiday ") on a weekday on which he would normally work for the employer, within the period of four weeks next ensuing.

(4) A worker who is required to work on a customary holiday shall be paid: —

(a) for all time worked thereon at the minimum rate then appropriate to the worker for work on a customary holiday ; and

(b) in respect of the holiday in lieu of the customary holiday, holiday remuneration in accordance with paragraph 6 of this Schedule.

PART III

ANNUAL HOLIDAY

3.—(1) Subject to the provisions of this paragraph and of paragraph 4, in addition to the holidays specified in Part II of this Schedule an employer shall, between the date on which this Schedule becomes effective and 30th September 1974, and in each succeeding year between 1st May and 30th September, allow a holiday (hereinafter referred to as an " annual holiday ") to every worker in his employment to whom this Schedule applies who has been employed by him during the 12 months immediately preceding the commencement of the holiday season for any of the periods of employment (calculated in accordance with the provisions of paragraph 10) set out in the table below and the duration of the annual holiday shall in the case of each such worker be related to his period of employment during that 12 months as follows: —

Period of employment	Duration of annual holiday for workers with a normal working week of:—	
	Five days	Four days or less
At least 48 weeks	15 days	12 days
,, ,, 44 ,, ...	13 ,,	11 ,,
,, ,, 40 ,, ...	12 ,,	10 ,,
,, ,, 36 ,, ...	11 ,,	9 ,,
,, ,, 32 ,, ...	10 ,,	8 ,,
,, ,, 28 ,, ...	8 ,,	7 ,,
,, ,, 24 ,, ...	7 ,,	6 ,,
,, ,, 20 ,, ...	6 ,,	5 ,,
,, ,, 16 ,, ...	5 ,,	4 ,,
,, ,, 12 ,, ...	3 ,,	3 ,,
,, ,, 8 ,, ...	2 ,,	2 ,,
,, ,, 4 ,, ...	1 day	1 day

(2) Notwithstanding the provisions of the last foregoing sub-paragraph the number of days of annual holiday which an employer is required to allow to a worker in respect of a period of employment during the 12 months immediately preceding 1st May 1974, and during the 12 months immediately preceding 1st May in any succeeding year, shall not exceed in the aggregate three times the number of days constituting the worker's normal working week.

(3) Where before the expiration of any holiday season a worker enters into an agreement in writing with his employer that the annual holiday or part thereof shall be allowed on a specified date or dates after the expiration of the holiday season but before the commencement of the next following holiday season, then any day or days of annual holiday so allowed shall for the purposes of this Schedule be treated as having been allowed during the holiday season.

(4) The duration of the workers' annual holiday during the holiday season ending on 30th September 1974 shall be reduced by any days of holiday with pay (not being days of customary holiday) which have been allowed to him by the employer under the provisions of Order V.(70), between 6th April 1974 and the date on which this Schedule becomes effective.

(5) In this Schedule the expression " holiday season " means in relation to the year 1974 the period commencing with the date on which the provisions of this Schedule become effective and ending on 30th September 1974, and in each succeeding year, the period commencing on 1st May and ending on 30th September of the same year.

4.—(1) Subject to the provisions of this paragraph, an annual holiday shall be allowed on consecutive working days, being days on which the worker is normally called upon to work for the employer, and days of annual holiday shall be treated as consecutive notwithstanding that a Sunday, a customary holiday on which the worker is not required to work for the employer or a holiday in lieu of a customary holiday intervenes.

(2)(*a*) Where the number of days of annual holiday for which a worker has qualified exceeds the number of days constituting his normal working week but does not exceed twice that number, the holiday may be allowed in two separate periods of consecutive working days ; so however that when a holiday is so allowed, one of the periods shall consist of a number of such days not less than the number of days constituting the worker's normal working week ;

(*b*) Where the number of days of annual holiday for which a worker has qualified exceeds twice the number of days constituting his normal working week the holiday may be allowed as follows : —

    (i) as to one or two periods of consecutive working days, comprising not more than twice the number of days constituting the worker's normal working week, during the holiday season : so however that one of such periods is not less than the period constituting the worker's normal working week ;

    (ii) as to any additional days, on working days which need not be consecutive, to be fixed by the employer, either during the holiday season or before the beginning of the next following holiday season.

(3) One day of annual holiday may be allowed on a non-consecutive working day (other than the worker's weekly short day) falling within the holiday season (or after the holiday season in the circumstances specified in sub-paragraph (2)(*b*)(ii) of this paragraph) where the annual holiday or, as the case may be, such separate period, is allowed immediately after a customary holiday or so that such a holiday intervenes.

(4) Any day of annual holiday under this Schedule may be allowed on a day on which the worker is entitled to a day of holiday or to a half-holiday under any enactment other than the Wages Councils Act 1959.

5. An employer shall give to a worker reasonable notice of the commencing date or dates and duration of the period or periods of his annual holiday. Such notice shall be given at least three months before the first day of the holiday and may be given individually to the worker or by the posting of a notice in the place where the worker is employed.

PART IV

HOLIDAY REMUNERATION

A.—CUSTOMARY HOLIDAYS AND HOLIDAYS IN LIEU OF
CUSTOMARY HOLIDAYS

6.—(1) Subject to the provisions of this paragraph, for each day of holiday to
which a worker is entitled under Part II of this Schedule he shall be paid
by the employer holiday remuneration equal to the amount to which he would
have been entitled, calculated at the appropriate rate of statutory minimum
remuneration, if the day had not been a day of holiday and he had worked on
that day on work for which statutory minimum remuneration is payable for
the time usually worked by him on that day of the week.

Provided, however, that payment of the said holiday remuneration is subject
to the condition that the worker presents himself for employment within one
hour of the usual starting hour on the first working day following the holiday
or, if he fails to do so, failure is by reason of the proved illness of the worker
or with the consent of the employer.

(2) The holiday remuneration in respect of any customary holiday shall be
paid by the employer to the worker not later than the pay day on which the
wages are paid for the first working day following the holiday.

(3) The holiday remuneration in respect of any holiday in lieu of a customary
holiday shall be paid not later than the pay day on which the wages are paid
for the first working day following the holiday in lieu of a customary holiday.
Provided that the said payment shall be made immediately upon the termination of the worker's employment in the case where he ceases to be employed
before being allowed a holiday in lieu of a customary holiday to which he is
entitled, and in that case the proviso contained in sub-paragraph (1) of this
paragraph shall not apply.

B.—ANNUAL HOLIDAY

7.—(1) Subject to the provisions of paragraph 8 of this Schedule, a worker
qualified to be allowed an annual holiday under this Schedule shall be paid
by his employer in respect thereof, on the last pay day preceding such annual
holiday, one day's holiday pay (as defined in paragraph 11 of this Schedule) in
respect of each day thereof.

(2) Where under the provisions of paragraph 4 of this Schedule an annual
holiday is allowed in more than one period, the holiday remuneration shall be
apportioned accordingly.

8. Where any accrued holiday remuneration has been paid by the employer to
the worker in accordance with paragraph 9 of this Schedule or in accordance
with the provisions of Order V. (70) in respect of employment during any of
the periods referred to in that paragraph or that Order respectively, the amount
of holiday remuneration payable by the employer in respect of any annual holiday
for which the worker has qualified by reason of employment during the said
period shall be reduced by the amount of the said accrued holiday remuneration
unless that remuneration has been deducted from a previous payment of holiday
remuneration made under the provisions of this Schedule.

ACCRUED HOLIDAY REMUNERATION PAYABLE ON TERMINATION OF EMPLOYMENT

9. Where a worker ceases to be employed by an employer after the provisions of this Schedule become effective the employer shall, immediately on the termination of the employment, pay to the worker as accrued holiday remuneration: —

(1) in respect of employment in the twelve months up to and including 30th April immediately preceding the termination date, a sum equal to the holiday remuneration for any days of annual holiday for which he has qualified, except days of annual holiday which he has been allowed or has become entitled to be allowed before leaving the employment; and

(2) in respect of any employment since 30th April immediately preceding the termination date, a sum equal to the holiday remuneration which would have been payable to him if he could have been allowed an annual holiday in respect of that employment at the time of leaving it.

PART V

GENERAL

10. For the purposes of calculating any period of employment qualifying a worker for an annual holiday or for any accrued holiday remuneration under this Schedule, the worker shall be treated: —

(1) as if he were employed for a week in respect of any week in which—
(a) he has worked for the employer for not less than sixteen hours and has performed some work for which statutory minimum remuneration is payable; or

(b) (i) he has been absent throughout the week, or

(ii) he has worked for the employer for less than sixteen hours solely by reason of the proved illness of, or accident to, the worker, provided that the number of weeks which may be treated as weeks of employment for such reason shall not exceed eight in the aggregate in the period of twelve months immediately preceding the commencement of the holiday season; or

(c) he is absent from work owing to suspension due to shortage of work, provided that the number of weeks which may be treated as weeks of employment for such reason shall not exceed eight in the aggregate in the period of twelve months last mentioned, and

(2) as if he were employed on any day of holiday allowed under the provisions of this Schedule or of the Schedule to Order V. (70), and for the purposes of the provisions of sub-paragraph (1) of this paragraph, a worker who is absent on such a holiday shall be treated as having worked thereon for the employer for the number of hours ordinarily worked by him on that day of the week on work for which statutory minimum remuneration is payable.

11. In this Schedule, unless the context otherwise requires, the following expressions have the meanings hereby respectively assigned to them, that is to say: —

" appropriate rate of statutory minimum remuneration " means—
(a) in the case of a time worker, the rate or rates of statutory minimum remuneration applicable to the worker, and

(b) in the case of a piece worker, the rate or rates of statutory minimum remuneration which would be applicable to the worker if he were a time worker.

"normal working week" means the number of days on which it has been usual for the worker to work in a week in the employment of the employer during the twelve months immediately preceding the commencement of the holiday season or, where under paragraph 9 of this Schedule accrued holiday remuneration is payable on the termination of the employment, during the twelve months immediately preceding the date of the termination of the employment.

Provided that—

(i) part of a day shall count as a day ;

(ii) no account shall be taken of any week in which the worker did not perform any work for which statutory minimum remuneration has been fixed.

"one day's holiday pay" means the appropriate proportion of the remuneration which the worker would be entitled to receive from his employer at the date of the annual holiday (or where the holiday is allowed in more than one period at the date of the first period) or at the termination date, as the case may require, for one week's work if working his normal working week and the number of daily hours normally worked by him (exclusive of overtime), and if paid at the appropriate rate of statutory minimum remuneration for work for which statutory minimum remuneration is payable and at the same rate for any work for which such remuneration is not payable, and in this definition "appropriate proportion" means—

where the worker's normal working week is five days ... one-fifth

where the worker's normal working week is four days or less ... ... one-quarter

"statutory minimum remuneration" means statutory minimum remuneration (other than holiday remuneration) fixed by a wages regulation order made by the Secretary of State to give effect to proposals submitted to him by the Wages Council.

"week" in paragraphs 3 and 10 means "pay week".

12. The provisions of this Schedule are without prejudice to any agreement for the allowance of any further holidays with pay or for the payment of additional holiday remuneration.

EXPLANATORY NOTE

(This Note is not part of the Order.)

This Order, which has effect from 3rd May 1974, sets out the holidays which an employer is required to allow to workers in relation to whom the Button Manufacturing Wages Council operates and the remuneration payable for those holidays. It also amends the provisions relating to customary holidays contained in the Wages Regulation (Button Manufacturing) (Holidays) Order 1970 (Order V.(70)) so as to take account of recent changes in the law and practice relating to public holidays. Order V.(70) is revoked.

New provisions are printed in italics.

STATUTORY INSTRUMENTS

1974 No. 676

CUSTOMS AND EXCISE
The Import Duties (Quota Relief) (No. 3) Order 1974

Made - - - -	*5th April* 1974
Laid before the House of Commons	*8th April* 1974
Coming into Operation	*9th April* 1974

The Secretary of State, in exercise of the powers conferred on him by section 5(1) and (4) of, and paragraph 8 of Schedule 3 to, the Import Duties Act 1958(a), as amended (b), and of all other powers enabling him in that behalf, hereby makes the following Order:

1.—(1) This Order may be cited as the Import Duties (Quota Relief) (No. 3) Order 1974 and shall come into operation on 9th April 1974.

(2) The Interpretation Act 1889(c) shall apply for the interpretation of this Order as it applies for the interpretation of an Act of Parliament.

2.—(1) Up to and including 30th June 1974 no import duty shall be charged on a quantity of 50,000 tonnes (hereinafter referred to as the "quota") of goods of heading 73.08 (iron or steel coils for re-rolling) of the Customs Tariff 1959.

(2) The following classes of goods shall not be treated as forming part of the quota, namely:

(*a*) goods on which, apart from this Order, no import duty would be chargeable;

(*b*) goods exempt from duty by virtue of Article 3 below.

(3) Goods shall be treated as forming part of the quota in the order in which they are entered for home use (within the meaning of the Customs and Excise Act 1952(d)) in the United Kingdom on or after the date of coming into operation of this Order.

3.—(1) So long as relief is available in respect of the quota, no import duty shall be charged on goods of the said heading 73.08 which satisfy the requisite conditions to benefit from Regulation (EEC) 385/73(e) (relating to goods entitled to benefit from the eventual abolition of customs duties in trade between the United Kingdom and the other Member States of the Communities).

(2) For the purpose of paragraph (1) above relief shall be treated as being available in respect of the quota until two days after the end of the last day on which goods of that heading are entitled to exemption from import duty by virtue of Article 2 above.

Peter Shore,
Secretary of State for Trade.

5th April 1974.

(a) 1958 c. 6.
(b) *See* paragraph 1 of Schedule 4 to the European Communities Act 1972 (c. 68).
(c) 1889 c. 63.   (d) 1952 c. 44.
(e) O.J. L 42, 14.2.1973, p. 1.

EXPLANATORY NOTE

(This Note is not part of the Order.)

This Order, which comes into operation on 9th April 1974, provides for the opening and administration of a tariff quota of 50,000 tonnes of iron and steel coils for re-rolling. This is a renewal of the tariff quota the opening and administration of which was provided for by the Import Duties (Quota Relief) Order 1974 (S.I. 1974/96).

The Order provides for exemption from import duty until 30th June 1974 for imports of such goods within the quota.

Goods are treated as forming part of the quota in the order in which they are entered for home use on or after the date of coming into operation of this Order.

The Order also provides that goods shall not constitute part of the quota if duty would not be chargeable apart from this Order, and that no duty shall be chargeable on goods satisfying the requisite conditions to benefit from the eventual abolition of customs duties between the United Kingdom and other Member States of the Communities until after the quota has been exhausted.

STATUTORY INSTRUMENTS

1974 No. 677

CUSTOMS AND EXCISE

The Customs Duties (Quota Relief) (No. 3) Order 1974

Made - - - -	*5th April* 1974
Laid before the House of Commons	*8th April* 1974
Coming into Operation	*1st May* 1974

The Secretary of State, in exercise of the powers conferred on him by section 5(1) and (4) of, and paragraph 8 of Schedule 3 to, the Import Duties Act 1958(a), as amended (b), and of all other powers enabling him in that behalf, hereby makes the following Order:

1.—(1) This Order may be cited as the Customs Duties (Quota Relief) (No. 3) Order 1974 and shall come into operation on 1st May 1974.

(2) The Interpretation Act 1889(c) shall apply for the interpretation of this Order as it applies for the interpretation of an Act of Parliament.

2.—(1) Up to and including 31st December 1974—

(a) any import duty for the time being chargeable or

(b) any additional amount of customs duty under the Hydrocarbon Oil (Customs and Excise) Act 1971(d) chargeable by virtue of column 2 of Schedule 1 to the Hydrocarbon Oil (Customs Duties) Order 1973(e)

on goods of a subheading of the Customs Tariff 1959 specified in column 1 of the Schedule hereto shall be reduced to the relevant rate shown in column 2 thereof if the goods are refined in Egypt and form part of the quota of goods which are to be subject to reduced rates of duty on import into the United Kingdom by virtue of Regulation (EEC) No. 369/74(f).

(2) Goods shall be treated as forming part of the quota referred to in paragraph (1) above in the order in which they are entered for home use (within the meaning of the Customs and Excise Act 1952(g)) in the United Kingdom on or after the date on which this Order comes into operation.

Peter Shore,
Secretary of State for Trade.

5th April 1974.

(a) 1958 c. 6.
(b) *See* section 5(5) of, and paragraph 1 of Schedule 4 to, the European Communities Act 1972 (c. 68).
(c) 1889 c. 63. (d) 1971 c. 12.
(e) S.I. 1973/1948 (1973 III, p. 6753). (f) O.J. No. L 48, 20.2.1974, p. 79.
(g) 1952 c. 44.

SCHEDULE

GOODS OF EGYPT SUBJECT TO REDUCTIONS IN DUTY WITHIN A QUOTA

Tariff Heading (1)	Rates of duty (2)
(Certain petroleum products in tariff headings 27.10–27.14)	
27.10 A III a) b) B III a) b) 1 C III d) 1	1%*
27.10 C I c) 1 C II c) 1	0·6%*
27.10 C III c) 1	0·7%*
27.10 B III b) 2 aa) C III d) 2 aa)	2·7%*
27.10 C III c) 2 aa)	1·8%*
27.10 B III b) 2 bb)	3%
27.10 C I c) 2 C II c) 2 C III c) 2 bb) C III d) 2 bb)	3%
27.11 B I c) 1 c) 2	4·8% 3%
27.12 A III a) A III b) B I B II	0·3%* 3% 1·2%* 3·1%
27.13 B I c) 1 c) 2 c) 3 B II a) b) c)	0·3% 6% 3% 1% 6% 3%
27·14 C II a) b)	0·3%* 3%

These goods are also subject to (non-protective) hydrocarbon oil duties.

EXPLANATORY NOTE

(This Note is not part of the Order.)

This Order, which comes into operation on 1st May 1974, provides for the implementation and administration of the United Kingdom's share of the tariff quota opened by the European Economic Community for certain petroleum products refined in Egypt under the provisions of Regulation (EEC) 369/74.

The Schedule to the Order specifies the reduced rates of customs duty—whether import duties or protective elements of revenue duties—applicable up to and including 31st December 1974 to imports of the relevant products within the United Kingdom's share of the quota.

The Order also provides that goods which constitute part of that share of the quota do so in the order in which they are entered for home use in the United Kingdom.

STATUTORY INSTRUMENTS

1974 No. 678

FOOD AND DRUGS

The Butter Subsidy Amendment Regulations 1974

Made - - -	8th April 1974
Laid before Parliament	10th April 1974
Coming into Operation	1st May 1974

The Secretary of State for Social Services and the Minister of Agriculture, Fisheries and Food, being Ministers designated (a) for the purposes of section 2(2) of the European Communities Act 1972(b) in relation to the Common Agricultural Policy of the European Economic Community, in exercise of the powers conferred on them by the said section 2(2) hereby make the following regulations : —

Citation, interpretation and commencement

1. These regulations which may be cited as the Butter Subsidy Amendment Regulations 1974 shall be read as one with the Butter Subsidy Regulations 1974(c) (hereinafter called "the principal regulations") and shall come into operation on 1st May 1974.

Amendment of the Butter Subsidy Regulations 1974

2.—(1) In regulations 3(2), 4(2) and 5(1) of the principal regulations for the words "4½ pence" in each place where they occur, there shall be substituted the words "6 pence".

(2) Nothing in this regulation shall affect the operation of the principal regulations in relation to a butter token issued for any period prior to the date of coming into operation of this regulation notwithstanding that it may have been accepted by a supplier after that date.

Barbara Castle,
Secretary of State for Social Services.
8th April 1974.

In witness whereof the official seal of the Minister of Agriculture, Fisheries and Food is hereunto affixed on 8th April 1974.

(L.S.)

Frederick Peart,
Minister of Agriculture, Fisheries and Food.

(a) S.I. 1972/1811 (1972 III, p. 5216).   (b) 1972 c. 68.
(c) S.I. 1974/54 (1974 I, p. 196).

EXPLANATORY NOTE

(This Note is not part of the Regulations.)

These Regulations amend the Butter Subsidy Regulations 1974 by increasing the amount of the subsidy with effect from 1st May 1974. Persons entitled to butter tokens will be able to purchase 2 one-half pounds of butter a month at a price of 6 pence a half pound below that at which it would otherwise have been sold (hitherto the rate was 4½ pence a half pound).

The Regulations take advantage of an increase in the amount of subsidy which may be granted in the United Kingdom under Commission Decision 73/10/EEC, OJ No. L 40, 13.2.1973 p.15 (as corrected by OJ No. L 78, 27.3.1973, p.26 and as amended by OJ No. L 77, 26.3.1973, p.46 and OJ No. L 30, 4.2.1974, p.23); this increase derives from a change in the compensatory amount applicable to trade in butter between the United Kingdom and the European Economic Community as originally constituted.

STATUTORY INSTRUMENTS

1974 No. 682

CUSTOMS AND EXCISE
The Import Duties (Temporary Reductions and Exemptions) (No. 5) Order 1974

Made - - - -	*8th April* 1974
Laid before the House of Commons	*19th April* 1974
Coming into Operation	*20th April* 1974

The Lords Commissioners of Her Majesty's Treasury, by virtue of the powers conferred on them by sections 1, 3(6) and 13 of the Import Duties Act 1958(a), as amended (b), and of all other powers enabling them in that behalf, on the recommendation of the Secretary of State (c), hereby make the following Order:

Citation, operation, interpretation

1.—(1) This Order may be cited as the Import Duties (Temporary Reductions and Exemptions) (No. 5) Order 1974 and shall come into operation on 20th April 1974.

(2) In this Order "the relevant date" in relation to goods of a descripton specified in column 2 of the Schedule hereto means 31st December 1974 or, if an earlier date is there specified in relation to the description, the date so specified.

(3) The Interpretation Act 1889(d) shall apply for the interpretation of this Order as it applies for the interpretation of an Act of Parliament.

Intra-Community trade

2. Up to and including the relevant date, no import duty shall be charged on goods of a heading of the Customs Tariff 1959 specified in column 1 of the Schedule hereto which are of a description specified in column 2 thereof if they satisfy the requisite conditions to benefit from Regulation (EEC) 385/73(e) (relating to goods entitled to benefit from the eventual abolition of customs duties in trade between member States of the European Communities).

The full rate

3.—(1) Up to and including the relevant date, in the case of goods which fall within a heading of the Customs Tariff 1959 specified in column 1 of the Schedule hereto which are of a description specified in column 2 thereof, if a rate of duty is shown in column 3 thereof in relation to the goods, import duty

---

(a) 1958 c. 6.
(b) *See* section 5(5) of, and paragraph 1 of Schedule 4 to, the European Communities Act 1972 (c. 68).
(c) *See* S.I. 1970/1537 (1970 III, p. 5293).
(d) 1889 c. 63.　　　　　　　　　　　(e) O.J. No. L 42, 14.2.1973, p. 1.

shall be charged at the rate so shown instead of any higher rate which would otherwise apply, and if the entry "free" appears in relation to them, no import duty shall be charged.

(2) If no entry appears in column 3 of the Schedule hereto in relation to goods of a description specified in column 2 thereof, no exemption from or reduction in duty applies to such goods by virtue of this Article.

(3) Paragraph (1) above shall operate without prejudice to the exemption provided for by Article 2 above or any greater reductions provided for by Article 4 below in the case of goods originating in Egypt or Cyprus.

Egypt and Cyprus

4.—(1) Up to and including the relevant date, any import duty for the time being chargeable on goods of a heading of the Customs Tariff 1959 specified in column 1 of the Schedule hereto which are of a description specified in column 2 thereof shall be charged:

(*a*) at the rate, if any, shown in column 4 thereof in relation to the description if the goods originate in Egypt and

(*b*) at the rate, if any, shown in column 5 thereof in relation to the description if the goods originate in Cyprus.

(2) For the purposes of paragraph (1) above goods shall be regarded as originating:

(*a*) in Egypt if they are to be so regarded under the Agreement, signed on 18th December 1972, between the European Economic Community and Egypt**(a)** and

(*b*) in Cyprus if they are to be so regarded under the Agreement, signed on 19th December 1972, between the Community and Cyprus **(b)**.

(3) If no entry appears in column 4 or 5 of the Schedule in relation to goods of a description specified in column 2 thereof, no reduction in duty applies by virtue of this Article to goods of that description originating in Egypt or Cyprus.

(4) This Article shall operate without prejudice to any greater reduction in, or to any exemption from, import duties which may be available apart from this Order in the case of goods herein referred to by virtue of their being goods of a developing country or goods qualifying for Commonwealth preference or otherwise.

Miscellaneous

5.—(1) Any description in column 2 of the Schedule hereto shall be taken to comprise all goods which would be classified under an entry in the same terms constituting a subheading (other than the final subheading) in the relevant heading in the Customs Tariff 1959.

(a) The Agreement is annexed to Regulation (EEC) 2409/73 (O.J. No. L 251, p. 1).
(b) The Agreement is annexed to Regulation (EEC) 1246/73 (O.J. No. L 133, p. 1).

(2) For the purposes of classification under the Customs Tariff 1959, insofar as that depends on the rate of duty, any goods to which this Order applies shall be treated as chargeable with the same duty as if this Order had not been made.

Donald R. Coleman,
James Hamilton,
Two of the Lords Commissioners
of Her Majesty's Treasury.

8th April 1974.

NOTE: *Where no rate of duty is shown in column 3 there is no reduction in the full rate and where no rate is shown in columns 4 and 5 there is no reduction in the case of goods of Egypt or Cyprus as such.*

SCHEDULE

GOODS SUBJECT TO TEMPORARY REDUCTION IN OR EXEMPTION FROM IMPORT DUTY

Tariff Heading (1)	Description (2)	Rates of Duty %		
		Full (3)	Egypt (4)	Cyprus (5)
27.11	Propene of a purity not less than 90 per cent. but less than 95 per cent. (up to and including 2nd September 1974)	1·5	0·7	0·4
29.01	Propene of a purity not less than 95 per cent. (up to and including 2nd September 1974)	Free	—	—
29.08	Digol	16	7·2	4·8
30.03	Bleomycin sulphate	—	6	4
73.18	Longitudinally welded steel tubes in lengths of not less than 1·5 metres and not more than 6 metres having an outside diameter of not less than 48 millimetres and not more than 50 millimetres; with a wall thickness of not less than 3·5 millimetres and not more than 5 millimetres; containing not more than 0·06 per cent. sulphur and not more than 0·06 per cent. phosphorus; having a tensile strength of not less than 34 Kgf/mm^2 and not more than 48 Kgf/mm^2 and a minimum yield stress of 21·3 Kgf/mm^2 (up to and including 1st July 1974).	10	4·5	3

EXPLANATORY NOTE

(This Note is not part of the Order.)

This Order provides for exemption from or reductions in import duty in the case of goods specified in the Schedule to the Order from 20th April 1974 until 31st December 1974 or any earlier date appearing in the Schedule.

There is exemption from import duties in the case of all goods in the Schedule if the goods satisfy the requisite conditions to benefit from the eventual abolition of customs duties in trade between member States of the European Communities.

In the case of other goods, where a rate of duty is specified in column 3 of the Schedule, duty is reduced to that rate, instead of any higher rate which would otherwise apply, and where "free" appears in column 3 in relation to the goods, they are exempt from duty.

In the case of goods originating in Egypt or Cyprus greater reductions in duty are available in a number of cases than those referred to above. These are shown respectively in columns 4 and 5 of the Schedule.

1974 No. 683

LOCAL GOVERNMENT, ENGLAND AND WALES

The Local Government Administration (Representative Body for England) Order 1974

Made - - -	*9th April* 1974	
Laid before Parliament	*10th April* 1974	
Coming into Operation	*1st May* 1974	

The Secretary of State for the Environment, in exercise of the powers conferred upon him by section 24(1) of the Local Government Act 1974(a) and of all other powers enabling him in that behalf, hereby makes the following order:—

Title and commencement

1. This order may be cited as the Local Government Administration (Representative Body for England) Order 1974 and shall come into operation on 1st May 1974.

Interpretation

2. The Interpretation Act 1889(b) shall apply for the interpretation of this order as it applies for the interpretation of an Act of Parliament.

Designation of representative body for England

3. For the purposes of section 24 of the Local Government Act 1974 (which provides for the designation of bodies representing the authorities to which are applied the provisions of the Act with regard to investigations of alleged maladministration) a body consisting of—

(*a*) 3 members appointed by the Association of County Councils,

(*b*) 3 members appointed by the Association of District Councils,

(*c*) 3 members appointed by the Association of Metropolitan Authorities,

(*d*) 1 member appointed by the Greater London Council
      and

(*e*) 1 member appointed by the National Water Council

is hereby designated as the representative body for England.

Anthony Crosland,
Secretary of State for
the Environment.

9th April 1974.

(a) 1974 c. 7.   (b) 1889 c. 63.

EXPLANATORY NOTE

(This Note is not part of the Order.)

Part III of the Local Government Act 1974 sets up machinery for the investigation of alleged maladministration by local and certain other authorities. Investigations in England are to be carried out by Local Commissioners who submit reports to the Commission for Local Administration in England, and the Commission in turn submit reports to the representative body for England, which represents the authorities to which Part III applies. This Order designates as the representative body for England a body consisting of members nominated by certain associations of local authorities, the Greater London Council and the National Water Council.

STATUTORY INSTRUMENTS

1974 No. 684

INDUSTRIAL TRAINING

The Industrial Training Levy (Hotel and Catering) Order 1974

Made - - - -	*9th April* 1974
Laid before Parliament	*23rd April* 1974
Coming into Operation	*16th May* 1974

The Secretary of State after approving proposals submitted by the Hotel and Catering Industry Training Board for the imposition of a further levy on employers in the hotel and catering industry and in exercise of powers conferred by section 4 of the Industrial Training Act 1964(a) as amended by paragraph 2(2) of Part I of Schedule 2 to the Employment and Training Act 1973 (b), and of all other powers enabling him in that behalf hereby makes the following Order:—

Title and commencement

1. This Order may be cited as the Industrial Training Levy (Hotel and Catering) Order 1974 and shall come into operation on 16th May 1974.

Interpretation

2.—(1) In this Order unless the context otherwise requires:—

(*a*) "agriculture" has the same meaning as in section 109(3) of the Agriculture Act 1947(c) or, in relation to Scotland, as in section 86(3) of the Agriculture (Scotland) Act 1948(d);

(*b*) "an appeal tribunal" means an industrial tribunal established under section 12 of the Industrial Training Act 1964;

(*c*) "assessment" means an assessment of an employer to the levy;

(*d*) "the Board" means the Hotel and Catering Industry Training Board;

(*e*) "British Airways Group" means the British Airways Board, the British Overseas Airways Corporation, the British European Airways Corporation and all subsidiaries and joint subsidiaries, and "member of the British Airways Group" shall be construed accordingly;

(*f*) "charity" has the same meaning as in section 360 of the Income and Corporation Taxes Act 1970(e);

(*g*) "the eighth base period" means the period of twelve months that commenced on 6th April 1973;

(*h*) "the eighth levy period" means the period commencing with the day upon which this Order comes into operation and ending on 31st March 1975;

(*i*) "emoluments" means all emoluments assessable to income tax under Schedule E (other than pensions), being emoluments from which tax

---

(**a**) 1964 c. 16. (**b**) 1973 c. 50.
(**c**) 1947 c. 48. (**d**) 1948 c. 45.
(**e**) 1970 c. 10.

under that Schedule is deductible, whether or not tax in fact falls to be deducted from any particular payment thereof;

(*j*) "employer" means a person who is an employer in the hotel and catering industry at any time in the eighth levy period;

(*k*) "establishment" (except in sub-paragraphs (*l*) and (*m*) of this paragraph) means an establishment comprising catering activities or a hotel and catering establishment;

(*l*) "establishment comprising catering activities" means an establishment in Great Britain at or from which persons were employed in the eighth base period in the supply of food or drink to persons for immediate consumption, but does not include—

(i) a hotel and catering establishment; or

(ii) an establishment in which the employer supplied for immediate consumption light refreshments to persons employed at or from the same where the employer was not otherwise engaged at or from the establishment in any activities to which paragraph 1 of the Schedule to the industrial training order applies or in the manufacture of any chocolate or flour confectionery so supplied as light refreshments;

(*m*) "hotel and catering establishment" means an establishment in Great Britain that was engaged in the eighth base period wholly or mainly in the hotel and catering industry;

(*n*) "hotel and catering industry" means any one or more of the activities which, subject to the provisions of paragraph 2 of the Schedule to the industrial training order, are specified in paragraph 1 of that Schedule as the activities of the hotel and catering industry;

(*o*) "the industrial training order" means the Industrial Training (Hotel and Catering Board) Order 1966(a), as amended by the Industrial Training (Hotel and Catering Board) Order 1969(b);

(*p*) "the levy" means the levy imposed by the Board in respect of the eighth levy period;

(*q*) "notice" means a notice in writing;

(*r*) "subsidiary" and "joint subsidiary" have the same meanings as in section 60(1) of the Civil Aviation Act 1971(c);

(*s*) "the supply of food or drink to persons for immediate consumption" means such a supply either by way of business or by a person carrying on a business to persons employed in the business;

(*t*) other expressions have the same meanings as in the industrial training order.

(2) In the case where an establishment is taken over (whether directly or indirectly) by an employer in succession to, or jointly with, another person, a person employed at any time in the eighth base period at or from the establishment shall be deemed, for the purposes of this Order, to have been so employed by the employer carrying on the said establishment on the day upon which this Order comes into operation, and any reference in this Order to persons employed by an employer in the eighth base period at or from an establishment shall be construed accordingly.

(3) Any reference in this Order to an establishment that ceases to carry on business shall not be taken to apply where the location of the establishment

(a) S.I. 1966/1347 (1966 III, p. 3669).   (c) 1971 c. 75.
(b) S.I. 1969/1405 (1969 III, p. 4132).

is changed but its business is continued wholly or mainly at or from the new location, or where the suspension of activities is of a temporary or seasonal nature.

(4) The Interpretation Act 1889(a) shall apply to the interpretation of this Order as it applies to the interpretation of an Act of Parliament.

Imposition of the levy

3.—(1) The levy to be imposed by the Board on employers in respect of the eighth levy period shall be assessed in accordance with the provisions of this and the next following Article.

(2) Subject to the provisions of the next following Article, the levy shall be assessed by the Board separately in respect of each establishment of an employer (not being an employer who is exempt from the levy by virtue of paragraph (3) of this Article), but in agreement with the employer one assessment may be made in respect of any number of hotel and catering establishments or of establishments comprising catering activities, in which case such establishments shall be deemed for the purposes of the assessment to constitute one establishment.

(3) There shall be exempt from the levy—

(*a*) an employer in whose case the sum of the emoluments of all the persons employed by him in the eighth base period in the hotel and catering industry at or from the establishment or establishments of the employer was less than £32,000.

(*b*) a charity.

Assessment of the levy

4.—(1) Subject to the provisions of this Article, the levy assessed in respect of an establishment shall be an amount equal to 0.7 per cent. of the sum of the emoluments of the following persons, being persons employed by the employer at or from the establishment in the eighth base period, that is to say—

(*a*) in the case of a hotel and catering establishment, all such persons;

(*b*) in the case of an establishment comprising catering activities, all such persons employed wholly or mainly in the supply of food or drink to persons for immediate consumption.

(2) The amount of the levy imposed in respect of an establishment that ceases to carry on business in the eighth levy period shall be in the same proportion to the amount that would otherwise be due under the foregoing provisions of this Article as the number of days between the commencement of the said levy period and the date of cessation of business (both dates inclusive) bears to the number of days in the said levy period.

(3) For the purposes of this Article, no regard shall be had to the emoluments of any person employed as follows—

(*a*) wholly in the supply (except at or in connection with an hotel, restaurant, café, snack bar, canteen, mess room or similar place of refreshment) of—

(i) ice cream, chocolate confectionery, sugar confectionery or soft drink;

(ii) shellfish or eels; or

(iii) food or drink by means of an automatic vending machine;

(a) 1889 c. 63.

    (b) wholly in agriculture;

    (c) otherwise than wholly in the supply of food or drink to persons for immediate consumption, where the employment is at or from an establishment engaged mainly in any activities of an industry specified in column 1 of the Schedule to this Order by virtue of the relevant industrial training order specified in column 2 of that Schedule or in any activities of two or more such industries;

    (d) as a member of the crew of an aircraft, or as the master or a member of the crew of a ship or, in the case of a person ordinarily employed as a seaman, in or about a ship in port by the owner or charterer thereof on work of a kind ordinarily done by a seaman on a ship while it is in port;

    (e) by a local authority in any activities mentioned in sub-paragraph (d) or (e) of paragraph 1 of the Schedule to the industrial training order, not being activities mentioned in head (ii) or head (iv) of paragraph 3(l) of that Schedule; or

    (f) in any activities mentioned in sub-paragraph (b), c(ii), (d) or (e) of paragraph 1 of the Schedule to the industrial training order when carried out by—

        (i) a harbour authority while acting in that capacity;

        (ii) the Electricity Council, the Central Electricity Generating Board or an Area Electricity Board;

        (iii) the North of Scotland Hydro-Electric Board or the South of Scotland Electricity Board;

        (iv) the British Gas Corporation;

        (v) statutory water undertakers within the meaning of the Water Act 1973(a) or regional water boards or water development boards within the meaning of the Water (Scotland) Act 1967(b), being the activities of such undertakers or boards in the exercise of their powers or duties as such;

        (vi) the British Airports Authority or a member of the British Airways Group;

        (vii) a marketing board; or

        (viii) the United Kingdom Atomic Energy Authority.

Assessment notices

5.—(1) The Board shall serve an assessment notice on every employer assessed to the levy, but one notice may comprise two or more assessments.

(2) An assessment notice shall state the Board's address for the service of a notice of appeal or of an application for an extension of time for appealing.

(3) An assessment notice may be served on the person assessed to the levy either by delivering it to him personally or by leaving it, or sending it to him by post, at his last known address or place of business in the United Kingdom or, if that person is a corporation, by leaving it, or sending it by post to the corporation, at such address or place of business or at its registered or principal office.

Payment of the levy

6.—(1) Subject to the provisions of this Article and of Articles 7 and 8, the amount of the levy payable under an assessment notice served by the Board

---

    (a) 1973 c. 37.   **(b)** 1967 c. 78.

shall be payable to the Board in two equal instalments, and the first such instalment shall be due one month after the date of the assessment notice and the second such instalment shall be due one month after the date (not being earlier than five months after the date of the assessment notice) of a notice requiring payment of that instalment, which notice shall be served by the Board on the person assessed to the levy in the same manner as an assessment notice.

(2) The amount of an instalment mentioned in the last foregoing paragraph may be rounded up or down by the Board to a convenient figure, but so that the aggregate amount of both instalments shall be equal to the amount of the levy stated in the assessment notice.

(3) An instalment of an assessment shall not be recoverable by the Board until there has expired the time allowed for appealing against the assessment by Article 8(1) of this Order and any further period or periods of time that the Board or an appeal tribunal may have allowed for appealing under paragraph (2) or (3) of that Article or, where an appeal is brought, until the appeal is decided or withdrawn.

Withdrawal of assessment

7.—(1) The Board may, by a notice served on the person assessed to the levy in the same manner as an assessment notice, withdraw an assessment if that person has appealed against that assessment under the provisions of Article 8 of this Order and the appeal has not been entered in the Register of Appeals kept under the appropriate Regulations specified in paragraph (5) of that Article, and such withdrawal may be extended by the Board to any other assessment appearing in the assessment notice.

(2) The withdrawal of an assessment shall be without prejudice—

(a) to the power of the Board to serve a further assessment notice in respect of any establishment to which that assessment related and, where the withdrawal is made by reason of the fact that an establishment has ceased to carry on business in the eighth levy period, the said notice may provide that the whole amount payable thereunder in respect of the establishment shall be due one month after the date of the notice; or

(b) to any other assessment included in the original assessment notice and not withdrawn by the Board, and such notice shall thereupon have effect as if any assessment withdrawn by the Board had not been included therein.

Appeals

8.—(1) A person assessed to the levy may appeal to an appeal tribunal against the assessment within one month from the date of the service of the assessment notice or within any further period or periods of time that may be allowed by the Board or an appeal tribunal under the following provisions of this Article.

(2) The Board by notice may for good cause allow a person assessed to the levy to appeal to an appeal tribunal against the assessment at any time within the period of four months from the date of the service of the assessment notice or within such further period or periods as the Board may allow before such time as may then be limited for appealing has expired.

(3) If the Board shall not allow an application for extension of time for appealing, an appeal tribunal shall upon application made to the tribunal by

the person assessed to the levy have the like powers as the Board under the last foregoing paragraph.

(4) In the case of an establishment that ceases to carry on business in the eighth levy period on any day after the date of the service of the relevant assessment notice, the foregoing provisions of this Article shall have effect as if for the period of four months from the date of the service of the assessment notice mentioned in paragraph (2) of this Article there were substituted the period of six months from the date of the cessation of business.

(5) An appeal or an application to an appeal tribunal under this Article shall be made in accordance with the Industrial Tribunals (England and Wales) Regulations 1965(a) as amended by the Industrial Tribunals (England and Wales) (Amendment) Regulations 1967(b) except where the establishment to which the relevant assessment relates is wholly in Scotland in which case the appeal or application shall be made in accordance with the Industrial Tribunals (Scotland) Regulations 1965(c) as amended by the Industrial Tribunals (Scotland) (Amendment) Regulations 1967(d).

(6) The powers of an appeal tribunal under paragraph (3) of this Article may be exercised by the President of the Industrial Tribunals (England and Wales) or by the President of the Industrial Tribunals (Scotland) as the case may be.

Evidence

9.—(1) Upon the discharge by a person assessed to the levy of his liability under an assessment the Board shall if so requested issue to him a certificate to that effect.

(2) The production in any proceedings of a document purporting to be certified by the Secretary of the Board to be a true copy of an assessment or other notice issued by the Board or purporting to be a certificate such as is mentioned in the foregoing paragraph of this Article shall, unless the contrary is proved, be sufficient evidence of the document and of the facts stated therein.

Signed by order of the Secretary of State.
9th April 1974.

Harold Walker,
Joint Parliamentary Under-Secretary of State,
Department of Employment.

(a) S.I. 1965/1101 (1965 II, p. 2805).   (b) S.I. 1967/301 (1967 I, p. 1040).
(c) S.I. 1965/1157 (1965 II, p. 3266).   (d) S.I. 1967/302 (1967 I, p. 1050).

Article 4

SCHEDULE

THE INDUSTRIES REFERRED TO IN ARTICLE 4(3)(*c*) OF THIS ORDER

Column 1	Column 2
The wool, jute and flax industry	The Industrial Training (Wool Industry Board) Order 1964 as amended by the Industrial Training (Wool, Jute and Flax Board) Order 1968(a)
The iron and steel industry	The Industrial Training (Iron and Steel Board) Order 1964 as amended by the Industrial Training (Iron and Steel Board) Order 1969(b)
The construction industry	The Industrial Training (Construction Board) Order 1964 as amended by the Industrial Training (Construction Board) Order 1973(c)
The engineering industry	The Industrial Training (Engineering Board) Order 1964 as amended by the Industrial Training (Engineering Board) Order 1971(d)
The shipbuilding industry	The Industrial Training (Shipbuilding Board) Order 1964 as amended by the Industrial Training (Shipbuilding Board) Order 1968(e)
The ceramics, glass and mineral products industry	The Industrial Training (Ceramics, Glass and Mineral Products Board) Order 1965 as amended by the Industrial Training (Ceramics, Glass and Mineral Products Board) Order 1969(f)

(a) S.I. 1964/907, 1968/898 (1964 II, p. 1928; 1968 II, p. 2376).
(b) S.I. 1964/949, 1969/884 (1964 II, p. 2127; 1969 II, p. 2517).
(c) S.I. 1964/1079, 1973/160 (1964 II, p. 2384; 1973 I, p. 654).
(d) S.I. 1964/1086, 1971/1530 (1964 II, p. 2402 ;1971 III, p. 4309).
(e) S.I. 1964/1782, 1968/1614 (1964 III, p. 3928; 1968 III, p. 4432).
(f) S.I. 1965/1391, 1969/689 (1965 II, p. 4062; 1969 II, p. 1860).

Column 1	Column 2
The furniture and timber industry	The Industrial Training (Furniture and Timber Industry Board) Order 1965 as amended by the Industrial Training (Furniture and Timber Industry Board) Order 1969, the Industrial Training (Furniture and Timber Industry Board) Order 1969 (Amendment) Order 1970 and the Industrial Training (Furniture and Timber Industry Board) Order 1965 (Amendment) Order 1973(a)
The man-made fibres producing industry	The Industrial Training (Man-made Fibres Producing Industry Board) Order 1966 as amended by the Industrial Training (Man-made Fibres Producing Industry Board) Order 1969(b)
The carpet industry	The Industrial Training (Carpet Board) Order 1966 as amended by the Industrial Training (Carpet Board) Order 1968(c)
The knitting, lace and net industry	The Industrial Training (Knitting, Lace and Net Industry Board) Order 1966(d)
The cotton and allied textiles industry	The Industrial Training (Cotton and Allied Textiles Board) Order 1966(e)
The agricultural, horticultural and forestry industry	The Industrial Training (Agricultural, Horticultural and Forestry Board) Order 1966 as amended by the Industrial Training (Agricultural, Horticultural and Forestry Board) Order 1970(f)
The road transport industry	The Industrial Training (Road Transport Board) Order 1966 as amended by the Industrial Training (Road Transport Board) Order 1972 and the Industrial Training (Road Transport Board) Order 1966 (Amendment) Order 1973(g)
The air transport and travel industry	The Industrial Training (Civil Air Transport Board) Order 1967 as amended by the Industrial Training (Air Transport and Travel Industry Board) Order 1970(h)
The petroleum industry	The Industrial Training (Petroleum Board) Order 1967 as amended by the Industrial Training (Petroleum Board) Order 1970(i)

(a) S.I. 1965/2028, 1969/1290, 1970/1634, 1973/1224 (1965 III, p. 5998; 1969 III, p. 3820; 1970 III, p. 5372; 1973 II, p. 3662).
(b) S.I. 1966/143, 1969/1210 (1966 I, p. 257; 1969 II, p. 3545).
(c) S.I. 1966/245, 1968/1882 (1966 I, p. 499; 1968 III, p. 5017).
(d) S.I. 1966/246 (1966 I, p. 506).   (e) S.I. 1966/823 (1966 II, p. 1907).
(f) S.I. 1966/969, 1970/1886 (1966 II, p. 2333; 1970 III, p. 6227).
(g) S.I. 1966/1112, 1972/772, 1973/860 (1966 III, p. 2712; 1972 II, p. 2471; 1973 II, p. 2663).
(h) S.I. 1967/263, 1970/252 (1967 I, p. 968; 1970 I, p. 983).
(i) S.I. 1967/648, 1970/205 (1967 I, p. 2032; 1970 I, p. 926).

Column 1	Column 2
The chemical and allied products industry	The Industrial Training (Chemical and Allied Products Board) Order 1967 as amended by the Industrial Training (Chemical and Allied Products Board) Order 1970(a)
The paper and paper products industry	The Industrial Training (Paper and Paper Products Board) Order 1968(b)
The printing and publishing industry	The Industrial Training (Printing and Publishing Board) Order 1968(c)
The distributive industry	The Industrial Training (Distributive Board) Order 1968 as amended by the Industrial Training (Distributive Board) Order 1970 and the Industrial Training (Distributive Board) Order 1970 (Amendment) Order 1971(d)
The food, drink and tobacco industry	The Industrial Training (Food, Drink and Tobacco Board) Order 1968 as amended by the Industrial Training (Food, Drink and Tobacco Board) Order 1971(e)
The footwear, leather and fur skin industry	The Industrial Training (Footwear, Leather and Fur Skin Board) Order 1968 as amended by the Industrial Training (Footwear, Leather and Fur Skin Board) Order 1968 (Amendment) Order 1972(f)
The clothing and allied products industry	The Industrial Training (Clothing and Allied Products Board) Order 1969(g)
The rubber and plastics processing industry	The Industrial Training (Rubber and Plastics Processing Board) Order 1967(h)

(a) S.I. 1967/1386, 1970/1743 (1967 III, p. 4049; 1970 III, p. 5706).
(b) S.I. 1968/787 (1968 II, p. 2194).   (c) S.I. 1968/786 (1968 II, p. 2185).
(d) S.I. 1968/1032, 1970/1053, 1971/1876 (1968 II, p. 2709; 1970 II, p. 3273; 1971 III, p. 5109).
(e) S.I. 1968/1033, 1971/648 (1968 II, p. 2721; 1971 I, p. 1709).
(f) S.I. 1968/1763, 1972/597 (1968 III, p. 4785; 1972 I, p. 1966).
(g) S.I. 1969/1375 (1969 III, p. 4094).
(h) S.I. 1967/1062 (1967 II, p. 3151).

EXPLANATORY NOTE

(This Note is not part of the Order.)

This Order gives effect to proposals submitted by the Hotel and Catering Industry Training Board to the Secretary of State for Employment for the imposition of a further levy upon employers in the hotel and catering industry for the purpose of raising money towards the expenses of the Board.

The levy is to be imposed in respect of the eighth levy period commencing with the day upon which this Order comes into operation and ending on 31st March 1975. The levy will be assessed by the Board and there will be a right of appeal against an assessment to an industrial tribunal.

STATUTORY INSTRUMENTS

1974 No. 685

WAGES COUNCILS

The Wages Regulation (Hollow-ware) Order 1974

Made - - -	*9th April* 1974
Coming into Operation	*7th May* 1974

Whereas the Secretary of State has received from the Hollow-ware Wages Council (Great Britain) the wages regulation proposals set out in the Schedule hereto;

Now, therefore, the Secretary of State in exercise of powers conferred by section 11 of the Wages Councils Act 1959(a), as modified by Article 2 of the Counter-Inflation (Modification of Wages Councils Act 1959) Order 1973(b), and now vested in him(c), and of all other powers enabling him in that behalf, hereby makes the following Order:—

1. This Order may be cited as the Wages Regulation (Hollow-ware) Order 1974.

2.—(1) In this Order the expression "the specified date" means the 7th May, 1974, provided that where, as respects any worker who is paid wages at intervals not exceeding seven days, that date does not correspond with the beginning of the period for which the wages are paid, the expression "the specified date" means, as respects that worker, the beginning of the next such period following that date.

(2) The Interpretation Act 1889(d) shall apply to the interpretation of this Order as it applies to the interpretation of an Act of Parliament and as if this Order and the Order hereby revoked were Acts of Paliament.

3. The wages regulation proposals set out in the Schedule hereto shall have effect as from the specified date and as from that date the Wages Regulation (Hollow-ware) Order 1973(e) shall cease to have effect.

Signed by order of the Secretary of State.
9th April 1974.

W. H. Marsh,
Assistant Secretary,
Department of Employment.

(a) 1959 c. 69.   (b) S.I. 1973/661 (1973 I, p. 2141).
(c) S.I. 1959/1769, 1968/729 (1959 I, p. 1795; 1968 II, p. 2108).
(d) 1889 c. 63.   (e) S.I. 1973/146 (1973 I, p. 592).

Article 3
SCHEDULE

The following minimum remuneration shall be substituted for the statutory minimum remuneration fixed by the Wages Regulation (Hollow-ware) Order 1973 (Order H.(104)).

STATUTORY MINIMUM REMUNERATION
PART I
GENERAL

1.—(1) *Subject to the provisions of paragraph 2* the minimum remuneration payable to a worker to whom this Schedule applies for all work except work to which a minimum overtime rate applies under Part IV is:—

    (*a*) in the case of a time worker, the hourly general minimum time rate payable to the worker under Part II or Part III of this Schedule;

    (*b*) in the case of a worker employed on piece work, piece rates each of which would yield, in the circumstances of the case, to an ordinary worker at least the same amount of money as the hourly *general minimum time rate* which would be payable to the worker under Part II or Part III of this Schedule if he were a time worker.

(2) In this Schedule, the expression "hourly general minimum time rate" means the weekly *general minimum time rate* applicable to the worker under Part II or Part III of this Schedule divided by 40.

2.—(*1*) *Up to and including 15th November 1974, in addition to the minimum remuneration specified in paragraph 1 of this Schedule, additional remuneration hereinafter referred to as a "cost of living payment" shall be payable to all workers to whom that paragraph applies in accordance with the following table:*—

		Retail Price Indices				
Cost of living payment to be paid from the first complete pay week following the publication by the Department of Employment of the Index of Retail Prices for All Items containing a figure which is	*not less than* .. 198·4	200·2	202·1	203·9	205·8
	and not more than .. 200·1	202·0	203·8	205·7	207·5
	£	£	£	£	£
Cost of living payment payable to full-time workers in respect of each complete pay week ..	0·40	0·80	1·20	1·60	2·00
Cost of living payment payable to part-time workers, in respect of each complete pay week, is the amount in the appropriate column multiplied by the number of hours worked (excluding overtime)	0·01	0·02	0·03	0·04	0·05

(2) *The cost of living payment shall not be treated as part of the general minimum time rate for the purposes of calculating payment for overtime under paragraph 5 of this Schedule.*

(3) *On and after 16th November 1974, the cost of living payment to be payable under this paragraph shall be that which was payable in respect of the last complete pay week before that date.*

(4) *In this paragraph—*

    "*full-time worker*" *means a worker who normally works for the employer for 40 hours or more a week;*

    "*part-time worker*" *means a worker who normally works for the employer for less than 40 hours a week.*

PART II

MALE WORKERS

TIME WORKERS

3. The general minimum time rates payable to male time workers are as follows:—

General
minimum
time rates
per week
of 40 hours
£

(1) Workers aged 21 years or over and employed in the enamel ware section of the trade as—

(a) Fusers' helpers who work in association with fusers   ..   ..
(b) Annealers, or ..   ..   } 18·17
(c) Scalers ..   ..

(2) All other workers

Aged 21 years or over	17·75
,, 20 and under 21 years	16·95
,, 19 ,, ,, 20 ,, ...	15·51
,, 18 ,, ,, 19 ,, ...	14·33
,, 17 ,, ,, 18 ,, ...	11·64
,, Under 17 years	9·04

PART III

FEMALE WORKERS

TIME WORKERS

4. The general minimum time rates payable to female time workers are as follows:—

General
minimum
time rates
per week
of 40 hours
£

Workers aged 21 years or over	17·05
,, ,, 20 and under 21 years	16·27
,, ,, 19 ,, ,, 20 ,, ...	15·02
,, ,, 18 ,, ,, 19 ,, ...	14·33
,, ,, 17 ,, ,, 18 ,, ...	11·64
,, ,, Under 17 years	9·04

PART IV

OVERTIME AND WAITING TIME

MINIMUM OVERTIME RATES

5.—(1) The following minimum overtime rates are payable to all workers other than male workers employed as fusers' helpers, dippers, annealers or scalers in the enamel ware section of the trade:—

    (a) on a Sunday or a customary holiday—
        for all time worked   ..   ..   double time

    (b) on a Saturday, not being a customary holiday—
        for all time worked in excess of 4 hours   ..   ..   time-and-a-half

    (c) in any week exclusive of any time in respect of which
        a minimum overtime rate is payable under the foregoing
        provisions of this sub-paragraph—
        for all time worked in excess of 40 hours   ..   ..   time-and-a-quarter

(2) The following minimum overtime rates are payable to male workers employed as fusers' helpers, dippers, annealers or scalers in the enamel ware section of the trade:—

    (a) on a Sunday or a customary holiday—
        for all time worked in excess of 2 hours   ..   ..   double time

    (b) in any week exclusive of any time in respect of which
        double time is payable under (a) of this sub-paragraph—
        for all time worked in excess of 40 hours   ..   ..   time-and-a-quarter

6. In this Part of this Schedule,

(1) the expression "customary holiday" means:—

    (a)   (i) In England and Wales—
            Christmas Day;
            26th December if it be not a Sunday, 27th December in a year when
            25th or 26th December is a Sunday;
            New Year's Day (*or, if New Year's Day falls on a Sunday, the following Monday*);
            Good Friday;
            Easter Monday;
            the last Monday in May;
            the last Monday in August (or, where a day is substituted for any of the above days by national proclamation, that day);

      (ii) in Scotland—
            New Year's Day (or, if New Year's Day falls on a Sunday, the following Monday);
            the local Spring holiday;
             the local Autumn holiday; and
            four other days (being days on which the worker normally works) in the course of a calendar year, to be fixed by the employer and notified to the worker not less than three weeks before the holiday;

or (b) in the case of each of the said days (other than a day fixed by the employer and notified to the worker as aforesaid), a day substituted therefor, being either a day recognised by local custom as a day of holiday in substitution for the said day, or a day fixed by agreement between the employer and the worker or his agent.

(2) the expressions "time-and-a-quarter", "time-and-a-half" and "double time" mean respectively—

    (a) in the case of a time worker, one and a quarter times, one and a half times and twice the general minimum time rate otherwise payable to the worker;

    (b) in the case of a piece worker, such piece rates as would each yield respectively, in the circumstances of the case, to an ordinary worker at least the same amount of money as one and a quarter times, one and a half times and twice the *general minimum time rate which would otherwise be payable to the worker under Part II or Part III of this Schedule if he were a time worker.*

WAITING TIME

7.—(1) A worker is entitled to payment of the minimum remuneration specified in this Schedule for all time during which he is present on the premises of his employer, unless he is present thereon in any of the following circumstances:—

(a) without the employer's consent, express or implied;

(b) for some purpose unconnected with his work and other than that of waiting for work to be given to him to perform;

(c) by reason only of the fact that he is resident thereon;

(d) during normal meal times in a room or place in which no work is being done and he is not waiting for work to be given to him to perform.

(2) The minimum remuneration payable under sub-paragraph (1) of this paragraph to a piece worker when not engaged in piece work, is that which would be payable if the worker were a time worker.

PART V

APPLICABILITY OF STATUTORY MINIMUM REMUNERATION

8.—(1) This Schedule does not apply to workers employed as watchmen, but save as aforesaid applies to workers in relation to whom the Hollow-ware Wages Council (Great Britain) operates, that is to say, workers employed in Great Britain in the operations in the Hollow-ware branch of the Hollow-ware making trade specified in the Schedule to the Trade Boards (Hollow-ware Trade, Great Britain) (Constitution and Proceedings) Regulations 1937(a), namely:—

(a) all work in connection with—

(i) the manufacture from sheet iron or sheet steel (hereinafter called black plate) of articles of hollow-ware or parts thereof;

(ii) the manufacture of baths and dustbins from black plate or from black plate coated with any metal, of an average thickness not exceeding ·0392 of an inch (20 Birmingham Gauge);

(iii) the manufacture from any iron or steel of forged, stamped or pressed mountings or fittings or parts thereof, for articles specified in (a) (i) and (ii) of this sub-paragraph when done by workers wholly or mainly so engaged, or in association or conjunction with the manufacture specified in (a) (i) and (ii) of this sub-paragraph;

(b) all work in connection with—

(i) the manufacture of kegs, drums, tapers, taper-necked cans and painters' pots, or parts thereof:

from black plate of an average thickness less than ·125 of an inch (10 Birmingham Gauge), or

from black plate coated with any metal and of an average thickness exceeding ·01745 of an inch (27 Birmingham Gauge) but less than ·125 of an inch (10 Birmingham Gauge),

and the repair thereof;

when done in a department mainly engaged on work specified in (a) of this sub-paragraph;

(ii) the manufacture from any iron or steel of forged, stamped or pressed mountings or fittings, or parts thereof, for the articles to the manufacture or repair of which (b) (i) of this sub-paragraph applies.

(a) S.R. & O. 1937/325 (1937, p. 2335).

(2) Work in connection with the manufacture specified in sub-paragraph (1) of this paragraph includes—

(a) finishing;

(b) the work of persons employed in the factory or workshop in counting or weighing materials handed to workers and articles or parts thereof received from workers;

(c) packing, warehousing, despatching, the work of inside messengers, yard-workers and stokers and work of a similar nature.

(3) Notwithstanding anything in this paragraph the following operations are not operations in the Hollow-ware branch of the Hollow-ware making trade:—

(a) work specified in sub-paragraph (1) of this paragraph when performed in an establishment, branch or department mainly engaged on other work and in which the jointing and finishing of the articles or parts of articles specified in sub-paragraph (1) of this paragraph are done by workers mainly employed in jointing and finishing other articles;

(b) finishing (other than enamelling) when performed in a department mainly engaged in the finishing of articles other than articles specified in sub-paragraph (1) of this paragraph and in which no manufacture specified in sub-paragraph (1) of this paragraph is carried on;

(c) packing, warehousing, despatching, the work of inside messengers, yard-workers and stokers, and work of a similar nature when performed in an establishment not otherwise engaged in operations in the hollow-ware branch of the hollow-ware making trade;

(d) the manufacture of baths or dustbins from black plate or from black plate coated with any metal, of an average thickness exceeding ·0392 of an inch (20 Birmingham Gauge);

(e) the manufacture referred to in (a) (ii) of sub-paragraph (1) of this paragraph in an establishment, branch or department mainly engaged in the operations specified in (d) of this sub-paragraph or in operations other than those specified in sub-paragraph (1) of this paragraph or both in such operations and such manufacture;

(f) the manufacture of component parts of motor vehicles, motor plants, aircraft, cycles or motor cycles;

(g) the manufacture of any article or part of any article when made in an establishment mainly engaged in the manufacture of motor vehicles, motor plants, aircraft, cycles or motor cycles or of component parts thereof;

(h) all clerical work other than work specified in (b) of sub-paragraph (2) of this paragraph;

(i) the manufacture of tin rollers, tin roller drums, card cases, coiler cans and other articles for use with textile or other machinery;

(j) all work in connection with the maintenance or upkeep of premises, machinery or plant;

(k) all work included under the Trade Boards (Keg and Drum Trade, Great Britain) (Constitution and Proceedings) Regulations 1928(a);

(l) all work included under the Trade Boards (Tin Box Trade, Great Britain) (Constitution and Proceedings) Regulations 1928(b).

(4) The expression "finishing" includes operations of coating (including the processes of galvanising, tinning, enamelling, painting, japanning, lacquering and varnishing), polishing and cleaning articles.

(a) S.R. & O. 1928/844 (1928, p. 1276).   (b) S.R. & O. 1928/847 (1928, p. 1289).

EXPLANATORY NOTE

(This Note is not part of the Order.)

This Order, which has effect from 7th May 1974, sets out the increased statutory minimum remuneration payable to workers in relation to whom the Hollow-ware Wages Council (Great Britain) operates, in substitution for that fixed by the Wages Regulation (Hollow-ware) Order 1973 (Order H.(104)). Order H.(104) is revoked.

New provisions are printed in italics.

STATUTORY INSTRUMENTS

1974 No. 686

WAGES COUNCILS

The Wages Regulation (Hollow-ware) (Holidays) Order 1974

Made - - -	*9th April* 1974
Coming into Operation	*7th May* 1974

Whereas the Secretary of State has received from the Hollow-ware Wages Council (Great Britain) the wages regulation proposals set out in the Schedule hereto;

Now, therefore, the Secretary of State in exercise of powers conferred by section 11 of the Wages Councils Act 1959(a), as modified by Article 2 of the Counter-Inflation (Modification of Wages Councils Act 1959) Order 1973(b), and now vested in him(c), and of all other powers enabling him in that behalf, hereby makes the following Order:—

1. This Order may be cited as the Wages Regulation (Hollow-ware) (Holidays) Order 1974.

2.—(1) In this Order the expression "the specified date" means the 7th May 1974, provided that where, as respects any worker who is paid wages at intervals not exceeding seven days, that date does not correspond with the beginning of the period for which the wages are paid, the expression "the specified date" means, as respects that worker, the beginning of the next such period following that date.

(2) The Interpretation Act 1889(d) shall apply to the interpretation of this Order as it applies to the interpretation of an Act of Parliament and as if this Order and the Order hereby revoked were Acts of Parliament.

3. The wages regulation proposals set out in the Schedule hereto shall have effect as from the specified date and as from that date the Wages Regulation (Hollow-ware) (Holidays) Order 1971(e) as amended by Schedule 2 to the Wages Regulation (Hollow-ware) Order 1973(f) shall cease to have effect.

Signed by order of the Secretary of State.

9th April 1974.

W. H. Marsh,
Assistant Secretary,
Department of Employment.

Article 3   SCHEDULE

The following provisions as to holidays and holiday remuneration shall be substituted for the provisions as to holidays and holiday remuneration set out in the Wages Regulation (Hollow-ware) (Holidays) Order 1971 (Order H. (102) as amended by Schedule 2 to the Wages Regulation (Hollow-ware) Order 1973 (Order H. (104)).

(a) 1959 c. 69.   (b) S.I. 1973/661 (1973 I, p. 2141).
(c) S.I. 1959/1769, 1968/729 (1959 I, p. 1795; 1968 II, p. 2108).
(d) 1889 c. 63.   (e) S.I. 1971/1697 (1971 III, p. 4628).
(f) S.I. 1973/146 (1973 I, p. 592).

Part I

APPLICATION

1. This Schedule applies to every worker for whom statutory minimum remuneration has been fixed.

Part II

CUSTOMARY HOLIDAYS

2.—(1) An employer shall allow to every worker in his employment to whom this Schedule applies a holiday (hereinafter referred to as a "customary holiday") in each year on the days specified in the next following sub-paragraph, provided that the worker:—

(a) was in his employment on the day immediately preceding the customary holiday;

(b) has performed some work for the employer during the period of 12 weeks immediately preceding the customary holiday; and

(c) (unless excused by the employer or absent by reason of the proved illness of the worker) has worked throughout the last working day on which work was available to him before the customary holiday.

(2) The said customary holidays are:—

(a) (i) in England and Wales—

Christmas Day;

26th December if it be not a Sunday, 27th December in a year when 25th or 26th December is a Sunday;

New Year's Day (or, if New Year's Day falls on a Sunday, the following Monday);

Good Friday;

Easter Monday;

the last Monday in May;

the last Monday in August;

(or where a day is substituted for any of the above days by national proclamation, that day);

(ii) in Scotland—

New Year's Day (or, if New Year's Day falls on a Sunday, the following Monday);

the local Spring holiday;

the local Autumn holiday; and

four other days (being days on which the worker normally works) in the course of a calendar year, to be fixed by the employer and notified to the worker not less than three weeks before the holiday,

or (b) in the case of each of the said days (other than a day fixed by the employer and notified to the worker as aforesaid), a day substituted therefor, being either a day recognised by local custom as a day of holiday in substitution for the said day, or a day fixed by agreement between the employer and the worker or his agent.

(3) Notwithstanding the preceding provisions of this paragraph, an employer may (except where in the case of a woman or young person such a requirement would be unlawful) require a worker who is otherwise entitled to any customary holiday under the foregoing provisions of this Schedule to work thereon, and, in lieu of any customary holiday on which he so works, the employer shall allow to the worker a day's holiday (hereinafter referred to as a "holiday in lieu of a customary holiday") on a weekday on which he would normally work for the employer within the period of four weeks next ensuing.

(4) A worker who is required to work on a customary holiday shall be paid:—

   (a) for all time worked thereon at the minimum rate then appropriate to the worker for work on a customary holiday; and

   (b) in respect of the holiday in lieu of the customary holiday, holiday remuneration in accordance with paragraph 6.

PART III

ANNUAL HOLIDAY

3.—(1) In addition to the holidays specified in Part II of this Schedule, and subject to the provisions of paragraph 4, an employer shall, between the date on which this Schedule becomes effective and 31st October, and in each succeeding year between 1st April and 31st October, allow a holiday (hereinafter referred to as an "annual holiday") to every worker in his employment to whom this Schedule applies who has been employed by him during the 12 months immediately preceding the commencement of the holiday season for any of the periods of employment (calculated in accordance with the provisions of paragraph 10) set out in the appropriate table below and the duration of the annual holiday shall, in the case of each such worker, be related to his period of employment during that 12 months as follows:—

Workers with a normal working week of six days

Column 1 Period of employment	Column 2 Duration of annual holiday
Not less than 48 weeks	20 days
Not less than 44 weeks but less than 48 weeks	18 "
" 40 " " " 44 "	16 "
" 36 " " " 40 "	15 "
" 32 " " " 36 "	13 "
" 28 " " " 32 "	11 "
" 24 " " " 28 "	10 "
" 20 " " " 24 "	8 "
" 16 " " " 20 "	6 "
" 12 " " " 16 "	5 "
" 8 " " " 12 "	3 "
" 4 " " " 8 "	1 day

Workers with a normal working week of five days or less

Column 1 Period of employment	Column 2 Duration of annual holiday
Not less than 48 weeks	17 days
Not less than 43 weeks but less than 48 weeks	15 "
" 38 " " " 43 "	13 "
" 33 " " " 38 "	11 "
" 28 " " " 33 "	9 "
" 24 " " " 28 "	8 "
" 19 " " " 24 "	6 "
" 14 " " " 19 "	4 "
" 9 " " " 14 "	3 "
" 4 " " " 9 "	1 day

(2) Notwithstanding the provisions of the last foregoing sub-paragraph the number of days of annual holiday which an employer is required to allow to a worker in respect of a period of employment during the 12 months immediately preceding 1st April 1974 and during the 12 months immediately preceding 1st April in any succeeding year shall not exceed in the aggregate three times the number of days constituting the worker's normal working week, *plus two days*.

(3) The duration of the worker's annual holiday during the holiday season ending on 31st October 1974 shall be reduced by any days of annual holiday duly allowed to him by the employer under the provisions of Order H. (102) between 1st April 1974 and the date on which this schedule becomes effective.

(4) In this Schedule the expression "holiday season" means in relation to an annual holiday during the year 1974 the period commencing with the date on which the provisions of this Schedule become effective and ending on 31st October 1974, and in relation to each subsequent year, the period commencing on 1st April and ending on 31st October in that year.

4.—(1) Subject to the provisions of this paragraph, an annual holiday under this Schedule shall be allowed on consecutive working days, being days on which the worker is normally called upon to work for the employer, and days of annual holiday shall be treated as consecutive notwithstanding that a customary holiday on which the worker is not required to work for the employer or a holiday in lieu of a customary holiday intervenes.

(2) (*a*) Where the number of days of annual holiday for which a worker has qualified exceeds the number of days constituting his normal working week but does not exceed twice that number, the holiday may be allowed in two separate periods of consecutive working days; so, however, that when a holiday is so allowed, one of the periods shall consist of a number of such days not less than the number of days constituting the worker's normal working week;

(*b*) Where the number of days of annual holiday for which a worker has qualified exceeds twice the number of days constituting his normal working week the holiday may be allowed as follows:—

(i) as to two periods of consecutive working days, each such period not being less than the period constituting the worker's normal working week, during the holiday season; and

(ii) as to any additional days, on working days which need not be consecutive, to be fixed by the employer after consultation with the worker, either during the holiday season or before the beginning of the next following holiday season.

(3) Where a day of holiday allowed to a worker under Part II of this Schedule immediately precedes a period of annual holiday or occurs during such a period then, notwithstanding the foregoing provisions of this paragraph, the duration of that period of annual holiday may be reduced by one day and in such a case one day of annual holiday may be allowed on any working day in the holiday season, or by agreement between the employer and the worker or his representative, on any working day before the beginning of the next following holiday season.

(4) Subject to the foregoing provisions of this paragraph, any day of annual holiday under this Schedule may be allowed on a day on which the worker is entitled to a day of holiday or to a half-holiday under any enactment other than the Wages Councils Act 1959.

5. An employer shall give to a worker reasonable notice of the commencing date or dates and duration of the period or periods of his annual holiday. Such notice may be given individually to the worker or by the posting of a notice in the place where the worker is employed.

PART IV

HOLIDAY REMUNERATION

A—CUSTOMARY HOLIDAYS AND HOLIDAYS IN LIEU OF
CUSTOMARY HOLIDAYS

6.—(1) For each day of holiday which a worker is allowed under Part II of this Schedule he shall be paid by the employer holiday remuneration equal to the amount, calculated at the general minimum time rate applicable to the worker (or which would be applicable if he were a time worker) increased by $17\frac{1}{2}$ per cent., to which he would have been entitled, if the day had not been a day of holiday and he had been employed on work entitling him to statutory minimum remuneration for the time normally worked by him on that day of the week:

Provided, however, that payment of the said holiday remuneration is subject to the condition that the worker presents himself for employment at the usual starting hour on the first working day following the holiday and works throughout that day or, if he fails to do so, failure is by reason of his proved illness or with the consent of the employer.

(2) The holiday remuneration in respect of any customary holiday shall be paid by the employer to the worker on the pay day on which the wages for the pay week including the first working day following the customary holiday are paid.

(3) The holiday remuneration in respect of any holiday in lieu of a customary holiday shall be paid on the pay day on which the wages for the pay week including the first working day following that holiday in lieu of a customary holiday are paid:

Provided that the said payment shall be made immediately upon the termination of the worker's employment in the case where he ceases to be employed before being allowed a holiday in lieu of a customary holiday to which he is entitled, and in that case the proviso contained in sub-paragraph (1) of this paragraph shall not apply.

B—ANNUAL HOLIDAY

7.—(1) Subject to the provisions of paragraph 8, a worker qualified to be allowed an annual holiday under this Schedule shall be paid by the employer in respect thereof, on the last pay day preceding such annual holiday, one day's holiday pay (as defined in paragraph 11) in respect of each day thereof.

(2) Where under the provisions of paragraph 4 an annual holiday is allowed in more than one period, the holiday remuneration shall be apportioned accordingly.

8. Where any accrued holiday remuneration has been paid by the employer to the worker in accordance with paragraph 9 or with Order H. (102) as amended, in respect of employment during any of the periods referred to in that paragraph or that Order, the amount of holiday remuneration payable by the employer in respect of any annual holiday for which the worker has qualified by reason of employment during the said period shall be reduced by the amount of the said accrued holiday remuneration unless that remuneration has been deducted from a previous payment of holiday remuneration made under the provisions of this Schedule or of Order H. (102) as amended.

ACCRUED HOLIDAY REMUNERATION PAYABLE ON
TERMINATION OF EMPLOYMENT

9. Where a worker ceases to be employed by an employer after the provisions of this Schedule become effective the employer shall, immediately on the termination of the employment (hereinafter referred to as the "termination date") pay to the worker as accrued holiday remuneration:—

(1) in respect of employment in the 12 months up to the preceding 31st March, a sum equal to the holiday remuneration for any days of annual holiday for

which he has qualified, except days of annual holiday which he has been allowed or has become entitled to be allowed before leaving the employment; and

(2) in respect of any employment since the preceding 31st March, a sum equal to the holiday remuneration which would have been payable to him if he could have been allowed an annual holiday in respect of that employment at the time of leaving it.

PART V

GENERAL

10. For the purposes of calculating any period of employment qualifying a worker for an annual holiday or for any accrued holiday remuneration under this Schedule, the worker shall be treated—

(1) as if he were employed for a week in respect of any week in which—

    (*a*) he has worked for the employer for not less than eight hours and has performed some work for which statutory minimum remuneration is payable;

    (*b*) he has been absent throughout the week or has worked for the employer for less than eight hours by reason of the proved illness of, or accident to, the worker, provided that the number of weeks which may be treated as weeks of employment for such reasons shall not exceed eight weeks at any one time in the period of 12 months immediately preceding the commencement of the holiday season;

    (*c*) he has been suspended throughout the week owing to shortage of work in the period of 12 months last mentioned; and

(2) as if he were employed on any day of holiday allowed under the provisions of this Schedule, or of Order H. (102) as amended, and for the purposes of the provisions of sub-paragraph (1) of this paragraph, a worker who is absent on such a holiday shall be treated as having worked thereon the number of hours ordinarily worked by him on that day of the week for the employer on work for which statutory minimum remuneration is payable.

11. In this Schedule, unless the context otherwise requires, the following expressions have the meanings hereby respectively assigned to them, that is to say:—

"normal working week" means the number of days on which it has been usual for the worker to work in a week in the employment of the employer in the 12 months immediately preceding the worker's first period of annual holiday or immediately preceding *8th* October if no part of the annual holiday has been allowed before that date or, where under paragraph 9 accrued holiday remuneration is payable on the termination of the employment, in the 12 months immediately preceding the date of the termination of the employment:

Provided that—

(1) part of a day shall count as a day;

(2) no account shall be taken of any week in which the worker did not perform any work for which statutory minimum remuneration has been fixed.

"one day's holiday pay" means the appropriate proportion of the remuneration which the worker would be entitled to receive from his employer at the date of the annual holiday (or where the holiday is allowed in more than one period at the date of the first period) or at the termination date, as the case may require, for one week's work if working his normal working week and the number of daily hours normally worked by him (exclusive of overtime) and if paid at the general minimum time rate applicable to the worker (or which would be applicable if he were a time worker), increased by $17\frac{1}{2}$ per cent., for work for which statutory minimum remuneration is payable and at the same rate (increased as aforesaid) for any work for which such remuneration is not payable, and in this definition "appropriate proportion" means—

where the worker's normal working week is six days .. .. one-sixth
where the worker's normal working week is five days .. .. one-fifth
where the worker's normal working week is four days or less.. one-quarter.

"statutory minimum remuneration" means minimum remuneration (other than holiday remuneration) fixed by a wages regulation order made by the Secretary of State to give effect to the proposals submitted to him by the Council.

"week" in paragraphs 3 and 10 means "pay week".

12. The provisions of this Schedule are without prejudice to any agreement for the allowance of any further holidays with pay or for the payment of additional holiday remuneration.

EXPLANATORY NOTE

(This Note is not part of the Order).

This Order, which has effect from 7th May 1974, sets out the holidays which an employer is required to allow to workers in relation to whom the Hollow-ware Wages Council (Great Britain) operates and the remuneration payable for those holidays in substitution for the holidays and holiday remuneration fixed by the Wages Regulation (Hollow-ware) (Holidays) Order 1971 (Order H. (102)) as amended by the Wages Regulation (Hollow-ware) Order 1973 (H. (104)). Order H. (102) is revoked.

New provisions are printed in italics.

STATUTORY INSTRUMENTS

1974 No. 688

MONOPOLIES AND MERGERS

The Restriction of Merger (No. 1) Order 1974

Made - - - -	10*th April* 1974
Laid before Parliament	10*th April* 1974
Coming into Operation	11*th April* 1974

Whereas the Secretary of State in exercise of powers conferred on her by sections 69(2) and 75 of the Fair Trading Act 1973(**a**) has referred to the Monopolies and Mergers Commission for investigation and report the matter of the proposed acquisition by Charter Consolidated Investments Limited (a subsidiary of Charter Consolidated Limited) of Sadia Limited:

Now, therefore, the Secretary of State with a view to preventing action which may prejudice the reference or impede the taking of any action under the Fair Trading Act 1973 which may be warranted by the Commission's Report on the reference and in exercise of powers conferred on her by section 74(1)(*d*) of, and paragraph 12 of Schedule 8 to, that Act hereby orders as follows:

1.—(1) This Order may be cited as the Restriction of Merger (No. 1) Order 1974 and shall come into operation on 11th April 1974.

(2) The Interpretation Act 1889(**b**) shall apply to the interpretation of this Order as it applies to the interpretation of an Act of Parliament.

2. It shall be unlawful for Charter Consolidated Limited or any subsidiary thereof to acquire any shares or any interest in shares of Sadia Limited if such acquisition would or might result in Charter Consolidated Investments Limited and Sadia Limited becoming interconnected bodies corporate:

Provided that this Article shall not apply to anything done in pursuance of a legally enforceable agreement to acquire shares made before the commencement of this Order other than an agreement made in pursuance of any general offer addressed to the members of Sadia Limited by Charter Consolidated Limited on behalf of Charter Consolidated Investments Limited.

Alan Williams,
Minister of State,
Department of Prices and Consumer
Protection.

10th April 1974.

(**a**) 1973 c. 41.   (**b**) 1889 c. 63.

EXPLANATORY NOTE

(This Note is not part of the Order.)

This Order imposes a standstill on any acquisition by Charter Consolidated Limited or its subsidiaries of shares of Sadia Limited which would or might result in Sadia Limited becoming a subsidiary of Charter Consolidated Investments Limited (a subsidiary of Charter Consolidated Limited). The proposed merger of these two companies has been referred to the Monopolies and Mergers Commission.

An exemption is provided for any acquisition of shares in pursuance of an agreement made before the commencement of this Order other than an agreement resulting from a general offer to acquire shares of Sadia Limited made by Charter Consolidated Limited on behalf of Charter Consolidated Investments Limited.

The Order, unless previously revoked, will cease to have effect—

(a) 40 days after the report of the Commission on the proposed merger is laid before Parliament; or

(b) on the failure of the Commission to report within the period allowed.

STATUTORY INSTRUMENTS

1974 No. 691

MINISTERS OF THE CROWN

The Ministry of Posts and Telecommunications (Dissolution) Order 1974

Laid before Parliament in draft

Made - - - -		10*th April* 1974
Coming into Operation		17*th April* 1974

At the Court at Windsor Castle, the 10th day of April 1974

Present,

The Queen's Most Excellent Majesty in Council

Whereas a draft of this Order has been laid before Parliament in pursuance of section 3(1) of the Ministers of the Crown (Transfer of Functions) Act 1946(a), and each House has presented an Address to Her Majesty praying that the Order be made:

Now, therefore, Her Majesty, in pursuance of section 1 of the Ministers of the Crown (Transfer of Functions) Act 1946(a) is pleased, by and with the advice of Her Privy Council, to order, and it is hereby ordered, as follows:—

Citation, interpretation and commencement

1.—(1) This Order may be cited as the Ministry of Posts and Telecommunications (Dissolution) Order 1974.

(2) In this Order " Minister " means the Minister of Posts and Telecommunications.

(3) The Interpretation Act 1889(b) applies for the interpretation of this Order as it applies for the interpretation of an Act of Parliament.

(4) Any reference in this Order to an enactment or instrument is a reference to that enactment or instrument as amended or extended by or under any other enactment or instrument; and in this Order " instrument " includes the judgment, decree or order of any court or tribunal.

(5) This Order shall come into operation 7 days after the date on which it is made.

Transfer of functions, and dissolution of Ministry

2. The Ministry of Posts and Telecommunications is hereby dissolved and all the functions of the Minister are hereby transferred to the Secretary of State.

(a) 1946 c. 31.   (b) 1889 c. 63.

Supplementary

3.—(1) This Order shall not affect the validity of anything done by or in relation to the Minister before the coming into operation of this Order; and anything which at the coming into operation of this Order is in process of being done by or in relation to that Minister may be continued by or in relation to the Secretary of State.

(2) Any authorisation given (by way of approval or otherwise), requirement imposed or appointment made by the Minister, or having effect as if so given, imposed or made shall, if in force at the coming into operation of this Order, have effect as if given, imposed or made by the Secretary of State, in so far as that is required for continuing its effect after the coming into operation of this Order.

(3) Subject to any specific provision made by this Order, any enactment, instrument or contract passed or made before the coming into operation of this Order shall have effect, so far as may be necessary for the purpose or in consequence of the transfer of functions effected by this Order, as if any reference to the Minister or to his department or an officer of his (including any reference which is to be construed as such a reference) were or included a reference to the Secretary of State or to his department or an officer of his, as the context may require.

(4) Documents or forms printed or duplicated for use in connection with any functions of the Minister transferred by this Order may be so used notwithstanding that they contain references to the Minister, and those references shall be construed as references to the Secretary of State; and similarly with references to the department or an officer of the Minister.

4.—(1) The enactments specified in the Schedule to this Order are hereby repealed to the extent specified in the third column thereof; but nothing in the repeals made in section 2 of the Post Office Act 1969(a) shall be taken to prejudice the transfer of functions effected by the foregoing provisions of this Order.

(2) Subject to the provisions of the Schedule to this Order, where in connection with any functions transferred by this Order any enactment or instrument provides for anything to be done by or in relation to both the Minister and the Secretary of State, it shall be read as providing for it to be done by or in relation to both the Secretary of State for the time being discharging those functions and such other Secretary of State (if any) as may be concerned.

(3) In section 40(3) of the Land Drainage Act 1930(b) for the reference to the Postmaster-General there shall be substituted a reference to the Post Office.

W. G. Agnew.

(a) 1969 c. 48.   (b) 1930 c. 44.

SCHEDULE

ENACTMENTS REPEALED

Chapter	Short Title	Extent of Repeal
5 & 6 Eliz. 2. c. 20.	The House of Commons Disqualification Act 1957.	In Schedule 2 the words " Minister of Posts and Telecommunications ".
1967 c. 13.	The Parliamentary Commissioner Act 1967.	In Schedule 2 the words " Ministry of Posts and Telecommunications ".
1969 c. 48.	The Post Office Act 1969.	Section 2, except subsection (6).
1972 c. 3.	The Ministerial and other Salaries Act 1972.	In Schedule 1, in Part II, the words " Minister of Posts and Telecommunications ".
1973 c. 9.	The Counter-Inflation Act 1973.	In section 21(1), in the definition of " the Minister ", the words " or the Minister of Posts and Telecommunications ".
1973 c. 41.	The Fair Trading Act 1973.	In section 51(3), the words "and the Minister of Posts and Telecommunications ".

EXPLANATORY NOTE

(This Note is not part of the Order.)

This Order provides for the dissolution of the Ministry of Posts and Telecommunications and the transfer to the Secretary of State of all functions of the Minister. As an incidental matter it also corrects (Article 4(3)) a statutory reference to the Postmaster-General which should have been amended when the Post Office Act 1969 (c. 48) abolished that Office. Without the amendment made by Article 4(3) the effect of the Order would, in relation to section 40(3) of the Land Drainage Act 1930 (c. 44), be uncertain.

STATUTORY   INSTRUMENTS

1974 No. 692

MINISTERS OF THE CROWN

The Secretary of State (New Departments) Order 1974

Made - - - -	10*th April* 1974
Laid before Parliament	11*th April* 1974
Coming into Operation	16*th April* 1974

At the Court at Windsor Castle, the 10th day of April 1974

Present,

The Queen's Most Excellent Majesty in Council

Her Majesty, in pursuance of section 1 of the Ministers of the Crown (Transfer of Functions) Act 1946(a) and section 4 of the Ministers of the Crown Act 1964(b), is pleased, by and with the advice of Her Privy Council, to order, and it is hereby ordered, as follows:—

Citation, interpretation and commencement

1.—(1) This Order may be cited as the Secretary of State (New Departments) Order 1974.

(2) The Interpretation Act 1889(c) applies for the interpretation of this Order as it applies for the interpretation of an Act of Parliament.

(3) Any reference in this Order to an enactment or instrument is a reference to that enactment or instrument as amended or extended by or under any other enactment or instrument.

(4) This Order shall come into operation on 16th April 1974.

Transfer of functions and property

2.—(1) The functions of the Secretary of State for Trade and Industry under the provisions in column 1 of Schedule 1 to this Order shall be transferred as follows—

Functions under provisions in respective Parts of the Schedule	Transferred to Secretary of State for—
Part I	Energy
Part II	Industry
Part III	Trade
Part IV	Prices and Consumer Protection

(2) The functions of the Secretary of State for Trade and Industry under any local Act passed before the making of this Order, other than a local Act in Part I of Schedule 1 to this Order, shall be transferred to the Secretary of State for Trade.

(a) 1946 c. 31.   (b) 1964 c. 98.   (c) 1889 c. 63.

(3) Subject to the preceding provisions of this Article, any functions conferred on the Secretary of State for Trade and Industry by any enactment or instrument passed or made before the coming into operation of this Order shall be transferred to the Secretary of State.

(4) With any functions transferred by this Order to a Secretary of State, or to the Secretary of State, there shall be transferred to him all property, rights and liabilities to which the Secretary of State for Trade and Industry is entitled or subject in connection with the relevant functions at the coming into operation of this Order.

Style, seal and acts of Secretary of State

3.—(1) The person who at the coming into operation of this Order is the Secretary of State for each one of the new Departments and his successors shall be, by the name of his office as Secretary of State for that new Department, a corporation sole (with a corporate seal), but so that anything done by or in relation to any other Secretary of State for the Secretary of State for that new Department as a corporation sole shall have effect as if done by or in relation to the Secretary of State for that new Department.

(2) The corporate seal of the Secretary of State for any of the new Departments shall be authenticated by the signature of a Secretary of State, or of a Secretary to that Department, or of a person authorised by a Secretary of State to act in that behalf.

(3) The corporate seal of the Secretary of State for any of the new Departments shall be officially and judicially noticed, and every document purporting to be an instrument made or issued by the Secretary of State for that Department, and to be sealed with that seal authenticated in the manner provided by paragraph (2) above, or to be signed or executed by a Secretary to that Department, or a person authorised as above, shall be received in evidence and be deemed to be so made or issued without further proof, unless the contrary is shown.

(4) A certificate signed by the Secretary of State for any of the new Departments that any instrument purporting to be made or issued by him was so made or issued shall be conclusive evidence of that fact.

(5) In this Article " new Department " means the Department of Energy, the Department of Industry, the Department of Trade and the Department of Prices and Consumer Protection.

4.—(1) In Schedule 2 to the Parliamentary Commissioner Act 1967(a) there shall be inserted at the appropriate places in alphabetical order the entries—

" Department of Energy ".

" Department of Industry ".

" Department of Trade ".

" Department of Prices and Consumer Protection ".

(2) In the said Schedule 2 the words " Department of Trade and Industry " shall be repealed.

Supplemental

5.—(1) This Order shall not affect the validity of anything done by or in relation to the Secretary of State for Trade and Industry before the coming into operation of this Order, and anything which at the coming into operation of this Order is in process of being done by or in relation to the Secretary of

---

(a) 1967 c. 13.

State for Trade and Industry (including in particular any legal proceedings to which he is a party) may be continued by or in relation to the Secretary of State.

(2) Any authorisation given (by way of approval or otherwise), requirement imposed or appointment made by the Secretary of State for Trade and Industry in connection with functions transferred by this Order, or having effect as if so given, imposed or made, shall, if in force at the coming into operation of this Order, have effect as if given, imposed or made by the Secretary of State in so far as that is required for continuing its effect after the coming into operation of this Order.

(3) Subject to any express amendment made by this Order any enactment, instrument or contract passed or made before the coming into operation of this Order shall have effect, so far as may be necessary for the purpose or in consequence of the transfers effected by this Order, as if any reference to the Secretary of State for Trade and Industry or to his Department or an officer of his (including any reference which is to be construed as such a reference) were or included a reference to the Secretary of State to whom the transfer is made or to his Department, or an officer of his, as the case may be.

(4) Documents or forms printed or duplicated for use in connection with any functions transferred by this Order may be so used notwithstanding that they contain references to the Secretary of State for Trade and Industry, and those references shall be construed as references to the Secretary of State to whom the functions are transferred; and similarly with references to the Department or an officer of the Secretary of State for Trade and Industry.

(5) Schedule 2 to this Order, which contains consequential amendments, shall have effect.

(6) In paragraph 1 of Schedule 3 to the Secretary of State for the Environment Order 1970(a) sub-paragraphs (1), (2), (3) and (5) (which are spent) shall be revoked.

W. G. Agnew.

●

SCHEDULE 1

Article 2

PART I

ENERGY

Enactment referring to Secretary of State for Trade and Industry	*Subject matter*
Section 49(2) of the Public Health Act 1961(b) as amended by paragraph 19(2) of Schedule 3 to the Secretary of State for the Environment Order 1970.	Use of local authority vehicles on paths and bridleways.
Section 5(1)(b) of the Science and Technology Act 1965(c) as amended by paragraph 7 of the Schedule to the Ministry of Aviation Supply (Dissolution) Order 1971(d).	Powers as respects scientific research.

(a) S.I. 1970/1681 (1970 III, p. 5551).   (b) 1961 c. 64.
(c) 1965 c. 4.   (d) S.I. 1971/719 (1971 II, p. 1943).

Enactment referring to Secretary of State for Trade and Industry	*Subject matter*
Section 18(4)(*b*) of the Local Government (Scotland) Act 1966(**a**) as amended by paragraph 16(1)(*b*) of Schedule 6 to the Gas Act 1972(**b**).	Rating of British Gas Corporation.

In the General Rate Act 1967(**c**)—

Paragraph 12 of Schedule 6 as amended by paragraph 2 of Schedule 5 to the Gas Act 1972.	Rating of British Gas Corporation.
Paragraph 15 of Schedule 7, as amended by paragraph 23(2) of Schedule 3 to the Secretary of State for the Environment Order 1970.	Rating of Electricity Boards.

The Town and Country Planning Act 1971(**d**)—

Section 224(1)(*a*)	Appropriate Minister for electricity, gas and hydraulic power.
Section 273(1)	Application of Act to National Coal Board.

The Town and Country Planning (Scotland) Act 1972(**e**)—

Section 213(1)(*a*)	Appropriate Minister for gas and hydraulic power.
Section 259(1)	Application of Act to National Coal Board.

The Gas Act 1972(**f**)—

Section 26(6)	Standards of quality for gas.
Section 29(8) (two references)	Supply of gas by persons other than Corporation.
Section 35(2)	Terms and conditions of employment.

In Schedule 3 to the Secretary of State for the Environment Order 1970, paragraph—

1(4). 6(1)(i). 6(2)(i). 9(2)(b).	Definitions of "appropriate Minister" in relation to electricity, gas or hydraulic power.

Local Acts

Section 54 of the Trent and Lincolnshire Water Act 1971(**g**).	Trial borings for water: functions of appropriate Minister.
Section 34 of the Cumberland River Authority Act 1971(**h**).	Trial borings for water: functions of appropriate Minister.
Section 10(8) of the Tyneside Metropolitan Railway Act 1973(**i**).	Approval of underground electric cable.

(**a**) 1966 c. 51.	(**b**) 1972 c. 60.	(**c**) 1967 c. 9.
(**d**) 1971 c. 78.	(**e**) 1972 c. 52.	(**f**) 1972 c. 60.
(**g**) 1971 c. xiii.	(**h**) 1971 c. xvi.	(**i**) 1973 c. xxxii.

Enactment referring to Secretary of State for Trade and Industry	*Subject matter*
The North Wales Hydro Electric Power Act 1973(**a**)—	
Section 21(2)	Approval of plans for generating station.
Section 49(6)	Determination of questions concerning amenities.

PART II

INDUSTRY

Section 5(1)(*b*) of the Science and Technology Act 1965 as amended by paragraph 7 of the Schedule to the Ministry of Aviation Supply (Dissolution) Order 1971.	Powers as respects scientific research.
The Industry Act 1971(**b**)	Functions as respects property, rights and liabilities vesting under the Act.
Section 265(1) of the Town and Country Planning Act 1971.	Modification of Mines (Working Facilities and Support) Act 1966(**c**).
Section 252(1) of the Town and Country Planning (Scotland) Act 1972.	Modification of Mines (Working Facilities and Support) Act 1966.

PART III

TRADE

Sections 1(1) and 2 of the Coastguard Act 1925(**d**), as amended by paragraph 1 of Schedule 2 to the Secretary of State for Trade and Industry Order 1970(**e**).	Control of coastguard.
Section 41(7) of the Land Drainage Act 1930(**f**) as amended by paragraph 13 of Schedule 3 to the Secretary of State for the Environment Order 1970.	Variation of navigation rights in tidal waters.
The Harbours, Piers and Ferries (Scotland) Act 1937(**g**), as amended by paragraph 2 of Schedule 2 to the Secretary of State for Trade and Industry Order 1970.	Construction of works.
In the Water Resources Act 1963(**h**), as amended by paragraph 9 of Schedule 3 to the Secretary of State for the Environment Order 1970—	
Section 19(4)(*d*)(*e*).	Minimum flows for inland waters.
Paragraphs 4(*e*)(*f*) and 17 of Schedule 7.	
Section 18(4) of the Airports Authority Act 1965(**i**), as amended by paragraph 22 of Schedule 3 to the Secretary of State for the Environment Order 1970.	Planning decisions.

(**a**) 1973 c. xxxvi.   (**b**) 1971 c. 17.   (**c**) 1966 c. 4.
(**d**) 1925 c. 88.   (**e**) S.I. 1970/1537 (1970 III, p. 5293).
(**f**) 1930 c. 44.   (**g**) 1937 c. 28.   (**h**) 1963 c. 38.   (**i**) 1965 c. 16.

Enactment referring to Secretary of State for Trade and Industry	*Subject matter*
Sections 6 and 8 of the Sea Fish (Conservation) Act 1967(**a**), as amended by paragraph 10 of Schedule 2 to the Secretary of State for Trade and Industry Order 1970.	Regulation of landing of sea fish.
The Development of Tourism Act 1969(**b**), as amended by paragraph 12 of the Schedule 2 mentioned above.	Relevant Minister in England.
Section 224(1)(*b*) of the Town and Country Planning Act 1971.	Appropriate Minister for lighthouses.
Section 213(1)(*b*) of the Town and Country Planning (Scotland) Act 1972.	Appropriate Minister for lighthouses.
In the Insurance Companies Amendment Act 1973(**c**) sections 22(1)(*b*), 23(1)(*b*), 33(3)(*b*) and 34(2)(*b*).	Powers of intervention and changes of director, controller or manager.
In Schedule 3 to the Secretary of State for the Environment Order 1970, paragraph—	
6(1)(ii). 6(2)(ii). 11(3)(*a*).	Definitions of "appropriate Minister" in relation to airports and light-houses.

PART IV

PRICES AND CONSUMER PROTECTION

Section 9(11) of the Agriculture Act 1967(**d**), as amended by Article 2(3) of the Secretary of State for Trade and Industry Order 1970.	Exception of certain agreements from Part I of the Restrictive Trade Practices Act 1956.

Note: The amendments noted in column 1 of this Schedule are those which introduced references to the Secretary of State for Trade and Industry.

Article 5(5)　　　　　　　　**SCHEDULE 2**

CONSEQUENTIAL AMENDMENTS

The Science and Technology Act 1965

1. For section 5(1)(*b*) of the Science and Technology Act 1965 substitute—

" (*b*) as regards the Secretary of State for Defence, the Secretary of State for Energy and the Secretary of State for Industry, in furthering the practical application of the results of scientific research.".

The Town and Country Planning Acts

2. In section 224(1) of the Town and Country Planning Act 1971 (definition of appropriate Minister)—

(*a*) in paragraph (*a*) for the words " Trade and Industry " substitute " Energy ",

(*b*) in paragraph (*b*) for the words " the said Secretary of State " substitute " the Secretary of State for Trade ".

3. In section 213(1) of the Town and Country Planning (Scotland) Act 1972 (definition of appropriate Minister)—

(*a*) in paragraph (*a*) for the words " Trade and Industry " substitute " Energy ",

(*b*) in paragraph (*b*) for the words " the said Secretary of State " substitute " the Secretary of State for Trade ".

(**a**) 1967 c. 84.　　　(**b**) 1969 c. 51.　　　(**c**) 1973 c. 58.　　　(**d**) 1967 c. 22.

The Local Employment Act 1972

4. In section 8(6) and section 9(1)(*c*) of the Local Employment Act 1972(**a**) the words " for Trade and Industry " shall be repealed.

The Insurance Companies Amendment Act 1973

5. In the Insurance Companies Amendment Act 1973, in sections 22(1)(*b*), 23(1)(*b*), 33(3)(*b*) and 34(2)(*b*), the words " and Industry " shall be repealed.

The Secretary of State for the Environment Order 1970

6. In paragraph 6 of Schedule 3 to the Secretary of State for the Environment Order 1970, in sub-paragraph (1)(ii) and paragraph 2(ii) for the words " that Secretary of State " substitute the words " the Secretary of State for Trade ".

EXPLANATORY NOTE

(This Note is not part of the Order.)

This Order transfers all functions conferred on the Secretary of State for Trade and Industry. Functions under the provisions in the four Parts of Schedule 1 go respectively to the Secretaries of State for Energy, Industry, Trade, and Prices and Consumer Protection. Functions under local Acts not specified in the Schedule go to the Secretary of State for Trade, and any other functions go to the Secretary of State.

(**a**) 1972 c. 5.

STATUTORY INSTRUMENTS

1974 No. 693

TAXES

The Capital Gains Tax (Exempt Gilt-edged Securities) Order 1974

Made - - - *10th April* 1974

The Treasury, in exercise of the powers conferred on them by Section 41(2) of the Finance Act 1969(**a**), hereby make the following Order:—

1. This Order may be cited as the Capital Gains Tax (Exempt Gilt-edged Securities) Order 1974.

2. The Interpretation Act 1889(**b**) shall apply for the interpretation of this Order as it applies for the interpretation of an Act of Parliament.

3. The following security, being a stock denominated in sterling and issued after 15th April 1969 under section 12 of the National Loans Act 1968(**c**), is hereby specified for the purposes of section 41 of the Finance Act 1969 (gilt-edged securities exempt from tax on capital gains if held for more than twelve months):—

12 per cent Treasury Loan 1983

> *John Golding,*
> *T. Pendry,*
> Two of the Lords Commissioners of
> Her Majesty's Treasury.

10th April 1974.

EXPLANATORY NOTE
(*This Note is not part of the Order.*)

This Order adds the following gilt-edged security to the category of stocks and bonds which are exempt from tax on capital gains if held for more than twelve months:—

12 per cent Treasury Loan 1983

(**a**) 1969 c.32.   (**b**) 1889 c.63.   (**c**) 1968 c.13.

STATUTORY INSTRUMENTS

1974 No. 695 (C. 12)

CHILDREN AND YOUNG PERSONS

The Guardianship Act 1973 (Commencement No. 1) Order 1974

Made - - - *9th April* 1974

In exercise of the powers conferred upon me by section 15(3) of the Guardianship Act 1973(a), I hereby make the following Order:—

1. This Order may be cited as the Guardianship Act 1973 (Commencement No. 1) Order 1974.

2. Parts I and III of the Guardianship Act 1973 (including Schedules 1 to 3 thereto) shall come into force on 8th May 1974.

Roy Jenkins,
One of Her Majesty's Principal
Secretaries of State.

Home Office,
Whitehall.

9th April 1974.

EXPLANATORY NOTE

(*This Note is not part of the Order.*)

This Order brings into force Parts I and III of the Guardianship Act 1973 (including Schedules 1 to 3 thereto) on 8th May 1974.

Accordingly, it brings into force on that date, as respects England and Wales, all the provisions of the Act which extend exclusively thereto and, as respects the whole of the United Kingdom, the consequential amendment of the Maintenance Orders Act 1950 (c.37) contained in section 9(3)(*b*).

(**a**) 1973 c. 29.

STATUTORY INSTRUMENTS

1974 No. 698

HOUSING, ENGLAND AND WALES

HOUSING, SCOTLAND

The Housing Corporation Advances (Increase of Limit) Order 1974

Laid before the House of Commons in draft

Made	-	-	*9th April* 1974
Coming into Operation			*10th April* 1974

The Secretary of State for the Environment, the Secretary of State for Scotland and the Secretary of State for Wales, acting jointly in exercise of their powers under section 9(2) of the Housing Act 1964(a), as amended by section 77(3) of the Housing Finance Act 1972(b), and of all other powers enabling them in that behalf, hereby make the following order in the terms of a draft approved by resolution of the Commons House of Parliament:—

Citation and commencement

1. This order may be cited as the Housing Corporation Advances (Increase of Limit) Order 1974 and shall come into operation on the day following the day on which it is made.

Interpretation

2. The Interpretation Act 1889(c) shall apply for the interpretation of this order as it applies for the interpretation of an Act of Parliament.

Increase of limit of advances

3. £300 million is hereby specified as the sum which advances made to the

---

(a) 1964 c. 56.   (b) 1972 c. 47.   (c) 1889 c. 63.

Housing Corporation under section 9(2) of the Housing Act 1964, as amended by section 77(3) of the Housing Finance Act 1972, shall not together exceed.

Anthony Crosland,
Secretary of State for the Environment.

4th April 1974.

William Ross,
Secretary of State for Scotland.

8th April 1974.

John Morris,
Secretary of State for Wales.

9th April 1974.

EXPLANATORY NOTE

(This Note is not part of the Order.)

Under section 9 of the Housing Act 1964, as amended by section 77(3) of the Housing Finance Act 1972, the three Secretaries of State respectively may make advances to the Housing Corporation to enable the Corporation to exercise and perform their functions. The total amount which may be advanced to the Corporation is limited to £150 million or such greater sum, not exceeding £300 million, as the three Secretaries of State jointly may by Order specify. This Order specifies that the total amount which may be so advanced shall not exceed £300 million.

STATUTORY INSTRUMENTS

1974 No. 701

SEA FISHERIES

BOATS AND METHODS OF FISHING

The Foreign Sea-Fishery Officers (International Commission for the Northwest Atlantic Fisheries Scheme) Variation Order 1974

Made - - - -	*9th April* 1974
Laid before Parliament	*23rd April* 1974
Coming into Operation	*14th May* 1974

The Minister of Agriculture, Fisheries and Food and the Secretaries of State respectively concerned with the sea fishing industry in Scotland and Northern Ireland, in exercise of the powers conferred on them by sections 7(4) and 18(3) of the Sea Fisheries Act 1968(a) and of all other powers enabling them in that behalf, hereby make the following Order:—

Citation and commencement

1. This Order may be cited as the Foreign Sea-Fishery Officers (International Commission for the Northwest Atlantic Fisheries Scheme) Variation Order 1974 and shall come into operation on 14th May 1974.

Interpretation

2.—(1) In this Order "Principal Order" means the Foreign Sea-Fishery Officers (International Commission for the Northwest Atlantic Fisheries Scheme) Order 1971(b) as amended (c).

(2) The Interpretation Act 1889(d) shall apply to the interpretation of this Order as it applies to the interpretation of an Act of Parliament.

Variation of Principal Order

3. Reservation (*a*) in Part 1 of Schedule 1 to the Principal Order shall be omitted.

(a) 1968 c. 77.   (b) S.I. 1971/1103 (1971 II, p. 3282).
(c) The amending Order is not relevant to the subject matter of this Order.
(d) 1889 c. 63.

In Witness whereof the Official Seal of the Minister of Agriculture, Fisheries and Food is hereunto affixed on 8th April 1974.

(L.S.) *Frederick Peart,*
Minister of Agriculture, Fisheries and Food.

William Ross,
Secretary of State for Scotland.
9th April 1974.

Merlyn Rees,
Secretary of State for Northern Ireland.
9th April 1974.

EXPLANATORY NOTE

(This Note is not part of the Order.)

This Order varies the Foreign Sea-Fishery Officers (International Commission for the Northwest Atlantic Fisheries Scheme) Order 1971. Russia has withdrawn its reservations to the Scheme of Joint Enforcement of the Northwest Atlantic Fisheries Commission (set out in Part I of Schedule 1 to the Order) and is now allowing inspection of gear below deck of Russian fishing vessels and of catch. This Order reciprocates these new arrangements entitling Russian inspectors to inspect gear below deck of British fishing boats and their catch.

STATUTORY INSTRUMENTS

1974 No. 702

DEFENCE

The Imprisonment and Detention (Army) (Amendment) Rules 1974

Made - - - -	10th April 1974
Laid before Parliament	23rd April 1974
Coming into Operation	14th May 1974

The Secretary of State, in exercise of the powers conferred upon him by sections 119, 122, 123, 124, 126, 127 and 129 of the Army Act 1955(a), and section 52 of the Courts-Martial (Appeals) Act 1968(b) and of all other powers enabling him in that behalf, hereby makes the following Rules:—

Citation, commencement and interpretation

1.—(1) These Rules may be cited as the Imprisonment and Detention (Army) (Amendment) Rules 1974 and shall come into operation on 14th May 1974.

(2) The Interpretation Act 1889(c) shall apply to the interpretation of these Rules as it applies to the interpretation of an Act of Parliament.

(3) In these Rules, "the Principal Rules" means the Imprisonment and Detention (Army) Rules 1956(d), as amended (e).

Amendments to the Principal Rules

2.—(1) In Rule 2(2) of the Principal Rules, in the interpretation of the expression "the Act" there shall be added after "Army Act 1955" the words "as amended from time to time" and for references to section 209 of that Act wherever they appear in the Principal Rules there shall be substituted references to sections 208A or 209 thereof.

(2) Rule 22(3) of the Principal Rules shall be deleted.

(3) In Rule 47 of the Principal Rules there shall be added at the end the following paragraphs:

"(8) A soldier under sentence who is a non-smoker shall be issued with sweets and chocolates of an equivalent value to the issue of cigarettes, as laid down in the ration scales or other instructions issued from time to time by the Defence Council, and the first day of issue shall be the day after the admission of the soldier to the military establishment.

(a) 1955 c. 18.   (b) 1968 c. 20.

(c) 1889 c. 63.   (d) S.I. 1956/1914 (1956 I, p. 310).

(e) The relevant amending Instrument is S.I. 1962/2387 (1962 III, p. 3291).

(9) Forfeiture of sweets or chocolates may not be ordered as a punishment, but sweets and chocolates may be withheld on the advice of a medical officer during any period of sickness, and soldiers under sentence who are in close confinement or on restricted diet as a punishment shall not be entitled to an issue of, or to have in their possession, sweets or chocolates."

(4) In Rule 50 of the Principal Rules for the words "soldiers under sentence" there shall be substituted "persons to whom this Rule applies" and "soldier" and "a soldier under sentence" shall be amended accordingly and there shall be added at the end the following paragraph:

"(5) This Rule applies to

(a) soldiers under sentence in a military establishment;

(b) persons detained in safe custody in a military establishment pursuant to Rule 27 of these Rules;

Provided that in relation to a person to whom this Rule applies by virtue of sub-paragraph (b) above:

(i) no letter, or any part of a letter, written by or addressed to such a person shall be withheld without reference to higher authority;

(ii) any confidential communication between such a person and his legal adviser shall be exempt from censorship unless the commandant has reason to believe it contains matter unrelated to the case in respect of which the person is detained in safe custody."

(5) In Rule 57 of the Principal Rules—

(a) for the words "soldier under sentence" there shall be substituted "person on whom a military sentence of imprisonment or detention has been passed";

(b) there shall be inserted after the word "conviction", in both places, "(or, where applicable, sentence)";

(c) in the proviso there shall be inserted after the words "a police station" the words "or, in the case of a person on whom a military sentence of detention has been passed, in a military, naval or air-force prison,".

(6) In Rule 63(2)(a) of the Principal Rules, specifying the authorities or persons to be notified by the commandant on an escape of a person serving a military sentence of imprisonment or detention, there shall be inserted after (ii) the following:

"(iii) The Central Criminal Record and Intelligence Office RMP (CCRIO);" and the remaining persons and authorities shall be renumbered accordingly.

Dated this 10th day of April 1974.

Roy Mason,

One of Her Majesty's Principal
Secretaries of State.

· EXPLANATORY NOTE

(This Note is not part of the Rules.)

These Rules further amend the Imprisonment and Detention (Army) Rules 1956 mainly by the introduction of an issue of sweets and chocolates to prisoners who are non-smokers and by a qualified extension of the censorship rules to other persons in military custody. Amendments are included to reflect changes made by the Armed Forces Act 1971 (c. 33) (affecting the application of the Rules to civilians and relating to their right of appeal to the Courts-Martial Appeal Court against sentence as well as against conviction) and changes in the command structure within the United Kingdom.

STATUTORY INSTRUMENTS

1974 No. 703 (S.63)

NURSES AND MIDWIVES

The Nurses (Area Nurse-Training Committees) (Scotland) Order 1974

Made - - - -	*4th April* 1974
Laid before Parliament	*24th April* 1974
Coming into Operation	*15th May* 1974

In exercise of the powers conferred on me by section 19(1) and (4) of and the Fourth Schedule to the Nurses (Scotland) Act 1951(a) as amended by Part II of Schedule 6 to the National Health Service (Scotland) Act 1972(b) and of all other powers enabling me in that behalf, and after consultation with the General Nursing Council for Scotland, I hereby make the following order:—

Citation and commencement

1. This order may be cited as the Nurses (Area Nurse-Training Committees) (Scotland) Order 1974 and shall come into operation on 15th May 1974.

Interpretation

2.—(1) In this order, unless the context otherwise requires, the following expressions have the respective meanings hereby assigned to them:—

"the Act of 1972" means the National Health Service (Scotland) Act 1972(b);

"Area Nursing and Midwifery Committee" means the committee of that name for a board area recognised under section 16 of the Act of 1972;

"Committee" means an Area Nurse-Training Committee;

"the Council" means the General Nursing Council for Scotland;

"board area" means an area for which a Health Board is for the time being constituted under section 13(1) of the Act of 1972 and known by the title set out in the Schedule to the National Health Service (Determination of Areas of Health Boards) (Scotland) Order 1974(c).

(2) The Interpretation Act 1889(d) applies for the interpretation of this order as it applies for the interpretation of an Act of Parliament.

Constitution and title of Committees

3.—(1) A Committee shall on 1st April 1974 be constituted for each of the board areas or combination of such areas set out in column (2) of the Schedule to this order.

(2) Each Committee shall be known by the title set out in column (1) of the Schedule to this order opposite the name of the board area or the names of the combination of such areas for which the Committee is constituted.

Appointment of members

4.—(1) Each Committee shall consist of thirteen members appointed as follows:—

(*a*) six persons appointed by the Health Board for the area for which the Committee is constituted, or, if that area consists of a combination of board areas, by the Health Boards for those areas acting jointly;

(b) four persons appointed by the Council;

(c) one person appointed by the Central Midwives Board for Scotland;

(d) two persons appointed by the Secretary of State after consultation with the education authorities for the area for which the Committee is constituted and with such universities as the Secretary of State thinks fit.

(2) One of the persons appointed under paragraph (1)(a) of this Article shall be so appointed after consultation by the Health Board or Health Boards concerned with the appropriate area nursing and midwifery committee or committees.

Qualifications of members

5.—(1) Of the members appointed to a Committee by a Health Board or by Health Boards acting jointly, four shall be registered nurses and one shall be a fully registered medical practitioner.

(2) Of the members appointed by the Council at least three shall be registered nurses of which one shall be a representative of community nursing interests.

(3) The member appointed by the Central Midwives Board for Scotland shall be a registered nurse and certified midwife.

(4) The members appointed by the Secretary of State shall be persons with experience in education.

Tenure of office of members

6.—(1) "Chairman" in relation to a Committee, means the chairman selected by the Committee from among their members in accordance with paragraph 6 of Schedule 4 to the Nurses (Scotland) Act 1951.

(2) The term of office of members of a Committee shall be four years expiring on 31st March in the relevant year, except that, in the case of persons appointed at the coming into operation of this order, two members appointed by a Health Board or Health Boards acting jointly, two members appointed by the Council and the two members appointed by the Secretary of State shall have a term of office expiring on 31st March 1976.

(3) The Chairman of a Committee may resign his membership on giving notice in writing to the Committee and to the authority or authorities which appointed him to the Committee, and any other member may resign on giving notice in writing to the Chairman, who shall immediately give written notice to the authority or authorities which appointed that member.

(4) A casual vacancy occurring at any time shall be filled as soon as may be by the authority or authorities which appointed the member who has vacated office and the person appointed to fill the vacancy shall hold office for the remainder of the period for which his predecessor was appointed.

(5) A member shall, on the expiration of his term of office, be eligible for re-appointment.

(6) The provisions of subsections (1) (except paragraph (a)), (2) and (3) of section 31 of the Local Government (Scotland) Act 1973 **(a)** (which relates to the disqualifications for nomination, election and holding office as a member of a local authority) shall apply to a Committee as if those provisions related to disqualifications for membership of a Committee.

(a) 1973 c. 65.

Procedure of Committees

7. A Committee shall make standing orders respecting its procedure, including the quorum (which shall not be less than three members), and may vary or revoke such standing orders.

Sub- committees

8.—(1) A Committee may appoint such sub-committees as it may think fit, consisting either wholly of members of the Committee or partly of members of the Committee and partly of other persons, in such proportion as it may determine.

(2) The Chairman of a sub-committee shall be appointed by the Committee.

(3) A Committee may delegate all or any of its functions to a sub-committee subject to such restrictions or conditions as it may think fit.

(4) A Committee appointing a sub-committee may make standing orders respecting the quorum, proceedings and place of meeting of the sub-committee, and may vary or revoke such standing orders.

Estimates of expenditure

9.—(1) Each Committee shall, not later than 31st August in each year or such later date as the Secretary of State may approve, submit to the Council an estimate of all expenditure during the following financial year.

(2) The estimate shall be submitted in such form as the Council, with the approval of the Secretary of State, may from time to time determine.

(3) The Council may approve the estimate with or without modification and the expenditure of a Committee in any financial year shall not, without the prior sanction of the Council, exceed the amount of the estimate approved by the Council.

Accounts

10.—(1) The financial year shall end on 31st March in each year, and a Committee shall make up its accounts of income and expenditure to that date.

(2) The accounts shall be made up in such form as the Council, with the approval of the Secretary of State, may from time to time determine.

Audit

11.—(1) Not later than 30th June in each year a Committee shall submit its accounts to an auditor appointed by the Secretary of State.

(2) The auditor shall have a right of access at all reasonable times to the books, accounts and vouchers of a Committee: he may, by writing under his hand, require the production before him of all books, deeds, contracts, accounts, vouchers, receipts and other documents and shall be entitled to require from the members and officers of the Committee such information or explanation as he may deem necessary for the purpose of the audit.

(3) Each Committee shall submit its audited accounts to the Council not later than 31st August in each year.

Revocation

12.—(1) The Nurses (Regional Nurse-Training Committees) (Scotland) Order 1963**(a)**, the Nurses (Regional Nurse-Training Committees) (Scotland) Amendment Order 1966**(b)** and the Nurses (Regional Nurse-Training Committees) (Scotland) Amendment Order 1969**(c)**, are hereby revoked.

(a) S.I. 1963/1342 (1963 II, p. 2325).   (b) S.I. 1966/919 (1966 II, p. 2203).
(c) S.I. 1969/849 (1969 II, p. 2381).

(2) Section 38 of the Interpretation Act 1889 shall apply as if this order were an Act of Parliament and as if the orders revoked by this order were Acts of Parliament repealed by an Act of Parliament.

(sgd.) *William Ross,*
One of Her Majesty's Principal
Secretaries of State.

St. Andrew's House,
Edinburgh.
4th April 1974.

SCHEDULE

(1)	(2)
Title of Committee	Area of Health Board or combination of Areas of Health Boards
Northern Area Nurse-Training Committee	Combination of the Areas of the Highland the Western Isles Health Boards
North-Eastern Area Nurse-Training Committee	Combination of the Areas of the Grampian, Orkney and Shetland Health Boards
Eastern Area Nurse-Training Committee	Area of the Tayside Health Board
Glasgow Area Nurse-Training Committee	Area of the Greater Glasgow Health Board
South-Eastern Area Nurse-Training Committee	Combination of the Areas of the Lothian, Fife and the Borders Health Boards
West Central Area Nurse-Training Committee	Combination of the Areas of the Argyll and Clyde and Forth Valley Health Boards
Western Area Nurse-Training Committee	Combination of the Areas of the Lanarkshire, Ayrshire and Arran and Dumfries and Galloway Health Boards

EXPLANATORY NOTE

(This Note is not part of the Order.)

This Order provides for the setting up of seven Area Nurse-Training Committees to replace five Regional Nurse-Training Committees following the reorganisation of the health service. The duty of these Committees is generally to supervise the training of nurses in accordance with the training rules laid down by the General Nursing Council for Scotland.

STATUTORY INSTRUMENTS

1974 No. 706 (L.13)

MAGISTRATES' COURTS

The Magistrates' Courts (Guardianship of Minors) Rules 1974

Made - - -	11*th April* 1974
Laid before Parliament	24*th April* 1974
Coming into Operation	8*th May* 1974

The Lord Chancellor, in exercise of the powers conferred on him by section 3 of the Marriage Act 1949(**a**) and by section 15 of the Justices of the Peace Act 1949(**b**), as extended by section 122 of the Magistrates' Courts Act 1952(**c**), section 16(5) of the Guardianship of Minors Act 1971(**d**) and that section as applied by sections 1(6), 3(3) and 4(3) of the Guardianship Act 1973(**e**), and section 3(4) of the said Act of 1973, after consultation with the Rule Committee appointed under the said section 15, hereby makes the following Rules:—

Citation and commencement

1. These Rules may be cited as the Magistrates' Courts (Guardianship of Minors) Rules 1974 and shall come into operation on 8th May 1974.

Interpretation

2.—(1) In these Rules, the following expressions have the meanings hereby respectively assigned to them, that is to say:—

"the Act of 1949" means the Marriage Act 1949;

"the Act of 1971" means the Guardianship of Minors Act 1971;

"the Act of 1973" means the Guardianship Act 1973;

"court" means a magistrates' court;

"the Rules of 1968" means the Magistrates' Courts Rules 1968(**f**), as amended(**g**);

"supervision order" means an order made by a magistrates' court under section 2(2)(*a*) of the Act of 1973 providing for the supervision of a minor by a probation officer or local authority.

(2) In these Rules, unless the context otherwise requires, any reference to a rule or to the Schedule shall be construed as a reference to a rule contained in these Rules or to the Schedule thereto; and any reference in a rule to a paragraph shall be construed as a reference to a paragraph of that rule.

(3) In these Rules, any reference to a form in the Schedule shall be construed as including a reference to a form to the like effect with such variations as the circumstances may require.

(**a**) 1949 c. 76.   (**b**) 1949 c. 101.   (**c**) 1952 c. 55.
(**d**) 1971 c. 3.   (**e**) 1973 c. 29.
(**f**) S.I. 1968/1920 (1968 III, p. 5175).
(**g**) The relevant amending instrument is S.I. 1973/790 (1973 I, p. 2500).

(4) In these Rules, unless the context otherwise requires, any reference to any enactment shall be construed as a reference to that enactment as amended, extended or applied by any subsequent enactment.

(5) The Interpretation Act 1889(a) shall apply for the interpretation of these Rules as it applies for the interpretation of an Act of Parliament.

Revocation

3. The Guardianship of Infants (Summary Jurisdiction) Rules 1925(b) and the Guardianship of Infants (Summary Jurisdiction) Rules 1944(c) are hereby revoked.

Applications under Guardianship of Minors Acts 1971 and 1973 to be by complaint

4. Except as provided in rule 8, an application to a court under any provision of the Act of 1971 or the Act of 1973 shall be made by way of complaint.

Procedure for applications for consent to marriage

5.—(1) An application for the consent of the court to the marriage of a minor under section 3 of the Act of 1949 (marriages of persons under 18) may be made, either orally or in writing, to a justice of the peace having jurisdiction in the place where the applicant or any respondent resides.

(2) Upon receiving such an application as is referred to in paragraph (1) the justice shall, where the application was in consequence of a refusal to give consent to the marriage, give to any person whose consent is required and who has refused consent a notice of the application and of the date, time and place appointed for the hearing thereof.

(3) Rule 82 of the Rules of 1968 (service of summons, etc.) shall apply in relation to the service of a notice given in accordance with paragraph (2) as it applies in relation to the service of a summons issued on a person other than a corporation.

(4) The provisions of Part II of the Magistrates' Courts Act 1952 relating to the hearing of a complaint and of rule 14 of the Rules of 1968 (order of evidence and speeches) shall apply to the hearing of such an application as is referred to in paragraph (1) as if it were made by way of complaint but as if for any reference therein to the complainant, the complaint, the defendant and his defence there were substituted references, respectively, to the applicant, the application, the respondent and his case.

Provisions for certain hearings to be in camera

6. If a court which hears an application under section 3 of the Act of 1949 or any provision of the Act of 1971 considers it expedient in the interests of the minor, it may decide to hear the proceedings in camera.

Notice to local authority of proposal to commit minor to its care

7. Where, on an application under section 9 of the Act of 1971 (orders for custody and maintenance), the court proposes to commit a minor to the care of a local authority under section 2(2)(b) of the Act of 1973, the court shall, at least ten days before making the order, cause a notice in the form numbered 1 in the Schedule to be delivered or sent by post to that authority.

(a) 1889 c. 63.　　　　　　(b) S. R. & O. 1925/960 (Rev. XIII, p. 245: 1925 p. 512).
(c) S. R. & O. 1944/1206 (Rev. XIII, p. 245: 1944 I, p. 327).

Substitution of new supervisor for minor

8.—(1) Where a supervision order is in force and the court is of the opinion, upon representations made to it orally or in writing—

(*a*) in the case of an order providing for the supervision of the minor by a probation officer appointed or assigned to a petty sessions area, by or on behalf of any probation officer appointed for or assigned to that area, or

(*b*) in the case of an order providing for the supervision of the minor by a local authority, by or on behalf of that authority,

that the child is or will be resident in a different petty sessions area or, as the case may be, in the area of another local authority, the court may vary the order by substituting a probation officer appointed for or assigned to the other petty sessions area or, as the case may be, by substituting the other local authority.

(2) Where the court varies a supervision order in accordance with this rule, the court shall cause a notice in the form numbered 2 in the Schedule to be delivered or sent by post—

(*a*) to the person who has for the time being the custody of the minor by virtue of an order under section 9 of the Act of 1971; and

(*b*) in duplicate, to the clerk to the justices for the petty sessions area or, as the case may be, the local authority substituted by the order made under this rule,

and shall cause the probation officer or local authority by or on whose behalf the representations were made to be informed that the order has been so varied.

Defendants to application for variation or discharge of order

9.—(1) The following paragraphs of this rule shall have effect for the purpose of making provision as to the persons (not being the applicant) who shall be made defendants on an application under the provisions of the Act of 1971 and the Act of 1973 therein mentioned.

(2) Where the application is made under section 1(5) of the Act of 1973 for the variation or discharge of an order under section 1(3) of that Act the persons to be made defendants shall be—

(*a*) the parent or parents of the minor;

(*b*) any person having the custody of the minor;

(*c*) where, under an order giving custody, the minor is for the time being under the supervision of a probation officer or local authority, that probation officer or, as the case may be, that authority;

(*d*) where, after the death of either of the parents, any guardian has been appointed or is acting under the Act of 1971, that guardian.

(3) Where the application is made under section 9 of the Act of 1971 for the variation or discharge of an order giving the custody of a minor to a person other than one of the parents the persons to be made defendants shall be—

(*a*) the persons specified in sub-paragraphs (*a*) and (*d*) of paragraph (2);

(*b*) the person for the time being having the custody of the minor by virtue of the order;

(*c*) where, under the order, the minor is for the time being under the supervision of a probation officer or local authority, that probation officer or, as the case may be, that authority.

The father of a minor who is illegitimate shall not be treated as a parent of that minor for the purposes of sub-paragraph (*a*) of this paragraph unless he has been adjudged by a court to be the father of that minor or unless he was a party to the proceedings in which the order was made.

(4) Where the application is made under section 3(3) of the Act of 1973 for the variation or discharge of a supervision order the persons to be made defendants shall be—

(*a*) the persons specified in sub-paragraphs (*a*) to (*c*) of paragraph (3); and

(*b*) if the application is for the variation of the order, any probation officer or local authority whom it is sought to substitute for the officer or local authority under whose supervision the minor is.

(5) Where the application is made under section 9 of the Act of 1971, as applied by section 4(3) of the Act of 1973, for the discharge of an order under section 2(2)(*b*) of the Act of 1973 committing a minor to the care of a local authority, the persons to be made defendants shall be—

(*a*) the persons specified in sub-paragraph (*a*) of paragraph (3); and

(*b*) the local authority to whose care the minor has been committed.

(6) Where the application is made for the variation or discharge of an order under section 9(2) of the Act of 1971 in a case where custody has been given by an order under sub-section (1) thereof to a person other than one of the parents the persons to be made defendants shall be—

(*a*) the person or persons by whom payment is required to be made under the order; and

(*b*) the person to whom payment falls to be made.

(7) Where the application is made for the variation or discharge of an order under section 2(3) of the Act of 1973 requiring payments to be made to the local authority to whom the care of the minor was committed by an order under section 2(2)(*b*) of that Act, the persons to be made defendants shall be—

(*a*) the person or persons by whom payment is required to be made; and

(*b*) the local authority to whose care the minor was committed.

Notice to defendant outside United Kingdom of complaint for revocation etc. of order

10.—(1) Where a complaint is made for the revocation, revival or variation of an order for the payment of sums towards the maintenance of a minor under section 9, 10 or 11 of the Act of 1971 and—

(*a*) the defendant does not appear at the time and place appointed for the hearing of the complaint, and

(*b*) the court is satisfied that there is reason to believe that the defendant has been outside the United Kingdom during the whole of the period beginning one month before the making of the complaint and ending with the date of the hearing,

the court may, subject to paragraph (2), if it thinks it reasonable in all the circumstances to do so, proceed to hear and determine the complaint at the time and place appointed for the hearing or for any adjourned hearing in like manner as if the defendant had appeared at that time and place if it has been proved to the satisfaction of the court that the complainant has taken any of the following steps to give notice to the defendant of the making of the complaint and of the time and place aforesaid, that is to say:—

(a) has caused a notice in the form numbered 3 in the Schedule to be delivered to the defendant or sent by post addressed to the defendant at his last known or usual place of abode or at his place of business or at such other address at which there is ground for believing that it will reach him; or

(b) has caused a notice summarising the matters dealt with in the form referred to in sub-paragraph (a) of this paragraph to be inserted in one or more newspapers on one or more occasions.

(2) Where it is proposed to take any of the steps referred to in paragraph (1) other than delivering the notice to the defendant, the complainant shall apply for directions to a justice of the peace acting for the same petty sessions area as that of the court by which the complaint is to be heard, and the taking of such steps shall be effective for the purposes of this rule only if they were taken in accordance with the directions given by the said justice.

(3) Rule 55(1) of the Rules of 1968 (proof of service, handwriting, etc.) shall apply for the purpose of proving the delivery of a written notice in pursuance of paragraph (1)(a) as it applies for the purpose of proving the service of a summons.

In relation to a solemn declaration made outside the United Kingdom, the said rule 55(1), as applied by this paragraph, shall have effect as if for the reference to the persons before whom the declaration is to be made there were substituted a reference to a consular officer of Her Majesty's Government in the United Kingdom, or any person for the time being authorised by law, in the place where the declarant is, to administer an oath for any judicial or other legal purpose.

(4) Rule 55(2) of the Rules of 1968 shall apply for the purpose of proving the sending by post of a written notice in pursuance of paragraph (1)(a), or the insertion of a notice in a newspaper in pursuance of paragraph (1)(b), as it applies for the purpose of proving the service of any process, provided, as respects the insertion of a notice in a newspaper, that a copy of the newspaper containing the notice is annexed to the certificate.

Certificate by clerk when maintenance payments are forwarded abroad

11. A complainant for the revocation or variation of an order under section 9, 10 or 11 of the Act of 1971 under which payments fall to be made by the complainant to the defendant through the clerk of a magistrates' court may apply to the clerk for such a certificate as is mentioned in section 9(4) of the Matrimonial Proceedings (Magistrates' Courts) Act 1960(a) and, if the facts warrant it, the clerk shall supply such a certificate to the complainant in the form numbered 4 in the Schedule.

Dated 11th April 1974.

Elwyn-Jones C.

(a) 1960 c. 48.

SCHEDULE

Rules 7, 8,
10 and 11

FORMS

1

Notice to local authority of proposal to commit a minor to their care
(G. of M. Act 1971, s. 9; G. Act 1973, ss. 2(2)(*b*), 4(2).)

....Magistrates' Court (*Code*)

To the council of the [non-metropolitan county] [metropolitan district] of

....

Proceedings are pending under section 9 of the Guardianship of Minors Act 1971, before this Court between A.B. of   , and B.B. of   .

Notice is hereby given that the Court proposes to commit the following minors to the care of the council, namely:—

C.B., D.B., and E.F.

If the Council wishes to make any representations in this matter, including representations about payments to the council towards the maintenance of the said minors, the Court will hear such representations on   , at   .m.

Dated: .

J.C.,
Justices' Clerk.

2

Notice of appointment of new supervisor for minor
(G. Act 1973, s. 3(4).)

....Magistrates' Court (*Code*)

To A.B., who has for the time being the custody of C.B. by virtue of an order under section 9 of the Guardianship of Minors Act 1971.

To the justices' clerk for the   petty sessions area [*or* to the council of the [non-metropolitan county] [metropolitan district] of   ].

By an order dated the   day of   , 19   , made under section 2(2)(*a*) of the Guardianship Act 1973, the said C.B., then of   , was placed under the supervision of a probation officer for the petty sessions area [*or* of the council of the [non-metropolitan county] [metropolitan district] of   ].

You are hereby given notice that the Court, being of the opinion that the said C.B. is now or will be resident in the   petty sessions area [*or* the area of the council of the [non-metropolitan county] [metropolitan district] of   at   ], has varied the order so that the said C.B., shall be under the supervision of a probation officer for that petty sessions area [or of that council].

Dated: .

J.C.,
Justices' Clerk.

3

Notice to defendant outside United Kingdom of complaint for revocation etc. of order for maintenance payments

(M.P.(M.C.) Act 1960, s.9(2) and (3); M.O.(R.E.) Act 1972, s.41(2).)

....Magistrates' Court *(Code)*

To A.B.

of

A complaint has been made by me, the undersigned, this day [*or* on   ] to the above Magistrates' Court sitting at under section 53 of the Magistrates' Court Act 1952, that the order made by that Court under the Guardianship of Minors Act 1971 for the payment of periodical sums towards the maintenance of C.B. on   , should be [revoked] [revived] [varied by   ].

The complaint will be heard by that Court on   , at   .m. You may appear in person or be represented by a barrister or solicitor at the hearing. If you do neither, the Court may, if it thinks it reasonable deal with the case in your absence.

[*To be completed in a case where the complaint is for the revocation or variation of a provision for the making of payments by the complainant to the defendant and is based on the defendant's prolonged absence abroad as mentioned in s.9(3) of the M.P. (M.C.) Act* 1960.

At the hearing I intend to satisfy the Court that there is reason to believe that during the period of six months immediately preceding the making of the complaint you were continuously outside the United Kingdom or were not in the United Kingdom on more than thirty days. If the Court is satisfied of this, it may, after having regard to any communication to the Court in writing from you, revoke the order for payments by me to you or reduce the amount of the payments. If you wish to make any written communication, you should do so by letter addressed to the Justices' Clerk at (*address*) so that it will reach him before the hearing.]

(Signed) B.B.

4

Certificate by clerk when maintenance payments are forwarded abroad

(M.P. (M.C.) Act 1960, s.9(4); M.O. (R.E.) Act 1972, s.41(2).)

I, J.C., the Clerk to the Magistrates' Court sitting at through whom payments fall to be made by A.B. to B.B. under an order under the Guardianship of Minors Act 1971 made by the Magistrates' Court sitting at   , on   , hereby certify that (*a*) during the period from   , to   , every payment made under the order has been forwarded by me to an address outside the United Kingdom, namely   ; and (*b*) during the period from   , to   , the said B.B. has not, to my knowledge, been in the United Kingdom at any time [*or* on more than thirty days, namely from   , to   .]

Date: .

J.C.

EXPLANATORY NOTE
(*This Note is not part of the Rules.*)

These Rules, which revoke the Guardianship of Infants (Summary Juris-diction) Rules of 1925 and 1944, contain provisions similar to those in the 1925 Rules relating to the procedure for hearing applications under the Guardianship of Minors Act 1971 and applications for consent to marriage under section 3 of the Marriage Act 1949 and also contain new provisions which take account of the amendments made to the 1971 Act by the Guardianship Act 1973 and of the application of section 9 of the Matrimonial Proceedings (Magistrates' Courts) Act 1960 to maintenance payments under the 1971 Act by section 41 of the Maintenance Orders (Reciprocal Enforcement) Act 1972(c.18).

Rule 4 provides for applications to a magistrates' court under the 1971 Act to be by way of complaint. Rule 5 relates to the procedure for applications for the consent of the court to the marriage of a minor under section 3 of the Marriage Act 1949. Rule 6 enables the court to hear proceedings under the 1971 Act or section 3 of the Marriage Act 1949 *in camera* if it considers it expedient in the interests of the minor.

Rule 7 provides for notice to be given to the local authority where a court hearing an application under section 9 of the 1971 Act proposes to commit a minor to the care of that authority under section 2(2)(*b*) of the 1973 Act in the form numbered 1 in the Schedule. Rule 8 enables the court to substitute a new local authority or probation officer as supervisor, upon representations by the existing supervisor, where a supervision order has been made under section 2(2)(*a*) of the 1973 Act and the minor has changed or is about to change his residence. In such a case the Rule provides for notice in form 2 to be given to the person who has custody of the minor and the local authority or (as the case may be) clerk to the justices of the petty sessions area substituted by the order.

Rule 9 makes provision as to the persons to be made defendants to applica-tions to vary or discharge an order under section 1(3) of the 1973 Act, an order under section 9 of the 1971 Act, in a case where custody is given to a person other than one of the parents, a supervision order or an order committing a minor to the local authority under section 2(2) of the 1973 Act (including any order for payments to a local authority under section 3(3) of the Act).

Rule 10 (together with form 3 in the Schedule) provides for notice to be given to a defendant outside the United Kingdom by a complainant for the revocation, revival or variation of an order under section 9, 10 or 11 of the 1971 Act providing for periodical payments towards the maintenance of a minor for the purpose of the hearing of the complaint in the absence of the defendant under section 9 of the Matrimonial Proceedings (Magistrates' Courts Act) 1960, as applied by section 41 of the Maintenance Orders (Reciprocal Enforcement) Act 1972. Rule 11 (with form 4) provides for a certificate by a clerk to a magistrates' court in a case where payments have been made by the clerk to the defendant at an address outside the United Kingdom.

STATUTORY INSTRUMENTS

1974 No. 707

LOCAL GOVERNMENT, ENGLAND AND WALES

The Local Government Administration (Representative Body for Wales) Order 1974

Made - - -	16*th April* 1974
Laid before Parliament	18*th April* 1974
Coming into Operation	1*st May* 1974

The Secretary of State for Wales, in exercise of the powers conferred upon him by section 24(1) of the Local Government Act 1974(**a**) and of all other powers enabling him in that behalf, hereby makes the following order:—

Title and commencement

1. This order may be cited as the Local Government Administration (Representative Body for Wales) Order 1974 and shall come into operation on 1st May 1974.

Interpretation

2. The Interpretation Act 1889(**b**) shall apply for the interpretation of this order as it applies for the interpretation of an Act of Parliament.

Designation of representative body for Wales

3. For the purposes of section 24 of the Local Government Act 1974 (which provides for the designation of bodies representing the authorities to which are applied the provisions of the Act with regard to investigations of alleged maladministration) the body consisting of—

(*a*) four members appointed by the committee consisting of representatives of county councils in Wales known as the Welsh Counties Committee,

(*b*) four members appointed by the council consisting of representatives of district councils in Wales known as the Council for the Principality,

(*c*) two members appointed by the Welsh National Water Development Authority, one of whom shall be the member of that Authority who has been appointed by the Secretary of State as a member of the Severn-Trent Water Authority under section 3(4) of the Water Act 1973(**c**),

is hereby designated as the representative body for Wales.

John Morris,
Secretary of State for Wales.

16th April 1974.

(**a**) 1974 c.7.   (**b**) 1889 c.63.   (**c**) 1973 c.37.

EXPLANATORY NOTE

(This Note is not part of the Order.)

Part III of the Local Government Act 1974 sets up machinery for the investigation of alleged maladministration by local and certain other authorities. Investigations in Wales are to be carried out by one or more Local Commissioners who submit reports to the Commission for Local Administration in Wales, and the Commission in turn submit reports to the representative body for Wales, which represents the authorities to which Part III applies. This Order designates as the representative body for Wales a body consisting of members appointed by—

(*a*) bodies representing county councils and district councils in Wales, and

(*b*) the Welsh National Water Development Authority.

STATUTORY INSTRUMENTS

1974 No. 708 (S.64)

EDUCATION, SCOTLAND
Milk and Meals (Education) (Scotland) Amendment Regulations 1974

Made - - -	11*th April* 1974
Laid before Parliament	25*th April* 1974
Coming into Operation	15*th May* 1974

In exercise of the powers conferred on me by sections 53(3) and 144(5) of the Education (Scotland) Act 1962(**a**), and of all other powers enabling me in that behalf, I hereby make the following regulations: —

Citation, commencement and interpretation

1.—(1) These regulations may be cited as the Milk and Meals (Education) (Scotland) Amendment Regulations 1974 and these regulations and the Milk and Meals (Education) (Scotland) Regulations 1971 to 1973 may be cited together as the Milk and Meals (Education) (Scotland) Regulations 1971 to 1974.

(2) These regulations shall come into operation on 15th May 1974.

(3) The Interpretation Act 1889(**b**) shall apply for the interpretation of these regulations as it applies for the interpretation of an Act of Parliament.

Amendment of principal regulations

2. The Milk and Meals (Education) (Scotland) Regulations 1971(**c**) as amended (**d**) shall have effect subject to—

(*a*) the substitution in regulation 2(1) for the words " 'medical officer of health' has the same meaning as in section 79(1) and 87(1) of the Local Government (Scotland) Act 1947" of the words " 'Health Board' means a board constituted under section 13 of the National Health Service (Scotland) Act 1972"(**e**);

(*b*) the substitution in regulation 3(1)(*b*) for the words "the education authority" of the words "a Health Board in the area of the authority";

(*c*) the substitution in proviso (*a*) to regulation 3(2) for the words "the medical officer of health for" of the words "a designated medical officer of a Health Board in"; and

(*d*) the substitution in regulation 3(3) for the words "and the expression" of the words "the expression" and the addition at the end of the regulation of the words "and the expression 'designated medical officer' means a medical officer designated under section 21 of the National Health Service (Scotland) Act 1972".

(**a**) 1962 c. 47. (**b**) 1889 c. 63.
(**c**) S.I. 1971/1537 (1971 III, p. 4340).
(**d**) S.I. 1972/1220, 1973/423, 1258 (1972 II, p. 3612; 1973 I, p. 1386; II, p. 3729).
(**e**) 1972 c. 58.

William Ross,
One of Her Majesty's Principal
Secretaries of State.

St. Andrew's House,
Edinburgh.
11th April 1974.

EXPLANATORY NOTE

(This Note is not part of the Regulations.)

These Regulations amend the Milk and Meals (Education) (Scotland) Regulations 1971 by substituting for the references therein to "medical officer of the education authority" and "the medical officer of health for the area of the authority" references to "medical officer of a Health Board in the area of the authority" and "a designated medical officer of a Health Board in the area of the authority" to take account of the changes brought about by the provisions of the National Health Service (Scotland) Act 1972.

1974 No. 709 (C.13)

LEGAL AID AND ADVICE, ENGLAND
The Legal Aid Act 1974 (Commencement No. 1) Order 1974

Made - - - *8th April* 1974

The Lord Chancellor, in exercise of the powers conferred on him by section 43(4)(*c*) of the Legal Aid Act 1974(**a**), hereby makes the following Order: —

1.—(1) The Interpretation Act 1889(**b**) shall apply to the interpretation of this Order as it applies to the interpretation of an Act of Parliament.

(2) This Order may be cited as the Legal Aid Act 1974 (Commencement No. 1) Order 1974.

2. Paragraph 3(*e*) of Part I of Schedule 1 to the Legal Aid Act 1974 shall come into operation on 8th May 1974.

Dated 8th April 1974.

Elwyn-Jones, C.

EXPLANATORY NOTE
(This Note is not part of the Order.)

This Order brings into operation on 8th May 1974 paragraph 3(*e*) of Part I of Schedule 1 to the Legal Aid Act 1974, which makes legal aid available in connection with proceedings under Part I of the Maintenance Orders (Reciprocal Enforcement) Act 1972 (c.18) relating to a maintenance order made by a court of a country outside the United Kingdom.

(**a**) 1974 c. 4.   (**b**) 1889 c. 63.

STATUTORY INSTRUMENTS

1974 No. 711

MEDICINES

The Medicines (Interim Prescription Only) (No. 1) Order 1974

Made	- - -	9th April 1974
Laid before Parliament		25th April 1974
Coming into Operation		19th May 1974

The Secretaries of State respectively concerned with health in England and in Wales, the Secretary of State concerned with health and with agriculture in Scotland, the Minister of Agriculture, Fisheries and Food, the Head of the Department of Health and Social Services for Northern Ireland and the Head of the Department of Agriculture for Northern Ireland, acting jointly, in exercise of powers conferred by section 62(1) of the Medicines Act 1968(a) and now vested in them (b) and of all other powers enabling them in that behalf, it appearing to them to be necessary in the interests of safety to make the following order, after consulting such organisations as appear to them to be representative of interests likely to be substantially affected by the order, and after consulting and taking into account the advice of the Committee on Safety of Medicines (c) and the Veterinary Products Committee (d), hereby make the following order:—

Citation, commencement and interpretation

1.—(1) This order may be cited as the Medicines (Interim Prescription Only) (No. 1) Order 1974 and shall come into operation on 19th May 1974.

(2) In this order, unless the context otherwise requires, "the Act" means the Medicines Act 1968, and other expressions have the same meanings as in the Act.

(3) Except in so far as the context otherwise requires, any reference in this order to any enactment (including any enactment of the Parliament of Northern Ireland), shall be construed as a reference to that enactment, as amended or extended by any other enactment, Measure of the Northern Ireland Assembly, regulation or order.

(4) The rules for the construction of Acts of Parliament contained in the Interpretation Act 1889(e) shall apply for the purposes of the interpretation of this order as they apply for the purposes of the interpretation of an Act of Parliament.

(a) 1968 c. 67.
(b) In the case of the Secretaries of State concerned with health in England and in Wales by virtue of Article 2(2) of, and Schedule 1 to, the Transfer of Functions (Wales) Order 1969 (S.I. 1969/388; (1969 I, p. 1070), and in the case of the Heads of the Northern Ireland Departments by virtue of section 40 of, and Schedule 5 to, the Northern Ireland Constitution Act 1973 (c. 36).
(c) S.I. 1970/1257 (1970 II, p. 4098).
(d) S.I. 1970/1304 (1970 III, p. 4335).   (e) 1889 c. 63.

Provisions prohibiting sale or supply

2.—(1) Subject to the exceptions specified in the following provisions of this order, the sale or supply of any medicinal product consisting of or containing any of the substances specified in the Schedule to this order is hereby prohibited.

(2) The retail sale or the supply in circumstances corresponding to retail sale of any medicinal product as aforesaid shall not, by virtue of the preceding paragraph, be prohibited where such sale or supply takes place on premises which are a registered pharmacy and is—

(*a*) by or under the supervision of a pharmacist in accordance with a prescription given by a practitioner, or

(*b*) by a pharmacist to the order of a practitioner who is by reason of some emergency unable to furnish a prescription immediately if the said practitioner undertakes to furnish such a prescription within the 24 hours next following the sale or supply and the sale or supply is not repeated until such a prescription has been furnished.

(3) The prohibition imposed by paragraph (1) of this Article shall be subject to the further exceptions that the sale or supply of any medicinal product as aforesaid shall not, by virtue of that paragraph, be prohibited—

(*a*) where the sale or supply is by a doctor or dentist to a patient of his or to a person under whose care such a patient is or by a veterinary surgeon or veterinary practitioner for administration by him or under his direction to an animal or herd which is under his care, or

(*b*) where the sale or supply is by a doctor or dentist to another doctor or dentist at the request of that other doctor or dentist for administration to a particular patient of that other doctor or dentist, or

(*c*) where the sale or supply is by a veterinary surgeon or veterinary practitioner to another veterinary surgeon or veterinary practitioner at the request of that other veterinary surgeon or veterinary practitioner for administration to a particular animal or herd which is under the care of that other veterinary surgeon or veterinary practitioner, or

(*d*) where the sale or supply is in the course of the business of a hospital or health centre and the sale or supply is for the purpose of administration, whether in the hospital or health centre or elsewhere, in accordance with the directions of a doctor or dentist, or

(*e*) where the sale is to a person who buys it for one or more of the purposes specified in section 131(2) of the Act (wholesale) and such sale is—

(i) to a person carrying on the business of selling by way of wholesale dealing, or

(ii) to a person lawfully conducting a retail pharmacy business, or

(iii) to a practitioner, or

(iv) for use in a hospital or health centre, or

(*f*) where the sale or supply is to any of the following persons:—

(i) a public analyst appointed under section 89 of the Food and Drugs Act 1955(**a**), section 27 of the Food and Drugs (Scotland) Act 1956(**b**) or section 31 of the Food and Drugs Act (Northern Ireland) 1958(**c**);

(ii) a sampling officer within the meaning of the Food and Drugs Act 1955, the Food and Drugs (Scotland) Act 1956 or the Food and Drugs Act (Northern Ireland) 1958;

(iii) a sampling officer within the meaning of Schedule 3 of the Act;

(iv) an inspector appointed by the Pharmaceutical Society of Great Britain under section 25 of the Pharmacy and Poisons Act 1933(**d**).

(4) The prohibition imposed by paragraph (1) of this Article shall be subject to the additional exception that the sale or supply of any medicinal product as aforesaid shall not be prohibited where the sale or supply involves, or is for the purpose of exporting the medicinal product.

(5) The prohibition imposed by paragraph (1) of this Article shall not apply to the sale or supply of any medicinal product consisting of or containing—

(*a*) clotrimazole where the medicinal product is in the form of a cream, or

(*b*) sodium cromoglycate where the medicinal product is manufactured sold or supplied for use by being administered through the nose.

Barbara Castle,
Secretary of State for Social Services.

2nd April 1974.

John Morris,
Secretary of State for Wales.

4th April 1974.

William Ross,
Secretary of State for Scotland.

4th April 1974.

In witness whereof the official seal of the Minister of Agriculture, Fisheries and Food is hereunto affixed on 5th April 1974.

(L.S.)

Frederick Peart,
Minister of Agriculture, Fisheries and Food.

Patrick J. Devlin,
Head of the Department of Health and
Social Services for Northern Ireland.

9th April 1974.

Leslie J. Morrell,
Head of the Department of Agriculture for
Northern Ireland.

9th April 1974.

(**a**) 1955 c. 16 (4 & 5 Eliz. 2). (**b**) 1956 c. 30.
(**c**) 1958 c. 27 (N.I.). (**d**) 1933 c. 25.

SCHEDULE

Article 2(1)

Alclofenac
Alphadolone Acetate
Alphaxalone
Amantadine Hydrochloride
Aminocaproic Acid

Baclofen
Benapryzine
Betahistine dihydrochloride
Bleomycin
Bretylium Tosylate
Bumetanide

Clofazimine
Clomipramine Hydrochloride
Clonidine Hydrochloride
Clotrimazole (a)
Colaspase
Cropropamide
Crotethamide
Cyclofenil
Cytarabine

Daunorubicin Hydrochloride
Diazoxide
Dinoprost
Dinoprostone
Disopyramide
Distigmine Bromide
Doxorubicin

Fluorouracil

Ibuprofen

Heparin Calcium

Ketamine Hydrochloride
Ketoprofen

Mazindol
Metolazone
Mithramycin

Naftidrofuryl Oxalate
Naloxone Hydrochloride
Naproxen
Natamycin
Niridazole

Oxprenolol Hydrochloride
Oxypertine Hydrochloride

Pancuronium Bromide
Practolol
Propranolol Hydrochloride

Sodium Cromoglycate (a)

Tamoxifen Citrate
Tranexamic Acid
L-Pyroglutamyl-L-histidyl-L-proline amide (Thyrotrophin-releasing Hormone)

(a) *See* Article 2(5) of this Order.

EXPLANATORY NOTE
(*This Note is not part of the Order.*)

This Order prohibits the sale or supply of certain medicinal products except where the sale or supply takes place in a registered pharmacy and is in accordance with a prescription given by a practitioner.

The Order provides for certain other exceptions from the prohibition. These include exceptions in the case of certain sales or supplies in hospitals or by practitioners, and in the case of certain wholesale dealings. The export of such medicinal products is also excepted.

STATUTORY INSTRUMENTS

1974 No. 713

PRISONS

The Prison (Amendment) Rules 1974

Made - - - - *12th April* 1974

Laid before Parliament 25th April 1974

Coming into Operation 1st June 1974

In pursuance of section 47(1) of the Prison Act 1952(a), I hereby make the following Rules:—

1.—(1) These Rules may be cited as the Prison (Amendment) Rules 1974 and shall come into operation on 1st June 1974.

(2) In these Rules, "the principal Rules" means the Prison Rules 1964(b) as amended by the Prison (Amendment) Rules 1968(c), the Prison (Amendment) Rules 1971(d) and the Prison (Amendment) Rules 1972(e).

2. For Rule 10 of the principal Rules (which relates to the determination of a prisoner's religious denomination) there shall be substituted the Rule set out in Part I of the Schedule to these Rules.

3. In Rule 33(3) of the principal Rules (which requires a prisoner's correspondence to be censored), for the word "shall" there shall be substituted the word "may".

4. A convicted prisoner shall be entitled under Rule 34(2)(*b*) of the principal Rules to receive a visit once in four weeks whether he is under the age of 21 or not, and accordingly the words in that sub-paragraph "if he is under the age of 21 years, and otherwise once in eight weeks" shall be omitted.

5. For Rules 50 to 56 of the principal Rules (which relate to disciplinary awards, and of which Rule 53 has already been omitted) there shall be substituted the Rules set out in Part II of the Schedule to these Rules.

Roy Jenkins,
One of Her Majesty's Principal
Secretaries of State.

Home Office,
 Whitehall.
12th April 1974.

(a) 1952 c. 52.
(c) S.I. 1968/440 (1968 I, p. 1149).
(e) S.I. 1972/1860 (1972 III, p. 5423).

(b) S.I. 1964/388 (1964 I, p. 591).
(d) S.I. 1971/2019 (1971 III, p. 5788).

SCHEDULE
RULES TO BE SUBSTITUTED FOR RULES 10 AND 50 TO 56 OF THE PRINCIPAL RULES

Rule 2   **PART I**

Religious denomination

10. A prisoner shall be treated as being of the religious denomination stated in the record made in pursuance of section 10(5) of the Prison Act 1952 but the governor may, in a proper case and after due enquiry, direct that record to be amended.

Rule 5   **PART II**

Governor's awards

50. Subject to Rules 51 and 52 of these Rules, the governor may make any one of more of the following awards for an offence against discipline:—

    (*a*) caution;
    (*b*) forfeiture for a period not exceeding 28 days of any of the privileges under Rule 4 of these Rules;
    (*c*) exclusion from associated work for a period not exceeding 14 days;
    (*d*) stoppage of earnings for a period not exceeding 28 days;
    (*e*) cellular confinement for a period not exceeding 3 days;
    (*f*) forfeiture of remission of a period not exceeding 28 days;
    (*g*) forfeiture for any period, in the case of a prisoner otherwise entitled thereto, of any of the following:—
        (i) the right to be supplied with food and drink under Rule 21(1) of these Rules; and
        (ii) the right under Rule 41(1) of these Rules to have the articles there mentioned;
    (*h*) forfeiture for any period, in the case of a prisoner otherwise entitled thereto who is guilty of escaping or attempting to escape, of the right to wear clothing of his own under Rule 20(1) of these Rules.

Graver offences

51.—(1) Where a prisoner is charged with any of the following offences against discipline:—

    (*a*) escaping or attempting to escape from prison or from legal custody,
    (*b*) assaulting an officer, or
    (*c*) doing gross personal violence to any person not being an officer,
the governor shall, unless he dismisses the charge, forthwith inform the Secretary of State and shall, unless otherwise directed by him, refer the charge to the board of visitors.

(2) Where a prisoner is charged with any serious or repeated offence against discipline (not being an offence to which Rule 52 of these Rules applies) for which the awards the governor can make seem insufficient, the governor may, after investigation, refer the charge to the board of visitors.

(3) Where a charge is referred to the board of visitors under this Rule, the chairman thereof shall summon a special meeting at which not more than five nor fewer than two members shall be present.

(4) The Board so constituted shall inquire into the charge and, if they find the offence proved, shall make one or more of the following awards:—

    (*a*) caution;
    (*b*) forfeiture for any period of any of the privileges under Rule 4 of these Rules;

(c) exclusion from associated work for a period not exceeding 56 days;

(d) stoppage of earnings for a period not exceeding 56 days;

(e) cellular confinement for a period not exceeding 56 days;

(f) forfeiture of remission of a period not exceeding 180 days;

(g) forfeiture for any period, in the case of a prisoner otherwise entitled thereto, of any of the following:—

   (i) the right to be supplied with food and drink under Rule 21(1) of these Rules; and

   (ii) the right under Rule 41(1) of these Rules to have the articles there mentioned;

(h) forfeiture for any period, in the case of a prisoner otherwise entitled thereto who is guilty of escaping or attempting to escape, of the right to wear clothing of his own under Rule 20(1) of these Rules.

(5) The Secretary of State may require any charge to which this Rule applies to be referred to him, instead of to the board of visitors, and in that case an officer of the Secretary of State (not being an officer of a prison) shall inquire into the charge and, if he finds the offence proved, make one or more of the awards listed in paragraph (4) of this Rule.

Especially grave offences

52.—(1) Where a prisoner is charged with one of the following offences:—

(a) mutiny or incitement to mutiny; or

(b) doing gross personal violence to an officer,

the governor shall forthwith inform the Secretary of State and shall, unless otherwise directed by him, refer the charge to the board of visitors.

(2) Where a charge is referred to the board of visitors under this Rule, the chairman thereof shall summon a special meeting at which not more than five nor fewer than three members, at least two being justices of the peace, shall be present.

(3) The board constituted as aforesaid shall inquire into the charge and, if they find the offence proved, shall make one or more of the awards listed in Rule 51(4) of these Rules, so however that, if they make an award of forfeiture of remission, the period forfeited may exceed 180 days.

Provisions in relation to particular awards

53.—(1) An award of stoppage of earnings may, instead of forfeiting all a prisoner's earnings for a specified period not exceeding 28 or as the case may be 56 days, be expressed so as to forfeit a proportion (not being less than one half) of his earnings for a specified period not exceeding a correspondingly greater number of days.

(2) No award of cellular confinement shall be made unless the medical officer has certified that the prisoner is in a fit state of health to be so dealt with.

Prospective forfeiture of remission

54.—(1) In the case of an offence against discipline committed by a prisoner who has attained the age of 21 years and is detained only on remand or to await trial or sentence, an award of forfeiture of remission may be made notwithstanding that the prisoner has not (or had not at the time of the offence) been sentenced to imprisonment.

(2) An award under paragraph (1) above shall have effect only in the case of a sentence of imprisonment being imposed which is reduced, by section 67 of the Criminal Justice Act 1967**(a)**, by a period which includes the time when the offence against discipline was committed.

_____

(a) 1967 c. 80.

Suspended awards

55.—(1) Subject to any directions of the Secretary of State, the power to make a disciplinary award (other than a caution) shall include power to direct that the award is not to take effect unless, during a period specified in the direction (not being more than 6 months from the date of the direction), the prisoner commits another offence against discipline and a direction is given under paragraph (2) below.

(2) Where a prisoner commits an offence against discipline during the period specified in a direction given under paragraph (1) above the person or board dealing with that offence may—

(*a*) direct that the suspended award shall take effect; or

(*b*) reduce the period or amount of the suspended award and direct that it shall take effect as so reduced; or

(*c*) vary the original direction by substituting for the period specified therein a period expiring not later than 6 months from the date of variation; or

(*d*) give no direction with respect to the suspended award.

Remission and mitigation of awards

56.—(1) The Secretary of State may remit a disciplinary award or mitigate it either by reducing it or by substituting another award which is, in his opinion, less severe.

(2) Subject to any directions of the Secretary of State, the governor may remit or mitigate any award made by a governor and the board of visitors may remit or mitigate any disciplinary award.

EXPLANATORY NOTE

(This Note is not part of the Rules.)

These Rules make a number of amendments to the Prison Rules 1964. The principal changes made are to abolish restricted diet as a punishment, to make provision for the forfeiture of remission where a prisoner is "earning" remission although not yet sentenced to imprisonment, and to make provision for suspended awards of punishment. The Rules also increase the power of a governor to award stoppage of earnings for a disciplinary offence, and allow any award of stoppage of earnings to be confined to a proportion of the earnings but for a correspondingly longer period.

STATUTORY INSTRUMENTS

1974 No. 714

WAGES COUNCILS

The Wages Regulation (Retail Bread and Flour Confectionery) (Scotland) Order 1974

Made - - - -		*17th April* 1974
Coming into Operation		*13th May* 1974

Whereas the Secretary of State has received from the Retail Bread and Flour Confectionery Trade Wages Council (Scotland) the wages regulation proposals set out in the Schedule hereto;

Now, therefore, the Secretary of State in exercise of powers conferred by section 11 of the Wages Councils Act 1959(a), as modified by Article 2 of the Counter-Inflation (Modification of Wages Councils Act 1959) Order 1973(b), and now vested in him (c), and of all other powers enabling him in that behalf, hereby makes the following Order:—

1. This Order may be cited as the Wages Regulation (Retail Bread and Flour Confectionery) (Scotland) Order 1974.

2.—(1) In this Order the expression "the specified date" means the 13th May 1974, provided that where, as respects any worker who is paid wages at intervals not exceeding seven days, that date does not correspond with the beginning of the period for which the wages are paid, the expression "the specified date" means, as respects that worker, the beginning of the next such period following that date.

(2) The Interpretation Act 1889(d) shall apply to the interpretation of this Order as it applies to the interpretation of an Act of Parliament and as if this Order and the Order hereby revoked were Acts of Parliament.

3. The wages regulation proposals set out in the Schedule hereto shall have effect as from the specified date and as from that date the Wages Regulation (Retail Bread and Flour Confectionery) (Scotland) Order 1972(e) shall cease to have effect.

Signed by order of the Secretary of State.

17th April 1974.

Anthony Sutherland,
Under Secretary,
Department of Employment.

(a) 1959 c. 69.　　　　　　　　　(b) S.I. 1973/661 (1973 I, p. 2141).
(c) S.I. 1959/1769, 1968/729 (1959 I, p. 1795; 1968 II, p. 2108).
(d) 1889 c. 63.　　　　　　　　　(e) S.I. 1972/1959 (1972 III, p. 5841).

ARRANGEMENT OF SCHEDULE

PART I
STATUTORY MINIMUM REMUNERATION

PART II
ANNUAL HOLIDAY AND HOLIDAY REMUNERATION

PART III
GENERAL

Article 3   SCHEDULE

The following minimum remuneration and provisions as to holidays and holiday remuneration shall be substituted for the statutory minimum remuneration and the provisions as to holidays and holiday remuneration fixed by the Wages Regulation (Retail Bread and Flour Confectionery) (Scotland) Order 1972 (hereinafter referred to as "Order B.F.C.S. (30)").

PART I: STATUTORY MINIMUM REMUNERATION
APPLICATION

1. Subject to the provisions of paragraphs 2, 2A, 8, 9 and 13, the minimum remuneration for workers to whom this Schedule applies shall be the remuneration set out in paragraphs 3, 4, 5 and 6:

Provided that any increase in remuneration payable under the provisions of paragraph 5 or 6 shall become effective on the first day of the first full pay week following the date upon which the increase would otherwise become payable under those provisions.

HOURS ON WHICH REMUNERATION IS BASED

2.—(1) *Up to and including 12th May 1975* the minimum remuneration specified in paragraphs 3, 4, 5 and 6 relates—

(a) in the case of a worker, other than a van salesworker, to a week of 40 hours exclusive of overtime;

(b) in the case of a van salesworker, to a week of 42 hours exclusive of overtime; and, except as provided in paragraph 13, is subject to a proportionate reduction according as the number of hours worked is less than 40 or 42, as the case may be.

(2) In calculating the remuneration for the purpose of this Schedule recognisep breaks for meal times shall, subject to the provisions of paragraph 10, be excluded.

2A.—(1) *On and after 13th May 1975* the minimum remuneration specified in paragraphs 3, 4, 5 and 6 relates to a week of 40 hours exclusive of overtime; and, except as provided in paragraph 13, is subject to a proportionate reduction according as the number of hours worked is less than 40.

(2) In calculating the remuneration for the purpose of this Schedule recognised breaks for meal times shall, subject to the provisions of paragraph 10, be excluded.

MANAGERS AND MANAGERESSES

3. The minimum remuneration for managers and manageresses shall be the amount appearing in Column 2 of the following table against the amount of weekly trade shown in Column 1 of the said table:—

Column 1	Column 2	
Weekly trade	Area 1	Area 2
	per week £	per week £
Under £160 ...	18·05	17·85
£160 and under £180	18·20	18·00
£180 „ „ £200	18·35	18·15
£200 „ „ £220	18·45	18·25
£220 „ „ £240	18·55	18·35
£240 „ „ £260	18·65	18·45
£260 „ „ £280	18·75	18·55
£280 „ „ £300	18·85	18·65
£300 „ „ £320	18·95	18·75
£320 „ „ £340	19·05	18·85
£340 „ „ £360	19·15	18·95
£360 „ „ £380	19·20	19·00
£380 „ „ £400	19·25	19·05
£400	19·35	19·15

The minimum remuneration for Managers and Manageresses employed in shops with a weekly trade in excess of £400 shall be the appropriate amount specified in the table above for a worker employed in a shop where the weekly trade is £400 and in addition 10p for every complete £20 of weekly trade in excess of that amount.

For the purposes of this paragraph, "weekly trade" shall be calculated half-yearly and based on the period of 12 months immediately preceding the commencement of each half-year in the following manner:—

(1) for the 26 pay weeks beginning with the fifth pay week following the last Saturday in February in any year, or for any part thereof, the weekly trade of a shop shall be one fifty-second of the amount of the total receipts for goods sold at that shop during the 52 weeks immediately preceding the last Saturday in February in that year;

(2) for the 26 pay weeks in any year immediately following (hereinafter called the "second period"), or for any part thereof, the weekly trade of a shop shall be one fifty-second of the amount of the total receipts in respect of goods sold at that shop during the 52 weeks immediately preceding the last Saturday in August of the same year as that in which the second period begins:

Provided that, so long as a shop has been under management for less than 52 weeks immediately preceding the last Saturday in February in any year or the last Saturday in August in any year, as the case may be, the weekly trade of that shop, for the purpose of calculating the weekly minimum remuneration payable in any pay week under the foregoing table, shall until such period of 52 weeks has elapsed be the amount of the total receipts for goods sold at that shop in the week immediately preceding such pay week and for the purpose of calculating such weekly minimum remuneration as aforesaid payable in respect of each of the first two pay weeks during which a shop is under management the weekly trade of that shop shall be the amount of the total receipts in respect of goods sold thereat in the first week during which the shop is under management.

TEMPORARY MANAGERS AND TEMPORARY MANAGERESSES

4.—(1) The minimum remuneration for temporary managers and temporary manageresses shall be—

(a) during the first two weeks of employment as such—the appropriate minimum remuneration for a manager or manageress, as the case may be, employed in a shop with a weekly trade of under £160; and

(b) thereafter—the appropriate minimum remuneration for a manager or manageress, as the case may be, at the shop in which the worker is employed.

(2) For the purposes of this paragraph where a worker commences a period of employment as a temporary manager or temporary manageress within six months of the termination of such a period of employment at the same shop, the two periods of employment shall be treated as continuous.

WORKERS OTHER THAN MANAGERS, MANAGERESSES, TEMPORARY MANAGERS, TEMPORARY MANAGERESSES, TRANSPORT WORKERS AND VAN SALESWORKERS

5. The minimum remuneration for workers of the classes specified in Column 1 of the following table, employed in Area 1 or Area 2, as the case may be, shall be the appropriate amount set out in Column 2:—

Column 1	Column 2	
	Area 1	Area 2
	per week £	per week £
Workers other than Managers, Manageresses, Temporary Managers, Temporary Manageresses, Transport Workers and Van Salesworkers—		
Aged 16 and under 17 years	9·90	9·65
„ 17 „ „ 18 „	10·30	10·05
„ 18 „ „ 19 „	11·70	11·40
„ 19 „ „ 20 „	12·05	11·70
„ 20 „ „ 21 „	13·05	12·75
„ 21 years or over	15·75	15·35

TRANSPORT WORKERS AND VAN SALESWORKERS

6. The minimum remuneration for transport workers and van salesworkers employed in Area 1 or Area 2, as the case may be, shall be the appropriate amount set out in Column 3 of the table below:—

Column 1	Column 2	Column 3	
Age of Worker	Vehicle with carrying capacity of	Area 1	Area 2
		per week £	per week £
Transport Worker:—			
21 years or over		19·05	18·50
20 and under 21 years	1 ton or less	16·35	16·10
19 „ „ 20 „		15·50	15·25
18 „ „ 19 „		14·50	14·35
Under 18 years		12·95	12·85
All ages	Over 1 ton	19·35	18·80
Van Salesworkers:—			
All ages	—	19·50	18·95

WORKERS WHO WORK IN TWO AREAS

7. The minimum remuneration applicable to a transport worker or to a van sales-worker in any week in which he works in two areas shall be the remuneration which would be applicable if the worker worked solely at the bakery or depot from which he operates.

MINIMUM OVERTIME RATES

8. Overtime rates shall be payable to workers to whom this Schedule applies as follows:—

(1) For work on a Sunday—

    (a) where time worked does not exceed 4 hours ... double time for 4 hours

    (b) where time worked exceeds 4 hours—for all time worked ... ... double time

    Provided that where it is, or becomes, the established practice in a Jewish undertaking for the employer to require attendance on Sunday instead of Saturday, the foregoing provisions of this paragraph shall apply in like manner as if in such provisions the word "Saturday" were substituted for "Sunday", except where such substitution is unlawful.

(2) In the case of workers other than transport workers or van salesworkers—for all time worked in excess of 40 hours in any week ... ... time-and-a-half

(3) In the case of transport workers—

    (a) for the first 6 hours worked in excess of 40 hours in any week ... ... time-and-a-quarter

    (b) thereafter ... ... time-and-a-half

(4) In the case of van salesworkers—

    (a) (i) up to and including 12th May 1975 for the first 6 hours worked in excess of 42 hours in any week; and
    (ii) on and after 13th May 1975 for the first 6 hours worked in excess of 40 hours in any week — time-and-a-quarter

    (b) thereafter ... ... time-and-a-half

Provided that—

(i) the periods of *40* hours specified in sub-paragraphs (2), (3) *and* (*4*)(*a*)(*ii*) and *42* hours specified in sub-paragraph (4)(*a*)(*i*) of this paragraph shall be reduced by 7 hours in any week which includes one customary holiday and by 14 hours in any week which includes two customary holidays;

(ii) for the purposes of sub-paragraphs (2), (3) and (4) of this paragraph, no account shall be taken of any time—

   (*a*) for which double time is payable under paragraph 9;

   (*b*) worked on a day of customary holiday; or

   (*c*) not exceeding 15 minutes on any day or one hour in the aggregate in any week worked by any worker (other than a transport worker or van salesworker) at a shop immediately after the closing of the shop to the public;

(iii) no overtime rate shall be payable to a manager or manageress except where the overtime worked was specifically authorised by the employer or his representative.

SPECIAL TIME

9. Where a worker who is a shop assistant within the meaning of the Shops Act 1950(a) works after 1 p.m. on a day which would have been his weekly half-holiday if the employer had not, under the proviso to sub-section (1) of section 17 or under subsection (3) of section 40 of that Act, (suspension of weekly half-holiday in week preceding a bank holiday and in holiday resorts), been relieved of his obligation to allow the worker a weekly half-holiday, he shall be paid double time for all time so worked.

WAITING TIME

10. A worker shall be entitled to payment of the minimum remuneration specified in this Part of this Schedule for all the time during which he is present on the premises of the employer, unless he is present thereon in any of the following circumstances, that is to say—

(1) without the employer's consent, express or implied;

(2) for some purpose unconnected with his work and other than that of waiting for work to be given to him to perform;

(3) by reason only of the fact that he is resident thereon; or

(4) during normal meal times in a room or place in which no work is being done, and he is not waiting for work to be given to him to perform.

WORKERS WHO ARE NOT REQUIRED TO WORK ON A CUSTOMARY HOLIDAY

11. Where a worker is not required to work on a customary holiday he shall be paid for the day of customary holiday not less than the amount to which he would have been entitled under the provisions of this Schedule had the day not been a customary holiday and had he worked the number of hours ordinarily worked by him on that day of the week.

WORKERS WHO WORK ON A CUSTOMARY HOLIDAY

12. Where a worker works on a customary holiday he shall be paid not less than the amount to which he would have been entitled under the other provisions of this Schedule had the day not been a customary holiday and had he worked the number of hours ordinarily worked by him on that day of the week and, in addition thereto—

(1) for any time worked not exceeding 4 hours   ...   double time for 4 hours

---

(a) 1950 c. 28.

(2) for any time worked in excess of 4 hours up to a total
of 8 hours   ...   .   hourly rate

(3) for all time worked in excess of 8 hours   ...   double time.

GUARANTEED WEEKLY REMUNERATION PAYABLE TO A FULL-TIME WORKER

13.—(1) Notwithstanding the other provisions of this Schedule, where in any week the total remuneration (including holiday remuneration) payable under those other provisions to a full-time worker is less than the guaranteed weekly remuneration provided under this paragraph, the minimum remuneration payable to that worker for that week shall be that guaranteed weekly remuneration:

Provided that no guaranteed remuneration under this paragraph shall be payable to a worker in any week during which the worker was not throughout his normal working hours (excluding any time allowed to him as a holiday or during which he was absent from work in accordance with sub-paragraph (3) of this paragraph) capable of and available for work.

(2) Subject to sub-paragraph (3) of this paragraph, the guaranteed weekly remuneration shall be the remuneration to which the worker would be entitled under paragraph 3, 4, 5 or 6 for work in his usual occupation for the number of hours specified in (a) or (b), as the case may be, of sub-paragraph (1) of paragraphs 2 and 2A:

Provided that where the worker normally works for the employer on work to which this Schedule applies for less than 40 hours in the week or in the case of a van salesworker—

(a) for 42 hours in the week *up to and including 12th May 1975,* and

(b) for 40 hours in the week *on and after 13th May 1975—*

by reason only of the fact that he does not hold himself out as normally available for work for more than the number of hours he normally works in the week, and the worker has informed the employer in writing that he does not so hold himself out, the guaranteed weekly remuneration shall be the remuneration to which the worker would be entitled (calculated as in paragraph 2 *or* 2A) for the number of hours in the week normally worked by the worker for the employer on work to which this Schedule applies.

(3) Where in any week a worker at his request and with the written consent of his employer is absent from work during any part of his normal working hours on any day (other than a day of annual holiday allowed under Part II of this Schedule or a customary holiday or a holiday allowed to all persons employed in the undertaking or branch of an undertaking in which the worker is employed), the guaranteed weekly remuneration payable in respect of that week shall be reduced in respect of each day on which he is absent as aforesaid by one-sixth where the worker's normal working week is six days or by one-fifth where his normal working week is five days.

PART II: ANNUAL HOLIDAY AND HOLIDAY REMUNERATION

ANNUAL HOLIDAY

14.—(1) Subject to the provisions of paragraphs 15 and 16, an employer shall, between the date on which this Schedule becomes effective and 31st October 1974 and in each succeeding year between 1st April and 31st October allow a holiday (hereinafter referred to as an "annual holiday") to every worker in his employment to whom this Schedule applies who has been employed by him during the 12 months immediately preceding the commencement of the holiday season for any one of the periods of employment (calculated in accordance with the provisions of paragraph 21) set out in the table below and the duration of the annual holiday shall in the case of each such worker be related to that period as follows:—

Period of employment	Duration of annual holiday
12 months	*18* days
not less than 11 months but less than 12 months	11 ,,
,, ,, ,, 10 ,, ,, ,, ,, 11 ,, ...	10 ,,
,, ,, ,, 9 ,, ,, ,, ,, 10 ,, ...	9 ,,
,, ,, ,, 8 ,, ,, ,, ,, 9 ,, ...	8 ,,
,, ,, ,, 7 ,, ,, ,, ,, 8 ,, ...	7 ,,
,, ,, ,, 6 ,, ,, ,, ,, 7 ,, ...	6 ,,
,, ,, ,, 5 ,, ,, ,, ,, 6 ,, ...	5 ,,
,, ,, ,, 4 ,, ,, ,, ,, 5 ,, ...	4 ,,
,, ,, ,, 3 ,, ,, ,, ,, 4 ,, ...	3 ,,
,, ,, ,, 2 ,, ,, ,, ,, 3 ,, ...	2 ,,
,, ,, ,, 1 month ,, ,, ,, 2 ,, ...	1 day

(2) Notwithstanding the provisions of the last foregoing sub-paragraph—

(*a*) the number of days of annual holiday which an employer is required to allow to a worker in any holiday season shall not exceed in the aggregate *three times* the number of days constituting the worker's normal working week;

(*b*) where before the expiration of any holiday season a worker enters into an agreement in writing with his employer that the annual holiday or part thereof shall be allowed on a specified date or dates after the expiration of the holiday season but before 1st January in the following year, then any day or days of annual holiday so allowed shall be treated as having been allowed during the holiday season;

(*c*) the duration of the worker's annual holiday in the holiday season ending on 31st October 1974, shall be reduced by any days of annual holiday duly allowed to him by the employer, under the provisions of Order B.F.C.S.(30) between 1st April 1974 and the date on which the provisions of this Schedule become effective.

(3) In this Schedule the expression "holiday season" means in relation to the year 1974, the period commencing on 1st April 1974 and ending on 31st October 1974 and, in each succeeding year, the period commencing on 1st April and ending on 31st October of the same year.

15. Where at the written request of the worker at any time preceding the commencement of the holiday season in any year, his employer allows him any day or days of annual holiday and pays him holiday remuneration in respect thereof calculated in accordance with the provisions of paragraphs 18 and 19, then the annual holiday to be allowed in accordance with paragraph 14 in the holiday season in that year shall be reduced by the day or days of annual holiday so allowed prior to the commencement of that holiday season.

16.—(1) Subject to the provisions of this paragraph an annual holiday shall be allowed on consecutive working days, being days on which the worker is normally called upon to work for the employer.

(2) (*a*) Where the number of days of annual holiday for which a worker has qualified exceeds the number of days constituting his normal working week, *but does not exceed twice that number*, the holiday may at the written request of the worker be allowed in two periods of consecutive working days; so however that when a holiday is so allowed, one of the periods shall consist of a number of such days not less than the number of days constituting the worker's normal working week.

(*b*) *Where the number of days of annual holiday for which a worker has qualified exceeds twice the number of days constituting his normal working week the holiday may be allowed as follows:—*

(*i*) *as to the number of days comprising twice the number of days constituting the worker's normal working week, in one or two periods of consecutive working days during the holiday season;*

(*ii*) *as to any additional days, either during the holiday season or before the beginning of the next following holiday season, such days to be consecutive unless otherwise agreed between the employer and the worker or his representative.*

(3) For the purposes of this paragraph, days of annual holiday shall be treated as consecutive notwithstanding that a customary holiday on which the worker is not required to work for the employer or a day on which he does not normally work for the employer intervenes.

(4) Where a customary holiday on which the worker is not required to work for the employer immediately precedes a period of annual holiday or occurs during such a period and the total number of days of annual holiday required to be allowed in the period under the foregoing provisions of this paragraph, together with any customary holiday, exceeds the number of days constituting the worker's normal working week then, notwithstanding the foregoing provisions of this paragraph, the duration of that period of annual holiday may be reduced by one day and in such a case one day of annual holiday may be allowed on a day on which the worker normally works for the employer (not being the worker's weekly short day) in the holiday season.

(5) No day of annual holiday shall be allowed on a customary holiday.

(6) A day of annual holiday under this Schedule may be allowed on a day on which the worker is entitled to a day of holiday (not being a customary holiday) or to a half-holiday under any enactment other than the Wages Councils Act 1959.

17. An employer shall give to a worker not later than 1st April in each year notice of the commencing date or dates and of the duration of his annual holiday. Such notice may be given individually to the worker or by the posting of a notice in the place where the worker is employed.

HOLIDAY REMUNERATION

18.—(1) Subject to the provisions of paragraph 19, a worker qualified to be allowed an annual holiday under this Schedule shall be paid by his employer, on the last pay day preceding such holiday, one day's holiday pay in respect of each day thereof.

(2) Where an annual holiday is taken in more than one period the holiday remuneration shall be apportioned accordingly.

19. Where any accrued holiday remuneration has been paid by the employer to the worker in accordance with paragraph 20 of this Schedule or with Order B.F.C.S. (30), in respect of employment during either or both of the periods referred to in paragraph 20, the amount of holiday remuneration payable by the employer in respect of any annual holiday for which the worker has qualified by reason of employment during the said period or periods shall be reduced by the amount of the said accrued holiday remuneration unless that remuneration has been deducted from a previous payment of holiday remuneration made under the provisions of this Schedule or of Order B.F.C.S. (30).

ACCRUED HOLIDAY REMUNERATION PAYABLE ON TERMINATION OF EMPLOYMENT

20. Where a worker ceases to be employed by an employer after the provisions of this Schedule become effective the employer shall, immediately on the termination of the employment, pay to the worker as accrued holiday remuneration:—

(1) in respect of employment in the 12 months up to the preceding 31st March, a sum equal to the holiday remuneration for any days of annual holiday for which he has qualified except days of annual holiday which he has been allowed or has become entitled to be allowed before leaving the employment; and

(2) in respect of any employment since the preceding 31st March, a sum equal to the holiday remuneration which would have been payable to him if he could

have been allowed an annual holiday in respect of that employment at the time of leaving it:

Provided that—

(a) no worker shall be entitled to the payment by his employer of accrued holiday remuneration if he is dismissed on the grounds of misconduct and is so informed by the employer at the time of dismissal;

(b) where, during the period or periods in respect of which the said accrued holiday remuneration is payable, the worker has at his written request been allowed any day or days of holiday (other than days of holiday allowed by the employer under paragraph 15) for which he had not qualified under the provisions of this Schedule, any accrued holiday remuneration payable as aforesaid may be reduced by the amount of any sum paid by the employer to the worker in respect of such day or days of holiday;

(c) where a worker is employed under a contract of service under which he is required to give not less than one week's notice before terminating his employment and the worker without the consent of his employer terminates his employment:—

(i) without having given not less than one week's notice, or

(ii) before one week has expired from the beginning of such notice,

the amount of accrued holiday remuneration payable to the worker shall be the amount payable under the foregoing provisions of this paragraph less an amount equal to one day's holiday pay multiplied in the case of (i) by the number of days constituting the worker's normal working week or, in the case of (ii), by the number of days which at the termination of the employment would complete a normal working week commencing at the beginning of the notice.

CALCULATION OF EMPLOYMENT

21. For the purposes of calculating any period of employment qualifying a worker for an annual holiday or for any accrued holiday remuneration, the worker shall be treated as if he were employed for a month in respect of any month throughout which he has been in the employment of the employer.

PART III: GENERAL

DEFINITIONS

22. In this Schedule, unless the context otherwise requires, the following expressions have the meanings hereby respectively assigned to them, that is to say:—

"AREA 1" means—

(1) all Burghs which, according to the Registrar-General's Preliminary Report on the Census of Scotland 1961, had a population of 5,000 or more;

(2) the following Special Lighting Districts, the boundaries of which have been defined, namely, Vale of Leven and Renton in the County of Dunbarton; and Larbert and Airth in the County of Stirling; and

(3) the following areas the boundaries of which were defined as Special Lighting Districts prior to 10th March 1943, namely, Bellshill and Mossend, Blantyre, Cambuslang, Larkhall and Holytown, New Stevenston and Carfin, all in the County of Lanark.

"AREA 2" means all localities other than those comprised in Area 1.

"CARRYING CAPACITY" means the weight of the maximum load normally carried by the vehicle, and such carrying capacity when so established shall not be affected either by variations in the weight of the load resulting from collections or deliveries or emptying of containers during the course of the journey, or by the fact that on any particular journey a load greater or less than the established carrying capacity is carried.

"CUSTOMARY HOLIDAY" means New Year's Day, if it be not a Sunday or, if it be a Sunday, 2nd January; the local Spring Holiday, the local Autumn Holiday, *Christmas Day, if it be not a Sunday or, if it be a Sunday, 26th December* and three other days, observed by local custom as holidays, to be fixed by the employer and notified to the worker and any day proclaimed as a public holiday throughout Scotland.

"FULL-TIME WORKER" means a worker who normally works for the employer for at least 36 hours in the week on work to which this Schedule applies.

"HOURLY RATE" means the amount obtained by dividing the minimum remuneration to which the worker is entitled under paragraph 3, 4, 5 or 6—

(1) *up to and including 12th May 1975,* by

    (*a*) *40* in the case of any worker other than a van salesworker;

    (*b*) *42* in the case of a van salesworker; and

(2) *on and after 13th May 1975,* by *40* in the case of all workers.

"MANAGER", "MANAGERESS" means a worker, other than a temporary manager or temporary manageress, who is in charge of a shop, and has immediate control of—

(1) one or more other workers being full-time workers; or

(2) two or more part-time workers,

not being workers solely engaged in cleaning premises.

"NORMAL WORKING WEEK" means the number of days on which it has been usual for the worker to work in a week while in the employment of the employer during the 12 months immediately preceding the commencement of the holiday season or, where accrued holiday remuneration is payable under (2) of paragraph 20 on the termination of the employment, during the 12 months immediately preceding the date of the termination of the employment:

Provided that—

(1) part of a day shall count as a day;

(2) no account shall be taken of any week in which the worker did not perform any work for which statutory minimum remuneration has been fixed.

"ONE DAY'S HOLIDAY PAY" means one-sixth of the remuneration which the worker would be entitled to receive from his employer at the date of the annual holiday (or, where the holiday is taken in more than one period, at the date of the first period) or at the date of the termination of the employment, as the case may be, for one week's work, if working his normal working week and the number of daily hours normally worked by him (exclusive of overtime) and if paid at the appropriate rate of statutory minimum remuneration for work for which statutory minimum remuneration is payable and at the same rate for any work for the same employer for which such remuneration is not payable.

"TEMPORARY MANAGER", "TEMPORARY MANAGERESS" means a worker who, during the temporary absence (for a period of not less than one day) of a manager or manageress, carries out the duties of the manager or manageress, whilst the worker is so carrying out the said duties.

"TIME-AND-A-QUARTER", "TIME-AND-A-HALF" and "DOUBLE TIME" mean respectively one and a quarter times, one and a half times and twice the hourly rate.

"TRANSPORT WORKER" means a male worker (other than a van salesworker) engaged wholly or mainly in driving a mechanically propelled or horse drawn road vehicle for the transport of goods and on work in connection with the vehicle and its load (if any) while on the road.

"VAN SALESWORKER" means a worker wholly or mainly employed in the sale of goods to customers from a vehicle of which he is in charge.

"WEEK" means the period of six days commencing at midnight on Sunday and ending at midnight on the following Saturday.

WORKERS TO WHOM THIS SCHEDULE APPLIES

23.—(1) Subject to the provisions of sub-paragraph (2) of this paragraph, the workers to whom this Schedule applies are all workers employed in Scotland in any undertaking or any branch or department of an undertaking, being an undertaking, branch or department, wholly or mainly engaged in the retail bread and flour confectionery trade:

Provided that if a branch or department of an undertaking is not so engaged, this Schedule shall not apply to workers employed in that branch or department (notwithstanding that the undertaking as a whole is so engaged) except as respects their employment in a department of that branch if that department is so engaged.

(2) This Schedule does not apply to any of the following workers in respect of their employment in any of the following circumstances, that is to say:—

    (i) workers in relation to whom either of the following Wages Councils operates in respect of any employment which is for the time being within the field of operation of that Wages Council, that is to say:—

        (a) the Milk Distributive Wages Council (Scotland);

        (b) the Road Haulage Wages Council;

    (ii) workers in relation to whom any Wages Council (which was immediately before 30th May 1959 a Wages Board established under the Catering Wages Act 1943(a)) operates in respect of any employment which is for the time being within the field of operation of that Wages Council;

    (iii) workers (other than workers employed as cleaners) employed in the maintenance or repair of buildings, plant, equipment or vehicles;

    (iv) workers employed in any ship (which includes every description of vessel used in navigation);

    (v) workers employed on post office business.

(3) For the purposes of this Schedule the retail bread and flour confectionery trade does not include the sale of biscuits or meat pastries or any sale for immediate consumption on the premises at which the sale is effected, but save as aforesaid consists of the sale by retail of bread (including rolls) or flour confectionery (including pastry) and operations connected with any such sale, including:—

    (i) operations in or about a shop or other place where the bread or flour confectionery is sold, being operations carried on for the purpose of or in connection with such sale;

    (ii) operations in connection with the transport of bread or flour confectionery when carried on in conjunction with its sale by retail;

    (iii) clerical or other office work carried on in conjunction with the sale by retail as aforesaid and relating to such sale or to any of the operations specified in (i) or (ii) of this sub-paragraph;

and for the purposes of this definition "sale by retail" includes any sale to a person for use in connection with a catering business carried on by him, when such sale takes place at or in connection with a shop engaged in the retail sale of bread or flour confectionery to the general public.

(a) 1943 c. 24.

EXPLANATORY NOTE

(This Note is not part of the Order.)

This Order, which has effect from 13th May 1974, sets out the increased statutory minimum remuneration and the holidays to be allowed to workers in relation to whom the Retail Bread and Flour Confectionery Trade Wages Council (Scotland) operates, in substitution for the statutory minimum remuneration and holidays and holiday remuneration fixed by the Wages Regulation (Retail Bread and Flour Confectionery) (Scotland) Order 1972 (Order B.F.C.S.(30)), which Order is revoked.

New provisions are printed in italics.

STATUTORY INSTRUMENTS

1974 No. 715

PENSIONS ·

The Pensions Increase (Civil Service Pensions) Regulations 1974

Made - - - -		*17th April* 1974
Laid before Parliament		*26th April* 1974
Coming into Operation		*18th May* 1974

The Minister for the Civil Service, in exercise of the powers conferred on him by sections 1(1), (2) and (4) and 4(1) and (3)(*a*) of the Pensions (Increase) Act 1974(**a**) and of all other powers enabling him in that behalf, hereby makes the following Regulations:—

1. These Regulations may be cited as the Pensions Increase (Civil Service Pensions) Regulations 1974, and shall come into operation on 18th May 1974.

2.—(1) In these Regulations—

"the 1974 Act" means the Pensions (Increase) Act 1974;

"civil service pension" means a pension payable under the principal civil service pension scheme;

"Class A pension" means any civil service pension payable in respect of service ending with—

(*a*) employment in which any pay increase normally takes effect on 1st January in any year, or

(*b*) employment in any capacity specified in column 1 of Schedule 1 to these Regulations, by the department or body specified in column 2 of that Schedule;

"Class B pension" means any civil service pension—

(*a*) which is payable in respect of service ending with employment, in any capacity specified in column 1 of Schedule 2 to these Regulations, by the department or body specified in column 2 of that Schedule, or

(*b*) which is not either such a pension as is specified in paragraph (*a*) above or a Class A pension;

"principal civil service pension scheme" has the meaning given by section 2(10) of the Superannuation Act 1972(**b**).

(2) The Interpretation Act 1889(**c**) shall apply for the interpretation of these Regulations as it applies for the interpretation of an Act of Parliament.

(**a**) 1974 c. 9.　　　　　　　　　(**b**) 1972 c. 11.
(**c**) 1889 c. 63.

3. Civil service pensions are hereby prescribed for the purposes of section 1(1) of the 1974 Act.

4. Class A pensions are pensions as respects which, in the opinion of the Minister for the Civil Service, increases in the emoluments relevant for the purpose of calculating the pensions were deferred during the period beginning with 6th November 1972 and ending with 31st March 1973 in consequence of provisions of the Counter-Inflation (Temporary Provisions) Act 1972**(a)**, and accordingly paragraph (a) of section 1(2) of the 1974 Act applies to such pensions.

5. The date on which, in the opinion of the Minister for the Civil Service, the emoluments relevant for the purpose of calculating a civil service pension were, or are expected to be, increased by the principal pay increase made or expected to be made, during the year ending with 6th November 1974, in accordance with the code in force under section 2 of the Counter-Inflation Act 1973**(b)** at the time of the increase, is—

(a) in the case of a Class A pension related to an employment specified in Schedule 1 to these Regulations, the date specified in relation to that employment in column 3 of that Schedule;

(b) in the case of any other Class A pension, 1st January 1974;

(c) in the case of a Class B pension related to an employment specified in Schedule 2 to these Regulations, the date specified in relation to that employment in column 3 of that Schedule; and

(d) in the case of any other Class B pension, 1st July 1974;

and accordingly those dates shall respectively be the relevant dates for those pensions.

6.—(1) The 1974 Act shall have effect, in relation to any civil service pension which by virtue of the principal civil service pension scheme is calculated by reference to the provisions of paragraph 2(2) or 6 of Schedule 1 to the Superannuation Act 1965**(c)** (which apply to certain persons who were civil servants on 27th June 1935), subject to the amendments specified in paragraph (2) below.

(2) In relation to such a pension as is described in paragraph (1) above, the Schedule to the 1974 Act shall have effect as if—

(a) in paragraph 5, for the words "before 1st April 1974" there were substituted the words "on or before the relevant date", and

(b) paragraphs 7 and 16 were omitted,

and accordingly such a pension, if it begins after the relevant date for the pension, shall not be increased under the 1974 Act.

7. Any increase of pension payable by virtue of these Regulations shall have effect in respect of any period beginning on or after 1st December 1973.

Given under the official seal of the Minister for the Civil Service on 17th April 1974.

(L.S.)

Robert Sheldon,
Minister of State
to the Civil Service Department.

(a) 1972 c. 74. (b) 1973 c. 9. (c) 1965 c. 74.

SCHEDULE 1

Employments to which certain Class A pensions are related, together with relevant dates

Regulations 2(1) and 5

Employment	Employer	Relevant date
1. Fire service officer or fire prevention officer	Ministry of Defence	7th November 1973
2. Member of the Fire Service Inspectorate	Home Office or Scottish Office	7th November 1973
3. Commandant or Deputy Commandant, Fire Service Technical College	Home Office	7th November 1973
4. Commandant, Fire Service Staff College	Home Office	7th November 1973
5. Fire service instructor, senior fire service instructor or chief fire service instructor	Home Office	7th November 1973
6. Member of film trade grades whose pay is linked to the agreement between the Kinematograph Renters Society and the National Association of Theatrical, Television and Kinematograph Employees	Central Office of Information	3rd December 1973
7. Special duty orderly at Artificial Limb and Appliance Centres	Department of Health and Social Security	13th December 1973
8. Member of ancillary health grades at Leopardstown Park Hospital, the Common Cold Unit or the Polish Home Sick Bay	Department of Health and Social Security	13th December 1973
9. Non-craft industrial employee at Royal Navy Hospital, Haslar or Plymouth	Ministry of Defence	13th December 1973
10. Assistant cook, cook, domestic, gardener, general labourer and gardener labourer, head porter, kitchen porter, medical orderly, porter, seamstress, storeman, waitress or ward orderly at the Hostel for Paraplegics, Duchess of Gloucester House, Isleworth or the Industrial Rehabilitation Unit, Egham	Department of Employment	13th December 1973
11. Chefs I or II in the Civil Service Catering Organisation	Civil Service Department	13th December 1973
12. Manager of a licensed public house in Carlisle and District State Management Scheme	Home Office	20th January 1974
13. Agricultural worker	Ministry of Agriculture, Fisheries & Food	22nd January 1974

Employment	Employer	Relevant date
14. Agricultural worker	Scottish Office	28th January 1974
15. Studio director	Central Office of Information	1st July 1974
16. Member of film trade grades whose pay is linked to the agreement between the Independent Television Companies Association and the Association of Cinematograph, Television and Allied Technicians	Central Office of Information	1st July 1974
17. Adviser on magistrates' courts	Home Office	1st July 1974
18. Member of the film trade grades other than those specified in paragraphs 6 and 16 above	Central Office of Information	2nd July 1974
19. Film Librarian	Imperial War Museum	2nd July 1974

SCHEDULE 2

Employments to which certain Class B pensions are related, together with relevant dates

Regulations 2(1) and 5

Employment	Employer	Relevant date
1. Fireman	Ministry of Defence	7th November 1973
2. Assistant at Reception or Re-establishment Centre	Department of Health & Social Security	7th November 1973
3. Care assistant at the Polish Home	Department of Health & Social Security	7th November 1973
4. Member of staff in off-licence sales branch, Carlisle and District State Management Scheme	Home Office	18th December 1973
5. Member of industrial staff employed on the reconstruction and maintenance of Alderney Breakwater	Department of the Environment (Property Services Agency)	3rd January 1974
6. Member of hotel and restaurant staff, Carlisle & District State Management Scheme	Home Office	4th February 1974
7. Traffic representative	Ministry of Defence	28th February 1974
8. Deputy Director at St Charles Youth Treatment Centre	Department of Health & Social Security	1st April 1974
9. Deputy chief nursing officer, principal nursing officer or nursing officer	Department of Health & Social Security	1st April 1974
10. Deputy chief nursing officer, chief nursing officer or nursing officer	Scottish Office	1st April 1974
11. Occupational therapy instructor	Department of Health & Social Security	1st April 1974
12. Director of studies or director of general studies	Home Office	1st April 1974
13. Head of civilian tutors, senior civilian tutor or civilian tutor	Home Office	1st April 1974
14. Head of Educational Methods Unit	Home Office	1st April 1974
15. Senior tutor or tutor I or II (Educational Methods)	Home Office	1st April 1974
16. Extra-mural tutor	Home Office	1st April 1974
17. Matron housekeeper or assistant matron housekeeper	Home Office	1st April 1974
18. Housekeeper caterer	Home Office	1st April 1974
19. Hostel warden	Home Office	1st April 1974
20. Home warden	Government Communications Headquarters	1st April 1974
21. Bookshop assistant (provincial)	Her Majesty's Stationery Office	1st April 1974
22. Civilian operating room assistant	Ministry of Defence	1st April 1974
23. Dental technician	Ministry of Defence	1st April 1974
24. Assistant housekeeper	Scottish Office	1st April 1974
25. Pharmacist	Ministry of Defence	1st April 1974
26. Member of Navy Department printing grades	Ministry of Defence	21st May 1974

Employment	Employer	Relevant date
27. Member of marine staff, Sea Fisheries Laboratory, Lowestoft or Torry Research Station, Aberdeen	Ministry of Agriculture, Fisheries & Food	1st June 1974
28. Scientific Staff in the Fisheries Research Service	Scottish Office	1st June 1974
29. Member of officer grades in ocean weather ship, cable ship or RMAS "Whitehead"	Ministry of Defence	1st June 1974
30. Printer	Department for National Savings	17th June 1974
31. Presser or bookbinder	Ministry of Overseas Development	17th June 1974
32. Binder or lady sewer	Office of Population Censuses and Surveys	19th June 1974
33. Bookbinder or sewer	Inland Revenue	19th June 1974
34. Member of the industrial grades in the Ordnance Board Press and Mapping and Charting Establishment who received a pay increase on 19th June 1973	Ministry of Defence	19th June 1974
35. Member of industrial staff in presses and binderies	Her Majesty's Stationery Office	19th June 1974
36. Royal Fleet Auxiliary contract officer	Ministry of Defence	2nd July 1974
37. Member of exhibition trade grades	Central Office of Information	2nd July 1974
38. Member of marine grades	Ministry of Agriculture, Fisheries and Food	2nd July 1974
39. Rating, Royal Maritime Auxiliary Service	Ministry of Defence	2nd July 1974
40. Member of crew of ocean weather ship	Ministry of Defence	2nd July 1974
41. Carpenter	Department for National Savings	2nd July 1974
42. Member of industrial marine staff	Department of Agriculture and Fisheries for Scotland	2nd July 1974
43. Member of industrial staff in warehouses	Her Majesty's Stationery Office	26th July 1974
44. Member of park keeping grades or park attendant	Department of the Environment	1st September 1974
45. Member of Ministry of Defence police	Ministry of Defence	1st September 1974
46. Member of constabulary, Royal Botanic Gardens, Kew	Ministry of Agriculture, Fisheries and Food	1st September 1974
47. Member of brewery staff, Carlisle and District State Management Scheme	Home Office	2nd September 1974
48. Member of sound recording grades	Central Office of Information	1st October 1974
49. Director of studies, Dartmouth or Sandhurst	Ministry of Defence	1st October 1974
50. Bookbinder or sewer	Scottish Record Office	3rd October 1974

EXPLANATORY NOTE

(This Note is not part of the Regulations.)

These Regulations apply the Pensions (Increase) Act 1974 to pensions payable under the Principal Civil Service Pension Scheme. Such pensions which begin after 1st January 1973 qualify for the special pensions increases under the 1974 Act. The Regulations specify those pensions under the scheme ("Class A pensions") which are payable in respect of service in a grade of the civil service which suffered deferment of a pay increase in consequence of the Counter-Inflation (Temporary Provisions) Act 1972 during the period 6th November 1972 to 31st March 1973; these pension will consequently be increased in accordance with Part I of the Schedule to the 1974 Act. All other pensions under the scheme ("Class B pensions") will be increased in accordance with Part II of the Schedule to the Act.

The Regulations also specify the "relevant date"—the date of the principal pay increase made or expected to be made during the year ending 6th November 1974—for the grades concerned.

The provisions of the 1974 Act are modified for pensions of those civil servants with a reserved right to the terms of the Superannuation Act 1859. Those pensions are calculated by reference to pay on the last day of service rather than the average salary over a 12-month period. The effect of the modification is that no increase is payable on such pensions which begin after the specified relevant date.

Under the powers in section 4 (3)(a) of the 1974 Act the Regulations provide for increases payable by virtue of the Regulations to take effect from 1st December 1973.

STATUTORY INSTRUMENTS

1974 No. 719

INDUSTRIAL TRAINING

The Industrial Training Levy (Clothing and Allied Products) Order 1974

Made - - -		18*th April* 1974
Laid before Parliament		30*th April* 1974
Coming into Operation		22*nd May* 1974

The Secretary of State after approving proposals submitted by the Clothing and Allied Products Industry Training Board for the imposition of a further levy on employers in the clothing and allied products industry and in exercise of powers conferred by section 4 of the Industrial Training Act 1964(a) as amended by paragraph 2(2) of Part I of Schedule 2 to the Employment and Training Act 1973(b), and of all other powers enabling him in that behalf hereby makes the following Order: —

Title and commencement

1. This Order may be cited as the Industrial Training Levy (Clothing and Allied Products) Order 1974 and shall come into operation on 22nd May 1974.

Interpretation

2.—(1) In this Order unless the context otherwise requires: —

(a) "agriculture" has the same meaning as in section 109(3) of the Agriculture Act 1947(c) or, in relation to Scotland, as in section 86(3) of the Agriculture (Scotland) Act 1948(d);

(b) "an appeal tribunal" means an industrial tribunal established under section 12 of the Industrial Training Act 1964;

(c) "assessment" means an assessment of an employer to the levy;

(d) "the Board" means the Clothing and Allied Products Industry Training Board;

(e) "business" means any activities of industry or commerce;

(f) "charity" has the same meaning as in section 360 of the Income and Corporation Taxes Act 1970(e);

(g) "clothing and allied products establishment" means an establishment in Great Britain engaged in the fifth base period wholly or mainly in the clothing and allied products industry for a total of twenty-seven or more weeks or, being an establishment that commenced to carry on business in the fifth base period, for a total number of weeks exceeding one half of the number of weeks in the part of the said period commencing with the day on which business was commenced and ending on the last day thereof;

(a) 1964 c. 16.	(b) 1973 c. 50.
(c) 1947 c. 48.	(d) 1948 c. 45.
(e) 1970 c. 10.	

(*h*) "the clothing and allied products industry" means any one or more of the activities which, subject to the provisions of paragraph 2 of Schedule 1 to the industrial training order, are specified in paragraph 1 of that Schedule as the activities of the clothing and allied products industry;

(*i*) "emoluments" means all emoluments assessable to income tax under Schedule E (other than pensions), being emoluments from which tax under that Schedule is deductible, whether or not tax in fact falls to be deducted from any particular payment thereof;

(*j*) "employer" means a person who is an employer in the clothing and allied products industry at any time in the fifth levy period;

(*k*) "the fifth base period" means the period of twelve months that commenced on 6th April 1973;

(*l*) "the fifth levy period" means the period commencing with the day upon which this Order comes into operation and ending on 31st March 1975;

(*m*) "the industrial training order" means the Industrial Training (Clothing and Allied Products Board) Order 1969(**a**);

(*n*) "the levy" means the levy imposed by the Board in respect of the fifth levy period;

(*o*) "notice" means a notice in writing.

(2) Any reference in this Order to an establishment that commences to carry on business or that ceases to carry on business shall not be taken to apply where the location of the establishment is changed but its business is continued wholly or mainly at or from the new location, or where the suspension of activities is of a temporary or seasonal nature.

(3) In the case where a clothing and allied products establishment is taken over (whether directly or indirectly) by an employer in succession to, or jointly with, another person, a person employed at any time in the fifth base period at or from the establishment shall be deemed, for the purposes of this Order, to have been so employed by the employer carrying on the said establishment on the day upon which this Order comes into operation, and any reference in this Order to persons employed by the employer at or from a clothing and allied products establishment in the fifth base period shall be construed accordingly.

(4) The Interpretation Act 1889(**b**) shall apply to the interpretation of this Order as it applies to the interpretation of an Act of Parliament.

Imposition of the levy

3.—(1) The levy to be imposed by the Board on employers in respect of the fifth levy period shall be assessed in accordance with the provisions of this Article.

(2) Subject to the provisions of this Article, the levy shall be assessed by the Board in respect of each employer and the amount thereof shall be equal to 0·8 per cent. of the sum (less £29,000) of the emoluments of all the persons employed by the employer at or from the clothing and allied products establishment or establishments of the employer in the fifth base period.

(**a**) S.I. 1969/1375 (1969 III, p. 4094).   (**b**) 1889 c. 63.

(3) There shall be exempt from the levy—

(*a*) an employer in respect of whom the sum of the emoluments of the persons mentioned in the last foregoing paragraphs is less than £30,250,

(*b*) a charity.

(4) Where any persons whose emoluments are taken into account for the purposes of this Article were employed at or from an establishment that ceases to carry on business in the fifth levy period, the sum of the emoluments of those persons shall be reduced for such purposes in the same proportion as the number of days between the commencement of the said levy period and the date of cessation of business (both dates inclusive) bears to the number of days in the said levy period.

(5) For the purposes of this Article, no regard shall be had to the emoluments of any person wholly engaged—

(*a*) in agriculture; or

(*b*) in the supply of food or drink for immediate consumption.

Assessment notices

4.—(1) The Board shall serve an assessment notice on every employer assessed to the levy.

(2) The amount of an assessment shall be rounded down to the nearest £1.

(3) An assessment notice shall state the Board's address for the service of a notice of appeal or of an application for an extension of time for appealing.

(4) An assessment notice may be served on the person assessed to the levy either by delivering it to him personally or by leaving it, or sending it to him by post, at his last known address or place of business in the United Kingdom or, if that person is a corporation, by leaving it, or sending it by post to the corporation, at such address or place of business or at its registered or principal office.

Payment of the levy

5.—(1) Subject to the provisions of this Article and of Articles 6 and 7, the amount of the assessment payable under an assessment notice served by the Board shall be due and payable to the Board one month after the date of the notice.

(2) The amount of an assessment shall not be recoverable by the Board until there has expired the time allowed for appealing against the assessment by Article 7(1) of this Order and any further period or periods of time that the Board or an appeal tribunal may have allowed for appealing under paragraph (2) or (3) of that Article or, where an appeal is brought, until the appeal is decided or withdrawn.

Withdrawal of assessment

6.—(1) The Board may, by a notice served on the person assessed to the levy in the same manner as an assessment notice, withdraw an assessment if that person has appealed against that assessment under the provisions of Article 7 of this Order and the appeal has not been entered in the Register of Appeals kept under the appropriate Regulations specified in paragraph (5) of that Article.

(2) The withdrawal of an assessment shall be without prejudice to the power of the Board to serve a further assessment notice on the employer.

Appeals

7.—(1) A person assessed to the levy may appeal to an appeal tribunal against the assessment within one month from the date of the service of the assessment notice or within any further period or periods of time that may be allowed by the Board or an appeal tribunal under the following provisions of this Article.

(2) The Board by notice may for good cause allow a person assessed to the levy to appeal to an appeal tribunal against the assessment at any time within the period of four months from the date of the service of the assessment notice or within such further period or periods as the Board may allow before such time as may then be limited for appealing has expired.

(3) If the Board shall not allow an application for extension of time for appealing, an appeal tribunal shall upon application made to the tribunal by the person assessed to the levy have the like powers as the Board under the last foregoing paragraph.

(4) In the case of an assessment that has reference to an establishment that ceases to carry on business in the fifth levy period on any day after the date of the service of the assessment notice, the foregoing provisions of this Article shall have effect as if for the period of four months from the date of the service of the assessment notice mentioned in paragraph (2) of this Article there were substituted the period of six months from the date of the cessation of business.

(5) An appeal or an application to an appeal tribunal under this Article shall be made in accordance with the Industrial Tribunals (England and Wales) Regulations 1965(**a**) as amended by the Industrial Tribunals (England and Wales) (Amendment) Regulations 1967(**b**) except where the assessment has reference to persons employed at or from one or more establishments that are wholly in Scotland and to no other persons, in which case the appeal or application shall be made in accordance with the Industrial Tribunals (Scotland) Regulations 1965(**c**) as amended by the Industrial Tribunals (Scotland) (Amendment) Regulations 1967(**d**).

(6) The powers of an appeal tribunal under paragraph (3) of this Article may be exercised by the President of the Industrial Tribunals (England and Wales) or by the President of the Industrial Tribunals (Scotland) as the case may be.

Evidence

8.—(1) Upon the discharge by a person assessed to the levy of his liability under an assessment the Board shall if so requested issue to him a certificate to that effect.

(2) The production in any proceedings of a document purporting to be certified by the Secretary of the Board to be a true copy of an assessment or other notice issued by the Board or purporting to be a certificate such as is mentioned in the foregoing paragraph of this Article shall, unless the contrary is proved, be sufficient evidence of the document and of the facts stated therein.

Signed by order of the Secretary of State.

18th April 1974.

John Fraser,
Joint Parliamentary Under Secretary of State,
Department of Employment.

(**a**) S.I. 1965/1101 (1965 II, p. 2805). (**b**) S.I. 1967/301 (1967 I, p. 1040).
(**c**) S.I. 1965/1157 (1965 II, p. 3266). (**d**) S.I. 1967/302 (1967 I, p. 1050).

EXPLANATORY NOTE

(This Note is not part of the Order.)

This Order gives effect to proposals submitted by the Clothing and Allied Products Industry Training Board to the Secretary of State for Employment for the imposition of a further levy upon employers in the industry for the purpose of raising money towards the expenses of the Board.

The levy is to be imposed in respect of the fifth levy period commencing with the day upon which this Order comes into operation and ending on 31st March 1975. The levy will be assessed by the Board and there will be a right of appeal against an assessment to an industrial tribunal.

STATUTORY INSTRUMENTS

1974 No. 721

ACQUISITION OF LAND
COMPENSATION

The Acquisition of Land (Rate of Interest after Entry) Regulations 1974

Made - - -		*19th April* 1974
Laid before Parliament		*29th April* 1974
Coming into Operation		*30th April* 1974

The Treasury, in exercise of the powers conferred upon them by section 32(1) of the Land Compensation Act 1961(**a**), and of all other powers enabling them in that behalf, hereby make the following Regulations:—

1. These Regulations may be cited as the Acquisition of Land (Rate of Interest after Entry) Regulations 1974, and shall come into operation on 30th April 1974.

2. The Interpretation Act 1889(**b**) shall apply for the interpretation of these Regulations as it applies for the interpretation of an Act of Parliament.

3. The rate of interest on any compensation in respect of the compulsory acquisition of an interest in any land on which entry has been made before the payment of the compensation shall be $14\frac{1}{2}$ per cent. per annum.

4. The Acquisition of Land (Rate of Interest after Entry) (No. 5) Regulations 1973(**c**) are hereby revoked.

Donald R. Coleman,
T. Pendry,
Two of the Lords Commissioners
of Her Majesty's Treasury.
19th April 1974.

EXPLANATORY NOTE
(This Note is not part of the Regulations.)

These Regulations increase from $13\frac{1}{2}$ per cent. to $14\frac{1}{2}$ per cent. per annum, in respect of any period after the coming into operation of these Regulations, the rate of interest payable where entry is made, before payment of compensation, on land in England and Wales which is being purchased compulsorily, and revoke the Acquisition of Land (Rate of Interest after Entry) (No. 5) Regulations 1973.

(**a**) 1961 c. 33.   (**b**) 1889 c. 63.   (**c**) S.I. 1973/2072 (1973 III, p. 7147).

STATUTORY INSTRUMENTS

1974 No. 722

ACQUISITION OF LAND

COMPENSATION

The Acquisition of Land (Rate of Interest after Entry) (Scotland) Regulations 1974

Made - - -	*19th April* 1974
Laid before Parliament	*29th April* 1974
Coming into Operation	*30th April* 1974

The Treasury, in exercise of the powers conferred upon them by section 40(1) of the Land Compensation (Scotland) Act 1963(**a**), and of all other powers enabling them in that behalf, hereby make the following Regulations:—

1.—(1) These Regulations may be cited as the Acquisition of Land (Rate of Interest after Entry) (Scotland) Regulations 1974, and shall come into operation on 30th April 1974.

(2) These Regulations shall extend to Scotland only.

2. The Interpretation Act 1889(**b**) shall apply for the interpretation of these Regulations as it applies for the interpretation of an Act of Parliament.

3. The rate of interest on any compensation in respect of the compulsory acquisition of an interest in any land on which entry has been made before the payment of the compensation shall be $14\frac{1}{2}$ per cent. per annum.

4. The Acquisition of Land (Rate of Interest after Entry) (Scotland) (No. 5) Regulations 1973(**c**) are hereby revoked.

Donald R. Coleman,
T. Pendry,
Two of the Lords Commissioners
of Her Majesty's Treasury.

19th April 1974.

(**a**) 1963 c. 51
(**b**) 1988 c. 63.
(**c**) S.I. 1973/2073 (1973 III. p. 7148).

EXPLANATORY NOTE

(This Note is not part of the Regulations.)

These Regulations increase from 13½ per cent. to 14½ per cent. per annum, in respect of any period after the coming into operation of these Regulations, the rate of interest payable where entry is made, before payment of compensation, on land in Scotland which is being purchased compulsorily, and revoke the Acquisition of Land (Rate of Interest after Entry) (Scotland) (No. 5) Regulations 1973.

1974 No. 723 (S.65)

HOUSING, SCOTLAND

The Rent Rebate and Rent Allowance Schemes (Scotland) Regulations 1974

Made - - -	*18th April* 1974
Laid before Parliament	*24th April* 1974
Coming into Operation	*16th May* 1974

In exercise of the powers conferred on me by section 17(2) of the Housing (Financial Provisions) (Scotland) Act 1972(a) and of all other powers enabling me in that behalf, and having consulted with such associations of local authorities as appear to me to be concerned, I hereby, with the consent of the Treasury, make the following regulations:—

Citation and commencement

1. These regulations which may be cited as the Rent Rebate and Rent Allowance Schemes (Scotland) Regulations 1974 shall come into operation on 16th May 1974.

Interpretation

2.—(1) The Interpretation Act 1889(b) shall apply for the interpretation of these regulations as it applies for the interpretation of an Act of Parliament.

(2) In these regulations—

"the Act" means the Housing (Financial Provisions) (Scotland) Act 1972;

"Schedule 2" means Schedule 2 to the Act; and

"Schedule 3" means Schedule 3 to the Act.

(3) In these regulations, unless the context otherwise requires, references to any enactment shall be construed as references to that enactment as amended varied extended or applied by or under any other enactment or by these regulations.

Effective date for variation of Schedules 2 and 3

3. Without prejudice to the making at any time before the beginning of the year 1974-75 of a scheme under Part II of the Act expressed to come into

---

(a) 1972 c. 46.   (b) 1889 c. 63.

operation from the beginning of that year, being a scheme taking account of the variations of the provisions of Schedule 2 and Schedule 3 made by these regulations, the said variations shall take effect from the beginning of that year and not before.

Variation of Schedule 2

4. In relation to any week in a rebate period or allowance period, being a week commencing after the beginning of the year 1974-75, paragraph 12(1)(*c*), (*d*) and (*e*) of Schedule 2 shall have effect with the substitution for each of the references therein to £0·70 of a reference to £0·60.

Variation of Schedule 3

5. In relation to any application for a further rebate or allowance made after the end of the year 1973-74, paragraph 10 of Schedule 3 shall have effect with the substitution for sub-paragraph (4) thereof of the following sub-paragraph—

"(4) If the application is made at any later date, the new rebate period or allowance period shall commence at the commencement of the rental period in which the application for a further rebate or allowance was received ("the relevant rental period"):

Provided that—

(i) Where a rebate period or allowance period terminates during the relevant rental period, the new rebate period or allowance period shall commence with the first rental period after the end of the former rebate period or allowance period; and

(ii) Where the commencement of the relevant rental period is later than the commencement of the first rental period after the end of the former rebate period or allowance period, the authority may, if in their opinion the circumstances are exceptional—

(*a*) allow the new period to commence at the commencement of the first rental period after the end of the former rebate or allowance period, or

(*b*) allow the new period to commence at such later date (not being a date later than the commencement of the relevant rental period) as they may determine.

William Ross,
One of Her Majesty's Principal
Secretaries of State.

St. Andrew's House,
Edinburgh.
11th April 1974.
We consent.

Donald R. Coleman,
T. Pendry,
Two of the Lords Commissioners
of Her Majesty's Treasury.

18th April 1974.

EXPLANATORY NOTE
(*This Note is not part of the Regulations.*)

These Regulations further vary the provisions of Schedules 2 and 3 to the Housing (Financial Provisions) (Scotland) Act 1972, as amended by the Furnished Lettings (Rent Allowances) Act 1973 (1973 c.6), with which, subject to the other provisions of the 1972 Act, every rent rebate scheme and rent allowance scheme under Part II of that Act must conform.

They provide firstly for a reduction of 10 pence per week in the deductions required to be made from a rebate or allowance for each week in respect of certain non-dependants.

They provide secondly for the substitution of a new sub-paragraph (4) in paragraph 10 (Application for further rebate or allowance) of Schedule 3, so that where applications for further rebates or allowances are made later than one month after the end of the former rebate period of allowance period, the further rebates or allowances will normally be granted from the commencement of the rental period in which the applications were made—as is the case where rebates or allowances are first granted. Provision is also made for backdating to an earlier date in certain cases, at the discretion of authorities, if in their opinion the circumstances are exceptional.

The variations have effect from the beginning of the local authority financial year 1974-75, although schemes taking account of them, and expressed to come into force then, may be made in advance.

STATUTORY INSTRUMENTS

1974 No. 724

CUSTOMS AND EXCISE

The Anti-Dumping Duty (Temporary Suspension) (No. 2) Order 1974

Made - - -	*22nd April* 1974
Laid before the House of Commons	*30th April* 1974
Coming into Operation	*24th May* 1974

The Secretary of State, in exercise of powers conferred by sections 1, 10(3) and 15(4) of the Customs Duties (Dumping and Subsidies) Act 1969(a) and now vested in him(b), and of all other powers enabling him in that behalf, hereby makes the following Order:—

1. This Order may be cited as the Anti-Dumping Duty (Temporary Suspension) (No. 2) Order 1974 and shall come into operation on 24th May 1974.

2. The Interpretation Act 1889(c) shall apply for the interpretation of this Order as it applies for the interpretation of an Act of Parliament.

3. The anti-dumping duty imposed by the Anti-Dumping and Countervailing Duties Order 1973(d) on zirconium dioxide originating in the Union of Soviet Socialist Republics shall not be chargeable on zirconium dioxide imported into the United Kingdom during a period of twelve months beginning with the date of coming into operation of this Order.

Eric Deakins,
Joint Parliamentary Under-Secretary of State for Trade,
Department of Trade.
22nd April 1974.

EXPLANATORY NOTE

(*This Note is not part of the Order.*)

This Order suspends for a period of twelve months the anti-dumping duty imposed by the Anti-Dumping and Countervailing Duties Order 1973 on zirconium dioxide originating in the Union of Soviet Socialist Republics.

(a) 1969 c. 16.
(b) *See* S.I. 1970/1537 (1970 III, p.5293).
(c) 1889 c. 63.
(d) S.I. 1973/2037 (1973 III, p.7059).

STATUTORY INSTRUMENTS

1974 No. 731

NURSES AND MIDWIVES

The Central Midwives Board (Constitution) Order 1974

Laid before Parliament in draft

Made - - - - -	22nd April	1974
Coming into Operation -	1st May	1974

The Secretary of State for Social Services in exercise of the powers conferred by section 1 (3) and (4) of the Midwives Act 1951(a), and now vested in her(b), and of all other powers enabling her in that behalf, after consultation with such bodies and persons as appear to her to be concerned, hereby makes the following Order in the terms of a draft which has been laid before Parliament: —

Citation and commencement

1. This Order may be cited as the Central Midwives Board (Constitution) Order 1974 and shall come into operation on 1st May 1974.

Interpretation

2.—(1) In this Order, unless the context otherwise requires, " the Board " means the Central Midwives Board.

(2) The rules for the construction of Acts of Parliament contained in the Interpretation Act(c) shall apply for the purposes of the interpretation of this Order as they apply for the purposes of the interpretation of an Act of Parliament.

Constitution of the Central Midwives Board

3.—(1) Subject to the provisions of article 4 of this Order, on the date of coming into operation of this Order, the Board shall be constituted in accordance with the following provisions of this article.

(2) The Board shall consist of seventeen persons of whom—

(*a*) Seven (of whom two shall be certified midwives and one shall be a fully registered medical practitioner engaged in general practice) shall be appointed by the Secretary of State after consultation with such bodies and persons as appear to him to be concerned;

(*b*) Four shall be fully registered medical practitioners appointed, as to one each, by the Royal College of Physicians of London, the Royal College of Surgeons of England, the Royal College of Obstetricians and Gynaecologists and the Society of Community Medicine;

(*c*) Four shall be certified midwives appointed by the Royal College of Midwives; and

---

(a) 1951 c. 53.　　(b) S.I. 1968/1699 (1968 III, p. 4585).　　(c) 1889 c. 63.

(d) Two (not being certified midwives) shall be appointed, as to one each, by the County Councils' Association and the Faculty of Community Medicine.

4.—(1) Nothing in this Order shall affect the term of office of any person who is a member of the Board on the date of coming into operation of this Order.

(2) When the member of the Board appointed by the Society of Medical Officers of Health ceases to hold office, the vacancy shall be filled by a person appointed by the Society of Community Medicine.

(3) When the member of the Board appointed by the Association of Municipal Corporations ceases to hold office, the vacancy shall be filled by a person appointed by the Faculty of Community Medicine.

Barbara Castle,
Secretary of State for Social Services.

22nd April 1974.

EXPLANATORY NOTE

(*This Note is not part of the Order.*)

This Order amends the Constitution of the Central Midwives Board with the effect that when the members of the Board appointed by the Society of Medical Officers of Health and the Association of Municipal Corporations cease to hold office they will be succeeded by persons appointed by the Society of Community Medicine and the Faculty of Community Medicine respectively.

STATUTORY INSTRUMENTS

1974 No. 732

WAGES COUNCILS

The Wages Regulation (Milk Distributive) (England and Wales) Order 1974

Made - - - - *22nd April* 1974

Coming into Operation *13th May* 1974

Whereas the Secretary of State has received from the Milk Distributive Wages Council (England and Wales) the wages regulation proposals set out in the Schedule hereto;

Now, therefore, the Secretary of State in exercise of powers conferred by section 11 of the Wages Councils Act 1959(a), as modified by Article 2 of the Counter-Inflation (Modification of Wages Councils Act 1959) Order 1973(b), and now vested in him(c), and of all other powers enabling him in that behalf, hereby makes the following Order:—

1. This Order may be cited as the Wages Regulation (Milk Distributive) (England and Wales) Order 1974.

2.—(1) In this Order the expression "the specified date" means the 13th May 1974, provided that where, as respects any worker who is paid wages at intervals not exceeding seven days, that date does not correspond with the beginning of the period for which the wages are paid, the expression "the specified date" means, as respects that worker, the beginning of the next such period following that date.

(2) The Interpretation Act 1889(d) shall apply to the interpretation of this Order as it applies to the interpretation of an Act of Parliament and as if this Order and the Order hereby revoked were Acts of Parliament.

3. The wages regulation proposals set out in the Schedule hereto shall have effect as from the specified date and as from that date the Wages Regulation (Milk Distributive) (England and Wales) Order 1973(e) shall cease to have effect.

Signed by order of the Secretary of State.
22nd April 1974.

W. H. Marsh,
Assistant Secretary,
Department of Employment.

(a) 1959 c. 69.   (b) S.I. 1973/661 (1973 I, p. 2141).
(c) S.I. 1959/1769, 1968/729 (1959 I, p. 1795; 1968 II, p. 2108).
(d) 1889 c. 63.   (e) S.I. 1973/122 (1973 I, p. 528).

ARRANGEMENT OF SCHEDULE
PART I
STATUTORY MINIMUM REMUNERATION

PART II
HOLIDAYS AND HOLIDAY REMUNERATION

PART III
GENERAL

Article 3

SCHEDULE

The following minimum remuneration and provisions as to holidays and holiday remuneration shall be substituted for the statutory minimum remuneration and the provisions as to holidays and holiday remuneration fixed by the Wages Regulation (Milk Distributive) (England and Wales) Order 1973 (Order M.D. (119)).

PART I
STATUTORY MINIMUM REMUNERATION
GENERAL

1. In this Schedule the expression "hourly general minimum time rate" means the general minimum time rate applicable to the worker under the provisions of paragraphs 4, 5 and 6 divided by 40.

2. Subject to paragraph 3, the minimum remuneration payable to a worker to whom this Schedule applies is the sum of the amounts calculated in accordance with the provisions of (a)(i) or (a)(ii) and (b) and (c) below:—

(*a*) For all work except overtime,

    (i) in the case of a time worker, the amount yielded by the hourly general minimum time rate applicable to the worker under the provisions of this Schedule; or

    (ii) in the case of a worker employed on piece work, the amount yielded by piece rates, each of which would yield, in the circumstances of the case, to an ordinary worker at least the same amount of money as the hourly general minimum time rate which would be applicable if the worker were a time worker.

(*b*) For all overtime including work on a customary holiday and any waiting time, the amount payable under paragraphs 7, 8, 9, 10 and 11; and

(*c*) Any further amount payable under paragraph 12.

SPECIAL PROVISIONS FOR CERTAIN ROUNDS SALESMEN AND ROUNDS SALESWOMEN

3. Where a rounds salesman or a rounds saleswoman is employed under a system of calculating remuneration which is not related to the general minimum time rate specified in relation to that worker in paragraph 4(4) or paragraph 5(1) the minimum remuneration payable to that worker for any week in which he works on not less than 5 days shall be whichever is the greater of the following amounts, that is to say:—

(*a*) the appropriate amount calculated in accordance with paragraph 2 for a time worker of the relevant class and description; or

(*b*) an amount equal to the general minimum time rate specified in relation to a worker of the relevant class and description under paragraph 4(4) or paragraph 5(1) increased by the following amount:—

	Per week
	p
in the case of a worker aged 21 years or over	80
,, ,, ,, ,, ,, ,, ,, 20 and under 21 years	74
,, ,, ,, ,, ,, ,, ,, 19 ,, ,, 20 ,,	68
,, ,, ,, ,, ,, ,, ,, 18 ,, ,, 19 ,,	62
,, ,, ,, ,, ,, ,, ,, under 18 years	48

GENERAL MINIMUM TIME RATES

MALE WORKERS

4. The general minimum time rates applicable to male workers employed in Area A, Area B or Area C are respectively as follows:—

	AREA A	AREA B	AREA C
	Per week	Per week	Per week
	£	£	£
(1) Foreman	21·65	21·90	22·25
(2) Sterilizers (other than assistant sterilizers), being workers aged 21 years or over	20·95	21·10	21·30
(3) Clerks, being workers aged:—			
21 years or over	20·95	21·10	21·30
20 and under 21 years	19·40	19·55	19·70
19 „ „ 20 „	17·80	17·95	18·10
18 „ „ 19 „	16·25	16·40	16·55
17 „ „ 18 „	12·55	12·65	12·75
Under 17 years	11·00	11·10	11·20
(4) Rounds Salesmen, being workers aged:—			
21 years or over	21·20	21·30	21·50
20 and under 21 years	19·60	19·70	19·90
19 „ „ 20 „	18·05	18·10	18·30
18 „ „ 19 „	16·45	16·55	16·70
Under 18 years	13·75	13·85	13·95
(5) Shop Assistants, Assistant Rounds Salesmen, Pasteurizers, Assistant Sterilizers, and Any Other Workers not specified in the foregoing provisions of this Table, being workers aged:—			
21 years or over	20·70	20·85	21·05
20 and under 21 years	19·15	19·30	19·50
19 „ „ 20 „	17·60	17·75	17·90
18 „ „ 19 „	16·05	16·20	16·35
17 „ „ 18 „	12·40	12·50	12·60
Under 17 years	10·85	10·95	11·05

FEMALE WORKERS

5. The general minimum time rates applicable to female workers employed in Area A, Area B or Area C are respectively as follows:—

	AREA A	AREA B	AREA C
	Per week	Per week	Per week
	£	£	£
(1) Rounds Saleswomen, being workers aged:—			
21 years or over	20·75	20·85	21·10
20 and under 21 years	19·15	19·25	19·50
19 ,, ,, 20 ,, ..	17·65	17·75	17·95
18 ,, ,, 19 ,, ..	16·05	16·15	16·35
Under 18 years	13·50	13·55	13·70
(2) Clerks, being workers aged:—			
21 years or over	19·20	19·25	19·55
20 and under 21 years	18·40	18·50	18·75
19 ,, ,, 20 ,, ..	17·00	17·05	17·30
18 ,, ,, 19 ,, ..	15·50	15·60	15·80
17 ,, ,, 18 ,, ..	12·55	12·55	12·70
Under 17 years	11·00	11·10	11·20
(3) All Other Workers, being workers aged:—			
21 years or over	19·15	19·20	19·40
20 and under 21 years	18·40	18·45	18·65
19 ,, ,, 20 ,, ..	16·95	17·00	17·20
18 ,, ,, 19 ,, ..	15·50	15·55	15·70
17 ,, ,, 18 ,, ..	12·40	12·50	12·60
Under 17 years	10·85	10·95	11·05

MALE OR FEMALE WORKERS IN TWO OR MORE AREAS

6. The general minimum time rate applicable to any worker in any week in which he works in Area A, Area B and Area C or in any two of those areas is:—

(1) in the case of a rounds salesman or rounds saleswoman, the rate which would be applicable if he worked solely in that Area in which is served the majority of the customers on his round;

(2) in the case of any other worker, the rate which would be applicable if he worked solely at his depot.

OVERTIME, WORK ON A CUSTOMARY HOLIDAY AND WAITING TIME
OVERTIME

7. Subject to the provisions of paragraph 11, the following minimum remuneration is payable to any worker for overtime:—

(1) On any week day, not being a rest day or a customary holiday, for all time worked in excess of 8 hours   ...   time-and-a-half

(2) On a Sunday, not being a rest day or a customary holiday—

(a) for any time worked not exceeding 5 hours ...	time-and-a-half for 5 hours
(b) for all time worked in excess of 5 hours ...	time-and-a-half

(3) On a Sunday, being also a rest day but not being a customary holiday—

(a) for any time worked not exceeding 6 hours ...	double time for 6 hours
(b) for all time worked in excess of 6 hours ...	double time

(4) On a rest day, not being a Sunday or a customary holiday, for all time worked ... ... time-and-a-half

WORK ON A CUSTOMARY HOLIDAY

8. Subject to the provisions of paragraphs 9 and 11, the following minimum remuneration is payable for work on a customary holiday:—

(1) To any worker who normally works for an employer for not less than 20 hours per week—

(a) On a customary holiday not being the worker's rest day—

(i) for any time worked not exceeding 6 hours	double time for 6 hours
(ii) for all time worked in excess of 6 hours ...	double time

(b) On a customary holiday being also the worker's rest day—

(i) for any time worked not exceeding 6 hours	treble time for 6 hours
(ii) for all time worked in excess of 6 hours ...	treble time

(2) To all other workers—

for all time worked ... ... double time

9. Where a worker to whom the provisions of paragraph 13 apply is required to work on a customary holiday, and it is mutually agreed between the employer and the worker (in accordance with the provisions of sub-paragraph (4) of paragraph 13) that a holiday in lieu of the customary holiday shall not be allowed to the worker, the minimum remuneration payable to the worker in respect of work on that day shall be:—

(1) the amount to which the worker is entitled in accordance with the provisions of paragraph 8 for working on a customary holiday, and in addition,

(2) an amount equal to the holiday remuneration to which the worker would have been entitled under the provisions of paragraph 18 had he been allowed a holiday on that day.

WAITING TIME

10.—(1) A worker is entitled to payment of the minimum remuneration specified in this Schedule for all time during which he is present on the premises of his employer, unless he is present thereon in any of the following circumstances—

(a) without the employer's consent, express or implied;

(b) for some purpose unconnected with his work and other than that of waiting for work to be given to him to perform;

(c) by reason only of the fact that he is resident thereon;

(d) during normal meal times in a room or place in which no work is being done, and he is not waiting for work to be given to him to perform.

(2) The minimum remuneration payable under sub-paragraph (1) of this paragraph to a piece worker when not engaged on piece work is that which would be applicable if he were a time worker.

OVERTIME BEING NIGHT WORK

11.—(1) In the application of the provisions of paragraphs 7, 8 and 9 to a worker to whom an additional minimum time rate is payable for night work under the provisions of paragraph 12—

(a) the minimum remuneration for overtime shall be payable only in respect of hours of overtime within the same turn of duty, and

(b) a day shall be deemed to be any period of 24 hours commencing at noon.

(2) Where a worker is ordinarily employed on a spell of duty which starts before and ends after midnight the provisions of paragraphs 8 and 9 shall be applicable to time worked during the period of 24 hours commencing at noon on the day prior to the customary holiday.

ADDITIONAL MINIMUM REMUNERATION
NIGHT WORK

12. In addition to the minimum remuneration payable to a worker under paragraphs 7, 8, 9, 10 and 11, minimum remuneration at the rate of 5p per hour is payable to a worker for any time worked between the hours of 9 p.m. and 5 a.m.:

Provided that where a worker commences a spell of work between the hours of 9 p.m. and 5 a.m. and works for less than 4 hours between those hours he shall be paid as remuneration under this paragraph the sum of 20p instead of at the rate of 5p per hour.

PART II
HOLIDAYS AND HOLIDAY REMUNERATION
CUSTOMARY HOLIDAYS

13.—(1) Subject to the provisions of this paragraph, and, except in the circumstances provided for in sub-paragraph (3) of this paragraph, the employer shall in each year on the days specified in the next following sub-paragraph or in sub-paragraph (5) of this paragraph, as the case may be, allow a holiday (hereinafter referred to as a "customary holiday") to any worker in his employment who—

(*a*) normally works for the employer for not less than 20 hours a week, and

(*b*) unless excused by the employer or absent by reason of proved illness or injury of the worker, worked for the employer throughout the last working day on which work was available to him immediately prior to the customary holiday.

(2) The said customary holidays are Christmas Day; *26th December, if it be not a Sunday, 27th December in a year when 25th or 26th is a Sunday; 1st January, if it be not a Sunday, or if it be a Sunday, 2nd January;* Good Friday; Easter Monday; *the last Monday in May; the last Monday in August; or where a day is substituted for any of the above days by national proclamation, that day,* and any day proclaimed as an additional Bank Holiday or as a public holiday, or where it is the custom in any locality instead of any of the said days to observe some other day as a holiday each such other day shall, for the purposes of this Schedule, be treated in that locality as a customary holiday instead of the day for which it is substituted.

(3) Notwithstanding the preceding provisions of this paragraph, an employer may (except where in the case of a woman or young person such a requirement would be unlawful) require a worker who is otherwise entitled to any customary holiday under the preceding provisions of this paragraph to work thereon and, in lieu of any customary holiday on which he so works, the employer shall (except in the case provided for in sub-paragraph (4) of this paragraph) allow to the worker a day's holiday (hereinafter referred to as "a holiday in lieu of a customary holiday") on a week day being:—

(*a*) a day mutually agreed between the employer and the worker,

(*b*) a day on which the worker would normally work, and

(*c*) a day before the commencement of the next holiday season or before the commencement of the holiday season in the next succeeding year:

Provided that in the absence of agreement between the employer and the worker a holiday in lieu of a customary holiday shall be allowed on the last day on which the worker would normally work prior to the commencement of the next holiday season or as the case may require the holiday season in the next succeeding year.

(4) Where a worker, otherwise entitled to be allowed a customary holiday or holiday in lieu thereof under the foregoing provisions of this paragraph, is required to work on a customary holiday and it is mutually agreed between the employer and the worker before the customary holiday on which the worker works (for which he is to receive not less than the remuneration calculated in accordance with paragraph 9) that a holiday in lieu thereof shall not be allowed, the employer shall not be required to allow the worker a holiday in lieu of the customary holiday.

(5) Where a worker is ordinarily employed on a spell on duty which starts before and ends after midnight he shall be allowed—

(*a*) as a customary holiday in his case the period of 24 hours commencing at noon on the day prior to the customary holiday;

(*b*) as a holiday in lieu of a customary holiday a period of 24 hours commencing at noon.

ANNUAL HOLIDAY

14.—(1) Subject to the provisions of this paragraph, an employer shall, between the date on which this schedule becomes effective and 31st October 1974, and in each succeeding year between 1st April and 31st October allow a holiday (hereinafter referred to as an "annual holiday") to every worker in his employment to whom this Schedule applies who was employed by him during the 12 months immediately preceding the commencement of the holiday season for any one of the periods of employment set out in the Table below and the duration of the annual holiday shall in the case of each such worker be related to that period as follows:—

Period of employment	Duration of annual holiday where the worker's normal working week is:—		
	5 days	4 days	3 days
At least 5 weeks but less than 6	1 day	—	—
" " 6 " " " " 7	1 "	1 day	—
" " 7 " " " " 8	1 "	1 "	—
" " 8 " " " " 10	1 "	1 "	1 day
" " 10 " " " " 11	2 days	1 "	1 "
" " 11 " " " " 12	2 "	1 "	1 "
" " 12 " " " " 14	2 "	2 days	1 "
" " 14 " " " " 15	2 "	2 "	1 "
" " 15 " " " " 16	3 "	2 "	1 "
" " 16 " " " " 18	3 "	2 "	2 days
" " 18 " " " " 20	3 "	3 "	2 "
" " 20 " " " " 21	4 "	3 "	2 "
" " 21 " " " " 24	4 "	3 "	2 "
" " 24 " " " " 25	4 "	4 "	3 "
" " 25 " " " " 28	1 normal working week	4 "	3 "
" " 28 " " " " 30	1 " " "	4 "	3 "
" " 30 " " " " 32	1 " " " and 1 day	5 "	3 "
" " 32 " " " " 35	1 " " " " " 1 "	5 "	4 "
" " 35 " " " " 36	1 " " " " " 2 days	5 "	4 "
" " 36 " " " " 39	1 " " " " " 2 "	6 "	4 "
" " 39 " " " " 40	1 " " " " " 2 "	6 "	4 "
" " 40 " " " " 42	1 " " " " " 3 "	6 "	5 "
" " 42 " " " " 44	1 " " " " " 3 "	7 "	5 "
" " 44 " " " " 45	1 " " " " " 3 "	7 "	5 "
" " 45 " " " " 46	1 " " " " " 4 "	7 "	5 "
" " 46 " " " " 48	1 " " " " " 4 "	7 "	5 "
" " 48 " " " " 49	1 " " " " " 4 "	8 "	6 "
" " 49 " " " " 50	1 " " " " " 4 "	8 "	6 "
" " 50	2 normal working weeks	8 "	6 "

(2) In this Schedule the expression "holiday season" means in relation to an annual holiday during the year 1974, the period commencing on 1st April 1974, and ending on 31st October 1974, and in relation to each subsequent year, the period commencing on 1st April and ending on 31st October in that year.

(3) Notwithstanding the provisions of sub-paragraph (1) of this paragraph:—

(a) the number of days of annual holiday which an employer is required to allow to a worker in any holiday season shall not exceed in the aggregate twice the number of days constituting the worker's normal working week;

(b) where before the expiration of any holiday season a worker enters into an agreement in writing with his employer that the annual holiday or part thereof shall be allowed on a specified date or dates after the expiration of the holiday season but before the commencement of the next following holiday season, then any day or days of annual holiday so allowed shall for the purposes of this Schedule be treated as having been allowed during the holiday season;

(c) the duration of the worker's annual holiday during the holiday season ending on 31st October 1974, shall be reduced by any days of annual holiday duly allowed to him by the employer under the provisions of Order M.D. (119) between 1st April 1974 and the date on which this Schedule becomes effective.

(4) A night worker shall be allowed as a day of annual holiday in his case, a period of 24 hours commencing at noon.

15.—(1) An annual holiday shall be allowed on consecutive working days, being days on which the worker is normally called upon to work for the employer, and days of annual holiday shall be treated as consecutive notwithstanding the intervention of a customary holiday on which the worker is not required to work or of some other holiday:

Provided that where the number of days of annual holiday for which a worker has qualified exceeds the number of days constituting his normal working week, the holiday may at the written request of the worker and with the agreement of the employer be allowed in two periods of consecutive working days; so however that when a holiday is so allowed, one of the periods shall consist of a number of such days not less than the number of days constituting the worker's normal working week.

(2) A day of annual holiday under this Schedule may be allowed on a day on which the worker is entitled to a day of holiday or to a half-holiday under any enactment other than the Wages Councils Act 1959.

ADDITIONAL ANNUAL HOLIDAY

16.—(1) In addition to the holidays specified in paragraphs 13 and 14 of this Schedule and subject to the provisions of this paragraph, an employer shall, during the relevant period of 12 months commencing on 1st April 1974 and during each succeeding relevant period of 12 months, allow an additional annual holiday amounting to one normal working week to every worker in his employment to whom this Schedule applies, who—

    (a) at 31st March immediately preceding the relevant period of 12 months has been continuously employed by him for not less than 12 months, and

    (b) during the 12 months ending on the said 31st March has worked for a period qualifying him in accordance with paragraph 14 for an annual holiday equal in duration to twice his normal working week.

(2) Days of additional annual holiday need not be consecutive and shall be allowed—

    (a) on days on which the worker is normally called upon to work for the employer, and

    (b) at any time after the holiday season but during the relevant period of 12 months either on dates agreed between the employer and the worker at any time before 21st March in that period, or during the remaining days of that period:

      Provided that where the employer so decides, any day or days of additional annual holiday may be allowed during the holiday season.

(3) The duration of the worker's additional annual holiday during the 12 months commencing on 1st April 1974, shall be reduced by any days of additional annual holiday duly allowed to him by the employer under the provisions of Order M.D. (119) between 1st April 1973 and the date on which the provisions of this Schedule become effective.

GENERAL

17. An employer shall give to a worker reasonable notice of the commencing date or dates and of the duration of his annual holiday and of any days of additional annual holiday not previously agreed. Such notice may be given individually to the worker or by the posting of a notice in the place where the worker is employed.

HOLIDAY REMUNERATION

18.—(1) (a) Subject to the provisions of this paragraph, for each customary holiday or day in lieu of a customary holiday, which a worker is entitled to be allowed under this Schedule, he shall be paid by the employer one day's holiday pay as defined in the appropriate part of paragraph 23:

Provided, however, that payment of the above-mentioned remuneration is subject to the condition that the worker presents himself for employment at the usual starting hour on the first working day following the holiday or day in lieu, or, if he fails to do so, failure is by reason of the proved illness or injury of the worker or with the consent of the employer, and

Provided also that when two customary holidays on both of which the worker is not required to work occur on successive days or so that no working day intervenes, the above proviso shall apply only to the second customary holiday.

(b) Subject to the provisions of this paragraph, holiday remuneration in respect of any customary holiday or day in lieu of a customary holiday shall be paid by the employer to the worker on the pay day on which the wages for the first working day following the holiday or day in lieu are paid:

Provided that if a worker ceases to be employed before being allowed a holiday in lieu of a customary holiday to which he is entitled the said payment shall be made immediately upon the termination of his employment.

(2) Subject to the provisions of paragraph 19, a worker qualified to be allowed an annual holiday or any days of additional annual holiday under this Schedule shall be paid by his employer one day's holiday pay as defined in the appropriate part of paragraph 23 in respect of each day thereof, and in the case of annual holiday such payment shall be made by the employer on the last pay day preceding such annual holiday.

(3) Where under the provisions of paragraph 15 an annual holiday is allowed in more than one period the holiday remuneration shall be apportioned accordingly.

19. Where any accrued holiday remuneration has been paid by the employer to the worker in accordance with paragraph 20 of this Schedule or with Order M.D. (119) in respect of employment during any of the periods referred to in that paragraph or that Order respectively, the amount of holiday remuneration payable by the employer in respect of any annual holiday or days of additional annual holiday for which the worker has qualified by reason of employment during the said period shall be reduced by the amount of the said accrued holiday remuneration unless that remuneration has been deducted from a previous payment of holiday remuneration made under the provisions of this Schedule or of Order M.D. (119).

ACCRUED HOLIDAY REMUNERATION PAYABLE ON TERMINATION OF EMPLOYMENT

20. Where a worker ceases to be employed by an employer after the provisions of this Schedule become effective the employer shall, immediately on the termination of the employment (hereinafter referred to as "the termination date"), pay to the worker as accrued holiday remuneration:—

(1) in respect of employment in the 12 months up to the end of the preceding March, a sum equal to the holiday remuneration for any days of annual holiday or additional annual holiday for which he has qualified, except days of annual holiday or additional annual holiday which he has been allowed or has become entitled to be allowed before leaving the employment; and

(2) in respect of any employment since the end of the preceding March—

(a) a sum equal to the holiday remuneration which would have been payable to him if he could have been allowed an annual holiday in respect of that period of employment at the time of leaving it; and

(b) in addition, in the case of a worker who has qualified for an additional annual holiday in accordance with the provisions of paragraph 16, one day's holiday pay in respect of each of the following periods occurring between the end of the preceding March and the termination date, in the case of a worker with a normal working week of—

5 days—a period of not less than 10 weeks;
4 „ —„   „   „   „   „   „   12   „
3 „ —„   „   „   „   „   „   16   „

Provided that—

(*a*) no worker shall be entitled to the payment by his employer of accrued holiday remuneration if he is dismissed on the grounds of misconduct and is so informed by the employer at the time of dismissal;

(*b*) where a worker is employed under a contract of service under which he is required to give not less than one week's notice before terminating his employment and the worker without the consent of his employer terminates his employment:—

(i) without having given not less than one week's notice, or

(ii) before one week has expired from the beginning of such notice, the amount of accrued holiday remuneration payable to the worker shall be the amount payable under the foregoing provisions of this paragraph, less an amount equal to one day's holiday pay multiplied, in the case of (i), by the number of days constituting the worker's normal working week or, in the case of (ii), by the number of days which at the termination date would complete a normal working week commencing at the beginning of the notice.

CALCULATION OF EMPLOYMENT

21. For the purposes of calculating any period of employment qualifying a worker for an annual holiday or days of additional annual holiday or for any accrued holiday remuneration under this Schedule, the worker shall be treated—

(1) as if he were employed for a week in respect of any week in which—

(*a*) he has worked for the employer for not less than 20 hours and has performed some work for which statutory minimum remuneration is payable; or

(*b*) he has worked for the employer for less than 20 hours, or has performed no work, solely by reason of the proved illness of, or accident to, the worker (provided that the number of weeks which may be treated as weeks of employment for such reason shall not exceed eight in any such period as aforesaid); and

(2) as if he were employed on any day of annual holiday or additional annual holiday allowed under the provisions of this Schedule and for the purpose of the provisions of sub-paragraph (1) of this paragraph, a worker who is absent on such a holiday shall be treated as having worked thereon for the employer for the number of hours ordinarily worked by him on that day of the week on work for which statutory minimum remuneration is payable.

OTHER HOLIDAY AGREEMENTS

22. The provisions of this Schedule are without prejudice to any agreement for the allowance of any further holidays with pay or for the payment of additional holiday remuneration.

PART III
GENERAL
DEFINITIONS

23. In this Schedule, the following expressions have the meanings hereby assigned to them respectively, that is to say—

(1) "AREA A" comprises each area in England and Wales which at the date of the 1961 census was administered by—

(*a*) a Rural District Council; or

(*b*) a Municipal Borough Council or an Urban District Council and which, according to the census had a population not exceeding 10,000 but does not include any area within the Metropolitan Police District.

(2) "AREA B" comprises the whole of England and Wales other than Area A and Area C.

(3) "AREA C" comprises the Metropolitan Police District, as defined in the London Government Act 1963(a), the City of London, the Inner Temple and the Middle Temple.

(4) "CLERK" means a person employed, wholly or mainly, on clerical work.

(5) "CUSTOMARY HOLIDAY" has the meaning assigned to it in sub-paragraph (2) of paragraph 13.

(6) "FOREMAN" means a person to whom is deputed the duty of exercising supervisory authority over workers exceeding 5 in number (exclusive of the foreman).

(7) "HOURLY GENERAL MINIMUM TIME RATE" has the meaning assigned to it in paragraph 1.

(8) "NIGHT WORKER" means a worker who is ordinarily employed on a spell of duty which starts before and ends after midnight.

(9) "NORMAL WORKING WEEK" means:—

> (*a*) in the case of a rota worker the total number of days (excluding rest days) on which the worker has ordinarily worked for the employer during the periods of rota during the 12 months immediately preceding the commencement of the holiday season, or where under paragraph 20 accrued holiday remuneration is payable, during the 12 months immediately preceding the termination date, divided by the total number of weeks in the said periods of rota;

> (*b*) in the case of any other worker the number of days (excluding rest days) on which it has been usual for the worker to work for the employer in a week during the 12 months immediately preceding the commencement of the holiday season, or where under paragraph 20 accrued holiday remuneration is payable, during the 12 months immediately preceding the termination date: provided that in either case—

>> (i) for the purpose of calculating the normal working week part of a day shall count as a day;

>> (ii) except in the case of a rota worker's rest days, no account shall be taken of any week in which the worker did not perform any work for which statutory minimum remuneration has been fixed;

>> (iii) in the case of a night worker a day is a period of 24 hours commencing at noon.

(10) "ONE DAY'S HOLIDAY PAY" means:—

in relation to customary holidays, the appropriate proportion of the remuneration which the worker would be entitled to receive from his employer at the date of the customary holiday for work for which statutory minimum remuneration is payable, either—

> (*a*) for the number of hours normally worked by him for the employer in his normal working week, or

> (*b*) for 40 hours,

whichever number of hours is the less, if paid at the appropriate hourly general minimum time rate for that number of hours' work; and

in relation to an annual holiday or additional annual holiday—

> (*a*) in the case of a worker who has at 31st March immediately preceding the commencement of the holiday season (or the last holiday season as the case may require) completed 12 months' service with the employer, the appropriate proportion of whichever of the following amounts is the greatest—

(a) 1963 c. 33.

(i) 85% of the average weekly earnings of the worker during the 12 months ended on 5th April immediately preceding the holiday or the termination date, as the case may be, such average weekly earnings to be determined by dividing the total remuneration paid to the worker by the employer during the said 12 months by the number of weeks in respect of which it has been paid; or

(ii) the holiday remuneration payable for a week of annual or additional annual holiday under the arrangement in force between the employer and the worker at the date of such holiday or at the termination date as the case may be; or

(iii) the remuneration which the worker would be entitled to receive from his employer at the date of the annual holiday or additional annual holiday or at the termination date, as the case may be, for work for which statutory minimum remuneration is payable, either—

for the number of hours normally worked by him for the employer in his normal working week, or
for 40 hours,

whichever number of hours is the less, if paid at the appropriate hourly general minimum time rate for that number of hours' work;

(b) in the case of any other worker, the appropriate proportion of a week's holiday remuneration as set out in (a)(iii) above.

In this definition "appropriate proportion" means where the worker's normal working week is

5 days—one-fifth; or

4 days—one-quarter; or

3 days—one-third.

(11) "OVERTIME" means work for which minimum remuneration is payable under paragraphs 7, 8, 9 and 10.

(12) "REST DAYS" means two days in each week which have been notified to the worker by the employer before the commencement of the week as rest days, or, failing such notification, the last two days in the week; and "REST DAY" means one of these days:

Provided that in the case of a rota worker "REST DAYS" means any such days calculated at the rate of two days for each week in the period of rota.

(13) "ROTA WORKER" means a worker employed under an agreement which provides that his rest days should be taken according to a rota over a period not exceeding 12 weeks.

(14) "ROUNDS SALESMAN" or "ROUNDS SALESWOMAN" means a person who is employed, wholly or mainly, as a salesman on a defined or established route, and is responsible for keeping account of his retail sales to customers and of any cash or tokens received in payment and is not accompanied, save in exceptional circumstances, by any other person who exercises control or supervision.

(15) "SHOP ASSISTANT" means a person employed, wholly or mainly, in a shop in serving customers or in checking in and out or in both such operations.

(16) "SPELL OF DUTY" means a period of work broken only by intervals for meals.

(17) "STATUTORY MINIMUM REMUNERATION" means minimum remuneration (other than holiday remuneration) fixed by a wages regulation order made by the Secretary of State to give effect to proposals submitted to him by the Milk Distributive Wages Council (England and Wales).

(18) "TIME-AND-A-HALF", "DOUBLE TIME" and "TREBLE TIME" mean respectively one and a half times, twice and three times the hourly general minimum time rate (exclusive of any amount payable under paragraph 12 in respect of time worked between 9 p.m. and 5 a.m.) which would be payable to the worker for work other than overtime.

(19) "WEEK" means "pay week".

WORKERS TO WHOM THE SCHEDULE APPLIES

24. This Schedule applies to workers in relation to whom the Milk Distributive Wages Council (England and Wales) operates, that is to say, workers employed in England and Wales in the trade specified in the Schedule to the Trade Boards (Milk Distributive Trade, England and Wales) (Constitution and Proceedings) Regulations 1928(a), which reads as follows:—

"1. Subject as hereinafter provided the Milk Distributive Trade shall consist of the following operations:—

  (i) the wholesale and retail sale of milk;

  (ii) the sale of other goods by workers mainly employed in the sale specified in paragraph 1(i) hereof;

  (iii) all work incidental to the sale specified in paragraph 1(i) hereof.

2. Work incidental to the sale specified in paragraph 1(i) hereof shall include, inter alia:—

  (a) collecting, delivering, despatching;

  (b) pasteurising, sterilising, homogenising, humanising, cooling, separating and all work performed in connection with any other processes in the preparation of milk;

  (c) blending, testing and sampling of milk;

  (d) cleaning of utensils, receptacles, vehicles, premises, plant, machinery;

  (e) stoking, attending to boiler, plant or machinery, fire lighting, portering of coal or other fuel;

  (f) horse keeping and harness cleaning;

  (g) portering, lift or hoist-operating, time-keeping, storing, stock-keeping, warehousing;

  (h) boxing, parcelling, labelling, weighing, measuring, checking, bottling, packing and unpacking;

  (i) clerical work or canvassing carried on in conjunction with the work specified in paragraph 1 hereof.

3. Notwithstanding any of the foregoing provisions, the Milk Distributive Trade shall not include any of the following operations:—

(a) S.R. & O. 1928/480 (1928, p. 1281).

(a) the wholesale sale of milk (and operations incidental thereto) from an establishment at which milk products are manufactured and from which unseparated milk is not ordinarily sold as such;

(b) the wholesale sale of milk direct from the farm where the milk was produced and all operations incidental thereto;

(c) the sale of milk in restaurants, shops or similar premises by waiters or shop assistants who are not mainly engaged upon such sale;

(d) the transport of goods by common carriers;

(e) carting and operations incidental thereto where the business carried on consists exclusively of such operations;

(f) work done by or on behalf of the Post Office.

4. For the purpose of this Schedule the expression 'milk' means milk other than dried or condensed milk."

EXPLANATORY NOTE

(*This Note is not part of the Order.*)

This Order, which has effect from 13th May 1974, sets out the increased statutory minimum remuneration payable and the additional customary holiday to be allowed to workers in relation to whom the Milk Distributive Wages Council (England and Wales) operates, in substitution for the statutory minimum remuneration and customary holidays fixed by the Wages Regulation (Milk Distributive) (England and Wales) Order 1973 (Order M.D. (119)), which Order is revoked.

New provisions are printed in italics.

STATUTORY INSTRUMENTS

1974 No. 733

JURIES

The Jurors' Allowances (Amendment) Regulations 1974

Made - - -	*24th April* 1974
Coming into Operation	*20th May* 1974

The Lord Chancellor, in exercise of the powers conferred on him by section 1 of the Juries Act 1949(**a**), as amended by section 1 of the Juries Act 1954(**b**), section 36 of the Courts Act 1971(**c**) and section 27 of the Criminal Justice Act 1972(**d**), and with the consent of the Minister for the Civil Service, hereby makes the following Regulations: —

1.—(1) These Regulations may be cited as the Jurors' Allowances (Amendment) Regulations 1974 and shall come into operation on 20th May 1974.

(2) In these Regulations "the principal Regulations" means the Jurors' Allowances Regulations 1972(**e**), as amended (**f**).

2. At the end of regulation 4(3) of the principal Regulations there shall be added the following proviso: —

"Provided that for such an absence overnight for the purpose of serving as a juror in Greater London the rate may be increased by a supplementary allowance not exceeding 80p a night.".

3. The Schedule to the principal Regulations shall be amended as follows: —
   (*a*) in paragraph 3(2)(i), for the expression "4·4p" there shall be substituted the expression "4·8p";
   (*b*) in paragraph 3(2)(ii), for the expression "5·5p" there shall be substituted the expression "6·0p";
   (*c*) in paragraph 3(2)(iii), for the expression "6.0p" there shall be substituted the expression "6·6p".

Dated 23rd April 1974.

Elwyn-Jones, **C.**

Consent of the Minister for the Civil Service given under his official seal on 24th April 1974.

(L.S.)

P. F. Clifton,
Authorised by the Minister
for the Civil Service.

(**a**) 1949 c. 27. (**b**) 1954 c. 41. (**c**) 1971 c. 23.
(**d**) 1972 c. 71. (**e**) S.I. 1972/1976 (1972 III, p. 5889).
(**f**) The relevant amending instrument is S.I. 1973/1601 (1973 III, p. 5040).

EXPLANATORY NOTE

(This Note is not part of the Regulations.)

These Regulations provide for a supplement to the overnight rate of the subsistence allowance where a juror serves in Greater London and for increases in the rates of travelling allowance payable where a juror travels by private motor car.

STATUTORY INSTRUMENTS

1974 No. 734

PENSIONS

The Pensions Commutation (Amendment) Regulations 1974

Made - - - -	11*th April* 1974
Coming into Operation	2*nd May* 1974

The Minister for the Civil Service, in exercise of the powers conferred on him by sections 4 and 7 of the Pensions Commutation Act 1871(a) and section 3 of the Pensions Commutation Act 1882(b) and of all other powers enabling him in that behalf, hereby makes the following Regulations:—

1. These Regulations may be cited as the Pensions Commutation (Amendment) Regulations 1974, and shall come into operation on 2nd May 1974.

2. The Interpretation Act 1889(c) shall apply for the interpretation of these Regulations as it applies for the interpretation of an Act of Parliament.

3. The Pensions Commutation Regulations 1968(d), as amended by the Pensions Commutation (Amendment) Regulations 1970(e), shall be further amended—

(*a*) by the deletion, in Regulation 5 thereof (which relates to the withdrawal of an application before medical examination), of the words "on payment of any expense (not exceeding £2 10s. 0d.) which may have been incurred by the Board".

(*b*) by the deletion, in Regulation 7(3) thereof (which relates to the withdrawal of an application), of the words "on payment of a fee of £2 10s. 0d.".

(*c*) by the substitution, for Regulation 8 thereof (which relates to the determination of the commutation rate), of the following Regulation:—

"8.—(1) Where the pension to be commuted is not qualified for an increase under the Pensions (Increase) Act 1971(f) or any corresponding increase by reason of the pension-holder not having attained the age of fifty-five years, the Table set out in Part I of the Schedule to these Regulations shall be used to determine the commutation rate in accordance with the following provisions:—

(*a*) the age of the applicant shall be reckoned as his age on his birthday next succeeding the date of his application;

(a) 1871 c. 36.
(c) 1889 c. 63.
(e) S.I. 1970/515 (1970 I, p. 1716).

(b) 1882 c. 44.
(d) S.I. 1968/1163 (1968 II, p. 3145).
(f) 1971 c. 56.

(*b*) in the case of unimpaired lives, column 2 shall apply; and

(*c*) in the case of impaired lives, column 3 shall apply according to the number of years added to the age of the pension-holder on account of his imparied life.

(2) In cases other than those covered by paragraph (1) above, the Table set out in Part II of the Schedule to these Regulations shall be used to determine the commutation rate and for that purposes the age of the applicant shall be reckoned as the aggregate of his age on his birthday next succeeding the date of his application and any years to be added to his age on account of his life being impaired.";

(*d*) by the substitution, in Regulation 9(1) thereof (which relates to the commutation fee), for the amount "£20" of the amount "£50";

(*e*) by the substitution for the Table set out in the Schedule thereto of the Tables set out in the Schedule to these Regulations.

4. The Pensions Commutation (Amendment) Regulations 1970 are hereby revoked.

Given under the official seal of the Minister for the Civil Service on 11th April 1974.

(L.S.)

Robert Sheldon,
Civil Service Department.

SCHEDULE

PART I

TABLE FOR DETERMINING THE COMMUTATION RATE FOR PENSIONS WHICH WILL BECOME QUALIFIED FOR PENSIONS INCREASE ON THE PENSION-HOLDER'S ATTAINING THE AGE OF 55

Col. 1 Age next birth-day	Col. 2 Rate for unim-paired lives	Col. 3 Rates for impaired lives according to the number of years added to the age of the pension-holder						
		1 year	2 years	3 years	4 years	5 years	6 years	7 years
20	11·16	11·10	11·04	10·98	10·91	10·84	10·77	10·70
21	11·24	11·18	11·12	11·05	10·98	10·91	10·83	10·76
22	11·33	11·26	11·20	11·12	11·05	10·98	10·89	10·82
23	11·42	11·35	11·28	11·20	11·12	11·05	10·96	10·88
24	11·51	11·44	11·36	11·28	11·20	11·12	11·03	10·94
25	11·60	11·53	11·45	11·36	11·28	11·19	11·10	11·00
26	11·70	11·62	11·54	11·45	11·36	11·26	11·16	11·06
27	11·80	11·71	11·63	11·54	11·44	11·33	11·23	11·12
28	11·90	11·81	11·72	11·62	11·52	11·41	11·30	11·18
29	12·00	11·91	11·81	11·71	11·60	11·49	11·37	11·25
30	12·11	12·01	11·91	11·80	11·69	11·57	11·45	11·32
31	12·22	12·11	12·00	11·89	11·77	11·65	11·52	11·39
32	12·33	12·21	12·09	11·98	11·86	11·73	11·59	11·46
33	12·44	12·31	12·19	12·07	11·94	11·80	11·66	11·52
34	12·54	12·42	12·29	12·16	12·02	11·88	11·73	11·58
35	12·65	12·53	12·39	12·25	12·10	11·95	11·79	11·63
36	12·76	12·63	12·49	12·34	12·18	12·02	11·85	11·68
37	12·87	12·73	12·58	12·42	12·25	12·08	11·90	11·72
38	12·98	12·83	12·67	12·50	12·32	12·14	11·95	11·76
39	13·08	12·92	12·75	12·57	12·39	12·20	12·00	11·80
40	13·17	13·00	12·83	12·64	12·45	12·25	12·04	11·83
41	13·26	13·08	12·90	12·71	12·51	12·30	12·08	11·86
42	13·34	13·16	12·96	12·76	12·56	12·34	12·11	11·88
43	13·41	13·22	13·01	12·80	12·59	12·36	12·13	11·89
44	13·47	13·27	13·05	12·83	12·61	12·38	12·14	11·89
45	13·52	13·31	13·08	12·86	12·62	12·38	12·13	11·88
46	13·55	13·33	13·10	12·87	12·62	12·37	12·11	11·85
47	13·57	13·34	13·10	12·86	12·61	12·35	12·08	11·81
48	13·57	13·33	13·08	12·83	12·58	12·31	12·03	11·75
49	13·54	13·30	13·04	12·78	12·52	12·25	11·96	11·67
50	13·50	13·24	12·98	12·71	12·43	12·15	11·86	11·56
51	13·42	13·15	12·88	12·60	12·31	12·02	11·73	11·43
52	13·30	13·03	12·75	12·46	12·17	11·87	11·57	11·27
53	13·14	12·86	12·58	12·28	11·98	11·68	11·38	11·08
54	12·94	12·65	12·36	12·06	11·76	11·46	11·16	10·86
55	12·68	12·38	12·08	11·78	11·48	11·18	10·88	10·58

Part II

Table for Determining the Commutation Rate in Cases other than those Covered by Part I

Age next birthday	Rate	Age next birthday	Rate
20	18·24	55	12·68
21	18·18	56	12·38
22	18·11	57	12·08
23	18·05	58	11·78
24	17·98	59	11·48
		60	11·18
25	17·90		
26	17·82	61	10·88
27	17·74	62	10·58
28	17·65	63	10·29
29	17·56	64	10·00
		65	9·71
30	17·46		
31	17·35	66	9·42
32	17·25	67	9·14
33	17·13	68	8·86
34	17·01	69	8·58
		70	8·31
35	16·88		
36	16·75	71	8·04
37	16·61	72	7·77
38	16·46	73	7·50
39	16·31	74	7·25
		75	7·00
40	16·14		
41	15·97	76	6·76
42	15·79	77	6·52
43	15·60	78	6·29
44	15·40	79	6·07
		80	5·86
45	15·19		
46	14·97	81	5·65
47	14·74	82	5·44
48	14·51	83	5·24
49	14·27	84	5·05
		85	4·87
50	14·03		
51	13·77	86	4·69
52	13·51	87	4·51
53	13·24	88	4·34
54	12·96	89	4·17
		90	4·00

EXPLANATORY NOTE

(This Note is not part of the Regulations.)

These Regulations further amend the Pensions Commutation Regulations 1968.
The main changes are as follows:—

1. The charges formerly payable by an applicant on withdrawal of his application are abolished.

2. New tables are substituted which give the rates for the calculation of the capital sum obtained in commutation and which take account of the effect of increases payable under the Pensions (Increase) Act 1971 or under a Prerogative Instrument relating to the Armed Forces. An interest rate of 11% per annum has been used where a pension is not qualified at the time of commutation for a pensions increase and 5% where the pension is so qualified.

3. The maximum fee payable on commutation is increased from £20 to £50.

1974 No. 735

RIGHTS OF WAY

The Walkways (Amendment) Regulations 1974

Made - - -	*22nd April* 1974
Laid before Parliament	*3rd May* 1974
Coming into Operation	*24th May* 1974

The Secretary of State for the Environment (as respects England) and the Secretary of State for Wales (as respects Wales) make these Regulations in exercise of powers conferred by section 18 of the Highways Act 1971(a), as read with section 188(6) of the Local Government Act 1972(b), and of all other enabling powers, after consultation with representative organisations in accordance with subsection (8) of the said section 18 : —

1. These Regulations shall come into operation on 24th May 1974, and may be cited as the Walkways (Amendment) Regulations 1974.

2. The Walkways Regulations 1973(c) shall have effect as if after Regulation 8 thereof the following regulation were inserted : —

"Application of Regulations to walkway agreements to which district councils are parties

9.—(1) Where by virtue of section 188(6) of the Local Government Act 1972 a walkway agreement is entered into by a district council but the highway authority are not a party to that agreement, then in relation to that agreement and to any walkway or proposed walkway to which that agreement applies these Regulations shall have effect with the following amendments : —

(a) In Regulation 1(2), Regulation 4(1)(a) and Regulation 6(3) and (4) for the words "the highway authority" substitute the words "the district council";

(b) in Regulation 5(3)(a) and Regulation 6(2)(a) for the words "the highway authority for the walkway" substitute the words "the district council"; and

(c) in Regulation 8,3) for the words "the highway authority for the former walkway" substitute the words "the district council (after consulting the highway authority for the former walkway)".

(2) Where by virtue of section 188(6) of the Local Government Act 1972 a walkway agreement is entered into by a district council but the highway authority are also a party to that agreement, then in relation to that agreement and to any walkway or proposed walkway to which that agreement

(a) 1971 c. 41. (b) 1972 c. 70.
(c) S.I. 1973/686 (1973 I, p. 2281).

applies these Regulations shall have effect with the following amendments:—

(a) in Regulation 1(2) and Regulation 4(1)(a) after the words "the highway authority" insert the words "and the district council";

(b) in Regulation 5(3)(a) after the words "to the highway authority for the walkway" insert the words "to the district council";

(c) in Regulation 6(2)(a) after the words "to the highway authority for the walkway" insert the words "and to the district council";

(d) in Regulation 6(4) for the words "If the highway authority themselves object to the proposed stopping up, or if they consider that" substitute the words "If the highway authority or the district council object to the proposed stopping up, or if the highway authority (after consulting the district council) consider that", and for the word "they", where secondly occurring, substitute the words "the highway authority"; and

(e) in Regulation 8(3) after the words "the highway authority for the former walkway" insert the words "(after consulting the district council)".

(3) In this Regulation and in the amendments made by this Regulation to the preceding Regulations the expression "the district council", in relation to a walkway or proposed walkway, means the council of the district in which the walkway or proposed walkway is, or (as the case may be) will be, situated."

Anthony Crosland,
Secretary of State for the Environment.

9th April 1974.

John Morris,
Secretary of State for Wales.

22nd April 1974.

EXPLANATORY NOTE

(This Note is not part of the Regulations.)

These Regulations add a new Regulation to the Walkways Regulations 1973 so as to adapt those Regulations to cases where, by virtue of section 188(6) of the Local Government Act 1972, district councils are parties to walkway agreements made under section 18 of the Highways Act 1971.

STATUTORY INSTRUMENTS

1974 No. 736

SEEDS

The Seeds (Fees) Regulations 1974

Made - - -	23rd April 1974
Laid before Parliament	2nd May 1974
Coming into Operation	23rd May 1974

The Minister of Agriculture, Fisheries and Food and the Secretary of State for Scotland, acting jointly, in exercise of the powers vested in them by section 16(1A)(e) of the Plant Varieties and Seeds Act 1964(a), as amended by section 4(1) of and paragraph 5(1) and (2) of Schedule 4 to the European Communities Act 1972(b), and of all other powers enabling them in that behalf, hereby make the following Regulations: —

Citation and commencement

1. These Regulations may be cited as the Seeds (Fees) Regulations 1974 and shall come into operation on 23rd May 1974.

Revocation of previous Regulations

2. The Seeds (Fees) Regulations 1973(c) are hereby revoked.

Interpretation

3. The Interpretation Act 1889(d) shall apply to the interpretation of these Regulations as it applies to the interpretation of an Act of Parliament and as if these Regulations and the Regulations hereby revoked were Acts of Parliament.

Fees

4. There shall be paid in respect of matters arising under regulations made under Part II of the Plant Varieties and Seeds Act 1964, as amended by the European Communities Act 1972, being the matters specified in the first column of the Schedule to these Regulations, the fees specified in the second column of the said Schedule opposite the respective references to such matters.

5. Any such fees in respect of matters arising—

    (*a*) in England and Wales shall be payable to the Minister of Agriculture, Fisheries and Food, and

    (*b*) in Scotland shall be payable to the Secretary of State.

(a) 1964 c. 14.   (b) 1972 c. 68.
(c) S.I. 1973/1050 (1973 II, p. 3161).   (d) 1889 c. 63.

In Witness whereof the official seal of the Minister of Agriculture, Fisheries and Food is hereunto affixed on 19th April 1974.

(L.S.)   *Frederick Peart,*
Minister of Agriculture, Fisheries and Food.

William Ross,
Secretary of State for Scotland.
23rd April 1974.

SCHEDULE

MATTERS ARISING UNDER THE VEGETABLE SEEDS REGULATIONS 1973(a)

Matter	Fee
	£
A. Certification of vegetable seeds to which the Regulations apply, other than seeds of cucumber, gherkin and tomato.	
Basic seeds:	
(*a*) initial fee, per acre or part of an acre	2·40
(*b*) final fee, per label	0·10
Certified seeds:	
(*a*) initial fee (excluding the cost of inspecting the crop), per acre or part of an acre	0·65
(*b*) final fee (excluding the cost of sampling and testing the seeds), per label	0·05
B. Certification of cucumber, gherkin or tomato seeds.	
Basic seeds, per crop	20·00
Certified seeds (excluding the cost of inspecting the crop and sampling and testing the seeds), per crop	20·00
C. Test of basic seeds of brassicas for *Phoma lingam*	4·25
D. Test of basic seeds of beets for *Phoma betae*	7·75
E. Test of basic seeds of lettuce for lettuce mosaic virus	10·25

Provided that if an application for certification of seeds is withdrawn prior to the inspection of the crop one half of the certification fee in the case of cucumber, gherkin or tomato seeds and one half of the initial fee in the case of other seeds will be repaid to the applicant.

EXPLANATORY NOTE

(*This Note is not part of the Regulations.*)

These Regulations supersede the Seeds (Fees) Regulations 1973 which are revoked. Fees are prescribed in respect of matters arising under the Vegetable Seeds Regulations 1973 in place of those in the earlier Fees Regulations.

(a) S.I. 1973/1049 (1973 II, p. 3142).

STATUTORY INSTRUMENTS

1974 No. 737

PENSIONS

The Pensions Increase (Federated Superannuation System for Universities) (Amendment) Regulations 1974

Made -	-	-	-	*24th April* 1974
Laid before Parliament				*9th May* 1974
Coming into Operation				*31st May* 1974

The Minister for the Civil Service, in exercise of the powers conferred on him by section 13(2) and (5) of the Pensions (Increase) Act 1971(a) and of all other powers enabling him in that behalf, hereby makes the following Regulations:—

1. These Regulations may be cited as the Pensions Increase (Federated Superannuation System for Universities) (Amendment) Regulations 1974, and shall come into operation on 31st May 1974.

2.—(1) In these Regulations "the principal Regulations" means the Pensions Increase (Federated Superannuation System for Universities) Regulations 1972(b).

(2) The Interpretation Act 1889(c) shall apply for the interpretation of these Regulations as it applies for the interpretation of an Act of Parliament.

3. The principal Regulations shall be amended, in Regulation 2, by adding at the end of the definition of "period of F.S.S.U. service" in paragraph (1) the following words:—

"and the said expression also includes any period of service in respect of which, by virtue of the provisions of any of the following:—

(i) the Federated Superannuation System for Universities (Temporary Service) Regulations 1949(d),

(ii) the Federated Superannuation System for Universities (War Service) Regulations 1949(e), or

(iii) Rule 11 of the Superannuation (Reckoning of Certain Previous Service) Rules 1949(f),

a contribution has been invested in his case in a single premium policy under an F.S.S.U. scheme;".

(a) 1971 c. 56.
(c) 1889 c. 63.
(e) S.I. 1949/1891 (1949 I, p. 3201).

(b) S.I. 1972/877 (1972 II, p. 2801).
(d) S.I. 1949/1890 (1949 I, p. 3196).
(f) S.I. 1949/1803 (1949 I, p. 3043).

4. The principal Regulations shall be amended, in Regulation 4, by substituting for paragraph (1) the following paragraph:—

"(1) There shall be ascribed to every person to whom these Regulations apply an appropriate pension rate calculated, subject to the provisions of this Regulation, by multiplying one seventy-fifth of his pensionable salary by forty or by the number of completed years of his period of F.S.S.U. service, whichever is the less; and in this Regulation "pensionable salary" means—

(a) in the case of a person who is subject to an F.S.S.U. scheme at the time of his retirement and either—

(i) was born on or before 1st April 1915 and retires from the civil service of the State on or after 1st April 1972 after attaining the age of sixty years, or

(ii) retires on or after 1st April 1972 in the circumstances described in Regulation 3(d)(iii) or (iv) above,

his salary in such period of one year during the last three years of his period of F.S.S.U. service as would be appropriate under the civil service pension scheme for the purpose of determining his pensionable pay if he were eligible for a pension under that scheme, and

(b) in the case of any other person, the average amount of his salary during the last three years of his period of F.S.S.U. service."

5. The principal Regulations shall be amended, in Regulation 4, by adding at the end the following paragraphs:—

"(6) Where a person's period of F.S.S.U. service includes service in respect of which, by virtue of any of the instruments referred to in sub-paragraphs (i) to (iii) in the definition of "period of F.S.S.U. service" in Regulation 2(1) above, a contribution has been invested in a single premium policy under an F.S.S.U. scheme, that service shall be taken into account at one half its actual length in calculating the number of completed years of his period of F.S.S.U. service for the purpose of paragraph (1) above.

(7) Where the salary of a person who is serving in the civil service of the State and subject to an F.S.S.U. scheme is reduced after he has attained the age of sixty years, his appropriate pension rate shall be calculated in accordance with paragraphs (8) to (11) below.

(8) There shall be ascribed to such a person as is referred to in paragraph (7) above—

(a) a basic pension rate of an amount equal to the appropriate pension rate which would have been ascribed to him in accordance with paragraph (1) above if he had retired on the day before the day on which the reduction of his salary took effect, and

(b) a supplemental pension rate calculated by multiplying one seventy-fifth of his pensionable salary by the number of completed years of that part of his period of F.S.S.U. service which followed the reduction of his salary, any period of not less than six months beyond a completed number of years being treated as a whole completed year.

(9) The appropriate pension rate of such a person as is referred to in paragraph (7) above shall be the aggregate of—

(a) his basic pension rate,

(b) the annual rate of any increase which would be payable to him under the 1971 Act at the time of his retirement from the civil service of the State if he were in receipt of a pension under the civil service pension scheme of an amount equal to his basic pension rate and beginning on the day on which the reduction of his salary took effect, and

(c) his supplemental pension rate.

(10) Where the salary of such a person as is referred to in paragraph (7) above is reduced more than once after he has attained the age of sixty years, there shall be ascribed to him a separate supplemental pension rate, calculated in accordance with paragraph (8)(b) above, in respect of that part of his period of F.S.S.U. service which falls between one reduction of salary and the next or, in the case of the last reduction of salary before his retirement from the civil service of the State, between that reduction and his retirement; and, in calculating his appropriate pension rate in accordance with paragraph (9) above, there shall be included in the aggregate therein mentioned—

(a) every supplemental pension rate so calculated in respect of him, and

(b) in the case of a supplemental pension rate so calculated in respect of any part of his period of F.S.S.U. service except the part immediately preceding his retirement from the civil service of the State, the annual rate of any increase which would be payable to him under the 1971 Act at the time of his retirement if he were in receipt of a pension under the civil service pension scheme of an amount equal to the supplemental pension rate in question and beginning on the last day of the period in respect of which the supplemental pension rate is calculated.

(11) For the purpose of calculating the supplemental pension rate in accordance with paragraph 8(b) above, in a case where a person's pensionable salary falls to be taken as the average annual amount of his salary during the last three years of his service, and that part of his period of F.S.S.U. service which followed the reduction of his salary was less than three years, his pensionable salary shall be taken to be the average annual amount of his salary during that part of his period of F.S.S.U. service; and in a case where a person's pensionable salary falls to be determined by reference to his salary in a period of one year, and such part of his period of F.S.S.U. service as aforesaid was less than one year, his pensionable salary shall be taken to be the average annual amount of his salary during such part of his period of F.S.S.U. service."

6. The principal Regulations shall be amended, in Schedule 2, by inserting after the entry relating to the Cambridge Institute of Education the words "Cancer Research Campaign", after the entry relating to the National Institute of Agricultural Botany the words "National Institute of Economic and Social Research" and after the entry relating to the Institute of Seaweed Research the words "Inter-University Council".

7. The principal Regulations shall be amended, in Schedule 3, by substituting for the words "Date F.S.S.U. service ended" at the head of column 1 the words "Period in which qualifying date falls".

8. Any increase of benefit attributable to Regulation 3 or 5 above shall take effect in respect of any period beginning on or after 1st September 1971, and any increase of benefit attributable to Regulation 4 above shall take effect in respect of any period beginning on or after 1st April 1972.

Given under the official seal of the Minister for the Civil Service on 24th April 1974.

(L.S.)

Robert Sheldon,
Minister of State to the
Civil Service Department.

EXPLANATORY NOTE

(*This Note is not part of the Regulations*).

These Regulations amend the Pensions Increase (Federated Superannuation System for Universities) Regulations 1972, which provide for the payment of allowances corresponding to pension increases under the Pensions (Increase) Act 1971 to persons who have been subject to the Federated Superannuation System for Universities (F.S.S.U.) and who have retired from the civil service.
    The principal changes are:—

(1) The Regulations provide that, in the case of certain persons who have retired on or after 1st April 1972, their "appropriate pension rate", on which their allowances are based, is to be calculated in accordance with the principal civil service pension scheme on the year's salary in their last three years of service which is most favourable to them, instead of on the average of their salary for such last three years.

(2) The Regulations provide for a more favourable method of calculation of a person's appropriate pension rate in a case where after attaining the age of sixty he continues to serve in the civil service under F.S.S.U. at a reduced rate of salary.

(3) The Regulations provide that certain war service and temporary service in the civil service, in respect of which a contribution has been invested in a single premium policy under F.S.S.U., is to be included, at half its actual length, in the service on which a person's appropriate pension rate is to be calculated.

In accordance with the power conferred by section 13(5) of the 1971 Act, the Regulations provide for any increase in benefit attributable to the change described in paragraph (1) above to take effect from 1st April 1972, and for any increase in benefit attributable to the changes described in paragraphs (2) and (3) above to take effect from 1st September 1971.

STATUTORY INSTRUMENTS

1974 No. 738

SEA FISHERIES

BOATS AND METHODS OF FISHING

The Herring (Celtic Sea) Licensing Order 1974

Made - - -	*24th April* 1974
Laid before Parliament	*3rd May* 1974
Coming into Operation	*24th May* 1974

The Minister of Agriculture, Fisheries and Food and the Secretaries of State respectively concerned with the sea fishing industry in Scotland and Northern Ireland, in exercise of the powers conferred on them by sections 4 and 15 of the Sea Fish (Conservation) Act 1967(a) as the latter section is amended by section 22(1) of, and paragraph 38 of Part II of Schedule 1 to, the Sea Fisheries Act 1968(b) and of all other powers enabling them in that behalf, being satisfied that substantially equivalent measures are being taken by governments of other countries concerned, hereby make the following Order: —

Citation and commencement

1. This Order may be cited as the Herring (Celtic Sea) Licensing Order 1974 and shall come into operation on 24th May 1974.

Interpretation

2.—(1) In this Order "the Act" means the Sea Fish (Conservation) Act 1967.

(2) The Interpretation Act 1889(c) shall apply to the interpretation of this Order as it applies to the interpretation of an Act of Parliament.

Appointed day

3. The appointed day for the purposes of section 4 of the Act (which provides for the licensing of British fishing boats in relation to fishing by way of trade or business in specified areas) in conjunction with this Order, is 24th May 1974.

Area, fish and period

4. This Order applies to fishing in the area of sea specified in the Schedule to this Order for herring (*Clupea harengus*) during the period 24th May 1974 to 31st March 1975 (both dates inclusive).

Enforcement

5. For the purpose of the enforcement of section 4 of the Act in conjunction with this Order, there are hereby conferred on every British sea-fishery officer the powers of a British sea-fishery officer under section 8(2) to (4) of the Sea Fisheries Act 1968.

(a) 1967 c. 84.   (b) 1968 c. 77.   (c) 1889 c. 63.

In Witness whereof the Official Seal of the Minister of Agriculture, Fisheries and Food is hereunto affixed on 19th April 1974.

(L.S.)   *Frederick Peart,*
                                Minister of Agriculture, Fisheries and Food.

                                               William Ross,
                                   Secretary of State for Scotland.
23rd April 1974.

                                               Merlyn Rees,
                                Secretary of State for Northern Ireland.
24th April 1974.

SCHEDULE   Article 4

Specified area to which the Order applies:—

The area of sea lying to the south-east of Eire bounded by a line beginning at a point on the coast of Eire in 52° 30′ N latitude, thence due east to the coast of Wales, thence in a south-westerly and southerly direction along the coast of Wales to a point in 5° W longitude; thence due south to 51° N latitude; thence due west to 6° W longitude; thence due south to 50° 30′ N latitude; thence due west to 7° W longitude; thence due south to 49° 30′ N latitude; thence due east to 5° W longitude; thence due south to 48° N latitude; thence due west to 9° W longitude; thence due north to the coast of Eire; thence in a north-easterly direction along the coast of Eire to the point of beginning.

EXPLANATORY NOTE

(This Note is not part of the Order.)

Section 4 of the Sea Fish (Conservation) Act 1967 provides that from a day appointed by an Order, no fishing boat registered in the United Kingdom shall be used by way of trade or business for fishing in any area specified in the Order except under the authority of a licence granted by one of the fisheries Ministers.

This Order, which implements a recommendation of the North-East Atlantic Fisheries Commission, appoints 24th May 1974 as the date from which no such fishing boat shall so fish for herring in the specified area of the Celtic Sea comprising the International Council for the Exploration of the Sea statistical divisions VII g and VII h and part of division VII a except under the authority of such a licence.

The Order shall cease to have effect on 1st April 1975.

STATUTORY INSTRUMENTS

1974 No. 743

WAGES COUNCILS

The Wages Regulation (Shirtmaking) Order 1974

Made - - - -   *24th April* 1974

Coming into Operation   *22nd May* 1974

Whereas the Secretary of State has received from the Shirtmaking Wages Council (Great Britain) the wages regulation proposals set out in the Schedule hereto;

Now, therefore, the Secretary of State in exercise of powers conferred by section 11 of the Wages Councils Act 1959(a), as modified by Article 2 of the Counter-Inflation (Modification of Wages Councils Act 1959) Order 1973(b), and now vested in him(c), and of all other powers enabling him in that behalf, hereby makes the following Order:—

1. This Order may be cited as the Wages Regulation (Shirtmaking) Order 1974.

2.—(1) In this Order the expression "the specified date" means the 22nd May 1974, provided that where, as respects any worker who is paid wages at intervals not exceeding seven days, that date does not correspond with the beginning of the period for which the wages are paid, the expression "the specified date" means, as respects that worker, the beginning of the next such period following that date.

(2) The Interpretation Act 1889(d) shall apply to the interpretation of this Order as it applies to the interpretation of an Act of Parliament and as if this Order and the Order hereby revoked were Acts of Parliament.

3. The wages regulation proposals set out in the Schedule hereto shall have effect as from the specified date and as from that date the Wages Regulation (Shirtmaking) Order 1973(e) shall cease to have effect.

Signed by order of the Secretary of State.

W. H. Marsh,
Assistant Secretary,
Department of Employment.

24th April 1974.

(a) 1959 c. 69.   (b) S.I. 1973/661 (1973 I, p. 2141).
(c) S.I. 1959/1769, 1968/729 (1959 I, p. 1795; 1968 II, p. 2108).
(d) 1889 c. 63.   (e) S.I. 1973/183 (1973 I, p. 743).

Article 3

SCHEDULE

The following minimum remuneration shall be substituted for the statutory minimum remuneration fixed by the Wages Regulation (Shirtmaking) Order 1973 (Order S. (79)).

STATUTORY MINIMUM REMUNERATION

PART I

GENERAL

1. The minimum remuneration payable to a worker to whom this Schedule applies for all work except work to which a minimum overtime rate applies under Part IV of this Schedule is:—

   (1) in the case of a time worker, the general minimum time rate payable to the worker under Part II or Part III of this Schedule;

   (2) in the case of a worker employed on piece work, piece rates each of which would yield in the circumstances of the case, to an ordinary worker at least the same amount of money as the general minimum time rate which would be payable if the worker were a time worker.

PART II

MALE WORKERS

GENERAL MINIMUM TIME RATES

2. Subject to the provisions of this Schedule, the general minimum time rates payable to male time workers are as follows:—

	General minimum time rates Per hour p
(1) SPECIAL OR MEASURE CUTTERS, PATTERN CUTTERS OR PATTERN TAKERS, who are employed as such during the whole or a substantial part of their time and have had after the age of 18 years not less than three years' employment as a cutter of any class specified in this or the next following sub-paragraph including not less than two years as a measure cutter	47·25
(2) CUTTERS, aged 21 years or over, who are employed as such during the whole or a substantial part of their time and have had not less than four years' employment as a cutter of any class specified in this or the last preceding sub-paragraph	46·50
(3) TIE CUTTERS, aged 22 years or over, who are employed during the whole or a substantial part of their time in tie cutting and have had at least five years' experience therein	47·25
(4) TIE CUTTERS (not being workers to whom sub-paragraph (3) applies) aged 21 years or over, who are employed during the whole or a substantial part of their time in tie cutting and have had at least four years' experience therein	46·50

(5) ALL OTHER WORKERS being aged—

21 years or over	44·75
20 and under 21 years	40·30
19 ,, ,, 20 ,,	38·36
18 ,, ,, 19 ,,	34·47
17 ,, ,, 18 ,,	28·91
Under 17 years	25·29

Part III

FEMALE WORKERS

GENERAL MINIMUM TIME RATES

3.—(1) Subject to the provisions of this Schedule, the general minimum time rates payable to female time workers are as follows:—

(a) LEARNERS during the following periods of employment in the trade:—

	First 6 months Per hour	Second 6 months Per hour	Second year Per hour
	p	p	p
Entering the trade			
Aged 15 and under 16 years	—	25·48	31·99
,, 16 ,, ,, 17 ,, ...	23·78	27·18	33·69
,, 17 ,, ,, 18 ,, ...	25·48	28·88	33·69
,, 18 years or over	30·86	32·84	38·50

(b) ALL OTHER WORKERS

(including home-workers) .. .. 40·50p per hour

(2) For the purpose of determining the period of a learner's employment in the trade and the date on which she ceases to be a learner, there shall be reckoned as employment in the trade any employment in any branch of the trade or in the making, wherever carried on, of overalls for male or female persons.

Part IV

OVERTIME AND WAITING TIME

NORMAL NUMBER OF HOURS

4. Subject to the provisions of this Part of this Schedule, the minimum overtime rates set out in paragraph 5 are payable to a worker in respect of any time worked—

(1) in excess of the hours following, that is to say,

    (a) in any week .. .. 40 hours

    (b) on any day other than a Saturday, Sunday or customary holiday—

        where the normal working hours exceed $8\frac{1}{2}$ .. .. 9 hours

        or

        where the normal working hours are more than 8, but not more than $8\frac{1}{2}$ .. .. $8\frac{1}{2}$ hours

        or

        where the normal working hours are not more than 8 .. 8 hours

(2) on a Saturday, Sunday or customary holiday.

MINIMUM OVERTIME RATES

5.—(1) Minimum overtime rates are payable to any worker as follows:—

    (a) on any day other than a Sunday or customary holiday—

        (i) for the first 2 hours of overtime worked .. time-and-a-quarter

        (ii) for the next 2 hours .. .. time-and-a-half

        (iii) thereafter .. .. double time

(*b*) on a Sunday or customary holiday—
for all time worked   ..   ..   double time

(*c*) in any week, exclusive of any time in respect of which
any minimum overtime rate is payable under the foregoing provisions of this sub-paragraph—
for all time worked in excess of 40 hours   ..   ..   time-and-a-quarter

(2) The minimum overtime rates set out in sub-paragraph (1)(*a*) or (*b*) of this paragraph are payable in any week whether or not the minimum overtime rate set out in sub-paragraph (1)(*c*) is also payable.

6. In this Part of this Schedule—

(1) the expression "CUSTOMARY HOLIDAY" means:—

    (*a*) (i) in England and Wales—

Christmas Day; 26th December if it be not a Sunday; 27th December in a year when 25th or 26th December is a Sunday; Good Friday; Easter Monday; the last Monday in May; the last Monday in August (or, where another day is substituted for any of the above days by national proclamation, that day); and one other day (being a day of the week on which the worker normally works for the employer) in the course of a calendar year, to be fixed by the employer and notified to the worker not less than three weeks before the holiday;

      (ii) in Scotland—

New Year's Day, if it be not a Sunday or, if it be a Sunday, 2nd January;
the local Spring holiday;
the local Autumn holiday; and
four other days (being days of the week on which the worker normally works for the employer) in the course of a calendar year, to be fixed by the employer and notified to the worker not less than three weeks before the holiday;

or (*b*) in the case of each of the said days a day substituted by the employer therefor, being a day recognised by local custom as a day of holiday in substitution for the said day.

(2) the expressions "TIME-AND-A-QUARTER", "TIME-AND-A-HALF" and "DOUBLE TIME" mean respectively—

    (*a*) in the case of a time worker, one and a quarter times, one and a half times and twice the general minimum time rate otherwise payable to the worker;

    (*b*) in the case of a worker employed on piece work—
      (i) a time rate equal respectively to one quarter, one half and the whole of the general minimum time rate which would be payable to him if he were a time worker and a minimum overtime rate did not apply and, in addition thereto,

      (ii) the piece rates otherwise payable to him under paragraph 1(2).

WAITING TIME

7.—(1) A worker is entitled to payment of the minimum remuneration specified in this Schedule for all time during which he is present on the premises of his employer unless he is present thereon in any of the following circumstances:—

(*a*) without the employer's consent, express or implied;

(*b*) for some purpose unconnected with his work and other than that of waiting for work to be given to him to perform;

(*c*) by reason only of the fact that he is resident thereon;

(d) during normal meal times in a room or place in which no work is being done, and he not waiting for work to be given to him to perform.

(2) The minimum remuneration payable under sub-paragraph (1) of this paragraph to a piece worker when not engaged on piece work is that which would be payable if he were a time worker.

PART V

INTERPRETATION

8. In this Schedule, unless the context otherwise requires, the following expressions have the meanings hereby expressly assigned to them:—

(1) A CUTTER is a worker (other than a special or measure cutter, a pattern cutter or a pattern taker) substantially employed in one or more of the following processes:—

    (a) marking-in or marking-out or marking-up materials;

    (b) laying-up or hooking-up or folding materials;

    (c) cutting materials; and

    (d) dividing, that is to say, the process ordinarily carried on by cutters or their assistants of dividing, parting or separating parts of garments which are being cut and of assembling them into suitable bundles for making-up;

(2) A LEARNER is a female worker who—

    (a) is employed during the whole or a substantial part of her time in learning any branch or process of the trade by an employer who provides her with reasonable facilities for such learning; and

    (b) does not work in a room used for dwelling purposes, except where she is in the employment of her parent or guardian;

(3) A SPECIAL OR MEASURE CUTTER is a worker who—

    (a) is able to take a complete set of measures and cut from model patterns; and

    (b) has sufficient technical knowledge to alter patterns (excluding stock patterns);

(4) "THE TRADE" means the shirtmaking trade as specified in paragraph 10.

EXPERIENCE UNDER THE GOVERNMENT VOCATIONAL TRAINING SCHEME

9. A worker who has completed his period of training under the Government Vocational Training Scheme as a male cutter or as a female machinist shall, for the purposes of this Schedule be treated—

(1) in the case of a male worker, as a cutter or a tie cutter as the case may be, aged 21 years or over who has had not less than four years' employment as a cutter or tie cutter;

(2) in the case of a female worker, as a worker who has worked for two years as a learner in the trade.

APPLICABILITY OF STATUTORY MINIMUM REMUNERATION

10. Subject to the provisions of paragraph 11, this Schedule applies to workers in relation to whom the Shirtmaking Wages Council (Great Britain) operates, that is to say, workers employed in Great Britain in any branch of the trade specified in the Trade Boards (Shirtmaking Trade, Great Britain) (Constitution and Proceedings)

Regulations 1929**(a)**, namely:—

(1) The making from textile fabrics of shirts, collars, cuffs, pyjamas, aprons, chefs' caps, hospital ward caps, and other washable clothing worn by male persons;

(2) the making of women's collars and cuffs and of nurses' washing belts where carried on in association with or in conjunction with the making of the before mentioned articles;

(3) the making of neckties worn by male persons, and of neckties worn by female persons where made in association with or in conjunction with the making of neckties worn by male persons;

including:—

Laundering, smoothing, folding, ornamenting, boxing, packing, warehousing, and all other operations incidental to or appertaining to the making of any of the above mentioned articles;

but excluding:—

(1) the making of articles which are knitted or are made from knitted fabrics;

(2) the making of handkerchiefs, mufflers, gloves, socks, stockings, spats, gaiters, bonnets, hats or caps (other than chefs' caps and hospital ward caps);

(3) the making of boys' washing suits;

(4) the making of washable clothing to be worn by children without distinction of sex;

(5) the making of any articles, the making of which is included in the Trade Boards (Tailoring) Order 1919**(b)**.

TRAINING UNDER THE GOVERNMENT VOCATIONAL TRAINING SCHEME

11. Notwithstanding anything hereinbefore contained, this Schedule shall not apply to—

(1) female workers employed as machinists, or

(2) male workers employed as cutters—

during any period in respect of which they are in receipt of allowances as provided under the Government Vocational Training Scheme for resettlement training if they are trainees who have been placed by the Department of Employment with the employer for a period of approved training and if the requirements of the said Scheme are duly complied with.

EXPLANATORY NOTE
(*This Note is not part of the Order.*)

This Order, which has effect from 22nd May 1974, sets out the increased statutory minimum remuneration payable to workers in relation to whom the Shirtmaking Wages Council (Great Britain) operates, in substitution for that fixed by the Wages Regulation (Shirtmaking) Order 1973 (Order S.(79)). Order S.(79) is revoked.

New provisions are printed in italics.

(a) S. R. & O. 1929/825 (1929, p. 1374).   **(b)** S. R. & O. 1919/1201 (1919 II, p. 528).

STATUTORY INSTRUMENTS

1974 No. 744

WAGES COUNCILS

The Wages Regulation (Shirtmaking) (Holidays) Order 1974

Made - - -	*24th April* 1974
Coming into Operation	*22nd May* 1974

Whereas the Secretary of State has received from the Shirtmaking Wages Council (Great Britain) the wages regulation proposals set out in the Schedule hereto;

Now, therefore, the Secretary of State in exercise of powers conferred by section 11 of the Wages Councils Act 1959(a), as modified by Article 2 of the Counter-Inflation (Modification of Wages Councils Act 1959) Order 1973(b), and now vested in him(c), and of all other powers enabling him in that behalf, hereby makes the following Order:—

1. This Order may be cited as the Wages Regulation (Shirtmaking) (Holidays) Order 1974.

2.—(1) In this Order the expression "the specified date" means the 22nd May 1974, provided that where, as respects any worker who is paid wages at intervals not exceeding seven days, that date does not correspond with the beginning of the period for which the wages are paid, the expression "the specified date" means, as respects that worker, the beginning of the next such period following that date.

(2) The Interpretation Act 1889(d) shall apply to the interpretation of this Order as it applies to the interpretation of an Act of Parliament and as if this Order and the Order hereby revoked were Acts of Parliament.

3. The wages regulation proposals set out in the Schedule hereto shall have effect as from the specified date and as from that date the Wages Regulation (Shirtmaking) (Holidays) Order 1973(e) shall cease to have effect.

Signed by order of the Secretary of State.
24th April 1974.

W. H. Marsh,
Assistant Secretary,
Department of Employment.

(a) 1959 c. 69. (b) S.I. 1973/661 (1973 I, p. 2141).
(c) S.I. 1959/1769, 1968/729 (1959 I, p. 1795; 1968 II, p. 2108).
(d) 1889 c. 63. (e) S.I. 1973/184 (1973 I, p. 749).

Article 3

SCHEDULE
HOLIDAYS AND HOLIDAY REMUNERATION

The following provisions as to holidays and holiday remuneration shall be substituted for the provisions as to holidays and holiday remuneration set out in the Wages Regulation (Shirtmaking) (Holidays) Order 1973 (hereinafter referred to as "Order S.(80)").

PART I
APPLICATION

1.—(1) This Schedule applies to every worker (other than a homeworker) for whom statutory minimum remuneration has been fixed.

(2) For the purposes of this Schedule a homeworker is a worker who works in his own home or in any other place not under the control or management of the employer.

PART II
CUSTOMARY HOLIDAYS

2.—(1) An employer shall allow to every worker in his employment to whom this Schedule applies a holiday (hereinafter referred to as a "customary holiday") in each year on the days specified in the following sub-paragraph, provided that the worker has been in his employment for a period of not less than eight weeks immediately preceding the customary holiday and has worked for the employer during the whole or part of that period and is in his employment on the day of the customary holiday.

(2) The said customary holidays are:—

(a) (i) in England and Wales—
    Christmas Day; 26th December if it be not a Sunday; 27th December in a year when 25th or 26th December is a Sunday; Good Friday; Easter Monday; the last Monday in May; the last Monday in August (or, where another day is substituted for any of the above days by national proclamation, that day); and one other day (being a day of the week on which the worker normally works for the employer) in the course of a calendar year, to be fixed by the employer and notified to the worker not less than three weeks before the holiday;

(ii) in Scotland—
    New Year's Day, if it be not a Sunday or, if it be a Sunday, 2nd January;
            the local Spring holiday;
            the local Autumn holiday; and
    four other days (being days of the week on which the worker normally works for the employer) in the course of a calendar year, to be fixed by the employer and notified to the worker not less than three weeks before the holiday; or

(b) in the case of each of the said days a day substituted by the employer therefor, being a day recognised by local custom as a day of holiday in substitution for the said day.

(3) Notwithstanding the preceding provisions of this paragraph, an employer may (except where in the case of a woman or young person such a requirement would be unlawful) require a worker who is otherwise entitled to any customary holiday under the foregoing provisions of this Schedule to work thereon and, in lieu of any such holiday on which he so works for the employer, the worker shall be entitled to be allowed a day's holiday (hereinafter referred to as a "holiday in lieu of a customary holiday") on a weekday within the period of four weeks next ensuing.

(4) A worker who is required to work on a customary holiday shall be paid:—

(a) for all time worked thereon at the minimum rate then appropriate to the worker for work on a customary holiday; and

(b) in respect of the holiday in lieu of the customary holiday, holiday remuneration in accordance with paragraph 6.

PART III
ANNUAL HOLIDAY

3.—(1) Subject to the provisions of this paragraph and of paragraph 4, in addition to the holidays specified in Part II of this Schedule, an employer shall between the date on which the provisions of this Schedule become effective and 30th September 1974, and in each succeeding year between 6th April and 30th September allow a holiday (hereinafter referred to as an "annual holiday") to every worker in his employment to whom this Schedule applies, who has been employed by him during the 12 months immediately preceding the commencement of the holiday season for any of the periods of employment (calculated in accordance with the provisions of paragraph 10) specified below, and the duration of the annual holiday shall in the case of each such worker be related to that period as follows:—

Period of Employment	Duration of annual holiday
At least 48 weks	17 days
„ „ 46 „	16 „
„ „ 44 „	15 „
„ „ 42 „	14 „
„ „ 40 „	13 „
„ „ 39 „	12 „
„ „ 38 „	12 „
„ „ 36 „	11 „
„ „ 33 „	10 „
„ „ 30 „	9 „
„ „ 27 „	8 „
„ „ 24 „	7 „
„ „ 21 „	6 „
„ „ 18 „	5 „
„ „ 15 „	4 „
„ „ 12 „	3 „
„ „ 8 „	2 „
„ „ 4 „	1 day

(2) Notwithstanding the provisions of the last foregoing sub-paragraph —

  (a) the number of days of annual holiday which an employer is required to allow to a worker in respect of a period of employment during the 12 months immediately preceding 6th April in any year shall not exceed in the aggregate three times the number of days constituting the worker's normal working week, plus 2 days;

  (b) where before 17th September in any holiday season a worker and his employer enter into an agreement in writing that the worker shall be allowed after the end of the holiday season and before 6th April next following, days of holiday not exceeding twice the number of days constituting his normal working week, being all or part of the annual holiday for which he has qualified under this paragraph, any such days of annual holiday may, subject to the provisions of paragraph 4, be allowed in accordance with the agreement and if so allowed shall be treated for the purposes of this Schedule as having been allowed during the holiday season;

  (c) the duration of the worker's annual holiday in the holiday season ending on 30th September 1974 shall be reduced by any days of annual holiday with pay duly allowed to him by the employer under the provisions of Order S.(80) between 6th April 1974, and the date on which the provisions of this Schedule become effective.

(3) In this Schedule the expression "holiday season" means in relation to the year 1974, the period commencing on 6th April 1974 and ending on 30th September 1974 and in relation to each subsequent year, the period commencing on 6th April and ending on 30th September in that year.

4.—(1) Subject to the provisions of this paragraph, an annual holiday under this Schedule shall be allowed on consecutive working days and days of holiday shall be treated as consecutive notwithstanding that a day of holiday allowed to a worker under Part II of this Schedule or a day upon which he does not normally work for the employer intervenes.

(2) (*a*) Where the number of days of annual holiday for which a worker has qualified exceeds the number of days constituting his normal working week, but does not exceed twice that number, the holiday may be allowed in two periods of consecutive working days; so, however, that when a holiday is so allowed, one of the periods shall consist of a number of such days not less than the number of days constituting the worker's normal working week;

(*b*) Where the number of days of annual holiday for which a worker has qualified exceeds twice the number of days constituting his normal working week the holiday may be allowed as follows:—

   (i) as to two periods of consecutive working days, each such period not being less than the period constituting the worker's normal working week, during the holiday season; and

   (ii) as to any additional days, on working days which need not be consecutive, to be fixed by the employer, either during the holiday season or within the period ending on 8th January immediately following the holiday season.

(3) Where a day of holiday allowed to a worker under Part II of this Schedule immediately precedes a period of annual holiday or occurs during such a period then, notwithstanding the foregoing provisions of this paragraph, the duration of that period of annual holiday may be reduced by one day and in such a case one day of annual holiday may be allowed on any working day in the holiday season, or by agreement between the employer and the worker or his representative, on any working day before the beginning of the next following holiday season.

(4) Subject to the provisions of this paragraph, any day of annual holiday under this Schedule may be allowed on a day on which the worker is entitled to a day of holiday or to a half-holiday under any enactment other than the Wages Councils Act 1959.

5. An employer shall give to a worker reasonable notice of the commencing date or dates and of the duration of his annual holiday. Such notice may be given individually to the worker or by the posting of a notice in the place where the worker is employed.

PART IV

HOLIDAY REMUNERATION

A—CUSTOMARY HOLIDAYS AND HOLIDAYS IN LIEU OF CUSTOMARY HOLIDAYS

6.—(1) For each day of holiday (including a holiday falling on a Saturday) to which a worker is entitled under Part II of this Schedule he shall be paid by the employer as holiday remuneration whichever of the following amounts is the greater:—

   (*a*) (i) in the case of workers other than tie workers, one-fifth of the average weekly earnings of the worker during the 12 months ended on 5th April immediately preceding the holiday, such average weekly earnings to be determined by dividing, by the number of weeks of employment with the employer during the said period, the total remuneration paid to him by the employer during that period:

   Provided that when Good Friday or Easter Monday in England and Wales or the local Spring holiday in Scotland (or days substituted therefor under the provisions of sub-paragraph (2)(*b*) of paragraph 2 or holidays in lieu of such customary holidays) fall after 5th April in any year, the holiday remuneration for any such holiday under this sub-paragraph shall be one-fifth of the average weekly earnings of the worker during the 12 months ended on 5th April in the preceding calendar year;

(ii) in the case of tie workers, one-fifth of the amount which the worker would be entitled to receive from his employer for a week's work under the arrangement current immediately prior to the holiday if he worked his normal working week and the number of daily hours usually worked by him (exclusive of overtime); or

(b) in the case of all workers, the appropriate statutory minimum remuneration to which he would have been entitled as a time worker if the day had not been a day of holiday and he had been employed on work for which statutory minimum remuneration is payable:—

(i) in the case of a worker normally employed for more than 30 hours a week, for 8 hours, or

(ii) in the case of a worker normally employed for 30 hours a week or less, for 4 hours.

(2) Notwithstanding the provisions of sub-paragraph (1) of this paragraph, payment of the said holiday remuneration is subject to the condition that the worker (unless excused by the employer or absent by reason of the proved illness of, or accident to, the worker) presents himself for employment at the usual starting hour on the first working day following the holiday:

Provided that when two customary holidays occur on successive days (or so that no working day intervenes) the said condition shall apply only to the second customary holiday.

(3) Where a worker normally works in the week on every week-day except Saturday, he shall be paid in respect of any Saturday on which he would have been entitled to a holiday under Part II of this Schedule if it had been a day on which he normally worked, a sum equivalent to the holiday remuneration he would have been entitled to receive had he been allowed a holiday on that day.

(4) Holiday remuneration in respect of any customary holiday shall be paid by the employer to the worker on the pay-day on which the wages for the first working day following the customary holiday are paid.

(5) Holiday remuneration in respect of any holiday in lieu of a customary holiday shall be paid on the pay-day on which the wages are paid for the first working day following the holiday in lieu of a customary holiday:

Provided that the said payment shall be made immediately upon the termination of the worker's employment if he ceases to be employed before being allowed such holiday in lieu of a customary holiday and in that case the condition specified in sub-paragraph (2) of this paragraph shall not apply.

B—ANNUAL HOLIDAY

7.—(1) Subject to the provisions of paragraph 8, a worker qualified to be allowed an annual holiday under this Schedule shall be paid as holiday remuneration by his employer in respect thereof, on the last pay-day preceding such annual holiday:—

(a) in the case of workers other than tie workers, whichever of the following amounts is the greater:

(i) an amount equal to *seventeen two-hundred-and-sixtieths* of the total remuneration paid by the employer to the worker in the 12 months ending on 5th April immediately preceding the holiday season; or

(ii) one day's holiday pay (as defined in paragraph 11) in respect of each day of annual holiday;

(b) in the case of tie workers in respect of each day of annual holiday:

(i) where the worker's normal working week is five days, one-fifth

(ii) where the worker's normal working week is four days or less, one-quarter

of the amount which the worker would be entitled to receive from his employer for a week's work under the arrangement current immediately prior to the holiday if he worked his normal working week and the number of daily hours usually worked by him (exclusive of overtime).

(2) Where, under the provisions of paragraph 4, an annual holiday is allowed in more than one period the holiday remuneration shall be apportioned accordingly.

8. Where any accrued holiday remuneration has been paid by the employer to the worker (in accordance with paragraph 9 of this Schedule or under the provisions of Order S. (80)) in respect of employment during any of the periods referred to in that paragraph or that Order, the amount of holiday remuneration payable by the employer in respect of any annual holiday for which the worker has qualified by reason of employment during the said period shall be reduced by the amount of the said accrued holiday remuneration unless that remuneration has been deducted from a previous payment of holiday remuneration made under the provisions of this Schedule or of Order S. (80).

ACCRUED HOLIDAY REMUNERATION PAYABLE ON TERMINATION OF EMPLOYMENT

9.—(1) Where a worker ceases to be employed by an employer after the provisions of this Schedule become effective, the employer shall, immediately on the termination of the employment, pay to the worker accrued holiday remuneration in accordance with this paragraph.

(2) Accrued holiday remuneration shall be payable in accordance with the following table if the worker has in the 12 months commencing on 6th April 1973, and thereafter in any period of 12 months commencing on 6th April been employed for any of the periods of employment specified in that table.

(3) Accrued holiday remuneration is not payable in respect of any period of employment for which the worker has been allowed or become entitled to be allowed an annual holiday under this Schedule.

(4) Subject to the provisions of sub-paragraph (5) hereof, where a worker has been allowed in a holiday season part only of the annual holiday for which he has qualified under this Schedule or under Order S. (80) and his employment is terminated before he becomes entitled to the rest of that holiday the accrued holiday remuneration payable shall be:—

(a) in the case of a worker who has qualified for days of annual holiday exceeding twice the number of days constituting his normal working week and who has been allowed as days of annual holiday not less than twice the number of days constituting his normal working week, or, where the circumstances in sub-paragraph (3) of paragraph 4 are applicable, that number of days reduced by one:—

(i) in respect of the days of holiday for which he has qualified during the 12 months ended on 5th April immediately preceding the termination of his employment, the holiday remuneration due in respect thereof calculated in accordance with the provisions of paragraph 7 less the amount received by him in respect of the part of the holiday which has been allowed; and

(ii) in respect of any period of employment since the said 5th April, the amount calculated in accordance with the following table;

(b) in the case of any other worker, the appropriate amount under the following table in respect of the qualifying period of employment less the amount received by the worker in respect of that part of the holiday which has been allowed.

(5) Any accrued holiday remuneration payable under the provisions of this paragraph shall be reduced by the amount of any accrued holiday remuneration already paid by the employer to the worker in pursuance of this Order or Order S. (80) in respect of the same period of employment or part thereof.

TABLE OF ACCRUED HOLIDAY REMUNERATION

Period of Employment calculated in accordance with the provisions of paragraph 10	ACCRUED HOLIDAY REMUNERATION 12 months commencing 6th April 1973 and each succeeding 12 months commencing on 6th April	COLUMN 2
COLUMN 1		
At least 48 weeks	Three and two-fifths times the amount in Col. 2	The amount which the worker would be entitled
„ „ 46 „	Three and one-fifth times the amount in Col. 2	to receive from his employer, at the date of the
„ „ 44 „	Three times the amount in Col. 2 ..	termination of his employment, for one week's work,
„ „ 42 „	Two and four-fifths times the amount in Col. 2	if working his normal
„ „ 40 „	Two and three-fifths times the amount in Col. 2	working week and the number of daily hours
„ „ 39 „	Two and two-fifths times the amount in Col. 2	normally worked by him (exclusive of overtime) and
„ „ 38 „	Two and two-fifths times the amount in Col. 2	if paid as a time worker at the appropriate rate of
„ „ 36 „	Two and one-fifth times the amount in Col. 2	statutory minimum remuneration for work for
„ „ 33 „	Twice the amount in Col. 2	which statutory minimum
„ „ 30 „	One and four-fifths times the amount in Col. 2	remuneration is payable and at the same rate for
„ „ 27 „	One and three-fifths times the amount in Col. 2	any work for which such remuneration is not payable.
„ „ 24 „	One and two-fifths times the amount in Col. 2	able.
„ „ 21 „	One and one-fifth times the amount in Col. 2	
„ „ 18 „	The amount in Col. 2	
„ „ 15 „	Four-fifths of the amount in Col. 2	
„ „ 12 „	Three-fifths of the amount in Col. 2	
„ „ 8 „	Two-fifths of the amount in Col. 2	
„ „ 4 „	One-fifth of the amount in Col. 2	

(6) Notwithstanding the provisions of the foregoing table, the accrued holiday remuneration payable to a worker who has been employed by the employer for the whole of the 12 months ended on 5th April immediately preceding the termination of his employment shall be as follows:—

(a) in respect of that 12 months an amount equal to the holiday remuneration for the days of annual holiday for which he has qualified, calculated in accordance with the provisions of sub-paragraph (1) of paragraph 7; and

(b) in respect of any period of employment since the said 5th April, the amount calculated in accordance with the foregoing table.

PART V

GENERAL

10. For the purpose of calculating any period of employment qualifying a worker for an annual holiday or for any accrued holiday remuneration under this Schedule, the worker shall be treated—

(1) as if he were employed for a week in respect of any week in which—

(a) in the case of a worker other than a part-time worker, he has worked for the employer for not less than 20 hours and has performed some work for which statutory minimum remuneration is payable;

(b) in the case of a part-time worker, he has worked for the employer and has performed some work for which statutory minimum remuneration is payable;

(c) in the case of any worker—

    (i) he has worked for the employer for less than 20 hours by reason of the proved illness of, or accident to, the worker or for a like reason has been absent throughout the week (provided that the number of weeks which may be treated as weeks of employment for such reason shall not exceed four in the aggregate in any such period); or

    (ii) he has been suspended throughout the week owing to shortage of work (provided that the number of weeks which may be treated as weeks of employment for such reason shall not exceed six in the aggregate in any such period).

(2) as if he were employed on any day of holiday allowed under the provisions of this Schedule, or of Order S. (80), and for the purposes of the provisions of sub-paragraph (1) of this paragraph, a worker who is absent on such holiday shall be treated as having worked thereon for the employer on work for which statutory minimum remuneration is payable—

    (a) where the holiday is a customary holiday, or a holiday in lieu of a customary holiday, for 8 hours if the worker is normally employed for more than 30 hours a week or for 4 hours if he is normally employed for 30 hours a week or less, or

    (b) where the holiday is a day of annual holiday or any other day of holiday, for the number of hours ordinarily worked by him on that day of the week.

11. In this Schedule, unless the context otherwise requires, the following expressions have the meanings hereby respectively assigned to them, that is to say:—

"NORMAL WORKING WEEK" means the number of days on which it has been usual for the worker to work in a week in the employment of the employer in the 12 months immediately preceding the commencement of the holiday season or, where under paragraph 9 accrued holiday remuneration is payable on the termination of the employment, in the 12 months immediately preceding the date of the termination of the employment:

Provided that—

    (1) part of a day shall count as a day;

    (2) no account shall be taken of any week in which the worker did not perform any work for which statutory minimum remuneration has been fixed.

"ONE DAY'S HOLIDAY PAY" means the appropriate proportion of the remuneration which the worker would be entitled to receive from his employer at the date of the annual holiday for one week's work if working his normal working week and the number of daily hours normally worked by him (exclusive of overtime) and if paid as a time worker at the appropriate rate of statutory minimum remuneration for work for which statutory minimum remuneration is payable and at the same rate for any work for which such remuneration is not payable, and in this definition "appropriate proportion" means—

where the worker's normal working week is five days ..   .. one-fifth
where the worker's normal working week is four days or less .. one-quarter

"PART-TIME WORKER" means a worker who normally works for the employer for less than 20 hours a week by reason only of the fact that he does not hold himself out as normally available for work for more than the number of hours he normally works in the week.

"STATUTORY MINIMUM REMUNERATION" means minimum remuneration (other than holiday remuneration) fixed by a wages regulation order.

"TIE WORKER" means a male worker employed wholly or mainly in the making of neckties—

(a) in the Metropolitan Police District, the City of London, the Inner Temple or the Middle Temple; or (*b*) in any other area, in an establishment engaged wholly or mainly in the making of neckties.

"WAGES REGULATION ORDER" means a wages regulation order made by the Secretary of State to give effect to proposals submitted to him by the Shirtmaking Wages Council (Great Britain).

"WEEK" means "pay week".

12. The provisions of this Schedule are without prejudice to any agreement for the allowance of any further holidays with pay or for the payment of additional holiday remuneration.

EXPLANATORY NOTE

(This Note is not part of the Order.)

This Order, which has effect from 22nd May 1974, sets out the holidays which an employer is required to allow to workers in relation to whom the Shirtmaking Wages Council (Great Britain) operates and the remuneration payable for those holidays in substitution for the holidays and holiday remuneration fixed by the Wages Regulation (Shirtmaking) Order 1973 (Order S. (80)), which Order is revoked.

New provisions are printed in italics.

STATUTORY INSTRUMENTS

1974 No. 746

PROBATION AND AFTER-CARE
The Probation (Allowances) (Amendment) Rules 1974

Made - - -	*24th April* 1974
Coming into Operation	*6th May* 1974

In exercise of the powers conferred upon me by Schedule 5 to the Criminal Justice Act 1948(**a**), as extended by section 36 of the Justices of the Peace Act 1949(**b**) (as amended by section 4 of the Justices of the Peace Act 1968(**c**) and applied by section 52(5) of the Criminal Justice Act 1972(**d**)), I hereby make the following Rules : —

1. These Rules may be cited as the Probation (Allowances) (Amendment) Rules 1974 and shall come into operation on 6th May 1974.

2. In paragraph 3(2) of Schedule 1 to the Probation (Allowances) Rules 1971(**e**) as amended (**f**) for the words "5·5p", "6·2p" and "6·9p" there shall be substituted the words "6·4p", "6·9p" and "7·8p" respectively.

Roy Jenkins,
One of Her Majesty's Principal
Secretaries of State.

Home Office,
 Whitehall.
6th May 1974.

EXPLANATORY NOTE
(This Note is not part of the Rules.)

These Rules amend the Probation (Allowances) Rules 1971 by increasing the rates of travelling allowance payable to members of probation and after-care committees, case committees and community service committees in respect of the use of a private motor car.

(**a**) 1948 c. 58.	(**b**) 1949 c. 101.
(**c**) 1968 c. 69.	(**d**) 1972 c. 71.
(**e**) S.I. 1971/414 (1971 I, p. 1225).	(**f**) S.I. 1972/1400 (1972 III, p. 4258).

STATUTORY INSTRUMENTS

1974 No. 747

EDUCATION, ENGLAND AND WALES

The Remuneration of Teachers (Primary and Secondary Schools) (Amendment) Order 1974

Made - - - -	*25th April* 1974
Coming into Operation	*26th April* 1974

Whereas—

(1) in pursuance of section 2(2) of the Remuneration of Teachers Act 1965**(a)** (hereinafter referred to as "the Act") the Committee constituted under section 1 thereof for the purpose of considering the remuneration payable to teachers in primary and secondary schools maintained by local education authorities (hereinafter referred to as "the Committee") have transmitted to the Secretary of State for Education and Science (hereinafter referred to as "the Secretary of State") recommendations agreed on by them with respect to the remuneration of such teachers;

(2) the Committee have, in pursuance of section 2(2) of the Act as modified by the Counter-Inflation (Modification of the Remuneration of Teachers Act 1965) Order 1973**(b)**, also transmitted to the Pay Board established under section 1(1) of the Counter-Inflation Act 1973**(c)** (hereinafter referred to as "the Pay Board") the proposals contained in those recommendations for increases in the remuneration of such teachers;

(3) the Pay Board have approved the said proposals;

(4) there is in force an Order made under section 2 of the Act with respect to the remuneration of teachers in primary and secondary schools maintained by local education authorities, namely, the Remuneration of Teachers (Primary and Secondary Schools) Order 1973**(d)**;

(5) it appears to the Secretary of State that effect can more conveniently be given to the recommendations of the Committee by amending the scales and other provisions set out in the document referred to in the said Order, namely, the document published by Her Majesty's Stationery Office on 24th May 1973 under the title "SCALES OF SALARIES FOR TEACHERS IN PRIMARY AND SECONDARY SCHOOLS, ENGLAND AND WALES, 1973" (hereinafter referred to as "the Document");

(6) in pursuance of Section 2(5) of the Act the Secretary of State has prepared a draft Order (being the draft of this Order) setting out the amendments of the scales and other provisions which, in his opinion, are requisite for giving effect to the recommendations of the Committee; and

---

(a) 1965 c. 3.
(c) 1973 c, 9,
(b) S.I. 1973/616 (1973 I, p. 1950).
(d) S.I. 1973/956 (1973 II, p. 2887).

(7) the Secretary of State, as required by section 2(6) of the Act, has consulted the Committee with respect to the draft Order and made such modifications thereof as were requisite for giving effect to representations made by the Committee.

Now therefore the Secretary of State, in pursuance of section 2(6) of the Act, hereby orders as follows:—

Citation and commencement

1. This Order may be cited as the Remuneration of Teachers (Primary and Secondary Schools) (Amendment) Order 1974 and shall come into operation on 26th April 1974.

Interpretation

2. The Interpretation Act 1889**(a)** shall apply for the interpretation of this Order as it applies for the interpretation of an Act of Parliament.

Amendment of Document

3. The scales and other provisions contained in the Document are hereby amended—

    (*a*) with effect from 1st April 1973, in the manner specified in Schedule 1 to this Order;

    (*b*) with effect from 1st April 1974, in the manner specified in Schedule 2 to this Order; and

    (*c*) with effect from 1st September 1974, in the manner specified in Schedule 3 to this Order.

SCHEDULE 1

AMENDMENTS EFFECTIVE FROM 1ST APRIL 1973

1. In Part IV of the Document (which relates to additional payments and allowances)—

    (*a*) the words "and 12(1)(*c*)" shall be deleted from sub-section 12(1)(*a*); and

    (*b*) the following sub-section shall be substituted for sub-section 12(1)(*b*):—

        "(*b*) Recognition of a school by the Secretary of State for the purposes of sub-section 12(1)(*a*) above shall cease on the closure or reorganisation of the school. Accordingly the payment to teachers in the school shall cease except in the case of an individual teacher who was in receipt of the payment immediately before the closure or reorganisation and who continues to be responsible substantially for the education of children who would have attended the school had it not been closed or reorganised."; and

    (*c*) the following sub-section shall be substituted for sub-section 12(1)(*c*):—

        "(*c*) The additional payments in sub-section 12(1)(*a*) above shall also apply to teachers who are appointed to a school provided for children who would have attended a school or schools formerly recognised by the Secretary of State as of exceptional difficulty if such school or schools had not been closed or reorganised."

(a) 1889 c. 63.

2. In Part V of the Document (which contains supplementary provisions relating to teachers' salaries) the following sub-section shall be substituted for sub-section 17(6):—

"(6) A teacher to whom sub-section (1) above applies shall not receive any additional payments or allowances under Part IV of this Document other than those to which he may be entitled by virtue of the post he held immediately before the closure or reorganisation except that:

(i) a teacher who subsequent to the closure or reorganisation is transferred to a special school or special class shall be entitled to receive the additional payment provided in section 11 for so long as the conditions of that section are satisfied and the teacher is not already in receipt of that additional payment, or a safeguarded salary as a head or deputy head teacher of a special school; and

(ii) a teacher who satisfies the conditions of sub-section 12(1)(b) or (c) may continue to receive the additional payment as provided therein."

3. In Appendix III to the Document—

(a) the words "or deputy head" shall be inserted after the word "head" in sub-paragraph 11(1)(e); and

(b) there shall be added to Annex E (which specifies the qualifications and/or courses entitling a qualified teacher to a payment of £78)—

(i) to paragraph 5 the following qualification in relation to the University of London:—

"Diploma in Secondary Education".

(ii) after paragraph 11 the following paragraph—

"11A. The satisfactory completion of a full or part-time course leading to the Diploma in Educational Technology of the National Committee for Audio-Visual Aids in Education."

(c) In Part II of Annex F (which specifies the qualifications which entitle a qualified teacher to be classed as a graduate for salary purposes)—

(a) paragraphs 38 and 42 shall be deleted; and

(b) for paragraph 56 there shall be substituted the following paragraph:—

"56. Associateship of the Institution of Metallurgists if obtained after examination held in or after August 1949 except where the qualification entitles the teacher to be classed as a good honours graduate under Part III of this annex."

(d) In Part III of Annex F (which specifies the qualifications which entitle a qualified teacher to be classed as a good honours graduate for salary purposes)—

(a) paragraph 11 shall be deleted; and

(b) the following qualifications shall be added after that specified in paragraph 10:—

"11. Membership of the Institute of Biology obtained by written examination first held in June 1966.

12. Master of Science (MSC) or Master of Business Administration (MBA) of Cranfield Institute of Technology.

13. (a) Graduateship of the Institution of Metallurgists obtained by the Institution's examination first held in 1972;

(b) Associateship of the Institution of Metallurgists obtained by examination held in 1963 or subsequently under the 1961/62 revised regulations of the Institution.

14. The Diploma in Medical Technology of the Institute of Medical Laboratory Technology obtained by the Institute's examination.

15. Such other qualifications as are accepted by the Burnham Committee."

SCHEDULE 2

AMENDMENTS EFFECTIVE FROM 1ST APRIL 1974

1. In section 1 of Part I of the Document there shall be inserted after the words "unattached teachers (section 16)" the words "safeguarding (section 17)".

2. In Part III of the Document (which relates to unqualified teachers)—

  (*a*) in sub-section 9(*c*) for the sum of "£158" there shall be substituted the sum of "£168";

  (*b*) in sub-section 10(*c*)(i) for the sum of "£330" there shall be substituted the sum of "£354"; and

  (*c*) in sub-section 10(*c*)(ii) for the sum of "£267" there shall be substituted the sum of "£285".

3. In Part IV of the Document (which relates to additional payments and allowances)—

  (*a*) in sub-section 11(*a*)(i) for the sum of "£175" there shall be substituted the sum of "£195";

  (*b*) in sub-section 11(*a*)(ii) for the sum of "£125" there shall be substituted the sum of "£141";

  (*c*) in sub-section 11(*b*) for the sum of "£180" there shall be substituted the sum of "£198";

  (*d*) in sub-section 12(1)(*a*)(i) for the sum of "£105" there shall be substituted the sum of "£114";

  (*e*) in sub-section 12(1)(*a*)(ii) for the sum of "£83" there shall be substituted the sum of "£87";

  (*f*) in sub-sections 15(2)(*a*) and 15(2)(*b*) for the sum of "£160" there shall be substituted the sum of "£171".

4. In Part V of the Document (which contains supplementary provisions relating to teachers' salaries), the following section shall be substituted for section 17:—

"17. SAFEGUARDING

  (1) (*a*) Subject as hereafter in this section provided, a teacher who loses his post, or whose salary would otherwise be diminished, as a result of the closure or reorganisation of an educational establishment, as defined in sub-section (3)(ii) below, and who continues in service as a full-time teacher in an educational establishment maintained by the same local education authority shall be deemed for all salary purposes to continue to hold the post he held immediately before the closure or reorganisation, save however that he shall not be entitled to continue to receive the additional payment applicable to teachers in primary and secondary schools recognised by the Secretary of State as of exceptional difficulty except as provided in sub-section 12(1)(*b*) or (*c*) of this Document.

  (*b*) sub-section (1)(*a*) above shall not apply or, as the case may be, shall cease to apply to a teacher:

  (i) who at any time unreasonably refuses to accept an alternative post in an educational establishment maintained by the same local education authority; or

  (ii) who leaves a post to which appointed after the closure or reorganisation except on movement to another teaching post under arrangements approved by the same local education authority, such approval not being unreasonably withheld; or

  (iii) who in the case of closure or reorganisation on or after 1st April 1969 had held for less than two years a teaching post to which he was appointed for a fixed period or on an acting or temporary basis unless in order to take up that post he had under arrangements made by the local education authority relinquished a regular full-time teaching post in one of their educational establishments, when sub-section (1)(*a*) above shall apply as if he were still in that regular full-time post immediately before the closure or reorganisation; or

(iv) whose salary under this section falls below that applicable to him under the other provisions of this document.

(*c*) The foregoing provisions of this section shall only apply:

(i) where the date of closure or reorganisation was 1st April 1974 or later; or

(ii) to a teacher who on 31st March 1974 was in receipt of a safeguarded salary under the provisions in force on that date of section 17 of this Document, or the corresponding sections of the Documents prepared by the Secretary of State for Education and Science under section 2 of the Remuneration of Teachers Act 1965(a) (as amended(b)) in relation to the scales of salaries for teachers in establishments in England and Wales for Further Education, or for the teaching staff of farm institutes and for teachers of agricultural (including horticultural) subjects. Where, however, in the case of a school teacher who at the time of the closure or reorganisation and before 1st April 1969 had held a post of head teacher or deputy head teacher for less than two years, having been appointed thereto for a fixed period or on an acting or temporary basis, the provisions of Appendix VII to the Primary and Secondary Salaries Document 1967 relating to the calculation of unit totals shall be deemed to continue in force in place of the corresponding provisions of the document now in force.

(*d*) A teacher to whom sub-section (1)(*a*) above applies shall not be paid any additional payments or allowances under Part IV of this Document other than those to which he may be entitled by virtue of the post he held immediately before the closure or reorganisation, except that:

(i) a teacher who subsequent to the closure or reorganisation is transferred to a special school or special class shall be entitled to receive the additional payment provided in section 11 for so long as the conditions of that section are satisfied and the teacher is not already in receipt of that additional payment, or a safeguarded salary as a head or deputy head teacher of a special school; and

(ii) a teacher who satisfies the conditions of sub-section 12(1)(*b*) or (*c*) may continue to receive the additional payment as provided therein.

(2) (*a*) Subject as hereafter in this section provided, a teacher who was formerly employed in a full-time teaching post in a college of education in England or Wales maintained by a local education authority or which was in receipt of grant from the Secretary of State and who on or after 1st April 1974 loses that post as a result of the closure or reorganisation of the college but continues in full-time teaching service in an educational establishment, as defined in sub-section (3)(ii) below, shall be deemed for all salary purposes to continue to hold the post he held immediately before the closure or reorganisation, save however that no London Area payment shall be payable except that payable under section 13 of this document where the conditions of that section are satisfied.

(*b*) Sub-section (2)(*a*) above shall not apply or, as the case may be, shall cease to apply to a teacher:

(i) who at any time unreasonably refuses to accept an alternative post in an educational establishment maintained by the employing authority; or

(ii) who leaves a post to which appointed after the closure or reorganisation except on movement to another teaching post under arrangements approved by the employing authority, such approval not being unreasonably withheld; or

(iii) who at the time of the closure or reorganisation had held for less than two years a teaching post in a college of education to which he had been appointed for a fixed period or on an acting or temporary basis unless

---

(a) 1965 c. 3. (b) S.I. 1973/616 (1973 I, p. 1950).

in order to take up that post he had under arrangements made by the college authority relinquished a regular full-time teaching post in a college of education, in which case, sub-section (2)(*a*) above shall apply as if he were still in that regular full-time post immediately before the closure or reorganisation; or

(iv) whose salary under this section falls below that applicable to him under the other provisions of this Document.

(*c*) A teacher in receipt of a salary under sub-section (2)(*a*) above shall not be paid any additional payments or allowances under Part IV of this Document other than:—

(i) the "special schools" addition under section 11 and/or

(ii) the "London Area" payment under section 13 where the conditions of the sections referred to are satisfied.

(3) For the purposes of section (1) and (2) above:

(i) a teacher shall be deemed to continue in the employment of the same local education authority if the educational establishment (or educational establishments in the case of an unattached school teacher) in which he is serving becomes maintained by another local education authority or joint committee of authorities; and

(ii) an "educational establishment" is a primary or secondary school or a farm institute or an establishment for further education (including a department of such an establishment) maintained by a local education authority in England or Wales."

5. For Appendix I to the Document (which sets out the salary scales for teachers) there shall be substituted the following Appendix:—

"APPENDIX I

Scales of Salaries for Teachers

1. Qualified Assistant Teachers

Incremental Point	Scales				
	1	2	3	4	5
	£	£	£	£	£
0	1449	1590	1863	2286	2718
1	1527	1668	1956	2382	2829
2	1605	1746	2049	2478	2940
3	1683	1827	2145	2577	3051
4	1761	1908	2238	2676	3162
5	1842	1989	2334	2775	3273
6	1923	2070	2430	2874	3384
7	2004	2154	2526	2973	3498
8	2085	2238	2622	3072	3612
9	2166	2322	2721	3171	
10	2250	2406	2820†	3270	
11	2334	2490			
12	2442*	2577			
13	2442	2688†			
14	2442				
15	2553				

*Where a teacher paid on scale 1 is entitled to be classed as a good honours graduate for salary purposes under the conditions set out in Parts I and III of Annex F to Appendix III, the salary rates from incremental point 12 shall be as follows:

Incremental Point	Salary Rate
	£
13	2529
14	2616
15	2616
16	2616
17	2733

†Where a teacher paid on scales 2 or 3 is likewise entitled to be classed as a good honours graduate for salary purposes, the appropriate scale shall be extended by two increments of £90 per annum as follows:

Scale	
2	3
£	£
2778	2910
2868	3000

2. Senior Teachers

Incremental Point	Scale
	£
0	2940
1	3051
2	3162
3	3273
4	3384
5	3498
6	3612
7	3726
8	3840

3. Qualified Deputy Head Teachers

(a) Schools, other than special schools

Incremental Point	Group						
	below 3	3	4	5	6	7	8
0	£	£	£	£	£	£	£
1	1782	1839	2100	2448	2988	3150	3300
2	1863	1920	2193	2547	3087	3249	3399
3	1944	2001	2286	2646	3186	3348	3501
4	2028	2082	2379	2745	3285	3450	3600
5	2112	2166	2472	2844	3387	3549	3699
6	2196	2250	2571	2943			
7	2280	2331	2670	3042			
8	2364	2415	2769	3144			
9	2448	2499	2868				
10	2532	2583	2970				
11	2616	2673					
	2724	2787					

Incremental Point	Group					
	9	10	11	12	13	14
0	£	£	£	£	£	£
1	3516	3702	3858	4023	4170	4332
2	3615	3801	3957	4122	4269	4431
3	3714	3900	4056	4224	4368	4530
4	3813	3999	4155	4323	4467	4629
	3915	4098	4254	4422	4566	4728

(b) Special Schools

Incremental Point	Group							
	2(S)	3(S)	4(S)	5(S)	6(S)	7(S)	8(S)	9(S)
0	£	£	£	£	£	£	£	£
	1962	2196	2424	2946	3141	3303	3468	3645
1	2043	2277	2520	3045	3240	3402	3567	3744
2	2124	2358	2619	3144	3339	3501	3666	3843
3	2205	2439	2718	3243	3438	3600	3765	3942
4	2289	2523	2817	3342	3537	3702	3867	4044
5	2373	2607	2916					
6	2457	2694	3015					
7	2541	2784	3117					
8	2631	2874						
9	2721	2964						
10	2811							
11	2922							

Where the unit total or review average of a special school exceeds 2100, the local education authority shall determine a deputy head teacher scale appropriately related to the scale in group 9(S).

4. Qualified Head Teachers

(a) Schools, other than special schools

Incremental Point	Group						
	1	2	3	4	5	6	7
	£	£	£	£	£	£	£
0	2565	2694	2850	3027	3282	3555	3855
1	2652	2781	2937	3126	3381	3654	3954
2	2739	2868	3024	3225	3480	3753	4053
3	2826	2958	3111	3324	3579	3852	4155
4	2916	3048	3201	3426	3681	3951	4254

Incremental Point	Group						
	8	9	10	11	12	13	14
	£	£	£	£	£	£	£
0	4140	4464	4788	5112	5433	5757	6078
1	4239	4563	4887	5211	5565	5889	6207
2	4338	4662	4986	5310	5697	6021	6330
3	4440	4761	5085	5409	5829	6150	6456
4	4539	4863	5184	5508			

(b) Special Schools

Incremental Point	Group							
	2(S)	3(S)	4(S)	5(S)	6(S)	7(S)	8(S)	9(S)
	£	£	£	£	£	£	£	£
0	2898	3078	3255	3546	3807	4113	4332	4539
1	2985	3165	3354	3645	3906	4212	4431	4644
2	3072	3252	3453	3744	4005	4311	4530	4749
3	3159	3339	3552	3843	4104	4410	4629	4854
4	3249	3429	3654	3945	4206	4512	4731	4959

Where the unit total or review average of a special school exceeds 2100 the local education authority shall determine a head teacher scale appropriately related to the scale in group 9(S).

Scales of Salaries for Unqualified Teachers

5. **Unqualified Assistant Teachers,** other than those to whom sub-section 8(2)(*a*) applies.

Incremental Point	Scales		
	A	B	C
	£	£	£
0	1194	1194	1302
1	1230	1230	1338
2	1266	1266	1377
3	1302	1302	1413
4	1338	1338	1449
5		1377	1527
6		1413	1605
7		1449	1683
8			1761
9			1842
10			1923
11			2004

(see below)

Scale C above may be extended by either one increment of £63 to a maximum of £2067 or by two increments of £63 to a maximum of £2130 in the case of a teacher who, in the opinion of the local education authority employing him, possesses a qualification of particular value in the performance of his duties.

Unqualified assistant teachers shall be placed on scales A, B or C in accordance with the following table:

Employment authorised under	Scale Applicable
Regulation 17(1) or 18 of the Schools Regulations 1959 **(a)**	A
Regulation 16(3) of the Schools Regulations 1959 or regulation 15(3)(*a*) or 15(3)(*b*) of the Handicapped Pupils and Special Schools Regulations 1959 **(b)**	B
Regulation 16A of the Handicapped Pupils and Special Schools Regulations 1959	C

6. **Unqualified Deputy Head Teachers of Special Schools,** to whom sub-section 9(*a*) applies.

Incremental Point	Group							
	2(S)	3(S)	4(S)	5(S)	6(S)	7(S)	8(S)	9(S)
	£	£	£	£	£	£	£	£
0	1740	1983	2223	2742	2952	3111	3276	3453
1	1821	2064	2316	2841	3051	3210	3375	3552
2	1902	2145	2412	2940	3150	3309	3474	3651
3	1986	2229	2505	3039	3249	3408	3573	3750
4	2070	2313	2604	3141	3348	3510	3675	3852
5	2154	2397	2703					
6	2238	2481	2802					
7	2322	2565	2904					
8	2406	2652						
9	2490	2742						
10	2574							
11	2682							

(a) S.I. 1959/364 (1959 I, p. 1584).   **(b)** S.I. 1959/365 (1959 I, p. 1024).

7. Unqualified Head Teachers of Special Schools, to whom sub-section 10(a) applies.

Incremental Point	Group							
	2(S)	3(S)	4(S)	5(S)	6(S)	7(S)	8(S)	9(S)
	£	£	£	£	£	£	£	£
0	2646	2835	3024	3324	3615	3921	4140	4350
1	2733	2922	3123	3423	3714	4020	4239	4452
2	2820	3009	3222	3522	3813	4119	4338	4554
3	2907	3096	3321	3621	3912	4218	4437	4659
4	2997	3186	3423	3723	4014	4320	4539	4764

"

6. In Appendix II to the Document (which relates to unit totals and review averages)—

(a) for paragraph 8 there shall be substituted the following paragraph—
"8. Where a local education authority has regarded a school as one of exceptional difficulty in accordance with sub-section 12(2) of this document, the maximum of the points score range otherwise applicable to the school may be increased by 1 point or up to 20 per cent., whichever is the higher. In the calculation of the percentage increase a fraction of a point shall be rounded up to the next higher point."

(b) In the Annex to the said Appendix—

(i) there shall be inserted the following additional footnote to the table relating to schools, other than special schools:—

"Where under the provisions of sub-section 12(2) of this document a school in Group 1 or Group 2 is regarded as of exceptional difficulty by the local education authority one assistant teacher may be placed on scale 2."

(ii) for the table relating to special schools there shall be substituted the following table:—

"Special Schools

Unit Total or Review Average	Points Score Range	Highest Scale for Assistant Teachers	Group of School for Head and Deputy Head Teacher purposes
up to 180	0–1	Scale 2	Group 2(S)
181–300	1–2	Scale 2	3(S)
301–360	2–3		
361–400	3–4	Scale 2	4(S)
401–500	3–5		
501–600	4–7	Scale 3	
601–700	6–8		5(S)
701–800	7–10	Scale 3	
801–900	8–11		
901–1000	10–14		6(S)
1001–1100	12–16	Scale 4	
1101–1200	13–17		
1201–1300	15–19		7(S)
1301–1400	17–21	Scale 4	
1401–1500	19–25		
1501–1600	19–25	Scale 4	8(S)
1601–1800	23–29		
1801–2000	27–33	Scale 4	9(S)
2001–2100	31–37	Scale 5	
2101–2200	31–37	Scale 5	
2201–2400	35–41		

Where in a particular case the maximum of the points score range is not considered adequate to meet the needs of a special school, the local education authority in their discretion may exceed that maximum. In such a case, the limitations on the highest scale for assistant teachers in the school set out in the table above may also be waived, provided that the maximum of the highest assistant teacher scale then paid shall not exceed the sum of the maximum of the scale applicable to the deputy head teacher of the school and any additional payment under sub-section 15(1)(i) of this document."

7. In Appendix III (which prescribes the method of determining the correct position of a teacher on the appropriate salary scale)—

(a) for paragraph 6 there shall be substituted the following paragraph:—
    "6.—(1) Subject to the provisions of section 19, a teacher who continues to be entitled to receive salary on a scale corresponding to that on which he was paid on 31st March 1974 shall enter the appropriate scale set out in Appendix I from 1st April 1974 at the incremental point or intermediate point of any twelfth of an increment corresponding to that on which he would

have received salary (excluding any "London Area" or other above scale payments) had the scale in operation on 31st March 1974 continued to apply.

(2) A teacher who on or after 1st April 1974 is re-appointed to a post for which the salary scale corresponds to that on which he was paid at any time between 1st April 1971 and 31st March 1974 shall enter the appropriate scale set out in Appendix I from the date of re-appointment:

(i) at the point corresponding to that applicable to him at the date of leaving the former post (based on service to that date and excluding any "London Area" or other above scale payments), or

(ii) the salary determined under paragraph 7 or 8 below as appropriate, whichever is the higher."

(b) for each reference in paragraphs 7, 8 and 11(1) to "1st April 1973" there shall be substituted a reference to "1st April 1974";

(c) in paragraph 7(3)(a)(i) for the sum of "£1696" there shall be substituted the sum of "£1842";

(d) for the table in sub-paragraph 8(2) there shall be substituted the following table:—

Promotion		Increase
From	To	
Scale 1	Scale 2	2 × £90
Scale 2	Scale 3	2 × £99
Scale 3	Scale 4	2 × £99
Scale 4	Scale 5	2 × £114
Scale 5	Senior Teacher	2 × £114 "

(e) in sub-paragraph 9(1)(a) for the sums of "£36", "£66", and "£72" there shall be substituted the sums of "£39", "£71", and "£77" respectively;

(f) in sub-paragraph 11(1)(c) for the sum of "£175" there shall be substituted the sum of "£195";

(g) for the table in sub-paragraph 11(2) specifying the promotion increases for head and deputy head teachers there shall be substituted the following table:—

Promotion to Group	Increase	
	Head	Deputy Head
1–3 2(S)–3(S)	2 × £90	2 × £90
4–11 4(S)–8(S)	2 × £100·50	2 × £100·50
9(S)	2 × £105	2 × £100·50
12 or above	2 × £126	2 × £100·50 "

(h) for sub-paragraph 12(2) there shall be substituted the following sub-paragraph:—

"(2) A teacher who has been so "promoted" or "demoted" may be paid in accordance with the following arrangements provided that the maximum of the scale to which he is transferred is not exceeded:

(i) a teacher who is "promoted" from one assistant teacher scale to another or to the Senior Teacher scale may be paid the salary applicable in the former post plus a promotion increase determined in accordance with sub-paragraph 8(2) above;

(ii) a teacher who is "promoted" to an assistant teacher scale or the Senior Teacher scale from a head or deputy head teacher scale may be paid the salary applicable in the former post plus an amount equivalent to two increments at the rates set out in sub-paragraph 8(2) above according to the scale to which promoted;

(iii) a head or deputy head teacher who is "promoted" in accordance with sub-paragraph 12(1) above may be paid the salary applicable in the former post plus the promotion increase specified in sub-paragraph 11(2) above;

(iv) a teacher who is "demoted" from the Senior Teacher scale or an assistant teacher scale to another assistant teacher scale may be paid the salary applicable in the former post less an amount equivalent to two increments on the scale previously applicable and two increments on each of any intervening scales. For this purpose increments on the scales shall be deemed to be at the rates set out in sub-paragraph 8(2) above;

(v) a teacher who is "demoted" to an assistant teacher scale or the Senior Teacher scale from a head or deputy head teacher scale may be paid the salary applicable in the former post less an amount equivalent to two increments at the rates set out in sub-paragraph 11(2) above according to the head or deputy head teacher scale previously applicable;

(vi) a teacher who is "demoted" to a head or deputy head teacher post in accordance with sub-paragraph 12(1) above may be paid the salary applicable to him in his former post less an amount equivalent to two increments on the scale previously applicable. For this purpose increments on the scale shall be deemed to be at the rates set out in sub-paragraph 8(2) or 11(2) above, according to the scale previously applicable,

subject, in the case of a teacher to whom (iv), (v) or (vi) above applies and who is reverting to a scale on which he previously received salary, that he should not receive less than he would have received had he remained on that scale."

SCHEDULE 3

AMENDMENTS EFFECTIVE FROM 1ST SEPTEMBER 1974

1. For Appendix III to the Document there shall be substituted the following Appendix :—

"APPENDIX III

Method of Determining Correct Position of a Teacher on the Appropriate Salary Scale

GENERAL

1.—(1) A uniform incremental date of 1st September shall be adopted for teacher salary purposes. In the calculation of a teacher's salary on 1st September or at any time during a year beginning on that date incremental credit shall be given for reckonable service or experience up to and including the previous 31st August, except where otherwise provided in this appendix.

A teacher in continuous service throughout an incremental year but placed on a different scale during that year shall, subject to the maximum of his new scale, receive a complete increment on that scale at the next uniform incremental date.

(2) Incremental credit under the provisions of this document in respect of teaching and other experience shall not include any period:

(a) undertaken before the age of 18 years;

(b) of absence from teaching service without pay except:

(i) in so far as the teacher's occupation during such period may otherwise be acceptable under the provisions of this document;

(ii) that where a period of such absence in any year beginning on 1st September results, or would otherwise result, in a teacher's annual increment being reduced, the first fifteen days of such absence shall count for salary increment purposes. This provision shall not apply in respect of any absence before 1st April 1969.

(3) Aggregation for incremental purposes of periods of—

(a) full-time service of less than one year shall be in accordance with the following arrangements:

(i) the complete calendar months shall be totalled;

(ii) other periods shall be totalled in days and the result divided by 30; and

(iii) the quotient shall be taken as complete months to be added to (i) above, and the remainder shall be counted as one month, or shall not count, according as it is 15 days or over, or less than 15 days.

(b) service, other than a full-time appointment, rendered on or after 1st July 1967 shall be calculated in accordance with the proportion that the service bears to full-time service (e.g. one increment for two years' half-time service) subject to the condition that not more than one increment shall, in the aggregate, be given in respect of each year of a teacher's life whether for service by itself or together with other experience which can be counted for incremental purposes. Service rendered before 1st July 1967 shall continue to be counted as hitherto.

2. No increment shall be withheld in respect of any year of teaching service unless the service in that year has been declared unsatisfactory by the local education authority. In such a case, payment of the increment shall be delayed only during the following year unless the local education authority otherwise expressly determines.

3. Where a teacher's salary calculated in accordance with the other provisions of this Appendix is an exact incremental point on the relevant salary scale, the teacher shall be paid at that point. In other cases, the teacher shall be paid at the next half incremental point or the next full incremental point, whichever is the nearer above the said salary, except where that salary results from an increase under sub-paragraph 5(1)(b) below and is an exact half incremental point on the relevant salary scale.

4. It shall be an overriding provision of this Appendix that once a teacher's incremental position on a salary scale has been correctly determined in a year beginning on 1st September that position shall apply throughout the year during any period that the teacher is entitled to salary on the same scale and is not entitled to receive a higher salary under the provisions of this document.

5.—(1) Any qualified teacher who, subsequent to being placed on a scale under this document, for the first time obtains any of the qualifications or completes any of the courses satisfying the conditions set out in annex E or annex F to this Appendix shall have the salary payable to him from the first day of service after obtaining the qualification or completing the course, as the case may be:

(a) re-calculated in accordance with sub-paragraph 7(1)(a) below in the case of a teacher on scale 1; or

(b) increased by:

(i) £84, where the qualification or course satisfies the conditions set out in annex E;

(ii) £168, where the qualification or course satisfies the conditions set out in parts I and II of annex F;

(iii) £336, where the qualification or course satisfies the conditions set out in parts I and III of annex F and the teacher was formerly paid as a non-graduate, or £168 where the salary was formerly as a graduate,

in the case of a teacher on scale 2 or a higher scale and subject to the maximum of the scale not being exceeded.

(2) The provisions of paragraph 3 of this Appendix shall be applied to the salary as re-calculated or increased under the terms of sub-paragraph 5(1) above.

TEACHERS CONTINUING ON OR RE-ENTERING A SCALE PREVIOUSLY APPLICABLE

6.—(1) Subject to the provisions of section 19 of this document, a teacher who was in service on 31st August 1974 and continues on the same salary scale shall have his salary on that scale re-calculated by adding incremental credit for reckonable service on the relevant scale between 1st April 1974 and 31st August 1974 to the rate of salary payable to the teacher on 31st August 1974 under the provisions of this document as in operation on that date. The salary so determined shall, subject to the provisions of paragraph 3 above, apply from 1st September 1974 (see annex G to this appendix).

(2) A teacher who on or after 1st September 1974 re-enters a salary scale which corresponds to that on which he was paid at any time between 1st April 1971 and 31st August 1974 shall enter the appropriate scale set out in appendix I:

> (i) at the point corresponding to that applicable to him at the date of leaving the former post (based on service to that date and excluding any "London Area" or other above scale payments); or

> (ii) at the salary rate determined under paragraphs 7 or 8 below as appropriate,

whichever is the higher.

TEACHERS TO WHOM PARAGRAPH 6 DOES NOT APPLY OR HAS CEASED TO APPLY

Qualified Assistant Teachers, including Senior Teachers

7.—(1) A teacher, other than one to whom sub-paragraph 7(2) cr 7(3) below applies, who is placed on scale 1 on or after 1st September 1974 shall, subject to the maximum of the scale not being exceeded, receive salary calculated as follows:

> (*a*) the minimum of the scale to which shall be added:

>> (i) one increment where the teacher holds any of the qualifications, or has satisfactorily completed any of the courses, satisfying the conditions set out in annex E of this appendix; plus

>> (ii) two increments where the teacher is entitled to be classed as a graduate under the conditions set out in Parts I and II of annex F to this appendix, or four increments where the teacher is entitled to be classed as a good honours graduate under the conditions set out in Parts I and III of annex F; plus

>> (iii) incremental credit in respect of previous service or experience in accordance with paragraph 9 below and annexes A, B, C and D to this appendix.

> For the purposes of (i) and (ii) above increments shall be at the rate of £78 per annum where the relevant conditions were satisfied before 1st September 1974 and at the rate of £84 per annum where the conditions were satisfied on or after that date.

> (*b*) the rate determined in accordance with paragraph 12 below, where the teacher was placed on scale 1 following service on a higher scale under this document;

or

> (*c*) at the salary, excluding any "London Area" payment, payable to the teacher in his former post under the relevant salaries document as in operation from 1st September 1974 where the teacher has been appointed on transfer from teaching service in a maintained establishment for further education, a maintained farm institute or a college of education in England or Wales,

whichever is the highest applicable.

(2) A teacher who is a qualified teacher by virtue of sub-paragraphs (*f*), (*g*) or (*h*) of paragraph 2 of regulation 16 of the Schools Regulations 1959 and is placed on scale 1 shall enter the scale at the minimum, or such higher point as the local

education authority may determine to be appropriate having regard to his qualifications and experience and the salary on scale 1 of a teacher with similar qualifications and experience.

(3) A teacher who became a qualified teacher on or after 1st September 1968 by virtue of sub-paragraph (c) or (d) of paragraph 2 of regulation 16 of the Schools Regulations 1959 and is placed on scale 1 shall enter the scale:

(a) (i) at £1842 per annum, or

    (ii) at the incremental point on scale 1 immediately above his former salary as an unqualified teacher, exclusive of any allowances or additional payments other than a payment made under section 15(1)(iii) of this document immediately before becoming a qualified teacher,

whichever is the higher in the case of a teacher appointed as a qualified teacher for the first time on or after 1st September 1974.

(b) at the minimum to which shall be added the same number of increments, at the rates specified in sub-paragraph 9(1) below, as he was eligible to receive above the minimum of the scale for qualified teachers applicable to him at the date of leaving his former post in the case of a teacher who is re-appointed after a break in service.

8.—(1) A teacher who is placed on scale 2, 3, 4 or 5 or the Senior Teacher scale for the first time on or after 1st September 1974 shall, subject to the maximum of the scale not being exceeded, enter the appropriate scale:

(a) at the minimum;

or

(b) at the salary applicable to him on scale 1 under sub-paragraph 7(1)(a) above plus a promotion increase determined in accordance with sub-paragraph 8(2) below;

or

(c) at a rate determined in accordance with paragraph 12 where the teacher has been placed on the scale following service on another scale for qualified teachers under this document;

or

(d) at the salary, excluding any "London Area" payment, payable to the teacher in his former post under the relevant salaries document as in operation from 1st September 1974 where the teacher has been appointed on transfer from teaching service in a maintained establishment for further education, a maintained farm institute or a college of education in England or Wales,

whichever is the highest applicable.

(2) The promotion increase for qualified assistant teachers placed on scales 2, 3, 4 or 5 or the Senior Teacher scale shall be as follows:

| Promotion | | Increase |
From	To	
Scale 1	Scale 2	2 × £90
Scale 2	Scale 3	2 × £99
Scale 3	Scale 4	2 × £99
Scale 4	Scale 5	2 × £114
Scale 5	Senior Teacher	2 × £114

Where a teacher is placed on a scale higher than that next above the scale previously applicable to him the promotion increase shall be the sum of the increases that he would have received had he moved up one scale at a time, subject, at each stage, to the maximum of the scale. The provisions of paragraph 3 of this appendix shall not be applied at the intermediate stages but shall apply at the final stage in determining the teacher's commencing salary on the scale to which promoted.

9.—(1) Incremental credit allowed under the terms of annexes A, B, C and D to this appendix shall be calculated according to whether it is in respect of pre- or post-1st April 1971 experience and counted on the following basis:

(a) subject to paragraph 10 below, experience undertaken before 1st April 1971 shall be counted for increments as set out below:

> 1st increment ⎤
> 2nd increment ⎦ shall each be £39
>
> 3rd increment ⎤
> 4th increment ⎥
> 5th increment ⎥
> 6th increment ⎥
> 7th increment ⎬ shall each be £71
> 8th increment ⎥
> 9th increment ⎥
> 10th increment ⎦
>
> 11th increment ⎤
> 12th increment ⎬ shall each be £77
> 13th increment ⎦
> 14th (final) increment shall be £77

(b) experience undertaken on or after 1st April 1971, except as provided in sub-paragraph 9(2) below, shall count for increments on scale 1 according to the incremental pattern of that scale.

(2) For the purposes of sub-paragraph 9(1) above, a year of study, training or research or a period of gainful employment accepted for an increment under annex A or C to this appendix shall be regarded as pre-1st April 1971 experience where:—

(i) the year of study, training or research accepted for an increment commenced before 1st April 1971 but ended after that date;

(ii) in the case of pre-qualified employment, one half or more of that period accepted for an increment was before 1st April 1971.

10. Incremental credit otherwise payable to a qualified teacher on scale 1 shall be reduced by one increment in the case of a teacher who, under the provisions of the Burnham Reports in operation before 31st March 1963 received salary on the scale for two year trained teachers (Scale A), except that this provision shall not apply to a teacher who:

(i) satisfactorily completed a shortened course of initial training of less than three years but not less than one year's duration entered upon on or after 1st September 1960 under the provisions of regulation 11(1)(b) of the Training of Teachers (Local Education Authorities) Regulations 1959(a) as amended by the Training of Teachers (Local Education Authorities) Amending Regulations 1960(b), or the corresponding regulations in force from time to time, or

(ii) received or would have received Scale C, D or E under the provisions of the amended Burnham Primary and Secondary Schools Report 1961, or

(iii) after the age of 18 years, has undertaken and satisfactorily completed not less than three years full-time study, training or research, excluding any period spent in repetition or any period taken into account for incremental purposes under the provisions of annexes A or D to this appendix. For this purpose a year of study, training or research shall be regarded as being after the age of 18 where the student attained that age in the first term of the year; the Spring, Summer and Autumn terms being deemed to end on 30th April, 31st August and 31st December respectively.

Qualified Head and Deputy Head Teachers, including Second Masters/Mistresses

11.—(1) A head (or deputy head) teacher appointed in that capacity on or after 1st September 1974 or to a school in a different group, or on re-appointment follow-

(a) S.I. 1959/395 (1959 I, p. 1590).   (b) S.I. 1960/708 (1960 II, p. 1857).

ing a break in service as a head or deputy head teacher shall, subject to the maximum of the scale not being exceeded, enter the appropriate scale:

(*a*) at the minimum;

or

(*b*) at the salary applicable to him on scale 1 for qualified assistant teachers under sub-paragraph 7(1)(*a*) above plus a promotion increase. The promotion increase shall be that applicable under sub-paragraph 11(2) below, or the sum that the teacher would have received under sub-paragraph 8(2) of this appendix had he been placed on the highest assistant teacher scale appropriate to the particular school including the additional payment under section 11(*a*) if the school is a special school, whichever is the greater;

or

(*c*) at the rate determined in accordance with paragraph 12 below where the head (or deputy head) teacher has been placed on the head (or deputy head) teacher scale following service on another scale for qualified teachers under this document, plus £195 per annum where the appointment is to a special school and the previous service was not as head or deputy head of a special school;

or

(*d*) at the salary payable in the former post, excluding any "London Area" payment, together with the promotion increase prescribed in paragraph 11(2) below in the case of a head (or deputy head) teacher appointed or re-appointed on transfer from teaching service in a maintained establishment for further education, a maintained farm institute or a college of education in England or Wales;

whichever is the highest applicable, or

(*e*) in the case of a teacher appointed as head or deputy head teacher on transfer from service other than from maintained schools or educational establishments and where the salary calculated under sub-paragraph 11(1)(*a*) or 11(1)(*b*) above is not considered adequate, at such point on the scale applicable as the local education authority deem appropriate having regard to the provisions of sub-paragraph 11(1)(*d*) above.

(2) The promotion increase for head and deputy head teachers shall be as follows:—

Promotion to Group	Increase	
	Head	Deputy Head
1–3 2(S)–3(S)	2 × £90	2 × £90
4–11 4(S)–8(S)	2 × £100·50	2 × £100·50
9(S)	2 × £105	2 × £100·50
12 or above	2 × £126	2 × £100·50

MOVEMENT BETWEEN SCALES

12.—(1) Movement between one qualified teacher scale and another shall be deemed for salary purposes to be a "promotion" or "demotion", as the case may be, according as the maximum of the new scale to which the teacher is transferred is greater or less than the maximum of the scale previously applicable in the former post by £100 or more.

(2) A teacher who has been so "promoted" or "demoted" may be paid in accordance with the following arrangements provided that the maximum of the scale to which he is transferred is not exceeded:

(i) a teacher who is "promoted" from one assistant teacher scale to another or to the Senior Teacher scale may be paid the salary applicable in the former post plus a promotion increase determined in accordance with sub-paragraph 8(2) above;

(ii) a teacher who is "promoted" to an assistant teacher scale or the Senior Teacher scale from a head or deputy head teacher scale may be paid the salary applicable in the former post plus an amount equivalent to two increments at the rates set out in sub-paragraph 8(2) above according to the scale to which promoted;

(iii) a head or deputy head teacher who is "promoted" in accordance with sub-paragraph 12(1) above may be paid the salary applicable in the former post plus the promotion increase specified in sub-paragraph 11(2) above;

(iv) a teacher who is "demoted" from the Senior Teacher scale or an assistant teacher scale to another assistant teacher scale may be paid the salary applicable in the former post less an amount equivalent to two increments on the scale previously applicable and two increments on each of any intervening scales. For this purpose increments on the scales shall be deemed to be at the rates set out in sub-paragraph 8(2) above;

(v) a teacher who is "demoted" to an assistant teacher scale or the Senior Teacher scale from a head or deputy head teacher scale may be paid the salary applicable in the former post less an amount equivalent to two increments at the rates set out in sub-paragraph 11(2) above according to the head or deputy head teacher scale previously applicable;

(vi) a teacher who is "demoted" to a head or deputy head teacher post in accordance with sub-paragraph 12(1) above may be paid the salary applicable to him in his former post less an amount equivalent to two increments on the scale previously applicable. For this purpose increments on the scale shall be deemed to be at the rates set out in sub-paragraph 8(2) or 11(2) above, according to the scale previously applicable,

subject, in the case of a teacher to whom (iv), (v) or (vi) above applies and who is reverting to a scale on which he previously received salary, that he should not receive less than he would have received had he remained on that scale.

(3) A teacher who moves from one scale to another, where the difference in the maxima of the scales is £99 or less, may be transferred at the salary applicable to him in his former post.

(4) For the purposes of this paragraph the salary applicable in the former post shall be deemed to be the rate of salary (excluding any additional payments under sections 11, 12(1), 13 and 14(1) of this document) payable to the teacher on the former scale as at the date of promotion or demotion, as the case may be.

(5) A head (or deputy head) teacher of a special school who while serving in that capacity becomes a qualified teacher by virtue of sub-paragraph (f), (g) or (h) of paragraph (2) of regulation 16 of the Schools Regulations 1959 shall be transferred from the unqualified head (or deputy head) teacher scale to the qualified head (or deputy head) teacher scale in the same group at the corresponding point.

Unqualified Teachers
Assistant Teachers

13.—(1) An unqualified teacher, other than one to whom sub-paragraph 13(2) below applies, shall enter the scale (A or B) applicable to him under sub-section 8(1)(a) of this document at the minimum to which shall be added, up to the maximum, incremental credit in respect of previous service or experience in accordance with annexes B and D to this appendix.

(2) An unqualified teacher:

(i) whose employment is authorised by regulation 16A of the Handicapped Pupils and Special Schools Regulations 1959 and who is placed on scale C under the provisions of sub-section 8(1)(a) of this document; or

(ii) who holds the Diploma in the Teaching of Mentally Handicapped Children or the Declaration of Recognition of Experience awarded by the National Council for the Training of Mentally Handicapped Children and is placed on scale 1 under the provisions of sub-section 8(2)(a) of this document;

shall enter the appropriate scale at the minimum or such higher point as the local education authority may determine to be appropriate having regard to his qualifications and experience and the salaries of teachers having similar qualifications and experience.

(3) An unqualified teacher who holds either of the qualifications described in sub-paragraph 13(2)(ii) above and who is placed on scale 2, 3, 4 or 5 under the provisions of sub-section 8(2)(a) of this document shall enter the appropriate scale at a point determined in accordance with the procedure set out in sub-paragraph 8(1) of this appendix.

Head and Deputy Head Teachers

14. An unqualified head (or deputy head) teacher of a special school who holds either of the qualifications described in sub-paragraph 13(2)(ii) of this appendix shall enter the appropriate scale applicable to him under this document at a point determined in accordance with the procedure set out in paragraph 11 of this appendix."

2. In Annex E to Appendix III to the Document (which sets out the qualifications and/or courses which entitle a qualified teacher to additional payment) where there occurs a reference to "a payment of £78" there shall be substituted a reference to "the payment specified in Appendix III."

3. To Appendix III of the Document the following Annex shall be added after Annex F:—

"ANNEX G to APPENDIX III

ABOLITION OF TWELFTHS OF INCREMENTS

TABLE OF ADJUSTMENTS ON 1ST SEPTEMBER 1974

Salary Point in Twelfths on 1st April, 1974	Salary point on 31st August 1974	Further Adjustment	Rounded up salary point at 1st September 1974
$\frac{1}{12}$	$+ \frac{5}{12} = \frac{6}{12}$	$+ \frac{6}{12}$ to	Whole incremental point
$\frac{2}{12}$	$+ \frac{5}{12} = \frac{7}{12}$	$+ \frac{5}{12}$ to	Whole incremental point
$\frac{3}{12}$	$+ \frac{5}{12} = \frac{8}{12}$	$+ \frac{4}{12}$ to	Whole incremental point
$\frac{4}{12}$	$+ \frac{5}{12} = \frac{9}{12}$	$+ \frac{3}{12}$ to	Whole incremental point
$\frac{5}{12}$	$+ \frac{5}{12} = \frac{10}{12}$	$+ \frac{2}{12}$ to	Whole incremental point
$\frac{6}{12}$	$+ \frac{5}{12} = \frac{11}{12}$	$+ \frac{1}{12}$ to	Whole incremental point
$\frac{7}{12}$	$+ \frac{5}{12} = 1$	$-$ to	Whole incremental point
$\frac{8}{12}$	$+ \frac{5}{12} = 1\frac{1}{12}$	$+ \frac{5}{12}$ to	Half incremental point
$\frac{9}{12}$	$+ \frac{5}{12} = 1\frac{2}{12}$	$+ \frac{4}{12}$ to	Half incremental point
$\frac{10}{12}$	$+ \frac{5}{12} = 1\frac{3}{12}$	$+ \frac{3}{12}$ to	Half incremental point
$\frac{11}{12}$	$+ \frac{5}{12} = 1\frac{4}{12}$	$+ \frac{2}{12}$ to	Half incremental point
No Twelfths	$+ \frac{5}{12} = \frac{5}{12}$	$+ \frac{1}{12}$ to	Half incremental point

N.B.—This table only refers to teachers in service on 1st April 1974, who continue in service on the same scale until 1st September 1974.

Teachers placed on a scale between 1st April 1974 and 31st August 1974 will have their salaries calculated from the date of such placing, and then will have their salaries rounded up according to the number of twelfths of increments to which they are entitled on 31st August 1974."

Given under the Official Seal of the Secretary of State for Education and Science on 25th April 1974.

(L.S.)

Reginald E. Prentice,
Secretary of State for Education
and Science.

EXPLANATORY NOTE

(This Note is not part of the Order.)

This Order amends the scales and other provisions relating to the remuneration of teachers in primary and secondary schools maintained by local education authorities, set out in a document published by Her Majesty's Stationery Office on 24th May 1973 under the title "SCALES OF SALARIES FOR TEACHERS IN PRIMARY AND SECONDARY SCHOOLS, ENGLAND AND WALES, 1973", which was brought into operation by the Remuneration of Teachers (Primary and Secondary Schools) Order 1973. The amendments specified in Schedule 1 and Schedule 2 to the Order take effect retrospectively on 1st April 1973 and 1st April 1974 respectively, by virtue of section 7(3) of the Remuneration of Teachers Act 1965.

STATUTORY INSTRUMENTS

1974 No. 750

REPRESENTATION OF THE PEOPLE
London Borough Councillors Order 1974

Made - - -	*25th April* 1974
Laid before Parliament	*29th April* 1974
Coming into Operation	*1st May* 1974

In exercise of the powers conferred upon me by section 254 of the Local Government Act 1972(**a**), I hereby make the following Order: —

1.—(1) This Order may be cited as the London Borough Councillors Order 1974.

(2) This Order shall come into operation on 1st May 1974.

2. The Interpretation Act 1889(**b**) shall apply to the interpretation of this Order as it applies to the interpretation of an Act of Parliament.

3. A London borough councillor in office on 1st May 1974 shall, unless he resigns his office or it otherwise becomes vacant, continue in office until the fourth day after the day of election on which his successor is elected.

Roy Jenkins,
One of Her Majesty's Principal
Secretaries of State.

Home Office,
  Whitehall.
25th April 1974.

EXPLANATORY NOTE
(This Note is not part of the Order.)

The provisions of the London Government Act 1963 (c.33) governing the retirement from office of London borough councillors who are at present in office were repealed by the Local Government Act 1972. This Order provides that they will continue in office until their successors come into office after the forthcoming elections.

(**a**) 1972 c. 70.   (**b**) 1889 c. 63.

STATUTORY INSTRUMENTS

1974 No. 752

DEFENCE

The Rules of Procedure (Air Force) (Amendment) Rules 1974

Made - - -	26th April 1974
Laid before Parliament	8th May 1974
Coming into Operation	29th May 1974

The Secretary of State in exercise of the powers conferred upon him by sections 103, 104, 105 and 106 of the Air Force Act 1955(a) and of all other powers enabling him in that behalf, hereby makes the following Rules:—

Citation and commencement

1. These Rules may be cited as the Rules of Procedure (Air Force) (Amendment) Rules 1974 and shall come into operation on 29th May 1974.

Interpretation

2. The Interpretation Act 1889(b) shall apply to the interpretation of these Rules as it applies to an Act of Parliament.

Amendments to the Rules of Procedure (Air Force) 1972(c)

3.—(1) The Rules of Procedure (Air Force) 1972 shall be amended in accordance with the following provisions of this Rule.

(2) In Rule 2, for the definition of "sexual offence" there shall be substituted the words:—

"means in relation to an offence against section 70 of the Act any offence under the Sexual Offences Act 1956(d) or the Indecency with Children Act 1960(e) or any attempt to commit such an offence and shall include any offence of an indecent or unnatural kind under section 66 of the Act or any attempt to commit such offence under section 68 of the Act or aiding, abetting, counselling, procuring or inciting the commission of such an offence under section 68A of the Act or an offence of an indecent kind under section 69 of the Act;"

(3) In paragraph 4 of Form (9) in the Fourth Schedule (Service Record of Accused) for the words "under the age of 16 years" there shall be substituted the words "dependent upon him".

Roy Mason,
One of Her Majesty's Principal
Secretaries of State.

Dated 26th April 1974.

(a) 1955 c. 19.   (b) 1889 c. 63.
(c) S.I. 1972/419 (1972 I, p. 1506).   (d) 1956 c. 69.
(e) 1960 c. 33.

EXPLANATORY NOTE

(This Note is not part of the Rules.)

These Rules amend the Rules of Procedure (Air Force) 1972 by revising the definition of sexual offence and by introducing a wider category of children to be referred to in the service record of accused.

STATUTORY INSTRUMENTS

1974 No. 754

WAGES COUNCILS

The Wages Regulation (Wholesale Mantle and Costume) Order 1974

Made - - -	*26th April* 1974
Coming into Operation	*24th May* 1974

Whereas the Secretary of State has received from the Wholesale Mantle and Costume Wages Council (Great Britain) the wages regulation proposals set out in the Schedule hereto ;

Now, therefore, the Secretary of State in exercise of powers conferred by section 11 of the Wages Councils Act 1959(a), as modified by Article 2 of the Counter-Inflation (Modification of Wages Councils Act 1959) Order 1973(b), and now vested in him(c), and of all other powers enabling him in that behalf, hereby makes the following Order:—

1. This Order may be cited as the Wages Regulation (Wholesale Mantle and Costume) Order 1974.

2.—(1) In this Order the expression "the specified date" means the 24th May 1974, provided that where, as respects any worker who is paid wages at intervals not exceeding seven days, that date does not correspond with the beginning of the period for which the wages are paid, the expression "the specified date" means, as respects that worker, the beginning of the next such period following that date.

(2) The Interpretation Act 1889(d) shall apply to the interpretation of this Order as it applies to the interpretation of an Act of Parliament and as if this Order and the Order hereby revoked were Acts of Parliament.

3. The wages regulation proposals set out in the Schedule hereto shall have effect as from the specified date and as from that date the Wages Regulation (Wholesale Mantle and Costume) Order 1973(e) shall cease to have effect.

Signed by order of the Secretary of State.

26th April 1974.

W. H. Marsh,
Assistant Secretary,
Department of Employment.

SCHEDULE
Article 3

The following minimum remuneration shall be substituted for the statutory minimum remuneration fixed by the Wages Regulation (Wholesale Mantle and Costume) Order 1973 (Order W.M. (90)).

(a) 1959 c. 69.
(b) S.I. 1973/661 (1973 I, p. 2141).
(c) S.I. 1959/1769, 1968/729 (1959 I, p. 1795; 1968 II, p. 2108).
(d) 1889 c. 63.
(e) S.I. 1973/190 (1973 I, p. 762).

STATUTORY MINIMUM REMUNERATION

PART I

GENERAL

1. The minimum remuneration payable to a worker to whom this Schedule applies for all work except work to which a minimum overtime rate applies under Part IV of this Schedule is:—

(1) in the case of a time worker, the general minimum time rate payable to the worker under Part II or Part III of this Schedule;

(2) in the case of a worker employed on piece work, piece rates each of which would yield, in the circumstances of the case, to an ordinary worker at least the same amount of money as the general minimum time rate otherwise applicable to the worker under Part II or Part III of this Schedule.

PART II

MALE WORKERS

GENERAL MINIMUM TIME RATES

2. Subject to the provisions of this Schedule, the general minimum time rates payable to male workers with the qualifications specified in Column 2 of the next following Table when employed on time work are those set out in Column 3 of the said Table.

Column 1	Column 2	Column 3
Class of Worker	Qualifying Period of Employment or Age of Worker	General Minimum Time Rates
		Per Hour
		p
(1) MEASURE CUTTER, that is to say, a person employed in any process of measure cutting who is capable of taking a complete set of measures and of cutting all garments for a female person from patterns.	Not less than three years' employment after the age of 18 years as a measure cutter, but excluding designing.	47·58

(2) CUTTER or TRIMMER, that is to say, a person substantially employed in one or more of the following processes:— (a) marking-in or marking-up cloth or linings or other materials; (b) laying-up, hooking-up or folding cloth or linings or other materials; (c) cutting cloth or linings or other materials or cutting out patterns of any description to be used afterwards for the cutting out of garments; and (d) dividing (that is to say, the process ordinarily carried on by cutters or their assistants of dividing, paring or separating the parts of garments after being cut and of assembling them into suitable bundles for making up), other than a measure cutter to whom the minimum rates specified in (1) of this Table apply or a knife cutter or knifeman.	Not less than three years' employment after the age of 18 years as a cutter of any of the classes specified in Column 1 or as a knifeman.	46·75
(3) KNIFE CUTTER or KNIFEMAN, that is to say, a person wholly or mainly employed on band, electric or hand-knife processes.	Not less than three years' employment after the age of 18 years as a cutter of any of the classes specified in Column 1 or as a knifeman.	46·75
(4) FITTER-UP, that is to say, a person employed in fitting-up (which is a process between that of cutting and that of sewing, baisting or machining, and which consists of preparing or fitting accurately the various parts of the garments before being baisted, sewn or machined, such work of preparing or fitting being always done by shears or knives or other cutting appliances—sewing, baisting or machining forming no part or process of fitting-up).	Not less than three years' employment after the age of 18 years as a fitter-up or tailor.	46·75
(5) TAILOR, that is to say, a person employed in sewing by hand in a process of:— (a) making a garment or portion of a garment, or (b) altering, repairing, renovating or re-making a garment or portion of a garment, when such process is carried out in a factory.	Not less than three years' employment after the age of 18 years as a tailor.	47·58

Column 1	Column 2	Column 3	
		General Minimum Time Rates	
Class of Worker	Qualifying Period of Employment or Age of Worker	Per Hour	
			p
(6) PRESSER, that is to say, a person employed in pressing-off by hand or by machine.	Not less than three years' employment after the age of 18 years in the processes of pressing-off or under-pressing.	46·75	
(7) MACHINIST, that is to say, a person employed in machining other than as a plain machinist and capable of machining any one garment or portion of a garment.	Not less than three years' employment after the age of 18 years as a machinist.	46·75	
(8) PASSER, that is to say, a person employed in examining garments, either in the course of being made up or upon completion.	Not less than three years' employment after the age of 18 years as a passer or tailor.	46·75	
(9) UNDER-PRESSER, that is to say, a person employed in pressing processes other than pressing-off.	Not less than three years' employment after the age of 18 years as an under-presser or presser.	45·29	
(10) PLAIN MACHINIST, that is to say, a person employed in the process of making up plain sleeves, facings, linings, inside pockets, quilting or padding.	Not less than three years' employment after the age of 18 years as a plain machinist or machinist.	45·29	
(11) WAREHOUSEMAN, that is to say, a person employed, wholly or mainly, upon one or more of the operations of assembling, keeping, storing and distributing stock, and cutting off lengths of cloth, linings or other materials.	Not less than three years' employment as a warehouseman after the age of 18 years.	45·92	
(12) PACKER, that is to say, a person employed, wholly or mainly, in packing goods and materials.	Not less than three years' employment as a packer after the age of 18 years.	45·92	

(13) LEARNERS (as defined in paragraph 10)

Aged 21 years or over ...	44·04
" 20 and under 21 years	40·59
" 19 " " 20 "	38·77
" 18 " " 19 "	34·80
" 17 " " 18 "	29·28
" under 17 years ...	25·87

Provided that the general minimum time rate payable during his first year's employment to a learner who enters or has entered the trade for the first time at or over the age of 19 years shall be ...

(a) Aged under 21 years ...	34·80
(b) " 21 years or over ...	38·77

PART III

FEMALE WORKERS

GENERAL MINIMUM TIME RATES

3. Subject to the provisions of this Schedule, the general minimum time rates payable to female workers are as follows:—

(1) LEARNERS (as defined in paragraph 10) during the following periods of employment in the trade—

	During 1st six months	During 2nd six months	During 2nd Year
	Per Hour	Per Hour	Per Hour
	p	p	p
Entering the trade:			
Aged 15 and under 16 years ...	—	25·71	32·01
" 16 " 17 " ...	23·79	27·63	33·93
" 17 " 18 " ...	25·71	29·54	33·93
" 18 years and over...	31·15	33·39	38·83

(2) ALL OTHER WORKERS ...   40·83 p per hour

Part IV

OVERTIME AND WAITING TIME

ALL WORKERS OTHER THAN ALTERATION HANDS WHO ARE NORMALLY REQUIRED TO ATTEND ON 6 DAYS IN THE WEEK

NORMAL NUMBER OF HOURS

4. Subject to the provisions of this Part of this Schedule, the minimum overtime rates set out in paragraph 5 are payable to workers other than alteration hands referred to in paragraphs 6 and 7 in respect of any time worked—

(1) in excess of the hours following, that is to say,

(a) in any week	40 hours
(b) on any day other than a Saturday, Sunday or customary holiday—	
where the normal working hours exceed 8½ ... ... or	9 hours
where the normal working hours are more than 8 but not more than 8½ ... ... or	8½ hours
where the normal working hours are not more than 8 ...	8 hours

(2) on a Saturday, Sunday or customary holiday.

MINIMUM OVERTIME RATES

5.—(1) Minimum overtime rates are payable to a worker other than an alteration hand referred to in paragraphs 6 and 7 as follows:—

(a) on any day other than a Sunday or customary holiday—

(i) for the first 2 hours of overtime worked	time-and-a-quarter
(ii) for the next 2 hours	time-and-a-half
(iii) thereafter	double time

(b) on a Sunday or customary holiday—

for all time worked ... ... double time

Provided that where it is the practice in a Jewish undertaking for the employer to require attendance on Sunday instead of Saturday the provisions of this paragraph shall apply as if in such provisions the word "Saturday" were substituted for "Sunday", except where such substitution is unlawful.

(c) in any week, exclusive of any time in respect of which any minimum overtime rate is payable under the foregoing provisions of this sub-paragraph—

for all time worked in excess of 40 hours ... ... time-and-a-quarter

(2) The minimum overtime rates set out in sub-paragraph (1)(a) or (b) of this paragraph are payable in any week whether or not the minimum overtime rate set out in sub-paragraph (1)(c) is also payable.

ALTERATION HANDS WHO ARE NORMALLY REQUIRED TO ATTEND ON 6 DAYS IN THE WEEK

NORMAL NUMBER OF HOURS

6. Subject to the provisions of this Part of this Schedule, the minimum overtime rates set out in paragraph 7 are payable to workers who are normally required to attend on 6 days in the week and who are employed solely in the alteration (including repairing and renovating) of any of the garments specified in inclusion (1) in paragraph 12 and who are employed in or about a shop engaged in the retail sale of the garments so specified in respect of any time worked—

(1) in excess of the hours following, that is to say,

(a) in any week	40 hours
(b) on any day other than a Saturday, Sunday or customary holiday	8 hours
(c) on a Saturday, not being a customary holiday	4 hours

(2) on a Sunday or customary holiday.

MINIMUM OVERTIME RATES

7.—(1) Minimum overtime rates are payable to a worker who is normally required to attend on 6 days in the week and who is employed solely in the alteration (including repairing and renovating) of any of the garments specified in inclusion (1) in paragraph 12 and who is employed in or about a shop engaged in the retail sale of the garments so specified as follows:—

(a) on any day other than a Saturday, Sunday or customary holiday—

     (i) for the first 2 hours worked in excess of 8 hours   ...   time-and-a-quarter

     (ii) for the next 2 hours   ...   .   time-and-a-half

     (iii) thereafter...   ...   .   double time

(b) on a Saturday, not being a customary holiday—

     (i) for the first 4 hours worked in excess of 4 hours   ...   time-and-a-half

     (ii) thereafter...   ...   .   double time

(c) on a Sunday or customary holiday—

     for all time worked   ...   .   double time

(d) in any week, exclusive of any time in respect of which any minimum overtime rate is payable under the foregoing provisions of this sub-paragraph—

     for all time worked in excess of 40 hours ...   .   time-and-a-quarter

(2) The minimum overtime rates set out in sub-paragraph (1)(a), (b) or (c) of this paragraph are payable in any week whether or not the minimum overtime rate set out in sub-paragraph (1)(d) is also payable.

(3) Where the employer normally requires the worker's attendance on Sunday and not on Saturday, for the purposes of this Part of this Schedule (except where such attendance is unlawful) Saturday shall be treated as a Sunday and, subject to the provisions of sub-paragraph (4) of this paragraph, Sunday shall be treated as a Saturday.

(4) Where an ordinary week-day is substituted for Saturday or, in a case where the provisions of sub-paragraph (3) of this paragraph apply, for Sunday, as the worker's weekly short day, for the purposes of this Part of this Schedule (except where such substitution is unlawful) that ordinary week-day shall be treated as a Saturday, and Saturday or Sunday, as the case may be, shall be treated as an ordinary week-day.

8. In this Part of this Schedule—

(1) The expression "customary holiday" means—

     (a) (i) In England and Wales—

         Christmas Day; 26th December if it be not a Sunday; 27th December in a year when 25th or 26th December is a Sunday; Good Friday; Easter Monday; the last Monday in May; the last Monday in August (or, where another day is substituted for any of the above days by national proclamation, that day); and one other day (being a day of the week on which the worker normally works for the employer) in the course of a calendar year, to be fixed by the employer and notified to the worker not less than three weeks before the holiday;

     (ii) In Scotland—

         New Year's Day, if it be not a Sunday or, if it be a Sunday, 2nd January;
         the local Spring holiday;
         the local Autumn holiday;

and four other days (being days of the week on which the worker normally works for the employer) in the course of a calendar year, to be fixed by the employer and notified to the worker not less than three weeks before the holiday; or

(b) in the case of each of the said days a day substituted by the employer therefor, being a day recognised by local custom as a day of holiday in substitution for the said day.

(2) The expressions "time-and-a-quarter", "time-and-a-half" and "double time" mean respectively—

(a) in the case of a time worker, one and a quarter times, one and a half times and twice the general minimum time rate otherwise payable to the worker;

(b) in the case of a worker who is employed on piece work,

(i) a time rate equal respectively to one quarter, one half and the whole of the general minimum time rate which would be payable if the worker were a time worker and a minimum overtime rate did not apply and in addition thereto,

(ii) the piece rates otherwise payable to the worker under paragraph 1(2).

WAITING TIME

9.—(1) A worker is entitled to payment of the minimum remuneration specified in this Schedule for all time during which he is present on the premises of his employer unless he is present thereon in any of the following circumstances:—

(a) without the employer's consent, express or implied;

(b) for some purpose unconnected with his work and other than that of waiting for work to be given to him to perform;

(c) by reason only of the fact that he is resident thereon;

(d) during normal meal times in a room or place in which no work is being done and he is not waiting for work to be given to him to perform.

(2) The minimum remuneration payable under sub-paragraph (1) of this paragraph to a piece worker when not engaged on piece work is that which would be payable if he were a time worker.

PART V

INTERPRETATION

10. In this Schedule—

(1) A LEARNER is a worker who:—

(a) is employed during the whole or a substantial part of his time in learning any branch or process of the trade by an employer who provides him with reasonable facilities for such learning; and

(b) does not work in a room used for dwelling purposes, except where he is in the employment of his parent or guardian.

(2) "THE TRADE" means the trade of wholesale mantle and costume making as specified in paragraph 12.

RECKONING OF EMPLOYMENT

11. For the purpose of determining whether a worker has completed any period of employment specified in paragraph 2 or paragraph 3, there shall be taken into account—

(1) any such employment as a worker in relation to whom there operated one or more of the following Wages Councils (or of the Trade Boards which respectively

preceded them), that is to say, the Wholesale Mantle and Costume Wages Council (Great Britain), the Retail Bespoke Tailoring Wages Councils for England and Wales and for Scotland and the Readymade and Wholesale Bespoke Tailoring Wages Council (Great Britain) and

(2) in the case of a male worker employed as a cutter of any description or as a knifeman any such employment in the rubberised waterproof trade.

APPLICABILITY OF STATUTORY MINIMUM REMUNERATION

12. This Schedule applies to workers in relation to whom the Wholesale Mantle and Costume Wages Council (Great Britain) operates, that is to say, workers employed in Great Britain in wholesale mantle and costume making as specified in the Regulations made by the Minister of Labour and dated 20th November 1919, with respect to the constitution and proceedings of the Trade Board for the Wholesale Mantle and Costume Trade (Great Britain)(a), namely:—

"Women's, girls' and children's ready-made and wholesale bespoke tailoring, and all women's, girls' and children's retail bespoke tailoring carried on in a factory where garments are made up for three or more retail establishments, and any other branch of women's, girls' and children's tailoring which is not included within the scope of the Trade Boards (Tailoring) Order 1919(b),

including:—

(1) All operations and processes of cutting, making or finishing by hand or machine of coats, costumes, tailored skirts, coat-frocks, mantles, service clothing or similar garments made by tailoring processes;

(2)(a) The altering, repairing, renovating or remaking of any of the above-mentioned tailored garments, except where included within the scope of the Retail Bespoke Tailoring Trade Board;

(b) The cleaning of such garments where carried out in association with or in conjunction with the altering, repairing, renovating or remaking of the garments;

(3) The lining with fur of any of the above-mentioned garments where carried out in association with or in conjunction with the making of such garments;

(4)(a) All processes of embroidery or decorative needlework where carried on in association with or in conjunction with the making, altering, repairing, renovating or remaking of any of the above-mentioned tailored garments other than hand-embroidery or hand-drawn thread work on garments made of linen or cotton or of mixed linen and cotton;

(b) The following processes if done by machine, namely, thread-drawing, thread clipping, top-sewing, scalloping, nickelling and paring;

(5) Warehousing, packing and all other operations incidental to or appertaining to any of the above-mentioned branches of tailoring,

but excluding:—

(1) Those branches of women's or girls' bespoke tailoring, and all operations or processes covered by the Trade Boards (Tailoring) Order 1919;

(2) The making of head-gear;

(3) The making of rubberised or oilskin garments;

(4) Warehousing, packing and other similar operations carried on in shops mainly engaged in the retail distribution of articles of any description that are not made on the premises."

(a) S.R. & O. 1919/2218 (1919 II, p. 576).   (b) S.R. & O. 1919/1201 (1919 II, p. 528).

EXPLANATORY NOTE

(This Note is not part of the Order.)

This Order, which has effect from 24th May 1974, sets out the increased statutory minimum remuneration payable to workers in relation to whom the Wholesale Mantle and Costume Wages Council (Great Britain) operates, in substitution for that fixed by the Wages Regulation (Wholesale Mantle and Costume) Order 1973 (Order W.M. (90)), which Order is revoked.

New provisions are printed in italics.

STATUTORY INSTRUMENTS

1974 No. 755

WAGES COUNCILS

The Wages Regulation (Wholesale Mantle and Costume) (Holidays) Order 1974

Made - - - -	26*th April* 1974
Coming into Operation	24*th May* 1974

Whereas the Secretary of State has received from the Wholesale Mantle and Costume Wages Council (Great Britain) the wages regulation proposals set out in the Schedule hereto;

Now, therefore, the Secretary of State in exercise of powers conferred by section 11 of the Wages Councils Act 1959(a), as modified by Article 2 of the Counter-Inflation (Modification of Wages Councils Act 1959) Order 1973(b), and now vested in him(c), and of all other powers enabling him in that behalf, hereby makes the following Order:—

1. This Order may be cited as the Wages Regulation (Wholesale Mantle and Costume) (Holidays) Order 1974.

2.—(1) In this Order the expression "the specified date" means the 24th May 1974, provided that where, as respects any worker who is paid wages at intervals not exceeding seven days, that date does not correspond with the beginning of the period for which the wages are paid, the expression "the specified date" means, as respects that worker, the beginning of the next such period following that date.

(2) The Interpretation Act 1889(d) shall apply to the interpretation of this Order as it applies to the interpretation of an Act of Parliament and as if this Order and the Order hereby revoked were Acts of Parliament.

3. The wages regulation proposals set out in the Schedule hereto shall have effect as from the specified date and as from that date the Wages Regulation (Wholesale Mantle and Costume) (Holidays) Order 1973(e) shall cease to have effect.

Signed by order of the Secretary of State.
26th April 1974.

W. H. Marsh,
Assistant Secretary,
Department of Employment.

(a) 1959 c. 69. (b) S.I. 1973/661 (1973 I, p. 2141).
(c) S.I. 1959/1769, 1968/729 (1959 I, p. 1795; 1968 II, p. 2108).
(d) 1889 c. 63. (e) S.I. 1973/191 (1973 I, p. 773).

Article 3   SCHEDULE

HOLIDAYS AND HOLIDAY REMUNERATION

The following provisions as to holidays and holiday remuneration shall be substituted for the provisions as to holidays and holiday remuneration set out in the Wages Regulation (Wholesale Mantle and Costume) (Holidays) Order 1973 (Order W.M. (91)).

PART I

APPLICATION

1.—(1) This Schedule applies to every worker (other than a homeworker) for whom statutory minimum remuneration has been fixed.

(2) For the purposes of this Schedule a homeworker is a worker who works in his own home or in any other place not under the control or management of the employer.

PART II

CUSTOMARY HOLIDAYS

2.—(1) An employer shall allow to every worker in his employment to whom this Schedule applies a holiday (hereinafter referred to as a "customary holiday") in each year on the days specified in the following sub-paragraph, provided that the worker has been in his employment for a period of not less than six weeks immediately preceding the customary holiday and has worked for the employer during the whole or part of that period and is in his employment on the day of the customary holiday.

(2) The said customary holidays are:—

(a) (i) in England and Wales—

Christmas Day; 26th December if it be not a Sunday; 27th December in a year when 25th or 26th December is a Sunday; Good Friday; Easter Monday; the last Monday in May; the last Monday in August (or, where another day is substituted for any of the above days by national proclamation, that day); and one other day (being a day of the week on which the worker normally works for the employer) in the course of a calendar year, to be fixed by the employer and notified to the worker not less than three weeks before the holiday;

(ii) in Scotland—

New Year's Day, if it be not a Sunday or, if it be a Sunday, 2nd January;

the local Spring holiday;

the local Autumn holiday; and

four other days (being days of the week on which the worker normally works for the employer) in the course of a calendar year, to be fixed by the employer and notified to the worker not less than three weeks before the holiday;

or (b) in the case of each of the said days a day substituted by the employer therefor, being a day recognised by local custom as a day of holiday in substitution for the said day.

(3) Notwithstanding the preceding provisions of this paragraph, an employer may (except where in the case of a woman or young person such a requirement would be unlawful) require a worker who is otherwise entitled to any customary holiday under the foregoing provisions of this Schedule to work thereon and, in lieu of any

such holiday on which he so works for the employer, the worker shall be entitled to be allowed a day's holiday (hereinafter referred to as a "holiday in lieu of a customary holiday") on a week-day within the period of four weeks next ensuing.

(4) A worker who is required to work on a customary holiday shall be paid:—

> (*a*) for all time worked thereon at the minimum rate then appropriate to the worker for work on a customary holiday; and

> (*b*) in respect of the holiday in lieu of the customary holiday, holiday remuneration in accordance with paragraph 6.

PART III

ANNUAL HOLIDAY

3.—(1) Subject to the provisions of this paragraph and of paragraph 4, in addition to the holidays specified in Part II of this Schedule, an employer shall between the date on which the provisions of this Schedule become effective and 30th September 1974 and between 6th April and 30th September in each succeeding year, allow a holiday (hereinafter referred to as an "annual holiday") to every worker in his employment to whom this Schedule applies, who has been employed by him during the 12 months immediately preceding the commencement of the holiday season in that year for any of the periods of employment (calculated in accordance with the provisions of paragraph 10) specified in the following table, and the duration of the annual holiday shall in the case of each such worker be related to that period as follows:—

Workers with a normal working week of 6 days		Workers with a normal working week of 5 days or less	
Period of employment	Duration of annual holiday	Period of employment	Duration of annual holiday
At least 48 weeks	20 *days*	At least 48 weeks	17 *days*
,, ,, 46 ,, ...	19 ,,	,, ,, 46 ,, ...	16 ,,
,, ,, 44 ,, ...	18 ,,	,, ,, 44 ,, ...	15 ,,
,, ,, 42 ,, ...	17 ,,	,, ,, 42 ,, ...	14 ,,
,, ,, 40 ,, ...	16 ,,	,, ,, 40 ,, ...	13 ,,
,, ,, 38 ,, ...	14 ,,	*n* ,, 38 ,, ...	12 ,,
,, ,, 36 ,, ...	13 ,,	,, ,, 36 ,, ...	11 ,,
,, ,, 34 ,, ...	12 ,,	,, ,, 33 ,, ...	10 ,,
,, ,, 32 ,, ...	11 ,,	,, ,, 30 ,, ...	9 ,,
,, ,, 30 ,, ...	10 ,,	,, ,, 27 ,, ...	8 ,,
,, ,, 28 ,, ...	9 ,,	,, ,, 24 ,, ...	7 ,,
,, ,, 25 ,, ...	8 ,,	,, ,, 21 ,, ...	6 ,,
,, ,, 22 ,, ...	7 ,,	,, ,, 18 ,, ...	5 ,,
,, ,, 19 ,, ...	6 ,,	,, ,, 15 ,, ...	4 ,,
,, ,, 16 ,, ...	5 ,,	,, ,, 12 ,, ...	3 ,,
,, ,, 13 ,, ...	4 ,,	,, ,, 8 ,, ...	2 ,,
,, ,, 10 ,, ...	3 ,,	,, ,, 4 ,, ...	1 day
,, ,, 7 ,, ...	2 ,,		
,, ,, 4 ,, ...	1 day		

(2) Notwithstanding the provisions of the last foregoing sub-paragraph—

> (*a*) the number of days of annual holiday which an employer is required to allow to a worker in respect of a period of employment during the 12 months immediately preceding 6th April in any year shall not exceed in the aggregate three times the number of days constituting the worker's normal working week, *plus two days;*

(b) where before 17th September in any holiday season a worker and his employer enter into an agreement in writing that the worker shall be allowed after the end of the holiday season and before 6th April next following, days of holiday not exceeding twice the number of days constituting his normal working week, being the whole or part of the annual holiday for which he has qualified under this paragraph, any such days of annual holiday may, subject to the provisions of paragraph 4, be allowed in accordance with the agreement and if so allowed shall be treated for the purposes of this Schedule as having been allowed during the holiday season;

(c) the duration of the worker's annual holiday during the holiday season ending on *30th September 1974* shall be reduced by any days of holiday with pay (not being days of customary holiday) which have been allowed to him by the employer under the provisions of Order WM(91), between 6th April 1974 and the date on which the provisions of this Schedule become effective.

(3) In this Schedule the expression "holiday season" means in relation to an annual holiday during the year 1974 and each subsequent year, the period commencing on 6th April and ending on 30th September in that year.

4.—(1) Subject to the provisions of this paragraph, an annual holiday under this Schedule shall be allowed on consecutive working days and days of holiday shall be treated as consecutive notwithstanding that a day of holiday allowed to a worker under Part II of this Schedule or a day upon which he does not normally work for the employer intervenes.

(2) (a) Where the number of days of annual holiday for which a worker has qualified exceeds the number of days constituting his normal working week, but does not exceed twice that number, the holiday may be allowed in two periods of consecutive working days; so, however, that when a holiday is so allowed, one of the periods shall consist of a number of such days not less than the number of days constituting the worker's normal working week.

(b) Where the number of days of annual holiday for which a worker has qualified exceeds twice the number of days constituting his normal working week the holiday may be allowed as follows:—

(i) as to two periods of consecutive working days, each such period not being less than the period constituting the worker's normal working week, during the holiday season; and

(ii) as to any additional days, on working days which need not be consecutive, to be fixed by the employer, either during the holiday season or within the period ending on 8th January immediately following the holiday season.

(3) Where a day of holiday allowed to a worker under Part II of this Schedule immediately precedes a period of annual holiday or occurs during such a period then, notwithstanding the foregoing provisions of this paragraph, the duration of that period of annual holiday may be reduced by one day and in such a case one day of annual holiday may be allowed on any working day (other than the worker's weekly short day) falling within the holiday season or, by agreement between the employer and the worker or his representative, after the holiday season but before the beginning of the next following holiday season.

(4) Subject to the foregoing provisions of this paragraph, any day of annual holiday under this Schedule may be allowed on a day on which the worker is entitled to a day of holiday or to a half-holiday under any enactment other than the Wages Councils Act 1959.

5. An employer shall give to a worker reasonable notice of the commencing date or dates and of the duration of his annual holiday. Such notice may be given individually to the worker or by the posting of a notice in the place where the worker is employed.

PART IV

HOLIDAY REMUNERATION

A—CUSTOMARY HOLIDAYS AND HOLIDAYS IN LIEU OF CUSTOMARY HOLIDAYS

6.—(1) For each day of holiday (including a holiday falling on a Saturday) to which a worker is entitled under Part II of this Schedule he shall be paid by the employer as holiday remuneration whichever of the following amounts is the greater:—

(a) one-fifth of the average weekly earnings of the worker during the 12 months ended on 5th April immediately preceding the holiday, such average weekly earnings to be determined by dividing, by the number of weeks of employment with the employer during the said period, the total remuneration paid to him by the employer during that period:

Provided that when Good Friday or Easter Monday in England and Wales or the local Spring holiday in Scotland (or days substituted therefor under the provisions of sub-paragraph (2)(b) of paragraph 2 or holidays in lieu of such customary holidays) fall after 5th April in any year, the holiday remuneration for any such holiday under this sub-paragraph shall be one-fifth of the average weekly earnings of the worker during the 12 months ended on 5th April in the preceding calendar year;

or (b) the appropriate statutory minimum remuneration to which he would have been entitled as a time worker if the day had not been a day of holiday and he had been employed on work for which statutory minimum remuneration is payable:

(i) in the case of a worker normally employed for more than 30 hours a week, for 8 hours, or

(ii) in the case of a worker normally employed for 30 hours a week or less, for 4 hours.

(2) Notwithstanding the provisions of sub-paragraph (1) of this paragraph, payment of the said holiday remuneration is subject to the condition that the worker (unless excused by the employer or absent by reason of the proved illness of, or accident to, the worker) presents himself for employment at the usual starting hour on the first working day following the holiday:

Provided that when two customary holidays occur on successive days (or so that no working day intervenes) the said condition shall apply only to the second customary holiday.

(3) Where a worker normally works in the week on every week-day except Saturday, he shall be paid in respect of any Saturday on which he would have been entitled to a holiday under Part II of this Schedule if it had been a day on which he normally worked, a sum equivalent to the holiday remuneration he would have been entitled to receive had he been allowed a holiday on that day.

(4) Holiday remuneration in respect of any customary holiday shall be paid by the employer to the worker on the pay-day on which the wages for the first working day following the customary holiday are paid.

(5) Holiday remuneration in respect of any holiday in lieu of a customary holiday shall be paid on the pay-day on which the wages are paid for the first working day following the holiday in lieu of a customary holiday: Provided that the said payment shall be made immediately upon the termination of the worker's employment if he ceases to be employed before being allowed such holiday in lieu of a customary holiday and in that case the conditions specified in sub-paragraph (2) of this paragraph shall not apply.

B—ANNUAL HOLIDAY

7.—(1) Subject to the provisions of paragraph 8, a worker qualified to be allowed an annual holiday under this Schedule shall be paid as holiday remuneration by his employer in respect thereof, on the last pay-day preceding such annual holiday, whichever of the following amounts is the greater:—

(a) an amount equal to *seventeen two-hundred-and-sixtieths* of the total remuneration paid by the employer to the worker during the 12 months ended on 5th April immediately preceding the holiday; or

(b) one day's holiday pay (as defined in paragraph 11) in respect of each day of annual holiday.

(2) Where, under the provisions of paragraph 4, an annual holiday is allowed in more than one period the holiday remuneration shall be apportioned accordingly.

8. Where any accrued holiday remuneration has been paid by the employer to the worker (in accordance with paragraph 9 of this Schedule or under the provisions of Order W.M. (91)) in respect of employment during any of the periods referred to in that paragraph or that Order, the amount of holiday remuneration payable by the employer in respect of any annual holiday for which the worker has qualified by reason of employment during the said period shall be reduced by the amount of the said accrued holiday remuneration unless that remuneration has been deducted from a previous payment of holiday remuneration made under the provisions of this Schedule or of Order W.M. (91).

ACCRUED HOLIDAY REMUNERATION PAYABLE ON TERMINATION OF EMPLOYMENT

9.—(1) Where a worker ceases to be employed by an employer after the provisions of this Schedule become effective, the employer shall, immediately on the termination of the employment, pay to the worker accrued holiday remuneration in accordance with this paragraph.

(2) Accrued holiday remuneration shall be payable in accordance with the following table if the worker has in the 12 months commencing on 6th April 1973, and thereafter in any period of 12 months commencing on 6th April been employed for any of the periods of employment specified in that table.

(3) Accrued holiday remuneration is not payable in respect of any period of employment for which the worker has been allowed or become entitled to be allowed an annual holiday under this Schedule.

(4) Subject to the provisions of sub-paragraph (5) hereof, where a worker has been allowed in a holiday season part only of the annual holiday for which he has qualified under this Schedule or under Order W.M. (91) and his employment is terminated before he becomes entitled to the rest of that holiday the accrued holiday remuneration payable shall be:—

(*a*) in the case of a worker who has qualified for days of annual holiday exceeding twice the number of days constituting his normal working week and who has been allowed as days of annual holiday not less than twice the number of days constituting his normal working week, or, where the circumstances in sub-paragraph (3) of paragraph 4 are applicable, that number of days reduced by one:—

    (i) in respect of the days of holiday for which he has qualified during the 12 months ended on 5th April immediately preceding the termination of his employment, the holiday remuneration due in respect thereof calculated in accordance with the provisions of paragraph 7 less the amount received by him in respect of the part of the holiday which has been allowed; and

    (ii) in respect of any period of employment since the said 5th April, the amount calculated in accordance with the following table;

(*b*) in the case of any other worker, the appropriate amount under the following table in respect of the qualifying period of employment less the amount received by the worker in respect of that part of the holiday which has been allowed.

(5) Any accrued holiday remuneration payable under the provisions of this paragraph shall be reduced by the amount of any accrued holiday remuneration already paid by the employer to the worker in pursuance of this Order or Order W.M. (91) in respect of the same period of employment or part thereof.

TABLE OF ACCRUED HOLIDAY REMUNERATION

A. Workers with a normal working week of 6 days.

Column 1 Period of employment calculated in accordance with the provisions of paragraph 10	Column 2 Accrued holiday remuneration	Column 3
At least 48 weeks	*Three and one-third times the amount in Column 3*	
„ „ *46* „	*Three and one-sixth times the amount in Column 3*	The amount which the worker would be en-
„ „ *44* „	*Three times the amount in Column 3*	titled to receive from his
„ „ *42* „	*Two and five-sixths times the amount in Column 3*	employer, at the date of the termination of his
„ „ *40* „	*Two and two-thirds times the amount in Column 3*	employment, for one week's work, if working
„ „ *38* „	*Two and one-third times the amount in Column 3*	his normal working week and the number
„ „ *36* „	*Two and one-sixth times the amount in Column 3*	of daily hours normally worked by him (exclu-
„ „ *34* „	*Twice the amount in Column 3*	sive of overtime) and if
„ „ *32* „	*One and five-sixths times the amount in Column 3*	paid as a time worker at the appropriate rate for
„ „ *30* „	*One and two-thirds times the amount in Column 3*	statutory minimum re-
„ „ *28* „	One and one-half times the amount in Column 3	muneration for work for which statutory mini-
„ „ *25* „	One and one-third times the amount in Column 3	mum remuneration is payable and at the same
„ „ *22* „	One and one-sixth times the amount in Column 3	rate for any work for which such remunera-
„ „ 19 „	The amount in Column 3	tion is not payable.
„ „ 16 „	Five-sixths of the amount in Column 3	
„ „ 13 „	Two-thirds of the amount in Column 3	
„ „ 10 „	One-half of the amount in Column 3	
„ „ 7 „	One-third of the amount in Column 3	
„ „ 4 „	One-sixth of the amount in Column 3	

B. Workers with a normal working week of 5 days or less.

Column 1 Period of employment calculated in accordance with the provisions of paragraph 10	Column 2 Accrued holiday remuneration	Column 3
At least 48 weeks	Three and two-fifths times the amount in Column 3	
„ „ 46 „	Three and one-fifth times the amount in Column 3	The amount which the worker would be en-
„ „ 44 „	Three times the amount in Column 3	titled to receive from his
„ „ 42 „	Two and four-fifths times the amount in Column 3	employer, at the date of the termination of his
„ „ 40 „	Two and three-fifths times the amount in Column 3	employment, for one week's work, if working
„ „ 38 „	Two and two-fifths times the amount in Column 3	his normal working week and the number of
„ „ 36 „	Two and one-fifth times the amount in Column 3	daily hours normally worked by him (exclu-
„ „ 33 „	Twice the amount in Column 3	sive of overtime) and
„ „ 30 „	One and four-fifths times the amount in Column 3	if paid as a time worker at the appropriate rate
„ „ 27 „	One and three-fifths times the amount in Column 3	of statutory minimum remuneration for work
„ „ 24 „	One and two-fifths times the amount in Column 3	for which statutory minimum remuneration
„ „ 21 „	One and one-fifth times the amount in Column 3	is payable and at the same rate for any work
„ „ 18 „	The amount in Column 3	for which such remun-
„ „ 15 „	Four-fifths of the amount in Column 3	eration is not payable.
„ „ 12 „	Three-fifths of the amount in Column 3	
„ „ 8 „	Two-fifths of the amount in Column 3	
„ „ 4 „	One-fifth of the amount in Column 3	

(6) Notwithstanding the provisions of the foregoing table, the accrued holiday remuneration payable to a worker who has been employed by the employer for the whole of the 12 months ended on 5th April immediately preceding the termination of his employment shall be as follows:—

   (a) in respect of that 12 months an amount equal to the holiday remuneration for the days of annual holiday for which he has qualified, calculated in accordance with the provisions of sub-paragraph (1) of paragraph 7; and

   (b) in respect of any period of employment since the said 5th April, the amount calculated in accordance with the foregoing table.

Part V

GENERAL

10. For the purpose of calculating any period of employment qualifying a worker for an annual holiday or for any accrued holiday remuneration under this Schedule, the worker shall be treated—

(1) as if he were employed for a week in respect of any week in which—

(*a*) in the case of a worker other than a part-time worker, he has worked for the employer for not less than 20 hours and has performed some work for which statutory minimum remuneration is payable;

(*b*) in the case of a part-time worker, he has worked for the employer and has performed some work for which statutory minimum remuneration is payable;

(*c*) in the case of any worker—

(i) he has worked for the employer for less than 20 hours by reason of the proved illness of, or accident to, the worker or for a like reason has been absent throughout the week (provided that the number of weeks which may be treated as weeks of employment for such reason shall not exceed four in the aggregate in any such period); or

(ii) he has been suspended throughout the week owing to shortage of work (provided that the number of weeks which may be treated as weeks of employment for such reason shall not exceed six in the aggregate in any such period);

(2) as if he were employed on any day of holiday allowed under the provisions of this Schedule, or of Order W.M. (91), and on any other day of holiday with pay, and for the purposes of the provisions of sub-paragraph (1) of this paragraph, a worker who is absent on such a holiday shall be treated as having worked thereon for the employer on work for which statutory minimum remuneration is payable,

(*a*) where the holiday is a customary holiday, or a holiday in lieu of a customary holiday, for 8 hours if the worker is normally employed for more than 30 hours a week or for 4 hours if he is normally employed for 30 hours a week or less, or

(*b*) where the holiday is a day of annual holiday or any other day of holiday with pay, for the number of hours ordinarily worked by him on that day of the week.

11. In this Schedule, unless the context otherwise requires, the following expressions have the meanings hereby respectively assigned to them, that is to say:—

"NORMAL WORKING WEEK" means the number of days on which it has been usual for the worker to work in a week in the employment of the employer in the 12 months immediately preceding the commencement of the holiday season or, where under paragraph 9 accrued holiday remuneration is payable on the termination of the employment, in the twelve months immediately preceding the date of the termination of the employment:

Provided that—

(1) part of a day shall count as a day;

(2) no account shall be taken of any week in which the worker did not perform any work for which statutory minimum remuneration has been fixed.

"ONE DAY'S HOLIDAY PAY" means the appropriate proportion of the remuneration which the worker would be entitled to receive from his employer at the date of the annual holiday or at the termination of the employment, as the case may require, for one week's work if working his normal working week and the number of daily hours normally worked by him (exclusive of overtime) and if paid as a time worker at the appropriate rate of statutory minimum remuneration for work for which statutory minimum remuneration is payable and at the same rate for any work for which such remuneration is not payable, and in this definition "appropriate proportion" means—

where the worker's normal working week is six days ...   .   one-sixth
where the worker's normal working week is five days   ...   ...   one-fifth
where the worker's normal working week is four days or less   one-quarter.

"PART-TIME WORKER" means a worker who normally works for the employer for less than 20 hours a week by reason only of the fact that he does not hold himself out as normally available for work for more than the number of hours he normally works in the week.

"STATUTORY MINIMUM REMUNERATION" means minimum remuneration (other than holiday remuneration) fixed by a wages regulation order.

"WAGES REGULATION ORDER" means a wages regulation order made by the Secretary of State to give effect to proposals submitted to him by the Wholesale Mantle and Costume Wages Council (Great Britain).

"WEEK" means "pay week".

12. The provisions of this Schedule are without prejudice to any agreement for the allowance of any further holidays with pay or for the payment of additional holiday remuneration.

EXPLANATORY NOTE

(This Note is not part of the Order.)

This Order, which has effect from 24th May 1974, sets out the holidays which an employer is required to allow to workers in relation to whom the Wholesale Mantle and Costume Wages Council (Great Britain) operates and the remuneration payable for those holidays in substitution for the holidays and holiday remuneration fixed by the Wages Regulation (Wholesale Mantle and Costume) (Holidays) Order 1973 (Order W.M. (91)), which Order is revoked.

New provisions are printed in italics.

STATUTORY INSTRUMENTS

1974 No. 756

CUSTOMS AND EXCISE

The Import Duties (Temporary Reductions and Exemptions) (No. 6) Order 1974

Made - - - -	*26th April* 1974
Laid before the House of Commons	*2nd May* 1974
Coming into Operation—	
for the purposes of Article 6(3)	*1st June* 1974
for all other purposes	*3rd May* 1974

The Lords Commissioners of Her Majesty's Treasury, by virtue of the powers conferred on them by sections 1, 2, 3(6) and 13 of the Import Duties Act 1958(a), as amended(b), and of all other powers enabling them in that behalf, on the recommendation of the Secretary of State(c), hereby make the following Order:

Citation, operation, interpretation

1.—(1) This Order may be cited as the Import Duties (Temporary Reductions and Exemptions) (No. 6) Order 1974 and shall come into operation for the purposes of Article 6(3) on 1st June 1974 and for all other purposes on 3rd May 1974.

(2) In this Order "the relevant date" in relation to goods of a description specified in column 2 of any Schedule hereto means the date there specified in relation to the description.

(3) The Interpretation Act 1889(d) shall apply for the interpretation of this Order as it applies for the interpreation of an Act of Parliament.

Intra-Community trade

2. Up to and including the relevant date, no import duty shall be charged on goods of a heading of the Customs Tariff 1959 specified in column 1 of Schedules 1, 2 or 4 hereto which are of a description specified in column 2 thereof if they satisfy the requisite conditions to benefit from Regulation (EEC) 385/73(e) (relating to goods entitled to benefit from the eventual abolition of customs duties in trade between member States of the European Communities).

(a) 1958 c. 6.

(b) *See* section 5(5) of, and paragraph 1 of Schedule 4 to, the European Communities Act 1972 (c. 68).   (c) *See* S.I. 1970/1537 (1970 III, p. 5293).

(d) 1889 c. 63.   (e) O.J. No. L42, 14.2.1973, p. 1.

The full rate

3.—(1) Up to and including the relevant date, in the case of goods which fall within a heading of the Customs Tariff 1959 specified in column 1 of any Schedule hereto which are of a description specified in column 2 thereof, if a rate of duty is shown in column 3 thereof in relation to the goods, import duty shall be charged at the rate so shown instead of any higher rate which would otherwise apply.

(2) If no entry appears in column 3 of any Schedule hereto in relation to goods of a description specified in column 2 thereof, no exemption from or reduction in duty applies to such goods by virtue of this Article.

(3) Paragraph (1) above shall operate without prejudice to the exemption provided for by Article 2 above or any greater reductions provided for by Articles 4 and 5 below in the case of goods originating in Egypt or Cyprus or goods qualifying for Commonwealth preference.

Egypt and Cyprus·

4.—(1) Up to and including the relevant date, any import duty for the time being chargeable on goods of a heading of the Customs Tariff 1959 specified in column 1 of any Schedule hereto which are of a description specified in column 2 thereof shall be charged:

  (*a*) at the rate, if any, shown in column 4 thereof in relation to the description if the goods originate in Egypt and

  (*b*) at the rate, if any, shown in column 5 thereof in relation to the description if the goods originate in Cyprus.

(2) For the purposes of paragraph (1) above goods shall be regarded as originating:

  (*a*) in Egypt if they are to be so regarded under the Agreement, signed on 18th December 1972, between the European Economic Community and Egypt**(a)** and

  (*b*) in Cyprus if they are to be so regarded under the Agreement, signed on 19th December 1972, between the Community and Cyprus**(b)**.

(3) If no entry appears in column 4 or 5 of the said Schedules in relation to goods of a description specified in column 2 thereof, no reduction in duty applies by virtue of this Article to goods of that description originating in Egypt or Cyprus.

(4) This Article shall operate without prejudice to any greater reduction in, or to any exemption from, import duties which may be available apart from this Order in the case of goods herein referred to by virtue of their being goods of a developing country or goods qualifying for Commonwealth preference or otherwise.

Goods qualifying for Commonwealth preference

5. Up to and including the relevant date, any import duty for the time being chargeable on goods of a heading of the Customs Tariff 1959 specified in column 1 of Schedules 3 or 4 hereto which are of a description specified in column 2 thereof and which qualify for Commonwealth preference shall be charged at the rate shown in column 6 of the said Schedules instead of any higher rate which would otherwise apply.

(a) The Agreement is annexed to Regulation (EEC) 2409/73 (O.J. No. L251, p. 1).

(b) The Agreement is annexed to Regulation (EEC) 1246/73 (O.J. No. L133, p. 1).

Miscellaneous

6.—(1) Any description in column 2 of any Schedule hereto shall be taken to comprise all goods which would be classified under an entry in the same terms constituting a subheading (other than the final subheading) in the relevant heading in the Customs Tariff 1959.

(2) For the purposes of classification under the Customs Tariff 1959, insofar as that depends on the rate of duty, any goods to which this Order applies shall be treated as chargeable with the same duty as if this Order had not been made.

(3) The exemption and reductions provided for in articles 2 to 5 above in relation to goods of a description specified in column 2 of Schedule 2 hereto and the reductions provided for in articles 3 to 5 above in relation to goods of a description specified in column 2 of Schedule 3 hereto shall begin on 1st June 1974.

(4) Schedule 2 to the Import Duties (Temporary Reductions and Exemptions) (No. 3) Order 1973(a) shall be amended by the deletion of the entries in columns 1 to 6 thereto in relation to goods of a description specified in column 2 of Schedule 4 hereto.

(5) The Schedule to the Import Duties (Temporary Reductions and Exemptions) (No. 5) Order 1974(b) shall be amended by the deletion of the entries in columns 1 to 5 thereto in relation to goods of heading 73.18 of the Customs Tariff 1959.

John Golding,

T. Pendry,

Two of the Lords Commissioners
of Her Majesty's Treasury.

26th April 1974.

(a) S.I. 1973/2152 (1973 III, p. 7434).   (b) S.I. 1974/682 (1974 I, p. 2675).

NOTE: *Where no rate of duty is shown in column 3 there is no reduction in the full rate and where no rate is shown in columns 4 and 5 there is no reduction in the case of goods in Egypt or Cyprus as such.*

SCHEDULE 1

GOODS SUBJECT TO TEMPORARY REDUCTION IN OR EXEMPTION FROM IMPORT DUTY FROM 3 MAY 1974

Tariff heading	Description	Rates of Duty %		
		Full	Egypt	Cyprus
(1)	(2)	(3)	(4)	(5)
39.02	Poly(vinyl chloride), in powder form and of natural colour, unplastisised (up to and including 1st July 1974)	—	5·5	3·7
73.18	Longitudinally welded steel tubes in lengths of not less than 1·5 metres and not more than 8 metres having an outside diameter of not less than 47·98 millimetres and not more than 50 millimetres; with a wall thickness of not less than 3·5 millimetres and not more than 5 millimetres; containing not more than 0·06 per cent sulphur and not more than 0·06 per cent phosphorus; having a tensile strength of not less than 34 Kgf/mm^2 and not more than 48 Kgf/mm^2 and a minimum yield stress of 21·3 Kgf/mm^2 (up to and including 1st July 1974)	10	4·5	3

SCHEDULE 2

GOODS ON WHICH TEMPORARY REDUCTION IN OR EXEMPTION FROM IMPORT DUTY IS EXTENDED

Tariff heading	Description	Rates of Duty %		
		Full	Egypt	Cyprus
(1)	(2)	(3)	(4)	(5)
29.15	Adipic acid (up to and including 2nd September 1974)	13·6	6·1	4

SCHEDULE 3

GOODS SUBJECT TO TEMPORARY REDUCTION IN IMPORT DUTY FROM 1 JUNE 1974

Tariff Heading	Description	Rates of Duty %			
		Full	Egypt	Cyprus	Common-wealth
(1)	(2)	(3)	(4)	(5)	(6)
08.02 Aia)	Sweet oranges, fresh (up to and including 30th September 1974)	£0·1400 per cwt. + 1%	—	—	1

SCHEDULE 4

GOODS HITHERTO SUBJECT TO TEMPORARY REDUCTION IN OR EXEMPTION FROM DUTY UNDER THE IMPORT DUTIES (TEMPORARY REDUCTIONS AND EXEMPTIONS) (NO. 3) ORDER 1973

		Rates of Duty %			
Tariff Heading (1)	Description (2)	Full (3)	Egypt (4)	Cyprus (5)	Common-wealth (6)
38.08 C	Colophony, hydrogenated, poly-merised, dimerised or oxidised (up to and including 30th June 1974)	1·6	0·7	0·4	1·6

EXPLANATORY NOTE

(*This Note is not part of the Order.*)

This Order provides for exemption from or reductions in import duty in the case of goods specified in Schedules 1 and 4 to the Order from 3rd May 1974 and in the case of goods specified in the other Schedules from 1st June 1974 until the dates appearing in the Schedules.

There is exemption from import duties in the case of all goods in Schedules 1, 2 or 4 if the goods satisfy the requisite conditions to benefit from the eventual abolition of customs duties in trade between member States of the European Communities.

In the case of other goods, where a rate of duty is specified in column 3 of any of the Schedules, duty is reduced to that rate, instead of any higher rate which would otherwise apply.

In the case of goods qualifying for Commonwealth preference or originating in Egypt or Cyprus greater reductions in duty are available in a number of cases than those referred to above. These are shown respectively in column 6 of Schedules 3 and 4 and columns 4 and 5, of Schedules 1, 2 and 4.

STATUTORY INSTRUMENTS

1974 No. 759

LOCAL GOVERNMENT, ENGLAND AND WALES
The Police (Compensation) Regulations 1974

Made - - - -	*25th April* 1974
Laid before Parliament	*9th May* 1974
Coming into Operation	*30th May* 1974

ARRANGEMENT OF REGULATIONS

Part V

Retirement Compensation and Payments on Death

Part VI

Adjustment, Review and Compounding of Compensation

Part VII

Procedure and Miscellaneous

Whereas the Secretary of State for the Home Department is the appropriate Minister for the purposes of section 259 of the Local Government Act 1972(a) in relation to members of police forces:

Now, therefore, in pursuance of the said section 259, I hereby make the following Regulations:—

PART I
PRELIMINARY

Title and commencement

1. These Regulations may be cited as the Police (Compensation) Regulations 1974 and shall come into operation on 30th May 1974.

Interpretation

2.—(1) In these Regulations, unless the context otherwise requires—

"the Act" means the Local Government Act 1972;

"age of compulsory retirement" means, in relation to a member of a police force, the age at which he would become liable to be required to retire on account of age under the Police Pensions Regulations;

"compensating authority" in relation to any person who suffers loss of office or loss or diminution of emoluments as a member of a police force as specified in Regulation 4, means the police authority which maintained the police force of which he was last a member prior to the loss or diminution or, if that authority has ceased to exist, the authority to whom the residue of their property and liabilities has been transferred under the Act;

"compensation question" means a question arising under these Regulations—

> (*a*) as to a person's entitlement to compensation for loss of office, or for loss or diminution of emoluments as a member of a police force; or

> (*b*) as to the manner of a person's employment or the comparability of his duties;

"emoluments" has the meaning given by Regulation 36(1) and "annual rate of emoluments" has the meaning given by Regulation 36(3);

"enactment" means any Act or any instrument made under an Act;

"existing authority" has the meaning given by section 270(1) of the Act;

"fund authority", in relation to any person, means the authority maintaining the superannuation fund or account in relation to that person;

"instrument" includes an Order in Council, regulation, order, rule, scheme or direction;

"interchange rules" means rules made under section 2 of the Superannuation (Miscellaneous Provisions) Act 1948(b) (which provides for the pensions of persons transferring to different employment) and includes any similar instrument made, or having effect as if made, under any other Act which makes similar provision;

"local authority" means—

> (*a*) the council of a county, county borough, borough (whether or not included in a rural district) and an urban or rural district; a county council and a district council described in section 2 or 21 of the Act; a parish council, a community council; a parish meeting, a representative body of a parish and a common parish council;

· (a) 1972 c. 70.　　　　(b) 1948 c. 33.

(b) the council of a metropolitan borough or London borough, the Common Council of the City of London, the Greater London Council and the Council of the Isles of Scilly;

(c) any burial board or joint burial board established under the Burial Acts 1852 to 1906;

(d) any joint board or joint body constituted by or under any enactment for the purpose of exercising the functions of two or more authorities described in (a), (b) or (c) above;

(e) any other authority or body, not specified in (a), (b), (c) or (d) above established by or under any enactment for the purpose of exercising the functions of or advising one or more of the authorities specified in (a), (b), (c) or (d) above;

(f) any committee (including a joint committee) established by or under any enactment for the purpose of exercising the functions of, or advising, two or more authorities described in (a), (b), (c) or (d) above;

(g) any two or more authorities described in (a), (b), (c), (d), (e) or (f) above acting jointly or as a combined authority;

(h) a police authority for a county, a borough or a combined area;

"long-term compensation" means compensation payable in accordance with the provisions of Part IV of these Regulations for loss of office or loss or diminution of emoluments;

"material date" means—

(a) in relation to any person affected by any provision of the Act, 1st April 1974 or the date on which the loss of office or loss or diminution of emoluments as a member of a police force occurred, whichever is the earlier;

(b) in relation to a person affected by any provision of an instrument made under the Act, the date on which the instrument was made or, if some other date is specified therein, that other date;

"national service", in relation to any person, means compulsory national service and service which is relevant service within the meaning of the Reserve and Auxiliary Forces (Protection of Civil Interests) Act 1951(a) and any similar service immediately following such service entered into with the consent of the authority or person under whom he held his last relevant employment, or, where appropriate, the authority by whom he was appointed, and service otherwise than as a member of a police force which is pensionable under the Police Pensions Regulations;

"office" includes any place, situation or employment, and the expression "officer" shall be construed accordingly;

"pensionable pay" and "average pensionable pay" have the same meanings, respectively, as in the Police Pensions Regulations;

"pension scheme", in relation to any person, means any form of arrangement associated with his employment for the payment of superannuation benefits, whether subsisting by virtue of an Act of Parliament, trust, contract or otherwise;

"pensionable service" has the same meaning as in the Police Pensions Regulations;

"Police Pensions Regulations" means the Regulations from time to time in force under the Police Pensions Act 1948(b);

(a) 1951 c. 65.   (b) 1948 c. 24.

"reckonable service", in relation to any person, means any period of whole-time or part-time employment in any relevant employment and includes any period of war service or national service undertaken on his ceasing to hold such an employment;

"relevant employment" means service or employment—

(a) under the Crown or by or under any person, authority or body for the purposes of the Crown or as a member of a police force;

(b) under any officer employed as mentioned in (a) above for the purposes of the functions of that person, authority or body;

(c) by any person, authority or body specified in the Schedule to these Regulations;

(d) preceding any of the foregoing employment which was reckonable for the purposes of the Police Pensions Regulations; or

(e) such other employment as the Secretary of State may, in the case of any named person, approve;

but, except for national service and war service, does not include service in the armed forces of the Crown;

"resettlement compensation" means compensation payable in accordance with Part III of these Regulations for loss of office;

"retirement compensation" means compensation payable in accordance with the provisions of Regulation 19, 20 or 21;

"tribunal" means a tribunal established under section 12 of the Industrial Training Act 1964(a);

"war service" means war service within the meaning of the Local Government Staffs (War Service) Act 1939(b), the Teacher's Superannuation (War Service) Act 1939(c), the Education (Scotland) (War Service Superannuation) Act 1939(d), the Police and Firemen (War Service) Act 1939(e) or employment for war purposes within the meaning of the Superannuation Schemes (War Service) Act 1940(f), and includes any period of service in the first world war in the armed forces of the Crown or in the forces of the Allied or Associated Powers if that service immediately followed a period of relevant employment and was undertaken either compulsorily or with the permission of the employer in that employment.

(2) The holder of any office, appointment, place, situation or employment shall, for the purposes of these Regulations, be regarded as an officer employed in that office, appointment, place, situation or employment, and the expressions "officer" and "employment" shall be construed accordingly.

(3) Where under any provision of these Regulations an annual value is to be assigned to a capital sum or a capital value to an annual amount, the annual or capital value shall be calculated by the Government Actuary.

(4) In these Regulations, unless the context otherwise requires, references to any enactment shall be construed as references thereto as amended, re-enacted, applied or modified by any subsequent enactment.

(5) References in these Regulations to a numbered Regulation shall, unless the reference is to a regulation of specified regulations, be construed as references to the Regulation bearing that number in these Regulations.

(a) 1964 c. 16.   (b) 1939 c. 94.   (c) 1939 c. 95.
(d) 1939 c. 96.   (e) 1939 c. 103.   (f) 1940 c. 26.

(6) References in any of these Regulations to a numbered paragraph shall, unless the reference is to a paragraph of a specified Regulation, be construed as references to the paragraph bearing that number in the first mentioned Regulation.

(7) The Interpretation Act 1889(a) shall apply for the interpretation of these Regulations as it applies for the interpretation of an Act of Parliament.

PART II

ENTITLEMENT TO COMPENSATION

Persons to whom the Regulations apply

3.—(1) Subject to the provisions of paragraph (2), these Regulations shall apply to any person who—

(a) was serving immediately before the material date in a police force as the chief constable or deputy chief constable thereof or in the rank of assistant chief constable; or

(b) would have been so serving at that time but for any national service on which he was then engaged.

(2) These Regulations shall not apply to a person duly entitled within the meaning of the Police (Retirement of Senior Officers) Regulations 1973(b).

Grounds of entitlement to compensation

4.—(1) Subject to the provisions of these Regulations, any person to whom these Regulations apply and who suffers loss of office as a member of a police force or loss or diminution of emoluments which is attributable to any provision of the Act or of any instrument made under the Act shall be entitled to have his case considered for the payment of compensation under these Regulations, and such compensation shall be determined in accordance with these Regulations.

(2) Without prejudice to the generality of these Regulations, paragraph (1) shall apply to a person who—

(a) for the purposes of accepting an appointment as a member of a police force described in sub-paragraph (b) of this paragraph, terminates his services as a member of a police force;

(b) at any time before 1st April 1974 accepted an appointment as a member of a police force for a police area as established on 1st April 1974;

(c) would, but for his acceptance of the appointment described in the said sub-paragraph (b), have become on 1st April 1974 in accordance with the provisions of section 255 of the Act a member of a police force;

and in determining the compensating authority for the purposes of these Regulations, any loss or diminution of emoluments suffered by him which is attributable thereto shall be assumed to have occurred on the day after that on which he enters the employment described in the said sub-paragraph (b).

National service

5.—(1) Where any person to whom these Regulations apply would have been serving immediately before the material date as a member of a police force but for any national service on which he was then engaged, then if before the expiry of two months after ceasing to be so engaged, or if prevented by sickness or other

---

(a) 1889 c. 63.   (b) S.I. 1973/1944 (1973 III, p. 6693).

reasonable cause, as soon as practicable thereafter, he gives notice to the compensating authority that he is available for employment, that person shall be entitled to have his case considered for the payment of compensation on the ground—

(a) if he is not serving, or offered an appointment, as a member of a police force in his former rank or in any reasonably comparable employment, of loss of office;

(b) if he is so serving with reduced emoluments as compared with the emoluments which he would have enjoyed had he contined to serve as a member of a police force in his former rank, of diminution of emoluments.

(2) The loss of office which is the ground of a claim for compensation under sub-paragraph (a) of paragraph (1) shall be treated as having occurred on the earlier of the two following dates, that is to say, the date of the refusal of an offer of an appointment or a date one month after the date on which the person gave notice that he was available for employment, and the claimant shall be deemed to have been entitled to the emoluments which he would have enjoyed at such earlier date had he continued to serve as a member of a police force in his former rank.

PART III

RESETTLEMENT COMPENSATION

Resettlement compensation for loss of office

6. The compensating authority shall, subject to the provisions of these Regulations, pay resettlement compensation to any person to whom these Regulations apply and who satisfies the conditions set out in Regulation 7.

Conditions for payment of resettlement compensation

7.—(1) Without prejudice to any other requirement of these Regulations the conditions for the payment of resettlement compensation to any person are that—

(a) he has suffered loss of office attributable to any provision of the Act or of any instrument made under the Act not later than 10 years after the material date;

(b) he had not at the date of the loss attained the age of compulsory retirement;

(c) he had been for a period of 2 years immediately before the material date continuously engaged (disregarding breaks not exceeding in the aggregate 6 months) for the whole or part of his time in relevant employment;

(d) he has made a claim for such compensation in accordance with the provisions of Part VII of these Regulations not later than 13 weeks after the loss of office which is the cause of his claim, or 13 weeks after the coming into operation of these Regulations, whichever is the later, or within any longer period which the compensating authority allow in any particular case where they are satisfied that the delay in making the claim was due to ill health or other circumstances beyond the claimant's control;

(e) the loss of office which is the cause of his claim has occurred for some reason other than misconduct or incapacity to perform the duties that, immediately before the loss, he was performing or might reasonably have been required to perform;

(*f*) he has not, subject to paragraphs (2) and (3), on or after the police authority either informs him in writing that his services are to be terminated or are likely to be terminated or gives him written notice of termination of his services, been offered in writing:—

(i) any relevant employment which is reasonably comparable with the office which he has lost, or

(ii) any employment by a police authority which is suitable for him and is at the same place or in the same locality as that where he held office immediately before the loss.

(2) In ascertaining for the purposes of this Regulation whether a person has been offered employment which is reasonably comparable with the office which he has lost, no account shall be taken of the fact that the duties of the employment offered are not employment for police purposes or are duties which involve a transfer from one place to another within England and Wales.

(3) For the purposes of this Regulation, where the compensating authority are satisfied—

(*a*) that acceptance of an offer could have involved undue hardship to the person,

(*b*) that he was prevented from accepting an offer by reason of ill-health or other circumstances beyond his control, or

(*c*) that, before the commencement of these Regulations, an offer—

(i) has not been accepted by him, and

(ii) has lapsed or otherwise terminated,

no account shall be taken of that offer.

Amount of resettlement compensation

8. The amount of resettlement compensation which may be paid to a person shall, subject to the provisions of Regulation 9, be the amount described in paragraph (*a*) or (*b*) of this Regulation whichever is the greater—

(*a*) an amount equal to 13 weeks' emoluments and, in the case of a person who has attained the age of 45 years, one additional week's emoluments for every year of his age after attaining the age of 45 years and before the loss of employment, subject to a maximum addition of 13 such weeks;

(*b*) subject to the provisions of Regulation 35, an amount equal to—

(i) $1\frac{1}{2}$ weeks' emoluments for each completed year of reckonable service in which the person was not below the age of 41 years,

(ii) 1 week's emoluments for each completed year of reckonable service (not falling within (i) of this paragraph) in which the person was not below the age of 22 years, and

(iii) $\frac{1}{2}$ week's emoluments for each completed year of reckonable service not falling within either (i) or (ii) of this paragraph.

Special factors relating to calculation of amount of resettlement compensation

9.—(1) For the purposes of paragraph (*a*) of Regulation 8, if the loss of office takes place within 3 years of the date on which he would have become entitled to retire with an ordinary pension under the Police Pensions Regulations, the amount shall be reduced by the fraction of which—

(*a*) the denominator is 6, and

(*b*) the numerator is the number of complete periods of 6 months in the period beginning with the date 3 years before that on which he would have become so entitled and ending on the date of loss of office;

but the amount payable to a person who, on the material date, has not been continuously engaged in relevant employment as described in Regulation 12(1)(c) shall not by this paragraph be reduced to less than the equivalent of 13 weeks' emoluments.

(2) For the purposes of paragraph (b) of Regulation 8—

(a) in the case of a person who has completed more than 20 years' reckonable service, only the period of 20 years immediately prior to the loss of employment shall be taken into account, and

(b) if the loss of office takes place within the period of one year prior to the date on which the person would have attained the age of compulsory retirement the amount shall be reduced by the fraction of which the denominator is 12 and of which the numerator is the number of whole months in the period commencing at the beginning of the said period of one year and ending with the date of loss of office.

(3) For the purposes of this Regulation and the preceding Regulation, the weekly rate of emoluments shall be deemed to be seven-three hundred and sixty-fifths of the annual rate of emoluments.

Adjustment of resettlement compensation

10. A person who is entitled to—

(a) a redundancy payment under the Redundancy Payments Act 1965**(a)**, or

(b) any similar payment in consequence of the loss of his office under any other enactment or under any contract or arrangement with the authority by whom he was employed (other than payments by way of a return of contributions under a pension scheme), or

(c) any payment under or by virtue of the provisions of any enactment relating to the reinstatement in civil employment of persons who have been in the service of the Crown, shall—

(i) if the amount of any resettlement compensation that would, apart from this Regulation, be payable exceeds the payment or payments specified in (a), (b) or (c) above, be entitled to resettlement compensation equal to that excess, or

(ii) if the amount of any resettlement compensation that would apart from this Regulation be payable is equal to or less than the said payment or payments, not be entitled to resettlement compensation.

PART IV

LONG-TERM COMPENSATION

Long-term compensation for loss of office or loss or diminution of emoluments

11. The compensating authority shall, subject to the provisions of these Regulations, pay long-term compensation to any person to whom these Regulations apply and who satisfies the conditions set out in Regulation 12.

Conditions for payment of long-term compensation

12.—(1) Without prejudice to any other requirement of these Regulations, the conditions for the payment of long-term compensation to any person are that—

(a) he has suffered loss of office as a member of a police force or loss or

---

(a) 1965 c. 62.

diminution of emoluments attributable to any provision of the Act or of any instrument under the Act not later than 10 years after the material date;

(b) he had not at the date of the loss or diminution attained the age of compulsory retirement;

(c) he had been, for a period of not less than 5 years immediately before the material date, continuously engaged (without a break of more than 12 months at any one time) for the whole or part of his time in relevant employment;

(d) he has made a claim for such compensation in accordance with the provisions of Part VII of these Regulations not later than 2 years after the loss or diminution which is the cause of the claim or 2 years after the coming into operation of these Regulations whichever is the later; and

(e) if the cause of the claim for compensation is loss of office as a member of a police force—

(i) the loss has occurred for some reason other than misconduct or incapacity to perform such duties as, immediately before the loss, he was performing or might reasonably have been required to perform; and

(ii) he has not, subject to paragraph (2), after the police authority either informed him in writing that his services were to be terminated or were likely to be terminated or gave him written notice of termination of services, been offered in writing any relevant employment which is reasonably comparable with the office which he has lost.

(2) Regulation 7(2) and (3) (which relate to offers of employment) shall apply for the purposes of this Regulation in ascertaining whether a person has been offered reasonably comparable employment.

(3) Claims for long-term compensation for loss of office shall in all respects be treated as claims for such compensation for the loss of emoluments occasioned thereby and the provisions of these Regulations shall apply to all such claims accordingly.

Factors to be considered in determining payment of long-term compensation

13.—(1) For the purpose of determining whether long-term compensation for loss or diminution of emoluments should be paid to any person and, if so, the amount of the compensation (subject to the limits set out in these Regulations) the compensating authority shall, subject to the provisions of paragraphs (2) and (3), have regard to such of the following factors as may be relevant, that is to say—

(a) the conditions upon which the person held the office which he has lost, including in particular its security of tenure, whether by law or practice;

(b) the emoluments and other conditions, including security of tenure, whether by law or practice, of any work or employment undertaken by the person as a result of the loss of office;

(c) the extent to which he has sought suitable employment and the emoluments he might have acquired by accepting other suitable employment which, after the police authority either informs him in writing that his services are to be terminated or are likely to be terminated or gives him written notice of termination of his services, has been offered to him in writing;

(d) all the other circumstances of his case;

but, subject to the provisions of Regulation 37, no account shall be taken of the fact that he entered the office which he has lost or the emoluments of which have been diminished after—

(i) 26th October 1972, where the loss or diminution was attributable to any provision of the Act, or

(ii) after the making of any instrument under the Act, where the loss or diminution was attributable to any provision of that instrument.

(2) In ascertaining for the purposes of paragraph (1)(*b*) and (1)(*c*) the emolument in respect of any work or employment that gives the employee or his widow, child or other dependant the right to benefit under a pension scheme under which the employee is not under an obligation to pay contributions, the amount of emoluments shall be increased by the amount of contributions which the employee would have to pay to secure equivalent benefits under a pension scheme in respect of which both the employer and the employee are under an obligation to pay equal contributions.

(3) Regulation 7(3) shall apply for the purposes of this Regulation in ascertaining whether a person has been offered suitable employment.

Amount of long-term compensation payable for loss of emoluments

14.—(1) Long-term compensation for loss of emoluments shall, subject to the provisions of these Regulations, be payable until the age of compulsory retirement or death of a person to whom it is payable, whichever first occurs, and shall not exceed a maximum annual sum calculated in accordance with the provisions of paragraphs (2) and (3).

(2) The said maximum annual sum shall, subject to the provisions of paragraph (3) and Regulation 35 as hereinafter provided, be the aggregate of the following sums, namely—

(*a*) for every year of the person's reckonable service, one sixtieth of the emoluments which he has lost; and

(*b*) in the case of a person who has attained the age of 40 years at the date of the loss, a sum calculated in accordance with the provisions of paragraph (3) appropriate to his age at that date, but the said maximum annual sum shall in no case exceed two thirds of the emoluments which the person has lost.

(3) The sum referred to in paragraph (2)(*b*) shall be—

(*a*) in the case of a person who has attained the age of 40 years but has not attained the age of 50 years at the date of the loss, the following fraction of the emoluments which he has lost—

(i) where his reckonable service is less than 10 years, one sixtieth for each year of that service after attaining the age of 40 years; or

(ii) where his reckonable service amounts to 10 years but is less than 15 years, one sixtieth for each year of that service after attaining the age of 40 years and an additional one sixtieth; or

(iii) where his reckonable service amounts to 15 years but is less than 20 years, one sixtieth for each year of that service after attaining the age of 40 years and an additional two sixtieths; or

(iv) where his reckonable service amounts to 20 years or more, one sixtieth for each year of that service after attaining the age of 40 years and an additional three sixtieths;

but the sum so calculated shall not in any case exceed one sixth of the said emoluments;

(b) in the case of a person who has attained the age of 50 years but has not attained the age of 60 years at the date of the loss, one sixtieth of the said emoluments for each year of his reckonable service after attaining the age of 40 years, up to a maximum of 15 years; and

(c) in the case of a person who has attained the age of 60 years at the date of the loss, one sixtieth of the said emoluments for each year of his reckonable service after attaining the age of 45 years.

(4) The amount of long-term compensation, which apart from this paragraph would become payable to a person, shall be reduced by the amount by which the aggregate of—

(a) the emoluments of any work or employment undertaken by him as a result of the loss of office, and

(b) the long-term compensation which, apart from this Regulation and any reduction under Regulation 26,

exceeds the emoluments of the employment which has been lost.

(5) Long-term compensation shall be payable to a person at intervals equivalent to those at which his emoluments as a member of a police force were previously paid or at such other intervals as may be agreed between the person and the compensating authority.

Long-term compensation for diminution of emoluments

15.—(1) Long-term compensation for diminution of emoluments in respect of any employment shall, subject to the provisions of these Regulations consist of an annual sum calculated in accordance with the provisions of paragraph (2).

(2) The said annual sum shall not exceed the sum that would be the annual sum under the provisions of Regulation 14(1) to (4) calculated on the assumptions—

(a) that there was a loss of office, and

(b) that emoluments after diminution were emoluments of any work or employment undertaken as a result of a loss of office within the meaning of Regulation 13(1)(b).

(3) Long-term compensation for diminution of emoluments shall be payable to a person at intervals equivalent to those at which his emoluments as a member of a police force are or were previously paid or at such other intervals as may be agreed between the person and the compensating authority.

Period during which long-term compensation is to be payable

16.—(1) Long-term compensation shall be payable with effect from the date of the claim or from any earlier date permitted by the succeeding provisions of this Regulation.

(2) Where a claim for long-term compensation is duly made within 13 weeks of the commencement of these Regulations or occurrence of the loss or diminution which is the cause of the claim (whichever is the later), the award shall be made retrospective to the date on which the loss or diminution occurred.

(3) Where a claim for long-term compensation is made after the expiry of the period mentioned in paragraph (2), the compensating authority may—

(a) in its discretion make the award retrospective to a date not earlier than 13 weeks prior to the date on which the claim was made, or

(b) if it is satisfied that the failure to make the claim within the period mentioned in paragraph (2) was due to ill-health or other circumstances beyond the claimant's control, make the award retrospective to a date not earlier than that on which the loss or diminution occurred.

(4) Long-term compensation shall not be payable to a person for any period in respect of which compensation under Part V of these Regulations is payable to him.

PART V

RETIREMENT COMPENSATION AND PAYMENTS ON DEATH

Entitlement to retirement compensation and other payments

17.—(1) The compensating authority shall, subject to the provisions of these Regulations, pay retirement compensation to any person to whom these Regulations apply and who satisfies the conditions set out in Regulation 12, and shall make the other payments for which provision is made in Regulation 24.

(2) Regulation 13 shall apply in relation to compensation under this Part of these Regulations as it applies in relation to compensation under Part IV.

Additional factors governing payment of retirement compensation

18.—(1) Where retirement compensation is payable under any one of Regulations 19, 20 and 21, compensation shall not be payable under any other of these Regulations.

(2) If a person has attained the age of 40 years at the date on which he lost office as a member of a police force or suffered a diminution of his emoluments, the compensating authority, in calculating the amount of the retirement compensation payable to him, shall credit him with an additional period of service on the following basis, namely—

(a) 2 years, whether or not he has completed any years of service after attaining the age of 40 years,

(b) 2 years for each of the first 4 completed years of his reckonable service between the date when he attained the age of 40 years and the date of the loss or diminution, and

(c) 1 year for each year of that reckonable service after the fourth,

but the additional period so credited shall not exceed the shortest of the following periods, namely—

(i) the number of years that, when added to his pensionable service, would amount to the maximum period of service which would have been reckonable by him had he continued to serve as a member of a police force until attaining the age of compulsory retirement, or

(ii) the period of his reckonable service, or

(iii) 15 years;

and in calculating the amount of any retirement compensation payable to him he shall be regarded as having served as a member of a police force, before 1st April 1972, for the additional period so credited and, for the purpose of determining the reduction (if any) falling to be made in that pension beyond the age of 65 years or, in the case of a woman, 60 years, if he had paid pension contributions as a regular policeman, in respect of that period at a rate related to 6p a week less than the appropriate percentage of his pensionable pay.

In this paragraph the expression "reckonable service" includes any period of service or employment which has been taken into account for the purposes of any award under the Police Pensions Regulations to which the person concerned has become entitled.

(3) The benefit in respect of the additional period described in paragraph (2) shall be calculated at the same rate as is applicable for the day immediately preceding the loss or diminution.

(4) When retirement compensation is awarded, or when an award is reviewed under Regulation 30, the additional compensation payable in consequence of any period credited to a person under paragraph (2) may be reduced or withheld to the extent that the compensating authority may think reasonable having regard to the pension scheme (if any) associated with any further employment obtained by him.

(5) The provisions of the Police Pensions Regulations relating to the allocation of a pension, that is to say to the surrender by a regular policeman of a portion of his pension in favour of his wife or such other person as is substantially dependent on him, shall, subject to any necessary modifications have effect in relation to any retirement compensation as they have effect in relation to an ordinary or ill-health pension under the Police Pensions Regulations; and without prejudice to the generality of the preceding provisions of this paragraph—

(a) where before the date of the loss or diminution a member of a police force has, under the Police Pensions Regulations, allocated an ordinary pension and the allocation has taken effect, the said provisions shall apply as if the retirement compensation were an ordinary pension; and

(b) the said provisions shall apply as if any reference to the police authority included a reference to the compensating authority and as if any reference to retirement included a reference to a person becoming entitled to retirement compensation.

(6) In calculating for the purpose of Regulation 19 or 20 the amount of a pension under the Police Pensions Regulations, no account shall be taken of any reduction falling to be made in that pension by reason of the provisions of any Act relating to National Insurance until the person concerned reaches the age at which under the Police Pensions Regulations the pension would have been so reduced.

Retirement compensation for loss of emoluments payable to a person on attainment of the age of compulsory retirement

19. Subject to the provisions of these Regulations, when a person to whom these Regulations apply reaches the age of compulsory retirement the retirement compensation payable to him for loss of emoluments shall be an annual sum equal to the amount of the short service pension which would have been payable under the provisions of the Police Pensions Regulations calculated in accordance with Regulation 18(2).

Retirement compensation payable to a person who would have become entitled to a pension

20.—(1) Where a person to whom these Regulations apply and who has suffered loss of office before attaining what would have been the age of compulsory retirement—

(a) becomes incapacitated in circumstances in which, if he had continued to serve as a member of a police force, he would have become entitled to retire with an ill-health pension under the Police Pensions Regulations, or

(b) attains the age at which, had he continued to serve as a member of a police force, he would have been entitled to retire with an ordinary pension, he shall be entitled on the happening of either event to claim—

    (i) in the case mentioned in head (a) of this paragraph,. an annual sum equal to the amount of the ill-health pension which would have been payable under the Police Pensions Regulations calculated in accordance with Regulation 18(2), and

    (ii) in the case mentioned in head (b) of this paragraph, an annual sum equal to the amount of the ordinary pension which would have been payable under the Police Pensions Regulations calculated in accordance with Regulation 18(2),

in both cases calculated by reference to his average pensionable pay immediately before he ceased to serve as a member of a police force, subject however to paragraph (6).

(2) On receipt of a claim under paragraph (1) the compensating authority shall consider whether the claimant is a person to whom that paragraph applies, and within 13 weeks after the date of the receipt of the claim—

    (a) if they are satisfied that he is not such a person, they shall notify him in writing accordingly, or

    (b) if they are satisfied that he is such a person, they shall assess the amount of compensation payable to him and notify him in writing accordingly:

and notification as described in (a) or (b) above shall, for the purposes of these Regulations, be deemed to be a notification by the authority of a decision on a claim for compensation.

(3) A compensating authority may require any person who makes a claim under paragraph (1)(a) to submit himself to a medical examination by a registered medical practitioner selected by that authority, and if they do so, they shall also offer the person an opportunity of submitting a report from his own medical adviser as a result of an examination by him, and the authority shall take that report into consideration together with the report of the medical practitioner selected by them.

(4) If a person wishes to receive compensation under this Regulation, he shall so inform the compensating authority in writing within one month from the receipt of a notification under paragraph (2) or, where the claim has been the subject of an appeal, from the decision of the tribunal thereon; and the compensation shall be payable as from the date on which the compensating authority received the claim.

(5) If the compensating authority so agree, in the case of a person who has not attained the age of 60 years but would have become entitled to retire with an ordinary pension, as aforesaid, if the police authority so decided, it shall be assumed for the purposes of this Regulation that they would have so decided.

(6) In calculating the amount of any compensation under this Regulation, where the compensating authority, by virtue of Regulation 18(2), have credited the person with an additional period of service, no account shall be taken of any additional period beyond the period which he could have served, had he not lost his employment, before the date on which the claim was received by the compensating authority.

Retirement compensation for diminution of emoluments

21.—(1) A person to whom these Regulations apply and who has suffered a diminution of his emoluments shall be entitled to receive retirement compensation in accordance with the provisions of this Regulation.

(2) The provisions of Regulations 19 and 20 shall apply to any such person as if he had suffered loss of office immediately before the diminution occurred; but the amount of retirement compensation payable shall be the amount which would have been payable in respect of loss of office multiplied by a fraction of which—

> (*a*) the numerator is the amount by which his pensionable emoluments have been diminished, and
>
> (*b*) the denominator is the amount of his pensionable emoluments immediately before they were diminished;

but in calculating, for the purpose of Regulation 19 or 20, the amount of a pension under the Police Pensions Regulations, no account shall be taken of any provision of those Regulations by which a pension would be reduced beyond the age of 65 years or, in the case of a woman, 60 years.

Superannuation contributions

22.—(1) A person entitled to retirement compensation under Regulation 19 or 20 shall pay to the compensating authority an amount equal to any award by way of repayment of aggregate contributions received by him under the Police Pensions Regulations on ceasing to be a member of a police force but, where he has made the said payment to the compensating authority before becoming entitled to retirement compensation as aforesaid, that authority may, at his request before he becomes so entitled, refund the payment to him; and if the said payment is not made to the compensating authority, or is refunded by them, the compensation shall be reduced by an annual amount the capital value of which is equal to the amount of the said award under the Police Pensions Regulations.

(2) In the case of a person who undertook, for the purposes of the Police Pensions Regulations, to make payments by regular instalments in respect of previous service, the compensating authority shall be empowered to deduct the balance of the sum outstanding under the undertaking when he ceased to serve as a member of a police force, if any, from any payments to him of retirement compensation.

(3) Any sums paid to a compensating authority under this Regulation, in respect of returned contributions under the Police Pensions Regulations shall be applied for the payment of compensation which the authority is liable to pay under this Part of these Regulations.

Retirement compensation of a person who obtains further pensionable employment

23.—(1) Where a person to whom these Regulations apply, after suffering loss of office or diminution of emoluments as a member of a police force, enters employment in which he is subject to a pension scheme and thereafter becomes entitled to reckon for the purposes of that scheme any service or period of contribution which falls to be taken into account for the purpose of assessing the amount of any retirement compensation payable to him, his entitlement to retirement compensation shall be reviewed, and, subject to the provisions of this Regulation, no retirement compensation shall be payable in respect of that service or period unless the annual rate of the emoluments to which he was entitled immediately before the loss or diminution exceeds the annual rate on entry of the emoluments of the new employment, and any retirement compensation so payable to him shall, insofar as it is calculated by reference to remuneration, be calculated by reference to the difference between the said annual rates.

(2) The provisions of this Regulation shall not operate to increase the amount of any retirement compensation payable in respect of diminution of emoluments beyond the amount which would have been payable if the person had attained

the age of compulsory retirement immediately before he ceased to hold the office in which he suffered the diminution of emoluments.

Compensation payable on the death of a claimant

24.—(1) Where a person to whom this part of these Regulations applies dies, payments in accordance with this Regulation shall be made to or for the benefit of his widow or child or to his personal representatives or as the case may be, to trustees empowered by him to stand possessed of any benefit under the Police Pensions Regulations.

(2) Where the widow or child has become, or but for the person's loss of office as a member of a police force would have become, entitled to benefits under the Police Pensions Regulations, the widow or child, as the case may be, shall (subject to the provisions of this Regulation) be entitled to compensation calculated from time to time in accordance with the methods prescribed by the Police Pensions Regulations modified as follows:—

(a) where the person dies before becoming entitled to receive retirement compensation, and the Police Pensions Regulations provide that when he dies in service his widow or child shall be entitled for any period to a benefit equal to his pensionable pay, the annual rate of compensation for that period shall be equal to the annual amount of his long-term compensation calculated in accordance with paragraphs (1) to (3) of Regulation 14;

(b) where the person dies before becoming entitled to receive retirement compensation and the Police Pensions Regulations provide that when he dies in service his widow or child shall be entitled for any period to a benefit calculated by reference to the pension or ill-health pension which would have been payable to him if he had retired immediately before his death, the compensation for that period shall be calculated by reference to the retirement compensation to which he would have been entitled under Regulation 20 if that Regulation had been applied to him immediately before his death;

(c) where a person dies after becoming entitled to receive retirement compensation and the Police Pensions Regulations provide that when he dies after having retired his widow or child shall be entitled for any period to a benefit equal to his pension, the annual rate of compensation for that period shall be equal to the anual amount of retirement compensation;

(d) where a person dies after he has become entitled to receive retirement compensation and the Police Pensions Regulations provide that when he dies after having retired his widow or child shall be entitled for any period to a benefit calculated by reference to his pension, the annual rate of compensation for that period shall be calculated by reference to the annual amount of retirement compensation that would have been payable to him but for any reduction or suspension under Regulation 28(1).

(3) Calculation of the amounts described in paragraph (2) shall be subject to the following adjustments, that is to say—

(a) where any retirement compensation has been surrendered under Regulation 18(5) or compounded under Regulation 31 any sum payable under paragraph (2)(b) or (d) shall be calculated as if such surrender or compounding had not taken place;

(b) if immediately before his death the person's long-term compensation was reduced under Regulation 14(4) or 30 or his retirement compensation was reduced or suspended under Regulation 28(1) by reason of employment in which he was subject to a pension scheme and the widow or child is entitled under that scheme for any period to a benefit equal to his pensionable renumeration, regard shall be had to any such reduction or suspension for the purpose of sub-paragraphs (*a*) and (*c*).

(4) If the person in question suffered a diminution of emoluments, the provisions of paragraph (2) shall apply with the substitution of references to diminution of emoluments for references to loss of employment, and the sums payable to his widow or child shall be calculated, as if he had suffered loss of employment and as if the loss of emoluments occasioned thereby had been equivalent to the amount of the diminution.

(5) Compensation payable in accordance with this Regulation shall be payable on the like conditions in all respects as a widow's pension or, as the case may be, a child's allowance under the Police Pensions Regulations and, accordingly, the provisions of those Regulations (including any provision for the commutation of a pension or allowance for a gratuity) shall apply, subject to any necessary modifications, in relation to such compensation as they apply in relation to such a pension or allowance.

(6) Except where retirement compensation payable to the deceased person has been reduced under Regulation 22(1), the payments by way of compensation under this Regulation shall, in the aggregate, be reduced by an amount the capital value whereof is equal to the amount of any award by way of repayment of aggregate contributions received by him under the Police Pensions Regulations and either not paid to the compensating authority in accordance with Regulation 22(1) or refunded to him by that authority; and, where payments under this Regulation are made to or for the benefit of two or more persons, the said reduction shall be apportioned between those payments according to the capital value thereof.

(7) Where a person to whom this part of these Regulations applies dies and, but for his loss of office as a member of a police force, the police authority would have had discretion to grant gratuity to a person who was substantially dependent on him immediately before his death, the compensating authority shall have a like discretion to grant a gratuity calculated in accordance with the methods prescribed by the Police Pensions Regulations.

(8) In this Regulation and in Regulation 26 the expression "child" has the same meaning as in the Police Pensions Regulations and related expressions shall be construed accordingly.

Intervals for payment of compensation under Part V

25. Any compensation awarded under this Part of these Regulations to or in respect of any person, shall be payable in advance at intervals equivalent to those at which the corresponding benefit would have been payable under the Police Pensions Regulations or at such other intervals as may be agreed between the person entitled to receive the compensation and the compensating authority.

PART VI

ADJUSTMENT, REVIEW AND COMPOUNDING OF COMPENSATION

Abatement of compensation by award under the Police Pensions Regulations

26.—(1) Where compensation under these Regulations is payable to a person who has lost office as a member of a police force or to or for the benefit of his widow or child and a pension or allowance under the Police Pensions Regulations is also so payable, the annual amount of the compensation shall be abated by the annual amount of the corresponding pension or allowance.

(2) For the purposes of this Regulation in its application to the payment of long-term compensation, where a pension has been reduced under the provisions of the Police Pensions Regulations—

(a) relating to the allocation of a portion of a pension and mentioned in Regulation 18(5), or

(b) relating to the commutation of a portion of a pension for a lump sum, or

(c) relating to payments under the Police Pensions Regulations for the purpose of qualifying for benefits in respect of previous service or for an improved widow's pension, the annual amount of that pension shall be deemed to be the annual amount which would have been payable but for the said reduction.

(3) For the purposes of this Regulation no account shall be taken of a pension payable to a widow or child under the Police Pensions Regulations by reason of the allocation by the husband or father of a portion of his pension.

Adjustment of compensation where superannuation benefit is also payable

27.—(1) Where any period of service of which account was taken in calculating the amount of any compensation payable under Part IV or V of these Regulations is subsequently taken into account for the purpose of calculating the amount of any superannuation benefit payable to or in respect of any person in accordance with a pension scheme associated with any employment undertaken subsequent to the loss of office as a member of a police force or diminution of emoluments which was the subject of the claim for compensation, the compensating authority may in accordance with this Regulation withhold or reduce the compensation payable.

(2) If the part of any superannuation benefit which is attributable to a period of service mentioned in paragraph (1) equals or exceeds the part of any compensation which is attributable to the same period, that part of the compensation may be withheld, or if the part of the superannuation benefit is less than the part of the compensation, the compensation may be reduced by an amount not exceeding that part of the superannuation benefit.

(3) In addition to any reduction authorised by paragraph (2), if, in the circumstances mentioned in paragraph (1), compensation is attributable in part to any provision of the Police Pensions Regulations for a minimum benefit, the compensation may be reduced by an amount not exceeding that part.

(4) Where any additional period of service has been credited to a person under Regulation 18(2), and that period is equal to or less than the period spent in the subsequent employment mentioned in paragraph (1), the compensation may be reduced (in addition to any other reduction authorised by this Regulation) by an amount not exceeding that attributable to the additional period of service credited or, if the period is greater than the period spent in the subsequent employment, by the proportion of that amount which the period spent in the subsequent employment bears to the additional period so credited.

(5) In making any reduction under paragraphs (2) to (4), the amount of pension to be taken into account relating to the subsequent employment shall be the amount of such pension reduced by a fraction of that pension, where—

(i) the numerator of the fraction is equivalent to the aggregate of the amount of increases which would have been awarded under the provisions of the Pensions (Increase) Act 1971(a), during the period beginning with the day following loss of office for which compensation is payable and ending on the day the subsequent employment terminated, on an official pension (within the meaning of that Act) of £100 a year which commenced from the first mentioned day, and

(ii) the denominator of the fraction is equivalent to the aggregate of an official pension of £100 a year and the amount of the increases so determined.

(6) Where compensation has been calculated in accordance with Regulation 23, the provisions of this Regulation shall only apply in relation to the part (if any) of the superannuation benefit which is attributable to annual emoluments in excess of those to which the person was entitled on entering the new employment referred to in Regulation 23.

(7) Where compensation is payable in respect of diminution of emoluments, the provisions of this Regulation shall apply only in relation to the part (if any) of the superannuation benefit which is attributable to annual emoluments in excess of those to which the person was entitled immediately prior to the diminution.

Reduction of compensation in certain cases

28.—(1) If under the Police Pensions Regulations any benefit payable to a person under those Regulations would have been subject to reduction or suspension on his taking up other specified employment, any retirement compensation to which he is entitled for loss of office as a member of a police force or diminution of emoluments shall, where such an employment is taken up, be reduced or suspended in the like manner and to the like extent.

(2) There shall be deducted from any long-term compensation or retirement compensation payable to any person any contributory payments remaining unpaid at the date when he suffered loss of office that are not recovered in accordance with the provisions of the Police Pensions Regulations.

(3) Where in any week a person entitled to long-term compensation for loss or diminution of emoluments is also entitled to a National Insurance benefit, there shall be deducted from the long-term compensation payable in respect of that week a sum equal to the amount by which the aggregate of—

(i) the National Insurance benefit that would be payable in respect of that week if calculated at the rate applicable at the date of loss or diminution, and

(ii) the weekly rate at which the long-term compensation would be payable but for this Regulation,

exceeds two-thirds of the weekly rate of the emoluments of the office which he has lost or in which the emoluments have been diminished.

(4) No deduction shall be made under paragraph (3) insofar as—

(*a*) an equivalent sum is deducted from the emoluments of his current employment, and

(*b*) that deduction from those emoluments has not occasioned an increase in his long-term compensation.

(5) (*a*) In paragraph (2) the expression "contributory payments" in relation to any person means any payments which he undertook to make under the Police Pensions Regulations for the purpose of qualifying for benefits in respect of previous service or for an improved widow's pension.

(a) 1971 c. 56.

(b) In paragraph (3) the expression "weekly rate" means seven-three hundred and sixty-fifths of the relevant annual rate, and the expression "National Insurance benefit" means any unemployment, sickness, invalidity or injury benefit or retirement pension payable under any enactment relating to National Insurance, other than a benefit claimable by him in respect of a dependant.

Notification of change of circumstances

29. Where a person to whom these Regulations apply—

- (a) after suffering loss of office or diminution of emoluments enters any employment referred to in Regulation 23 or becomes entitled to any superannuation benefit on ceasing to hold such an employment, or

- (b) being entitled to long-term compensation, whilst that compensation is liable to review in accordance with the provisions of Regulation 30, enters any employment, or ceases to hold an employment, or receives any increase in his emoluments in an employment, or

- (c) being entitled to retirement compensation, enters employment in which the compensation is subject to reduction or suspension under Regulation 28 or ceases to hold such an employment, or

- (d) being entitled to long-term compensation, starts to receive any benefit, any increase in benefit or any further benefit, under any enactment relating to National Insurance,

he shall forthwith in writing inform the compensating authority of that fact.

Review of awards of long-term or retirement compensation

30.—(1) The compensating authority shall—

- (a) on the expiry of 6 months from the decision date, or

- (b) on the occurrence of any material change in the circumstances of the case,

whichever shall first occur, and thereafter within a period of 2 years after the decision date, or within any longer period specified in the subsequent provisions of this Regulation, and at intervals of not more than 6 months, review its decision or, where the claim has been the subject of an appeal, the decision of the tribunal, and (subject to paragraph (7)) these Regulations shall apply in relation to such a review as they apply in relation to the initial determination of the claim; and on such a review, in the light of any material change in the circumstances of the case, compensation may be awarded, or compensation previously awarded may be increased, reduced or discontinued, subject to the limits set out in these Regulations.

(2) The person to whom the decision relates may require the compensating authority to carry out the review mentioned in paragraph (1) at any time mentioned in that paragraph if he considers that there has been a change in the circumstances of his case which is material for the purposes of these Regulations.

(3) The compensating authority shall carry out a review in accordance with paragraph (1), notwithstanding the expiration of the period of 2 years mentioned in that paragraph, if—

- (a) the emoluments of employment or work undertaken as a result of the loss of office had been taken into account in determining the amount of any compensation awarded, and

- (b) that employment or work has been lost or the emoluments thereof reduced, otherwise than by reason of misconduct or incapacity to perform the duties which the person might reasonably have been required to perform, and

(c) the compensating authority is satisfied that the loss or reduction is causing him hardship,

and where any decision is so reviewed, the decision shall be subject to further review in accordance with paragraph (1) as if the review carried out under this paragraph had been the initial determination of the claim.

(4) Paragraphs (1) and (2) shall apply in relation to any decision on a claim for long-term or retirement compensation in respect of diminution of emoluments as they apply in relation to any decision mentioned in paragraph (1) and as if in paragraph (1) "decision date" means the date on which any decision on a claim for long-term compensation for diminution of emoluments is notified to the claimant, but—

(a) where the person to whom the decision relates ceases to hold the office in which his emoluments were diminished, a review shall be held within 3 months after that date, but no further review shall be held after the expiry of that period, and

(b) while that person continues to hold that office, there shall be no limit to the period within which a review may take place.

(5) Notwithstanding anything contained in the foregoing provisions of this Regulation, the compensating authority shall review a decision, whether of the authority or the tribunal, on a claim for long-term compensation for loss of office or diminution of emoluments as a member of a police force after the expiration of any period within which a review is required to be made if at any time—

(a) the person to whom the decision relates becomes engaged in any employment (hereinafter referrred to as "his current employment") the emoluments of which are payable out of public funds and which he had undertaken subsequent to the loss or diminution, and

(b) the aggregate of the emoluments of his current employment, any pension under the Police Pensions Regulations and the long-term compensation payable to him exceeds the emoluments of the office which he has lost or, as the case may be, of which the emoluments have been diminished.

(6) The compensating authority shall further review any decision reviewed under paragraph (5) whenever the emoluments of the person's current employment are increased.

(7) If on any review under this Regulation the compensation is reduced it shall not be reduced below the amount by which the emoluments of the work or employment undertaken as a result of the loss of employment or diminution of emoluments, together with any pension under the Police Pensions Regulations falls short of the emoluments of the office which he has lost, or, as the case may be, in which the emoluments have been diminished.

(8) The compensating authority shall give to a person to whom a decision relates not less than 14 days' notice of any review of that decision to be carried out under this Regulation unless the review is carried out at his request.

(9) In this Regulation the expression "decision date" means the date on which any decision on a claim for long-term or retirement compensation for loss of employment is notified to a claimant under Regulation 32.

(10) For the purpose of Regulations 14(4), 23(1) and 27(6) and (7) and any review under this Regulation, no account shall be taken of any increase in the emoluments of any work or employment undertaken as a result of the loss of office or diminution of emoluments, or of any superannuation benefit attributable to such an increase, if any such increase is effective from any date after the date of the loss or diminution, and is attributable to a rise in the cost of living.

(11) Nothing in this Regulation shall preclude the making of any adjustment of compensation required by Regulation 27 or 28.

Compounding of awards

31.—(1) In the case where an annual sum which has been or might be awarded under these Regulations does not exceed £35, the compensating authority may, at its discretion, compound its liability in respect thereof by paying a lump sum equivalent to the capital value of the annual sum.

(2) In any other case, if the person who has been awarded long-term or retirement compensation requests it to do so, the compensating authority may after having regard to the state of health of that person and the other circumstances of the case, compound up to one quarter of their liability to make payments under the award (other than payments to a widow, child or other dependant under Regulation 24) by the payment of an equivalent amount as a lump sum.

(3) The making of a composition under paragraph (2) in relation to an award of long-term or retirement compensation shall not prevent the subsequent making of a composition under paragraph (1) in relation to that award but, subject as aforesaid, not more than one composition may be made in relation to any award.

Part VII

Procedure and Miscellaneous

Procedure on making claims

32.—(1) Every claim for compensation under these Regulations and every request for a review of an award of long-term or retirement compensation shall be made in accordance with this Regulation.

(2) Every such claim or request shall be made to the compensating authority in writing and shall state whether any other claim for compensation has been made by the claimant under these Regulations.

(3) Resettlement compensation shall be claimed separately from any other form of compensation claimable under these Regulations.

(4) The compensating authority shall consider any such claim or request in accordance with the relevant provisions of these Regulations and shall notify the claimant in writing of their decision—

    (*a*) in the case of a claim for resettlement compensation, not later than 1 month after the receipt of the claim,

    (*b*) in the case of a claim for, or request for a review of an award of, compensation under Part IV or V of these Regulations, not later than 1 month after the receipt of the claim or request, and

    (*c*) in any other case, as soon as possible after the decision;

but the decision of the compensating authority shall not be invalidated by reason of the fact that notice of the decision is given after the expiry of the period mentioned in this paragraph.

(5) Every notification of a decision by the compensating authority (whether granting or refusing compensation or reviewing an award, or otherwise affecting any compensation under these Regulations) shall contain a statement—

(a) giving reasons for the decision;

(b) showing how any compensation has been calculated and, in particular, if the amount is less than the maximum which could have been awarded under these Regulations, showing the factors taken into account in awarding that amount; and

(c) directing the attention of the claimant to his right under Regulation 39, if he is aggrieved by the decision, to institute proceedings before a tribunal and giving him the address to which any application instituting those proceedings should be sent.

Claimants to furnish information

33.—(1) Any person claiming or receiving compensation or whose award of compensation is being reviewed shall furnish all such information that the compensating authority may at any time reasonably require; and he shall verify that information in such manner, including the production of documents in his possession or control, as may be reasonably so required.

(2) Such a person shall, on receipt of reasonable notice, present himself for interview at any place that the compensating authority may reasonably require; and any person who attends for interview may, if he so desires be represented by his adviser.

Procedure on death of claimant

34.—(1) In the event of the death of a claimant or of a person who, if he had survived, could have been a claimant, a claim for compensation under these Regulations may be continued or made, as the case may be, by his personal representatives.

(2) Where any such claim is continued or made as aforesaid by personal representatives, the personal representatives shall, as respects any steps to be taken or thing to be done by them in order to continue or make the claim, be deemed for the purposes of these Regulations to be the person entitled to claim, but, save as aforesaid, the person in whose right they continue or make the claim shall be deemed for the purposes of these Regulations to be that person, and the relevant provisions of these Regulations shall be construed accordingly.

(3) The compensating authority may in any case where a person who, if he had survived could have been a claimant, has died, extend the period within which a claim under Regulation 7 or 12 is to be made by his personal representatives.

Calculation of service

35. For the purpose of making any calculation under these Regulations in respect of a person's reckonable service, all periods of that service shall be aggregated, and except where reference is made to completed years of service if the aggregated service includes a fraction of a year, that fraction shall, if it equals or exceeds 6 months, be treated as a year, and shall, in any other case be disregarded.

Emoluments

36.—(1) In these Regulations, subject to the provisions of paragraph (2) and Regulation 37 (temporary variation of emoluments) the expression "emoluments" means all salary, wages, fees and other payments paid or made to an officer as such for his own use, and also the money value of any accommodation or other allowances in kind appertaining to his employment, but does not include payments for overtime which are not a usual incident of his employment, or any allowances payable to him to cover the cost of providing office accommodation or clerical or other assistance, or any travelling or subsistence allowance or other moneys to be spent, or to cover expenses incurred, by him for the purposes of his employment.

(2) Where fees or other variable payments were paid to an officer as part of his emoluments during any period immediately preceding the loss or diminution the amount in respect of fees or other variable payments to be included in the annual rate of emoluments shall be the annual average of the fees or other payments paid to him during the period of 5 years immediately preceding the loss or diminution, or such other period as the compensating authority may think reasonable in the circumstances.

(3) For the purpose of these Regulations the annual rate of emoluments in relation to any employment which has been lost or the emoluments whereof have been lost or diminished shall be the amount described in (*a*), (*b*) or (*c*) of this paragraph, whichever is the greater—

    (*a*) the emoluments received by him in the period of 12 months immediately preceding the loss or diminution;

    (*b*) in the case of emoluments payable monthly, the emoluments payable in respect of the last complete month immediately preceding the loss or diminution multiplied by 12; or

    (*c*) in the case of emoluments payable weekly, the emoluments payable in respect of the last complete week immediately preceding the loss or diminution multiplied by 52.

Temporary variation of emoluments

37. In calculating for the purposes of these Regulations the amount of any emoluments lost, or the amount by which any emoluments have been diminished and in determining the resettlement and long-term compensation of any person who has suffered such a loss or diminution—

    (*a*) no account shall be taken of any temporary increase or decrease in the amount of the person's emoluments which is attributable to the passing or making of any provision mentioned in Regulation 4 and otherwise than in the ordinary course of his employment, and

    (*b*) in any case where an office becomes vacant by reason of the last holder thereof either becoming a person duly entitled, in respect of the same employment, to benefits payable under regulations made under section 260(3) of the Local Government Act 1972(**a**) (early retirement of Chief Officers) or entering an employment to which Article 10 of the Local Government (New Council's etc.) Order 1973(**b**) applies, any increase in the amount of a person's emoluments which is, after the date of com-

---

    (a) 1972 c. 70.   (b) S.I. 1973/444 (1973 I, p. 1535).

mencement of the Regulations or the Order relating to that person, attributable to—

(i) his filling that office in an acting or temporary capacity, or

(ii) his performance of, or responsibility for, the duties of that office, shall be disregarded.

Compensation not assignable

38.—(1) Subject to any statutory provision in that behalf, any compensation under these Regulations shall be paid by the compensating authority and (except in the case of compensation payable in accordance with Regulation 24(4)) shall be payable to, or in trust for, the person who is entitled to receive it, and shall not be assignable.

(2) Without prejudice to any other right of recovery, any compensation paid in error may be recovered by the compensating authority by deduction from any compensation payable under these Regulations.

Right of appeal from decision of compensating authority

39.—(1) Every person who is aggrieved by any decision of the compensating authority with respect to a compensation question or by any failure on the part of the compensating authority to notify him of any such decision within the appropriate time prescribed by these Regulations, may within 13 weeks of the notification to him of the decision or the expiry of the prescribed time, as the case may be, institute proceedings for the determination of the question by a tribunal in accordance with the Industrial Tribunals (Industrial Relations, etc.) Regulations 1972**(a)** and these Regulations; and the tribunal shall determine the question accordingly.

(2) Every interested authority aggrieved by any decision of the compensating authority with respect to a compensation question may, within 13 weeks of the notification to them of the decision, institute proceedings for the determination of the question by a tribunal in accordance with the Industrial Tribunals (Industrial Relations, etc.) Regulations 1972 and these Regulations; and the tribunal shall determine the question accordingly.

(3) For the purpose of any proceedings described in paragraph (1) a person or persons may be appointed to sit with the tribunal as assessor or assessors.

(4) The compensating authority shall give effect to the decision of a tribunal subject to any modifications that may be required in consequence of any appeal from that decision on a point of law.

Roy Jenkins,
One of Her Majesty's Principal
Secretaries of State.

Home Office,
Whitehall.
25th April 1974.

(a) S.I. 1972/38 (1972 I, p. 91).

Regulation 2. **SCHEDULE**

1. An officer of a local authority.

2. An officer of a water authority.

3. An officer of an association—

  (i) which is representative of local authorities,

  (ii) which is established by one or more of the associations described in (i) above for the purpose of disseminating information concerning local government, or

  (iii) being the Association of River Authorities or the British Waterworks Association.

4. The holder of the office of justices' clerk or a person employed in assisting the holder of such an office in the performance of his duties.

5. An officer of a probation and after-care committee.

6. An officer of a Local Valuation Panel.

7. A person employed by managers of an approved school, remand home, approved probation hostel or approved probation home (which has not been taken over by a local authority or by a joint committee representing two or more local authorities) to whom a certificate of approval under section 79 of the Children and Young Persons Act 1933(a) has been issued by the Secretary of State for Health and Social Security.

8. A person employed by a voluntary organisation described in section 30 of the National Assistance Act 1948(b).

9. A person employed by the Central Council for the Education and Training in Social Work and the Courses for the Education and Training of Health Visitors.

10. A person employed by a Passenger Transport Executive.

11. A person employed by or under (and for the purpose of the functions of) any person described in paragraphs 1–3 and 5–10 above.

EXPLANATORY NOTE
(This Note is not part of the Regulations.)

1. These Regulations provide for the payment of compensation to or in respect of chief constables, deputy chief constables or assistant chief constables who suffer loss of office or loss or diminution of emoluments in consequence of the provisions of the Local Government Act 1972 or any instrument made thereunder.

2. Part I of the Regulations contains definitions. Part II specifies the persons to whom the Regulations apply and the grounds of entitlement to compensation.

3. The compensation payable is—

  (*a*) resettlement compensation for loss of office (Part III);

  (*b*) long-term compensation for loss of office or loss or diminution of emoluments (Part IV);

  (*c*) retirement compensation for loss of office or loss or diminution of emoluments (Part V);

  (*d*) compensation payable on the death of a claimant (Part V).

(a) 1933 c. 12.   (b) 1948 c. 29.

4. Resettlement compensation is payable in a lump sum to persons with at least 2 years' service in relevant employment. The qualifying conditions and factors to be considered are set out in Regulation 7 and the methods of calculation are set out in Regulations 8, 9 and 10.

5. Long-term and retirement compensation is payable to persons with at least 5 years' service in relevant employment. The qualifying conditions and factors to be considered are set out in Regulations 12 and 13.

6. The method of calculating the amount of long-term compensation is laid down in Regulations 14 (loss of emoluments) and 15 (diminution of emoluments).

The compensation is payable from the date determined under Regulation 16, but is not payable for any period in respect of which retirement compensation is payable.

7. Retirement compensation is based upon accrued pension rights (Regulations 18 and 20) supplemented in the case of persons aged 40 years or over at the date of the loss or diminution by the addition of notional years of service (Regulation 18). Retirement compensation is ordinarily payable from the age of compulsory retirement but in certain circumstances is payable earlier (Regulations 19 and 20).

8. Compensation is payable to the widow, child or other dependant or to the personal representatives or trustees of a claimant who dies where such persons would have benefited under the relevant pension scheme (Regulation 24).

9. Part VI provides for long-term and retirement compensation to be reviewed and for awards to be varied in the light of changing circumstances. It also contains provisions for the adjustment, suspension and compounding of compensation in certain circumstances.

10. Part VII contains provisions relating to the procedure for making claims and notifying decisions. A right is given to a claimant who is aggrieved by a decision on a compensation question or the failure of the compensating authority to notify its decision to refer the question for determination by a tribunal in accordance with the Industrial Tribunals (Industrial Relations, etc.) Regulations 1972.

STATUTORY INSTRUMENTS

1974 No. 760

SEEDS

The Seeds (Registration and Licensing) Regulations 1974

Made - - - -		*29th April* 1974
Laid before Parliament		*7th May* 1974
Coming into Operation		*28th May* 1974

The Minister of Agriculture, Fisheries and Food and the Secretary of State, acting jointly, in exercise of the powers vested in them by sections 16(1), (1A), (3) and (8) and 36 of the Plant Varieties and Seeds Act 1964(a) as amended by section 4(1) of and paragraph 5(1), (2), (3) and (5) of Schedule 4 to the European Communities Act 1972(b) and of all other powers enabling them in that behalf, after consultation with the Council on Tribunals in accordance with section 10(1) of the Tribunals and Inquiries Act 1971(c) as applied to the Plant Varieties and Seeds Tribunal and with representatives of such interests as appear to them to be concerned, hereby make the following Regulations.

Citation and commencement

1. These Regulations, which apply to Great Britain, may be cited as the Seeds (Registration and Licensing) Regulations 1974 and shall come into operation on 28th May 1974.

Interpretation

2.—(1) In these Regulations, unless the context otherwise requires—

"the Act" means the Plant Varieties and Seeds Act 1964 as amended by section 43 of and Schedule 7 to the Agriculture (Miscellaneous Provisions) Act 1968(d) and by section 4(1) of and paragraph 5 of Schedule 4 to the European Communities Act 1972;

"marketing" includes, as the context shall permit, the offering for sale, exposing for sale, sale and possession with a view to sale of seeds, and any transaction in the course of business under which the property in seeds is transferred from one person to another and "marketed" shall be construed accordingly;

"the Minister" means, as respects England and Wales, the Minister of Agriculture, Fisheries and Food and, as respects Scotland, the Secretary of State;

"seed merchant" means a person engaged in the business of trading in seeds other than trading only in small packages of seeds as defined in seeds regulations or in unpacketed seeds which may be marketed in accordance with seeds regulations;

(a) 1964 c. 14.   (b) 1972 c. 68.
(c) 1971 c. 62.   (d) 1968 c. 34.

"seed packer" means a person engaged in the business of re-packing seeds or a person who in accordance with the requirements of seeds regulations labels or marks packages of standard seeds of vegetables;

"seed processor" means a person engaged in the business of cleaning, treating or otherwise processing seeds intended for sale;

"seeds" means seeds of any kind to which, for the time being, seeds regulations apply but does not include seed potatoes or silvicultural propagating or planting material;

"seeds regulations" means regulations made under section 16 of the Act and for the time being in force;

"the Tribunal" means the Plant Varieties and Seeds Tribunal established by section 10 of and Schedule 4 to the Act, as respectively amended by paragraph 5(5) of Schedule 4 to the European Communities Act 1972.

(2) The Interpretation Act 1889(a) shall apply to the interpretation of these Regulations as it applies to the interpretation of an Act of Parliament.

Registration of seed merchants, seed packers and seed processors

3.—(1) No person shall after the 31st August 1974 carry on the business of a seed merchant, of a seed packer or of a seed processor unless he has by not later than that date applied to the Minister for registration as a seed merchant, seed packer or seed processor, as the case may be, for the purposes of these Regulations and the Minister has not refused so to register him or unless he is for the time being so registered by the Minister.

(2) A person desirous of being so registered shall make an application to the Minister in writing and shall give to the Minister such information and particulars relating to his business or proposed business as the Minister may require.

(3) The Minister shall register a person if he is satisfied that there are available to such person such premises, machinery, equipment and facilities and the services of such persons as appear to the Minister to be adequate to enable such person to carry on the business to which the application relates.

(4) A person so registered shall keep proper records of his transactions in seeds and of the transport, treatment, testing and other operations undertaken by him or on his behalf in relation to any seeds and shall give to the Minister such information as he shall require and when required to do so shall permit an officer authorised by the Minister to inspect and take copies of any such records and to inspect the premises, machinery, equipment and facilities available for the carrying on of the business in respect of which such person is registered.

(5) The registration of a person shall be effective for a period not exceeding three years: Provided that the Minister may at any time revoke such registration if it appears to him that there are no longer available to such person such premises, machinery, equipment, facilities and services as are adequate to enable him to carry on the business in respect of which he is registered, or if such person has failed to comply with the obligations imposed by paragraph (4) of this Regulation.

(a) 1889 c. 63.

Prohibition of marketing of seeds

4.—(1) If it shall appear to the Minister that seeds of a particular category, kind or variety marketed by a person registered in accordance with Regulation 3 of these Regulations have been shown to fail to satisfy the requirements of seeds regulations he may prohibit for either an indeterminate or for a specified period the further marketing of seeds of that category, kind or variety by such person from such premises, if any, as may be indicated and thereafter such seeds may not be marketed by such person from such premises, if any, until the prohibition is terminated.

(2) If the Minister during the period whilst the marketing of seeds is so prohibited becomes satisfied that it is no longer likely that such seeds when marketed by such person will fail to satisfy the said requirements he shall terminate the prohibition imposed by this Regulation.

Representations and hearings

5.—(1) The Minister shall, before making a decision to refuse to register a person on the ground that he is not satisfied as to one or more of the matters referred to in Regulation 3(3) of these Regulations, to revoke the registration of a person in accordance with the proviso to Regulation 3(5) of these Regulations or to prohibit in accordance with Regulation 4(1) of these Regulations the marketing by a person of seeds of a particular category, kind or variety, give to such a person a notice in writing of his proposed decision with particulars of the grounds upon which it is founded and shall afford to such person, subject to the payment of any fee imposed by seeds regulations, an opportunity of making representations to him in writing or of being heard by a person appointed by him for the purpose or of both making such representations and being so heard.

(2) The said notice shall inform the person affected of his right to make written representations, of the manner in which and the time (not being less than 21 days from the giving of the notice) within which such representations may be made and of his right to be heard and of the manner in which and the time (not being less than 21 days from the giving of the notice) within which he may apply for an opportunity to be heard.

(3) If the person affected shall make no written representations nor apply to be heard the Minister shall proceed to make his decision.

(4) A person making written representations to the Minister shall with the representations, and a person applying to be heard shall not later than 7 days before the day appointed for the hearing, deliver to the Minister two copies of any documents upon which such person proposes to rely.

(5) If a person so entitled shall apply to be heard the Minister shall, subject to the payment of any fee imposed by seeds regulations, appoint a time and place for the hearing.

(6) In appointing such time and place the Minister shall have regard to the convenience of the person who is to be heard and of his witnesses, the situation of any premises to be viewed in connection with the matter and to the other circumstances of the case.

(7) The Minister shall give to the person who is to be heard not less than 21 days notice in writing of the time and place of the hearing.

(8) The hearing may be adjourned from time to time.

(9) The person who is to be heard may be represented at the hearing by a person chosen by him.

(10) The person who is to be heard may give evidence and he or his representative may call witnesses and produce documents: Provided that except with the leave of the person conducting the hearing no document shall be produced unless copies were delivered to the Minister in accordance with paragraph (4) of this Regulation.

(11) The person conducting the hearing may require any witness to give his evidence on oath or affirmation and may for that purpose administer an oath or affirmation in due form.

(12) The hearing shall be in public unless the person conducting the hearing after consulatation with the person who is to be heard or his representative otherwise directs.

(13) The Minister shall make his decision after taking into account any written representations made to him and the submissions made and evidence adduced at the hearing and shall give the person affected notice thereof, and, if his decision is adverse to such person, with his reasons for his decision together with an indication of the time within which and the manner in which an appeal may be brought.

Extension of time

6. Where any document is to be delivered or given or any act is to be done within a time prescribed by these Regulations such time may, if in all the circumstances of the case he consideres it reasonable to do so, be extended by the Minister for such period and upon such terms, if any, as he thinks fit.

Appeal

7.—(1) An appeal shall lie to the Tribunal against a decision of the Minister to refuse to register a person, to revoke the registration of a person or to prohibit the marketing by a person of seeds of a particular category, kind or variety.

(2) The hearing of an appeal by the Tribunal shall be held in such place as shall be determined by the Chairman of the Tribunal who shall have regard to the matters referred to in Regulation 5(6) of these Regulations as well as to the convenience of the members of the Tribunal.

(3) Where an appeal is brought against any decision of the Minister to refuse to register a person who applied for registration by not later than 31st August 1974, to revoke the registration of a person or to prohibit the marketing by a person of seeds of a particular category, kind or variety the operation of the decision shall be suspended pending the final determination of the appeal.

(4) The Minister shall take such steps as may be necessary to give effect to any decision given on the final determination of the appeal.

Seed testing stations

8.—(1) The Minister may by licence granted to any person authorise him to maintain for a period specified in the licence an establishment for the testing of seeds for the purposes of seeds regulations.

(2) A licence granted in accordance with paragraph (1) of this Regulation may impose such conditions as the Minister shall deem appropriate having

regard to the kinds of seeds to be tested, the kinds of tests to be made and the procedure to be followed in connection therewith and may require the keeping and production of records.

(3) The Minister may withdraw a licence granted in accordance with paragraph (1) of this Regulation if it appears to him that there has been a breach of any of the conditions referred to in paragraph (2) of this Regulation.

(4) A breach of any of the conditions referred to in paragraph (2) of this Regulation shall be an offence against these Regulations.

(5) Upon the granting of a licence in accordance with paragraph (1) of this Regulation there shall be payable to the Minister the appropriate fee prescribed in seeds regulations.

Crop inspectors and seed samplers

9.—(1) The Minister upon being satisfied that a person has undergone an appropriate course of instruction and is otherwise qualified for the purpose may grant him a licence for a period specified therein to be a crop inspector or a seed sampler.

(2) A person so licensed may for the purposes of seeds regulations perform such functions and in such manner, if any, as the Minister may direct.

(3) The Minister may at any time withdraw a licence granted to a person under paragraph (1) of this Regulation if he is satisfied that such person is no longer qualified or is otherwise unfit to perform the functions of a crop inspector or a seed sampler, as the case may be.

Publication

10. The Minister shall be at liberty to publish in such manner as he thinks fit the names and addresses of person for the time being registered or licensed in pursuance of these regulations.

In Witness whereof the Official Seal of the Minister of Agriculture, Fisheries and Food is hereunto affixed on 26th April 1974.

(L.S.)   *Frederick Peart,*
                      Minister of Agriculture, Fisheries and Food.

                                                        William Ross,
                                    Secretary of State for Scotland.

29th April 1974.

EXPLANATORY NOTE

(This Note is not part of the Regulations.)

These Regulations, which apply to Great Britain are made under Part II of the Plant Varieties and Seeds Act 1964 as amended by the European Communities Act 1972.

The Regulations provide that after the 31st August 1974 no person shall carry on the business of a seed merchant, seed packer or seed processor unless he is either registered or has before that date applied for registration and his application has not been refused. A seed merchant is so defined as to exclude persons trading only in small packages of seeds or loose seeds under the relevant seeds Regulations.

Registration in England and Wales is effected with the Minister of Agriculture, Fisheries and Food and in Scotland with the Secretary of State and continues for a period not exceeding three years. The appropriate Minister is to be satisfied that persons to be registered have available to them adequate premises, machinery equipment, facilities and services and he may revoke a registration if these do not continue to be available. He may also revoke the registration of a person who fails to maintain proper records and make them available for inspection by the Minister. Further, the Minister may temporarily prohibit the marketing, by a person registered, of seeds of a particular category, kind or variety which have fallen short of the requirements of seed Regulations.

Provision is made for oral and written representations to the Minister before he refuses to register a person, revokes a registration or prohibits the marketing of seeds and an appeal against his decision may be made to the Plant Varieties and Seeds Tribunal.

The Regulations also provide for the licensing by the appropriate Minister of seed testing stations, which will be required to observe such conditions as to procedure and keeping of records as are imposed by the licence, and of crop inspectors and seed samplers.

STATUTORY INSTRUMENTS

1974 No. 761

DEFENCE

The Rules of Procedure (Army) (Amendment) Rules 1974

Made - - -	*30th April* 1974
Laid before Parliament	*8th May* 1974
Coming into Operation	*29th May* 1974

The Secretary of State in exercise of the powers conferred upon him by sections 103, 104, 105 and 106 of the Army Act 1955(a) and of all other powers enabling him in that behalf hereby makes the following rules: —

Citation and commencement

1. These Rules may be cited as the Rules of Procedure (Army) (Amendment) Rules 1974 and shall come into operation on the 29th day of May 1974.

Interpretation

2. The Interpretation Act 1889(b) shall apply to the interpretation of these Rules as it applies to an Act of Parliament.

Amendment to the Rules of Procedure (Army) 1972(c)

3.—(1) The Rules of Procedure (Army) 1972 shall be amended in accordance with the following provisions of this Rule.

(2) In Part (2) of the Second Schedule (Statements of Offences), for the Statement of Offence relating to Section 65(*b*) there shall be substituted: —

$$\left.\begin{array}{l}\text{Striking}\\\text{Ill-}\\\text{treating}\end{array}\right\}\left\{\begin{array}{l}\text{a warrant officer}\\\text{a non-commissioned}\\\text{officer}\\\text{a soldier}\end{array}\right\}\left\{\begin{array}{l}\text{of inferior rank}\\\text{of less seniority}\end{array}\right\}$$

contrary to Section 65(*b*) of the Army Act 1955

(3) In paragraph 4 of Form (9) in the Fourth Schedule (Service Record of Accused), for the words "under the age of 16 years" there shall be substituted the words "dependent upon him".

(4) In Part (2) of the Sixth Schedule (Oaths At Courts-Martial), in the Oath for Shorthand Writer, for the words "take down" there shall be substituted the word "record".

Roy Mason,
One of Her Majesty's Principal
Secretaries of State.

Dated 30th April 1974.

(a) 1955 c. 18.   **(b)** 1889 c. 63.   **(c)** S.I. 1972/316 (1972 I, p. 965).

EXPLANATORY NOTE

(This Note is not part of the Rules.)

These Rules amend the Rules of Procedure (Army) 1972 so that reference to the accused's family commitments in the service record of the accused considered by a Court Martial before deliberation on sentence will now include a reference to all children dependent upon him rather than only to children under the age of 16 years. They further amend the principal Rules by making a technical correction in the form of Statement of Offence provided in respect of Section 65(*b*) of Army Act 1955. A further amendment changes the form of oath to be administered to the shorthand writer to enable electronic or mechanical means of recording to be used.

STATUTORY INSTRUMENTS

1974 No. 762

CLEAN AIR

The Smoke Control Areas (Exempted Fireplaces) (Variation) Order 1974

Made - - - -	30*th April* 1974
Laid before Parliament	8*th May* 1974
Coming into Operation	29*th May* 1974

The Secretary of State for the Environment, in exercise of the powers conferred by section 11(8) of the Clean Air Act 1956**(a)** and now vested in him **(b)** and of all other powers enabling him in that behalf, hereby orders as follows:—

Title and commencement

1. This order may be cited as the Smoke Control Areas (Exempted Fireplaces) (Variation) Order 1974 and shall come into operation on 29th May 1974.

Interpretation

2. The Interpretation Act 1889**(c)** shall apply for the interpretation of this order as it applies for the interpretation of an Act of Parliament.

Variation of conditions for classes of fireplace exempted from section 11 *of the Clean Air Act* 1956

3. For the conditions set out in column 2 of the Schedule to each of the orders specified in the Schedule hereto, being the conditions upon which certain fireplaces are exempted from the provisions of section 11 of the Clean Air Act 1956 (which empowers a local authority to declare the whole or any part of their district to be a smoke control area), there shall be substituted the following:—

"The fireplace shall be installed, maintained and operated so as to minimise the emission of smoke and in accordance with the manufacturer's instructions. No fuel shall be used other than selected washed coal marketed under the name "Housewarm" by agreement with the National Coal Board.".

(a) 1956 c. 52.   **(b)** S.I. 1970/1681 (1970 III, p. 5551).
(c) 1889 c. 63.

SCHEDULE

The Smoke Control Areas (Exempted Fireplaces) Order 1970(a)
The Smoke Control Areas (Exempted Fireplaces) (No. 2) Order 1970(b)
The Smoke Control Areas (Exempted Fireplaces) Order 1971(c)
The Smoke Control Areas (Exempted Fireplaces) Order 1972 (d)
The Smoke Control Areas (Exempted Fireplaces) (No. 2) Order 1972 (e)
The Smoke Control Areas (Exempted Fireplaces) Order 1973 (f)

30th April 1974.

Anthony Crosland,
Secretary of State
for the Environment.

EXPLANATORY NOTE

(This Note is not part of the Order.)

Section 11 of the Clean Air Act 1956 empowers local authorities to declare the whole or any part of their district to be a smoke control area, in which the emission of smoke is, generally, prohibited. This Order alters the conditions, by extending them, upon which the fireplaces in the Orders listed are exempted, namely the Housewarmer manufactured for the National Coal Board by Ideal Standard Ltd; the Triancomatic T80 manufactured by Trianco Limited; the Rayburn CB 34 manufactured by Glynwed Foundries Ltd; the Parkray Coalmaster manufactured by Radiation Parkray Limited; the Trianco TGB17 manufactured by Trianco Limited; the Rayburn Prince 101 manufactured by Glynwed Foundries Limited and the Rayburn Prince 301 manufactured by Glynwed Foundries Limited.

(a) S.I. 1970/615 (1970 I, p. 1948). (b) S.I. 1970/1667 (1970 III, p. 5438).
(c) S.I. 1971/1265 (1971 II, p. 2630). (d) S.I. 1972/438 (1972 I, p. 1640).
(e) S.I. 1972/955 (1972 II, p. 2980). (f) S.I. 1973/2166 (1973 II, p.7568).

STATUTORY INSTRUMENTS

1974 No. 763

ROAD TRAFFIC

The Motor Vehicles (Type Approval) (Amendment) (No. 2) Regulations 1974

Made	-	-	-	-	*5th April* 1974
Laid before Parliament					*9th May* 1974
Coming into Operation					*30th May* 1974

The Secretary of State for the Environment, as the designated Minister under the European Communities (Designation) Order 1972(a), in exercise of his powers under section 2 of the European Communities Act 1972(b) and of all other enabling powers, hereby makes the following Regulations:—

1. These Regulations may be cited as the Motor Vehicles (Type Approval) (Amendment) (No. 2) Regulations 1974 and shall come into operation on 30th May 1974.

2. The Motor Vehicles (Type Approval) Regulations 1973(c) shall be amended in accordance with the following provisions of these Regulations.

3. Regulation 3 (Interpretation) shall have effect as though in paragraph (1)—

(*a*) for the definition of "information document" there were substituted the following:—

" "information document"—

   (i) in relation to an application, not being an application within sub-paragraph (iii) below, for the approval of a motor vehicle to which these Regulations apply, means a document in the form set out in Part I of Schedule 1 to these Regulations;

  (ii) in relation to an application, not being an application within sub-paragraph (iii) below, for the approval of a trailer to which these Regulations apply, means a document in the form set out in Part II of that Schedule, and

 (iii) in relation to an application for the approval of a vehicle to which these Regulations apply and for which the type approval requirements are contained in a single Community Directive or Regulation, or for the approval of a component of a vehicle to which these Regulations apply, means a document in a form issued for the purpose of such applications by or on behalf of the Secretary of State;";

(**a**) S.I. 1972/1811 (1972 III, p. 5216).   (**b**) 1972 c. 68.

(**c**) S.I. 1973/1199 (1973 II, p. 3610).

(b) for the definition of "the type approval requirements" there were substituted the following—

" "the type approval requirements", in relation to a vehicle or component, means such of the requirements with respect to the design, construction, equipment and marking of vehicles or their components contained in the Community Directives or Community Regulations as are for the time being applicable in relation to a vehicle or component of that type;";

(c) in the definition of "the Community Directives" after the words "the Council Directives" there were inserted the words "and Commission Directives", and before the words "Schedule 2" there were inserted the words "Part I of";

(d) after the definition of "the Community Directives" there were inserted the following definition:—

" "the Community Regulations" means the Council Regulations mentioned in Part II of Schedule 2 to these Regulations concerning the harmonisation of certain social legislation relating to road transport;"; and

(e) after the definition of "member State" there were inserted the following definition:—

" "the relevant approval mark" in relation to the marking of a component of a vehicle means the marking designated pursuant to section 63 of the Road Traffic Act 1972(a) as an approval mark applicable to such a component;".

4. Regulation 5 shall have effect as though—

(a) in paragraph (1)(a)(ii), for the words "such of the type approval requirements as apply in relation to vehicles or vehicle components of that type;" there were substituted the words "the type approval requirements;"; and

(b) in paragraph (2) the words "applicable to vehicles of that type" were omitted.

5. After Regulation 6 there shall be inserted the following Regulation:—

"Marking of vehicle components

6A. A manufacturer of a type vehicle component in respect of which a type approval certificate is in force may mark each component which is manufactured by him and which conforms with the type vehicle component in such of the relevant aspects of design, construction, equipment and marking as are mentioned in the type approval certificate with the relevant approval mark.".

6. Regulation 11 shall have effect as though—

(a) for the head note to that Regulation there were substituted the following:—

(a) 1972 c. 20.

"Suspension of type approval certificates where vehicles or vehicle components are altered", and

(b) in paragraph (1) after the word "force" there were inserted the words "or of a vehicle component marked with the relevant mark", after the words "made to the vehicle" there were inserted the words "or vehicle component", and after the words "the manufacturer of the vehicle" there were inserted the words "or the component".

7. Regulation 12 (Notice of cancellation, suspension or modification of type approval certificates) shall have effect as though in paragraph (3) after the words "previously issued" there were inserted the words "or any relevant approval mark applied".

8. Schedule 1 shall have effect as though—

(a) in the heading to Part I the words *"or to a component of such a motor vehicle"*, and

(b) in the heading to Part II the words *"or to a component of such a trailer"*

were omitted.

9. Schedule 2 shall have effect as though—

(a) after the words "Schedule 2" there were inserted the words "Part I";

(b) in Part I of Schedule 2—

   (i) in column 3, at the end of the first entry, there were added the words "as amended by Commission Directive 73/350/EEC dated 7th November 1973", and

   (ii) in column 4, at the end of the first entry, there were added the words "O.J. L321, 22.11.1973, p.33"; and

(c) at the end of Part I of Schedule 2 there were added the following Part—

"PART II

The Council Regulations on the harmonisation of certain social legislation relating to road transport

Community Reference No.	Date of Regulation	Subject Matter	Official Journal Reference
(EEC) No. 1463/70	20th July 1970	The introduction of recording equipment in road transport	O.J. L164, 27.7.1970, p.1 (S.E. 1970 (II) p. 482)"

Signed by authority of the Secretary of State.

Fred Mulley,

Minister for Transport,

Department of the Environment.

5th April 1974.

EXPLANATORY NOTE

(This Note is not part of the Regulations.)

These Regulations amend the Motor Vehicles (Type Approval) Regulations 1973 which make provision for the type approval of certain motor vehicles and trailers and their components where the Secretary of State is satisfied that the vehicle or vehicle component is of a type which conforms with the requirements as to design, construction, equipment and marking which are applicable thereto by virtue of certain Council Directives (EEC). The principal changes are as follows:—

(a) the forms of information document in Part I of Schedule 1 to the 1973 Regulations are now applicable only to applications in respect of motor vehicles and trailers; the information document to be used in connection with applications for approval of vehicles in relation to which all the requirements for approval are contained within one Community Directive or Regulation or for approval of vehicle components will be in a form to be issued by or on behalf of the Secretary of State;

(b) a new Regulation 6A empowers the manufacturer of a vehicle component in respect of which a type approval certificate is in force to apply an approval mark to components which are manufactured by him and which conform to the type vehicle components;

(c) the existing Schedule 2 becomes Part I of Schedule 2 and a reference is inserted to Commission Directive No. 73/350/EEC of 7th November 1973 (which amends Council Directive No. 70/157/EEC relating to the permissible sound level and the exhaust system of motor vehicles and which requires the refusal after 30th September 1974 of a type approval certificate in respect of a motor vehicle which does not comply with the amended provisions);

(d) a new Part II in Schedule 2 provides for reference to Regulations of the Council of the European Communities, on the harmonisation of certain social legislation relating to road transport, and providing for type approval of vehicles and components; and

(e) provision is made for the type approval of recording equipment in vehicles used for the carriage of passengers or goods by road in accordance with Council Regulation (EEC) No. 1463/70 of 20th July 1970.

STATUTORY INSTRUMENTS

1974 No. 764

MERCHANDISE MARKS

The Motor Vehicles (Designation of Approval Marks) Regulations 1974

Made - - - -	*5th April* 1974
Laid before Parliament	*9th May* 1974
Coming into Operation	*30th May* 1974

The Secretary of State for the Environment, in exercise of his powers under section 63(1) of the Road Traffic Act 1972**(a)**, as amended by the Designation of Approval Marks (European Communities) Regulations 1973**(b)** and of all other enabling powers, and after consultation with representative organisations in accordance with the provisions of section 199(2) of that Act, hereby makes the following Regulations:—

1.—(1) These Regulations may be cited as the Motor Vehicles (Designation of Approval Marks) Regulations 1974 and shall come into operation on 30th May 1974.

(2) In these Regulations the expression "the International Agreement of 1958" means the Agreement concerning the adoption of uniform conditions of approval and reciprocal recognition of approval for motor vehicle equipment and parts concluded at Geneva on 20th March 1958**(c)**, as amended**(d)**, to which the United Kingdom is a party**(e)**.

(3) The Interpretation Act 1889**(f)** shall apply for the interpretation of these Regulations as it applies for the interpretation of an Act of Parliament.

2. The Secretary of State hereby designates as an approval mark a marking which, subject to Part II of Schedule 1 to these Regulations, is in the form and of a size not less than the marking shown in the diagram in column 1 of Part I of that Schedule, the said marking being a marking for which the International Agreement of 1958, by virtue of the Regulation annexed to that Agreement specified in column 2 of Part I of the Schedule in relation to that marking, makes such provision as is mentioned in section 63(1)(a) and (b) of the Road Traffic Act 1972 in connection with a motor vehicle part being an advance-warning triangle.

3. The Secretary of State hereby designates as an approval mark a marking which, subject to Part II of Schedule 2 to these Regulations, is in the form and of a size not less than the marking shown in the diagram in Part I of that Schedule and is such that the ratios between the dimensions of the said marking are maintained, the said marking being a marking for which provision is made by the Regulation adopted under the EEC treaty and specified in column 2 of Part I of that Schedule, being such provision as is mentioned in section 63(1)(a) and (b) of the Road Traffic Act 1972 in connection with the motor vehicle part being road transport recording equipment and model record sheets.

(a) 1972 c. 20.　　　　　　　　　　　(b) S.I. 1973/1193 (1973 II, p.3571).
(c) Cmnd. 2535.　　　　　　　　　　　(d) Cmnd. 3562.
(e) By instrument of accession dated 14th January 1963 deposited with the Secretary-General of the United Nations on 15th January 1963.
(f) 1889 c. 63.

Signed by authority of the Secretary of State.

Fred Mulley,
Minister for Transport,
Department of the Environment.

5th April 1974.

SCHEDULE 1

Part I—*Diagram*

(1) Diagram showing marking	(2) Regulation annexed to International Agreement of 1958
 a › 8 millimetres	Regulation No. 27 (UNIFORM PROVISIONS FOR THE APPROVAL OF ADVANCE-WARNING TRIANGLES WHICH ENTERED INTO FORCE ON 15th SEPTEMBER 1972)

Part II—*Variations of Marking*

1. The number inside the circle in a marking in the diagram shown in column 1 of Part I above will be varied, where appropriate, so as to be the number assigned to each Contracting State party to the International Agreement of 1958 and applying the Regulation specified in column 2 of that part in relation to that marking.

2. The number outside the circle in such a marking will be varied, where appropriate, so as to be the number allotted by a competent authority to distinguish the manufacturer of the type of motor vehicle part concerned, namely an advance-warning triangle.

3. The said number will be close to and outside the circle in any position relative thereto, so however that it shall read in the same direction as the number inside the circle.

SCHEDULE 2
PART I—*Diagram*

(1) Diagram showing marking	(2) Regulation adopted under the EEC treaty
THE DIMENSIONS OF THE APPROVAL MARK ARE IN MILLIMETRES; THEY ARE MINIMUM DIMENSIONS AND THE RATIOS MUST BE MAINTAINED. e 4 1471	Regulation (EEC) No. 1463/70 of 20th July 1970 of the European Communities Council(a) on the introduction of recording equipment in road transport

PART II—*Variation of Marking*

1. The number shown inside the rectangle will be varied, where appropriate, so as to be the distinguishing symbol assigned to the country which has granted the approval, that is to say 1 for Germany, 2 for France, 3 for Italy, 4 for the Netherlands, 6 for Belgium, 11 for the United Kingdom, 12 for Luxembourg, IRL for Ireland and DK for Denmark.

2. The number shown outside and immediately below the rectangle will be varied, where appropriate, to correspond to the number of the approval document issued for the prototype vehicle component concerned, namely road transport recording equipment and model record sheets.

(a) O.J. L164, 27.7.1970, p. 1 (S.E. 1970 (II) p. 482).

EXPLANATORY NOTE

(This Note is not part of the Regulations.)

Section 63(1) of the Road Traffic Act 1972, as amended by the Designation of Approval Marks (European Communities) Regulations 1973, enacts that where any international agreement to which the United Kingdom is a party provides—

(a) for markings to be applied to motor vehicle parts of any description to indicate conformity with a type approved by any country, and

(b) for motor vehicle parts bearing those markings to be recognised as complying with the requirements imposed by the law of another country,

the Secretary of State may by Regulations designate the markings as approval marks.

Section 63 of the Road Traffic Act 1972 also provides that any markings so designated shall be deemed for the purpose of the Trades Description Act 1968 (c.29) to be a trade description and that it shall be an offence under that Act to apply an approval mark without proper authority.

These Regulations designate for the purposes of section 63 as approval marks, markings complying with the provisions of the Schedules to these Regulations and in respect of which either—

(i) the International Agreement of 1958 (referred to in these Regulations) and the Regulation specified in the Schedule to these Regulations and annexed to that Agreement make such provision as is mentioned in (a) and (b) above as respects a motor vehicle part being an advance-warning triangle, or

(ii) a regulation of the European Communities Council (EEC) No. 1463/70 of 20th July 1970 makes such provision as is mentioned in (a) and (b) above as respects motor vehicle parts being road transport recording equipment and model record sheets.

1974 No. 765

ROAD TRAFFIC

The Motor Vehicles (Construction and Use) (Amendment) (No. 2) Regulations 1974

Made - - - -	*5th April* 1974
Laid before Parliament	*9th May* 1974
Coming into Operation	*30th May* 1974

The Secretary of State for the Environment, in exercise of his powers under section 40(1) of the Road Traffic Act 1972(a) and of all other enabling powers, and after consultation with representative organisations in accordance with the provisions of section 199(2) of the Act, hereby makes the following Regulations:—

  1. These Regulations may be cited as the Motor Vehicles (Construction and Use) (Amendment) (No. 2) Regulations 1974 and shall come into operation on 30th May 1974.

  2. The Motor Vehicles (Construction and Use) Regulations 1973(b), as amended(c), shall be further amended so as to have effect in accordance with the following provisions of these Regulations.

  3. In Regulation 4A—
in the table, after the entry relating to Council Directive 70/157/EEC there shall be inserted the following item:—

"Council Directive 70/157/EEC of 6th February 1970(d), as amended by Commission Directive 73/350/EEC of 7th November 1973(e) (relating to the permissible sound level and exhaust system of motor vehicles)	1st March 1974	29 .."

  4. In Regulation 4B the words "or any other community instrument" shall be omitted.

  (a) 1972 c.20.   (b) S.I. 1973/24 (1973 I, p. 93).
  (c) The relevant amending instruments are S.I. 1973/1347, 1974/64
         (1973 II, p. 4133; 1974 I, p. 208).
  (d) O.J. L42, 23.2.1970, p. 16 (S.E. 1970 (I) p. 111).
  (e) O.J. L321, 22.11.1973, p. 33.

Signed by authority of the Secretary of State.

Fred Mulley,
Minister for Transport,
Department for the Environment.

5th April 1974.

EXPLANATORY NOTE

(This Note is not part of the Regulations.)

Regulation 4A of the Motor Vehicles (Construction and Use) Regulations 1973 exempts from compliance with the requirements of certain of the Regulations motor vehicles and trailers in respect of which a type approval certificate has been issued by the Secretary of State, or by the competent authority in another member state of the European Economic Community, and a certificate of conformity has been issued by the manufacturer of the vehicle. These Regulations provide for the exemption from compliance with Regulation 29 (which relates to permissible noise levels) vehicles in respect of which a type approval certificate and a certificate of conformity have been issued by reason of the vehicles' complying with the technical requirements of the relevant Community Directive as amended by a further Directive coming into operation on 1st March 1974. The vehicles which comply with the technical requirements of the Community Directive before amendment will continue to be exempted.

APPENDIX
OF CERTAIN INSTRUMENTS
NOT REGISTERED AS S.I.

Orders in Council,
Letters Patent
and Royal Instructions

relating to the Constitutions etc. of
Overseas Territories or to appeals to the Judicial
Committee,

Royal Proclamations, etc.

BY THE QUEEN

A PROCLAMATION

ELIZABETH R.

MARGARET

Whereas Her Majesty, in pursuance of the Regency Acts 1937 to 1953, was pleased, by Letters Patent dated the 24th day of January 1974, to delegate to the six Counsellors of State therein named or any two or more of them full power and authority during the period of Her Majesty's absence from the United Kingdom to summon and hold on Her Majesty's behalf Her Privy Council, to approve and sign on Her Majesty's behalf any proclamation relating to the affairs of the United Kingdom, to do on Her Majesty's behalf anything required to be done in relation to any such proclamation, and further to do on Her Majesty's behalf anything which, by virtue of any statutory or other power, Her Majesty is authorised to do for the safety or good government of the United Kingdom:

And whereas by section 1 of the Emergency Powers Act 1920, as amended by the Emergency Powers Act 1964, it is enacted that if it appears to Her Majesty that there have occurred or are about to occur events of such a nature as to be calculated, by interfering with the supply and distribution of food, water, fuel or light, or with the means of locomotion, to deprive the community, or any substantial portion of the community, of the essentials of life, Her Majesty may, by proclamation, declare that a state of emergency exists:

And, whereas, on the 9th day of January, 1974, Her Majesty made, in pursuance of the said Act of 1920, as so amended, a proclamation declaring that the industrial disputes affecting persons employed in the coal mines and on the railways and the reduction of oil supplies reaching Great Britain did, in Her Majesty's opinion, constitute a state of emergency within the meaning of that Act:

And whereas, by virtue of section 1 of the said Act of 1920, a proclamation issued in pursuance thereof does not remain in force for more than one month:

And whereas the continuance of the said industrial disputes and the continued reduction in those oil supplies do, in Our opinion, constitute a state of emergency within the meaning of the said Act of 1920:

Now, therefore, We, Elizabeth The Queen Mother and Margaret, Countess of Snowdon, being authorised thereto by the said Letters Patent, in pursuance of the said Act of 1920, and by and with the advice of Her Majesty's Privy Council, do on Her Majesty's behalf hereby declare that a state of emergency exists.

Given at the Court of Saint James this seventh day of February in the year of our Lord nineteen hundred and seventy-four, and in the twenty-third year of Her Majesty's Reign.

GOD SAVE THE QUEEN

PACIFIC ISLANDS

The Gilbert and Ellice Islands Colony (Electoral Provisions) Order 1974

At the Court of Saint James, the 20th day of February 1974

Present,

The Counsellors of State in Council

Whereas Her Majesty, in pursuance of the Regency Acts 1937 to 1953, was pleased, by Letters Patent dated the 24th day of January 1974, to delegate to the six Counsellors of State therein named or any two or more of them full power and authority during the period of Her Majesty's absence from the United Kingdom to summon and hold on Her Majesty's behalf Her Privy Council and to signify thereat Her Majesty's approval for anything for which Her Majesty's approval in Council is required;

And whereas it is proposed that in due course there shall be established for the Gilbert and Ellice Islands Colony (hereinafter referred to as "the Colony") a House of Assembly (in this Order referred to as "the proposed House of Assembly") comprising 28 elected members as well as certain other members;

Now, therefore, Her Majesty Queen Elizabeth The Queen Mother and Her Royal Highness The Princess Margaret, Countess of Snowdon, being authorised thereto by the said Letters Patent, and in exercise of the powers enabling Her Majesty in that behalf, and by and with the advice of Her Majesty's Privy Council, do on Her Majesty's behalf order, and it is hereby ordered, as follows:—

1.—(1) This Order may be cited as the Gilbert and Ellice Islands Colony (Electoral Provisions) Order 1974. *Citation and interpretation.*

(2) The Interpretation Act 1889(a) shall apply, with the necessary adaptations, for the purpose of interpreting this Order and otherwise in relation thereto as it applies for the purpose of interpreting, and in relation to, Acts of Parliament of the United Kingdom.

2.—(1) The Governor may by regulations make provision for the election of the elected members of the proposed House of Assembly, and in particular, and without prejudice to the generality of the foregoing power, may provide for— *Provision for election of members of proposed House of Assembly.*

(a) the qualifications and disqualifications of voters;

(b) the registration of voters;

(c) the nomination of candidates for election (including the number of persons required to support nominations);

(a) 1889 c. 63.

(*d*) the ascertainment of the qualifications of the voters and of candidates for election;

(*e*) the establishment in the Colony of electoral districts (by whatever name called) for the purpose of returning members to the proposed House of Assembly and the division of such electoral districts for any purpose connected with elections;

(*f*) the holding of elections;

(*g*) the determination of any question whether any person has been validly elected an elected member of the proposed House of Assembly or whether an elected member thereof has vacated his seat therein; and

(*h*) the definition and trial of offences connected with elections and the imposition of penalties therefor, including disqualification for membership of the proposed House of Assembly, or for registration as a voter, or for voting at elections, of any person concerned in any such offence.

(2) Elections of elected members of the proposed House of Assembly may be held under regulations made under this section notwithstanding that provision for the establishment of that House has not been made by Order of Her Majesty in Council.

(3) Regulations made under this section shall be published in the Colony by exhibition at the Public Office of the Governor and shall be printed in the Gazette as soon as may be after the date of such publication.

(4) In this section "the Governor" means the Governor of the Colony, and includes any person for the time being performing the functions of the office of Governor.

Qualifications for election to proposed House of Assembly.

3. Subject to the provisions of the next following section a person shall be qualified to be elected as a member of the proposed House of Assembly if, and shall not be so qualified unless—

(*a*) he is a British subject or a British protected person;

(*b*) he has attained the age of twenty-one years; and

(*c*) he has resided in the Colony during the three years immediately preceding the date of his election for a period or periods amounting in the aggregate to not less than thirty months, or is domiciled in the Colony and is resident there at that date.

Disqualifications for elected membership.

4.—(1) No person shall be qualified to be elected as an elected member of the proposed House of Assembly who—

(*a*) is, by virtue of his own act, under any acknowledgement of allegiance, obedience or adherence to a foreign power or state;

(*b*) has been adjudged or otherwise declared bankrupt under any law for the time being in force in any part of the Commonwealth and has not been discharged;

(*c*) is certified to be insane or otherwise adjudged to be of unsound mind under any law for the time being in force in the Colony;

(*d*) is under sentence of death imposed on him by a court in any part of the Commonwealth, or is serving a sentence of imprisonment (by whatever name called) for a term of or exceeding twelve months, imposed on him by such a court or substituted by competent authority for some other sentence imposed on him by such a court, or is under a sentence of imprisonment the execution of which has been suspended;

(*e*) is disqualified from membership of the proposed House under any provision of regulations made under section 2 of this Order relating to offences connected with elections;

(*f*) holds, or is acting in, any office the functions of which involve any responsibility for, or in connection with, the conduct of any election or the compilation or revision of any electoral register; or

(*g*) subject to such exemptions as may be prescribed by any law in force in the Colony, holds, or is acting in, any public office.

(2) For the purposes of paragraph (*d*) of the last preceding subsection—

(*a*) two or more terms of imprisonment that are required to be served consecutively shall be regarded as a single term of imprisonment for the aggregate period of those terms; and

(*b*) no account shall be taken of a sentence of imprisonment imposed as an alternative to or in default of the payment of a fine.

N. E. Leigh.

EXPLANATORY NOTE

(This Note is not part of the Order.)

This Order empowers the Governor of the Gilbert and Ellice Islands Colony to make regulations providing for the election of the elected members of a House of Assembly which it is proposed should be established in due course for that Colony and enables elections to the proposed House of Assembly to be held before an Order in Council establishing that House has been made and to make provision with respect to qualifications and disqualifications for election.

BY THE QUEEN
A PROCLAMATION

ELIZABETH R.

Whereas by section 1 of the Emergency Powers Act 1920, as amended by the Emergency Powers Act 1964, it is enacted that if it appears to Us that there have occurred or are about to occur events of such a nature as to be calculated, by interfering with the supply and distribution of food, water, fuel or light, or with the means of locomotion, to deprive the community, or any substantial portion of the community, of the essentials of life, We may, by Proclamation, declare that a state of emergency exists:

And, whereas on the 7th day of February, 1974, Her Majesty Queen Elizabeth The Queen Mother and Her Royal Highness The Princess Margaret, Countess of Snowdon, being authorised thereto by Letters Patent in pursuance of the Regency Acts, 1937 to 1953, did on Our behalf make, in pursuance of the said Act of 1920, as so amended, a Proclamation declaring that the industrial dispute then affecting (among others) persons employed in the coal mines did, in their opinion, constitute a state of emergency within the meaning of that Act:

And whereas, by virtue of section 1 of the said Act of 1920, a Proclamation issued in pursuance thereof does not remain in force for more than one month:

And whereas the continuance of the said industrial dispute does, in Our opinion, constitute a state of emergency within the meaning of the said Act of 1920:

Now, therefore, in pursuance of the said Act of 1920, We do by and with the advice of Our Privy Council, hereby declare that a state of emergency exists.

Given at Our Court at Buckingham Palace this sixth day of March in the year of our Lord One thousand nine hundred and seventy-four, and in the twenty-third year of Our Reign.

GOD SAVE THE QUEEN

BY THE QUEEN

A PROCLAMATION

REVOKING A PROCLAMATION, DATED THE 6TH DAY OF MARCH, 1974
DECLARING THE EXISTENCE OF A STATE OF EMERGENCY

ELIZABETH R.

Whereas by Our Proclamation, dated the 6th day of March 1974, We declared that the continuance of the industrial dispute affecting persons employed in the coal mines did, in Our opinion, constitute a state of emergency within the meaning of the Emergency Powers Act 1920, as amended by the Emergency Powers Act 1964:

And Whereas it appears to Us that the state of emergency has now ceased to exist and that it is expedient that the said Proclamation should be revoked accordingly:

Now, Therefore, We, by and with the advice of Our Privy Council, hereby proclaim that the said Proclamation is revoked.

Given at Our Court at Buckingham Palace this eleventh day of March in the year of our Lord One thousand nine hundred and seventy-four, and in the twenty-third year of Our Reign.

GOD SAVE THE QUEEN

PACIFIC ISLANDS

The Gilbert and Ellice Islands Order 1974.

At the Court at Windsor Castle, the 26th day of March 1974

Present,

The Queen's Most Excellent Majesty in Council

Her Majesty, by virtue and in exercise of the powers in Her Majesty vested, is pleased, by and with the advice of Her Privy Council, to order, and it is hereby ordered, as follows:—

ARRANGEMENT OF ORDER

CHAPTER I
INTRODUCTORY

CHAPTER II

PROTECTION OF FUNDAMENTAL RIGHTS AND FREEDOMS OF THE INDIVIDUAL

CHAPTER III
THE GOVERNOR

CHAPTER IV
THE EXECUTIVE
Composition

General Provisions Relating to Procedure

CHAPTER V
HOUSE OF ASSEMBLY
Composition

SCHEDULE 1

ELECTION OF CHIEF MINISTER

SCHEDULE 2

OATHS AND AFFIRMATIONS

CHAPTER I

INTRODUCTORY

1.—(1) This Order may be cited as the Gilbert and Ellice Islands Order 1974 and shall be construed as one with the Gilbert and Ellice Islands Order in Council 1915(a), and that Order and this Order may be cited together as the Gilbert and Ellice Islands Orders 1915 and 1974. _Citation, construction and commencement._

(2) This Order shall be published in the Colony by exhibition at the Public Office of the Governor and printed in the Gazette as soon as may be after the date of such publication and shall come into operation on such date as the Governor acting in his discretion, by notice published and printed in like manner respectively, shall appoint.

2.—(1) In this Order, unless the context otherwise requires— _Interpretation._

" the appointed day " means the date appointed under section 1(2) of this Order;

" the Chief Justice " means the Chief Justice of the Western Pacific;

" the Colony " means the Gilbert and Ellice Islands Colony;

" functions " include rights, duties and powers;

" the Gazette " means the official Gazette of the Colony;

" general election " means a general election of the elected members of the House of Assembly;

" High Court " means the High Court of the Western Pacific as re-constituted by the Western Pacific (Courts) Order in Council 1961(b);

" local enactment " means any law made under this Order, any subsidiary instrument made under any such law and any existing law for the purposes of section 77 of this Order;

" Minister " and " Ministers " mean those members of the Council of Ministers referred to in section 32(b) of this Order;

" oath " includes affirmation;

" public office " means an office of emolument in the public service;

" public officer " means a person holding or acting in any public office;

" the public seal " means the public seal of the Colony;

" public service " means the service of the Crown in a civil capacity in respect of the government of the Colony;

(a) Rev. IX, p. 655 (1915 III, p. 315).   (b) S.I. 1961 1506 (1961 II, p. 3066).

" session " means the sittings of the House of Assembly commencing when the House first meets after the appointed day or after its prorogation or dissolution at any time and ending when the House is prorogued or is dissolved without having been prorogued;

" sitting " means, in relation to the House of Assembly, a period during which the House is sitting continuously without adjournment and includes any period during which the House is in committee;

" subsidiary instrument " means any proclamation, regulation, order, rule or other like instrument having the force of law.

(2) In this Order, unless the context otherwise requires, a reference to the holder of an office by the term designating his office shall be construed as including a reference to any person who is for the time being lawfully acting in or performing the functions of that office.

(3) For the purposes of this Order a person shall not be treated as holding, or acting in, a public office by reason only that he—

(a) is on leave of absence pending relinquishment of a public office, or is on leave of absence without salary from a public office;

(b) is receiving a pension or other like allowance from the Crown;

(c) is receiving any remuneration or allowance as a member of the Council of Ministers or of the House of Assembly;

(d) is a retired or reserve member of Her Majesty's forces or a special constable;

(e) is a member, officer or servant of any Island Council or other local government council, or of any Island Court or Lands Court established under any law for the time being in force in the Colony; or

(f) is the holder of an office in the service or appointment of the Crown, or is performing any functions on behalf of the Crown, if the only payments he receives in respect of that office or those functions are by way of travelling or subsistence allowances or a refund of out-of-pocket expenses.

(4) Where any power is conferred by this Order to make any proclamation, regulation, order or rule, or to give any direction or instructions, the power shall be construed as including the power, exercisable in like manner, to amend or revoke any such proclamation, regulation, order, rule, direction or instructions.

(5) The Interpretation Act 1889(a) shall apply, with the necessary adaptations, for the purpose of interpreting the Gilbert and Ellice Islands Order in Council 1915 and this Order, and otherwise in relation thereto, as it applies for the purpose of interpreting and in relation to Acts of Parliament of the United Kingdom.

Revocations. **3.** The Gilbert and Ellice Islands Order 1970(b) and the Gilbert and Ellice Islands (Amendment) Order 1971(c) are revoked.

(a) 1889 c. 63.   (c) S.I. 1971 III, p. 6330.
(b) S.I. 1970 III, p. 6765.

CHAPTER II

PROTECTION OF FUNDAMENTAL RIGHTS AND FREEDOMS OF THE INDIVIDUAL

4. Whereas every person in the Colony is entitled to the fundamental rights and freedoms of the individual, that is to say, the right, whatever his race, place of origin, political opinions, colour, creed or sex, but subject to respect for the rights and freedoms of others and for the public interest, to each and all of the following, namely— *Fundamental rights and freedoms of the individual.*

(*a*) life, liberty, security of the person and the protection of the law;

(*b*) freedom of conscience, of expression and of assembly and association; and

(*c*) protection for the privacy of his home and other property and from deprivation of property without compensation,

the provisions of this Chapter shall have effect for the purpose of affording protection to those rights and freedoms subject to such limitations on that protection as are contained in those provisions, being limitations designed to ensure that the enjoyment of the said rights and freedoms by any individual does not prejudice the rights and freedoms of others or the public interest.

5.—(1) No person shall be deprived of his life intentionally save in execution of the sentence of a court in respect of a criminal offence under the law in force in the Colony of which he has been convicted. *Protection of right to life.*

(2) A person shall not be regarded as having been deprived of his life in contravention of this section if he dies as the result of the use, to such extent and in such circumstances as are permitted by law, of such force as is reasonably justifiable—

(*a*) for the defence of any person from violence or for the defence of property;

(*b*) in order to effect a lawful arrest or to prevent the escape of a person lawfully detained;

(*c*) for the purpose of suppressing a riot, insurrection or mutiny; or

(*d*) in order to prevent the commission by that person of a criminal offence,

or if he dies as the result of a lawful act of war.

6.—(1) No person shall be deprived of his personal liberty save as may be authorised by law in any of the following cases, that is to say— *Protection of right to personal liberty.*

(*a*) in consequence of his unfitness to plead to a criminal charge;

(*b*) in execution of the sentence or order of a court, whether established for the Colony or some other country, in respect of a criminal offence of which he has been convicted;

(*c*) in execution of the order of a court of record punishing him for contempt of that court or of a court inferior to it;

(*d*) in execution of the order of a court made to secure the fulfilment of any obligation imposed on him by law;

(*e*) for the purpose of bringing him before a court in execution of the order of a court;

(*f*) upon reasonable suspicion of his having committed, or being about to commit, a criminal offence under the law in force in the Colony;

(*g*) in the case of a person who has not attained the age of eighteen years, under the order of a court or with the consent of his parent or guardian, for the purpose of his education or welfare;

(*h*) for the purpose of preventing the spread of an infectious or contagious disease;

(*i*) in the case of a person who is, or is reasonably suspected to be, of unsound mind, addicted to drugs or alcohol, or a vagrant, for the purpose of his care or treatment or the protection of the community;

(*j*) for the purpose of preventing the unlawful entry of that person into the Colony, or for the purpose of effecting the expulsion, extradition or other lawful removal of that person from the Colony or for the purpose of restricting that person while he is being conveyed through the Colony in the course of his extradition or removal as a convicted prisoner from one country to another; or

(*k*) to such extent as may be necessary in the execution of a lawful order requiring that person to remain within a specified area within the Colony or prohibiting him from being within such an area, or to such extent as may be reasonably justifiable for the taking of proceedings against that person relating to the making of any such order, or to such extent as may be reasonably justifiable for restraining that person during any visit that he is permitted to make to any part of the Colony in which, in consequence of any such order, his presence would otherwise be unlawful.

(2) Any person who is arrested or detained shall be informed as soon as reasonably practicable, and in a language that he understands, of the reasons for his arrest or detention.

(3) Any person who is arrested or detained—

(*a*) for the purpose of bringing him before a court in execution of the order of a court; or

(*b*) upon reasonable suspicion of his having committed, or being about to commit, a criminal offence under the law in force in the Colony,

and who is not released, shall be brought without undue delay before a court; and if any person arrested or detained upon reasonable suspicion of his having committed or being about to commit a criminal offence is not tried within a reasonable time, then, without prejudice to any further proceedings that may be brought against him, he shall be released either unconditionally or upon reasonable conditions, including in particular such conditions as are reasonably necessary to ensure that he appears at a later date for trial or for proceedings preliminary to trial.

(4) Any person who is unlawfully arrested or detained by any other person shall be entitled to compensation therefor from that other person.

Protection from slavery and forced labour.

7.—(1) No person shall be held in slavery or servitude.

(2) No person shall be required to perform forced labour.

(3) For the purposes of this section, the expression " forced labour " does not include—

(a) any labour required in consequence of the sentence or order of a court;

(b) any labour required of any person while he is lawfully detained that, though not required in consequence of the sentence or order of a court, is reasonably necessary in the interests of hygiene or for the maintenance of the place at which he is detained;

(c) any labour required of a member of a disciplined force in pursuance of his duties as such or, in the case of a person who has conscientious objections to service as a member of a naval, military or air force, any labour that that person is required by law to perform in place of such service;

(d) any labour required during any period of public emergency or in the event of any other emergency or calamity that threatens the life and well-being of the community, to the extent that the requiring of such labour is reasonably justifiable in the circumstances of any situation arising or existing during that period or as a result of that other emergency or calamity, for the purpose of dealing with that situation; or

(e) any labour reasonably required as part of reasonable and normal communal or other civic obligations.

8.—(1) No person shall be subjected to torture or to inhuman or degrading punishment or other treatment. Protection from inhuman treatment.

(2) Nothing contained in or done under the authority of any law shall be held to be inconsistent with or in contravention of this section to the extent that the law in question authorises the infliction of any description of punishment that was lawful in the Colony immediately before the coming into operation of this Order.

9.—(1) No property of any description shall be compulsorily taken possession of, and no interest in or right over property of any description shall be compulsorily acquired, except where the following conditions are satisfied, that is to say— Protection from deprivation of property.

(a) the taking of possession or acquisition is necessary or expedient in the interests of defence, public safety, public order, public morality, public health, town or country planning or the development or utilisation of any property in such a manner as to promote the public benefit; and

(b) there is reasonable justification for the causing of any hardship that may result to any person having an interest in or right over the property; and

(c) provision is made by a law applicable to that taking of possession or acquisition—

(i) for the prompt payment of adequate compensation; and

(ii) securing to any person having an interest in or right over the property a right of access to the High Court, whether direct or on appeal from any other authority, for the determination of his interest or right, the legality of the taking of possession or acquisition of the property, interest or right and the amount of any compensation to which he is entitled, and for the purpose of obtaining prompt payment of that compensation

(2) Nothing contained in or done under the authority of any law shall be held to be inconsistent with or in contravention of this section—

(*a*) to the extent that the law in question makes provision for the taking of possession or acquisition of any property—

(i) in satisfaction of any tax, rate or duty;

(ii) by way of penalty for breach of the law or forfeiture in consequence of a breach of the law;

(iii) as an incident of a lease, tenancy, mortgage, charge, bill of sale, pledge or contract;

(iv) in the execution of judgments or orders of a court in proceedings for the determination of civil rights or obligations;

(v) in circumstances where it is reasonably necessary so to do because the property is in a dangerous state or injurious to the health of human beings, animals or plants;

(vi) in consequence of any law with respect to the limitation of actions or acquisitive prescription; or

(vii) for so long only as may be necessary for the purposes of any examination, investigation, trial or inquiry or, in the case of land, the carrying out thereon—

(A) of work of soil conservation or of conservation of other natural resources; or

(B) of work relating to agricultural development or improvement which the owner or occupier of the land has been required, and has without reasonable excuse refused or failed, to carry out,

except so far as that provision or, as the case may be, the thing done under the authority thereof is shown not to be reasonably justifiable in a democratic society; or

(*b*) to the extent that the law in question makes provision for the taking of possession or acquisition of—

(i) enemy property;

(ii) property of a deceased person, a person of unsound mind, a person who has not attained the age of twenty-one years or a person who is absent from the Colony, for the purpose of its administration for the benefit of the persons entitled to the beneficial interest therein;

(iii) property of a person declared to be insolvent or a body corporate in liquidation, for the purpose of its administration for the benefit of the creditors of the insolvent or body corporate and, subject thereto, for the benefit of other persons entitled to the beneficial interest in the property; or

(iv) property subject to a trust, for the purpose of vesting the property in persons appointed as trustees under the instrument creating the trust or by a court or, by order of a court, for the purpose of giving effect to the trust.

(3) Nothing in this section shall be construed as affecting the making or operation of any law for the compulsory taking of possession in the public interest of any property, or the compulsory acquisition in the public interest of any interest in or right over property, where that property, interest or right is held by a body corporate established for public purposes by any law and in which no moneys have been invested other than moneys provided by the Government of the Colony.

10.—(1) Except with his own consent, no person shall be subjected to the search of his person or his property or the entry by others on his premises.

Protection for privacy of home and other property.

(2) Nothing contained in or done under the authority of any law shall be held to be inconsistent with or in contravention of this section to the extent that the law in question makes provision—

(a) in the interests of defence, public safety, public order, public morality, public health, town and country planning, the development and utilisation of mineral resources, or the development or utilisation of any other property in such a manner as to promote the public benefit ;

(b) for the purpose of protecting the rights or freedoms of other persons ;

(c) for the purpose of authorising an officer or agent of the Government of the Colony, a local government authority or a body corporate established by law for a public purpose to enter on the premises of any person in order to inspect those premises or anything thereon for the purpose of any tax, rate or duty or in order to carry out work connected with any property that is lawfully on those premises and that belongs to that Government, authority or body corporate, as the case may be ;

(d) for the purpose of authorising the entry upon any premises in pursuance of an order of a court for the purpose of enforcing the judgment or order of a court in any proceedings ; or

(e) for the purpose of authorising the entry upon any premises for the purpose of preventing or detecting criminal offences,

and except so far as that provision or, as the case may be, anything done under the authority thereof is shown not to be reasonably justifiable in a democratic society.

11.—(1) If any person is charged with a criminal offence, then, unless the charge is withdrawn, the case shall be afforded a fair hearing within a reasonable time by an independent and impartial court established by law.

Provisions to secure protection of law.

(2) Every person who is charged with a criminal offence—

(a) shall be presumed to be innocent until he is proved or has pleaded guilty ;

(b) shall be informed as soon as reasonably practicable, in detail and in a language that he understands, of the nature of the offence charged ;

(c) shall be given adequate time and facilities for the preparation of his defence ;

(*d*) shall be permitted to defend himself before the court in person or, at his own expense, by a legal representative of his own choice ;

(*e*) shall be afforded facilities to examine in person or by his legal representative the witnesses called by the prosecution before the court, and to obtain the attendance and carry out the examination of witnesses to testify on his behalf before the court on the same conditions as those applying to witnesses called by the prosecution ; and

(*f*) shall be permitted to have without payment the assistance of an interpreter if he cannot understand the language used at the trial of the charge,

and, except with his own consent, the trial shall not take place in his absence unless he so conducts himself as to render the continuance of the proceedings in his presence impracticable and the court has ordered him to be removed and the trial to proceed in his absence.

(3) When a person is tried for any criminal offence, the accused person or any person authorised by him in that behalf shall, if he so requires and subject to payment of such reasonable fee as may be prescribed by law, be given within a reasonable time after judgment a copy for the use of the accused person of any record of the proceedings made by or on behalf of the court.

(4) No person shall be held to be guilty of a criminal offence on account of any act or omission that did not, at the time it took place, constitute such an offence, and no penalty shall be imposed for any criminal offence that is severer in degree or description than the maximum penalty that might have been imposed for that offence at the time when it was committed.

(5) No person who shows that he has been tried by a competent cour for a criminal offence and either convicted or acquitted shall again be tried for that offence or for any other criminal offence of which he could have been convicted at the trial for that offence, save upon the order of a superior court in the course of appeal or review proceedings relating to the conviction or acquittal.

(6) No person shall be tried for a criminal offence if he shows that he has been pardoned for that offence.

(7) No person who is tried for a criminal offence shall be compelled to give evidence at the trial.

(8) Any court or other adjudicating authority prescribed by law for the determination of the existence or extent of any civil right or obligation shall be established or recognised by law and shall be independent and impartial ; and where proceedings for such a determination are instituted by any person before such a court or other adjudicating authority, the case shall be given a fair hearing within a reasonable time.

(9) Except with the agreement of all the parties thereto, all proceedings of every court and proceedings for the determination of the existence or extent of any civil right or obligation before any other adjudicating authority, including the announcement of the decision of the court or other authority, shall be held in public.

(10) Nothing in the last preceding subsection shall prevent the court or other adjudicating authority from excluding from the proceedings persons other than the parties thereto and their legal representatives to such extent as the court or other authority—

(*a*) may by law be empowered so to do and may consider necessary or expedient in circumstances where publicity would prejudice the interests of justice or in interlocutory proceedings or in the interests of decency, public morality, the welfare of persons under the age of eighteen years or the protection of the private lives of persons concerned in the proceedings ; or

(*b*) may by law be empowered or required so to do in the interests of defence, public safety or public order.

(11) Nothing contained in or done under the authority of any law shall be held to be inconsistent with or in contravention of—

(*a*) subsection (2)(*a*) of this section to the extent that the law in question imposes upon any person charged with a criminal offence the burden of proving particular facts ;

(*b*) subsection (2)(*e*) of this section to the extent that the law in question imposes reasonable conditions that must be satisfied if witnesses called to testify on behalf of an accused person are to be paid their expenses out of public funds ; or

(*c*) subsection (5) of this section to the extent that the law in question authorises a court to try a member of a disciplined force for a criminal offence notwithstanding any trial and conviction or acquittal of that member under the disciplinary law of that force, so, however, that any court so trying such a member and convicting him shall in sentencing him to any punishment take into account any punishment awarded him under that disciplinary law.

(12) in this section—

" criminal offence " means a criminal offence under the law in force in the Colony ;

" legal representative " means a person lawfully in, or entitled to be in, the Colony and entitled to practise in the Colony as an advocate or, except in relation to proceedings before a court in which a solicitor has no right of audience, as a solicitor.

12.—(1) Except with his own consent, no person shall be hindered in the enjoyment of his freedom of conscience, and for the purposes of this section the said freedom includes freedom of thought and of religion, freedom to change his religion or belief, and freedom, either alone or in community with others, and both in public and in private, to manifest and propagate his religion or belief in worship, teaching, practice and observance. *Protection of freedom of conscience.*

(2) Every religious community shall be entitled, at its own expense, to establish and maintain places of education and to manage any place of education which it wholly maintains.

(3) No religious community shall be prevented from providing religious instruction for persons of that community in the course of any education provided at any place of education which it wholly maintains or in the course of any education which it otherwise provides.

(4) Except with his own consent (or, if he is a person who has not attained the age of twenty-one years, the consent of his guardian) no person attending any place of education shall be required to receive religious instruction or to take part in or attend any religious ceremony or observance if that instruction, ceremony or observance relates to a religion other than his own.

(5) No person shall be compelled to take any oath which is contrary to his religion or belief or to take any oath in a manner which is contrary to his religion or belief.

(6) Nothing contained in or done under the authority of any law shall be held to be inconsistent with or in contravention of this section to the extent that the law in question makes provision which is reasonably required—

(*a*) in the interests of defence, public safety, public order, public morality or public health ; or

(*b*) for the purpose of protecting the rights and freedoms of other persons, including the right to observe and practise any religion without the unsolicited intervention of members of any other religion,

and except so far as that provision or, as the case may be, the thing done under the authority thereof is shown not to be reasonably justifiable in a democratic society.

(7) References in this section to a religion shall be construed as including references to a religious denomination, and cognate expressions shall be construed accordingly.

Protection of freedom of expression. **13.**—(1) Except with his own consent, no person shall be hindered in the enjoyment of his freedom of expression, and for the purposes of this section the said freedom includes the freedom to hold opinions without interference, freedom to receive ideas and information without interference, freedom to communicate ideas and information without interference and freedom from interference with his correspondence.

(2) Nothing contained in or done under the authority of any law shall be held to be inconsistent with or in contravention of this section to the extent that the law in question makes provision—

(*a*) in the interests of defence, public safety, public order, public morality or public health ;

(*b*) for the purpose of protecting the reputations, rights and freedoms of other persons or the private lives of persons concerned in legal proceedings, preventing the disclosure of information received in confidence, maintaining the authority and independence of the courts, or regulating the administration or the technical operation of telephony, telegraphy, posts, wireless, broadcasting or television ; or

(*c*) that imposes restrictions upon public officers,

and except so far as that provision or, as the case may be, the thing done under the authority thereof is shown not to be reasonably justifiable in a democratic society.

14.—(1) Except with his own consent, no person shall be hindered Protection of in the enjoyment of his freedom of assembly and association, that is freedom of to say, his right to assemble freely and associate with other persons association. and in particular to form or belong to political parties or to form or belong to trade unions or other associations for the protection of his interests.

(2) Nothing contained in or done under the authority of any law shall be held to be inconsistent with or in contravention of this section to the extent that the law in question makes provision—

(*a*) in the interests of defence, public safety, public order, public morality or public health ;

(*b*) for the purpose of protecting the rights or freedoms of other persons ; or

(*c*) that imposes restrictions upon public officers,

and except so far as that provision or, as the case may be, the thing done under the authority thereof is shown not to be reasonably justifiable in a democratic society.

15.—(1) No person shall be deprived of his freedom of movement, Protection of and for the purposes of this section the said freedom means the right to freedom of move freely throughout the Colony, the right to reside in any part of movement. the Colony, the right to enter the Colony and immunity from expulsion from the Colony.

(2) Any restriction on a person's freedom of movement that is involved in his lawful detention shall not be held to be inconsistent with or in contravention of this section.

(3) Nothing contained in or done under the authority of any law shall be held to be inconsistent with or in contravention of this section to the extent that the law in question makes provision—

(*a*) for the imposition of restrictions on the movement or residence within the Colony of any person or on any person's right to leave the Colony that are reasonably required in the interests of defence, public safety or public order ;

(*b*) for the imposition of restrictions on the movement or residence within the Colony or on the right to leave the Colony of persons generally or any class of persons that are reasonably required in the interests of defence, public safety, public order, public morality, public health or environmental conservation ;

(*c*) for the imposition of restrictions on the movement or residence within the Colony of any person who does not belong to the Colony or the exclusion or expulsion from the Colony of any such person ;

(*d*) for the imposition of restrictions on the acquisition or use by any person of land or other property in the Colony ;

(*e*) for the imposition of restrictions upon the movement or residence within the Colony of public officers that are reasonably required for the purpose of ensuring the proper performance of their functions ;

(*f*) for the removal of a person from the Colony to be tried or punished in some other country for a criminal offence under the law of that other country or to undergo imprisonment in that other country in execution of the sentence of a court in respect of a criminal offence under the law in force in the Colony of which he has been convicted ;

(*g*) for the imposition of restrictions, by order of a court, on the movement or residence within the Colony of any person or on any person's right to leave the Colony either in consequence of his having been found guilty of a criminal offence under the law of the Colony or for the purpose of ensuring that he appears before a court at a later date for trial or for proceedings relating to his extradition or lawful removal from the Colony ; or

(*h*) for the imposition of restrictions on the right of any person to leave the Colony in order to secure the fulfilment of any obligations imposed upon that person by law, except so far as the provision or, as the case may be, the thing done under the authority thereof is shown not to be reasonably justifiable in a democratic society.

(4) If any person whose freedom of movement has been restricted by virtue only of such a provision as is referred to in subsection (3)(*a*) of this section so requests at any time during the period of that restriction not earlier than six months after he last made such a request during that period, his case shall be reviewed by an independent and impartial tribunal presided over by a person, qualified to be admitted to practice as an advocate or solicitor in the Colony, appointed by the Chief Justice.

(5) On any review by a tribunal in pursuance of the last preceding subsection of the case of a person whose freedom of movement has been restricted, the tribunal may make recommendations concerning the necessity or expediency of continuing the restriction to the authority by which it was ordered but, unless it is otherwise provided by law, that authority shall not be obliged to act in accordance with any such recommendations.

Protection from discrimination on the grounds of race, etc. **16.**—(1) Subject to the provisions of subsections (4), (5) and (8) of this section, no law shall make any provision that is discriminatory either of itself or in its effect.

(2) Subject to the provisions of subsections (6), (7) and (8) of this section, no person shall be treated in a discriminatory manner by any person acting by virtue of any written law or in the performance of the functions of any public office or any public authority.

(3) In this section, the expression " discriminatory " means affording different treatment to different persons attributable wholly or mainly to their respective descriptions by race, place of origin, political opinions, colour or creed whereby persons of one such description are subjected to disabilities or restrictions to which persons of another such description are not made subject or are accorded privileges or advantages which are not accorded to persons of another such description.

(4) Subsection (1) of this section shall not apply to any law so far as that law makes provision—

(*a*) for the imposition of taxation or the appropriation of revenue by the Government of the Colony or any local authority or body for local purposes ;

(*b*) with respect to persons who do not belong to the Colony ;

(*c*) for the application, in the case of persons of any such description as is mentioned in the last preceding subsection (or of persons connected with such persons), of the law with respect to adoption, marriage, divorce, burial, devolution of property on death or other like matters that is the personal law applicable to persons of that description ;

(d) with respect to land, the tenure of land, the resumption and acquisition of land and other like purposes ; or

(e) whereby persons of any such description as is mentioned in subsection (3) of this section may be subjected to any disability or restriction or may be accorded any privilege or advantage which, having regard to its nature and to special circumstances pertaining to those persons or to persons of any other such description, is reasonably justifiable in a democratic society.

(5) Nothing contained in any law shall be held to be inconsistent with or in contravention of subsection (1) of this section to the extent that it makes provision with respect to standards or qualifications (not being standards or qualifications specifically relating to race, place of origin, political opinions, colour or creed) to be required of any person who is appointed to any office in the public service, any office in a disciplined force, any office in the service of a local authority or any office in a body corporate established directly by any law for public purposes.

(6) Subsection (2) of this section shall not apply to anything which is expressly or by necessary implication authorised to be done by any such provision of law as is referred to in subsection (4) or (5) of this section.

(7) Subsection (2) of this section shall not affect any discretion relating to the institution, conduct or discontinuance of civil or criminal proceedings in any court that is vested in any person by or under this Order or any other law.

(8) Nothing contained in or done under the authority of any law shall be held to be inconsistent with or in contravention of this section to the extent that the law in question makes provision whereby persons of any such description as is mentioned in subsection (3) of this section may be subjected to any restriction on the rights and freedoms guaranteed by sections 10, 12, 13, 14 and 15 of this Order, being such a restriction as is authorised by section 10(2), 12(6), 13(2), 14(2) or 15(3), as the case may be.

(9) Nothing contained in or done under the authority of any law shall be held to be inconsistent with the provisions of this section—

(a) if that law was in force immediately before the coming into operation of this Order and has continued in force at all times since the coming into operation of this Order ; or

(b) to the extent that the law repeals and re-enacts any provision which has been contained in any enactment at all times since immediately before the coming into operation of this Order.

17.—(1) Nothing contained in or done under the authority of any regulation made under the Emergency Powers Order in Council 1939(a), as amended(b), shall be held to be inconsistent with or in contravention Provisions for periods of public emergency.

(a) See S.I. 1952 I, at p. 621.
(b) The relevant amending instruments are S.I. 1956/731; 1963/88 (1956 I, p. 512; 1963 I, p. 105) and S.I. 1971 III, p. 6330.

of section 6, 7(2), 10, 12, 13, 14, 15 or 16 of this Order to the extent that the regulation in question makes in relation to any period of public emergency provision, or authorises the doing during any such period of anything, that is reasonably justifiable in the circumstances of any situation arising or existing during the period for the purpose of dealing with that situation.

(2) Where any person who is lawfully detained in pursuance only of such a regulation as is referred to in the last preceding subsection so requests at any time during the period of that detention not earlier than six months after he last made such a request during that period, his case shall be reviewed by an independent and impartial tribunal established by law and presided over by a person, qualified to be admitted to practise as an advocate or solicitor in the Colony, appointed by the Chief Justice.

(3) On any review by a tribunal in pursuance of this section of the case of a detained person, the tribunal may make recommendations concerning the necessity or expediency of continuing his detention to the authority by which it was ordered but, unless it is otherwise provided by law, that authority shall not be obliged to act in accordance with any such recommendations.

Enforcement of protective provisions.

18.—(1) Subject to the provisions of subsection (6) of this section, if any person alleges that any of the provisions of sections 4 to 17 (inclusive) of this Order has been, is being or is likely to be contravened in relation to him (or, in the case of a person who is detained, if any other person alleges such a contravention in relation to the detained person) then, without prejudice to any other action with respect to the same matter which is lawfully available, that person (or that other person) may apply to the High Court for redress.

(2) The High Court shall have original jurisdiction—

(*a*) to hear and determine any application made by any person in pursuance of the last preceding subsection;

(*b*) to determine any question arising in the case of any person which is referred to in pursuance of the next following subsection.

and may make such orders, issue such writs and give such direction, as it may consider appropriate for the purpose of enforcing or securing the enforcement of any of the provisions of sections 4 to 17 (inclusive) of this Order:

Provided that the High Court may decline to exercise its powers under this subsection if it is satisfied that adequate means of redress for the contravention alleged are or have been available to the person concerned under any other law.

(3) If in any proceedings in any subordinate court any question arises as to the contravention of any of the provisions of sections 4 to 17 (inclusive) of this Order, the person presiding in that court may, and shall if any party to the proceedings so requests, refer the question to the High Court unless, in his opinion, the raising of the question is merely frivolous or vexatious.

(4) Any person aggrieved by any determination of the High Court under this section may appeal therefrom to the Fiji Court of Appeal:

Provided that no appeal shall lie from a determination of the High Court under this section dismissing an application on the ground that it is frivolous or vexatious.

(5) A law made under section 53 of this Order may confer upon the High Court powers additional to those conferred by this section for the purpose of enabling that court more effectively to exercise the jurisdiction conferred upon it by this section.

(6) Rules of court making provision with respect to the practice and procedure of the High Court in relation to the jurisdiction conferred on it by or under this section (including rules with respect to the time within which any application or reference shall or may be made or brought) may be made by the person or authority for the time being having power to make rules of court with respect to the practice and procedure of that court generally.

19.—(1) In this Chapter, unless the context otherwise requires— *Interpre-tation and*

" contravention ", in relation to any requirement, includes a *savings.* failure to comply with that requirement, and cognate expressions shall be construed accordingly;

" court " means any court of law having jurisdiction in the Colony, other than a court established by a disciplinary law, and includes Her Majesty in Council and in sections 5 and 7 of this Order a court established by a disciplinary law;

" disciplinary law " means a law regulating the discipline of any disciplined force;

" disciplined force " means—

    (*a*) any naval, military or air force;

    (*b*) the Gilbert and Ellice Islands Constabulary Force; or

    (*c*) any other constabulary or police force established by a law made under section 53 of this Order;

" member ", in relation to a disciplined force, includes any person who, under the law regulating the discipline of that force, is subject to that discipline.

(2) In this Chapter " a period of public emergency " means any period during which Part II of the Emergency Powers Order in Council 1939, as amended, is in force in the Colony or any part thereof.

(3) For the purposes of this Chapter a person shall be deemed to belong to the Colony if he is a British subject or a British protected person and—

    (*a*) was born in the Colony or of parents who at the time of his birth were ordinarily resident in the Colony; or

    (*b*) has been ordinarily resident in the Colony continuously for a period of seven years or more and since the completion of such period of residence has not been ordinarily resident continuously for a period of seven years or more in any other part of the Commonwealth or in the Republic of Ireland; or

    (*c*) has obtained the status of a British subject by reason of having been naturalised in the Colony before the British Nationality Act 1948(**a**) came into force or by reason of his having been naturalised in the Colony as a citizen of the United Kingdom and Colonies under that Act or registered in the Colony as such under any provision of that Act; or

(**a**) 948 c. 56.

(*d*) is the wife of a person to whom any of the foregoing sub-paragraphs applies not living apart from such person under a decree of a court or a deed of separation ; or

(*e*) is the child, stepchild, or child adopted in a manner recognised by law under the age of eighteen years of a person to whom any of the foregoing paragraphs applies ; or

(*f*) is a member of any other class of persons that may be prescribed by any law enacted under this Order:

Provided that for the purpose of calculating the period for which any person has been ordinarily resident in the Colony (but not of determining whether he has been continuously so resident) no account shall be taken—

(i) of any period during which he was serving a sentence of imprisonment exceeding six months imposed on him by a court or substituted by competent authority for some other sentence imposed upon him by a court ; or

(ii) of any period during which any adjudication that he was of unsound mind was in force under the law of the Colony or during which he was lawfully detained in the Colony as a criminal lunatic ; or

(iii) of any period during which his presence in the Colony was unlawful.

(4) In relation to any person who is a member of a disciplined force raised under a law made under section 53 of this Order, nothing contained in or done under the authority of the disciplinary law of that force shall be held to be inconsistent with or in contravention of any of the provisions of this Chapter other than sections 5, 7 and 8.

(5) In relation to any person who is a member of a disciplined force raised otherwise than as aforesaid and lawfully present in the Colony, nothing contained in or done under the authority of the disciplinary law of that force shall be held to be inconsistent with or on contravention of any of the provisions of this Chapter.

CHAPTER III

THE GOVERNOR

The Governor, his functions and emoluments.

20.—(1) There shall be a Governor for the Colony who shall be appointed by Her Majesty by commission under Her Sign Manual and Signet and shall hold office during Her Majesty's pleasure.

(2) The Governor shall have such functions as may be conferred upon him by or under this Order or any other law for the time being in force in the Colony and such other functions as Her Majesty may assign to him and, subject to the provisions of this Order (and, in the case of functions conferred upon him by or under any other law, subject to the provisions of that law or any law amending that law) shall perform all the functions of his office, including those he exercises in his discretion, according to such instructions as may be given to him by Her Majesty:

Provided that the question whether or not the Governor has in any matter complied with any such instructions shall not be inquired into in any court.

(3) The holder of the office of Governor shall receive such emoluments as may be prescribed from time to time by a Secretary of State and which are hereby charged on and shall be paid out of the Consolidated Fund.

21. Every person appointed to the office of Governor shall, before assuming the functions of his office— *Publication of commission and making of oaths.*

(a) cause the commission appointing him to be Governor to be read and published in the presence of the Chief Justice, or such person as the Chief Justice may designate for the purpose, and of such members of the Council of Ministers as can conveniently attend ; and

(b) make before the above-mentioned persons the oaths of allegianc and for the due execution of his office in the forms set out in Schedule 2 to this Order, which oaths the Chief Justice, or person designated by him, shall administer.

22. There shall be a Deputy Governor, who shall be appointed by the Governor in pursuance of instructions given by Her Majesty through a Secretary of State and shall hold office during Her Majesty's pleasure. *Office of Deputy Governor.*

23.—(1) Whenever the office of Governor is vacant or the Governor is absent from the Colony or is for any other reason unable to discharge the functions of his office— *Succession to Government.*

(a) the Deputy Governor ; or

(b) if the office of Deputy Governor is vacant or the Deputy Governor is absent from the Colony or is for any other reason unable to discharge the functions of his office, such person as Her Majesty may habe designated by instructions given through a Secretary of State (hereinafter referred to as "the person designated"),

shall, during Her Majesty's pleasure, discharge the functions of the office of Governor and administer the government of the Colony accordingly.

(2) Before assuming the administration of the government of the Colony, the Deputy Governor or the person designated shall take and subscribe oaths of allegiance and for the due execution of the office of Governor in the forms set out in Schedule 2 to this Order.

(3) The Deputy Governor shall not continue to administer the government after the Governor has informed him that he is about to assume or resume the administration of the government, and the person designated shall not continue to administer the government after the Governor or the Deputy Governor has so informed him.

(4) For the purposes of subsection (1) of this section, the Governor or Deputy Governor shall not be regarded as absent from the Colony or as unable to discharge the functions of the office of Governor—

(a) by reason only of the fact that he is in passage from one part of the Colony to another ; or

(b) at any time when there is a subsisting appointment of a deputy under the next following section.

(5) In this section, " the Governor " means the person holding the office of Governor.

Discharge of
Governor's
functions by
temporary
deputy.

24.—(1) Whenever the Governor—

(a) has occasion to be absent from Tarawa but not from the Colony ; or

(b) has occasion to be absent from the Colony for a period that in his opinion will be of short duration ; or

(c) is suffering from an illness which he has reason to believe will be of short duration,

he may, acting in his discretion, by instrument under the public seal, appoint any public officer in the Colony to be his deputy during his absence or illness and in that capacity to perform on his behalf such of the functions of the office of Governor as may be specified in the instrument, other than functions conferred upon the Governor by any Act of Parliament or by any Order of Her Majesty in Council or other instrument made under any such Act.

(2) The powers and authority of the Governor shall not be in any way affected by the appointment of a deputy under this section otherwise than as Her Majesty may from time to time direct by instructions to the Governor through a Secretary of State and the deputy shall conform to and observe such instructions relating to the exercise by him of any of the functions of the office of Governor as the Governor, acting in his discretion, may from time to time address to him:

Provided that the question whether or not the deputy has in any matter complied with any such instructions shall not be enquired into in any court.

(3) A person appointed as deputy under this section shall hold that office for such period as may be specified in the instrument by which he is appointed but his appointment may be revoked at any time by Her Majesty by instructions given to the Governor through a Secretary of State or by the Governor, acting in his discretion.

(4) In this section, " the Governor " means the person holding the office of Governor or the person discharging the functions of that office under the immediately preceding section.

Discharge of
Governor's
functions by
Deputy
Governor.

25.—(1) The Governor, acting in his discretion, may, by writing under his hand, authorise the Deputy Governor to exercise for and on behalf of the Governor, subject to such exceptions and conditions as the Governor may from time to time specify, any or all of the functions fo the office of Governor.

(2) The powers and authority of the Governor shall not be in any way affected by any authority of the Deputy Governor under the preceding subsection otherwise than as Her Majesty may from time to time direct by instructions to the Governor through a Secretary of State, and the Deputy Governor shall conform to and observe such instructions relating to the exercise by him of any of the functions of the office of Governor as the Governor, acting in his discretion, may from time to time address to him:

Provided that the question whether or not the Deputy Governor has in any matter complied with any such instructions shall not be enquired into in any court.

(3) Any authority given under subsection (1) of this section may at any time be varied or revoked by Her Majesty by instructions given to the Governor through a Secretary of State or by the Governor, acting in his discretion, by writing under his hand.

(4) In subsection (1) of this section the reference to any functions of the office of Governor does not include a reference to—

(*a*) the functions conferred upon the Governor by this section ; or

(*b*) any functions conferred upon the Governor by any Act of Parliament or by any Order of Her Majesty in Council or other instrument made under any such Act.

(5) In this section, " the Governor " means the person holding the office of Governor.

26. The Governor shall be responsible for the conduct (subject to the provisions of this Order and of any other law) of any business of the Government of the Colony, including the administration of any department of government, with respect to the following matters—

Governor's special responsi- bilities.

(*a*) external affairs ;

(*b*) defence, including armed forces ;

(*c*) internal security, including the Police Force ;

(*d*) the appointment (including the appointment on promotion or transfer, appointment on contract and appointment to act in an office) of any person to any public office, the suspension, termination of employment, dismissal or retirement of any public office or taking of disciplinary action in respect of any public officer, the application to any public officer of the terms or conditions of employment of the public service (including salary scales, allowances, leave, passages or pensions) for which financial provision has been made, or the organisation of the public service to the extent that it does not involve new financial provision :

Provided that the Governor, acting in his discretion, or, in the case of a Minister, after consultation with the Chief Minister, may assign to any member of the Council of Ministers responsibility for the conduct on behalf of the Governor of any business in the House of Assembly with respect to any of the said matters.

27.—(1) Subject to the provisions of this section, the Governor shall consult the Council of Ministers in the exercise of all powers conferred upon him by or under this Order or any other law for the time being in force in the Colony, except—

Governor to consult Council of Ministers.

(*a*) any power conferred upon him by this Order which he is empowered to exercise in his discretion ;

(*b*) any power conferred upon him by any other law which he is empowered, either expressly or by implication, to exercise without consulting the Council ;

(*c*) any power conferred upon him by this Order or any other law which he is required or authorised to exercise after consultation with or on the advice of a person or authority other than the Council ;

(*d*) any power conferred upon him by any law where, in his opinion, the exercise of the power relates to, or would affect, any of the matters specified in the immediately preceding section.

(2) The Governor shall not be required to consult the Council of Ministers in any case in which, in his judgment—

(*a*) the service of Her Majesty would sustain material prejudice thereby ;

(*b*) the matters to be decided are too umimportant to require such consultation ; or

(*c*) the urgency of the matter requires him to act before the Council can be consulted :

Provided that before acting in pursuance of paragraph (*c*) of this subsection the Governor shall, if practicable, consult the Chief Minister, and shall in any case at the next convenient opportunity communicate to the Council them easures he has adopted and the reasons for those measures.

Governor to act in accordance with the advice of Council of Ministers.
28.—(1) In exercising any power in the exercise of which he is obliged by the immediately preceding section of this Order to consult the Council of Ministers, the Governor shall act in accordance with the advice of the Council with the exception only of those cases where he thinks it right not to do so.

(2) Where the Governor acts, in accordance with the provisions of the preceding subsection, against the advice of the Council of Ministers, he shall at the first convenient opportunity report the matter to the Secretary of State with the reasons for his action :

Provided that he shall not be obliged to so report the matter in any case in which he so acts for the purposes of—

(*a*) maintaining or securing the financial or economic stability of the Colony ; or

(*b*) ensuring that a condition attached to a financial grant or loan made by the United Kingdom Government to the Government of the Colony is complied with.

(3) Whenever the Governor acts against the advice of the Council of Ministers any member of the Council may require that there shall be recorded in the minutes any advice or opinion he may give upon the question at issue and his reasons.

(4) The question whether the Governor has exercised any power after consultation with the Council of Ministers or the Chief Minister, or in accordance with the advice of the Council, shall not be inquired into in any court of law.

Governor's powers as respects offices.
29.—(1) Subject to the provisions of this Order and of any other law for the time being in force in the Colony, the Governor shall have power, in Her Majesty's name and on Her Majesty's behalf—

(*a*) to constitute such offices as may lawfully be constituted by Her Majesty and abolish any office so constituted by him ;

(*b*) to make appointments (including appointments on promotion or transfer) to any office so constituted by him ; and

(*c*) to terminate the appointment of or dismiss any person so appointed, or suspend him from performing the functions of his office, or take such other disciplinary action with respect to him as may be necessary.

(2) A person appointed to an office constituted under this section shall, unless it is otherwise provided by law, hold office during Her Majesty's pleasure.

(3) The Governor may delegate to any public officer, in such manner and on such conditions as he may think fit, any of the powers conferred upon him by this section.

(4) The posers conferred upon the Governor by this section shall, with the exception of the powers referred to in subsection 1(a) of this section, be exercised by him in his discretion.

30.—(1) The Governor, acting in his discretion, may, in Her Majesty's name and on Her Majesty's behalf— *Prerogative of mercy.*

(a) grant to any person concerned in or convicted of any offence against the law in force in the Colony a pardon, either free or subject to lawful conditions ;

(b) grant to any person a respite, either indefinite or for a specified period, of the execution of any punishment imposed on that person for any offence ;

(c) substitute a less severe form of punishment for any punishment imposed on any person for any offence ; and

(d) remit the whole or part of any punishment imposed on any person for an offence or of any penalty or forfeiture otherwise due to the Crown on account of any offence.

(2) The provisions of this section shall not apply in relation to any conviction by a court-martial established under any Act of Parliament of the United Kingdom, any punishment imposed in respect of any such conviction or any penalty or forfeiture due under any such Act.

31. The Governor shall keep and use the public seal. *Public seal.*

CHAPTER IV

The Executive

Composition

32. There shall be a Council of Ministers in and for the Colony which shall consist of— *Council of Ministers.*

(a) the Chief Minister, who shall be elected as such in accordance with the provisions of Schedule 1 ot this Order ;

(b) not less than four nor more than six Ministers, as the Chief Minister shall determine, appointed in accordance with the provisions of the next following section from among the elected members of the House of Assembly :

Provided that at least one of such Ministers shall be a member who has been elected to represent an electoral district in the Ellice Islands ; and

(c) the Deputy Governor, the Attorney-General and the Financial Secretary.

Appointment of Ministers. **33.** Ministers shall be appointed by the Governor, in accordance with the advice of the Chief Minister, by instrument under the public seal.

Tenure of office of Chief Minister and Ministers. **34.**—(1) The office of the Chief Minister shall become vacant—

(a) upon the happening of any of the events specified in paragraphs (a), (b), (c) or (e) of subsection (2) of this section; or

(b) if a motion of no confidence in the Chief Minister receives in the House of Assembly the affirmative votes of a majority of all the elected members.

(2) The office of a Minister shall become vacant—

(a) when, after a general election ,the elected members of the House of Assembly meet, in accordance with the provisions of paragraph 1 of Schedule 1 to this Order, to elect the Chief Minister;

(b) if he ceases to be an elected member of the House of Assembly for any reason other than a dissolution of the House;

(c) if he resigns such office by writing under his hand addressed to the Governor;

(d) if his appointment to the office of Minister is revoked by the Governor, acting on the advice of the Chief Minister, by instrument under the public seal;

(e) if he is absent from the Colony for a period of more than four weeks without the written permission of the Governor, acting in his discretion;

(f) if the office of Chief Minister becomes vacant and the Minister is elected in accordance with the provisions of paragraph 1(1)(b) of Schedule 1 to this Order to be Chief Minister; or

(g) if the office of Chief Minister becomes vacant pursuant to subsection (1)(b) of this section.

(3) Any question whether the office of Chief Minister or of a Minister has become vacant shall be determined by the Governor, acting in his discretion

Temporary Ministers. **35.**—(1) Whenever a Minister is, by reason of his illness or absence from the Colony or for any other reason, incapable of performing his functions as a member of the Council of Ministers, or has been elected, in accordance with the provisions of paragraph 2 of Schedule 1 to this Order, to act as Chief Minister, the Governor, acting in accordance with the advice of the Chief Minister, may, by instrument under the public seal, appoint an elected member of the House of Assembly, who is not already a Minister, to be temporarily a Minister:

Provided that, if occasion arises for making an appointment under this section between a dissolution of the House of Assembly and the date appointed for the completion of the voting in the next following general election, a person who was an elected member of the House immediately before the dissolution may be appointed as if he were still a member of the House.

(2) Subject to the provisions of this section, the provisions of this Order shall apply to a person appointed under this section as they apply in relation to the Minister in whose place he has been temporarily appointed.

(3) A person appointed under subsection (1) of this section to be temporarily a Minister shall vacate his seat if the Governor, acting in accordance with the advice of the Chief Minister, revokes his appointment, or when he is informed by the Governor that the circumstances given rise to the appointment have ceased to exist.

36. Before assuming the functions of his office every member of the Council of Ministers shall make before the Governor, or some person authorised in that behalf by the Governor, an oath of allegiance and an oath for the due execution of his office in the form set out in Schedule 2 of this Order. Oath by members.

General Provisions Relating to Procedure

37. The Governor shall summon the Council of Ministers if the Chief Minister so requests but it shall not otherwise be summoned except by authority of the Governor acting in his discretion. Summoning of Council of Ministers.

38. There shall preside at meetings of the Council of Ministers— Presiding in Council of Ministers.

(*a*) the Governor;

(*b*) in his absence, the Deputy Governor;

(*c*) in the absence of the Governor and the Deputy Governor, such member of the Council as may generally or specially appointed by the Governor, acting in his discretion, for that purpose.

39.—(1) No business except that of adjournment shall be transacted in the Council of Ministers if objection is taken by any member present that there are less than four members present besides the Governor or members presiding. Proceedings in Council of Ministers.

(2) Subject to the provisions of subsection (1) of this section, the Council of Ministers shall not be disqualified for the transaction of business by reason of any vacancy in its membership, and any proceedings in the Council shall be valid notwithstanding that some person who was not entitled to do so took part in those proceedings.

40.—(1) The Governor shall, after consultation with the Chief Minister, decide what business shall be considered at any meeting of the Council of Ministers. Agenda.

(2) If the Governor declines to submit a matter to the Council of Ministers when requested by any member of the Council to do so that person may require that the request and the reply of the Governor be reported in the minutes of the Council.

41. The Governor, or the member presiding, may summon any person to a meeting of the Council of Ministers, notwithstanding that that person is not a member of the Council, when in his opinion the business before the Council makes the presence of that person desirable: Summoning of persons to attend Council of Ministers.

Provided that a person shall not be under any obligation to answer any question put to him by any member of the Council, or by the Governor, at such meeting.

Attorney-General.

42.—(1) The Attorney-General shall be the principal legal adviser to the Government of the Colony.

(2) The Attorney-General shall have power in any case in which he considers it desirable to do so—

(a) to institute and undertake criminal proceedings against any person before any court (other than a court-martial) in respect of any offence alleged to have been committed by that person;

(b) to take over and continue any such criminal proceedings that have been instituted or undertaken by any other person or authority; and

(c) to discontinue at any stage before judgement is delivered any such criminal proceedings instituted or undertaken by himself or any other person or authority.

(3) The powers of the Attorney-General under the last foregoing subsection may be exercised by him in person or by officers subordinate to him acting in accordance with his general or specific instructions.

(4) The powers conferred on the Attorney-General by subsection (2)(b) and (c) of this section shall be vested in him to the exclusion of any other person or authority:

Provided that where any other person or authority has instituted criminal proceedings, nothing in that subsection shall prevent the withdrawal of those proceedings by or at the instance of that person or authority and with the leave of the court.

(5) In the exercise of the functions vested in him by subsection (2) of this section the Attorney-General shall not be subject to the direction and control of any other person or authority.

(6) For the purposes of this section, any appeal from any judgment in any criminal proceedings before any court, or any case stated or question of law reserved for the purpose of any such proceedings, to any other court (including the Judicial Committee of Her Majesty's Privy Council) shall be deemed to be part of those proceedings:

Provided that the power conferred on the Attorney-General by sub-section (2)(c) of this section shall not be exercised in relation to any appeal by a person convicted in any criminal proceedings or to any case stated or question of law reserved at the instance of such a person.

Assignment of respon-sibilities to Ministers.

43.—(1) The Governor, acting in accordance with the advice of the Chief Minister, may, by direction in writing, assign to any Minister responsibility for the conduct (subject to the provisions of this Order and of any other law) of any business of the Government of the Colony, including responsibility for the administration of any department of government:

Provided that a Minister shall not be charged with responsibility under this section for finance or for any of the matters mentioned in section 26 of this Order.

(2) The Governor, acting in his discretion, may at any time call for any official papers or seek any official information or advice available to a Minister with respect to a matter for which that Minister is responsible under this Section.

(3) Without prejudice to the generality of the provisions of section 77 of this Order, the Governor, acting in his discretion, may, by order published at the Public Office of the Governor, provide that, subject to such limitations and conditions as may be prescribed in the order, any of the functions of the Governor or of any public officer under any local enactment that are specified in the order shall be performed by the Minister charged with responsibility for the matter to which those functions relate.

(4) Where an order under subsection (3) of this section in relation to any functions is in force—

(a) the Governor or public officer, as the case may be, shall not perform those functions; and

(b) the Minister performing those functions may vary or rescind anything previously done in the performance thereof to the same extent as the Governor or public officer, as the case may be, could have done.

(5) Where, by reason of the revocation or amendment of a direction under subsection (1) of this section, functions cease to be performed by a Minister anything done by him in the performance thereof and having effect immediately before the revocation or amendment shall continue to have effect, but without prejudice to the power of the Governor or public officer or any other Minister authorised under this section to perform the functions to rescind or vary the same.

(6) Nothing in this section shall apply to—

(a) any functions relating to the making of any subsidiary instrument; or

(b) the functions of any judge, magistrate or court of law.

(7) The Governor shall cause a copy of every order made under subsection (3) of this section to be laid before the House of Assembly at its sitting next following the date on which the order was made.

44. The members of the Council of Ministers shall be collectively responsible to the House of Assembly for any advice given to the Governor in the exercise of their functions under this Order and for all things done by or under the authority of any member of the Council in the exercise of his functions; *Collective responsibility*

Provided that the provisions of this section shall not apply to any advice given by the Chief Minister under subsection (1) of the immediately preceding section.

CHAPTER V

HOUSE OF ASSEMBLY

Composition

45. There shall be a House of Assembly which shall consist of— *House of Assembly.*

(a) twenty-eight elected members who shall be directly elected in such manner as may be prescribed by regulations made by the Governor, acting in his discretion; and

(b) the Deputy Governor, the Attorney-General and the Financial Secretary.

Election of
elected
members.

46. For the purpose of the election of the elected members of the House of Assembly, electoral districts shall be established within the Colony having such boundaries and such number of elected representatives as may be prescribed by or under regulations made under the immediately preceding section.

Qualifi-
cations for
elected
membership.

47. Subject to the provisions of the next following section, a person shall be qualified to be elected as an elected member of the House of Assembly if, and shall not be so qualified unless,—

(*a*) he is a British subject or a British protected person;

(*b*) he has attained the age of twenty-one years; and

(*c*) he has resided in the Colony during the three years immediately preceding the date of his election for a period or periods amounting in the aggregate to not less than thrity months, or is domiciled in the Colony and is resident there at that date.

Disqualifi-
cations for
elected
membership.

48.—(1) No person shall be qualified to be elected as an elected member of the House of Assembly who—

(*a*) is, by virtue of his own act, under any acknowledgement of allegiance, obedience of adherence to a foreign power or state;

(*b*) has been adjudged or otherwise declared bankrupt under any law for the time being in force in any part of the Commonwealth and has not been discharged;

(*c*) is certified to be insane or otherwise adjudged to be of unsound mind under any law for the time being in force in the Colony;

(*d*) is under sentence of death imposed on him by a court in any part of the Commonwealth, or is serving a sentence of imprisonment (by whatever name called) for a term of or exceeding twelve months, imposed on him by such a court or substituted by competent authority for some other sentence imposed on him by such a court, or is under a sentence of imprisonment the execution of which has been suspended;

(*e*) is disqualified from membership of the House under any law for the time being in force in the Colony relating to offences connected with elections;

(*f*) holds, or is acting in, any office the functions of which involve any responsibility for, or in connection with, the conduct of any election or the compilation or revision of any electoral register; or

(*g*) subject to such exemptions as may be prescribed by any law in force in the Colony, holds, or is acting in, any public office.

(2) For the purposes of paragraph (*d*) of the last preceding subsection—

(*a*) two or more terms of imprisonment that are required to be served consecutively shall be regarded as a single term of imprisonment for the aggregate period of those terms; and

(*b*) no account shall be taken of a sentence of imprisonment imposed as an alternative to or in default of the payment of a fine.

49. The seat of an elected member of the House of Assembly shall become vacant— Tenure of office of elected members.

(*a*) on a dissolution of the House;

(*b*) if he is absent from the sittings of the House for such period and in such circumstances, as may be prescribed in the rules of procedure of the House;

(*c*) if he resigns his seat by writing under his hand addressed to the Governor;

(*d*) if any circumstances arise which, if he were not a member of the House would cause him not to be qualified for election thereto under paragraph (*a*) of section 47 of this Order or to be disqualified for election thereto by virtue of paragraph (*a*), (*b*), (*c*), (*e*), (*f*) or (*g*) of subsection (1) of the immediately preceding section; or

(*e*) in the circumstances specified in the next following section.

50.—(1) Subject to the provisions of this section. if an elected member of the House of Assembly is sentenced by a court in any part of the Commonwealth to death or to imprisonment (by whatever name called) for a term of or exceeding twelve months, he shall forthwith cease to discharge his functions as a member of the House, and his seat in the House shall become vacant at the expiration of a period of thirty days thereafter: Vacation of seat on sentence.

Provided the Governor, acting in his discretion, may, at the request of the member, from time to time extend that period of thirty days to enable the member to pursue any appeal in respect of his conviction or sentence, so however that extensions of time exceeding in the aggregate one hundred and fifty days shall not be granted without the approval of the House signified by resolution.

(2) If at any time before the member vacates his seat he receives a free pardon of his conviction is set aside or his sentence is reduced to a term of imprisonment less than twelve months or a punishment other than imprisonment is substituted, his seat in the House of Assembly shall not become vacant under the provisions of the immediately preceding subsection and he may again discharge his functions as a member of the House.

(3) For the purposes of this section—

(*a*) two or more terms of imprisonment that are required to be served consecutively shall be regarded as a single term of imprisonment for the aggregate period of those terms; and

(*b*) no account shall be taken of a sentence of imprisonment imposed as an alternative to or in default of the payment of a fine.

51.—(1) The High Court shall have jurisdiction to hear and determine any question whether— Determination of questions as to membership.

(*a*) any person has been validly elected as a member of the House of Assembly; or

(*b*) any elected member of the House has vacated his seat therein or is required by virtue of the immediately preceding section to cease to perform his functions as a member.

(2) An application to the High Court for the determination of—

(*a*) any question under paragraph (*a*) of the immediately preceding subsection may be made by any person entitled to vote in the electoral district, and at the election, to which the application relates or by any person who was a candidate in that district at that election or by the Attorney-General ;

(*b*) any question under paragraph (*b*) of the immediately preceding subsection may be made by any person entitled to vote at an election in the electoral district for which the member concerned was returned or by any elected member of the House of Assembly or by the Attorney-General :

Provided that if such an application is made by a person other than the Attorney-General, the Attorney-General may intervene and may then appear or be represented in the proceedings.

(3) Regulations made under section 45(*a*) of this Order may make provision with respect to—

(*a*) the circumstances and manner in which and the imposition of conditions upon which any application may be made to the High Court for the determination of any question under subsection (1) of this section ; and

(*b*) the powers, practice and procedure of the High Court in relation to any such application.

(4) No appeal shall lie from any decision of the High Court in proceedings under subsection (1) of this section.

Penalty for sitting or voting whilst unqualified.

52.—(1) Any person who sits or votes in the House of Assembly knowing or having reasonable grounds for knowing that he is not entitled to do so shall be liable to a penalty not exceeding twenty dollars for each day upon which he so sits or votes.

(2) Any such penalty shall be recoverable by civil action in the High Court at the suit of the Attorney-General.

Legislation

Power to make laws.

53.—(1) Subject to the provisions of this Order, the Governor, with the advice and consent of the House of Assembly, may make laws for the peace, order and good government of the Colony.

(2) In the making of laws the Governor and the House of Assembly shall conform as nearly as may be to the directions contained in any Instructions given under Her Majesty's Sign Manual and Signet which may from time to time be addressed to the Governor in that behalf.

Rules of procedure.

54. Subject to the provisions of this Order, the House of Assembly may make rules of procedure for the regulation and orderly conduct of its proceedings and the discharge of business at meetings of the House and for the passing, intituling and numbering of Bills and for the presentation thereof to the Governor for assent ; but no such rules shall have effect until approved by the Governor, acting in his discretion.

Introduction of Bills, etc.

55.—(1) Subject to the provisions of this Order and of the rules of procedure of the House of Assembly, any member may introduce any Bill or propose any motion for debate in, or may present any petition to, the House, and the same shall be debated and disposed of according to the rules of procedure of the House.

(2) Except on the recommendation of the Governor, the House of Assembly shall not—

(*a*) proceed upon any Bill (including any amendment to a Bill) which, in the opinion of the person presiding in the House—

(i) makes provision for imposing or increasing any tax, for imposing or increasing any charge on the revenues or other funds of the Colony, or for altering any such charge otherwise than by reducing it, or for compounding or remitting any debt due to the Government of the Colony ; or

(ii) would effect any alteration in the salary, allowances or other conditions of service (including leave, passages and promotion) of any public officer or in the law, regulations or practice governing the payment of pensions, gratuities or other like benefits to any public officer or former public officer or his widow, children, dependants or personal representatives ; or

(*b*) proceed upon any motion (including any amendment to a motion) the effect of which in the opinion of the person presiding in the House is that provision would be made for any of the purposes aforesaid.

56.—(1) A Bill passed by the House of Assembly shall not become a law until— Assent to Bills.

(*a*) the Governor has assented to it in Her Majesty's name and on Her Majesty's behalf and has signed it in token of his assent ; or

(*b*) Her Majesty has given Her assent to it through a Secretary of State, and the Governor has signified that assent by proclamation published together with the law by exhibition at the Public Office of the Governor.

(2) When a Bill is presented to the Governor for his assent, he shall, acting in his discretion, declare that he assents or refuses to assent to it, or that he reserves the Bill for the signification of Her Majesty's pleasure.

57.— A law made under section 53 of this Order— Publication and commencement of laws.

(*a*) shall be published in the Colony by exhibition at the Public Office of the Governor ; and

(*b*) shall come into operation on the date of such publication or, if it is enacted either in the law or in some other law that it shall come into operation on some other date, on that date.

58.—(1) Any law to which the Governor has given his assent may be disallowed by Her Majesty through a Secretary of State. Disallowance of laws

(2) Whenever any law has been disallowed by Her Majesty the Governor shall cause notice of the disallowance to be published by exhibition at the Public Office of the Governor.

(3) A law disallowed by Her Majesty shall be annulled with effect from the date of the publication of the notice of the disallowance.

(4) Section 38(2) of the Interpretation Act 1889 shall apply to the annulment of any law under this section as it applies to the repeal of an Act of Parliament, save that any enactment amended or repealed by or in pursuance of that law shall have effect as from the date of the annulment as if that law had not been made.

Governor's reserved power.

59.—(1) If the Governor considers that it is expedient in the interests of public order, public faith or good government (which expressions shall, without prejudice to their generality, include the responsibility of the Colony as a territory within the Commonwealth, and all matters pertaining to the creation or abolition of any public office, or to the salary or other conditions of service of any public officer) that any Bill introduced or any motion proposed at any meeting of the House of Assembly held in accordance with the provisions of this Chapter should have effect, then, if the House fails to pass the Bill or to carry the motion within such time and in such form as the Governor thinks reasonable and expedient, the Governor may, at any time that he thinks fit, and notwithstanding any provisions of this Order or of any rules of procedure of the House, declare that the Bill or motion shall have effect as if it had been passed or carried by the House either in the form in which it was introduced or proposed or with such amendments as the Governor thinks fit that have been moved or proposed in the House, including any committee thereof; and the Bill or motion shall be deemed thereupon to have been so passed or carried, and the provisions of this Order, and in particular the provisions relating to assent to Bills and disallowance of laws, shall have effect accordingly.

(2) The Governor shall forthwith report to a Secretary of State every case in which he makes any such declaration and the reasons for it.

(3) If any member of the House of Assembly objects to any declaration made under this section, he may, within seven days of the making thereof, submit to the Governor a statement in writing of his reasons for so objecting and, if he furnishes a copy of that statement and requests the Governor to do so, the Governor shall as soon as practicable forward the copy to a Secretary of State.

(4) Any declaration made under this section, other than a declaration relating to a Bill, may be revoked by a Secretary of State and the Governor shall forthwith cause notice of the revocation to be published in the Colony by exhibition at the Public Office of the Governor; and from the date of such publication any motion that is deemed to have been carried by virtue of the declaration shall cease to have effect and section 38(2) of the Interpretation Act 1889 shall apply to the revocation as it applies to the repeal of an Act of Parliament.

(5) The powers conferred upon the Governor by this section shall be exercised by him in his discretion.

(6) The motions to which this section applies are—

(*a*) any motion relating to or for the purposes of a Bill ;

(*b*) any motion proposing or amending a resolution which, if passed by the House of Assembly, would have the force of law ; and

(*c*) any motion proposing or amending a resolution upon which the coming into force or continuance in force of a subsidiary instrument depends.

Procedure

Oath of allegiance.

60. No member of the House of Assembly shall be permitted to take part in the proceedings of the House (other than proceedings necessary for the purpose of this section) until he has made before the House an oath of allegiance in the form set out in Schedule 2 to this Order.

61.—(1) There shall be a speaker of the House of Assembly who The Speaker. shall be appointed by the Governor, acting after consultation with the Chief Minister, from among persons who are not members of the House.

(2) The Speaker shall hold office during Her Majesty's pleasure and, subject thereto, for such period as may be specified in the instrument by which he is appointed, and shall not vacate his office by reason only of a dissolution of the House of Assembly.

(3) Any appointment made under subsection (1) of this section shall be by instrument under the public seal.

(4) No person shall be appointed as Speaker if—

(*a*) he is not a British subject or a British protected person; or

(*b*) he is a person disqualified for election as an elected member of the House of Assembly by virtue of any provision of section 48 of this Order.

(5) A person shall vacate the office of Speaker—

(*a*) if he announces the resignation of his office to the House of Assembly or if, by writing under his hand addressed to the House and received by the Clerk of the House, he resigns that office;

(*b*) if he ceases to be a British subject or a British protected person;

(*c*) if any circumstances arise that would cause him to be disqualified for election as an elected member by virtue of any provision of section 48 of this Order; or

(*d*) if he was at the date of his appointment a party to (or a partner in a firm or a director or manager of a company which was a party to) any contract with the Government of the Colony for or on account of the public service and if, before the expiration of a period of thirty days from the date of his appointment, he has not disclosed to the House the nature of such contract and his interest, or the interest of such firm or company, therein and the House has not exempted him from vacating his office under this paragraph.

62.—(1) Subject to the provisions of subsection (2) of this section, Presiding in House of Assembly. the Speaker or, in his absence or when his office is vacant, a member of the House of Assembly (not bieng a member of the Council of Ministers) elected by the House for that sitting, shall preside at each sitting of the House.

(2) Until such time as a person is appointed to the office of Speaker, the Governor (or, in his absence, such member of the House of Assembly as the Governor, acting in his discretion, may generally or specially designate) shall preside at each sitting of the House.

63.—(1) Subject to the provisions of this Order, all questions Voting. proposed for decision in the House of Assembly shall be determined by a majority of the votes of the members present and voting.

(2) If the person presiding is:

(*a*) the Speaker or the Governor, he shall have neither an original nor a casting vote;

(b) a member elected in accordance with the provisions of subsection (1) of the immediately preceding section, or designated by the Governor in accordance with the provisions of subsection (2) of that section, he shall not have an original vote but shall have and shall exercise a casting vote if on any question the votes are equally divided.

Quorum.

64. If objection is taken by any member of the House of Assembly present that there are present in the House (besides the person presiding) less than fifteen members of the House and, after such interval as may be prescribed in the rules of procedure of the House, the person presiding ascertains that the number of members present is still less than fifteen, he shall thereupon adjourn the House.

Summoning of persons to attend House of Assembly.

65. At the request of a member of the Council of Ministers, the person presiding in the House of Assembly may summon any person to a sitting of the House, notwithstanding that that person is not a member of the House, and a person so summoned shall be entitled to take part in the proceedings of the House as if he were a member but shall not have a vote.

Provided that a person shall not be under any obligation to answer any question put to him by any member of the House, or by the person presiding, at such sitting.

Governor may address House of Assembly.

66. Notwithstanding any other provision of this Order, the Governor may address the members of the House of Assembly at any time and call a sitting of the House for that purpose.

Proceedings in House of Assembly.

67. The House of Assembly shall not be disqualified for the transaction of business by reason of any vacancy in its membership, and any proceedings in the House shall be valid notwithstanding that some persons who was not entitled to do so took part in those proceedings.

Privileges etc. of House of Assembly.

68.—(1) Subject to the provisions of subsections (2) and (3) of this section, a law made under section 53 of this Order may determine the privileges, immunities and powers of the House of Assembly and of its members.

(2) No civil or criminal proceedings may be instituted against any member of the House of Assembly for words spoken before, or written in a report to, the House or a committee of the House, or by reason of any matter or thing brought by him in the House or in a committee of the House.

(3) No process issued by any court in the exercise of its civil jurisdiction shall be served or executed within the precincts of the House of Assembly while the House is sitting.

Summoning, Prorogation and Dissolution

Sessions of House of Assembly.

69.—(1) Subject to the provisions of this section, each session of the House of Assembly shall be held at such place within the Colony and shall commence at such time as the Governor, acting in his discretion, may appoint by proclammation published by exhibition at the Public Office of the Governor.

(2) The first session of the House of Assembly shall be held within six months after the appointed day, and thereafter sessions shall be held so that a period of twelve months does not intervene between the end of one session and the first sitting of the House in the next session.

70.—(1) The Governor, acting in his discretion, may at any time Prorogation prorogue or dissolve the House of Assembly by proclamation published and dissolution. by exhibition at the Public Office of the Governor.

(2) The Governor shall dissolve the House of Assembly at the expiration of four years from the date when the House first sits after any general election unless the House has been sooner dissolved under the last preceding subsection.

71. If before the appointed day a general election has not been held General elections. pursuant to the provisions of section 2(2) of the Gilbert and Ellice Islands Colony (Electoral Provisions) Order 1974, there shall be a general election at such time within three months after the appointed day, and thereafter within three months of every dissolution of the House of Assembly, as the Governor acting in his discretion, shall appoint by proclamation published by exhibition at the Public Office of the Governor.

CHAPTER VI

PUBLIC ACCOUNTS COMMITTEE

72.—(1) There shall be a Public Accounts Committee of the House Public of Assembly which shall consist of three elected members of the House: Accounts Committee.

Provided that no such person shall be qualified for appointment as a member of the Committee if he holds, or is acting in, the office of a Minister or of Chief Minister.

(2) The members of the Committee shall be appointed by the Governor by instrument in writing under his hand.

(3) A member of the Committee shall hold his seat thereon for such period as may be specified in the instrument by which he was appointed:

Provided that his seat shall become vacant—

(a) if he ceases to be an elected member of the House of Assembly;

(b) if he is elected as Chief Minister or to act as such;

(c) if he is appointed to the office of a Minister or to be temporarily a Minister; or

(d) if the Governor by instrument under his hand, so directs.

(4) In the exercise of the powers conferred on him by subsections (2) and (3) of this section the Governor shall act after consultation with the Chief Minister.

(5) The functions of the Committee shall be—

(a) to consider the accounts of the Government in conjunction with the report of the Director of Audit;

(b) to report to the House of Assembly, in the case of any excess or unauthorised expenditure of funds, the reasons for such expenditure;

(c) to propose any measures it considers necessary to ensure that the funds of the Government are properly and economically spent; and

(d) where a report on the examination and audit of the accounts of any corporation, statutory board, body or commission is required by law to be laid before the House of Assembly, to consider, report on and make recommendations to the House in respect of such accounts.

CHAPTER VII

MISCELLANEOUS AND TRANSITIONAL PROVISIONS

Concurrent appointments.

73.—(1) When the holder of any office constituted or deemed to be constituted by or under this Order is on leave of absence pending relinquishment of his office, it shall be lawful for another person to be appointed substantively to the same office.

(2) When two or more persons are holding the same office by reason of an appointment made pursuant to subsection (1) of this section, then for the purpose of any function conferred upon the holder of that office the person last appointed to the office shall be deemed to be the holder of the office.

Executive Council.

74. Notwithstanding the revocation by this Order of the Gilbert and Ellice Islands Order 1970, the Executive Council established by that Order—

(a) shall continue on and after the appointed day to exist as if the provisions of sections 26 and 27, and Chapter V, of that Order were still in force, until such time as the Council of Ministers established by this Order first meets; and

(b) shall until that time perform its functions and be consulted by the Governor in accordance with the provisions of that Order and of the Instructions given under Her Majesty's Sign Manual and Signet in relation to that Order.

Governor's interim legislative power.

75. Subject to the provisions of this Order, the Governor, acting in his discretion, may make laws for the peace, order and good government of the Colony during the period beginning with the appointed day and ending when the House of Assembly first sits.

Existing offices and officers.

76.—(1) Any office constituted, or deemed to be constituted, for the Colony by the Governor under section 28 of the Gilbert and Ellice Islands Order 1970 and subsisting immediately before the appointed day shall, on and after that day, be deemed to be an office constituted by the Governor under section 29 of this Order.

(2) Any person who, immediately before the appointed day, holds or is acting in any such office shall, on and after that day, continue to hold or to act in his office as if he had been appointed to it in accordance with the provisions of this Order.

(3) Any person to whom the immediately preceding subsection applies who, before the appointed day, has made any oath required to be made by him before assuming the functions of his office shall not, by reason only of that subsection, be required to make a like oath.

77.—(1) The existing laws shall, as from the appointed day, be construed with such adaptations and modifications as may be necessary to bring them into conformity with the provisions of this Order.

Existing laws.

(2) (*a*) The Governor, acting in his discretion, may, by order published by exhibition at the Public Office of the Governor, at any time within twelve months after the appointed day provide that any existing law shall be read and construed with such adaptations and modifications as may appear to him to be necessary or expedient for bringing that law into conformity with the provisions of this Order or otherwise for giving effect or enabling effect to be given to those provisions; and any existing law shall have effect accordingly from such date as may be specified in the order.

(*b*) An order made under this subsection may be amended or revoked in relation to any law affected thereby by the authority competent to amend or revoke that law.

(3) In this section " existing law " means any law made for the Colony by the Governor or any subsidiary instrument made thereunder, that has effect as part of the law of the Colony immediately before the appointed day.

78. The rules of procedure of the Legislative Council constituted by the Gilbert and Ellice Islands Order 1970 as in force immediately before the appointed day shall, until it is otherwise provided under section 54 of this Order, be the rules of procedure of the House of Assembly but shall be construed with such modifications, adaptations, qualifications and exceptions as may be necessary to bring those rules into conformity with this Order.

Rules of procedure of Legislative Council.

79. Where in this Order it is provided that any proclamation, notice, law, regulation or order shall be published by exhibition at the Public Office of the Governor then such proclamation, notice, law or order shall be printed in the Gazette as soon as may be after the date of such publication.

Proclamations, etc. to be printed in the Gazette.

80. Until such time as it is otherwise provided by regulations made under section 45(*a*) of this Order, any regulations made under the Gilbert and Ellice Islands Colony (Electoral Provisions) Order 1974 and in force immediately before the appointed day shall have effect on and after that day as if they were a law made in pursuance of that section:

Electoral Regulations.

Provided that, until such time as the Council of Ministers established by this Order first meets, the Governor, acting in his discretion, may by regulations amend or revoke those regulations.

81. There is reserved to Her Majesty full power to make laws from time to time for the peace, order and good government of the Colony, including, without prejudice to the generality of the foregoing, laws amending or revoking this Order.

Power reserved to Her Majesty.

W. G. Agnew.

Section 32(a)   SCHEDULE 1

ELECTION OF CHIEF MINISTER

1.—(1) The Governor shall cause an election of the Chief Minister to be held—

(a) in the case of a general election, as soon as practicable after the holding of a general election of the members of the House of Assembly and before the House first sits after that general election; and

(b) in the case of a bye-election to the office of Chief Minister, as soon as practicable after that office has become vacant.

(2) In respect of any election of the Chief Minister, any elected member of the House of Assembly shall be entitled to nominate from among the elected members of the House, one candidate for election as Chief Minister.

(3) Any meeting of the elected members of the House of Assembly held for the purpose of electing the Chief Minister shall be summoned by the Governor, and the proceedings at any such meeting shall be valid notwithstanding any vacancy among the elected members of the House or the absence of any such member.

(4) A list of the candidates nominated for election under sub-paragraph (2) of this paragraph shall be prepared, and each elected member of the House of Assembly present at the meeting shall have one vote and shall be entitled to cast it for one candidate on the list so constituted.

(5) The vote of every such elected member shall be given by ballot in such a manner as not to disclose how that member voted.

(6) No other business than the holding of the election of the Chief Minister may be transacted at any meeting of the elected members of the House of Assembly summoned under sub-paragraph (3) of this paragraph and such a meeting shall not be regarded as a sitting of the House of Assembly for the purposes of any other provision of this Order.

(7) The candidate on the list constituted in accordance with the foregoing paragraphs who receives the greatest number of votes shall, subject to the provisions of the next following sub-paragraph, be deemed to have been elected.

(8) When two or more candidates equally receive the greatest number of votes, no candidate shall be deemed to have been elected and a further ballot or, if necessary, ballots, shall be held in accordance with the provisions of this Schedule:

Provided that—

(i) for the purposes of any such further ballot only those candidates who received the greatest number of votes in the preceding ballot may stand as candidates; and

(ii) where in two successive ballots the same two or more candidates equally receive the greatest number of votes, the Governor may determine by lot which of those candidates is deemed to be elected instead of holding a further ballot.

2.—(1) If the office of the Chief Minister becomes vacant or the person holding that office is, by reason of his illness or absence from the Colony or for any other reason, in the opinion of the Governor incapable of performing the functions of such office, the Governor shall summon a meeting of the Ministers for the election by them of one of their number to act as Chief Minister during the said vacancy or, as the case may be, during the said incapacity.

(2) The proceedings at any such meeting shall be conducted by the Governor in such manner as he may direct and shall be valid notwithstanding any vacancy or the absence of any Minister.

(3) The Minister who receives the greatest number of votes cast at any such meeting shall be declared to have been elected to act as Chief Minister; and if two Ministers equally receive the greatest number of votes, the Governor may, if he thinks fit, determine by lot which of them shall be deemed to have been so elected.

(4) A person elected or deemed to have been elected under the preceding sub-paragraph shall cease to act as Chief Minister when a person has been elected, or deemed to have been elected, in accordance with paragraph 1 of this Schedule as Chief Minister, or when he has been informed by the Governor that the Chief Minister is again able to perform the functions of his office, as the case may be.

3. The powers conferred upon the Governor by this Schedule shall be exercised by him in his discretion.

SCHEDULE 2   Sections 21, 36 and 60

OATHS AND AFFIRMATIONS

1. Oath of Allegiance

I, ..., do swear [or solemnly affirm] that I will be faithful and bear true allegiance to Her Majesty Queen Elizabeth II, Her Heirs and Successors, according to law. [So help me God.]

2. Oath for the due execution of the office of Governor

I, ..., do swear [or solemnly affirm] that I will well and truly serve Her Majesty Queen Elizabeth II, Her Heirs and Successors, in the office of Governor of the Gilbert and Ellice Islands Colony. [So help me God.]

3. Oath for the due execution of the office of member of the Council of Ministers

I, ..., being a member of the Council of Ministers, do swear [or solemnly affirm] that I will do the best of my judgment, at all times when so required, freely give my counsel and advice to the Governor of the Gilbert and Ellice Islands Colony (or any other person for the time being lawfully performing the functions of the office of Governor) for the good management of the public affairs of the Gilbert and Ellice Islands Colony, and I do further swear [or solemnly affirm] that I will not on any account, at any time whatsoever, disclose the counsel, advice, opinion or vote of any particular member of the Council of Ministers, and that I will not, except with the authority of the Governor and to such extent as may be required for the good management of the affairs of the Gilbert and Ellice Islands Colony, directly or indirectly reveal the business or proceedings of the Council of Ministers or any matter coming to my knowledge in my capacity as a member of the Council and that in all things I will be a true and faithful member of the Council. [So help me God.]

EXPLANATORY NOTE

(*This Note is not part of the Order.*)

This Order makes new provision for the Government of the Gilbert and Ellice Islands Colony. In particular it replaces the existing Executive and Legislative Councils by a Council of Ministers and a House of Assembly, and provides for a Public Accounts Committee.

PACIFIC ISLANDS

The Gilbert and Ellice Islands Royal Instructions 1974

Dated: 24th April, 1974. *ELIZABETH* R.

INSTRUCTIONS to Our Governor in and over Our Colony of the Gilbert and Ellice Islands or other Officer Administering the Government of the Colony.

We do hereby direct and enjoin and declare Our will and pleasure as follows:—

Citation, publication, commencement and revocation.

1.—(1) These Instructions may be cited as the Gilbert and Ellice Islands Royal Instructions 1974.

(2) These Instructions shall be published by exhibition at the Public Office of the Governor and thereafter as soon as may be in the Gazette and shall take effect on the day on which the Gilbert and Ellice Islands Order 1974 (in these Instructions referred to as "the Order of 1974") comes into operation.

(3) Without prejudice to anything lawfully done thereunder, the Gilbert and Ellice Islands Royal Instructions 1971(a) shall cease to have effect on the taking effect of these Instructions.

Interpretation.

2. The provisions of section 2 of the Order of 1974 shall apply for the purpose of interpreting these Instructions as they apply for the purpose of interpreting that Order.

Instructions to be observed by Deputy Governor.

3.—(1) These Instructions, so far as they apply to any functions to be performed by the Deputy Governor under section 25 of the Order of 1974 shall be deemed to be addressed to, and shall be observed by, the Deputy Governor.

(2) The Deputy Governor may, if he thinks fit, apply to Us through a Secretary of State for instructions in any matter; but he shall forthwith transmit to the Governor a copy of every despatch or other communication so addressed to Us.

Rules for the making of laws.

4. In the making of laws under the powers conferred by section 53 of the Order of 1974 the following rules shall be observed as far as practicable:—

(*a*) All laws shall be styled "Ordinances" and the words of enactment shall be—

"Enacted by the Governor with the advice and consent of the House of Assembly":

Provided that in the case of any law made by the Governor under section 59 of the Order of 1974 the words of enactment shall be "Enacted by the Governor in accordance with the provisions of section 59 of the Gilbert and Ellice Islands Order 1974".

(a) S.I. 1971 III, p. 6336.

(*b*) All Ordinances shall be distinguished by titles, and shall be divided into successive sections consecutively numbered, and to every section there shall be annexed in the margin or at its head a short indication of its contents.

(*c*) All Ordinances shall be numbered consecutively in a separate series for each year, commencing with the number one, so that—

(i) an Ordinance passed by the House of Assembly (or deemed to have been so passed under section 59 of the Order of 1974) and assented to by the Governor is included in the series for the year in which it is so passed, and its position in the series is determined with reference to the day on which the Governor has assented to it;

(ii) an Ordinance assented to by Us through a Secretary of State is included in the series for the year in which the Governor has signified Our assent by proclamation, and its position in the series is determined with reference to the day on which Our assent has been so signified.

(*d*) Matters having no proper relation to each other shall not be provided for by the same Ordinance; no Ordinance shall contain anything foreign to what the title of the Ordinance imports; and no provision having indefinite duration shall be included in any Ordinance expressed to have limited duration.

5. Without having previously obtained Our Instructions through a Secretary of State, the Governor shall not assent to any Bill within any of the following classes, unless the Bill contains a provision suspending its operation until the signification of Our pleasure, that is to say, any Bill— Certain Bills not to be assented to without instructions.

(*a*) for the divorce of married persons;

(*b*) whereby any grant of land or money or other donation be made to himself;

(*c*) affecting the currency of the Colony or relating to the issue of bank notes;

(*d*) establishing any banking association, or altering the constitution, powers or privileges of any banking association;

(*e*) imposing differential duties;

(*f*) affecting the discipline or control of Our naval, military or air forces;

(*g*) the provisions of which appear to him to be inconsistent with obligations imposed on Us by treaty, convention, agreement or arrangement relating to any country or international or similar organisation outside the Colony;

(*h*) of an extraordinary nature and importance whereby Our prerogative, or the rights or property of Our subjects not residing in the Colony, or the trade, transport or communications of any part of Our dominions or any territory under Our protection or in which We have for the time being jurisdiction, may be prejudiced;

(*i*) the provisions of which appear to him as likely to cause a financial liability which the Government of the Colony might find difficulty in meeting out its own resources; or (*j*) containing provisions to which Our assent has been refused or which have been disallowed by Us;

Provided that if the Governor is satisfied that it is urgently necessary in the public interest that a Bill falling within any of the said classes (other than a Bill falling within paragraph (*g*) of this clause) be brought into immediate operation, he may assent to that Bill without such instructions as aforesaid and although the Bill contains no provision as aforesaid; but he shall forthwith transmit to Us the Bill together with his reasons for so assenting to it.

Ordinances and Bills to be sent through a Secretary of State.

6. When any Ordinance has been enacted or any Bill has been reserved for the signification of Our pleasure, the Governor shall forthwith transmit to Us through a Secretary of State for the signification of Our pleasure, a transcript in duplicate of the Ordinance or Bill, duly authenticated by his own signature, together with an explanation of the reasons and occasion for the enactment of the Ordinance or the passing of the Bill.

Collection of Ordinances to be published annually.

7. As soon as practicable after the commencement of each year the Governor shall cause a complete collection of all Ordinances enacted during the preceding year to be published for general information.

Purchase of property by Governor.

8. The Governor shall not, directly or indirectly, purchase for himself any land or building in the Colony to Us belonging without Our special permission given through a Secretary of State.

Oath of allegiance by public officers, etc.

9. The Governor may, whenever he thinks fit, require any person in the public service of the Colony or holding any office constituted by or under the Order of 1974 to make an oath or affirmation of allegiance in the form set out in Schedule 2 to the Order of 1974 together with any other oath or affirmation that may be prescribed in relation to his office by any law for the time being in force in the Colony.

Given at Our Court at St. James's this twenty-fourth day of April 1974 in the twenty-third year of Our Reign.

PACIFIC ISLANDS

The Ellice Islands (Referendum) Order 1974

At the Court at Buckingham Palace, the 21st day of May 1974

Present,

The Queen's Most Excellent Majesty in Council

Her Majesty, by virtue and in exercise of all the powers enabling Her in that behalf, is pleased, by and with the advice of Her Privy Council, to order, and it is hereby ordered, as follows:—

1.—(1) This Order may be cited as the Ellice Islands (Referendum) Order 1974.

Citation and commencement.

(2) This Order shall be published by exhibition at the Public Office of the Governor and shall come into operation on the date of such publication and shall be printed in the Gazette as soon as may be after such date.

2.—(1) This Order shall be construed as one with the Gilbert and Ellice Islands Order 1974.

Interpretation.

(2) In this Order "prescribed" means prescribed by regulations made under section 4 of this Order.

(3) In the exercise of the powers conferred upon him by this Order the Governor shall not be obliged to consult the Council of Ministers.

3.—(1) There shall be a referendum for the purpose of enabling the Ellice people of the Colony to state which of the following courses they support:—

Referendum to be held.

(a) the establishment of a separate Ellice Islands Colony in accordance with the conditions set out in the statement by the Government of the United Kingdom set out in the Schedule to this Order; or

(b) the Ellice Islands remaining part of the Gilbert and Ellice Islands Colony.

(2) Without prejudice to any provisions which may be made for voting by post, the referendum shall be held on such day or days and during such hours as the Governor, after consultation with the Referendum Administrator, shall appoint by notice published at the Public Office of the Governor and different days may be appointed for different islands or districts.

(3) The period between the date of publication of the notice in accordance with the provisions of subsection (2) of this section and the day or the first of the days, as the case may be, appointed thereunder shall not be less than twenty-eight days.

(4) The Referendum Administrator shall take all practicable steps to publicise in the island or district concerned the day and hours appointed for voting in that island or district in accordance with the provisions of subsection (2) of this section.

(5) Voting may take place after the date or hour so appointed if in the opinion of the Referendum Administrator circumstances make it impossible or impracticable to hold the referendum on the date or at the hour appointed and the Referendum Administrator publishes as soon as possible by exhibition in the island or district concerned a notice specifying the new date or time, as the case may be.

Governor may make regulations.

4.—(1) Subject to the provisions of this Order, the Governor may by regulation make provision for the conduct and organisation of the referendum, all matters incidental or ancillary thereto, and generally for the purposes of this Order.

(2) Regulations made under this section shall make provision—

(a) for the registration as voters of persons qualified to be so registered by virtue of the provisions of section 5 of this Order;

(b) for the procedure to be followed at the holding of the referendum, including the manner in which votes shall be cast;

(c) for ascertaining and publishing the result of the voting;

(d) for affording facilities to observe the conduct and organisation of the referendum to any persons selected for that purpose by the Secretary-General of the United Nations or by any other international organisation or Government invited to do so by the Government of the United Kingdom;

(e) for the presentation to the High Court of petitions relating to any dispute concerning the result of the voting and for the time and manner in which such petitions shall be heard and determined by that Court;

(f) for giving effect to any directions given under section 9(2) of this Order; and

(g) for the definition and trial of offences relating to the referendum and the imposition of penalties therefor:

Provided that the penalty for such an offence shall not exceed a fine of one hundred pounds or a term of imprisonment of twelve months or both such fine and imprisonment.

(3) Regulations made under this section shall be published by exhibition at the Public Office of the Governor, and unless otherwise provided therein shall take effect and come into operation on the date of such publication and may be amended or revoked by subsequent regulations so made.

Qualifications for registration as a voter.

5.—(1) Subject to the provisions of subsection (2) of this section, a person shall be qualified to be registered as a voter if, and shall not be so qualified unless, on the prescribed date—

(a) he is of the age of eighteen years or upwards; and

(*b*) he is a citizen of the United Kingdom and Colonies or a British Protected Person; and

(*c*) he is domiciled in the Colony:

Provided that he is wholly or partly of Ellice descent in that one or more of his ancestors was born in the Ellice Islands before 1 January 1900.

(2) No person shall be qualified to be registered as a voter who, on the prescribed date—

(*a*) has at any time been sentenced by a court in any part of the Commonwealth to death or to imprisonment (by whatever name called) for a term exceeding twelve months and has not been granted a free pardon:

Provided that if three years or more have elapsed since the termination of the imprisonment the person convicted shall not be disqualified from registration as a voter by reason only of having been so sentenced; or

(*b*) is a person certified to be insane or otherwise adjudged to be of unsound mind under any law in force in the Colony; or

(*c*) is disqualified for registration as an elector for, or disqualified from voting at, elections of members of the House of Assembly by any law in force in the Colony relating to offences connected with elections.

6.—(1) Any person who is registered as a voter shall be entitled to cast a vote in the manner prescribed for the purpose of indicating which of the alternatives specified in section 3(1) of this Order he prefers: | Entitlement to vote of registered voters.

Provided that no such person shall be entitled so to vote if on the date appointed for voting he is in lawful custody or (except in so far as may be otherwise prescribed) he is for any other reason unable to attend in person at the place and time appointed for voting.

(2) Subject to the provisions of section 9(2) of this Order, no person shall be entitled to vote more than once in the referendum.

7.—(1) There shall be a Referendum Administrator who shall, subject to the provisions of section 8(1) and (3) of this Order, be responsible for the conduct of the referendum. | Appointment, etc. of Referendum Administrator and other officers.

(2) The Referendum Administrator shall be appointed by the Governor in puruance of instructions given by Her Majesty through a Secretary of State:

Provided that no person shall be appointed who is qualified to be registered as a voter or who is in the service of the Crown in respect of the government of the Colony.

(3) The Governor may, in Her Majesty's name and on Her Majesty's behalf, constitute such other offices as he may consider necessary for the purposes of this Order and any regulations made thereunder, and appoint persons to those offices and exercise disciplinary control over and dismiss persons appointed to those offices.

(4) The Referendum Administrator and the other officers appointed under this section shall hold office at Her Majesty's pleasure.

Directions to Referendum Administrator and other officers, and exercise of Administrator's functions.

8.—(1) The Governor may give the Referendum Administrator such directions with respect to the exercise of his functions under this Order or any regulations made thereunder as he may consider desirable; and the Referendum Administrator shall comply with those directions or cause them to be complied with.

(2) Subject to the provisions of subsection (1) of this section, the Referendum Administrator may give the officers appointed under section 7(3) of this Order such directions with respect to the exercise of their functions under this Order or any regulations made thereunder as he may consider desirable; and those officers shall comply with those directions or shall cause them to be complied with.

(3) Until the Referendum Administrator has been appointed and has assumed the functions of his office, the functions of the Referendum Administrator under this Order or any regulations made thereunder, including the power to give directions under subsection (2) of this section, may be exercised by the Governor.

Result of voting may be declared invalid and fresh votes taken.

9.—(1) The decision of the High Court in respect of any petition for which provision is made by regulations made in pursuance of paragraph (e) of section 4(2) of this Order, including the findings of the Court upon the facts of the case, shall be transmitted to the Referendum Administrator. ˙

(2) The Referendum Administrator may, if he considers it desirable so to do in the light of any decision of the High Court relating to any dispute concerning the result of the voting, declare that the result of the voting, either generally or at a particular place, is invalid, and direct that the voters or, as the case may be, the voters entitled to vote at that place shall be given a further opportunity of voting for the purposes of the referendum.

W. G. Agnew.

THE SCHEDULE　　　　　　　Section 3(1)(a)

Statement by the Government of the United Kingdom

1. In a statement read by His Excellency the Governor to the Legislative Council of the Gilbert and Ellice Islands Colony on 27 November 1973, the Government of the United Kingdom announced that before a referendum is held to determine whether the majority of Ellice islanders support the separation of the Ellice Islands from the Colony, a statement of the conditions governing separation would be circulated to all Ellice islanders eligible to vote.

2. The conditions governing the separation of the Ellice Islands from the Colony are as follows:—

   (a) the Ellice Islands would become a separate dependent territory of the United Kingdom;

   (b) the Ellice Islands would receive no part of the Revenue Equalisation Reserve Fund of the Gilbert and Ellice Islands Colony;

   (c) the Ellice Islands would receive no part of present or future phosphate royalties;

(d) the Ellice Islands would have no claim to any of the assets (whether fixed, moveable or in cash) belonging to the Gilbert and Ellice Islands Colony and situated outside the Ellice Islands themselves, except for one ship which would be transferred from the Gilbert and Ellice Islands Development Authority; and

(e) an Ellice Islands Colony would be limited to the Ellice Islands Group and would have no right to any other territory of the Gilbert and Ellice Islands Colony.

3. As stated in the announcement to the Legislative Council, if the referendum shows a majority of Ellice islanders to be in favour of separation, and if the Government of the Gilbert and Ellice Islands Colony also wishes it, the Government of the United Kingdom will invite the Government of the Colony and representatives of the Ellice islanders to discuss:—

(a) the future constitution and form of administration of an Ellice Island Colony;

(b) questions relating to access in the future by Ellice islanders to training establishments in Tarawa (including the King George VI School, the Merchant Marine Training School, and the Teachers' Training College);

(c) questions relating to the future employment of Ellice islanders now working in the public and private sectors in the Gilbert and Ellice Islands Colony outside the Ellice Islands Group,

(d) questions relating to the level of and future employment of Ellice islanders outside the Gilbert and Ellice Islands Colony; and

(e) the level of British aid, both current and development, needed to maintain a separate Ellice Islands Colony.

EXPLANATORY NOTE

(This Note is not part of the Order.)

This Order makes provision for a referendum to be held for the purpose of enabling the Ellice people of the Gilbert and Ellice Islands Colony to state whether they support the establishment of a separate Ellice Islands Colony or the Ellice Islands remaining part of the Gilbert and Ellice Islands Colony.

MODIFICATIONS TO LEGISLATION
PART I
MODIFICATIONS TO GENERAL ACTS AND GENERAL INSTRUMENTS
PART II
MODIFICATIONS TO LOCAL ACTS
PART I

Year and Number (or date)	Act or instrument	How affected
1542	Laws in Wales Act (c. 26)	s. 61**r.**, 1974/595
1863	Telegraph Act (c. 112)	s. 9 replaced, 21, 23, ss. **am.**, 1974/595
1880	Burial Laws Amdt. Act (c. 41) ...	ss. 1, 10, 12 **am.** (exc. Is. of Scilly), 1974/628
1882	Electric Lighting Act (c. 56)	s. 31 **am.**, 1974/595
1888	Local Government Act (c. 41) ...	s. 64(5) **r.**, 1974/595
1892	Telegraph Act (c. 59)	ss. 3, 5(2) (b), 9 **am.**, 1974/595
1897		
6	Friendly Society Regs. (Rev. VIII. p. 815)	**am.**, 1974/474
1898		
552	Compulsory Registration of title to land in City of London—O. in C. (Rev. XII, p. 79)	**r.**, 1974/250
1069	Land Registration (E.)—Amdg. O. in C.	**r.**, 1974/250
1899		
858	Land Registration (E.)—Amdg. O. in C.	**r.**, 1974/250
1900	Burial Act (c. 15)	ss. 1, 2, 7-11 **r.** (exc. Is. of Scilly), 1974/628
1901		
203	Land Registration (E.)—Amdg. Regs.	**r.**, 1974/250
986	Land Registration (E.)—Amdg. O. in C.	**r.**, 1974/250
1902		
209	Land Registration (E.)—Amdg. O. in C.	**r.**, 1974/250
1903	Patriotic Fund Reorganisation Act (c.20)	sch. 1 para. 1 replaced (E. and W.), 1974/595
1906	Prevention of Corruption Act (c.34)	s. 1(3) **am.**, 1974/595
1907		
1020	Limited Partnerships Rules (Rev. XVII, p. 15)	**am.**, 1974/560
1908	Telegraph (Construction) Act (c.33)	s. 2 **replaced**, 1974/595
1925	Coastguard Act (c. 88)	ss. 1(1), 2 functions transfd. Secy. of State for Trade, 1974/692
960	Guardianship of Infants (Summary Jurisdiction) Rules (Rev. XIII, p. 245)	**r.**, 1974/706
1262	Registration of Title, Eastbourne—O. in C. (Rev. XII, p. 50)	**r.**, 1974/250
1927		
1184	Supreme Ct. Funds Rates (Rev. X, p. 889)	**am.**, 1974/207
1928		
253	Registration of land at Hastings—O. in C. (Rev. XII, p. 186)	**r.**, 1974/250

Year and Number (or date)	Act or instrument	How affected
1930	Land Drainage Act (c. 44)	s. 23 (1) **am.,** 1974/595 s. 40 (3) **am.,** 1974/691 s.41(7) functions transfd. Secy. of State for Trade, 1974/692
1934 619	Local Authies. (Stock) Regs. (Rev. XII, p. 482)	**r.,** 1974/519
620	Local Govt. (Form of Mortgages and Transfers) Regs. (Rev. XII, p. 502)	**r.,** 1974/518
1346	London Cab O. (Rev. XIV, p. 795) ...	**am.,** 1974/601
1936 626	County Ct. Rules (1936 I, p. 282) ...	**am.,** 1974/178, 636
689	Registration of Land in Middlesex—O. in C. (Rev. XII, p. 186)	**r.,** 1974/250
1937	Harbours, Piers and Ferries (S.) Act (c. 28)	certain functions transfd. Secy. of State for Trade, 1974/692
1938 32	Public Health (Nursing Homes Registration Form) Regs. (Rev. XVI. p. 1097)	**r.,** 1974/22
611	Sanitary Accommodation (Factories) Regs. (Rev. VII, p. 109)	**am.,** 1974/426
1569	Registration of Land, Croydon—O. in C. (Rev. XII, p. 185)	**r.,** 1974/250
1939 54	Local Govt. Superannuation (Sum in lieu of Transfer Value) Regs. (Rev¹ XVII, p. 839)	**r.,** 1974/520
57	Local Govt. Superannuation (Service of Registration Officers) Regs. (Rev. XVII, p. 834)	**r.,** 1974/520
1944	Education Act (c. 31)	s. 114(1) **am.,** 1974/595
1206	Guardianship of Infants (Summary Jurisdiction) Rules (Rev. XIII, p. 245)	**r.,** 1974/706
1946	National Health Service Act (c. 81) ...	s. 15(1) **am.,** 1974/248
1947	Electricity Act (c. 54)	s. 67(1) **am.,** 1974/595
1948	National Assistance Act (c. 29) ...	sch. 6 paras. 6-8 **am.,** 1974/248 7(5) **replaced,** 1974/248
575	National Health Service (Central Health Services Council and Standing Advisory Ctees.) Regs. (Rev. XV, p. 503)	**r.,** 1974/187

Year and Number (or date)	Act or instrument	How affected
1948		
1257	National Health Service (General Dental Services) (S.) Regs. (Rev. XV, p. 910)	r., 1974/504
1259	National Health Service (Medical and Pharmaceutical Service Ctees. and Tribunal) (S.) Regs. (Rev. XV, p. 887)	r., 1974/504
1450	National Health Service (Supplementary Ophthalmic Services) (S.) Regs. (Rev. XV, p. 955)	r., 1974/507
1505	National Health Service (Charges for Appliances) Regs. (Rev. XV. p. 560)	r. (saving), 1974/284
1677	National Health Service (Local Health Authy., Charges) (S.) Regs. XV, p. 1030)	r., 1974/548
1949	Representation of the People Act (c. 68)	ss. 36(2), 116(5), 118(2), 167(1), 172(1) **am.**, 1974/595 sch. 8 para. 2. **am.**, 1974/595
628	Local Govt. Superannuation (Break of Service) Regs. (1949 I, p. 3054)	r., 1974/520
1432	Civil Defence (General) Regs. (1949 I, p. 637)	**am.**, 1974/68
1562	Local and Other Authies. (Transfer of Stock) Regs. (1949 I, p. 2482)	r., 1974/519
2145	Civil Defence (Burial) Regs. (1949 I, p. 648)	r., 1974/70
2147	Civil Defence (Evacuation and Care of the Homeless) Regs. (1949 I, p. 654)	r., 1974/70
2368	Designs Rules (1949 I, p. 1417) ...	**am.**, 1974/86
1950	Public Utilities Street Works Act (c. 39)	sch. 5 **am.**, 1974/595
1251	National Health Service (Expenses in attending Hospitals (S.) Regs. (1950 I, p. 1442)	r., 1974/486
1258	Civil Defence (Demolition and Repair Services) Regs. (1950 I, p. 346)	r., 1974/70
1603	National Health Service (Supplementary Ophthalmic Services) (S.) Amdt. Regs. (1950 I, p. 1559)	r., 1974/507
1945	National Health Service (General Dental Services and Fees) (S.) Amdt. Regs. (1950 I, p. 1443)	r., 1974/504
1951	Mineral Workings Act (c. 60) ...	s.1(1), 16(5) **am.**, 1974/ 595 sch. 1 **replaced**, 1974/482

Year and Number (or date)	Act or instrument	How affected
1951		
843	National Health Service (Charges for Appliances) Regs. (1951 I, p. 1389)	r. (saving), 1974/284
861	National Health Service (General Dental and Supplementary Ophthalmic Services) (S.) Regs. (1951 I, p. 1412)	r., 1974/507
862	National Health Service (Charges for Appliances) (S.) Regs. (1951 I, p. 1411)	r., 1974/522
1223	Civil Defence (Emergency Feeding) Regs. (1951 I, p. 258)	r., 1974/70
1464	National Health Service (Local Health Authy. Charges) (S.) Amdt. Regs. (1951 I, p. 1426)	r., 1974/548
1465	National Health Service (Remuneration and Conditions of Service) (S.) Regs. (1951 I, p. 1429)	r., 1974/276
2057	National Health Service (General Dental Services) (S.) Amdt. Regs. (1951 I. p. 1415)	r., 1974/504
1952		
395	Registration of Title (Surrey) O. (1952 I, p. 1250)	r., 1974/250
1869	Marriage (Authorised Persons) Regs. (1952 II, p. 1691)	am., 1974/573
2113	Bankruptcy Rules (1952 I, p.213) …	am., 1974/205
2138	Civil Defence (Billeting) Regs. (1952 I, p. 581)	r., 1974/70
1953		
1777	Civil Defence (Grant) Regs. (1953 I, p. 281)	am., 1974/69
1954		
796	Non-Contentious Probate Rules (1954 II, p. 2202)	am., 1974/597
879	Local Govt. Superannuation (Surrender of Superannuation Allowances) Rules (1954 II, p. 1701)	r., 1974/520
1048	Local Govt. Superannuation (Benefits) Regs. (1954 II, p. 1595)	am., 1974/520
1049	Probation Officers and Clerks (Superannuation) Regs. (1954 II, p. 1749)	r. (saving), 1974/520
1050	Justices Clerks and Assistants (Superannuation) Regs. (1954 II, p. 1525)	r. (saving), 1974/520
1192	Local Govt. Superannuation (Administration) Regs. (1954 II, p. 1570)	r., 1974/520
1224	Local Govt. Superannuation (Actuarial Valuations) Regs. (1954 II, p. 1537)	r., 1974/520
1229	Local Govt. (Teachers) Regs. (1954 II, p. 1715)	r., 1974/520

Year and Number (or date)	Act or instrument	How affected
1954		
1237	Local Govt. Superannuation (Limitation on Service) Regs. (1954 II, p. 1672)	r., 1974/520
1238	Local Govt. Superannuation (Reduction and Adjustment of Superannuation Allowances) Regs. (1954 II, p. 1683)	r., 1974/520
1955		
120	Midwives Rules Approval Instrt. (1955 I, p. 1145)	am., 1974/496
1041	Local Govt. Superannuation (Benefits) (Amdt.) Regs. (1955 II, p. 1825)	am., 1974/520
1956		
41	National Health Service (Supplementary Ophthalmic Services) (S.) Amdt. Regs. (1956 I, p. 1612)	r., 1974/507
327	Local Authies. (Stock) Regs. (1956 I, p. 1171)	r., 1974/519
328	Local and Other Authies. (Transfer of Stock) Regs. (1956 I, p. 1172)	r., 1974/519
1077	National Health Service (Service Ctees. and Tribunal) Regs. (1956 I, p. 1554)	r. (saving), 1974/455
1078	National Health Service (Supplementary Ophthalmic Services) Regs. (1956 I, p. 1524)	r , 1974/287
1914	Imprisonment and Detention (Army) Rules (1956 I, p. 310)	am., 1974/702
1957	House of Commons Disqualification Act (c. 20)	sch. 2 am., 1974/691
488	National Health Service (Designation of London Teaching Hospitals) O. (1957 I, p. 1452)	r., 1974/32
1958		
505	National Health Service (Designation of London Teaching Hospitals) Amdt. O. (1958 II, p. 1543)	r., 1974/32
519	Independent Schools Tribunal Rules (1958 I, p. 1006)	am., 1974/563
1273	Local Govt. Superannuation (Benefits) (New Towns Staffs) Regs. (1958 II, p. 1806)	r., 1974/520
2024	National Health Service (Supplementary Ophthalmic Services) Amdt. Regs. (1958 II, p. 1548)	r., 1974/287
2048	National Health Service (Qualifications of Supplementary Ophthalmic Services) (S.) Regs. (1958 II, p. 1562)	r., 1974/507
1959	Dog Licences Act (c. 55)	ss. 10(1), 13 am., 1974/595

Year and Number (or date)	Act or instrument	How affected
1959		
81	Agricultural Land Tribunals and Notices to Quit O. (1959 I, p. 91)	**am.,** 1974/67
83	Agriculture (Areas for Agricultural Land Tribunals) O. (1959 I, p. 38)	**r.,** 1974/66
363	School Health Service Regs. (1959 I, p. 1582)	**r.,** 1974/259
377	Maintenance Orders (Facilities for Enforcement) O. (1959 I, p. 1666)	**r.,** certain territories *see* 1974/557
518	National Health Service (Designation of London Teaching Hospitals) (Amdt.) (No. 1) O. (1959 I, p. 1817)	**r.,** 1974/32
766	National Health Service (Designation of London Teaching Hospitals) (Amdt.) (No. 2) O. (1959 I, p. 1821)	**r.,** 1974/32
956	General Optical Council (Education Ctee. Rules) O. (1959 II, p. 1983)	**r.,** 1974/149
962	Public Health Officers Regs. (1959 I, p. 1605)	**r.,** 1974/595
963	Public Health Officers (Port Health Districts) Regs. (1959 II, p. 2125)	**r.,** 1974/595
1960		
119	Nurses (Area Nurse-Training Ctees.) O. (1960 II, p. 2618)	**r.** (saving), 1974/235
122	Plant and Machinery (Rating) O. (1960 III, p. 2825)	**r.,** 1974/413
180	Agricultural Wages Ctees. (Areas) O. (1960 I, p. 69)	**r.,** 1974/514
250	Cycle Racing on Highways Regs. ...	**am.** (temp.), 1974/401
502	Civil Defence (Disease) Regs. (1960 I, p. 754)	**r.,** 1974/70
1139	Mental Health Review Tribunal Rules (1960 II, p. 1962)	**am.,** 1974/241
1241	Mental Health (Hospital and Guardianship) Regs. (1960 II, p. 1903)	**am.,** 1974/24, 241
1794	Factories (Cleanliness of Walls and Ceilings) O. (1960 II, p. 1415)	**am.,** 1974/427
1885	Agriculture (Areas for Agricultural Land Tribunals) (Amdt.) O. (1960 I, p. 89)	**r.,** 1974/66
2284	Local Govt. (Compulsory Purchase) Regs. (1960 I, p. 65)	**r.,** 1974/423
1961	Public Health Act (c. 64)	s.49(2) functions transfd. Secy. of State for Energy, 1974/692
368	Authorised Officers (Meat Inspection) Regs.	**r.,** 1974/391
577	Double Taxation Relief (Taxes on Income) (Sweden) O.	**am.,** 1974/558

Year and Number (or date)	Act or instrument	How affected
1961		
656	Landing of Unbarked Coniferous Timber O.	r., 1974/2
908	National Health Service (Supplementary Ophthalmic Services (No. 1) Regs.	r., 1974/287
909	National Health Service (Charges for Appliances) Regs.	r. (saving), 1974/284
915	National Health Service (Supplementary Ophthalmic Services) (S.) Amdt. Regs.	r., 1974/507
917	National Health Service (Charges for Appliances) (S.) Amdt. Regs.	r., 1974/522
947	National Health Service (Supplementary Ophthalmic Services) (No. 2) Regs.	r., 1974/287
973	National Health Service (Qualifications for Supplementary Ophthalmic Services (S.) Amdt. Regs.	r., 1974/507
1398	National Health Service (Superannuation) (S.) Regs.	am., 1974/441
1441	National Health Service (Superannuation) Regs.	am., 1974/223
2271	National Health Service (Designation of London Teaching Hospitals) O.	r., 1974/32
1962	Pipe-lines Act (c. 58)	s. 35(6) am., 1974/595
687	National Health Service (Designation of London Teaching Hospitals) O.	r., 1974/32
1977	National Health Service (S.) (Service of Documents) Regs.	r., 1974/504
2682	Local Govt. Superannuation (Benefits) (New Towns Staffs) Regs.	r., 1974/520
1963	London Govt. Act (c. 33)	s. 49(1) (c) am., 1974/70 sch. 14 para. 11, 1974/595
	Water Resources Act (c. 38)	am., 1974/607 gen. s. 19(4)(d)(e), sch. 7 paras. 4(e)(f), 17 functions transfd. Secy. of State for Trade, 1974/692. 56(5), 135(1) am., 1974/607
749	Land Compensation Development O.	r., 1974/539
926	Civil Defence (Training in Nursing) Regs.	r., 1974/70
1342	Nurses (Regional Nurse-Training Ctees.) (S.) O.	r., 1974/703
1571	Milk (Special Designation) Regs. ...	am., 1974/62

Year and Number (or date)	Act or instrument	How affected
1963		
1833	Radioactive Substances (Hospitals' Waste) Exemption O.	**am.,** 1974/501
1834	Radioactive Substances (Thorium-X) Exemption O.	**am.,** 1974/500
1879	Radioactive Substances (Hospitals' Waste) Exemption (S.) O.	**am.,** 1974/487
1880	Radioactive Substances (Thorium-X) Exemption (S.) O.	**am.,** 1974/488
1927	Consular Conventions (Republic of Austria) O.	**r.,** 1974/538
1964	Police Act (c. 48)	sch. 9 **r.,** 1974/595
23	National Health Service (Council on Tribunals) (S.) Regs.	**r.,** 1974/504
388	Prison Rules	**am.,** 1974/713
453	National Health Service (Designation of London Teaching Hospitals) O.	**r.,** 1974/32
983	Local Authy. Bonds Regs.	**r.,** 1974/519
986	National Health Service (Designation of London Teaching Hospitals) (No. 2) O.	**r.,** 1974/32
997	National Health Service (Speech Therapists) (S.) Regs.	**r.,** 1974/667
1126	Local Authies. (Appropriate Superannuation Funds) O.	**r.,** 1974/520
1965	Science and Technology Act (c. 4) ...	s. 5(1)(b) **replaced,** 1974/692
		s. 5(1)(b) certain functions transfd. Secy. of State for Energy, 1974/692
		s. 5(1)(b) certain functions transfd. to Secy. of State for Industry, 1974/692
	Airport Authority Act (c. 16) ...	s. 18(4) functions transfd. Secy. of State for Trade, 1974/692
	Severn Bridge Tolls Act (c. 24) ...	s. 3(7) **am.,** 1974/595
	Gas Act (c. 36)	s. 28(1) **am.,** 1974/595
261	Rate-demands Rules	**r.,** 1974/363
362	Civil Defence (Emergency Feeding) (Amdt.) Regs.	**r.,** 1974/70
422	Probation Officers and Clerks (Superannuation) (Amdt.) Regs.	**r.** (saving), 1974/520
534	Water Resources (Licences) Regs. ...	**am.,** 1974/607
537	Superannuation (Inner London Magistrates' Cts.) Regs.	**r.** (saving), 1974/520

Year and Number (or date)	Act or instrument	How affected
1965		
579	Town and Country Planning (Greater London) Development O.	r., 1974/418
621	London Authies. (Superannuation) O.	am., 1974/520
645	London Cts. and Probation (Superannuation) O.	am., 1974/520
655	London County Council Stock O. ...	r. (saving), 1974/519
679	Town and Country Planning (Local Planning Authies. in Greater London) Regs.	am., 1974/450
899	National Insurance (Industrial Injuries) (Medical Certification) Regs.	am., 1974/464
1288	Local Govt. Superannuation (Administration) (Amdt.) Regs.	am., 1974/520
1366	National Health Service (Service Ctees. and Tribunal) Amdt. Regs.	r. (saving), 1974/455
1500	County Ct. Funds Rules	am., 1974/206
1776	Rules of Supreme Ct. (Revision) ...	am., 1974/295
1819	National Health Service (Designation of London Teaching Hospitals) O.	r., 1974/32
2121	Importation of Forest Trees (Prohibition) (G.B.) O.	am., 1974/1
1966	Docks and Harbours Act (c. 28) ...	sch. 1 am., 1974/595
	Local Govt., (S.) Act (c. 51)	s. 18(4)(b) functions transfd. Secy. of State for Energy, 1974/692
95	Construction (Health and Welfare) Regs.	am., 1974/209
277	National Health Service (Designation of London Teaching Hospitals) O.	r., 1974/32
288	National Health Service (Designation of London Teaching Hospitals) (No. 2) O.	r., 1974/32
579	Local Land Charges Rules	am., 1974/424
794	Agricultural Lime Scheme	am., 1974/595
919	Nurses (Regional Nurse-Training Ctees.) (S.) Amdt. O.	r., 1974/703
1164	London Transport (Male Wages Grades Pensions) O.	am., 1974/526
1216	London Authies. (Staff) O.	am., 1974/520
1449	National Health Service (General Dental Services) (S.) Regs.	r. (saving), 1974/505
1967	General Rate Act (c. 9)	schs. 6 para. 12, 7 para. 15 functions transfd. to Secy. of State for Energy, 1974/692
	Forestry Act (c. 10)	s.40(2)(c) am., 1974/595

Year and Number (or date)	Act or instrument	How affected
1967		
	Parliamentary Comm. Act (c. 13) ...	sch. 2 **am.**, 1974/691, 692
	Agriculture Act (c.22)	s. 9 (11) certain functions transfd. Secy. of State for Prices and Consumer Protection, 1974/692
	Sea Fish (Conservation) Act (c. 84)	ss. 6, 8 functions transfd. Secy. of State for Trade, 1974/692
330	National Insurance (Unemployment and Sickness Benefit) Regs.	**am.**, 1974/593
372	Fishing Vessels (Acquisition and Improvement) (Grants) Scheme	**am.**, 1974/194
489	Teachers' Superannuation Regs. ...	**am.**, 1974/260
520	National Insurance (Medical Certification) Regs.	**am.**, 1974/416
947	National Health Service (General Dental Services (S.) Amdt. Regs.	**r.** (saving), 1974/505
1104	Civil Defence (Casualty Services) Regs.	**r.**, 1974/70
1114	Civil Defence (Public Protection) Regs.	**r.**, 1974/70
1330	London Authies. (Superannuation) (Amdt.) O.	**am.**, 1974/520
1965	Rate-demands (Amdt.) Rules	**r.**, 1974/363
1968	Pastoral Measure 1968 No. 1	s. 52(1)(a) **am.**, 1974/306
357	Ancillary Dental Workers Regs. ...	**am.**, 1974/544
488	London Authies. (Staff) O.	**am.**, 1974/520
490	National Health Service (Designation of London Teaching Hospitals, etc.) O.	**r.**, 1974/32
491	Rate Product Rules	**r.**, 1974/364
545	National Health Service (Hydestile Hospital) O.	**r.**, 1974/32
557	National Health Service (Charges for Dental Treatment) (S.) Regs.	**r.** (saving), 1974/505
759	National Health Service (Charges for Drugs and Appliances) Regs.	**r.**, 1974/285
818	National Health Service (Charges for Drugs and Appliances) (S.) Regs.	**r.**, 1974/508
1048	Agricultural Land Tribunals (Transitional Provns.) O.	**r.**, 1974/67
1163	Pensions Commutation Regs. ...	**am.**, 1974/734
1334	National Health Service (Designation of London Teaching Hospitals) Amdt. (No. 1) O.	**r.**, 1974/32
1366	Public Health (Infectious Diseases) Regs.	**am.**, 1974/274

Year and Number (or date)	Act or instrument	How affected
1968		
1389	Patents Rules	**am.** 1974/87
1588	National Health Service (Charges for Drugs and Appliances) (Amdt.) Regs.	**r.,** 1974/285
1607	National Health Service (Charges for Drugs and Appliances) (S.) (Amdt.) Regs.	**r.,** 1974/508
1610	Wages Regulation (Dressmaking and Women's Light Clothing) (S.) (Holidays) (No. 2) O.	**r.,** 1974/211
1642	National Health Service (Veneral Diseases) Regs.	**superseded,** 1974/29
1919	Magistrates Ct. (Forms) Rules ...	**am.,** 1974/444
1927	Wages Regulation (Ostrich and Fancy Feather and Artificial Flowers) (Holidays) O.	**r.,** 1974/538
1945	National Health Service (Designation of London Teaching Hospitals) Amdt. (No. 2) O.	**r.,** 1974/32
1952	Town and Country Planning Appeals (Determination by Appointed Persons) (Inquiry Procedure) Rules	**r.,** 1974/420
2049	Registration of Births, Deaths and Marriages Regs.	**am.,** 1974/571
1969	Finance Act (c. 32)	s. 41(2), sch. 18 Pt. I **am.,** 1974/693
	Post Office Act (c. 48)	s. 2(1)-(5) (7), **r.,** 1974/691 s. 14(1) **am.,** 1974/595
	Development of Tourism Act (c. 51)	certain functions transfd. Secy. of State for Trade, 1974/692.
18	Conveyance in Harbours of Military Explosives Regs.	**am.,** 1974/479
163	National Health Service (Appointment of Consultants) Regs.	**r.,** 1974/361
203	Registration of Births, Still-births and Deaths (Welsh Language) Regs.	**am.,** 1974/572
254	National Health Service General Dental Services) (S.) Amdt. Regs.	**r.** (saving), 1974/505 **am.,** 1974/506
286	Town and Country Planning General Regs.	**r.** 1974/596
351	National Health Service (General Ophthalmic Services) (Amdt.) Regs.	**r.,** 1974/287
354	National Health Service (Service Ctees. and Tribunal) (Amdt.) Regs.	**r.** (saving), 1974/455
413	London Authies. (Superannuation) (Amdt.) O.	**r.,** 1974/520

Year and Number (or date)	Act or instrument	How affected
1969		
436	National Health Service (General Dental Services) (S.) Amdt. (No. 2) Regs.	**r.** (saving), 1974/505
438	River Authies. (Precepts of Internal Drainage Bds.) Regs.	**r.,** 1974/375
513	Public Trustee (Fees) O.	**am.,** 1974/310
519	Companies (Bd. of Trade) Fees O.	**am.,** 1974/638
785	Teachers Superannuation Account (Rates of Interest) (S.) Regs.	**am.,** 1974/376
793	National Insurance (Modification of Local Govt. Superannuation Schemes) Regs.	**r.** (saving), 1974/520
849	Nurses (Regional Nurse-Training Ctees.) (S.) Amdt. O.	**r.,** 1974/703
863	Registration of Title O.	**r.,** 1974/250
904	Representation of the People Regs.	**r.** (saving), 1974/648
906	National Health Service (Charges for Appliances) Regs.	**r.** (saving), 1974/284 **am.,** 1974/287
912	Representation of the People (S.) Regs.	**am.,** 1974/651
918	National Health Service (Charges for Appliances) (S.) Regs.	**r.,** 1974/522
1092	Town and Country Planning (Inquiries Procedure) Rules	**r.,** 1974/419
1161	National Health Service (Nottingham University Hospital Designation) O.	**am.,** 1974/6
1296	Statutory Harbour Undertakings (Form of Accounts etc.) (Local Authies.) Regs.	**am.,** 1974/595
1440	Midwives (Disciplinary Ctee.) Rules Approval Instrt.	**am.,** 1974/496
1532	Town and Country Planning (Control of Advertisements) Regs.	**am.,** 1974/185
1581	National Health Service (Executive Councils and Dental Estimates Bd.) Financial Regs.	**am.,** 1974/282, 541
1611	National Health Service (Hospital Accounts and Financial Provns. (S.) Regs.	**r.,** 1974/468
1612	National Health Service (Executive Councils and Scottish Dental Estimates Bd.) (S.) Financial Regs.	**r.,** 1974/468
1654	Industrial Assurance (Collecting Societies' Deposits) Regs.	**am.,** 1974/493
1676	General Nursing Council] (Election Scheme) Rules Approval Instrt.	**r.,** 1974/320
1970	Sea Fish Industry Act (c. 11)	ss. 22(1), 23(1), 24(2), 35(1), 36(1,) 37(2) **am.,** 1974/88

Year and Number (or date)	Act or instrument	How affected
1970		
	Parish Councils and Burial Authties. (Misc. Provns.) Act (c. 29)	s. 1(1) **am.** (exc. Is. of Scilly), 1974/628
107	Local Govt. (Travelling Allowances, etc.) (S.) Regs.	**am.,** 1974/652
197	Rural Borough Council Election Rules	**r.,** 1974/595
198	Fixed Penalty (Procedure) Regs. ...	**r.,** 1974/476
298	Returning Officers' Expenses (E. and W.) Regs.	**r.,** 1974/179
299	Returning Officers' Expenses (N.I.) Regs.	**r.,** 1974/181
300	Returning Officers' Expenses (S.) Regs.	**r.,** 1974/180
335	Children and Young Persons (Planning Areas) O.	**r.,** 1974/163
515	Pensions Commutation (Amdt.) Regs.	**r.,** 1974/734
615	Smoke Control Areas (Exempted Fireplaces) O.	**am.,** 1974/762,855
850	Returning Officers' Expenses (E. and W.) (Amdt.) Regs.	**r.,** 1974/179
851	Returning Officers' Expenses (S.) (Amdt.) Regs.	**r.,** 1974/180
852	Returning Officers' Expenses (N.I.) (Amdt.) Regs.	**r.,** 1974/181
1047	Corn Returns Regs.	**r.,** 1974/399
1051	Smallholdings (Contributions Toward Losses) Regs.	**am.,** 1974/396
1125	Local Govt. Superannuation (Teachers) (Amdt.) Regs.	**r.,** 1974/520
1228	Wages Regulation (Made-up Textiles) (Holidays) O.	**r.,** 1974/632
1288	Export of Goods (Control) O. ...	**am.,** 1974/134, 213,909
1340	National Health Service (General Dental Services) (S.) Amdt. (No. 2) Regs.	**r.** (saving), 1974/505
1478	Wages Regulation (Button Manufacturing) O.	**r.,** 1974/674
1479	Wages Regulation (Button Manufacturing (Holidays) O.	**r.,** 1974/675
1667	Smoke Control Areas (Exempted Fireplaces) (No. 2) O.	**am.,** 1974/762
1681	Secretary of State for the Environment O.	**am.,** 1974/692
1880	Public Health (Aircraft) Regs. ...	**am.,** 1974/268
1881	Public Health (Ships) Regs.	**am.,** 1974/269
2007	Bankruptcy Fees O.	**am.,** 1974/637
1971	Vehicles (Excise) Act (c. 10)	s. 4(1) para. (L) **inserted,** (E. and W.), 1974/168

Year and Number (or date)	Act or instrument	How affected
1971		
	Industry Act (c. 17)	s. 1(1) (b) (ii) functions transfd. Secy. of State for Industry, 1974/692
	Cts. Act (c. 23)	sch. 3 **am.**, 1974/595
	Fire Precautions Act (c.40)	s. 43(1) **am.**, 1974/595
	Pensions Increase Act (c. 56)	sch. 3 para. 6(1) (a) **replaced**, 1974/595
	Town and Country Planning Act (c. 78)	s. 224(1) (a) (b) **am.**, 1974/692
		ss. 224(1) (a), 273(1) functions transfd. Secy. of State for Energy, 1974/692
		s. 265(1) functions transfd. Secy. of State for Industry, 1974/692
		s. 224(1) (b) functions transfd. Secy. of State for Trade, 1974/692
		sch. 13 **replaced**, 1974/482
129	Registration of Marriages (Welsh Language) Regs.	**am.**, 1974/572
156	Police Regs.	**am.**, 1974/649,1217,1365
220	Juror's Allowances (S.) Regs.	**am.**, 1974/666
249	Residential Establishments (Payments by Local Authies.) (S.) O.	**am.**, 1974/169
304	Therapeutic Substances (Supply of Antibiotics and Chemo-therapeutic Substances for Agricultural Purposes) Regs.	**am.**, 1974/242
340	National Health Service (Charges) Regs.	**am.**, 1974/285,307,1377
352	Goods Vehicles (Plating and Testing) Regs.	**am.**, 1974/99
413	Justices' Allowances Regs.	**am.**, 1974/530
414	Probation (Allowances) Rules ...	**am.**, 1974/746
420	National Health Service (Charges) (S.) Regs.	**r.**, 1974/522
469	Rate Support Grant (S.) O.	**am.**, 1974/613
472	National Health Service (General Medical and Pharmaceutical Services) (S.) Amdt. Regs.	**r.**, 1974/506
490	Justices' Allowances (S.) Regs. ...	**am.**, 1974/673
547	Rural Borough Council Election Rules	**r.**, 1974/595
621	National Insurance (Attendance Allowance) Regs.	**am.**, 1974/416

Year and Number (or date)	Act or instrument	How affected
1971		
1037	Milk (N.I.) O.	**am.,** 1974/566
1038	Milk (G.B.) O.	**am.,** 1974/565
1103	Foreign Sea-Fishery Officers (International Commn. for the North-west Atlantic Fisheries Scheme) O.	**am.,** 1974/701
1117	Employers' Liability (Compulsory Insurances) General Regs.	**am.,** 1974/208
1135	Civil Aviation (Navigation Services Charge) Regs.	**am.,** 1974/564,1132
1172	Fishing Nets (North-west Atlantic) O.	**am.,** 1974/192
1237	Commonwealth Countries and Republic of Ireland Immunities and Privileges) O.	**am.,** 1974/109
1265	Smoke Control Areas (Exempted Fireplaces) O.	**am.,** 1974/762
1394	Wages Regulation (Toy Manufacturing) (Holidays) O.	**am.,** 1974/234
1537	Milk and Meals (Education) (S.) Regs.	**am.,** 1974/708,1134
1569	Wages Regulation (Paper Box) (Holidays) O.	**r.,** 1974/42
1679	Wages Regulation (Paper Box) O. ...	**r.,** 1974/41
1697	Wages Regulation (Hollow-ware) (Holidays) O.	**r.,** 1974/686
1775	Teachers Superannuation (Family Benefits) (S.) Regs.	**am.,** 1974/376
1933	Employers' Liability (Compulsory Insurance) Exemption Regs.	**am.,** 1974/208
2029	Gaming Club (Permitted Areas) (Amdt) Regs.	**r.,** 1974/595
1972	Ministerial and other Salaries Act (c. 3)	sch. 1 Pt. II **am.,** 1974/691
	Local Employment Act (c. 5)	ss. 8 (6), 9(1) (c) **am.,** 1974/692
	Finance Act (c. 41)	sch. 4 group 2, 7 **replaced,** 1974/542
	Road Traffic Act (c. 20)	Pt. VI s. 144 (2) para. (f) **inserted,** 1974/168
	Housing (Financial Provns.) (S.) Act (c. 46)	sch. 2 para. 12(1) (c)-(e) **am.,** 1974/723
		sch. 3 para. 10(4) **replaced,** 1974/723

Year and Number (or date)	Act or instrument	How affected
1972	Housing Finance Act (c. 47)	ss. 62, 64, 66(4) **mod.,** 1974/381
		s. 35(2) **am.,** 1974/615
		sch. 3 para. 12(1) (c)-(e), **am.,** 1974/516
		sch. 4 para. 10(4) **replaced,** 1974/516
		sch. 9 para. 2(1) (2) **am.,** 1974/595
	Town and Country Planning (S.) Act (c. 52)	s. 213(1) (a) (b), **am.,** 1974/692
		ss. 213(1) (a), 259(1) functions transfd. Secy. of State for Energy, 1974/692
		s. 252(1) functions transfd. Secy. of State for Industry, 1974/692
		s. 213(1) (b) functions transfd. Secy. of State for Trade, 1974/693
	Gas Act (c. 60)	ss. 26(b), 29(8), 35(2) functions transfd. Secy. of State for Energy, 1974/692
		s. 39(3), **am.,** 1974/595
	Local Government Act (c. 70)... ...	s. 250 (5), **am.,** 1974/455
		sch. 26 para. 10 **am.,** 1974/595
		sch. 26 paras. 12, 13, 18-23 **r.** (exc. Is. of Scilly), 1974/628
		sch. 26 para. 25 **am.** (exc. Is. of Scilly), 1974/628
96	National Health Service (General Dental Services) (S.) Amdt. Regs.	**r.** (saving), 1974/505
129	Air Navigation O.	**am.,** 1974/111,1114
154	Fiduciary Note Issue (Extension of Period) O.	**r.,** 1974/405
321	Rules of the Air and Air Traffic Control Regs.	**am.,** 1974/150,1401
333	Fixed Penalty (Procedure) (Amdt.) Regs.	**am.,** 1974/476
419	Rules of Procedures (Air Force) ...	**am.,** 1974/752
438	Smoke Control Areas (Exempted Fireplaces) O.	**am.,** 1974/762
466	Residential Establishments (Payments by Local Authies.) (S.) Amdt. O.	**superseded,** 1974/169

Year and Number (or date)	Act or instrument	How affected
1972		
518	Combined Probation and After-Care Areas O.	**r.,** 1974/529
519	Combined Probation and After-Care Areas (No. 2) O.	**r.,** 1974/529
555	National Insurance (Classification) Regs.	**am.,** 1974/10, 416,1036
568	Teachers' Superannuation (Financial Provns.) Regs.	**am.,** 1974/390
603	National Insurance (Hospital In-Patients) Regs.	**am.,** 1974/416,1128
604	National Insurance (Overlapping Benefits) Regs.	**am.,** 1974/593
641	Savings Certificate Regs.	**am.,** 1974/552
764	National Savings Bank Regs.	**am.,** 1974/553
777	Police (S.) Regs.	**am.,** 1974/489 ,1348
827	National Health Service (Tribunal for General Ophthalmic Services) (S.) Regs.	**r.,** 1974/504
828	National Health Service (Joint Ophthalmic Services Ctees.) (S.) Regs	**am.,** 1974/503, 504
869	Wages Regulation (Industrial and Staff Canteen) O.	**r.,** 1974/45
877	Pensions Increase (Federated Superannuation System for Universities) Regs.	**am.,** 1974/737
943	Wages Regulation (Licensed Non-residential Establishment) O.	**r.,** 1974/11
944	Wages Regulation (Licensed Non-residential Establishment) (Managers and Club Stewards) O.	**r.,** 1974/12
1087	Wages Regulation (Stamped or Pressed Metal-Wares) O.	**r.,** 1974/439
1088	Wages Regulation (Stamped or Pressed Metal-Wares) (Holidays) O.	**r.,** 1974/440
1200	Medicines (Exemption from Licences) (Speical Cases and Misc. Provns.) O.	**mod.,** 1974/498
1245	Corn Returns (Amdt.) Regs.	**r.,** 1974/399
1313	Compulsory Purchase of Land Regs.	**am.,** 1974/423
1348	National Health Service (General Dental Services) (S.) Amdt. (No. 2) Regs.	**r.** (saving), 1974/505
1399	Fixed Penalty (Procedure) (Amdt.) (No. 2) Regs.	**r.,** 1974/476
1432	National Insurance (Industrial Injuries) (Insurable and Excepted Employments) Regs.	**am.,** 1974/8, 464
1484	Wages Regulation (Licensed Non-residential Establishment) (Amdt.) O.	**r.,** 1974/11

Year and Number (or date)	Act or instrument	How affected
1972		
1485	Wages Regulation (Licensed Non-residential Establishment) Managers and Club Stewards) (Amdt.) O.	**r.,** 1974/12
1566	Local Govt. (Allowances to Members) Regs.	**r.,** 1974/595
1602	National Health Service (General Medical and Pharmaceutical Services) Regs.	**r.,** 1974/160
1728	Combined Probation and After-Care Areas (Amdt.) O.	**r.,** 1974/529
1771	Wages Regulation (Hairdressing) O.	**r.,** 1974/478
1819	Wages Regulation (Retail Bookselling and Stationery) O.	**r.,** 1974/139
1820	Wages Regulation (Toy Manufacturing) O.	**r.,** 1974/234
1862	National Health Service (General Dental Services-Seniority Payments) (S.) Regs.	**r.** (saving), 1974/505
1938	Poisons List O.	**am.,** 1974/80
1939	Poisons Rules ... ... \...	**am.,** 1974/81,595
1959	Wages Regulation (Retail Bread and Flour Confectionery) (S.) O.	**r.,** 1974/714
1960	Superannuation (Teachers and Teachers' Families) (Amdt.) Regs.	**am.,** 1974/260
1976	Jurors' Allowances Regs.	**am.,** 1974/733,1461
1988	Wages Regulation (Retail Newsagency, Tobacco and Confectionery) (E. and W.) O.	**r.,** 1974/305
2018	Wages Regulation (Retail Bread and Flour Confectionery) (E. and W.) O.	**r.,** 1974/46
1973	Counter-Inflation Act (c. 9)	s. 21 (1) **am.,** 1974/691
	National Health Service Reorganisation Act (c. 32)	s. 35 (4) **am.,** 1974/247
	Fair Trading Act (c. 41)	s. 51(3) **am.,** 1974/691
	Insurance Companies Amdt. Act (c. 58)	ss. 21(1)(b), 23(1) (b), 33(8)(b), 34(2)(b) **am.,** 1974/692
		ss. 21(1)(b), 23(1))b), 33(3)(b), 34(2)(b), functions transfd. Secy. of State for Trade, 1974/692
24	Motor Vehicles (Construction and Use) Regs.	**am.,** 1974/64,765,973
31	Town and Country Planning General Development O.	**am.,** 1974/418
39	Wages Regulation (Retail Food) (E. and W.) O.	**r.,** 1974/261

Year and Number (or date)	Act or instrument	How affected
1973		
63	National Health Service (Qualifications of Health Visitors) (S.) Regs.	**r.,** 1974/485
122	Wages Regulation (Milk Distribution) (E. and W.) O.	**r.,** 1974/734
131	Land Registration (District Registries) O.	**r.,** 1974/445
146	Wages Regulation (Hollow-ware) O.	**r.,** 1974/685
147	Wages Regulation (Retail Newsagency, Tobacco and Confectionery) (S.) O.	**r.,** 1974/174
156	Wages Regulation (Rubber Proofed Garment) O.	**r.,** 1974/331
157	Wages Regulation (Rubber Proofed Garment) (Holidays) O.	**r.,** 1974/332
175	Wages Regulation (Made-up Textiles) O.	**r.,** 1974/631
183	Wages Regulation (Shirtmaking) O.	**r.,** 1974/743
184	Wages Regulation (Shirtmaking) (Holidays) O.	**r..** 1974/744
190	Wages Regulation (Wholesale Mantle and Costume) O.	**r.,** 1974/754
191	Wages Regulation (Wholesale Mantle and Costume) (Holidays) O.	**r.,** 1974/755
218	Wages Regulation (Corset) O. ...	**r.,** 1974/437
219	Wage Regulation (Corset) (Holidays) O.	**r.,** 1974/438
229	Rural Borough Council Election (Amdt.) Rules	**r.,** 1974/595
264	Wages Regulation (Unlicensed Place of Refreshment) O.	**r.,** 1974/278
311	Wages Regulation (Dressmaking and Women's Light Clothing) (E. and W.) O.	**r.,** 1974/574
312	Wages Regulation (Dressmaking and Women's Light Clothing) (E. and W.) (Holidays) O.	**r.,** 1974/575
313	Local Govt. Superannuation (Misc. Provns.) Regs.	**r.,** 1974/520
319	Fixed Penalty (Procedure) (Amdt.) Regs.	**r.,** 1974/476
386	Added Value Tax (Food) O.	**r.,** 1974/542
389	Saving Certificates (Amdt.) Regs.	**r.,** 1974/552
410	Sugar Beet (Research and Education) O.	**superseded,** 1974/370
427	Representation of the People Regs.	**r.** (saving), 1974/648

Year and Number (or date)	Act or instrument	How affected
1973		
484	Wages Regulation (Retail Bookselling and Stationery) (Amdt.) O.	r., 1974/139
519	London Cab O.	r., 1974/601
521	Wages Regulation (Ostrich and Fancy Feather and Artificial Flower) O.	r., 1974/537
539	Wages Regulation (Dressmaking and Women's Light Clothing) (S.) O.	r., 1974/210
558	Approved Schools and Classifying Centres (Contributions by Local Authies.) Regs.	r., 1974/497
666	Rate Support Grant (S.) O.	am., 1974/614
686	Waterways Regs.	am., 1974/735
691	National Health Service (Determination of Areas of Health Bds.) (S.) O.	r., 1974/266
748	Motor Vehicles (Speed Limits on Motorways) Regs.	r., 1974/619
797	Misuse of Drugs Regs....	am., 1974/402
936	Teachers' Superannuation (Family Benefits) (Amdt.) Regs.	am., 1974/260
1047	Local Govt. (Financial Loss Allowance) Regs.	r., 1974/595
1050	Seeds (Fees) Regs.	r., 1974/736
1063	National Health Service (General Medical and Pharmaceutical Services) (S.) Amdt. Regs.	r., 1974/506
1159	Wages Regulation (Pin, Hook and Eye, and Snap Fastener) O.	r., 1974/655
1160	Wages Regulation (Pin, Hook and Eye, and Snap Fastener) (Holidays) O.	am., 1974/655
1189	Carriage by Air (Sterling Equivalents) O.	superseded, 1974/528
1190	Merchant Shipping (Limitation of Liability) (Sterling Equivalents) O.	r., 1974/536
1199	Motor Vehicles (Type Approval) Regs.	am., 1974/65, 763
1218	Wages Regulation (Retail Food) (E. and W.) (Amdt.) O.	r., 1974/261
1237	Wages Regulation (Retail Bread and Flour Confectionary) (E. and W.) (Amdt.) O.	r., 1974/46
1261	Wages Regulation (Retail Newsagency, Tobacco and Confectionery) (E. and W.) (Amdt.) O.	r., 1974/205
1311	Hydrocarbon Oil Regs.	am., 1974/379
1468	National Health Service (General Dental Services) Regs.	am., 1974/53
1495	Cessation of Approved Institutions (Eastmore House) O.	r., 1974/414
1536	National Health Services (General Dental Services) (S.) Amdt. Regs.	r. (saving), 1974/505

Year and Number (or date)	Act or instrument	How affected
1973		
1593	Local Govt. (Petty Sessional Divisions etc.) O.	am., 1974/403
1613	Cessation of Approved Institutions (Eastmore House) (Amdt.) O.	r., 1974/414
1764	Registration of Title O.	r., 1974/250
1785	Counter-Inflation (Price and Pay Code) (No. 2) O.	am., 1974/661
1786	Counter-Inflation (Notification of Increases in Price and Charges) (No. 3) O.	am., 1974/543
1845	Import Duties (General) (No. 8) O.	am., 1974/166, 167, 475, 570, 608, 610, 611, 677, 682
1847	Local Govt. (Staff Transfer Schemes) O.	am., 1974/147
1861	Local Authies. (E.) (Property etc.) O.	am., 1974/406
1863	Local Authies. (W.) (Property etc.) O.	am., 1974/404
1910	Local Elections (Parishes and Communities) Rules	am., 1974/84
1946	Customs Duties and Drawbacks (Revenue Duties) O.	am., 1974/143
1949	Exchange Control (Authorised Dealers and Depositaries) (No. 2) O.	am., 1974/588
1996	Local Govt. Superannuation (Misc. Provns.) (No. 2 Regs.)	r., 1974/520
2037	Anti-Dumping and Countervailing Duties O.	susp. (temp.), 1974/724
2058	Motor Vehicles (Speed Limits on Motorways) (Amdt.) Regs.	r., 1974/619
2059	Motorways Traffic (Speed Limit) Regs.	r., 1974/502
2063	Employment and Training Act 1973 (Commencement No. 1) O.	am., 1974/398
2068	Fuel and Electricity (Heating) (Control) O.	r., 1974/511
2072	Acquisition of Land (Rate of Interest after Entry) (No. 5) Regs.	r., 1974/721
2073	Acquisition of Land (Rate of Interest after Entry) (S.) (No. 5) Regs.	r., 1974/722
2078	Teachers Superannuation (Family Benefits) (S.) Amdt. Regs.	am., 1974/376
2080	Electricity (Lighting) (Control) O. ...	r., 1974/511
2087	Motor Fuel (Restriction of Acquisition) O.	am., 1974/245
2089	Emergency (No. 2) Regs.	superseded, 1974/33
2091	Electricity (Advertising, Display, etc.) (Control) O.	r., 1974/511
2092	Electricity (Heating) (Control) O.	r., 1974/511
2119	Motor Fuel (Maximum Retail Prices) O.	am., 1974/197, 420

Year and Number (or date)	Act or instrument	How affected
1973		
2120	Electricity (Industrial and Commercial Use) (Control) O.	r., 1974/78
2131	Electricity (Lighting) (Control) (N.I.) O.	r., 1974/512
2132	Fuel and Electricity (Heating) (Control) (N.I.) O.	r., 1974/512
2137	Electricity (Industrial and Commercial Use) (Control) (Amdt.) O.	r., 1974/78
2146	Electricity (Industrial and Commercial Use) (Control) (Second Amdt.) O.	r., 1974/78
2150	Value Added Tax (Finance and Insurance) (No. 2) O.	am., 1974/554
2151	Value Added Tax (General) (No. 2) O.	am., 1974/554
2152	Import Duties (Temp. Reductions and Exemptions) (No. 3) O.	am., 1974/756
2153	Army Air Force and Naval Discipline Acts (Continuation) O.	am., 1974/161
2166	Smoke Control Areas (Exempted Fireplaces) O.	am., 1974/762
2172	Electricity (Industrial and Commercial Use) (Control) (No. 2) O.	r., 1974/377
2188	Paraffin (Maximum Retail Prices) O.	am., 1974/198
2208	Import Duties (Certain Mediterranean Countries) (Reductions and Exemptions) O.	am., 1974/167
2209	Import Duties (Turkey) (Reductions and Exemptions) O.	am., 1974/166
2210	Import Duties (Temp. Reductions and Exemptions) (No. 2) O.	am., 1974/132
2219	Import Duties (Temp. Reductions and Exemptions) (No. 4) O.	am., 1974/161
1974	Pensions (Increase) Act (c.9)	sch. para. 5 am., paras. 7-17 r., 1974/715
32	National Health Service (Designation of London Teaching Hospitals) O.	am., 1974/341
33	Emergency Regs.	superseded, 1974/175
35	National Health Service (Staff Transfer Schemes) O.	am., 1974/378
44	Judicial Pensions (Widows' and Children's Benefits) Regs.	am., 1974/229
54	Butter Subsidy Regs.	am., 1974/678
96	Import Duties (Quota Relief) O. ...	expired (31.3.74)
125	Local Govt. (Allowances to Members) (Amdt.) Regs.	r., 1974/595
143	Customs Duties and Drawbacks (Revenue Duties) (Morocco) O.	expired (1.1.75)

Year and Number (or date)	Act or instrument	How affected
1974		
175	Emergency (No. 2) Regs.	**superseded,** 1974/350
184	Counter-Inflation (Rents) (E. and W.) O.	**r.,** 1974/381
282	National Health Service Financial Regs.	**r.,** 1974/541
284	National Health Service (Charges for Appliances) Regs.	**am.,** 1974/609
285	National Health Service (Charges for Drugs and Appliances) Regs.	**am.,** 1974/627
287	National Health Service (General Ophthalmic Services) Regs.	**am.,** 1974/527
381	Counter-Inflation (Public Sector Residential Rents) (E. and W.) O.	**am.,** 1974/434
419	Town and Country Planning (Inquiries Procedure) Rules	**mod.** (Greater London), 1974/419
420	Town and Country Planning Appeals (Determination by Appointed Persons) (Inquiries Procedure) Rules	**mod.** (Greater London), 1974/420
483	Local Authies. etc. (Staff Transfer and Protection) O.	**am.,** 1974/595
508	National Health Service (Charges for Drugs and Appliances) (S.) Regs.	**am.,** 1974/647
682	Import Duties (Temporary Reductions and Exemptions) (No. 5) O.	**am.,** 1974/756

HMSO
£27.00
set